Rethinking *the* Color Line

Rethinking *the* Color Line

Readings in Race and Ethnicity

FIFTH EDITION

CHARLES A. GALLAGHER
La Salle University

Mc Graw Hill

Connect
Learn
Succeed™

The McGraw·Hill Companies

RETHINKING THE COLOR LINE: READINGS IN RACE AND ETHNICITY, FIFTH EDITION

Published by McGraw-Hill, a business unit of The McGraw-Hill Companies, Inc., 1221 Avenue of the Americas, New York, NY 10020. Copyright © 2012 by The McGraw-Hill Companies, Inc. All rights reserved. Previous editions © 2009, 2007, and 2003. Printed in the United States of America. No part of this publication may be reproduced or distributed in any form or by any means, or stored in a database or retrieval system, without the prior written consent of The McGraw-Hill Companies, Inc., including, but not limited to, in any network or other electronic storage or transmission, or broadcast for distance learning.

Some ancillaries, including electronic and print components, may not be available to customers outside the United States.

This book is printed on acid-free paper.

2 3 4 5 6 7 8 9 0 DOC/DOC 1 0 9 8 7 6 5 4 3 2

ISBN 978-0-07-802663-8
MHID 0-07-802663-6

Vice President & Editor-in-Chief: *Michael Ryan*
Vice President of Specialized Publishing: *Janice M. Roerig-Blong*
Sponsoring Editor: *Jessica Cannavo*
Marketing Manager: *Patrick Brown*
Lead Project Manager: *Jane Mohr*
Design Coordinator: *Brenda A. Rolwes*
Cover Design: *Studio Montage, St. Louis, Missouri*
Cover Image: *Black House, © Alex Kanevsky*
Buyer: *Sandy Ludovissy*
Media Project Manager: *Sridevi Palani*
Compositor: *Laserwords Private Limited*
Typeface: *10/12 Perpetua Std Regular*
Printer: *R.R. Donnelley*

All credits appearing on page or at the end of the book are considered to be an extension of the copyright page.

Library of Congress Cataloging-in-Publication Data

Rethinking the color line : readings in race and ethnicity / [edited by] Charles A. Gallagher.—5th ed.
    p. cm.
  Includes bibliographical references.
  ISBN 978-0-07-802663-8 (alk. paper)
    1. United States—Race relations. 2. United States—Ethnic relations. 3. Minorities—Civil rights—United States.
I. Gallagher, Charles A. (Charles Andrew), 1962–
    E184.A1R4485 2012
    305.800973—dc23
                                                                      2011030547

www.mhhe.com

To my daughters Sophia and Talia.

About the Author and Rethinking the Color Line

An old saying suggests that if you "scratch" at any creative endeavor you will uncover personal biography. The genealogy of *Rethinking the Color Line* reflects this adage. As a boy I grew up in Overbrook Park, an all-white, working- and lower-middle-class neighborhood in Philadelphia. My world was a mix of first- and second-generation immigrants from Poland, Russia, Ireland, and Italy. Race was something I experienced when we left our completely self-contained, row house community and went "downtown." Race was typically presented to me in terms of geography: blacks lived in North and West Philly, Asians clustered in Chinatown, and Latinos resided off of N. Broad Street. The "race as geography" analogy was cemented as I got older and was taken on class trips to museums of art and natural history. The dioramas in the museums had each of the "major races of mankind" frozen in a variety of daily, primitive routines: some were engaged in tepee making, others were spearing fish or seals, farmers tended rice paddies, peasants worked the land. Typically there was a map that explained that black people were from this continent, brown people from there, and so on, until all the racial groups had been repatriated back to their "original" homeland.

I saw parallels to the representations of race I experienced as a boy and the textbooks available to me as a student teacher almost twenty years ago. Race and ethnicity readers and textbooks typically presented each group's history as discrete events that took place in a social vacuum, rather than weaving a narrative that reflects the constant interaction within and between racial and ethnic groups. Race relations play out in housing, the economy, criminal justice, schooling, love, culture, and politics. This perspective shows the social relations that link all racial and ethnic groups together, rather than an approach in which week four is dedicated to African Americans and week seven to American Indians. What I have attempted to do in this book is take the study of race out of the museum and into the spaces we live in and share across the color line.

Contents

Part II
PREJUDICE, DISCRIMINATION, AND RACISM 115

Part III
RACIALIZED OPPORTUNITY IN SOCIAL INSTITUTIONS 209

Preface

When it comes to race and ethnic relations in the United States, we are two nations: the nation we imagine ourselves to be as depicted in the media and the nation we actually inhabit. Reflect for a moment about how race is depicted in popular culture. Turn on the television and you enter a fantasyland where whites, blacks, Latinos, and Asians gather together to shop, eat, work, and interact in spaces where race is meaningless. In this racial utopia, a car packed with young adults from *every* racial group drives through a Checkers fast-food take-out window as the hip-hop voice-over tells us "Ya gotta eat." Car commercials as well as advertisements for ant-acids, snack foods, soda, and fast-food restaurants routinely show an America that is integrated, assimilated, and color-blind. In this carefully manufactured racial utopia, television commercials depict actors of different races interacting in race-neutral environments like Chili's or Applebee's. In Hollywood's version of U.S. race relations, one of your best friends is always from a different race. In this racial nirvana, handsome, middle-class men of varying races relax in upper-middle-class living rooms backslapping and bonding over football, Coors beer, and Domino's pizza. America's racial "presentation of self" in the media is overwhelmingly depicted as an environment that is inte-grated, multiracial, and for the most part color-blind. The media now present America as a kind of United Nations reunion party where everyone has equal social standing and equal opportunity, and everyone is middle class.

These representations of a color-blind America seri-ously misrepresent the extent to which race continues to shape the life chances of racial minorities in the United States. Consider, for example, racial diversity in corpo-rate America. Significant movement into the upper ranks of top management would indicate that racial barriers have fallen. Progress has been made in the upper ranks of corporate America, but the proportion of racial minorities now in these positions is minuscule. "The Glass Ceiling Report" produced by the U.S. Department of Labor found that "97 percent of the senior managers of Fortune 1000 industrial and Fortune 500 are white; 95 to 97 percent are male." Racial minorities make up about 30 percent of the U.S. population. All things being equal, we should expect to see about 30 percent of the top jobs going to racial minorities. What we see, however, is that only 3 percent *not* 30 percent of senior managers at Fortune 1000 and Fortune 500 companies are members of racial minorities. What does this figure say about the notion that we are now a color-blind nation?

The United States Senate provides a rather good test of the fit between how groups are presented in television dramas like *CSI* or in films at the multiplex and the politi-cal power these groups have achieved. Since there are 100 members in the U.S. Senate and racial minorities in the United States account for about 30 percent of the popula-tion, all things being equal, the Senate should have about 30 members from racial minorities. When we look at the members of the 112th Congress, however, we find only 4 racial minority members, which means that 96 senators are white. Since whites constitute about 70 percent of the pop-ulation, proportional representation suggests that whites should hold 70 Senate seats not 96. There are currently no American Indians in the U.S. Senate. Although women comprise 52 percent of the adult population (which means we should see 52 women in the Senate), there are only 17 female U.S. Senators.

It is difficult to think about life in America without directly confronting issues of race and ethnicity. Reflect for a moment on how recent events and trends both domi-nate and alter American social and cultural life: White rac-ists tie a black Texan to the back of a pickup truck and drag him to his death, while white rapper Eminem wins three Grammy awards; challenges to the University of Michigan's affirmative action program move up to the Supreme Court, creating a national dialogue on the extent to which the racial "playing field" is level; after 9/11 politicians called for tougher immigration laws, while U.S. farmers and agribusiness discuss institution of a new *bracero* farm labor program that would ease restrictions on seasonal immigrant farmworkers; Oprah Winfrey has a net worth of more than a billion dollars, while almost of a quarter of the total black population lives below the poverty line; racial profiling brings about a new term, DWB (driving while black), while Colin Powell, Denzel Washington, and Tiger Woods are consistently voted among America's most celebrated and respected people; white suburban teenagers continue to be the largest consumers of rap and hip-hop, yet racially motivated hate crimes continue to happen on campuses throughout the country; Latinos now outnumber the black population, yet each group is significantly underrepresented in Congress and in corporate America. The readings in *Rethinking the Color Line* will allow students to examine the contradictions of race and ethnicity and prepare them to live in an increasingly racially and ethnically diverse society.

Although the media have seized on a U.S. Census Bureau figure predicting that by the year 2060 whites will be outnumbered by Asians, blacks, Hispanics, and American Indians, this rather simplistic demographic forecast misses the conflicts, contradictions, and cultural convergences that currently define race and ethnic relations in the United States. *Rethinking the Color Line* is designed to help make sense of how race and ethnicity influence aspects of social life in ways that are often made invisible by culture, politics, and economics. This theoretically informed, empirically grounded reader uses a social constructionist perspective to frame and define the concepts of race and ethnicity in the United States. The selections should stimulate conversation in the classroom and allow students to think through solutions to what often seem intractable problems. As a pedagogical strategy, this text raises a number of questions in the part introductions that guide students through the readings by providing an overview of how each reading is conceptually linked to the others. Each chapter starts with "Questions to Consider," asking students to focus their attention on specific themes, issues, or questions raised in the reading. It is important to me that my students be exposed to the classic paradigms in the study of race and ethnic relations in the United States. However, just as important is my desire that students be exposed to and explore new theories and paradigms that are challenging, supplanting, and redefining the classic race and ethnicity "canon," which itself changes over time. The biologically based, pseudoscientific assumptions

that defined and guided race and ethnicity scholarship for much of this and the previous century have been debunked, discredited, and discarded. What has emerged in the last 30 years are competing narratives of what race and ethnic identity mean and the social pressures that shape those meanings. Postcolonial, postmodern, postethnic, class-based, and primordialist perspectives all claim to elucidate how race and ethnicity have been, and continue to be, thoroughly rethought.

The readings in the first part of this text provide students with the theoretical framework and analytical tools they will use throughout the book. Students come to understand what is meant by race and ethnicity as social constructions. The news, situation comedies, MTV, and racial topography of neighborhoods all become subjects for sociological scrutiny. *Rethinking the Color Line* allows students to learn how race and ethnicity influence life in ways that many students routinely take for granted. It has been my experience that a majority of students who read these articles internalize a version of the "sociological imagination" that forever changes how they understand race and ethnic relations. Raising consciousness about how each of us influences and in turn is influenced by race and ethnic relations is an explicit goal of this book.

Over the last decade I have had the luxury of testing a large number of varied readings on hundreds of students in dozens of race and ethnic relations classes at large public universities as well as small, elite liberal arts colleges. The readings in this book represent the final outcome of classroom "hits and misses." I have used classroom experiences, the results of examinations, and how easily students were able to integrate the readings into research papers to gauge (1) the extent to which the reading contributed to students' understanding of a particular theory or concept, (2) if the reading was intellectually engaging, and (3) if it lent itself to active learning in the classroom. If a reading could pass these hurdles in at least three of my classes, then it made it into this book. Teaching at both public universities and private colleges also provided me with the opportunity to observe how students from different regions, class backgrounds, and racial and ethnic identities reacted to the assigned readings. The articles speak to, challenge, and find common ground among students from racially, ethnically, culturally, and economically diverse backgrounds. *Rethinking the Color Line* is a response to my students' calls for a book that was user-friendly but did not sacrifice intellectual or theoretical rigor.

This book has been designed to be relevant for students on an individual level while also helping them understand that race and ethnic relations are embedded in the institutions that structure their lives. The readings require students to constantly negotiate the tensions between individual agency and the often determined constraints of social structure. The common thread that links these readings is the ongoing debate about the relationship between agency and structure. It is this conceptual framework that will allow students to think about race and ethnicity in fluid rather than static terms.

Changes in the Fifth Edition

The fifth edition contains ten new articles that explore a number of topics that are timely, topical, and explore how the idea of race is being refashioned by various social, political, and cultural forces. C. Matthew Snipp (reading 4) examines how institutions like the government and the U.S. Census have changed their definition of race and ethnicity every decade since the definition came into "official" use in the first census of 1790. His astute observations chronicling the ever-changing definition of race provide clear evidence of how race is indeed a social construction. David Williams and Michelle Sternthal (reading 6) examine the contributions sociologists have made to our understanding of race-based health disparities. They argue that because sociologists focus on a multiplicity of social factors that shape health outcomes, sociology as a field of inquiry provides a unique window into the reasons health outcomes vary by race. James Sterba (reading 16) provides a succinct overview of the extent to which racial and gender discrimination continues to shape the experiences of racial minorities and women. While most Americans subscribe to the idea that racial equality should be the norm, Sterba's research suggests that this is not always the case in how individuals are treated. The Arab American population is growing at a time when here in the United States there is animosity toward certain Arab nations because of the complicated geo political times in which we find ourselves. What is it like to grow up Arab American in a post-9/11, post-Osama bin-Laden era? In reading 17 Moustafa Bayoumi addresses what it is like to navigate

being Arab *and* being American in a time when many people in the United States are wary of individuals of Arab descent. In reading 27 Michelle Alexander makes a shocking assertion: The explosion in the numbers of young brown and black men who have been incarcerated since 1980 has many parallels to how racial minorities were controlled for the century that followed the end of slavery. Calling this "The New Jim Crow," she describes in detail how and why such social control maintains racial inequality. Lawrence Bobo and Victor Thompson (reading 28) examine how and why such increases in black and brown incarceration took place and what the community and societal implications of these policies have been. Everyone has watched a crime show in which DNA evidence is used to definitively demonstrate the guilt or innocence of a suspect. Sheldon Krimsky and Tania Simoncelli (reading 30) suggest that such certitude may be misplaced because there is some likelihood that racial bias may be at work in how DNA is used to locate suspects. Three new readings appear in the section on representations of race in the media. The first (reading 36), by Danielle Dirks and Jennifer Mueller, examines how derogatory ethnic and racial images are created and disseminated by the mainstream media and how these representations then become part of the American psyche. They argue that once these images become part of popular culture, they take on a life of their own, becoming the "common sense" understanding of that group. In reading 37 Marci Bounds Littlefield looks at the intersection of racial imagery in the media through the lens of gender stereotypes and how this process sexualizes African American women. In reading 38 Alicia Edison and George Yancey examine how and why biracial characters with light skin are portrayed in a positive manner while actors with dark skin tend to have negative attributes.

Appendix

The appendix, "Race by the Numbers: America's Racial Report Card," is meant to capture almost every quality-of-life measure (income, education, health, etc.) by race and ethnicity. The appendix is linked to each reading in the "Seeing the Big Picture" questions at the end of each chapter. It was designed for faculty and students to have a ready comparative reference of racial and ethnic social statistics relevant for classroom discussions and research assignments.

Supplements

Visit our Online Learning Center Web site at www.mhhe .com/Gallagher5e for robust student and instructor resources.

For students: Student resources include multiple-choice quizzes for each reading, Web links, and other study tools.

For instructors: The password-protected instructor portion of the Web site includes the instructor's manual, a comprehensive test bank, and other instructor resources.

Acknowledgments

Many thanks go to the following reviewers who provided suggestions about the form and content of *Rethinking the Color Line:* Kholoud Al-Qubbaj, Southern Utah University; Patrick C. Archer, Iowa State University; Rod Golden, Mesa Community College; Kevin Lamarr James, University of Illinois at Chicago; Demetrius Semien, University of North Carolina at Chapel Hill; Victor Thompson, San Jose State University; Will Tyson, University of South Florida; and Kathy Westman, Waubonsee Community College.

I welcome any comments, suggestions, or criticism concerning this reader. Please feel free to contact me about which readings work, which do not, or readings I might include in future editions. Please send any comments directly to me. I look forward to your feedback.

CHARLES A. GALLAGHER
Professor of Sociology and Chair
Department of Sociology and Criminal Justice
La Salle University
1900 W. Olney Ave.
Phila, PA 19141

THE SOCIOLOGICAL PROMISE IMPLICIT IN THE TITLE *RETHINKING THE COLOR LINE* IS THAT WE WILL EXPLORE THE CONTEMPORARY MEANINGS OF RACE AND ETHNICITY AND EXAMINE HOW SOCIAL, POLITICAL, ECONOMIC, AND CULTURAL FORCES SHAPE THOSE MEANINGS. This may seem like a straightforward task. It is not. Race and ethnicity are slippery concepts because they are always in a state of flux. Imagine for a moment the shape of the United States as analogous to a definition of race or ethnicity. It may appear that an outline or sketch of the U.S. border, like a definition of race or ethnicity, can be neatly described or mapped out; that is, just as we can imagine the borders of the United States, we can, with reasonable certainty, identify someone as black, white, Asian, or American Indian. We place people in these racial categories because we have been trained to focus on a combination of traits like skin color, hair texture, and eye shape. After we have placed individuals in racial categories, we typically use cultural markers, such as their ethnic background or ancestry, to further sort them. For instance, if a white person walks into a room, we *see* that individual's race. What happens when he or she starts talking and we pick up on an Irish brogue or a New York City accent or a southern dialect? What happens when the brown woman in front of us in the supermarket talks to the cashier and we recognize her accent as Jamaican or English? We tend to sort first by color and then by cultural background.

Since the founding of the United States more than two hundred years ago, the lines that have defined the nation's borders have been redrawn dozens of times. Just as there was no United States of America prior to 1776, the idea of race as it is currently understood did not exist until the Europeans colonized the Americas, Africa, and parts of Asia. The mental map we conjure up of the United States today is only about fifty years old. The map was last redrawn in 1959 when Hawaii was admitted into the Union as the fiftieth state. Previously, the map had been

RETHINKING THE COLOR LINE ~ *Understanding How Boundaries Shift*

redrawn after the Louisiana Purchase of 1803 and again after the Missouri Compromise of 1820, as well as after the admittance of every new state to the Union. And we will have to redraw our mental map yet again if the Commonwealth of Puerto Rico votes to enter the Union as the fifty-first state.

The problem with definitions of race and ethnicity, as with the shape of the United States, is that the borders or contours that give form and meaning to these concepts change over time. A person defined as white in the year 2010 might have been defined as black or Irish or Italian at various times in American history. For example, around the turn of the twentieth century, Irish and Italian immigrants were *not* viewed as white when they first arrived in the United States. At that time, members of those groups did not easily fit into the existing racial hierarchy; they were in a racial limbo—not white, not black, not Asian. Their ethnic background—that is, the language, culture, and religious beliefs that distinguished these Irish and Italian immigrants from the dominant group—was used in various ways to define them as a racial group. Within a generation or two, these so-called Irish and Italian racial groups assimilated and were absorbed into the category we now know as white. The journey from being considered not white or racially ambiguous to white was rather swift. It may seem odd, and may even shock our racial sensibilities, to think of Supreme Court Justice Antonin Scalia's or Senator Ted Kennedy's parents or grandparents as possibly being defined as nonwhite Italians or nonwhite Irish at different times in American history. But is a nonwhite Italian or nonwhite Irish any less curious an idea than a black-Irish American or an Asian-Italian American? If one's ethnic identity is subsumed or taken over by a racial identity, the question we need to ask as sociologists is, why?

Just as the shape of the United States has changed over time, so have the definitions of race and ethnicity. Do you think your view of race and ethnicity is different from that of your parents or grandparents? How you understand race and ethnicity reflects a definition specific to this moment in time, one that, in all likelihood, will look quite different in three or four decades. *Rethinking the Color Line* will provide you with a theoretical framework for understanding how and why definitions of race and ethnicity change over time, what sociological forces bring about these changes, and what these categories might look like in the future.

What these examples suggest, and what many of the readings in *Rethinking the Color Line* consciously explore, is how race and ethnicity are socially constructed. When we say that something is "socially constructed," we mean that *the characteristics deemed relevant to that definition are based on societal and cultural values.* Race and ethnicity are social constructions because their meanings are derived by focusing on arbitrary characteristics that a given society deems important. Race and ethnicity are social products based on cultural values, not scientific facts.

Think for a moment about gravity. If you push this book off your desk, do you expect it to fall to the ground? Obviously, you do. If you lived in Brazil or South Africa or Puerto Rico, would you expect the same thing to happen to your book? Of course you would, because you know that gravity is a universal constant. However, someone defined as black in the United States could be defined as white in Brazil, Trigueno (intermediate) in Puerto Rico, and "coloured" in South Africa. Gravity is the same everywhere, but racial classifications vary across place and time because definitions of race and ethnicity are based on the physical traits a society chooses to value or devalue. Because each society's values are based on a different set of historical experiences, cultural circumstances, and political definitions, ideas about race and ethnicity can vary quite a bit, not only between countries

but within them as well. For example, historically, it was not uncommon for someone to have been socially and legally defined as black in the southern part of the United States but to "pass" for white after migrating north. The beliefs and definitions that undergird the idea of race are very unstable and, as we will see in the readings, quite susceptible to political manipulation.

Racial and ethnic identity is culturally meaningful only because we define and understand it in that way. In other words, race exists because we say race exists. And because the characteristics that make up the idea of race and ethnicity reflect a social process, it is possible to imagine these concepts in a different way. Instead of looking at skin color, facial features, or hair texture as a way to sort individuals, we could create a racial category based on the size of people's feet. People with shoe sizes between 4 and 7 would be labeled the Petite Race, those with sizes 8–11 would be designated the Bigger Race, and the 12–15 shoe size crowd would be categorized as the Monster Foot Race. Those with feet smaller or larger than the existing categories would be the "Other" Race. Likewise, we could use eye color, height, glove size, or nose length to create racial categories. Because the physical markers we use to define race are arbitrary and have no basis in genetics, biology, anthropology, or sociology, using shoe size as the criterion to fashion a new definition of race would be just as valid as the system currently in place. Similarly, we could redefine ethnicity by changing the focus from language, culture, religion, or nationality as a method of sorting people and instead create categories of people based on the amount of meat they eat or the way they style their hair.

What complicates our ability to accurately and easily map these definitions of race and ethnicity is that the definitions are constantly changing. Are the 40+ million Latinos in the United States an ethnic group because they are defined by the U.S. Census Bureau as such, or are Latinos a racial group? If the current census categories of white, black, Asian, and American Indian do not adequately reflect what Latinos experience or how Latinos are viewed by non-Latinos, should a "brown" category be added to the census? Would a newly created "brown" category link Puerto Ricans in New York City with Cuban Americans in Miami and Mexican Americans in San Diego? Why or why not? How should we define the race of a child whose father is Mexican-African American and whose mother is Japanese-Irish American? What is this child's ethnicity? For that matter, how and in what ways are race and ethnicity related?

In 1903, sociologist W. E. B. Du Bois wrote "the problem of the twentieth century is the problem of the color-line." It appears that a key problem of the twenty-first century, while different in degree and context from the one Du Bois chronicled, will still be the color line. A topic or issue may not initially seem to be linked to race or ethnicity, but on closer sociological scrutiny, patterns often emerge that make it clear that race and ethnicity matter quite a bit. How do you see race and ethnicity being connected to who gets a good education or adequate health care, who is likely to be poor, where toxic waste sites are built, who gets hired or promoted, or who is more likely to be sentenced to death and executed? Race and ethnicity are intertwined in every aspect of our lives.

Rethinking the Color Line will provide you with the tools necessary to navigate the complicated and often contradictory meanings of race and ethnicity in the United States. The readings will take you on a sociological journey and explore how you, your classmates, your family, and your friends fit into the racial and ethnic mosaic of the United States. If you focus carefully on the readings, the "Questions to Consider" that introduce them, and the "Seeing the Big Picture" discussion at the end of most chapters, your perspective on race and ethnic relations in the United States will be changed forever. ✳

WHO TAUGHT YOU HOW TO "BE" BLACK or American Indian or white or Asian? Did you learn to "do" your race by watching sitcoms on television or by watching your peers in the schoolyard? Was it your parents or an older sibling or cousin who taught you how to act both your age and your race? In what social situations do you think about your racial identity? Is it only when you interact with an individual from a different racial background? Do you think about your race, about other racial groups, or about race relations when you watch football games or MTV or the nightly news? Do you think about your race while you are in your neighborhood or only when you drive through an area with a different racial population? Were you ever in a social setting in which you were the only person of your color? How did that make you feel?

How did you learn to "be" Korean or Jamaican or German? In what situations do you think about your ancestry? Is it during the holidays or when you spend time with your family? Or has your family been in the United States for so many generations that the family tree linking you to the homeland is unimportant, nonexistent, or untraceable? Does that mean you have a racial identity but not an ethnic identity? Or does "American" best mirror your social identity?

The readings in Part I answer these questions by exposing you to the social theories used to define and understand the dynamics of race and ethnicity. The first five readings, in **Race and Ethnicity: Sociohistoric Constructions,** examine how the natural variation in human skin color has been used as a way to sort people into groups, create a racial hierarchy, and justify exploitation based on skin color. Marvin Harris explains why gradations of color, from black to white, are "beautiful" sociocultural responses to the environment. Howard Zinn charts the evolution of the idea of race in early U.S. history and how the idea of racial categories was synonymous with who would be free and who would be enslaved. Michael Omi and Howard Winant explain the emergence of racial categories as a "sociohistoric" process

SORTING BY COLOR ~
Why We Attach Meaning to Race

they call racial formation; that is, the way we define ourselves racially reflects a political and social process that was hundreds of years in the making. C. Matthew Snipp provides an overview of the theories central to ethnic and racial studies, theories that will reemerge throughout the book. Eduardo Bonilla-Silva suggests that race, like class or gender, takes on a "life of its own," creating hierarchical social relations that are exploitive and coercive. As you will see throughout the text, many of the articles in this reader draw on one or more of these theories to explain a particular aspect of racial inequality and race and ethnic relations.

The next two readings, in **Race and Ethnicity: Contemporary Socioeconomic Trends,** draw on theories outlined in the first section while emphasizing socioeconomic disparities between racial and ethnic groups. David Williams and Michelle Sternthal examine racial and ethnic inequalities in health and how sociology's unique focus on social structure provides insight into the factors that lead to racial differences in disease. Not only are racial minorities worse off compared to whites on almost every health measure, but it is likely this gap will continue to grow as the United States limits access to public health care for the poor. Using national data on wealth, Thomas Shapiro examines the racial dynamics of how transformative assets, the financial assistance one gets from families, shapes life chances.

In **Race as Chameleon: How the Idea of Race Changes over Time and Place,** F. James Davis uses the "one-drop rule" to map the ever changing definition of race by focusing on the various "status and identity positions"

5

that emerged as groups mixed across the color line. What is important to note is that the definitions forced on mixed race groups reflected power relations and the desire to fashion various social buffers that maintained white supremacy.

Both David Wilkins and Yen Le Espiritu demonstrate how, why, and in what situations racial and ethnic identities are used to organize politically. It is often the case that those in power thrust a racial identity upon a group even though there may be enormous cultural diversity within that group. Chinese, Japanese, and Koreans "became" Asian through the racialization process.

Throughout this book I will be arguing that the idea of race is not static. Jennifer Lee and Frank Bean suggest that we are yet again at a crossroads in the construction of how we think about racial categories as the number of individuals who define themselves as "multiracial" grows. As these readings demonstrate, the creation of racial categories is as much a historical process as it is a political one.

The next three readings, in **Color-Blind America: Fact, Fantasy, or Our Future,** focus on how different social conditions can exacerbate racial and ethnic relations and what might be done at both the macro and micro levels to ameliorate racial inequality. Professor Charles A. Gallagher notes that current trends in popular culture have blurred the color line by linking the consumption of products across racial groups to racial harmony. If groups from various races now share and consume the same products (hip-hop, McDonalds, reality TV), Gallagher asks, has racial equality been achieved? Lani Guinier and Gerald Torres make the case that descriptions of the United States as a color-blind nation are quite premature, and Herbert Gans argues that a "beige-ing" of America is taking place that will incorporate some parts of the Latino and Asian populations but not blacks. The color line will shift, Gans argues, but not necessarily in a way that is inclusive. Each of these readings points to the various social, economic, and cultural barriers to racial equality and the rather lofty goal of becoming a truly color-blind nation. ✳

How Our Skins Got Their Color
Marvin Harris

The late MARVIN HARRIS spent a portion of his life teaching in the anthropology department at Columbia University, where he served as department chair. He published sixteen books, including *Cannibals and Kings; Culture, People, and Nature;* and *Our Kind.*

Questions to Consider   Cultural anthropologist Marvin Harris links the variations in skin color one can observe in traveling around the world to the human body's ability to adapt physically to changes in exposure to solar radiation. How do you explain his assertion that "white was beautiful because white was healthy" and "black was beautiful because black was healthy"?

MOST HUMAN BEINGS ARE NEITHER VERY fair nor very dark, but brown. The extremely fair skin of northern Europeans and their descendants, and the very black skins of central Africans and their descendants, are probably special adaptations. Brown-skinned ancestors may have been shared by modern-day blacks and whites as recently as 10,000 years ago. Human skin owes its color to the presence of particles known as **melanin.** The primary function of melanin is to protect the upper levels of the skin from being damaged by the sun's ultraviolet rays. This radiation poses a critical problem for our kind because we lack the dense coat of hair that acts as a sunscreen for most mammals. . . . Hairlessness exposes us to two kinds of radiation hazards: ordinary sunburn, with its blisters, rashes, and risk of infection; and skin cancers, including malignant melanoma, one of the deadliest diseases known. Melanin is the body's first line of defense against these afflictions. The more melanin particles, the darker the skin, and the lower the risk of sunburn and all forms of skin cancer. This explains why the highest rates for skin cancer are found in sun-drenched lands such as Australia, where light-skinned people of European descent spend a good part of their lives outdoors wearing

melanin The pigment that gives the skin its color. Melanin protects the skin from the ultraviolet rays associated with various skin cancers. Populations living near the equator have darker skin to protect them from the harsh effects of the sun.

scanty attire. Very dark-skinned people such as heavily pigmented Africans of Zaire seldom get skin cancer, but when they do, they get it on depigmented parts of their bodies—palms and lips.

If exposure to solar radiation had nothing but harmful effects, natural selection would have favored inky black as the color for all human populations. But the sun's rays do not present an unmitigated threat. As it falls on the skin, sunshine converts a fatty substance in the epidermis into vitamin D. The blood carries vitamin D from the skin to the intestines (technically making it a hormone rather than a vitamin), where it plays a vital role in the absorption of calcium. In turn, calcium is vital for strong bones. Without it, people fall victim to the crippling diseases rickets and osteomalacia. In women, calcium deficiencies can result in a deformed birth canal, which makes childbirth lethal for both mother and fetus.

Vitamin D can be obtained from a few foods, primarily the oils and livers of marine fish. But inland populations must rely on the sun's rays and their own skins for the supply of this crucial substance. The particular color of a human population's skin, therefore, represents in large degree a trade-off between the hazards of too much versus too little solar radiation: acute sunburn and skin cancer on the one hand, and rickets and osteomalacia on the other. It is this trade-off that largely accounts for the preponderance of brown people in the world and for the general tendency for skin color to be darkest among **equatorial populations** and lightest among populations dwelling at higher latitudes.

At middle latitudes, the skin follows a strategy of changing colors with the seasons. Around the Mediterranean basin, for example, exposure to the summer sun brings high risk of cancer but low risk for rickets; the body produces more melanin and people grow darker (i.e., they get suntans). Winter reduces the risk of sunburn and cancer; the body produces less melanin, and the tan wears off.

The correlation between skin color and latitude is not perfect because other factors—such as the availability of foods containing vitamin D and calcium, regional cloud cover during the winter, amount of clothing worn, and cultural preferences—may work for or against the predicted relationship. Arctic-dwelling Eskimo, for example, are not as light-skinned as expected, but their habitat and economy afford them a diet that is exceptionally rich in both vitamin D and calcium.

Northern Europeans, obliged to wear heavy garments for protection against the long, cold, cloudy winters, were always at risk for rickets and osteomalacia from too little vitamin D and calcium. This risk increased sometime after 6000 B.C., when pioneer cattle herders who did not exploit marine resources began to appear in northern Europe. The risk would have been especially great for the brown-skinned Mediterranean peoples who migrated northward along with the crops and farm animals. Samples of Caucasian skin (infant penile foreskin obtained at the time of circumcision) exposed to sunlight on cloudless days in Boston (42°N) from November through February produced no vitamin D. In Edmonton (52°N) this period extended from October to March. But further south (34°N) sunlight was effective in producing vitamin D in

the middle of the winter. Almost all of Europe lies north of 42°N. Fair-skinned, nontanning individuals who could utilize the weakest and briefest doses of sunlight to synthesize vitamin D were strongly favored by **natural selection.** During the frigid winters, only a small circle of a child's face could be left to peek out at the sun through the heavy clothing, thereby favoring the survival of individuals with translucent patches of pink on their cheeks characteristic of many northern Europeans. (People who could get calcium by drinking cow's milk would also be favored by natural selection.)

If light-skinned individuals on the average had only 2 percent more children survive per generation, the changeover in their skin color could have begun 5,000 years ago and reached present levels well before the beginning of the Christian era. But natural selection need not have acted alone. **Cultural selection** may also have played a role. It seems likely that whenever people consciously or unconsciously had to decide which infants to nourish and which to neglect, the advantage would go to those with lighter skin, experience having shown that such individuals tended to grow up to be taller, stronger, and healthier than their darker siblings. White was beautiful because white was healthy.

To account for the evolution of black skin in equatorial latitudes, one has merely to reverse the combined effects of natural and cultural selection. With the sun directly overhead most of the year, and clothing a hindrance to work and survival, vitamin D was never in short supply (and calcium was easily obtained from vegetables). Rickets and osteomalacia were rare. Skin cancer was the main problem, and what nature started, culture amplified. Darker infants were favored by parents because experience showed that they grew up to be freer of disfiguring and lethal malignancies. Black was beautiful because black was healthy.

equatorial populations Populations living near the equator.

natural selection In his 1859 book *The Origin of Species*, Charles Darwin describes the process by which nature "selects" the best-adapted varieties of animals for survival.

cultural selection The idea that, in ways that mirror natural selection, society "selects" those cultural traits that will enhance the survival of a particular civilization.

2 Drawing the Color Line

Howard Zinn

The late **HOWARD ZINN** professor, activist, and author, dedicated his life to the notion that the knowledge of history is important to people's everyday lives and can be a powerful force for social change.

A BLACK AMERICAN WRITER, J. SAUNDERS Redding, describes the arrival of a ship in North America in the year 1619:

> Sails furled, flag drooping at her rounded stern, she rode the tide in from the sea. She was a strange ship, indeed, by all accounts, a frightening ship, a ship of mystery. Whether she was trader, privateer, or man-of-war no one knows. Through her bulwarks black-mouthed cannon yawned. The flag she flew was Dutch; her crew a motley. Her port of call, an English settlement, Jamestown, in the colony of Virginia. She came, she traded, and shortly afterwards was gone. Probably no ship in modern history has carried a more portentous freight. Her cargo? Twenty slaves.

There is not a country in world history in which racism has been more important, for so long a time, as the United States. And the problem of "the color line," as W. E. B. Du Bois put it, is still with us. So it is more than a purely historical question to ask: How does it start?—and an even more urgent question: How might it end? Or, to put it differently: Is it possible for whites and blacks to live together without hatred?

If history can help answer these questions, then the beginnings of slavery in North America—a continent where we can trace the coming of the first whites and the first blacks—might supply at least a few clues.

Some historians think those first blacks in Virginia were considered as servants, like the white **indentured servants** brought from Europe. But the strong probability is

indentured servant Historically, a laborer under contract to an employer for some period of time, usually seven years, in exchange for travel, food, and accommodations. Servants often became indebted to their employer and were often subject to violence.

Questions to Consider In this article Howard Zinn chronicles the beginning of slavery in North America. How did law, custom, and culture reconcile the emergence of chattel slavery with Christian precepts, which reject the idea that one human can own or forcibly control another human being? What arguments were used to justify slavery? List which groups profited from the slave trade.

that, even if they were listed as "servants" (a more familiar category to the English), they were viewed as being different from white servants, were treated differently, and in fact were slaves. In any case, slavery developed quickly into a regular institution, into the normal labor relation of blacks to whites in the New World. With it developed that special racial feeling—whether hatred, or contempt, or pity, or patronization—that accompanied the inferior position of blacks in America for the next 350 years—that combination of inferior status and derogatory thought we call racism.

Everything in the experience of the first white settlers acted as a pressure for the enslavement of blacks.

The Virginians of 1619 were desperate for labor, to grow enough food to stay alive. Among them were survivors from the winter of 1609–1610, the "starving time," when, crazed for want of food, they roamed the woods for nuts and berries, dug up graves to eat the corpses, and died in batches until five hundred colonists were reduced to sixty.

In the *Journals* of the House of Burgesses of Virginia is a document of 1619 which tells of the first twelve years of the Jamestown colony. The first settlement had a hundred persons, who had one small ladle of barley per meal. When more people arrived, there was even less food. Many of the people lived in cavelike holes dug into the ground, and in the winter of 1609–1610, they were driven thru insufferable hunger to eat those things which nature most abhorred, the flesh and excrements of man as well of our own nation as of an Indian, digged by some out of his grave after he had lain buried three days and wholly devoured him; others, envying the better state of body of any whom hunger has not yet so much wasted as their own, lay wait and threatened to kill and eat them; one among them slew his wife as she slept in his bosom, cut her in pieces, salted her and fed upon her till he had clean devoured all parts saving her head.

A petition by thirty colonists to the House of Burgesses, complaining against the twelve-year governorship of Sir Thomas Smith, said:

In those 12 years of Sir Thomas Smith, his government, we aver that the colony for the most part remained in great want and misery under most severe and cruel laws. . . . The allowance in those times for a man was only eight ounces of meale and half a pint of peas for a day . . . mouldy, rotten, full of cobwebs and maggots, loathsome to man and not fit for beasts, which forced many to flee for relief to the savage enemy, who being taken again were put to sundry deaths as by hanging, shooting and breaking upon the wheel . . . of whom one for stealing two or three pints of oatmeal had a bodkin thrust through his tongue and was tied with a chain to a tree until he starved.

The Virginians needed labor, to grow corn for subsistence, to grow tobacco for export. They had just figured out how to grow tobacco, and in 1617 they sent off the first cargo to England. Finding that, like all pleasurable drugs tainted with moral disapproval, it brought a high price, the planters, despite their high religious talk, were not going to ask questions about something so profitable.

They couldn't force Indians to work for them, as Columbus had done. They were outnumbered, and while, with superior firearms, they could massacre Indians, they would face massacre in return. They could not capture them and keep them enslaved; the Indians were tough, resourceful, defiant, and at home in these woods, as the transplanted Englishmen were not.

White servants had not yet been brought over in sufficient quantity. Besides, they did not come out of slavery, and did not have to do more than contract their labor for a few years to get their passage and a start in the New World. As for the free white settlers, many of them were skilled craftsmen, or even men of leisure back in England, who were so little inclined to work the land that John

Smith, in those early years, had to declare a kind of martial law, organize them into work gangs, and force them into the fields for survival.

There may have been a kind of frustrated rage at their own ineptitude, at the Indian superiority at taking care of themselves, that made the Virginians especially ready to become the masters of slaves. Edmund Morgan imagines their mood as he writes in his book *American Slavery, American Freedom:*

If you were a colonist, you knew that your technology was superior to the Indians'. You knew that you were civilized, and they were savages. . . . But your superior technology had proved insufficient to extract anything. The Indians, keeping to themselves, laughed at your superior methods and lived from the land more abundantly and with less labor than you did. . . . And when your own people started deserting in order to live with them, it was too much. . . . So you killed the Indians, tortured them, burned their villages, burned their cornfields. It proved your superiority, in spite of your failures. And you gave similar treatment to any of your own people who succumbed to their savage ways of life. But you still did not grow much corn.

Black slaves were the answer. And it was natural to consider imported blacks as slaves, even if the institution of slavery would not be regularized and legalized for several decades. Because, by 1619, a million blacks had already been brought from Africa to South America and the Caribbean, to the Portuguese and Spanish colonies, to work as slaves. Fifty years before Columbus, the Portuguese took ten African blacks to Lisbon—this was the start of a regular trade in slaves. African blacks had been stamped as slave labor for a hundred years. So it would have been strange if those twenty blacks, forcibly transported to Jamestown, and sold as objects to settlers anxious for a steadfast source of labor, were considered as anything but slaves.

Their helplessness made enslavement easier. The Indians were on their own land. The whites were in their own European culture. The blacks had been torn from their land and culture, forced into a situation where the heritage of language, dress, custom, family relations, was bit by bit obliterated except for the remnants that blacks could hold on to by sheer, extraordinary persistence.

Was their culture inferior—and so subject to easy destruction? Inferior in military capability, yes—vulnerable to whites with guns and ships. But in no other way—except that cultures that are different are often taken as inferior, especially when such a judgment is practical and profitable. Even militarily, while the Westerners could secure forts on the African coast, they were unable to subdue the interior and had to come to terms with its chiefs.

The African civilization was as advanced in its own way as that of Europe. In certain ways, it was more admirable; but it also included cruelties, hierarchical privilege, and the readiness to sacrifice human lives for religion or profit. It was a civilization of 100 million people, using iron implements and skilled in farming. It had large urban centers and remarkable achievements in weaving, ceramics, sculpture.

European travelers in the sixteenth century were impressed with the African kingdoms of Timbuktu and Mali, already stable and organized at a time when European states were just beginning to develop into the modern nation. In 1563, Ramusio, secretary to the rulers in Venice, wrote to the Italian merchants: "Let them go and do business with the King of Timbuktu and Mali and there is no doubt that they will be well-received there with their ships and their goods and treated well, and granted the favours that they ask."

A Dutch report, around 1602, on the West African kingdom of Benin, said: "The Towne seemeth to be very great, when you enter it. You go into a great broad street, not paved, which seemeth to be seven or eight times broader than the Warmoes Street in Amsterdam. . . . The Houses in this Towne stand in good order, one close and even with the other, as the Houses in Holland stand."

The inhabitants of the Guinea Coast were described by one traveler around 1680 as "very civil and good-natured people, easy to be dealt with, condescending to what Europeans require of them in a civil way, and very ready to return double the presents we make them."

Africa had a kind of **feudalism,** like Europe based on agriculture, and with hierarchies of lords and vassals. But African feudalism did not come, as did Europe's, out of the slave societies of Greece and Rome, which had destroyed ancient tribal life. In Africa, tribal life was still powerful, and some of its better features—a communal spirit, more kindness in law and punishment—still existed. And because the lords did not have the weapons that European lords had, they could not command obedience as easily.

feudalism A medieval European political system in which land was leased through the king to barons and knights who engaged serfs to work the land in return for military protection. The system was based on military, social, and economic obligations and enforced through law, custom, and religion.

In his book *The African Slave Trade,* Basil Davidson contrasts law in the Congo in the early sixteenth century with law in Portugal and England. In those European countries, where the idea of private property was becoming powerful, theft was punished brutally. In England, even as late as 1740, a child could be hanged for stealing a rag of cotton. But in the Congo, communal life persisted, the idea of private property was a strange one, and thefts were punished with fines or various degrees of servitude. A Congolese leader, told of the Portuguese legal codes, asked a Portuguese once, teasingly: "What is the penalty in Portugal for anyone who puts his feet on the ground?"

Slavery existed in the African states, and it was sometimes used by Europeans to justify their own slave trade. But, as Davidson points out, the "slaves" of Africa were more like the serfs of Europe—in other words, like most of the population of Europe. It was a harsh servitude, but they had rights which slaves brought to America did not have, and they were "altogether different from the human cattle of the slave ships and the American plantations." In the Ashanti Kingdom of West Africa, one observer noted that "a slave might marry; own property; himself own a slave; swear an oath; be a competent witness and ultimately become heir to his master. . . . An Ashanti slave, nine cases out of ten, possibly became an adopted member of the family, and in time his descendants so merged and intermarried with the owner's kinsmen that only a few would know their origin."

One slave trader, John Newton (who later became an antislavery leader), wrote about the people of what is now Sierra Leone:

The state of slavery, among these wild barbarous people, as we esteem them, is much milder than in our colonies. For as, on the one hand, they have no land in high cultivation, like our West India plantations, and therefore no call for that excessive, unintermitted labour, which exhausts our slaves: so, on the other hand, no man is permitted to draw blood even from a slave.

African slavery is hardly to be praised. But it was far different from plantation or mining slavery in the Americas, which was lifelong, morally crippling, destructive of family ties, and without hope of any future. African slavery lacked two elements that made American slavery the most cruel form of slavery in history: the frenzy for limitless profit that comes from capitalistic agriculture; the reduction of the slave to less than human status by the use of racial hatred, with that relentless clarity based on color, where white was master, black was slave.

In fact, it was because they came from a settled culture, of tribal customs and family ties, of communal life and traditional ritual, that African blacks found themselves especially helpless when removed from this. They were captured in the interior (frequently by blacks caught up in the slave trade themselves), sold on the coast, then shoved into pens with blacks of other tribes, often speaking different languages.

The conditions of capture and sale were crushing affirmations to the black African of his helplessness in the face of superior force. The marches to the coast, sometimes for 1,000 miles, with people shackled around the neck, under whip and gun, were death marches, in which two of every five blacks died. On the coast, they were kept in cages until they were picked and sold. One John Barbot, at the end of the seventeenth century, described these cages on the Gold Coast:

> As the slaves come down to Fida from the inland country, they are put into a booth or prison . . . near the beach, and when the Europeans are to receive them, they are brought out onto a large plain, where the ship's surgeons examine every part of everyone of them, to the smallest member, men and women being stark naked. . . . Such as are allowed good and sound are set on one side . . . marked on the breast with a red-hot iron, imprinting the mark of the French, English, or Dutch companies. . . . The branded slaves after this are returned to their former booths where they await shipment, sometimes 10–15 days.

Then they were packed aboard the slave ships, in spaces not much bigger than coffins, chained together in the dark, wet slime of the ship's bottom, choking in the stench of their own excrement. Documents of the time describe the conditions:

> The height, sometimes, between decks, was only eighteen inches; so that the unfortunate human beings could not turn around, or even on their sides, the elevation being less than the breadth of their shoulders; and here they are usually chained to the decks by the neck and legs. In such a place the sense of misery and suffocation is so great, that the Negroes . . . are driven to frenzy.

On one occasion, hearing a great noise from below decks where the blacks were chained together, the sailors opened the hatches and found the slaves in different stages of suffocation, many dead, some having killed others in desperate attempts to breathe. Slaves often jumped overboard to drown rather than continue their suffering.

To one observer a slave-deck was "so covered with blood and mucus that it resembled a slaughter house."

Under these conditions, perhaps one of every three blacks transported overseas died, but the huge profits (often double the investment on one trip) made it worthwhile for the slave trader, and so the blacks were packed into the holds like fish.

First the Dutch, then the English, dominated the slave trade. (By 1795 Liverpool had more than a hundred ships carrying slaves and accounted for half of all the European slave trade.) Some Americans in New England entered the business, and in 1637 the first American slave ship, the *Desire,* sailed from Marblehead. Its holds were partitioned into racks, 2 feet by 6 feet, with leg irons and bars.

By 1800, 10 to 15 million blacks had been transported as slaves to the Americas, representing perhaps one-third of those originally seized in Africa. It is roughly estimated that Africa lost 50 million human beings to death and slavery in those centuries we call the beginnings of modern Western civilization, at the hands of slave traders and plantation owners in Western Europe and America, the countries deemed the most advanced in the world.

In the year 1610, a Catholic priest in the Americas named Father Sandoval wrote back to a church functionary in Europe to ask if the capture, transport, and enslavement of African blacks was legal by church doctrine. A letter dated March 12, 1610, from Brother Luis Brandaon to Father Sandoval gives the answer:

> Your Reverence writes me that you would like to know whether the Negroes who are sent to your parts have been legally captured. To this I reply that I think your Reverence should have no scruples on this point, because this is a matter which has been questioned by the Board of Conscience in Lisbon, and all its members are learned and conscientious men. Nor did the bishops who were in Sao Thome, Cape Verde, and here in Loando—all learned and virtuous men—find fault with it. We have been here ourselves for forty years and there have been among us very learned Fathers . . . never did they consider the trade as illicit. Therefore we and the Fathers of Brazil buy these slaves for our service without any scruple.

With all of this—the desperation of the Jamestown settlers for labor, the impossibility of using Indians and the difficulty of using whites, the availability of blacks offered in greater and greater numbers by profit-seeking dealers in human flesh, and with such blacks possible to control because they had just gone through an ordeal which if it did not kill them must have left them in a state of psychic and physical helplessness—is it any wonder that such blacks were ripe for enslavement?

And under these conditions, even if some blacks might have been considered servants, would blacks be treated the same as white servants?

The evidence, from the court records of colonial Virginia, shows that in 1630 a white man named Hugh Davis was ordered "to be soundly whipt . . . for abusing himself . . . by defiling his body in lying with a Negro." Ten years later, six servants and "a negro of Mr. Reynolds" started to run away. While the whites received lighter sentences, "Emanuel the Negro to receive thirty stripes and to be burnt in the cheek with the letter R, and to work in shackle one year or more as his master shall see cause."

Although slavery was not yet regularized or legalized in those first years, the lists of servants show blacks listed separately. A law passed in 1639 decreed that "all persons except Negroes" were to get arms and ammunition—probably to fight off Indians. When in 1640 three servants tried to run away, the two whites were punished with a lengthening of their service. But, as the court put it, "the third being a negro named John Punch shall serve his master or his assigns for the time of his natural life." Also in 1640, we have the case of a Negro woman servant who begot a child by Robert Sweat, a white man. The court ruled "that the said negro woman shall be whipt at the whipping post and the said Sweat shall tomorrow in the forenoon do public penance for his offense at James citychurch."

This unequal treatment, this developing combination of contempt and oppression, feeling and action, which we call "**racism**"—was this the result of a "natural" antipathy of white against black? The question is important, not just as a matter of historical accuracy, but because any emphasis on "natural" racism lightens the responsibility of the social system. If racism can't be shown to be natural, then it is the result of certain conditions, and we are impelled to eliminate those conditions.

We have no way of testing the behavior of whites and blacks toward one another under favorable conditions—with no history of subordination, no money incentive for

racism The assigning of attitudes, behaviors, and abilities to individuals or groups based on skin color; includes the institutional arrangements that privilege one group over another and the ideological apparatus that perpetuates and makes those arrangements possible.

exploitation and enslavement, no desperation for survival requiring forced labor. All the conditions for black and white in seventeenth-century America were the opposite of that, all powerfully directed toward antagonism and mistreatment. Under such conditions even the slightest display of humanity between the races might be considered evidence of a basic human drive toward community.

Sometimes it is noted that, even before 1600, when the slave trade had just begun, before Africans were stamped by it—literally and symbolically—the color black was distasteful. In England, before 1600, it meant, according to the *Oxford English Dictionary:* "Deeply stained with dirt; soiled, dirty, foul. Having dark or deadly purposes, malignant; pertaining to or involving death, deadly; baneful, disastrous, sinister. Foul, iniquitous, atrocious, horribly wicked. Indicating disgrace, censure, liability to punishment, etc." And Elizabethan poetry often used the color white in connection with beauty.

It may be that, in the absence of any other overriding factor, darkness and blackness, associated with night and unknown, would take on those meanings. But the presence of another human being is a powerful fact, and the conditions of that presence are crucial in determining whether an initial prejudice, against a mere color, divorced from humankind, is turned into brutality and hatred.

In spite of such preconceptions about blackness, in spite of special subordination of blacks in the Americas in the seventeenth century, there is evidence that where whites and blacks found themselves with common problems, common work, common enemy in their master, they behaved toward one another as equals. As one scholar of slavery, Kenneth Stampp, has put it, Negro and white servants of the seventeenth century were "remarkably unconcerned about the visible physical differences."

Black and white worked together, fraternized together. The very fact that laws had to be passed after a while to forbid such relations indicates the strength of that tendency. In 1661 a law was passed in Virginia that "in case any English servant shall run away in company of any Negroes" he would have to give special service for extra years to the master of the runaway Negro. In 1691, Virginia provided for the banishment of any "white man or woman being free who shall intermarry with a negro, mulatoo, or Indian man or woman bond or free."

There is an enormous difference between a feeling of racial strangeness, perhaps fear, and the mass enslavement of millions of black people that took place in the Americas. The transition from one to the other cannot be explained easily by "natural" tendencies. It is not hard to understand as the outcome of historical conditions.

Slavery grew as the plantation system grew. The reason is easily traceable to something other than natural racial repugnance: the number of arriving whites, whether free or indentured servants (under four to seven years contract), was not enough to meet the need of the plantations. By 1700, in Virginia, there were 6,000 slaves, one-twelfth of the population. By 1763, there were 170,000 slaves, about half the population.

Blacks were easier to enslave than whites or Indians. But they were still not easy to enslave. From the beginning, the imported black men and women resisted their enslavement. Ultimately their resistance was controlled, and slavery was established for 3 million blacks in the South. Still, under the most difficult conditions, under pain of mutilation and death, throughout their two hundred years of enslavement in North America, these Afro-Americans continued to rebel. Only occasionally was there an organized insurrection. More often they showed their refusal to submit by running away. Even more often, they engaged in sabotage, slowdowns, and subtle forms of resistance which asserted, if only to themselves and their brothers and sisters, their dignity as human beings.

The refusal began in Africa. One slave trader reported that Negroes were "so wilful and loth to leave their own country, that they have often leap'd out of the canoes, boat and ship into the sea, and kept under water till they were drowned."

When the very first black slaves were brought into Hispaniola in 1503, the Spanish governor of Hispaniola complained to the Spanish court that fugitive Negro slaves were teaching disobedience to the Indians. In the 1520s and 1530s, there were slave revolts in Hispaniola, Puerto Rico, Santa Marta, and what is now Panama. Shortly after those rebellions, the Spanish established a special police for chasing fugitive slaves.

A Virginia statute of 1669 referred to "the obstinacy of many of them," and in 1680 the Assembly took note of slave meetings "under the pretense of feasts and brawls" which they considered of "dangerous consequence." In 1687, in the colony's Northern Neck, a plot was discovered in which slaves planned to kill all the whites in the area and escape during a mass funeral.

Gerald Mullin, who studied slave resistance in eighteenth-century Virginia in his work *Flight and Rebellion,* reports:

> The available sources on slavery in 18th-century Virginia—plantation and county records, the newspaper advertisements for runaways—describe rebellious slaves and few others. The slaves described were lazy and thieving; they feigned illnesses, destroyed crops, stores, tools, and sometimes attacked or killed overseers. They operated blackmarkets in stolen goods. Runaways were defined as various types, they were truants (who usually returned voluntarily), "outlaws" . . . and slaves who were actually fugitives: men who visited relatives, went to town to pass as free, or tried to escape slavery completely, either by boarding ships and leaving the colony, or banding together in cooperative efforts to establish villages or hide-outs in the frontier. The commitment of another type of rebellious slave was total; these men became killers, arsonists, and insurrectionists.

Slaves recently from Africa, still holding on to the heritage of their communal society, would run away in groups and try to establish villages of runaways out in the wilderness, on the frontier. Slaves born in America, on the other hand, were more likely to run off alone, and, with the skills they had learned on the plantation, try to pass as free men.

In the colonial papers of England, a 1729 report from the lieutenant governor of Virginia to the British Board of Trade tells how "a number of Negroes, about fifteen . . . formed a design to withdraw from their Master and to fix themselves in the fastnesses of the neighboring Mountains. They had found means to get into their possession some Arms and Ammunition, and they took along with them some Provisions, their Cloths, bedding and working Tools. . . . Tho' this attempt has happily been defeated, it ought nevertheless to awaken us into some effectual measures."

Slavery was immensely profitable to some masters. James Madison told a British visitor shortly after the American Revolution that he could make $257 on every Negro in a year, and spend only $12 or $13 on his keep. Another viewpoint was of slaveowner Landon Carter, writing about fifty years earlier, complaining that his slaves so neglected their work and were so uncooperative ("either cannot or will not work") that he began to wonder if keeping them was worthwhile.

Some historians have painted a picture—based on the infrequency of organized rebellions and the ability of the

South to maintain slavery for two hundred years—of a slave population made submissive by their condition; with their African heritage destroyed, they were, as Stanley Elkins said, made into "Sambos," "a society of helpless dependents." Or as another historian, Ulrich Phillips, said, "by racial quality submissive." But looking at the totality of slave behavior, at the resistance of everyday life, from quiet noncooperation in work to running away, the picture becomes different.

In 1710, warning the Virginia Assembly, Governor Alexander Spotswood said:

> freedom wears a cap which can without a tongue, call together all those who long to shake off the fetters of slavery and as such an Insurrection would surely be attended with most dreadful consequences so I think we cannot be too early in providing against it, both by putting our selves in a better posture of defence and by making a law to prevent the consultations of those Negroes.

Indeed, considering the harshness of punishment for running away, that so many blacks did run away must be a sign of a powerful rebelliousness. All through the 1700s, the Virginia slave code read:

> Whereas many times slaves run away and lie hid and lurking in swamps, woods, and other obscure places, killing hogs, and commiting other injuries to the inhabitants . . . if the slave does not immediately return, anyone what soever may kill or destroy such slaves by such ways and means as he . . . shall think fit. . . . If the slave is apprehended . . . it shall . . . be lawful for the county court, to order such punishment for the said slave, either by dismembering, or in any other way . . . as they in their discretion shall think fit, for the reclaiming any such incorrigible slave, and terrifying others from the like practices.

Mullin found newspaper advertisements between 1736 and 1801 for 1,138 men runaways, and 141 women runaways. One consistent reason for running away was to find members of one's family—showing that despite the attempts of the slave system to destroy family ties by not allowing marriages and by separating families, slaves would face death and mutilation to get together.

In Maryland, where slaves were about one-third of the population in 1750, slavery had been written into law since the 1660s, and statutes for controlling rebellious slaves were passed. There were cases where slave women killed their masters, sometimes by poisoning them, sometimes by burning tobacco houses and homes. Punishments ranged from whipping and branding to execution, but the trouble continued. In 1742, seven slaves were put to death for murdering their master.

Fear of slave revolt seems to have been a permanent fact of plantation life. William Byrd, a wealthy Virginia slave owner, wrote in 1736:

> We have already at least 10,000 men of these descendants of Ham, fit to bear arms, and these numbers increase every day, as well by birth as by importation. And in case there should arise a man of desperate fortune, he might with more advantage than Cataline kindle a servile war . . . and tinge our rivers wide as they are with blood.

It was an intricate and powerful system of control that the slaveowners developed to maintain their labor supply and their way of life, a system both subtle and crude, involving every device that social orders employ for keeping power and wealth where it is. As Kenneth Stampp puts it:

> A wise master did not take seriously the belief that Negroes were natural-born slaves. He knew better. He knew that Negroes freshly imported from Africa had to be broken into bondage; that each succeeding generation had to be carefully trained. This was no easy task, for the bondsman rarely submitted willingly. Moreover, he rarely submitted completely. In most cases there was no end to the need for control—at least not until old age reduced the slave to a condition of helplessness.

The system was psychological and physical at the same time. The slaves were taught discipline, were impressed again and again with the idea of their own inferiority to "know their place," to see blackness as a sign of subordination, to be awed by the power of the master, to merge their interest with the master's, destroying their own individual needs. To accomplish this there was the discipline of hard labor, the breakup of the slave family, the lulling effects of religion (which sometimes led to "great mischief," as one slaveholder reported), the creation of disunity among slaves by separating them into field slaves and more privileged house slaves, and finally the power of law and the immediate power of the overseer to invoke whipping, burning, mutilation, and death. Dismemberment was provided for in the Virginia Code of 1705. Maryland passed a law in 1723 providing for cutting off the ears of blacks who struck whites, and that for certain serious crimes, slaves should be hanged and the body quartered and exposed.

Still, rebellions took place—not many, but enough to create constant fear among white planters. The first large-scale revolt in the North American colonies took place in New York in 1712. In New York, slaves were 10 percent of the population, the highest proportion in the northern states, where economic conditions usually did not require large numbers of field slaves. About twenty-five blacks and two Indians set fire to a building, then killed nine whites who came on the scene. They were captured by soldiers, put on trial, and twenty-one were executed. The governor's report to England said: "Some were burnt, others were hanged, one broke on the wheel, and one hung alive in chains in the town." One had been burned over a slow fire for eight to ten hours—all this to serve notice to other slaves.

A letter to London from South Carolina in 1720 reports:

> I am now to acquaint you that very lately we have had a very wicked and barbarous plot of the designe of the negroes rising with a designe to destroy all the white people in the country and then to take Charles Town in full body but it pleased God it was discovered and many of them taken prisoners and some burnt and some hang'd and some banish'd.

Around this time there were a number of fires in Boston and New Haven, suspected to be the work of Negro slaves. As a result, one Negro was executed in Boston, and the Boston Council ruled that any slaves who on their own gathered in groups of two or more were to be punished by whipping.

At Stono, South Carolina, in 1739, about twenty slaves rebelled, killed two warehouse guards, stole guns and gunpowder, and headed south, killing people in their way, and burning buildings. They were joined by others, until there were perhaps eighty slaves in all and, according to one account of the time, "they called out Liberty, marched on with Colours displayed, and two Drums beating." The militia found and attacked them. In the ensuing battle perhaps fifty slaves and twenty-five whites were killed before the uprising was crushed.

Herbert Aptheker, who did detailed research on slave resistance in North America for his book *American Negro Slave Revolts,* found about 250 instances where a minimum of ten slaves joined in a revolt or conspiracy.

From time to time, whites were involved in the slave resistance. As early as 1663, indentured white servants and black slaves in Gloucester County, Virginia, formed a conspiracy to rebel and gain their freedom. The plot was betrayed, and ended with executions. Mullin reports that the newspaper notices of runaways in Virginia often warned "ill-disposed" whites about harboring fugitives. Sometimes slaves and free men ran off together, or cooperated in crimes together. Sometimes, black male slaves ran off and joined white women. From time to time, white ship captains and watermen dealt with runaways, perhaps making the slave a part of the crew.

In New York in 1741, there were ten thousand whites in the city and two thousand black slaves. It had been a hard winter and the poor—slave and free—had suffered greatly. When mysterious fires broke out, blacks and whites were accused of conspiring together. Mass hysteria developed against the accused. After a trial full of lurid accusations by informers, and forced confessions, two white men and two white women were executed, eighteen slaves were hanged, and thirteen slaves were burned alive.

Only one fear was greater than the fear of black rebellion in the new American colonies. That was the fear that discontented whites would join black slaves to overthrow the existing order. In the early years of slavery, especially, before racism as a way of thinking was firmly ingrained, while white indentured servants were often treated as badly as black slaves, there was a possibility of cooperation. As Edmund Morgan sees it:

> There are hints that the two despised groups initially saw each other as sharing the same predicament. It was common, for example, for servants and slaves to run away together, steal hogs together, get drunk together. It was not uncommon for them to make love together. In Bacon's Rebellion, one of the last groups to surrender was a mixed band of eighty negroes and twenty English servants.

As Morgan says, masters, "initially at least, perceived slaves in much the same way they had always perceived servants . . . shiftless, irresponsible, unfaithful, ungrateful, dishonest." And "if freemen with disappointed hopes should make common cause with slaves of desperate hope, the results might be worse than anything Bacon had done."

And so, measures were taken. About the same time that slave codes, involving discipline and punishment, were passed by the Virginia Assembly,

> Virginia's ruling class, having proclaimed that all white men were superior to black, went on to offer their social (but white) inferiors a number of benefits previously

denied them. In 1705 a law was passed requiring masters to provide white servants whose indenture time was up with ten bushels of corn, thirty shillings, and a gun, while women servants were to get 15 bushels of corn and forty shillings. Also, the newly freed servants were to get 50 acres of land.

Morgan concludes: "Once the small planter felt less exploited by taxation and began to prosper a little, he became less turbulent, less dangerous, more respectable. He could begin to see his big neighbor not as an extortionist but as a powerful protector of their common interests."

We see now a complex web of historical threads to ensnare blacks for slavery in America: the desperation of starving settlers, the special helplessness of the displaced African, the powerful incentive of profit for slave trader and planter, the temptation of superior status for poor whites, the elaborate controls against escape and rebellion, the legal and social punishment of black and white collaboration.

The point is that the elements of this web are historical, not "natural." This does not mean that they are easily disentangled, dismantled. It means only that there is a possibility for something else, under historical conditions not yet realized. And one of these conditions would be

the elimination of that class exploitation which has made poor whites desperate for small gifts of status, and has prevented that unity of black and white necessary for joint rebellion and reconstruction.

Around 1700, the Virginia House of Burgesses declared:

> The Christian Servants in this country for the most part consists of the Worser Sort of the people of Europe. And since . . . such numbers of Irish and other Nations have been brought in of which a great many have been soldiers in the late warrs that according to our present Circumstances we can hardly governe them and if they were fitted with Armes and had the Opertunity of meeting together by Musters we have just reason to fears they may rise upon us.

It was a kind of **class consciousness**, a class fear. There were things happening in early Virginia, and in the other colonies, to warrant it.

class consciousness Karl Marx argued that the working classes were not conscious of the ways in which the ruling class oppressed them. Class consciousness refers to the ability of the laboring class (the proletariat) to challenge the reasons given to them by economic elites as to why they were impoverished.

3 Racial Formations
Michael Omi • Howard Winant

MICHAEL OMI is a professor in the Department of Ethnic Studies at the University of California, Berkeley, and the co-author of *Racial Formation in the United States from the 1960s to the 1980s* (1986). He has also written about racial theory and politics, right-wing political movements, Asian Americans and race relations, and race and popular culture. In 1990, he was the recipient of Berkeley's Distinguished Teaching Award.

HOWARD WINANT is a professor of sociology at the University of California, Santa Barbara. He is the author of numerous books and articles, including *Racial Formation in the United States from the 1960s to the 1990s* (1994) (with Michael Omi), *Racial Conditions: Politics, Theory, Comparisons* (1994), and *Stalemate: Political Economic Origins of Supply-Side Policy* (1988).

Questions to Consider If race is not "real" in a scientific sense, why can I look around the classroom or campus and see that someone is black or Asian or white? What is the difference between something being "real" (like the book in front of you) and something being a "social construction" (like race or gender)? Use Omi and Winant's theory of racial formation to explain how and why we "see" race as we do.

IN 1982–83, SUSIE GUILLORY PHIPPS unsuccessfully sued the Louisiana Bureau of Vital Records to change her racial classification from black to white. The descendant of an eighteenth-century white planter and a black slave, Phipps was designated "black" in her birth certificate in accordance with a 1970 state law which declared anyone with at least one-thirty-second "Negro blood" to be black. The legal battle raised intriguing questions about the concept of **race,** its meaning in contemporary society, and its use (and abuse) in public policy. Assistant Attorney General Ron Davis defended the law by pointing out that some type of racial classification was necessary to comply with federal record-keeping requirements and to facilitate programs for the prevention of genetic diseases. Phipps's attorney, Brian Begue, argued that the assignment of racial categories on birth certificates was unconstitutional and that the one-thirty-second designation was inaccurate. He called on a retired Tulane University professor who cited research indicating that most whites have one-twentieth "Negro" ancestry. In the end, Phipps lost. The court upheld a state law which quantified racial identity, and in so doing affirmed the legality of assigning individuals to specific racial groupings.[1]

The Phipps case illustrates the continuing dilemma of defining race and establishing its meaning in institutional life. Today, to assert that variations in human physiognomy are racially based is to enter a constant and intense debate. *Scientific* interpretations of race have not been alone in sparking heated controversy; *religious* perspectives have done so as well.[2] Most centrally, of course, race has been a matter of *political* contention. This has been particularly true in the United States, where the concept of race has varied enormously over time without ever leaving the center stage of US history.

What Is Race?

Race consciousness, and its articulation in theories of race, is largely a modern phenomenon. When European explorers in the New World "discovered" people who looked

race Sociologists view race as a social concept because the idea of race has changed over time, the categories of race are not discrete (they blend into one another), and the definition of race changes from country to country. We tend to think about race in terms of skin color, but the reason we place human beings into skin color categories is as arbitrary as grouping individuals by height, blood type, weight, eye color, or finger length.

different than themselves, these "natives" challenged then existing conceptions of the origins of the human species, and raised disturbing questions as to whether *all* could be considered in the same "family of man."[3] Religious debates flared over the attempt to reconcile the Bible with the existence of "racially distinct" people. Arguments took place over creation itself, as theories of polygenesis questioned whether God had made only one species of humanity ("monogenesis"). Europeans wondered if the natives of the New World were indeed human beings with redeemable souls. At stake were not only the prospects for conversion, but the types of treatment to be accorded them. The expropriation of property, the denial of political rights, the introduction of slavery and other forms of coercive labor, as well as outright extermination, all presupposed a worldview which distinguished Europeans—children of God, human beings, etc.—from "others." Such a worldview was needed to explain why some should be "free" and others enslaved, why some had rights to land and property while others did not. Race, and the interpretation of racial differences, was a central factor in that worldview.

In the colonial epoch science was no less a field of controversy than religion in attempts to comprehend the concept of race and its meaning. Spurred on by the classificatory scheme of living organisms devised by Linnaeus in *Systema Naturae,* many scholars in the eighteenth and nineteenth centuries dedicated themselves to the identification and ranking of variations in humankind. Race was thought of as a *biological* concept, yet its precise definition was the subject of debates which, as we have noted, continue to rage today. Despite efforts ranging from Dr. Samuel Morton's studies of cranial capacity[4] to contemporary attempts to base racial classification on shared gene pools,[5] the concept of race has defied biological definition. . . .

Attempts to discern the *scientific meaning* of race continue to the present day. Although most physical anthropologists and biologists have abandoned the quest for a scientific basis to determine racial categories, controversies have recently flared in the area of genetics and educational psychology. For instance, an essay by Arthur Jensen argued that hereditary factors shape intelligence not only revived the "nature or nurture" controversy, but raised highly volatile questions about racial equality itself.[6] Clearly the attempt to establish a *biological* basis of race has not been swept into the dustbin of history, but is being resurrected in various scientific arenas. All such attempts seek to remove the concept of

race from fundamental social, political, or economic determination. They suggest instead that the truth of race lies in
the terrain of innate characteristics, of which skin color and
other physical attributes provide only the most obvious, and
in some respects most superficial, indicators.

Race as a Social Concept

The social sciences have come to reject biologistic notions
of race in favor of an approach which regards race as a *social*
concept. Beginning in the eighteenth century, this trend has
been slow and uneven, but its direction clear. In the nineteenth century Max Weber discounted biological explanations for racial conflict and instead highlighted the social and
political factors which engendered such conflict.[7] The work
of pioneering cultural anthropologist Franz Boas was crucial
in refuting the scientific racism of the early twentieth century by rejecting the connection between race and culture,
and the assumption of a continuum of "higher" and "lower"
cultural groups. Within the contemporary social science literature, race is assumed to be a variable which is shaped by
broader societal forces.

Race is indeed a pre-eminently *sociohistorical* concept.
Racial categories and the meaning of race are given concrete expression by the specific social relations and historical context in which they are embedded. Racial meanings
have varied tremendously over time and between different societies.

In the United States, the black/white color line has historically been rigidly defined and enforced. White is seen
as a "pure" category. Any racial intermixture makes one
"nonwhite." In the movie *Raintree County,* Elizabeth Taylor
describes the worst of fates to befall whites as "havin' a
little Negra blood in ya'—just one little teeny drop and a
person's all Negra."[8] This thinking flows from what Marvin
Harris has characterized as the principle of *hypo-descent:*

> By what ingenious computation is the genetic tracery of
> a million years of evolution unraveled and each man [sic]
> assigned his proper social box? In the United States, the
> mechanism employed is the rule of hypo-descent. This
> descent rule requires Americans to believe that anyone
> who is known to have had a Negro ancestor is a Negro.
> We admit nothing in between. . . . "Hypo-descent"
> means affiliation with the subordinate rather than the
> superordinate group in order to avoid the ambiguity
> of intermediate identity. . . . The rule of hypo-descent

is, therefore, an invention, which we in the United
States have made in order to keep biological facts from
intruding into our collective racist fantasies.[9]

The Susie Guillory Phipps case merely represents the contemporary expression of this racial logic.

By contrast, a striking feature of race relations in
the lowland areas of Latin America since the abolition of
slavery has been the relative absence of sharply defined
racial groupings. No such rigid descent rule characterizes
racial identity in many Latin American societies. Brazil,
for example, has historically had less rigid conceptions of
race, and thus a variety of "intermediate" racial categories
exist. Indeed, as Harris notes, "One of the most striking
consequences of the Brazilian system of racial identification is that parents and children and even brothers and
sisters are frequently accepted as representatives of quite
opposite racial types."[10] Such a possibility is incomprehensible within the logic of racial categories in the US.

To suggest another example: the notion of "passing"
takes on new meaning if we compare various American
cultures' means of assigning racial identity. In the United
States, individuals who are actually "black" by the logic of
hypo-descent have attempted to skirt the discriminatory
barriers imposed by law and custom by attempting to "pass"
for white.[11] Ironically, these same individuals would not be
able to pass for "black" in many Latin American societies.

Consideration of the term "black" illustrates the
diversity of racial meanings which can be found among
different societies and historically within a given society.
In contemporary British politics the term "black" is used
to refer to all nonwhites. Interestingly this designation
has not arisen through the racist discourse of groups such
as the National Front. Rather, in political and cultural
movements, Asian as well as Afro-Caribbean youth are
adopting the term as an expression of self-identity.[12] The
wide-ranging meanings of "black" illustrate the manner in
which racial categories are shaped politically.

The meaning of race is defined and contested
throughout society, in both collective action and personal
practice. In the process, racial categories themselves are
formed, transformed, destroyed and reformed. We use
the term **racial formation** to refer to the process by

---

racial formation The process in which race operates as a central axis of social relations, which then determine social, economic, and political institutions and practices.

which social, economic and political forces determine the content and importance of racial categories, and by which they are in turn shaped by racial meanings. Crucial to this formulation is the treatment of race as a *central axis* of social relations which cannot be subsumed under or reduced to some broader category or conception.

Racial Ideology and Racial Identity

The seemingly obvious, "natural" and "common sense" qualities which the existing racial order exhibits themselves testify to the effectiveness of the racial formation process in constructing racial meanings and racial identities.

One of the first things we notice about people when we meet them (along with their sex) is their race. We utilize race to provide clues about *who* a person is. This fact is made painfully obvious when we encounter someone whom we cannot conveniently racially categorize—someone who is, for example, racially "mixed" or of an ethnic/racial group with which we are not familiar. Such an encounter becomes a source of discomfort and momentarily a crisis of racial meaning. Without a racial identity, one is in danger of having no identity.

Our compass for navigating race relations depends on preconceived notions of what each specific racial group looks like. Comments such as, "Funny, you don't look black," betray an underlying image of what black should be. We also become disoriented when people do not act "black," "Latino," or indeed "white." The content of such stereotypes reveals a series of unsubstantiated beliefs about who these groups are and what "they" are like.[13]

In US society, then, a kind of "racial etiquette" exists, a set of interpretative codes and racial meanings which operate in the interactions of daily life. Rules shaped by our perception of race in a comprehensively racial society determine the "presentation of self,"[14] distinctions of status, and appropriate modes of conduct. "Etiquette" is not mere universal adherence to the dominant group's rules, but a more dynamic combination of these rules with the values and beliefs of subordinated groupings. This racial "subjection" is quintessentially ideological. Everybody learns some combination, some version, of the rules of racial classification, and of their own racial identity, often without obvious teaching or conscious inculcation. Race becomes "common sense"—a way of comprehending, explaining and acting in the world.

Racial beliefs operate as an "amateur biology," a way of explaining the variations in "human nature."[15] Differences in skin color and other obvious physical characteristics supposedly provide visible clues to differences lurking underneath. Temperament, sexuality, intelligence, athletic ability, aesthetic preferences and so on are presumed to be fixed and discernible from the palpable mark of race. Such diverse questions as our confidence and trust in others (for example, clerks or salespeople, media figures, neighbors), our sexual preferences and romantic images, our tastes in music, films, dance, or sports, and our very ways of talking, walking, eating and dreaming are ineluctably shaped by notions of race. Skin color "differences" are thought to explain perceived differences in intellectual, physical and artistic temperaments, and to justify distinct treatment of racially identified individuals and groups.

The continuing persistence of racial ideology suggests that these racial myths and stereotypes cannot be exposed as such in the popular imagination. They are, we think, too essential, too integral, to the maintenance of the US social order. Of course, particular meanings, stereotypes and myths can change, but the presence of a *system* of racial meanings and stereotypes, of racial ideology, seems to be a permanent feature of US culture.

Film and television, for example, have been notorious in disseminating images of racial minorities which establish for audiences what people from these groups look like, how they behave, and "who they are."[16] The power of the media lies not only in their ability to reflect the dominant racial ideology, but in their capacity to shape that ideology in the first place. D.W. Griffith's epic *Birth of a Nation*, a sympathetic treatment of the rise of the Ku Klux Klan during Reconstruction, helped to generate, consolidate and "nationalize" images of blacks which had been more disparate (more regionally specific, for example) prior to the film's appearance.[17] In US television, the necessity to define characters in the briefest and most condensed manner has led to the perpetuation of racial caricatures, as racial stereotypes serve as shorthand for scriptwriters, directors and actors, in commercials, etc. Television's tendency to address the "lowest common denominator" in order to render programs "familiar" to an enormous and diverse audience leads it regularly to assign and reassign racial characteristics to particular groups, both minority and majority.

These and innumerable other examples show that we tend to view race as something fixed and immutable—something rooted in "nature." Thus we mask the historical construction of racial categories, the shifting meaning of race, and the crucial role of politics and ideology in shaping race relations. Races do not emerge full-blown. They are the results of diverse historical practices and are continually subject to challenge over their definition and meaning.

Racialization: The Historical Development of Race

In the United States, the racial category of "black" evolved with the consolidation of racial slavery. By the end of the seventeenth century, Africans whose specific identity was Ibo, Yoruba, Fulani, etc., were rendered "black" by an ideology of exploitation based on racial logic—the establishment and maintenance of a "color line." This of course did not occur overnight. A period of indentured servitude which was not rooted in racial logic preceded the consolidation of racial slavery. With slavery, however, a racially based understanding of society was set in motion which resulted in the shaping of a specific *racial* identity not only for the slaves but for the European settlers as well. Winthrop Jordan has observed: "From the initially common term *Christian,* at mid-century there was a marked shift toward the terms *English* and *free.* After about 1680, taking the colonies as a whole, a new term of self-identification appeared—*white.*"[18]

We employ the term **racialization** to signify the extension of racial meaning to a previously racially unclassified relationship, social practice or group. Racialization is an ideological process, an historically specific one. Racial ideology is constructed from pre-existing conceptual (or, if one prefers, "dis-cursive") elements and emerges from the struggles of competing political projects and ideas seeking to articulate similar elements differently. An account of racialization processes that avoids the pitfalls of US ethnic history[19] remains to be written.

Particularly during the nineteenth century, the category of "white" was subject to challenges brought about by the influx of diverse groups who were not of the same

racialization The social process by which a racial identity is attached to a group and that group is placed in a race-based social hierarchy. Upon their arrival in America, for example, Europeans labeled the hundreds of indigenous tribal populations "Indians" and placed them in a single group in a racial hierarchy.

Anglo-Saxon stock as the founding immigrants. In the nineteenth century, political and ideological struggles emerged over the classification of Southern Europeans, the Irish and Jews, among other "nonwhite" categories.[20] Nativism was only effectively curbed by the institutionalization of a racial order that drew the color line *around,* rather than *within,* Europe.

By stopping short of racializing immigrants from Europe after the Civil War, and by subsequently allowing their assimilation, the American racial order was reconsolidated in the wake of the tremendous challenge placed before it by the abolition of racial slavery.[21] With the end of Reconstruction in 1877, an effective program for limiting the emergent class struggles of the later nineteenth century was forged: the definition of the working class *in racial terms*—as "white." This was not accomplished by any legislative decree or capitalist maneuvering to divide the working class, but rather by white workers themselves. Many of them were recent immigrants, who organized on racial lines as much as on traditionally defined class lines.[22] The Irish on the West Coast, for example, engaged in vicious anti-Chinese race-baiting and committed many pogrom-type assaults on Chinese in the course of consolidating the trade union movement in California.

Thus the very political organization of the working class was in important ways a racial project. The legacy of racial conflicts and arrangements shaped the definition of interests and in turn led to the consolidation of institutional patterns (e.g., segregated unions, dual labor markets, exclusionary legislation) which perpetuated the color line *within* the working class. Selig Perlman, whose study of the development of the labor movement is fairly sympathetic to this process, notes that:

> The political issue after 1877 was racial, not financial, and the weapon was not merely the ballot, but also "direct action"—violence. The anti-Chinese agitation in California, culminating as it did in the Exclusion Law passed by Congress in 1882, was doubtless the most important single factor in the history of American labor, for without it the entire country might have been overrun by Mongolian [sic] labor and *the labor movement might have become a conflict of races instead of one of classes.*[23]

More recent economic transformations in the US have also altered interpretations of racial identities and meanings. The automation of southern agriculture and the augmented labor demand of the postwar boom transformed blacks from a largely rural, impoverished labor force to a largely urban, working-class group by 1970.[24] When boom became bust and liberal welfare statism moved rightwards, the majority of blacks came to be seen, increasingly, as part of the "underclass," as state "dependents." Thus the particularly deleterious effects on blacks of global and national economic shifts (generally rising unemployment rates, changes in the employment structure away from reliance on labor intensive work, etc.) were explained once again in the late 1970s and 1980s (as they had been in the 1940s and mid-1960s) as the result of defective black cultural norms, of familial disorganization, etc.[25] In this way new racial attributions, new racial myths, are affixed to "blacks."[26] Similar changes in racial identity are presently affecting Asians and Latinos, as such economic forces as increasing Third World impoverishment and indebtedness fuel immigration and high interest rates, Japanese competition spurs resentments, and US jobs seem to fly away to Korea and Singapore.[27] . . .

Once we understand that race overflows the boundaries of skin color, super-exploitation, social stratification, discrimination and prejudice, cultural domination and cultural resistance, state policy (or of any other particular social relationship we list), once we recognize the racial dimension present to some degree in *every* identity, institution and social practice in the United States—once we have done this, it becomes possible to speak of *racial formation*. This recognition is hard-won; there is a continuous temptation to think of race as an *essence,* as something fixed, concrete and objective, as (for example) one of the categories just enumerated. And there is also an opposite temptation: to see it as a mere illusion, which an ideal social order would eliminate.

In our view it is crucial to break with these habits of thought. The effort must be made to understand race as *an unstable and "decentered" complex of social meanings constantly being transformed by political struggle.*

4   Defining Race and Ethnicity
C. Matthew Snipp

C. MATTHEW SNIPP is Burnet C. and Milfred Finley Professor of Sociology at Stanford University.

———————

THERE ARE FEW TERMS THAT ARE MORE deeply embedded within the conversations of everyday life than the descriptors of "race and ethnicity." Applications for jobs, scholarships, drivers' licenses, and other modern privileges routinely request this information. As we encounter others in our everyday world, we instantly and unconsciously assess their age, sex, and race or ethnicity. Race and ethnicity are relevant considerations when choosing our friends, future mates, and clandestinely, when we choose our neighbors and co-workers. To settle any doubt about the pervasive presence of race and ethnicity in modern society, a Google search is one powerful measure of popular discourse. Using the phrase "race and ethnicity" yields a list consisting of 47,500,000 entries—a considerable number. This number is even more imposing

Questions to Consider   C. Matthew Snipp demonstrates how race is a social construction by examining the ways in which the definitions of race and ethnicity have changed from one decade to the next and from one location to another. If race were "real" in the sense that gravity or a glass of water is "real," how is it possible that the definition of race is constantly in a state of flux? What role do institutions play in the social construction of race? How do these shifting definitions of race and ethnicity benefit some groups and harm others? Why do we continue to treat race as a "real" category when the very definition of what constitutes race is constantly changing?

when, and for the sake of comparison, searches for personalities in popular culture such as "Britney Spears" produce lists that are impressive in number yet are still significantly smaller than the number of entries for race and ethnicity.

Historical Origins

It is impossible to discuss the meaning of race and ethnicity in American society, or in any society, without taking note of the intellectual roots of the ideas we hold about them. Most scholars agree that race and ethnicity exist mainly as a means for accentuating or highlighting differences that may exist between groups (Omi and Winant 1994; Fredrickson 2002). The terms serve as shorthand for designating people belonging to some groups as "others" or "not one of us." The practice of identifying some people as "like us" and others as "not like us" is one that predates written history and quite possibly was present in the earliest forms of human societies.

In its modern usage, race often has been used to reflect some set of biological properties, and the Spanish Inquisition is credited with being the first to connect biological qualities with social and cultural habits. The Inquisition linked "blood" and "blood purity" with the Jewish faith by presenting the question of whether it was possible to cleanse the Jewish blood from Jews who converted to Christianity (Fredrickson 2002). This connection has provided a vocabulary for racial discourse framed in terms of blood and blood purity that persists into the twenty-first century.

The concept of race, and its association with blood and other biological traits, remained an ill-formed idea for at least three centuries. However, the Enlightenment embedded the concept of race within modern secular thought in several ways. The Swedish naturalist and one of the founders of modern biology, Carl Linnaeus, introduced in 1735 a classification to describe the several varieties of *Homo sapiens*. Linnaeus differentiated Europeans, American Indians, Asians and Africans, and a residual category of "monstrous" races that later proved to be nonexistent (Fredrickson 2002). Forty years later, Johann Friedrich Blumenbach, a founder of physical anthropology, published *On the Natural Varieties of Mankind* (1776). This work proved to be an authoritative classification of the known races and introduced the terms "Caucasian," "Mongolian," "Ethiopian," "American," and "Malay" to describe them.

Although many of the founding fathers of the United States, especially Thomas Jefferson, were deeply influenced by Enlightenment thinking, it is not clear how much they were influenced by the work of Linnaeus and Blumenbach. Nonetheless, the crafting of the U.S. Constitution took special notice of race and incorporated it into the political framework of the United States as a category of civil status. The necessity of recognizing race stemmed from the controversies surrounding slavery and a tacit acknowledgment that American Indian tribes were sovereigns beyond the jurisdiction of the U.S. government. Specifically, Article I, Section 2, of the Constitution stipulates that

> Representatives and direct Taxes . . . shall be determined by adding to the whole Number of free Persons, including those bound to Service for a Term of Years, and excluding Indians not taxed, three fifths of all other Persons. . . . The actual Enumeration shall be made . . . within every subsequent Term of ten Years, in such Manner as they shall by Law direct.

Thus, for purposes of determining political representation and taxes—the two issues most critical in the American Revolution—African slaves were counted as 60 percent (3/5) of a whole person and American Indians were excluded. In this manner, race was used to determine civil status in the most fundamental legal document of the nation.

In the nineteenth century, race and racial differences were the preeminent concerns of the racial sciences, **eugenics** and **ethnology,** better known today as scientific racism. Scholars such as Lewis Henry Morgan, Francis Galton, and Arthur de Gobineau labored to identify and catalog racial differences and to establish a biological basis for why some races were superior or inferior to others. By the late nineteenth century, others scholars such as Franz Boas and his students began to challenge key tenets in scientific racism, such as the presumption of cultural inferiority or superiority. This challenge also led scholars critical of scientific racism to embrace the concept of ethnicity as an alternative to the concept of race (McKee 1993).

The term "ethnicity" is derived from the Greek word "ethnikos" or "ethnos," meaning people or nation (Peterson 1980). As an alternative to the concept of race, ethnicity

---

eugenics a branch of science that attempted to restrict certain groups, typically immigrants and racial minorities, from having children because they were deemed socially and intellectually inferior.

ethnology the study of racial groups, their language and culture.

is rooted in national identity or in behavior sets connected with subgroups within nations. An ethnic group may share a common language, religion, family structure, diet, and lifestyle—to name only a few traits associated with ethnic differences. Most significantly, ethnicity connotes a group's differences that are wholly disconnected from biology, and further, does not imply invidious judgments about these differences.

In the twentieth century, the popularity of the term "ethnicity" grew slowly and coincided with the growing presence and influence of the social sciences within the academy. After World War II, the social sciences vigorously undertook the task of debunking ideas that for many years served as the conventional wisdom of scientific racism. In 1942, Ashley Montagu published his groundbreaking work *Race: Man's Most Dangerous Myth.* Montagu's work laid the foundation for understanding race as purely a social construction that can change over time and from one social environment to another. In the years after World War II, a consensus has grown behind the idea that race is nothing more than a social construct and that ethnicity is tied to social, as opposed to biological distinctions. By the late twentieth century, the terms "race" and "ethnicity" had come to be used interchangeably. Clearly, however, the two terms have very different intellectual pedigrees and as the discussion to follow will show, these ideas involve considerably different social and political implications.

Alternative Approaches to Defining Race and Ethnicity

In the early years of the twentieth century, social scientists seemed content to agree that ethnic differences represented cultural and behavioral differences that were uniquely social in nature; however, debates about the content and quality of racial characteristics continued to rage (McKee 1993). A recurring issue within these debates was how best to define and understand the fundamental content of the concept of race. Was race fundamentally a biological characteristic, a product of the social environment, or both? How did the biology of race connect with the sociology of race and how did biological characteristics come to have social consequences?

For much of the twentieth century, social scientists, especially those in sociology and anthropology, struggled to define the meaning of race. But after decades of debate, dozens if not hundreds of different definitions for the concept of race could be found in the social scientific literature. By 1953 it was clear to at least two sociologists, George Simpson and Milton Yinger, that efforts to define race were at an intellectual dead end; countless inquiries had yielded countless variations on themes about which little or no consensus existed. However, they noted that while an absence of consensus existed about the true meaning of race, certain themes seemed to emerge from these disparate accounts. Simpson and Yinger argued that while it might not be possible to obtain a single conceptual definition of race that would be widely accepted, it was possible to classify racial definitions into several different types of concepts. Specifically, they suggested that there are at least three types of racial definitions: *mystical definitions, biological definitions,* and *administrative definitions* (Simpson and Yinger 1953). Understanding these definitional types provides some useful insights about the way that race is defined in the United States.

Mystical definitions of race are rooted in folklore, religious beliefs and other traditions such as origin stories that are largely outside of empirical experience. They represent attempts to explain variations in the human race by ascribing them to the actions of gods, spirits, and other mythological beings that transcend everyday human experience. One noteworthy example from the 1930s is the creation of the mythological race of Aryans by Nazi propagandists to justify the extermination of "lesser" races, especially European Jews. Needless to say, while mystical definitions may be interesting, they are of little value for most purposes in scientific inquiry.

Biological definitions of race are perhaps best known owing to more than a century of publications on the subjects of eugenics and ethnology. Following Linnaeus and Blumenbach, biologists, geneticists, physical anthropologists, and others debated intensely the exact number of races into which human beings could be classified. Advances in modern genetics in the late nineteenth and early twentieth centuries allowed the argument to progress to the point that a race could be defined as a "homogeneous gene pool." The discovery of various genetic markers enabled scientists to develop tests that could be used to assign individuals to a particular race. For example, earwax texture and fingerprint patterns could be used to identify certain "races" (Snipp 1989). However, as the numbers of these markers proliferated, they often yielded contradictory results that could only be reconciled by increasing the numbers of possible races. That is, as more markers became available, the more difficult it was to identify gene pools that could be considered truly homogeneous.

By the late twentieth century, scientists were beginning to seriously question whether race was a meaningful scientific construct, and many were skeptical about its utility (Gould 1996; Cavalli-Sforza 2001). However, recent discoveries connected to the mapping of the human genome have allowed geneticists to reliably assay the continental origins of genetic material. This has paved the way for a resurrection of biological interpretations of race associated with continental origins insofar as unique patterns of genes can be identified with Europe, Asia, Africa, and the Americas. This research and its nascent implications for a revitalized biology of race has been the object of intense controversy since its discovery (Erlich and Feldman 2003). The social and political implications of this work remain highly ambiguous.

Administrative definitions of race are constructions promulgated by government agencies and other bureaucratic institutions for the purpose of realizing a political agenda or completing an administrative task. This type of definition is the most commonplace insofar as administrative definitions of race are encountered in applications for employment, scholarships, and a variety of other situations for which government agencies require information about race or ethnicity to be collected from a particular constituency. Administrative definitions of race can vary a great deal over time and from one nation-state to another.

The reason for the variability in administrative definitions of race over time and across nation-states should be obvious. As governments and the agendas they pursue change, so do the racial classifications that they use. Classifications change in response to evolving conditions in the social and political environment. For example, as new ethnic groups immigrate en masse from one nation-state to another, national governments often seek to monitor their movement and deploy various kinds of surveillance to estimate their numbers, locations, movements, and other details. Obtaining this information requires some sort of method for determining membership within the ethnic group of interest. This entails, of course, devising a new ethnic classification system that may replace or modify any existing systems already in place.

There are many examples of administrative definitions of race. In the eighteenth century, the authorities responsible for the Spanish colonies in what is now Mexico promulgated an elaborate system of *castas* to describe the various combinations of racial and ethnic mixing taking place among Europeans, Native Americans, and Africans. This classification included the term "mestizo" to describe the offspring of Spanish and Indian parents, and labeled the children of Spanish and African parents as "mulattos." The *castas* included fourteen other possible combinations and they were preserved for posterity in a series of paintings depicting the physical features of each racial/ethnic admixture.

Besides the *castas,* another noteworthy administrative definition of race was devised by South Africa during the era of **racial apartheid.** Unlike the *castas,* the South African system was relatively simple. It consisted of three categories: black, white, and colored. However, the South African system illustrates the arbitrary and sometimes nonsensical nature of administrative definitions. Specifically, the South African system classified as "Colored" persons who were neither black nor white. This included most persons from Asia, except for the Japanese, who were considered white. This was a concession to Japanese business representatives, with whom the South African government was trying to curry favor during the years when South Africa was boycotted by the international community.

Defining Race and Ethnicity in America

As indicated above, counting people by race is a tradition deeply embedded within the governing framework of the United States. Indeed, some notation of race has been taken since the first census in 1790. As mandated by the Constitution, the first administrative definition of race used by the United States took note of African slaves and American Indians subject to taxation who were living under the jurisdiction of the United States. The implementation of this classification in the decennial census is significant because for most of this nation's history—at least throughout the nineteenth century and into the first half of the twentieth century—the census was the only reliable source of information about race and ethnicity in the United States.

racial apartheid the political system in South Africa from 1948 to 1994 organized around white supremacy and the economic, social and political disenfranchisement of the black majority population.

In the nineteenth century, the official racial and ethnic classification used by the federal government evolved in response to the changing composition of the population and in response to political concerns of the era. In 1820, for example, the census began collecting information about the foreign-born population as concerns mounted about the national "stock" of new immigrants. The 1820 census also was noteworthy because for the first time enumerators were instructed to take note of each person's "color" and record whether they were white, black, or American Indian.

In the second half of the nineteenth century, scientific racism was virtually unassailable as a scientific doctrine, and hostility to foreigners—especially from Asia—was an established norm. These attitudes and beliefs were reflected in the approach of the United States to counting its inhabitants in each decennial census and in its efforts to articulate a racial cosmology more complex than one that distinguished only between whites, blacks, and American Indians. The 1850 census acknowledged for the first time the existence of black–white and black–American Indian sexual relations by adding a category for mulatto to the census questionnaire. In the 1860 census, categories were added to include Chinese and Asian Indians, reflecting concerns about immigrant railroad workers. Ten years later, a category for Japanese was added to the 1870 census (Snipp 2003).

The 1890 census followed the **Chinese Exclusion Act** (1882), the cessation of the Indian Wars in the West, and a growing concern among politicians over racial purity. To address these concerns, the census counted Chinese and Japanese, and American Indians (both taxed and not taxed), and it subdivided the mulatto population into "**Quadroons**" and "**Octoroons**." It responded to nativist concerns about the impact of immigration on the nation by showing that a substantial amount of the growth in the U.S. population was due to immigration from Europe, particularly southern and eastern Europe. This finding provided potent fuel to the anti-immigration movement and others concerned with the "degradation" of American stock (Anderson 1988).

Chinese Exclusion Act Law passed by Congress in 1882 that banned Chinese immigration to the United States.

Quadroons and **Octoroons** A onetime U.S. Census description of individuals who were one quarter white and three quarters black. Octoroons were those thought to be one eight white and seven-eighths black.

The official classification of race in the early decades of the twentieth century continued to evolve with changes in immigration and changing ideas about the nature of race. For example, in 1922 the Supreme Court was challenged to define the meaning of "white" in *Takao Ozawa v. US,* a case involving a man of Japanese descent who claimed a right to become a naturalized citizen. The Court concluded that only persons of the white race were eligible for membership. In trying to establish the meaning of white, the Court said:

> Manifestly the test afforded by the mere color of the skin of each individual is impracticable, as that differs greatly among persons of the same race, even among Anglo-Saxons, ranging by imperceptible gradations from the fair blond to the swarthy brunette, the latter being darker than many of the lighter hued persons of the brown or yellow races. Hence to adopt the color test alone would result in a confused overlapping of races and a gradual merging of one into the other, without any practical line of separation. Beginning with the decision of Circuit Judge Sawyer, . . . the federal and state courts, in an almost unbroken line, have held that the words "white person" were meant to indicate only a person of what is popularly known as the Caucasian race. . . . With the conclusion reached in these several decisions we see no reason to differ. . . . The determination that the words "white person" are synonymous with the words "a person of the Caucasian race" simplifies the problem, although it does not entirely dispose of it. Controversies have arisen and will no doubt arise again in respect of the proper classification of individuals in border line cases. The effect of the conclusion that the words "white person" means a Caucasian is not to establish a sharp line of demarcation between those who are entitled and those who are not entitled to naturalization, but rather a zone of more or less debatable ground outside of which, upon the one hand, are those clearly eligible, and outside of which, upon the other hand, are those clearly ineligible for citizenship. (*Ozawa v. U.S. 1922*)

As it happened, the Court was called upon to clarify its tortured logic in *U.S. v. Bhagat Singh Thind.* This 1923 case involved an Asian Indian man, Bhagat Singh Thind, who claimed the right to naturalization. Thind argued that because he was born in a northwestern region of India that many ethnologists considered part of the Caucasus, he was eligible for citizenship as a Caucasian. Trying to clarify its use of the term "Caucasian" in the Ozawa case, Justice Sutherland delivered the opinion:

> The word "Caucasian," not means [*sic*] clear, and the use of it in its scientific [*sic*] probably wholly unfamiliar to the original framers of the statute in 1790. When we employ it, we do so as an aid to the ascertainment of the legislative intent and not as an invariable substitute for the statutory words. Indeed, as used in the science of ethnology, the connotation of the word is by no means clear, and the use of it in its scientific sense as an equivalent. . . . But in this country, during the last half century especially, the word by common usage has acquired a popular meaning, not clearly defined to be sure, but sufficiently so to enable us to say that its popular as distinguished from its scientific application is of appreciably narrower scope. It is in the popular sense of the word, therefore, that we employ is as an aid to the construction of the statute, for it would be obviously illogical to convert words of common speech used in a statute into words of scientific terminology when neither the latter nor the science for whose purposes they were coined was within the contemplation of the framers of the statute or of the people for whom it was framed. . . . They imply, as we have said, a racial test; but the term "race" is one which, for the practical purposes of the statute, must be applied to a group of living persons now possessing in common the requisite characteristics, not to groups of persons who are supposed to be or really are descended from some remote, common ancestor, but who, whether they both resemble him to a greater or less extent, have, at any rate, ceased altogether to resemble one another. It may be true that the blond Scandinavian and the brown Hindu have a common ancestor in the dim reaches of antiquity, but the average man knows perfectly well that there are unmistakable and profound differences between them to-day; and it is not impossible, if that common ancestor could be materialized in the flesh, we should discover that he was himself sufficiently differentiated from both of his descendants to preclude his racial classification with either. (*U.S. v. Thind* 1923)

For African Americans, the ascendancy of Jim Crow legislation in the late nineteenth century and early twentieth century institutionalized the so-called one-drop rule. The one-drop rule held that even the smallest amount of black heritage was sufficient to warrant the designation of "black." In the 1930 census, enumerators received the instruction that

> a person of mixed White and Negro blood was to be returned as Negro, no matter how small the percentage

of Negro blood; someone part Indian and part Negro also was to be listed as Negro, unless the Indian blood predominated. (Snipp 2003)

This instruction, of course, relies on terminology (blood) rooted in medieval beliefs about race.

In addition to institutionalizing the **one-drop rule,** the 1930 census also added categories for Mexicans, Hindus, Koreans, and Filipinos. These groups were beginning to immigrate to the West Coast, mostly as agricultural labor, in sufficient numbers to attract the attention of politicians and their constituencies. In California, for example, there was considerable public concern about the numbers of Filipinos entering the state.

Defining Race and Ethnicity in Postwar America

From 1940 to 1960, the federal government published relatively little information about racial and ethnic minorities. The information that was available was produced once a decade in reports from the decennial census usually titled *Nonwhite Population by Race*. The racial and ethnic landscape of early postwar America consisted of whites, blacks, American Indians, and a polyglot category of Asians and other races. Latinos were absent from consideration insofar as Mexican American advocacy groups, including the Mexican government, had lobbied to have Mexicans counted as white for statistical purposes (Snipp 2003).

In the 1950 census, as in previous censuses, enumerators ascribed race on the basis of physical appearances. Because census enumerators received no instructions from their supervisors about how to code race on their questionnaires, we can presume that the ascription of race was regarded as a self-evident exercise. However, in 1960, in an effort to reduce the cost of the census, the Census Bureau drastically reduced the number of enumerators it used and replaced them with a form that was delivered through the mail and was to be completed and returned to the Census Bureau by the nominal head of the household. This meant that race was no longer ascribed by enumerators on the basis of physical appearance. Instead, race became a matter of personal identification, based on self-reports provided by the person completing the census

one drop rule the belief that if an individual had any black ancestry, even the preverbal "one drop", that person was legally and socially a member of the black race and as such could be defined as a slave.

form. Race in the 1960 census was now based instead on subjective judgments about the self-identification of racial and ethnic ancestry. Wittingly or unwittingly, Census Bureau planners devised a statistical measure of race that was wholly consistent with constructionist theories. That is, race is purely a matter of subjective experience in the everyday social environment—race meant whatever an individual understood it to mean. One by-product of this change was a dramatic increase in the American Indian population, especially in urban areas where they had been misidentified in earlier censuses as white, black, or possibly Asian (Snipp 1989).

After the 1960 census, federal efforts involving the collection of information about race proliferated. This development was largely in response to the passage of civil rights and other race-based legislation and the desires of Congress to ensure that the laws, policies, and programs it was creating were having the intended effect. Throughout the executive branch of the federal government, agencies began to collect and monitor information about the racial composition of the constituencies and to widely disseminate this information (Table 1).

As the volume of race-based data increased exponentially, problems connected with the comparability and coverage of this information soon became apparent. For example, some agencies produced reports showing information about "Whites" and "Nonwhites." These reports could not be compared to the reports of other agencies showing information about "Whites," "Blacks,"

TABLE 1   Federal Agencies That Collect and Report Information about Race and Ethnicity

- Commerce
- Education
- Equal Employment Opportunity Commission (EEOC)
- Federal Reserve
- Health and Human Services (HHS)
- Housing and Urban Development (HUD)
- Justice
- Labor
- Agriculture
- Veterans Affairs

and "Others" without sacrificing the detailed information about blacks in the latter report. Of course, neither of these approaches was satisfactory for persons seeking information about Latinos, American Indians, Asians, or any other group subsumed under the "Other" category.

By 1974, the Office of Management and Budget (OMB) set about the task of creating a standard classification for the production of statistical information about race. The Federal Interagency Committee on Education (FICE) was assigned the task of devising a standard taxonomy and set of definitions for racial and ethnic groups of particular interest to the federal government. After months of deliberation, the committee adopted a recommendation late in 1976 that the federal government should collect information about five more or less distinct groups: (1) American Indians and Alaska Natives; (2) Asians and Pacific Islanders; (3) Non-Hispanic Blacks; (4) Non-Hispanic Whites; and (5) Hispanics, of any race. This recommendation became official policy when OMB adopted it and designated it as OMB Directive No. 15. Although this document stipulated the groups for whom information should be collected, it did not try to define the meaning of these designations beyond to state simply, "These classifications should not be interpreted as being scientific or anthropological in nature" (OMB 1977).

The importance of the adoption of OMB Directive No. 15 should not be underestimated. Because this document became the standard for all agencies of the federal government, including its grantees and contractors, its five mandated categories became, in effect, a racial cosmology for the United States. Directive No. 15 stipulated the categories by which most Americans would identify themselves on job applications, college scholarship applications, census forms, and virtually every other form and application that requested information about race. This directive also constrained social scientific inquiry insofar as it made government data available about some groups but not others. For example, as a result of Directive No. 15, information about births and deaths is readily available for blacks but not for Arab Americans because the latter are not included in the directive. In short, OMB Directive No. 15 defined the known racial and ethnic landscape in the late twentieth century.

Conveniently, the categories mandated by Directive No. 15 closely coincided with those used by the census.

The 1980 census was administered under the mandate of this directive and it included categories for race and a new question designed to obtain information about persons of Hispanic origins. The Census Bureau also introduced a new open-ended question requesting information about ethnic ancestry. Although these new questions posed a number of difficulties, they were used again in the 1990 census (Snipp 2003).

The 1990 census proved to be a pivotal event in the way that public perception focused on the meaning of race.

Two sets of controversies surfaced from the 1990 census questionnaire and the way that it solicited information about race. One set of complaints was lodged by groups who were omitted from the race question. For example, advocacy groups representing Taiwanese and Arab American interests argued that each of these groups should be included as an option on the race question. Native Hawaiians also complained that they should not be grouped with Asians and other Pacific Islanders (see Figure 1). Another set of complaints stemmed from the instruction that

4. Race
Fill ONE circle for the race that the person considers himself/herself to be.

    If Indian (Amer.), print the name of the enrolled or principal tribe. ⟶

    If Other Asian or Pacific Islander (API), print one group, for example: Hmong, Fijian, Laotian, Thai, Tongan, Pakistani, Cambodian, and so on. ⟶

    If Other race, print race. ⟶

○ White
○ Black or Negro
○ Indian (Amer.) (Print the name of the enrolled or principal tribe.)

    ○ Eskimo
○ Aleut

      Asian or Pacific Islander (API)
○ Chinese   ○ Japanese
○ Filipino   ○ Asian Indian
○ Hawaiian   ○ Samoan
○ Korean   ○ Guamanian
○ Vietnamese   ○ Other API

○ Other race (Print race)

7. Is this person of Spanish/Hispanic origin?
Fill ONE circle for each person.

    If Yes, other Spanish/Hispanic, print one group. ⟶

○ No (not Spanish/Hispanic)
○ Yes, Mexican, Mexican-Am., Chicano
○ Yes, Puerto Rican
○ Yes, Cuban
○ Yes, other Spanish/Hispanic
(Print one group, for example: Argentinean, Colombian, Dominican, Nicaraguan, Salvadoran, Spaniard, and so on.)

FIGURE 1 **Facsimile of the Race Question from the 1990 Decennial Census.** *Source:* U.S. Census Bureau.

respondents should mark only one race for each person in the household. Representatives of multiracial family organizations argued that by forcing parents to choose only one race for their children, they were causing multiracial couples to privilege the race of one parent over another when identifying the racial heritage of their children. They claimed that this was a source of marital stress and that it did not adequately capture the true multiracial heritage of children who have parents of different races.

Defining Race and Ethnicity in Twenty-First-Century America

These complaints caused the Office of Management and Budget to begin a thorough review *of* Directive No. 15 in 1993. This review included consultation with expert social scientists, hearings held around the country, numerous meetings of a large interagency committee, and a program of testing by the Census Bureau to find alternative approaches to measuring the racial and ethnic composition of the United States. In October 1997, OMB issued a revised standard for Directive No. 15 that attempted to address the concerns raised by the various groups who objected to this rule.

Specifically, the revised standard for the collection of data about race and ethnicity mandated a new set of categories and a new set of instructions. The new categories included whites, blacks, American Indians and Alaska Natives, Asians, and Native Hawaiians and Other Pacific Islanders. It also stipulated that Hispanics should be regarded as an ethnic group to be identified separately from the categories of race, suggesting that the Hispanic ethnic group included people of different races and that the identification of groups such as non-Hispanic whites and Hispanic blacks should be retained.

The new categories were a modest departure from past practices and at most represent a significant gain by Native Hawaiians insofar as they were able to obtain recognition as a group distinct from Asians and other Pacific Islanders. A more far-reaching modification was the new language instructing agencies to allow multiple entries for the identification of racial heritage. Specifically, questions soliciting information about racial heritage should include an instruction permitting respondents to "mark one or more" or to "select one or more." This change allowed individuals to identify themselves with multiple races, and

it was first implemented in the 2000 census. A facsimile of the question used in the 2000 census to obtain information about race is shown in Figure 2.

Although the vast majority of Americans (274.6 million persons) reported only one race in the 2000 census, 6.8 million persons reported two or more races. The modified race question created a number of complex problems, including some that still remain unsolved. One of the first dilemmas to arise in connection with the new question was how to report the information that was generated from the 2000 census. There are sixty-three unique racial combinations that can be constructed from the choices offered in the 2000 census form. When these sixty-three racial designations are combined with the Hispanic/non-Hispanic distinction, the census yields 126 possible categories. This number of categories produces unwieldy tabulations. In response to this problem, the Census Bureau publishes subsets of the data for persons who identify with one race only and for persons who report two or more races. The OMB also has offered guidance for possible aggregations of these categories for the purposes of civil rights enforcement (Snipp 2003).

Several vexing and still unresolved problems involve how to compare these numbers with statistics collected earlier in time given the fact that some multiracial persons may change the way they report their race from one time to another. Comparisons over time are particularly problematic since only one race was reported in the past; consequently, persons who report more than one race today must be reallocated to a single racial category as in previous reports. There is no agreed-upon way regarding how this should be done or whether such a reallocation is even possible. Another problem is that when persons have two or more races that they can report, they do not always report this information consistently. Sometimes they may report two or more races and other times they may selectively report only one race. Statistics from the American Community Survey, a precise, nationally representative sample collected in conjunction with the decennial census, show about two million fewer multiracial persons than were enumerated in the census. Ostensibly, these two numbers should have been approximately the same. Finally, how to obtain accurate third party reports from employers or school administrators about the complex multiracial heritages of employees or students also has been a significant and unresolved problem.

→ **NOTE: Please answer BOTH Questions 5 and 6.**

5. Is this person Spanish/Hispanic/Latino? *Mark ☒ the*
   *"No" box if **not** Spanish/Hispanic/Latino.*
   ☐ **No,** not Spanish/Hispanic/Latino   ☐ Yes, Puerto Rican
   ☐ Yes, Mexican, Mexican Am., Chicano   ☐ Yes, Cuban
   ☐ Yes, other Spanish/Hispanic/Latino—*Print group.* ⤵

   | | | | | | | | | | | | | | | | | | | | |

6. What is this person's race? *Mark ☒ **one or more races** to*
   indicate what this person considers himself/herself to be.
   ☐ White
   ☐ Black, African Am., or Negro
   ☐ American Indian or Alaska Native—*Print name of enrolled or principal tribe.* ⤵

   | | | | | | | | | | | | | | | | | | | | |

   ☐ Asian Indian   ☐ Japanese   ☐ Native Hawaiian
   ☐ Chinese   ☐ Korean   ☐ Guamanian or Chamorro
   ☐ Filipino   ☐ Vietnamese   ☐ Samoan
   ☐ Other Asian—*Print race.* ⤵   ☐ Other Pacific Islander—*Print race.* ⤵

   | | | | | | | | | | | | | | | | | | | | |

   ☐ Some other race—*Print race.* ⤵

   | | | | | | | | | | | | | | | | | | | | |

FIGURE 2   **Facsimile of the Race Question from the 2000 Decennial Census.** *Source:* U.S. Census Bureau.

Conclusion: Defining Race and Ethnicity in the United States and Beyond

As this essay has attempted to show, the business of defining race and ethnicity is a tricky one. In some respects, pinpointing the meaning of ethnicity is an easier task than trying to define race. This is only because the concept of ethnicity is a relatively new idea that was developed with a specific reference in mind and for many years remained within the confines of scholarly discourse.

In contrast, the notion of race is an old idea that dates back to medieval Europe and possibly earlier. At different times, it has referred to differences in blood, differences in a variety of biological characteristics, differences in character, and lately, to a set of social categories constructed to achieve some set of legal and political objectives. These different meanings are rooted in mythology, pseudo-science, and the intentions of governments and other institutions with particular agendas in mind. Under these circumstances, the muddle and confusion attached to the idea of race and what it means is hardly surprising. What is perhaps more surprising is that we often act as if none of this confusion exists. Laws are written, policies are enacted, and judges render opinions as if the meaning of race is both well understood and the subject of great agreement.

Assuming that the meaning of race is fixed and unchanging is a convenient fiction that anchors a great deal of our everyday thinking and an even larger amount of public policy. But despite the convenience of this sort of thinking, the conceptual content of the term "race" has evolved tremendously over the centuries. It continues to be a shorthand expression for describing "otherness," but how we understand and deal with others has shifted over time. We understand that enslaving and mistreating others simply because they are different is no longer acceptable in civilized society. We are beginning to understand that because people are different, they are not inherently superior or inferior to one another.

5 Racialized Social System Approach to Racism
Eduardo Bonilla-Silva

EDUARDO BONILLA-SILVA is professor of sociology at Duke University. He is best known for his 1997 piece in the *American Sociological Review* entitled "Rethinking Racism: Toward a Structural Interpretation." He is the author of three books: *White Supremacy and Racism in the Post–Civil Rights Era* (2001), *Racism Without Racists: Color-Blind Racism and the Persistence of Racial Inequality in the United States* (2003), and *Whiteout: The Continuing Significance of Racism* (with Ashley Doane, 2003).

Questions to Consider   Eduardo Bonilla-Silva argues that "after a society becomes racialized, racialization develops a life of its own." What does this mean? How does society become "racialized," and how is it possible that the idea of race can develop a "life" of its own? How, according to the author, is the United States characterized by racialized social systems?

IN ORDER TO CAPTURE THE SOCIETY-WIDE, organized, and institutional character of racism I build my alternative theory around the notion of **racialized social systems**.[1] This term refers to societies in which economic, political, social, and ideological levels are partially structured by the placement of actors in racial categories or races. Races typically are identified by their phenotype, but (as we see later) the selection of some human traits to designate a racial group is always socially rather than biologically based.

racialized social systems The idea that society is organized along racial lines and that economic, political, social, and even psychological rewards differ according to one's placement in a racial hierarchy. Once established, the system of racial hierarchy takes on a life of its own.

These systems are structured partially by race because modern social systems incorporate two or more forms of hierarchical patterns. Although processes of racialization are always embedded in other forms of hierarchy, they acquire autonomy and have independent social effects. This implies that the phenomenon that has been conceived as a free-floating ideology in fact has its own structural foundation.

In all racialized social systems the placement of actors in racial categories involves some form of hierarchy[2] that produces definite social relations among the races. The race placed in the superior position tends to receive greater economic remuneration and access to better occupations and prospects in the labor market, occupies a primary position in the political system, is granted higher social estimation (e.g., is viewed as "smarter" or "better looking"), often has the license to draw physical (segregation) as well as social (racial etiquette) boundaries between itself and other races, and receives what W. E. B. Du Bois called a "psychological wage."[3] The totality of these racialized social relations and practices constitutes the racial structure of a society.

Although all racialized social systems are hierarchical, the particular character of the hierarchy, and, thus, of the racial structure, is variable. For example, the domination of blacks in the United States was achieved through dictatorial means during slavery, but in the post–civil rights period this domination has been *hegemonic,* that is in the Gramscian sense of the term, achieved through consent rather than coercion.[4] Similarly, the form of securing domination and white privilege is variable too. For instance, the racial practices and mechanisms that kept blacks subordinated changed from overt and eminently racist in the Jim Crow era to covert and indirectly racist in the contemporary period. The unchanging element of these systems is racial inequality—that the subordinated races' life chances are significantly lower than those of the dominant race. This is the feature that ultimately distinguishes this form of hierarchical social organization. Generally, the higher the level of racial inequality, the more racialized the social system, and vice versa.

Because the races receive different social rewards at all levels, they develop different interests, which can be detected in their struggles to either transform or maintain a particular racial order. These interests are collective rather than individual, are based on relations among races rather than on particular group needs, and are practical; that is, they are related to concrete struggles. Although one race's general interest may ultimately lie in the complete elimination of a society's racial structure, its array of alternatives may not include that possibility. For instance, the historical struggle against chattel slavery led not to the development of race-free societies but to the establishment of social systems with a different kind of racialization. Race-free societies were not among the available alternatives because the nonslave populations had the capacity to preserve some type of racial privilege. The historical "exceptions" occurred in racialized societies in which the nonslaves' power was almost completely superseded by that of the slave population.[5]

A simple criticism of the argument I have advanced so far is that it ignores the internal divisions of the races along class and gender lines. Such criticism, however, does not deal squarely with the issue at hand. The fact that not all members of the dominant race receive the same level of rewards and (conversely) that not all members of the subordinate race or races are at the bottom of the social order does not negate the fact that races, as social groups, are in either a superordinate or a subordinate position in a social system. Historically the racialization of social systems did not imply the exclusion of other forms of oppression. In fact, racialization occurred in social formations also structured by class and gender. Hence, in these societies, the racialization of subjects is fragmented along class and gender lines. The important question—Which interests move actors to struggle?—is historically contingent and cannot be ascertained a priori.[6] Depending on the character of racialization in a social order, class interests may take precedence over racial interests as in contemporary Brazil, Cuba, and Puerto Rico. In other situations, racial interests may take precedence over class interests as in the case of blacks throughout most of U.S. history.

In general, the systemic salience of class in relation to race increases when the economic, political, and social inequality among the races decreases substantially. Yet this broad argument generates at least one warning: The narrowing of within-class differences among racial actors usually causes *more* rather than *less* racial conflict, at least in the short run, as the competition for resources increases. More significantly, even when class-based conflict becomes more salient in a social order, this cannot be interpreted as prima facie evidence that race has subsided as a social factor. For instance, because of the way in which Latin American racial formations rearticulated race and racial discourse in the nineteenth-century post-emancipation era,[8] these societies silenced from above the political space for public racial contestation. Yet more than 100 years after these societies developed the myth of racial democracy, they have more rather than less racial inequality than countries such as the United States.[9]

Because racial actors are also classed and gendered (that is, they belong to class and gender groups), analysts must control for class and gender to ascertain the material advantages enjoyed by a dominant race. In a racialized society such as the United States, the independent effects of race are assessed by analysts who (1) compare data between whites and nonwhites in the *same* class and gender positions, (2) evaluate the proportion as well as the general character of the races' participation in some domain of life, and (3) examine racial data at all levels—social, political, economic, and ideological—to ascertain the general position of racial groups in a social system.

The first of these procedures has become standard practice in sociology. No serious sociologist would present racial statistics without controlling for gender and class (or at least the class of persons' socioeconomic status). By doing this, analysts assume they can measure the unadulterated effects of "discrimination" manifested in unexplained "residuals." Despite its usefulness, however, this technique provides only a partial account of the "race effect" because (1) a significant amount of racial data cannot be retrieved through surveys and (2) the technique of "controlling for" a variable neglects the obvious—why a group is over- or underrepresented in certain categories of the control variables in the first place.[10] Moreover, these analysts presume that it is possible to analyze the amount of discrimination in one domain (e.g., income, occupational status) "without analyzing the extent to which discrimination also affects the factors they hold constant."[11] Hence to evaluate "race effects" in any domain, analysts must attempt to make sense of their findings in relation to a race's standing in other domains.

But what is the nature of races or, more properly, of racialized social groups? Omi and Winant state that races are the outcome of the racialization process, which they define as "the extension of racial meaning to a previously racially unclassified relationship, social practice, or group."[12] Historically the classification of a people in racial terms has been a highly political act associated with practices such as conquest and colonization, enslavement, peonage, indentured servitude, and, more recently, colonial and neocolonial labor immigration. Categories such as "Indians" and "Negroes" were invented in the sixteenth and seventeenth centuries to justify the conquest and exploitation of various peoples.[13] The invention of such categories entails a dialectical process of construction; that is, the creation of the category "Other" involves the creation of a category "Same." If "Indians" are depicted as "savages," Europeans are characterized as "civilized";

if "blacks" are defined as natural candidates for slavery, "whites" are defined as free subjects.[14] Yet although the racialization of peoples was socially invented and did not override previous forms of social distinction based on class or gender, it did not lead to imaginary relations but generated new forms of human association with definite status differences. After the process of attaching meaning to a "people" is instituted, race becomes a real category of group association and identity.[15]

Because racial classifications partially organize and limit actors' life chances, racial practices of opposition emerge. Regardless of the form of racial interaction (overt, covert, or inert), races can be recognized in the realm of racial relations and positions. Viewed in this light, races are the effect of racial practices of opposition ("we" versus "them") at the economic, political, social, and ideological levels.[16]

Races, as most social scientists acknowledge, are not biologically but socially determined categories of identity and group association. In this regard, they are analogous to class and gender.[17] Actors in racial positions do not occupy those positions because they are of X or Y race, but because X or Y has been socially defined as a race. Actors' **phenotypic** (i.e., biologically inherited) characteristics, such as skin tone and hair color and texture, are usually, although not always, used to denote racial distinctions.[18] For example, Jews in many European nations and the Irish in England have been treated as racial groups.[19] Also, Indians in the United States have been viewed as one race despite the tremendous phenotypic and cultural variation among nations. Because races are socially constructed, both the meaning and the position assigned to races in the racial structure are always contested. Who is to be black or white or Indian reflects and affects the social, political, ideological, and economic struggles among the races. The global effects of these struggles can change the meaning of the racial categories as well as the position of a racialized group in a social formation.

This latter point is illustrated clearly by the historical struggles of several "white ethnic" groups in the United States in their efforts to become accepted as legitimate whites or "Americans."[20] Neither light-skinned nor, for

phenotype A biological term that refers to how we look (skin color, facial features, hair texture, etc.).

that matter, dark-skinned immigrants necessarily came to this country as members of X or Y race. Light-skinned Europeans, after brief periods of "not-yet white," became "white" but did not lose their "ethnic" character.[21] Their struggle for inclusion had specific implications: racial inclusion as members of the white community allowed Americanization and class mobility. On the other hand, among dark-skinned immigrants from Africa, Latin America, and the Caribbean, the struggle was to avoid classification as "black." These immigrants challenged the reclassification of their identity for a single reason: In the United States "black" signified a subordinate status in society. Hence many of these groups struggled to keep their own ethnic or cultural identity, as denoted in expressions such as "I am not black; I am Jamaican," or "I am not black; I am Senegalese."[22] Yet eventually many of these groups resolved this contradictory situation by accepting the duality of their situation: In the United States, they were classified socially as black yet they retained and nourished their own cultural or ethnic heritage—a heritage deeply influenced by African traditions.

Although the content of racial categories changes over time through manifold processes and struggles, race is not a secondary category of group association. The meaning of black and white, the "racial formation," changes within the larger racial structure. This does not mean that the racial structure is immutable and completely independent of the action of racialized actors. It means only that the social relations among the races become institutionalized (form a structure as well as a culture) and affect social life whether or not individual members of the races want it to. In Frederick Barth's words, "Ethnic identity implies a series of constraints on the kinds of roles an individual is allowed to play [and] is similar to sex and rank, in that it constrains the incumbent in all his activities."[23] For instance, free blacks during the slavery period struggled to change the meaning of "blackness," specifically to dissociate it from slavery. Yet they could not escape the larger racial structure that restricted their life chances and their freedom.[24]

The placement of a group of people in a racial category stemmed initially [25] from the interests of powerful actors in the social system (e.g., the capitalist class, the planter class, and colonizers). After racial categories were employed to organize social relations in societies,

however, race became an independent element of the operation of the social system.

What are the dynamics of racial issues in racialized systems? Most important, after a social formation is racialized, its "normal" dynamics always include a racial component. Societal struggles based on class or gender contain a racial component because both of these social categories are also racialized; that is, both class and gender are constructed along racial lines. In 1922, for example, white South African workers in the middle of a strike inspired by the Russian revolution rallied under the slogan "Workers of the world unite for a white South Africa." One of the state's "concessions" to this "class" struggle was the passage of the Apprenticeship Act of 1922, "which prevented Black workers acquiring apprenticeships."[26] In another example, the struggle of women in the United States to attain their civil and human rights has always been plagued by deep racial tensions.[27]

Nonetheless, some of the strife that exists in a racialized social formation has a distinct racial character; I call such strife *racial contestation*—the struggle of racial groups for systemic changes regarding their position at one or more levels. Such a struggle may be social (Who can be here? Who belongs here?), political (Who can vote? How much power should they have? Should they be citizens?), economic (Who should work, and what should they do? They are taking our jobs!), or ideological (Black is beautiful!).

Although much of this contestation is expressed at the individual level and is disjointed, sometimes it becomes collective and general and can effect meaningful systemic changes in a society's racial organization. The form of contestation may be relatively passive and subtle (e.g., in situations of fundamental overt racial domination such as slavery and apartheid) or more active and overt (e.g., in quasi-democratic situations such as the contemporary United States). As a rule, however, fundamental changes in racialized social systems are accompanied by struggles that reach the point of overt protest.[28] This does not mean that a violent racially based revolution is the only way of accomplishing effective changes in the relative position of racial groups. It is simply an extension of the argument that social systems and their supporters must be "shaken" if fundamental transformations are to take place.[29] On this structural foundation rests the phenomenon labeled racism by social scientists.

I reserve the term *racial ideology* for the segment of the ideological structure of a social system that crystallizes racial notions and stereotypes. Racial ideology provides the rationalization for social, political, and economic interactions among the races. Depending on the particular character of a racialized social system and on the struggles of the subordinated races, racial ideology may be developed highly (as in apartheid) or loosely (as in slavery) and its content expressed in overt or covert terms.

Although racial ideology originates in race relations, it acquires relative autonomy in the social system and performs practical functions.[30] In Paul Gilroy's words, racial ideology "mediates the world of agents and the structures which are created by their social praxis."[31] Racism crystallizes the changing "dogma" on which actors in the social system operate and becomes "common sense"; it provides the rules for perceiving and dealing with the Other in a racialized society. In the United States, for instance, because racial notions about what blacks and whites are or ought to be pervade their encounters, whites still have difficulty in dealing with black bankers, lawyers, professors, and doctors.[32] Thus, although racist ideology is ultimately false, it fulfills a practical role in racialized societies.

At this point it is possible to sketch the framework of the racialized social system. First, racialized social systems are societies that allocate differential economic, political, social, and even psychological rewards to groups along racial lines, lines that are socially constructed. After a society becomes racialized, a set of social relations and practices based on racial distinctions develops at all societal levels. I designate the aggregate of those relations and practices as the racial structure of a society. Second, races historically are constituted according to the process of racialization; they become the effect of relations of opposition among racialized groups at all levels of a social formation. Third, on the basis of this structure, a racial ideology develops. This ideology is not simply a "superstructural" phenomenon (a mere reflection of the racialized system) but becomes the organizational map that guides actions of racial actors in society. It becomes as real as the racial relations it organizes. Fourth, most struggles in a racialized social system contain a racial component, but sometimes they acquire or exhibit a distinct racial character. Racial contestation is the logical outcome of a society with a racial hierarchy. A social formation that includes some form of racialization will always exhibit some form of racial contestation. Finally, the process of racial contestation reveals the different objective interests of the races in a racialized social system.

Conclusion

My central argument in this chapter is that the common-sense understanding of racism, which is not much different than the definition developed by mainstream social scientists or even by many critical analysts, does not provide an adequate theoretical foundation for understanding racial phenomena. With notable exceptions,[33] analysts in academia are still entangled in ungrounded ideological interpretations of racism. Lacking a structural view, they tend to reduce racial phenomena to a derivation of the class structure (as Marxist interpreters do) or the result of an irrational ideology (as mainstream social scientists do).

In the racialized social system framework, I suggest, as do Omi and Winant, that racism should be studied from the viewpoint of racialization. I contend that after a society becomes racialized, racialization develops a life of its own.[34] Although racism interacts with class and gender structurations in society, it becomes an organizing principle of social relations in itself. Race, as most analysts suggest, is a social construct, but that construct, like class and gender, has independent effects in social life. After racial stratification is established, race becomes an independent criterion for vertical hierarchy in society. Therefore different races experience positions of subordination and superordination in society and develop different interests. This framework has the following advantages over traditional views of racism:

Racial phenomena are regarded as the "normal" outcome of the racial structure of a society. Thus we can account for all racial manifestations. Instead of explaining racial phenomena as deriving from other structures or from racism (conceived of as a free-floating ideology), we can trace cultural, political, economic, social, and even psychological racial phenomena to the racial organization of that society.

The changing nature of what analysts label "racism" is explained as the normal outcome of racial contestation in a racialized social system. In this framework, changes in racism are explained rather than described. Changes are due to specific struggles at different levels among the races, resulting from differences in interests. Such changes may transform the nature of racialization and the global character of racial relations in the system (the racial structure). Therefore, change is viewed as a normal component of the racialized system.

The racialized social system framework allows analysts to explain overt as well as covert racial behavior. The covert or overt nature of racial contacts depends on how the process of racialization is manifested; this in turns depends on how race originally was articulated in a social formation and on the process of racial contestation. This point implies that rather than conceiving of racism as a universal and uniformly orchestrated phenomenon, analysts should study "historically-specific racisms."[35] This insight is not new: Robert Park, Oliver Cox, Pierre van den Bergue, and Marvin Harris described varieties of "situations of race relations" with distinct forms of racial interaction.

Racially motivated behavior, whether or not the actors are conscious of it, is regarded as "rational"—that is, based on the given race's individual interests.[36] This framework accounts for Archie Bunker–type racial behavior as well as for more "sophisticated" varieties of racial conduct. Racial phenomena are viewed as systemic; therefore all actors in the system participate in racial affairs. Some members of the dominant racial group tend to exhibit less virulence toward members of the subordinated races because they have greater control over the form and outcome of their racial interactions. When they cannot control that interaction—as in the case of revolts or blacks moving into "their" neighborhood—they behave much like other members of the dominant race.

The reproduction of racial phenomena in contemporary societies is explained in this framework not by reference to a long-distant past but in relation to its contemporary structure. Because racism is viewed as systemic (possessing a racial structure) and as organized around the races' different interests, racial aspects of social systems today are viewed as fundamentally related to hierarchical relations among the races in those systems. Elimination of the racialized character of a social system entails the end of racialization, and hence of races altogether. This argument clashes with social scientists' most popular policy prescription for "curing" racism, namely education. This "solution" is the logical outcome of defining racism as a belief. Most analysts regard racism as a matter of individuals subscribing to an irrational view, thus the cure is educating them to realize that racism is wrong. Education is also the choice pill prescribed by Marxists for healing workers from racism. The alternative theory offered here implies that because the phenomenon has structural consequences for the races, the only way to cure society of racism is by eliminating its systemic roots. Whether this can be accomplished democratically or only through revolutionary means is an open question, and one that depends on the particular racial structure of the society in question.

A racialization framework accounts for the ways in which racial and ethnic **stereotypes** *emerge, are transformed, and disappear.* Racial stereotypes are crystallized at the ideological level of a social system. These images ultimately indicate—although in distorted ways—and justify the stereotyped group's position in a society. Stereotypes may originate out of (1) material realities or conditions endured by the group, (2) genuine ignorance about the group, or (3) rigid, distorted views on the group's physical, cultural, or moral nature. Once they emerge, however, stereotypes must relate—although not necessarily fit perfectly—to the group's true social position in the racialized system if they are to perform their ideological function. Stereotypes that do not tend to reflect a group's situation do not work and are bound to disappear. For example, notions of the Irish as stupid or of Jews as athletically talented have all but vanished since the 1940s, as the Irish moved up the educational ladder and Jews gained access to multiple routes of social mobility. Generally, then, stereotypes are reproduced because they reflect a group's distinct position and status in society. As a corollary, racial or ethnic notions about a group disappear only when the group's status mirrors that of the dominant racial or ethnic group in the society.

The framework of the racialized social system is not a universal theory explaining racial phenomena in societies. It is intended to trigger a serious discussion of how race shapes social systems. Moreover, the important question of how race interacts and intersects with class and gender has not yet been addressed satisfactorily. Provisionally I maintain that a nonfunctionalist reading of the concept of social system may give us clues for comprehending societies *structured in dominance,* to use Stuart Hall's term. If

stereotype A simplfied picture we paint of an entire group of people. The tendency is to generalize about everyone in that group based on ignornance, limited information, or prejudice. Examples of racial stereotypes: all Asians are good at math, white people can't jump, and all black people have rhythm.

societies are viewed as systems that articulate different structures (organizing principles on which sets of social relations are systematically patterned), it is possible to claim that race—as well as gender—has both individual and combined (interactive) effects in society.

To test the usefulness of the racialized social system framework as a theoretical basis for research, we must perform comparative work on racialization in various societies. One of the main objectives of this comparative work should be to determine the specific mechanisms, practices, and social relations that produce and reproduce racial inequality at all levels—that is, uncover the society's racial structure. Unlike analysts who believe that "racism" has withered away, I argue that the persistent inequality experienced by blacks and other racial minorities in the United States today is due to the *continued* albeit *changed* existence of a racial structure. In contrast to race relations in the Jim Crow period, however, racial practices that reproduce racial inequality in contemporary America are (1) increasingly covert, (2) embedded in normal operations of institutions, (3) void of direct racial terminology, and (4) invisible to most whites.

Seeing the Big Picture   The Social Construction of Race, 1790–2000

The Appendix provides the official racial definitions used by the U.S. Census. Figure 1 shows how racial and ethnic categories changed from 1790 to 2000. How do these changing definitions reflect the idea that race is a "social construction"?

6 Understanding Racial-Ethnic Disparities in Health: Sociological Contributions

David R. Williams • Michelle Sternthal

DAVID R. WILLIAMS is the Florence and Laura Norman Professor of Public Health and professor of African and African American studies and of sociology at Harvard University. His scholarly interests focus on the trends and determinants of socioeconomic and racial disparities in health, the effects of racism on health, and the ways in which religious involvement can affect health. He recently served as the staff director of the Robert Wood Johnson Foundation Commission to Build a Healthier America.

MICHELLE STERNTHAL is a postdoctoral research fellow in the Department of Environmental Epidemiology at the Harvard School of Public Health. Her research uses a life course perspective and focuses on social determinants of physical and mental health, and their connection to racial and socioeconomic health disparities. Her most recent research explores the biosocial pathways through which cumulative exposure to stress affects childhood asthma susceptibility and onset.

Questions to Consider David R. Williams and Michelle Sternthal use sociological theory to understand and discuss racial disparities in health. As you read this article, take note of the socioeconomic status various groups occupy and how that status is related to the relative health of the group. How do these authors use sociological theory to understand social inequality as a means to identify health disparities? What role do ethnicity, class, race, and immigration status play in racial differences in disease and health?

The most difficult social problem in the matter of Negro health is the peculiar attitude of the nation toward the well-being of the race. There have . . . been few other cases in the history of civilized peoples where human suffering has been viewed with such peculiar indifference.

—W. E. B. DU BOIS, 1899 [1967], 163

RACIAL DIFFERENCES IN HEALTH DATE BACK to some of our earliest health records in the United States, with blacks (or African Americans) having poorer health than whites across a broad range of health status indicators. This article highlights some of the important contributions of sociologists to understanding racial

inequities in health. It begins with a brief description of the findings of a seminal study conducted by the African American sociologist W. E. B. Du Bois in the late nineteenth century. It shows how later sociologists have built on this work by elaborating on the ways in which socioeconomic status (SES), racism, and migration affect racial differences in health. We also consider the implications of this sociological research for policies to reduce disparities in health.

Du Bois's Early Research on Race and Health

In his classic 1899 book, *The Philadelphia Negro*, W. E. B. Du Bois provided a detailed characterization of the "negro problem" in America (Du Bois [1899] 1967). His insightful analysis indicated that the higher level of poor health for blacks was one important indicator of racial inequality in the United States. In the late nineteenth and early twentieth centuries the dominant medical paradigm attributed any observed racial difference in health to innate biological differences between racial groups (Krieger 1987). In contrast, Du Bois saw racial differences in health as reflecting differences in "social advancements," the "vastly different conditions" under which blacks and whites lived. He argued that, although the causes of racial differences in health were multifactorial, they were nonetheless primarily social. The list of contributing factors included poor heredity, neglect of infants, bad dwellings, poor food, and unsanitary living conditions. For example, consumption (tuberculosis) was the leading cause of death for blacks in Philadelphia, and Du Bois ([1899] 1967) indicated that the causal factors were primarily environmental. He stated that "bad ventilation, lack of outdoor life for women and children, poor protection against dampness and cold are undoubtedly the chief causes of the excessive death rate" (p. 152). Du Bois also noted that the health of blacks varied within Philadelphia by neighborhood of residence. Death rates were higher in the Fifth Ward, "the worst Negro slum in the city and the worst part of the city in respect to sanitation," than in the Thirtieth Ward, which had "good houses and clean streets" (Du Bois [1899] 1967:150–51).

Du Bois reported that black men had poorer health than black women and that the gender differences in health were larger for blacks than for whites. These patterns were also attributed to "the social condition of the sexes in the city" (Du Bois [1899] 1967:151). He indicated that, although domestic work was the only option for black women, work was more available for black women than for their male counterparts. In addition, the conditions of work for black women were more conducive to health than those for black men. The domestic servant had access to a good house, good food, and proper clothing. In contrast, black males lived in poorer housing, lived on poorly prepared or irregular food, and had jobs that provided greater exposure to adverse weather conditions. Du Bois also speculated that migration and urbanization were influences on black health. He noted, though, that because the migration of blacks from the south to the north was recent, its full impact on black health was not known. However, he documented that in Philadelphia

wards with a high proportion of immigrants, death rates were reduced because of the demographic composition of the population ("the absence of old people and children," see Du Bois [1899] 1967, p. 155).

For much of the twentieth century, as reflected by publications in the two leading journals in American sociology, the health of the black population has not been a central focus of the discipline. To illustrate, we searched the phrases "race and health," "health inequality and race," "health inequality and ethnicity," and "health disparity" in the *American Journal of Sociology (AJS)* and the *American Sociological Review (ASR)* from the earliest dates available electronically (1895 for *AJS* and 1934 for *ASR*) to identify articles addressing racial-ethnic disparities in health. We identified only 18 relevant articles published by the year 1989 (ten in *AJS* and eight in *ASR*). However, there was considerably more recent interest in the topic. There were 14 articles published from 1990 to 2008 (six in *AJS* and eight in *ASR*). Although we argue that racial disparities in health were not a central focus of the top journals of the discipline, sociologists have made and continue to make seminal contributions to our understanding of racial disparities in health. Examples include Williams and Collins (1995) in the *Annual Review of Sociology*, Link and Phelan (1995) in the *Journal of Health and Social Behavior*, and Markides and Coreil (1986) in *Public Health Reports*. Sociologists have also been contributors to several landmark publications on race in the last several decades. These include *A Common Destiny: Blacks and American Society* (Jaynes and Williams 1989), *Unequal Treatment* (Smedley, Stith, and Nelson 2002), and *America Becoming: Racial Trends and Their Consequences* (Smelser, Wilson, and Mitchell 2001). As we indicate below, much of the sociological research on race and health has built and elaborated on many of the insights that were present in Du Bois's seminal work.

The Persistence of Racial Differences in Health

There is abundant evidence of the continued existence of racial differences in health. Table 1 provides an example of the magnitude and trends of these inequities. It shows racial differences in life expectancy at birth for men and women from 1950 to the present. Gender is an important social status category, and there is need for increased

TABLE 1   **Racial Differences in Years of Life Expectancy at Birth: 1950–Present**

Year	Men			Women			Gender Difference	
	White	*Black[a]*	*Difference*	*White*	*Black[a]*	*Difference*	*White*	*Black[a]*
1950	66.5	59.1	7.4	72.2	62.9	9.3	5.7	3.8
1960	67.4	61.1	6.3	74.1	66.3	7.8	6.7	5.2
1970	68.0	60.0	8.0	75.6	68.3	7.3	7.6	8.3
1980	70.7	63.8	6.9	78.1	72.5	5.6	7.4	8.7
1990	72.7	64.5	8.2	79.4	73.6	5.8	6.7	9.1
2000	74.7	68.2	6.5	79.9	75.1	4.8	5.2	6.9
2006	75.7	69.7	6.0	80.6	76.5	4.1	4.9	6.8
Change from 1950 to 2006	9.2	10.6		8.4	13.6			

[a]From 1950 to 1960, includes all non-white races.

Source: Heron et al. 2009

attention to how health is distributed by multiple social status categories simultaneously. The racial gap in health is large and persistent over time. White men and women outlived their black counterparts by 7.4 and 9.3 years, respectively, in 1950. Although life expectancy has increased for all groups over the last half-century, in 2006 white men still lived six years longer than African American men and white women had a four year advantage over their black peers. And as Du Bois ([1899] 1967) noted over a century ago, the patterns are gendered. The racial gap in health is larger for men than for women, and there have been larger reductions in the racial gap in life expectancy for women than for men over time, reflecting the fact that, of the four race-gender groups considered, black women have had the largest absolute gains in life expectancy between 1950 and 2006. Moreover, since 1970, the gender difference in life expectancy has been larger for blacks than for whites, with African American women enjoying a higher level of life expectancy than white men.

Other research reveals that African Americans and American Indians have higher age-specific death rates than whites from birth through retirement (Williams et al. 2010). Hispanics (or Latinos) have elevated rates of some leading causes of death, such as diabetes, **hypertension,** liver cirrhosis, and homicide. Moreover, the elevated rates of disease and death for minorities compared to whites

hypertension having high blood pressure

reflect the earlier onset of illness, greater severity of disease, and poorer survival (Williams et al. 2010). Even when African Americans have a lower rate of illness than whites, they have a prognosis that is considerably worse than those of their white counterparts. For example, a recent national study found that, although blacks have lower current and lifetime rates of major depression than whites, the cases of depression among blacks were more likely to be persistent, severe, disabling, and untreated (Williams et al. 2007a).

What Is Race?

Sociological research seeking to understand how and why these large racial differences in health persist has attempted to delineate what "race" is. The U.S. Government's Office of Management and Budget (OMB) currently recognizes five racial categories (white; black or African American; American Indian or Alaskan Native; Asian; and Native Hawaiian and other Pacific Islander), as well as Hispanic or Latino, an ethnic category. Early research on racial differences in health viewed all observed disparities as reflecting biological differences between racial groups (Krieger 1987). Recent scientific research reveals that human genetic variation does not naturally aggregate into subgroups that match human conceptions of racial categories, and that "race" is in large part a social rather than a biological category (Cooper, Kaufman, and Ward 2003).

Sociologists have long shown that established racial classification systems are arbitrary and evolved from systems of stratification, power, and ideology (Frazier 1947; Blauner 1972; Omi and Winant 1994). In critiques of the conceptual, methodological, and practical implications of using race as a variable in health research, sociologists have rejected the dominant view of the last century that racial disparities in health primarily reflect biological differences between racial groups (Wilkinson and King 1987; Williams 1997; American Sociological Association 2003). Duster and Garrett (1984), for example, have shown how an emphasis on the genetic sources of racial disparities in health can serve important ideological functions in society. Views of race that focus on biology can divert attention from the social origins of disease, reinforce social norms of racial inferiority, and promote the maintenance of the status quo. If racial differences in health are caused by inherent genetic differences, then social policies and structures that initiate and sustain the production of disease are absolved from responsibility. Sociologists have also emphasized that science is not **value-free** and that preconceived opinions, political agendas, and cultural norms, consciously or unconsciously, can shape scientific research by determining which research questions are asked and which projects are funded (Duster and Garrett 1984).

Sociologists have also noted a recent trend on the part of some geneticists to use current racial categories to capture genetic differences between population groups (Frank 2008). These researchers argue that data from multiple loci on the human genome can provide fairly accurate characterization of individuals into continental ancestral groups that approximate our current racial categories (Risch et al. 2002). These data on "continental ancestry" have been used to suggest that there is enormous practical value in using race as a biological category. However, Serre and Paabo (2004) have shown that sampling biases play a key role in conclusions regarding the continental clustering of populations. Thus, although genetic markers can uniquely identify most individuals, variations in biological characteristics relevant for health risks are not inherently structured into meaningful "racial" categories such that identifying ancestry provides little direct information regarding whether an individual has a specific genetic characteristic (Cooper et al. 2003). Sociologist Reanne Frank (2008) has noted the worrying trend in

value-free to be completely and totally objective

health disparities research of keeping the logic of genetic racial differences intact but substituting the language of "ancestral background" for the language of "race."

Sociologists also emphasize that, although the contribution of genetics to racial variations in major chronic diseases is likely to be small, research on racial differences in health should seek to understand how social exposures combine with biology to affect the social distribution of disease (Williams et al. 2010). However, all conclusions about the contribution of genetics should be based on explicit tests of genetic traits. In addition, researchers should pay more attention to issues of population sampling when making inferences to larger populations about observed genetic variation, and they should also be more mindful both of genetic variation within race and differences across racial groups. Most importantly, sociologists and other social scientists need to devote more concerted and systematic attention to developing valid and reliable measures of the relevant aspects of the social environment for the study of gene–environment interactions.

Research indicates that, even in the case of single gene disorders, the severity and timing of genetic expression are affected by environmental triggers, and that established genetic risks can be exacerbated or become protective in the presence of specific environmental exposures (Shields, Fullerton, and Olden 2009). Recent sociological research illustrates how gene–environment interactions can potentially shed light on the mechanisms linking the social environment to disease. For example, an analysis of data from adolescents in the Add Health Study found that genetic traits interacted with family processes (e.g., daily family meals), school processes (e.g., repeating a grade), and friendship network variables (e.g., friend delinquency) to predict delinquency and violence among male adolescents (Guo and Roettger 2008).

In contemporary society, racial groups differ on a broad range of social, behavioral, nutritional, psychological, residential, occupational, and other variables. And, given that biology is not static but is adaptive to the environmental conditions in which the human organism exists, there are likely to be interactions of the social environment with both innate and acquired biological factors. Thus, although variation in gene frequency is unlikely to play a major role in accounting for racial disparities, differences in gene expression linked to the occupancy of different environmental contexts could play a critical role.

Epigenetics refers to changes in gene expression that are not caused by changes in the nucleotide sequences of the DNA. Recent research reveals that exposure to risk factors and resources in the social environment can produce changes in gene expression (Williams et al. 2010). Future research on racial inequities in health needs to more systematically explore the extent to which the distinctive residential and occupational environments of racial minorities give rise to patterns of social exposures that can produce epigenetic changes in gene expression and tissue and organ function (Kuzawa and Sweet 2009).

Social Structure and Race

Sociological research has long explored the role of social structure and social stratification as a key determinant of health. Social structure refers to enduring patterns of social life that shape an individual's attitudes and beliefs, behaviors and actions, and material and psychological resources. Among the social structures investigated within sociology, social class, usually operationalized as socioeconomic status (SES), has proven particularly relevant for understanding racial disparities in health. In a seminal study in the 1840s, Engels ([1844] 1984) showed how life expectancy in Liverpool, England varied by the occupation of the residents. Moreover, he showed how specific exposures in both occupational and residential environments were related to the elevated risk of particular diseases. More recent sociological research has found that SES is associated with high quality health care, stress, exposure to social and physical toxins, social support, and healthy behaviors. Accordingly, SES remains one of the strongest known determinants of variations in health status (Williams and Collins 1995).

Sociological work on class informs the study of racial disparities in health, because, as Du Bois ([1899] 1967) noted at the turn of the century, race is strongly intertwined with SES. Recent research continues to find that SES differences among the races account for a substantial component of the racial-ethnic differences in health (Hayward et al. 2000; Williams and Collins 1995; Hummer 1996). However, sociologists have emphasized that race and SES are two related but distinct systems of social ordering that jointly contribute to health risks (Navarro 1990; Williams and Collins 1995). Accordingly, attention needs to be given to both race-based and class-based factors that undergird racial health disparities.

Table 2 illustrates the complex relationship between race and SES by presenting national data on life expectancy at age 25 across categories of race and education. It shows that there is a five-year racial difference in life expectancy at age 25, but an even larger difference within each race by education. It also indicates that the racial differences in health cannot be simply reduced to SES, because there are residual racial differences at every level of education. These data illustrate the notion of the potential "double jeopardy" facing those in nondominant racial groups who experience health risks associated with both their stigmatized racial status and low SES (Ferraro and Farmer 1996). The life expectancy data at age 25 also reveal that the racial gap in life expectancy is greater at the higher levels of education compared to the lowest level. This is generally consistent with the "diminishing returns" hypothesis, which argues that racial minorities receive declining health returns as SES increases (Farmer and Ferraro 2005). This pattern exists for some but not all health outcomes. Sociologists have also shown that race and SES can combine with gender and other social statuses in complex ways to create patterns of interaction and intersectionality (Schulz and Mullings 2006).

Sociological work on social class has also contributed to our understanding of racial disparities by underscoring the multidimensionality of SES indicators (Hauser 1994). Sociologists have shown that it requires assessing the multiple dimensions of SES to fully characterize its contribution to racial disparities in health. Moreover, all of the indicators of SES are nonequivalent across race. For example, compared to whites, blacks and some other racial minorities have lower income at every level of education; less wealth (net assets) at every level of income; higher rates of unemployment at all levels of education; higher exposure to occupational hazards, even after adjusting for job experience and education; and less purchasing power because of higher costs of goods and services in their residential contexts (Williams and Collins 1995). Sociological research has also highlighted the role of SES at the community level, as captured by neighborhood-level markers of economic hardship, social disorder, and concentrated disadvantage (Wilson 1990; Massey and Denton 1993). Other sociological research has called attention to large racial-ethnic inequalities in wealth, and they have documented that these gaps reflect, at least in part, the historical legacy of institutional discrimination

TABLE 2   **Years of Life Expectancy at Age 25, United States**

Group	White	Black	Difference
All (1998)[a]	53.4	48.4	5.0
By Education (1988–1998)[b]			
0–12 Years	50.1	47.0	3.1
12 Years	54.1	49.9	4.2
Some College	55.2	50.9	4.3
College Graduate	56.5	52.3	4.2
Difference	6.4	5.3	

[a]Murphy National Vital Statistics Survey 2000.
[b]Braveman et al. 2010, National Longitudinal Mortality Study 1988–1998.

(Conley 1999; Oliver and Shapiro 2006). While income captures the flow of economic resources (such as wages) into the household, wealth captures the economic reserves that are reflected in savings, home equity, and other financial assets. National data reveal that, for every dollar of wealth that white individuals have, blacks have 9 cents and Hispanics have 12 cents (Orzechowski and Sepielli 2003). These striking disparities exist at every level of income. For example, for every dollar of wealth that poor whites in the lowest **quintile** of income have, poor blacks have one penny and poor Latinos have two pennies.

Racism and Health

Sociological research has also shed important light on how factors linked to race contribute to racial differences in health. This work has identified multiple ways in which racism initiates and sustains health disparities (Williams and Mohammed 2009). This research explicitly draws on the larger sociology literature on racism and conceptualizes it as a multilevel construct, encompassing institutional and individual discrimination, racial prejudice and stereotypes, and internalized racism (Feagin and McKinney 2003; Bonilla-Silva 1997; Massey and Denton 1993).

At the institutional level, sociological research has underscored the role of residential racial segregation as a primary institutional mechanism of racism and a fundamental cause of racial disparities in health (Massey and Denton 1993; LaVeist 1989; Williams and Collins 2001),

quintile to divide a population into five equal parts

and it has helped shape local and federal policies. Sociologists have documented how segregation produces the concentration of poverty, social disorder, and social isolation, and how it creates pathogenic conditions in residential environments (Massey 2004; Schulz et al. 2002; Williams and Collins 2001). For example, an examination of the 171 largest U.S. cities found that the worst urban context in which white individuals lived was better than the average context of black neighborhoods (Sampson and Wilson 1995). These differences in neighborhood quality and community conditions are driven by residential segregation by race, a neglected but enduring legacy of institutional racism in the United States. Considerable evidence suggests that, because of segregation, the residential conditions under which African Americans, American Indians, and an increasing proportion of Latinos live are distinctive from those of the rest of the population.

Sociologists have also identified multiple pathways through which segregation can adversely affect health (Morenoff 2003; Williams and Collins 2001; Schulz et al. 2002). First, segregation restricts SES attainment by limiting access to quality elementary and high school education, preparation for higher education, and job opportunities. Second, the residential conditions of concentrated poverty and social disorder created by segregation make it difficult for residents to eat nutritiously, exercise regularly, and avoid advertising for tobacco and alcohol. For example, concerns about personal safety and the lack of recreation facilities can discourage leisure time physical exercise. Third, the concentration of poverty can lead to exposure to elevated levels of financial stress and hardship, as well as other chronic and acute stressors at the individual, household, and neighborhood levels. Fourth, the weakened community and neighborhood infrastructure in segregated areas can also adversely affect interpersonal relationships and trust among neighbors. Fifth, the institutional neglect and disinvestment in poor, segregated communities contributes to increased exposure to environmental toxins, poor quality housing, and criminal victimization. Finally, segregation adversely affects both access to care and the quality of care. Research has linked residential segregation to an elevated risk of illness and death, and it has shown that segregation contributes to the racial disparities in health (Williams and Collins 2001; Acevedo-Garcia et al. 2003).

Segregation probably has a larger impact on the health of African Americans than other groups because blacks currently live under a level of segregation that is higher than that of any other immigrant group in U.S. history (Massey and Denton 1993). In addition, the association between segregation and SES varies by minority racial group. For Latinos and Asians, segregation is inversely related to household income, but segregation is high at all levels of SES for blacks (Massey 2004). The highest SES blacks (incomes greater than $50,000) in the 2000 Census were more segregated than the poorest Latinos and Asians (incomes less than $15,000) (Massey 2004).

At the individual level, experiences of discrimination have been shown to be a source of stress that adversely affect health (Williams and Mohammed 2009). Research has documented elevated levels of exposure to both chronic and acute measures of discrimination for socially stigmatized racial and immigrant groups in the United States, Europe, Africa, Australia, and New Zealand (Williams and Mohammed 2009). Exposure to discrimination has been shown to be associated with increased risk of a broad range of indicators of physical and mental illness. In addition, discrimination, like other measures of social stress, adversely affects patterns of health care utilization and adherence behaviors, and it is predictive of increased risk of using multiple substances to cope with stress, including tobacco, alcohol, and illicit drugs. Several studies have found that, in multiple national contexts, racial discrimination makes an incremental contribution to SES in accounting for observed racial disparities in health (Williams and Mohammed 2009).

While much research has focused on the pervasive role of racism in perpetuating health disparities, sociologists have also enhanced our understanding of the complex ways communities respond to discrimination. Some research has explored the harmful health effects of internalized racism, in which minority groups accept the dominant society's ideology of their inferiority (Williams and Mohammed 2009). Other research has identified cultural and psychosocial resources that foster resilience. For example, sociological research has found that religious involvement can enhance health in the face of racial discrimination, and that it can also buffer the negative effects of interpersonal discrimination on health (Bierman 2006; Ellison, Musick, and Henderson 2008). Other research indicates that ethnic identity can serve as a resource in the face of discrimination (Mossakowski 2003). Having a sense of ethnic pride and engaging in ethnic practices can enhance mental health directly, and the strength of ethnic identification can reduce the stress of discrimination on mental health.

Migration and Health

Du Bois's ([1899] 1967) insight that immigrant status affects the health profile of a population is relevant to understanding contemporary patterns of health. Asians and Latinos have lower overall age-adjusted mortality rates than whites. In the 2000 U.S. Census, 67 percent of Asians and 40 percent of Latinos were foreign-born (Malone et al. 2003). Processes linked to migration make an important contribution to the observed mortality rates for these groups. National data reveal that immigrants of all racial groups have lower rates of adult and infant mortality than their native-born counterparts (Hummer et al. 1999; Singh and Miller 2004; Singh and Yu 1996). Moreover, across multiple immigrant groups, with increasing exposure to American society, health tends to decline. This pattern is especially surprising for Latinos. Hispanic immigrants, especially those of Mexican background, have high rates of poverty and low levels of access to health insurance in the United States. However, their levels of health are equivalent and sometimes superior to that of the white population. This pattern has been called the Hispanic paradox (Markides and Eschbach 2005).

Sociological research has shed important light on the complex association between migration and health. First, research has shown that when a broad range of health outcomes are considered, a complex pattern emerges. For example, although Hispanics have comparable levels of infant mortality to whites, women of all Hispanic groups have a higher risk of low birth weight and prematurity than whites (Frisbie, Forbes, and Hummer 1998). Similarly, in the California Health Interview Survey (CHIS), virtually all immigrants reported better physical health status than the native-born (Williams and Mohammed 2008). In contrast, for psychological distress, many immigrant groups (most Latino groups, Pacific Islanders, and Koreans) reported worse health than the native-born, while other immigrants groups (blacks, Puerto Ricans, and Filipinos) had better health, and still others (Vietnamese, Japanese, and Chinese) did not differ from their native-born counterparts.

Second, sociological research has shown that migration status combines in complex ways with SES to affect health. Immigrant populations differ markedly in SES upon arrival in the United States (Rumbaut 1996). For example, Asian and African immigrants have markedly higher levels of education than other immigrant groups and U.S.-born whites. In contrast, immigrants from Mexico have low levels of education at the time of migration to the United States, and they face major challenges with socioeconomic mobility in the second generation. Sociological research has shown that these differences in SES affect patterns and trajectories of health in important ways. For immigrant populations largely made up of low SES individuals, traditional indicators of SES tend to be unrelated to health in the first generation, but they exhibit the expected associations in health by the second generation (Angel, Buckley, and Finch 2001). In addition, the socioeconomic status of immigrants upon arrival to the United States appears to be a determinant of the immigrant group's trajectory of health. For example, the gap in mortality between immigrants and the native-born is smaller for Asians than for whites, blacks, and Hispanics (Singh and Miller 2004), and recent national data reveal that declines in mental health for subsequent generations were less marked for Asians (Takeuchi et al. 2007) than for blacks (Williams et al. 2007b) and Hispanics (Alegria et al. 2007). Thus, although black, Latino, and Asian first generation immigrants all have lower disorder rates than the general population of blacks and whites, by the third generation the disorder rates of Latino and black but not Asian immigrants are higher (Alegria et al. 2007; Takeuchi et al. 2007; Williams et al. 2007b; Miranda et al. 2008). One of the factors contributing to the good health profile of immigrants is their selection on the basis of health. Recent

sociological research has shown that differences in the SES of immigrant streams is the key determinant of variation in health selection among immigrants, with immigrants to the United States from Mexico having lower levels of positive health selection than immigrants from all other regions of the world (Akresh and Frank 2008). That is, the surprisingly good health of immigrants from Mexico is not primarily due to the better health of Mexican immigrants relative to Mexicans who did not migrate. Future research is needed to clearly identify the relative contribution of various factors to the health status of immigrants and how these may vary across various immigrant populations.

Third, sociological research has begun to characterize how risk factors and resources in immigrant populations can affect the health of immigrants. Specifically, stressors and strains associated with migration and adaptation, inadequate health care in the country of origin, and factors linked to larger social structures and context (e.g., institutional racism and interpersonal discrimination) can affect health among immigrants (Angel and Angel 2006). For example, a study of adult migrant Mexican workers in California found that stressors linked to discrimination, legal status, and problems speaking English were inversely related to self-reported measures of physical and mental health, and that they partially accounted for the declines in these health indicators with increasing years in the United States (Finch, Frank, and Vega 2004).

Finally, sociologists have also shown that a full understanding of the health effects of migration requires an assessment of the ways in which migration impacts the health of sending communities. For example, a study of infant health in two high-migration sending states in Mexico found that infants born to fathers who had migrated to the United States had a lower risk of low birth weight and prematurity compared to infants born to fathers who had never migrated (Frank 2005). This study also found that women with partners in the United States had lower levels of social support and higher levels of stress during pregnancy than women with nonimmigrant partners, but the benefits of the receipt of remittances and the practice of better health behaviors led to improved infant health outcomes. These findings highlight the importance of attending to the bidirectional effects of migration processes.

At the same time, the good health profile of immigrants highlights how much we still need to learn regarding the determinants of health and the policies needed to improve the health of all Americans and to reduce inequities in health across population groups. Especially striking and intriguing are the data for Mexican immigrants. Despite having levels of poverty comparable to those of African Americans, and despite having among the lowest levels of access to health care of any racial-ethnic group in the United States, Mexican immigrants nonetheless have levels of health that are often equivalent and sometimes superior to those of whites (Williams et al. 2010). These data emphasize that health is not primarily driven by medical care but by other social-contextual factors. However, precisely what these social determinants of health are, and how they may operate in the absence of high levels of SES, and why they change over time is less clear. Accordingly, for both research and policy reasons, there is an urgent need to identify the relevant factors that shape the association between migration status and health for Mexicans and other immigrants. Moreover, we need to identify and implement the interventions, if any, that can avert or reverse the downward health trajectory of immigrants with increasing length of stay in the United States.

Conclusions and Policy Implications

Sociological research on racial disparities in health has many important lessons for policies that seek to address social inequities in health. First, there are implications for how data on social inequalities in health are reported. For over 100 years, the U.S. public health system has routinely reported national health data by race. Instructively, although SES differences in health are typically larger than racial ones, health status differences by SES are seldom reported, and only very rarely are data on health status presented by race and SES simultaneously. Moreover, striking differences are also evident by sex. Given the patterns of social inequalities and the need to raise awareness among the public and policy makers of the magnitude of these inequities and their social determinants, we strongly urge that health data should be routinely collected, analyzed, and presented simultaneously by race, SES, and gender. This will highlight the fundamental contribution of SES to the health of the nation and to racial disparities in health. Failure to routinely present racial data by stratifying them by SES within racial groups can obscure the social factors that affect health and reinforce negative racial stereotypes. The inclusion of gender must be accompanied by research

that seeks to identify how biological factors linked to sex and social factors linked to gender relate to each other and combine with race and SES to create new identities at the convergence of multiple social statuses that predict differential access to societal resources.

Sociological research indicates that race and SES combine in complex ways to affect health. There has been some debate regarding the advisability of race-specific versus universal initiatives to improve outcomes for vulnerable social groups. Extant research that clearly documents residual effects of race at every level of SES suggests that race-specific strategies are needed to improve outcomes for disadvantaged racial groups. The research reviewed here indicates that both the legacies of racism and its continued manifestations matter for health. For example, unless and until serious attention is given to addressing institutional racism such as residential segregation, reducing racial inequities in health will likely prove elusive. More research and policy attention should be given to identifying and implementing individual and, especially, institutional interventions that would be effective in reducing the levels and consequences of racism in society. For instance, state or federal policies that expand the stock of safe, stable, low-income and mixed-income housing or funding for section 8 vouchers could increase access to high-opportunity neighborhoods, while more robust enforcement of housing and financial regulations could help curb predatory lending and housing discrimination practices in minority or underserved neighborhoods.

There are many good reasons for reducing societal racism and improving the racial climate of the United States. The substantial health benefits of such interventions are an important benefit that is not widely recognized. Similarly, some evidence suggests that many of the most promising efforts to improve health are likely to widen disparities because the most advantaged social groups are likely to extract the greatest benefit from them (Mechanic 2002). Accordingly, policies are needed that improve the health of vulnerable social groups more rapidly than that of the rest of the population so that health gaps can be narrowed.

The evidence documenting that race is primarily a social rather than a biological category provides insight into the types of interventions that are needed to improve the health of disadvantaged racial populations. Effective interventions will be those that are targeted not at internal biological processes, but those that seek to improve the quality of life in the places where Americans spend most of their time: their homes, schools, workplaces, neighborhoods, and places of worship (Williams, McClellan and Rivlin 2010). For example, incentive programs for farmers' markets and full-service grocery stores, along with more stringent regulations on fast food and liquor stores, could increase availability of nutritious, affordable foods in underserved areas. Other potential interventions include (1) restructured land-use and zoning policies that reduce the concentration of environmental risks (e.g., close proximity of bus depots to schools or daycares); (2) public transportation options that encourage physical activity and minimize pollution risks; (3) the creation of public green spaces that promote walking, exercise, and community cohesion; and (4) educational initiatives aimed at equalizing access to K–12 education and higher education, improving teacher quality, raising graduation rates, and reducing the achievement gap.

Historically, sociological research on racial disparities in health has directly contributed to action and debate in the policy arena. For example, informed by Robert Bullard's groundbreaking research on environmental racism (Bullard 2000; Bullard and Johnson 2000), President Clinton signed an executive order which required federal agencies to ensure that their policies and programs did not disproportionally adversely affect minorities or the poor (Clinton 1994). More recently, an influential report co-authored by sociologist Thomas LaVeist (LaVeist, Gaskin, and Richard 2009) is helping to transform the policy debate about racial disparities in health by emphasizing that these differences in health have substantial economic costs for society. This report estimated that the medical care and lost productivity costs for racial disparities in health amount to a $309 billion annual loss to the economy. These economic costs are a compelling additional policy justification for eliminating health inequities. Sociologist David Williams also recently served as the staff director for the Robert Wood Johnson Foundation Commission to Build a Healthier America, a national bipartisan initiative focused on improving Americans' health and reducing socioeconomic and racial disparities in health. The recommendations of this commission have shaped recent federal spending and budget priorities on nutrition and investments in early developmental support for children (Williams, McClellan and Rivlin 2010).

Since health is embedded in policies far removed from traditional health policy, success will depend on integrative and collaborative efforts across multiple sectors of society that seek to leverage resources to enhance health. It was earlier noted that black women experienced a large decline in life expectancy between 1950 and 2006. This success was likely due to improvements in the SES of African American women. A review of studies of the health effects of the civil rights movement found that black women experienced larger economic gains than black men during the 1960s and 1970s. Further, the study showed that during this period of the narrowing of the income gap between blacks and whites, blacks, especially black women, experienced larger improvements in health, relatively and absolutely, than whites (Williams et al. 2008).

The magnitude and persistence of racial inequities in health call on U.S. policy makers to seriously confront what Du Bois ([1899] 1967) referred to as the "peculiar indifference" to the magnitude of human suffering that racial disparities in health reflect. Policy makers need to identify the real and perceived barriers to implementing comprehensive societal initiatives that are necessary to eliminating racial differences in health. More systematic and sustained attention should be given to how to frame such efforts in ways that resonate with dominant American ideals. Widely cherished norms of equal opportunity and the dignity of the individual could be creatively harnessed to build the needed political support to improve the health of all Americans, including those that currently live shorter and sicker lives than the rest of the population.

Seeing the Big Picture   How Race Can Be Hazardous to Your Health

Look at Section III in the Appendix on race and health. What trends do you observe? Why do certain diseases affect one group more than others? Are you able to discern the role of race and class in these health disparities?

7 | Transformative Assets, the Racial Wealth Gap, and the American Dream

Thomas M. Shapiro

THOMAS M. SHAPIRO is the Pokross Professor of Sociology at Brandeis University. Shapiro and Melvin L. Oliver have been awarded the C. Wright Mills Award and the American Sociological Association's Distinguished Scholarly Publication Award for *Black Wealth/White Wealth.* Shapiro's books include *Population Control Politics: Women, Sterilization, and Reproductive Choice* and *Great Divides: Readings in Social Inequality in the United States.*

Questions to Consider There is a saying that the color of America is green (money!). But using income as a way to measure the relative success of racial groups does not, according to Professor Tom Shapiro, paint an accurate portrait of social inequality or who is likely to achieve the American Dream. What are "transformative assets," who is likely to have them, and how are these intergenerational perks a form of unearned privilege? Are these intergenerational transfers of wealth throughout the life course "fair"? Are they racist? Do these transfers of wealth undermine the deeply held belief that individuals should pull themselves up by their own bootstraps?

Race and Wealth

Racial inequality remains a festering public and private issue in American society. After dismantling the most oppressive racist policies and practices of its past, many have come to believe that the United States has moved beyond race and that our most pressing racial concerns should center now on race-neutrality and color blindness. Proclaiming the successes of the civil rights agenda and the dawning of a postracial age in America, books by Shelby Steele, Abigail and Stephan Thernstrom, and others influenced not only the academic debates but elite, media, and popular opinion as well.[1] Indeed, a review of the record shows impressive gains since the mid-1960s, most particularly in the areas of law, education, jobs, and earnings. During the 2004 Presidential election, for instance, and into the second term of the Bush Administration, politicians and the media treat racial inequality as a non-issue, or as if it no longer existed. Even though progress is real, this new political sensibility about racial progress and equality incorporates illusions that mask an enduring and robust racial hierarchy and continue to hinder efforts to achieve our ideals of democracy and justice.

In fact, we can consider seriously the declining economic significance of race because the measures we have traditionally used to gauge racial inequality focus almost exclusively on salaries and jobs. The black-white earning gap narrowed considerably throughout the 1960s and 1970s. The earnings gap has remained relatively stable since then, with inequality rising again in the 1980s and closing once more during tight labor markets in the 1990s. The average black family earned 55 cents for every dollar earned by the average white family in 1989; by 2000, it reached an all-time high of 64 cents on the dollar. For black men working full-time, the gains are more impressive, as their wages reached 67 percent of those of fully employed white men, up from 62 percent in 1980 and only 50 percent in 1960. How much the racial wage gap has closed, why it has closed, and what it means are the subjects of academic and political debate. One study, for example, argues that the racial wage gap is really 23 percent higher than the official figures because incarceration rates hide low wages and joblessness among blacks. In any case, it takes more African American family members to work to earn the same money as white families. For example, middle-income black families worked the equivalent of 12 more weeks than white families to earn the same family income in 2000.[2]

The tremendous growth of the black middle class often is cited as the triumphant sign of progress toward racial equality. The raw numbers appear to justify celebration: In 1960, a little more than three-quarters of a million black men and women worked in middle class occupations. By 1980, the number increased to nearly three and a half million and nearly seven million African Americans worked in middle class jobs in 1995. This impressive growth in achieving middle class status, however, does not tell the whole story, as one can point out that stagnating economic conditions and blacks' lower middle class occupational profile have stalled the march into the great American middle class since the mid-1970s.

The case I want to make is that the real story of the meaning of race in modern America, however, must include a serious consideration of how one generation passes advantage and disadvantage to the next—how individuals' starting points are determined. While ending the old ways of outright exclusion and violence, our nation continues to reproduce racial inequality, racial hierarchy, and social injustice that is very real and formidable for those who experience [it]. This contribution will explore the bedrock of racial inequality in modern America.

The racial wealth gap—which has more to do with race than with merit or accomplishments—translates into different worlds, opportunities, and rewards for black and white families. My argument is grounded in three big ideas. First, I argue that family inheritance and continuing discrimination in really vital areas like homeownership are reversing gains earned in schools and on the job and making racial inequality worse. In addition to money passed at death, family inheritance includes paying for college education, substantial down payment assistance in buying a first home, and other continuing parental financial assistance. Consequently, it is virtually impossible for people of color to earn their way to equal wealth through wages. No matter how much blacks earn, they cannot pass their occupational status along to their children; they cannot outearn the wealth gap. Many believe that African Americans do not do as well as whites, other minorities, or immigrants because they spend too much money rather than save and invest in the future of their

families. They are unable to defer gratification, do not sacrifice for the future, and consume excessively. The facts speak otherwise. Second, these inheritances amount to **transformative assets.** This involves the capacity of unearned, inherited wealth to lift a family economically and socially beyond where their own achievements, jobs, and earnings would place them. Since the vast majority of African Americans were first excluded and later precluded from the kind of occupations, investments, and government policies and programs that lead to wealth generation, transformative assets typically apply to whites from financial advantaged families and not blacks. These head-start assets set up different starting lines, establish different rules for success, fix different rewards for accomplishments, and ultimately perpetuate racial inequality. Third, the way families use head-start assets to transform their own lives—within current structures that reward them for doing so—has racial and class consequences for the homes they buy, the communities they live in, and the quality of schools their children attend. The same set of processes typically advantages whites while disadvantaging African Americans.

These big ideas help us understand one of the most important issues facing America as we start the twenty-first century. African American were frozen out of the mainstream of American life over the first half of the last century, but since 1954 the civil rights movement has won many battles against racial injustice, and America has reached a broad national consensus in favor of a more tolerant, more inclusive society. Yet we live with a great paradox: Why is racial inequality increasing in this new era?

The Racial Wealth Gap

The typical black household makes 59 cents earned by the typical white household. This income comparison is the most widely used indicator of current racial and ethnic material inequality.[3] However, changing the lens of analysis to wealth dramatically shifts the perspective. For example,

---

transformative assets Assets that individuals receive, typically from parents and grandparents, that socially and economically "transform" their lives. For example, getting a down payment for a house in a neighborhood you could not afford on your own, having your parents pay for your college education so you start life without college debt, or receiving an inheritance.

the 1999 net worth (all assets minus all liabilities) of typical white families is $81,000 compared to $8,000 for black families. This baseline racial wealth gap, then, shows the black families possess only 10 cents for every dollar of wealth held by white families. The socioeconomic yardstick is no longer how to get from 59 cents on the dollar to parity but how to think about going from 10 cents on the dollar to a figure approaching parity. In dollars, the baseline racial wealth gap is robust: The typical white family's wealth is almost $74,000 more than the typical black family's. Even though both white and black families increased their net worth between 1988 and 1999, the black-white gap actually grew by $16,000 (in 1999 dollars). During this period, typical white and black families improved financially but inequality grew. The figures for net financial assets (excluding home equity and vehicles) do not paint a better picture. Later we will examine the impact of the recession and jobless recovery that started in the late 1990s.

The classic argument is that racial inequality in significant areas like family wealth represents huge disparities in education, jobs, and income. Once these disparities are alleviated, our traditional understanding and theory lead to an expectation that racial inequality will be diminished to a great extent.[4] Confounding this traditional understanding, and demonstrating the need for new thinking about civil rights in the twenty-first century, examining middle class families demonstrates that even black and white families with equal accomplishments are separated by a dramatic wealth gap. Defining middle class by income, we see a reduction in the baseline racial wealth gap to $44,500 for whites and $17,000 for blacks. Clearly, income is important to wealth accumulation. At the same time, however, middle class black families with similar incomes to white own only 26 cents of wealth for every dollar owned by whites. Defining middle class by occupation changes the ratio to 22 cents on the dollar. And, using a college education as a hallmark of middle class status moves the wealth ratio to 27 cents on the dollar. One needs to be asking how it is that blacks with equal accomplishments in income, jobs, and degrees possess only about a quarter of the wealth of their white counterparts.

The black middle class that emerged between the mid-1960s and early 1980s is a success story written in the accomplishments of education, occupation, and earnings. An asset perspective, however, shows that the white middle class stands for the most part on the two legs of good earning and substantial financial assets while the black middle class stands for the most part on the earning of one leg alone. Middle class status is thus more precarious for blacks than it is for whites; blacks are more susceptible to falling from middle class grace, less capable of cushioning hard times, and less able to retool careers or change directions. And, of course, they are far less able to pass along their hard-earned successes to their children.

We can examine the relationship between family wealth and what we think predicts wealth, such as education, income, age, marital status, family size, region, and job. To make our findings more graphic, we can estimate the cost of being African American, that is, the wealth difference between typical white and black families with equal accomplishments on all the factors that we think lead to wealth accumulation. The cost of being black amounts to $136,174. This is a measure of the accumulative disadvantage of being African American. Flipping the perspective, the accumulative advantage or the legacy of whiteness for the typical white family also is $136,174.[5]

Is the Racial Wealth Gap Narrowing or Growing?

Among the crucial issues facing families today is how the recent recession and jobless recovery have affected family economic security. My recent research argues that a widening wealth gap between minorities and whites is reversing gains earned in schools and on jobs and making inequality worse. A 2004 report from the Pew Hispanic Center provides new data on family wealth and offers a sobering assessment of the precarious and fragile status of middle class families, including whites, but most particularly Hispanics and African Americans.[6]

In the years prior to the 2001 recession, white, Hispanic, and African American families were generating wealth through savings, investment, and homeownership. More families were acquiring assets and family portfolios were growing. In this context of wealth accumulation, however, the wealth gap between minority and white families was widening. The recession and recovery brought wealth growth to an abrupt halt for millions of American families. During the recession and jobless recovery, Hispanic and African American families lost over one-quarter of their wealth while the wealth of white families grew slowly. In 2002, a typical Hispanic family owned 11 cents of wealth for every dollar owned by a typical white family, and African American families owned only 7 cents.

Net wealth losses illustrate how Hispanic and African American families, and low-to-middle income families in general, have shouldered the burden of tightening economic times in the Bush administration. And the wealth data show that the current combination of recession and recovery has tightened the financial vice on millions of American families. Over one in four Hispanic and African American families are asset-poor, having no liquid financial assets, compared to 6 percent of whites. Families with small or moderate amounts of wealth drew down their meager stockpile of savings to use as private safety nets. In addition to making tough choices like giving up health insurance or spacing out medical appointments and refilling prescriptions, this is the real story of how families are adapting to the recession, jobless recovery, stagnating wages, outsourcing, and dwindling federal commitment to important safety nets like unemployment benefits and the minimum wage, which are not keeping pace with inflation.

For example, interest-earning assets like savings bonds, IRA and Keogh accounts, 401(k) and thrift accounts, stocks and mutual funds, and business capital declined precipitously in Hispanic families with assets. In African American families, stock and mutual fund investments plummeted by nearly two-thirds. Surely, this reflects investment losses, but it also represents families tapping accounts to cover insecurities about employment and losses of job-related income. These families are adapting by eating the acorns they were storing for their future economic mobility and security. These setbacks will not be made up easily or in a short time span.

While the income, educational achievement, and job gaps among Hispanics, African Americans and whites remain steady or show some slight narrowing, the wealth gap increases. I made this argument in my recent book, *The Hidden Cost of Being African American*. The report and current data from the Pew Hispanic Center further corroborate how a growing wealth gap reverses gains in schools, on jobs, and in paychecks. An added compounding change is that the financial portfolios of Hispanics and African Americans have been shrinking in the current economy.

More than any other economic attribute, wealth represents the sedimentation of historical inequalities in the American experience, in a sense the accumulation of advantages and disadvantages for different racial, class, and ethnic groups. In this way, it allows us a window to explore how our past influences realities today.

This is not simply a story about counting money, because families think about using wealth first as a private safety net, and then as a vehicle to launch mobility into middle class status, homeownership, business development, or a more secure retirement. The recent recession and recovery—along with public policies—are a real step backward for the self-reliance and independence of Hispanics, African Americans, and other low-to-middle income families. They are a double blow against equality and family well-being in America. Missing from the current national political scene is a serious conversation about the economic status of America's families and the role of government in enabling families to build a wealth pillar for their mobility, stability, and well-being. Finally, family wealth is not a story about counting dollars to determine who has played the game best. Far more importantly, family wealth is crucial to opportunities and success in a way that allows families to launch their own social mobility in a self-reliant and independent manner. Closing the racial wealth gap needs to be at the forefront of the civil rights agenda moving into the twenty-first century.

Seeing the Big Picture   The Color of Money

Section VI in the Appendix lists households making more than $250,000 and those in poverty, which the government defines as $19,484 for a family of four (2004). Using these two income categories as your reference points, explain how race is linked to transformative assets and upward mobility.

RACE AS CHAMELEON~
How the Idea of Race Changes
over Time and Place

8   Defining Race: Comparative Perspectives
F. James Davis

F. JAMES DAVIS is professor emeritus of sociology at Illinois State University. Dr. Davis conducted research for the Air Force at the University of Washington during the years 1951–1952. He is the author of the classic work *Who Is Black? One Nation's Definition,* as well as *Society and the Law, Social Problems,* and *Minority-Dominant Relations.*

A BLACK PERSON IN THE UNITED STATES HAS long been defined as a person with any known African black ancestry, no matter how little or how distant. The aphorism for this so-called one-drop rule is that "one drop of black blood makes you black." So deeply rooted in the American psyche is this rule that a person can have predominantly white ancestry and even look white, yet unquestionably be defined as black. Such people as Halle Berry, Lena Horne, Julian Bond, or Muhammad Ali come to mind. Is it any wonder that foreign visitors and television viewers have trouble understanding why we define such people as black? No other nation defines blacks in this way, and our one-drop rule does not apply to any minority other than African Americans.

Walter White, president of the National Association for the Advancement of Colored People (NAACP) from 1931 to 1955, had blue eyes, blond hair, and fair skin, and his ancestry was no more than one sixty-fourth African black (Ottley 1943). He had been raised in Georgia in the black community and had been subjected to white discrimination and violence (White 1948). He passed as white in order to investigate lynchings in the Jim Crow South. White's second marriage, to a brunette white woman, provoked outrage from the black press for his betrayal. He had married outside the black community, across the ethnic barrier. When the White family made an international goodwill tour and were

Questions to Consider   For most of U.S. history the "one-drop" rule defined someone as black if he or she had a single "drop" of black blood—that is, any African ancestry. This "rule" was designed to maintain white supremacy by keeping the color line rigid and guaranteed there would be a constant source of slaves even after the importation of enslaved Africans was banned in 1808 (slavery wouldn't end until 1865). Professor F. James Davis makes the point that for many in the United States the law of hypodescent placed individuals within the black community even if they did not phenotypically "look" black. What Professor Davis brings to light is that there are many other identities (he outlines six) that mixed-raced individuals occupy. Are these categories still relevant today?

publicized as an interracial couple, White was often asked how he happened to marry a black woman (Cannon 1956).

A former law professor, now a university president, grew up in a white, middle-class neighborhood in Virginia and had always thought he was white until he was ten years old. He certainly looks white. His father, after a financial collapse and a broken marriage, took him and his younger brother to live in his home community in Muncie, Indiana, in the 1950s. While en route there by bus, their father told the boys that he had passed as white and they would be living in a black neighborhood. There the boys were discriminated against and harassed by both whites and blacks. Against all odds, this older brother's abilities, both in the classroom and in athletics, enabled him to achieve outstanding success. When asked why he does not pass as white, he answers that he has been taught through bitter experience that in the United States he is black (G. H. Williams 1995).

Although there are average differences in visible physical traits in human populations, there are no pure races. When I use the term "unmixed African black," I mean someone whose entire ancestry derives from populations in sub-Saharan Africa. Originally the term "mulatto" meant half African black and half white, but it came to mean any degree of mixture. Often people now say that a child of an African American and a white is "half and half," which correctly describes the child's racial background. However, one such child may have a parent whose ancestry is three-fourths African, whereas another's is one-fourth. The ancestry of the first child would be three-eighths black, the second one-eighth. Regardless of the ancestral fractions and physical appearances, both children are black under the American one-drop rule. Due to strong social conditioning, most light-hued African Americans identify themselves as black, but as we shall see, some do not.

Because of the one-drop rule, mixed offspring with any African ancestry are assigned to the black community. The result of over 350 years of **miscegenation** in the United States is a "new people," derived predominantly from African black populations but with a large infusion of genes from European whites and a substantial amount from Native Americans (Reed 1969; Williamson 1980). Estimates of the number of African Americans who have some white ancestry range from three-fourths to above 90 percent, and as many as one-fourth have Native American ancestry. The color spectrum in the black community ranges from ebony to lighter than most whites, and other visible physical traits show a similar range of variation.

The one-drop rule is unique in the world because it has resulted from our particular experiences with slavery and racial segregation in the United States. The social statuses and identities of racially mixed people are determined by group power dynamics, just as those of their parent groups are. The varying social structures and histories of societies around the globe have produced sharply contrasting status

miscegenation The social and intimate "mixing" of different racial groups and the children resulting from such unions.

positions and terms of identity for mixed-race people. Seven different status positions are identified here to help readers gain perspective on current issues of racial identity in the United States. First, we need to examine further the development and effects of the one-drop rule.

The Hypodescent Status

Anthropologists call our one-drop rule a hypodescent rule because mixed black/white children are assigned the status position of the lower status parent group—that of blacks. Evidently this first occurred in the mid-1600s in the Chesapeake area of Maryland and Virginia, where miscegenation between white indentured servants and slaves from Africa became widespread. The mixed persons generally were assigned the status of slaves and the same racial identity as African blacks (Williamson 1980). By the early 1700s, the one-drop rule had become the social definition of a black person in the upper South, and from there it spread southward.

Also in the 1600s, a competitor to the one-drop rule emerged. In Louisiana and South Carolina, free mulattoes came to have an in-between, buffer status. These free mulattoes were allied with whites and not considered to be blacks (Williamson 1980). Until the 1840s in South Carolina, mulattoes could become white by behavior and reputation and could marry into white families (Catterall 1926–1937). Louisiana also rejected the one-drop rule, accepting miscegenation and the intermediate status of mulattoes until 1808, when the Louisiana Civil Code prohibited "free people of color" from marrying either whites or blacks (Domínguez 1986).

In a number of states before the Civil War, there were court cases in which persons who had as much African ancestry as one-fourth were declared to be white. The United States had not yet lined up solidly behind the one-drop rule. Finally in the 1850s, in order to preserve slavery, the South came together in firm support of the one-drop rule (Williamson 1980). Although the competing rule was put down, for several decades there were statutes and court decisions that limited the definition of a black person to at least one-fourth, one-eighth, or some other fraction of ancestry.

The Civil War and Reconstruction accelerated the alienation of mulattoes from whites, who made it clear that mulattoes of all shades would be defined as blacks. The one-drop rule gained support in the North as well as the South and was further strengthened at the turn of the twentieth century by the passage of Jim Crow laws in the southern states. These segregation laws were reinforced by extralegal threats and terrorism. Light blacks were as likely as darker ones to pay the ultimate price for alleged violations of the master-servant etiquette for "getting out of their place" (Vander Zanden 1972). The lynching of blacks peaked from 1885 to 1909, and the peak of passing also occurred during this period, although most of those who could pass permanently did not do so (Burma 1946; Eckard 1947). By World War I, the one-drop rule was backed uniformly by US whites.

The one-drop rule was crucial to maintaining Jim Crow segregation, in which widespread miscegenation, not racial "purity," prevailed. The racial double standard of sexual relations gave white men access to black women but protected white women from black men. The entire system of white domination would be threatened by a mixed child living in a white home. Mixed children fathered by white males, defined as black by the one-drop rule, stayed with the mother in the black community (Blaustein and Ferguson 1957; Myrdal, Sterner, and Rose 1944; Rose 1956). US senator Theodore Bilbo of Mississippi trumpeted in a 1947 book that protecting white women from black men was preventing "**mongrelization**," keeping the white race pure (Bilbo 1947).

By 1925, the African American community had fully accepted the one-drop rule and was giving it strong support. The black community had developed a vested interest in a rule used for centuries to preserve slavery and legalized segregation. The rule had forced all shades of mixed persons into the black community, where, over time, white oppression and other common experiences created a common culture and a sense of ethnic unity and pride. Lighter mulattoes, discriminated against and terrorized by whites, allied themselves more firmly than ever with blacks. Many leaders of the Harlem Renaissance of the 1920s, including Langston Hughes and A. Philip Randolph, were light mulattoes.

The civil rights movement of the 1950s and 1960s put an end to the Jim Crow laws and saw major civil rights legislation passed in Washington, D.C. At the same time, white backlash to the movement strengthened African American support for the one-drop rule. In the 1960s, lighter blacks often felt heavy pressure to affirm their blackness (Williamson 1980). In 1972, the National Association of Black Social Workers (NABSW) strongly endorsed the one-drop rule by passing a resolution against the adoption of black children by white parents (Day 1979). Rejecting the terms "biracial" and "racially mixed," the Association insisted

mongrelization Used as a pejorative, a blending of different populations as a result of widespread miscegenation.

that mixed children be taught to acknowledge their blackness and raised to survive as blacks (Ladner 1977). By the mid-1970s, "cross-racial" adoption had almost stopped, and by 1987, thirty-five or more states had a policy against it. Although the issue has been revived, the NABSW has not changed its position.

In general the one-drop rule has had the support of law. The rule was challenged often in court in the nineteenth century and earlier but not much in the twentieth. State laws defining who is black in terms of fractions of ancestry, or an explicit one-drop rule, have generally been rescinded in recent decades. However, the courts have not invalidated the one-drop rule. In 1983, the rule was upheld by a district court in Louisiana in a lawsuit brought by Susie Phipps (*Jane Doe v. Louisiana*), whose application for a passport was denied because she checked "white" as her race. She looks white, had always lived as white, and thought she was white (Trillin 1986). Lawyers for the state produced evidence that Mrs. Phipps was three thirty-seconds black, and by a 1970 statute, one thirty-second was enough. Before 1970, a "traceable amount" was enough in Louisiana. In 1986 the US Supreme Court refused to review this decision on the ground that no substantial federal question was involved (107 Sup.Ct.Reporter, interim ed. 638). Louisiana has abolished the one thirty-second criterion, but its courts have not ruled against the one-drop rule.

Despite the general support for the one-drop rule by both whites and blacks, there are long-standing examples of rejection of it in both communities (Daniel 1992). Some of the African American children adopted by whites and some children of mixed marriages are socialized to reject the black-only identity. Many Creoles of color in New Orleans and vicinity still reject both the black and the white identity (Domínguez 1986: 163–164). Many Hispanic Americans with some black ancestry resist the rule if they can and embrace a Latino identity. Although a majority of Puerto Rican immigrants have some African ancestry, few of them were identified as black when they were still on the island (Jorge 1979).

Native Americans with some African ancestry generally try to avoid the one-drop rule, usually by staying on a reservation (Bennett 1962). Those who leave the reservation are often treated as blacks. In Virginia, persons who are one-fourth or more Native American and less than one-sixteenth African black have been defined as Indians while on the reservation but as blacks when they leave (Berry 1965). States and tribes differ in their definitions of who is Indian. In the East and South, there are 200 or so small triracial communities that have long evaded the rule by remaining isolated (Berry 1963).

The most common response to deviations from the rule in both the black and the white communities is to condemn the deviations and affirm the rule. Deviant acts and rhetoric call attention to a violated rule and can strengthen the consensus that supports it (Durkheim 1960). For most African Americans of all hues, apparently, the rule gets such constant reinforcement that it provides a clear sense of black ethnic identity. After the US Census Bureau offered respondents the opportunity to designate their own race in 1960, the percentage who checked "black" did not decline significantly.

Problems engendered by the rule, some of them painfully distressing, are borne primarily by the black community. Public concern about these problems does not rise very high because the one-drop rule is so taken for granted by both blacks and whites. All the problems stem from defining as black a mixed population with a rainbow of physical characteristics. The ambiguity of the racial identity of very light blacks often leads to everyday strains and embarrassments, even to traumatic experiences and deep dilemmas of identity.

The rule has other costs, including conflicts in black families and communities over differences in color, hair, and other traits. Darker and "nappier" blacks often receive stinging criticism of their appearance, and the lightest ones are also often harassed and humiliated (Gwaltney 1980). As filmmaker Spike Lee has shown in *School Daze* and later in *Jungle Fever,* intense conflicts among blacks over color and hair accompany dating, sexual relations, and marriage. Color discrimination among blacks also occurs in the workplace, in the media, and elsewhere (Russell, Wilson, and Hall 1992). Is discrimination based on racial traits not a violation of civil rights laws?

Among still other problems are collective anxieties of whites about "invisible blackness" (Williamson 1980) and of blacks about persons who "deny their color." Many white parents of mixed children worry about the suppression of their white ancestry. There is profound anxiety about the rare resort to passing to gain opportunities. There are complex administrative and legal problems in implementing the one-drop rule. The rule causes gross misperceptions of the racial classification of very large populations in Asia, the Middle East, Latin America, and elsewhere. It poses problems of sampling and interpretation in medical and scientific research on racial differences (Davis 1991).

Elsewhere in the world, persons whose ancestry is part African black are perceived as mixed, not as just black. However, the status positions of mixed-race persons vary greatly from one society to another, reflecting different group power dynamics. We now examine six other status and identity positions.

The In-Between Status

Remember that the one-drop rule assigns to mixed-race persons the identical status position occupied by the lower status parent group. A second rule assigns persons of mixed heritage a status between that of the parent groups, as occupied by the mulattoes of South Carolina and Louisiana before 1850. Such groups are seen as marginal to both parent groups, but often there is a firmer tie with one than the other. Some middle groups develop a strong separate identity.

Many, if not most, in-between minorities, whether racial hybrid groups or not, meet special occupational needs the dominant community is unable or unwilling to meet. "Middleman minorities," as the economists call them, may or may not have had previous experience with such work. Often the work is onerous, highly stigmatized, or very risky, or it involves long hours. This in-between group serves as a buffer between the groups above and below it. Political and economic changes, especially when they eliminate the group's special occupations, can have drastic consequences for the middle minority. When crises come, the dominant group rarely protects the middle group from the animosity of lower-status groups (Blalock 1967). The vulnerability of the middle minority is especially great when it is occupied by a mixed-race group because of special problems with identity and group acceptance.

Under the apartheid system in the Republic of South Africa, there were two buffer groups between the dominant whites and the native blacks: the Asians and the Coloureds. This system of fourfold segregation was legalized in 1948 (Van den Berghe 1971) and lasted for half a century. During the prolonged crisis that preceded the downfall of the system and of white domination in 1994, the two buffer groups experienced much harassment and violence. Major adjustments in group statuses in recent years are complex and have been proceeding with much less conflict than was expected.

The definitions of the four "race groups" in South Africa remain essentially as they were under the apartheid system. Blacks are unmixed Africans. South African whites often explain who the Coloureds are by saying they are not black and not Asian. Coloureds are any "mixed-blood" persons, including children and descendants of black/Asian and white/Asian unions, not just those of black/white and black/Coloured unions. The bulk of the Coloureds are mulattoes, ranging from very dark to very light, and thus are very similar to most African Americans. Under apartheid, both legal and informal controls were designed to prevent or punish all white/nonwhite sexual contacts, not just those involving white women. There was no double standard. White men were punished as severely for white/nonwhite sexual contacts as black, Asian, and Coloured men were.

Under apartheid, passing as white was facilitated by the infinite gradations of racial traits among the Coloureds, with many mixed persons appearing white. However, far from being secret as in the United States, passing was open, legalized, and administered by a complex bureaucracy. Passing required official reclassification to a different "racial" category, usually from Coloured to white. Some individuals and couples were reclassified more than once, and different members of a family were sometimes classified differently (Watson 1970). Such reclassification could not occur under a one-drop rule.

Bottom of the Ladder

By a third rule, persons of mixed race are assigned a status lower than that of either parent group. Not accepted on equal terms by either of the parent race groups, such people are defined as a separate and lowly people, as outcasts. In East Africa, mulattoes among the Ganda peoples of Uganda are regarded with condescension and contempt by the Ganda and not accepted by the English or other whites. For a time there was discussion of a plan to remove all the mulattoes to an island in Lake Victoria where they could be completely isolated (Berry 1965). A similar position is occupied by the métis in Canada, the Anglo-Indians in India, Korean Americans in Korea, and Vietnamese Americans in Vietnam.

The métis population originated in the seventeenth century from unions in the Canadian wilderness between Indian women and French and Scottish trappers. At first, the children were called métis if they spoke French, or "half-breeds" if they spoke English, but eventually all racial hybrids were known as métis. They were regarded as neither white nor Indian. They felt superior to the Indians and would not marry them. They became valued middlemen—buffalo hunters, interpreters, and transporters of supplies and furs by canoe or carts. They plummeted from middle to bottom-of-the-ladder status when white settlement and the coming of the railroads in the latter half of the nineteenth century ended the need for their special occupations.

After the métis rebelled against the Canadian government in 1879 and 1884, they dispersed throughout the Canadian West, despised by whites and Indians alike. Some managed to get accepted on Indian reservations, but most lived as outcasts in poor, isolated areas or moved to towns and cities to become an urban underclass. There may be as many as 750,000 métis now in Canada, more than the number of full Indians. They remain a broken, desperately poor people.

Similarly, the mixed Anglo-Indian population in India went from a relatively secure middle minority status under British colonial rule to a precarious and lowly position, especially after India became independent in 1947 (Gist and Dean 1973). Anthropologists classify South Asians as "Hindu Caucasoids," but the British consider all dark-skinned "native peoples" to be nonwhite, and race is what people believe it to be. There is no place for "mixed-blood" people in the Hindu caste tradition (Ballhatchet 1980). Many Anglo-Indians fled to Australia or England as Indian nationalism grew (Berry 1965), but around a quarter of a million remain in India. Caste has been legally abolished, but the traditions still have force, and the Eurasians remain a despised out-group.

Thousands of Korean American children were born to women in Korea during the Korean War, some fathered by white servicemen and some by African Americans, and many more have been born since. Mixed children face extreme difficulties in Korea, where there is a strong prejudice against marrying someone of a different racial or ethnic group. Citizenship there is paternal, so the mixed children have been defined not as Koreans but as Americans. Children of American males are not granted US citizenship if born out of wedlock outside the United States. The great majority of the children thus have had no country and have been denied the rights of Korean citizens. These children are seen as debased and polluted, and some Korean families have refused to accept them. Mixed children under fifteen years of age can be adopted if the mothers give them up and register them with the Korean government as orphans.

The 80,000 or so mixed children fathered in Vietnam by white and black American military personnel during the war there are called the "dust of life" and treated with contempt. They are virtual outcasts in their own society, where, as in Korea, the child's identity and citizenship rights derive from the father. The US approach to this contrasts sharply with that of the French, who took 25,000 mixed children with them when they left in 1954 and offered them French citizenship. In 1982, the United States began allowing the mixed children to emigrate, provided that Americans adopt the younger ones and sponsor the older ones. Although many of these mixed children in both Vietnam and Korea have been adopted in the United States in recent years, most of them and their descendants remain lowly outcasts (Valverde 1992).

Top of the Ladder

Sometimes racially mixed people have achieved a higher status than that of either parent group, as experienced by the mulattoes of Haiti, Liberia, and Namibia, and the mestizos of Mexico (Nicholls 1981; Stoddard 1973). The two examples discussed here required a successful political revolution. In the wealthy French colony on Saint Domingue (Hispaniola), later called Haiti, a slave named Toussaint L'Ouverture began a revolution in 1791 that ended slavery. Previously there had been some 30,000 whites exercising extremely harsh control over half a million black slaves, with about 24,000 free blacks and mulattoes occupying an in-between status. After the rebels achieved independence in 1804, the mulattoes emerged as the economically and politically dominant elites and retained their ascendancy for more than a century and a half. They maintained tight kinship ties among mulatto families, preventing intermarriage with both whites and African blacks. They looked down on both unmixed Africans and the small white population, although the Lebanese, Syrians, and other whites performed valuable middle minority commercial functions (Nicholls 1981). The mulattoes lost control to the Duvalier regime in 1957, later regained it, and lost it again, and the volatile struggle for political power goes on.

The Spanish ruled Mexico for three centuries. During the long colonial period, there was massive miscegenation between the Spanish and Indian populations and some that involved African blacks. At first the term "mestizo" meant half-Spanish and half-Indian, but it came to refer to the entire mixed population, regardless of the degree of mixture. Under Spanish rule, mestizos occupied a middle status position, with Indians on the bottom. The mestizos took pride in their Spanish ancestry and played down their Indian backgrounds (Stoddard 1973). Mestizos became the rulers when Spanish control was overthrown in 1821, and today they are by far the largest group in Mexico. Some Spanish and other whites have retained considerable wealth and influence, but political power remains chiefly in mestizo hands. The overwhelming size of the mestizo group would appear to be a major factor in its political dominance, yet in Haiti the mulatto elites retained control for a long time with relatively small numbers.

Highly Variable Status: Latin America

Under a fourth rule, mixed-race persons are assigned a status that may vary from quite low to very high, depending more on education and wealth than on color or other racial traits. In Brazil and lowland Latin America generally, the upper class is called white, but it also includes light mulattoes and mestizos. The middle class is a long ladder with many rungs and is composed mainly of mulattoes, although in some countries it also includes many mestizos. The lower class includes most of the unmixed blacks and Indians, along with a few whites and some mulattoes and mestizos.

Race influences class placement, but it is only one factor, and it may be overcome by wealth and education. A plethora of terms is used for the innumerable gradations of racial mixture, but the color designations depend more on the place on the class ladder than on actual racial traits. As people use educational and economic success to climb the class ladder, their racial designations often change. No secrecy is needed to "pass" to another racial identity (Wagley 1963).

Latin Americans can accept light mulattoes and mestizos as whites, referring to any visible traces of African traits in such euphemistic terms as "brunette" or "a little mulatto" (Solaun and Kronus 1973). In Brazil it is class rather than racial discrimination that is pervasive, sharp, and persistent, even involving class-segregated public facilities and a class-based master-servant etiquette (Harris 1964). The expression "money whitens" indicates that class can have more weight than physical traits in determining racial classification. Census estimates of the number of people in different racial categories can be very misleading when compared with the estimates in the United States or other nations.

In Puerto Rico, as in Latin America generally, miscegenation of whites, native Indians, and African blacks has produced the entire range of skin color and other racial features. A substantial proportion of the mixed population is considered white, including many who are quite dark. Individuals are allowed some choice and room to negotiate for a racial identity (Domínguez 1986). Around 10 percent of Puerto Rican migrants to the United States are unmixed blacks, and half or more of the remainder have some African ancestry. Therefore, some three-fifths of the migrants are perceived as black in the United States, whereas on the island most of them were known either as whites or by one of the many color designations other than black. It comes as a shock to the majority of the migrants to be defined as black in the United States. Some manage to become known as Hispanic whites by emphasizing their Spanish language and heritage, but others fail. Parents in the Puerto Rican immigrant community pressure their young to "whiten" the family in order to succeed, which puts them in conflict with the African American community.

On the Caribbean islands colonized by the Spanish and Portuguese, Iberian whites have readily married lighter mulattoes with visible African traits. Iberian colonists brought with them an ideal image of beauty known as Morena (meaning Moorish) and the acceptance of marriage with mulattoes. By contrast, whites on the Caribbean islands colonized by the English, French, and Dutch have accepted intermarriage only with those mulattoes who look white (Hoetink 1967). It is appearance that counts, however, not known African ancestry, so there is no one-drop rule. The Iberian approach seems to be the general rule in southern Europe and the Near and Middle East. The intermarriage rule on the English, French, and Dutch islands was brought from northern Europe. The one-drop rule is not inherent in British culture, then, or in northwestern Europe generally. It emerged on US soil.

Egalitarian Pluralism for the Racially Mixed: Hawai'i

As in Latin America, the status of mixed-race people in Hawai'i can range from quite low to very high, depending on educational and economic achievement. However, color and other racial traits do not affect the class placement in Hawai'i as they do to some extent in Latin America. There is no preoccupation with race in Hawai'i and no color ladder

with a preferred hue at the top. Hawai'i has a long tradition of treating the racially mixed in an egalitarian manner that contrasts sharply with the hypodescent status on the US mainland. Despite the eventual wresting of political and economic power from the original Hawaiians by US economic interests in the 1890s, the competitive struggles and occasional conflicts have essentially been those of class and ethnicity, not race.

The Polynesian settlers in the Hawaiian Islands some 1,500 years ago were probably a racial blend of Mongoloid peoples from Southeast Asia and Caucasoid stocks from Indonesia and South Asia (Howard 1980). Further miscegenation with many different peoples began when the first **haoles** (non-Polynesians) came. Captain Cook found in 1778 that Hawaiian hospitality included openness to sexual relations and marriage with outsiders. The haoles never stopped coming, first for a way station for the fur trade; next for sandalwood; then for whales; then for sugarcane, pineapples, and other agricultural products; and finally as tourists. Many white traders and planters took Hawaiian wives, and eventually some of the children of Congregational missionaries from New England took native Hawaiian wives.

The demand for sugarcane workers escalated in the 1850s, and large numbers were brought from China and later from Portugal, other European countries, and Japan. By 1900 the Japanese were the largest ethnic group in Hawai'i. Migrants then came from Puerto Rico, Korea, and the Philippines. Still later, more came from South and East Asia, other Pacific Islands, Mexico, the Middle East, Europe, the United States, and elsewhere. Miscegenation never stopped. By 1930 there were more part-Hawaiians than unmixed ones, and by 1960 nine times as many. By the 1970s, Hawaiians and part-Hawaiians (one-eighth or more) were not quite one-fifth of the population, behind whites and Japanese (Howard 1980: 449–451). Native chiefs had made overly generous trade concessions and had lost much of their land. Revival of traditional culture began in the 1970s, along with charges of past and present discrimination against Hawaiians and part-Hawaiians by wealthy whites and other haole groups. This has been an ethnic and class protest, not a racial one. Clearly the native Hawaiians have been badly exploited, but the basis for it has been greed, not racism. The rhetoric of racist ideology is absent.

haoles The Hawaiian word for whites.

There has been no systematic racial segregation and discrimination, either de jure or de facto, and the various peoples in Hawai'i generally are scornful of anyone who exhibits racial prejudice. Many of the Pacific Island peoples are relatively dark-skinned, and the class status of the mixed people in Hawai'i seems to be unaffected by color or other racial traits. Ethnic and racial intermarriages are common, and many people can identify ancestry in several groups. It is considered bad manners to express disapproval of miscegenation. The tolerant, egalitarian balance of pluralism and assimilation extends to racially mixed persons, whose status is no lower or higher than that of the parent groups involved. The first racial hybrids in Hawai'i were highly respected, and this model has had a lasting impact (Adams 1969; Berry 1965).

Assimilating Minority Status

The seventh rule accounts for the status of persons in the United States who are partly descended from racial minorities other than African American. The children of the first generation of miscegenation may experience ambiguity or be identified as members of the minority group. However, when the proportion of minority ancestry becomes one-fourth or less in the next generation of mixture, the children are accepted unambiguously as assimilating Americans. There is no need for them to "pass" in order to hide the minority background. In fact, they can be proud of having ancestry that is part Native American, Mexican, Chinese, Japanese, Filipino, Vietnamese, or other Asian, and they find little opposition to intermarriage with whites. There is no one-drop rule to deter their further miscegenation and full assimilation into the dominant Anglo-American community.

For many decades, Chinese immigrants in the United States were despised and did not have the benefit of the status of an assimilating minority. Neither did the earlier Japanese Americans, especially during the days of their relocation to prison camps as enemy aliens during World War II. The operating rule was that everyone with one-eighth or more Japanese ancestry was to be removed to the camps. Since the Japanese had been immigrating to the United States only since 1885, this one-eighth criterion was a sure way to intern everyone with any known Japanese ancestry (T. K. Williams 1996). During the war years, then, what was in effect a one-drop rule was used for Japanese Americans.

The foregoing comparative discussion dramatizes the uniqueness of America's one-drop rule. It also shows that the status occupied by mixed-race people in a society can change in response to major shifts in racial group power relations. Experiences in other societies can provide valuable perspective on current issues about racial identity and the one-drop rule. They also suggest the need for caution in extrapolating to other societies the findings on the dynamics of the personal identity of mixed-race people in the United States.

The Multiracial Identity Movement

In recent years, new challenges to the one-drop rule have emerged. In the 1980s and 1990s, a movement to allow mixed-race persons to adopt a biracial or multiracial identity rapidly gained momentum. Campus groups were organized at many colleges and universities. A national organization called the Association of Multiethnic Americans (AMEA) was created to coordinate groups in thirty or more cities (Grosz 1989). The emphasis, rather than a frontal attack on the one-drop rule, has been on the freedom to acknowledge all of one's ancestries, including black (Nakashima 1992). The movement includes all racial blends, not just those with African black ancestry.

Mixed-race people with no black ancestry, although not subject to a one-drop rule, have been well aware that the rule for blacks has been responsible for the "check only one" instruction. Until the 2000 census, this rendered persons with Native American, Mexican, Asian, or Pacific Islander forebears unable to acknowledge two or more ancestries. Mexican Americans, the majority of whom are mestizos, had to check "black," "white," or "other." In 1990, 48 percent of them checked "other," and 97 percent of all Americans who checked "other" were Hispanics, who may be of any race or blend.

The marked increase in interracial marriages, although still a small proportion of all marriages, is one argument for recognizing the multiracial identity. The trend that began in the 1960s has accelerated, especially since the *Loving* case, in which the US Supreme Court in 1967 held the Virginia statute prohibiting interracial marriage to be unconstitutional. From 1970 to 1991, mixed-race marriages in the United States tripled. During this same period, births for one black and one white parent increased more than fivefold, and increases almost this large occurred in marriages involving one white and one Asian-American parent (Page 1996).

The vast majority of black/white sexual unions over 350 years have not had the benefit of marriage and have involved white males and black females. By contrast, a large majority of black/white marriages in recent decades have been between a black man and a white woman. One estimate is that at least 30 percent of these couples want to identify their children as biracial or multiracial. Many of these wives do not want their children to have to deny their mother's ancestry.

The multiracial identity movement has faced determined opposition. Many blacks fear that persons who want to affirm their European, Native American, or Asian ancestry want to deny their African roots. There is also fear that the movement will divide the black community, reduce its numbers, weaken black political power, and undermine civil rights remedies (Daniel 1992). Some fear that whites want to create a buffer class with a status above that of blacks or a system of "colorism" like the one in lowland Latin America.

Despite the opposition, the movement has had some successes. PROJECT RACE (Reclassify All Children Equally) has persuaded a number of states to require the multiracial option on some official forms, and school districts in several states have added the option (Graham 1995). In 1993, both PROJECT RACE and the AMEA testified in favor of the multiracial option before the Subcommittee on Census, Statistics, and Postal Personnel of the US House of Representatives. These organizations later gave similar testimony to the US Office of Management and Budget (OMB), which defines racial categories for all levels of government in the country, including the public schools (Fernandez 1995).

The policy debate centered mainly on the possible use of the multiracial category on the Census Bureau forms for 2000, an option strongly opposed by the NAACP and other black leaders (Daniel 2000). The OMB decided to reject the multiracial category but to change the traditional instruction, "check only one," to "check one or more." This compromise was approved by the NAACP, the Urban League, the Congressional Black Caucus, and other black groups (Daniel 2000). Although it was only a partial victory for the multiracial identity movement, the federal government had finally acknowledged the reality of multiple racial ancestries. To counter the fears of civil rights leaders, the OMB instruction was that persons who check "white" and any minority race are to be counted as members of that minority for the purpose of enforcing

civil rights laws. Also, the term "multiracial" was not to be used in interpreting the responses. The plan received unanimous support from thirty federal agencies and was adopted for the collection of all governmental data on race, not just census data (Lew 2000).

The percentage of Americans who checked more than one race in the 2000 census was 2.3. That percentage varies according to age group, however. Among African Americans over the age of fifty, 2.3 percent checked more than one race. However, for blacks eighteen years of age or younger, the percentage was 8.3. This age difference is probably due in part to the increase in the number of young interracial parents, in part to the multiracial identity movement, but also to the public rejection of the one-drop rule by a number of black celebrities. These rejections have been a prominent part of the increased publicity about mixed-race experiences in the past two decades. Issues of identity have been featured in books, articles, films, and newscasts and on talk shows.

One of the most dramatic news stories of the 1990s was the DNA testing that showed the high likelihood that Thomas Jefferson was the father of the last son of his slave Sally Hemmings (Foster 1998). Alex Haley's 1976 book *Roots* and the television series based on it had demonstrated how fully both African Americans and whites accept the one-drop rule. It seemed perfectly natural for Haley to pursue his African roots. In his 1993 book *Queen,* however, Haley focused on his white-appearing grandmother, played by Halle Berry in the television series. In 1990, when Renee Tenison was hailed as the first black woman to be Playboy's "Playmate of the Year," she protested that it was unfair for her to have to deny her white mother (Russell, Wilson, and Hall 1992). When Chelsi Smith was portrayed as the first black winner of the Miss USA pageant in 1995, she insisted that she is both black and white. (The first black winner was actually Carole Gist, in 1990.) It seems unlikely that such celebrities would so publicly reject the one-drop rule without the encouragement of the multiracial identity movement and the heightened awareness in the media.

Shirley Haizlip and her book *The Sweeter the Juice* (1994) were featured on the Oprah Show in 1994. The family members on the show all looked white, but some had passed while others had not. The author appeared on the show to explain how this can happen. In subsequent years, there have been other Oprah shows featuring similar experiences with the color line.

When Tiger Woods won the Masters Championship in 1997 and sports reporters asked how it felt to be the first black winner, he replied that he is not only black. He pointed out that his mother is from Thailand. Evidently he is one-fourth Thai, one-fourth Chinese, one-fourth black, one-eighth Native American, and one-eighth white. In the fall of 2003 in South Africa, US television reporters repeatedly referred to both Tiger and Vijay Singh as blacks. Tiger says he checks "Asian" on forms calling for race, and Singh is from India, not Africa. In South Africa, Tiger would be defined as Coloured, Singh as Asian, and neither one as black.

Whither the One-Drop Rule?

Do the successes of the multiracial identity movement, along with the increased media attention, foreshadow the end of the one-drop rule? Or will they join the several patterned deviations that point to the rule and reinforce it? Some states that have passed statutes to legitimate a multiracial category are finding them difficult to implement. It remains to be seen how much the states will follow the OMB's instruction to "check one or more" in collecting governmental data. Evidently it will take a lot to convince most African Americans that they have more to gain than to lose by backing away from the one-drop rule, especially in the face of continuing prejudice and discrimination.

Exceptions can become so blatant, however, that a rule becomes conspicuously obsolete. Significant further changes might be a long time coming, yet the fall of the apartheid system in South Africa in 1994 shows that momentum sometimes builds to a point at which major change can occur very fast. Increasing global awareness puts a spotlight on the US one-drop rule and its uniqueness in the world. Since national origins immigration quotas were abolished in the 1960s, the United States has increasingly become a multiracial, multiethnic society. How rapidly might the view grow that persons with partly black ancestry have a human right to have both or all of their racial backgrounds recognized?

If and when the one-drop rule loses its hold, what then? Of the six other status positions for mixed-race people discussed here, which one might incur the least opposition from most whites and most blacks? Is there one that would be accompanied by problems that are less serious than those resulting from the one-drop rule? Some of the six

alternatives could not possibly fit conditions in the United States, especially the bottom-of-the-ladder and the top-of-the-ladder statuses. The idea of a return to the in-between, buffer status would arouse intense hostility in the black community. Light mulatto leaders are highly valued and are held tightly in the embrace of black pride. African Americans also disdain the "colorism" of the Latin American pattern, and most whites would abhor very frequent intermarriage between whites and persons with visibly African traits.

The northern European status for mixed-race people would appear to be the closest alternative to the US hypo-descent position. To some whites, marriage with persons with known black ancestry but who look white might seem but a limited and beneficial exception to the one-drop rule. After all, "white blacks" carry very few genes from African ancestors, and many common beliefs about miscegenation are false and racist. Other whites, however, would be dominated by irrational fears of massive miscegenation, widespread passing, and "invisible blackness." As for the black community, few would likely consider it a good thing that those wishing to be assimilated could do so without having to pass secretly and abandon their black families and community. It would require the belief that very few persons would be lost to the white community and that black unity would not be impaired. This leap of faith seems highly unlikely so long as fully equal treatment of blacks is still an elusive goal.

Opposition to the assimilating minority status for the racially mixed would no doubt be very strong. That alternative would require acceptance of widespread intermarriage between whites and persons with one-fourth or less African ancestry. This process has helped visible minorities other than blacks to climb the class ladder and achieve equal treatment. To many, if not most, whites, it would probably seem to be an extreme departure from the one-drop rule, which has been designed to prevent total assimilation of persons with invisible as well as visible black ancestry.

Most blacks want equal treatment and economic and political integration, not total assimilation. Some barriers to opportunities have been lowered, but there is still considerable opposition by both whites and blacks to more informal contacts. Churches are as segregated as ever, urban housing segregation has been increasing, and pressures for black unity have limited social contacts between blacks and whites. Neither the black nor the white community exhibits any enthusiasm for complete assimilation.

Unlikely as it may now seem, the mainland United States might someday move toward the Hawaiian approach as most feasible. Mainlanders who move to Hawai'i have seemed able to accept the island pattern, different though it is, within a few months (Adams 1969). The implicit

rule for mixed-race status in Hawai'i is consistent with egalitarian pluralism, an outcome that African Americans and Hispanics generally prefer to full assimilation (Davis 1995). Although that may not be the road taken sooner or even later, we have seen that the status of racially mixed people can be changed by shifts in group power relations. Deeply rooted as it has been, then, the one-drop rule may not be perpetuated forever.

Seeing the Big Picture   **What Was *Your* Race in 1890?**
Look at Figure 1 in the Introduction of the Appendix. What parallels do you see between the six "status and identity" positions described by F. James Davis and the changing categories used by the U.S. Census? What do you make of the census categories in 1790 and 2000? Why are they so different?

---

9   A Tour of Indian Peoples and Indian Lands

David E. Wilkins

DAVID E. WILKINS is an associate professor of American Indian studies, political science, and law at the University of Minnesota, Twin Cities Campus. He has authored several books and a number of articles dealing with the political/legal relationship between indigenous nations and the United States and state governments. His most recent book is *American Indian Politics and the American Political System* (2002).

Questions to Consider   Why has it been so difficult to find a political and cultural definition of who is an American Indian, what constitutes a tribe, and what criteria need to be met to claim tribal membership? How are race, culture, identity, and politics linked in Wilkins's discussion of American Indians?

One of the greatest obstacles faced by the Indian today in his desire for self-determination . . . is the American public's ignorance of the historical relationship of the United States with Indian tribes and the lack of general awareness of the status of the American Indian in our society today.

—AMERICAN INDIAN POLICY REVIEW
COMMISSION, 1977[1]

THIS CHAPTER PROVIDES DESCRIPTIONS, definitions, and analysis of the most important concepts necessary for a solid foundation for the study of Indian politics. I will attempt to clarify how indigenous peoples, variously grouped, are defined, and discuss why such definitions are necessary. I will then analyze how the term Indian is defined and discuss what constitutes a reservation or Indian Country. Finally, I will conclude the chapter with a description of the basic demographic facts and socioeconomic data that applies throughout Indian lands.

What Is an Indian Tribe?

American Indians, tribal nations, Indian **tribes,** indigenous nations, Fourth World peoples, Native American peoples, aboriginal peoples, First Nations, and native peoples— these are just a sample of current terms that are used to refer to indigenous peoples in the continental United States in a collective sense. Alaska Natives, including Aleuts, Inuit, and Indians, and Native Hawaiians are the indigenous people of those respective territories. While I will provide some descriptive details about Alaska Natives, I will have less to say about Native Hawaiians because their legal status is unique among aboriginal peoples of the United States.[2]

This was brought to light in the Supreme Court's 2000 ruling in *Rice v. Cayetano*.[3] In that case, the Court struck down restrictions that had allowed only persons with Native Hawaiian blood to vote for the trustees of the Office of Hawaiian Affairs, a state agency created to better the lives of Hawaii's aboriginal people. While *Cayetano* did not specifically address the political relationship of the Native Hawaiians to the federal government, it called into question the status of the more than 150 federal statutes that recognize that Hawaii's native peoples do, in fact, have a unique legal status.

The departments of the Interior and Justice issued a preliminary report of August 23, 2000, that recommended that Congress "enact further legislation to clarify Native Hawaiians' political status and to create a framework for recognizing a government-to-government relationship with a representative Native Hawaiian governing body."[4] If Congress acts to create such a framework, and a bill was introduced on July 20, 2000 (S. 2898), by Senator Daniel K. Akaka (D-HI), then Hawaii's Natives would have a political relationship with the federal government similar to that of federally recognized tribes. The sovereignty movement in Hawaii is very complex, however, and some segments of the population desire more than mere federal recognition of their status because of their nation's preexisting sovereign status.[5]

Indigenous communities expect to be referred to by their own names—Navajo or Diné, Ojibwe or Anishinabe, Sioux or Lakota, Suquamish, or Tohono O'odham—since they constitute separate political, legal, and cultural entities. In fact, before Europeans arrived in the Americas, it is highly doubtful whether any tribes held a "conception of that racial character which today we categorize as 'Indian.' People recognized their neighbors as co-owners of the lands given to them by the Great Spirit and saw themselves sharing a basic status within creation as a life form."[6] However, when discussing Indian people generically, *American Indian tribes* and *Native Americans* remain the most widely used terms despite the inherent problems with both. For instance, America's indigenous people are not *from* India, and the term *Native American* was "used during the nativist (anti-immigration, anti-foreign) movement (1860s–1925) and the anti-black, anti-Catholic, and anti-Jewish Ku Klux Klan resurgence during the early 1900s."[7]

There is no universally agreed upon definition of what constitutes an Indian tribe, in part because each tribal community defines itself differently and because the U.S. government in its relations with tribes has operated from conflicting sets of cultural and political premises across time. Although no universal definition exists, many statutes give definitions for purposes of particular laws, federal agencies like the Bureau of Indian Affairs generate their own definitions, numerous courts have crafted definitions, and the term *tribe* is found—though not defined—in the Constitution's commerce clause.

For example, the Indian Self-Determination Act of 1975 (as amended) defines an Indian tribe as "any Indian tribe, band, nation, or other organized group or community . . . which is recognized as eligible for the special programs and services provided by the United States to Indians because of their status as Indians." By contrast, the Supreme Court in *Montoya v. United States* (1901) even more ambiguously said that "by a 'tribe' we understand a body of Indians of the same or a similar race united in a community under one leadership or government, and inhabiting a particular though sometimes ill-defined territory."[8]

Broadly, the term *tribe* can be defined from two perspectives—**ethnological** and *political-legal*.[9] From

tribe A social unit organized around ancestry, ethnicity, race, or a common culture.

ethnology The branch of anthropology that compares human cultures; includes the study of the origin and history of racial groupings.

an ethnological perspective, a tribe may be defined as a group of indigenous people connected by biology or blood; kinship, cultural, and spiritual values; language; political authority; and a territorial land base. But for our purposes, it is the political-legal definition (since there is no single definitive legal definition) of tribe, especially by the federal government, which is crucial since whether or not a tribal group is *recognized* as a tribe by the federal government has important political, cultural, and economic consequences, as we shall see shortly.

Federally Recognized Tribal and Alaska Native Entities

The extension of federal recognition by the United States to a tribal nation is the formal diplomatic acknowledgment by the federal government of a tribe's legal status as a sovereign. This is comparable to when the United States extended "recognition" to the former republics of the Soviet Union after that state's political disintegration. It is the beginning point of a government-to-government relationship between an indigenous people and the U.S. government.[10] The reality is that an American Indian tribe is not a legally recognized entity in the eyes of the federal government unless some explicit action by an arm of the government (i.e., congressional statute, administrative ruling by the BIA, presidential executive order, or a judicial opinion) decides that it exists in a formal manner.

Federal recognition has historically had two distinctive meanings. Before the 1870s, "recognize" or "recognition" was used in the cognitive sense. In other words, federal officials simply acknowledged that a tribe existed, usually by negotiating treaties with them or enacting specific laws to fulfill specific treaty pledges.[11] During the 1870s, however, "recognition," or more accurately, "acknowledgment," began to be used in a formal jurisdictional sense. It is this later usage that the federal government most often employs to describe its relationship to tribes. In short, federal acknowledgment is a formal act that establishes a political relationship between a tribe and the United States. It affirms a tribe's sovereign status. Simultaneously, it outlines the federal government's responsibilities to the tribe.

More specifically, federal acknowledgment means that a tribe is not only entitled to the immunities and privileges available to other tribes, but is also subject to the same federal powers, limitations, and other obligations of recognized tribes. What this means, particularly the "limitations" term, is that "acknowledgment shall subject the Indian tribe to the same authority of Congress and the United States to which other federally acknowledged tribes are subjected."[12] In other words, tribes are informed that they are now subject to federal plenary power and may, ironically, benefit from the virtually unlimited and still largely unreviewable authority of the federal government. For example, recognized tribes have exemptions from most state tax laws, enjoy sovereign immunity, and are not subject to the same constitutional constraints as are the federal and state governments.

Until 1978, federal recognition or acknowledgment was usually bestowed by congressional act or presidential action. But in 1978 the BIA, the Department of the Interior agency primarily responsible for carrying out the federal government's treaty and trust obligations to tribal nations, published regulations which contained specific criteria that unacknowledged or nonrecognized tribal groups had to meet in order to be formally recognized by the United States. The set of guidelines was based mainly on confirmation by individuals and groups outside the petitioning tribe that members of the group were Indians. The mandatory criteria were the following: the identification of the petitioners "from historical times until the present on a substantially continuous basis, as 'American Indian' or 'Aboriginal' by the federal government, state or local governments, scholars, or other Indian tribes; the habitation of the tribe on land identified as Indian; a functioning government that had authority over its members; a constitution; a roll of members based on criteria acceptable to the secretary of the interior; not being a terminated tribe, and members not belonging to other tribes.[13]

These criteria largely were designed to fit the **"aboriginal"** or "mythic" image of the western and already recognized tribes. They were problematic for many eastern tribes who sought recognition, since they paid little heed to the massive historical, cultural, economic, and legal barriers those tribes had to endure merely to survive as tribes into the late twentieth century, lacking any semblance of federal support or protection.

---

aboriginal Usually refers to the first people to inhabit a particular region; often used as shorthand for native groups who were geographically displaced, mistreated, or slaughtered by settlers, as in the case of the indigenous population of Australia.

Since the late 1970s there has been tension between those who support BIA or administrative recognition versus those who believe that only the Congress has authority to recognize tribes. The debate over administrative versus legislative recognition rages on, with some advocates from each camp asserting their exclusive right to extend or withhold recognition. This raises an important question: Is there a qualitative difference between the two types of recognition? There are two important differences. First, tribes that opt for administrative variety must meet the formalized set of criteria mentioned earlier. Tribes that pursue congressional recognition, provided they can muster enough proof that they are a legitimate group composed of people of Indian ancestry, have only to make a compelling case to the congressional representative(s) of the state they reside in. The congressional sponsor(s) then make(s) the case for the tribe via legislation.

The second major difference involves the administrative law component known as "subordinate delegation." The major grant of authority the Congress has delegated to the secretary of the interior is located in title 25—*Indians*—of the *U.S. Code*. Section 1 states that the head of Indian affairs, formerly the commissioner of Indian Affairs, today the assistant secretary of Indian Affairs, is "appointed by the President, by and with the advice and consent of the Senate."[14] In section 2, the head is authorized to "have the management of all Indian affairs and of all matters arising out of Indian relations."[15] As William Quinn states, this law "would arguably not authorize the Secretary or Commissioner to establish a perpetual government-to-government relationship via federal acknowledgment with an Indian group not already under the Department's aegis."[16] Nevertheless, Quinn asserts that the secretary of the interior, with the U.S. Supreme Court's approval, has historically exercised the authority to "recognize" tribes "when a vacuum of responsibility existed over decades, resulting in a gradual and unchallenged accretion of this authority."[17]

The problem, however, is not that the secretary is usurping unused congressional authority; instead, it is the manner and degree to which secretarial discretion and interpretation of federal laws have been discharged by BIA officials. As Felix Cohen said more than forty years ago, "Indians for some decades have had neither armies nor lawyers to oppose increasingly broad interpretations of the power of the Commissioner of Indian Affairs, and so little by little 'the management of all Indian affairs' has come to

be read as 'the management of all the affairs of Indians.'"[18] This statement has relevance today, notwithstanding the federal government's policy of Indian self-determination and the more recent policy of tribal self-governance.

The Congress's track record is problematic as well. Generally speaking, however, tribes with explicit congressional acknowledgment have found their status less subject to the whims of BIA officials, though even that is no guarantee of smooth affairs, because BIA oversees and administers most of the government's political relationship with tribes.

A prime example involves the Pascua Yaqui tribe of southern Arizona. The Yaqui were legislatively recognized in 1978. However, in the late 1980s, when they solicited the approval of the BIA on some changes in their constitution, they were informed by bureau officials that they were limited in what governmental powers they could exercise because they were not a "historic tribe," but were instead merely a "created adult Indian community":

> A historic tribe has existed since time immemorial. Its powers derive from its unextinguished, inherent sovereignty. Such a tribe has the full range of governmental powers except where it has been removed by Federal law in favor of either the United States or the state in which the tribe is located. By contrast, a community of adult Indians is composed simply of Indian people who reside together on trust land. A community of adult Indians may have a certain status which entitles it to certain privileges and immunities. . . . However, that status is derived as a necessary scheme to benefit Indians, not from some historical inherent sovereignty.[19]

The bureau's attempt to create two categories of recognized tribes, a novel and disturbing approach to determining tribal identity, was halted by Congress, which declared that no department or agency of the government could develop regulations that negated or diminished the privileges and immunities of any federally recognized tribes.[20] The Congress has, moreover, in recent years tried to reassert its constitutional authority in the field by introducing legislation that would transfer administrative and congressional consideration of applications for federal recognition to an independent commission.[21]

Congress's actions, along with the increasing politicization of the administrative recognition process because of Indian gaming operations and state concerns, compelled Kevin Gover, the assistant secretary of Indian Affairs (head of the BIA), in May 2000 to testify before Congress that his agency was no longer able to do the job of recognizing tribes. Gover admitted that he had been unable to streamline the recognition process, which in some cases had taken years to resolve, but he placed larger blame on the fact that Indian gaming revenues had enabled some groups to wage protracted legal battles that often involved nonrecognized tribes, non-Indian citizens and towns, and recognized tribes.[22]

As of 2001, the Department of the Interior officially recognizes 561 indigenous entities—332 are Indian nations, tribes, bands, organized communities, or Pueblos in the lower forty-eight states; 229 are Alaska Native villages or corporations—on a list annually prepared by the BIA. These constitute the indigenous people eligible for special programs and services provided by the United States to indigenous communities because of their status as Indians or Alaska Natives.

The situation of Alaska Native villages and corporations is complicated not only by distinctive ethnological differences but also by their unique political and legal status. Although Alaska Natives are eligible to receive services from the BIA, their political sovereignty as self-governing bodies has been questioned and at times constrained by the federal government. A recent Supreme Court case, *Alaska v. Native Village of Venetie Tribal Government* (1998),[23] cast some doubts on the sovereign status of Alaskan villages. *Venetie* dealt with the jurisdictional status of Alaska Native villages and whether or not lands owned in fee simple by these communities—a type of ownership defined by the Alaska Native Claims Settlement Act of 1971—constituted "Indian Country."

In a major victory for Alaskan state authorities and a blow to the sovereignty of the village of Venetie, an Alaskan community of some 350 people, Justice Clarence Thomas for a unanimous court held that Venetie's 1.8 million acres of fee-simple lands did not qualify as "Indian Country" because they had not been set aside by the federal government for tribal use and were not "under federal supervision." Thus, the tribal government lacked the inherent authority to impose a 5 percent business tax on a contractor building a state-funded school in the village. In denying Venetie, and by extension every other Alaskan village, the power to tax, this ruling called into question what the actual political status of these villages was.

In addition, the indigenous people of Hawaii, who prefer to be called Hawaiians, Hawaiian Natives, or Native Hawaiians, although they are treated as Native Americans for some legal purposes, are not on the Department of the Interior's list of federally recognized tribal entities and have a unique status under federal law.[24]

But there are other indigenous people in the United States who are *not federally recognized,* who had their recognized status *terminated* by the federal government, or who have *state recognition* only. I will discuss these three categories briefly.

Nonrecognized or Unacknowledged Groups

These are groups exhibiting a tremendous degree of racial, ethnic, and cultural diversity. In some cases, they are descendants of tribes who never fought the United States, had no resources desired by the federal government, or lived in geographic isolation and were simply ignored, and hence may never have participated in a treaty or benefited from the trust relationship which forms the basis of most contemporary recognized tribes' status. Despite these circumstances, some of these groups retain their aboriginal language, hold some lands in common, and in some cases have retained some degree of traditional structures of governance. These groups feel entitled to recognition status and have petitioned the United States to be so recognized.[25]

In other cases, groups have questionable genealogical connections to legitimate historical tribes but, for varying reasons, have chosen to self-identify as particular tribes and desire to be recognized by the federal government.[26] As of 2000, the BIA had received a total of 237 letters of intent and petitions for federal recognition. The acknowledgment process, established in 1978 and administered by the Branch of Acknowledgment and Research (BAR) in the BIA, proved to be an extremely slow, expensive, and politicized process that required excessive historical documentation and was greatly influenced by already recognized tribes who were reluctant to let other groups, regardless of their historical legitimacy, gain politically recognized status.[27] Because of these and other problems, the bureau surrendered its power to administratively recognize tribal groups in the fall of 2000. Between 1978 and 2000, the BIA officially recognized only fifteen tribes (e.g., Grand Traverse Band of Ottawa & Chippewa and Jamestown S'Klallam) and denied the petitions of fifteen groups (e.g., Lower Muscogee Creek Tribe east of Mississippi, Kaweah Indian Nation, Southeastern Cherokee Confederacy).[28]

Terminated Tribes

From 1953 to the mid-1960s, the federal government's Indian policy was called "termination" because the United States wanted to sever the trust relationship and end federal benefits and support services to as many tribes, bands, and California rancherias as was feasible in an effort to expedite Indian assimilation and to lift discriminatory practices and policies that negatively affected indigenous peoples.[29] This policy was exemplified by House Concurrent Resolution No. 108, passed in 1953. This measure declared that,

> Whereas it is the policy of Congress, as rapidly as possible, to make the Indians within the territorial limits of the United States subject to the same laws and entitled to the same privileges and responsibilities as are applicable to other citizens of the United States, to end their status as wards of the United States, and to grant them all the rights and prerogatives pertaining to American citizenship; and Whereas the Indians within the territorial limits of the United States should assume their full responsibilities as American citizens: Now, therefore, be it resolved . . . that it is declared to be the sense of Congress that, at the earliest possible time, all of the Indian tribes and the individual members thereof located within the States of California, Florida, New York . . . should be freed from Federal supervision and control and from all disabilities and limitations specially applicable to Indians.[30]

Over one hundred tribes, bands, and California rancherias—totaling a little more than eleven thousand Indians—were "terminated" and lost their status as "recognized" and sovereign Indian communities. Termination thus subjected the tribes and their members to state law, their trust assets were usually individualized and either sold or held by the banks, and they were no longer eligible for the other benefits and exemptions recognized tribes enjoy.

The terminated tribes, other tribes faced with termination, and Indian and non-Indian interest groups began to lobby Congress to end this disastrous policy, because of the economic and political hardships it was causing. By the mid-1960s, the policy was stifled. Gradually, terminated tribes began to push for "restoration" of their recognized status. The first tribe terminated, the Menominee of Wisconsin (terminated in 1954), was also the first tribe to be legislatively "restored," in 1973.

Although discredited as policy by the mid-1960s, and rejected by presidents Nixon and Reagan in their Indian policy statements, termination was not officially rejected by Congress until 1988 in a largely symbolic gesture that declared that "the Congress hereby repudiates and rejects HCR 108 of the 83rd Congress and any policy of unilateral termination of federal relations with any Indian nation."[31]

State-Recognized Tribes

Some Indian tribes have been recognized by their host states since the colonial era (e.g., Pamunkey Tribe of Virginia), although others have been recognized by state decrees (governor's action or state statute) in contemporary times. There are currently over fifty state-recognized tribes in Alabama, Connecticut, Georgia, Louisiana, Massachusetts, Michigan, Montana, New Jersey, North Carolina, New York, Oklahoma, Virginia, Washington, and West Virginia. See Table 1 for a list of these tribes. Depending on the policy established by the individual state, state recognition may or may not depend on prior federal recognition. Importantly, state recognition is not a prerequisite for federal recognition, although a long-standing relationship with a state is one factor in the federal recognition criteria that the BIA weighs in its determination of whether a group has historical longevity in a particular place.

For example, the Lumbee Tribe of North Carolina was legislatively recognized by the state in 1953.[32] Confident, the Lumbee leadership two years later asked Representative Frank Carlyle (D-NC) to introduce a bill before Congress that would extend federal recognition to the Lumbee. On June 7, 1956, the Congress passed an act which provided a measure of recognition to the Lumbee Nation,[33] without giving them the full range of benefits and services other federally recognized tribes received because federal policy at the time was focused on terminating the unique trust relationship between tribes and the United States. To date, the Lumbee Tribe is still not considered a federally recognized tribe by the BIA or the Indian Health Service, though they qualify for and receive other federal services as a recognized tribe.[34]

Who Is an American Indian?

Having established the complexity of determining what an Indian tribe is from a legal-political perspective, we now turn to a brief but necessary examination of the equally if not more cumbersome question of "Who is an Indian?" This is important, as McClain and Stewart note, because "the question of who is an Indian is central to

TABLE 1   State Recognized Tribes

Alabama	Nansemond Indian Tribe
Echota Cherokee	Pamunkey Indian Tribe
Northeast Alabama Cherokee	United Rappahannock Tribe
MaChis Lower Creek	Upper Mattaponi Indian Tribe
Southeast Alabama Cherokee	**West Virginia**
Star Muscogee Creek	Appalachian American Indians of West Virginia
Mowa Band of Choctaw	**Connecticut**
Georgia	Golden Hill Paugussett
Georgia Eastern Cherokee	Paucatuck Eastern Pequot
Cherokee of Georgia	Schagticoke
Lower Muskogee Creek	**Louisiana**
Tama Tribal Town	Choctaw-Apache of Ebarb
New Jersey	Caddo Tribe
Nanticoke Lenni-Lanape	Clifton Choctaw
Powhatan Renape	Four Winds Cherokee
Ramapough Mountain	United Houma Nation
Michigan	**New York**
Burt Lake Band of Ottawa & Chippewa Indians	Shinnecock
Gun Lake Band of Grand River Ottawa Indians	Poospatuk
Grand River Band of Ottawa Indians	**Montana**
Swan Creek Black River Confederated Tribes	Little Shell Tribe of Chippewa
North Carolina	**Oklahoma**
Coharie Intra-Tribal Council	Delaware Tribe of East Oklahoma
Haliwa-Saponi Tribe	Loyal Shawnee Tribe
Lumbee	Yuchi Tribe
Meherrin Tribe	**Washington**
Person County Indians	Chinook Indian Tribe
Waccamaw-Siouan Tribe	Duwamish Tribe
Virginia	Kikiallus Indian Nation
Chickahominy Indian Tribe	Marietta Band of Nooksack Indians
Eastern Chickahominy Indian Tribe	Steilacoom Indian Tribe
Mattaponi Indian Tribe	Snohomish Tribe of Indians
Monacan Indian Tribe	

Source: http://www.thespike.com/tablest.htm.

any discussion of American Indian politics."[35] The political relationship that exists between tribes and the federal government, bloated with issues of disparate power, **cultural biases,** and race and ethnicity, makes this so. Of course, like the concept of "Indian tribe," before Columbus arrived in 1492 there were no peoples in the Americas known as "Indians" or "Native Americans." Each

cultural bias The assumption that one's own cultural practices or beliefs are better and as such should be the norm by which other cultures are measured.

indigenous community had its own name relating to the character of its people and the lands they inhabited.

With the political status of Indian nations defined, the question of deciding just "who is an Indian" would not appear to be a difficult one to answer. The decision rests with the tribal nations who retain, as one of their inherent sovereign powers, the power to decide who belongs in their nation. Unless this right has been expressly ceded in a treaty, it remains probably the most essential component of self-government. If tribes were to lose the right to decide who their citizens/members were, then it would logically follow that any government could dictate or influence what the tribe's membership should entail.

Since the identification of individuals as Indians depends upon or coincides with their association in a unique body politic and distinctive cultural and linguistic systems, historically, at least, "allegiance rather than ancestry per se [was] the deciding factor" in determining who was an Indian.[36] In other words, historically, to be considered an Indian one had to meet certain basic tribally defined criteria, including the social, cultural, linguistic, territorial, sociopsychological, and ceremonial. These criteria, of course, varied from tribal nation to tribal nation. However, as the federal government's power waxed by the late nineteenth century, with the corresponding waning of tribal power, indigenous cultural-social-territorial–based definitions of tribal identity were sometimes ignored and replaced by purely legal and frequently race-based definitions often arbitrarily articulated in congressional laws, administrative regulations, or court cases.

Congress, in particular, began to employ and still uses ethnological data, including varying fractions of blood quantum. In fact, blood quantum remains one of the most important criteria used by the federal government and tribal governments to determine Indian status, despite the fact that its continued use "poses enormous conceptual and practical problems" since blood is not the carrier of genetic material and cultural traits as was thought in the nineteenth century.[37]

When blood quantum was first used in the Indian context in the early part of the twentieth century as a mechanism to reduce federal expenditures for Indian education, it "was meant to measure the amount of Indian blood possessed by an individual. Because racial blood types could not be observed directly, Indian blood quantum was inferred from the racial backgrounds of parents. If both parents were reputed to have 'unadulterated' Indian blood, then the blood quantum of their children was fixed at 100 percent. For children of racially mixed parents, their Indian blood quantum might be some fractional amount such as ¾, ½, or ⅛."[38]

The federal government's principal function in formulating definitions of "Indian," since like the concept "tribe" there is no single constitutional or universally accepted definition, is to "establish a test whereby it may be determined whether a given individual is to be excluded from the scope of legislation dealing with Indians."[39] The most

widely accepted "legal" definition of "Indian" is from Felix Cohen, who wrote in 1943 that:

> The term "Indian" may be used in an ethnological or in a legal sense. Ethnologically, the Indian race may be distinguished from the Caucasian, Negro, Mongolian, and other races. If a person is three-fourths Caucasian and one-fourth Indian, it is absurd, from the ethnological standpoint, to assign him to the Indian race. Yet legally such a person may be an Indian. From a legal standpoint, then, the biological question of race is generally pertinent, but not conclusive. Legal status depends not only upon biological, but also upon social factors, such as the relation of the individual concerned to a white or Indian community. . . . Recognizing the possible diversity of definitions of "Indianhood," we may nevertheless find some practical value in a definition of "Indian" as a person meeting two qualifications: (a) That some of his ancestors lived in America before its discovery by the white race, and (b) That the individual is considered an "Indian" by the community in which he lives.[40]

Because of the Constitution's silence on the issue of who is an Indian, Congress, the BIA, and the federal courts have had great latitude in developing specific meanings for specific situations which only sometimes reflect the definitions of particular tribes. But because of the plenary power doctrine and the trust doctrine, these federal actors, but especially the Congress, have vested themselves with the right to define "who an Indian is" for purposes relating to legislation and have sometimes established base rolls which actually identify who a tribe's members are. This was done in the case of the so-called Five Civilized Tribes of present-day Oklahoma. Congress, in 1893, enacted a law that all but secured to the federal government the right to determine membership of these tribes.[41]

Over thirty "legal" definitions have been promulgated by various agencies, departments, and congressional committees and subcommittees that explain who is and is not an Indian eligible for federal services.[42] These definitions can be grouped into six categories. First, and most common, are those definitions that require a specific blood quantum, with one-fourth being the most widely accepted fraction. Second, there is a set of definitions clustered under the requirement that the individual be a member of a federally recognized indigenous community.

A third category includes definitions that mandate residence "on or near" a federal Indian reservation. A fourth class includes definitions grouped under descendancy.

These entail definitions that extend eligibility not only to tribal members but also to their descendants up to a specified degree. For example, the definition of Indian found in a 1998 bill, Indian Trust-Estate Planning and Land Title Management Improvement Act, declares that "the term 'Indian' means any individual who is a member, or a descendant of a member, of a North American tribe, band, pueblo, or other organized group of natives who are indigenous to the continental U.S., or who otherwise has a special relationship with the U.S. through a treaty, agreement, or other form of recognition." The bill's sponsors described an "Alaska Native" as "an individual who is an Alaskan Indian, Eskimo, Aleut, or any combination thereof, who are indigenous to Alaska."

Under the fifth grouping are several definitions that rely on self-identification. The U.S. Census Bureau, for example, allows individuals to simply declare that they are Indian. Finally, the sixth class is a miscellaneous category that includes definitions which do not easily fit in the other categories.[43]

Defining "Indian" and "tribe" are not simple tasks in part because of the political and economic resources involved and because of the number and power of the respective actors: tribal governments, individual Indians, Congress, the president, the Department of the Interior, the BIA, federal courts and, increasingly, state governments and the various agencies and individuals who constitute those sovereigns. But who does the defining and how these emotionally laden terms are defined are crucial in expanding our understanding of the politics of individual tribes, intertribal relations, and intergovernmental relations.

For example, in terms of identity, high outmarriage rates, steadily decreasing federal dollars, and an intensified tribal-state relationship have prompted questions about "whether the rules defining Indianness and tribal membership should be relaxed or tightened—that is, made more inclusionary or more exclusionary."[44] For instance, some tribes are eliminating **blood quantum** and adopting descent criteria, while others are pursuing an "ethnic purification strategy" by adopting a stricter set of blood quantum rules concerning tribal enrollment.

blood quantum The idea of counting the percentage of racial heritage, which comes from racist laws that were used to place American Indians on reservations. The laws asked the question, in terms of a percentage, how black, or Indian, or white you were.

These decisions impact tribes and their political relationship with the federal government.

While tribes retain the right to establish their own membership criteria, the BIA in August 2000 published proposed regulations on the documentation requirements and standards necessary for Indians to receive a "certificate of degree of Indian blood" (CDIB), which is the federal government's way of determining whether individuals possess sufficient Indian blood to be eligible for certain federal programs and services provided exclusively to American Indians or Alaska Natives.[45]

But a number of Indian leaders, like W. Ron Allen, chairman of the Jamestown S'Klallam Tribe of Washington, charged that the federal government should not be in the business of determining who is Indian. The proposed regulations, he argued, by requiring applicants to show a relationship to an enrolled member of a federally recognized tribe, would potentially exclude members or descendants of terminated tribes, state-recognized tribes, and nonrecognized tribes.

Since the BIA's standard blood quantum is one-fourth, and with the high rates of out-marriage, Russell Thornton, an anthropologist, suggests that sometime in this century the proportion of the Indian population with less than one-fourth blood quantum will rise to 60 percent. If this trend is correct, from the federal government's standpoint "decreasing blood quanta of the total Native American population may be perceived as meaning that the numbers of Native Americans to whom it is obligated have declined."[46] This will not mean the extinction of Indian tribes, but it will mean a new form of federal termination of Indians who are eligible for federal aid and services.

Questions around whether a tribe is federally recognized, state-recognized, nonrecognized, or terminated have direct bearing on the internal and external political dynamics of tribes, and directly affect intergovernmental relations, since only recognized tribes may engage in gaming operations that are not directly subject to state law, may exercise criminal jurisdiction over their members and a measure of civil jurisdiction over nonmembers, and are exempt from a variety of state and federal taxes.

What Are Indian Lands?

The first and most obvious difference between Indian peoples and all other groups in the United States is that Indians were here before anyone else. All the land in the continental United States, Alaska, and Hawaii was inhabited and revered by the over six hundred distinctive indigenous peoples who dwelt here. Gradually, however, from 1492 forward, various foreign nations—Russia, Holland, Spain, Great Britain, France, Sweden, and later the United States—competed for an economic foothold in North America. For the three most dominant European states, France, Spain, and Great Britain (and later the United States, as Britain's successor), this usually included efforts to secure title to indigenous lands through formal treaties, which were sometimes coercive and occasionally fraudulent, while some were fairly negotiated.[47]

When the United States declared independence in 1776, it wisely opted to continue the policy of negotiating treaties with tribes, which it continued to do until 1871, when Congress unilaterally declared that "hereafter no Indian nation or tribe within the territory of the United States shall be acknowledged or recognized as an independent nation, tribe, or power with whom the United States may contract by treaty."[48] However, this stance proved unworkable and within a short period the United States was again negotiating *agreements* with tribal nations that were often referred to and accorded the legal status of treaties. The negotiation of agreements continued until 1912.

Many of these documents were primarily viewed as land cession arrangements by the federal government, in which the United States purchased varying amounts of tribal lands in exchange for monies, goods, and services. In addition, tribes "reserved" their remaining lands, or agreed to relocate to new lands, which were usually designated as reservations. These reserved lands were to be held "in trust" by the United States on behalf of the tribe(s), who were deemed the beneficiaries. As the tribes' "trustee," the federal government theoretically exercised the responsibility to assist the tribes in the protection of their lands, resources, and cultural heritage and pledged that it would hold itself to the highest standards of good faith and honesty in all its dealings with the tribes.

For example, article 1 of a treaty the Kickapoo signed on October 24, 1832, contained a cession of land:

> The Kickapoo tribe of Indians, in consideration of the stipulations hereinafter made, do hereby cede to the United States, the lands assigned to them by the treaty of Edwardsville, and concluded at St. Louis . . . and all other claims to lands within the State of Missouri.[49]

The second article, however, described the lands the tribe had secured for their land cessions:

> The United States will provide for the Kickapoo tribe, a country to reside in, southwest of the Missouri river, as their permanent place of residence as long as they remain a tribe . . . [and] it is hereby agreed that the country within the following boundaries shall be assigned, conveyed, and forever secured . . . to the said Kickapoo tribe.[50]

In this case the Kickapoo agreed to relocate to a little over 700,000 acres of new lands in Kansas that were to serve as their permanent "reservation."

In short, a reservation is an area of land—whether aboriginal or new—that has been reserved for an Indian tribe, band, village, or nation. Generally, the United States holds, in trust for the tribe, legal title to the reserved territory. The tribe in these instances holds a beneficial title to the lands, or, in other words, an exclusive right of occupancy. Of course, reservations were not all created by treaty. Congress established a number of reservations by statute.

The president, through the use of executive order power, established many other reservations. For instance, the state of Arizona has twenty-one reservations—twenty of which were created by presidents. The core foundation of the Navajo Reservation (the largest in the country), was treaty-established in 1868, though the many additions to it were mostly by executive orders. In 1919, Congress forbade the president from establishing any more reservations via executive order. Finally, the secretary of the interior is empowered under the 1934 Indian Reorganization Act to establish, expand, or restore reservations.

As of 1998, there were 314 reservations and other restricted and trust lands in the United States. These reserved lands are located in thirty-one states, mostly in the West. There are also twelve state-established reservations in Connecticut, Massachusetts, Michigan, New York, New Jersey, South Carolina, Georgia, and Virginia. Despite the large number of federally recognized Alaska Native groups, there is only one reservation, the Annette Island Indian Reserve.[51]

At present, the indigenous land base in the United States, including Alaska, is approximately 100 million acres—fifty-six million in the continental United States, forty-four million in Alaska. This represents approximately 4 percent of all lands in the United States. Map 1 graphically shows the rapid and enormous loss of aboriginal

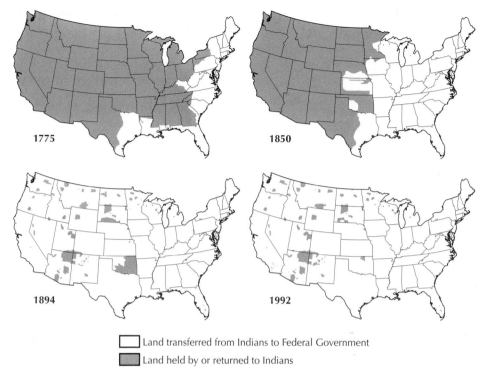

1775

1850

1894

1992

☐ Land transferred from Indians to Federal Government

■ Land held by or returned to Indians

MAP 1   American Indian Land Losses. *Source: Encyclopedia of North American Indians,* edited by Frederick E. Hoxie. Copyright © 1996 by Houghton Mifflin Company. All rights reserved.

territory to the United States from the birth of the American republic to the present day.

The roughly 100 (per previous paragraph) million acres constitutes territory over which tribal governments and Alaska Native villages and corporations exercise varying amounts of governmental jurisdiction, and where state laws are generally inapplicable, with exceptions.

In 1999, 1,397,931 Indians were identified in a BIA report out of the total U.S. Indian population in 2000 of 2,475,956 (individuals self-identifying as single race American Indian or Alaska Native).

What Is Indian Country?

For an indigenous government to be able to exercise criminal or civil jurisdiction over their territory, their own members, and, in some limited cases, non-Indians, the land in question must be designated as *Indian Country.* In the colonial era, Indian Country encompassed all the lands beyond the frontier lands "populated by tribes and bands

of Indians who rejected contact with 'civilized' populations."[52] Today, however, the concept "has been elevated by federal law above other ideas because it transcends mere geographical limitations and represents that sphere of influence in which Indian traditions and federal laws passed specifically to deal with the political relationship of the United States to American Indians have primacy."[53]

Indian Country: Beyond the Reservation

Broadly, the term "Indian Country" means land within which Indian laws and customs and federal laws relating to Indians are generally applicable. But it is also defined as all the land under the supervision and protection of the federal government that has been set aside primarily for the use of Indians. Federal law defines it, first, as all land within the boundaries of an Indian reservation, whether owned by Indians or non-Indians. Second, it includes all "dependent Indian communities" in the United States.

These are lands—pueblos of New Mexico, Oklahoma Indian tribal lands, and California rancherias—previously recognized by European nations and now by the successor government, the United States, as belonging to the tribes or as set aside by the federal government for use and benefit of the Indians.

Pueblo lands, because they were previously recognized as belonging to the pueblos under Spanish, Mexican, and later U.S. law, are not, strictly speaking, reservations, but are considered Indian lands and are held in trust by the federal government because they are held in communal ownership with fee-simple title residing in each pueblo. Some Pueblo Indian lands are held in equitable ownership by various pueblos, with the United States holding legal title. These lands include reservations created by congressional statute and executive order reservations established by the president.

Oklahoma's numerous Indian tribes also have a distinctive history, though their lands also constitute Indian Country. It is important to note that the tribes in the eastern part of the state, what was called "Indian Territory," home of the Five Civilized Tribes, have a somewhat different history from tribes in the western part of the state, or what was called "Oklahoma Territory," home of the Cheyenne, Arapaho, Kiowa, Comanche, etc. Although the BIA and the Bureau of the Census have asserted that there are no Indian reservations in Oklahoma, except for the Osage, John Moore argues that the reservation status of Oklahoma tribes persists, notwithstanding allotment and other policies designed to terminate Indian communal land holdings.[54]

Some California tribes, because of heavy Spanish influence dating from 1769, live on rancherias, a Spanish term meaning "small reservation" and originally applied to Indians who had not been settled in Christian mission communities. The history of death and dispossession visited upon California's indigenous population may well be the worst of any aboriginal peoples in the United States. From a population of well over 300,000 at the time of contact, California Indians experienced a staggering rate of decline from diseases, outright **genocide,** and displacement.[55] That they have retained any lands at all is a remarkable testimony to their fortitude.

Finally, the Indian Country designation includes all individual Indian allotments (I will discuss the allotment

genocide The systematic wholesale killing of individuals because of their race, religion, ethnicity, or political affiliation. The idea behind genocide is the total eradication of a group, motivated by hatred.

policy shortly) that are still held in trust or restricted status by the federal government—whether inside or outside an Indian reservation.[56]

For political and legal purposes, the designation of Indian Country is crucial because the reach of a tribal nation's jurisdiction is generally restricted to lands so designated. And it is Indian Country where most jurisdictional disputes arise between tribes and their members, tribes and non-Indians, and tribes and the local, county, state, or federal governments.

For example, this was the central question in the recent U.S. Supreme Court case involving indigenous people, *Alaska v. Native Village of Venetie Tribal Government* (1998). In this case, the court had to decide whether the village of Venetie constituted Indian Country. If so, then the tribal government had the right to impose a tax on a construction company; if not, then it lacked such taxing power. In a harmful ruling for Alaska Native sovereignty, the Supreme Court held that the village's fee-simple lands did not constitute Indian Country, thus depriving Alaska villages and corporations of the power to exercise a number of governmental powers that tribal nations in the lower forty-eight states exercise routinely. The Supreme Court, however, need not have relied so exclusively on the question of whether or not Venetia constituted "Indian Country" since the statutes articulating this concept clearly did not encompass Alaska at the time they were enacted.

Demography and Indian Country

According to a report, *Changing America,* prepared by the Council of Economic Advisers for President Clinton's Race Initiative in 1998, the population of the United States is increasingly diverse. In recent years the four major racial/ethnic minority groups—Latinos, Asian Americans, African Americans, and American Indians—have each grown faster than the population as a whole. Whereas in 1970 the combination of these four groups represented only 16 percent of the entire population, by 1998 this had increased to 27 percent.[57] The Bureau of the Census, the report noted, projects that by 2050, these groups will account for "almost half of the U.S. Population." Early data from the 2000 U.S. census, which shows a total population of 281,421,906, indicate the continuing transformation of race and ethnicity in America. While the categories of white (211,460,626), Hispanic or Latino (35,305,818), black or African American (34,658,190), American Indian

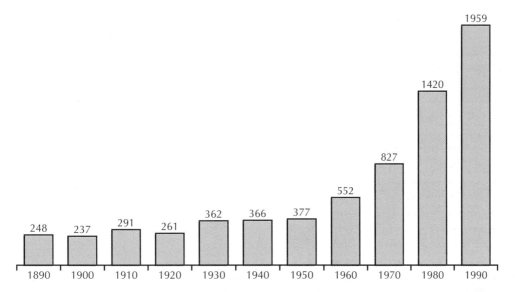

FIGURE 1   **American Indian Population, 1890–1990 (thousands).** *Source:* Larry Hajime Shinagawa and Michael Jang, *Atlas of American Diversity* (Walnut Creek, Calif.: AltaMira, 1998), 107–8. *Notes:* 1900, partially estimated; 1940 Eskimo and Aleut populations are based on 1939 counts.

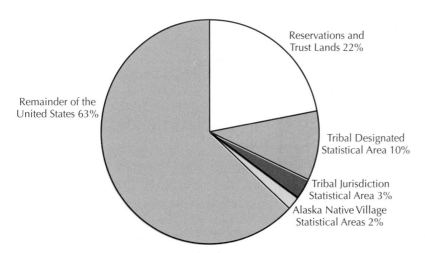

FIGURE 2   **American Indian Population by Type of Area, 1990 (percent).** *Source:* Larry Hajime Shinagawa and Michael Jang, *Atlas of American Diversity* (Walnut Creek, Calif.: AltaMira, 1998), 107–8.

or Alaska Native (2,475,956), Asian (10,242,998), and Native Hawaiian or other Pacific Islander (398,835) were familiar, for the first time in history individuals could choose self-identify as having more than one race. Some 6,826,228 people, 2.4 percent of the total population, claimed affiliation with two or more races.[58]

While this projected growth has potentially staggering political and economic implications, the fact is that the total indigenous population, despite the large number of indigenous nations—561 and counting—is comparatively quite small (see Figures 1–5). In 2000, there were a reported 2,475,956 self-identified Indians and Alaska

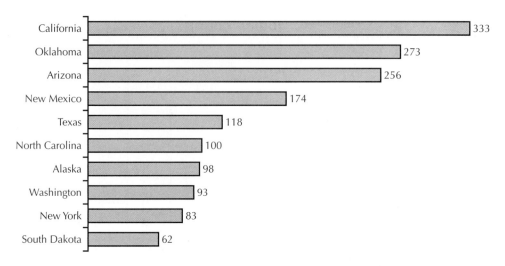

FIGURE 3   **States with the Ten Largest American Indian Populations, 2000 (thousands).** *Source:* www.census.gov/clo/www/redistricting.html.

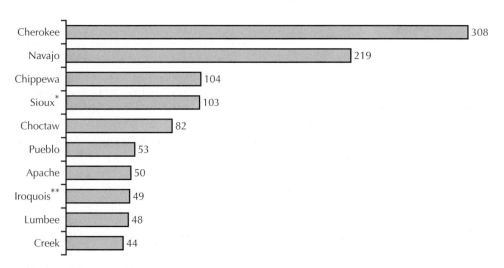

FIGURE 4   **Ten Largest American Indian Tribes, 1990 (thousands).** *Source:* Larry Hajime Shinagawa and Michael Jang, *Atlas of American Diversity* (Walnut Creek, Calif.: AltaMira, 1998), 107–8. *Any entry with the spelling "Siouan" was miscoded to Sioux in North Carolina. **Reporting and/or processing problems have affected the data for this tribe.

Natives, a 26 percent increase since 1990. This is a drastic decline from pre-European figures of over seven million, but it is far more than the nadir of perhaps only 250,000 around 1900.[59] The 2000 figure represents only 0.9 percent of the total U.S. population of 281,421,906.

Although the overall population of self-identified American Indians and Alaska Natives is still quite small, because of the new category allowing individuals to identify as belonging to more than one race (sixty-three racial options were possible), the 2000 census data are not

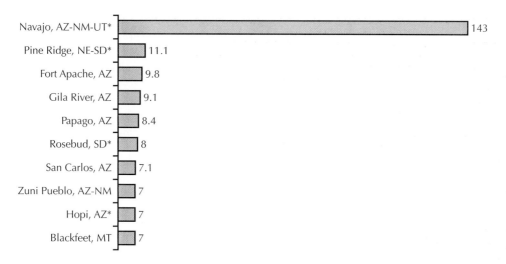

FIGURE 5 **Reservations with the Largest Numbers of American Indians, 1990 (thousands).** *Source:* Larry Hajime Shinagawa and Michael Jang, *Atlas of American Diversity* (Walnut Creek, Calif.: AltaMira, 1998), 107–8. *Includes trust lands.

directly comparable with data from the 1990 census or previous censuses. Thus, while approximately 2.5 million individuals identified themselves as American Indian and Alaska Native alone, an additional 1.6 million people reported themselves as being indigenous and belonging to "at least one other race." Within this group, the most common combinations were "American Indian and Alaska Native *and* White" (66 percent of the population reported this); "American Indian and Alaska Native *and* Black or African American" (11 percent of the population); and "American Indian and Alaska Native *and* White *and* Black or African American" (7 percent). In sum, approximately 4.1 million people reported themselves as being American Indian and Alaska Native "alone or in combination with one or more other races."[60] The wide diversity within this population will be discussed in greater detail in forthcoming Census reports not yet available.

Suffice it to say, the amount of racial mixing acknowledged in the American Indian context is extreme when compared to that of other racial/ethnic groups. As Russell Thorton, a Cherokee anthropologist, noted in his analysis of the 2000 census data, American Indians have a racial mixture of 37 percent, which "far exceeds percentages for other groups." Thornton noted that only about 5 percent of African Americans reported mixed ancestry.[61]

In Alaska, there is only one small reservation, Annette Island Reserve, though for census purposes lands are designated as "Alaska Native Village Statistical areas" that are inhabited and recognized as indigenous areas. Approximately 47,244 Alaska Natives live on these lands. In sum, more than 60 percent, over one million, of all Indian people do not live on Indian reservations.[62] A majority of indigenous peoples, in fact some 56.2 percent, live in metropolitan or suburban areas. And roughly half of all urban Indians can be found in as few as sixteen cities, largely as a result of the 1950s and 1960s termination, relocation, and educational programs of the federal government.

In the early days of relocation, the BIA generally helped send Indians to Chicago, Los Angeles, Denver, or Salt Lake City. By 1990, Indians had migrated to a number of other metropolitan areas. Cities with the largest Indian populations in 1990 were Tulsa, Oklahoma (48,348); Oklahoma City, Oklahoma (46,111); Los Angeles–Long Beach, California (43,689); Phoenix, Arizona (38,309); and Seattle-Tacoma, Washington (32,980).[63] The vast majority of Indians still live in the western half of the United States.

The states with the ten largest indigenous populations are shown in Figure 3. The District of Columbia had the fewest Indians, 1,466.

There is also great variation in the population of individual tribes (see Figure 5). The largest tribe is the Cherokee Nation of Oklahoma, with 369,035 members. The smallest tribes have fewer than one hundred members. The indigenous population is also a young population, with more than 35 percent younger than age seventeen. In fact, the median age for reservation Indians is more than ten years younger than that of the general U.S. population. The Indian population, like that of the Jews and the Japanese Americans in Hawaii, is also one that experiences an extremely high level of intergroup marriage (marriage between persons of different races). Although intergroup marriage couples accounted for only 4 percent of all married couples in the United States in 1990, American Indians had a 53 percent intergroup marriage rate. Potentially, this figure could have severe cultural and political implications for indigenous nations.[64]

As Snipp mused:

> The extraordinarily high level of racial intermarriage for American Indians provides a good reason to expect that growing numbers of American Indians and their descendants will choose non-Indians for spouses and to a greater or lesser degree become absorbed into the dominant culture. Some of these Indians will abandon their cultural heritage altogether, while others may make only minor accommodations as a result of having a non-Indian spouse. This raises a question that is extremely controversial within many quarters of the American Indian community: Are American Indians assimilating so quickly through racial intermarriage that they will eventually, in the not to distant future, marry themselves out of existence?[65]

Predicting the future is an impossible task and I will not hazard a guess as to whether this intermarriage rate will continue. Suffice it to say, this is viewed as a serious predicament by some tribes and raises some important questions. For instance, will Indians, like many intermarried Jews, be able to show a propensity for combining extensive intermarriage with a surge in ethnic and religious pride? For while the rate of Jewish intermarriage is higher today than at any other point, American Jewish culture and community life appear to be flourishing, including a resurgent interest in Yiddish.[66]

Other questions confront tribes as well. Will they continue to use blood quantum as their primary definitional criteria? Will the federal government claim that its legal and moral obligations to Indians dissipate if a tribal nation's blood quantum falls below a certain percentage? Will tribes be able to exercise jurisdiction over a multiracial citizenry? These are questions some tribes are beginning to address as we begin the new millennium.

Conclusion

The power to define—what is a tribe, who is an Indian, what constitutes Indian Country, which group gets recognized—along with the power to decide whether or not to act in a colonial capacity in relation to indigenous nations are important means by which the federal government has gained and retains a dominant position vis-à-vis tribal groups. While on one hand supporting the right of indigenous polities to exercise self-determination, the United States on the other hand still insists that it has the power and the right to trump important tribal governmental decisions regarding identity and has shown throughout its history that it will so act if it deems it necessary to further its own economic, political, and cultural interests.

The demographic data presented glaringly show that diversity and uncertainty are hallmarks of Indian Country, with more than half the indigenous population living off reservations and Indians outmarrying at increasing rates. What the impact of such movement and marriage rates will be on tribal national identity, federal Indian policy, and the government-to-government relationship is, however, impossible to predict.

Seeing the Big Picture   **From Riches to the "Res" (Reservation System)**

Map 1 in this reading shows land held by Indians in 1775 and 1992. Glance at the quality-of-life indicators in the Appendix. Do you believe that socioeconomic standing and the loss of Indian lands are connected? How?

10 Asian American Panethnicity: Contemporary National and Transnational Possibilities

Yen Le Espiritu

YEN LE ESPIRITU is professor of ethnic studies at the University of California, San Diego.

———

IN AN ARTICLE PUBLISHED IN *GIDRA*, AN activist Asian American news magazine, Naomi Iwasaki (1999, under "Asian American or Not") writes, "You know, the hardest thing about pan-Asian solidarity is the 'pan' part. It forces us all to step outside of our comfort zones, whether they be constructed by ethnicity, class, home city, identity, whatever." Iwasaki's statement calls attention to the social constructedness of panethnicity—panethnic identities are self-conscious products of political choice and actions, not of inherited phenotypes, bloodlines, or cultural traditions. . . . Employing a racial formation perspective (Omi and Winant 1986), I argue that the racialist constructions of Asians as homogeneous and interchangeable spawn important alliances and affiliations among ethnic and immigrant groups of Asian origin. Adopting the dominant group's categorization of them, Asian Americans have institutionalized pan-Asianism as their political instrument, thereby enlarging their own capacities to challenge and transform the existing structure of power. In other words, Asian Americans did not just adopt the pan-Asian concept but also transformed it to conform to their political, economic, and ideological needs.

Though powerful, pan-Asianism is not unproblematic: it can mask salient divisions, subsume nondominant groups, and create marginalities, all of which threatens the legitimacy and effectiveness of pan-Asianism and bolsters (however inadvertently) the racist discourses and practices that construct Asians as homogeneous. In the three decades since the emergence of the pan-Asian concept in the late 1960s, Asian American communities have changed in dramatic ways. No longer constrained by race-based exclusion laws, Asian immigrants began arriving in much larger numbers than before. Many of the post-1965 immigrants have little direct experience with the Asian American movement and little reason to think of

Questions to Consider   Most non-Asian Americans have the tendency to "lump" Asians into a single, culturally homogeneous racial category even though this population is, as Espiritu points out, quite diverse culturally and linguistically. Complicating perceptions of this group is that a significant number of immigrants Asians have been here for many generations and have undergone extensive assimilation while others, much larger in number, have arrived in the last few decades. What are the implications, according to Professor Yen Le Espiritu, of having new and old immigrants sharing social space and navigating the politics of race?

themselves as Asian American rather than as immigrants, as low-wage workers, or as members of different national and ethnic groups (Espiritu et al. 2000, 131). Moreover, recent immigration has further diversified Asian Americans along cultural, generational, economic, and political lines—all of which have compounded the difficulties of forging pan-Asian identities and institutions.

This chapter reviews the history of Asian American panethnicity in the United States *then to now,* paying particular attention to the ways in which pan-Asian identities and institutions have been transformed by the post-1965 immigration and by changes in the global economy. The first section documents the social, political, and demographic factors that led to the emergence of pan-Asianism in the late 1960s and early 1970s. The second details how the post-1965 immigration has diversified the Asian American population and made it more difficult for groups to imagine shared origins and destinies. The third establishes that the construction of Asian American identities not only is a response to conditions in the United States but also is deeply bound to U.S. colonial and imperialist practices that propel the contemporary migration of Asians to the United States in the first place. The fourth discusses the political importance of cross-group affiliation, not only among Asians but also with other groups across class, ethnic, racial, and national lines. Of the four sections, the third conveys the chapter's central argument: pan-Asianism in the United States has been determined not exclusively by events and population changes in the United States but also by U.S. colonialism and imperialism in Asia. Much of the published work in the field of U.S. immigration studies has remained "America-centric," focusing on the immigrants' "modes of incorporation" and the process of their "becoming American." In contrast, this chapter takes a *critical transnational approach* to the study of Asian Americans, calling attention to the deep historical entanglements of immigration and imperialism.[1]

Coming Together: The Emergence of Pan-Asianism

Arriving in the United States, nineteenth-century immigrants from Asian countries did not think of themselves as "Asians." Coming from specific districts and provinces in different nations, Asian immigrant groups did not even think of themselves as Chinese, Japanese, Korean, and so forth, but rather as people from Toishan, Hoiping, or some other district in Guandong Province in China or from Hiroshima, Yamaguchi, or some other prefecture in Japan. Members of each group considered themselves culturally and politically distinct. Historical enmities between their countries of origin further separated the groups even before their arrival in the United States. However, non-Asians had little understanding or appreciation of these distinctions. For the most part, outsiders accorded to people from Asia certain common characteristics and traits that were essentially supranational. Indeed, the exclusion acts and quotas limiting Asian immigration to the United States relied on racialist constructions of Asians as homogeneous (Lowe 1991, 28).

The development of panethnicity among Asian Americans has a short history. It was not until the late 1960s,

transnational The movement of individuals, families, culture, and ideas back and forth between one's country of origin and a new place of residence.

with the advent of the Asian American movement, that a pan-Asian consciousness and constituency were first formed. Before the 1960s, Asians in the United States frequently practiced ethnic disidentification: distancing one's group from another group so as not to be mistaken for a member of that group and to avoid suffering the blame for its presumed misdeeds (Hayano 1981, 161, 162; Daniels 1988, 113). For example, in the late nineteenth century, aware of Chinese exclusion, Japanese immigrant leaders did everything possible to distinguish themselves from the Chinese immigrants (Ichioka 1988, 250). In the end Japanese attempts at disidentification failed. With the passage of the 1924 Immigration Act, the Japanese joined the Chinese as a people deemed unworthy of becoming Americans. Less than two decades later, after the bombing of Pearl Harbor, it was the turn of the Chinese to disassociate themselves from the Japanese. Fearful that they would be targets of anti-Japanese activities, many Chinese immigrants took to wearing buttons that proclaimed positively, "I'm Chinese." Some Chinese immigrants—and also Korean and Filipino migrants—even joined the white persecution with buttons that added, "I hate Japs worse than you do" (Daniels 1988, 205; Takaki 1989, 370–71). These two examples are instructive not only as evidence of ethnic disidentification but also as documentation of the pervasiveness of racial lumping. Precisely because of racial lumping, persons of Asian ancestry found it necessary to disassociate themselves from other Asian groups.

The development of a pan-Asian consciousness and constituency reflected broader societal developments and demographic changes as well as the group's political agenda. Before World War II, pan-Asian unity was not feasible because the predominantly foreign-born Asian population did not share a common language. During the postwar years, owing to immigration restrictions and the growing dominance of the second and even third generations, U.S.-born Asians outnumbered immigrants. By 1960 approximately two-thirds of the Asian population in California had been born in the United States (Ong 1989, 5–8). With English as the common language, persons from different Asian backgrounds were able to communicate with one another (Ling 1984, 73) and in so doing to create a common identity associated with the United States. Also, the breakdown of economic and residential barriers during the postwar period provided the first opportunity for an unprecedented number of Asian Americans to come into intimate, sustained contact with the larger society—and with one another. Formerly homogeneous, the Asian ethnic enclaves started to house mixed-Asian communities, as well as non-Asian groups. Multigroup suburban centers also emerged. Paul Wong (1972, 34) reported that since the early 1960s Asian Americans of diverse national origins had moved into the suburbs outside the major Asian communities such as Berkeley and San Mateo, California. Although a small proportion of the local population, these Asian Americans tended to congregate in pockets; consequently, in some residential blocks a majority of the residents were Asian Americans.

Although broader social struggles and internal demographic changes provided the impetus for the Asian American movement, it was the Asian Americans' politics—explicitly radical, confrontational, and pan-Asian—that shaped the movement's content. Inspired by anticolonial revolutions in Asia and by black and Chicano revolutionary nationalism, college students of Asian ancestry sought to transcend inter-Asian ethnic divisions and to ally themselves with other "Third World" minorities (Blauner 1972, ch. 2; Omatsu 1994). Through pan-Asian organizations, publications, and Asian American studies programs, Asian American activists forged a pan-Asian consciousness by highlighting their shared resistance to Western imperialism and to U.S. racism. The pan-Asian concept enabled diverse Asian American groups to understand their "unequal circumstances and histories as being related" (Lowe 1991, 30). By the mid-1970s, "Asian American" had become a familiar term (Lott 1976, 30). Although first coined by college activists, the pan-Asian concept began to be used extensively by professional and community spokespersons to lobby for the health and welfare of Americans of Asian descent. Commenting on the "literally scores of pan-Asian organizations" in the mid-1970s, William Liu (1976, 6) asserted that "the idea of pan-Asian cooperation [was] viable and ripe for development."

The advent of state-sponsored affirmative action programs provided another material reason for Asian American subgroups to consolidate their efforts. Because the welfare state bureaucracy often treats all Asian Americans as a single administrative unit in distributing economic and political resources, it imposes a pan-Asian structure on persons and communities dependent on government support. As dealings with government bureaucracies increased, political organization along a pan-Asian line became necessary, not only because numbers confer power but also because the

pan-Asian category is the institutionally relevant category in the political and legal system. Administratively treated as a homogeneous group, Asian Americans found it necessary—and even advantageous—to respond as a group. The pan-Asian strategy has led to some political victories. For example, Asian American legislators, community leaders, and organizations united to fight the Census Bureau's proposal to collapse all Asian racial codes into one summary category for the 1980 and 1990 censuses. Partly in response to the strength of their political lobbying, the Census Bureau finally conceded to the coalition's demand for a detailed enumeration of Asian subgroups.[2] Indeed, the emergence of the pan-Asian entity may be one of the most significant political developments in Asian American affairs.

Changing Demographic and Economic Characteristics

The post-1965 immigration surge from Asia has transformed Asian America—and thus the feasibility of pan-Asian ethnicity—in dramatic ways. The share of immigrants to the United States from Asia as a proportion of total admission grew from a tiny 5 percent in the 1950s to 11 percent in the 1960s and 33 percent in the 1970s, and it has remained at 35 percent since 1980 (Zhou and Gatewood 2000, 9). In sheer numbers, the Asian American population grew from a total of 1.4 million in 1970 to 7.3 million in 1990, to 10.2 million in 2000.[3] According to Zhou and Gatewood (2000, 14), immigration accounted for more than two-thirds of this spectacular population growth. For the new national origins groups (Indians, Koreans, Vietnamese, Cambodians, Laotians, and the Hmong), population growth can be attributed almost entirely to immigration (Zhou and Gatewood 2000, 14). Projections from the Census Bureau suggest that the Asian American population will increase from 9 million in 1995 to 34 million in 2050, growing from 3 percent to 8 percent of the total U.S. population (Smith and Edmonston 1997). The dramatic growth in the absolute numbers of Asian Americans has been accompanied by increasing ethnic, generational, and socioeconomic diversity within Asian America, all of which has important implications for pan-Asian identities and practices. As Michael Omi (1993, 205) succinctly states, "The irony is that the term ["Asian American"] came into vogue at precisely the historical moment when new Asian groups were entering the U.S. who would render the term problematic."

Ethnic Diversification

Before the post-1965 immigration surge, the Asian American population was composed mainly of three ethnic groups: Japanese, Chinese, and Filipino. In 1970 Japanese Americans constituted the single largest group (41 percent of the Asian American population), followed by Chinese Americans (30 percent) and Filipino Americans (24 percent). Members of other national origins groups (mostly Koreans) represented less than 5 percent of the Asian American population total (Zhou and Gatewood 2000, 13). Coming of age in the 1960s, U.S.-born Japanese and Chinese Americans formed the core force of the Asian American movement on West Coast college campuses and in the Northeast (Espiritu 1992). In contrast, in 2000 the U.S. census recorded twenty-four national origins groups, and no single group accounted for more than one-quarter of the Asian American population. Although Japan has sent very few immigrants to the United States, the Philippines, China and Taiwan, Korea, India, and Vietnam have been on the list of the top ten sending countries since 1980 (USINS 1997). Reflecting these changing immigration patterns, in 2000 the Japanese American share of the Asian American population fell to only 8 percent, and the five largest Asian American groups were Chinese and Taiwanese (24 percent), Filipino (18 percent), Asian Indian (17 percent), Korean (11 percent), and Vietnamese (11 percent) (Barnes and Bennett 2002).[4] The new Asian American demographics have complicated the delicate pan-Asian alignments created in the 1960s and 1970s among the then-largest Asian American groups: Japanese, Chinese, and, to a lesser extent, Filipino Americans.

Generational Diversification

Between the 1940s and 1960s, when immigration from Asia was restricted, U.S.-born Asian Americans dominated the Asian American population. By the 1970s the foreign-born reemerged as a large majority. In 2000, 7.2 million Asian Pacific Americans—approximately 70 percent of the total Asian American population—were foreign-born (U.S. Department of Commerce 2002). The foreign-born component dominated all Asian American groups except for Japanese Americans; over 60 percent of Filipinos and nearly 80 percent of Vietnamese and other Asians were foreign-born (Zhou and Gatewood 2000, 14). Because of legal exclusion in the past, it is only among the two oldest immigrant groups—the Japanese and Chinese Americans—that a sizable third or fourth generation exists. Among Asian American children under eighteen years of age, more than 90 percent are either foreign-born or children of foreign-born parents (Zhou and Greenwood 2000, 23). Paul Ong and Suzanne Hee (1993) have predicted that the foreign-born segment will still be a majority in the year 2020.

Class Diversification

Post-1965 immigration has also increased the economic diversity of Asian Americans. In contrast to the largely unskilled immigrant population of the pre–World War II period, the new arrivals include not only low-wage service-sector workers but also significant numbers of white-collar professionals. According to the 1990 U.S. census, more than 60 percent of immigrants (age twenty-five or older) from India and Taiwan reported having attained a college degree (three times the proportion of average Americans), but fewer than 5 percent of those from Cambodia and Laos made such a report. Among the employed workers, about 45 percent of immigrants from India and Taiwan held managerial or professional occupations, more than twice the proportion of average American workers, but fewer than 5 percent of those from Laos and only about 10 percent of those from Cambodia held such a position. Further, immigrants from India, the Philippines, and Taiwan reported a median household income of about $45,000, compared to $30,000 for average American households; those from Cambodia and highland Laos reported a median household income below $20,000. Poverty rates for Asian immigrants ranged from a low of 7 percent for Filipinos, Indians, and Japanese to a high of more than 60 percent for Hmongs and 42 percent for Cambodians, compared to about 10 percent for average American families (Zhou 1999). Given the diversity of economic background, Asian Americans can be found throughout the income spectrum of the United States. In other words, today's Asian Americans join whites in the well-paid, educated, white-collar service sector of the workforce as well as Latino immigrants in lower-paying service and manufacturing jobs (Ong and Hee 1994). Responding to limited job opportunities for highly skilled immigrants, a large number of Asian immigrants have also turned to self-employment (Ong and Hee 1994).

Implications for Panethnicity in Contemporary Asian America

By most accounts, the expanding diversity of Asian Americans has brought into question the very definition of Asian America—and along with it, the feasibility and appropriateness of pan-Asian identities and practices. In a major public policy report on the state of Asian America, editor Paul Ong (2000) suggests that the pan-Asian identity is "fragile," citing as evidence the group's ethnic and economic diversity as well as the growing population of bi- and multiracial Asian Americans who want to acknowledge their combined racial heritage.[5] Similarly, in the introduction to their substantial multidisciplinary reader on contemporary Asian America, editors Min Zhou and James Gatewood (2000, 27) caution that "differences in class background among the immigrant generation and divergent modes of incorporation of that generation can deter the formation of panethnicity." Comparing the experiences of affluent Chinese immigrants and Cambodian refugees, Aihwa Ong (1996, 751) concludes that the category "Asian American" "must confront the contradictions and instabilities within the imposed solidarity, brought about by the group's internal class, ethnic, and racial stratifications." In Asian American studies, many scholars have critically pointed to the field's privileging of East Asians (the "old" Asian Americans) over South and Southeast Asians (the "new" Asian Americans)—a clear indictment of the suppression of diverse histories, epistemologies, and voices within the pan-Asian framework. For example, in an edited volume on South Asians in Asian America aptly titled *A Part, Yet Apart*, Rajiv Shankar (1998, x) laments that South Asians "find themselves so unnoticed as an entity that they feel as if they are merely a crypto-group, often included but easily marginalized within the house of Asian America.". . .

Pan-Asian National and Transnational Possibilities

As we begin the twenty-first century, the Asian American community is at a crossroads: how is it to build pan-Asian solidarity amid increasing internal diversities and amid an increasingly racially polarized U.S. society? As I have argued here, Asian American panethnicity is a socially constructed identity that emerged in large part from the violence of racism and imperialism to contest and disrupt these structures of inequality and domination. But

it is also a contested category, encompassing not only cultural differences but also social, political, and economic inequalities. In the past two decades underrepresented groups within the pan-Asian coalition have decried the dangers of an Asian American cultural and political agenda that erases differences or tokenizes and patronizes its less dominant members (Strobel 1996; Misir 1996; Nguyen 2002). But pan-Asian possibilities also abound. Since panethnic identities are self-conscious products of political choice and actions, I provide here examples of instances where Asian Americans have made conscious choices to organize politically across difference.

The growing population of bi- and multiracial Asian Americans poses an immediate challenge to pan-Asianism. On the other hand, some existing evidence suggests that the growth in the population of multiracial Asians need not spell the end of pan-Asianism. For example, in their analyses of Asian American intermarriages from 1980 and 1990 census data, Larry Hajime Shinagawa and Gin Yong Pang (1996, 140–41) report a prominent countertrend toward pan-Asian interethnic marriages, regardless of gender, nativity, region, and generation: "For a span of ten years (1980 to 1990), nationally and for California, the number of Asian interethnic marriages approaches or now exceeds interracial marriages. Meanwhile, interethnic marriages for Asian Pacific men increased from 21.1 percent in 1980 to 64 percent in 1990, and for women from 10.8 percent to 45.5 percent." They attribute this rise to a combination of factors, including the large population increases and concentrations of Asian Americans, their growing similarities in socioeconomic attainment and middle-class orientation, and their growing racial consciousness in an increasingly racially stratified U.S. society.

But what of the multiracial children? According to the 2000 U.S. census, approximately 850,000 people reported that they were Asian and white, and 360,000 reported that they were two or more Asian groups (Barnes and Bennett 2000, table 4). While there exist no comprehensive data on the racial identification of multiracial Asians, the close contact with Asian American advocacy groups maintained by the Hapa Issues Forum (HIF)—a national multiracial Asian American organization—suggests that multiracial Asian and pan-Asian identities need not be mutually exclusive. From its inception, HIF has pursued a double political mission: pushing for recognition of multiracial Asians as well as for the civil rights agendas of existing Asian American groups.

These two goals are most evident in the group's response to the controversy over the classification of multiracials in the 2000 census. Denouncing the government's past attempts to wedge mixed-race Americans into one rigid racial category, most mainstream multiracial groups favored adding a "multiracial" category to the 2000 census. However, most civil rights groups, including many pan-Asian groups, argued that such a category would dilute the numbers of people who identify with a particular race and cause their respective communities to lose hard-won gains in civil rights, education, and electoral arenas (Espiritu 2001, 31). Refusing this "splitting" of their multiple personal and political identities, HIF's board of directors rejected the "stand-alone multiracial" category and endorsed the "check more than one" format, contending that the latter option would allow them to identify as multiracial *and* "still be counted with their Asian American brethren and sisters" (King 2000, 202). In other words, the "check more than one" format would allow the data to be collected in a way that recognized the existence of multiracial Asians and still make it possible to use the data in "the five racial category format to track discrimination against Asian Americans" (King 2000, 202).

Asian American activists have also engaged in *proactive* efforts to draw together Asian Americans of different classes to organize against anti-Asian racism, defined not as random attacks against Asians but as a product of structural oppression and everyday encounters (Kurashige 2000, 15). The activities of the Asian Americans United, a panethnic community-based organization in Philadelphia, provide an example (Kurashige 2000). When large numbers of Southeast Asian immigrants began experiencing problems in Philadelphia with racist violence, educational inequality, and poor housing, a small group of educated East and South Asian American activists responded. Modeling themselves after the militant Yellow Seeds organization in the 1970s, group members insisted on anti-imperialist politics, a critique of racism as institutional and structural, and a focus on activist organizing and politics. They organized a successful rent strike and were part of a victorious legal campaign to institute bilingual education in the local schools. Most important, they sought to build relationships with working-class Southeast Asian communities by creating a youth leadership training program organized around a pan-Asian identity and radical politics. When a violent attack on Southeast Asian youths in that city by a group of white youths led to a fight

that left one of the white attackers dead, city police and prosecutors portrayed the attackers as victims and laid the responsibility for the violence at the hands of the Southeast Asians. Although unable to secure full justice in the court cases that ensued, Asian Americans United seized on the incident as a means of educating its constituency about institutionalized racism. The group succeeded in mobilizing parts of the Asian American community around these efforts, and its success enabled it to move from panethnic to interethnic affiliation through an alliance with a Puerto Rican youth group also plagued by hate crimes, police brutality, and prosecutorial racism (Espiritu et al. 2000, 132). This example suggests that class need not be a source of cleavage among Asian Americans, and that the concerns of working-class Asian Americans *can* unite people at the grassroots level with class-conscious members of the intellectual and professional strata (Kurashige 2000).

Given our globalizing world and the resultant demographic changes, the construction of an Asian American identity is no longer situated—if indeed it ever was—only within Asian America but also through relations and struggles with other communities of color. Today working-class immigrants of diverse backgrounds coexist with African American and U.S.-born Latinos in urban communities across the country. This "social geography of race" has produced new social subjects and new coalitions. For example, young Laotian women in northern California joined Chinese and Japanese Americans in panethnic struggles against anti-Asian racism and also against the "neighborhood race effects" of underfunded schools, polluted air and water, and low-wage jobs that they and their families share with their African American, Latino, Arab American, and poor white neighbors (Espiritu et al. 2000; Shah 2002). In the same way, recognizing their common histories of political fragmentation and disfranchisement, Japanese, Chinese, and Mexicans in the San Gabriel Valley of Los Angeles County formed political alliances to work together on the redistricting and reapportionment process in the Valley (Saito 1998, 10).

Finally, given the internationalization and feminization of the labor force in recent decades, some Asian women in the United States *and* in Asia have begun to conceive of themselves as similarly situated racial, gendered, and classed subjects. The dominance of women in contemporary immigration reflects the growth of female-intensive industries in the United States, particularly in services, health care, microelectronics, and apparel manufacturing. To escape the tightening labor market, employers in the United States have opted either to shift labor-intensive processes to less-developed countries or to import migrant labor, especially female, to fill low-wage, insecure assembly and service-sector jobs (Lim 1983; Hossfeld 1994). Women thus have become a rapidly growing segment of the world's migratory and international workforce (Sacks and Scheper-Hughes 1987).

For post-1965 immigrant women from Asia, their politically insecure status as "alien" and their limited English proficiency have interacted with geographical segregation, racist and sexist hiring practices, and institutional barriers to recertification by U.S. professional boards to narrow greatly their occupational choices. Consequently, many Asian immigrant women, instead of gaining access to a better, more modern, and more liberated life in the United States, have been confined to low-paying service jobs and factory assembly-line work, especially in the garment and microelectronics industries. The similarities in the labor conditions for Asian women here and in Asia, brought about by global capitalism, constitute the "situating grounds for a strategic transnational affiliation" (Kang 1997, 415). Moreover, examples abound of collaboration amongst capitalists *across* geopolitical boundaries. In the case of the garment industry, the small Asian immigrant garment factories in New York and Los Angeles are significant and fairly well integrated components in a globalized production process (Kang 1997). In other words, Asian women working in the garment and electronics factories in major cities in the United States are virtually part of the same labor force as those employed in export-processing zones in Asia or Latin America. Such simultaneous, transnational linkages in Asian women's working conditions—the similarities between exploitive labor conditions for Asian women in Asia and Asian American women in the United States—could disrupt the First World–Third World binary and call attention to their shared lives across geopolitical boundaries (Kang 1997, 429). Since this is the case, the focus on women's labor within the global economy provides *one* means for linking Third World women, immigrant women, and U.S. women of color. The racialized feminization of labor gives rise to a "common context of struggle" among Asian women within, outside, and across the borders of the United States and has resulted in the establishment of numerous cross-border and transnational women's organizations, such as

Gabriela, the support committee for Maquiladora workers, and Asian Immigrant Women Advocates (Lowe 1996).

These cross-racial and cross-border alliances and the radical mobilization around gender issues underscore the centrality of "unlikely coalitions" in contemporary political organizing. As Angela Davis (1997, 322) points out, we can accomplish important things in the struggle for social justice if we focus on the creation of "unpredictable or unlikely coalitions grounded in political projects." A complex world requires a complex set of alliances. These unlikely coalitions, including pan-Asian coalitions, along with the antiglobal organizations that are seeking to impose workplace and environmental restraints on multinational corporations and capital, could prove a potent force for social change at both the national and global levels.

Conclusion

Since the pan-Asian concept was forged in the late 1960s, the Asian American population has become much more variegated. The post-1965 immigration surge from Asia has fragmented Asian America more clearly than in the past along ethnic, generational, and class lines. This increasing diversity has brought into question the very feasibility and appropriateness of pan-Asian identities and practices, challenging Asian Americans to take seriously the social, political, and economic inequalities that exist within their communities. My main contention in this chapter is that we cannot examine Asian American panethnicity solely in terms of racial politics within the framework of the U.S. nation-state. While important, this framework narrowly focuses on identity politics within Asian America, not on the global politics and power that produced massive displacements and migrations of Asians in the first place. Calling for a critical transnational perspective on the study of panethnicity, I argue instead that different circumstances of exit—the product of different types of U.S. engagement in different Asian countries—have shaped the size and timing of migration and the socioeconomic profile of different Asian groups and thus have profoundly affected their group formation and differentiation in the United States. This approach expands the discussion on pan-Asian ethnicity by viewing it as an integral part not only of Asian American studies or American studies but also of international and transnational studies. In all, the examples cited in this chapter confirm the plural and ambivalent nature of panethnicity: it is a highly contested terrain on which Asian Americans merge and clash over terms of inclusion but also an effective site from which to forge crucial alliances with other groups both within and across the borders of the United States in their ongoing efforts to effect larger social transformation.

Seeing the Big Picture   **Panethnic Fortunes: Riches *and* Rags**

Look at Asians relative to other groups in Sections VI (Income, Wealth, and Poverty), VII (Employment), and VIII (Occupations) in the Appendix. Might panethnic identity formation as a political strategy explain the relative success of Asians? How?

---

11 Beyond Black and White: Remaking Race in America

Jennifer Lee • Frank D. Bean

JENNIFER LEE is an associate professor in the department of sociology at the University of California, Irvine, and received her B.A. and Ph.D. degrees from Columbia University. She is author of *Civility in the City: Blacks, Jews, and Koreans in Urban America* (2002) and co-editor (with Min Zhou) of *Asian American Youth: Culture, Identity, and Ethnicity* (2004).

FRANK D. BEAN is a professor of sociology at the University of California, Irvine, and the co-director of the Center for Research on Immigration, Population and Public Policy. He is former director of the Center for U.S./Mexico Border and Migration Research at the University of Texas, Austin. His current research examines four areas: the intersection of race/ethnicity in the United States, immigration and U.S. welfare patterns, migration within and from Mexico, and the effects of immigration on labor markets. He is the author of *America's Newcomers and the Dynamics of Diversity* (2003).

STARTING WITH THE 2000 CENSUS, AMERICANS could officially label themselves and their children as members of more than one race. Nearly 7 million Americans, 2.4 percent of the nation's population, were recorded as being multiracial. This option and these

Questions to Consider   Much has been made of recent U.S. Census reports that Latinos are now the largest racial minority in the United States. Equally important but not as widely addressed in the media has been the relative explosion of individuals who self-identify as "multiracial." Tiger Woods (Cablinasian: Caucasian-Black-Indian-Asian), Vin Diesel (white Italian-American and African American) and Halle Berry (white mother and African American father) each have made a point to publicly celebrate and affirm their hybrid ethnic and racial identities. What do Lee and Bean say these trends mean for the future of the color line as the children of mixed-race unions age out and have their own children? Will racial categories as we know them blur into one another or are we likely to see new categories emerge that serve to maintain racial hierarchy and inequality?

numbers signal a profound loosening of the rigid racial and ethnic boundaries that have so long divided the country. The immigration patterns behind these changes also point to potentially important realignments in America's color lines.

How might a black father and a white mother fill out official government documents, like U. S. Census forms, requiring them to designate the race of their child? Before 2000, such an intermarried couple had no alternative but to list their child as either black or white. Similarly, a child born to a white father and an Asian mother had to be listed as either Asian or white, but not Asian and white. Not any more. Americans can now officially identify themselves and their children as black and white, or white and Asian. Indeed, respondents can now choose a combination of up to six different categories of races, including "Other." The 2000 Census reported one in every forty Americans was registered as belonging to two or more racial groups. Many sociologists think this ratio could soar to one in five Americans by the year 2050.

Why does this checking of additional boxes matter? For one thing, how people report themselves racially provides information needed to implement and enforce important legislation, such as the **Voting Rights Act.** The Department of Justice uses the statistics to identify places where substantial minority populations exist and may be subject to disenfranchisement. For another, the counts document social and economic disparities among racial groups in America. Countries like France that do not collect data on race cannot verify the existence and effects of racial discrimination even when other evidence suggests such discrimination is a major problem. These data also signal the official recognition and hence the influence of groups that define themselves on the basis of common national origin, skin color or ancestry. Americans of Pacific Islander origin, for example, recently asked to be separately classified. On the other hand, critics worry that official data on race perpetuate rather than eliminate racial identities and divisions. A ballot initiative being circulated in California, for example, would largely ban the state's collection of racial information.

Voting Rights Act Civil rights legislation signed into law by President Lyndon Johnson in 1965, making obstacles to voting (poll taxes and literacy tests) illegal. These measures had been used in the South to disenfranchise blacks.

But the new opportunity to mark more than one race is also important because it indicates that people can now officially recognize the mixing of racial backgrounds in American society. If the United States was once thought of as a black-and-white society, this is certainly no longer so. Continued immigration from Latin America and Asia, the rise in intermarriage over the past 30 years, and the formal recognition of the multiracial population are moving America far beyond black and white. Yet while America's increasing diversity implies that racial divisions may be weakening, it does not mean that race has become irrelevant. Instead, new kinds of color lines may be emerging. For now, however, the rearrangement seems to leave African Americans facing a new black-nonblack, instead of the old black-white, racial divide.

Why There Are More Multiracial Americans

The growth of the multiracial population is a result both of increasing intermarriage between whites and nonwhites and of people's increasing willingness to report their multiracial backgrounds. The number of racial intermarriages in the United States grew from 150,000 in 1960 to 1.6 million in 1990—a tenfold increase over three decades. It is still the exception rather than the rule for whites and blacks in this country, however. Just 6 percent of whites and 10 percent of blacks marry someone of a different race. By contrast, more than one-quarter of all native-born Asians and Latinos marry someone of a different race. (For this discussion, we will speak of Latinos as if they were a "race," although government forms count Hispanic background separately, so that people who say they are Latino can report themselves as belonging to any racial group, such as white, black, or Asian.) Even more striking is that two of every five young Latinos and two of every three young Asians born in the United States marry someone of a different race, and the majority marry whites. Asians and Latinos—many of whom are either immigrants or the children of immigrants—are three times as likely to marry whites as blacks are to marry whites.

Coinciding with the rise in intermarriage has been the growth of a new immigrant stream from Latin America and Asia. Today, immigrants and their children total more than 60 million people, approximately 22 percent of the U.S. population. The increase in immigration from non-European countries over the past 35 years has converted the United States from a largely white and black society into one that is comprised of numerous racial and ethnic groups. This, plus increasing intermarriage, and the increasing willingness of Americans to call themselves multiracial has changed the way race is measured in America.

Constructing Race

Social scientists generally agree that race is not a biological category, but a social and cultural construction, meaning that racial distinctions have not existed since time immemorial, are not rooted in biology and are not fixed. Rather, they have changed and been reinterpreted throughout our nation's history. For instance, when the Irish, Italians, and Jews first arrived in the United States in the 19th century, Anglo Americans considered them racially distinct and inferior. They were not considered white. However, they successfully achieved "whiteness" by deliberately and forcefully distinguishing themselves from African Americans. Today, few would contest the claim that the Irish, Italians and Jews are white.

Race and racial boundaries have changed for other groups as well. For example, Asian ethnic groups like the Chinese in Mississippi have changed their racial status from almost black to almost white. Sociologist James Loewen details how the Chinese there achieved near-white status by becoming as economically successful as whites, copying their cultural and social practices, and distancing themselves from African Americans and Chinese Mississippians who married African Americans.

As historian Gary Gerstle explains, whiteness as a category "has survived by stretching its boundaries to include Americans—the Irish, eastern and southern Europeans—who had been deemed nonwhite. Contemporary evidence suggests that the boundaries are again being stretched as Latinos and Asians pursue whiteness much as the Irish, Italians, and Poles did before them." Given the change in racial boundaries over time, it is likely that the boundaries may continue to stretch to include newer groups. For instance, some sociologists argue that Asians are the next in line to become white. Whether or not they do, we should understand that race is a cultural product that has changed over time, rather than a fixed, primordial category rooted in biology.

The Origin of "Mark One or More Races"

Since its inception in 1790, the decennial U.S. Census has determined taxation, the numbers of representatives from each state, and the boundaries of Congressional districts. And it has always counted the U.S. population by race. The way that race is measured and even the racial categories themselves, however, have changed considerably. For example, in 1850, the Census added the category "mulatto," and in 1890, it added the categories "quadroon" and "octoroon" in an effort to more precisely measure the representation of black mixtures in the population. ("Mulatto" refers to people of mixed black and white "blood," "quadroon" to people with one-fourth black blood, and "octoroon" to those with one-eighth black blood.) However, "quadroon" and "octoroon" were promptly removed in 1900 because they caused countless statistical inaccuracies. The Census Board determined that the "mulatto" category provided clearer data on the U.S. population with mixed blood, but eventually dropped this category in 1930. By that time, the law of the country, with the census following suit, had adopted the "one-drop rule" of hypodescent (by which all persons with any trace of black ancestry were labeled racially black) as an appropriate criterion by which to attempt to measure race. Importantly, census enumerators classified the people they interviewed by race.

In the 1960s, racial categories came under scrutiny once again, and the Civil Rights Movement prompted one of the most significant changes in the political context and purpose of racial categorization. The argument spread that Americans should be able to mark their own race to identify themselves and their children rather than leaving this to enumerators. Some politicians and experts asserted that the racial categories should more accurately reflect America's diversity and lobbied for new categories, distinguishing among categories of whites, and substituting the term "ethnic" in place of "race." Changes in the 1970 Census reflected some of these currents, with self-identification replacing enumerator identification in order to satisfy public sentiments. By the mid-1970s, groups wanting to be recognized as racial minorities organized advisory committees to seek official statistical representation so that they could participate in federal programs designed to assist racial "minorities." These advisory committees lobbied for the adoption of five racial categories—white, black, Asian,

Native American, and other—by the Census and all federal agencies. In 1980, the Census categories changed yet again, this time including the category of Hispanic origin separately from race, and modifying one of the racial categories to Asian–Pacific Islander.

During the early 1990s, new advocacy groups arose with a different agenda. These groups criticized the government standards for not accurately reflecting the diversity in the country brought about by increases in immigration and interracial marriage. In particular, advocates from groups such as the Association for Multi-Ethnic Americans (AMEA) and Project RACE (Reclassify All Children Equally) lobbied the Census Bureau to adopt a "multiracial" category. Advocates argued that it was an affront to force them or their children into a single racial category. Furthermore, they argued that forced mono-racial identification was inaccurate because it denies the existence of interracial marriages, and is ultimately discriminatory. A year later in 1994, the Office of Management and Budget (OMB), which managed this issue, acknowledged that the racial categories were of decreasing value and considered an alternate strategy: allowing respondents to identify with as many races as they wished. While the spokespeople for the multiracial movement were not entirely satisfied with this option, they conceded that it was an improvement over forced mono-racial identification.

Not everyone favored adding a multiracial category or allowing Americans to mark more than one race. Civil rights groups—and in particular, black civil rights groups such as the NAACP—strongly objected. They feared that those who would otherwise be counted as black or Hispanic would now choose to identify as multiracial, and, depending on how such persons were counted, diminish their official counts. This, in turn, could undermine enforcement of the Voting Rights Act and potentially reduce the size and effectiveness of government programs aimed at helping minorities.

On October 30, 1997 the Census Bureau announced its final decision that all persons would have the option to identify with two or more races, starting with the 2000 Census and extending to all federal data systems by the year 2003. The racial options on the 2000 Census included "White," "Black," "Asian," "Native Hawaiian or Other Pacific Islander," "American Indian and Alaska Native," and "Other." While "Latino" or "Hispanic" was not a racial category on the 2000 Census, OMB mandated two distinct questions: one on race and a second asking whether a person is "Spanish/Hispanic/Latino." Because those who classify themselves as "Spanish/Hispanic/Latino" can be of any race, the Census asks both questions in order to identify the Latino population in the United States.

The Census Bureau's decision to allow Americans to "mark one or more races" is a landmark change in the way the U.S. government collects data on race. Perhaps even more importantly, it gives official status and recognition to individuals who see themselves or their children as having mixed racial heritage—an acknowledgement that speaks volumes about how far the country has come since the days when the "one-drop rule" enjoyed legal legitimacy. Moreover, such changes may mean that old racial divides are beginning to fade. Multiracial reporting, however, has not been equally distributed across all racial and ethnic groups. Rather, those who choose to mark two or more races are distinctive.

Who Are the Multiracials?

As we noted, in 2000, 6.8 million people, or 2.4 percent of the population, were reported as multiracial. While these figures may not appear large, a recent National Academy of Science study estimated that the multiracial population could rise to 21 percent by the year 2050 because of rising intermarriage, when as many as 35 percent of Asians and 45 percent of Hispanics could claim a multiracial background. Of the multiracial population in 2000, 93 percent reported two races, 6 percent reported three races, and 1 percent reported four or more races.

As Table 1 illustrates, the groups with high percentages of multiracial persons include "Native Hawaiian or Other Pacific Islander," "American Indian and Alaska Native," "Other," and "Asian." The categories with the lowest proportion of persons who claim a multiracial background are "White" and "Black."

The proportion of blacks who identify as multiracial is quite small, accounting for just 4.2 percent of the total black population. These figures stand in sharp contrast to those among American Indian/Alaska Natives and Native Hawaiian or other Pacific Islanders who have the highest percentage of multiracials as a proportion of their populations at 36.4 and 44.8 percent, respectively. The particular combinations are of interest. Among those identified as black, Asian, or Latino, 2 percent, 7 percent, and

TABLE 1   Multiracial Identification by Race: People Recorded as One Race Who Are Also Recorded as One or More Other Races

	Racial Identification (millions)	Multiracial Identification (millions)	Percent Multiracial
White	216.5	5.1	2.3%
Black	36.2	1.5	4.2
Asian	11.7	1.4	12.4
Other	18.4	3.0	16.4
American Indian and Alaska Native	3.9	1.4	36.4
Native Hawaiian or other Pacific Islander	0.7	0.3	44.8

Source: U.S. Census 2000.

5 percent, respectively, also claim a white identity. Among Asians, the Asian-white multiracial combination is about three and a half times more likely to occur, and among Latinos, the Latino-white combination is more than two and a half times more likely to occur, as the black-white combination occurs among blacks. Why this is so is particularly perplexing when we consider that the Census Bureau has estimated that at least three-quarters of black Americans have some white ancestry and thus could claim a multiracial identity on this basis alone.

The tendency of black Americans not to report multiracial identifications undoubtedly owes in part to the legacy of slavery, lasting discrimination, and both the legal and de facto invocation of the "one-drop rule." For no other racial or ethnic group in the United States does the one-drop rule limit identity choices and options. Recent sociological studies find that about 50 percent of American Indian–white and Asian-white intermarried couples report a white racial identity for their children. In a study of multiracial Hispanic students, we found that 44 percent chose a Hispanic identity. Without the imposition of the "one-drop rule" that historically imposed a black racial identity on multiracial black Americans, multiracial Asians, Latinos, and American Indians appear to have much more leeway to choose among different racial options.

In addition, because a significant proportion of Latinos and Asians in the United States are either immigrants

or the children of immigrants, their understanding of race, racial boundaries, and the black-white color divide is shaped by a different set of circumstances than those of African Americans. Most importantly, Latinos' and Asians' experiences are not rooted in the same legacy of slavery with its systematic and persistent patterns of legal and institutional discrimination and inequality through which the tenacious black-white divide was formed and cemented. For these reasons, racial and ethnic boundaries appear more fluid for the newest immigrants than for native-born blacks, providing multiracial Asians and Latinos more racial options than their black counterparts.

Remaking Race and Redrawing the Color Line

What do current trends and patterns in immigration, intermarriage, and multiracial identification tell us about the remaking of race in America? It appears that increases in intermarriage and the growth of the multiracial population reflect a blending of races and the shifting of color lines. Because interracial marriage and multiracial identification indicate a reduction in social distance and racial prejudice, these phenomena provide evidence of loosening racial boundaries. At first glance, these patterns offer an optimistic portrait of the weakening of color lines. For instance, interracial marriage was illegal in 16 states as recently as 1967, but today, about 13 percent of American marriages involve persons of different races. If we go back even further to 1880, the rates of intermarriage among Asians and Latinos in this country were close to zero, but now, more than a quarter of all native-born Asians and Latinos marry someone of a different racial background, mostly whites.

Yet, upon closer examination, we find that patterns of intermarriage and multiracial identification are not similar across all groups. Not only are Latinos and Asians more likely to intermarry than blacks, they are also more likely to report a multiracial identification. These different rates suggest that while racial boundaries may be fading, they are not disappearing at the same pace for all groups.

What is crucial here is how we interpret the intermarriage and multiracial identification rates for Latinos and Asians. If we consider Latinos and Asians as discriminated-against racial minorities, closer to blacks than whites in their social disadvantages, then their high levels of multiracial identification suggest that racial border lines might be fading for all nonwhite groups. Latinos and Asians look more, however, like immigrant groups whose disadvantages derive from their not having had time to join the economic mainstream, but who soon will. Their high levels of intermarriage and multiracial reporting therefore signal an experience and trajectory different from that of blacks. Their situations do not necessarily indicate that similar assimilation can be expected among blacks.

Based on the patterns of intermarriage and multiracial identification noted above, the color line appears less rigid for Latinos and Asians than blacks. Asians and Latinos have high rates of intermarriage and multiracial reporting because they were not and are not treated as blacks have been. While the color line may also be shifting for blacks, this shift is occurring more slowly, leaving Asians and Latinos socially nearer to whites. Much of America's racial history has revolved around who was white and who was not; the next phase may revolve instead around who is black and who is not.

The emergence of a black-nonblack divide in a context where diversity is increasing and other racial and ethnic boundaries are diminishing represents a good news–bad news outcome for America. That a white-nonwhite color line does not seem to be enduring is the good news. But that newer nonwhite immigrant groups appear to be jumping ahead of African Americans in a hierarchy still divided by race is the bad news. Based on immigration, intermarriage, and multiracial identification, it appears that Latinos and Asians are closer to whites than to blacks, and consequently may be participants in a new color line that continues to disadvantage blacks.

As a final matter, one might ask: What does all of this imply for the future of measuring race in the census? Critics of racial labels argue that if racial and ethnic boundaries are loosening, we should abandon the use of racial categories in the census altogether and learn to get along without them in our policy making. They argue that if racial labels could be eliminated, racial discrimination itself would be eradicated. However, in the United States today, because the practice of discrimination based on physical characteristics such as skin color continues to persist, at least for African Americans, eradicating racial labels would simply put us in a position where we know less about the disadvantages experienced by blacks and can do less about it.

Seeing the Big Picture **Check All That Apply (Finally!): The Institutionalization of Mixed Race Identity**

Section X in the Appendix lists the percentage of Americans who identify with more than one race. How might you interpret the fact that Latino and American Indians are more likely than whites or blacks to claim more than one race?

12 Color-Blind Privilege: The Social and Political Functions of Erasing the Color Line in Post-Race America

Charles A. Gallagher

CHARLES A. GALLAGHER is professor and chair of the Department of Sociology, Social Work and Criminal Justice at La Salle University in Philadelphia. His research focuses on racial and social inequality, immigration, urban sociology, and the ways in which the media, the state, and popular culture construct, shape, and disseminate ideas of race. He has published articles on the sociological functions of color-blind political narratives, how racial categories expand and contract within the context of interracial marriages, race theory, racial innumeracy, and how one's ethnic history shapes perceptions of privilege. Professor Gallagher can be reached at gallagher@lasalle.edu.

Questions to Consider The dominant view in the United States is that we are now a color-blind nation. Rap and hip-hop are thoroughly mainstream commodities available for sale in every mall across the country. Celebrities, CEOs, high-level politicians, and opinion makers are drawn from every racial and ethnic group. Race, the mainstream media would have us believe, no longer matters. Charles A. Gallagher argues that the story of color blindness promoted in the mass media disguises a more troubling reality: continued racial inequality. How does presenting the United States as a color-blind nation serve various political, ideological, and social functions?

Introduction

An adolescent white male at a bar mitzvah wears a FUBU[1] shirt while his white friend preens his tightly set, perfectly braided corn rows. A black model dressed in yachting attire peddles a New England yuppie boating look in Nautica advertisements. It is quite unremarkable to observe whites, Asians, or African Americans with dyed purple, blond, or red hair. White, black, and Asian students decorate their bodies with tattoos of Chinese characters and symbols. In cities and suburbs, young adults across the color line wear hip-hop clothing and listen to white rapper Eminem and black rapper Jay-Z. A north Georgia branch of the NAACP installs a white biology professor as its president. The music of Jimi Hendrix is used to sell Apple Computers. Du-Rag kits, complete with bandana headscarf and elastic headband, are on sale for $2.95 at hip-hop clothing stores and family-centered theme parks like Six Flags. Salsa has replaced ketchup as the best-selling condiment in the United States.

Companies as diverse as Polo, McDonald's, Tommy Hilfiger, Walt Disney World, MasterCard, Skechers sneakers, IBM, Giorgio Armani, and Neosporin antibiotic ointment have each crafted advertisements that show a balanced, multiracial cast of characters interacting and consuming their products in a post-race, color-blind world.[2]

Americans are constantly bombarded by depictions of race relations in the media which suggest that discriminatory racial barriers have been dismantled. Social and cultural indicators suggest that America is on the verge, or has already become, a truly color-blind nation. National polling data indicate that a majority of whites now believe discrimination against racial minorities no longer exists. A majority of whites believe that blacks have as good a chance as whites in procuring housing and employment or achieving middle-class status while a 1995 survey of white adults found that a majority of whites (58%) believed that African Americans were better off finding jobs than whites.[3] Much of white America now sees a level playing field, while a majority of black Americans see a field which is still quite uneven. Best-selling books like *The End of Racism*[4] and *Color-Blind: Seeing Beyond Race in a Race-Obsessed World* suggest the United States is not very far from making **color blindness** a social and political reality.[5] The color-blind or race neutral perspective holds that in an environment where institutional racism and discrimination have been replaced by equal opportunity, one's qualifications, not one's color or ethnicity, should be the mechanism by which upward mobility is achieved. Whites and blacks differ significantly, however, on their support for affirmative action, the perceived fairness of the criminal justice system, the ability to acquire the "American Dream," and the extent to which whites have benefited from past discrimination.[6]

This article examines the social and political functions color blindness serves for whites in the United States. Drawing on information compiled from interviews and focus groups with whites around the country, I argue that color blindness maintains white privilege by negating racial inequality. Embracing a post-race, color-blind perspective provides whites with a degree of psychological comfort by allowing them to imagine that being white or black or brown has no bearing on an individual's or a group's relative place in the socioeconomic hierarchy. My research included interviews with seventeen focus groups and thirty individual whites around the country. While my sample is not representative of the total white population, I used personal contacts and snowball sampling to purposively locate respondents raised in urban, suburban, and rural environments. Twelve of the seventeen focus groups were conducted in a university setting, one in a liberal arts college in the Rocky Mountains and the others at a large urban university in the Northeast. Respondents in

these focus groups were selected randomly from the student population. The occupational range for my individual interviews was quite eclectic and included a butcher, construction worker, hair stylist, partner in a prestigious corporate law firm, executive secretary, high school principal, bank president from a small town, retail workers, country lawyer, and custodial workers. Twelve of the thirty individual interviews were with respondents who were raised in rural and/or agrarian settings. The remaining respondents lived in suburbs of large cities or in urban areas.

What linked this rather disparate group of white individuals together was their belief that race-based privilege had ended. As a majority of my respondents saw it, color blindness was now the norm in the United States. The illusion of racial equality implicit in the myth of color blindness was, for many whites, a form of comfort. This aspect of pleasure took the form of political empowerment ("what about whites' rights") and moral gratification from being liberated from "oppressor" charges ("we are not responsible for the past"). The rosy picture that color blindness presumes about race relations and the satisfying sense that one is part of a period in American history that is morally superior to the racist days of the past is, quite simply, a less stressful and more pleasurable social place for whites to inhabit.

The Norm of Color Blindness

The perception among a majority of white Americans that the socioeconomic playing field is now level, along with whites' belief that they have purged themselves of overt racist attitudes and behaviors, has made color blindness the dominant lens through which whites understand contemporary race relations. Color blindness allows whites to believe that segregation and discrimination are no longer an issue because it is now illegal for individuals to be denied access to housing, public accommodations, or jobs because of their race. Indeed, lawsuits alleging institutional racism against companies like Texaco, Denny's, Coca-Cola, and Cracker Barrel validate what many whites know at a visceral level is true; firms which deviate from the color-blind norms embedded in **classic liberalism** will be punished. As a political ideology, the commodification and mass marketing of products that signify color

---

color blindness This term can be understood in two ways: the idea that we *should* live in a society where people are treated equally regardless of their skin color, or the belief that we *are now* a color-blind society where race no longer shapes life chances.

classic liberalism A school of thought stressing individual freedom and limited government.

but are intended for consumption across the color line further legitimate color blindness. Almost every household in the United States has a television that, according to the U.S. Census, is on for seven hours every day.[7] Individuals from any racial background can wear hip-hop clothing, listen to rap music (both purchased at Wal-Mart) and root for their favorite, majority black, professional sports team. Within the context of racial symbols that are bought and sold in the market, color blindness means that one's race has no bearing on who can purchase an SUV, live in an exclusive neighborhood, attend private schools, or own a Rolex.

The passive interaction whites have with people of color through the media creates the impression that little, if any, socioeconomic difference exists between the races. Research has found that whites who are exposed to images of upper-middle-class African Americans, like the Huxtable family in *The Cosby Show,* believe that blacks have the same socioeconomic opportunities as whites.[8] Highly visible and successful racial minorities like Secretary of State Colin Powell and National Security Advisor Condoleezza Rice are further proof to white America that the nation's efforts to enforce and promote racial equality have been accomplished. Reflecting on the extent to which discrimination is an obstacle to socioeconomic advancement and the perception of seeing African Americans in leadership roles, Tom explained:

> If you look at some prominent black people in society today, and I don't really see [racial discrimination], I don't understand how they can keep bringing this problem onto themselves. If they did what society would want them to, I don't see that society is making problems for them. I don't see it.

The achievement ideology implicit in the color-blind perspective is also given legitimacy and stripped of any racist implications by black neoconservatives like anti–affirmative action advocate Ward Connerly, Shelby Steele, and Clarence Thomas, and Asian American Secretary of Labor Elaine Chou.[9] Each espouses a color-blind, race neutral doctrine that treats race-based government programs as a violation of the sacrosanct belief that American society only recognizes the rights of individuals. These individuals also serve as an important public example that in a post-race, color-blind society climbing the occupational ladder is now a matter of individual choice.

The new color-blind ideology does not, however, ignore race; it acknowledges race while ignoring racial hierarchy by taking racially coded styles and products and

reducing these symbols to commodities or experiences which whites and racial minorities can purchase and share. It is through such acts of shared consumption that race becomes nothing more than an innocuous cultural signifier. Large corporations have made American culture more homogenous through the ubiquity of fast food, television, and shopping malls but this trend has also created the illusion that we are all the same through consumption. Most adults eat at national fast-food chains like McDonald's, shop at mall anchor stores like Sears and J. C. Penney's, and watch major league sports, situation comedies, or television dramas. Defining race only as cultural symbols that are for sale allows whites to experience and view race as nothing more than a benign cultural marker that has been stripped of all forms of institutional, discriminatory or coercive power. The post-race, color-blind perspective allows whites to imagine that depictions of racial minorities working in high status jobs and consuming the same products, or at least appearing in commercials for products whites desire or consume, is the same as living in a society where color is no longer used to allocate resources or shape group outcomes. By constructing a picture of society where racial harmony is the norm, the color-blind perspective functions to make white privilege invisible while removing from public discussion the need to maintain any social programs that are race-based.

How then is color blindness linked to privilege? Starting with the deeply held belief that America is now a meritocracy, whites are able to imagine that the socioeconomic success they enjoy relative to racial minorities is a function of individual hard work, determination, thrift, and investments in education. The color-blind perspective removes from personal thought and public discussion any taint or suggestion of white supremacy or white guilt while legitimating the existing social, political, and economic arrangements that whites are privileged to receive. This perspective insinuates that class and culture, and not institutional racism, are responsible for social inequality. Color blindness allows whites to define themselves as politically progressive and racially tolerant as they proclaim their adherence to a belief system that does not see or judge individuals by the "color of their skin." This perspective ignores, as Ruth Frankenberg puts it, how whiteness is a "location of structural advantage societies structured in racial dominance."[10] Frankenberg uses the term "color and power evasiveness" rather than color blindness to convey how the ability to ignore race by members of the dominant group reflects a position of power and privilege. Color blindness hides white privilege behind a mask of assumed meritocracy while rendering invisible the institutional arrangements that perpetuate racial inequality. The veneer of equality implied in color blindness allows whites to present their place in the racialized social structure as one that was earned.

Given the pervasiveness of color blindness, it was not surprising that respondents in this study believed that using race to promote group interests was a form of racism.

Joe, a student in his early twenties from a working-class background, was quite adamant that the opportunity structure in the United States did not favor one racial group over another.

> I mean, I think that the black person of our age has as much opportunity as me, maybe he didn't have the same guidance and that might hurt him. But I mean, he's got the same opportunities that I do to go to school, maybe even more, to get more money. I can't get any aid. . . . I think that blacks have the same opportunities as whites nowadays and I think it's old hat.

Not only does Joe believe that young blacks and whites have similar educational experiences and opportunity but it is his contention that blacks are more likely or able to receive money for higher education. The idea that race matters in any way, according to Joe, is anachronistic; it is "old hat" in a color-blind society to blame one's shortcomings on something as irrelevant as race.

Believing and acting as if America is now color-blind allows whites to imagine a society where institutional racism no longer exists and racial barriers to upward mobility have been removed. The use of group identity to challenge the existing racial order by making demands for the amelioration of racial inequities is viewed as racist because such claims violate the belief that we are a nation that recognizes the rights of individuals, not rights demanded by groups. Sam, an upper-middle-class respondent in his twenties, draws on a pre– and post–civil rights framework to explain racial opportunity among his peers:

> I guess I can understand my parents' generation. My parents are older, my dad is almost sixty and my mother is in her mid-fifties, ok? But the kids I'm going to school with, the minorities I'm going to school with, I don't think they should use racism as an excuse for not getting a job. Maybe their parents, sure, I mean they were discriminated against. But these kids have *every* opportunity that I do to do well.

In one generation, as Sam sees it, the color line has been erased. Like Sam's view that there are opportunities for all, there is, according to Tara, a reason to celebrate the current state of race relations.

> I mean, like you are not the only people that have been persecuted—I mean, yeah, you have been, but so has every group. I mean, if there's any time to be black in America, it's now.

Seeing society as race neutral serves to decouple past historical practices and social conditions from present-day racial inequality. A number of respondents viewed society this way and pointed out that job discrimination had ended. Michelle was quite direct in her perception that the labor market is now free of discrimination, stating that "I don't think people hire and fire because someone is black and white now." Ken also believed that discrimination in hiring did not occur since racial minorities now have legal recourse if discrimination occurs.

> I think that pretty much we got past that point as far as jobs. I think people realize that you really can't discriminate that way because you will end up losing . . . because you will have a lawsuit against you.

Critical race theorist David Theo Goldberg sees this narrative as part of the "continued insistence on implementing an ideal of color blindness [that] either denies historical reality and its abiding contemporary legacies, or serves to cut off any claims to contemporary entitlements."[11] It also means that whites can picture themselves as victims of reverse discrimination and racism, as Anne, a woman in a focus group, explained:

> Why is it so important to forget about, you know, white people's rights? I mean, not that, not being racist or anything, but why is it such a big deal that they have to have it their way or no way when it should be a compromise between the two, and the whites should be able to voice their opinions as much as the blacks do.

There is the belief that whites have been silenced by race politics and as Jodie explains, "The tables have turned where they're getting more rights than we have. Like it never balanced out."

The logic inherent in the color-blind approach is circular; since race no longer shapes life opportunities in a color-blind world, there is no need to take race into account when discussing differences in outcomes between racial groups. This approach erases America's racial hierarchy by implying that social, economic, and political power and mobility are equally shared among all racial groups. Ignoring the extent or ways in which race shapes life opportunities validates whites' social location in the existing racial hierarchy while legitimating the political and economic arrangements that perpetuate and reproduce racial inequality and privilege.

Color Is Now a Matter of Choice

Leslie Carr suggests "the roots of color-blind ideology are found in classic liberal doctrines of freedom—the freedom of the individual created by the free capitalist marketplace."[12] Within the context of a free-market model, color blindness has come to mean that ignoring or attending to one's racial identity is a matter of individual choice, much like the ways in which whites can choose whether or not to emphasize part of their ethnic background. Many whites, for example, claim to be Irish on St. Patty's Day. Some Italian Americans feel purchasing a meal at the Olive Garden Restaurant is an ethnic dining experience that reconnects them to their immigrant past or fictive ethnic family tree. Some whites don kilts at Highlander Fairs or dress as medieval artisans or knights at Renaissance Festivals. These individuals experience their ethnicity as an option. There is no social cost to "being ethnic" for a day, nor does this voluntary behavior circumscribe opportunities in life. The color-blind narrative holds that affirming racial identity is, like whites who have the luxury of an **optional ethnicity,** an individual, voluntary decision.[13] If pride in one's ethnicity and by extension one's color is a matter of choice, then race no longer matters as an independent force which organizes social life, allocates resources, or creates obstacles to upward mobility.[14] In **post-race,** color-blind America, one can now consume images and products for, from, and about any racial or ethnic group. Racial styles, like clothing fashion, food choices, or musical preferences, are like interchangeable, mix-and-match commodities for sale at the mall.

The color-blind narrative allows racial identity to be acknowledged in individual and superficial ways but using

optional ethnicity A form of ethnicity that one can pick and choose. There is little or no social cost to engaging in optional ethnicity, as in someone is being "Irish" on St. Patrick's Day even though this person does not think about being Irish during the rest of the year.

post-race The notion that race is no longer relevant in politics, culture, or economics. The post-race perspective posits that racism no longer shapes individuals' life chances.

race to assert group demands violates the cherished notion that as a nation we recognize the rights of individuals rather than group rights. Within the color-blind perspective, it is understood that one does not choose one's race, but one should be conscious, or at least cautious, not to make race more than background cultural information. In a post-race, color-blind world, race can be seen, but pointing out race-based inequities should not be heard. The idea of identity, race, and the fluidity of individual choices was part of Jeff's explanation of race relations:

> It just seems like a gap's been bridged, where people don't have like separate things. You know, like in past generations there were things that each group had to itself, but now it's like there are plenty of things you can find in, like, black people that white people do. You know, there's music; rap music is no longer, . . . it's not a black thing anymore. . . . When it first came out, it was black music, but now it's just music. It's another choice, just like country music can be considered like white hick music or whatever. You know, it's just a choice.

Tom makes the point that race categories exist, but assimilation allows any individual to become an American, if they so choose:

> Blacks don't seem, poor blacks seem like they're more immigrant than we are.
> Interviewer: In what way?
> Because they try to keep pushing the differences. You know, like I said, the Asians just meld in a little bit better than the blacks. . . . Why do they have to be caught up in being African American? They've been in America all their lives. They were born here. They're not African Americans. That's just separate.

There was the perception that Asians did not embrace identity politics or use their racial identity to promote group rights. As Mike, a young white man in a focus group told me:

> It's just becoming like really, really popular for black students to be black and proud and racist. But with Asians, it's not that way. I mean there is a magazine *Ebony* for strictly black people—I've never really read it. I mean there is no magazine for just Asian people. There's nothing saying, like, "Asian power."

Comedian Chris Rock points to how erasing the color line and color blindness are linked when he asked rhetorically "What does it say about America when the greatest golfer in the world [Tiger Woods] is black and the greatest rapper [Eminem] is white." Rock's message is clear: No role or occupation (at least in sports and music) is now determined by skin color. By allowing anyone to claim ownership of racial styles, color-blind narratives negate the ways in which race continues to circumscribe opportunities in life. The color-blind approach requires that these preferences, while racially bracketed, be available to all for purchase or consumption. At its core, the color-blind philosophy holds that racial minorities can succeed if they rid themselves of any notion that their race entitles them to special treatment. Racial identity can still be expressed or acknowledged, but one's race should mean nothing more than a tendency towards individualistic expressions, like music, foods, or clothes.

Within the color-blind perspective, it is not race per se which determines upward mobility, but how much an individual *chooses* to pay attention to race that determines one's fate. According to this perspective, race is only as important as you allow it to be, as Kevin, a 33-year-old white male custodial worker in Colorado told me:

> I never really look at anyone as a color, you know. Your skin's a color, but that doesn't mean, . . . I don't know, I never look at someone being black or Chinese. Yeah, you're Chinese because of the way your eyes are slanted, but you talk just like me. You're just like me. I don't look at you any different than you being me. You know, that's how I've always looked at it. You know.

Implicit in this expression of color blindness is that color does not matter as long as blacks and Chinese assimilate to the point where they are "just like" Kevin. As a member of the dominant group, Kevin has the privilege of defining color blindness as the expectation that racial minorities will mirror his own cultural and social experiences while denying how racism shapes the experiences of racial minorities.[15]

When racial identity shifts from being an individual expression to one that is used to organize politically or make group-based grievances, whites view it as racist. Mary believes that race is used to force whites to think about color and inequality:

> I think that they are making it worse for themselves. I think that anybody can see in this country—I think it's you [blacks]. It doesn't matter what color you are. I mean, sure there are black things but why put it on a T-shirt? Why not just have a plain black T-shirt? Why would you have to make such a big statement that pushes people away, that threatens people. I would never want to threaten anybody.

As Mary's comments make clear, embracing racial symbols that serve to socially isolate and challenge the racial status quo is a "threat." Implicit in this exchange is that it is not very pleasurable for Mary to interact with those who would use race to promote a political agenda.

The respondents below were bothered by what they saw as a double standard concerning beauty pageants; blacks could have their own pageant but whites could not. Their anger is based, at least in part, on an understanding that the norm of color blindness has been violated. Jodie lamented that:

> You know, it's amazing. Like, even, like even, like the Miss America pageants. There's a black Miss America pageant. But there's also black contestants in the Miss America pageant and then there's a separate pageant for blacks only. And if we had a separate pageant for whites only I just think that things would be . . . more hell would be raised.

Michelle was also bothered by her perception that the idea of race was taken too seriously by blacks:

> You know, it just seems, even for silly things, even the fact that you have to have black women in the Miss America pageant but then they have their own Miss Black America pageant. You know, like that type of thing, and it's like, come on. . . .

John, a 22-year-old male from New Jersey, also felt that whites were held to a different set of social expectations than blacks:

> I watch Miss America and we've had what, a black Miss America three out of the last five years, yet they do have a black Miss America [contest]. They don't have white contestants, they only have black contestants. Now, I'm not saying that a black person can't enter the white contest, but it's just kind of ironic that here a black woman enters a predominately white contest and, you know, usually a Miss America's supposed to be representative of the whole population, yet only 12% of the population is black. . . . It just kind of seems strange that if a white person tried to enter a black contest, forget it, you'd have mayhem.

Viewed within the color-blind perspective, the Miss Black America pageant is a form of institutional racism because it denies all racial groups full access to participation. The Miss Black America pageant is, as suggested above, racist for excluding whites because of the color of their skin. The long history of racial minorities being excluded from white organizations and institutions as the reason behind why black, Latino, and Asian organizations were formed in the first place is now only viewed as irrelevant.

Like the anger expressed over what was perceived as a racial double standard concerning the Miss America pageant, Malcolm X also came to represent challenges to the color-blind perspective, which were viewed as illegitimate because they advocate group solutions to race-based inequities. As one respondent told me about Malcolm X:

> He got into Buddha [sic] and changed his violence. When he was younger, I think that's when he was violent but in the years before he was killed I think he definitely went towards peace, like Martin Luther King. I don't know why they can't wear Martin Luther King hats [instead of Malcolm X hats].

Color blindness has emerged as America's newest racial mythology because it provides a level-playing-field narrative that allows whites to inhabit a psychological space that is free of racial tension. This new era of color blindness is a respite from the racial identity movements which often result in white guilt, defensiveness, or the avoidance of racially charged issues. Color blindness provides whites with the belief that they live in an era that is free of racism. Convinced that these racist attitudes and practices are over, whites today are able to define themselves as racially progressive and tolerant. Within this universe where racial differences are almost meaningless, whites are able to claim that their privileged social position relative to racial minorities reflects individual achievement rather than the fruits of white supremacy. The constant barrage of color-blind messages and messengers reinforces and confirms that the egalitarian and meritocractic norms that undergird American culture are intact. Embracing color blindness allows whites to be blind to or ignore the fact that racial and ethnic minorities lag behind whites on almost every measure of quality of life. Color-blind pleasure means whites are able to think about contemporary race relations as a clean slate where the crimes of slavery, Jim Crow, institutional racism, and white privilege have been ended and the racist sins of their grandparents have been erased.

Our Survey Says— "Color-Blind Nation"

National survey data suggest that a majority of whites view race relations through the lens of color blindness. A 1997 Gallup poll found that a majority of whites believe that blacks have "as good a chance as whites" in their community in procuring employment (79%).[16] A Kaiser Family Poll (1997) found that a majority of whites believe that blacks are doing at least as well or better than whites in income and educational attainment. The poll found that "almost two-thirds (64%) of whites do NOT believe that whites have benefited from past and present discrimination against African Americans."[17] In their study on racial attitudes, Schuman and associates found that when white Americans are asked to account for black disadvantage, the most popular explanation is that of black people's lack of motivation or willpower to get ahead.[18] These surveys suggest a majority of whites view the opportunity structure as being open to all, regardless of color. Not only do whites see parity compared to blacks in access to housing, employment, education, and achieving a middle-class life style, but where differences do exist, whites attribute racial inequities to the individual shortcomings of blacks.

Reflecting on affirmative action, Monica articulates an all-is-now-equal argument as to why color should no longer matter in hiring decisions or school admissions:

> I think all the backgrounds have come a long way to where they don't need it any more. Basically everyone has equal opportunity to get a certain job, to get into a certain school, and now it should be based on your performance and not for what you are.

Drawing on an ideology of egalitarianism and meritocracy, Monica believes, as most white Americans do, that color is no longer a factor in obtaining employment or a quality education. Given the premise that racial equality has now been achieved, Monica is able to argue that achievement and not skin color should shape the allocation of resources. In other words, since the playing field is now level, any group claims to address real or imagined inequities are illegitimate. Joan voiced the anger that whites should in some way be held accountable for past or present racial inequities.

> That's what bothers me. They say "we" have been oppressed. They have not. The students here at the university right now have not been oppressed. They did not experience the Watts riot, they didn't experience physically being hosed down by police. Granted, the white population was responsible for that, but we are not. We are not responsible. Therefore, we should not be put out because of that. We didn't do it. We're not doing it now, therefore they have no right to say, well, we've been oppressed.

Neither Joan, nor the white race, should be "put out" for past racist practices. The color-blind perspective is a historical rendering of the actions of the near and distant past as events which are disconnected from contemporary racial inequality.

James expresses a number of the trends found in the surveys cited earlier. After stating that "hey, everybody's got the same opportunity" when asked about what his views were on the idea of white privilege, James countered that:

> They say that I have white privileges. Uh, and if they say it's like because where I live, I live in a big house or something like that, they're wrong, because that's not a privilege. That's something my parents worked for. And if they don't live in a big fancy houses that's something that their parents didn't work for. And if they want to change that . . . I've got black people living across from me. Uh, they're no different than me. They're different from the black people down here because they worked for what they wanted. These people [blacks in a poor segregated part of the city], they don't have to live here. There's no one holding them back. They can get into school as well as everybody else can. I was lucky my parents could pay for school and I didn't need financial aid. . . . You know, the opportunity is there. You've just got to take hold of it.

James suggests that when class background is taken into account whites and blacks are the same. The blacks who are unable to leave poor, segregated neighborhoods reflect individual shortcomings on the part of blacks, not structural obstacles. Rob implies that it is hard work and individual merit, not one's skin color that matters. Examining his own mobility, Rob remarks, "I don't know if their situation is any different than mine. I mean, I can only gauge on the fact that I've been busting my ass for the last ten years to get to where I want to be."

How Color-Blind a Nation?

The beliefs voiced by whites in national survey data and my own interviews raise an empirical question: to what extent are we now a color-blind nation? If educational opportunity, occupational advancement, health, upward mobility, and equal treatment in the public sphere can be used as indicators of how color-blind we are as a nation, then we have failed. U.S. census figures present a picture of America that is far from color-blind. In 1999, over 73% of white households owned their own homes compared to 46% for blacks, 45% for Hispanics, 53% for Asians, and 56% for American Indians.[19] In 1993, whites had about ten times more in assets than blacks or Latinos.[20] Median family income in 1998 was $42,439 for whites, $25,351

for blacks, $27,330 for Latinos, and $46,637 for Asians. In 1997, almost 25% of whites over the age of 25 had four years of college or more compared to less than 14% for blacks and Latinos. In 1997, 8.6% of whites compared to 26.5% blacks, 27% of Latinos, and 14% of Asians lived at or below the poverty line.[21] A national study found that even after controlling for individual credit history, blacks in 33 states were charged more for car loans than whites.[22] Health statistics tell a similar tale. Whites have lower rates of diabetes, tuberculosis, pregnancy-related mortality, and sudden infant death syndrome (SIDS), and are more likely to have prenatal care in the first trimester than blacks, Latinos, or Asians. In 1997, 15% of whites did not have public or private health care coverage compared to 21.5% for blacks, 34% for Latinos, and 20.7% for Asians.[23]

In 1998, blacks and Latinos were also underrepresented as lawyers, physicians, professors, dentists, engineers, and registered nurses. A Glass Ceiling study commissioned by the federal government found that when one reaches the level of vice president and above at *Fortune* 1000 industrial companies and *Fortune* 500 service industries, 96.6% of the executives are white males. Nationally, white men comprise 90% of the newspaper editors and 77% of television news directors.[24] In 1999, the Department of Justice found that blacks and Latinos were twice as likely as whites to be subject to force when they encounter a police officer, were more likely to be subjected to car searches during a traffic stop, and were more likely to be ticketed than whites. Although blacks and whites are just as likely to use drugs, almost two-thirds of those convicted on drug charges are black.[25] Congress does not represent the racial and ethnic diversity of this country. In 2000, blacks were 13% of the population, Asians and Pacific Islanders 4%, and Latinos 12%. Yet the House of Representatives was only 9% black, 4% Latino, and 0.9% Asian. The U.S. Senate was 97% white and only 2% Asian and 1% American Indian, and therefore had no black or Latino members.[26] In early 2003, there were no black or Latino governors. According to another report, if you were black and living in Florida, you were four times as likely as whites to have your ballot invalidated in the 2000 presidential election.[27] We are not now, nor have we ever been, a color-blind nation.

The Cost of Racialized Pleasures

Being able to ignore or being oblivious to the ways in which almost all whites are privileged in a society cleaved on race has a number of implications. Whites derive pleasure in being told that the current system for allocating resources is fair and equitable. Creating and internalizing a color-blind view of race relations reflects how the dominant group is able to use the mass media, immigration stories of upward mobility, rags-to-riches narratives, and achievement ideology to make white privilege invisible. Frankenberg argues that whiteness can be "displaced," as is the case with whiteness hiding behind the veil of color blindness. It can also be made "normative" rather than specifically "racial," as is the case when being white is defined by white respondents as being no different than being black or Asian.[28] Lawrence Bobo and associates have advanced a theory of laissez-faire racism that draws on the color-blind perspective. As whites embrace the equality of opportunity narrative they suggest that

> laissez-faire racism encompasses an ideology that blames blacks themselves for their poorer relative economic standing, seeing it as a function of perceived cultural inferiority. The analysis of the bases of laissez-faire racism underscores two central components: contemporary stereotypes of blacks held by whites, and the denial of societal (structural) responsibility for the conditions in black communities.[29]

As many of my respondents make clear, if the opportunity structure is open ("It doesn't matter what color you are"), there must be something inherently wrong with racial minorities or their culture that explains group-level differences.

Leslie Carr argues "that color blindness is not the opposite of racism; it is another form of racism."[30] I would add that the form color blindness takes as the nation's hegemonic political discourse is a variant of laissez-faire racism. Historian David Roediger contends that in order for the Irish to have been absorbed into the white race in the mid-nineteenth century "the imperative to define themselves as whites came from the particular public and psychological wages whiteness offered" these new immigrants.[31] There is still a "wage" to whiteness, that element of ascribed status whites automatically receive because of their membership in the dominant group. But within the framework of color blindness the imperative has switched from whites overtly defining themselves or their interests as white, to one where they claim that color is irrelevant; being white is the same as being black, yellow, brown, or red. Some time ago, Ralph Ellison asked this important question about race relations that continues to go unanswered:

> What, by the way, is one to make of a white youngster who, with a transistor radio glued to his ear, screaming a Stevie Wonder tune, shouts racial epithets at black youngsters trying to swim at a public beach. . . . ?[32]

My interviews with whites around the country suggest that in this post-race era of color-blind ideology Ellison's keen observations about race relations need modification. The question now is what are we to make of a young white man from the suburbs who listens to hip-hop, wears baggy hip-hop pants, a baseball cap turned sideways, unlaced sneakers, and an oversized shirt emblazoned with a famous NBA player who, far from shouting racial epithets, lists a number of racial minorities as his heroes? It is now possible to define oneself as not being racist because of the clothes you wear, the celebrities you like, or the music you listen to while believing that blacks or Latinos are disproportionately poor or overrepresented in low-pay, dead-end jobs because they are part of a debased, culturally deficient group. Having a narrative that smooths over the cognitive dissonance and ofttimes schizophrenic dance that whites must do when they navigate race relations is likely an invaluable source of pleasure.

13   The Ideology of Color blindness
Lani Guinier • Gerald Torres

LANI GUINIER is the Bennett Boskey Professor of Law at Harvard University. She was nominated by President Clinton to be the first black woman to head the civil rights division of the Department of Justice. She has authored ninety-seven publications, many examining the intersection of race, gender, and the law.

GERALD TORRES is the H.O. Head Centennial Professor of Real Property Law at the University of Texas. He was previously professor of law and associate dean at the University of Minnesota Law School and also served in the U.S. Department of Justice, first as deputy assistant attorney general for Environment and Natural Resources and then as counsel to Attorney General Janet Reno. His publications include *Environmental Justice: The Legal Meaning of a Social Movement* (1996), *Understanding Environmental Racism* (1992), and *Critical Race Theory: The Decline of the Universalist Ideal and the Hope of Plural Justice* (1991).

Questions to Consider   Dr. Martin Luther King Jr.'s plea that one day his children would be judged "not by the color of their skin, but by the content of their character" is perhaps the single most quoted statement about the goals of the modern civil rights movement. There is, however, a huge gap between the expressed societal goals of what we "ought to be" and what we are. Guinier and Torres suggest that the very idea of color blindness has become a way to turn a blind eye toward glaring racial inequality. What purpose is served by turning MLK's statement on color blindness on its head? How and in what ways has the idea of color blindness been appropriated by individuals or groups who believe race no longer matters in shaping individual or group socioeconomic outcomes?

THE DISCOURSE OF COLORBLINDNESS focuses on managing the appearance of formal equality without worrying overmuch about the consequences of real-world inequality. Proponents of a colorblind ethos define freedom and equality exclusively in terms of the autonomous—some would say atomized—individual. This individual has no historical antecedents, no important social relationships, and no political commitments. By structuring the primary concerns around the idea of freedom for an everyman or everywoman, proponents of colorblind analysis locate that atomized individual in an abstract universe of rights and preferences rather than within an obdurate social structure that may limit or even predetermine a person's choices. In relationship to the state and to the market, the paramount virtue of the colorblind universe resides in treating each abstract individual the same as every other. By subjecting rules to this metric of simple sameness, people are legitimized through the appearance of abstract fairness.

Three rules seem to govern this colorblind universe. First, race is all about skin color. It is not a marker for social status, history, or power but is simply a false construction of phenotype that relies improperly on ascriptive physical identifiers of "blood" or ancestry. This is what some commentators call "formal race." Others refer to it as "biological race." Formal or biological race treats all race as pigmentation and grants all racial classifications symmetrical status. When race is only pigmentation, all racial classifications are equally bad, despite hierarchies of privilege or disadvantage that accompany the racial assignation.

Thus, the second rule of colorblindness is that recognizing race is the equivalent of holding onto unscientific notions of racial biology. If race is essentially "made up," with no scientific basis, then critics of race argue that treating people differently based on these made-up categories is unacceptable. Even if members of different "races" are treated "the same," each person so identified is denied his or her essential individual humanity. Moreover, when one notices race, one is implicitly manifesting racial enmity or racial preference. Since racial classification enabled a Jim Crow legal system to perpetuate false assumptions about biological inferiority, noticing race is in essence a throwback to racism.

The third rule is that racism is a personal problem. Unlike capitalism or socialism which are economic systems, or democracy which is a political arrangement, racism, racial hierarchy, or any institutionalized racial discrimination is not an economic or historic system, political arrangement, or social structure. Under the third rule of colorblindness, racism lacks any necessary nexus to power or privilege, and any observed connection is incidental, merely a result of the actions of people with a bad heart. Racism is a psychological disease of individuals, not a social plague. Racism is not produced by environmental toxins, nor is it reinforced by cultural forms or institutional practice. It is simply an irrational defect of the individual mind. It afflicts the aberrant soul who is vulnerable to prejudice or even self-hatred. The challenge for the judiciary, therefore, is to discern and eliminate to the greatest extent possible any public identification of race, since the identification is per se stigmatizing.

For those who believe we are already close to a colorblind society, formal fairness outweighs other concerns. They prefer rules like colorblindness even when such rules hide or reinforce relationships of privilege and subordination. The dangers of continuing to notice race are so profound that they justify doing nothing about the historic and present effects of the nexus between race and political and economic power. Not only is it wrong for the government to notice race, it is wrong for the political system to permit racially affected groups to mobilize in either their own self-interest or the larger public good.

• • •

In response to the claims of those who take a colorblind approach, we argue, as a practical matter, that it is impossible to be colorblind in a world as color-conscious as ours. Moreover, efforts to be colorblind are undesirable because they inhibit racialized minorities from struggling against their marginalized status. The rule of colorblindness disguises (sometimes deliberately) or normalizes (sometimes unwittingly) relationships of privilege and subordination. It gives those who have enjoyed little power in our society no mechanisms for understanding and challenging the systemic nature of their oppression. It affirms the existing imbalance in power relations; all that must change is for the privileged within the society to learn to tolerate on an individual basis those who were previously raced black or brown. Racial difference is relegated to celebratory holidays that capture the nostalgia of a time when we once thought we were different, but whose celebration reaffirms how essentially "the same" we truly are. This approach does not involve any fundamental rethinking of how race has socially and politically constructed privilege. The way race has been used both to distribute resources and to camouflage the unfairness in that distribution remains invisible. And the political space, where groups come together to give voice to their collective experience and mobilize to engage in fundamental social change, vanishes.

• • •

Racial Inequality Is Not a Problem of Individuals

Most people who oppose racism today believe that it is a psychological condition which distorts a person's thinking about people of a different "racial" phenotype. They believe in the changing-people's-thinking approach to racism. This approach, we argue, poses several dangers.

First, it reaffirms an essentialist view of race as merely a biological holdover from a less enlightened time that lacks any present political or social meaning. It suggests that racism is simply an inappropriate way that some individuals categorize groups of people who are in fact phenotypically different but whose physical differences amount to nothing important. This approach does not leave any space for other kinds of differences that people of color do in fact experience. These experiences are written off as some aberrational individual commitment to racialism that is obsessive and negative.

Second, the changing-people's-thinking approach not only locates the problem in the individual but it locates the remedy there as well. All that is necessary to overcome racism is for an individual to become better informed about different racial groups.

Third, in the changing-people's-thinking approach, either not speaking of race at all or speaking of it as a uniformly bad thing trumps all other options. This so-called neutral stance becomes almost inevitable after one has defined racism solely as an individual problem and an aberrant one at that. Racism is chased into the closet, and we are surprised when someone openly expresses intolerant views. Conservatives and progressives alike get caught in this trap and end up as speaking police, monitoring what people may say but feeling no compulsion to do anything about the racial hierarchy that shelters the root sources of bigotry. What surprises us about open bigotry is that it is public, not that it exists.

If we do not shift the locus of conversation to make visible the effects of such deeply held but unspoken attitudes, they will tend to normalize inequality. We will all then be tempted to explain the terrible condition of people of color as resulting from the behavior of the victims themselves. Having cleansed the social discourse of any mention of race and having policed expressions of bigotry, we will come to view any remaining racial dimension to observed injustices and inequities as a function of the way "those people" of color conceive of and structure their social life.

Colorblindness Masks Entrenched Racial Inequality

The colorblindness doctrine assumes that race is an individual attribute that should be of no consequence. For that reason, those advocating colorblindness as both means and end fail to recognize patterns of racial inequality and perceive no need to look more closely at data associated with these collective accidents of birth. They fail to see that an economy which is largely unaccountable to democratic institutions and principles of justice merely compounds inequality through the generations.

Stripped of concrete features like race, a black family earning $50,000 a year, for example, seems financially identical to a white family with the same income. Yet, this assumption of sameness does not take into account the effects of structural inequality compounded over time. Data on the generational effects of inequality show that blacks earning $50,000 or more have a **median** net worth that is barely one-half the median net worth of their white counterparts.

median If you were to line up a list of numbers from the smallest to the largest, the median would be the place where half of the numbers were above and half were below the number in the middle.

Most Americans have difficulty accumulating wealth. Income, understood principally as wages and salaries, does not easily convert into wealth because immediate necessities deplete available resources. Although income is distributed in a highly unequal manner in the United States (the top 20 percent of earners receives 43 percent of all income, while the poorest 20 percent of the population receives 4 percent of the total income), the distribution of wealth is even more unequal, and that inequality grows with each succeeding generation. In 1900, 39 percent of the wealthiest men in America emerged from wealthy families; by 1950, 68 percent of the wealthiest were born into wealth. By 1970, this figure climbed to 82 percent. That same year, only 4 percent of the richest men came from modest origins.

Income has been used as a surrogate for wealth at least in part due to the existence of little reliable data on wealth accumulation. But income alone offers an incomplete, skewed assessment of the inequality in life chances among different individuals and groups. The reality for most families is that while income may supply basic necessities, wealth is a critical resource for improving life chances, securing prestige, passing status along to the next generation, and influencing the political process. Wealth also provides financial stability during times in which needs overwhelm income.

Even at a time when the economy is good and when the unemployment rate for people of color is at an all-time low, blacks will not be able to sustain their economic gains until they can convert income into asset accumulation. Yet as the sociologist Dalton Conley points out: "At the lower end of the income spectrum (less than $15,000 per year), the median African American family has no assets, while the equivalent white family holds $10,000 worth of equity. At upper income levels (greater than $75,000 per year), white families have a median net worth of $308,000, almost three times the figure for upper-income African American families ($114,600)." The median net worth of whites is twelve times that of blacks. Similarly, the average white household controls $6,999 in net financial assets while the average black household retains no net financial assets whatsoever.

Owning a home is the primary method of equity accumulation for most families in the United States. Not surprisingly, disparities in home-ownership rates contribute to the black-white wealth disparity. As of 1997, only 44 percent of blacks owned their homes, in contrast with 71 percent of whites. Not only are blacks less likely to own homes, but when they do own homes, their asset is less likely to accumulate value than that of white home-owners. The value of housing in black neighborhoods increases at a lower rate compared with similar units in predominantly white neighborhoods. Black households are less likely than white households to have their wealth invested in financial assets, rental property, and businesses or farms that are likely to produce income. Black assets more often are tied up in a home and consumables, such as a car or household goods. As a result, black families are less able to expand their income than white families, and thus the disparity in wealth perpetuates itself.

What these comparisons of income and wealth illustrate is not just the effects of historical discrimination in particular cases but the effects of an entire complex of social relations, reflected in poorer housing markets, less adequate schools, reduced access to banks and other sources of capital, hostile relations with police authority, and increased crime. The cumulative impact of these disparities requires an explanation that does not merely excuse the current distribution of assets.

Efforts to pass these effects off to class are unavailing. When trying to explain the wealth gap between blacks and whites, Melvin Oliver and Thomas Shapiro used a large number of controls in their work—income, age, sex, marriage, children, number of working people within the household, education, occupation, work history, and region. With these controls, Oliver and Shapiro confirmed that nonracial factors standing alone cannot explain the black-white wealth gap.

The status of both the black poor and the black middle class is much more precarious and unstable than that of their white peers. Between 1980 and 1996 the absolute incomes of the poorest blacks declined dramatically, as compared with a small decline in the income of the poorest white families. Even as poverty in the black community declined overall, those who remained poor became poorer still. The percentage of black men between ages 25 and 34 who earn less than the poverty line for a family of four jumped from about 20 percent in 1969 to just over 50 percent in 1991.

Even among blacks and whites who both start at low socioeconomic positions as measured by parental occupation, whites who make it into the middle class accumulate more wealth than blacks who have traveled the same path. Blacks' middle-class status entirely depends on income,

whereas the status of the white middle class rests on the stability and security of assets. The writer DeNeen L. Brown illustrates this marginality and fragility when she explains what it means to be first-generation black middle-class: "To me that term doesn't mean anything other than someone who is one step out of poverty and two paychecks from being broke. I have income but not true wealth."

The average net worth of middle-class whites is nearly four times that of comparably situated blacks, and their average net financial assets are nearly 55 times greater than that of their black counterparts. This is true even within the context of real economic success. As Oliver and Shapiro note: "No matter how high up the mobility ladder blacks climb, their asset accumulation remains capped at inconsequential levels, especially when compared to that of equally mobile whites." As a result, each generation passes on a form of "asset poverty" regardless of the level of mobility or occupational attainment achieved. Social mobility does not fully counteract the effects of the intergenerational transmission of wealth.

Access to higher education has always been an indicator of both social mobility and the capacity of families to transfer wealth across generations. What we find when we compare the opportunities of white and black people is a continuing gap in access to higher education between these two groups. Because of the dramatic changes occurring in our economy, what this differential means is that the distribution of access to our knowledge-based economy will be color-coded.

Most people believe (and the data confirm) that education positively affects wealth accumulation: high educational achievement typically leads to better-paying jobs, which in turn result in greater wealth accumulation. What is less clear is the effect that wealth has upon education. While ample research has explored the effect of family and neighborhood income upon student performance and attainment, few studies have focused on wealth. The studies that do exist provide some insight into this relationship. Conley found that financial contributions of parents to their children's educational expenses have strong effects upon children's educational expectations. Yet African-American young adults receive less financial help from their parents and return more money to their parents' households than their white counterparts during the period immediately following high school. These data suggest that African-American young adults are substituting work for schooling.

Conley found that the most significant wealth-based predictor of educational performance is parents' liquid assets. (The most significant *overall* predictor, according to Conley, is parental educational level—another instance of the compounding of wealth over generations.) From this he infers that family-based educational financing is "probably more important than the differences in school districts associated with housing values." Conley states that wealth-based resource disparities at the district level (created by reliance on local property taxes, which fund the schools) account for approximately 10 percent of the gap in black and white standardized test scores. Furthermore, a decline in our social commitment to providing access to higher education for people of color is widening the gap. The declining support for public education compounds the problems in higher education. Black and other non-white communities feel the impact of this decreased support first and most powerfully, but it will affect all poor communities, regardless of color, in the long run. Everyone who depends on public education for upward mobility will suffer. Recent dramatic changes in the economy promise to magnify this disadvantage.

When Conley incorporated wealth factors into traditional educational analyses, a number of important elements in the cultural-deficit model for explaining educational disparities disappear. These include the pathologies supposedly created by female heads of households, receipt of welfare payments, parental age, parental occupational prestige, and parental income level. As the economist Marcellus Andrews puts it: "Working-class black people are muddling through an economy that no longer offers the prospect of middle-class life to hard working but modestly educated adults." There is a simple way to look at the confluence of these facts. Black people as a group not only have lower incomes than whites but also reduced access to the major avenue of wealth creation and transfer in the middle and working classes, namely high-quality higher education. Race in this society tracks wealth, wealth tracks education, and education tracks access to power.

Race provides an analytic tool for understanding significant dynamics of American economic life, such as the largely unremarked upon absence of any automatic escalator from one class to the next, despite the Horatio Alger myth. The linkages between race and black poverty tell us more about race than they do about individual black people. Moreover, the linkage between race and poverty tells us as much about white people as it does about black people. It tells us that the most potent determinant of economic success lies in the accumulated assets that are passed on from one generation to the next. Racial disparities cannot be explained by reference to any simple binary in which blacks are poor and whites are not. Instead, the mechanisms making it so hard for black people to accumulate assets in a way that changes their life chances are the same mechanisms that keep poor whites poor. These mechanisms are compounded by race, but they are not totally explained by race. Race is instructive in identifying the workings of class, but it cannot be swallowed up into class.

Hugh Price, President of the National Urban League, challenged us in his 1999 State of Black America address to look at race as "endogenous," that is, "something that is defined within a political-economic system and not at all natural or immutable." Race cannot be defined outside the economic or political system; "it is defined by the economic system, to grant or deny access to wealth accumulation." For the individual who is raced black, Price is pointing out links in a chain that may provide an important context for what otherwise might be interpreted as individual deficits, behavioral flaws, or cultural pathology.

Seeing the Big Picture   Color-Blind or Blind to Color?

Briefly glance through the Appendix. Based on your observations of statistics on race in this section, can you make an argument that the United States is now color-blind? How might you reconcile the ideal of color blindness with the trends in the data?

14   The Possibility of a New Racial Hierarchy in the Twenty-First-Century United States

Herbert J. Gans

HERBERT J. GANS is the Robert Lynd Professor of Sociology at Columbia University. He received his Ph.D. from the University of Pennsylvania. He has worked as a research planner for public and private agencies, and prior to coming to Columbia taught at the University of Pennsylvania, MIT, and Teachers College of Columbia University. He is the author of nine books and more than 160 articles. His first book was *The Urban Villagers* (1962). Recent works include *War Against the Poor* (1995), *Making Sense of America* (1999), and *Democracy and the News* (2003).

Questions to Consider   In a timely and provocative article, Herbert Gans suggests that racial categories, as currently understood, are undergoing fundamental changes. He argues that the current racial hierarchy will collapse into two categories: black and nonblack. How will this happen? Which racial and ethnic groups will be placed in each of these two categories, and why?

OVER THE LAST DECADE, A NUMBER OF social scientists writing on race and ethnicity have suggested that the country may be moving toward a new racial structure (Alba 1990; Sanjek 1994; Gitlin 1995). If current trends persist, today's multiracial hierarchy could be replaced by what I think of as a dual or bimodal one consisting of "nonblack" and "black" population categories, with a third, "residual," category for the groups that do not, or do not yet, fit into the basic dualism.[1]

More important, this hierarchy may be based not just on color or other visible bodily features, but also on a distinction between undeserving and deserving, or stigmatized and respectable, races.[2] The hierarchy is new only insofar as the old white-nonwhite dichotomy may be replaced by a nonblack-black one, but it is hardly new for blacks, who are likely to remain at the bottom once again. I fear this hierarchy could develop even if more blacks achieve educational mobility, obtain professional and managerial jobs, and gain access to middle-class incomes, wealth, and other "perks." Still, the hierarchy could also end, particularly if the black distribution of income and wealth resembles that of the then-dominant races, and if interracial marriage eliminates many of the visible bodily features by which Americans now define race.

Since no one can even guess much less model the many causal factors that will influence the future, the observations that follow are not intended to be read as a prediction but as an exercise in speculative analysis. The weakness of such an analysis is its empirical reliance on the extrapolation of too many current trends and the assumed persistence of too many current phenomena. The analysis becomes a justifiable exercise, however, because it aims only to speculate about what future "scenarios" are possible, and what variables might shape these.

Obviously, the observations about such a hierarchy are not meant to suggest that it is desirable. Indeed, I wrote the paper with the hope that if such a future threatens to become real, it can be prevented.

The remainder of this paper elaborates the basic scenario, adds a set of qualifications, and considers the variables and alternative scenarios now most likely to be significant for the future. The paper concludes with observations about the contemporary construction of race in the United States raised by my analysis about a possible future.

The Dual Racial Hierarchy

Before what is now described, somewhat incorrectly, as the post-1965 immigration, the United States was structured as a predominantly Caucasian, or white, society, with a limited number of numerically and otherwise inferior races, who were typically called Negroes, Orientals, and American Indians—or blacks, yellows, and reds to go with the pinkish-skinned people called whites. There was also a smattering of groups involving a huge number of people who were still described by their national or geographic origins rather than language, including Filipinos, Mexicans and Puerto Ricans, Cubans, etc.[3]

After 1965, when many other Central and Latin American countries began to send migrants, the Spanish-speaking groups were all recategorized by language and called Hispanics. Newcomers from Southeast Asia were classified by continental origin and called Asians, which meant that the later Indian, Pakistani, and Sri Lankan newcomers had to be distinguished regionally, and called South Asians.

At the end of the twentieth century, the country continues to be dominated by whites. Nevertheless, both the immigrants who started to arrive after the end of World War II and the political, cultural, and racial changes that took place in the wake of their arrival have further invalidated many old racial divisions and labels. They have also set into motion what may turn out to be significant transformations in at least part of the basic racial hierarchy.

These transformations are still in an early phase but one of the first has been the elevation of a significant, and mostly affluent, part of the Asian and Asian-American population into a **"model minority"** that also bids to eradicate many of the boundaries between it and whites. Upward socioeconomic mobility and increasing intermarriage with whites may even end up in eliminating the boundary that now constructs them as a separate race. Thus, one possible future trend may lead to all but poor Asians and Asian-Americans being perceived and even treated so much like whites that currently visible bodily differences will no longer be judged negatively or even noticed, except when and where Asians or Asian-Americans threaten white interests (e.g., Newman 1993). The same treatment as quasi whites may spread to other successfully mobile and intermarrying immigrants and their descendants, for example Filipinos and white Hispanics.[4]

What these minorities have in common now with Asians, and might have in common even more in the future, is that they are all nonblack, although not as many are currently as affluent as Asians. Nonetheless, by the middle of the twenty-first century, as whites could perhaps become, or will worry about becoming, a numerical minority in the country, they might cast about for political and cultural allies.[5] Their search for allies, which may not even be conscious or deliberate, could hasten the emergence of a new, nonblack racial category, whatever it is named, in which

model minority A minority ethnic or racial group that has been socioeconomically successful relative to other racial minorities. The media typically frame this group as a "model" that other racial and ethnic groups should emulate.

skin color, or in the case of "Hispanics," racially constructed ethnic differences, will be ignored, even if whites would probably remain the dominant subcategory.

The lower part of the emerging dual hierarchy will likely consist of people classified as blacks, including African-Americans, as well as Caribbean and other blacks, dark skinned or black Hispanics, Native Americans, and anyone else who is dark skinned enough and/or possessed of visible bodily features and behavior patterns, actual or imagined, that remind nonblacks of blacks. Many of these people will also be poor, and if whites and other nonblacks continue to blame America's troubles on a low-status scapegoat, the new black category will be characterized as an undeserving race.

In effect, class will presumably play nearly as much of a role in the boundary changes as race, but with some important exceptions. For example, if a significant number of very poor whites remain as the twenty-first-century equivalent of today's "white trash," they will probably be viewed as less undeserving than equally poor blacks simply because they are whites.[6]

Furthermore, the limits of class are indicated, at least for today, by the continued stigmatization of affluent and otherwise high-status blacks, who suffer some of the same indignities as poor blacks (Feagin and Sykes 1994).[7] So, of course, do moderate and middle-income members of the working class, who constitute the majority of blacks in America even if whites do not know it. The high visibility of "black" or Negroid physical features renders class position invisible to whites, so that even affluent blacks are suspected of criminal or pathological behavior that is actually found only among a minority of very poor blacks.

Despite continuing white hatreds and fears of blacks that continue almost 150 years after the Civil War, racial classification systems involving others have been more flexible. When the first Irish immigrants came to New York, they were so poor that they were perceived by Anglo-Saxon whites as the black Irish and often treated like blacks. Even so, it did not take the Irish long to separate themselves from blacks, and more important, to be so separated by the city's Anglo-Saxons. A generation later, the Irish were whites (Roediger 1991; Ignatiev 1995).

Perhaps their new whiteness was reinforced by the arrival of the next set of newcomers: people from Eastern and Southern Europe who were often described as members of "swarthy races." Even though the word *race* was used the way we today use *ethnicity*, the newcomers were clearly not white in the Anglo-Saxon sense, and Southern Italians were sometimes called "guineas" because of their dark skin.

Nonetheless, over time, they too became white, thanks in part to their acculturation, their integration into the mainstream economy, and after World War II, their entry into the middle class. Perhaps the disappearance of their swarthiness was also reinforced by the arrival in the cities of a new wave of Southern blacks during and after World War II.

A less typical racial transformation occurred about that time in Mississippi, where whites began to treat the Chinese merchants who provided stores for poor blacks as near whites. As Loewen (1988) tells the story, increased affluence and acculturation were again relevant factors. Although whites neither socialized nor intermarried with the Chinese, they accorded them greater social deference and political respect than when they had first arrived. They turned the Chinese into what I previously called a residual category, and in the process created an early version of the nonblack-black duality that may appear in the United States in the next century.

As the Mississippi example suggests, changes in racial classification schemes need not require racial or class equality, for as long as scarce resources or positions remain, justifications for discrimination also remain and physical features that are invisible in some social settings can still become visible in others. **Glass ceilings** supply the best example, because they seem to change more slowly than some other hierarchical boundaries. Even ceilings for Jews, non-Irish Catholics, and others long classified as whites are still lower than those for **WASPs** in the upper reaches of the class and prestige structures.

I should note that the racial hierarchy I have sketched here, together with the qualifications that follow, are described both from the perspective of the (overtly) detached social scientist, and also from the perspective of the populations that end up as dominant in the structure. A longer paper would analyze how very differently the people who are fitted into the lower or residual parts of the hierarchy see it.[8]

Qualifications to the Dual Hierarchy

Even if the country would someday replace its current set of racial classifications, the result would not be a simple dual structure, and this model needs to be qualified in at least three ways.

glass ceiling A situation in which the advancement of a qualified person within the hierarchy of an organization is curtailed at a particular point due to sexist or racist discrimination. One is able to "see" the corporate path to the top but hits an imaginary "glass ceiling" where advancement stops.

WASP White Anglo-Saxon Protestant.

Residuals

The first qualification is the near certainty of a residual or middle category that includes groups placed in a waiting position by the dominant population until it becomes clear whether they will be allowed to become nonblack, face the seemingly permanent inferiority that goes with being black, or become long-term residuals.

If such a structure were to develop in the near future, those likely to be placed in a residual category would include the less affluent members of today's Asian, Hispanic and Filipino, Central and South American Indian, and mixed Indian-Latino populations. The future of the dark-skinned members of the South Asian newcomers is harder to predict. Indeed, their treatment will become an important test of how whites deal with the race-class nexus when the people involved are very dark skinned but are not Negroid—and when their class position is so high that in 1990 it outranked that of all other immigrants (Rumbaut 1997, table 1.4).[9]

Who is classified as residual will, like all other categorizations, be shaped by both class and race. To borrow Milton Gordon's (1964) useful but too rarely used notion of "ethclass," what may be developing are "race-classes," with lower-class members of otherwise racially acceptable groups and higher-class members of racially inferior ones being placed in the residual category.

It is also possible for two or more residual categories to emerge, one for nonwhite and Hispanic populations of lower- and working-class position, and another for nonwhites and Hispanics of higher-class position, with the latter more likely to be eligible eventually to join whites in the nonblack portion of a dual hierarchy. Yet other variations are conceivable, however, for white America has not yet given any clues about how it will treat middle-class Latinos of various skin colors and other bodily features. Perhaps today's ad hoc solution, to treat nonblack Hispanics as a quasi-racial ethnic group that is neither white nor black, may survive for another generation or more, particularly if enough Hispanics remain poor or are falsely accused of rejecting linguistic Americanization.

Being placed in a residual classification means more than location in a middle analytic category; it is also a socially enforced, even if covert, category, and it will be accompanied by all the social, political, and emotional uncertainties that go with being placed in a holding pattern and all the pains these create (Marris 1996). True, residuals may not know they are waiting, but then the second-generation white ethnic "marginal men" identified by Stonequist (1937) did not know they were waiting for eventual acculturation and assimilation.

Multiracials

A second qualification to the dual model is created by the emergence of biracials or multiracials that result from the rising intermarriage rates among Asian, Hispanic, and black and white immigrants as well as black and white native-born Americans.[10] Interracial marriages increased from 1 percent of all marriages in 1960 to 3 percent in 1990 (Harrison and Bennett 1995, 165).[11] They are expected to increase much faster in the future, particularly Asian-white ones, since even now, about a third of all Asian marriages, and more than half of all Japanese ones, are intermarriages.[12] If Hispanic-white marriages were also counted, they would exceed all the rest in current number and expected growth, but these are usually treated as ethnic rather than racial intermarriages.

Another set of recruits for a residual position includes the light-skinned blacks, once called mulattos, who today dominate the African-American upper class, some of whom may be sufficiently elite and light skinned to be viewed as nonblack. Even now, the most prominent among the light-skinned black-white biracials, including business and civic leaders, celebrities and entertainers, are already treated as honorary whites, although many refuse this option and take special pride in their blackness and become "race leaders."[13]

Meanwhile, "multiracial" is in the process of slowly becoming a public racial category, and someday it could become an official one codified by the U.S. Census.[14] At this writing, however, many people of mixed race are not ready to define themselves publicly as such, and those who can choose which racial origin to use are sometimes flexible on instrumental grounds, or may choose different racial origins on different occasions.[15] How people of various racial mixtures construct themselves in the longer run is impossible to tell, since issues of their identification and treatment by others, their own identity, and the social, occupational, financial, and political benefits and costs involved cannot be predicted either.

As far as the country's long-term future racial structure is concerned, however, what matters most is how whites will eventually view and treat multiracial people. This will be affected by the variations in class and visible physical features among multiracial people—for example, how closely they resemble whites or other deserving races.

Another question is the future of the traditional identification of race with "blood," which counts all nonwhites in halves, quarters, or even eighths, depending on how many and which ancestors intermarried with whom.[16] If the late-twentieth-century belief in the power of genes continues, blood might simply be replaced by genes someday.

Mixed race is a particularly complex category, for several reasons. In any racial intermarriage with more than one offspring, each sibling is likely to look somewhat different racially from the others, ranging from darker to lighter or more and less nonwhite. Thus, one black-white sibling could be viewed as black and another as nonblack—even before they decide how they view themselves. What happens in subsequent generations is virtually unimaginable, since even if mixed-race individuals marry others of the same mixture, their children will not resemble their grandparents and some may barely resemble their parents. Eventually, a rising number will be treated as, and will think of themselves as, white or nonblack, but this is possible only when people of multiracial origin can no longer bear children who resemble a black ancestor.

Empirical evidence about the effects of racial intermarriage from countries where it has taken place for a long time is unfortunately not very relevant. The closest case, the Caribbean islands, are for the most part, tiny. They are also former plantation societies, with a small number of white and light-skinned elites, and a large number of nonwhites—and a differential conception of white and nonwhite from island to island.[17] Caribbean nonwhites appear to intermarry fairly freely but skin color does count and the darkest-skinned peoples are invariably lowest in socioeconomic class and status (Mintz 1989; Rodriguez 1989).

The only large country, Brazil, also began as a plantation society, and it differs from the United States particularly in that the Brazilian state eschewed racial legislation. As a result, Brazil never passed Jim Crow laws, but as of this writing (January 1998) it has not passed civil rights legislation either. Racial stratification, as well as discrimination and segregation, has persisted nonetheless, but it has been maintained through the class system. Drastic class inequalities, including a high rate of illiteracy among the poor, have enabled whites to virtually monopolize the higher class and status positions.

The absence of state involvement has given Brazil an undeserved reputation as a society that encourages intermarriage but ignores racial differences, a reputation the state has publicized as "racial democracy." The reality is not very different from that of the United States, however, for while there has been more intermarriage, it appears to have taken place mainly among blacks and black-white biracials, who together make up about half the country's population. Moreover, biracials gain little socioeconomic advantage from their lighter skins, even as the darkest-skinned blacks are kept at the bottom, forced into slums and prisons as in the United States.[18]

In effect, the Brazilian experience would suggest an empirical precedent for my hypothesis that blacks will remain a separate, and discriminated-against, population in the United States of the future. Indeed, in just about every society in which blacks first arrived as slaves, they are still at the bottom, and the political, socioeconomic, and cultural mechanisms to keep them there remain in place. Although blacks obtain higher incomes and prestige than Asians or white Hispanics in a number of American communities, the descendants of nonblack immigrants are, with some notable exceptions, still able to overtake most blacks in the long run.

Since parts of the United States were also a plantation society in which the slaves were black, the leftovers of the racial stratification pattern will likely continue here as well. Thus, children of black-white intermarriages who turn out to be dark skinned are classified as blacks, even if the United States is on the whole kinder to light-skinned biracials than Brazil.

The future of Asian-white biracials remains more unpredictable, in part because no empirical data exist that can be used to shore up guesses about them. The same observation applies to the endless number of other multiracial combinations that will be created when the children of multiracial parents intermarry with yet other multiracials. There will be few limits to new variations in bodily features, though which will be visible or noticed, and which of the latter will be stigmatized or celebrated as exotic cannot be guessed now.[19] Most likely, however, the larger the number of multiracials and of multiracial variations, the more difficult it will be for nonblacks to define and enforce racial boundaries, or to figure out which of the many darker-skinned varieties of multiracials had black ancestors. In that case, an eventual end to racial discrimination is possible.

If future racial self-identification patterns will also resemble today's ethnic ones, the racial equivalent of today's voluntary white ethnicity and its associated lack of ethnic loyalty may mean that many future triracial, quadriracial, and other multiracial people may eventually know little, and care even less, about the various racial mixtures they have inherited. It is even conceivable that this change will extend to black multiracials, and should race become voluntary for them as well, the possibility of an end to racial discrimination will be increased. Unfortunately, at the moment such extrapolations are far closer to utopian thinking than to sociological speculation.

Regional Variations

A third qualification to the dual model is that the portrait I have drawn is national, but given the regional variations in old racial groups and new immigrant populations, it fits no single U.S. region. Moreover, some parts of the country are now still so devoid of new immigrants, with the exception of the handful who come to establish "ethnic" restaurants, that the present racial hierarchies, categories, and attitudes, many of them based on stereotypes imported from elsewhere, could survive unchanged for quite a while in such areas. Furthermore, some areas that have experienced heavy immigration from Asia and Latin America are currently seeing an outmigration of whites, especially lower-income ones (Frey 1996). Thus, even current patterns in the racial makeup of U.S. regions could change fairly quickly.

In addition, regional differences remain in the demography of the lowest strata. The racial hierarchy of the Deep South will probably continue to bear many direct marks of slavery, although the de facto black experience elsewhere in the country has so far not been totally different. Moreover, in some regions, Latin American and other poor nonblack immigrants have already been able to jump over the poor black population economically and socially, partly because whites, including institutions such as banks, are less hostile—or less necessary—to them than they are to blacks.

In the Southwest, Mexicans and other Hispanics remain at the socioeconomic bottom, although in California, they may be joined by the Hmong, Laotians, and other very poor Asians. And Native Americans still occupy the lowest socioeconomic stratum in the handful of mostly rural parts of the country where they now live, although tribes with gambling casinos may be able to effect some changes in that pattern.

Even though some of the new immigrants can by now be found just about everywhere in America, the Los Angeles and New York City areas not only remain the major immigrant arrival centers but also contain the most diverse populations. As a result, a number of the issues discussed in this paper will be played out there, even as they are barely noticeable in the many smaller American cities that may have attracted only a handful of the newcomers. Since these two cities are also the country's prime creators of popular culture, however, their distinctive racial and ethnic characteristics will probably be diffused in subtle ways through the country as a whole.

Alternative Scenarios

Speculating about the future also requires some explicit consideration of the variables that could affect the guesses I have made here, which in turn could lead to alternative scenarios. Generally speaking these variables are macrosociological—major changes in the economy, demographic patterns including internal migration and immigration, as well as political realignments and racial divisions of labor, among others. These in turn can result in changes in racial and ethnic relations as well as in classification systems.

As noted earlier, dominant groups can alter racial categories and constructions. Model minorities are "chosen" by the dominant population precisely because they appear to share, and thereby to uphold, that population's behavior or values. If new behavior or values need to be upheld, new model minorities may be recruited. Scapegoats are populations that can be blamed for social problems, although the dominant populations choose, or even create, the social problems for which scapegoats will be blamed. Scapegoats, or targets for blame, generally come in two varieties: *higher* scapegoats, usually recruited from higher status minority groups that can be blamed for obtaining too much economic or cultural power; and *lower* ones, typically the undeserving poor, who can be accused of deviant behavior or values said to hold back economic growth, require public expenditures that could bankrupt governmental budgets, threaten familial and sexual norms, or impair the moral fabric of the rest of society. Blaming both types of scapegoats is a politically easy way of responding to a crisis, particularly one for which immediate and feasible solutions are lacking.

During the long Cold War, the Soviets and other foreign scapegoats could be blamed for American problems, but now, domestic scapegoats have again become the primary target. While illegal and even legal American immigrants are once again joining poor blacks as the country's principal lower scapegoats, only a few states have sufficient immigrants to serve as targets for blame, which may help to explain why conservative politicians, particularly Republicans, have more often demonized poor blacks.

The most likely candidates for change in current racial categories, other than of model minorities, are the people whites now call Hispanics, as well as descendants of some now

officially nonwhite populations in the new immigration. They will have to be allowed into the higher-status occupations in larger number if and when the supply of whites runs out, and in that case, today's forms of racial and ethnic discrimination against them, particularly those shaped by class considerations, would have to give way. In fact, by the middle of the twenty-first century, demographers and journalists may be amazed that fifty years earlier, whites expected to be swamped in 2050 by an aggregate of diverse peoples then all called Hispanics.

Two macrosocial factors are probably most important in thinking about alternative scenarios. One is the set of geopolitical and economic demographics that can be produced by cross-national population movements, including the one that has fueled the immigration from Central and Latin America, as well as Russia, Asia, and now Africa, during the last half century. These movements were controlled at least in part by U.S. government legislation, but world catastrophes could take place that could force even the United States to open its borders to much larger numbers of people who might alter the racial distribution significantly.

National demographics can also be changed by domestic political considerations, however, which could lead to a new search for white—and non-Hispanic—immigrants. The United States found its late-nineteenth-century industrial workforce in white Europe rather than among the newly freed slaves in the South. Likewise, Australia has recently looked for European immigrants to discourage the arrival of further Asians.

The second major factor is the state of the domestic economy. If late-twentieth-century trends in the world economy and on Wall Street continue in their present forms, the further disappearance of American firms, jobs, and high wages, as well as related changes in the country's economy, would persist too.

Suppose, for example, that unemployment, or the decline of real income, or both, worsened in the first quarter of the twenty-first century, and Americans in large numbers conclude that the country's economy can never again supply full-time jobs paying a living wage for everyone. While the descendants of the poorer immigrants would be the first to experience what I once called "second generation decline" (Gans 1992), other immigrants can also be dispatched into persistent poverty when not enough jobs are available, with the appropriate racial stereotypes invented or reinvented to justify their downward mobility. Even some middle-class descendants of Asian, Russian, and other newcomers could be transformed into lower scapegoats. Then, the dual racial hierarchy I have described would look very different or might not come to pass at all.

Should economic crises result in political crises as well, or raise religious and culture "wars" to more feverish pitches, the current movement toward a dual racial structure could also end quickly. Then, a modern version of the nineteenth-century American monoracial pattern might reappear, with the children of white newcomers joining older white ethnics and WASPs as the only acceptable race. Some members of the newly scapegoated races would probably react in turn, inaugurating political protest, intensifying identity politics and slowing down on intermarriage and other forms of acculturation and assimilation. Some descendants of today's newcomers might return to the old country.

What if a very different economic scenario were assumed, involving a return of old-style economic growth accompanied by a stronger U.S. position in the global economy, a shortage of domestic workers, and an upward trend in real income? In that case, the trend toward a dual structure might be hastened, and the erosion of perceived racial differences speeded up as well.

At that point, the now still visible bodily differences of Asian-Americans and their descendants might no longer be noticed, and these groups would repeat the post–World War II pattern by which Southern and Eastern European "races" were redefined as "ethnic groups." The reclassification of Hispanics, including the treatment of third-generation Central and Latin Americans, would probably move in the same direction.

The fate of blacks is more difficult to imagine. If the economy created a seller's market for people with job skills at all levels from blue collar to professional and managerial, all poverty would decline sharply, including that of blacks. Moreover, blacks would be able to enter the upper middle and middle classes in such numbers as to disturb white America's long association of poverty with blackness. Indeed, in an economy with enough decent jobs for all, private and public affirmative action policies to assure the spread of blacks at all levels of the occupational and socioeconomic structure would be likely as well.

Under such conditions, those aspects of white racism due to fear of and anger at black poverty would begin to decline, and if the federal government was committed to fight racial discrimination and segregation, so would the construction of blacks as an undeserving race. Black-white intermarriage rates might also rise more quickly.

If the prosperity were long term, and it as well as other events in the society and the world reduced the country's resort to domestic scapegoats, a dual racial hierarchy might be replaced by the beginnings of a multiracial structure in which the boundaries of all races would become fuzzier and weaker. Since now-stigmatized visible bodily differences would then lose their negative connotations, they might not only be ignored but even come to be celebrated as positive contributions to American diversity, just as current ethnic differences among Europeans provide the country with nonthreatening cultural diversities.

Prosperity alone does not necessarily solve a society's other problems, however, and political, cultural, and religious conflicts could remain, encouraging dominant groups to choose and stigmatize an undeserving race, even if it is not a poor one. Anti-Semitic activities, for example, have occurred in prosperous times and societies, and in nations with minuscule Jewish populations.

Likewise, more economic prosperity and other positive economic tendencies alone do not necessarily produce more acculturation and assimilation of immigrants. Even the acculturation of large numbers of immigrants and their descendants does not automatically preclude identity politics, for today's college and university campuses are rife with rapidly acculturating newcomers who nevertheless feel strongly enough about their racial identity to become active in identity politics.

It is even possible that in a multiracial America, some latter-day descendants of WASPs and white ethnics will resort to identity politics as an attempt to retain or restore their political and cultural dominance.[20] And if a global economy also produced pressures toward global cultural and political homogeneities, nation-states or their successors might develop now unimagined forms of national identity politics or cultural revivals to maintain some kind of national distinctiveness. Immigrants and their descendants might be victimized by such developments more than blacks, however.

Three Tendencies in the Contemporary Construction of Race

Biological Constructions

The first tendency is the continuing construction of race from biological as well as social building blocks. Most scientific experts agree that there are no biologically definable races, and that race is therefore not a useful biological concept. The lay public, however, which is not ready to accept expert opinion, sees differences in visible bodily features, mostly facial, between people and treats them as racial differences caused by differences in "blood." People also racialize differences in personality traits such as "soul"—and national character in the case of immigrants.

The visible bodily differences are not imaginary, for people do differ by skin color, and the shapes or other characteristics of various body parts, including heads, eyelids, noses, hair, and others. To cite just a few examples, even in third-generation white ethnic America, one can find Irish and Welsh (or "Celtic") faces, southern Italian and Sicilian ones, and Slavic as well as Scandinavian ones.

What people notice are not scientifically defined races or subraces, but the descendants of once-isolated peoples who had been inbreeding for centuries.[21] Since most have now stopped doing so as a result of rural to urban and other migrations, their distinctiveness is disappearing with each new generation, but it has by no means disappeared.

Some of the variations in personality and social characteristics that laypeople correlate with race or "blood" can undoubtedly be traced in part to the societies and economies, as well as the racial hierarchies, in which these once-isolated peoples lived. The occupational and other social roles that immigrants play in their new societies also play a part, one reason why immigrant shopkeepers in "middlemen" roles are often seen as "clannish" by the populations they serve, for example.

Some visible bodily features that distinguish people are noticed and judged; some are noticed but not judged one way or another; and yet others are not even noticed, seeming to be virtually invisible. Although how features are judged can be traced in part to the popular Darwinisms of the last two centuries, in general, the bodily features of the most prestigious peoples are usually adopted as ideals of physical perfection, while features found among the lower social classes are judged pejoratively.[22]

Variations in skin color, as well as in head shapes, noses, eyes, lips, and hair, have been noticed in many societies, but differences in some bodily parts have been ignored, for example, the size of fingers and the shapes of ears and earlobes.[23] Yet other bodily features are not noticed because they are hidden by clothes; while a few are not noticed because people wear clothes to hide them. These often spur fantasies, for example about black penis size and other imagined racial differences in reproductive and other organs.[24]

A major ingredient of the social construction of race is the determination of which visible bodily features are noticed and used to delineate race and which remain unnoticed. In the process shaping that construction, various social constructors, including laypersons, experts, and, when relevant, commercial and political decision makers, take part. Unless explicit ideological, commercial, or political reasons are involved, the constructors may not be aware of the process in which they are involved, or the causes that shape the final determination. Usually, whites are the major constructors, but increasingly, representatives of the racial minorities to be constructed participate when they can politicize the process, or can frighten manufacturers or advertisers of national consumer goods.[25]

Strictly speaking, a biological construction should make racial characteristics and classifications relatively fixed, but lay biological construction is almost as flexible as social construction. The reason for the lack of fixity is not hard to find, for the choice of which visible bodily features are to be noticed has almost nothing to do with race and everything to do with stratification.

As the Brazilian and United States experiences indicate, the race of the lowest class became the lowest race because slaves were almost by definition the lowest class and race. That captured blacks were the only population economically and otherwise powerless to prevent their becoming enslaved in recent centuries led whites to use their distinguishable skin color and facial features to translate their class inferiority into a racial one (Fields 1990). Similarly, the stigmatization of "yellow" skin resulted from the serflike status of Chinese "coolies" on railroad construction gangs; the stigmatization of "swarthiness" followed from the low status of the Southern and Eastern European newcomers; and a century later, white Hispanic immigrants are sometimes called a race because of their low class position.[26] That the ancestors of now-respected Americans were once damned for their swarthy skins has been quietly forgotten, both among their descendants and among the peoples who "invented" the original stigma.

Ethnicity as Racial

The second, and related, tendency is the continuing lay practice of identifying ethnic and national differences as racial, particularly in private self-naming. Census analysts have discovered that in the 1990 census, respondents to open-ended questions claimed membership in nearly three hundred races or ethnic groups, including seventy Hispanic categories (Morganthau 1995, 64). In many instances, they equated their race with their nationality—or with their tribes in the case of Native Americans.[27] As Eleanor Gerber and Manuel de la Puente pointed out in reporting on a study of test questions for the 2000 census: "Most respondents recognized the term 'ethnic group' but . . . would indicate it was 'the same thing' as race . . . [and] often coined the term 'ethnic race' during our discussions" (Gerber and de la Puente 1996, 21).

The two Bureau of Census researchers suggest lack of education as the causal factor in this conflation, indicating that only the college educated could distinguish ethnic group from race. However, as long as Americans notice visible bodily differences among people of the same official race, they will hold on to *private* constructions of race that differ from the official definitions.[28] Even among the third- and fourth-generation white multiethnics whose "ethnic options" Mary Waters (1990) studied, some chose their ethnicities on the basis of racial conceptions of national origin.[29] In effect, ethnicity continues to be a matter of "blood."[30]

Racial Tolerance

The third and perhaps most important tendency is the apparently increasing white tolerance for racial differences, except with respect to blacks. At the same time, whites seem to use race less often as an indicator of class, except when they are considering poor blacks. This trend may become more widespread as racial intermarriage among people of similar class increases further. Today, class homogamy is apparently outranking racial homogamy among college-educated young people (Kalmijn 1991).

If this pattern spreads to other Americans of the same age and if it becomes permanent, and if whites were willing and able to see that their hatreds and fears of blacks and other very poor nonwhites are so often reactions to their extreme and persistent poverty rather than their race, class could become more important and more overt as a boundary and a principle of stratification in the future. If Americans could also realize that class is more than a matter of "lifestyle" differences among near equals, class stratification might someday become a matter of general public discussion. In that case, the myth of a class-less America might eventually be laid to rest.[31]

Even a more modest increase in awareness of class would be desirable, because class is after all an achieved status, while race is not, even in its reasonably flexible lay construction. However, the shift from race to class would also require Americans to develop a more fundamental understanding of the United States and to invent a new conception of the American dream and its underlying myth to replace that of the classless society. So far, there is no indication of this happening.

In fact, it would probably not happen until events in the political economy make it possible to achieve a drastic reduction of joblessness and poverty, so that the correlation of poverty with blackness is significantly lowered. If and when blacks become roughly equal economically to nonblacks, blacks can no longer be treated as an undeserving race.

If poverty and inequality are not lessened, however, and if more poor blacks are condemned to work for nothing but their welfare benefits, they could be treated as an ever more undeserving race, and other populations who cannot enter, or stay in, the middle class, including poor Hispanics and Asians, might join them. In that case, the racial hierarchy of the next century's United States would look very different from the one I have sketched here.

Conclusion

A society's reconstruction of racial categories appears to require at least the following conditions: (1) an influx of immigrants who do not fit the existing racial categories and their associated class backgrounds; (2) a healthy economy with sufficient opportunity for upward mobility even for poorer immigrants; (3) a lack of demand for new lower (and higher) racial scapegoats; and (4) an at least temporary demand for model minorities.

If these conditions are met, existing racial definitions and categories will be altered, sometimes even quickly if there is a proliferation of interracial marriages. However, in a society with a history of slavery, one possible effect is a dual racial hierarchy, in which one part consists mostly of ex-slaves. However, since even the effects of slavery should eventually be eliminated, at least in theory, the United States could become a predominantly interracial or multiracial society someday.

Even then, the more prestigious racial mixtures are apt to remain somewhat whiter for a while than the rest, and the less prestigious ones darker. But if the country's racial mixing ever became so thorough that skin color and other currently used bodily features were sufficiently unrecognizable or no longer of sufficient interest to be noticed, race would no longer be associated with social ranking. If Americans then still needed to rank each other, new criteria would have to be found.

PREJUDICE, DISCRIMINATION, AND RACISM

I MAGINE YOU ARE A 57-YEAR-OLD WHITE VICE president with Friendly Bank. You earn a considerable amount of money, have large mortgage and car payments, and support four kids, two of whom are in college. You are the primary breadwinner in your family. At lunch, your boss asks you about the new manager you will be hiring. He hints to you in a subtle way, a way you could never prove in court, that he has had bad experiences working with Asian Americans and would be extremely upset if one was hired. You are not racist toward Asians. In fact, one of your best friends is an Asian American. You do, however, need this job, your family needs to eat, two of your children are in college, and you are at an age at which moving from one job to another would be very difficult and extremely costly. Of the three hundred people who apply for this position, several Asian American candidates appear to be highly qualified, and one unquestionably would make an excellent bank manager. Would you turn a blind eye to the resumes of the Asian Americans, or would you hire the most qualified person, even if that meant hiring an Asian American and being marginalized or conveniently downsized by your boss?

How do feelings of antipathy toward or dislike of a group of people because of their skin color, ethnicity, or religion culminate in actions against members of that group? As the preceding example indicates, individuals may act in discriminatory ways and not be prejudiced or racist. Conversely, someone may be prejudiced and racist toward a group and not discriminate. The Asian or black shoe salesperson who does not like whites may still sell a white customer a pair of shoes in order to earn a commission.

Prejudice and **discrimination** are linked in complicated ways. Since World War II, whites' views on integration, interracial marriage, voting for nonwhite politicians,

prejudice To "prejudge"; having preconceived notions, attitudes, or negative beliefs about a group.

discrimination The denial of goods or services to an individual or group for arbitrary reasons, such as a person's race, religion, or nationality.

and sharing social space with blacks and Asians suggest that whites are gradually embracing the idea of a color-blind society. However, things, particularly attitudes through surveys, are not always as they seem. Such survey findings are encouraging only if you believe that respondents' answers are an accurate reflection of what they really think or feel. Perhaps these trends reflect pressure to conform to what respondents believe is a socially desirable attitude. Typically, individuals want to present themselves to others in a positive way. This pressure to conform may lead respondents to conveniently forget or tightly monitor racist or prejudiced beliefs. Are answers to questions about racial attitudes merely a reflection of what takes place in the abstract, unnatural interview setting, or are these responses a valid and reliable window into Americans' racial attitudes? Frankly, social scientists are not always sure. To further complicate matters, it's not clear what connection, if any, exists between attitudes and action or between prejudice and discrimination. Demonstrating a strong, consistent causal link between attitudes and actions has proved elusive in the social sciences. The proposition that actions flow from attitudes may seem straightforward, but as we will see in the readings, it is not. It seems logical that individuals would behave in a manner consistent with their attitudes, opinions, or beliefs about a particular topic. If, for example, you define yourself as not being racist, you would not engage in racial discrimination. But as the example about the vice president of Friendly Bank suggests, various social and economic pressures mediate what we would like to do, what we should do, and what we actually do.

Prejudice and discrimination take many forms. The first five readings, in **Understanding Racism,** examine those forms and the way certain social and structural conditions can create an environment in which prejudice and discrimination are likely to emerge. In an insightful and classic piece of sociology, Herbert Blumer explains race prejudice (racism) as a reflection of how individuals place themselves in a racial hierarchy relative to other racial groups they encounter; that is, individuals attempt to maintain privilege and status by reserving the "prerogatives" of their racial group, even if they are not consciously aware of it. Many believe that race based discrimination is a part of our nation's past. Citing various government statistics James Sterba demonstrates that discrimination directed at racially defined minorities continues to happen with great frequency. Robert Merton provides examples of the social context in which a nonprejudiced individual like our vice president at Friendly Bank might act in a discriminatory fashion. Like Blumer, Merton outlines how prejudice and discrimination are often rooted in efforts to maintain privileges or advantages that accrue to individuals because of their skin color. Moustafa Bayoumi discusses what it was like growing up as an Arab American in the United States in an environment that was hostile to this ethnic group. The discriminatory treatment this group has been subjected to has however, mirrored the treatment of most immigrant groups to the United States. Unfortunately the events surrounding 9/11 created the situation where Arab Americans had to prove that they were loyal Americans and not potential terrorists, creating a scenario where the "American" part of their Arab American identity is suspect. George Lipsitz chronicles how racism by the federal government in housing, bank lending, and huge subsidies to spur suburbanization (and white flight from the cities) after World War II should be understood as institutional practices that resulted in substantial long-term, intergenerational "investments" in the white population. Lawrence Bobo argues that the old-style Jim Crow racism of the past has been replaced by laissez-faire racism. This theory suggests that since the government and institutions can no longer legally engage in overt discrimination, individuals can no longer claim that racism affects upward mobility.

The five articles in **How Space Gets Raced** reveal a nation highly segregated by race and ethnicity. Douglas Massey argues that residential segregation results in a loss of occupational and educational mobility for racial minorities and cuts off communities from "mainstream" America. Elijah Anderson explains how many poor, young African Americans use fear and intimidation as a way to gain respect among their peers. Robert Bullard details how poor and nonwhite neighborhoods are disproportionately exposed to toxic waste, perhaps the most obvious way in which social space gets raced to the detriment of a racial minority.

The Reverend Martin Luther King commented, "The church is the most segregated institution in America . . . and Sunday service is the most segregated hour in the nation." Michael Emerson asks why this is the case and, perhaps more important, what are the social characteristics of racially integrated congregations. Finally, Shannon Zenk and associates expose the extent to which space gets raced in their study of which neighborhoods have access to large supermarkets and which ones must rely on the corner store or bodega for their groceries. ✳

15 Race Prejudice as a Sense of Group Position

Herbert Blumer

The late **HERBERT BLUMER** spent most of his professional career at the University of Chicago and the University of California, Berkeley. Blumer established symbolic interactionism as a major sociological perspective in American sociology.

Questions to Consider   Herbert Blumer writes, "to characterize another racial group is, by opposition, to define one's own group." How does a "sense of group position" shape how we see other racial and ethnic groups? Have you ever defined your racial group membership in such a way as to heighten your group's status at the expense of another? What was the context?

IN THIS PAPER I AM PROPOSING AN APPROACH to the study of race prejudice different from that which dominates contemporary scholarly thought on this topic. My thesis is that race prejudice exists basically in a sense of group position rather than in a set of feelings which members of one racial group have toward the members of another racial group. This different way of viewing race prejudice shifts study and analysis from a preoccupation with feelings as lodged in individuals to a concern with the relationship of racial groups. It also shifts scholarly treatment away from individual lines of experience and focuses interest on the collective process by which a racial group comes to define and redefine another racial group. Such shifts, I believe, will yield a more realistic and penetrating understanding of race prejudice.

There can be little question that the rather vast literature on race prejudice is dominated by the idea that such prejudice exists fundamentally as a feeling or set of feelings lodged in the individual. It is usually depicted as consisting of feelings such as antipathy, hostility, hatred, intolerance, and aggressiveness. Accordingly, the task of scientific inquiry becomes two-fold. On one hand, there is a need to identify the feelings which make up race prejudice—to see how they fit together and how they are supported by other psychological elements, such as mythical beliefs. On the other hand, there is need of showing how the feeling complex has come into being. Thus, some scholars trace the complex feelings back chiefly to innate dispositions; some trace it to personality composition, such as authoritarian personality; and others regard the feelings of prejudice as being formed through social experience. However different may be the contentions regarding the makeup of racial prejudice and the way in which it may come into existence, these contentions are alike in locating prejudice in the realm of individual feeling. This is clearly true of the work of psychologists, psychiatrists, and social psychologists, and tends to be predominantly the case in the work of sociologists.

Unfortunately, this customary way of viewing race prejudice overlooks and obscures the fact that race prejudice is fundamentally a matter of relationship between racial groups. A little reflective thought should make this very clear. Race prejudice presupposes, necessarily, that racially prejudiced individuals think of themselves as belonging to a given racial group. It means, also, that they assign to other racial groups those against whom they are prejudiced. Thus, logically and actually, a scheme of racial identification is necessary as a framework for racial prejudice. Moreover, such identification involves the formation of an image or a conception of one's own racial group and of another racial group, inevitably in terms of the relationship of such groups. To fail to see that racial prejudice is a matter (a) of the racial identification made of oneself and of others, and (b) of the way in which the identified groups are conceived in relation to each other, is to miss what is logically and actually basic. One should keep clearly in mind that people necessarily come to identify themselves as belonging to a racial group; such identification is not spontaneous or inevitable but a result of experience. Further, one must realize that the kind of picture which a racial group forms of itself and the kind of picture which it may form of others are similarly products of experience. Hence, such pictures are variable, just as the lines of experience which produce them are variable.

The body of feelings which scholars, today, are so inclined to regard as constituting the substance of race prejudice is actually a resultant of the way in which given racial groups conceive of themselves and of others. A basic understanding of race prejudice must be sought in the process by which racial groups form images of themselves and of others. This process, as I hope to show, is fundamentally *a collective process*. It operates chiefly through the public media in which individuals who are accepted as the spokesmen of a racial group characterize publicly another racial group. To characterize another racial group is, by opposition, to define one's own group. This is equivalent to placing the two groups in relation to each other, or defining their positions *vis-à-vis* each other. It is the *sense of social position* emerging from this collective process of characterization which provides the basis of race prejudice. The following discussion will consider important facets of this matter.

I would like to begin by discussing several of the important feelings that enter into race prejudice. This discussion will reveal how fundamentally racial feelings point to and depend on a positional arrangement of the racial groups. In this discussion I will confine myself to such feelings in the case of a dominant racial group.

There are four basic types of feeling that seem to be always present in race prejudice in the dominant group. They are **(1) a feeling of superiority, (2) a feeling that the subordinate race is intrinsically different and alien, (3) a feeling of proprietary claim to certain areas of privilege and advantage, and (4) a fear and suspicion that the subordinate race harbors designs on the prerogatives of the dominant race.** A few words about each of these four feelings will suffice.

In race prejudice there is a self-assured feeling on the part of the dominant racial group of being naturally superior or better. This is commonly shown in a disparagement of the qualities of the subordinate racial group. Condemnatory or debasing traits, such as laziness, dishonesty, greediness, unreliability, stupidity, deceit and immorality, are usually imputed to it. The second feeling, that the subordinate race is an alien and fundamentally different stock, is likewise always present. "They are not of our kind" is a common way in which this is likely to be expressed. It is this feeling that reflects, justifies, and promotes the social exclusion of the subordinate racial group. The combination of these two feelings of superiority and of distinctiveness can easily give rise to feelings of aversion and even antipathy. But in themselves they do not form prejudice. We have to introduce the third and fourth types of feeling.

The third feeling, the sense of proprietary claim, is of crucial importance. It is the feeling on the part of the dominant group of being entitled to either exclusive or prior rights in many important areas of life. The range of such exclusive or prior claims may be wide, covering the ownership of property such as choice lands and sites; the right to certain jobs, occupations or professions; the claim to certain kinds of industry or lines of business; the claim to certain positions of control and decision-making as in government and law; the right to exclusive membership in given institutions such as schools, churches and recreational institutions; the claim to certain positions of social prestige and to the display of the symbols and accoutrements of these positions; and the claim to certain areas of intimacy and privacy. The feeling of such proprietary claims is exceedingly strong in race prejudice. Again, however, this feeling even in combination with the feeling of superiority and the feeling of distinctiveness does not explain race prejudice. These three feelings are present frequently in societies showing no prejudice, as in certain forms of feudalism, in caste relations, in societies of chiefs and commoners, and under many settled relations of conquerors and conquered. Where claims are solidified into a structure which is accepted or respected by all, there seems to be no group prejudice.

The remaining feeling essential to race prejudice is a fear or apprehension that the subordinate racial group is threatening, or will threaten, the position of the dominant group. Thus, acts or suspected acts that are interpreted as an attack on the natural superiority of the dominant group, or an intrusion into their sphere of group exclusiveness, or an encroachment on their area of proprietary claim are crucial in arousing and fashioning race prejudice. These acts mean "getting out of place."

It should be clear that these four basic feelings of race prejudice definitely refer to a positional arrangement of the racial groups. The feeling of superiority places the subordinate people *below;* the feeling of alienation places them *beyond;* the feeling of proprietary claim excludes them from the prerogatives of position; and the fear of encroachment is an emotional recoil from the endangering of group position. As these features suggest, the positional relation of the two racial groups is crucial in race prejudice. The dominant group is not concerned with the subordinate group as such but it is deeply concerned with its position *vis-à-vis* the subordinate group. This is epitomized in the key and universal expression that a given race is all right in "its place." The sense of group position is the very heart of the relation of the dominant to the subordinate group. It supplies the dominant group with its framework of perception, its standard of judgment, its patterns of sensitivity, and its emotional proclivities.

It is important to recognize that this sense of group position transcends the feelings of the individual members of the dominant group, giving such members a common orientation that is not otherwise to be found in separate feelings and views. There is likely to be considerable difference between the ways in which the individual members of the dominant group think and feel about the subordinate group. Some may feel bitter and hostile, with strong antipathies, with an exalted sense of superiority and with a lot of spite; others may have charitable and protective feelings, marked by a sense of piety and tinctured by benevolence; others may be condescending and reflect mild contempt; and others may be disposed to politeness and considerateness with no feelings of truculence. These are only a few of many different patterns of feeling to be found among members of the dominant racial group. What gives a common dimension to them is a sense of the social position of their group. Whether the members be humane, or callous, cultured or unlettered, liberal or reactionary, powerful or impotent, arrogant or humble, rich or poor, honorable or dishonorable—all are led, by virtue of sharing the sense of group position, to similar individual positions.

The sense of group position is a general kind of orientation. It is a general feeling without being reducible to specific feelings like hatred, hostility or antipathy. It is also a general understanding without being composed of any set of specific beliefs. On the social psychological side it cannot be equated to a sense of social status as ordinarily conceived, for it refers not merely to vertical positioning but to many other lines of position independent of the vertical dimension. Sociologically it is not a mere reflection of the objective relations between racial groups. Rather, it stands for "what ought to be" rather than for "what is." It is a sense of where the two racial groups *belong.*

In its own way, the sense of group position is a norm and imperative—indeed a very powerful one. It guides, incites, cows, and coerces. It should be borne in mind that this sense of group position stands for and involves a fundamental kind of group affiliation for the members of the dominant racial group. To the extent they recognize or feel themselves as belonging to that group they will automatically come under the influence of the sense of position held by that group. Thus, even though given individual members may have personal views and feelings different from the sense of group position, they will have to conjure with the sense of group position held by their racial group. If the sense of position is strong, to act contrary to it is to risk a feeling of self-alienation and to face the possibility of ostracism. I am trying to suggest, accordingly, that the locus of race prejudice is not in the area of individual feeling but in the definition of the respective positions of the racial groups.

The source of race prejudice lies in a felt challenge to this sense of group position. The challenge, one must recognize, may come in many different ways. It may be in the form of an affront to feelings of group superiority; it may be in the form of attempts at familiarity or transgressing the boundary line of group exclusiveness; it may be in the form of encroachment at countless points of proprietary claim; it may be a challenge to power and privilege; it may take the form of economic competition. Race prejudice is a defensive reaction to such challenging of the sense of group position. It consists of the disturbed feelings, usually of marked hostility, that are thereby aroused. As such, race prejudice is a protective device. It functions, however short-sightedly, to preserve the integrity and the position of the dominant group.

It is crucially important to recognize that the sense of group position is not a mere summation of the feelings of position such as might be developed independently by separate individuals as they come to compare themselves with given individuals of the subordinate race. The sense of group position refers to the position of group to group, not to that of individual to individual. Thus, *vis-à-vis* the subordinate racial group the unlettered individual with low status in the dominant racial group has a sense of group position common to that of the elite of his group. By virtue of sharing this sense of position such an individual, despite his low status, feels that members of the subordinate group, however distinguished and accomplished, are somehow inferior, alien, and properly restricted in the area of claims. He forms his conception as a representative of the dominant group; he treats individual members of the subordinate group as representative of that group.

An analysis of how the sense of group position is formed should start with a clear recognition that it is an historical product. It is set originally by conditions of initial contact. Prestige, power, possession of skill, numbers, original self-conceptions, aims, designs and opportunities are a few of the factors that may fashion the original sense of group position. Subsequent experience in the relation of the two racial groups, especially in the area of claims, opportunities and advantages, may mold the sense of group position in many diverse ways. Further, the sense of group position may be intensified or weakened, brought to sharp focus or dulled. It may be deeply entrenched and tenaciously resist change for long periods of time. Or it may never take root. It may undergo quick growth and vigorous expansion, or it may dwindle away through slow-moving erosion. It may be firm or soft, acute or dull, continuous or intermittent. In short, viewed comparatively, the sense of group position is very variable.

However variable its particular career, the sense of group position is clearly formed by a running process in which the dominant racial group is led to define and redefine the subordinate racial group and the relations between them. There are two important aspects of this process of definition that I wish to single out for consideration.

First, the process of definition occurs obviously through complex interaction and communication between the members of the dominant group. Leaders, prestige bearers, officials, group agents, dominant individuals and ordinary laymen present to one another characterizations of the subordinate group and express their feelings and ideas on the relations. Through talk, tales, stories, gossip, anecdotes, messages, pronouncements, news accounts, orations, sermons, preachments and the like definitions are presented and feelings are expressed. In

this usually vast and complex interaction separate views run against one another, influence one another, modify each other, incite one another and fuse together in new forms. Correspondingly, feelings which are expressed meet, stimulate each other, feed on each other, intensify each other and emerge in new patterns. Currents of view and currents of feeling come into being; sweeping along to positions of dominance and serving as polar points for the organization of thought and sentiment. If the interaction becomes increasingly circular and reinforcing, devoid of serious inner opposition, such currents grow, fuse and become strengthened. It is through such a process that a collective image of the subordinate group is formed and a sense of group position is set. The evidence of such a process is glaring when one reviews the history of any racial arrangement marked by prejudice.

Such a complex process of mutual interaction with its different lines and degrees of formation gives the lie to the many schemes which would lodge the cause of race prejudice in the makeup of the individual—whether in the form of innate disposition, constitutional makeup, personality structure, or direct personal experience with members of the other race. The collective image and feelings in race prejudice are forged out of a complicated social process in which the individual is himself shaped and organized. The scheme, so popular today, which would trace race prejudice to a so-called authoritarian personality shows a grievous misunderstanding of the simple essentials of the collective process that leads to a sense of group position.

The second important aspect of the process of group definition is that it is necessarily concerned with *an abstract image* of the subordinate racial group. The subordinate racial group is defined as if it were an entity or whole. This entity or whole—like the Negro race, or the Japanese, or the Jews—is necessarily an abstraction, never coming within the perception of any of the senses. While actual encounters are with individuals, the picture formed of the racial group is necessarily of a vast entity which spreads out far beyond such individuals and transcends experience with such individuals. The implications of the fact that the collective image is of an abstract group are of crucial significance. I would like to note four of these implications.

First, the building of the image of the abstract group takes place in the area of the remote and not of the near. It is not the experience with concrete individuals in daily association that gives rise to the definitions of the extended, abstract group. Such immediate experience is usually regulated and orderly. Even where such immediate experience is disrupted the new definitions which are formed are limited to the individuals involved. The collective image of the abstract group grows up not by generalizing from experiences gained in close, first-hand contacts but through the transcending characterizations that are made of the group as an entity. Thus, one must seek the central stream of definition in those areas where the dominant group as such is characterizing the subordinate group as such. This occurs in the "public arena" wherein the spokesmen appear as representatives and agents of the dominant group. The extended public arena is constituted by such things as legislative assemblies, public meetings, conventions, the press, and the printed word. What goes on in this public arena attracts the attention of large numbers of the dominant group and is felt as the voice and action of the group as such.

Second, the definitions that are forged in the public arena center, obviously, about matters that are felt to be of major importance. Thus, we are led to recognize the crucial role of the "big event" in developing a conception of the subordinate racial group. The happening that seems momentous, that touches deep sentiments, that seems to raise fundamental questions about relations, and that awakens strong feelings of identification with one's racial group is the kind of event that is central in the formation of the racial image. Here, again, we note the relative unimportance of the huge bulk of experiences coming from daily contact with individuals of the subordinate group. It is the events seemingly loaded with great collective significance that are the focal points of the public discussion. The definition of these events is chiefly responsible for the development of a racial image and of the sense of group position. When this public discussion takes the form of a denunciation of the subordinate racial group, signifying that it is unfit and a threat, the discussion becomes particularly potent in shaping the sense of social position.

Third, the major influence in public discussion is exercised by individuals and groups who have the public ear and who are felt to have standing, prestige, authority and power. Intellectual and social elites, public figures of prominence, and leaders of powerful organizations are likely to be the key figures in the formation of the sense of group position and in the characterization of the subordinate group. It is well to note this in view of the not infrequent tendency of students to regard race prejudice as growing out of the multiplicity of experiences and attitudes of the bulk of the people.

Fourth, we also need to perceive the appreciable opportunity that is given to strong interest groups in directing the lines of discussion and setting the interpretations that arise in such discussion. Their self-interests may dictate the kind of position they wish the dominant racial group to enjoy. It may be a position which enables them to retain certain advantages, or even more to gain still greater advantages. Hence, they may be vigorous in seeking to manufacture events to attract public attention and to set lines of issue in such a way as to predetermine interpretations favorable to their interests. The role of strongly organized groups seeking to further special interest is usually central in the formation of collective images of abstract groups. Historical records of major instances of race relations, as in our South, or in South Africa, or in Europe in the case of the Jew, or on the West Coast in the case of the Japanese, show the formidable part played by interest groups in defining the subordinate racial group.

I conclude this highly condensed paper with two further observations that may throw additional light on the relation of the sense of group position to race prejudice. Race prejudice becomes entrenched and tenacious to the extent the prevailing social order is rooted in the sense of social position. This has been true of the historic South in our country. In such a social order race prejudice tends to become chronic and impermeable to change. In other places the social order may be affected only to a limited extent by the sense of group position held by the dominant racial group. This I think has been true usually in the case of anti-Semitism in Europe and this country. Under these conditions the sense of group position tends to be weaker and more vulnerable. In turn, race prejudice has a much more variable and intermittent career, usually becoming pronounced only as a consequence of grave disorganizing events that allow for the formation of a scapegoat.

This leads me to my final observation which in a measure is an indirect summary. The sense of group position dissolves and race prejudice declines when the process of running definition does not keep abreast of major shifts in the social order. When events touching on relations are not treated as "big events" and hence do not set crucial issues in the arena of public discussion; or when the elite leaders or spokesmen do not define such big events vehemently or adversely; or where they define them in the direction of racial harmony; or when there is a paucity of strong interest groups seeking to build up a strong adverse image for special advantage—under such conditions the sense of group position recedes and race prejudice declines.

The clear implication of my discussion is that the proper and fruitful area in which race prejudice should be studied is the collective process through which a sense of group position is formed. To seek, instead, to understand it or to handle it in the arena of individual feeling and of individual experience seems to me to be clearly misdirected.

Seeing the Big Picture   Racism: Group Position or Individual Belief?

Blumer explains that four "feelings" make up race prejudice. Are you able to come up with an example of each of these four feelings for a specific racial or ethnic group? Are you convinced by his argument that racism is "a fundamental matter of relationship between racial groups" rather than individual-level feelings of animosity?

---

16   Race and Gender Discrimination: Contemporary Trends

James Sterba

JAMES STERBA is Professor of Philosophy at the University of Notre Dame.

———

SURVEYS IN THE UNITED STATES TODAY SHOW that white Americans overwhelmingly publicly ascribe to principles of racial equality and integration.[1] At the same time, 80 percent of whites recently surveyed deny that racial discrimination against people of color is a significant problem.[2] In another survey, 70 percent of whites believe that blacks are treated equally in their communities. In this survey, 80 percent of whites also thought that underrepresented groups, such as blacks and Latinos, receive equal, if not preferred, treatment in education.[3] Another recent survey found that 68 percent of whites think that blacks have the same or more opportunities than whites to be "really successful and wealthy." According to this survey, a majority of whites think that educationally the average black American is just as well off as, or better off than, the average white

Questions to Consider   There is a tendency to think of race- or ethnicity-based discrimination as a thing of the past. Indeed polling data now tell us that a majority of Americans believe that these types of behaviors are anomalies. In the abstract Americans believe in equality, but survey research, matching studies, and ethnographic research suggest that discrimination against racial minorities and women is still commonly practiced. How can we espouse the idea that everyone should be treated as equals when discrimination remains a fact of life for so many Americans? Why does it appear that race-based discriminatory treatment remains such an entrenched facet of American society?

American; 47 percent think that blacks and whites enjoy the same standard of living. Still another survey found that most Americans believe that "reverse discrimination" is the predominant type of discrimination in the United States.[4]

Surprisingly, however, similar views were expressed in a poll taken in 1962, two years before the Civil Rights Act overcame a historic eighty-three-day filibuster in the Senate and made its way through the U.S. Congress. In that poll, more than nine in ten whites said that whites and blacks had just as good a chance for a quality education.[5] They said so even though at that time, despite two *Brown v. Board a/Education* Supreme Court decisions, **de jure segregation** still held sway throughout most of the South. In the 1963–64 school year in the eleven states of the former Confederacy, only 1.17 percent of black students were attending schools with white students.[6]

Nevertheless, many today would hold that the view shared by a large majority of white Americans in 1962 was at the time fundamentally mistaken and grounded in underlying racial prejudice. But what about the views of the greater majority of white Americans today, as reflected in the surveys I have just cited? Might not they also be mistaken for somewhat similar reasons?

Consider the following data: In the United States today almost half of all black children live in poverty. Black unemployment is twice that of white, and the median net worth of white families is ten times that of black families. The infant mortality rate in many black communities is twice that of whites. Blacks are twice as likely as whites to be robbed, seven times more likely to be murdered or to die of tuberculosis. A male living in the Harlem neighborhood of New York City is less likely to reach age sixty-five than a resident of Bangladesh. According to a United Nations study, white Americans, when considered as a separate nation, rank first in the world in well-being (a measure that combines life expectancy, educational achievements, and income). African Americans rank twenty-seventh, and Hispanic Americans even lower at thirty-second.[7]

Yet these particular disparities between blacks and whites could be just the result of past discrimination. They do not necessarily provide evidence of current ongoing

racial discrimination, although they do undercut the view that blacks and whites enjoy the same standard of living. Consider then the following data:

- According to a recent study of the U.S. Federal Reserve Board, the loan rejection rate for blacks in the highest income bracket is identical to the rejection rate of whites in the lowest income bracket. In another study, minority applicants are 50 percent more likely to be denied a loan than white applicants of equivalent economic status.[8]

- According to a study done at the University of Colorado at Boulder, blacks seeking business loans were two to three times more likely to be rejected than whites, and blacks were twelve times more likely to be rejected than whites at the highest levels of assets and collateral.[9]

- In a study by the Urban Institute equally qualified, identically dressed, white and African American applicants for jobs were used to test for bias in the job market for newspaper-advertised positions. White and African Americans were matched identically for age, work experience, speech patterns, personal characteristics, and physical build. The study found repeated discrimination against African American male applicants. The white men received three times as many job offers as equally qualified African Americans who interviewed for the same positions.[10]

- According to a 1998 study conducted by the Fair Housing Council in Washington, DC, minorities in the United States are discriminated against 40 percent of the time when they attempt to rent apartments or buy homes.[11]

- Another study revealed that African American and Hispanic American job applicants suffer blatant and easily identifiable discrimination one in every five times they apply for a job.[12]

- African American men with bachelor's degrees earn as much as $15,180 less than their white counterparts. Although native-born white males make up only 41 percent of the U.S. population, they comprise 80 percent of all tenured professors, 97 percent of all school superintendents, and 97 percent of senior managerial positions in Fortune 1000 industrial and Fortune 500 service companies. African Americans hold only 0.6 percent, Hispanic Americans 0.4 percent, and Asian Americans 0.3 percent of the senior managerial positions.[13]

De Jure Segregation Segregation sanctioned and enforced by law.

- Many blacks are overqualified for the jobs they hold. It has been estimated that the failure to employ blacks in jobs for which they are overqualified resulted in a $241 billion loss to the U.S. economy in 1993.[14]
- In resume-only tests, whites were almost twice as likely as blacks to be blatantly preferred, despite their having less objective experience and fewer credentials.[15]
- In studies done in New York City and Milwaukee whites with prison records were more likely to be hired than black men without prison records.[16]
- A study of Bay Area employment agencies found that white job applicants were preferred three times as often to equally matched black applicants.[17]
- One study done in the Los Angeles area found that race and skin color affected the probability of obtaining employment by as much as 52 percent. Though whites and light-skinned African Americans were relatively likely to find employment when searching for a job, dark-skinned men were not. In fact, dark-skinned men were twice as likely as others to remain unemployed. According to another study only 10.3 percent of light-skinned African Americans men with thirteen or more years of schooling were unemployed, compared with 19.4 percent of their dark-skinned counterparts. Among men who had participated in job-training programs, light-skinned blacks actually had a lower jobless rate than their white counterparts—11.1 percent, compared with 14.5 percent. Yet the rate for dark-skinned African American men with job training was 26.8 percent.[18]
- The bipartisan Glass Ceiling Commission found that Asian American men earned between 83 and 90 percent of what white men with the same credentials earned. The figure was about 60 percent for Asian American women.[19]
- In elementary and high schools, according to a national study, even when blacks demonstrate equal ability with whites, they are still far less likely to be placed in advanced classes. Even when children from lower income families, who are disproportionately of color, answer correctly all the math questions on a standardized test, it turns out that they are still less likely to be placed in advanced tracks than kids from upper income families who miss one-fourth of the questions on that test.[20]

- In a study of medical care racial and ethnic minorities were given poorer care than whites even when their income levels and insurance were the same.[21]
- Although blacks are more susceptible to kidney disease than whites, they are only half as likely as whites to be given a transplant, and those approved for a transplant have to wait twice as long as whites.[22]
- Blacks constitute about 13 percent of drug users in the United States but they make up 58 percent of those sent to prison for drug possession.[23] In Illinois, blacks are jailed for selling or using drugs at fifty-seven times the rate of whites.[24]
- Convicted murderers of whites are eleven times more likely to be condemned to death than convicted murderers of blacks.[25] Although approximately 50 percent of murder victims each year are black, 80 percent of victims in death row cases are white and only 14 percent are black.[26]

There is also evidence of considerable race-based environmental inequities. Consider the following data:

- Penalties under hazardous waste laws at sites having the greatest white population were 500 percent higher than penalties at sites with the greatest minority population, averaging $335,566 in white areas, compared with $55,318 in minority areas.[27]
- The disparity under toxic waste law occurs by race and not by income. The average penalty in areas with the lowest median income is only 3 percent higher or lower than the average penalty in areas with the highest median income.[28]
- For all the federal environmental laws aimed at protecting citizens from air, water, and waste pollution, penalties in white communities were 46 percent higher than in minority communities.[29]
- Under the giant Superfund cleanup program, abandoned hazardous waste sites in minority areas take 20 percent longer to be placed on the national priority action list than those in white areas.[30]
- In Tacoma, Washington, where paper mills and other industrial polluters ruined the salmon streams and the way of life of a Native American tribe, the government did not include the tribe in assessing the pollution's impact on residents' health.[31]

- Three of every five African and Hispanic Americans live in a community with uncontrolled toxic waste sites.[32]

Surely, this data provides plenty of evidence that, at least in the United States, African Americans and other minorities currently experience considerable discrimination. Surely, this data also radically undercuts the view of the greater majority of white Americans today that racial discrimination is a thing of the past.

Unfortunately, in this respect white Americans today may not be all that different from their counterparts in 1962 despite the fact that they now judge their 1962 counterparts to have been grossly mistaken in their views. This is because white Americans today, or at least a majority of them, when faced with the hard-to-ignore evidence of current racial discrimination, have yet to reach a similar conclusion about their own views on the subject.

With respect to sexual discrimination, the situation is more difficult to assess because it is harder to find surveys indicating what the majority of men think about the prevalence of sexual discrimination in the United States. Yet there are a number of self-styled experts on gender relations—like Warren Farrell, author of the best-selling *The Myth of Male Power*—who argue that women have now achieved equality with men. According to these experts, the real problem we encounter today is that feminists want to push beyond equality to secure special advantages for women, which have the effect of discriminating against men.[33] Yet whether most men would agree with Farrell that it is now they who are primarily being discriminated against based on their sex, many men—especially after the nearly successful campaign of Hilary Clinton for the 2008 Democratic Party presidential nomination—would surely agree with Farrell that discrimination against women has become, for all practical purposes, a thing of the past.

Yet consider the following data:

- Comparing the annual income of full-time workers with four-year degrees or more, women in the United States earn, on average, only 72 cents for every dollar men earn. Put another way, a college-educated women working full-time earns $44,200 a year compared to $61,800 for her male counterpart—a difference of $17,600. For a woman working thirty years, the difference exceeds half a million dollars.[34] Moreover, if part-time workers are included in this comparison, the gap in the United States rises, with women earning only about half of what men earn.[35]

- Women now hold 70 percent of white-collar positions but only 10 percent of management positions. There are only two women CEOs in Fortune 1000 companies.[36]

- College-educated Hispanic women annually earn $1,600 less than white male high school graduates and nearly $16,000 less than college-educated white men. College-educated black women annually earn only $1,500 more than white male high school graduates and almost $13,000 less than college-educated white men.[37]

- College-educated white women earn only $3,000 more than white male high school graduates and $11,500 less than college-educated white men. Women with identical credentials are also promoted at approximately one-half the rate of their male counterparts.[38]

- A National Bureau of Economic Research project sent equally qualified pairs of male and female applicants to seek jobs at a range of Philadelphia restaurants. This "audit" found that high-priced restaurants offering good pay and tips were twice as likely to offer jobs to the male applicants over their equally qualified female counterparts.[39]

There is also a high incidence of sexual harassment in the workplace in the United States.

- In research conducted by psychologists 50 percent of women questioned in the workplace said they had been sexually harassed.[40]

- According to the U.S. Merit Systems Protection Board, within the federal government, 56 percent of 8,500 female civilian workers surveyed claimed to have experienced sexual harassment.[41]

- According to the *National Law Journal,* 64 percent of women in "pink-collar" jobs reported being sexually harassed and 60 percent of 3,000 women lawyers at 250 top law firms said that they had been harassed at some point in their careers.[42]

- In a survey by *Working Women* magazine 60 percent of high-ranking corporate women said they have been harassed; 33 percent more knew of others who had been.[43]

- Similarly, in a survey of 90,000 female soldiers, sailors, and pilots, 60 percent said they had been sexually harassed. Only 47 percent of the Army women surveyed said that they believed their leaders were serious about putting a stop to sexual harassment.[44]
- According to another study, 66 percent of women in the military experienced at least one form of sexual harassment in the past year.[45]
- Another study found that 50 percent of women at the U.S. Naval Academy, 59 percent at the U.S. Air Force Academy, and 76 percent at the U.S. Military Academy experienced some form of sexual harassment at least twice a month.[46]
- According to a 2002 study by the U.S. Department of Defense over 60 percent of women in the military experienced some type of sexual harassment, down from 78 percent in 1995.[47]

There have also been legal cases brought for sexual harassment where large settlements have been paid out. For example, in 1998 Dupont Corporation paid out $3.53 million in a jury award to a peroxide departmental operator who was driven out of her job because of her sex. In 2002, the New York City Police Department paid $1.85 million in a jury award to a police officer who was forced out in retaliation for a sexual harassment complaint. In 2004, Home Depot paid a $5.5 million settlement to an employee for hostile environment sexual harassment and retaliation.[48]

There is plenty of evidence that women have also been neglected in medical research. For example, the Multiple Risk Factor Intervention Trial (MR. FIT)—a study to evaluate the impact of various activities on the risk of heart attack—was conducted with 12,866 men and 0 women. Other examples include the Health Professionals Follow-Up Study examining the relation of coffee consumption and heart disease, which was done with 45,589 men and 0 women; and the Physicians' Health Study on the effects of aspirin on the risk of heart attack, which was done with 22,071 male but no female physicians.[49] In addition, women had not been included in drug trials in the United States, even though they consume roughly 80 percent of pharmaceuticals. Drugs such as Valium were not tested on women, even though 2 million women took the drug each year.[50]

The General Accounting Office report found that fewer than half of publicly available prescription drugs in the United States had been analyzed for gender-related differences in response.[51] As a result, frequently prescribed drugs and dosages were based on men's conditions and average weights and metabolisms. This led to twice as many adverse reactions to drugs in women as in men.[52] For example, some clot-dissolving drugs that are useful for treating heart attacks in men were found to cause bleeding problems in women, and some drugs that are commonly used to treat high blood pressure tended to lower men's mortality from heart attack while raising women's. Other drugs (for example, antidepressants) varied in their effects over the course of a women's menstrual cycle such that a constant dosage of an antidepressant may be too high at some points in a woman's cycle and too low at others. Still other drugs (for example, acetaminophen, an ingredient in many pain relievers) are eliminated in women at slower rates than they are eliminated in men. Not only were drugs developed for men that turned out to be potentially dangerous for women, but also drugs that were potentially beneficial for women may have been eliminated in early testing because the test group did not include women.[53]

Similar problems plagued AIDS research. As late as 1991, neither of the two U.S. institutions that distributed funds for AIDS research had funded a major project to address whether women with AIDS experienced different symptoms than men.[54] As a result, the official definition of AIDS did not originally include many of the HIV-related conditions in women because what was known about the disease was derived principally from research on men. In fact, most early studies on women were largely restricted to preventing the transmission of HIV from mother to child.[55] This resulted in little information on the progress of the disease in women themselves. Consequently, most health-care workers were unable to diagnose AIDS in women until the disease had advanced significantly. On average, men died thirty months after diagnosis, while women died only fifteen weeks after diagnosis.[56] All of this data surely indicates that women are still being discriminated against in a variety of ways.[57]

It is in the face of this considerable evidence of existing racial and sexual discrimination that we now turn to the question of the justification for affirmation action.

One of the reasons frequently offered for rejecting affirmative action is that racial and sexual discrimination is a thing of the past, and so affirmative action is no longer needed. Confronted with all the evidence of existing racial and sexual discrimination surveyed in this chapter, we know that this reason for rejecting affirmative action is not credible. Of course, there may be other telling reasons against affirmative action, but it is important to recognize that as we now turn to the question of whether affirmative action can be justified, by first examining the history of the practice, we do so for a society where various forms of racial and sexual discrimination are still widespread.

17 Discrimination and the American Creed

Robert K. Merton

The late ROBERT K. MERTON was an eminent sociological theorist and a well-known defender of sociology as a genuine science. His publications include *On the Shoulders of Giants: A Shandean Postscript* (1965) and *The Sociology of Science: Theoretical and Empirical Investigations* (1973).

Questions to Consider   Have you ever been in a situation in which social, economic, or peer pressure forced you to treat someone from a different racial group in an inappropriate way? Robert Merton suggests that individuals who are *not* prejudiced often act in bigoted and discriminatory ways. How and why does this happen? Is it possible to live our lives in the category Merton calls the "unprejudiced non-discriminator"?

THE PRIMARY FUNCTION OF THE SOCIOLOGIST is to search out the determinants and consequences of diverse forms of social behavior. To the extent that he succeeds in fulfilling this role, he clarifies the alternatives of organized social action in a given situation and of the probable outcome of each. To this extent, there is no sharp distinction between pure research and applied research. Rather, the difference is one between research with direct implications for particular problems of social action and research which is remote from these problems. Not infrequently, basic research which has succeeded only in clearing up previously confused concepts may have an immediate bearing upon the problems of men in society to a degree not approximated by applied research oriented exclusively to these problems. At least, this is the assumption underlying the present paper: clarification of apparently unclear and confused concepts in the sphere of race and ethnic relations is a step necessarily prior to the devising of effective programs for reducing intergroup conflict and for promoting equitable access to economic and social opportunities. . . .

The American Creed: As Cultural Ideal, Personal Belief and Practice

The American **creed** as set forth in the Declaration of Independence, the preamble of the Constitution and the Bill of Rights has often been misstated. This part of the cultural heritage does *not* include the patently false assertion that all men are created equal in capacity or endowment. It does *not* imply that an Einstein and a moron are equal in intellectual capacity or that Joe Louis and a small, frail

creed In the context of this article, the belief system that a people share.

Columbia professor (or a Mississippian Congressman) are equally endowed with brawny arms harboring muscles as strong as iron bands. It does *not* proclaim universal equality of innate intellectual or physical endowment.

Instead, the creed asserts the indefeasible principle of the human right to full equity—the right of equitable access to justice, freedom and opportunity, irrespective of race or religion or ethnic origin. It proclaims further the universalist doctrine of the dignity of the individual, irrespective of the groups of which he is a part. It is a creed announcing full moral equities for all, not an absurd myth affirming the equality of intellectual and physical capacity of all men everywhere. And it goes on to say that though men differ in innate endowment, they do so as individuals, not by virtue of their group memberships.

Viewed sociologically, the creed is a set of values and precepts embedded in American culture, to which Americans are expected to conform. It is a complex of affirmations, rooted in the historical past and ceremonially celebrated in the present, partly enacted in the laws of the land and partly not. Like all creeds, it is a profession of faith, a part of cultural tradition sanctified by the larger traditions of which it is a part.

It would be a mistaken sociological assertion, however, to suggest that the creed is a fixed and static cultural constant, unmodified in the course of time, just as it would be an error to imply that as an integral part of culture, it evenly blankets all subcultures of the national society. It is indeed dynamic, subject to change and in turn promoting change in other spheres of culture and society. It is, moreover, unevenly distributed throughout the society, being institutionalized as an integral part of local culture in some regions of the society and rejected in others.

. . . Learned men and men in high public positions have repeatedly observed and deplored the disparity between ethos and behavior in the sphere of race and ethnic relations. In his magisterial volumes on the American Negro, for example, Gunnar Myrdal called this gulf between creed and conduct "an American dilemma," and centered his attention on the prospect of narrowing or closing the gap. The President's Committee on Civil Rights, in their report to the nation, and . . . President [Truman] himself, in a message to Congress, have called public attention to this "serious gap between our ideals and some of our practices."

But as valid as these observations may be, they tend so to simplify the relations between creed and conduct as to be seriously

misleading both for social policy and for social science. All these high authorities notwithstanding, the problems of racial and ethnic inequities are not expressible as a discrepancy between high cultural principles and low social conduct. It is a relation not between two variables, official creed and private practice, but between three: first, the cultural creed honored in cultural tradition and partly enacted into law; second, the beliefs and attitudes of individuals regarding the principles of the creed; and third, the actual practices of individuals with reference to it.

Once we substitute these three variables of cultural ideal, belief and actual practice for the customary distinction between the two variables of cultural ideals and actual practices, the entire formulation of the problem becomes changed. We escape from the virtuous but ineffectual impasse of deploring the alleged hypocrisy of many Americans into the more difficult but potentially effectual realm of analyzing the problem in hand.

To describe the problem and to proceed to its analysis, it is necessary to consider the official creed, individuals' beliefs and attitudes concerning the creed, and their actual behavior. Once stated, the distinctions are readily applicable. Individuals may *recognize* the creed as part of a cultural tradition, *without having any private conviction of its moral validity or its binding quality.* Thus, so far as the beliefs of individuals are concerned, we can identify two types: those who genuinely believe in the creed and those who do not (although some of these may, on public or ceremonial occasions, profess adherence to its principles). Similarly, with respect to actual practices: conduct may or may not conform to the creed. But, and this is the salient consideration: *conduct may or may not conform with individuals' own beliefs concerning the moral claims of all men to equal opportunity.*

Stated in formal sociological terms, this asserts that attitudes and overt behavior vary independently. *Prejudicial attitudes need not coincide with discriminatory behavior.* The implications of this statement can be drawn out in terms of a logical syntax whereby the variables are diversely combined, as can be seen in the following typology.

By exploring the interrelations between prejudice and discrimination, we can identify four major types in terms of their attitudes toward the creed and their behavior with respect to it. Each type is found in every region and social class, though in varying numbers. By examining each type, we shall be better prepared to understand their interdependence and the appropriate types of action for curbing ethnic discrimination. The folklabels for each type are intended to aid in their prompt recognition.

Type I: The Unprejudiced Non-Discriminator or All-Weather Liberal

These are the racial and ethnic liberals who adhere to the creed in both belief and practice. They are neither prejudiced nor given to discrimination. Their orientation toward the creed is fixed and stable. Whatever the environing situation, they are likely to abide by their beliefs: hence, the *all-weather* liberal.

This is, of course, the strategic group which *can* act as the spearhead for the progressive extension of the creed into effective practice. They represent the solid foundation both for the measure of ethnic equities which now exist and for the future enlargement of these equities. Integrated with the creed in both belief and practice, they would seem most motivated to influence others toward the same democratic outlook. They represent a reservoir of culturally legitimatized goodwill which can be channeled into an active program for extending belief in the creed and conformity with it in practice.

Most important, as we shall see presently, the all-weather liberals comprise the group which can so reward others for conforming with the creed, as to transform deviants into conformists. They alone can provide the positive social environment for the other types who will no longer find it expedient or rewarding to retain their prejudices or discriminatory practices.

But though the ethnic liberal is a *potential* force for the successive extension of the American creed, he does not fully realize this potentiality in actual fact, for a variety of reasons. Among the limitations on effective action are several fallacies to which the ethnic liberal seems peculiarly subject. First among these is the *fallacy of group soliloquies.* Ethnic liberals are busily engaged in talking to themselves. Repeatedly, the same groups of like-minded liberals seek each other out, hold periodic meetings in which they engage in mutual exhortation and thus lend social and psychological support to one another. But however much these unwittingly self-selected audiences may reinforce the creed among themselves, they do not thus appreciably diffuse the creed in belief or practice to groups which depart from it in one respect or the other.

More, these group soliloquies in which there is typically wholehearted agreement among fellow-liberals tend to promote another fallacy limiting effective action. This is the *fallacy of unanimity.* Continued association with like-minded individuals tends to produce the illusion that a large measure of consensus has been achieved in the community at large. The unanimity regarding essential cultural axioms which obtains in these small groups provokes an overestimation of the strength of the movement and of its effective inroads upon the larger population which does not necessarily share these creedal axioms. Many also mistake participation in the groups of like-minded individuals for effective action. Discussion accordingly takes the place of action. The reinforcement of the creed for oneself is mistaken for the extension of the creed among those outside the limited circle of ethnic liberals.

Arising from adherence to the creed is a third limitation upon effective action, the *fallacy of privatized solutions* to the problem. The ethnic liberal, precisely because he is at one with the American creed, may rest content with his own individual behavior and thus see no need to do anything about the problem at large. Since his own spiritual house is in order, he is not motivated by guilt or shame to work on a collective problem. The very freedom of the liberal from guilt thus prompts him to secede from any *collective* effort to set the national house in order. He essays a *private* solution to a *social* problem. He assumes that numerous individual adjustments will serve in place of a collective adjustment. His outlook, compounded of good moral philosophy but poor sociology, holds that each individual must put his own house in order and fails to recognize that privatized solutions cannot be effected for problems which are essentially social in nature. For clearly, if each person *were* motivated to abide by the American creed, the problem would not be likely to exist in the first place. It is only when a social environment is established by conformists to the creed that deviants can in due course be brought to modify their behavior in the direction of conformity. But this "environment" can be constituted only through collective effort and not through private adherence to a public creed. Thus we have the paradox that the clear conscience of many ethnic liberals may promote the very social situation which permits deviations from the creed to continue unchecked. Privatized liberalism invites social inaction. Accordingly, there appears the phenomenon of the inactive or passive liberal, himself at spiritual ease, neither prejudiced nor discriminatory, but in a measure tending to contribute to the persistence of prejudice and discrimination through his very inaction.

The fallacies of group soliloquy, unanimity and privatized solutions thus operate to make the potential strength of the ethnic liberals unrealized in practice.

It is only by first recognizing these limitations that the liberal can hope to overcome them. With some hesitancy, one may suggest initial policies for curbing the scope of the three fallacies. The fallacy of group soliloquies can be removed only by having ethnic liberals enter into organized groups not comprised merely by fellow-liberals. This exacts a heavy price on the liberal. It means that he faces initial opposition and resistance rather than prompt consensus. It entails giving up the gratifications of consistent group support.

The fallacy of unanimity can in turn be reduced by coming to see that American society often provides large rewards for those who express their ethnic prejudice in discrimination. Only if the balance of rewards, material and psychological, is modified will behavior be modified. Sheer exhortation and propaganda are not enough. Exhortation verges on a belief in magic if it is not supported by appropriate changes in the social environment to make conformity with the exhortation rewarding.

Finally, the fallacy of privatized solutions requires the militant liberal to motivate the passive liberal to collective effort, possibly by inducing in him a sense of guilt for his unwitting contribution to the problems of ethnic inequities through his own systematic inaction.

One may suggest a unifying theme for the ethnic liberal: goodwill is not enough to modify social reality. It is only when this goodwill is harnessed to social-psychological realism that it can be used to reach cultural objectives.

Type II: The Unprejudiced Discriminator or Fair-Weather Liberal

The fair-weather liberal is the man of expediency who, despite his own freedom from prejudice, supports discriminatory practices when it is the easier or more profitable course. His expediency may take the form of holding his silence and thus implicitly acquiescing in expressions of ethnic prejudice by others or in the practice of discrimination by others. This is the expediency of the timid: the

liberal who hesitates to speak up against discrimination for fear he might lose status or be otherwise penalized by his prejudiced associates. Or his expediency may take the form of grasping at advantages in social and economic competition deriving solely from the ethnic status of competitors. This is the expediency of the self-assertive: the employer, himself not an anti-Semite or Negrophobe, who refuses to hire Jewish or Negro workers because "it might hurt business"; the trade union leader who expediently advocates racial discrimination in order not to lose the support of powerful Negrophobes in his union.

In varying degrees, the fair-weather liberal suffers from guilt and shame for departing from his own effective beliefs in the American creed. Each deviation through which he derives a limited reward from passively acquiescing in or actively supporting discrimination contributes cumulatively to this fund of guilt. He is, therefore, peculiarly vulnerable to the efforts of the all-weather liberal who would help him bring his conduct into accord with his beliefs, thus removing this source of guilt. He is the most amenable to cure, because basically he wants to be cured. His is a split conscience which motivates him to cooperate actively with those who will help remove the source of internal conflict. He thus represents the strategic group promising the largest returns for the least effort. Persistent re-affirmation of the creed will only intensify his conflict; but a long regimen in a favorable social climate can be expected to transform the fair-weather liberal into an all-weather liberal.

Type III: The Prejudiced Non-Discriminator or Fair-Weather Illiberal

The fair-weather illiberal is the reluctant conformist to the creed, the man of prejudice who does not believe in the creed but conforms to it in practice through fear of sanctions which might otherwise be visited upon him. You know him well: the prejudiced employer who discriminates against racial or ethnic groups until a Fair Employment Practice Commission, able and willing to enforce the law, puts the fear of punishment into him; the trade union leader, himself deeply prejudiced, who does away with Jim Crow in his union because the rank-and-file demands that it be done away with; the businessman who forgoes his own prejudices when he finds a profitable market among the very people he hates, fears or despises; the timid **bigot** who will not express his prejudices when he is in the presence of powerful men who vigorously and effectively affirm their belief in the American creed.

It should be clear that the fair-weather illiberal is the precise counterpart of the fair-weather liberal. Both are men of expediency, to be sure, but expediency dictates different courses of behavior in the two cases. The timid bigot conforms to the creed only when there is danger or loss in deviations, just as the timid liberal deviates from the creed when there is danger or loss in conforming. *Superficial similarity in behavior of the two in the same situation should not be permitted to cloak a basic difference in the meaning of this outwardly similar behavior,* a difference which is as important for social policy as it is for social science. Whereas the timid bigot is under strain when he conforms to the creed, the timid liberal is under strain when he deviates. For ethnic prejudice has deep roots in the character structure of the fair-weather bigot, and this will find overt expression unless there are powerful countervailing forces, institutional, legal and interpersonal. He does not accept the moral legitimacy of the creed; he conforms because he must, and will cease to conform when the pressure is removed. The fair-weather liberal, on the other hand, is effectively committed to the creed and does not require strong institutional pressure to conform; continuing interpersonal relations with all-weather liberals may be sufficient.

This is the one critical point at which the traditional formulation of the problem of ethnic discrimination as a departure from the creed can lead to serious errors of theory and practice. Overt behavioral deviation (or conformity) may signify importantly different situations, depending upon the underlying motivations. Knowing simply that ethnic discrimination is rife in a community does not, therefore, point to appropriate lines of social policy. It is necessary to know also the distribution of ethnic prejudices and basic motivations for these prejudices as well. Communities with the same amount of overt discrimination may represent vastly different types of problems, dependent on whether the population is comprised by a large nucleus of fair-weather liberals ready to abandon their discriminatory practices under slight interpersonal pressure or a large nucleus of fair-weather illiberals who will abandon discrimination only if major changes in the local institutional

bigot Someone deeply committed to his or her own prejudices, distortions, or biases regarding other people. Bigots are intolerant of difference.

setting can be effected. Any statement of the problem as a gulf between creedal ideals and prevailing practice is thus seen to be overly simplified in the precise sense of masking this decisive difference between the type of discrimination exhibited by the fair-weather liberal and by the fair-weather illiberal. That the gulf-between-ideal-and-practice does not adequately describe the nature of the ethnic problem will become more apparent as we turn to the fourth type in our inventory of prejudice and discrimination.

Type IV: The Prejudiced Discriminator or the All-Weather Illiberal

This type, too, is not unknown to you. He is the confirmed illiberal, the bigot pure and unashamed, the man of prejudice consistent in his departure from the American creed. In some measure, he is found everywhere in the land, though in varying numbers. He derives large social and psychological gains from his conviction that "any white man (including the village idiot) is 'better' than any nigger (including George Washington Carver)." He considers differential treatment of Negro and white not as "discrimination," in the sense of unfair treatment, but as "discriminating," in the sense of showing acute discernment. For him, it is as clear that one "ought" to accord a Negro and a white different treatment in a wide diversity of situations, as it is clear to the population at large that one "ought" to accord a child and an adult different treatment in many situations.

This illustrates anew my reason for questioning the applicability of the unusual formula of the American dilemma as a gap between lofty creed and low conduct. For the confirmed illiberal, ethnic discrimination does *not* represent a discrepancy between *his* ideals and *his* behavior. His ideals proclaim the right, even the duty, of discrimination. Accordingly, his behavior does not entail a sense of social deviation, with the resultant strains which this would involve. The ethnic illiberal is as much a conformist as the ethnic liberal. He is merely conforming to a different cultural and institutional pattern which is centered, not about the creed, but about a doctrine of essential inequality of status ascribed to those of diverse ethnic and racial origins. To overlook this is to overlook the well-known *fact* that our national culture is divided into a number of local subcultures which are not consistent among themselves in all respects. And again, to fail to take this fact of different subcultures into account is to open the door for all manner of errors of social policy in attempting to control the problems of racial and ethnic discrimination.

This view of the all-weather illiberal has one immediate implication with wide bearing upon social policies and sociological theory oriented toward the problem of discrimination. The extreme importance of the social surroundings of the confirmed illiberal at once becomes apparent. For as these surroundings vary, so, in some measure, does the problem of the consistent illiberal. The illiberal, living in those cultural regions where the American creed is widely repudiated and is no effective part of the subculture, has his private ethnic attitudes and practices supported by the local mores, the local institutions and the local power-structure. The illiberal in cultural areas dominated by a large measure of adherence to the American creed is in a social environment where he is isolated and receives small social support for his beliefs and practices. In both instances, the *individual* is an illiberal, to be sure, but he represents two significantly different *sociological types*. In the first instance, he is a *social conformist,* with strong moral and institutional reinforcement, whereas in the second, he is a *social deviant,* lacking strong social corroboration. In the one case, his discrimination involves him in further integration with his network of social relations; in the other, it threatens to cut him off from sustaining interpersonal ties. In the first cultural context, personal change in his ethnic behavior involves alienating himself from people significant to him; in the second context, this change of personal outlook may mean fuller incorporation in groups meaningful to him. In the first situation, modification of his ethnic views requires him to take the path of greatest resistance whereas in the second, it may mean the path of least resistance. From all this, we may surmise that any social policy aimed at changing the behavior and perhaps the attitudes of the all-weather illiberal will have to take into account the cultural and social structure of the area in which he lives. . . .

Implications of the Typology for Social Policy

. . . In approaching problems of policy, two things are plain. First, these should be considered from the standpoint of the militant ethnic liberal, for he alone is sufficiently motivated to engage in positive action for the reduction of ethnic discrimination. And second, the fair-weather liberal, the fair-weather illiberal and the

all-weather illiberal represent types differing sufficiently to require diverse kinds of treatment.

Treatment of the Fair-Weather Liberal

The fair-weather liberal, it will be remembered, discriminates only when it appears expedient to do so, and experiences some measure of guilt for deviating from his own belief in the American creed. He suffers from this conflict between conscience and conduct. Accordingly, he is a relatively easy target for the all-weather liberal. He represents the strategic group promising the largest immediate returns for the least effort. Recognition of this type defines the first task for the militant liberal who would enter into a collective effort to make the creed a viable and effective set of social norms rather than a ceremonial myth. . . .

Since the fair-weather liberal discriminates only when it seems rewarding to do so, the crucial need is so to change social situations that there are few occasions in which discrimination proves rewarding and many in which it does not. This would suggest that ethnic liberals self-consciously and deliberately seek to draw into the social groups where they constitute a comfortable majority a number of the "expedient discriminators." This would serve to counteract the dangers of self-selection through which liberals come to associate primarily with like-minded individuals. It would, further, provide an interpersonal and social environment for the fair-weather liberal in which he would find substantial social and psychological gains from abiding by his own beliefs, gains which would more than offset the rewards attendant upon occasional discrimination. It appears that men do not long persist in behavior which lacks social corroboration.

We have much to learn about the role of numbers and proportions in determining the behavior of members of a group. But it seems that individuals generally act differently when they are numbered among a minority rather than the majority. This is not to say that minorities abdicate their practices in the face of a contrary-acting majority, but only that the same people are subjected to different strains and pressures according to whether they are included in the majority or the minority. And the fair-weather liberal who finds himself associated with militant ethnic liberals may be expected to forgo his occasional deviations into discrimination; he may move from category II into category I. . . .

Treatment of the Fair-Weather Illiberal

Because his *beliefs* correspond to those of the full-fledged liberal, the fair-weather liberal can rather readily be drawn into an interpersonal environment constituted by those of a comparable turn of mind. This would be more difficult for the fair-weather illiberal, whose beliefs are so fully at odds with those of ethnic liberals that he may, at first, only be alienated by association with them. If the initial tactic for the fair-weather liberal, therefore, is a change in interpersonal environment, the seemingly most appropriate tactic for the fair-weather illiberal is a change in the institutional and legal environment. It is, indeed, probably this type which liberals implicitly have in mind when they expect significant changes in behavior to result from the introduction of controls on ethnic discrimination into the legal machinery of our society.

For this type—and it is a major limitation for planning policies of control that we do not know his numbers or his distribution in the country—it would seem that the most effective tactic is the institution of legal controls administered with strict efficiency. This would presumably reduce the amount of *discrimination* practiced by the fair-weather illiberal, though it might *initially* enhance rather than reduce his *prejudices*. . . .

A second prevalent tactic for modifying the prejudice of the fair-weather illiberal is that of seeking to draw him into interethnic groups explicitly formed for the promotion of tolerance. This, too, seems largely ineffectual, since the deeply prejudiced individual will not enter into such groups of his own volition. As a consequence of this process of self-selection, these tolerance groups soon come to be comprised by the very ethnic liberals who initiated the enterprise.

This barrier of self-selection can be partially hurdled only if the ethnic illiberals are brought into continued association with militant liberals in groups devoted to significant common values, quite remote from objectives of ethnic equity as such. Thus, as our Columbia-Lavanburg researches have found, many fair-weather illiberals *will* live in interracial housing projects in order to enjoy the rewards of superior housing at a given rental. And some of the illiberals thus brought into personal contact with various ethnic groups under the auspices of prestigeful militant liberals come to modify their prejudices. It is, apparently, only through interethnic collaboration, initially enforced by pressures of the situation, for immediate and significant objectives (other than tolerance) that the self-insulation of the fair-weather illiberal from rewarding interethnic contacts can be removed.

But however difficult it may presently be to affect the *prejudicial sentiments* of the fair-weather illiberal, his *discriminatory practices* can be lessened by the uniform, prompt and prestigeful use of legal and institutional sanctions. The critical problem is to ascertain the proportions of fair-weather and all-weather illiberals in a given local population in order to have some clue to the probable effectiveness or ineffectiveness of anti-discrimination legislation.

Treatment of the All-Weather Illiberal

It is, of course, the hitherto confirmed illiberal, persistently translating his prejudices into active discrimination, who represents the most difficult problem. But though he requires longer and more careful treatment, it is possible that he is not beyond change. In every instance, his social surroundings must be assiduously taken into account. It makes a peculiarly large difference whether he is in a cultural region of bigotry or in a predominantly "liberal" area, given over to verbal adherence to the American creed, at the very least. As this cultural climate varies, so must the prescription for his cure and the prognosis for a relatively quick or long delayed recovery.

In an unfavorable cultural climate—and this does not necessarily exclude the benign regions of the Far South—the immediate resort will probably have to be that of working through legal and administrative federal controls over extreme discrimination, with full recognition that, in all probability, these regulations will be systematically evaded for some time to come. In such cultural regions, we may expect nullification of the law as the common practice, perhaps as common as was the case in the nation at large with respect to the Eighteenth Amendment, often with the connivance of local officers of the law. The large gap between the new law and local mores will not *at once* produce significant change of prevailing practices; token punishments of violations will probably be more common than effective control. At best, one may assume that significant change will be fitful, and excruciatingly slow. But secular changes in the economy may in due course lend support to the new legal framework of control over discrimination. As the economic shoe pinches because the illiberals do not fully mobilize the resources of industrial manpower nor extend their local markets through equitable wage-payments, they may slowly abandon some discriminatory practices as they come to find that these do not always pay—even the discriminator. So far as discrimination is concerned, organized counteraction is possible and some small results may be expected. But it would seem that wishes father thoughts, when one expects basic changes in the immediate future in these regions of institutionalized discrimination.

The situation is somewhat different with regard to the scattered, rather than aggregated, ethnic illiberals found here and there throughout the country. Here the mores and a social organization oriented toward the American creed still have some measure of prestige and

the resources of a majority of liberals can be mobilized to isolate the illiberal. In these surroundings, it is possible to move the all-weather illiberal toward Type III—he can be brought to conform with institutional regulations, even though he does not surrender his prejudices. And once he has entered upon this role of the dissident but conforming individual, the remedial program designed for the fair-weather illiberal would be in order.

18   How Does It Feel to Be a Problem?
Being Young and Arab in America
Moustafa Bayoumi

MOUSTAFA BAYOUMI is an associate professor of English at Brooklyn College, the City University of New York.

WHAT DOES IT MEAN TO BE YOUNG AND Arab in America today? The popular image we hold of American youth in general is one of carefree innocence, living out a time of breezy self-indulgences and creative self-inventions. This is a stage of life to be treasured, we are told, because it lies far away from the pressures of adult responsibilities and the burdens of politics. But the stories here suggest that being young and Arab in America can never be so simple, as the "war on terror" encroaches on young Arab and Muslim Americans and complicates their lives in ways that are often invisible to the general public. Far away from the headlines of the moment, young Arab and Muslim Americans face a volatile mixture of fear, suspicion, curiosity, and misunderstanding, all the while seeking to discover who they are. In this environment they have to deal with a slew of new realities uncomfortably born out of the age. National security can mean fundamental disruptions of their family life, where they may have to take care of their parents instead of the other way around. Jobs and careers become more worrisome, as they must now be concerned that the ring of their names or the misbegotten assumptions people carry about them will shove them down opportunity's ladder. In the hostilities they encounter is the lingering possibility of outright violence. The upheavals in the Middle East can dictate the direction of their lives, as can the pendulum

Questions to Consider   Imagine you are like any other "normal" teenager in your community. You like McDonald's, baseball, video games, and are reasonably popular at your school. Now imagine it's 9/11 and the World Trade Centered is destroyed in the deadliest act of terrorism the United States has ever experienced. Overnight you go from being the well-liked, nice Arab American student to being viewed by many in your community as a terrorist, a potential terrorist, or a terrorist sympathizer. You are told that you are not an American. Later in the week you learn that your house of worship has been vandalized. Sadly, this has been the reality for many Arab Americans. What were the experiences of immigrants coming from Arab nation states who came to make a home in the United States at the turn of the twentieth century? How and in what ways has the treatment of this diverse group changed since 9/11 and the United States' greater military involvement in the Middle East? Is it the case, as discussed in this reading, that "repression and inclusion [of Arab Americans] may be happening at the same time"?

swings of federal law enforcement, now completely over-hauled to terrorism prevention. Even high school, with all its highs and lows, becomes not merely a popularity contest but a political trial of tolerance and respect.

In this rocky terrain, young Arab and Muslim Americans are forging their lives as the newest minorities in the American imagination. In their circumstances and out of their actions, they are also shaping the contours of a future American society. And though they don't always succeed in their efforts, the human drama of their predicament has now become a part of what it means to be an American.

The burning question really is whether American society will treat them as equals. The answer is not entirely clear. Simply put, the general public seems divided about the Arabs and Muslims in our midst. On the one hand, the last few years have seen a spirit of inclusion and desire for mutual cooperation spread across the country. Arab and Muslim organizations have matured in this environment, as they engage the general public more openly and fully than before, and the results are evident. Islam is increasingly understood as an American religion—in 2006 the first American Muslim, Keith Ellison, was elected to Congress—and Arab Americans are now frequently acknowledged to be an integral part of the United States. Despite an unwarranted controversy, the first dual-language Arabic-English New York City public high school opened its doors in Brooklyn in 2007. Arabs and Muslims are successfully integrating themselves into the institutional framework of American society.

Yet too many people continue to see Arabs and Muslims in America—particularly the young generation—through narrowed eyes, as enemies living among us. Key members of the political class, an often shrill news media, and a law-enforcement establishment that succumbs to ethnic and religious profiling lead the charge, and Muslims and Arabs are scrutinized for sedition at every turn. Even the most mundane facts of their lives, such as visiting mosques and *shisha* cafés, are now interpreted as something sinister and malevolent. On any given day, popular feelings seem to swing wildly between these poles of fear and acceptance, illustrating what the sociologist Louise Cainkar has called "the apparent paradox of this historical moment: repression and inclusion may be happening at the same time."

Shisha café a coffee shop like business that serves tobacco for use in a communal hookah or waterpipe

It's a strange place to inhabit, and it reveals not only the bifurcated nature of contemporary American society but also the somewhat precarious condition of Arab and Muslim Americans. Because their situation here is ultimately dependent less on what happens on the home front and more on what happens in the Middle East, Muslim and Arab Americans know that their own domestic security and their ability to live full American lives turn on the winds of global conflicts and on America's posture in the world and its policies abroad.

In *The Souls of Black Folk*, W.E.B. Du Bois observed that the treatment of African Americans stands as "a concrete test of the underlying principles of the great republic." In fact, the same can be said about Arabs and Muslims today. However, the principles currently at stake revolve not only around issues of full equality and inclusion, but fundamentally around the consequences that American foreign policy has on domestic civil rights. This condition is not new, and the history is important to remember.

Islam was practiced in this land centuries ago. As far back as the colonial era, many West African Muslims were sold into slavery, making Muslim-American history older than the republic itself. Mustapha, historians tell us, was actually a fairly common name among slaves in colonial South Carolina. For their part, Arabs have been arriving on these shores since the latter part of the nineteenth century, when mostly Christian Arabs from Mount Lebanon packed up their belongings and landed on Ellis Island with an average of $31.85 in their pockets, more than the $12.26 that Polish immigrants carried or the $21.32 of the Greeks. The migrations of both Arabs and Muslims have ebbed and flowed over the years for many reasons, primarily because of the vicissitudes of American immigration law.

In the late nineteenth century, a few years after they began arriving in the United States, Arab Americans established themselves on Washington Street in Lower Manhattan (dubbed "Little Syria"), where they opened stores, published lots of newspapers, lived closely, fought among themselves, and worried about being too different from other Americans or about becoming too American. (The move to Brooklyn happened mostly in the 1940s, with the construction of the Brooklyn Battery Tunnel, which razed much of Little Syria.) The early community thrived mostly as pack peddlers who, after stocking up on jewelry and notions from the stores on Washington Street, would then set off to sell their Holy Land wares, crisscrossing the country, often on foot.

The Washington Street shops spawned a certain amount of nineteenth-century exotic curiosity. An 1892 *New York Tribune* article noted that in them were boxes piled high with gossamer silks, olivewood trinkets, and luxurious satins. "In the midst of all this riot of the beautiful and odd," the article says, "stands the dealer, the natural gravity of his features relaxed into a smile of satisfaction at the wonder and delight expressed by his American visitor. But the vision ends, and with many parting 'salaams' one goes back to the dust and dirt, the noise and bustle" of Washington Street.

The early Arab-American community also encountered ethnic bigotry typical of the period. An 1890 *New York Times* article, for example, manages to illustrate this in a few words, while insulting a few others along the way. "The foreign population in the lower part of this city has of late years been increased by the Arabic-speaking element from the Lebanon, in Syria," it begins. "In clannishness and outlandish manners these people resemble the Chinese and what are called the Diego Italians. Nearly all of them are Maronite [Christians], and in many respects they are inferior to the Chinese and Italians, who do possess a certain amount of self-respect and are willing to work honestly and work hard for a living." The comments seem antiquarian today ("Diego Italians"?), but what we find here, between exoticism and chauvinism, is precisely the nation's early-twentieth-century spirit, which welcomed and reviled foreigners simultaneously. (Like any ethnic story, really, Arab-American history reveals as much or more about American culture as it does about immigrant ethnic mores.)

The second phase of Arab-American history dates from around 1909 until 1944. During this period the main issue plaguing the Arab-American community, beside the growing unrest in Palestine, was whether Arabs could naturalize as American citizens. According to the citizenship laws of the period (and until 1952), only "free white persons" could qualify for naturalization, and laws were passed explicitly to bar "Asiatics" from American citizenship. Confronted with this reality, the Arab-American community from across the nation mobilized to prove that they were indeed "free white people," and a series of court rulings eventually affirmed this position. A close examination of these years similarly reveals much less about the genetic makeup of Arabs and much more about America's domestic racial politics between the wars.

When an immigration judge ruled in 1942 that the Yemeni Ahmed Hassan—perhaps the first Arab Muslim to face the court (the others had been Arab Christians)—could not petition for citizenship, the community faced a setback. "Arabs are not white persons within the meaning of the [Immigration] Act," wrote Judge Arthur Tuttle, who heard Hassan's petition, citing Hassan's Muslim background as proof of his racial difference. "Apart from the dark skin of the Arabs," he explained, "it is well known that they are . . . a part of the Mohammedan world and that a wide gulf separates their culture from that of the predominately [*sic*] Christian peoples of Europe."

Yet less than a year and a half later, the court changed its mind. In 1944, Mohamed Mohriez, "an Arab born in Sanhy, Badan, Arabia," who had been in the United States since 1921, succeeded in his case. Why the change? District Judge Charles E. Wyzanski explained. The "vital interest [of the United States] as a world power" required granting Mohriez's petition, wrote the judge, because it was now necessary "to promote friendlier relations between the United States and other nations and so as to fulfill the promise that we shall treat all men as created equal." Part of these warmer ties included a controversial aid package made in February 1943 under the Lend-Lease Act to Saudi Arabia, as the United States was now eager to secure access to the kingdom's massive oil reserves. In other words, as the United States assumed its leadership role on the world stage, the domestic understandings of America's racial-classification system and where Arabs fit within it altered alongside. The exigencies of international politics changed the supposedly immutable facts of the Arab "race," all within the span of seventeen months.

The decision was significant, but it had little effect on the Arab-American community, since immigration was still mostly a closed door until 1965. But when the immigration laws changed again in that year, abandoning the quota system that had favored European immigrants, the community grew substantially with new arrivals. This is also a period when two other important things were happening in the United States: the civil-rights movement and, after 1967, the deepening role of the United States in the Middle East in the wake of the 1967 Arab-Israeli War. Now, unlike in the earlier periods of Arab-American history, it will be American foreign policy and its designs on the Middle East—and not America's domestic ethnic or racial hierarchies—that define the parameters of Arab-American life.

And what are those parameters? They include substantial government surveillance and repression, a history that is generally little known outside the Arab-American community. In October 1972, Abdeen Jabara—a Michigan civil-rights attorney and one of the founders of the Association of Arab American University Graduates, the first politically active Arab-American organization created after the 1967 war—suspected that his phone was being tapped. He filed a lawsuit against the FBI, only to discover that his communications had been monitored since 1967. Jabara's suit also led to the disclosure of a secret Nixon plan dubbed "Operation Boulder," a series of presidential directives demanding that every person with an Arabic surname undergo a security check before receiving a visa to the United States. Operation Boulder further authorized the FBI to spy on the Arab-American community through compiling dossiers on people's lawful political activities and even monitoring the magazines they read, resulting in the general harassment of the community. The FBI's Mark Felt, later revealed to have been Woodward and Bernstein's **Deep Throat,** also approved an illegal burglary at the Bureau of the Arab Information Center in the fall of 1972, in the middle of the Watergate scandal. And government intimidation and repression continued throughout the 1970s and 1980s. By 1986, the same year President Reagan claimed that Libyan "hit squads" had entered the country to assassinate him (a charge later revealed as a "complete fabrication" by FBI assistant director Oliver Revell), the Immigration and Naturalization Service (INS) circulated an internal document titled "Alien Terrorists and Undesirables: A Contingency Plan." The program called for the wide-scale registration and detention of nationals from Iran and seven Arab nations in an Oakdale, Louisiana, camp that had already been prepared with fencing and sanitation facilities in the event of a major conflict in the Middle East. With shades of Japanese internment (and a precursor to post-September 11 policies), the INS contemplated housing large numbers of people on the camp's thousand acres, conceding in the memo that the plan "indiscriminately lumps together individuals of widely differing political opinions solely on the basis of nationality."

The disclosure of the Contingency Plan came in the wake of the arrests of eight student activists, seven Palestinians and one Kenyan woman, in Los Angeles in 1987. The L.A. 8, as they came to be known, were arrested not for criminal or terrorist activity but explicitly for their political opinions. The FBI had been monitoring the group for years, even renting an apartment adjacent to one couple and drilling a hole in their bedroom wall to spy on them, but by the government's own admission it never discovered any criminal activity. Still, the government ordered their arrest and then sought their deportation, manipulating **McCarthy**-era laws to show that the L.A. 8 promoted "the doctrines of world communism." The group was distributing literature of the Popular Front for the Liberation of Palestine, but the same pamphlets and newspapers were commonly found in public libraries around the country. Such activities would normally be constitutionally protected by the First Amendment, but the eight were not U.S. nationals, and FBI director William Webster himself later admitted that "if these individuals had been United States citizens, there would not have been a basis for their arrest."

Then, in the 1990s, immigration courts expanded their use of "secret evidence" in key deportation cases. Since the Constitution guarantees people the right to confront the evidence against them, including the right to examine exculpatory information, evidence cannot be kept secret from defendants (except perhaps in extraordinary circumstances). But immigration courts are not held to the same standard, and the INS pursued at least two dozen deportation cases based on "secret evidence" in this period. Although it claimed it was not engaged in selectively prosecuting Arab or Muslim immigrants, the agency was unable to name a single "secret evidence" case that didn't involve an Arab or a Muslim.

All these actions stemmed neither from domestic race relations nor from how Arab Americans fit into America's enduring ethnic hierarchies. Rather, they originated from U.S. foreign-policy interests in the Middle East. At times such policies and programs were reactions to nationalist terrorism (before "Islamic" terrorism was the foe), but—as with the L.A. 8—they were more often used to limit the speech of Arab Americans in order to cement U.S. policy on the Israeli-Palestinian conflict.

Deep Throat the name used by the tipster who provided damaging information about President Nixon's involvement in break-in to the Democratic National Committee headquarters in the Watergate office complex in Washington, D.C..

McCarthy a reference to Senator Joe McCarthy and his tactic of accusing individuals of disloyalty or subversion with little or no evidence.

With the terrorist attacks of 2001, a new era began and the "war on terror" was launched. There is a crucial difference between this earlier period and today. Before 2001 the government focused its efforts almost exclusively on a handful of immigrants and activists and especially on immigrant activists. Today everyone—immigrant and citizen, activist and spectator—has become vulnerable. Group membership alone, through national origin, religion, or ethnicity, suffices as grounds for broad legal and cultural suspicion as a new category of "the Muslim," resembling with more than a few brushstrokes the image of "the Jew" in classical anti-Semitism, has been painted into existence in the wake of our policies and fears.

Osama bin Laden and al-Qaeda are to blame for the terrorist attacks, but we are responsible for the kind of society we live in, and since September 11, 2001, Arab- and Muslim-American civil rights have been even further eroded. First there was the preventive detention of at least 5,000 men and a few women and entire families, grabbed almost exclusively because of birthplace. The government then sought 19,000 "voluntary" interviews between the wars in Afghanistan and Iraq. They instituted the program of "Special Registration," begun a year after 9/11, which required the interviewing, fingerprinting, and photographing of more than 170,000 men from twenty-four Muslim-majority countries (and North Korea). Special Registration initiated deportation proceedings for almost 14,000 people, many times more than the 556 foreign nationals deported between 1918 and 1921, during the infamous Palmer Raids that followed several bombings in the country, including one on the house of Attorney General A. Mitchell Palmer. None of these policies produced a single terrorism conviction.

At least five major Muslim charities in the United States have been shut down by the government, even though the authorities have never shown any significant evidence of terror financing by any United States–based charity, according to the nonpartisan OMB Watch. Spies and government informants have penetrated Muslim-American communities, "material witness" warrants have led to the prolonged and indefinite incarceration of individuals without charge, immigration hearings were routinely held behind closed doors, and there has been the dangerous expansion of the use of "secret evidence" in our courts. There was also the ruling by Brooklyn District Court judge John Gleeson in 2006 stating that the U.S. government has the right to detain immigrants on the basis of their race, religion, or national origin and that it can legally imprison immigrants indefinitely as long as their eventual removal from the country is "reasonably foreseeable." This is a district court's decision, and it is currently on appeal, but if the judgment is allowed to stand as good law, the implications are profound and chilling, paving the way for future selective prosecutions and incarcerations of any immigrant community based solely on its collective attributes.

Seeing the Big Picture   **America's New Public Enemy?**

The statistics on hate crimes in the Appendix (Section IV) show patterns that are analogous to the attacks on Arab Americans and Muslims in the United States. How is the disproportionate number of hate crimes committed against racial minorities similar to what has happened to Arab Americans and Muslims since the 9/11 terrorist attacks?

The Possessive Investment in Whiteness: Racialized Social Democracy

19

George Lipsitz

GEORGE LIPSITZ researches racialization in U.S. society, including the racialization of space, urban culture, collective memory, and movements for social change. He is the author of *American Studies in a Moment of Danger* (2001) and *The Possessive Investment in Whiteness: How White People Profit from Identity Politics* (1998).

Questions to Consider   What does George Lipsitz mean by a "possessive investment in whiteness"? How is it possible that being a member of a particular racial group could confer social and economic privileges (or disadvantages) that are both institutional and intergenerational? How many specific programs does Lipsitz identify as being party to institutional racism?

SHORTLY AFTER WORLD WAR II, A FRENCH reporter asked expatriate Richard Wright his opinion about the "Negro problem" in the United States. The author replied "There isn't any Negro problem; there is only a white problem."[1] By inverting the reporter's question, Wright called attention to its hidden assumptions—that racial polarization comes from the existence of blacks rather than from the behavior of whites, that black people are a "problem" for whites rather than fellow citizens entitled to justice, and that unless otherwise specified "American" means whites.[2] But Wright's formulation also placed political mobilization by African Americans in context, attributing it "to the systemic practices of aversion, exploitation, denigration, and discrimination practiced by people who think of themselves as white."

Whiteness is everywhere in American culture, but it is very hard to see. As Richard Dyer argues, "white power secures its dominance by seeming not to be anything in particular."[3] As the unmarked category against which difference is constructed, whiteness never has to speak its name, never has to acknowledge its role as an organizing principle in social and cultural relations.[4]

To identify, analyze, and oppose the destructive consequences of whiteness, we need what Walter Benjamin called "presence of mind." Benjamin wrote that people visit fortune-tellers not so much out of a desire to know the future but rather out of a fear of not noticing some important aspect of the present. "Presence of mind," he argued, "is an abstract of the future, and precise awareness of the present moment more decisive than foreknowledge of the most distant events."[5] In our society at this time, precise awareness of the present moment requires an understanding of the existence and the destructive consequences of "white" identity.

In recent years, an important body of American studies scholarship has started to explore the role played by cultural practices in creating "whiteness" in the United States. More than the product of private prejudices, whiteness emerged as a relevant category in American life largely because of realities created by slavery and segregation, by immigration restriction and Indian policy, by conquest and colonialism. A fictive identity of "whiteness" appeared in law as an abstraction, and it became actualized in everyday life in many ways. American economic and political life gave different racial groups unequal access to citizenship and property, while cultural practices including Wild West shows, minstrel shows, racist images in advertising, and Hollywood films institutionalized racism by uniting ethnically diverse European-American audiences into an imagined community—one called into being through inscribed appeals to the solidarity of white supremacy.[6] Although cross-ethnic identification and pan-ethnic antiracism in culture, politics, and economics have often interrupted and resisted racialized white supremacist notions of American identity, from colonial days to the present, successful political coalitions serving dominant interests have often relied on exclusionary concepts of whiteness to fuse unity among otherwise antagonistic individuals and groups.[7]

In these accounts by American studies scholars, cultural practices have often played crucial roles in prefiguring, presenting, and preserving political coalitions based on identification with the fiction of "whiteness." Andrew Jackson's coalition of the "common man," Woodrow Wilson's "New Freedom," and Franklin D. Roosevelt's New Deal all echoed in politics the alliances announced on stage and screen by the nineteenth-century minstrel show, by D. W. Griffith's cinema, and by Al Jolson's ethnic and racial imagery.[8] This impressive body of scholarship helps us understand how people who left Europe as Calabrians or Bohemians became something called "whites" when they got to America and how that designation made all the difference in the world.

Yet, while cultural expressions have played an important role in the construction of white supremacist political alliances, the reverse is also true (i.e., political activity has also played a constitutive role in racializing U.S. culture). Race is a cultural construct, but one with sinister structural causes and consequences. Conscious and deliberate actions have institutionalized group identity in the United States, not just through the dissemination of cultural stories but also through systematic efforts from colonial times to the present to create a possessive investment in whiteness for European Americans. Studies of culture too far removed from studies of social structure leave us with inadequate explanations for understanding racism and inadequate remedies for combatting it.

From the start, European settlers in North America established structures encouraging possessive investment in whiteness. The colonial and early-national legal systems authorized attacks on Native Americans and encouraged the appropriation of their lands. They legitimated racialized chattel slavery, restricted naturalized citizenship to "white" immigrants, and provided pretexts for exploiting labor, seizing property, and denying the franchise to Asian Americans, Mexican Americans, Native Americans, and African Americans. Slavery and "Jim Crow" segregation institutionalized possessive identification with whiteness visibly and openly, but an elaborate interaction of largely *covert* public and private decisions during and after the days of slavery and segregation also produced a powerful legacy with enduring effects on the racialization of experience, opportunities, and rewards in the United States. Possessive investment in whiteness pervades public policy in the United States past and present—not just long ago during slavery and segregation but in the recent past and present as well—through the covert but no less systematic racism inscribed within U.S. social democracy.

Even though there has always been racism in American history, it has not always been the same racism. Political and cultural struggles over power shape the contours and dimensions of racism in any era. Mass mobilizations against racism during the Civil War and civil rights eras meaningfully curtailed the reach and scope of white supremacy, but in each case reactionary forces then engineered a renewal of racism, albeit in new forms, during successive decades. Racism changes over time, taking on different forms and serving different social purposes in different eras.

Contemporary racism is not just a residual consequence of slavery and **de jure segregation** but rather something that has been created anew in our own time by many factors including the putatively race-neutral liberal social democratic reforms of the past five decades. Despite hard-fought battles for change that secured important concessions during the 1960s in the form of civil rights legislation, the racialized nature of social democratic policies in the United States since the Great Depression has, in my judgment, actually increased the possessive investment in whiteness among European Americans over the past half-century.

The possessive investment in whiteness is not a simple matter of black and white; all racialized minority groups have suffered from it, albeit to different degrees and in different ways. Most of my argument here addresses relations between European Americans and African Americans because they contain many of the most vivid oppositions and contrasts, but the possessive investment in whiteness always emerges from a fused sensibility drawing on many sources at once—on antiblack racism to be sure, but also on the legacies of racialization left by federal, state, and local policies toward Native Americans, Asian Americans, Mexican Americans, and other groups designated by whites as "racially other."

During the New Deal, both the Wagner Act and the Social Security Act excluded farm workers and domestics from coverage, effectively denying those disproportionately minority sectors of the work force protections and benefits routinely channeled to whites. The Federal Housing Act of 1934 brought home ownership within

de jure segregation Segregation that is imposed by law; versus de facto segregation, which exists "in fact" or practice but is not specified by law.

reach of millions of citizens by placing the credit of the federal government behind private lending to home buyers, but overtly racist categories in the Federal Housing Administration's (FHA's) "confidential" city surveys and appraisers' manuals channeled almost all of the loan money toward whites and away from communities of color.[9] In the post–World War II era, trade unions negotiated contract provisions giving private medical insurance, pensions, and job security largely to the mostly white workers in unionized mass-production industries rather than fighting for full employment, universal medical care, and old age pensions for all or for an end to discriminatory hiring and promotion practices by employers.[10]

Each of these policies widened the gap between the resources available to whites and those available to aggrieved racial communities, but the most damaging long-term effects may well have come from the impact of the racial discrimination codified by the policies of the FHA. By channeling loans away from older inner-city neighborhoods and toward white home buyers moving into segregated suburbs, the FHA and private lenders after World War II aided and abetted the growth and development of increased segregation in U.S. residential neighborhoods. For example, FHA appraisers denied federally supported loans to prospective home buyers in the racially mixed Boyle Heights neighborhood of Los Angeles because it was a "'**melting pot**' area literally honeycombed with diverse and subversive racial elements."[11] Similarly, mostly white St. Louis County secured five times as many FHA mortgages as the more racially mixed city of St. Louis between 1943 and 1960. Home buyers in the county received six times as much loan money and enjoyed per capita mortgage spending 6.3 times greater than those in the city.[12]

In concert with FHA support for segregation in the suburbs, federal and state tax monies routinely provided water supplies and sewage facilities for racially exclusive suburban communities in the 1940s and 1950s. By the 1960s, these areas often incorporated themselves as independent municipalities in order to gain greater access to federal funds allocated for "urban aid."[13] At the same time that FHA loans and federal highway building projects subsidized the growth of segregated suburbs, urban renewal programs in cities throughout the country devastated minority neighborhoods.

melting pot The blending or "melting" of different racial, cultural, and ethnic groups into a new configuration.

During the 1950s and 1960s, federally assisted **urban renewal** projects destroyed 20 percent of the central city housing units occupied by blacks, as opposed to only 10 percent of those inhabited by whites.[14] Even after most major urban renewal programs had been completed in the 1970s, black central city residents continued to lose housing units at a rate equal to 80 percent of what had been lost in the 1960s. Yet white displacement declined back to the relatively low levels of the 1950s.[15] In addition, the refusal first to pass, then to enforce, fair housing laws, has enabled realtors, buyers, and sellers to profit from racist collusion against minorities without fear of legal retribution.

During the decades following World War II, urban renewal helped construct a new "white" identity in the suburbs by helping destroy ethnically specific European-American urban inner-city neighborhoods. Wrecking balls and bulldozers eliminated some of these sites, while others became transformed by an influx of minority residents desperately competing for a declining number of affordable housing units. As increasing numbers of racial minorities moved into cities, increasing numbers of European-American ethnics moved out. Consequently, ethnic differences among whites became a less important dividing line in American culture, while race became more important. The suburbs helped turn European Americans into "whites" who could live near each other and intermarry with relatively little difficulty. But this "white" unity rested on residential segregation and on shared access to housing and life chances largely unavailable to communities of color.[16]

During the 1950s and 1960s, local "pro-growth" coalitions led by liberal mayors often justified urban renewal as a program designed to build more housing for poor people, but it actually destroyed more housing than it created. Ninety percent of the low-income units removed for urban renewal were never replaced. Commercial, industrial, and municipal projects occupied more than 80 percent of the land cleared for these projects, with less than 20 percent allocated for replacement housing. In addition, the loss of taxable properties and tax abatements granted to new enterprises in urban renewal zones often meant serious tax increases for poor, working-class, and

urban renewal Also known as slum clearance, these policies attempted to renew blighted urban areas by redeveloping the land. Many have viewed these policies as a way to dislocate the urban poor and working classes, seize the land, and create development opportunity for the elites.

middle-class home owners and renters.[17] Although the percentage of black suburban dwellers also increased during this period, no significant desegregation of the suburbs took place. From 1960 to 1977, four million whites moved out of central cities, while the number of whites living in suburbs increased by twenty-two million.[18] During the same years, the inner-city black population grew by six million, but the number of blacks living in suburbs increased by only 500,000 people.[19] By 1993, 86 percent of suburban whites still lived in places with a black population below 1 percent. At the same time, cities with large numbers of minority residents found themselves cut off from loans by the FHA; in 1966, because of their growing black and Puerto Rican populations, Camden and Paterson, New Jersey, received no FHA-sponsored mortgages between them.[20]

Federally funded highways designed to connect suburban commuters with downtown places of employment destroyed already scarce housing in minority communities and often disrupted neighborhood life as well. Construction of the Harbor Freeway in Los Angeles, the Gulf Freeway in Houston, and the Mark Twain Freeway in St. Louis displaced thousands of residents and bisected previously connected neighborhoods, shopping districts, and political precincts. The process of urban renewal and highway construction set in motion a vicious cycle: population loss led to decreased political power, which made minority neighborhoods more likely to be victimized by further urban renewal and freeway construction, not to mention more susceptible to the placement of prisons, waste dumps, and other projects that further depopulated these areas.

In Houston, Texas—where blacks make up slightly more than one-quarter of the local population—more than 75 percent of municipal garbage incinerators and 100 percent of the city-owned garbage dumps are located in black neighborhoods.[21] A 1992 study by staff writers for the *National Law Journal* examined the Environmental Protection Agency's response to 1,177 toxic waste cases and found that polluters of sites near the greatest white population received penalties 500 percent higher than penalties imposed on polluters in minority areas—an average of $335,566 for white areas contrasted with $55,318 for minority areas. Income did not account for these differences—penalties for low-income areas on average actually exceeded those for areas with the highest median incomes by about 3 percent. The penalties for violating all federal environmental laws about air, water, and waste pollution in minority communities were 46 percent lower than in white communities. In addition, **Superfund** remedies left minority communities with longer waiting times for being placed on the national priority list, cleanups that begin from 12 to 42 percent later than at white sites, and a 7 percent greater likelihood of "containment" (walling off a hazardous site) than cleanup, while white sites experienced treatment and cleanup 22 percent more often than containment.[22]

Urban renewal failed as a program for providing new housing for the poor, but it played an important role in transforming the U.S. urban economy away from factory production and toward producer services. Urban renewal projects subsidized the development of downtown office centers on land previously used for residences, and they frequently created buffer zones of empty blocks dividing poor neighborhoods from new shopping centers designed for affluent commuters. In order to help cities compete for corporate investment by making them appealing to high-level executives, federal urban aid favored construction of luxury housing units and cultural centers, such as symphony halls and art museums, over affordable housing for workers. Tax abatements granted to these producer-services centers further aggravated the fiscal crisis that cities faced, leading to tax increases on existing industries, businesses, and residences.

Workers from aggrieved racial minorities bore the brunt of this transformation. Because the 1964 Civil Rights Act came so late, minority workers who received jobs because of it found themselves more vulnerable to seniority-based layoffs when businesses automated or transferred operations overseas. Although the act initially made real progress in reducing employment discrimination, lessened the gaps between rich and poor and black and white, and helped bring minority poverty to its lowest level in history in 1973, that year's recession initiated a reversal of minority progress and a reassertion of white privilege.[23] In 1977, the U.S. Civil Rights Commission reported on the disproportionate impact of layoffs on minority workers. In cases where minority workers made up only 10 to 12 percent of the work force in their area, they accounted for from 60 to 70 percent of those laid off in 1974. The principle of seniority, a social democratic triumph, in this case worked

Superfund Aid to communties for cleanup and abatement of the effects of living near abandoned industrial waste sites.

to guarantee that minority workers would suffer most from technological changes because the legacy of past discrimination by their employers left them with less seniority than white workers.[24]

When housing prices doubled during the 1970s, white home owners who had been able to take advantage of discriminatory FHA financing policies received increased equity in their homes, while those excluded from the housing market by earlier policies found themselves facing higher costs of entry into the market in addition to the traditional obstacles presented by the discriminatory practices of sellers, realtors, and lenders. The contrast between European Americans and African Americans is instructive in this regard. Because whites have access to broader housing choices than blacks, whites pay 15 percent less than blacks for similar housing in the same neighborhood. White neighborhoods typically experience housing costs 25 percent less expensive than would be the case if the residents were black.[25]

A recent Federal Reserve Bank of Boston study showed that minority applicants had a 60 percent greater chance of being denied home loans than white applicants with the same credit-worthiness. Boston bankers made 2.9 times as many mortgage loans per one thousand housing units in neighborhoods inhabited by low-income whites than they did to neighborhoods populated by low-income blacks.[26] In addition, loan officers were far more likely to overlook flaws in the credit records of white applicants or to arrange creative financing for them than they were with black applicants.[27]

A Los Angeles study found that loan officers more frequently used dividend income and underlying assets criteria for judging black applicants than they did for whites.[28] In Houston, the NCNB Bank of Texas disqualified 13 percent of middle-income white loan applicants but disqualified 36 percent of middle-income black applicants.[29] Atlanta's home loan institutions gave five times as many home loans to whites as to blacks in the late 1980s. An analysis of sixteen Atlanta neighborhoods found that home buyers in white neighborhoods received conventional financing four times as often as those in black sections of the city.[30] Nationwide, financial institutions get more money in deposits from black neighborhoods than they invest in them in the form of home mortgage loans, making home lending a vehicle for the transfer of capital away from black savers and toward white investors.[31]

In many locations, high-income blacks were denied loans more often than low-income whites.[32]

Federal home loan policies have placed the power of the federal government behind private discrimination. Urban renewal and highway construction programs have enhanced the possessive investment in whiteness directly through government initiatives. In addition, decisions about the location of federal jobs have also systematically supported the subsidy for whiteness. Federal civilian employment dropped by 41,419 in central cities between 1966 and 1973, but total federal employment in metropolitan areas grew by 26,558.[33] While one might naturally expect the location of government buildings that serve the public to follow population trends, the federal government's policies in locating offices and records centers in suburbs helped aggravate the flight of jobs to suburban locations less accessible to inner-city residents. Since racial discrimination in the private sector forces minority workers to seek government positions disproportionate to their numbers, these moves exact particular hardships on them. In addition, minorities who follow their jobs to the suburbs generally encounter increased commuter costs because housing discrimination makes it harder and more expensive for them to relocate than for whites.

The racialized aspects of fifty years of these social democratic policies became greatly exacerbated by the anti-social democratic policies of neoconservatives in the Reagan and Bush administrations during the 1980s and 1990s. They clearly contributed to the reinforcement of possessive investments in whiteness through their regressive policies in respect to federal aid to education and their refusal to challenge segregated education, housing, and hiring, as well as their cynical cultivation of an antiblack, counter-subversive consensus through attacks on affirmative action and voting rights legislation. In the U.S. economy, where 86 percent of available jobs do not appear in classified advertisements and where personal connections provide the most important factor in securing employment, attacks on affirmative action guarantee that whites will be rewarded for their historical advantages in the labor market rather than for their individual abilities or efforts.[34]

Yet even seemingly race-neutral policies supported by both neoconservatives and social democrats in the 1980s and 1990s have also increased the absolute value of being white. In the 1980s, changes in federal tax laws decreased the value of wage income and increased the value of investment income—a move harmful to minorities who suffer from an even greater gap between their total wealth and that of whites than in the disparity between their income and white income. Failure to raise the minimum wage between 1981 and 1989 and the more than one-third decline in value of Aid for Families with Dependent Children payments hurt all poor people, but they exacted special costs on nonwhites facing even more constricted markets for employment, housing, and education than poor whites.[35]

Similarly, the "tax reforms" of the 1980s made the effective rate of taxation higher on investment in actual goods and services than it was on profits from speculative enterprises. This encouraged the flight of capital away from industrial production with its many employment opportunities and toward investments that can be turned over quickly to allow the greatest possible tax write-offs. Consequently, government policies actually discouraged investments that might produce high-paying jobs and encouraged investors to strip companies of their assets in order to make rapid short-term profits. These policies hurt almost all workers, but they exacted particularly high costs from minority workers who, because of employment discrimination in the retail and small business sectors, were overrepresented in blue-collar industrial jobs.

On the other hand, while neoconservative tax policies created incentives for employers to move their enterprises elsewhere, they created disincentives for home owners to move. Measures such as California's Proposition 13 granting tax relief to property owners badly misallocate housing resources because they make it financially unwise for the elderly to move out of large houses, further reducing the supply of housing available to young families. While one can well understand the necessity for protecting senior citizens on fixed incomes from tax increases that would make them lose their homes, the rewards and punishments provided by Proposition 13 are so extreme that they prevent the kinds of generational succession that have routinely opened up housing to young families in the past. This reduction works particular hardships on those who also face discrimination by sellers, realtors, and lending institutions.

Subsidies to the private sector by government agencies also tend to reward the results of past discrimination. Throughout the country, tax increment redevelopment programs give tax-free, low-interest loans to developers whose projects use public services, often without having to pay taxes to local school boards or county governments. Industrial development bonds resulted in a $7.4 billion tax loss in 1983, a loss that ordinary tax payers had to make up through increased payroll taxes. Compared to white Americans, people of color, who are more likely to be poor or working class, suffer disproportionately from these changes as tax payers, as workers, and as tenants. A study by the Citizens for Tax Justice found that wealthy Californians spend less than eleven cents in taxes for every dollar earned, while poor residents of the state paid fourteen cents out of every dollar in taxes. As groups overrepresented among the poor, minorities have been forced to shoulder this burden in order to subsidize the tax breaks given to the wealthy.[36] While holding property tax assessments for businesses and some home owners to about half of their market value, California's Proposition 13 deprived cities and counties of $13 billion a year in taxes. Businesses alone avoided $3.3 billion to $8.6 billion in taxes per year under this statute.[37]

Because they are ignorant of even the recent history of the possessive investment in whiteness—generated by slavery and segregation but augmented by social democratic reform—Americans produce largely cultural explanations for structural social problems. The increased possessive investment in whiteness generated by disinvestment in America's cities, factories, and schools since the 1970s disguises the general problems posed to our society by de-industrialization, economic restructuring, and **neoconservative** attacks on the welfare state as *racial* problems. It fuels a discourse that demonizes people of color for being victimized by these changes, while hiding the privileges of whiteness by attributing them to family values, fatherhood, and foresight—rather than to favoritism.

The demonization of black families in public discourse since the 1970s is particularly instructive in this regard. During the 1970s, the share of low-income households headed by blacks increased by one-third, while black family income fell from 60 percent of white family income in 1971 to 58 percent in 1980. Even when adjusting

neoconservatism A response to the liberalism of the 1960s, this political philosophy is an attempt to return to the conservatism of the 1950s. The movement is characterized by privatizing public goods, nation building through military intervention abroad, and minimum government regulation.

for unemployment and for African-American disadvantages in life-cycle employment (more injuries, more frequently interrupted work histories, confinement to jobs most susceptible to layoffs), the wages of full-time year-round black workers fell from 77 percent of white workers' income to 73 percent by 1986. In 1986, white workers with high school diplomas earned three thousand dollars per year more than African Americans with the same education.[38] Even when they had the same family structure as white workers, blacks found themselves more likely to be poor.

Among black workers between the ages of twenty and twenty-four, 46 percent held blue-collar jobs in 1976, but that percentage fell to only 20 percent by 1984. Earnings by young black families had reached 60 percent of the amount secured by white families in 1973, but by 1986 they fell back to 46 percent. Younger African-American families experienced a 50 percent drop in real earnings between 1973 and 1986, with the decline in black male wages particularly steep.[39]

Many recent popular and scholarly studies have explained clearly the causes for black economic decline over the past two decades.[40] Deindustrialization has decimated the industrial infrastructure that formerly provided high-wage jobs and chances for upward mobility to black workers. Neoconservative attacks on government spending for public housing, health, education, and transportation have deprived African Americans of needed services and opportunities for jobs in the public sector. A massive retreat from responsibility to enforce anti-discrimination laws at the highest levels of government has sanctioned pervasive overt and covert racial discrimination by bankers, realtors, and employers.

Yet public opinion polls conducted among white Americans display little recognition of these devastating changes. Seventy percent of whites in one poll said that African Americans "have the same opportunities to live a middle-class life as whites."[41] Nearly three-fourths of white respondents to a 1989 poll believed that opportunities for blacks had improved during the Reagan presidency.[42]

Optimism about the opportunities available to African Americans does not necessarily demonstrate ignorance of the dire conditions facing black communities, but, if not, it then indicates that many whites believe that blacks suffer deservedly, that they do not take advantage of the opportunities offered them. In the opinion polls, favorable assessments of

black chances for success often accompanied extremely negative judgments about the abilities, work habits, and character of black people. A National Opinion Research Report in 1990 disclosed that more than 50 percent of American whites viewed blacks as innately lazy and less intelligent and less patriotic than whites.[43] Furthermore, more than 60 percent of whites questioned in that survey said that they believed that blacks suffer from poor housing and employment opportunities because of their own lack of willpower. Some 56.3 percent of whites said that blacks preferred welfare to employment, while 44.6 percent contended that blacks tended toward laziness.[44] Even more important, research by Mary and Thomas Byrne Edsall indicates that many whites structure nearly all of their decisions about housing, education, and politics in response to their aversions to black people.[45]

The present political culture in this country gives broad sanction for viewing white supremacy and antiblack racism as forces from the past, as demons finally put to rest by the passage of the 1964 Civil Rights Act and the 1965 Voting Rights Act.[46] Jurists, journalists, and politicians have generally been more vocal in their opposition to "quotas" and to "reverse discrimination" mandating race-specific remedies for discrimination than to the thousands of well-documented incidents every year of routine, systematic, and unyielding discrimination against blacks.

It is my contention that the stark contrast between black experiences and white opinions during the past two decades cannot be attributed solely to ignorance or intolerance on the part of individuals but stems instead from the overdetermined inadequacy of the language of liberal individualism to describe collective experience.[47] As long as we define social life as the sum total of conscious and deliberate individual activities, then only *individual* manifestations of personal prejudice and hostility will be seen as racist. Systemic, collective, and coordinated behavior disappears from sight. Collective exercises of group power relentlessly channeling rewards, resources, and opportunities from one group to another will not appear to be "racist" from this perspective because they rarely announce their intention to discriminate against individuals. But they work to construct racial indentities by giving people of different races vastly different life chances.

The gap between white perceptions and minority experiences can have explosive consequences. Little more than a year after the 1992 Los Angeles rebellion, a sixteen-year-old high school junior shared her opinions with a reporter from the *Los Angeles Times*. "I don't think white people owe anything to black people," she explained. "We didn't sell them into slavery, it was our ancestors. What they did was wrong, but we've done our best to make up for it."[48] A seventeen-year-old senior echoed those comments, telling the reporter:

> I feel we spend more time in my history class talking about what whites owe blacks than just about anything else when the issue of slavery comes up. I often received dirty looks. This seems strange given that I wasn't even alive then. And the few members of my family from that time didn't have the luxury of owning much, let alone slaves. So why, I ask you, am I constantly made to feel guilty?[49]

More ominously, after pleading guilty to bombing two homes and one car, to vandalizing a synagogue, and attempting to start a race war by murdering Rodney King and bombing Los Angeles's First African Methodist Episcopal Church, twenty-year-old Christopher David Fisher explained that "sometimes whites were picked on because of the color of their skin. . . . Maybe we're blamed for slavery."[50] Fisher's actions were certainly extreme, but his justification of them drew knowingly and precisely on a broadly shared narrative about the victimization of innocent whites by irrational and ungrateful minorities.

The comments and questions raised about the legacy of slavery by these young whites illumine broader currents in our culture that have enormous implications for understanding the enduring significance of race in our country. These young people associate black grievances solely with slavery, and they express irritation at what they perceive as efforts to make them feel guilty or unduly privileged in the present because of things that happened in the distant past. Because their own ancestors may not have been slave owners or because "we've done our best to make up for it," they feel that it is unreasonable for anyone to view them as people who owe "anything" to blacks. On the contrary, Fisher felt that his discomfort with being "picked on" and "blamed" for slavery gave him good reason to bomb homes, deface synagogues, and plot to kill black people.

Unfortunately for our society, these young whites accurately reflect the logic of the language of liberal individualism and its ideological predispositions in discussions of race. They seem to have no knowledge of the disciplined, systemic, and collective *group* activity that has structured white identities in American history. They

are not alone in their ignorance; in a 1979 law journal article, future Supreme Court Justice Antonin Scalia argued that affirmative action "is based upon concepts of racial indebtedness and racial entitlement rather than individual worth and individual need" and is thus "racist."[51]

Yet liberal individualism is not completely color-blind on this issue. As Cheryl I. Harris demonstrates, the legacy of liberal individualism has not prevented the Supreme Court from recognizing and protecting the group interests of *whites* in the Bakke, Croson, and Wygant cases.[52] In each case, the Court nullified affirmative action programs because they judged efforts to help blacks as harmful to whites: to white expectations of entitlement, expectations based on the possessive investment in whiteness they held as members of a group. In the Bakke case, for instance, neither Bakke nor the court contested the legitimacy of medical school admissions standards that reserved five seats in each class for children of wealthy donors to the university or that penalized Bakke for being older than most of the other applicants. The group rights of not-wealthy people or of people older than their classmates did not compel the Court or Bakke to make any claim of harm. But they did challenge and reject a policy designed to offset the effects of past and present discrimination when they could construe the medical school admission policies as detrimental to the interests of whites as a group—and as a consequence they applied the "strict scrutiny" standard to protect whites while denying that protection to people of color. In this case, as in so many others, the language of liberal individualism serves as a cover for coordinated collective group interests.

Group interests are not monolithic, and aggregate figures can obscure serious differences within racial groups. All whites do not benefit from the possessive investment in whiteness in precisely the same way; the experiences of members of minority groups are not interchangeable. But the possessive investment in whiteness always affects individual and group life chances and opportunities. Even in cases where minority groups secure political and economic power through collective mobilization, the terms and conditions of their collectivity and the logic of group solidarity are always influenced and intensified by the absolute value of whiteness in American politics, economics, and culture.[53]

In the 1960s, members of the Black Panther Party used to say that "if you're not part of the solution, you're part of the problem." But those of us who are "white" can only become part of the solution if we recognize the degree to which we are already part of the problem—not because of our race, but because of our possessive investment in it. Neither conservative **"free market"** policies nor liberal social democratic reforms can solve the "white problem" in America because both of them reinforce the possessive investment in whiteness. But an explicitly antiracist pan-ethnic movement that acknowledges the existence and power of whiteness might make some important changes. Pan-ethnic, antiracist coalitions have a long history in the United States—in the political activism of John Brown, Sojourner Truth, and the Magon brothers, among others—but we also have a rich cultural tradition of pan-ethnic antiracism connected to civil rights activism of the kind detailed so brilliantly in rhythm and blues musician Johnny Otis's recent book, *Upside Your Head! Rhythm and Blues on Central Avenue.*[54] These efforts by whites to fight racism, not out of sympathy for someone else but out of a sense of self-respect and simple justice, have never completely disappeared; they remain available as models for the present.[55]

Walter Benjamin's praise for "presence of mind" came from his understanding of how difficult it may be to see the present. But more important, he called for presence of mind as the means for implementing what he called "the only true telepathic miracle"—turning the forbidding future into the fulfilled present.[56] Failure to acknowledge our society's possessive investment in whiteness prevents us from facing the present openly and honestly. It hides from us the devastating costs of disinvestment in America's infrastructure over the past two decades and keeps us from facing our responsibilities to reinvest in human capital by channeling resources toward education, health, and housing—and away from subsidies for speculation and luxury. After two decades of disinvestment, the only further disinvestment we need is to disinvest in the ruinous pathology of whiteness that has always undermined our own best instincts and interests. In a society suffering so badly from an absence of mutuality, an absence of responsibility, and an absence of simple justice, presence of mind might be just what we need.

free market A system of exchange in which buyers and sellers come to agreement about pricing with no outside influences. The idea of a free market is that there is little or no government intervention in the private transactions of individuals.

Seeing the Big Picture   Race as an Investment

How do rates of homeownership (Section II in the Appendix) and occupations by race (Section VIII) point to historic investments that have privileged one group over another?

20 Laissez-Faire Racism, Racial Inequality, and the Role of the Social Sciences

Lawrence D. Bobo

LAWRENCE BOBO is the W. E. B. Du Bois Professor of the Social Sciences at Harvard University. He holds appointments in the Department of Sociology and the Department of African and African American Studies. His research focuses on the intersection of social inequality, politics, and race.

Questions to Consider

There is the tendency, particularly in the media, to frame racism as a practice and belief system of the past. We like to tell ourselves that the racism of yesterday, which was a core feature and organizing principle of the United States, has been laid to rest. In his discussion of laissez-faire racism, Professor Bobo suggests that racism hasn't gone away; it's merely morphed into a new discourse in which nonracial reasons or rationalizations (social class, culture, work ethic) are used to explain away continued institutional racism and discrimination. How is laissez-faire racism different from "old-fashioned" racism, and why is this new type of racism more problematic?

AS PART OF RESEARCH ON THE INTERSECTION of poverty, crime, and race, I conducted two focus groups in a major eastern city in early September 2001, just prior to the tragic events of September 11. The dynamics of the two groups, one with nine white participants and another with nine black participants, drove home for me very powerfully just how deep but also just how sophisticated, elusive, and enduring a race problem the United States still confronts. An example from each group begins to make the point that the very nature of this problem and our vocabularies for discussing it have grown very slippery, very difficult to grasp, and therefore extremely difficult to name and to fight.

First let's consider the white focus group. In response to the moderator's early question, "What's the biggest problem facing your community?" a young working-class white male eagerly and immediately chimed in, "Section 8 housing." "It's a terrible system," he said. The racial implications hung heavy in the room until a middle-aged white bartender tried to leaven things a bit by saying:

> All right. If you have people of a very low economic group who have a low standard of living who cannot properly feed and clothe their children, whose speech patterns are not as good as ours [and] are [therefore] looked down upon as a low class. Where I live most of those people happen to be black. So it's generally perceived that blacks are inferior to whites for that reason.

The bartender went on to explain: "It's not that way at all. It's a class issue, which in many ways is economically driven. From my perspective, it's not a racial issue at all. I'm a bartender. I'll serve anybody if they're a class [act]." At this,

the group erupted in laughter, but the young working-class male was not finished. He asserted, a bit more vigorously:

> Why should somebody get to live in my neighborhood that hasn't earned that right? I'd like to live [in a more affluent area], but I can't afford to live there so I don't. . . . So why should somebody get put in there by the government that didn't earn that right?

And then the underlying hostility and stereotyping came out more directly when he said: "And most of the people on that program are trashy, and they don't know how to behave in a working neighborhood. It's not fair. I call it unfair housing laws."

Toward the end of the session, when discussing why the jails are so disproportionately filled with blacks and Hispanics, this same young man said: "Blacks and Hispanics are more violent than white people. I think they are more likely to shoot somebody over a fender bender than a couple of white guys are. They have shorter fuses, and they are more emotional than white people."

In fairness, some members of the white group criticized antiblack prejudice. Some members of the group tried to point out misdeeds done by whites as well. But even the most liberal of the white participants never pushed the point, rarely moved beyond abstract observations or declarations against prejudice, and sometimes validated the racial stereotypes more overtly embraced by others. In an era when everyone supposedly knows what to say and what not to say and is artful about avoiding overt bigotry, this group discussion still quickly turned to racial topics and quickly elicited unabashed negative stereotyping and antiblack hostility.

When asked the same question about the "biggest problem facing your community," the black group almost in unison said, "Crime and drugs," and a few voices chimed in, "Racism." One middle-aged black woman reported: "I was thinking more so on the lines of myself because my house was burglarized three times. Twice while I was at work and one time when I returned from church, I caught the person in there."

The racial thread to her story became clearer when she later explained exactly what happened in terms of general police behavior in her community:

> The first two robberies that I had, the elderly couple that lived next door to me, they called the police. I was at work when the first two robberies occurred. They called the police two or three times. The police never even showed up. When I came in from work, I had to go . . . file a police report. My neighbors went with me, and they had called the police several times and they never came. Now, on that Sunday when I returned from church and caught him in my house, and the guy that I caught in my house lives around the corner, he has a case history, he has been in trouble since doomsday. When I told [the police] I had knocked him unconscious, oh yeah, they were there in a hurry. Guns drawn. And I didn't have a weapon except for the baseball bat, [and] I wound up face down on my living room floor, and they placed handcuffs on me.

The moderator, incredulous, asked: "Well, excuse me, but they locked you and him up?" "They locked me up and took him to the hospital."

Indeed, the situation was so dire, the woman explained, that had a black police officer who lived in the neighborhood not shown up to help after the patrol car arrived with sirens blaring, she felt certain the two white police officers who arrived, guns drawn, would probably have shot her. As it was, she was arrested for assault, spent two days in jail, and now has a lawsuit pending against the city. Somehow I doubt that a single, middle-aged, churchgoing white woman in an all-white neighborhood who had called the police to report that she apprehended a burglar in her home would end up handcuffed, arrested, and in jail alongside the burglar. At least, I am not uncomfortable assuming that the police would not have entered a home in a white community with the same degree of apprehension, fear, preparedness for violence, and ultimate disregard for a law-abiding citizen as they did in this case. But it can happen in black communities in America today.

To say that the problem of race endures, however, is not to say that it remains fundamentally the same and essentially unchanged. I share the view articulated by historians such as Barbara Fields (1982) and Thomas Holt (2000) that race is both socially constructed and historically contingent. As such, it is not enough to declare that race matters or that racism endures. *The much more demanding challenge is to account for how and why such a social construction comes to be reconstituted, refreshed, and enacted anew in very different times and places.* How is it that we can find a working-class white man who is convinced that many blacks are "trashy people" controlled by emotions and clearly more susceptible to violence? How is it that a black woman defending herself and her home against a burglar ends up apprehended as if she were one of the "usual suspects"? Or cast more broadly, how do we have a milestone like the *Brown* decision and pass a Civil Rights Act, a Voting Rights Act, a Fair Housing Act, and numerous acts of enforcement and amendments to all of these, including the pursuit of affirmative action policies, and yet still continue to face a significant racial divide in America?

The answer I sketch here is but a partial one, focusing on three key observations. First, as I have argued elsewhere and elaborate in important ways here, I believe that we are witnessing the crystallization of a new racial ideology here in the United States. This ideology I refer to as laissez-faire racism. We once confronted a slave labor economy with its inchoate ideology of racism and then watched it evolve in response to war and other social, economic, and cultural trends into an explicit Jim Crow racism of the de jure segregation era. We have more recently seen the biological and openly segregationist thrust of twentieth-century Jim Crow racism change into the more cultural, free-market, and ostensibly color-blind thrust of laissez-faire racism in the new millennium. But make no mistake—the current social structure and attendant ideology reproduce, sustain, and rationalize enormous black-white inequality (Bobo and Kluegel 1997).

Second, race and racism remain powerful levers in American national politics. These levers can animate the electorate, constrain and shape political discourse and campaigns, and help direct the fate of major social policies. From the persistently contested efforts at affirmative action through a historic expansion of the penal system and the recent dismantling of "welfare as we know it," the racial divide has often decisively prefigured and channeled core features of our domestic politics (Bobo 2000).

Third, social science has played a peculiar role in the problem of race. And here I wish to identify an intellectual and scholarly failure to come to grips with the interrelated phenomena of white privilege and black agency. This failure may present itself differently depending on the ideological leanings of scholars. I critique one line of analysis on the left and one on the right. On the left, the problem typically presents as a failure of sociological imagination. It manifests itself in arguments that seek to reduce racialized social dynamics to some ontologically more fundamental nonracialized factor. On the right, the problem is typically the failure of explicit victim-blaming. It manifests itself in a rejection of social structural roots or causation of racialized social conditions. I want to suggest that both tactics—the left's search for some structural force more basic than race (such as class or skill levels or child-rearing practices) and the right's search for completely volitional factors (cultural or individual dispositions) as final causes of "race" differences—reflect a deep misunderstanding of the dynamics of race and racism. Race is not just a set of categories, and racism is not just a collection of individual-level anti–minority group attitudes. Race and racism are more fundamentally about sets of intertwined power relations, group interests and identities, and the ideas that justify and make sense out of (or challenge and delegitimate) the organized racial ordering of society (Dawson 2000). The latter analytic posture and theory of race in society is embodied in the theory of laissez-faire racism.

On Laissez-Faire Racism

. . . Laissez-faire racism involves persistent negative stereotyping of African Americans, a tendency to blame blacks themselves for the black-white gap in socioeconomic status, and resistance to meaningful policy efforts to ameliorate U.S. racist social conditions and institutions. It represents a critical new stage in American racism. As structures of racial oppression became less formal, as the power resources available to black communities grew and were effectively deployed, as other cultural trends paved the way for an assault on notions of biologically ranked "races," the stage was set for displacing Jim Crow racism and erecting something different in its place. . . .

The second point to emphasize here is that this is an argument about general patterns of group relations and ideology—not merely about variation in views among individuals from a single racial or ethnic category. As such, our primary concern is with the central tendency of attitudes and beliefs within and between racial groups and the social system as such, not within and between individuals. It is the collective dimensions of social experience that I most intend to convey with the notion of laissez-faire racism—not a singular attitude held to a greater or lesser degree by particular individuals. The intellectual case for such a perspective has been most forcefully articulated by the sociologist Mary R. Jackman (1994, 119). We should focus an analysis of attitudes and ideology on group-level comparisons, she writes, because doing so

> draws attention to the structural conditions that encase an intergroup relationship and it underscores the point that individual actors are not free agents but caught in an aggregate relationship. Unless we assume that the individual is socially atomized, her personal experiences constitute only one source of information that is evaluated against the backdrop of her manifold observations of the aggregated experiences (both historical and contemporaneous) of the group as a whole.

The focus is thus more on the larger and enduring patterns and tendencies that distinguish groups than on the individual sources of variation.

With this in mind, I want to focus on three pieces of data, the first of which concerns the persistence of negative stereotypes of African Americans. Figure 1 reports data from a national Web-based survey I recently conducted using eight of Paul Sniderman's stereotype questions

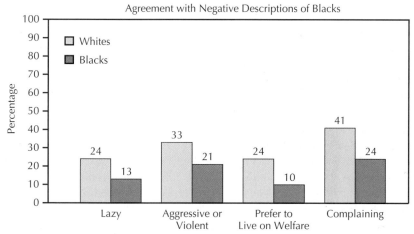

FIGURE 1 **Stereotype Items, by Race.** *Source:* Race, Crime, and Public Opinion Study (2001).

(four dealing with positive social traits and four dealing with negative social traits) (Sniderman and Piazza 1993). Several patterns stand out. It is easier for both blacks and whites to endorse the positive traits when expressing views about the characteristics of blacks than the negative traits. However, African Americans are always more favorable and less negative in their views than whites. Some of the differences are quite large. For instance, there is a thirty-percentage-point difference between white and black perceptions on the trait of intelligence and a thirty-three-percentage-point difference on the "hardworking" trait. . . .

Negative stereotypes of African Americans are common, though not uniform, and to a distressing degree they exist among both blacks and whites and presumably influence perceptions and behaviors for both groups. However, there is a sharp difference in central tendency within each group, in predictable directions. One cannot escape the conclusion that most whites have different and decidedly lesser views of the basic behavioral characteristics of blacks than do blacks themselves. And that generally these patterns indicate that African Americans remain a culturally dishonored and debased group in the American psyche. . . .

On the Peculiar Role of Social Science

Mainstream scholars on the left tend to treat race as a categorical designation that affects the outcomes that matter to us for reasons that have nothing to do with race as a sociological phenomenon. If African Americans have lower employment chances or earnings than whites, this is not a function of race but rather of purely "statistical discrimination" or other factors, such as different levels of education and skill, that somehow "explain" the extraneous influence of race. Since we do not believe in race as an inherent biological or primordial cultural factor that produces social outcomes, there must be other nonracial social conditions that account for any effect of race on outcomes that matter. The analog to this line of reasoning in examinations of political attitudes and public opinion is the treatment of African Americans as an out-group attitude object, an object toward which individual whites have been socialized to hold more or less negative attitudes.

To the credit of liberal social analysts, both approaches reject biological and inflexible cultural understandings of race and racial differences. Yet both approaches fail to come to grips with the condition of embedded white privilege and the import of constrained but quite real black agency. That is, there are sociologically meaningful "imagined communities," communities of identity as well as of typical residence, interaction, family connection, and larger interest defined as black and white that exist in relation to one another in the United States. And indeed, race has been used at various points and in various ways as one of the fundamental principles in organizing an array of conditions that define the relationship between those sociological units or imagined communities. Hence, its effects are not reducible to other, putatively more fundamental causes.

Let me be more specific by taking an example from the realm of racial attitudes and public opinion. The theory of symbolic racism contends that a new form of antiblack prejudice has arisen among whites reflecting a blend of early learned traditional values (for example, individualism and the Protestant work ethic) and early learned negative feelings and beliefs about blacks. This new attitude is an amalgamation. It consists of a resentment of demands made by blacks, a resentment of special favors received, especially from government, by blacks, and a denial of the contemporary relevance of discrimination. These views

constitute a coherent attitude, an attitude not bearing any functional relation to white advantage or privilege or to real-world black challenge and resistance to white privilege. Rather, the attitude is a learned ideation of centrally unreasoned, emotion-laden content. When political issues arise that make race and African Americans salient, this underlying psychological disposition becomes the basis of whites' political response. Hence, prejudice *intrudes* into politics.

What I want to suggest is that prejudice is *in and of* politics—not an ideational intrusion of the individual's emotionally expressive and irrational impulses upon the political sphere (Bobo and Tuan, forthcoming). As I have argued elsewhere, intergroup attitudes are not principally individual-level judgments of like and dislike (Bobo, Kluegel, and Smith 1997; Bobo and Smith 1998). Instead, following the inspiration of Herbert Blumer (1958), I argue that these attitudes centrally involve beliefs and feelings about the proper relation between groups. Racial attitudes capture aspects of the preferred group positions and those patterns of belief and affect that undergird, mobilize as needed, and make understandable the prevailing racial order.

These remarks have specific meaning with regard to the conceptualization and measurement of a notion like symbolic racism. Beliefs and feelings about whether blacks receive special treatment, favors, or an unfair advantage or have leaders and a political agenda that demand too much are not merely ventilations of atomistic feelings of resentment or hostility. These are highly political judgments about the status, rights, and resources that members of different *groups* are rightly entitled to enjoy or make claims on.

This difference in conceptualization is an important one and is directly linked to my concern with white privilege and black agency. From the vantage point of symbolic racism theory, there is no instrumental or rational objective whatsoever behind the intrusion of prejudice into politics. Whites are neither seeking the maintenance of privilege nor responding in any grounded fashion to real social, political, and economic demands arising from the black community and its leaders. Instead, the theory holds, a mixture of emotions, fears, anxieties, and resentments combines with important social values to occasion a hostile response when African Americans and their concerns are made politically salient (Kinder and Sanders 1996; Sears, van Laar, and Kosterman 1997).

Although not intended as such, this view trivializes African Americans' political activism and struggle that put issues like desegregation, antidiscrimination, affirmative action, and increasingly the matter of reparations on the national political agenda. Real political actors pursued deliberate strategies and waged hard-fought legal, electoral, and protest-oriented battles to advance the interests of black communities. These actions had powerful effects on the larger dynamics of politics and public opinion (Lee 2002). And however imperfect and imbued with exaggerated apprehensions they may have been, white Americans nonetheless perceived and responded to these very substantively political struggles (Bobo 1988). Hence, to classify white attitudes and beliefs about black demands, black leadership, and black responses to disadvantage as some sort of "pre-political," completely emotional ideation is to trivialize black America, to infantilize white America, and to skirt serious engagement with the many powerful "wages" that still accrue to whiteness.

Empirically and in terms of measurement, this argument raises serious doubts about how to understand the meaning of responses to the questions used to tap symbolic racism. For example, my own research suggests that when many whites say that blacks (or any other minority group) are "taking unfair advantage of privileges given to them by the government," these are not vague resentments (Bobo 1999). These sentiments are almost certainly not precisely calculated assessments of real risks and actual losses, but they are still expressly political judgments about the quality of life and about important resources, at once material and symbolic, that groups may get from the state.

In particular, whites who answer in the affirmative to this sort of survey question frequently speak of their tax dollars and their work effort going to support others, in the concrete language of a zero-sum resource transfer. A good illustration of the point comes from the cultural sociologist Michele Lamont's important new book, *The Dignity of Working Men: Morality and the Boundaries of Race, Class, and Immigration* (2000, 60–61). She writes of one of her subjects:

> Vincent is a workhorse. He considers himself "top gun" at his job and makes a very decent living. His comments on blacks suggest that he associates them with laziness and

welfare and with claims to receiving special treatment at work through programs such as affirmative action. He says: "Blacks have a tendency to . . . try to get off doing less, the least possible . . . to keep the job where whites will put in that extra oomph. I know this is a generality and it does not go for all, it goes for a portion. It's this whole unemployment and welfare gig. A lot of the blacks on welfare have no desire to get off it. Why should they? It's free money. I can't stand to see my hard-earned money [*said with emphasis*] going to pay for someone who wants to sit on his ass all day long and get free money."

As Lamont (2000, 62) concludes about a number of the white working-class men she interviewed: "They underscore a concrete link between the perceived dependency of blacks, their laziness, and the taxes taken from their own paychecks."

This is not an isolated finding of Lamont's in-depth interviews. For example, the sociologist Mary Waters (1999, 177) observed a very similar pattern among the white managers and employers she studied. She writes:

> Most white respondents were much more able to tap into their negative impressions of black people, especially "underclass" blacks whom they were highly critical of. These opinions were not just based on disinterested observation. There was a direct sense among many of the whites that they personally were being taken advantage of and threatened by the black population.

The language used is one of traits (laziness) and violations of values (hard work and self-reliance) coupled with moral condemnation, but the group comparison, sense of threat, and identity-engaging element is equally clear. Indeed, as the experimental social psychologist Eliot Smith (1993, 308–9) has persuasively argued, it is exactly this blend of important group identity and resource threat to the group that *should* be emotionally arousing: "These items and the definition all involve appraisals of an outgroup as violating ingroup norms or obtaining illegitimate advantages, leading to the emotion of anger." Conceptualizing such responses as the ventilation of resentment distorts the critical point that "the focus in the model advanced here is not the intrinsically negative qualities attributed to blacks themselves (which are the theoretical key in concepts of prejudice as a negative attitude) but *appraisals of the threats posed by blacks to the perceiver's own group*" (309, emphasis in original).

The substance of the theory and the interpretation of the measures of symbolic racism thus suffer from a failure of sociological imagination. The theory pushes out of analytical view the real and substantial linkage between the facts of white privilege and the facts of active black challenge to it. In their place, the theory gives us but the phantasms of racial resentments in the minds of individual whites. These phantasms somehow—but apparently unintentionally—enter politics, take note of black agitation and disruption, and then release in a spasm of reaction against race-targeted social policies. I would like to suggest that there is something decidedly wrong with the theory and conceptualization, even though the many sentiments identified in the concepts of symbolic racism and racial resentment are indeed at the heart of the contemporary political struggle over race (Krysan 2000).

On the right side of the political spectrum, the example I wish to draw attention to is the mounting speculation, most prominently offered by Stephan and Abigail Thernstrom (1997), that the pervasive patterns of racial segregation we observe in the United States are a function of "black self-segregation." In this case, African Americans are credited with agency, but that agency is said to be exercised in a manner that continues to disadvantage blacks. Only this time it is blacks themselves who, by choosing a self-handicapping preference, are responsible. The argument is a troubling one for anyone who believes that neighborhoods vary in school quality, safety, social services and amenities, and all that goes into the phrase "quality of life." It says that blacks are, perforce and of their own free will, placing racial solidarity above social mobility and a better quality of life.

The failure here is twofold. First, the Thernstroms' argument is contingent on the rejection of compelling empirical evidence of racial bias and discrimination in the housing market (for an authoritative review, see Charles 2003). It is clear that a powerful racial hierarchy continues to permeate thinking about communities, neighborhoods, and where to live. Using experimental data, Camille Z. Charles and I show that white Americans are systematically more open to residential contact with Asians and Latinos than with blacks—holding every other consideration constant (Zubrinsky and Bobo 1996). Several studies have now made it clear

that antiblack racial stereotypes are direct predictors of willingness to live in more integrated communities (Farley et al. 1994; Bobo and Zubrinsky 1996; Charles 2000).

These results are consistent with other demographic and behavioral data (Yinger 1998). Researchers at the State University of New York at Albany document the very small changes in high rates of black-white residential segregation between 1990 and 2000. Indeed, HUD auditing studies in 1989 found overall rates of discrimination in access to housing for African Americans that were only trivially different from those observed a decade earlier.

Second, the theory of black self-segregation treats black choice and action as if it exists in a vacuum. That is, it ignores altogether what are almost surely important feedback mechanisms that prompt many blacks to self-select into black neighborhoods out of the reasonable expectation that they would encounter hostility from some white neighbors. As formulated by the Thernstroms and others, the self-segregation hypothesis fails to address the immediately relevant question of whether African Americans would self-select into predominantly black communities in the absence of historic experience, current collective memory, and ongoing encounters with contemporary racism. The best available empirical evidence suggests that blacks as a group are the people who are the most likely to prefer integration and to comfortably accept living in minority group status in a neighborhood (Charles 2000).

Part of the message here concerning theoretical interpretation on the right and the left is that variables and data never speak for themselves. It is the questions we pose (and those we fail to ask) as well as our theories, concepts, and ideas that bring a narrative and meaning to marginal distributions, correlations, regression coefficients, and statistics of all kinds. If we suffer from failures of sociological imagination, if we conceive of race and racism in ways that disassociate them from white privilege, black agency, and the interrelations between the two phenomena, then we are bound to get things wrong however much we may have followed formal statistical criteria and other normative canons of science. Or, as the sociologist Tukufu Zuberi (2001, 144) puts it in his new book, *Thicker Than Blood: How Racial Statistics Lie:* "Most racial statistics lack a critical evaluation of racist structures that encourage pathological interpretations. These pathological interpretations have had a profound impact on our causal theories and statistical methods. Our theories of society, not our empirical evidence, guide how we interpret racial data."

Indeed, it is that perspective on racist structures, or what the political scientists Michael Dawson (2001) and Claire Jean Kim (2000) call the American racial order, that informs a very different reading of the import of white privilege and black agency.

Caveats

A series of interpretative caveats should be borne in mind here. First, although I have spoken extensively about black-white relations, I am mindful of the extent to which this is an increasingly partial view of American race relations. The rapid and continuing expansion of the Asian and Latino populations in the United States and the unique experiences and issues faced by members of these internally diverse communities will inevitably reshape the American social landscape. However, it is not at all clear that the continued diversification of the United States in any way fundamentally destabilizes the historic black-white divide. The urban sociologist Herbert Gans (1999) has written a provocative and I think more than suggestive essay arguing that we are evolving as a nation toward a new major racial dichotomy: the black versus the non-black. Accordingly, we would still have racial hierarchy and some degree of heterogeneity, especially within the nonblack category (which include whites and those effectively earning the title of honorary whites, such as successful middle-class Asians). And much of the arsenal of analytical tools and perspectives that long helped to make sense of the black-white divide would have applicability in such a new context. Similarly, my colleague Mary Waters's (1999) powerful recent book, *Black Identities: West Indian Immigrant Dreams and American Realities*, makes clear just how salient the black-white divide remains even for an immigrant population that arrived committed to transcending race.

Second, wartime and the social upheaval occasioned by war can present a powerful opportunity for reshaping the landscape of race relations. Indeed, the political scientists Philip Klinkner and Rogers Smith (1999) craft a persuasive claim that war is a necessary but not sufficient precondition for improvements in the status of blacks. They argue that far-reaching qualitative changes in the status of African Americans have typically involved the convergence of three factors: a major wartime mobilization that ultimately required a large number of black troops; an enemy viewed as profoundly antidemocratic, thereby heightening the claims for fuller realization of democratic ideals at home; and significant internal political mobilization and contestation from below demanding reform.

Viewed in this light, the terrorist attacks on the United States of September 11, 2001, and the subsequent military actions in Afghanistan against the al Qaeda network and the ruling Taliban regime and the later war in Iraq raise again the possibility of this convergence of circumstances. That the early televised images of the devastation at the World Trade Center in New York were so thoroughly multiracial and multiethnic only heightens this potential. And that African Americans in the persons of Colin Powell and Condoleezza Rice occupy such high leadership posts adds to the salutary import of the moment. Certainly we are already witnessing journalistic accounts of a nation pulling together and uniting in ways that may heal otherwise deep racial divisions.

Yet at this moment there are no strong indications that these events will seriously shift the landscape of black-white relations. Not all wartime moments do, as Klinkner and Smith note with regard to the Spanish-American War, the Korean War, and the Vietnam War.

Third, I have scarcely touched upon the matter of class divisions within the African American community and the growth of the black middle class. Nor, for that matter, have I wrestled with the ways in which gender and sexuality also condition life along the color line. It must be stressed that class, gender, and sexuality all become dividing lines within the African American community (and outside it) in ways that shape agendas, the capacity for mobilization, and even ideas about who is a full member of the community (Cohen 1999; Dawson 1994, 2001). My objective has been to focus on those aspects of contemporary race relations that largely cut across these cleavages and thus are centrally experienced as "race," rather than examine the intersection of race with

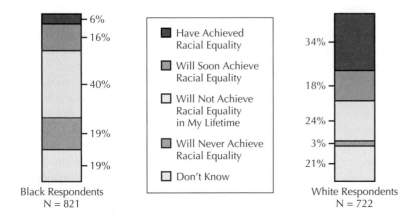

Do you think that blacks have achieved racial equality,
will soon achieve racial equality, will not achieve racial
equality in your lifetime, or will never achieve racial equality?

FIGURE 2   Respondents Race and Beliefs About Racial Equality.

Source: National African American Election Study (2000).

other statuses and identities. I do not mean to dismiss or disregard these other factors, but rather to stress that there remain social conditions we must understand and engage as a distinctive racial divide.

Conclusion

I opened with the words of a young, angry white male who saw "trashy" Section 8 blacks coming into his neighborhood with government subsidies and diminishing what he perceived as a standard of life that he had earned and that set him above and apart from them. And with the words of a middle-aged, churchgoing black woman who returned to her home one Sunday morning not only to do battle with a burglar but later with the racially biased police and criminal justice system. As these two cases attest, race remains a deep divide in America.

Of course, black and white Americans could scarcely be further apart in their own judgments about the severity of the racial divide. As part of an election study in 2000, Michael Dawson and I asked a large national sample of blacks and whites about the likelihood of achieving racial equality in America. Figure 2 shows the results. A full one-third of whites said that we had already achieved it, in

contrast to a mere 6 percent of African Americans. One in five blacks said that we never would achieve it, and another two out of five said that it would never happen in their lifetimes. Blacks see a deep and lingering social ill, and whites see a problem that is just about resolved. Without claiming to "know" the answer, I interpret responses of "have already achieved racial equality" and perhaps even of "will soon achieve racial equality" to constitute a deliberate evasion of responsibility more than a thoughtful assessment or response to social realities (Kluegel and Smith 1986; Kluegel and Bobo 2001). Too many friction points, inequalities, and signs of discrimination remain to take such views at face value.

Indeed, it is fair to still speak of white supremacy in America and of racism in America (Bonilla-Silva 2001; Feagin 2001). The persistence of white supremacy and the enduring potency of racism, I believe, trace to the adaptive capacity of racial ideologies. As Thomas Holt (2000, 27–28) has explained: "Race is ideological, but, being embedded in political economies that are quite historically specific, it cannot long survive changes in the material base from which it draws sustenance." The defeat of Jim Crow racism and the victories of the civil rights era did not eradicate black-white economic inequality, labor market discrimination, or gargantuan disparities in accumulated wealth; they did not end residential segregation by race and randomly disperse people in physical space; they did not reallocate political power; and they did not completely repudiate the racist stereotypes and other elements of American political culture and whites' sense of entitlement that feed and sustain racism.

These victories did, however, fundamentally restructure the terrain on which racism is now enacted, understood, and reproduced. This new regime of laissez-faire racism is more fluid and permeable than the Jim Crow regime. It works in ways that permit, on the one hand, the carefully delimited and controlled success of a Colin Powell, a Condoleezza Rice, or even an Oprah Winfrey, but that, on the other hand, do not eliminate the ghetto, black joblessness, and poverty and do not even wince at a despicable effort at black voter disenfranchisement. Indeed, it works in ways that allow a young working-class white man to seethe with anger at a social policy effort to extend a step up for poor blacks and in ways that allow a churchgoing black woman to endure the tragic burden of fighting a black burglar and the white police. These are all manifestations of our continued entrapment in the snare of racism.

I have no battle plan for defeating laissez-faire racism. What we can do as scholars is, first, to struggle to conceptualize, name, and understand as accurately as possible what is happening and to make those ideas widely available. Let's tell the story of enduring inequality in its fullness and according to the highest standards that we can attain.

Second, we can push for changes and social policies that speak to what our analyses tell us are the central structural and cultural problems. In that regard, the push for a serious dialogue about race—for truth and reconciliation, for an apology, and most of all for reparations—is a major element of the next stage of the struggle (Dawson and Popoff 2004). Liberal and progressive voices must turn away from the demand that the black political agenda be entirely suppressed in favor of a race-neutral, purely universalistic or centrist political agenda (see Thompson 1998).

And third, I do not believe it is possible to accomplish a recognition of one's full humanity without demanding it as such. Careful political thinking and organizing is necessary, to be sure. Strategic coalitions reaching across lines of class, color, and ethnicity will be essential. Working through conventional legal and political channels will be necessary too. But I remain doubtful that hidden agendas and half-measures will do what it takes to finally crush the legacy of white supremacy in America, to dislodge laissez-faire racism, and to lead us to that mountaintop that Martin Luther King spoke of the night before he was assassinated.

21 Residential Segregation and Neighborhood Conditions in U.S. Metropolitan Areas

Douglas S. Massey

DOUGLAS S. MASSEY is the Henry G. Bryant Professor of Sociology and Public Affairs at Princeton University. His book *American Apartheid* (co-authored with Nancy A. Denton) won the 1995 Distinguished Scholarly Publication Award from the American Sociological Association.

Questions to Consider Douglas Massey points out that almost all racial and ethnic groups are highly segregated in the United States. Racially integrated neighborhoods are an anomaly. Why is residential segregation the norm rather than the exception? Why are blacks subject to the most severe discrimination in the housing market?

SOCIAL SCIENTISTS HAVE LONG STUDIED patterns of racial and ethnic segregation because of the close connection between a group's spatial position in society and its socioeconomic well-being. Opportunities and resources are unevenly distributed in space; some neighborhoods have safer streets, higher home values, better services, more effective schools, and more supportive peer environments than others. As people and families improve their socioeconomic circumstances, they generally move to gain access to these benefits. In doing so, they seek to convert past socioeconomic achievements into improved residential circumstances, yielding tangible immediate benefits and enhancing future prospects for social mobility by providing greater access to residentially determined resources.

Throughout U.S. history, racial and ethnic groups arriving in the United States for the first time have settled in enclaves located close to an urban core, in areas of mixed land use, old housing, poor services, and low or decreasing socioeconomic status. As group members build up time in the city, however, and as their socioeconomic status rises, they have tended to move out of these enclaves into areas that offer more amenities and improved conditions—areas in which majority members are more prevalent—leading to their progressive spatial assimilation into society.

The twin processes of immigrant settlement, on the one hand, and spatial assimilation, on the other, combine to yield a diversity of segregation patterns across groups and times, depending on the particular histories of inmigration and socioeconomic mobility involved (Massey, 1985). Groups experiencing recent rapid inmigration and slow socioeconomic mobility tend to display relatively high levels of segregation, whereas those with rapid rates of economic mobility and slow rates of immigration tend to be more integrated.

When avenues of spatial assimilation are systematically blocked by prejudice and discrimination, however, residential segregation increases and persists over time. New minorities arrive in the city and settle within enclaves, but their subsequent spatial mobility is stymied, and ethnic concentrations increase until the enclaves are filled, whereupon group members are forced into adjacent areas, thus expanding the boundaries of the enclave (Duncan and Duncan, 1957). In the United States, most immigrant groups experienced relatively few residential barriers, so levels of ethnic segregation historically were not very high. Using a standard segregation index (the **index of dissimilarity**), which varies from 0 to 100,

index of dissimilarity: An index or measure used to represent the level of residential segregation in region or city.

European ethnic groups rarely had indexes of more than 60 (Massey, 1985; Massey and Denton, 1992).

Blacks, in contrast, traditionally experienced severe prejudice and discrimination in urban housing markets. As they moved into urban areas from 1900 to 1960, therefore, their segregation indices rose to unprecedented heights, compared with earlier times and groups. By mid-century, segregation indices exceeded 60 virtually everywhere; and in the largest Black communities they often reached 80 or more (Massey and Denton, 1989b, 1993).

Such high indices of residential segregation imply a restriction of opportunity for Blacks compared with other groups. Discriminatory barriers in urban housing markets mean individual Black citizens are less able to capitalize on their hard-won attainments and achieve desirable residential locations. Compared with Whites of similar social status, Blacks tend to live in systematically disadvantaged neighborhoods, even within suburbs (Schneider and Logan, 1982; Massey et al., 1987; Massey and Fong, 1990; Massey and Denton, 1992).

In a very real way, barriers to spatial mobility are barriers to social mobility; and a racially segregated society cannot logically claim to be "color-blind." The way a group is spatially incorporated into society is as important to its socioeconomic well-being as the manner in which it is incorporated into the labor force. It is important, therefore, that levels and trends in residential segregation be documented so that this variable can be incorporated fully into research and theorizing about the causes of urban poverty. To accomplish this, presented here is an overview and interpretation of historical trends in the residential segregation of Blacks, Hispanics, and Asians.

Long-Term Trends in Black Segregation

Blacks and Whites were distinctly segregated from one another across state boundaries early in the twentieth century. In 1900, for example, 64 percent of all Blacks would have had to move to a different state to achieve an even distribution across state lines, and most Blacks lived in a state that was 36 percent Black. These figures simply state the obvious, that in 1900, some 90 percent of Blacks lived in a handful of southern states, which contained only 25 percent of all Whites (U.S. Bureau of the Census, 1979).

In the South, most Blacks lived in rural counties that were approximately 45 percent Black, yielding a high degree of segregation and racial isolation at the county level as well. The dissimilarity index for 1900 reveals that nearly 70 percent of all Blacks would have had to shift their county of residence to achieve an even racial distribution across county lines.

At the beginning of the twentieth century, for Blacks, the typical residential setting was southern and rural; for Whites it was northern and urban. Under conditions of high state- and county-level segregation, race relations remained largely a regional problem centered in the South. Successive waves of Black migration out of the rural South into the urban North transformed the geographic structure of Black segregation during the twentieth century, however, ending the regional isolation and rural confinement of Blacks.

The movement of Blacks out of rural areas, however, was accompanied by their progressive segregation within cities. Although we lack indices of Black-White dissimilarity for 1900, research has demonstrated that Blacks were not particularly segregated in northern cities during the nineteenth century. Ward-level dissimilarity for Blacks in 11 northern cities circa 1860 had average indices of approximately 46 (Massey and Denton, 1993).

By 1910, however, the eight cities had an average index of 56, and the level of Black-White dissimilarity increased sharply during each decade after 1910, suggesting the progressive formation of black ghettos in cities throughout the nation. As Lieberson (1980) has shown, the growth of Black populations in urban areas triggered the imposition of higher levels of racial segregation within cities. Before the U.S. Supreme Court declared them unconstitutional in 1916, many U.S. cities actually passed apartheid laws establishing separate Black and White districts. Thereafter, however, segregation was achieved by less formal means (see Massey and Denton, 1993:26–42). Whatever the mechanism, the end result was a rapid increase in Black residential segregation, with the neighborhood segregation index rising from 56 to 78 between 1910 and 1940, a remarkable increase of 39 percent in just three decades.

The combination of growing urban Black populations and higher levels of segregation could only produce one possible outcome—higher levels of Black isolation. In 1900, the relatively small number of urban Blacks and the rather low level of Black-White segregation resulted in a low degree of racial isolation within neighborhoods. Urban Blacks early in the century were quite likely to know and interact socially with Whites (Massey and Denton, 1993:19–26). Indeed, on average they were more likely to share a neighborhood with a White person than with a Black person.

By 1930, however, the geographic structure of segregation had changed dramatically, shifting from state and county levels to the neighborhood level. The average isolation index was now 39 in neighborhoods, indicating that most Black residents in the cities under study lived in a ward that was almost 40 percent Black. In some cities, the degree of racial isolation reached truly extreme levels. The transformation was most dramatic in Chicago, where the isolation index went from 10 in 1900 to 70 in 1930, by which time, moreover, the dissimilarity index had reached 85. Similar conditions of intense Black segregation occurred in Cleveland, which by 1930 displayed a dissimilarity index of 85 and an isolation index of 51.

• • •

Despite the relative stability of segregation achieved by 1970 at the state, county, and neighborhood levels, a remarkable change was occurring at the city level. From 1950 onward, Blacks and Whites were becoming more and more segregated across *municipal* boundaries. After 1950, Blacks and Whites not only tended to live in different neighborhoods; increasingly they lived in different municipalities as well. After 1950, in other words, Blacks and Whites came to reside in wholly different towns and cities. From 1950 to 1980, the index of Black-White dissimilarity increased from 35 to 49 at the municipal level, a change of 40 percent in just 30 years, a shift that was remarkably similar to the rapid change observed in neighborhood-level segregation during the early period of ghetto formation. Black isolation went from an index of 19 to 35 at the municipal level, an increase of 84 percent. By the end of the 1970s, the average Black urban dweller lived in a municipality that was 35 percent Black; and one-half of all urban Blacks would have had to exchange places with Whites to achieve an even municipal distribution.

The emergence of significant municipal-level segregation in the United States reflects demographic trends that occurred in all parts of the urban hierarchy—in nonmetropolitan areas as well as central cities and suburbs. In 1950, there were no predominantly Black central cities in the United States. Among cities with more than 100,000 inhabitants, none had a Black percentage in excess of 50 percent. By 1990, however, 14 cities were at least 50 percent Black,

including Atlanta, Baltimore, Detroit, Gary, Newark, New Orleans, and Washington; together they were home to 11 percent of all Blacks in the United States. In addition, another 11 cities were approaching Black majorities by 1990, with percentages ranging from 40 percent to 50 percent, including Cleveland, St. Louis, and Oakland. Among cities with populations of 25,000 or more, only two municipalities in the entire United States were more than 50 percent Black in 1950, both in the South; but by 1990 the number had increased to 40. Some of these cities—such as Prichard, Alabama; Kinston, North Carolina; and Vicksburg, Mississippi—were located in nonmetropolitan areas of the South. Others—such as Maywood, Illinois; Highland Park, Michigan; and Inglewood, California—were suburbs of large central cities in the North and West.

Recent Trends in Black Segregation

Table 1 shows indicators of Black residential segregation for the 30 U.S. metropolitan areas with the largest Black populations. These data are used to evaluate racial segregation from two vantage points. The first three columns show trends in the indices of spatial separation between Blacks and Whites using the index of dissimilarity, and the next three columns show trends in indices of Black residential isolation. The indices for 1970 and 1980, from Massey and Denton (1987), are metropolitan areas based on 1970 boundaries. Indices for 1990, from Harrison and Weinberg (1992), are based on 1990 geographic definitions. White and Black Hispanics were excluded, by both sets of researchers, from their subject sets of Whites and Blacks, and both sets of researchers computed indices using tracts as units of analysis.

Among the northern metropolitan areas shown, there is little evidence of any trend toward Black residential integration. Black segregation indices averaged about 85 in 1970, 80 in 1980, and 78 in 1990, a decline of only 8 percent in 20 years. Dissimilarity indices more than 60 are generally considered high, whereas those between 30 and 60 are considered moderate (Kantrowitz, 1973). At the rate of change observed between 1970 and 1990, the average level of Black-White segregation in northern areas would not reach the lower limits of the high range until the year 2043. At the slower rate of change prevailing from 1970 to 1980, it would take until 2067. As of 1990, no large northern Black community approached even a moderate level of residential segregation.

TABLE 1 **Trends in Black Segregation and Isolation in the 30 Metropolitan Areas with the Largest Black Populations, 1970 to 1990**

Metropolitan	Dissimilarity Indices			Isolation Indices		
	1970[a]	1980[a]	1990[b]	1970[a]	1980[a]	1990[b]
Northern						
Boston, MA	81.2	77.6	68.2	56.7	55.1	51.2
Buffalo, NY	87.0	79.4	81.8	71.2	63.5	68.1
Chicago, IL	91.9	87.8	85.8	85.8	82.8	83.9
Cincinnati, OH	76.8	72.3	75.8	59.1	54.3	61.0
Cleveland, OH	90.8	87.5	85.1	81.9	90.4	80.8
Columbus, OH	81.8	71.4	67.3	63.5	57.5	52.5
Detroit, MI	88.4	86.7	87.6	75.9	77.3	82.3
Gary-Hammond-E. Chicago, IL	91.4	90.6	89.9	80.4	77.3	84.2
Indianapolis, IN	81.7	76.2	74.3	64.5	62.3	61.0
Kansas City, MO	87.4	78.9	72.6	74.2	69.0	61.6
Los Angeles-Long Beach, CA	91.0	81.1	73.1	70.3	60.4	69.3
Milwaukee, WI	90.5	83.9	82.8	73.9	69.5	72.4
New York, NY	81.0	82.0	82.2	58.8	62.7	81.9
Newark, NJ	81.4	81.6	82.5	67.0	69.2	78.6
Philadelphia, PA	79.5	78.8	77.2	68.2	69.6	72.2
Pittsburgh, PA	75.0	72.7	71.0	53.5	54.1	53.1
St. Louis, MO	84.7	81.3	77.0	76.5	72.9	69.5
San Francisco-Oakland, CA	80.1	71.7	66.8	56.0	51.1	56.1
Average	84.5	80.1	77.8	68.7	66.1	68.9
Southern						
Atlanta, GA	82.1	78.5	67.8	78.0	74.8	66.5
Baltimore, MD	81.9	74.7	71.4	77.2	72.3	70.6
Birmingham, AL	37.8	40.8	71.7	45.1	50.2	69.6
Dallas-Ft. Worth, TX	86.9	77.1	63.1	76.0	64.0	58.0
Greensboro-Winston Salem, NC	65.4	56.0	60.9	56.1	50.1	55.5
Houston, TX	78.1	69.5	66.8	66.4	59.3	63.6
Memphis, TN	75.9	71.6	69.3	78.0	75.9	75.0
Miami, FL	85.1	77.8	71.8	75.2	64.2	47.1
New Orleans, LA	73.1	68.3	68.8	71.3	68.8	71.9
Norfolk-Virginia Beach, VA	75.7	63.1	50.3	73.5	62.8	55.9
Tampa-St. Petersburg, FL	79.9	72.6	69.7	58.0	51.5	51.0
Washington, DC	81.1	70.1	66.1	77.2	68.0	66.7
Average	75.3	68.3	66.5	69.3	63.5	64.9

[a]Indices are from Massey and Denton (1987).
[b]Indices are from Harrison and Weinberg (1992).

Indeed, in most metropolitan areas, racial segregation remained very high throughout the 20-year period. Dissimilarity indices were essentially constant in seven metropolitan areas—Cincinnati, Detroit, Gary, New York, Newark, and Philadelphia; in seven others—Buffalo, Chicago, Cleveland, Indianapolis, Milwaukee, Pittsburgh, and St. Louis—small declines still left Blacks extremely segregated. All the latter metropolitan areas had dissimilarity indices exceeding 70 in 1990, and in four cases, the index was more than 80. No other ethnic or racial group in the history of the United States has ever, even briefly, experienced such high levels of residential segregation (Massey and Denton, 1993).

A few metropolitan areas experienced significant declines in the level of Black-White segregation between 1970 and 1990, although the pace of change slowed considerably during the 1980s, compared with the 1970s. In Columbus, Ohio, for example, Black-White dissimilarity fell by more than 10 index points from 1970 to 1980 (from 82 to 71), but then dropped by only 4 points through 1990. Likewise, San Francisco dropped from 80 to 72 during the 1970s, but went to just 68 by 1990.

The only areas that experienced a sustained decline in Black-White segregation across both decades were Los Angeles and Boston; but in each case, the overall index of segregation remained well within the high range. The drop in Los Angeles probably reflects the displacement of Blacks by the arrival of large numbers of Asian and, particularly, Hispanic immigrants (Massey and Denton, 1987). By 1990, for example, Watts, the core of the 1960s Black ghetto, had become predominantly Hispanic (Turner and Allen, 1991). The arrival of more than a million new immigrants in Los Angeles County between 1970 and 1980 put substantial pressure on the housing stock, and increased intergroup competition for residential units, especially at the low end of the market, leading to considerable neighborhood flux and residential mixing (Frey and Farley, 1996).

When large Black communities are subject to high levels of segregation, intense racial isolation is inevitable. In 1990, six metropolitan areas—Chicago, Cleveland, Detroit, Gary, New York, and Newark—had isolation indices of 80 or more, meaning that most Black people lived in neighborhoods that were more than 80 percent Black. Detailed analyses of neighborhoods show, however, that this overall average is misleading, because it represents a balance between a small minority of Blacks who

reside in highly integrated neighborhoods and a large majority of Blacks who live in all-Black neighborhoods (Denton and Massey, 1991). Moreover, in four of the six metropolitan areas, the level of Black isolation actually increased between 1970 and 1990.

In other northern areas, the prevailing pattern of change in racial isolation was one of stability, with shifts of less than 5 percent from 1970 to 1990. The average isolation index of 68.9 in 1990 was virtually identical to the index of 68.7 observed two decades earlier; in other words, 20 years after the Fair Housing Act, Blacks were still unlikely to come into residential contact with members of other groups. The large ghettos of the North have remained substantially intact and were largely unaffected by civil rights legislation of the 1960s.

Trends in Black segregation and isolation are somewhat different in the South, where segregation levels traditionally have been lower because of the distinctive history and character of southern cities. With social segregation enforced by Jim Crow legislation, Blacks and Whites before 1960 often lived in close physical proximity, with Black-inhabited alleys being interspersed between larger, White-occupied avenues (Demerath and Gilmore, 1954). During the postwar housing boom, moreover, rural Black settlements were often overtaken by expanding White suburbs, thereby creating the appearance of racial integration. For these and other reasons, Black-White segregation scores in the South traditionally have averaged about 10 points lower than in the North (Massey and Denton, 1993).

This regional differential is roughly maintained, but southern areas display considerably greater diversity, despite the regional averages, than in the North. In some metropolitan areas, such as Baltimore, Houston, and Tampa, significant declines in segregation occurred during the 1970s, but declines slowed during the 1980s. In others, such as Dallas, Miami, and Norfolk, steady declines occurred throughout both decades. In Memphis and New Orleans, relatively small changes occurred, no matter which decade one considers. Two southern areas displayed increasing levels of Black-White segregation—Birmingham, where the increase was very sharp after 1970, and Greensboro, where an initial decline during the 1970s was reversed during the 1980s.

In general, then, Black-White segregation scores in the South appear to be converging on indices from 60 to 70, yielding an average of 67 and maintaining the traditional differential compared with the North. Metropolitan areas with segregation indices higher than the 60 to 70 range in 1970 experienced decreasing segregation, whereas those with indices less than 60 to 70 displayed increasing segregation; and those with indices within that range did not change much.

Only Norfolk differed from this pattern, with a significant and sustained decline in segregation during both decades, producing by 1990 a level of Black-White dissimilarity well within the moderate range. Many Norfolk residents are in the military, which has been more successfully integrated than other institutions in American life (Moskos and Butler, 1996). Frey and Farley (1994) demonstrated that areas dominated, economically, by military bases have significantly lower levels of Black-White segregation than others, controlling for a variety of other factors.

Although indices of Black-White dissimilarity may be lower in the South, the relative number of Blacks in urban areas is greater; so the average level of racial isolation within neighborhoods is not much different than in the North. From 1970 to 1990, there was relatively little change in the overall degree of Black isolation, with the average index decreasing from 69 in 1970 to 65 in 1990. In four southern areas—Baltimore, Memphis, Miami, and New Orleans—the Black isolation index was more than 70 in both decades; and in Birmingham, the index of Black isolation rose from 45 to 70 between 1970 and 1990. Only in Norfolk, which was rapidly desegregating, and in Tampa, which had relatively few Blacks, did isolation scores fall below 60. In most cities in the South, as in the North, Blacks were relatively unlikely to share neighborhoods with members of other racial or ethnic groups.

Thus, despite evidence of change in the South, Blacks living within the nation's largest urban Black communities are still highly segregated and spatially isolated from the rest of American society. Of the 30 northern and southern areas examined here, 19 still had Black-White dissimilarity indices in excess of 70 in 1990, and 12 had isolation indices in excess of 70. Either in absolute terms or in comparison to other groups, Blacks remain a very residentially segregated and spatially isolated people.

Recent Trends in Hispanic Segregation

Based on the historical experience of Blacks, recent demographic trends of Hispanics would be expected to have produced increasing levels of segregation during the 1970s

and 1980s. In this period, there has been a remarkable resurgence of Hispanic immigration, yielding rapidly growing Hispanic populations in many metropolitan areas. In the Los Angeles metropolitan area, for example, the Hispanic population increased by 1.3 million between 1970 and 1990; Hispanics went from being 28 percent of the population to 38 percent. Because migrant networks channel new arrivals to neighborhoods where immigrants have already settled, such rapid in-migration could be expected to increase the concentration of Hispanics within enclaves and raise overall levels of isolation and segregation (Massey, 1985).

Although spatial assimilation may occur as income rises and the generations succeed one another, these socioeconomic mechanisms occur at a much slower pace than immigration and settlement. During periods of rapid immigration, therefore, segregation levels tend to rise; and the greater and more rapid the immigration, the more pronounced the increase in segregation.

Table 2 presents indicators of Hispanic-White dissimilarity and Hispanic residential isolation for the 30 metropolitan areas containing the largest Hispanic communities in the United States. In a significant subset of these metropolitan areas, Hispanics constitute an absolute majority of the total population, a condition that does not hold for any of the Black communities listed in Table 1. Because large minority populations increase the demographic potential for isolation, and because theorists hypothesize that high minority percentages foment greater discrimination on the part of majority members (Allport, 1958; Blalock, 1967), indices are tabulated separately for areas where Hispanics comprise a majority or near-majority (48 to 49 percent) of the population.

Despite the fact that demographic conditions in these metropolitan areas operate to maximize the potential for segregation, the degree of Hispanic-White residential dissimilarity proved to be quite moderate, and actually decreases over the two decades, going from an average of 55 in 1970 to 47 in 1990. Indices of Hispanic-White segregation were essentially constant in El Paso and Miami, and changed little in San Antonio and Corpus Christi. In Brownsville and McAllen, there were pronounced declines in segregation; but in no case was there an increase in Hispanic segregation from Whites within Hispanic-majority areas.

Indices of isolation, in contrast, were high and rose somewhat from 1970 to 1990. The increases did not stem from an increasing tendency for Whites and Hispanics to live apart, however, but from the large size and rapid growth of the Hispanic population. Isolation indices of 85 and 87 in Brownsville and McAllen mainly reflect the fact that Hispanics represent 82 and 85 percent of the metropolitan populations, respectively. Even if Hispanics were evenly distributed, high levels of Hispanic-White contact are impossible to achieve in areas that are so predominantly Hispanic.

Among Blacks, however, isolation indices in the 80s, as in Chicago and Detroit, generally reflect the intense segregation of Blacks, rather than high Black population percentages; in both these metropolitan areas, Blacks constitute about 22 percent of the population. The contrast in the indices between Hispanics and Blacks is put into perspective by comparing indices for Hispanics in San Antonio with indices for Blacks in northern areas. Although

TABLE 2   Trends in Hispanic Segregation and Isolation in the 30 Metropolitan Areas with the Largest Hispanic Populations, 1970 to 1990

Metropolitan Area	Dissimilarity Indices			Isolation Indices		
	1970[a]	1980[a]	1990[b]	1970[a]	1980[b]	1990[b]
Hispanic majority						
Brownsville-Harlingen, TX	54.0[c]	42.0[d]	39.8	NA	NA	85.2
Corpus Christi, TX	55.9	51.6	47.5	63.5	63.6	67.8
El Paso, TX	49.6	51.2	49.7	71.5	74.1	80.0
McAllen-Pharr, TX	62.0[c]	48.0[d]	37.9	NA	NA	87.4
Miami, FL	50.4	51.9	50.3	46.5	58.3	73.4
San Antonio, TX	59.1	57.2	53.7	67.5	67.5	69.1
Other metropolitan						
Albuquerque, NM	45.7	42.5	41.9	54.4	50.6	53.4
Anaheim-Santa Ana, CA	32.0	41.6	49.9	19.4	31.0	50.1
Bakersfield, CA	5.8	54.5	55.4	34.9	42.1	55.7
Chicago, IL	58.4	63.5	63.2	25.1	38.0	51.3
Dallas-Ft. Worth, TX	42.5	47.8	49.5	18.6	24.0	41.1
Denver-Boulder, CO	47.4	47.4	46.5	27.4	27.5	33.8
Fresno, CA	40.8	45.4	47.8	37.6	44.6	58.7
Houston, TX	45.3	46.4	49.3	26.9	32.8	49.3
Jersey City, NJ	54.8	48.8	42.9	34.5	46.5	56.0
Los Angeles, CA	46.8	57.0	61.0	37.8	50.1	71.5
Nassau-Suffolk, NY	29.1	36.2	42.3	6.0	9.6	22.1
New York, NY	64.9	65.6	65.8	36.1	40.0	66.6
Newark, NJ	60.4	65.6	66.7	16.7	26.3	48.5
Oxnard-Simi Valley, CA	NA	NA	52.3	NA	NA	51.2
Philadelphia, PA	54.0	62.9	62.6	10.6	21.6	42.9
Phoenix, AZ	48.4	49.4	48.1	32.1	32.1	39.8
Riverside-San Bernardino, CA	37.3	36.4	35.8	30.2	31.6	42.7
Sacramento, CA	34.7	36.4	37.0	16.3	16.5	23.9

TABLE 2 (Continued)

Metropolitan Area	Dissimilarity Indices			Isolation Indices		
	1970[a]	1980[a]	1990[b]	1970[a]	1980[b]	1990[b]
San Diego, CA	33.1	42.1	45.3	19.8	26.9	43.6
San Francisco-Oakland, CA	34.7	40.2	43.9	19.2	19.3	41.1
San Jose, CA	40.2	44.5	47.8	29.6	31.7	47.1
Tampa, FL	56.0	48.4	45.3	25.0	18.2	21.5
Tucson, AZ	52.6	51.9	49.7	46.7	43.1	48.8
Washington, DC	31.8	30.5	40.9	4.3	5.4	22.5
Average	45.3	48.0	49.6	26.5	30.8	45.1

Note: The Massey-Denton computations did not include several metropolitan areas that housed large Hispanic populations in 1990; therefore, additional indices have been taken from Lopez (1981) and Hwang and Murdock (1982). These figures, however, were computed for central cities rather than metropolitan areas and are therefore somewhat higher, thus underestimating increases and overestimating declines in the level of Hispanic-White segregation.

[a] Indices are from Massey and Denton (1987).

[b] Indices from Harrison and Weinberg (1992).

[c] Indices are from Lopez (1981).

[d] Indices are from Hwang and Murdock (1982).

Hispanics constitute 48 percent of San Antonio's population, its Hispanic-White dissimilarity index of 54 is less than that for Black-White indices in any northern area; and San Antonio's Hispanic isolation index of 69 is less than it is for 7 of the 18 black isolation indices.

A better indication of what happens to Hispanics in U.S. cities can be seen by examining segregation measures computed for metropolitan areas where Hispanics do not constitute such a large percentage of the population. On average, indices of Hispanic-White dissimilarity changed little in these areas, moving upward slightly from 45 in 1970 to 50 in 1990. In about one-third of these metropolitan areas—Chicago, Denver, Houston, New York, Phoenix, Riverside, Sacramento, and Tucson—Hispanic segregation remained nearly constant from 1970 to 1990; and in three cases—Albuquerque, Jersey City, and Tampa—indices of Hispanic-White dissimilarity decreased somewhat over the decades. In the remainder of the areas, indices of Hispanic segregation increased. In most cases, the increases were modest; but in several instances, segregation increased substantially over the two decades. In Los Angeles, for example, indices of Hispanic-White segregation increased from 47 to 61; in Anaheim the increase was from 32 to 50. Large increases were also recorded in Nassau-Suffolk,

San Diego, San Francisco, and Washington, D.C. In all these metropolitan areas there were rapid rates of Hispanic population growth and immigration from 1970 to 1990.

Despite these increases, indices of Hispanic-White segregation still remained moderate in 1990. Only 5 of the 24 metropolitan areas displayed indices in excess of 60. In 3 of these—New York, Newark, and Philadelphia—Puerto Ricans predominated; and since 1970, this group has stood apart from other Hispanic populations in displaying uniquely high levels of segregation (Jackson, 1981; Massey, 1981), a pattern largely attributable to the fact that many Puerto Ricans are of African ancestry (Massey and Bitterman, 1985; Massey and Denton, 1989a). The two remaining areas are Los Angeles, which experienced more Hispanic immigration than any other metropolitan area in the country, and Chicago, which contained a large population of Puerto Ricans in addition to a rapidly growing Mexican immigrant community.

Reflecting the increase in the proportion of Hispanics in most metropolitan areas, Hispanic isolation indices rose markedly throughout the nation. In those few areas where rates of Hispanic population increase were relatively slow—Albuquerque, Denver, Phoenix, and Tucson—the level of Hispanic isolation hardly changed;

but as the rate of Hispanic immigration increased, so did the extent of spatial isolation. Given the area's popularity as a destination for Hispanic immigration, Hispanic isolation rose most strongly in Southern California cities, going from 19 to 50 in Anaheim, 38 to 72 in Los Angeles, and 20 to 40 in San Diego.

By the 1990s, isolation indices equaled or exceeded 50 in about half of the metropolitan areas under consideration, but in only two cases—New York and Los Angeles, the two metropolitan areas with the largest Hispanic communities—did the index exceed 60. By way of contrast, only 8 of the 30 Black communities examined earlier had Black isolation indices less than 60. Although contemporary demographic conditions suggest trends toward high segregation and rising isolation among Hispanics, they still do not display the high index ratings characteristic for Blacks in large urban areas.

Recent Trends in Asian Segregation

Although Asian immigration into U.S. urban areas accelerated rapidly after 1970, Asian populations are still quite small compared with either Black or Hispanic populations. Moreover, Asians are more highly concentrated regionally and found in a relatively small number of metropolitan areas. Table 3, therefore, presents indices of Asian segregation and isolation only for the 20 largest Asian communities, rather than the 30 largest.

Again demographic conditions for Asians favor substantial increases in segregation and isolation. In most metropolitan areas, immigration led to the rapid expansion of a rather small 1970 population base. In some areas, the number of post-1970 migrants actually exceeds the size of the original Asian community severalfold. Only 25,000 Asians lived in the Anaheim-Santa Ana metropolitan area in 1970, for example, but by 1990, their number had multiplied ten times, to 249,000. Over the same period, the Asian community of Los Angeles quadrupled, going from 243,000 to 943,000; and Chicago's Asian population grew from 62,000 to 230,000. In such cases where a sudden massive in-migration overwhelms a small, established community, indices of segregation often decrease initially as new arrivals distribute themselves widely, and then increase as these pioneers attract subsequent settlers to the same residential areas.

Such a pattern of decreasing and then increasing Asian segregation is the most common pattern of change among

the metropolitan areas shown in Table 3. The Asian-White dissimilarity index averaged 44 in 1970, decreased to 36 in 1980, and then increased to 41 in 1990. This basic trend occurred in 12 of the 20 metropolitan areas. In three more areas, an initial decline was followed by no change from 1980 to 1990. Only one area—San Jose—experienced a sustained increase in Asian segregation; but it began from a very low level of segregation in 1970. Four areas displayed uninterrupted declines in segregation across both decades—Boston, Nassau-Suffolk, Newark, and Paterson.

Despite rapid immigration and population growth, Asian segregation indices remained quite moderate in 1990. Increases observed between 1980 and 1990 simply restored the indices to their 1970 levels, yielding little net change over the two decades. Thus, Asian-White dissimilarity indices ranged from the low 30s in Anaheim, Nassau-Suffolk, Newark, Riverside, and Washington to 50 in San Francisco-Oakland. In no metropolitan area did the index of Asian segregation approach the high levels characteristic of Blacks in the nation's largest metropolitan areas.

Rapid Asian immigration into moderately segregated communities did produce rather sharp increases in the extent of Asian isolation, however, consistent with a process of enclave consolidation. The most pronounced increases occurred in areas where Southeast Asian refugees settled in large numbers—Anaheim, where the isolation index rose from 3 in 1970 to 22 in 1990; Fresno, where the increase was from 6 to 33; and San Diego, where the increase was from 6 to 29. Despite these increases, however, Asians still are not very isolated anywhere, including San Francisco-Oakland, where they constitute a higher percentage of the population (21 percent) than in any other metropolitan area. The isolation index of 46 means that Asians in the Bay Area are more likely to share a neighborhood with non-Asians than with each other; and in Los Angeles, which received the highest number of Asian immigrants between 1970 and 1990, the isolation index rose to just under 41. Thus, the largest and most segregated Asian communities in the United States are much less isolated than the most integrated Black communities.

Black Hypersegregation

Despite their apparent clarity, the above data actually understate the extent of Black isolation in U.S. society, because the data only incorporate two dimensions of segregation: evenness, as measured by the dissimilarity

TABLE 3 Trends in Asian Segregation and Isolation in the 20 Metropolitan Areas with the Largest Asian Populations, 1970 to 1990

Metropolitan Area	Dissimilarity Indices			Isolation Indices		
	1970[a]	1980[a]	1990[b]	1970[a]	1980[a]	1990[b]
Anaheim, CA	27.4	24.9	33.3	2.6	7.7	22.4
Boston, MA	49.9	47.4	44.8	8.0	10.5	12.9
Chicago, IL	55.8	43.9	43.2	7.6	8.7	15.9
Dallas, TX	43.9	29.1	40.5	1.7	2.6	9.6
Fresno, CA	35.1	22.9	43.4	5.7	5.3	33.1
Houston, TX	42.7	34.6	45.7	1.5	4.5	15.7
Los Angeles, CA	53.1	43.1	46.3	12.3	15.2	40.5
Minneapolis, MN	45.2	36.9	41.2	3.0	6.2	15.1
Nassau-Suffolk, NY	42.2	34.5	32.4	1.0	2.2	5.9
New York, NY	56.1	48.1	48.4	11.6	14.3	32.8
Newark, NJ	50.2	34.4	29.6	1.5	2.9	7.5
Paterson-Clifton-Passaic, NJ	46.6	40.4	34.4	1.3	3.1	12.1
Philadelphia, PA	49.1	43.7	43.2	2.4	4.0	11.0
Riverside-San Bernardino, CA	31.9	21.5	32.8	2.5	4.1	10.2
Sacramento, CA	47.6	35.5	47.7	11.8	11.6	23.6
San Diego, CA	41.3	40.5	48.1	5.9	11.1	29.1
San Francisco-Oakland, CA	48.6	44.4	50.1	21.0	23.2	46.0
San Jose, CA	25.4	29.5	38.5	5.3	11.6	36.6
Seattle, WA	46.6	33.3	36.5	11.7	12.4	20.0
Washington, DC	36.5	26.8	32.3	2.2	5.7	12.6
Average	43.8	35.8	40.6	6.0	8.3	20.6

[a] Indices are from Massey and Denton (1987).
[b] Indices are from Harrison and Weinberg (1992).

index, and isolation, as measured by the P* index. Massey and Denton (1988, 1989b), however, conceptualize segregation as a multidimensional construct. They contend there are five dimensions of spatial variation; in addition to evenness and isolation, residential segregation should be conceptualized in terms of clustering, concentration, and centralization. This five-dimensional conceptualization of segregation recently has been updated and revalidated with 1990 data (Massey et al., 1996).

Clustering is the extent to which minority areas adjoin one another spatially. It is maximized when Black neighborhoods form one large, contiguous ghetto; and it is minimized when they are scattered, as in a checkerboard pattern. *Centralization* is the degree to which Blacks are

distributed in and around the center of an urban area, usually defined as the central-business district. *Concentration* is the relative amount of physical space occupied by Blacks; as segregation increases, Blacks are increasingly confined to smaller, geographically compacted areas.

A high level of segregation on any single dimension is problematic because it isolates a minority group from amenities, opportunities, and resources that affect socioeconomic well-being. As high levels of segregation accumulate across dimensions, however, the deleterious effects of segregation multiply. Indices of evenness and isolation (i.e., dissimilarity and P*), by themselves, cannot capture this multidimensional layering of segregation; therefore, there is a misrepresentation of the nature of Black segregation and an understatement of its severity. Blacks are not only more segregated than other groups on any single dimension of segregation; they are more segregated across all dimensions simultaneously.

Massey and Denton (1993) identified a set of 16 metropolitan areas that were highly segregated—i.e., had an index higher than 60—on at least four of the five dimensions of segregation, a pattern they called "hypersegregation." These metropolitan areas included Atlanta, Baltimore, Buffalo, Chicago, Cleveland, Dallas, Detroit, Gary, Indianapolis, Kansas City, Los Angeles, Milwaukee, New York, Newark, and St. Louis. Within this set of areas, the Black-White dissimilarity index averaged 82, the average isolation index was 71, the mean clustering index was 58, the mean centralization index was 88, and the average concentration index was 83. By way of contrast, neither Hispanics nor Asians were hypersegregated within *any* metropolitan area.

These 16 metropolitan areas are among the most important in the country, incorporating 6 of the 10 largest urban areas in the United States. Blacks in these areas live within large, contiguous settlements of densely inhabited neighborhoods packed tightly around the urban core. Inhabitants typically would be unlikely to come into contact with non-Blacks in the neighborhood where they live. If they were to travel to an adjacent neighborhood, they would still be unlikely to see a White face. If they went to the next neighborhood beyond that, no Whites would be there either. People growing up in such an environment would have little direct experience with the culture, norms, and behaviors of the rest of American society, and have few social contacts with members of other racial groups.

Denton (1994) reexamined the issue of hypersegregation using data from the 1990 Census. According to her analysis, not only has Black hypersegregation continued, in many ways it has grown worse. Of the 16 metropolitan areas defined as hypersegregated in 1980, 14 remained so in 1990. In Atlanta the index of spatial concentration decreased to 59, just missing the criteria for hypersegregation, and in Dallas the isolation index decreased to 58. But both these figures are *just* below the threshold index of 60. All other metropolitan areas that were hypersegrated in 1980 showed an increase on at least one dimension by 1990. In 10 areas, isolation increased; concentration grew more acute in 9 areas; and clustering increased in 8. In Newark and Buffalo, segregation increased in all five dimensions simultaneously; and in Detroit, segregation increased on all dimensions but one.

In short, areas that were hypersegregated in 1980 generally remained so in 1990, and there was little evidence of movement away from this extreme pattern. On the contrary, hypersegregation appears to have spread to several new urban areas during the 1980s. Of the 44 nonhypersegregated metropolitan areas studied by Massey and Denton in 1980, Denton (1994) found that 6 had come to satisfy the criteria by 1990—Birmingham, Cincinnati, Miami, New Orleans, Oakland, and Washington, D.C.—bringing the total number of hypersegregated metropolitan areas to 20. Taken together, these 20 contain roughly 11 million Blacks and constitute 36 percent of the entire U.S. Black population. As already pointed out, the percentage of Hispanics and Asians who are hypersegregated is zero.

Explaining the Persistence of Racial Segregation

A variety of explanations have been posited to account for the unusual depth and persistence of Black segregation in American cities. One hypothesis is that racial segregation reflects class differences between Blacks and Whites—i.e., because Blacks, on average, have lower incomes and fewer socioeconomic resources than Whites, they cannot afford to move into White neighborhoods in significant numbers. According to this hypothesis, Black-White segregation, to some extent, reflects segregation on the basis of income, with poor households, which happen to be predominantly Black, living in different neighborhoods than affluent households, which happen to be disproportionately White.

This explanation has not been sustained empirically, however. When indices of racial segregation are computed within categories of income, occupation, or education, researchers have found that levels of Black-White segregation do not vary by social class (Farley, 1977; Simkus, 1978; Massey, 1979, 1981; Massey and Fischer, 1999). According to Denton and Massey (1988), Black families annually earning at least $50,000 were just as segregated as those earning less than $2,500. Indeed, Black families annually earning more than $50,000 were more segregated than Hispanic or Asian families earning less than $2,500. In other words, the most affluent Blacks appear to be more segregated than the poorest Hispanics or Asians; and in contrast to the case of Blacks, Hispanic and Asian segregation levels fall steadily as income rises, reaching low or moderate levels at incomes of $50,000 or more (Denton and Massey, 1988).

Another explanation for racial segregation is that Blacks prefer to live in predominantly Black neighborhoods, and that segregated housing simply reflects these preferences. This line of reasoning does not square well with survey evidence on Black attitudes, however. Most Blacks continue to express strong support for the ideal of integration. When asked on opinion polls whether they favor "desegregation, strict segregation, or something in-between," Blacks answer "desegregation" in large numbers (Schuman et al., 1985). Blacks are virtually unanimous in agreeing that "Black people have a right to live wherever they can afford to," and 71 percent would vote for a community-wide law to enforce this right (Bobo et al., 1986).

Black respondents are not only committed to integration as an ideal; survey results suggest they also strongly prefer it in practice. When asked about specific neighborhood racial compositions, Blacks consistently select racially mixed areas as most desirable (Farley et al., 1978, 1979, 1994; Clark, 1991). Although the most popular choice is a neighborhood that is half-Black and half-White, as late as 1992, nearly 90 percent of Blacks in Detroit would be willing to live in virtually any racially mixed area (Farley et al., 1994).

Although Blacks express a reluctance about moving into all-White neighborhoods, this apprehension does not indicate a rejection of White neighbors per se, but stems from well-founded fears of hostility and rejection. Among Black respondents to a 1976 Detroit survey who expressed a reluctance to moving into all-White areas, 34 percent thought that White neighbors would be unfriendly and make them feel unwelcome, 37 percent felt they could be made to feel uncomfortable, and 17 percent expressed a fear of outright violence (Farley et al., 1979). Moreover, 80 percent of all Black respondents rejected the view that moving into a White neighborhood constituted a desertion of the Black community. More recently, Jackson (1994) linked the reluctance of Blacks to "pioneer" White areas not only to fears of rejection by White neighbors, but also to an *expectation* of discrimination by real estate agents and lenders.

Thus evidence suggests that racial segregation in urban America is not a voluntary reflection of Black preferences. If it were up to them, Blacks would live in racially mixed neighborhoods. But it is not up to them only, of course; their preferences interact with those of Whites and, thus,

produce the residential configurations actually observed. Even though Blacks may prefer neighborhoods with an even racial balance, integration will not occur if most Whites find this level of racial mixing unacceptable.

On the surface, Whites seem to share Blacks' ideological commitment to open housing. The percentage of Whites on national surveys who agree that "Black people have a right to live wherever they can afford to" approached 90 percent in the late 1970s; and the percentage who disagreed with the view that "White people have a right to keep Blacks out of their [Whites'] neighborhoods," reached 67 percent in 1980. At present, few Whites openly call for the strict segregation of American society (Schuman et al., 1985, 1998; Sniderman and Piazza, 1993; Hochschild, 1995).

However, Whites remain quite uncomfortable with the implications of open housing in practice; only 40 percent, in 1980, said they would be willing to vote for a community-wide law stating that "a homeowner cannot refuse to sell to someone because of their race or skin color" (Schuman and Bobo, 1988). In other words, 60 percent of Whites would vote *against* an open housing law, which, in fact, has been federal law for 25 years.

White support for open housing generally declines as the hypothetical number of Blacks in their neighborhood increases. Whereas 86 percent of Whites in 1978 said they would not move if "a Black person came to live next door," only 46 percent stated they would not move if "Black people came to live in large numbers," and only 28 percent of Whites would be willing to live in a neighborhood that was half-Black and half-White (Schuman et al., 1985). Likewise, the severity of White prejudice toward Blacks increases as the percentage of Blacks in the area increases, a relationship that is *not* observed for Hispanics or Asians (Taylor, 1998).

When questions are posed about specific neighborhood compositions, moreover, it becomes clear that White tolerance for racial mixing is quite limited. According to Farley et al. (1994), 16 percent of Whites responding to a 1992 Detroit survey said they would feel uncomfortable in a neighborhood where only 7 percent of the residents were Black; 13 percent would be unwilling to enter such an area. When the Black percentage reaches 20 percent, one-third of all Whites say they would be unwilling to enter, 30 percent would feel uncomfortable, and 15 percent would seek to leave. A neighborhood about 30 percent Black exceeds the limits of racial tolerance for most Whites; 59 percent would be unwilling to move in, 44 percent would feel uncomfortable, and 29 percent would try to leave. Beyond a 50:50 balance, a neighborhood becomes unacceptable to all except a small minority of Whites; 73 percent said they would not wish to move into such a neighborhood, 53 percent would try to leave, and 65 percent would feel uncomfortable. As was stated, most Blacks feel a 50:50 racial mixture is desirable. This fundamental disparity between the two races has been confirmed by surveys conducted in Milwaukee, Omaha, Cincinnati, Kansas City, and Los Angeles (Clark, 1991).

The discrepancy between Whites' acceptance of open housing in principle and their reluctance to live among Blacks in practice yields a rather specific hypothesis about the nature of trends in Black-White segregation over the past 20 years. Hypothetically, declines in Black-White segregation should be confined primarily to metropolitan areas with relatively small Black populations, because in these places, desegregation can occur without Whites having to share their neighborhoods with too many Black people (Massey and Gross, 1991). If Black people make up 3 percent of the metropolitan population, for example, then complete desegregation yields an average of 3 percent Black within every neighborhood, which is well within most Whites' tolerance limits. If, however, Black people make up 20 percent of the metropolitan population, desegregation would produce neighborhoods that are 20 percent Black, on average, which exceeds the tolerance limits of many Whites, creates instability, and fuels a process of neighborhood turnover. In keeping with this hypothesis, Krivo and Kaufman (1999) show that desegregation between 1980 and 1990 was quite likely where the Black population was small but very unlikely where it was large. As a result, observed declines in segregation during the 1980s were confined largely to metropolitan areas that contained very few Blacks.

Over the last three decades, U.S. metropolitan areas have been transformed by immigration and many have moved well beyond the simple Black-White dichotomy of earlier years, necessitating new approaches to the measurement of racial attitudes. A recent survey in Los Angeles sought to replicate the Detroit survey within an ethnically diverse metropolis. Analysis of these data by Zubrinsky and Bobo (1996) showed that all non-Black groups—Whites, Asians, and Hispanics—attribute a variety of negative traits to Blacks and consider Blacks to be the least desirable

neighbors (see, also, Bobo and Zubrinsky, 1996). Blacks experience by far the greatest likelihood of hostility from other groups, and are universally acknowledged to face the most severe housing discrimination. The end result is a clear hierarchy of neighborhood racial preferences in Los Angeles, with Whites at the top, followed by Asians and Hispanics, and Blacks at the bottom. Segregation does not result from Black ethnocentrism so much as from avoidance behavior by other groups, all of whom seek to circumvent potential coresidence with Blacks.

These contrasting racial attitudes create large intergroup disparities in the demand for housing in racially mixed neighborhoods. Given the violence, intimidation, and harrassment that historically have followed their entry into White areas, Blacks express reluctance at being first across the color line. After one or two Black families have moved into a neighborhood, however, Black demand grows rapidly, given the high value placed on integrated housing. This demand escalates as the Black percentage rises toward 50 percent, the most preferred neighborhood configuration; beyond this point, Black demand stabilizes and then falls off as the Black percentage rises toward 100 percent.

The pattern of White, Asian, and Hispanic demand for housing in racially mixed areas follows precisely the opposite trajectory. Demand is strong for homes in all-White areas, but once one or two Black families enter a neighborhood, demand begins to falter as some non-Black families leave and others refuse to move in. The acceleration in residential turnover coincides with the expansion of Black demand, making it likely that outgoing White, Hispanic, or Asian households are replaced by Black families. As the Black percentage rises, overall demand drops ever more steeply, and Black demand rises at an increasing rate. By the time Black demand peaks at the 50 percent mark, practically no other groups are willing to enter and most are trying to leave. Thus, racial segregation appears to be created by a process of racial turnover fueled by the persistence of significant anti-Black prejudice on the part of virtually every other group.

This model of racial change was proposed two decades ago by Schelling (1971), who argued that integration is an unstable outcome because Whites prefer lower minority proportions than Blacks—even though Whites might accept some Black neighbors. Yet by itself, Schelling's explanation is incomplete. Whites can only avoid coresidence with Blacks if mechanisms exist to keep Blacks out of neighborhoods to which they might otherwise be attracted. Whites can only flee a neighborhood where Blacks have entered if there are other all-White neighborhoods to go to, and this escape will only be successful if Blacks are unlikely or unable to follow.

Racial discrimination was institutionalized in the real estate industry during the 1920s and well established in private practice by the 1940s (Massey and Denton, 1993). Evidence shows that discriminatory behavior was widespread among realtors at least until 1968, when the Fair Housing Act was passed (Helper, 1969; Saltman, 1979). After that, outright refusals to rent or sell to Blacks became rare, given that overt discrimination could lead to prosecution under the law.

Black home seekers now face a more subtle process of exclusion. Rather than encountering "White only" signs, they encounter a covert series of barriers. Blacks who inquire about an advertised unit may be told that it has just been sold or rented; they may be shown only the advertised unit and told that no others are available; they may only be shown houses in Black or racially mixed areas and led away from White neighborhoods; they may be quoted a higher rent or selling price than Whites; they may be told that the selling agents are too busy and to come back later; their phone number may be taken but a return call never made; they may be shown units but offered no assistance in arranging financing; or they simply may be treated brusquely and discourteously in hopes that they will leave.

Although individual acts of discrimination are small and subtle, they have a powerful cumulative effect in lowering the probability of Black entry into White neighborhoods. Because the discrimination is latent, however, it is not easily observable, and the only way to confirm whether or not it has occurred is to·compare the treatment of both Black and White clients that have similar social and economic characteristics. If White clients receive systematically more favorable treatment, then one can safely conclude that discrimination has taken place (Fix et al., 1993).

Differences in the treatment of White and Black home seekers are measured by means of a housing audit. Teams of White and Black auditors are paired and sent to randomly selected realtors to pose as clients seeking a home or apartment. The auditors are trained to present comparable housing needs and family characteristics, and to express similar tastes; they are assigned equivalent social and economic

traits by the investigator. After each encounter, the auditors fill out a detailed report of their experiences and the results are tabulated and compared to determine the nature and level of discrimination (Yinger, 1986, 1989).

Local fair-housing organizations began to conduct such studies at the end of the 1960s. These efforts revealed that discrimination was continuing despite the Fair Housing Act. A 1969 audit of realtors in St. Louis, for example, documented a pattern and practice of discrimination sufficient to force four realty firms to sign a consent decree with the U.S. Department of Justice wherein they agreed to desist from certain biased practices (Saltman, 1979). Likewise, a 1971 audit study carried out in Palo Alto, California, found that Blacks were treated in a discriminatory fashion by 50 percent of the area's apartment complexes; and a 1972 audit of apartments in suburban Baltimore uncovered discrimination in more than 45 percent of the cases (Saltman, 1979).

Racial discrimination clearly persisted through the 1980s. In one 1983 Chicago study, suburban realtors showed homes to 67 percent of White auditors but only 47 percent of Black auditors (Hintzen, 1983). Another Chicago study done in 1985 revealed that Whites were offered financial information at nearly twice the rate it was offered to Blacks (Schroeder, 1985). One developer working in Chicago's south suburbs refused to deal with Blacks at all; Blacks were always told that no properties were available, even though 80 percent of Whites were shown real estate (Bertram, 1988). In the same study, realtors told 92 percent of Whites that apartments were available but gave this information to only 46 percent of Blacks.

Audit studies of other metropolitan areas reveal similar levels of racial discrimination. According to Yinger's (1986) review of studies conducted in metropolitan Boston and Denver during the early 1980s, Black home seekers had between a 38 percent and a 59 percent chance of receiving unfavorable treatment, compared to Whites, on any given real estate transaction. Through various lies and deceptions, Blacks were informed of only 65 of every 100 units presented to Whites, and they inspected fewer than 54 of every 100 shown to Whites.

• • •

Realtors were approached by auditors who inquired about the availability of the advertised unit; they also asked about other units that might be on the market. Based on the results, HDS provided evidence that discrimination against Blacks had declined little since 1977. Indeed, it appears the 1977 HUD study may have understated both the incidence and severity of housing discrimination in American cities (Yinger, 1995). According to HDS data, housing was made more available to Whites in 45 percent of the transactions in the rental market and in 34 percent of those in the sales market. Whites received more favorable credit assistance in 46 percent of sales encounters, and were offered more favorable terms in 17 percent of rental transactions. When housing availability and financial assistance were considered together, the likelihood of experiencing racial discrimination was 53 percent in both the rental and sales markets.

• • •

Compared with Blacks, relatively few studies of prejudice and discrimination against Hispanics have been conducted, and there are no national studies that examine attitudes and behaviors concerning Asians. Hakken (1979) found that discrimination against Hispanics in the rental housing market of Dallas was as likely as that against Blacks, and similar results were reported by Feins and colleagues for Boston (Feins et al., 1981). James and Tynan (1986) replicated these results in a study of Denver's sales market, but they found a substantially lower probability of discrimination against Hispanics in the rental market; and despite the relatively high likelihood of discrimination in home sales, in reality, severity of discrimination against Hispanics was not great; the average number of housing units offered to Hispanics was not significantly different than the number offered to non-Hispanic Whites (James and Tynan, 1986).

As with Blacks, however, discrimination against Hispanics appears to have a racial basis. Hakken (1979) found that dark-skinned Chicanos were more likely to experience discriminatory treatment than Blacks, whereas light-skinned Hispanics were less likely to experience such treatment. Consistent with this finding, Massey and Denton (1992) found that Mexicans who identified themselves as mestizos (people of mixed European and Indian origin) were less likely to achieve suburban residence than those who identified themselves as White.

The extent of the racial effect is greater among Caribbean Hispanics, particularly Puerto Ricans, among whom the racial continuum runs from European to African. Denton and Massey (1989) showed that for Puerto Ricans who identified themselves as Black, housing was as

segregated as for U.S. Blacks, whereas those who identified themselves as White experienced low-to-moderate levels of separation. Discrimination was mixed for Caribbean Hispanics who said they were of mixed Black-White origins, but were much closer to the high level of Black segregation. The degree of segregation experienced by racially mixed Caribbean Hispanics was generally greater than that experienced by racially mixed Mexicans, suggesting greater White antipathy toward Africans than Amerindians.

The most complete and systematic data on the treatment of Hispanics in urban real estate markets comes from HUD's 1988 HDS (Yinger, 1995). Results from this study indicate that the overall incidence of housing discrimination was greater for Hispanics than Blacks in the sale market (42 versus 34 percent), but less for Hispanics than Blacks in the rental market (32 versus 45 percent), replicating the earlier results of James and Tynan (1986) in Denver. Also in keeping with the findings of James and Tynan was the fact that the severity of discrimination in the sales market was considerably lower for Hispanics than for Blacks; whereas the marginal probability that an additional housing unit was denied to Blacks was 88 percent, it was only 66 percent for Hispanics. As in earlier research, in the 1988 HDS, race figured prominently in the treatment of Hispanics—dark-skinned Hispanics were much more likely to experience discrimination in the sales market than light-skinned Hispanics (Yinger, 1995). Paradoxically, therefore, recent research on discrimination involving Hispanics reaffirms the conclusion that race remains the dominant organizing principle in U.S. urban housing markets.

Segregation and the Concentration of Poverty

The past two decades have been hard on the socioeconomic well-being of many Americans. The structural transformation of the U.S. economy from goods production to service provision generated a strong demand for workers with high and low levels of schooling, but offered few opportunities for those with modest education and training. In the postindustrial economy that emerged after 1973, labor unions withered, the middle class bifurcated, income inequality grew, and poverty spread; and this new stratification between people was accompanied by a growing spatial separation between them. The stagnation of income proved to be remarkably widespread, and inequality rose not only for minorities—Blacks, Hispanics, and Asians—but also for non-Hispanic Whites (Danziger and Gottschalk, 1995; Levy, 1995; Morris et al., 1994). As a result of their continued racial segregation, however, the spatial concentration of poverty was especially severe for Blacks (Massey and Eggers, 1990; Massey et al., 1991; Krivo et al., 1998). High levels of income inequality paired with high levels of racial or ethnic segregation result in geographically concentrated poverty, because the poverty is localized in a small number of densely settled, racially homogenous, tightly clustered areas, often in an older, urban core abandoned by industry. Had segregation not been in place, the heightened poverty would be distributed widely throughout the metropolitan area (Massey, 1990; Massey and Denton, 1993). By 1990, 83 percent of poor inner-city Blacks lived in neighborhoods that were at least 20 percent poor (Kasarda, 1993).

In a recent paper, Massey and Fischer (2000) broadened this theoretical perspective by arguing that racial segregation interacts with any structural shift that affects the distribution of income, or the spatial configuration of the classes, to concentrate poverty spatially. Specifically, they hypothesize that as racial segregation increases, decreasing incomes, increasing inequality, increasing class segregation, and increasing immigration are more strongly translated into geographic isolation of the poor. Thus, these structural trends produce high and increasing concentrations of poverty for highly segregated groups, but low and falling concentrations of poverty among nonsegregated groups.

Because more than 70 percent of urban Blacks are highly segregated, but 90 percent of all other groups are not, the population of poor experiencing high concentrations of poverty is overwhelmingly Black (Massey and Fischer, 2000). Given the interaction between racial segregation and the changing socioeconomic structure of American society, the issue of race cannot be set aside to focus on the politics of race versus class. Although the implementation of policies that raise average incomes, lower income inequality, and reduce class segregation would lower the spatial isolation of the urban poor, policies to promote the desegregation of urban society would probably have an even greater effect, given segregation's critical role in determining how these factors generate concentrated poverty.

The Consequences of Concentrated Poverty

The argument that the prevalence of concentrated poverty among Blacks decisively undermines the life chances of the Black poor was first made forcefully by Wilson (1987). He argued that class isolation, through a variety of mechanisms, reduced employment, lowered incomes, depressed marriage, and increased unwed childbearing *over and above any effects of individual or family deprivation*. At the time Wilson made this argument, relatively little evidence existed to support it (Jencks and Mayer, 1990), but over the past decade a growing number of studies have accumulated to sustain the basic thrust of Wilson's hypothesis.

In 1988, the Rockefeller and Russell Sage Foundations funded the Social Science Research Council (SSRC) to establish a program of research into the causes and consequences of persistent urban poverty. One SSRC subcommittee—the Working Group on Communities and Neighborhoods, Family Processes, and Individual Development—met regularly over the next eight years to conceptualize and then implement a program of research to determine how concentrated poverty affected social and cognitive development. The ultimate product was a recently published series of studies (Brooks-Gunn et al., 1997) examining the effect of neighborhood conditions on cognitive and social development at three points in the life cycle—early childhood (ages 3–7), late childhood/early adolescence (ages 11–15), and late adolescence (ages 16–19).

The empirical analyses clearly show that socioeconomic inequality is perpetuated by mechanisms operating at the neighborhood level, although the specific pathways are perhaps more complex than Wilson or others imagined. Not only do neighborhood effects vary in their nature and intensity at different stages of the life cycle, they are often conditioned by gender, mediated by family processes, and possibly interactive in how they combine with individual factors to determine social outcomes. Despite these complexities, however, research permits three broad generalizations.

- First, neighborhoods seem to influence individual development most powerfully in early childhood and late adolescence.

- Second, the spatial concentration of affluence appears to be more important in determining cognitive development and academic achievement than the concentration of poverty.

- Third, the concentration of male joblessness affects social behavior more than cognitive development, particularly among Blacks.

These effects persist even after controlling for unobserved heterogeneity. Thus, Wilson's (1987) theory is basically correct—there is something to the hypothesis of neighborhood effects.

One of the most important disadvantages transmitted through prolonged exposure to the ghetto is educational failure. Datcher (1982) estimates that moving a poor Black male from his typical neighborhood (66 percent Black with an average annual income of $8,500) to a typical White neighborhood (86 percent White with a mean income of $11,500) would raise his educational attainment by nearly a year. Corcoran and colleagues (1989) found similar results. Crane (1991) likewise shows that the dropout probability for Black teenage males increases dramatically as the percentage of low-status workers in the neighborhood increases. Residence in a poor neighborhood also decreases the odds of success in the labor market. Datcher (1982) found that growing up in a poor Black area lowered male earnings by at least 27 percent, although Corcoran and colleagues (1989) put the percentage at about 18 percent.

Exposure to conditions typical of the ghetto also dramatically increases the odds of pregnancy and childbirth among teenage girls. According to estimates by Crane (1991), the probability of a teenage birth increases dramatically as the percentage of low-status workers in the neighborhood increases. Similarly, Hogan and Kitagawa (1985) found that living in a very poor neighborhood raised the monthly pregnancy rate among Black adolescents by 20 percent and lowered the age at which they became sexually active. Furstenberg et al. (1987) have shown that attending school in integrated, rather than segregated, classrooms substantially lowers the odds that 15- to 16-year-old Black girls will experience sexual intercourse. Brooks-Gunn et al. (1993) found that the probability of giving birth before age 29 rose markedly as the percentage of high-income families fell.

In a dynamic **longitudinal analysis** that followed young Black men and women from ages 15 to 30, Massey and Shibuya (1995) found that young men who live in neighborhoods of concentrated male joblessness are more likely to be jobless themselves, controlling for individual and family characteristics, and that Black women in such neighborhoods were significantly less likely to get married.

Massey and Shibuya (1995) also linked concentrated disadvantage to higher probabilities of criminality, a link well-documented by Krivo and Peterson (1996) using aggregate data. The concentration of criminal activity that accompanies the concentration of deprivation accelerates the process of neighborhood transition and, for Blacks, resegregation (Morenoff and Sampson, 1997); it also helps drive up rates of Black-on-Black mortality, which have reached heights unparalled for any other group (Almgren et al., 1998; Guest et al., 1998). The spatial concentration of crime presents special problems for the Black middle class, who must adopt extreme strategies to insulate their children from the temptations and risks of the street (Anderson, 1990; Patillo, 1998).

The quantitative evidence thus suggests that any process that concentrates poverty within racially isolated neighborhoods will simultaneously increase the odds of socioeconomic failure within the segregated group. People who grow up and live in environments of concentrated poverty and social isolation are more likely to become teenage parents, drop out of school, achieve low educations, earn lower adult incomes, and become involved with crime—either as perpetrator or victim.

One study has directly linked the socioeconomic disadvantages suffered by individual minority members to the degree of segregation they experience in society. Using individual, community, and metropolitan data from the 50 largest U.S. metropolitan areas in 1980, Massey et al. (1991) showed that group segregation and poverty rates interacted to concentrate poverty geographically within neighborhoods, and that exposure to neighborhood poverty subsequently increased the probability of male joblessness and single motherhood among group

longitudinal analysis Research conducted over many years so outcomes over time can be observed.

members. In this fashion, they linked the structural condition of segregation to individual behaviors widely associated with the underclass through the intervening factor of neighborhood poverty, holding individual and family characteristics constant. As the structural factor controlling poverty concentration, segregation is directly responsible for the perpetuation of socioeconomic disadvantage among Blacks.

The Road Ahead

This review yields several well-supported conclusions about residential segregation in the United States at the end of the twentieth century.

- First, the extreme segregation of Blacks continues unabated in the nation's largest metropolitan areas, and is far more severe than anything experienced by Hispanics or Asians.
- Second, this unique segregation can in no way be attributed to class.
- Third, although Whites now accept open housing in principle, they have yet to come to terms with its implications in practice. Whites still harbor strong anti-Black sentiments and are unwilling to live with more than a small percentage of Blacks in the neighborhood. As a result, declines in Black-White segregation have been confined almost entirely to metropolitan areas where few Blacks live.
- Fourth, color prejudice apparently extends to dark-skinned Hispanics, and discrimination against both Blacks and Afro-Hispanics is remarkably widespread in U.S. housing markets. Through a variety of deceptions and exclusionary actions, Black access to housing in White neighborhoods is systematically reduced.

- Fifth, White biases and discrimination apparently do not extend to Asians or light-skinned Hispanics, at least to the same degree. In no metropolitan area are Asians or Hispanics hypersegregated; and despite the recent arrival of large numbers of immigrants and rapid rates of population growth, they display levels of segregation and isolation that are far below those of Blacks.
- Sixth, as a result of segregation, poor Blacks are forced to live in conditions of intensely concentrated poverty. Recent shifts in U.S. socioeconomic structure and patterns of class segregation have interacted with Black segregation to produce unusual concentrations of poverty among Blacks. Poor Blacks are far more likely to grow up and live in neighborhoods surrounded by other poor people than poor Whites, Hispanics, or Asians.
- Finally, as a result of their prolonged exposure to high rates of neighborhood poverty, Blacks experience much higher risks of educational failure, joblessness, unwed childbearing, crime, and premature death compared with other groups.

Given the central role that residence plays in determining one's life chances, these results suggest the need to incorporate the effects of racial segregation more fully into theories about the perpetuation of poverty and the origins of the urban underclass. These results also suggest the need to incorporate desegregation efforts more directly into public policies developed to ameliorate urban poverty. All too often, U.S. policy debates have devolved into arguments about the relative importance of race versus class. The issue, however, is not whether race *or* class perpetuates the urban underclass, but how race *and* class *interact* to undermine the social and economic well-being of Black Americans.

Seeing the Big Picture   **How Integrated Is Your Neighborhood?**

The index of dissimilarity is a measure of how residentially segregated one population is from another. A score of 0 would mean groups are randomly distributed throughout a particular area while a score of 100 would mean groups share no social space with one another. What do the index of dissimilarity numbers in Section II of the Appendix tell us about residential segregation in the United States?

The Code of the Streets

22

Elijah Anderson

ELIJAH ANDERSON is William K. Lanman, Jr. Professor of Sociology at Yale University. He is author of *Streetwise: Race, Class and Change in an Urban Community* (1990) and *The Code of the Streets* (1999).

Questions to Consider   In "The Code of the Streets" Elijah Anderson chronicles how an individual's environment can create a set of expectations that are at odds with the "dominant" culture. How is "oppositional culture" often detrimental to children and young adults in these communities? How is oppositional culture linked to Anderson's discussion of "street" and "decent" families?

OF ALL THE PROBLEMS BESETTING THE POOR inner-city black community, none is more pressing than that of interpersonal violence and aggression. It wreaks havoc daily with the lives of community residents and increasingly spills over into downtown and residential middle-class areas. Muggings, burglaries, carjackings, and drug-related shootings, all of which may leave their victims or innocent bystanders dead, are now common enough to concern all urban and many suburban residents. The inclination to violence springs from the circumstances of life among the ghetto poor—the lack of jobs that pay a living wage, the stigma of race, the fallout from rampant drug use and drug trafficking, and the resulting alienation and lack of hope for the future.

Simply living in such an environment places young people at special risk of falling victim to aggressive behavior. Although there are often forces in the community which can counteract the negative influences, by far the most powerful being a strong, loving, "decent" (as inner-city residents put it) family committed to middle-class values, the despair is pervasive enough to have spawned an oppositional culture, that of "the streets," whose norms are often consciously opposed to those of mainstream society. These two orientations—decent and street—socially organize the community, and their coexistence has important consequences for residents, particularly children growing up in the inner city. Above all, this environment means that even youngsters whose home lives reflect mainstream values—and the majority of homes in the community do—must be able to handle themselves in a street-oriented environment.

This is because the street culture has evolved what may be called a code of the streets, which amounts to a set of informal rules governing interpersonal public behavior, including violence. The rules prescribe both a proper comportment and a proper way to respond if challenged. They regulate the use of violence and so allow those who are inclined to aggression to precipitate violent encounters in an approved way. The rules have been established and are enforced mainly by the street-oriented, but on the streets the distinction between street and decent is often irrelevant; everybody knows that if the rules are violated, there are penalties. Knowledge of the code is thus largely defensive; it is literally necessary for operating in public. Therefore, even though families with a decency orientation are usually opposed to the values of the code, they often reluctantly encourage their children's familiarity with it to enable them to negotiate the inner-city environment.

At the heart of the code is the issue of respect—loosely defined as being treated "right," or granted the deference one deserves. However, in the troublesome public environment of the inner city, as people increasingly feel buffeted by forces beyond their control, what one deserves in the way of respect becomes more and more problematic and uncertain. This in turn further opens the issue of respect to sometimes intense interpersonal negotiation. In the street culture, especially among young people, respect is viewed as almost an external entity that is hard-won but easily lost, and so must constantly be guarded. The rules of the code in fact provide a framework for negotiating respect. The person whose very appearance—including his clothing, demeanor, and way of moving—deters transgressions feels that he possesses, and may be considered by others to possess, a measure of respect. With the right amount of respect, for instance, he can avoid "being bothered" in public. If he is bothered, not only may he be in physical danger but he has been disgraced or "dissed" (disrespected). Many of the forms that dissing can take might seem petty to middle-class people (maintaining eye contact for too long, for example), but to those invested in the street code, these actions become serious indications of the other person's intentions. Consequently, such people become very sensitive to advances and slights, which could well serve as warnings of imminent physical confrontation.

This hard reality can be traced to the profound sense of alienation from mainstream society and its institutions felt by many poor inner-city black people, particularly the young. The code of the streets is actually a cultural adaptation to a profound lack of faith in the police and the judicial system. The police are most often seen as representing the dominant white society and not caring to protect inner-city residents. When called, they may not respond, which is one reason many residents feel they must be prepared to take extraordinary measures to defend themselves and their loved ones against those who are inclined to aggression. Lack of police accountability has in fact been incorporated into the status system: the person who is believed capable of "taking care of himself" is accorded a certain deference, which translates into a sense of physical and psychological control. Thus the street code emerges where the influence of the police ends and personal responsibility for one's safety is felt to begin. Exacerbated by the proliferation of drugs and easy access to guns, this volatile situation results in the ability of the street-oriented minority (or those who effectively "go for bad") to dominate the public spaces.

Decent and Street Families

Although almost everyone in poor inner-city neighborhoods is struggling financially and therefore feels a certain distance from the rest of America, the decent and the street family in a real sense represent two poles of value orientation, two contrasting conceptual categories. The labels "decent" and "street," which the residents themselves use, amount to evaluative judgments that confer status on local residents. The labeling is often the result of a social contest among individuals and families of the neighborhood. Individuals of the two orientations often coexist in the same extended family. Decent residents judge themselves to be so while judging others to be of the street, and street individuals often present themselves as decent, drawing distinctions between themselves and other people. In addition, there is quite a bit of circumstantial behavior—that is, one person may at different times exhibit both decent and street orientations, depending on the circumstances. Although these designations result from so much social jockeying, there do exist concrete features that define each conceptual category.

Generally, so-called decent families tend to accept mainstream values more fully and attempt to instill them in their children. Whether married couples with children or single-parent (usually female) households, they are generally "working poor" and so tend to be better off financially than their street-oriented neighbors. They value hard work and self-reliance and are willing to sacrifice for their children. Because they have a certain amount of faith in mainstream society, they harbor hopes for a better future for their children, if not for themselves. Many of them go to church and take a strong interest in their children's schooling. Rather than dwelling on the real hardships and inequities facing them, many such decent people, particularly the increasing number of grandmothers raising grandchildren, see their difficult situation as a test from God and derive great support from their faith and from the church community.

Extremely aware of the problematic and often dangerous environment in which they reside, decent parents tend to be strict in their child-rearing practices, encouraging children to respect authority and walk a straight moral line. They have an almost obsessive concern about trouble of any kind and remind their children to be on the lookout for people and situations that might lead to it. At the same time, they are themselves polite and considerate of others, and teach their children to be the same way. At home, at work, and in church, they strive hard to maintain a positive mental attitude and a spirit of cooperation.

So-called street parents, in contrast, often show a lack of consideration for other people and have a rather superficial sense of family and community. Though they may love their children, many of them are unable to cope with the physical and emotional demands of parenthood, and find it difficult to reconcile their needs with those of their children. These families, who are more fully invested in the code of the streets than the decent people are, may aggressively socialize their children into it in a normative way. They believe in the code and judge themselves and others according to its values.

In fact the overwhelming majority of families in the inner-city community try to approximate the decent-family model, but there are many others who clearly represent the worst fears of the decent family. Not only are their financial resources extremely limited, but what little they have may easily be misused. The lives of the street-oriented are often marked by disorganization. In the most desperate circumstances people frequently have a limited understanding of priorities and consequences, and so frustrations mount over bills, food, and, at times, drink, smoke cigarettes, and do drugs. Some tend toward self-destructive behavior; many street-oriented women are crack-addicted ("on the pipe"), alcoholic, or involved in complicated relationships with men who abuse them. In addition, the seeming intractability of their situation, caused in large part by the lack of well-paying jobs and the persistence of racial discrimination, has engendered deep-seated bitterness and anger in many of the most desperate and poorest blacks, especially young people. The need both to exercise a measure of control and to lash out at somebody is often reflected in the adults' relations with their children. At the least, the frustrations of persistent poverty shorten the fuse in such people—contributing to a lack of patience with anyone, child or adult, who irritates them.

In these circumstances a woman—or a man, although men are less consistently present in children's lives—can be quite aggressive with children, yelling at and striking them for the least little infraction of the rules she has set down. Often little if any serious explanation follows the verbal and physical punishment. This response teaches children a particular lesson. They learn that to solve any kind of interpersonal problem one must quickly resort to hitting or other violent behavior. Actual peace and quiet, and also the appearance of calm, respectful children conveyed to her neighbors and friends, are often what the young mother most desires, but at times she will be very aggressive in trying to get them. Thus she may be quick to beat her children, especially if they defy her law,

not because she hates them but because this is the way she knows to control them. In fact, many street-oriented women love their children dearly. Many mothers in the community subscribe to the notion that there is a "devil in the boy" that must be beaten out of him or that socially "fast girls need to be whupped." Thus much of what borders on child abuse in the view of social authorities is acceptable parental punishment in the view of these mothers.

Many street-oriented women are sporadic mothers whose children learn to fend for themselves when necessary, foraging for food and money any way they can get it. The children are sometimes employed by drug dealers or become addicted themselves. These children of the street, growing up with little supervision, are said to "come up hard." They often learn to fight at an early age, sometimes using short-tempered adults around them as role models. The street-oriented home may be fraught with anger, verbal disputes, physical aggression, and even mayhem. The children observe these goings-on, learning the lesson that might makes right. They quickly learn to hit those who cross them, and the dog-eat-dog mentality prevails. In order to survive, to protect oneself, it is necessary to marshal inner resources and be ready to deal with adversity in a hands-on way. In these circumstances physical prowess takes on great significance.

In some of the most desperate cases, a street-oriented mother may simply leave her young children alone and unattended while she goes out. The most irresponsible women can be found at local bars and crack houses, getting high and socializing with other adults. Sometimes a troubled woman will leave very young children alone for days at a time. Reports of crack addicts abandoning their children have become common in drug-infested inner-city communities. Neighbors or relatives discover the abandoned children, often hungry and distraught over the absence of their mother. After repeated absences, a friend or relative, particularly a grandmother, will often step in to care for the young children, sometimes petitioning the authorities to send her, as guardian of the children, the mother's welfare check, if the mother gets one. By this time, however, the children may well have learned the first lesson of the streets: survival itself, let alone respect, cannot be taken for granted; you have to fight for your place in the world.

Campaigning for Respect

These realities of inner-city life are largely absorbed on the streets. At an early age, often even before they start school, children from street-oriented homes gravitate to the streets, where they "hang"—socialize with their peers. Children from these generally permissive homes have a great deal of latitude and are allowed to "rip and run" up and down the street. They often come home from school, put their books down, and go right back out the door. On school nights eight- and nine-year-olds remain out until nine or ten o'clock (and teenagers typically come in whenever they want to). On the streets they play in groups that often become the source of their primary social bonds. Children from decent homes tend to be more carefully supervised and are thus likely to have curfews and to be taught how to stay out of trouble.

When decent and street kids come together, a kind of social shuffle occurs in which children have a chance to go either way. Tension builds as a child comes to realize that he must choose an orientation. The kind of home he comes from influences but does not determine the way he will ultimately turn out—although it is unlikely that a child from a thoroughly street-oriented family will easily absorb decent values on the streets. Youths who emerge from street-oriented families but develop a decency orientation almost always learn those values in another setting—in school, in a youth group, in church. Often it is the result of their involvement with a caring "old head" (adult role model).

In the street, through their play, children pour their individual life experiences into a common knowledge pool, affirming, confirming, and elaborating on what they have observed in the home and matching their skills against those of others. And they learn to fight. Even small children test one another, pushing and shoving, and are ready to hit other children over circumstances not to their liking. In turn, they are readily hit by other children, and the child who is toughest prevails. Thus the violent resolution of disputes, the hitting and cursing, gains social reinforcement. The child in effect is initiated into a system that is really a way of campaigning for respect.

In addition, younger children witness the disputes of older children, which are often resolved through cursing and abusive talk, if not aggression or outright violence. They see that one child succumbs to the greater physical and mental abilities of the other. They are also alert and attentive witnesses to the verbal and physical fights of adults, after which they compare notes and share their interpretations of the event. In almost every case the victor is the person who physically won the altercation, and this person often enjoys the esteem and respect of onlookers. These experiences reinforce the lessons the children have learned at home: might makes right, and toughness is a virtue, while humility is not. In effect they learn the social meaning of fighting. When it is left virtually unchallenged, this understanding becomes an ever more important part of the child's working conception of the world. Over time the code of the streets becomes refined.

Those street-oriented adults with whom children come in contact—including mothers, fathers, brothers, sisters, boyfriends, cousins, neighbors, and friends—help them along in forming this understanding by verbalizing the messages they are getting through experience: "Watch your back." "Protect yourself." "Don't punk out." "If somebody messes with you, you got to pay them back." "If someone disses you, you got to straighten them out." Many parents actually impose sanctions if a child is not sufficiently aggressive. For example, if a child loses a fight and comes home upset, the parent might respond, "Don't you come in here crying that somebody beat you up; you better get back out there and whup his ass. I didn't raise no punks! Get back out there and whup his ass. If you don't whup his ass, I'll whup your ass when you come home." Thus the child obtains reinforcement for being tough and showing nerve.

While fighting, some children cry as though they are doing something they are ambivalent about. The fight may be against their wishes, yet they may feel constrained to fight or face the consequences—not just from peers but also from caretakers or parents, who may administer another beating if they back down. Some adults recall receiving such lessons from their own parents and justify repeating them to their children as a way to toughen them up. Looking capable of taking care of oneself as a form of self-defense is a dominant theme among both street-oriented and decent adults who worry about the safety of their children. There is thus at times a convergence in their child-rearing practices, although the rationales behind them may differ.

Self-Image Based on "Juice"

By the time they are teenagers, most youths have either internalized the code of the streets or at least learned the need to comport themselves in accordance with its rules, which chiefly have to do with interpersonal communication. The code revolves around the presentation of self. Its basic requirement is the display of a certain predisposition to violence. Accordingly, one's bearing must send the unmistakable if sometimes subtle message to "the next person" in public that one is capable of violence and mayhem when the situation requires it, that one can take care of oneself. The nature of this communication is largely determined by the demands of the circumstances but can include facial expressions, gait, and verbal expressions—all of which are geared mainly to deterring aggression. Physical appearance, including clothes, jewelry, and grooming, also plays an important part in how a person is viewed; to be respected, it is important to have the right look.

Even so, there are no guarantees against challenges, because there are always people around looking for a fight to increase their share of respect—or "juice," as it is sometimes called on the street. Moreover, if a person is assaulted, it is important, not only in the eyes of his opponent but also in the eyes of his "running buddies," for him to avenge himself. Otherwise he risks being "tried" (challenged) or "moved on" by any number of others. To maintain his honor he must show he is not someone to be "messed with" or "dissed." In general, the person must "keep himself straight" by managing his position of respect among others; this involves in part his self-image, which is shaped by what he thinks others are thinking of him in relation to his peers.

Objects play an important and complicated role in establishing self-image. Jackets, sneakers, gold jewelry, reflect not just a person's taste, which tends to be tightly regulated among adolescents of all social classes, but also a willingness to possess things that may require defending. A boy wearing a fashionable, expensive jacket, for example, is vulnerable to attack by another who covets the jacket and either cannot afford to buy one or wants the added satisfaction of depriving someone else of his. However, if the boy forgoes the desirable jacket and wears one that isn't "hip," he runs the risk of being teased and possibly even assaulted as an unworthy person. To be allowed to hang with certain prestigious crowds, a boy must wear a different set of expensive clothes—sneakers and athletic suit—every day. Not to be able to do so might make him appear socially deficient. The youth comes to covet such items—especially when he sees easy prey wearing them.

In acquiring valued things, therefore, a person shores up his identity—but since it is an identity based on having things, it is highly precarious. This very precariousness gives a heightened sense of urgency to staying even with peers, with whom the person is actually competing. Young men and women who are able to command respect through their presentation of self—by allowing their possessions and their body language to speak for them—may not have to campaign for regard but may, rather, gain it by the force of their manner. Those who are unable to command respect in this way must actively campaign for it—and are thus particularly alive to slights.

One way of campaigning for status is by taking the possessions of others. In this context, seemingly ordinary objects can become trophies imbued with symbolic value that far exceeds their monetary worth. Possession of the trophy can symbolize the ability to violate somebody—to "get in his face," to take something of value from him, to "dis" him, and thus to enhance one's own worth by stealing someone else's. The trophy does not have to be something material. It can be another person's sense of honor, snatched away with a derogatory remark. It can be the outcome of a fight. It can be the imposition of a certain standard, such as a girl's getting herself recognized as the most beautiful. Material things, however, fit easily into the pattern. Sneakers, a pistol, even somebody else's girlfriend, can become a trophy. When a person can take something from another and then flaunt it, he gains a certain regard by being the owner, or the controller, of that thing. But this display of ownership can then provoke other people to challenge him. This game of who controls what is thus constantly being played out on inner-city streets, and the trophy—extrinsic or intrinsic, tangible or intangible—identifies the current winner.

An important aspect of this often violent give-and-take is its zero-sum quality. That is, the extent to which one person can raise himself up depends on his ability to put another person down. This underscores the alienation that permeates the inner-city ghetto community. There is a generalized sense that very little respect is to be had, and therefore everyone competes to get what affirmation he can of the little that is available. The craving for respect that results gives people thin skins. Shows of deference by others can be highly soothing, contributing to a sense of security, comfort, self-confidence, and self-respect. Transgressions by others which go unanswered diminish these feelings and are believed to encourage further transgressions. Hence one must be ever vigilant against the transgressions of others or even *appearing* as if transgressions will be tolerated. Among young people, whose sense of self-esteem is particularly vulnerable, there is an especially heightened concern with being disrespected. Many inner-city young men in particular crave respect to such a degree that they will risk their lives to attain and maintain it.

The issue of respect is thus closely tied to whether a person has an inclination to be violent, even as a victim. In the wider society people may not feel required to retaliate physically after an attack, even though they are aware that they have been degraded or taken advantage of. They may feel a great need to defend themselves *during* an attack, or to behave in such a way as to deter aggression (middle-class people certainly can and do become victims of street-oriented youths), but they are much more likely than street-oriented people to feel that they can walk away from a possible altercation with their self-esteem intact. Some people may even have the strength of character to flee, without any thought that their self-respect or esteem will be diminished.

In impoverished inner-city black communities, however, particularly among young males and perhaps increasingly among females, such flight would be extremely difficult. To run away would likely leave one's self-esteem in tatters. Hence people often feel constrained not only to stand up and at least attempt to resist during an assault but also to "pay back"—to seek revenge—after a successful assault on their person. This may include going to get a weapon or even getting relatives involved. Their very identity and self-respect, their honor, is often intricately tied up with the way they perform on the streets during and after such encounters. This outlook reflects the circumscribed opportunities of the inner-city poor. Generally people outside the ghetto have other ways of gaining status and regard, and thus do not feel so dependent on such physical displays.

By Trial of Manhood

On the street, among males these concerns about things and identity have come to be expressed in the concept of "manhood." Manhood in the inner city means taking the prerogatives of men with respect to strangers, other men, and women—being distinguished as a man. It implies physicality and a certain ruthlessness. Regard and respect are associated with this concept in large part because of its practical application: if others have little or no regard for a

person's manhood, his very life and those of his loved ones could be in jeopardy. But there is a chicken-and-egg aspect to this situation: one's physical safety is more likely to be jeopardized in public *because* manhood is associated with respect. In other words, an existential link has been created between the idea of manhood and one's self-esteem, so that it has become hard to say which is primary. For many inner-city youths, manhood and respect are flip sides of the same coin; physical and psychological well-being are inseparable, and both require a sense of control, of being in charge.

The operating assumption is that a man, especially a real man, knows what other men know—the code of the streets. And if one is not a real man, one is somehow diminished as a person, and there are certain valued things one simply does not deserve. There is thus believed to be a certain justice to the code, since it is considered that everyone has the opportunity to know it. Implicit in this is that everybody is held responsible for being familiar with the code. If the victim of a mugging, for example, does not know the code and so responds "wrong," the perpetrator may feel justified even in killing him and may feel no remorse. He may think, "Too bad, but it's his fault. He should have known better."

So when a person ventures outside, he must adopt the code—a kind of shield, really—to prevent others from "messing with" him. In these circumstances it is easy for people to think they are being tried or tested by others even when this is not the case. For it is sensed that something extremely valuable is at stake in every interaction, and people are encouraged to rise to the occasion, particularly with strangers. For people who are unfamiliar with the code—generally people who live outside the inner city—the concern with respect in the most ordinary interactions can be frightening and incomprehensible. But for those who are invested in the code, the clear object of their demeanor is to discourage strangers from even thinking about testing their manhood. And the sense of power that attends the ability to deter others can be alluring even to those who know the code without being heavily invested in it—the decent inner-city youths. Thus a boy who has been leading a basically decent life can, in trying circumstances, suddenly resort to deadly force.

Central to the issue of manhood is the widespread belief that one of the most effective ways of gaining respect is to manifest "nerve." Nerve is shown when one takes another person's possessions (the more valuable the better), "messes with" someone's woman, throws the first punch, "gets in someone's face," or pulls a trigger. Its proper display helps on the spot to check others who would violate one's person and also helps to build a reputation that works to prevent future challenges. But since such a show of nerve is a forceful expression of disrespect toward the person on the receiving end, the victim may be greatly offended and seek to retaliate with equal or greater force. A display of nerve, therefore, can easily provoke a life-threatening response, and the background knowledge of that possibility has often been incorporated into the concept of nerve.

True nerve exposes a lack of fear of dying. Many feel that it is acceptable to risk dying over the principle of respect. In fact, among the hard-core street-oriented, the clear risk of violent death may be preferable to being "dissed" by another. The youths who have internalized this attitude and convincingly display it in their public bearing are among the most threatening people of all, for it is commonly assumed that they fear no man. As the people of the community say, "They are the baddest dudes on the street." They often lead an existential life that may acquire meaning only when they are faced with the possibility of imminent death. Not to be afraid to die is by implication to have few compunctions about taking another's life. Not to be afraid to die is the quid pro quo of being able to take somebody else's life—for the right reasons, if the situation demands it. When others believe this is one's position, it gives one a real sense of power on the streets. Such credibility is what many inner-city youths strive to achieve, whether they are decent or street-oriented, both because of its practical defensive value and because of the positive way it makes them feel about themselves. The difference between the decent and the street-oriented youth is often that the decent youth makes a conscious decision to appear tough and manly; in another setting—with teachers, say, or at his part-time job—he can be polite and deferential. The street-oriented youth, on the other hand, has made the concept of manhood a part of his very identity; he has difficulty manipulating it—it often controls him.

Girls and Boys

Increasingly, teenage girls are mimicking the boys and trying to have their own version of "manhood." Their goal is the same—to get respect, to be recognized as capable of setting or maintaining a certain standard. They try to achieve this end in the ways that have been established by the boys, including posturing, abusive language, and the use of violence to resolve disputes, but the issues for the girls are different. Although conflicts over turf and status exist among the girls, the majority of disputes seem rooted in assessments of beauty (which girl in a group is "the cutest"), competition over boyfriends, and attempts to regulate other people's knowledge of and opinions about a girl's behavior or that of someone close to her, especially her mother.

A major cause of conflicts among girls is "he say, she say." This practice begins in the early school years and continues through high school. It occurs when "people," particularly girls, talk about others, thus putting their "business in the streets." Usually one girl will say something negative about another in the group, most often behind the person's back. The remark will then get back to the person talked about. She may retaliate or her friends may feel required to "take up for" her. In essence this is a form of group gossiping in which individuals are negatively assessed and evaluated. As with much gossip, the things said may or may not be true, but the point is that such imputations can cast aspersions on a person's good name. The accused is required to defend herself against the slander, which can result in arguments and fights, often over little of real substance. Here again is the problem of low self-esteem, which encourages youngsters to be highly sensitive to slights and to be vulnerable to feeling easily "dissed." To avenge the dissing, a fight is usually necessary.

Because boys are believed to control violence, girls tend to defer to them in situations of conflict. Often if a girl is attacked or feels slighted, she will get a brother, uncle, or cousin to do her fighting for her. Increasingly, however, girls are doing their own fighting and are even asking their male relatives to teach them how to fight. Some girls form groups that attack other girls or take things from them. A hard-core segment of inner-city girls inclined toward violence seems to be developing. As one thirteen-year-old girl in a detention center for youths who have committed violent acts told me, "To get people to leave you alone, you gotta fight. Talking don't always get you out of stuff." One major difference between girls and boys: girls rarely use guns. Their fights are therefore not life-or-death struggles. Girls are not often willing to put their lives on the line for "manhood." The ultimate form of respect on the male-dominated inner-city street is thus reserved for men.

"Going for Bad"

In the most fearsome youths such a cavalier attitude toward death grows out of a very limited view of life. Many are uncertain about how long they are going to live and believe they could die violently at any time. They accept this fate; they live on the edge. Their manner conveys the message that nothing intimidates them; whatever turn the encounter takes, they maintain their attack—rather like a pit bull, whose spirit many such boys admire. The demonstration of such tenacity "shows heart" and earns their respect.

This fearlessness has implications for law enforcement. Many street-oriented boys are much more concerned about the threat of "justice" at the hands of a peer than at the hands of the police. Moreover, many feel not only that they have little to lose by going to prison but that they have something to gain. The toughening-up one experiences in prison can actually enhance one's reputation on the streets. Hence the system loses influence over the hard core who are without jobs, with little perceptible stake in the system. If mainstream society has done nothing *for* them, they counter by making sure it can do nothing *to* them.

At the same time, however, a competing view maintains that true nerve consists in backing down, walking away from a fight, and going on with one's business. One fights only in self-defense. This view emerges from the decent philosophy that life is precious, and it is an important part of the socialization process common in decent homes. It discourages violence as the primary means of resolving disputes and encourages youngsters to accept nonviolence and talk as confrontational strategies. But "if the deal goes down," self-defense is greatly encouraged. When there is enough positive support for this orientation, either in the home or among one's peers, then nonviolence has a chance to prevail. But it prevails at the cost of relinquishing a claim to being bad and tough, and therefore sets a young person up as at the very least alienated from street-oriented peers and quite possibly a target of derision or even violence.

Although the nonviolent orientation rarely overcomes the impulse to strike back in an encounter, it does introduce a certain confusion and so can prompt a measure of soul-searching, or even profound ambivalence. Did the person back down with his respect intact or did he back down only to be judged a "punk"—a person lacking manhood? Should he or she have acted? Should he or she have hit the other person in the mouth? These questions beset many young men and women during public confrontations. What is the "right" thing to do? In the quest for honor, respect, and local status—which few young people are uninterested in—common sense most often prevails, which leads many to opt for the tough approach, enacting their own particular versions of the display of nerve. The presentation of oneself as rough and tough is very often quite acceptable until one is tested. And then that presentation may help the person pass the test, because it will cause fewer questions to be asked about what he did and why. It is hard for a person to explain why he lost the fight or why he backed down. Hence many will strive to appear to "go for bad," while hoping they will never be tested. But when they are tested, the outcome of the situation may quickly be out of their hands, as they become wrapped up in the circumstances of the moment.

An Oppositional Culture

The attitudes of the wider society are deeply implicated in the code of the streets. Most people in inner-city communities are not totally invested in the code, but the significant minority of hard-core street youths who have to maintain the code in order to establish reputations, because they have—or feel they have—few other ways to assert themselves. For these young people the standards of the street code are the only game in town. The extent to which some children—particularly those who through upbringing have become most alienated and those lacking in strong and conventional social support—experience, feel, and internalize racist rejection and contempt from mainstream society may strongly encourage them to express contempt for the more conventional society in turn. In dealing with this contempt and rejection, some youngsters will consciously invest themselves and their considerable mental resources in what amounts to an oppositional culture to preserve themselves and their self-respect. Once they do, any respect they might be able to garner in the wider system pales in comparison with the respect available in the local system; thus they often lose interest in even attempting to negotiate the mainstream system.

At the same time, many less alienated young blacks have assumed a street-oriented demeanor as a way of expressing their blackness while really embracing a much more moderate way of life; they, too, want a nonviolent setting in which to live and raise a family. These decent people are trying hard to be part of the mainstream culture, but the racism, real and perceived, that they encounter helps to legitimate the oppositional culture. And so on occasion they adopt street behavior. In fact, depending on the demands of the situation, many people in the community slip back and forth between decent and street behavior.

A vicious cycle has thus been formed. The hopelessness and alienation many young inner-city black men and women feel, largely as a result of endemic joblessness and persistent racism, fuels the violence they engage in. This violence serves to confirm the negative feelings many whites and some middle-class blacks harbor toward the ghetto poor, further legitimating the oppositional culture and the code of the streets in the eyes of many poor young blacks. Unless this cycle is broken, attitudes on both sides will become increasingly entrenched, and the violence, which claims victims black and white, poor and affluent, will only escalate.

23 Environmental Justice in the 21st Century: Race Still Matters

Robert D. Bullard

ROBERT D. BULLARD is Ware Professor of Sociology and director of the Environmental Justice Resource Center at Clark Atlanta University. He is the author of numerous articles, monographs, and scholarly papers that address environmental justice and public participation concerns. His book, *Dumping in Dixie: Race, Class and Environmental Quality* (1990, 1994, 2000), has become a standard text in the environmental justice field.

> **Questions to Consider** Where is the trash dump, the water treatment plant, or the power plant in your community? In this reading Robert Bullard argues that in all likelihood these environmental dangers are in low-income, black and brown neighborhoods. Why do some communities get "dumped on" while others remain free of any toxic waste sites?

HARDLY A DAY PASSES WITHOUT THE MEDIA discovering some community or neighborhood fighting a landfill, incinerator, chemical plant, or some other polluting industry. This was not always the case. Just three decades ago, the concept of environmental justice had not registered on the radar screens of environmental, civil rights, or social justice groups.[1] Nevertheless, it should not be forgotten that Dr. Martin Luther King, Jr., went to Memphis in 1968 on an environmental and economic justice mission for the striking black garbage workers. The strikers were demanding equal pay and better work conditions. Of course, Dr. King was assassinated before he could complete his mission.

Another landmark garbage dispute took place a decade later in Houston, when African-American homeowners in 1979 began a bitter fight to keep a sanitary landfill out of their suburban middle-income neighborhood.[2] Residents formed the Northeast Community Action Group or NECAG. NECAG and their attorney, Linda McKeever Bullard, filed a class-action lawsuit to block the facility from being built. The 1979 lawsuit, *Bean v. Southwestern Waste Management, Inc.,* was the first of its kind to challenge the siting of a waste facility under civil rights law.

The landmark Houston case occurred three years before the environmental justice movement was catapulted into the national limelight in the rural and mostly African-American Warren County, North Carolina. The environmental justice movement has come a long way since its humble beginning in Warren County, North Carolina, where a PCB landfill ignited protests and over 500 arrests. The Warren County protests provided the impetus for a U.S. General Accounting Office study, *Siting of Hazardous Waste Landfills and Their Correlation with Racial and Economic Status of Surrounding Communities.*[3] That study revealed that three out of four of the off-site, commercial hazardous waste landfills in Region 4 (which comprises eight states in the South) happen to be located in predominantly African-American communities, although African Americans made up only 20 percent of the region's population. More important, the protesters put "environmental racism" on the map. Fifteen years later, the state of North Carolina is required to spend over $25 million to clean up and detoxify the Warren County PCB landfill.

The Warren County protests also led the Commission for Racial Justice to produce *Toxic Wastes and Race,*[4] the first national study to correlate waste facility sites and demographic characteristics. Race was found to be the most potent variable in predicting where these facilities were located—more powerful than poverty, land values, and home ownership. In 1990, *Dumping in Dixie: Race, Class, and Environmental Quality* chronicled the convergence of two social movements—social justice and environmental movements—into the environmental justice movement. This book highlighted African Americans' environmental activism in the South, the same region that gave birth to the modern civil rights movement. What started out as local and often isolated community-based struggles against toxics and facility siting blossomed into a multi-issue, multiethnic, and multiregional movement.

The 1991 First National People of Color Environmental Leadership Summit was probably the most important single event in the movement's history. The Summit broadened the environmental justice movement beyond its early antitoxics focus to include issues of public health, worker safety, land use, transportation, housing, resource allocation, and community empowerment.[5]

The meeting also demonstrated that it is possible to build a multiracial grassroots movement around environmental and economic justice.[6]

Held in Washington, DC, the four-day Summit was attended by over 650 grassroots and national leaders from around the world. Delegates came from all fifty states including Alaska and Hawaii, Puerto Rico, Chile, Mexico, and as far away as the Marshall Islands. People attended the summit to share their action strategies, redefine the environmental movement, and develop common plans for addressing environmental problems affecting people of color in the United States and around the world.

On September 27, 1991, Summit delegates adopted 17 "Principles of Environmental Justice." These principles were developed as a guide for organizing, networking, and relating to government and nongovernmental organizations (NGOs). By June 1992, Spanish and Portuguese translations of the Principles were being used and circulated by NGOs and environmental justice groups at the Earth Summit in Rio de Janeiro.

In response to growing public concern and mounting scientific evidence, President Clinton on February 11, 1994 (the second day of the national health symposium), issued Executive Order 12898, "Federal Actions to Address Environmental Justice in Minority Populations and Low-Income Populations." This Order attempts to address environmental injustice within existing federal laws and regulations.

Executive Order 12898 reinforces the 35-year-old Civil Rights Act of 1964, Title VI, which prohibits discriminatory practices in programs receiving federal funds. The Order also focuses the spotlight back on the National Environmental Policy Act (NEPA), a twenty-five-year-old law that set policy goals for the protection, maintenance, and enhancement of the environment. NEPA's goal is to ensure for all Americans a safe, healthful, productive, and aesthetically and culturally pleasing environment. NEPA requires federal agencies to prepare a detailed statement on the environmental effects of proposed federal actions that significantly affect the quality of human health.

The Executive Order calls for improved methodologies for assessing and mitigating impacts, health effects from multiple and cumulative exposure, collection of data on low-income and minority populations who may be disproportionately at risk, and impacts on subsistence fishers and wildlife consumers. It also encourages participation of the impacted populations in the various phases of assessing impacts—including scoping, data gathering, alternatives, analysis, mitigation, and monitoring.

The Executive Order focuses on "subsistence" fishers and wildlife consumers. Everybody does not buy fish at the supermarket. There are many people who are subsistence fishers, who fish for protein, who basically subsidize their budgets, and their diets, by fishing from rivers, streams, and lakes that happen to be polluted. These subpopulations may be underprotected when basic assumptions are made using the dominant risk paradigm.

Many grassroots activists are convinced that waiting for the government to act has endangered the health and welfare of their communities. Unlike the federal EPA, communities of color did not first discover environmental inequities in 1990. The federal EPA only took action on environmental justice concerns in 1990 after extensive prodding from grassroots environmental justice activists, educators, and academics.[7]

People of color have known about and have been living with inequitable environmental quality for decades—most without the protection of the federal, state, and local governmental agencies. Environmental justice advocates continue to challenge the current environmental protection apparatus and offer their own framework for addressing environmental inequities, disparate impact, and unequal protection.

An Environmental Justice Framework

The question of environmental justice is not anchored in a debate about whether or not decision makers should tinker with risk management. The framework seeks to prevent environmental threats before they occur.[8] The environmental justice framework incorporates other social movements that seek to eliminate harmful practices (discrimination harms the victim) in housing, land use, industrial planning, health care, and sanitation services. The impact of redlining, economic disinvestments, infrastructure decline, deteriorating housing, lead poisoning, industrial pollution, poverty, and unemployment are not unrelated problems if one lives in an urban ghetto or barrio, rural hamlet, or reservation.

The environmental justice framework attempts to uncover the underlying assumptions that may contribute to and produce unequal protection. This framework brings to the surface the ethical and political questions of "who gets what, why, and how much." Some general characteristics of the framework include:

1. *The environmental justice framework incorporates the principle of the "right" of all individuals to be protected from environmental degradation.* The precedents for this framework are the Civil Rights Act of 1964, Fair Housing Act of 1968 and as amended in 1988, and Voting Rights Act of 1965.

2. *The environmental justice framework adopts a public health model of prevention (elimination of the threat before harm occurs) as the preferred strategy.* Impacted communities should not have to wait until causation or conclusive "proof" is established before preventive action is taken. For example, the framework offers a solution to the lead problem by shifting the primary focus from *treatment* (after children have been poisoned) to *prevention* (elimination of the threat via abating lead in houses).

Overwhelming scientific evidence exists on the ill effects of lead on the human body. However, very little action has been taken to rid the nation of childhood lead poisoning in urban areas. Former Health and Human Services Secretary Louis Sullivan tagged this among the "number one environmental health threats to children."[9]

The Natural Resources Defense Council, NAACP Legal Defense and Educational Fund, ACLU, and Legal Aid Society of Alameda County joined forces in 1991 and won an out-of-court settlement worth $15–20 million for a blood-lead testing program in California. The *Matthews v. Coye* lawsuit involved the State of California not living up to the federally mandated testing of some 557,000 poor children for lead who receive Medicaid. This historic agreement triggered similar actions in other states that failed to live up to federally mandated screening.[10]

Lead screening is an important element in this problem. However, screening is not the solution. Prevention is the solution. Surely, if termite inspections can be mandated to protect individual home investment, a lead-free home can be mandated to protect public health. Ultimately, the lead abatement debate, public health (who is affected) vs. property rights (who pays for cleanup), is a value conflict that will not be resolved by the scientific community.

3. *The environmental justice framework shifts the burden of proof to polluter/dischargers who do harm, discriminate, or who do not give equal protection to racial and ethnic minorities, and other "protected" classes.* Under the current system, individuals who challenge polluters must "prove" that they have been harmed, discriminated against, or disproportionately impacted. Few impacted communities have the resources to hire lawyers, expert witnesses, and doctors needed to sustain such a challenge.

The environmental justice framework would require the parties that are applying for operating permits (landfills, incinerators, smelters, refineries, chemical plants, etc.) to "prove" that their operations are not harmful to human health, will not disproportionately impact racial and ethnic minorities and other protected groups, and are nondiscriminatory.

    4.   *The environmental justice framework would allow disparate impact and statistical weight, as opposed to "intent," to infer discrimination.* Proving intentional or purposeful discrimination in a court of law is next to impossible, as demonstrated in *Bean v. Southwestern Waste.* It took nearly a decade after *Bean v. Southwestern Waste* for environmental discrimination to resurface in the courts.

    5.   *The environmental justice framework redresses disproportionate impact through "targeted" action and resources.* This strategy would target resources where environmental and health problems are greatest (as determined by some ranking scheme but not limited to risk assessment). Reliance solely on "objective" science disguises the exploitative way the polluting industries have operated in some communities and condones a passive acceptance of the status quo.

Human *values* are involved in determining *which* geographic areas are worth public investments. In the 1992 EPA report, *Securing Our Legacy,* the agency describes geographic initiatives as "protecting what we love."[11]

The strategy emphasizes "pollution prevention, multimedia enforcement, research into causes and cures of environmental stress, stopping habitat loss, education, and constituency building."[12] Geographic initiatives are underway in the Chesapeake Bay, Great Lakes, Gulf of Mexico programs, and the U.S.-Mexican Border program. Environmental justice targeting would channel resources to "hot spots," communities that are overburdened with more than their "fair" share of environmental and health problems.

The dominant environmental protection paradigm reinforces instead of challenges the stratification of people (race, ethnicity, status, power, etc.), place (central cities, suburbs, rural areas, unincorporated areas, Native American reservations, etc.), and work (i.e., office workers are afforded greater protection than farm workers). The dominant paradigm exists to manage, regulate, and distribute risks. As a result, the current system has (1) institutionalized unequal enforcement, (2) traded human health for profit, (3) placed the burden of proof on the "victims" and not the polluting industry, (4) legitimated human exposure to harmful chemicals, pesticides, and hazardous substances, (5) promoted "risky" technologies such as incinerators, (6) exploited the vulnerability of economically and politically disenfranchised communities, (7) subsidized ecological destruction,

(8) created an industry around risk assessment, (9) delayed cleanup actions, and (10) failed to develop pollution prevention as the overarching and dominant strategy.[13]

The mission of the federal EPA was never designed to address environmental policies and practices that result in unfair, unjust, and inequitable outcome. EPA and other government officials are not likely to ask the questions that go to the heart of environmental injustice: What groups are most affected? Why are they affected? Who did it? What can be done to remedy the problem? How can the problem be prevented? Vulnerable communities, populations, and individuals often fall between the regulatory cracks.

Impetus for a Paradigm Shift

The environmental justice movement has changed the way scientists, researchers, policy makers, and educators go about their daily work. This bottom-up movement has redefined environment to include where people live, work, play, go to school, as well as how these things interact with the physical and natural world. The impetus for changing the dominant environmental protection paradigm did not come from within regulatory agencies, the polluting industry, academia, or the "industry" that has been built around risk management. The environmental justice movement is led by a loose alliance of grassroots and national environmental and civil rights leaders who question the foundation of the current environmental protection paradigm.

Despite significant improvements in environmental protection over the past several decades, millions of Americans continue to live, work, play, and go to school in unsafe and unhealthy physical environments.[14] During its 30-year history, the U.S. EPA has not always recognized that many of our government and industry practices (whether intended or unintended) have adverse impact on poor people and people of color. Growing grassroots community resistance emerged in response to practices, policies, and conditions that residents judged to be unjust, unfair, and illegal. Discrimination is a fact of life in America. Racial discrimination is also illegal.

The EPA is mandated to enforce the nation's environmental laws and regulations equally across the board. It is also required to protect all Americans—not just individuals or groups who can afford lawyers, lobbyists, and experts. Environmental protection is a right, not a privilege reserved for a few who can vote with their feet and escape or fend off environmental stressors that address environmental inequities.

Equity may mean different things to different people. Equity is distilled into three broad categories: procedural, geographic, and social equity.

Procedural equity refers to the "fairness" question: the extent that governing rules, regulations, evaluation criteria, and enforcement are applied uniformly across the board and in a nondiscriminatory way. Unequal protection might result from nonscientific and undemocratic decisions, exclusionary practices, public hearings held in remote locations and at inconvenient times, and use of English-only material as the language to communicate and conduct hearings for non-English speaking publics.

Geographic equity refers to location and spatial configuration of communities and their proximity to environmental hazards, noxious facilities, and locally unwanted land uses (LULUs) such as landfills, incinerators, sewer treatment plants, lead smelters, refineries, and other noxious facilities. For example, unequal protection may result from land-use decisions that determine the location of residential amenities and disamenities. Unincorporated, poor, and communities of color often suffer a "triple" vulnerability of noxious facility siting.

Social equity assesses the role of sociological factors (race, ethnicity, class, culture, life styles, political power, etc.) on environmental decision making. Poor people and people of color often work in the most dangerous jobs, live in the most polluted neighborhoods, and their children are exposed to all kinds of environmental toxins on the playgrounds and in their homes.

The nation's environmental laws, regulations, and policies are not applied uniformly—resulting in some individuals, neighborhoods, and communities being exposed to the elevated health risks. A 1992 study by staff writers from the *National Law Journal* uncovered glaring inequities in the way the federal EPA enforces its laws. The authors write:

> There is a racial divide in the way the U.S. Government cleans up toxic waste sites and punishes polluters. White communities see faster action, better results and stiffer penalities than communities where blacks, Hispanics and other minorities live. This unequal protection often occurs whether the community is wealthy or poor.[15]

These findings suggest that unequal protection is placing communities of color at special risk.

The *National Law Journal* study supplements the findings of earlier studies and reinforces what many grassroots leaders have been saying all along: not only are people of color differentially impacted by industrial pollution, they can expect different treatment from the government. Environmental decision-making operates at the juncture of science, economics, politics, special interests, and ethics. This current environmental model places communities of color at special risk.

The Impact of Racial Apartheid

Apartheid-type housing, development, and environmental policies limit mobility, reduce neighborhood options, diminish job opportunities, and decrease choices for millions of Americans.[16] The infrastructure conditions in urban areas are a result of a host of factors including the distribution of wealth, patterns of racial and economic discrimination, redlining, housing and real estate practices, location decisions of industry, differential enforcement of land use and environmental choices, and diminished job communities for African Americans.

Race still plays a significant part in distributing public "benefits" and public "burdens" associated with economic growth. The roots of discrimination are deep and have been difficult to eliminate. Housing discrimination contributes to the physical decay of inner-city neighborhoods and denies a substantial segment of the African-American community a basic form of wealth accumulation and investment through home ownership.[17] The number of African-American homeowners would probably be higher in the absence of discrimination by lending institutions.[18] Only about 59 percent of the nation's middle-class African Americans own their homes, compared with 74 percent of whites.

Eight out of every ten African Americans live in neighborhoods where they are in the majority. Residential segregation decreases for most racial and ethnic groups with additional education, income, and occupational status. However, this scenario does not hold true for African Americans. African Americans, no matter what their educational or occupational achievement or income level, are exposed to higher crime rates, less effective educational systems, higher mortality risks, more dilapidated surroundings, and greater environmental threats because of their race. For example, in the heavily populated South

Coast air basin of the Los Angeles area, it is estimated that over 71 percent of African Americans and 50 percent of whites live in highly polluted areas.[19]

It has been difficult for millions of Americans in segregated neighborhoods to say "not in my backyard" (NIMBY) if they do not have a backyard.[20] Nationally, only about 44 percent of African Americans own their homes compared to over two-thirds of the nation as a whole. Homeowners are the strongest advocates of the NIMBY positions taken against locally unwanted uses or LULUs such as the construction of garbage dumps, landfills, incinerators, sewer treatment plants, recycling centers, prisons, drug treatment units, and public housing projects. Generally, white communities have greater access than people-of-color communities when it comes to influencing land use and environmental decision making.

The ability of an individual to escape a health-threatening physical environment is usually related to affluence. However, racial barriers complicate this process for many Americans.[21] The imbalance between residential amenities and land uses assigned to central cities and suburbs cannot be explained by class factors alone. People of color and whites do not have the same opportunities to "vote with their feet" and escape undesirable physical environments.

Institutional racism continues to influence housing and mobility options available to African Americans of all income levels—and is a major factor that influences quality of neighborhoods they have available to them. The "web of discrimination" in the housing market is a result of action and inaction of local and federal government officials, financial institutions, insurance companies, real estate marketing firms, and zoning boards. More stringent enforcement mechanisms and penalties are needed to combat all forms of discrimination.

Uneven development between central cities and suburbs combined with the systematic avoidance of inner-city areas by many businesses have heightened social and economic inequalities. For the past two decades, manufacturing plants have been fleeing central cities and taking their jobs with them. Many have moved offshore to Third-World countries where labor is cheap and environmental regulations are lax or nonexistent.

Industry flight from central cities had left behind a deteriorating urban infrastructure, poverty, and pollution. What kind of replacement industry can these communities attract? Economically depressed communities do not have a lot of choices available to them. Some workers have become so desperate that they see even

a low-paying hazardous job as better than no job at all. These workers are forced to choose between unemployment and a job that may result in risks to their health, their family's health, and the health of their community. This practice amounts to "economic blackmail." Economic conditions in many people-of-color communities make them especially vulnerable to this practice.

Some polluting industries have been eager to exploit this vulnerability. Some have even used the assistance of elected officials in obtaining special tax breaks and government operating permits. Clearly, economic development and environmental policies flow from forces of production and are often dominated and subsidized by state actors. Numerous examples abound where state actors have targeted cities and regions for infrastructure improvements and amenities such as water irrigation systems, ship channels, road and bridge projects, and mass transit systems. On the other hand, state actors have done a miserable job in protecting central city residents from the ravages of industrial pollution and nonresidential activities valued as having a negative impact on quality of life.[22]

Racial and ethnic inequality is perpetuated and reinforced by local governments in conjunction with urban-based corporations. Race continues to be a potent variable in explaining urban land use, streets and highway configuration, commercial and industrial development, and industrial facility siting. Moreover, the question of "who gets what, where, and why" often pits one community against another.[23]

Zoning and Land Use

Some residential areas and their inhabitants are at a greater risk than the larger society from unregulated growth, ineffective regulation of industrial toxins, and public policy decisions authorizing industrial facilities that favor those with political and economic clout.[24] African Americans and other communities of color are often victims of land-use decision making that mirrors the power arrangements of the dominant society. Historically, exclusionary zoning (and rezoning) has been a subtle form of using government authority and power to foster and perpetuate discriminatory practices.

Zoning is probably the most widely applied mechanism to regulate urban land use in the United States. Zoning laws broadly define land for residential, commercial, or industrial uses, and may impose narrower land-use restrictions (e.g., minimum and maximum lot size, number of dwellings per acre, square feet and height of buildings, etc.). Zoning ordinances, deed restrictions, and other land-use mechanisms have been widely used as a "NIMBY" tool, operating through exclusionary practices. Thus, exclusionary zoning has been used to zone against something rather than for something. With or without zoning, deed restrictions or other devices, various groups are unequally able to protect their environmental interests. More often than not, people-of-color communities get shortchanged in the neighborhood protection game.

In Houston, Texas, a city that does not have zoning, NIMBY was replaced with the policy of PIBBY (place in black's back yard).[25] The city government and private industry targeted landfills, incinerators, and garbage dumps for Houston's black neighborhoods for more than five decades. These practices lowered residents' property values, accelerated physical deterioration, and increased disinvestment in the communities. Moreover, the discriminatory siting of landfills and incinerators stigmatized the neighborhoods as "dumping grounds" for a host of other unwanted facilities, including salvage yards, recycling operations, and automobile "chop shops."[26]

The Commission for Racial Justice's landmark *Toxic Wastes and Race* study found race to be the single most important factor (i.e., more important than income, home ownership rate, and property values) in the location of abandoned toxic waste sites.[27] The study also found that (1) three out of five African Americans live in communities with abandoned toxic waste sites; (2) sixty percent of African Americans (15 million) live in communities with one or more abandoned toxic waste sites; (3) three of the five largest commercial hazardous waste landfills are located in predominately African American or Latino communities and accounts for 40 percent of the nation's total estimated landfill capacity; and (4) African Americans are heavily overrepresented in the population of cities with the largest number of abandoned toxic waste sites, which include Memphis, St. Louis, Houston, Cleveland, Chicago, and Atlanta.

Waste facility siting imbalances that were uncovered by the U.S. General Accounting Office (GAO) in 1983 have not disappeared.[28] The GAO discovered three out of four of the off-site commercial hazardous waste landfills in Region IV (Alabama, Florida, Georgia, Kentucky, Mississippi, North Carolina, South Carolina, and Tennessee) were located in predominately African-American communities. African Americans still made up about one-fifth of the population in EPA Region IV. In 2000, 100 percent of the off-site commercial hazardous wastes landfills in the region is dumped in two mostly African-American communities.

Environmental Racism

Many of the differences in environmental quality between black and white communities result from institutional racism, which influences local land use, enforcement of environmental regulations, industrial facility siting, and where people of color live, work and play. The roots of institutional racism are deep and have been difficult to eliminate. Discrimination is a manifestation of institutional racism and causes life to be very different for whites and blacks. Historically, racism has been and continues to be a major part of the American sociological system, and as a result, people of color find themselves at a disadvantage in contemporary society.

Environmental racism is real. It is just as real as the racism found in the housing industry, educational institutions, employment arena, and judicial system. What is environmental racism and how does one recognize it? *Environmental racism refers to any policy, practice, or directive that differentially affects or disadvantages (whether intended or unintended) individuals, groups, or communities based on race or color.* Environmental racism combines with public policies and industry practices to provide benefits for whites while shifting costs to people of color.[29] Environmental racism is reinforced by government, legal, economic, political, and military institutions.

Environmental decision making and policies often mirror the power arrangements of the dominant society and its institutions. Environmental racism disadvantages people of color while providing advantages or privileges for whites. A form of illegal "exaction" forces people of color to pay costs of environmental benefits for the public at large. The question of who *pays* and who *benefits* from the current environmental and industrial policies is central to this analysis of environmental racism and other systems of domination and exploitation.

Racism influences the likelihood of exposure to environmental and health risks as well as accessibility to health care.[30] Many of the nation's environmental policies distribute the costs in a regressive pattern while providing disproportionate benefits for whites and individuals who fall at the upper end of the education and income scale. Numerous studies, dating back to the seventies, reveal that people of color have borne greater health and environmental risk burdens than the society at large.[31]

Elevated public health risks are found in some populations even when social class is held constant. For example, race has been found to be independent of class in the distribution of air pollution,[32] contaminated fish consumption,[33] location of municipal landfills and incinerators,[34] toxic waste dumps,[35] cleanup of superfund sites,[36] and lead poisoning in children.[37]

Lead poisoning is a classic example of an environmental health problem that disproportionately impacts children of color at every class level. Lead affects between 3 million and 4 million children in the United States—most of whom are African-American and Latinos who live in urban areas. Among children 5 years old and younger, the percentage of African-American children who have excessive levels of lead in their blood far exceeds the percentage of whites at all income levels.

In 1988, the federal Agency for Toxic Substances Disease Registry (ATSDR) found that for families earning less than $6,000, 68 percent of African-American children had lead poisoning, compared with 36 percent for white children. In families with income exceeding $15,000, more than 38 percent of African-American children suffer from lead poisoning compared with 12 percent of whites. The average blood-lead level has dropped for all children with the phasing out of leaded gasoline. Today, the average blood-lead level for all children in the U.S. is under 6 ug/dl.[38] However, these efforts have not had the same positive benefits on all populations. There is still work to be done to address the remaining problem. The lead problem is not randomly distributed across the nation. The most vulnerable populations are low-income African-American and Hispanic-American children who live in older urban housing.[39]

Figures reported in the July 1994 *Journal of the American Medical Association* on the Third National Health and Nutrition Examination Survey (NHANES III) revealed that 1.7 million children (8.9 percent of children aged 1 to 5) are lead poisoned, defined as blood-lead levels equal to or above 10 ug/dl.[40] Lead-based paint (chips and dust) is the most common source of lead exposure for children. Children may also be exposed through soil and dust contamination built up from vehicle exhaust, lead concentration in soils in urban areas, lead dust brought into the home on parents' work clothes, lead used in ceramics and pottery, folk medicines, and lead in plumbing.

The Right to Breathe Clean Air

Urban air pollution problems have been with us for some time now. Before the federal government stepped in, issues related to air pollution were handled primarily by states and local government. Because states and local governments did such a poor job, the federal government set out to establish national clean air standards. Congress enacted the Clean Air Act (CAA) in 1970 and mandated the U.S. Environmental Protection Agency (EPA) to carry out this law. Subsequent amendments (1977 and 1990) were made to the CAA that form the current federal program. The CAA was a response to states' unwillingness to protect air quality. Many states used their lax enforcement of environmental laws as lures for business and economic development.[41]

Central cities and suburbs do not operate on a level playing field. They often compete for scarce resources. One need not be a rocket scientist to predict the outcome between affluent suburbs and their less affluent central city competitors.[42] Freeways are the lifeline for suburban commuters, while millions of central-city residents are dependent on public transportation as their primary mode of travel. But recent cuts in mass transit subsidies and fare hikes have reduced access to essential social services and economic activities. Nevertheless, road construction programs are booming—even in areas choked with automobiles and air pollution.[43]

The air quality impacts of transportation are especially significant to people of color who are more likely than whites to live in urban areas with reduced air quality. National Argonne Laboratory researchers discovered that 437 of the 3,109 counties and independent cities failed to meet at least one of the EPA ambient air quality standards.[44] Specifically, 57 percent of whites, 65 percent of African Americans, and 80 percent of Hispanics live in 437 counties with substandard air quality. Nationwide, 33 percent of whites, 50 percent of African Americans, and 60 percent of Hispanics live in the 136 counties in which two or more air pollutants exceed standards. Similar patterns were found for the 29 counties designated as nonattainment areas for three or more pollutants. Again, 12 percent of whites, 20 percent of African Americans, and 31 percent of Hispanics resided in the worse nonattainment areas.

Asthma is an emerging epidemic in the United States. The annual age-adjusted death rate from asthma increased by 40 percent between 1982 and 1991, from 1.34 to 1.88 per 100,000 population,[45] with the highest rates being consistently reported among blacks aged 15–24 years of age during the period 1980–1993.[46] Poverty and minority status are important risk factors for asthma mortality.

Children are at special risk from ozone.[47] Children also represent a considerable share of the asthma burden. It is the most common chronic disease of childhood. Asthma affects almost 5 million children under 18 years. Although the overall annual age-adjusted hospital discharge rate for asthma among children under 15 years old decreased slightly from 184 to 179 per 100,000 between 1982 and 1992, the decrease was slower compared to other childhood diseases,[48] resulting in a 70 percent increase in the proportion of hospital admissions related to asthma during the 1980s.[49] Inner-city children have the highest rates for asthma prevalence, hospitalization, and mortality.[50] In the United States, asthma is the fourth leading cause of disability among children aged less than 18 years.[51]

The public health community has insufficient information to explain the magnitude of some of the air pollution–related health problems. However, they do know that persons suffering from asthma are particularly sensitive to the effects of carbon monoxide, sulfur dioxide's particulate matter, ozone, and nitrogen oxides. Ground-level ozone may exacerbate health problems such as asthma, nasal congestion, throat irritation, respiratory tract inflammation, reduced resistance to infection, changes in cell function, loss of lung elasticity, chest pains, lung scarring, formation of lesions within the lungs, and premature aging of lung tissues.[52]

Nationally, African Americans and Latino Americans have significantly higher prevalence of asthma than the general population. A 1996 report from the federal Centers for Disease Control shows hospitalization and deaths rates from asthma increasing for persons twenty-five years or less.[53] The greatest increases occurred among African Americans. African Americans are two to six times more likely than whites to die from asthma.[54] Similarly, the hospitalization rate for African Americans is three to four times the rate for whites.

A 1994 CDC-sponsored study showed that pediatric emergency department visits at Atlanta Grady Memorial Hospital increased by one-third following peak ozone levels. The study also found that asthma rate among African-American children is 26 percent higher than the asthma rate among whites.[55] Since children with asthma in Atlanta may not have visited the emergency department for their care, the true prevalence of asthma in the community is likely to be higher.

Exploitation of Land, Environment, and People

Environmental decision making and local land-use planning operate at the juncture of science, economics, politics, and special interests that place communities of color at special risk.[56] This is especially true in America's Deep South. The Deep South has always been thought of as a backward land based on its social, economic, political, and environmental policies. By default, the region became a "sacrifice zone," a dump for the rest of the nation's toxic waste.[57] A colonial mentality exists in the South where local government and big business take advantage of people who are politically and economically powerless. Many of these attitudes emerged from the region's marriage to slavery and the plantation system—a brutal system that exploited humans and the land.[58] The Deep South is stuck with this unique legacy—the legacy of slavery, Jim Crow, and white resistance to equal justice for all. This legacy has also affected race relations and the region's ecology. Southerners, black and white, have less education, lower incomes, higher infant mortality, and lower life expectancy than Americans elsewhere. It should be no surprise that the environmental quality that Southerners enjoy is markedly different from that of other regions of the country.

The South is characterized by "look-the-other-way environmental policies and giveaway tax breaks."[59] It is our nation's Third World where "political bosses encourage outsiders to buy the region's human and natural resources at bargain prices."[60] Lax enforcement of environmental regulations has left the region's air, water, and land the most industry-befouled in the United States.

Toxic waste discharge and industrial pollution are correlated with poorer economic conditions. Louisiana typifies this pattern. Nearly three-fourths of Louisiana's population—more than 3 million people—get their drinking water from underground aquifers. Dozens of the aquifers are threatened by contamination from polluting industries.[61] The Lower Mississippi River Industrial Corridor has over 125 companies that manufacture a range of products including fertilizers, gasoline, paints, and plastics. This corridor has been dubbed "Cancer Alley" by environmentalists and local residents.[62] Ascension Parish typifies what many people refer to as a toxic "sacrifice zone." In two parish towns of Geismer and St. Gabriel, 18 petrochemical plants are crammed into a nine-and-a-half-square-mile area. Petrochemical plants discharge millions of pounds of pollutants annually into the water and air.

Louisiana citizens subsidize this corporate welfare with their health and the environment. Tax breaks given to polluting industries have created a few jobs at high cost. Nowhere is the polluter-welfare scenario more prevalent than in Louisiana. The state is a leader in doling out corporate welfare to polluters. A 1998 *Time Magazine* article reported that in the 1990s, Louisiana wiped off the books $3.1 billion in property taxes to polluting companies.[63] The state's top five worse polluters received $111 million dollars over the past decade.

Global Dumping Grounds

There is a direct correlation between exploitation of land and exploitation of people. It should not be a surprise to anyone to discover that Native Americans have to contend with some of the worst pollution in the United States.[64] Native American nations have become prime targets for waste trading.[65] More than three dozen Indian reservations have been targeted for landfills, incinerators, and other waste facilities.[66] The vast majority of these waste proposals were defeated by grassroots groups on the reservations. However, "radioactive colonialism" is alive and well.[67] The legacy of institutional racism has left many sovereign Indian nations without an economic infrastructure to address poverty, unemployment, inadequate education and health care, and a host of other social problems. In 1999, Eastern Navajo reservation residents filed suit against the Nuclear Regulatory Commission to block uranium mining in Church Rock and Crown Point communities.

Hazardous waste generation and international movement of hazardous waste pose some important health, environmental, legal, and ethical dilemmas. It is unlikely that many of the global hazardous waste proposals can be effectuated without first addressing the social, economic, and political context in which hazardous wastes are produced (industrial processes), controlled (regulations, notification and consent documentation), and managed (minimization, treatment, storage, recycling, transboundary shipment, pollution prevention, etc.). The "unwritten" policy of targeting Third-World nations for waste trade received international

media attention in 1991. Lawrence Summers, at the time he was chief economist of the World Bank, shocked the world and touched off an international scandal when his confidential memorandum on waste trade was leaked. Summers writes: "'Dirty' Industries: Just between you and me, shouldn't the World Bank be encouraging MORE migration of the dirty industries to the LDCs?"[68]

Consumption and production patterns, especially in nations with wasteful "throw-away" life styles as the United States, and the interests of transnational corporations create and maintain unequal and unjust waste burdens within and between affluent and poor communities, states, and regions of the world. Shipping hazardous wastes from rich communities to poor communities is not a solution to the growing global waste problem. Not only is it immoral, but it should be illegal. Moreover, making hazardous waste transactions legal does not address the ethical issues imbedded in such transactions.[69] The practice is a manifestation of power arrangements and a larger stratification system where some people and some places are assigned greater value than others.

In the real world, all people, communities, and nations are not created equal. Some populations and interests are more equal than others. Unequal interests and power arrangements have allowed poisons of the rich to be offered as short-term remedies for poverty of the poor. This scenario plays out domestically (as in the United States where low-income and people-of-color communities are disproportionately impacted by waste facilities and "dirty" industries) and internationally (where hazardous wastes from OECD states flow to non-OECD states).

The conditions surrounding the more than 1,900 maquiladoras, assembly plants operated by American, Japanese, and other foreign countries, located along the 2,000-mile U.S.-Mexico border may further exacerbate the waste trade.[70] The industrial plants use cheap Mexican labor to assemble imported components and raw material and then ship finished products back to the United States. Nearly a half million Mexican workers are employed in the maquiladoras.

A 1983 agreement between the United States and Mexico required American companies in Mexico to return waste products to the United States. Plants were required to notify the federal EPA when returning wastes. Results from a 1986 survey of 20 of the plants informed the U.S. EPA that they were returning waste to the United States, even though 86 percent of the plants used toxic chemicals in their manufacturing process. Much of the waste ends up being illegally dumped in sewers, ditches, and the desert. All along the Lower Rio Grande River Valley maquiladoras dump their toxic wastes into the river, from which 95 percent of the region's residents get their drinking water.[71]

The disregard for the environment and public safety has placed border residents' health at risk. In the border cities of Brownsville, Texas, and Matamoras, Mexico, the rate of anecephaly—babies born without brains—is four times the national average. Affected families have filed lawsuits against 88 of the area's 100 maquiladoras for exposing the community to xylene, a cleaning solvent that can cause brain hemorrhages, and lung and kidney damage.

Contaminated well and drinking water looms as a major health threat. Air pollution has contributed to a raging asthma and respiratory epidemic. The Mexican environmental regulatory agency is understaffed and "ill-equipped to adequately enforce its environmental laws."[72] Only time will tell if the North American Free Trade Agreement (NAFTA) will "fix" or exacerbate the public health, economic, and environmental problems along the U.S.-Mexico border.

Setting the Record Straight

The environmental protection apparatus is broken and needs to be fixed. The environmental justice movement has set out clear goals of eliminating unequal enforcement of environmental, civil rights, and public health laws. Environmental justice leaders have made a difference in the lives of people and the physical environment. They have assisted public decision makers in identifying "at-risk" populations, toxic "hot spots," research gaps, and action models to correct existing imbalances and prevent future threats. However, impacted communities are not waiting for the government or industry to get their acts together. Grassroots groups have taken the offensive to ensure that government and industry do the right thing.

Communities have begun to organize their own networks and force their inclusion into the mainstream of public decision making. They have also developed communication channels among environmental justice leaders, grassroots groups, professional associations (i.e., legal, public health, education, etc.), scientific groups, and public policy makers to assist them in identifying "at-risk" populations, toxic "hot spots," and research gaps, and work to correct imbalances.

In response to growing public concern and mounting scientific evidence, President Clinton signed Executive Order 12898. The Executive Order is not a new law. It only reinforces what has been the law of the land for over three decades. Environmental justice advocates are calling for vigorous enforcement of civil rights laws and environmental laws.

The number of environmental justice complaints is expected to escalate against industry, government, and institutions that receive funds. Citizens have a right to challenge discrimination—including environmental discrimination. It is a smokescreen for anyone to link Title VI or other civil rights enforcement to economic disinvestment in low-income and people-of-color communities. There is absolutely no empirical evidence to support the contention that environmental justice hurts **brownfields** redevelopment efforts.

The **EPA** has awarded over 200 Brownfields grants. In 1998, the agency had received some five dozen Title VI complaints. It is worth noting that not a single Title VI complaint involves a Brownfields site. On the other hand, two decades of solid empirical evidence documents the impact of racial redlining by banks, savings and loans, insurance companies, grocery chains, and even pizza delivery companies in thwarting economic vitality in black communities—not enforcement of civil rights laws. Racial redlining was such a real problem that Congress passed the Community Reinvestment Act in 1977.

States have had three decades to implement Title VI of the Civil Rights Act of 1964. Most states have chosen to ignore the law. States need to do a better job assuring nondiscrimination in the application and the implementation of permitting decisions, enforcement, and investment decisions. Environmental justice also means sharing in the benefits. Governments must live up to their mandate of protecting all people and the environment. Anything less is unacceptable. The solution to environmental injustice lies in the realm of equal protection of all individuals, groups, and communities. No community, rich or poor,

---

brownfield An industrial or commercial site that is idle or underused because of real or perceived environmental pollution.
EPA U.S. Environmental Protection Agency. The EPA's Brownfields Program provides direct funding for brownfields assessment, cleanup, revolving loans, and environmental job training.

urban or suburban, black or white, should be allowed to become a "sacrifice zone" or the dumping ground.

Hazardous wastes and "dirty" industries have followed the "path of least resistance." Poor people and poor communities are given a false choice of "no jobs and no development" versus "risky low-paying jobs and pollution." Industries and governments (including the military) have often exploited the economic vulnerability of poor communities, poor states, poor regions, and poor nations for their "risky" operations.

24 Race, Religion, and the Color Line (Or Is That the Color Wall?)
Michael O. Emerson

MICHAEL O. EMERSON is the Allyn and Gladys Cline Professor of Sociology and the Funding Director of the Center on Race, Religion, and Urban Life at Rice University. He has authored many papers and several books on the relationships between race and religion, as well as on neighborhood segregation and immigration issues.

A COUPLE OF YEARS AGO, BISHOP FRED Caldwell, pastor of Shreveport, Louisiana's Greenwood Acres Full Gospel Baptist Church, a large African American congregation, offered a unique proposal. He was offering to *pay* nonblacks to attend his church. So adamant that his church should not be segregated, Bishop Caldwell said that for at least one month he would pay nonblacks five dollars per hour to attend the multiple-hour Sunday morning service, and ten dollars an hour to attend the church's Thursday night service. And he would pay this money out of his own pocket. Bishop Caldwell told the Associated Press, "This idea is born of God. God wants a rainbow in his church." He said the inspiration came to him during a sermon. "The most segregated hour in America is Sunday morning at 11 o'clock. The Lord is tired of it, and I'm certainly tired of it. This is not right."[1]

This story was first reported in the local Shreveport, Louisiana, newspaper, but was soon picked up by papers across the country. The day the story appeared in *USA Today,* ten people sent me online links to the article, often with an e-mail subject heading like "You've got to see

> **Questions to Consider**   Michael O. Emerson points out that among the most segregated institutions in the United States are our houses of worship. How much racial separation is there in American religion? Why? Does this racial separation matter, and if so, how? What do we know about multiracial congregations? Why are these racially integrated congregations of interest for understanding race in the United States?

this!" The story was soon the talk on radio airwaves and television outlets. Internet chat rooms were talking about it, and people were debating it at the proverbial water cooler.

Pay people to attend worship services? To many, paying people to worship seemed outrageous. Others thought the idea was brilliant, highlighting the racial segregation in houses of worship across the nation. Still others thought the bishop should not focus on the race of those who attended his church, but merely minister to whoever attended. They found his "religious affirmative action" deeply troubling. Discussion spread beyond this simple offer to pay people to attend one church, and turned to whether the racial makeup of congregations matters.

Shortly after this story hit the national news, I was a guest on a two-hour radio call-in show in Baltimore. The show's hosts opened by discussing Bishop Caldwell's offer to pay nonblacks to come to his church, and featured the more general topic of congregational segregation. The issue touched a hot button among the listeners. The hosts kept commenting that their lines were lit up, jammed full. I could hear and feel that the callers were passionate about this topic.

When the first "post-pay-to-attend-offer" Sunday service was held, reporters were eager to see the results. The headlines told the story: "Few take pastor up on offer," said one headline. A year later, a small bit of change had happened. According to a report in one magazine, a year after the offer, about two dozen whites were attending this congregation of thousands, and five whites had become members.[2]

How Segregated Are Religious Congregations?

For a long time, when people studied race relations and inequality, they did not think of religion. But when well over 100 million Americans are attending religious congregations each week, and when 90 percent of Americans say they have a religious faith and believe in a higher being, it seems like a gross oversight not to consider the role of religion. It seems even more of a mistake given that the early giants in the field, such as W. E. B. DuBois, thought it so important that they actually wrote books about it. And like Bishop Caldwell, Martin Luther King, probably the best known advocate for racial equality, called religion the most segregated institution in the nation.

I wanted to piggyback on these giants, so I have spent a number of years researching the relationship between religion and race, and I am delighted to share some of what has been learned with you. One of my first questions was: How segregated are religious congregations? This question did not have an answer other than "very." So my colleagues and I set out to find a more precise answer.

To do so, we decided to study the segregation in two ways. First, we defined homogeneous congregations (80 percent or more of a congregation is of the same race) and mixed race congregations (no one racial group is 80 percent or more of the congregation). We used this cutoff of 80 percent because research done on other

organizations—such as businesses—has found that until another group or groups make up 20 percent or more of an organization, they lack the critical mass to make any significant changes in the organization.

Armed with this definition, we used data collected from a national random sample of congregations. We found that *more than 90 percent* of congregations are racially homogeneous (Figure 1). You have to look hard to find a racially mixed congregation in the United States.

But where you look is important. As Figure 2 shows, the faith tradition matters. Because of the sample size, unfortunately I had to combine all non-Christian congregations—such as Buddhist temples, Muslim mosques, and Jewish synagogues—into one category. When I do that, more than a quarter of all non-Christian congregations are racially mixed. Among Catholic congregations, 15 percent of them are mixed, and among Protestants, just 5 percent are mixed. Why this variation? We found that the larger the religious tradition—the number of people involved in that faith and the number of congregations to chose from—the more segregated it is. To put it most bluntly, the more choices people have of where to worship, the more they choose to be with people who are racially similar to themselves.

We have a more sophisticated way to study the level of congregational segregation. Instead of just studying whether a congregation is or is not racially mixed, we can ask how diverse congregations are by asking: *What is the probability that any two randomly selected people in the congregation will be of different races?* In other words, if you were to walk into a congregation, write the name of each person in attendance on a little slip of paper, put those slips of paper into your hat, mix them up, and then, with your eyes closed, draw out two names, how often would those two people be of different socially defined racial groups? Fifty percent of the time, perhaps, or maybe 30 percent of the time?

Rather than using a hat and slips of paper, we did this process with a statistical formula and a computer. We found that that the average (median) diversity of a congregation in the United States is *just .02*. That means that the probability that any two randomly selected people in a congregation will be of a different races is only 2 percent.

To put that number in context, we did the same calculations for the nation's neighborhoods and schools, both of which are highly segregated, and found that religious

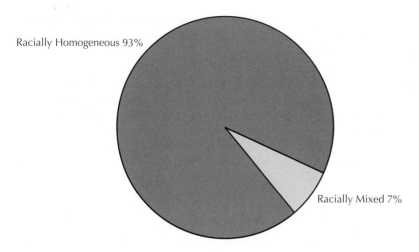

FIGURE 1   **Racial Composition of U.S. Congregations.**
Source: National Congregations Study.

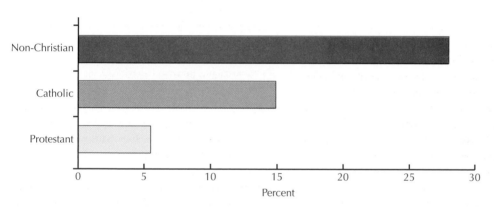

FIGURE 2   **Percentage of Congregations That Are Racially Mixed, by Faith Tradition.**
Source: National Congregations Study.

congregations are *10 times less diverse* than the neighborhoods in which they reside, and *20 times less diverse* than the nation's public schools. When Martin Luther King said that religious congregations are the most segregated institution in the United States, he wasn't kidding. Forget the color line. When it comes to religion in the United States, we have a color wall. Just as China has its great wall, so too does the United States.[3]

So What If Religious Congregations Are Segregated?

Having found out more precisely how segregated religious congregations are, I wondered if it made any difference for race relations and inequality. It does, dramatically so.

Religion has much potential for mitigating racial division and inequality. Most religions teach love, respect, and equality of all peoples. They usually teach of the errors inherent in racial prejudice and discrimination. They often proclaim the need to embrace all people. They speak of the need for fairness and justice. They often teach that selfishness and acting in self-interested ways are counter to the will of the divine.

In the United States, religious faith motivated the fight against slavery. It played an essential role in the Civil Rights movement. It currently is motivating many believers to attempt to reduce the racial divide and injustice. It directs people to value openness and diversity. It guides some to vote in ways that will overcome racial inequality. It motivates others to volunteer in groups working against racial hate and discrimination. For still others, it motivates them to form organizations intent on reducing inequality and strengthening justice. Others are motivated to donate money to such organizations.

Stories of positive actions of religious people and organizations to combat racial division and inequality abound. But in this section, focusing on the structural arrangement of racially segregated religious congregations, I demonstrate the powerful countervailing influences of religion on racialization.

To reflect on this issue properly, let's keep in mind the distinction between macro and micro effects. Part of the irony of religion's role is that in strengthening micro bonds between individuals, religion contributes to within-group sameness, heightens isolation from different groups, and reduces the opportunity to form macro bonds—that is, bonds between groups that serve to integrate a society. The lack of social ties between religious groups across race inhibits movement between them, increasing the importance of group boundaries and social differences. This means that racially segregated congregations lower the probability of intergroup mobility (such as through intermarriage) and heighten the importance of racial boundaries, separate racial identities, and other differences between groups. So though many in the religious community call and work for an end to racial division, the organization of religion into segregated congregations often undercuts their efforts.

The separate groups that are reproduced through religious division result in categorization, for separate groups must be categorized by something—in this case, by race and often by religious and other views. According to scholars Hamilton and Trolier, categorization has important implications:

> The social categories we develop are more than convenient groupings of individuals that simplify the actual diversities among the people we observe and encounter. They are also categories that can bias the way we process information, organize and store it in memory, and make judgments about members of those social categories.[4]

We all consistently engage in social comparison (Am I smart? Who is good-looking? Who has money?), and research links categorization to at least seven biases:

1. Our brains exaggerate the similarities of ingroup members and their differences from outgroup members.

2. Because people know the outgroup by its perceived differences, outgroup members are identified by these differences, overly homogenizing them.

3. Ingroup favoritism: Even when performing exactly the same actions, ingroup members are evaluated more positively and outgroup members more negatively.

4. We attribute positive behavior of ingroup members to internal traits such as intelligence, and negative behavior to external causes such as a poor home life. We do the exact opposite for outgroup members.

5. Cognitive psychologists find that we have better memories for negative outgroup behaviors than for negative ingroup behaviors.

6. Because our brains tend to overly homogenize outgroups, a negative behavior of an outgroup member is likely to be perceived as characteristic of the entire outgroup. We appear to make the leap from James of Group X shoplifted to people of Group X shoplift.

7. Once people have preconceived stereotypes of an outgroup, they tend to recall only information that confirms their stereotypes, while contradictory evidence is dismissed as an exception. A relative of mine, for example, knew for sure that African Americans were lazy, shiftless, and liars, even though one my relative's closest friends was African American. My relative's explanation? Her friend was not like other African Americans; she was the exception.[5]

Religion contributes to racial division and inequality, then, in that it increases racial categorization, which is a by-product of congregational segregation.

Given human limitations, racially exclusive identities and congregations necessitate another bias. We can call this the ethical paradox of group loyalty. The paradox is that even if made up of loving, unselfish individuals, the group transmutes individual unselfishness into group selfishness.

What does that mean in English? Imagine two groups. Each member of each group is a deeply committed religious person, full of love and concern for others, and has even developed a friendship or two with people of other groups. For historical reasons, one group has more social goods—income, wealth, education, power—than the other group. Despite being made up entirely of unselfish individuals, the two groups will continue to be divided and unequal. How can this be?

Reinhold Niebuhr explored this question way back in 1932 in his book *Moral Man and Immoral Society*.[6] For one thing, he wrote, direct contact with members of other groups is limited, always less than with members of one's own group. People thus know the members of their own group and their needs more deeply, fully, and personally than the members and needs of other groups. Therefore, they attend to the needs of their own group first, precisely because they are moral and loving. How can they turn their backs on the needs of their own group in favor of another group? At the individual level, selfishness is usually considered negative, but at the group level, it is considered moral and just. Indeed, at the group level, it is not selfishness, but morality, service, sacrifice, and loyalty.

We find evidence of this every day. Consider the family. Although we are selfish if we always look out for our individual needs first, it is considered wrong and immoral if we do not consider the needs of our family first, ahead of other families. Your parents would be considered immoral if they did not help pay for their own children's college first. Only if they had extra money (at college prices today, that would be rare!) would they even consider helping other children, but even then, there would be so many other family needs to be met.

So, the approximately 350,000 congregations in the United States, are busy creating group identity and forming moral persons. Those moral persons, acting morally, are aware of and help their families and the members of their own congregations first, making sure those needs are met before looking to help elsewhere. Because of segregation, this means we help people of our own race—whites helping whites, African Americans helping African Americans, Asians helping Asians, Latinos helping Latinos, and so on.

The problem with this pattern is that the inequality between groups is maintained. Members of groups with the most share it with others of their group. Members of groups with the least are busy trying to meet the needs of others in their group, which because the group has less, are typically bigger needs, trying to be met with less. It is a nasty cycle, even though the people involved are themselves not acting nasty.

We also have another problem, according to Niebuhr. Because the members of a group cannot understand and feel the needs of another group as completely and deeply as those of their own group, reliance on love, compassion, and persuasion to overcome group divisions and inequalities is practically impossible. For this reason, relations between groups are always mainly political rather than ethical or moral (wow, reflect on this statement—it's a doozy). As Niebuhr says, "They will always be determined by the proportion of power which each group possesses at least as much as by any rational and moral appraisal of the comparative needs and claims of each group."[7]

The facts just considered have considerable implications for the perpetuation of racial inequality and stratification. The logic is straightforward: (1) In the United States there is racial inequality in access to valued resources. (2) Access to valued resources—such as jobs, prestige, wealth, and power—is gained in significant part through social ties.[8] (3) For reasons such as social categorization, comparison, and the paradox of ingroup loyalty, people have positive bias for their ingroup and negative bias for outgroups. These three facts suggest that, other factors being equal, any social structure or process that both increases the saliency of group boundaries and reduces interracial ties necessarily reproduces racial inequality. Because the organization of religion in the United States heightens the salience of racial boundaries and reduces interracial ties, it necessarily reproduces racial inequality.[9]

Can We Find a Solution?

So is that it? Must we then conclude that religion really can only entrench and amplify the racial divisions and inequalities that already exist? For the millions of religious people, that would be a pretty disappointing conclusion. But that is not it. If you give it some thought, how could religion change to actually move toward reducing racial division and inequality?

If the whole edifice of evidence against positive effects of religion is built upon the foundation of segregated congregations, what if congregations were not segregated? Could positive changes for racial division and inequality result?

My colleagues and I spent a number of years trying to figure this out. We did so by studying multiracial congregations (those 7 percent of congregations from Figure 1) and, for comparative purposes, racially homogeneous congregations. We conducted telephone interviews, mail surveys, and face-to-face interviews, and we spent lots of time in congregations across the country. I even spent nearly six years in one congregation as it transformed from an all-white congregation to one that no longer had a majority racial group and had people from well over forty nations in attendance.

Social Ties

The first difference we noticed in studying these congregations was the extensive amount of friendships across race that people in these racially mixed congregations had. As an African American woman from Chicago who was a member of a multiracial congregation called Crosstown told us:

> I grew up in a predominantly black church and neighborhood. Crosstown has taught me about other races of people. [The diversity at Crosstown] helped me to develop relationships with people outside my race where I felt they were my friend and we share Christ in our life and that they have the same struggles as I do. . . . I've gotten to know other people on that more personal level.

To test whether this is true more systematically, we conducted a national survey and asked people several questions about the racial composition of their friends and acquaintances. We classified Americans into three groups: those attending racially homogeneous congregations, those attending racially mixed congregations, and those not attending any congregation. One of the questions we asked them was to think of their circle of friends, those people they like to spend time with and keep in regular contact (whether friends from their congregation, neighborhood, work, childhood, etc.). Were all, most, about half, some, or none of their circle of friends the same race as them?

What did we find? Of those attending racially homogeneous congregations, 83 percent said that most or all of their friends were the same race as them. Among those not attending any congregation, 70 percent said most or all of their friends were the same race as them. Here we see a general pattern I often find in my studies. Religion typically serves to intensify general patterns in the larger society. If society is segregated, religion can intensify that segregation through a variety of ways, but most certainly by providing yet another plane of segregation—its congregations.

What is the case, though, for people attending racially mixed congregations? We found a dramatic difference not only from people attending racially homogeneous congregations, but from people not attending congregations. Whereas 83 percent and 70 percent of those two groupings said most or all of their friends were the same race as them, only 36 percent of people attending racially mixed congregation said most or all of their friends were the same race as them. And we found that those 36 percent who did say most of their friends were the same race as them were relatively recent arrivals to their racially mixed congregation.

We found this same pattern for every question we asked about relationships with other people. People not attending congregations are more likely to be interracially married, have best friends who are of a different race, and have more diverse social networks than are those who attend racially homogeneous congregations. But both groups' level of racial diversity in relationships greatly pales compared to that of people in racially mixed congregations.

In terms of creating holes in the color wall, racially mixed congregations seem a promising avenue. But we cannot get ahead of ourselves. For all we know at this point, the folks attending these types of congregations formed their friendships before they started attending their mixed congregation. In fact, perhaps they ended up in such congregations precisely because they had racially diverse friendships to begin with.

So my colleagues and I again set out to find the answer. We went around the country and interviewed about two hundred people attending racially mixed congregations and, for comparison, people attending racially homogeneous congregations. We found two answers. People who attend racially mixed congregations are somewhat more likely to have at some time in their lives attended a racially mixed school or lived in a racially mixed neighborhood. But more than 80 percent of the people in racially mixed congregations said that most of the racial diversity in their friendships came *because of* their involvement in their racially mixed congregation. Indeed, when we did a fancy statistical analysis called logistic regression, we found that by far the most important factor in people's having racially diverse relationships is whether they attend a racially mixed congregation. Representative of this finding, a Salvadorian immigrant living in Los Angeles and attending a racially mixed congregation said that that perhaps 10 percent of the people she new before she started attending her church were of different races, but now, "since I have been at this church the majority of my friends are of different races."

This pattern happens for a couple of reasons. First, of course, people make friends with others in their racially mixed congregation. But the diversity effect of these types of congregations goes even further. After making interracial friends in their congregation, people were often introduced to others in their new friends' networks. For example, Chanel, an African American who attends a racially mixed congregation in the South, met Rosita, a Latina who attends the same congregation, through a women's group at the congregation. They soon became friends. Over time, Rosita would invite Chanel over to her place, for birthday parties or other gatherings, where Chanel would meet and get to know an extended network of other Hispanics. And vice versa. Chanel would invite Rosita to her place for family gatherings, were Rosita met and became friends with an extended network of other African Americans. Their children too became fast friends, and so they often got together so their children could play. And we found that this sort of pattern made people more confident and comfortable getting to know still others of different racial groups. As one man from the Northeast who attends a racially mixed congregation said: "Being in this church has really opened me up to people of all different backgrounds. Now when I meet people of different races at work, I don't just say hello

and move on. I am comfortable to get to know them. I've made new friends at work this way."

Attitudes

At a celebration service culminating a weekend of youth events at a Baptist church in the Deep South, families and friends of the youths who had attended were invited for the service. Chase, white, 16 years of age, and due to an accident, in a wheelchair for life, was in attendance that weekend. Not attending any congregation prior to this event, he was invited to this youth weekend by a white classmate who did belong to the church. That Sunday, moved by what he had experienced over the past few days of the youth event, he shared with the congregation that he had found a purpose in this congregation—he had made friends with youth of many different races, and who didn't seem to care at all that he was in a wheelchair. Having talked it over with his parents the day before, he announced, through tears, that he had found a home and that he wanted to become a member of the congregation.

Also in attendance that day were his parents and his brother, Tre. Tre was a longtime devout skinhead. His head shaved nearly clean, he had swastika tattoos all around his upper arms. He had a skinhead symbol tattooed on his chest. And he had a noose tattooed on the full length of this left thigh. He didn't at all like nonwhites: "they're whiners, they steal jobs that belong to us, they're lazy, steal, and they have the government always givin' 'em stuff." He was particularly upset at this church he had come to in support of his brother, Chase. The senior pastor was African American, the associate pastor Hispanic. The entire congregation, in fact, was, in his view, a sickening mix of the different races—black, Hispanic, Asian, and worst of all, whites. What are whites doing here with these people? he thought. He felt ill at the sight. Why hadn't his brother told him who was at this church? And now there was his brother, up front, saying he wanted to become part of this God-forsaken place, even with the support of his parents. Unbelievable! he thought. He was angry, feeling claustrophobic. He just wanted out of this place. But as he described it to me, something happened, something broke inside of him.

> Seein' the people all come up to hug my brother, seein' his happy face, seein' all these different people singin' together, feelin' the power in that, it was somethin'

I ain't never seen or felt before. Not sure how to describe it, just that it felt real, like it was the way things was supposed to be. I felt like some real bad stuff broke inside of me that day. These people weren't all bad people. They were carin' for my brother.

Two weeks later, through tears of his own, Tre joined the church as well, and asked if the African American pastor would come with him later that week to get his white supremacy tattoos removed.

Few stories of change in racial attitudes are as dramatic as this one. But we found a strong pattern of change in the direction of more positive racial attitudes of people that attend these mixed congregations. We found change in all racial groups, but especially among whites. They were the ones who most often had significant changes in their views, and they are the ones who differ the most from their white peers not in mixed race congregations. These changes in attitudes seemed to come about as a result of the newly formed friendships, through preaching and teaching, and through observing those of different races involved in common tasks.

We found these differences across religious traditions. At a multiracial mosque in the Midwest, they had a serious problem. The mosque had people from nations who thought you must *always* remove your shoes when entering the mosque, and people from others nations who thought you must *never* insult Allah by removing your shoes when entering the mosque. Pretty easy to see we've got a problem here. Folks take the shoe issue very seriously, because it is tied to their religion and the proper way to worship. And because the shoe issue was related to nationality, ethnicity, and race, the problem quickly became destructive. People took such offense at the other groups that the mosque leaders decided to put up a screen to divide the shoe removers from the shoe wearers, even though this also divided people by ethnicity and race. But they did not intend to keep it there permanently. After they put it up, the imam began to teach that Allah calls all Muslims to be together, across race, ethnicity, and worship approach. They therefore must find a way to do so in their mosque. Either they would all have to remove their shoes or all wear their shoes, or, the solution he proposed, they would have to accept that whichever people do, they do it out of reverence for Allah, not as a reflection of an inferior ethnicity or culture. Reverence for Allah is what must unite them. Over time, the worshippers came to accept this view, and the screen was eventually removed, even though some continued to remove their shoes, and some continued to wear their shoes. Friendships across cultures formed, and attitudes about the different groups became more favorable.

Raised Status

This leads to yet another difference we found in these mixed congregations. The congregation I spent years studying made a commitment to go on mission and service trips to each of the nations that members of the congregation were from. When they went on these trips, the appointed leaders were always the people from that country. As the senior pastor of the congregation told me, this worked wonders on the views of his congregants. A Guatemalan cleaning lady who can barely speak English is easy to marginalize in the U.S. context, but when she was the leader on the trip to Guatemala, when she became the person who was fluent in the language, who knew the lay of the land, who had the social connections, who knew what to eat and what to avoid, she came to be seen, this pastor and his congregants told me, in a substantially new light. She was important, she had skills they did not have, and they were dependent upon her. Through evening discussions while on these trips, the congregants came to conclude that social context, not a person's essence, shapes views of their worth and skills. Multiracial congregations, we found, often raise the status of racially different others in the eyes of their members.

As you will recall, segregated congregations contribute to socioeconomic inequality. But we found a different pattern in many mixed race congregations. Because of the social ties between people and changed attitudes, the average education, income, and occupational status of people in these congregations—especially for marginalized groups—were higher than their counterparts not in such congregations. Again, was this the case before or after they came to the congregation? We found that a great deal happened in these congregations that led to increased socioeconomic status after they arrived. Connections were made, child care was provided, and funding was often found that allowed for further schooling. People were hired into jobs that they otherwise might never have known about or had a chance at, because of their connections to others in the congregation well placed in the labor market. It also seems that such congregations help people accrue resources that can gain them access to better heath care, neighborhoods, schools, and other social goods. Mixed race congregations, then, seem to actually reduce the racial divide in inequality.

Bridge Organizations and Sixth Americans

Mixed race congregations are what I call bridge organizations; that is, they gather and facilitate cross-race social ties, creating a "natural" setting where people of different racial groups meet and form relationships, pursuing a common purpose (if you have ever studied contact theory, these types of congregations meet well the conditions necessary for forming friendships and reducing prejudice). So different is the average person in a mixed race congregation compared to the average American outside of these congregations that I call them Sixth Americans. The United States, writes David Hollinger, is really five melting pots;[10] that is, people come from hundreds if not thousands of ethnic backgrounds, but in the United States, they are expected to meld into one of five racial groupings: Indian/Native American, African American/Black, White/Caucasian, Hispanic/Latino/a, or Asian/Asian American.

But people in mixed race congregations, although phenotypically often part of one of these five melting pots, seem to operate outside of their melting pot in most aspects of their social relations. Sixth Americans live in multiple melting pots simultaneously. Minorities among Americans to be sure, Sixth Americans live in a world of primary relationships and associations that are racially diverse. Like other Americans, the Sixth American may work in a racially diverse setting, see racially different others at the grocery store, or perhaps have a friend of a different race. But unlike other Americans, the Sixth American's "world of racial diversity" does not stop here. It is not a racially homogenous world with some diversity sprinkled in; the Sixth American's world is a racially diverse world with some homogeneity sprinkled in. In my book, *People of the Dream,* I argue that these Sixth Americans are a different kind of American. And their congregations, where they gather together to worship, serve, and support one another, despite the failures along the way (which I detail in Chapter 6 of the book), may be harbingers of what is to come.[11]

Conclusion

Religion in the United States is divided by a vast, thick, massive color wall. That color wall has had and has severe implications for racial division and racial stratification. We have ignored the impact of religion on race for too long. Through studying not segregated congregations, but the small percentage of congregations that are racially mixed, I found that despite risks, the overall trends work to reduce racial division and inequality. These findings serve to further amplify the deleterious effects that segregated congregations have on American race relations.

Changing the organization of American religion is not the sole answer to destructive race relations, but it is part of the answer. To that end, several scholars are now pursuing studies of how multiracial congregations form, how to minimize costs and accentuate positives, and how people come to be in these congregations. If you are interested, we invite you to read further by searching out books and other articles on this topic. Humans create their social structures, so change is possible when humans decide their current social structures will no longer do. Will enough decide to make a change, and put enough holes in the color wall to eventually collapse it? Time will tell.

25 Why Are There No Supermarkets in My Neighborhood? The Long Search for Fresh Fruit, Produce, and Healthy Food

Shannon N. Zenk (et al.)

SHANNON N. ZENK is assistant professor in the department of public health, mental health, and administrative nursing at the University of Illinois at Chicago.

FOUR OF THE 10 LEADING CAUSES OF DEATH in the United States are chronic diseases for which diet is a major risk factor.[1] Racial disparities in the burden of these chronic, diet-related diseases are well documented, with African Americans often having the highest morbidity and mortality.[2–5] Because health risks and resources are spatially and socially structured and African Americans disproportionately live in economically disadvantaged neighborhoods, increased attention has been focused on how residential environments shape health and contribute to racial disparities in health.[6–9] An extensive body of literature now associates residence in economically disadvantaged neighborhoods, after control for individual socioeconomic status, with a variety of adverse diet-related health outcomes.[10–12]

Despite numerous research efforts that have examined neighborhood variations in health, relatively little is known about the mechanisms by which neighborhood environments affect health.[13–15] One hypothesis is that economically and socially disadvantaged neighborhoods have inadequate access to healthy foods, thus negatively affecting dietary quality and health. Although the presence of supermarkets may not always be beneficial for neighborhood residents (e.g., if supermarkets displace smaller stores with owners who had positively contributed to and invested in the neighborhood), such large stores can be neighborhood health resources providing generally better availability and selection, higher quality, and lower cost of foods compared with smaller food stores.[16] These food resource factors influence dietary patterns.[17–24] Previous studies have found that fewer supermarkets are located in

Questions to Consider In a typical middle- to upper-middle-class white suburban neighborhood it is not uncommon to find two, three, or even four supermarkets within a mile or two of one another. Because of their close proximity these stores engage in cutthroat competition. The result is a cheap abundance of fresh fruits, vegetables, and a staggering array of healthy foods. Now think about a poor neighborhood in an inner city. Corner stores, not supermarkets, are the source for grocery shopping. How, according to Professor Zenk and associates, is race and class implicated in having access to large supermarkets? What are the health consequences of having to purchase groceries from corner stores or bodegas rather than a huge supermarket?

African American neighborhoods compared with White neighborhoods[25,26] and are located in economically disadvantaged neighborhoods compared with affluent neighborhoods.[16,26–29] Other studies have found no differences in the accessibility of supermarkets according to racial or socioeconomic characteristics of neighborhoods.[30–32] This discrepancy could reflect either differences in the definition of supermarkets or true variability in results across time and place that may be caused by differences in the degree of racial or economic segregation. Lower purchasing power is an often-cited but disputed explanation for the relative scarcity of supermarkets in economically disadvantaged neighborhoods.[33–35]

Analysis of the role of race without regard to poverty and of poverty without regard to race offers an incomplete picture of the potential importance of these factors in shaping the spatial accessibility of supermarkets. Understanding these relationships is critical for informing intervention and policy efforts. Such an understanding is particularly important, given the roles of racial residential segregation and economic restructuring in concentrating poverty in African American neighborhoods of older industrial cities of the Northeast and Upper Midwest.[36–40] Therefore, we sought to determine whether supermarkets are located at farther distances from the center of African American neighborhoods compared with White neighborhoods regardless of neighborhood economic conditions or if racial disparities in supermarket accessibility occur only in higher poverty contexts.

Methods

Setting and Sample

The setting for this study was the Detroit metropolitan area in Michigan. Metropolitan Detroit is characterized by extreme economic inequalities across neighborhoods.[36] Economic inequalities can be traced to the period just after World War II, when highway construction and cheap land outside the city led many industries to relocate to the suburbs.[39,41–43] Between 1950 and 1990, the city of Detroit lost approximately 350,000 jobs,[41,43,44] largely owing to the relocation of industries to the suburbs, deindustrialization, and other facets of economic restructuring. At the same time, discriminatory federal housing policies and lending practices, racial steering (the act of real estate agents systematically showing African Americans to different neighborhoods than Whites), restrictive covenants, and violence created and reinforced racial residential segregation in metropolitan Detroit. In effect, African Americans were confined to the least desirable, older residential neighborhoods of the city, whereas Whites were able to move to more desirable, newer suburban locations.[35,37,41,44–47] The city of Detroit shifted from 16.2% African American in 1950 to 81.2% African American in 2000,[43,48] a sharp contrast with the 84.8% of metropolitan Detroit residents outside the city limits who identified as non-Hispanic White in 2000.[48] Metropolitan Detroit remains one of the most racially segregated areas in the United States— ranked second overall in residential segregation of African

Americans in 2000.[49] The sample for this study was 869 neighborhoods (we used census tracts as proxies) in the tricounty Detroit metropolitan area. These neighborhoods are located in the city of Detroit and in the tricounty Detroit metropolitan area (Wayne, Oakland, Macomb counties) within a 10-mile buffer of Detroit.

Measures

We used 2000 decennial census data to characterize the neighborhoods. Population density was computed as the total population per square mile (median = 5367.44). Racial composition was defined as the percentage of non-Hispanic African American residents (median = 6.06%). Neighborhood poverty was defined as the percentage of residents below the poverty line (median = 8.21%). . . . Given that 92% of residents in tricounty metropolitan Detroit were either non-Hispanic White (67.3%) or non-Hispanic African American (24.9%), neighborhoods with low proportions of African Americans generally correspond with predominately White neighborhoods.

Supermarkets were defined as supercenters (e.g., Meijer, Super Kmart) and full-line grocery stores (e.g., Farmer Jack, Kroger) associated with a national or regional grocery chain, i.e., a chain with 11 or more retail stores.[50] To identify supermarkets, we obtained a 2001 list of grocery stores from the Michigan Department of Agriculture. We used 2001–2002 paper telephone directories, as well as online telephone directories and company Web sites, in the fall of 2002 to verify the addresses of these supermarkets and to identify additional supermarkets. We confirmed the address of any supermarket not on the Michigan Department of Agriculture list by telephoning the store. One hundred and sixty supermarkets were identified in Detroit and in the metropolitan area within a 15-mile buffer of Detroit. . . . The additional 5-mile buffer of supermarkets around the sampled neighborhoods helped to ensure that we could calculate supermarket accessibility for neighborhoods at the periphery.

• • •

The nearest supermarket was significantly further away in neighborhoods with a high proportion of African Americans and in the most impoverished neighborhoods compared with neighborhoods with a low proportion of African Americans and the least impoverished neighborhoods, respectively. (These results were adjusted for population density.)

• • •

Among the most impoverished neighborhoods, distance to the nearest supermarket varied considerably by percentage African American, with the nearest supermarket averaging 1.10 to 1.15 miles farther in neighborhoods with medium . . . and high . . . proportions of African Americans, respectively, than in neighborhoods with low proportions of African Americans. . . .

Discussion

Disparities in Supermarket Accessibility

The relationship between neighborhood racial composition and supermarket accessibility varied according to neighborhood poverty level in metropolitan Detroit. The distance to the nearest supermarket was similar among the least impoverished neighborhoods across the 3 tertiles of percentage African American. However, disparities in supermarket accessibility on the basis of race were evident among the most impoverished neighborhoods: the most impoverished neighborhoods in which African Americans resided, on average, were 1.1 miles farther from the nearest supermarket than were the most impoverished White neighborhoods. Most African Americans in tricounty metropolitan Detroit reside in neighborhoods that are in the upper tertile for percentage poor and that have either a high proportion of African Americans (60%) or a medium proportion of African Americans (20%), as defined in this study.

Inadequate accessibility to supermarkets may contribute to less-nutritious diets and hence to greater risk for chronic, diet-related diseases. In a recent qualitative study, Detroit residents reported that lack of access to supermarkets was a barrier to healthy eating.[50] At least 3 previous quantitative studies, all of which examined chain supermarkets, have suggested that closer proximity to supermarkets is associated with better-quality diets.[51–53] The observation that the nearest supermarket averaged 1.1 miles further in the most impoverished neighborhoods in which African Americans resided . . . compared with the most impoverished White neighborhoods . . . is particularly salient, given that 23% and 28% . . . of households in the most impoverished neighborhoods in which African Americans resided did not own a car in 2000.

We began the study with 3 measures of supermarket accessibility: distance to the nearest supermarket, number of supermarkets within a 3-mile radius (considered reachable by car), and potential supermarket accessibility. . . .[54] Because the patterns of these relationships were similar, we present only distance to the nearest supermarket. For all 3 measures, supermarket accessibility was comparable among the least impoverished neighborhoods regardless of neighborhood racial composition, whereas disparities were evident among the most impoverished neighborhoods. The most impoverished neighborhoods in which African Americans resided . . . averaged 2.3 and 2.7 (respectively) fewer supermarkets within a 3-mile radius and had lower potential supermarket accessibility relative to the most impoverished White neighborhoods. . . .

Race appears to be an important factor with respect to supermarket accessibility in the context of more impoverished neighborhoods; 76% of neighborhoods with a high proportion of African Americans were among the most impoverished. The disproportionate representation of African Americans in more impoverished neighborhoods in Detroit can be traced historically. Until the 1940s—a decade in which Detroit's African American population doubled from 149,119 to 300,506 because of the influx of African Americans from the South for manufacturing jobs—African Americans generally resided in central Detroit and east central Detroit.[35,36] Facing overcrowded and substandard housing, African Americans began moving to other parts of the city.[39,55,56] Nevertheless, institutional racism—specifically racial residential segregation—confined African Americans to Detroit neighborhoods that began losing employment opportunities, particularly in the manufacturing industry, in the 1950s.[39,41,44] Between 1948 and 1967, Detroit lost nearly 130,000 manufacturing jobs.[39]

Often confronting strong resistance from Whites, African Americans first moved to nearby neighborhoods in central Detroit.[46,57] Hence, many neighborhoods located in central Detroit[56] transitioned from White to African American in the 1950s and 1960s when African Americans moved in and Whites moved out to newly constructed housing in northeast and northwest Detroit and the suburbs. Businesses closed soon thereafter, particularly after the 1967 racial discord, further compounding the adverse economic impact of the loss of manufacturing jobs.[39,44,58] Hence, the number of abandoned homes and businesses, including grocery stores, grew, and poverty increased substantially.

This pattern of White flight and economic divestment was repeated during several decades across Detroit neighborhoods. Residential patterns of African Americans generally expanded outward in a stepwise progression from central and east central Detroit toward the northern city boundaries and eventually to Southfield, a suburb adjacent to northwest Detroit.[39,44,57] Neighborhoods located in the northernmost portion of Detroit near Eight Mile Road, the infamous African American–White racial dividing line of metropolitan Detroit, and particularly in northwest and northeast Detroit were among the most recent neighborhoods to transition from White to African American. Some neighborhoods, such as those in the far northwest Detroit community of Redford, shifted to African American as late as the 1990s.[44,57,59,60] Similarly, in the suburb of Southfield, the African American population has grown tremendously, from 102 people (0.1% of the population) in 1970 to 42,259 people (54%) in 2000.[57] The number of African Americans in Southfield increased by 48% between 1990 and 2000 alone, despite an increase of only 3% in the city's total population.

This social history of metropolitan Detroit neighborhoods is relevant to our study because, among the least impoverished neighborhoods, all but 1 of the predominately African American neighborhoods with supermarket accessibility equivalent to that of their predominately White counterparts were located in northwest and north central Detroit and in Southfield. An optimistic interpretation of our findings is that supermarkets have newly opened or have remained open in or nearby these middle-income, yet racially transitioning, neighborhoods. This interpretation provides hope that supermarkets will invest or stay invested in African American neighborhoods as long as the residents have sufficient purchasing power to make these outlets profitable. An alternative interpretation of the findings is that among the least impoverished neighborhoods, African American neighborhoods have supermarket accessibility equivalent to that of predominantly White neighborhoods only because the supermarkets located in and nearby are remnants of historically White neighborhoods. Longitudinal data are needed to empirically test

these different theories. If these areas remain African American, if they maintain a middle-income population, and if supermarkets remain open in or near these neighborhoods, then economic development may be a key intervention strategy to improve supermarket accessibility in African American neighborhoods. If, conversely, supermarkets close or do not open new sites in these economically stable African American neighborhoods, then factors associated with race are a more likely cause of disparities in supermarket accessibility. Indeed, our finding of disparate supermarket accessibility among the most impoverished neighborhoods by neighborhood racial composition warrants further investigation to identify contributing factors.

• • •

Practice and Policy Implications

The results of the study have several practice and policy implications. Pursuit of these strategies would benefit from a partnership approach between public health professionals and community members to ensure the local relevance of intervention strategies and to enhance community capacity for future intervention efforts.[61] In the first of these implications, the results suggest the critical importance of working to redress fundamental inequalities between African Americans and Whites in order to reduce chronic, diet-related diseases among African Americans.[62] For example, the economic development of African American neighborhoods could be enhanced by policies of creating jobs that pay a fair wage, to improve educational quality and opportunities for adults to increase job skills, to subsidize child care, and to attract new businesses. Second, working to attract supermarkets to economically disadvantaged African American neighborhoods in Detroit is a specific economic development strategy that may directly improve food access. Supermarket development can enhance local economic vitality by (1) providing jobs for residents, (2) increasing the local tax base, (3) making foods available at lower prices, thereby increasing the spending power of residents, and (4) attracting other forms of retail.[34,35,63] Supporting African American ownership of and employment at these supermarkets may be critical to their acceptance and success.[64]

Third, a metropolitanwide planning approach to the food system needs to be pursued.[65] Ideally, the food system would be evaluated holistically to ensure that all communities are served equitably. Fourth, in the short term, inadequate transportation is a significant barrier for residents of economically disadvantaged African American neighborhoods' gaining access to supermarkets.[50] Affordable public transportation needs to be improved by integrating transportation routes with supermarket locations.[66,67]

Fifth, on the basis of our findings of disparate access to supermarkets among the most impoverished neighborhoods by percentage African American residents, efforts to expand the Community Reinvestment Act, a law designed to combat discrimination in commercial real estate lending, may be warranted. Finally, given that racial ideologies are likely to shape the political will to pursue these intervention strategies, public health researchers and practitioners need to work to challenge racial stereotypes in public discourse.[42,43,68]

Helping to contextualize the plight of African Americans historically and spatially and to identify its ramifications for health were the primary intents of this study. We found that the historically influenced concentration of African Americans in higher-poverty neighborhoods in Detroit adversely affects spatial access to supermarkets, a resource of potential great importance in promoting the health of African Americans.

Seeing the Big Picture   **Urban Food Deserts: Race, Health, and the Lack of "Real" Food**

Compare health outcomes by race in Section III (diabetes, obesity, hypertension) with rates of poverty by race in Section VI of the Appendix. What role do poverty and residential segregation by racial groups play in having access to "healthy foods" found in a supermarket compared to the processed, salty, and fatty foods that dominate corner stores or bodegas?

Answer the questions that follow.

1. As of 2011, what percentage of the U.S. population do you think was:

   a. Black _____ %

   b. White _____ %

   c. Asian _____ %

   d. American Indian _____ %

   e. Latino _____ %

2. Who are your three best friends? 1) _____ 2) _____ 3) _____

3. Does the unemployment rate in the United States vary by color or ethnicity? _____

Each of your answers, whether you realize it or not, reflects how you have been shaped by social institutions. Compare your answers on item 1 to the correct percentages as enumerated by the U.S. Bureau of the Census: 12.4 percent black, 67 percent white, 4.4 percent Asian/Pacific Islander, 0.8 percent American Indian, and 14.8 percent Latino.

Did your estimates of the size of these groups differ from the actual numbers? If you said that the black population was around 30 percent or that the Asian population was 10 percent, your answer was similar to the average American response. How do you explain the fact that most people in the United States almost triple-count the black and Asian population? From a sociological perspective, what does the overcounting of the nonwhite population mean?

Item 2 asked you to list your three best friends. How many of the people you listed are from a different race? How many are the same sex as you? If you don't have any best friends who are from a racial background different from your own, why not? Is it that you do not like people from other races? Does this mean you are a racist? Do you only have friends of the same sex? Why?

With regard to item 3, the unemployment rate in the United States does vary by color or ethnicity, with blacks and Latinos twice as likely as whites to be unemployed.

RACIALIZED OPPORTUNITY IN SOCIAL INSTITUTIONS

How is the unemployment rate linked to how close people live to areas of high job growth, and how are both of these factors linked to race and ethnicity?

The answers to these questions reflect the ways in which institutions shape how we view the world. Your beliefs, opinions, and attitudes, and the "commonsense" knowledge that guides your moment-to-moment understanding of the world—all may seem to be highly individualistic. Upon closer sociological inspection, however, we see that institutions and other social arrangements influence, mediate, and structure how we think about and come to understand the world in which we live. Think for a moment about your answers to the preceding questions. People of all colors typically overestimate the nonwhite population and underestimate the white population. Perhaps you overestimated the nonwhite population because you live in an all-black or all-Latino neighborhood. When you look out the window or walk down the street, you see that everyone in your neighborhood is like you. That local information is then used to make a judgment about the rest of the United States. But what if you are white and you overestimated the nonwhite population? How do you explain doubling or tripling the black or Asian population? Do you get your information about other racial groups secondhand, from watching television? Might there be a difference between the media's portrayal of race and ethnic relations and what is actually taking place in society? Do you watch professional sports, music videos, or the local television news? Might your estimates reflect something about your television viewing habits? If you live in a racially segregated neighborhood, might that explain why your best friends are all the same color as you? Do you think you might have close friends from different racial backgrounds if your high school or neighborhood were racially integrated? Why is it that compared to white areas or the suburbs, jobs are often not as plentiful or as well paying in black or Latino neighborhoods?

In Part III, we focus on how race and ethnic identity intersect with the criminal justice system, the labor market, where individuals live and why, and how the media shape our views on race and ethnic relations. The five readings in **Race and Criminal Justice: Oxymoron or an American Tragedy?** examine the influence of race and class in the American justice system. Law professor David Cole examines racial disparities in capital punishment sentencing. His research found that courts are more likely to sentence someone to death if the killer is black and the victim white than if the killer is white and the victim black. Who is likely to live or die, controlling for the type of crime committed, varies by race. Michelle Alexander examines the disproportionate impact government policies like the "War on Drugs" and "Three Strikes and You're Out" have had on communities of color. She does not see these trends as the unintended consequences of poorly designed public policy but rather a continuation of Jim Crow laws of the past that ultimately resulted in the control and incarceration of male black and brown populations. Examining the increased trends toward incarceration in greater detail, Lawrence Bobo and Victor Thomas examine how the US compares to other countries in terms of imprisonment rates and how these criminal justice policies reflect racial bias. Krimsky and Simoncelli argue that because certain racial groups are more likely to have undergone a DNA test, bias can creep into how DNA information is used to round up the "usual" suspects.

The next section, **How Race Shapes the Workplace,** examines the sociological reasons why economic and occupational outcomes vary by race and ethnicity. The short research summary by Amy Braverman details how a name can signal racial identity and how employers use this information. Roger Waldinger provides historical and contemporary examples of how employment opportunities have changed over time by examining the different occupational niches that ethnic and racial groups occupied in New York City and the conditions that allowed upward mobility for some and economic stagnation for others. Katherine Newman and Catherine Ellis document the work strategies used by fast-food workers in Harlem. The "McJob" experiences of two hundred black and brown respondents in their study challenge a number of "commonsense" assumptions about work at a fast-food restaurant and workers' attitudes about upward mobility. First, Xiaolan Bao and then William Kandel and Emilio Parrado chronicle the ways in which two newly arrived immigrant groups, Chinese laborers in the sweatshops of New York City and Latinos working in poultry plants in the South, are part of an unregulated and exploited workforce that is becoming all too common.

The third section, **Race, Representations, and the Media,** explores how the media shape our views on race and ethnicity. In the first subsection *Racism and Popular Culture* Danielle Dirks and Jennifer Mueller discuss how racist images are articulated and "consumed" by the public through the media. Marci Bounds-Littlefield uses the theory of racialization discussed in an earlier reading to frame how sexist and racist images are a staple in the media but are uncontested because many individuals believe these stereotypes to be true. Alicia Edison and George Yancey take on the topic of racial hybridity (mixed race individuals) in the media by asking the question if skin color and social class follow any patterns in who gets casted for which parts in Hollywood movies. These readings ask us to consider how representations of race and ethnicity on the nightly news or on situation comedies shape our worldview.

The final section, **Crazy Horse Malt Liquor and Athletes: The Tenacity of Stereotypes,** takes two examples of stereotypes that refuse to go away: the image of the savage Indian and the violent black athlete. Debra Merskin deconstructs the meaning of American Indians in popular culture and the consequences of such stereotypical and racist imagery. Finally, Richard Lapchick reports on one unintended consequence of America's romance with professional sports: the cementing of racial stereotypes. Athletes, particularly college athletes, are often subjected to a double standard because their lives are so closely scrutinized by the media. ✳

26 No Equal Justice: The Color of Punishment

David Cole

DAVID COLE was named one of the forty-five outstanding lawyers under the age of forty-five by *The American Lawyer*. He is a professor at Georgetown University Law Center, an attorney with the Center for Constitutional Rights, the chief litigator for *Karen Finley v. National Endowment for the Arts*, and a regular contributor to NPR's *All Things Considered*, *The Nation*, and op-ed pages in major newspapers nationwide. He is the author of *No Equal Justice* (1999).

TONYA DRAKE, A TWENTY-FIVE-YEAR-OLD mother of four on welfare, needed the money. So when a man she hardly knew gave her a $100 bill and told her she could keep the change if she mailed a package for him, she agreed, even though she suspected it might contain drugs. The change amounted to $47.40. The package contained crack cocaine. And for that, Tonya Drake, whose only prior offenses were traffic violations, received a ten-year mandatory minimum prison sentence. When federal judge Richard A. Gadbois, Jr., sentenced her, he said, "This woman doesn't belong in prison for 10 years for what I understand she did. That's just crazy, but there's nothing I can do about it." Had the cocaine in the package been in powder rather than crack form, she would have faced a prison sentence of less than three years, with no mandatory minimum.[1]

Tonya Drake is joined by thousands of prisoners serving lengthy mandatory prison terms for federal crack cocaine violations.[2] What unites them is skin color. About 90 percent of federal crack cocaine defendants are black. Indeed, a 1992 U.S. Sentencing Commission study found

> **Questions to Consider**
>
> In *McClesky v. Kemp,* the Supreme Court ruled that even though sentencing disparities were found to be significantly correlated with the race of the defendant, those findings did not necessarily mean there was racist intent in the sentencing. David Cole's research, however, challenges the deeply held belief that the rule of law should be and is applied to all citizens without regard to race, creed, status, or lineage. How do *you* explain differences in sentencing by race? What would happen if there were a "war on drugs" and the suburbs, rather than the city, were the target? What would white America's response be if millions of young, white, middle-class suburbanites were arrested, sentenced, and put in jail for an extended period of time for recreational marijuana or ecstasy use?

that in seventeen states, not a single white had been prosecuted on federal crack cocaine charges.[3]

Crack cocaine is nothing more than powder cocaine cooked up with baking soda. Wholesalers deal in powder; retailers deal in crack. But under the federal sentencing guidelines, a small-time crack "retailer" caught selling 5 grams of crack receives the same prison sentence as a large-scale powder cocaine dealer convicted of distributing 500 grams of powder cocaine. The U.S. Sentencing Commission has estimated that 65 percent of crack users are white.[4] In 1992, however, 92.6 percent of those convicted for crimes involving crack cocaine were black, while only 4.7 percent were white; at the same time, 45.2 percent of defendants convicted for powder cocaine crimes were white, and only 20.7 percent were black.[5] In Minnesota, where state sentencing guidelines drew a similar distinction between crack and powder cocaine, African Americans made up 96.6 percent of those charged with possession of crack cocaine in 1988, while almost 80 percent of those charged with possession of powder cocaine were white.[6] Sentencing guidelines were ostensibly adopted to eliminate disparity in sentencing, yet the crack/powder distinction has ensured that significant racial inequities remain.

Black defendants have challenged the crack/powder disparity on constitutional grounds, but every federal challenge has failed.[7] The courts, echoing the Supreme Court in *McCleskey,* have held that "mere" statistical disparities do not prove that Congress or the Sentencing Commission adopted the disparities for the purpose of harming African Americans. And it is not wholly irrational to treat crack as more harmful than powder cocaine, because crack is more often associated with violence, is more potent as typically ingested, and is more accessible to low-income people. Accordingly, even though black cocaine offenders in the federal system serve sentences on average five years longer than white cocaine offenders, the courts see no constitutional problem.

In 1995, however, the U.S. Sentencing Commission, which administers the federal sentencing guidelines, concluded that the disparities could not be justified by qualitative differences between the two drugs, particularly as powder cocaine distributors provide the raw material for crack. It proposed to reduce the differential, noting the racial disparities and their corrosive effect on criminal justice generally.[8] Congress and President Clinton responded like politicians; they reframed the issue as whether we should be "tough on crime," and opposed any change. For the first time since the sentencing guidelines were created in 1984, Congress passed a law overriding a Sentencing Commission recommendation to alter the guidelines.[9]

In 1995, the Georgia Supreme Court very briefly took a different approach. Georgia has a "two strikes and you're out" sentencing scheme that imposes life imprisonment for a second drug offense. As of 1995, Georgia's district attorneys, who have unfettered discretion to decide whether to seek this penalty, had invoked it against only 1 percent of white defendants facing a second drug conviction, but against more than 16 percent of eligible black defendants. The result: 98.4 percent of those serving life sentences under the provision were black. On March 17, 1995, the Georgia Supreme Court ruled, by a 4–3 vote, that these figures presented a threshold case of discrimination, and required prosecutors to explain the disparity.[10]

Instead of offering an explanation, however, Georgia Attorney General Michael Bowers took the unusual step of filing a petition for rehearing signed by every one of the state's forty-six district attorneys, all of whom were white. The petition warned that the court's approach was a "substantial step toward invalidating" the death penalty, and would "paralyze the criminal justice system," presumably because racial disparities in other areas might also have to be explained. Thirteen days later, the Georgia Supreme Court took the highly unusual step of reversing itself, and held that the figures established no discrimination and required no justification. The court's new decision relied almost exclusively on the U.S. Supreme Court's decision in *McCleskey.*[11]

The crack/powder differential and the Georgia experience with "two strikes and you're out" life sentences are but two examples of the widespread racial disparities caused by the war on drugs. Between 1986 and 1991, arrests of members of racial and ethnic minorities for all crimes increased by twice as much as nonminority arrests.[12] Yet when that figure is broken down by type of crime, drug offenses were the *only* area in which minority arrests actually increased more than nonminority arrests. The five-year increase in arrests of minorities for drug offenses was *almost ten times* the increase in arrests of white drug offenders.[13]

In 1992, the United States Public Health Service estimated, based on self-report surveys, that 76 percent of illicit drug users were white, 14 percent black, and 8 percent Hispanic—figures which roughly match each group's share of the general population.[14] Yet African Americans make up 35 percent of all drug arrests, 55 percent of all drug convictions, and 74 percent of all sentences for drug offenses.[15] In Baltimore, blacks are five times more likely than whites to be arrested for drug offenses.[16] In Columbus, Ohio, black males are less than 11 percent of the population, but account for 90 percent of drug arrests; they are arrested at a rate eighteen times greater than white males.[17] In Jacksonville, Florida, black males are 12 percent of the population, but 87 percent of drug arrests.[18]

And in Minneapolis, black males are arrested for drugs at a rate twenty times that for white males.[19]

Similar racial disparities are found in incarceration rates for drug offenses. From 1986 to 1991, the number of white drug offenders incarcerated in state prisons increased by 110 percent, but the number of black drug offenders increased by 465 percent.[20] In New York, which has some of the most draconian drug laws in the country—selling two ounces of cocaine receives the same sentence as murder—90 percent of those incarcerated for drugs each year are black or Hispanic.[21] The "war on drugs" is also responsible for much of the growth in incarceration since 1980. Federal prisoners incarcerated for drug offenses increased nearly tenfold from 1980 to 1993, and that increase accounted for nearly three-quarters of the total increase in federal prisoners.[22] The number of state prisoners incarcerated for drug offenses during the same period increased at a similar rate.[23]

The same pattern emerges in the treatment of juveniles. Between 1986 and 1991, arrests of minority juveniles (under age eighteen) for drug offenses increased by 78 percent, while arrests of nonminority juveniles for drugs actually *decreased* by 34 percent.[24] As with adults, black youth are also treated progressively more severely than whites at each successive stage of the juvenile justice process. In 1991, white youth were involved in 50 percent of all drug-related cases, while black youth accounted for 48 percent.[25] Yet blacks were detained for drug violations at nearly twice the rate of whites.[26] Four times as many black juvenile drug cases were transferred to criminal courts for adult prosecution as white cases.[27] And black youth involved in drug-related cases were placed outside the home almost twice as often as white youth. These disparities are only getting worse: from 1987 to 1991, such placement for black juveniles in drug cases increased 28.5 percent, while placement for whites *decreased* 30 percent.[28] The situation in Baltimore is illustrative. In 1980, eighteen white juveniles and eighty-six black juveniles were arrested for selling drugs—already a fairly stark five-to-one disparity. In 1990, the number of white juveniles arrested on drug charges fell to thirteen, while the number of black juveniles arrested grew to 1,304—a disparity of more than one hundred to one.[29]

Thus, the victims of the war on drugs have been disproportionately black. Some argue that this is neither surprising nor problematic, but simply reflects the unfortunate fact that the drug problem itself disproportionately burdens the black community.[30] If more blacks are using and selling drugs, equal enforcement of the drug laws will lead to disproportionate arrests and incarceration of African Americans. Even if that were the case, the fact that the disparities increase at each successive stage of both the criminal and juvenile justice processes suggests that greater drug use by blacks is not the whole story. In addition, as noted earlier, official estimates of drug use by race do not reflect the disparities evident in the criminal justice system, and in fact suggest very little racial disparity in drug use.

The effects of the drug war are difficult to measure. Critics contend that drugs are just as prevalent and cheap today as they were before the crackdown began in the mid-1980s. Proponents point to signs that crack use has declined, and that teen use of drugs generally has also fallen. But it is extremely difficult to say whether these trends are a result of the war on drugs. Scholars find that drug use goes in cycles, but they have never been able to find a correlation between fluctuations in drug use and criminal-law enforcement. One thing is certain, however: the stigmatization and incarceration of such a high proportion of young African-American males for drug crimes will have significant adverse long-term effects on the black community. A criminal record makes it much more difficult to find a legitimate job. We are disabling tens of thousands of young black men at the outset of their careers. The short-term "benefits" of removing offenders from the community may well come back to haunt us in the long term.

Three Strikes

Not so long ago, "three strikes and you're out" was just a baseball slogan. Today, it passes for a correctional philosophy. And here again, African Americans are disproportionately the losers. Between 1993 and 1995, twenty-four states and the federal government adopted some form of **"three strikes and you're out"** legislation, under which repeat offenders face life sentences for a third felony conviction.[31] (Georgia and South Carolina went even further, adopting "two strikes and you're out" laws.) California's three-strikes law, one of the first, was sparked by a repeat offender's

"three strikes and you're out" Laws that require judges to adhere to mandatory minimum sentencing guidelines for a third criminal offense.

abduction and murder of twelve-year-old Polly Klaas in Petaluma in 1993.[32] Under California's version, a second felony conviction doubles the sentence otherwise authorized, and a third felony conviction receives a mandatory twenty-five-year-to-life term, no matter how insubstantial the third conviction, so long as the prior convictions were for "violent" or "serious" crimes. The "three strikes" idea has been wildly popular; 72 percent of California's voters approved it in a popular referendum, and President Clinton himself jumped on the three-strikes bandwagon during the 1994 mid-term election campaign.[33] But the implementation of the laws has led to many problems.

First, the laws lead to draconian results. Jerry Dewayne Williams, for example, received a twenty-five-year sentence for stealing a slice of pizza from four young men at a Los Angeles beach.[34] Another defendant's third strike consisted of stealing five bottles of liquor from a supermarket.[35] In its first two years, California's law led to life sentences for twice as many marijuana users as murderers, rapists, and kidnappers combined.[36] A California Department of Corrections study reported that 85 percent of those sentenced under the law were convicted most recently of a nonviolent crime.[37] Some have argued that focusing on the third strike is an unfair basis for criticism, because most offenders sentenced under the law have long criminal histories.[38] But the law is triggered even where a defendant's prior offenses are in the distant past, the third conviction is for a minor offense, and there is little likelihood that public safety required anything like a life sentence. Robert Wayne Washington, for example, received twenty-five years to life for a minor cocaine possession charge; his prior offenses were two eight-year-old burglaries and an intervening conviction for possession of contraband.[39]

Second, if the purpose of the law is to incapacitate those who would otherwise repeatedly prey on society, it is overinclusive. Most violent criminals have a relatively limited "criminal career," tailing off after ten years or so.[40] An individual's third strike often will not occur until his criminal career is on the wane. Thus, the three-strikes laws will impose life sentences on many offenders who pose little future danger to the community.

Third, such laws increase the costs of administering the criminal justice system. They make police work more dangerous, because a repeat offender facing a life sentence, in the words of Los Angeles Police Department spokesman Anthony Alba, is like "a cornered animal. If he knows

he is going to get life in jail, he is definitely going to up the ante in eluding his captors."[41] Once apprehended, many defendants facing a third strike are unwilling to plead guilty, leading to a marked increase in criminal trials. Michael Judge, the chief public defender for Los Angeles County, said, "The law has created the single greatest increase in workload in the thirty years since I've been associated with the criminal justice system."[42] Two years into the California law's existence, an auditor estimated that it had cost Los Angeles County alone an extra $169 million.[43] The increase in criminal trials causes backlogs in the civil justice system, as the courts must increasingly devote themselves to criminal trials; as of 1996, 47 of California's 125 civil courts had to be diverted to hearing criminal cases.[44]

Three-strikes and other mandatory minimum laws have contributed to startling growth in our prison population. From 1980 to 1994, the national prison and jail population increased 195.6 percent.[45] By comparison, the general population increased from 1980 to 1990 by only 9.8 percent.[46] If the prison population continues to grow at the rate of increase from 1995–96, it would top 3.2 million in 2009. California alone has built seventeen new jails in the last fifteen years. Its prison spending has increased over that period from 2 percent to almost 10 percent of its state budget, and it now spends more on corrections than on higher education.[47]

Despite these problems, the three-strikes approach remains extraordinarily popular. Why? One possibility is that, as with many other "get tough" policies, its direct burdens fall disproportionately on minorities. The Georgia case discussed above involving racially disparate application of a two-strikes law is not unique. In California, for example, blacks make up only 7 percent of the general population, yet as of 1996 they accounted for 43 percent of the third-strike defendants sent to state prison. Whites, by contrast, make up 53 percent of the general population in California, but only 24.6 percent of third-strike prisoners. This means that blacks are being imprisoned under California's three-strikes law at a rate 13.3 times that of the rate for whites. And because three-strikes convicts serve such long sentences, their proportion of the prison population will steadily increase; third-strikers comprised 8 percent of the total prison population in 1996, but the California Department of Corrections estimates that by 2024 they will amount to 49 percent.[48] Without a change in direction, the already stark racial disparities in our nation's prisons will only get worse. Yet it is precisely for that reason that there is unlikely to be a change in direction. As long as the effects of this get-tough measure are felt principally in minority communities, there is not likely to be sufficient political pressure for change.

When Is Disparity Discrimination?

As the figures above illustrate, it is beyond dispute that criminal sentencing is marked by stark racial *disparities.* But does this amount to *discrimination*? Everyone agrees that black defendants should not receive harsher penalties simply because they are black, and that criminals who attack white victims should not be punished more severely because the victims were white. But the disparities identified above may be attributable to factors other than race discrimination. Perhaps blacks commit more serious crimes per capita than whites. Social scientists and criminologists have long sought to determine through statistical analysis whether criminal sentencing is impermissibly affected by race, and have reached contradictory conclusions.

In the death penalty setting, as we have seen, most studies conclude that there is discrimination based on the race of the victim, even after controlling for other possible factors. In non–death penalty cases, however, the results are more mixed. In a 1993 study of the racial impact of the federal sentencing guidelines, for example, the U.S. Justice Department's Bureau of Justice Statistics found that although blacks on average received sentences that were almost two years longer than whites, the bulk of this disparity was due to the crack/cocaine sentencing disparity.[49] The study concluded that other racial differences in sentencing for drug trafficking, fraud, and embezzlement could be explained by nonracial factors such as prior prison records, guilty pleas, and severity of offense.[50] But the study also found that even after controlling for such factors, black offenders were 50 percent to 60 percent more likely to be sentenced for larceny than white offenders, and twice as likely as whites to be sentenced for weapons offenses.[51] Several other studies have concluded that racial disparities in sentencing are largely attributable to race-neutral factors, such as offense severity or prior criminal record.[52] Most criminologists agree that a substantial part—but not all—of sentencing disparity is attributable to blacks committing more serious

crimes than whites.[53] However, all of these findings—both those that find discrimination and those that do not—are plagued by several inescapable problems.

First, in order to determine whether a racial *disparity* is the result of racial *discrimination,* one must compare similar cases. Where defendants similar in all respects but race are treated differently, one may reasonably conclude that discrimination has occurred. The rub lies in defining "similar." As Barbara Meierhoefer has argued,

> There is no disagreement that similar offenders should be sentenced similarly. The problem . . . is that there is no consensus as to what defines "similar offenders." Even outwardly empirical assessments of whether unwarranted disparity has been reduced will be strongly influenced by which offense and offender characteristics are selected to define "similarly situated" offenders.[54]

Thus, for example, critics of the Baldus study used in *McCleskey* have argued that it did not sufficiently identify "similar" cases, and that therefore its conclusion that the remaining disparities were racial in nature was flawed.[55]

Second, even if we could identify and agree on all relevant race-neutral factors that might conceivably explain a disparity, no study can possibly measure all such factors.[56] Some of the most important factors, such as strength of evidence, credibility of witnesses, or the effectiveness of a lawyer's representation, are simply not susceptible to quantification. Quantifiable factors may be missing from available data. No study can absolutely eliminate the possibility that some unaccounted-for race-neutral variable that correlates with race has caused the apparent racial disparity.

Third, statistical studies may also err in the opposite direction, by concealing racial discrimination. A study of sentencing decisions that found that all racial disparities could be explained by offense severity and prior criminal records, for example, might conceal racial discrimination in police or prosecutorial practices. If police officers observe, stop, and arrest blacks at a higher rate than whites because of their race, blacks are more likely to develop criminal records, all other things being equal. Similarly, if prosecutors offer more generous plea bargains to white than black defendants because of their race, black defendants' sentencing reports will reflect higher "offense severity" and more serious criminal records. By focusing only on one stage of the criminal justice system, a statistician may miss discrimination occurring at another stage. At the same time, statistical studies may miss discrimination if, in the aggregate, two forms of discrimination cancel each other out. For example, some biased sentencers might assign a longer sentence for a black-on-black crime because the *defendant* is black; others might impose a shorter sentence because the *victim* is black. If these biases cancel each other out in the aggregate, statistics may conceal actual discrimination.

For these reasons, statistical studies can rarely prove intentional discrimination. But even if none of the sentencing disparities outlined above is attributable to discrimination as the Supreme Court has defined it, they nonetheless raise serious questions about the racial fairness of our criminal justice policy. To see that this is so, one need only imagine the public response if the current racial disparities in criminal justice were reversed. Imagine what kind of pressure legislatures would feel, for example, if one in three young *white* men were in prison or on probation or parole. Imagine what the politics of the death penalty would look like if prosecutors sought the death penalty 70 percent of the time when whites killed blacks, but only 19 percent of the time when blacks killed whites. Or imagine what our juvenile justice policies would be like if white youth charged with drug offenses were four times as likely as black youth to be tried as adults, and twice as likely to be placed outside the home. One thing is certain: the nation would not accept such a situation as "inevitable."

Indeed, turning the tables on some of these statistics is almost beyond comprehension. If the per capita incarceration rate for whites were equal to that for blacks, more than 3.5 million white people would be incarcerated today, instead of 570,000, and we would need more than three times the prison capacity (and prosecution and court capacity) that we currently have. And because white people comprise about 80 percent of the general population, it would be literally impossible for whites to be overrepresented in the prison population to the same degree that black people currently are—four times their representation in the general population.

To see what happens when the criminal law begins to affect large numbers of white middle- and upper-class people, one need only look at the history of marijuana laws. The country's first marijuana users were largely nonwhite, mostly Mexicans.[57] By 1937, every state had criminalized marijuana. In the 1950s, federal penalties for the sale of marijuana ranged from two to five years imprisonment;

a second offense brought a sentence of five to ten years; and a third brought ten to twenty years. State penalties followed suit. In 1956, Congress imposed mandatory minimum sentences for marijuana possession and sale.

In the 1960s, however, marijuana spread to the white middle and upper classes. By 1970, some college campuses reported that at least 70 percent of their student population had tried marijuana. As one author wrote in 1970, "Vast numbers of people have recently adopted the drug as their principal euphoriant; however, by all estimates, the new users are the sons and daughters of the middle class, not the ethnic minorities and ghetto residents formerly associated with marijuana."[58] The harsh penalties imposed when their effect was primarily felt by minorities were no longer acceptable, and marijuana laws were liberalized. As Dr. Stanley Yolles explained in 1970,

> Nobody cared when it was a ghetto problem. Marijuana—well, it was used by jazz musicians or the lower class, so you didn't care if they got 20 years. But when a nice, middle-class girl or boy in college gets busted for the same thing, then the whole community sits up and takes notice. And that's the name of the game today. The problem has begun to come home to roost—in all strata of society, in suburbia, in middle-class homes, in the colleges. Suddenly, the punitive, the vindictive approach was touching all classes of society. And now the most exciting thing that's really happening is the change in attitude by the people. Now we have a willingness to examine the problem, as to whether it's an experimentation, or an illness rather than an "evil."[59]

Police and prosecutors began to leave users alone, and instead targeted dealers and sellers. The courts limited enforcement, using their discretion to invalidate convictions on a variety of grounds. And the legislatures amended the laws, eliminating strict penalties for possession. As one commentator described the development, "In response to the extraordinary explosion in marijuana consumption and the penetration of its use into the mainstream of American life, every state amended its penalties in some fashion between 1969 and 1972, the overall result being a massive downward shift in penalties for consumption-related offenses. Simple possession of less than one ounce was classified as a misdemeanor in all but eight states by the end of 1972."[60] In 1973, Oregon went further and actually decriminalized possession of small amounts of marijuana, and by 1981 ten other states had followed suit.[61]

When the effects of a criminal law reach the sons and daughters of the white majority, our response is not to get tough, but rather to get lenient. Americans have been able to sustain an unremittingly harsh tough-on-crime attitude precisely because the burden of punishment falls disproportionately on minority populations. The white majority could not possibly maintain its current attitude toward crime and punishment were the burden of punishment felt by the same white majority that prescribes it.

Seeing the Big Picture   **How Race Tips the Scales of Justice**

Look at Juvenile Drug Offenses in the section on Crime in Section IV of the Appendix. How might Cole explain the huge difference in arrest statistics between blacks and other racial groups?

---

27   The New Jim Crow
Michelle Alexander

MICHELLE ALEXANDER won the 2005 Soros Justice Fellowship and holds a joint appointment at the Kirman Institute for the Study of Race and Ethnicity and is a Professor of Law at Ohio State University.

THE LAW AND ORDER PERSPECTIVE, FIRST introduced during the peak of the Civil Rights Movement by rabid segregationists, had become nearly hegemonic two decades later. By the mid-1990s, no serious alternatives to the War on Drugs and "get tough" movement were being entertained in mainstream political discourse. Once again, in response to a major disruption in the prevailing racial order—this time the civil rights gains of the 1960s—a new system of racialized social control was created by exploiting the vulnerabilities and racial resentments of poor and working-class whites. More than 2 million people found themselves behind bars at the turn of the twenty-first century, and millions more were relegated to the margins of mainstream society, banished to a political and social space not unlike **Jim Crow,** where

Jim Crow Laws put in place throughout the US, but particularly in the South in the 19th century that institutionalized racism and discrimination towards blacks.

Questions to Consider   If one were to look at who is incarcerated in the United States for drug crimes, one might conclude that black and Latino men are more likely to carry, use, and distribute illegal drugs. What we learn from Michelle Alexander, however, is that national studies on drug use find that whites are in fact more likely to carry and use drugs like cocaine, marijuana, and heroin. If it is the case that whites have more contact with illegal drugs, why are African Americans and Latinos overrepresented in our prisons? Why is it that certain racial and ethnic groups are more likely to be stopped, searched, or arrested by the police? How might the very act of policing be linked to rates of incarceration?

discrimination in employment, housing, and access to education was perfectly legal, and where they could be denied the right to vote. The system functioned relatively automatically, and the prevailing system of racial meanings, identities and ideologies already seemed natural. Ninety percent of those admitted to prison for drug offenses in many states were black or Latino, yet the mass incarceration of communities of color was explained in race-neutral terms, an adaptation to the needs and demands of the current political climate. The New Jim Crow was born.

Imagine you are Emma Faye Stewart, a thirty-year-old, single African American mother of two who was arrested as part of a drug sweep in Hearne, Texas.[1] All but one of the people arrested were African American. You are innocent. After a week in jail, you have no one to care for your two small children and are eager to get home. Your court-appointed attorney urges you to plead guilty to a drug distribution charge, saying the prosecutor has offered probation. You refuse, steadfastly proclaiming your innocence. Finally, after almost a month in jail, you decide to plead guilty so you can return home to your children. Unwilling to risk a trial and years of imprisonment, you are sentenced to ten years' probation and ordered to pay $1,000 in fines, as well as court and probation costs. You are also now branded a drug felon. You are no longer eligible for food stamps; you may be discriminated against in employment; you cannot vote for at least twelve years; and you are about to be evicted from public housing. Once homeless, your children will be taken from you and put in foster care.

A judge eventually dismisses all cases against the defendants who did not plead guilty. At trial, the judge finds that the entire sweep was based on the testimony of a single informant who lied to the prosecution. You, however, are still a drug felon, homeless, and desperate to regain custody of your children.

Now place yourself in the shoes of Clifford Runoalds, another African American victim of the Hearne drug bust.[2] You returned home to Bryan, Texas, to attend the funeral of your eighteen-month-old daughter. Before the funeral services begin, the police show up and handcuff you. You beg the officers to let you take one last look at your daughter before she is buried. The police refuse. You are told by prosecutors that you are needed to testify against one of the defendants in a recent drug bust. You deny witnessing any drug transaction; you don't know what they are talking about. Because of your refusal to cooperate, you are indicted on felony charges.

After a month of being held in jail, the charges against you are dropped. You are technically free, but as a result of your arrest and period of incarceration, you lose your job, your apartment, your furniture, and your car. Not to mention the chance to say good-bye to your baby girl.

This is the War on Drugs. The brutal stories described above are not isolated incidents, nor are the racial identities or Emma Faye Stewart and Clifford Runoalds random or accidental. In every state across our nation, African Americans—particularly in the poorest neighborhoods—are subjected to tactics and practices that would result in public outrage and scandal if committed in middle-class white neighborhoods. In the drug war, the enemy is racially defined. The law enforcement methods described [earlier] have been employed almost exclusively in poor communities of color, resulting in jaw-dropping numbers of African Americans and Latinos filling our nation's prisons and jails every year. We are told by drug warriors that the enemy in this war is a thing—drugs—not a group of people, but the facts prove otherwise.

Human Rights Watch reported in 2000 that, in seven states, African Americans constitute 80 percent to 90 percent of all drug offenders sent to prison.[3] In at least fifteen states, blacks are admitted to prison on drug charges at a rate from twenty to fifty-seven times greater than that of white men.[4] In fact, nationwide, the rate of incarceration for African American drug offenders dwarfs the rate of whites. When the War on Drugs gained full steam in the mid-1980s, prison admissions for African Americans skyrocketed, nearly quadrupling in three years, and then increasing steadily until it reached in 2000 a level *more than twenty-six times* the level in 1983.[5] The number of 2000 drug admissions for Latinos was twenty-two times the number of 1983 admissions.[6] Whites have been admitted to prison for drug offenses at increased rates as well—the number of whites admitted for drug offenses in 2000 was eight times the number admitted in 1983—but their relative numbers are small compared to blacks' and Latinos'.[7] Although the majority of illegal drug users and dealers nationwide are white, three-fourths of all people imprisoned for drug offenses have been black or Latino.[8] In recent years, rates of black imprisonment for drug offenses have dipped somewhat—declining approximately 25 percent from their zenith in the mid-1990s—but it remains the case that African Americans are incarcerated at grossly disproportionate rates throughout the United States.[9]

There is, of course, an official explanation for all of this: crime rates. This explanation has tremendous appeal—before you know the facts—for it is consistent with, and reinforces, dominant racial narratives about crime and criminality dating back to slavery. The truth, however, is that rates and patterns of drug crime do not explain the glaring racial disparities in our criminal justice system. People of all races use and sell illegal drugs at remarkably similar rates.[10] If there are significant differences in the surveys to be found, they frequently suggest that whites, particularly white youth, are more likely to engage in illegal drug dealing than people of color.[11] One study, for example, published in 2000 by the National Institute on Drug Abuse reported that white students use cocaine at seven times the rate of black students, use crack cocaine at eight times the rate of black students, and use heroin at seven times the rate of black students.[12] That same survey revealed that nearly identical percentages of white and black high school seniors use marijuana. The National Household Survey on Drug Abuse reported in 2000 that white youth aged 12–17 are more than a third more likely to have sold illegal drugs than African American youth.[13] Thus the very same year Human Rights Watch was reporting that African Americans were being arrested and imprisoned at unprecedented rates, government data revealed that blacks were no more likely to be guilty of drug crimes than whites and that white youth were actually the *most likely* of any racial or ethnic group to be guilty of illegal drug possession and sales. Any notion that drug use among blacks is more severe or dangerous is belied by the data; white youth have about three times the number of drug-related emergency room visits as their African American counterparts.[14]

The notion that whites comprise the vast majority of drug users and dealers—and may well be more likely than other racial groups to commit drug crimes—may seem implausible to some, given the media imagery we are fed on a daily basis and the racial composition of our prisons and jails. Upon reflection, however, the prevalence of white drug crime—including drug dealing—should not be surprising. After all, where do whites get their illegal drugs? Do they all drive to the ghetto to purchase them from somebody standing on a street corner? No. Studies consistently indicate that drug markets, like American society generally, reflect our nation's racial and socioeconomic boundaries. Whites tend to sell to whites; blacks to blacks.[15] University students tend to sell to each other.[16] Rural whites, for their part, don't make a special trip to the 'hood to purchase marijuana. They buy it from somebody down the road.[17] White high school students typically buy drugs from white classmates, friends, or older relatives. Even Barry McCaffrey, former director of the White House Office of National Drug Control Policy, once remarked, if your child bought drugs, "it was from a student of their own race generally."[18] The notion that most illegal drug use and sales happens in the ghetto is pure fiction. Drug trafficking occurs there, but it occurs everywhere else in America as well. Nevertheless, black men have been admitted to state prison on drug charges at a rate that is more than thirteen times higher than white men.[19] The racial bias inherent in the drug war is a major reason that 1 in every 14 black men was behind bars in 2006, compared with 1 in 106 white men.[20] For young black men, the statistics are even worse. One in 9 black men between the ages of twenty and thirty-five was behind bars in 2006, and far more were under some form of penal control—such as probation or parole.[21] These gross racial disparities simply cannot be explained by rates of illegal drug activity among African Americans.

What, then, does explain the extraordinary racial disparities in our criminal justice system? Old-fashioned racism seems out of the question. No politicians and law enforcement officials today endorse racially biased practices, and most of them fiercely condemn racial discrimination of any kind. When accused of racial bias, police and prosecutors—like most Americans—express horror and outrage. Forms of race discrimination that were open and notorious for centuries were transformed in the 1960s and 1970s into something unAmerican—an affront to our newly conceived ethic of color-blindness. By the early 1980s, survey data indicated that 90 percent of whites thought black and white children should attend the same schools, 71 percent disagreed with the idea that whites have a right to keep blacks out of their neighborhoods, 80 percent indicated they would support a black candidate for president, and 66 percent opposed laws prohibiting intermarriage.[22] Although far fewer supported specific policies designed to achieve racial equality or integration (such as busing), the mere fact that large majorities of whites were, by the 1980s, supporting the antidiscrimination principle reflected a profound shift in racial attitudes.

The margin of support for color-blind norms has only increased since then.

This dramatically changed racial climate has led defenders of mass incarceration to insist that our criminal justice system, whatever its past sins, is now largely fair and nondiscriminatory. They point to violent crime rates in the African American community as a justification for the staggering number of black men who find themselves behind bars. Black men, they say, have much higher rates of violent crime; that's why so many of them are locked in prisons.

Typically, this is where the discussion ends.

The problem with this abbreviated analysis is that violent crime is *not* responsible for the prison boom. As numerous researchers have shown, violent crime rates have fluctuated over the years and bear little relationship to incarceration rates—which have soared during the past three decades regardless of whether violent crime was going up or down.[23] Today violent crime rates are at historically low levels, yet incarceration rates continue to climb.

Murder convictions tend to receive a tremendous amount of media attention, which feeds the public's sense that violent crime is rampant and forever on the rise. But like violent crime in general, the murder rate cannot explain the prison boom. Homicide convictions account for a tiny fraction of the growth in the prison population. In the federal system, for example, homicide offenders account for 0.4 percent of the past decade's growth in the federal prison population, while drug offenders account for nearly 61 percent of that expansion.[24] In the state system, less than 3 percent of new court commitments to state prison typically involve people convicted of homicide.[25] As much as a third of state prisoners are violent offenders, but that statistic can easily be misinterpreted. Violent offenders tend to get longer prison sentences than nonviolent offenders, and therefore comprise a much larger share of the prison population than they would if they had earlier release dates. The uncomfortable reality is that convictions for drug offenses—not violent crime—are the single most important cause of the prison boom in the United States, and people of color are convicted of drug offenses at rates out of all proportion to their drug crimes.

These facts may still leave some readers unsatisfied. The idea that the criminal justice system discriminates in such a terrific fashion when few people openly express or endorse racial discrimination may seem far-fetched, if not absurd. How could the War on Drugs operate in a discriminatory manner, on such a large scale, when hardly anyone advocates or engages in explicit race discrimination? That question is the subject of this chapter. As we shall see, despite the **color-blind rhetoric** and fanfare of recent years, the design of the drug war effectively guarantees that those who are swept into the nation's new undercaste are largely black and brown.

This sort of claim invites skepticism. Nonracial explanations and excuses for the systematic mass incarceration of people of color are plentiful. It is the genius of the new system of control that it can always be defended on nonracial grounds, given the rarity of a noose or a racial slur in connection with any particular criminal case. Moreover, because blacks and whites are almost never similarly situated (given extreme racial segregation in housing and disparate life experiences), trying to "control for race" in an effort to evaluate whether the mass incarceration of people of color is really about race or something else—anything else—is difficult. But it is not impossible.

A bit of common sense is overdue in public discussions about racial bias in the criminal justice system. The great debate over whether black men have been targeted by the criminal justice system or unfairly treated in the War on Drugs often overlooks the obvious. What is painfully obvious when one steps back from individual cases and specific policies is that the system of mass incarceration operates with stunning efficiency to sweep people of color off the streets, lock them in cages, and then release them into an inferior second-class status. Nowhere is this more true than in the War on Drugs.

The central question, then, is how exactly does a formally color-blind criminal justice system achieve such racially discriminatory results? Rather easily, it turns out. The process occurs in two stages. The first step is to grant law enforcement officials extraordinary discretion regarding whom to stop, search, arrest, and charge for drug offenses, thus ensuring the conscious and unconscious racial beliefs and stereotypes will be given free reign. Unbridled discretion inevitably creates huge racial disparities. Then, the damning step: Close the courthouse doors to all claims by defendants and private litigants that the criminal justice system operates in a racially discriminatory fashion. Demand that anyone who wants to challenge

color-blind rhetoric the tendency by the news media and Hollywood to define racism as a problem of the past.

racial bias in the system offer, in advance, clear proof that the racial disparities are the product of intentional racial discrimination—i.e., the work of a bigot. This evidence will almost never be available in the era of color-blindness, because everyone knows—but does not say—that the enemy in the War on Drugs can be identified by race. This simple design has helped to produce one of the most extraordinary systems of racialized social control the world has ever seen.

Race as a Factor

The dirty little secret of policing is that the Supreme Court has actually granted the police license to discriminate. This fact is not advertised by police departments, because law enforcement officials know that the public would not respond well to this fact in the era of colorblindness. It is the sort of thing that is better left unsaid. Civil rights lawyers—including those litigating racial profiling cases—have been complicit in this silence, fearing that any acknowledgment that race-based policing is authorized by law would legitimate in the public mind the very practice they are hoping to eradicate.

The truth, however, is this: At other stages of the criminal justice process, the Court has indicated that overt racial bias necessarily triggers strict scrutiny— a concession that has not been costly, as very few law enforcement officials today are foolish enough to admit bias openly. But the Supreme Court has indicated that in policing, race can be used as a factor in discretionary decision making. In *United States v. Brignoni-Ponce* the Court concluded it was permissible under the equal protection clause of the Fourteenth Amendment for the police to use race as a factor in making decisions about which motorists to stop and search. In that case, the Court concluded that the police could take a person's Mexican appearance into account when developing reasonable suspicion that a vehicle may contain undocumented immigrants. The Court said that "the likelihood that any person of Mexican ancestry is an alien is high enough to make Mexican appearance a relevant factor."[26] Some commentators have argued that *Brignoni-Ponce* may be limited to the immigration context; the Court might not apply the same principle to drug-law enforcement. It is not obvious what the rational basis would be for limiting overt race discrimination by police to immigration. The likelihood that a person of Mexican

ancestry is an "alien" could not be significantly higher than the likelihood that any random black person is a drug criminal.

The Court's quiet blessing of race-based traffic stops has led to something of an Orwellian public discourse regarding racial profiling. Police departments and highway patrol agencies frequently declare, "We do not engage in racial profiling," even though their officers routinely use race as a factor when making decisions whom to stop and search. The justification for the implicit doublespeak— "we do not racial-profile; we just stop people based on race"—can be explained in part by the Supreme Court's jurisprudence. Because the Supreme Court has authorized the police to use race as a factor when making decisions regarding whom to stop and search, police departments believe that racial profiling exists only when race is the *sole* factor. Thus, if race is one factor but not the only factor, then it doesn't really count as a factor at all.

The absurdity of this logic is evidenced by the fact that police almost never stop anyone because of race. A young black male wearing baggy pants, standing in front of his high school surrounded by a group or similarly dressed black friends, may be stopped and searched because police believe he "looks like" a drug dealer. Clearly, race is not the only reason for that conclusion. Gender, age, attire, and location play a role. The police would likely ignore an eighty-five-year-old black man standing in the same spot surrounded by a group of elderly black women.

The problem is that although race is rarely the sole reason for a stop or search, it is frequently a *determinative* reason. A young white male wearing baggy pants, standing in front of his high school and surrounded by his friends, might well be ignored by police officers. It might never occur to them that a group of white kids might be dealing dope in front of their high school. Similarly situated people inevitably are treated differently when police are granted permission to rely on racial stereotypes when making discretionary decisions.

Equally important, though, the sole-factor test ignores the ways in which seemingly race-neutral factors—such as location—operate in a highly discriminatory fashion. Some law enforcement officials claim that they would stop and search white kids wearing baggy jeans in the ghetto (that would be suspicious)—it just so happens they're rarely there. Subjecting people to stops and searches because they live in "high crime" ghettos cannot be said to be truly race-neutral, given that the ghetto itself was constructed to contain and control groups of people defined by race.[27] Even seemingly race-neutral factors such as "prior criminal history" are not truly race-neutral. A black kid arrested twice for possession of marijuana may be no more of a repeat offender than a white frat boy who regularly smokes pot in his dorm room. But because of his race and his confinement to a racially segregated ghetto, the black kid has a criminal record, while the white frat boy, because of his race and relative privilege, does not. Thus, when prosecutors throw the book at black repeat offenders or when police stalk ex-offenders and subject them to regular frisks and searches on the grounds that it makes sense to "watch criminals closely," they are often exacerbating racial disparities created by the discretionary decision to wage the War on Drugs almost exclusively in poor communities of color.

Defending against claims of racial bias in policing is easy. Because race is never the only reason for a stop or search, any police officer with a fifth-grade education will be able to cite multiple nonracial reasons for initiating an encounter, including any number of the so-called "indicators" of drug trafficking discussed [previously], such as appearing too nervous or too calm. Police officers (like prosecutors) are highly adept at offering race-neutral reasons for actions that consistently disadvantage African Americans. Whereas prosecutors claim they strike black jurors not because of their race but because of their hairstyle, police officers have their own stock excuses—e.g., "Your honor, we didn't stop him because he's black; we stopped him because he failed to use his turn signal at the right time," or "It wasn't just because he was black; it was also because he seemed nervous when he saw the police car." Judges are just as reluctant to second-guess an officer's motives as they are to second-guess prosecutors'. So long as officers refrain from uttering racial epithets and so long as they show the good sense not to say "the only reason I stopped him was because he's black," courts generally turn a blind eye to patterns of discrimination by the police.

Studies of racial profiling have shown that police do, in fact, exercise their discretion regarding whom to stop and search in the drug war in a highly discriminatory manner.[28] Not only do police discriminate in their determinations regarding where to wage the war, but they also discriminate in their judgments regarding whom to target outside of the ghetto's invisible walls.

The most famous of these studies were conducted in New Jersey and Maryland in the 1990s. Allegations of racial profiling in federally funded drug interdiction operations resulted in numerous investigations and comprehensive data demonstrating a dramatic pattern of racial bias in highway patrol stops and searches. These drug interdiction programs were the brainchild of the DEA, part of the federally funded program known as Operation Pipeline.

In New Jersey, the data showed that only 15 percent of all drivers on the New Jersey Turnpike were racial minorities, yet 42 percent of all stops and 73 percent of all arrests were of black motorists—despite the fact that blacks and whites violated traffic laws at almost exactly the same rate. While radar stops were relatively consistent with the percentage of minority violators, discretionary stops made by officers involved in drug interdiction resulted in double the number of stops of minorities.[29] A subsequent study conducted by the attorney general of New Jersey found that searches on the turnpike were even more discriminatory than the initial stops—77 percent of all consent searches were of minorities. The Maryland studies produced similar results: African Americans comprised only 17 percent of drivers along a stretch of I-95 outside of Baltimore, yet they were 70 percent of those who were stopped and searched. Only 21 percent of all drivers along that stretch of highway were racial minorities (Latinos, Asians, and African Americans), yet those groups comprised nearly 80 percent of those pulled over and searched.[30]

What most surprised many analysts was that, in both studies, whites were actually *more likely* than people of color to be carrying illegal drugs or contraband in their vehicles. In fact, in New Jersey, whites were almost twice as likely to be found with illegal drugs or contraband as African Americans, and five times as likely to be found with contraband as Latinos.[31] Although whites were more likely to be guilty of carrying drugs, they were far less likely to be viewed as suspicious, resulting in relatively few stops, searches, and arrests of whites. The former New Jersey attorney general dubbed this phenomenon the "circular illogic of racial profiling." Law enforcement officials, he explained, often point to the racial composition of our prisons and jails as a justification for targeting racial minorities, but the empirical evidence actually suggested the opposite conclusion was warranted. The disproportionate imprisonment of people of color was, in part, a product of racial profiling—not a justification for it.[32]

In the years following the release of the New Jersey and Maryland data, dozens of other studies of racial profiling have been conducted. A brief sampling:

- In Volusia County, Florida, a reporter obtained 148 hours of video footage documenting more than 1,000 highway stops conducted by state troopers. Only 5 percent of the drivers on the road were African American or Latino, but more them 80 percent of the people stopped and searched were minorities.

- In Illinois, the state police initiated a drug interdiction program known as Operation Valkyrie that targeted Latino motorists. While Latinos comprised less than 8 percent of the Illinois population and took fewer than 3 percent of the personal vehicle trips in Illinois, they comprised approximately 30 percent of the motorists stopped by drug interdiction officers for discretionary offenses, such as failure to signal a lane change.[33] Latinos, however, were significantly less likely than whites to have illegal contraband in their vehicles.

- A racial profiling study in Oakland, California, in 2001 showed that African Americans were approximately twice as likely as whites to be stopped, and three times as likely to be searched.[34]

Pedestrian stops, too, have been the subject of study and controversy. The New York Police Department released statistics in February 2007 showing that during the prior year its officers stopped an astounding 508,540 people—an average of 1,393 per day—who were walking down the street, perhaps on their way to the subway, grocery store, or bus stop. Often the stops included searches for illegal drugs or guns—searches that frequently required people to lie face down on the pavement or stand spread-eagled against a wall while police officers aggressively groped all over their bodies while bystanders watched or walked by. The vast majority of those stopped and searched were racial minorities, and more than half were African American.[35]

The NYPD began collecting data on pedestrian stops following the shooting of Amadou Diallo, an African immigrant who died in a hail of police bullets on the front steps of his own home in February 1999. Diallo was followed to his apartment building by four white police officers—members of the elite Street Crime Unit—who viewed him as suspicious and wanted to interrogate him. They ordered him to stop, but, according to the officers, Diallo did not respond immediately. He walked a bit further to his apartment building, opened the door, and retrieved his wallet—probably to produce identification. The officers said they thought the wallet was a gun, and fired forty-one times. Amadou Diallo died at the age of twenty-two. He was unarmed and had no criminal record.

Diallo's murder sparked huge protests, resulting in a series of studies commissioned by the attorney general of New York. The first study found that African Americans were stopped six times more frequently than whites, and that stops of African Americans were less likely to result in arrests than stops of whites—presumably because blacks were less likely to be found with drugs or other contraband.[36] Although the NYPD attempted to justify the stops on the grounds that they were designed to get guns off the street, stops by the Street Crime Unit—the group of officers who supposedly are specially trained to identify gun-toting thugs—yielded a weapon in only 2.5 percent of all stops.[37]

Rather than reducing reliance on stop-and-frisk tactics following the Diallo shooting and the release of this disturbing data, the NYPD dramatically *increased* its number of pedestrian stops and continued to stop and frisk African Americans at grossly disproportionate rates. The NYPD stopped five times more people in 2005 than in 2002—the overwhelming majority of whom were African American or Latino.[38]

In Los Angeles, mass stops of young African American men and boys resulted in the creation of a database containing the names, addresses, and other biographical information of the overwhelming majority of young black men in the entire city. The LAPD justified its database as a tool for tracking gang or "gang-related" activity. However, the criterion for inclusion in the database is notoriously vague and discriminatory. Having a relative or friend in a gang and wearing baggy jeans is enough to put youth on what the ACLU calls a Black List. In Denver, displaying any two of a list of attributes—including slang, "clothing of a particular color," pagers, hairstyles, or jewelry—earns youth a spot in the Denver Police's gang database. In 1992, citizen activism led to an investigation, which revealed that eight out of every ten people of color in the entire city were on the list of suspected criminals.[39]

The End of an Era

The litigation that swept the nation in the 1990s challenging racial profiling practices has nearly vanished. The news stories about people being stopped and searched on their way to church or work or school have faded from evening news. This is not because the problem has been solved or because the experience of being stopped, interrogated, and searched on the basis of race has become less humiliating, alienating, or demoralizing as time has gone by. The lawsuits have disappeared because, in the a little noticed case called *Alexander v. Sandoval*, decided in 2001, the Supreme Court eliminated the last remaining avenue available for challenging racial bias in the criminal justice system.[40]

Sandoval was not, on its face, even about criminal justice. It was a case challenging the Alabama Department of Public Safety's decision to administer state driver's license examinations only in English. The plaintiffs argued that the department's policy violated Title VI of the Civil Rights Act of 1964 and its implementing regulations, because the policy had the effect of subjecting non–English speakers to discrimination based on their national origin. The Supreme Court did not reach the merits of the case, ruling instead that the plaintiffs lacked the legal right even to file the lawsuit. It concluded that Title VI does not provide a "private right of action" to ordinary citizens and civil rights groups, meaning that victims of discrimination can no longer sue under the law.

The *Sandoval* decision virtually wiped out racial profiling litigation nationwide. Nearly all of the cases alleging racial profiling in drug-law enforcement were brought pursuant to Title VI of the Civil Rights Act of 1964 and its implementing regulations. Title VI prohibits federally funded programs or activities from discriminating on the basis of race, and the regulations employ a "disparate impact test" for discrimination—meaning that plaintiffs could prevail in claims of race discrimination without proving discriminatory intent. Under the regulations, a federally funded law enforcement program or activity is unlawful if it has a racially discriminatory impact and if that impact cannot be justified by law enforcement necessity. Because nearly all law enforcement agencies receive federal funding in the drug war, and because drug war tactics—such as pretext stops and consent searches—have a grossly discriminatory impact and are largely ineffective,

plaintiffs were able to argue persuasively that the tactics could not be justified by law enforcement necessity.

In 1999, for example, the ACLU of Northern California filed a class action lawsuit against the California Highway Patrol (CHP), alleging that its highway drug interdiction program violated Title VI of the Civil Rights Act because it relied heavily on discretionary pretext stops and consent searches that are employed overwhelmingly against African American and Latino motorists. During the course of the litigation, the CHP produced data that showed African Americans were twice as likely, and Latinos three times as likely, to be stopped and searched by its officers as were whites. The data further showed that consent searches were ineffective; only a tiny percentage of the discriminatory searches resulted in the discovery of drugs or other contraband, yet thousands of black and brown motorists were subjected to baseless interrogations, searches, and seizures as a result of having committed a minor traffic violation. The CHP entered into a consent decree that provided for a three-year moratorium on consent searches and pretext stops statewide and the collection of comprehensive data on the race and ethnicity of motorists stopped and searched by the police, so that it would be possible to determine whether discriminatory practices were continuing. Similar results were obtained in New Jersey, as a result of landmark litigation filed against the New Jersey State Police. After *Sandoval*, these cases can no longer be brought under Title VI by private litigants. Only the federal government can sue to enforce Title VI's antidiscrimination provisions— something it has neither the inclination nor the capacity to do in most racial profiling cases due to its limited resources and institutional reluctance to antagonize local law enforcement. Since the War on Drugs, private litigants represented by organizations such as the ACLU have been at the forefront of racial profiling litigation. Those days, however, have come to an end. The racial profiling cases that swept the nation in the 1990s may well be the last wave of litigation challenging racial bias in the criminal justice system that we see for a very long time.

The Supreme Court has now closed the courthouse doors to claims of racial bias at every stage of the criminal justice process, from stops and searches to plea bargaining and sentencing. The system of mass incarceration is now, for all practical purposes, thoroughly immunized from claims of racial bias. Staggering racial disparities in the drug war continue but rarely make the news. The Obama administration has indicated it supports abolition of the hundred-to-one disparity in sentencing for crack versus powder cocaine–the most obvious and embarrassing example of racial bias in a system that purports to be colorblind. But that disparity is just the tip of the iceberg. This system depends primarily on the prison label, not prison time. What matters most is who gets swept into this system of control and then ushered into an undercaste. The legal rules adopted by the Supreme Court guarantee that those who find themselves locked up and permanently locked out due to the drug war are overwhelmingly black and brown.

28 Racialized Mass Incarceration: Rounding Up the Usual Suspects

Lawrence D. Bobo • Victor Thompson

LAWRENCE D. BOBO is the W. E. B. Du Bois Professor of the Social Sciences at Harvard University. He holds appointments in the Department of Sociology and the Department of African and African American Studies. His research focuses on the intersection of social inequality, politics, and race.

VICTOR THOMPSON is a doctoral candidate in the Department of Sociology at Stanford University.

A**N ENORMOUS SOCIAL CHANGE HAS** steadily occurred in the arena of criminal justice. The United States is generally a far more punitive society today than it was just three decades ago. This change has been marked or designated with several different labels. These designations include the emergence of a "prison industrial complex," of a "carceral state," or the "mass incarceration society." All of these terms refer to a large-scale shift toward formal incarceration as our collective social response to crime.

The full reach of this change was captured in headlines from the *New York Times* in February 2008 that declared, "1 in 100 U.S. Adults behind Bars, New Study Says." The meaning of such a declaration is hard to judge without some more complete context for interpretation. As Figure 1 shows, since 1981 there has been a steady rise in the number of people in jail or prison, on parole, or on probation, with the numbers on probation or actually in prison undergoing the sharpest increase. In 1980, for

> **Questions to Consider** President Eisenhower warned the American public to beware of the "military industrial complex," or the unethical and self-serving relationship between the politicians in charge of the military (and waging wars) and the multinational corporations that make the weapons used to carry out those military actions. In a similar way, the "prison industrial complex" refers to the relationship between get-tough-on-crime laws (mostly directed at minor illegal drug offenses) and the fortunes that have been made building, maintaining, and staffing prisons. If crime rates have been heading down in recent years, as is argued in this reading, why have the number of prisoners and rates of incarceration skyrocketed? Why is it that other developed countries have similar challenges with illegal drugs but have far fewer of their citizens in prison?

instance, fewer than 300,000 people were in prison. By 2000, however, that number had risen to over 1 million. And by 2007 that number had reached above 1.5 million. If you include the number of people in jails, the total

There were 7,328,200 adults under correctional supervision in 2007.

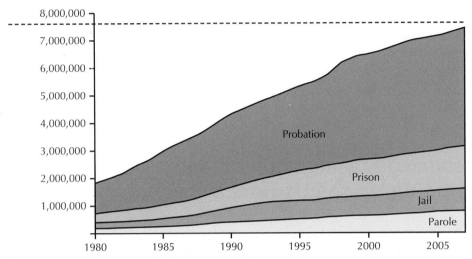

FIGURE 1   Adult Correctional Population, 1980–2007. *Source:* U.S. Bureau of Justice Statistics Correctional Surveys; totals for 1998–2007 exclude probationers in jail or prison.

population behind bars in the United States was more than 2.3 million. All told, as the figure shows, by 2007 there were more than 7.3 million people under some form of "state supervision," a figure more than three times the rate observed in 1980. Recent reports by the Bureau of Justice Statistics suggest that trend for growth continues, though at a slightly slower rate of increase.

The trend in Figure 1 is striking but it also understates the magnitude of the change. Not evident in this figure is the fact that a prison population below 300,000 characterized most of the twentieth century in the United States. Starting as it does in 1980, this figure does not fully capture the extreme and abrupt character of the underlying social change, which can be traced mainly to post-1980 policy reforms. The sharp rise in reliance upon incarceration is more readily visualized in Figure 2, which traces just the number of male prison inmates in the United States from 1925 to 2007. A more than fifty-year period of relative stability in the rate of male incarceration in the United States is followed by a sharp and largely unabated climb in the post-1980 period.

The headline from the *New York Times* noted above ("1 in 100 U.S. Adults behind Bars") signals, first, the high absolute number of people now swept up by the criminal justice system and second, the dramatic break with a very long stretch of prior practice that the recent period represents. Crime policy scholars Henry Ruth and Kevin Reitz help put these trends in perspective in their recent book *The Challenge of Crime.*

> Over a one hundred year period, 1880 to 1980, the nation added a total of about 285,000 inmates to the prison systems. During just the ensuing twenty years, from 1980 to 2000, the nation added about 1.1 million inmates. From 1850 through 2000, the nation's prison system expanded about 206 times over, during a period of only about twelve-fold population growth. Total people on probation or parole status rose almost nine-fold between 1965 and 2000. (Ruth and Reitz 2003, 283)

Not captured by these numbers is also a lengthening of the average amount of time served. Mandatory minimum sentencing guidelines, three-strikes laws, various special enhancements (i.e., selling drugs near a school), and truth in sentencing provisions ensure that people convicted of crimes are not only more likely to end up in prison but are there for much longer periods of time. Likewise, the number of prisoners incarcerated under extremely harsh conditions, such as isolation and severely limited hours of

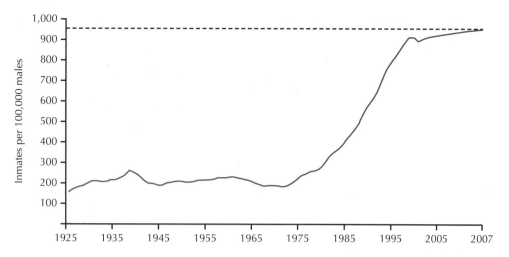

FIGURE 2   **Prison Inmates per 100,000 Males, 1925–2007.** *Sources:* Data from
Pastore, Ann L., and Kathleen Maguire, eds. 2005. *Sourcebook of Criminal Justice Statistics.* www.albany.edu/
sourcebook/pdf/t6282007.pdf

physical mobility, has also risen while access to rehabilitative programs and educational opportunities has declined (Whitman 2003; Irwin 2007).

The U.S. rate of incarceration is now also arguably of historic proportions for a developed modern democracy. On an international scale, as Figure 3 shows, the rate of incarceration per 100,000 citizens in the United States far exceeds that of all other Western industrial nations. The ratio ranges from a low of roughly four to one when compared to our closest neighbor, Mexico, to very nearly twelve to one when compared to places like Sweden and Japan. Only Russia comes close, where the most recent data show an incarceration rate of 626 per 100,000 as compared to a U.S. rate of 762 per 100,000 in 2008. Even the Communist regime in Cuba, at 531 per 100,000, fails to reach the U.S. standard when it comes to incarcerating its population. As the *New York Times* editorial declared on March 10, 2008, "Nationwide, the prison population hovers at almost 1.6 million, which surpasses all other countries for which there are reliable figures. The 50 states last year spent about $44 billion in tax dollars on corrections, up from nearly $11 billion in 1987. Vermont, Connecticut, Delaware, Michigan, and Oregon devote as much money or more to corrections as they do to higher

education. These statistics . . . point to a terrible waste of money and lives."

From one vantage point of observation this transformation can be accurately labeled "mass incarceration." Legal scholar and sociologist David Garland defined the mass imprisonment society as having two features: first, "a rate of imprisonment that is markedly above the historical and comparative norm for societies of this type," and second, "the social concentration of imprisonment effects," such that incarceration "ceases to be incarceration of individual offenders and becomes the systematic imprisonment of whole groups of the population" (Garland 2001, 5–6).

From a different vantage point, however, the label "mass incarceration" obscures the role of race in this social concentration of imprisonment. The "1 in 100" headline we quoted could just as easily, drawing figures from the same Pew Center report (2008), have been "1 in 15 African Americans behind Bars," or even more distressing, "1 in 9 Black Men, age 20 to 34 behind Bars." That is, while the overall U.S. rate of incarceration is up very substantially, this shift has fallen with radically disproportionate severity on African Americans, particularly low-income and poorly educated blacks.

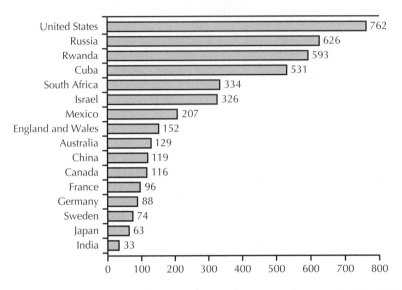

FIGURE 3   **International Incarceration Rates (per 100,000), 2008.**
Source: U.S. data from U.S. Bureau of Justice Statistics. West, Heather C. and William J. Sabol. 2008. *Prison and Jail Inmates at Midyear, 2008.* International data from the International Centre for Prison Studies. 2008. *World Prison Brief* (online version).

Indeed, the end result has been a sharp overrepresentation of blacks in jails and prisons. In 2007, as Figure 4 shows, black males constituted roughly 39 percent of incarcerated males in state, federal, and local prisons or jails, though representing only 12 percent of the total adult male population. White males, on the other hand, constituted just 36.1 percent of the male inmate population in 2007, well under their 65.6 percent of the total male population. The Hispanic population, which constitutes about 20 percent of the total inmate population, is also overrepresented but is much closer to its relative share of the total population of about 16 percent.

Again, these "one slice in time" numbers, even as extreme as they are, may fail to convey the enormity of the transformation that has taken place. In both absolute number and in terms of over-time change, the incarceration of African Americans has reached extraordinary levels. In 1954, there were only about 98,000 African Americans in prisons or jail (Mauer and King 2004). By 2002 the numbers had risen to 884,500, an increase of 900 percent. Today the number is nearly 1 million (913,800). In some states, such as California, blacks are incarcerated at a rate

of 2,992 per 100,000 compared to 460 per 100,000 for non-Hispanic whites and 782 per 100,000 Hispanics.

To state the matter differently, current rates of incarceration are a recent phenomenon. As distinguished criminologist Alfred Blumstein (2001) has documented, the black incarceration rate nearly tripled between 1980 and 2000 and is now over eight times that for non-Hispanic whites. Indeed, fully 2 percent of the black population was incarcerated in 1999 and one in ten black males in their twenties were under some form of criminal justice supervision. This change has reached such a level that a black male born in the 1990s faced almost one in three lifetime odds of ending up in jail or prison as compared to well under one in ten lifetime chances for non-Hispanic white males (Blumstein 2001). This is not merely a story of mass incarceration: it is one of racialized mass incarceration.

More than a decade ago Michael Tonry (1995) argued that it was completely foreseeable that the War on Drugs would be waged in a racially biased manner. This was so, he maintained, because much of the rhetoric and ambition of the drug war focused on cocaine and especially the trade in crack cocaine. This emphasis almost foreordained

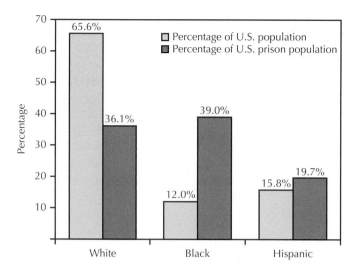

FIGURE 4   **Total Population and Prison Percentages by Race for Males, 2007.** *Source:* Data from U.S. Bureau of Justice Statistics. West, Heather C. and William J. Sabol. 2008 *Prison and Jail Inmates at midyear, 2007.*

a heavy focus on urban, black environments as the front line of this new anti-crime crusade. Furthermore, it would be a much simpler task for police to pursue open-air, public space drug trafficking than the drug trade that took place behind closed doors, since the former is much more readily observable by police than the latter. Likewise, police would have a much easier task of inserting themselves into personal and community networks of interaction in disadvantaged black communities than in relatively stable and densely networked working- and middle-class white communities. And given political pressure to "show results," police could more and more rapidly show evidence of arrests by focusing on low-income black communities where the drug trade was more often done in more easily penetrated public spaces.

Carefully designed research by sociologist Katherine Beckett and her colleagues has yielded some of the most compelling evidence on just how substantial and institutionalized this racial bias is in actual practice (Beckett et al. 2005; Beckett, Nyrop, and Pfingst 2006). Specifically, they argue that the highly racialized discourse and politics that led to the War on Drugs has become institutionalized

in street-level law enforcement practices. To wit, police selectively focus their attention on enforcement and arrests on the public space drug trade of crack among blacks and Latinos. Their own systematic observation of known drug-trading locations showed that police are more likely to pursue the black and Latino suspects in the area than the white ones. As Beckett and colleagues explain:

> Our findings indicate that the majority of those who deliver methamphetamine, ecstasy, powder cocaine, and heroin in Seattle are white; blacks are the majority of those who deliver only one drug: crack. Yet 64 percent of those arrested for delivering one of these five drugs is black. . . . Predominantly white outdoor drug markets received far less attention than racially diverse markets located downtown. . . . The overrepresentation of blacks and under-representation of whites among those arrested for delivering illegal narcotics does not appear to be explicable in race-neutral terms. (2006, 129)

Or, as criminologists Janet Lauritsen and Robert Sampson put it: "while 'crack' cocaine has generated an intense law enforcement campaign in our nation's black ghettos, 'powder' cocaine use among whites is quietly neglected (perhaps even portrayed as fashionable). These differences cannot be attributed to objective levels of criminal danger, but rather to the way in which minority behaviors are symbolically constructed and subjected to official social control" (1998, 79).

Some scholars suggest that anti-black racial bias is a key element in the emergence of the new law and order regime (Marable 2002; Soss, Fording, and Schram 2008). For example, David Jacobs and colleagues have shown that those states and jurisdictions with larger numbers of blacks—a condition that arguably fosters a greater

sense among many whites of competition and threat from minorities irrespective of the actual crime rate—adopt more punitive crime and social spending policies (Jacobs and Carmichael 2000; Jacobs and Tope 2007; see also Soss, Fording, and Schram 2008). Loic Wacquant (2001) has eloquently argued, in fact, that the emergence of the carceral state constitutes a fourth stage of racial oppression in the United States following on the legacy of first, slavery; second, Jim Crow racism; and third, the creation of the modern urban ghetto. He sees each institution as a distinctive way of controlling, regulating, and in a word, "oppressing" the black population.

Seeing the Big Picture   The Color of Incarceration Rates

Look at Figure 18 in the Appendix and observe the racial distribution of who is likely to be searched in a traffic stop. Now look at Figures 14 and 16. How might the trends you observe in Figures 14 and 16 be related to Figure 18?

The Mark of a Criminal Record
29
Devah Pager

DEVAH PAGER is an associate professor of sociology and faculty associate of the Office of Population Research at Princeton University. Her research focuses on institutions affecting racial stratification, including education, labor markets, and the criminal justice system. Pager's current research has involved a series of field experiments studying discrimination against minorities and ex-offenders in the low-wage labor market.

AMONG THOSE RECENTLY RELEASED FROM prison, nearly two-thirds will be charged with new crimes and 40 percent will return to prison within three years. Those who are not reincarcerated have poorer employment and incomes than those without criminal records. But there is strong disagreement over the reasons that ex-offenders do so poorly after release. Does

Questions to Consider   The rate of recidivism (convicts who return to jail) is extremely high in the United States. Poverty, a lack of formal education, and the disappearance of employment opportunities in the inner city that pay a living wage create conditions that researchers believe are linked to criminal activity. How difficult is it for someone with a criminal record, a "mark" as this author describes it, to secure employment? Furthermore, how might race play out among those with and without a criminal "mark"? Devah Pager's research findings are shocking.

incarceration itself actually lead to lower employment and income? Or do the poor outcomes of ex-offenders merely arise from the environmental and personal histories that sent them to prison in the first place—the broken families, the poor neighborhoods, the lack of education and absence of legitimate opportunities, the individual tendencies toward violence or addiction?[1]

Survey research has consistently shown their incarceration is linked to lower employment and income. Many hypotheses have been proposed for this relationship: the labeling effects of criminal stigma, the disruption of social and family networks, the loss of human capital, institutional trauma, and legal barriers to employment. It is, however, difficult, using survey data, to determine which of these mechanisms is at work and whether, for any given mechanism, the results are due to the effect of imprisonment or to preexisting characteristics of people who are convicted. A further issue, given racial disparities in imprisonment rates, is whether the effect of a criminal record is more severe for African American than it is for white ex-offenders.

In the research reported here I sought to answer three primary questions about the mechanisms driving the relationship between imprisonment and employment.[2] First, to what extent do employers use information about criminal histories to make hiring decisions? Second, does race, by itself, remain a major barrier to employment? Its continued significance has been questioned in recent policy debates.[3] Third, does the effect of a criminal record differ for black and white applicants? Given that many Americans hold strong and persistent views associating race and crime, does a criminal record trigger a more negative response for African American than for white applicants?

The Employment Audit

Just as a college degree may serve as a positive credential for those seeking employment, a prison term attaches a "negative credential" to individuals, certifying them in ways that may qualify them for discrimination or social exclusion. Using an experimental audit design, I have been able to isolate that institutional effect, holding constant many background and personal characteristics that otherwise make it very difficult to disentangle cause and effect.[4]

In an employment audit, matched pairs of individuals ("testers") apply for real job openings to see whether employers respond differently to applicants on the basis

of selected characteristics. The methodology combines experimental methods with real-life contexts. It is particularly valuable for those with an interest in discrimination, and has primarily been used to study characteristics such as race, gender, and age that are protected under the Civil Rights Act.

Several states, including Wisconsin, have expanded fair employment legislation to protect individuals with criminal records from discrimination by employers, because of their concern about the consequences of the rapid expansion and the skewed racial and ethnic composition of the ex-offender population over the last three decades. Under this legislation, employers are warned that past crimes may be taken into account only if they closely relate to the specific duties required by the job—as, for example, if a convicted embezzler applies for a bookkeeping position, or a sex offender for a job at a day care center. Because of the Wisconsin legislation barring discrimination on the basis of a criminal record, we might expect circumstances to be, if anything, more favorable to the employment of ex-offenders than in states without legal protections.

This audit was conducted between June and December, 2001, in Milwaukee, Wisconsin, which in population, size, racial composition, and employment rate is typical of many major American cities. At the time, the local economy was moderately strong and unemployment rates ranged between 4 percent and 5.2 percent.[5]

I used two audit teams of 23-year-old male college students, one consisting of two African Americans and the other of two whites. All were bright and articulate, with appealing styles of self-presentation. Characteristics that were not already identical, such as education and work experience, were made to appear identical for the purposes of the audit. Within each team, one auditor was randomly assigned a "criminal record" for the first week; then week by week auditors took turns playing the ex-offender role. The "criminal record" consisted of a nonviolent, felony drug conviction (possession of cocaine with intent to distribute). If the employment application did not request information about previous convictions, ways were found to include that information—for example, by reporting work experience in the correctional facility and citing a parole officer as a reference.

The audit teams applied to separate sets of jobs drawn from the Sunday classified section of the city's major daily newspaper, the *Milwaukee Journal Sentinel,* and from Jobnet, a state-sponsored Web site for employment listings. Since nearly 90 percent of state prisoners have no more than a high school diploma, the job openings chosen were for entry-level positions requiring no previous experience and no education beyond high school (see Figure 1). All openings were within 25 miles of downtown Milwaukee; a majority were in the suburbs or surrounding counties.[6] The survey audited 350 employers, 150 by the white audit team and 200 by the black team.

The audit study focused only on the first stage in the employment process—the stage most likely to be affected by the barrier of a criminal record. Auditors visited the employers, filled out applications, and went as far as they could during that first interview. They did not return for a second visit. Thus our critical variable of interest was the proportion of cases in which employers called the applicant after the first visit. Reference checks were included as an outcome, in the belief that it would be important to have a former employer or parole officer vouch for applicants with criminal records. As it turned out, employers paid virtually no attention to references; only 4 out of 350 actually checked.

Even though employers are not allowed to use criminal background information to make hiring decisions, about three-quarters of employers in this sample explicitly asked if the applicant had ever been convicted of a crime and, if so, for details. A much smaller proportion, just over a quarter, indicated that they would perform a background check (employers are not required to say if they intend to, and this doubtless represents a lower-bound estimate). The use of background checks by employers has been increasing steadily, however, because of greater ease of access to criminal history information and growing concerns over security.

To what extent are applicants with criminal backgrounds dropped at the beginning of the process? For answers, we turn to the results of the audit.

The Effects of a Criminal Record and Race on Employment

Given that all testers presented nearly identical credentials, the different responses they encountered can be attributed fully to the effects of race and criminal background.

The results in Figure 2 suggest that a criminal record has severe effects. Among whites, applicants with criminal records were only half as likely to be called back as equally qualified applicants with no criminal record.

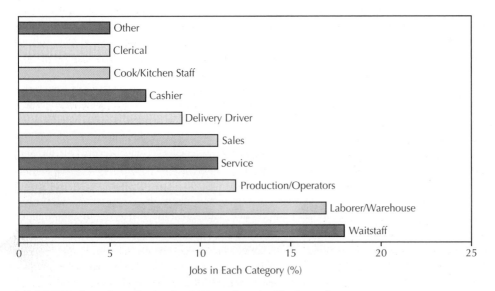

FIGURE 1 **The Jobs in the Milwaukee Audit Sample.**

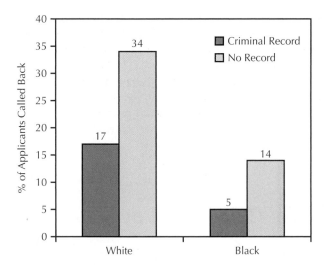

FIGURE 2   **The Effect of a Criminal Record in the Milwaukee Audit Sample.**

The second question involved the significance of race, by itself, in shaping black men's employment prospects, and here too the audit offered an unequivocal answer (Figure 2). The effect of race was very large, equal to or greater than the effect of a criminal record. Only 14 percent of black men without criminal records were called back, a proportion equal to or less than even than the number of whites *with* a criminal background. The magnitude of the race effect found here corresponds very closely to effects found in previous audit studies directly measuring racial discrimination.[7] Since 1994, when the last major audit was reported, very little has changed in the reaction of employers to minority applicants, at least in Milwaukee.

In addition to the strong independent effects of race and criminal record, evidence suggests that the combination of the two may intensify the negative effects: black ex-offenders are one-third as likely to be called as black applicants without a criminal record. It seems that employers, already reluctant to hire blacks, are even more wary of those with proven criminal involvement. None of our white testers was asked about a criminal record before submitting his application, yet on three occasions black testers were questioned. Our testers were bright, articulate young men, yet the cursory review that entry-level applicants receive leaves little room for these qualities to be noticed.

In some cases, testers reported that employers' levels of responsiveness changed dramatically once they had glanced down at the criminal record questions. Employers seemed to use the information as a screening mechanism, without probing further into the context or complexities of the applicant's situation. But in a few circumstances employers expressed a preference for workers who had recently been released from prison because (in one case) "they tend to be more motivated and are more likely to be hard workers" and (in the case of a janitorial job) the job "involved a great deal of dirty work." Despite these cases, the vast majority of employers were reluctant to take a chance on applicants with a criminal record.

The evidence from this audit suggests that the criminal justice system is not a peripheral institution in the lives of young disadvantaged men. It has become a dominant presence, playing a key role in sorting and stratifying labor market opportunities for such men. And employment is only one of the domains affected by incarceration. Further research is needed to understand its effects on housing, family formation, and political participation, among others, before we can more fully understand its collateral consequences for social and economic inequality.

Seeing the Big Picture   **The Link between Race, Education, Employment, and Crime**

In the Appendix look at the unemployment statistics in Section VII, the bachelor's degrees conferred by race in Section I, and the crime statistics in Section IV. How do you think these trends are linked?

30 Using DNA for Justice: Color-Blind or Biased?

Sheldon Krimsky • Tania Simoncelli

SHELDON KRIMSKY is a professor of environmental policy and planning at Tufts University.

TANIA SIMONCELLI has worked at the American Civil Liberties Union and currently works at the U.S. Food and Drug Administration.

One of the fears is that expanded genome profiling will lead to reification of the belief of the biological basis of race. In particular, the use of expanded genome profiling may lend credence to the opinion that criminal activity is associated with a particular genetic make-up prevalent in certain males and/or individuals.
—SUSANNE HAGA[1]

IT IS WELL DOCUMENTED THAT THE AMERICAN criminal justice system is heavily racialized. By this we mean that racial disparities have been identified in all parts of the system, from arrest, trial, and access to legal services to conviction, sentencing, parole, execution, and exoneration. For example, in regard to prison demographics, New York University sociologist Troy Duster reported that African Americans are currently incarcerated at a rate approximately seven times greater than that of Americans of European descent.[2] Duster's data show that the disparity in black versus white incarceration has grown significantly in recent years: in the 1930s blacks were incarcerated at a rate that was less than three times that of whites. Explanations that have been provided for

Questions to Consider   We have all watched the dramatic television moment on a CSI-type police show when someone bursts into room and announces "The DNA came back from the lab and we were wrong—the race of the murderer is (fill in the blank)". We tend to believe that, like the speed of light or any universal constant, the forensic science behind criminal justice is objective, irrefutable, and incontrovertible. In this article we learn that this is not always the case because the process often involves "a close, but not exact match . . . between a crime-scene profile" and an individual DNA profile. How does being included in the CODIS (Combined DNA Index System) data bank create the possibility that you might be accused of a crime you did not commit? How might someone who maintains his innocence challenge the results of a DNA match? If DNA is supposed to take the bias out of law enforcement, why is there concern that a new kind of bias might emerge with the expansion of DNA databases?

this change range from musings on the decline of the moral character of African American males to a society rife with racial prejudice and economic injustice against people of color. Although vigorous controversy remains whether differential criminal involvement or differential criminal justice selection and processing are to blame for racial disparities in the system, most criminologists agree that racial discrimination cannot be dismissed.[3] Indeed, a large body of empirical data supports the notion that racial bias plays a key role in driving these disparities.

Will the technology of DNA analysis and DNA data banks exacerbate or improve the racialized criminal justice system? One response suggests that DNA science trumps racial prejudice. DNA testing provides us with a means to identify suspects that—even if not impervious to error— is more objective than, say, eyewitness identification. The claimed neutrality of **forensic DNA** technology implies that its introduction would shed light on racial disparities and pave the way toward a more just and equitable criminal justice system. Cases where DNA exclusions have exonerated minorities falsely convicted as a result of racial bias support this view. Another response, however, suggests that race trumps science. In this view science and technology must be understood within their broader social context. In a racially polarized society rife with racial disparities, it is a reasonable expectation that DNA testing will be used to reinforce the bias in criminal justice.

Racial Disparities in the Criminal Justice System

To understand the nature and persistence of racial disparities in the criminal justice system, one has to begin with the laws that classify and then define crimes. For example, for many years the federal system punished those convicted of crack cocaine offenses much more severely than those convicted of powder cocaine offenses, even though studies showed that the difference in the danger of the drugs is minor.[4] Crack is far more likely to be sold and used by blacks, while powder cocaine is more likely to be sold and used by whites.[5] From 1986 to 1990, the height of the Reagan administration's "War on Drugs," the average prison sentence for blacks compared with that for whites for drug offenses rose from 11 percent to 49 percent.[6] But

forensic DNA the collection of DNA evidence at crime scenes for use in legal proceedings.

the problem goes well beyond sentencing guidelines. The Justice Policy Institute, citing national survey statistics, reported that in 2002, 24 percent of crack cocaine users were African American and 72 percent were white or Hispanic, but more than 80 percent of defendants sentenced for crack cocaine offenses were African American.

Part of the explanation of how these gross disparities arise can be found at the place where individuals tend to first come into contact with the criminal justice system—that of detention and arrest. Study after study has demonstrated that people of color are disproportionately arrested for drug offenses, automobile theft, and driving under the influence.

Data reported by sociologist Harry Levine on marijuana-possession arrests shed light on this phenomenon. From 1997 to 2006, on average, 100 people were arrested every day in New York City for marijuana possession. Each year, on average, New York City police arrested approximately 20,000 blacks for marijuana possession, compared with 5,000 whites. Adjusting for population, arrest rates for blacks have been approximately eight times as high as those for whites. This rate would be acceptable if it were true that blacks were eight times as likely as whites to use marijuana. But, in fact, U.S. national survey data have consistently shown that more whites use more marijuana than blacks.[7] In other words, "Since Whites use marijuana more than Blacks or Hispanics, and since there are more Whites than Blacks or Hispanics in New York City, on any given day significantly more Whites possess and use marijuana than either of the other two groups. But every day the New York Police Department arrests far more Blacks than Whites, and far more Hispanics than Whites, just for possessing marijuana."[8] This pattern is not true only for New York City, nor does it hold only for marijuana. A study of arrestees in Maryland found that while 28 percent of the population is comprised of African Americans, 68 percent of the arrests for drug abuse are African Americans.[9]

Some of the disparity in arrest rates might be explained by disparate policing practices—for example, where police focus their efforts on low-income or ethnic-minority neighborhoods.[10] Data from the Justice Mapping Center show that more than 50 percent of the men sent to prison from New York are from districts that represent only 17 percent of the adult male residents.[11] Pilar Ossorio and Troy Duster observed that the few DNA dragnets carried out in the United States have disproportionately targeted blacks. For example, San Diego police, in search of a serial killer in the early 1990s, identified and genetically profiled 750 African American men on the basis of eyewitness reports that the perpetrator was a black male.[12]

Some of the disparity in arrest rates might also be explained through racial profiling by individual officers. Michael Risher notes:

> Studies have shown that some mixture of unconscious racism, conscious racism, and the middle-ground use of criminal profiles leads law enforcement to focus its attention and authority on people of color. This can include everything from police officers disproportionately selecting people of color to approach, question and ask consent to search, to discriminatory enforcement of traffic laws, and detaining and arresting people of color without sufficient individualized suspicion.[13]

Police officers have significant discretion in making arrests, particularly when it comes to "victimless" crimes, such as drug use or "public order" crimes, and rarely face any consequences in cases where a person is improperly arrested without probable cause. In a study by Aleksandar Tomic and Jahn Hakes, the authors found that when police had broad discretion in making on-scene arrests, blacks were treated more aggressively than whites:

> Our model of racial bias in arrests predicts, and our empirical results suggest, that the policing of blacks has been disproportionately aggressive for crimes associated with high levels of police discretion to make on-scene arrests. . . . The resulting increases in the proportion of Blacks in the criminal justice system can affect the perception of officers in subsequent cases, perpetuating the imbalances even in the absence of racial differences in underlying criminality.[14]

A similar pattern of racial bias is seen in the makeup of the prison population. According to a 2007 report issued by the Justice Policy Institute, despite similar patterns of drug use, African Americans are far more likely to be incarcerated for drug offenses than whites. As of 2003, twice as many African Americans as whites were incarcerated for drug offenses in state prisons in the United States. African Americans made up 13 percent of the total U.S. population but accounted for 53 percent of sentenced drug offenders in state prisons in 2003. In 2002 African Americans were admitted to prison for drug offenses at 10 times the rate of whites in 198 large-population counties in the United States.[15]

According to data from the Innocence Project, an organization dedicated to the use of DNA to exonerate falsely convicted persons, racism is also a significant factor in wrongful convictions. African Americans make up 29 percent of people in prison for rape and 64 percent of those who were found to have been wrongfully convicted of rape. This suggests that there are disproportionately more false convictions for rape of blacks than of whites. Also, most sexual assaults nationwide are committed by men of the same race as the female victim. Only 12 percent of sexual assaults are cross-racial. This fact, in conjunction with data that show that two-thirds of African American men exonerated by DNA evidence were wrongfully convicted of raping white women,[16] reveals the subtext of racial bias in false conviction. The vestigial fears and prejudice held by whites of black-on-white rapes, whose roots go back to slavery, become expressed in our current society by trumped-up accusations, mistaken identification, and false convictions.

Racial Composition of CODIS

Because of the disproportionately high rates of arrest and incarceration of people of color,[17] it can be inferred that the U.S. Combined DNA Index System (CODIS), which, according to the FBI, is not coded by race, is also disproportionately composed of racial minorities. If CODIS, by and large, contains the profiles of past and present incarcerated felons, and minorities are disproportionately represented in prison, then it follows that they will be disproportionately represented in CODIS. Moreover, if Tomic and Hakes's results are corroborated, the mere appearance of innocent blacks in DNA data banks, even if they are never charged with a crime, will impose a penumbra of bias by law-enforcement officials toward those individuals. If DNA databases are superimposed on traditional racial profiling and other forms of bias toward African Americans, the combination could lead to greater degrees of racial disparity in criminal justice. Troy Duster observes:

> Indeed, racial disparities penetrate the whole system and are suffused throughout it, all the way up to and through racial disparities in seeking the death penalty for the same crime. If the DNA database is primarily composed of those who have been touched by the criminal justice system, and that system has provided practices that routinely select more from one group, there will be an obvious skew or bias toward this group.[18]

There has been a rapid expansion of DNA data banks in certain states where the criteria have evolved from violent offenders and felons to arrestees who have not been charged with or convicted of crimes. Let us assume that this policy continues beyond the dozen or so states that have lowered the threshold of inclusion in their forensic DNA data banks, and that "being arrested" becomes the standard within the criminal justice system for requiring a biological sample and a DNA profile. How will that affect the racial composition of CODIS?

To contextualize this question, we first examine the racial composition of those who are serving sentences in federal and state prisons. According to a report published by the Pew Charitable Trusts in 2008, 1 in every 15 black males aged 18 or over, compared with 1 in 106 white males of the same age group, is in prison or jail. The highest rate of incarceration is among young black men. One in 9 black men aged 20 to 34 is behind bars.[19] Although African Americans make up 12.8 percent of the U.S. population, they constitute between 41 and 49 percent of the prison population.[20] Sixty-two percent of all prisoners incarcerated in the United States are either African American or Latino, but those groups constitute only one-quarter of the nation's entire population.

There is no published information on the racial and/or ethnic composition of individuals who have DNA profiles contained in CODIS. The FBI does publish annual crime reports broken down into racial categories, but states may upload only names and DNA profiles to CODIS without personal information such as a racial or ethnic identifier. Each state retains the personal information associated with the profiles placed in the national DNA forensic database, but as far as we can tell, that information is not aggregated.

It is reasonable to assume that the racial composition of CODIS mirrors the racial composition of the prison population. The racial composition of CODIS can also be estimated indirectly. Henry Greely and colleagues use a crude measure of felony convictions to estimate the number of African Americans in CODIS, since the vast majority of states currently retain and upload to CODIS DNA from all felons:

> African-Americans constitute about thirteen percent of the U.S. population, or about thirty-eight million people. In an average year, over forty percent of people convicted of felonies in the United States are African-American. . . . We assume, based on the felony

conviction statistics, that African-Americans make up at least forty percent of the CODIS Offender Index.[21]

If we assume that the racial composition of CODIS mirrors the current prison population, we arrive at a similar estimate, with African Americans constituting 41 to 49 percent of CODIS.

According to the FBI, the National DNA Index System (NDIS) held 8,201,707 "offender" DNA profiles as of April 2010.[22] On the presumption of 40 percent African American entries, they would constitute 3,280,683 entries in CODIS. This means that approximately 8.6 percent of the entire African American population is currently in the database, compared with only 2 percent of the white population.

Suppose that we asked this question: how would the composition of the database change if all states collected DNA profiles of arrestees? If blacks in American society continue to be stopped, searched, arrested, and charged at a rate in excess of nonminorities, and if collecting DNA samples from arrestees becomes the norm, then it would seem that the racial disparity of blacks in CODIS would continue to grow. D. H. Kaye and Michael Smith make the case for strong racial skewing of U.S. DNA data banks as the system currently exists:

> There can be no doubt that any database of DNA profiles will be dramatically skewed by race if the sampling and typing of DNA becomes a routine consequence of criminal conviction. Without seismic changes in Americans' behavior or in the criminal justice system, nearly 30% of black males, but less than 5% of white males will be imprisoned on a felony conviction at some point in their lives. . . . A black American is five times more likely to be in jail

The authors estimate that the profiles of about 90 percent of urban black males would be found in DNA data banks if all states required DNA samples from arrestees. At the same time, they contend that racial disparities would be diminished by expanding the databases to include arrestees because many more whites would be brought into the databases: "Racial skewing of the DNA databases will be reduced somewhat if the legal authority to sample and type offenders' DNA continues to expand and come to include the multitudes convicted of lesser, but more numerous, felonies and misdemeanors."[23]

Because blacks represented in CODIS and in prisons at a much higher percentage than their relative composition in the general population and at a higher percentage relative to nonminorities, if we expand the use of forensic DNA technology to the existing disparity, it will produce downstream effects that will further exacerbate racial prejudice. This is illustrated by the use of familial searching, as in the case when a close, but not exact, match is made between a crime-scene profile and an individual who has a DNA profile in CODIS. When arrestees who have not been convicted of a crime are added, their families are also brought under the surveillance lens of criminal justice. This conclusion was reached by Greely and colleagues:

> Assume that, either using the current CODIS markers or an expansion to roughly twice as many markers, partial matches of crime scene DNA samples to the CODIS Offender Index could generate useful leads from an offender's first degree relatives—parents, siblings and children. . . . Using some additional sampling assumptions, the percentage of African-Americans who might be identified as suspects through this method would be roughly four to five times as high as the corresponding percentage of U.S. Caucasians. . . . More than four times as much of the African-American population as the U.S. Caucasian population would be "under surveillance" as a result of family forensic DNA and the vast majority of those people would be relatives of offenders, not offenders themselves. . . . African-Americans are disproportionately harmed by crimes committed by other African-Americans.[24]

In the United Kingdom, England and Wales have the largest per capita forensic DNA data bank in the world. At the end of March 2009 there were 4.8 million DNA profiles in the database, representing about 7 percent of the population in England and Wales, compared with the national DNA data bank in the United States, which contains 2.6 percent of its population. Recent data reveal that more than one-third of black men in the United Kingdom have DNA profiles in the national DNA data bank, which includes three out of four black males between the ages of 15 and 34.[25] If the United States were to reach that percentage, CODIS would have 13 million DNA profiles of African American males.

Rounding Up the Usual Suspects

Human DNA is shed continuously in all the environments in which people interact. Our saliva is left on paper cups we discard in a coffee shop or empty soda cans we leave behind at a park. We leave hair fragments in bathrooms of

restaurants or on shirts we bring to the cleaners. Swabbing for DNA at a crime scene has become almost as common as screening for fingerprints. Newer techniques allow investigators to retrieve trace DNA samples from touched objects. Obtaining profiles of DNA left at a crime scene may sometimes be useful to investigators, but it also may be irrelevant without other forms of evidence. With massive DNA data banks, every DNA sample found at a crime scene that matches someone in the data bank will become grounds for investigation—for no other reason than that the evidence shows that either the person or his or her discarded objects were once at the place of interest.

Let us suppose that there is a robbery and shooting at a Starbucks coffee shop. An employee at the coffee shop believes that the hooded robber had a cup of coffee before the robbery. Police obtain all the discarded cups for DNA samples on the premises. Once the profiling of the DNA is completed, investigators submit the profiles to the national and state DNA data banks, which by 10 years from today may have more profiles of innocent people, including juveniles, than of convicted felons.

If African Americans are disproportionately overrepresented in CODIS, not because of prior convictions, but because blacks are stopped and arrested more frequently than whites, then they are more likely to become suspects in any crime that involves a DNA sweep (see Figure 1). An old adage claims that crime-scene investigators will go where the evidence takes them. In this technological era we can say with some degree of confidence that crime-scene investigators will go where the DNA takes them. The greater the disparity in the percentage of African American DNA profiles in CODIS, the greater will be the disparity in suspicion of blacks, false arrests, and false convictions.

In the hypothetical Starbucks shooting, perhaps there were a dozen cups in the trash with sufficient cells for DNA analysis. If only two profiles showed up in CODIS that matched the DNA profiles on the cups, those would be the people the police would investigate, interrogate, and follow around for the reason that one pursues the leads one has even though what the police have became potential evidence because the database used to match "abandoned" DNA to profiles in CODIS was weighted disproportionately toward minorities. Given the racial composition of the data bank it would be no surprise to learn that both of the profiles were from black males.

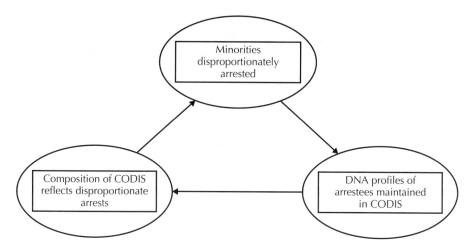

FIGURE 1   The Cycle of Racial Disparity in DNA Data Banks. This flowchart depicts the increasing and compounding racialization of CODIS under a system of expanded criteria collection and retention of DNA profiles in state and federal databases. Minorities, more likely to be arrested, are disproportionately represented on the database. Racial disparities in the criminal justice system are then further exacerbated, since, once in the database, these individuals are more likely to be arrested again in the future.

The forensic DNA data banks in the United States and the United Kingdom contain a disproportionately high number of people of color because of the demographics of crime and criminal arrests. Even if the purpose of DNA data banks remains true to its original mission of matching the identity of samples, the significant racial skewing of the database, combined with a well-established systemic racial bias in the overall system, means that people of color who commit crimes are more likely to be identified in a DNA match, while white individuals will be more likely to escape detection. The expansion of databases to arrestees will worsen this situation, since decisions concerning who is arrested are highly discretionary and therefore especially prone to bias. Since minorities are arrested disproportionately to their contribution to criminal activity, these communities will be placed under greater DNA surveillance and subjected to greater stigmatization.

In an effort to develop "profiles" of perpetrators from DNA left at a crime scene, the criminal justice community will inadvertently reify race as a scientific term, even though it has been widely discredited and undefined scientifically. From this, new consequences of abuse are likely to result. One of these consequences involves picking up the usual minority suspect from weak probabilistic assignments of skin color from DNA through ancestry analysis. Skin pigmentation is a continuous spectrum from albino to dark brown and every shade in between, with no clear breaks. Race, however, is socially constructed as a two-value concept—black or nonblack (white). When DNA is used to determine pigmentation, the outcome, as interpreted by police investigators, will most likely be that the perpetrator was black or nonblack. If the science remains weak, this type of inference can exacerbate the racialization of criminal justice because society still operates under the one-drop rule. If the forensic investigator estimates that a DNA sample from an individual shows 90 percent European and 10 percent African ancestry, does the one-drop rule imply that he or she should be looking for a person of color? Or does the melanin index (with its poor predictive power) trump ancestry? Although the introduction of these techniques in the courtroom is unlikely, there are no restrictions on their use by police in generating suspects. That is where we can see the confluence of expanded data banks of innocent people, disproportionate numbers of minorities in the data banks, and the use of not-ready-for-prime-time science to invade the privacy of people's lives.

31 Kristen v. Aisha; Brad v. Rasheed: What's in a Name and How It Affects Getting a Job

Amy Braverman

AMY BRAVERMAN is a reporter for *University of Chicago Magazine.*

Questions to Consider   We tend to think of racial discrimination as the denial of rights or opportunities to someone because of his or her race. Is it possible that race discrimination could also include denying someone employment opportunities because that person has a black-sounding name?

COULD THE NAME AT THE TOP OF A RÉSUMÉ prompt racial discrimination? According to Marianne Bertrand, associate professor in the Graduate School of Business, and MIT economist Sendhil Mullainathan, it can. Answering more than 1,300 help-wanted ads in Boston and Chicago, the researchers sent four résumés— two higher quality, two lower quality, one of each with a black-sounding name—to companies seeking sales, administrative-support, clerical, and customer-service employees. Overall, "white" applicants were called back 50 percent more often than "black" applicants. Brad and Kristen were the top performing white-sounding names, while Jermaine and Ebony got the most callbacks among black-sounding names. Neil, Emily, Rasheed, and Aisha received the fewest callbacks.

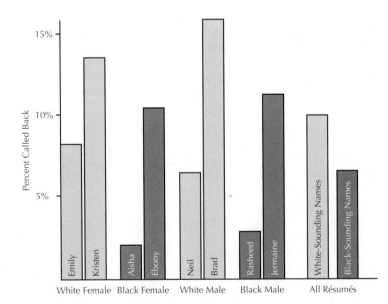

FIGURE 1   Why Brad and Kristen Beat Out Jermaine and Ebony.

32 When the Melting Pot Boils Over: The Irish, Jews, Blacks, and Koreans of New York
Roger Waldinger

ROGER WALDINGER is a professor of race/ethnic/minority relations, urban sociology, and migration and immigration at the University of California, Los Angeles. He is the author of *Still the Promised City? New Immigrants and African-Americans in Post-Industrial New York* (1996) and *Ethnic Los Angeles,* co-edited with Medhi Bozorgmehr (1996).

Questions to Consider   Roger Waldinger makes a number of astute observations about how racial and ethnic groups get sorted into certain occupations. How and in what ways does the historical timing of a group's entry (for example, Irish, Jews, Italians, and Afro-Caribbeans) into the United States affect its economic and social mobility? How does one group come to monopolize one trade or occupation? How are race, ethnicity, upward mobility, and control of local politics linked to upward mobility?

ASSIMILATION IS THE GRAND THEME OF American immigration research. The classic sociological position provided an optimistic counter to the dim assessments of the new immigrants prevalent at the early part of the century. Notwithstanding the marked differences that impressed contemporaries, Robert Park, Ernest Burgess, W. I. Thomas, and others contended that the new immigrant groups would lose their cultural distinctiveness and move up the occupational hierarchy. Milton Gordon's now classic volume distilled the essence of the sociological view: immigrant-ethnic groups start at the bottom and gradually move up; their mobility takes place through individual advancement, not group collective action; in the process of moving up, ethnic groups lose their distinctive social structure; and as ethnics become like members of the core group, they become part of the core group, joining it in neighborhoods, in friendship, and eventually in marriage.

But the image of immigrants moving onward and upward is hard to reconcile with the darker, conflictual side of American ethnic life. Conflict, often of the fiercest kind, runs like a red thread through the history of American ethnic groups. Certainly New Yorkers evince an extraordinary propensity to come to blows over racial and ethnic differences. The latest conflicts pitting blacks against Hasidim and Koreans in Brooklyn or Chinese against Puerto Ricans in Manhattan are but the latest episodes in a longer saga, extending from the anti-Catholic crusades of the 1850s to the school conflicts of the 1890s, to the controversies engendered by the Coughlinites and the German Bund of the 1930s, to the school integration struggles of the 1960s, right up to this day.

The contradiction between ethnic assimilation and ethnic conflict is more apparent than real. Where the classic sociological model goes wrong is not in its depiction of an upward trajectory, but rather in its individualistic assumptions about the process of ethnic change. The story of ethnic progress in America can be better thought of as a collective search for mobility, in which the succession of one migrant wave after another ensures a continuous competitive conflict over resources. Groups move up from the bottom by specializing in and dominating a particular branch of economic life; that specialization goes unchallenged as long as the newest arrivals are content to work in the bottom-level jobs for which they were initially recruited. This [reading] develops the story in the form of brief episodes from the New York experience of four ethnic groups—Irish, Jews, African Americans, and Koreans. Each group is associated with the four successive waves of migration that have swept over New York in the past two hundred years.

The Irish

Nearly one and a half million Irish flocked to the United States between 1846 and 1855 in flight from famine; they converged on the eastern port cities of Boston, Philadelphia, and New York, where, lacking resources, about a quarter stayed. Low levels of education, lack of exposure to industrial or craft work, and lack of capital led the Irish into the lower ranges of manual work, with women taking domestic work and men engaging in insecure, low-paid itinerant employment, especially in construction. Irish progress from the bottom proceeded at a slow pace.

By 1900, however, the Irish had already established themselves in public employment. At the time, the public sector provided relatively few jobs, but this was soon to change. Irish employment in New York City government almost quadrupled between 1900 and 1930, increasing from just under 20,000 to 77,000, while the total number of city workers climbed from 54,000 to 148,000 less than a factor of three.[1]

Irish penetration into the public sector reflected the growing political power of the Democratic machine, which remained Irish dominated. But the machine's hold on local government was met by opposition from WASP reformers. Seeking to break the machine's power by severing the link between political activity and government employment, the reformers installed a civil service system—to little avail. The Irish encountered few effective competitors for city jobs. There was never any serious threat that WASPs would dislodge the Irish. Moreover, the increasingly numerous Poles, Jews, Italians, and others who were just off the boat had little chance of doing well in essay-type exams against the Irish, who were, after all, native English speakers.

The liabilities of the new immigrants lasted hardly a generation; with the Jews' rapid educational and occupational advancement, another competitor entered the scene. But as long as the Irish, through Tammany Hall's grip over city government, could control municipal hiring, interethnic competition posed little threat. Competition was structured in such a way as to minimize the value of Jews' educational advantages. The patronage system functioned unencumbered throughout Tammany's dominance between 1917 and 1933.

The depression severely challenged Irish control over public jobs; LaGuardia's election in 1933 delivered the coup de grace. Keeping control of City Hall required LaGuardia to undermine the material base of Tammany's power and consolidate his support among groups not firmly under Tammany's tow—the most important of which were the Jews, who had split between LaGuardia and his Tammany opponent in 1933. Both goals could be accomplished in the same way, namely pursuing the administrative changes long championed by the reformers.[2]

The depression and LaGuardia's reforms made city jobs more attractive to highly educated workers, which, under the circumstances, mainly meant Jews. One door at which Jewish competitors knocked was teaching, previously an Irish reserve (as the 1900 statistics show). If Jewish entrance into teaching produced antagonism, far more explosive was the situation in the police force. Twenty-nine thousand men sat for the exam held in April 1939, from whom three hundred were selected to enter the department in 1940. Of these, over one-third were Jews. Not surprisingly, this class of 1940 constituted the first significant proportion of Jews to enter the police.[3]

Jewish-Irish competition produced some other episodes, but conflict between them abated, thanks to the prosperity of the postwar era and the new opportunities it provided. Outmigration to the suburbs and the Sun Belt and mobility into the middle class depleted the ranks of the city's Irish population. By the late 1950s, as Nathan Glazer and Daniel Moynihan noted, so profound was the sense of displacement that the remaining Irish New Yorkers reminded themselves, "There are still some of us left."[4]

Those who are left have kept up the long-established Irish occupational ways. Although the commissioners of the police and fire departments are black and Puerto Rican, respectively, the top brass retains a strongly Irish cast, as does the rank and file. Indeed, the fire department presents a glimpse of New York gone by, with a workforce that is 93 percent white and 80 percent Catholic. Some unions still have a distinctly Irish makeup.[5]

In the 1980s, some of the old niches at last gained new blood, as an influx of new, illegal Irish immigrants fled unemployment in the Republic of Ireland for better times in New York. Whereas black Americans still found the doors of construction unions closed, the new arrivals, dubbed "JFK carpenters," were warmly welcomed by their aging compatriots. Women also retraced the steps of the past, as could be seen from the classified pages of the *Irish Echo,* with its columns of ads for nannies, babysitters, and housekeepers.

The Jews

Although the Jewish presence in New York extends far back, almost to the city's founding, Jews did not become an important, visible element in the city's economic life until the 1880s. Rising anti-Semitism, combined with the pressures of modernization, led to a huge outflow of Jews from Eastern Europe. By 1920, New York, with two million Jews, had become the world's largest Jewish city.

The new arrivals came just when the demand for factory-made clothing began to surge. Many had been tailors in the old country, and although most had worked with needle and thread, they quickly adapted themselves to machine production. As the various components of the clothing industry grew in synergistic fashion, the opportunities for mobility through the ethnic economy multiplied. Through rags, some immigrants found riches; the sweatshop workers who moved to contracting and then to manufacturing, or possibly careers in retailing, filled the newly formed ranks of New York's *alrightniks.*[6]

The Jewish concentration in commerce and clothing manufacture defined their initial place in the ethnic division of labor. Jewish specializations seldom overlapped with the Irish: domestic service and general labor were rarities among the Russians but were common Irish pursuits; by the same token, tailoring and retailing, whether by merchant or peddler, were far more likely to engage Russians than Irish.

As Jews sought to move beyond the ethnic economy, interethnic competition and antagonism grew more intense. The relatively rapid educational progress of younger immigrants and of the second generation prepared them to work outside the ethnic economy, but gentile employers were rarely eager to hire Jews. One study, completed just before the Great Depression, found that the doors of New York's large, corporate organizations— "railroads, banks, insurance companies, lawyers' offices, brokerage houses, the New York Stock Exchange, hotels . . . and the home offices of large corporations of the first rank"—were infrequently opened to Jews.[7] The surge into the schools, and through the schools into the professions, met with resistance from the older, largely Protestant population that dominated these institutions.

In the 1930s, depression and discrimination outside the ethnic economy led many second-generation Jews to seek an alternative in public employment. Although the quest for government jobs, and in particular teaching positions, had started earlier, the straitened circumstances of the 1930s accelerated this search. The quality and quantity of Jews vying for government employment increased, heightening the competitive pressure on the Irish and yielding the antagonism we've already observed.

Jewish-Irish conflict reached its height in the late 1930s; it gradually subsided, replaced by a more explosive, deeply antagonistic relationship with blacks. Although black occupations were more similar to those of the Irish than they were to the Jews', the economic pursuits of Jews put them at odds with blacks on various counts. The Jews dominated small retail activity throughout the city and were particularly prominent in Harlem. The Jewish storeowners in Harlem sold to blacks but preferred not to employ them until protests in the mid-1930s finally forced them to relent. Antagonism toward Jewish shopkeepers in Harlem rose during the 1930s, fueled by the depression and by Jews' broader role as middlemen in the Harlem economy. Frustration boiled over in the riot of 1943, when black Harlemites burned down the stores of Jews in a fury that presaged events to come.[8] Hostility simmered thereafter, reaching the boiling point during the 1960s.

The transformation of the ethnic economy also engendered black-Jewish conflict, rapid Jewish social mobility meant a dwindling Jewish working class; the diminishing supply of Jewish workers had a particularly notable effect on the garment industry, where Jewish factory owners were forced to hire outsiders in growing numbers—first Italians, then blacks. In World War II, desperate for workers, Jewish employers hired blacks in great numbers. By 1950, there were 25,000 African American garment workers, 20,000 more than were working in clothing factories ten years before.[9]

But relations between blacks and Jews proved uneasy. Blacks moved into less-skilled, poorer-paying positions, from which mobility into better-remunerated positions proved difficult. Although the garment unions made explicit efforts to organize black workers and integrate them into union structures, few blacks moved up to elected offices, and none high up in the union hierarchy. To protect jobs from southern competitors, the unions adopted a policy of wage restraint, which inevitably meant a softened stance on union employers at home—much to the dismay of black New York garment workers.[10]

The garment business was the Jewish enclave of the past; Jewish mobility into the middle class had made teaching the Jewish niche of the mid-1960s. As the schools came to serve a growing black population, their role was increasingly contested by black students, parents, and protest organizations. The complaints were various, and not all directly linked to the Jews' prominent role in the school system; but the situation in which so many Jews were teachers and so many schools in black neighborhoods were staffed by Jews inevitably led to conflict. In 1968, a black-dominated school board in Brooklyn dismissed a group of white, largely Jewish teachers and replaced them with a mainly black staff; these actions set off a three-month-long strike by the Jewish-led teachers' union. Although the union eventually won, its victory was pyrrhic, at least concerning black-Jewish relations. Memory of the strike and the resentments it fueled have not significantly changed, even a generation later.[11]

What has altered, however, is the economic position of the Jews. The ethnic economy of the immigrant days remains, but in vestigial form. Although Jews are still active in the garment industry, they mainly concentrate in the designing and merchandising ends. "Goldberg" no longer runs clothing factories; his place has been taken by "Kim" and "Wong," who only employ compatriots, not blacks. The same transformations have changed the face of petty retailing and small landlording—the older flash points of black-Jewish conflict. The Jewish presence in the public sector is also fading fast: working as a city engineer or accountant used to be a Jewish occupation; now these careers engage far many more Patels than Cohens.[12] Only in teaching and in higher education do the Jewish concentrations of the past remain in full force.[13]

A distinctive Jewish role in New York's economy still lives on. It is to be found in the professions, in the persistently high rate of Jewish self-employment, in the prominence of Jews in law, real estate, finance, and the media. But the current Jewish pursuits differ crucially from the older ethnic economy in that they are detached from the dynamics of interethnic composition that characterized earlier periods. In a sense, the material basis that underlay anti-Semitic currents in New York for most of the twentieth century is gone. But its legacy and the many other resources around which groups can compete—status, politics, and territory—ensure continued conflict between Jews and their ethnic neighbors.

The Blacks

In 1890, the black share of the New York population was 1.6 percent—just about what it had been on the eve of the Civil War. But in the 1890s the South started losing blacks due to outmigration, and that loss quickly translated into New York's gain. By 1920, New York housed 150,000 black residents—who, although only 3 percent of the city's population, made New York the country's largest black urban concentration. In the next twenty years, as European immigration faltered and then stopped, and bad conditions in the rural South provided additional reasons to leave, the number of black New Yorkers tripled. Postwar prosperity and a new wave of mechanization down South launched a final, massive flow northward: by 1960, the African American population of New York numbered 1,088,000, of whom approximately 320,000 had moved to the city from other areas (mainly the South) in the previous ten years.[14]

It was not until 1940 that black New Yorkers moved out of the peripheries of the New York economy. At the turn of the century, blacks mainly found work in domestic labor, with 90 percent of black women and 55 percent of black men working in some type of domestic service occupation. Blacks' confinement to domestic service reflected, in part, the unfavorable terms of competition with immigrants, who had evicted them from trades where they had previously been accepted. The continued expansion of New York's economy slowly opened doors in a few manufacturing industries; the shutoff of immigration during World War I and its permanent demise after 1924 further accelerated dispersion into other fields.[15]

But the depression largely put an end to these gains. By 1940, 40 percent of blacks still worked in personal service—a far greater proportion than among the workforce overall.[16] With the advent of World War II doors to other jobs were finally unlocked; manufacturing, in particular, saw very large black employment gains. Yet unlike the case in Chicago or Detroit, the black sojourn in New York's manufacturing sector proved short-lived. Lacking auto factories or steel mills, New York's goods-producing sector was a concentration of low-wage jobs; white workers remained ensconced in the better-paying, more skilled positions. Opportunities for blacks were more easily found in the burgeoning service sector—for example, health care—and in government; hence, blacks quickly dispersed into other fields.

Government, where 35 percent of native-born black New Yorkers worked in 1990,[17] has become the black niche par excellence. The history of black employment in the public sector provides yet another example of the continuing, interethnic competitive conflicts over jobs and economic resources in which New York's ethnic groups have been engaged.

In the early years of the twentieth century, local government, like most other New York employers, closed its doors to blacks: in 1911, the city only employed 511 blacks, almost all of whom were laborers. In the early 1920s, Tammany installed the leader of its black client organization, the United Colored Democracy, as a member of the three-person Civil Service Commission, but black access to public jobs changed marginally. By the late 1920s, the city counted 2,275 black workers on its payroll of whom 900 were in laboring jobs and an additional 700 were in other noncompetitive or per diem positions.[18] The reform regime did more for blacks, pushing black employment above parity by 1940.[19] But these effects occurred as a result of the government's burgeoning payrolls, and they were mainly felt in the black concentrations of hospitals, sanitation, and public works, where more than 80 percent of the city's black job holders worked in 1935.[20] Moreover, blacks remained vulnerable to discriminatory practices, as in the city-owned subway system, where blacks only worked as porters, with the exception of a few stations in Harlem. Most important, the employment system that emerged during the depression put blacks at a structural disadvantage in competition with whites. Lacking the educational skills and credentials needed to qualify for most city jobs, blacks and Puerto Ricans found themselves channeled into noncompetitive positions, of which the single largest concentration was found in the municipal hospital system. From here there were few routes of movement upward, as these bottom-level positions were disconnected from the competitive system, which promoted from within.

Race didn't reach the top of government's agenda until 1965, when John Lindsay arrived in office, the first reformer elected mayor since LaGuardia.[21] Elected with the votes of liberals and minorities, Lindsay lacked his predecessors' commitments to the interests of the largely white, civil service workforce and pledged to increase black and Puerto Rican employment in city agencies. But the new mayor quickly discovered that the civil service structure was not easily amenable to change. Lindsay gradually made progress in reducing the inflated eligibility requirements inherited from the depression, but resistance proved severe when his reforms threatened established white ethnic workers in the better-paid ranks.

Lindsay's main focus, in contrast to earlier reform administrations, was to evade the civil service system and its unionized defenders. The Lindsay administration created new, less-skilled positions for which minority residents could be more easily hired. But this approach never involved large numbers and, more important, left existing eligibility requirements unchallenged, shunting minority recruits into dead-end jobs, where they were marooned.

Lindsay backed off from his confrontations with the civil service system and its defenders in the aftermath of the disastrous 1968 teachers' strike. Where the mayor could both accommodate the unions and pursue his earlier goals of increasing minority employment, he did—mainly by tripling the number of exempt workers and shifting them from agency to agency to avoid the requirement of taking an examination. But in other instances, pressure from civil service interests proved overwhelming. With Abraham Beame's accession to City Hall in 1973, followed in 1977 by Edward Koch, mayoral support for black employment gains vanished for the next sixteen years.

The 1970s and 1980s nevertheless saw dramatic gains in black government employment. Like earlier white ethnic groups that had developed a concentration in public jobs, blacks benefited from simultaneous shifts in the structure of employment and in the relative availability of competing groups.

Changes in the structure of employment came from a variety of sources. The Equal Employment Opportunity (EEO) Act of 1972 prohibited discrimination in local government. By requiring local governments to maintain records on all employees by race and gender and to submit them to the Equal Employment Opportunity Commission, with the clear expectation that governments would show improvement over time, the act also led to institutional changes. As EEO functions were established in each city agency, recruitment and personnel practices changed in ways that benefited previously excluded groups, as recruitment became focused on minority and immigrant communities.

Moreover, the 1972 act provided minority employees with levers to act on more recalcitrant agencies, which they used with greatest effectiveness in the uniformed services. For example, in 1973 the Vulcan Society (the organization of black firefighters) successfully challenged the results of a 1971 exam, leading to an imposition of a 1:3 quota for the duration of that list (1973–79). In 1979, the Guardians and the Hispanic Society challenged the 1979 police officer's exam; court findings of disparate impact led to the imposition of a 33.3 percent minority quota for the duration of the list.

While the advent of affirmative action helped increase access for blacks and other minorities, other changes on the supply side hastened the growth of black employment. Although the city's attraction to its traditional white ethnic labor force had begun to diminish by the 1960s, the fiscal crisis of the mid-1970s decisively exacerbated and extended the city's recruitment difficulties among its traditional workforce. By the time large-scale hiring resumed in the early 1980s, public employment had become a less attractive option than before. Moreover, municipal salaries and benefits took a severe beating during the fiscal crisis; although compensation edged back upward during the 1980s, real gains never recaptured the losses endured during the 1970s. The strength enjoyed by New York's private sector during the 1980s pulled native white workers up the hiring queue and out of the effective labor supply for many city agencies.[22]

In a situation where "the City was hiring a great deal and not turning away anyone who was qualified," as one deputy commissioner told me in an interview, the disparity in the availability of minority and white workers led to rapid recruitment of minority workers. Minorities had constituted only 40 percent of the new workers hired in 1977, making up the majority in only two low-paid occupational categories. By 1987, minorities made up 56 percent of all hires, dominating the ranks of new recruits in five out of eight occupational categories.[23]

Thus, the Koch years of 1977 to 1989 saw the ethnic composition of the municipal workforce completely transformed, notwithstanding the mayor's opposition to affirmative action and the disfavor with which minority leaders greeted his hiring policies. By 1990, whites constituted 48 percent of the 375,000 people working for the city and just slightly more—50 percent—of the 150,000 people working in the agencies that the mayor directly controlled.[24] The declining white presence in municipal employment chiefly benefited blacks. Blacks constituted 25 percent of the city's population and a still smaller proportion of residents who were older than eighteen and thus potentially employable, but made up 36 percent of the city's total workforce and 38 percent of those who worked in the mayoral agencies. Although blacks were still underrepresented in some of the city's most desirable jobs, the earlier pattern of concentration at the bottom was overcome. The municipal hospital system, which employed two-thirds of the city's black employees in the early 1960s, in 1990 employed less than one-fifth, reflecting the dispersion of blacks throughout the municipal sector. And higher-level jobs showed clusters of considerable black overrepresentation as well, with blacks accounting for 40 percent of the administrators and 36 percent of the professionals employed in the direct mayoral agencies.

By 1990, when David Dinkins became New York's first black mayor, the phase of black-for-white succession in municipal employment was nearly complete. Blacks held just over 35 percent of all city jobs; although unevenly represented among the city's many agencies, they were often a dominant presence, accounting for more than 40 percent of employment in six of the ten largest agencies, and more than 50 percent of employment in three of the largest ten.

The comparison with Latinos underlines blacks' advantage in the new ethnic division that has emerged in city government. Whereas the city's Latinos and black populations are equal in number, Latinos hold one-third as many municipal jobs as do blacks. The discrepancies are even greater as one moves up the occupational hierarchy into the ranks of managers and professionals. And blacks have been far more successful than Latinos in gaining new permanent civil service jobs, rather than the provisional appointments on which Latinos have mainly relied. The disparity has not gone unnoticed, as the Commission on Hispanic Concerns pointed out in a 1986 report.[25] Of course, other answers might be invoked to explain Latinos' municipal jobs deficit relative to blacks'. But whatever the precise explanation, Mayor Dinkins's continuing conflicts with the Hispanic community suggest that earlier patterns of interethnic competition over municipal jobs remain alive and well.

The Koreans

In the mid-1960s, just when New York could no longer retain its native population, it reverted back to its role as an immigrant mecca. Immigrants began flocking to New York immediately after the liberalization of U.S. immigration laws in 1965. Their arrival has been the principal driving force of demographic and ethnic change in New York ever since—and will continue to be for the foreseeable future.

In 1965, what no one expected was the burgeoning of Asian immigration. The reforms tilted the new system toward immigrants with kinship ties to permanent residents or citizens. Since there had been so little Asian immigration in the previous fifty years, how could Asian newcomers find settlers with whom to seek reunification? The answer is that kinship connections were helpful, but not essential. The 1965 reforms also created opportunities for immigrants whose skills—as engineers, doctors, nurses, pharmacists—were in short supply. Along with students already living in the United States and enjoying easy access to American employers, these professionals made up the first wave of new Asian immigrants, creating the basis for the kinship migration of less well-educated relatives.

Thus, well-educated, high-skilled immigrants have dominated the Korean influx to the United States and to New York in particular. Although Koreans constitute a small portion of New York's new immigrants—rarely more than 3 percent of the eighty thousand to ninety thousand legal immigrants who come to New York each year—they play an important and very visible role. As middle-aged newcomers with poor English-language skills and often lacking professional licenses, relatively few Koreans have managed to steer a route back into the fields for which they trained. Instead they have turned to small business, setting up new businesses at a rate that few other groups can rival.

Koreans started in fruit and vegetable stores, taking over shops in all areas of the city, regardless of neighborhood composition or customer clientele. From there, Koreans moved on to other retail specialties—dry cleaning, fish stores, novelty shops, and nail salons. By 1980, a third of New York Korean males were already self-employed. The *1991 Korean Business Directory* provides a ready indicator of commercial growth over the 1980s, listing over 120 commercial specialties in which Korean firms are to be found.[26]

The roots of the Korean ethnic economy are found in several sources. The competitive field was open. By the middle to late 1960s, the sons and daughters of Jewish and Italian storekeepers had better things to do than mind a store, and their parents, old, tired, and scared of crime, were ready to sell out to the newcomers from Korea. By the 1980s, the supply of new, native-born white entrepreneurs had virtually dried up. One survey of neighborhood businesses in Queens and Brooklyn found that almost half of the white-owned shops were run by immigrants and that most white businesses were long-established entities, in contrast to the newly founded Korean shops with which they competed.[27]

Another spur to growth came from within the ethnic community. Koreans, like every other immigrant group, have special tastes and needs that are best served by an insider: the growth of the Korean population has created business for Korean accountants, doctors, brokers, hair stylists, and restaurant owners. Although the Korean community is too small to support a huge commercial infrastructure oriented to ethnic needs, the community has utilized its ethnic connections to Korea to develop commercial activities oriented toward non-Korean markets. Active trade relations between South Korea and the United States have provided a springboard for many Korean-owned import-export businesses, of which 119 are listed in the *1991 Korean Business Directory.*

Finally, the social structure of the Korean community itself generates advantages for business success that few other immigrant groups share. Many Koreans emigrate with capital, and those who are cash poor can raise money through rotating credit associations known as *gae.* Because Koreans migrate in complete family units, family members provide a supply of cheap and trusted labor. The prevalence of self-employment means that many Koreans have close ties to other business owners, who in turn are a source of information and support, and the high organizational density of the Korean community—which is characterized by an incredible proliferation of alumni clubs, churches, businessmen's associations—provides additional conduits for the flow of business information and the making of needed contacts. These community resources distinguish the Koreans from their competitors, who are less likely to be embedded in ethnic or family ties that can be drawn upon for help with business information, capital assistance, or staffing problems.

The Koreans have discovered that conflict *need not* be interethnic; there are other sources of threat, and in the 1980s they mobilized Korean merchants on a considerable scale. Like other small business owners, Koreans were unhappy with local government, usually with something that government was doing or was threatening to do. Fruit and vegetable store owners felt that sanitation officials were too conscientious about sidewalk cleanliness, especially since the result of the officials' demands was often a fine that the Korean store owner had to pay. Pressuring the city to relax inspections became a high priority for Korean organizations. In the late 1980s, as the city's fiscal crisis led it to search for new sources of revenue, fiscal planners thought of placing a special tax on dry cleaners. So Korean dry cleaners entered an unusual coalition with the white owners of commercial laundries, and the union that represented the laundryworkers, to roll back the planned tax. Like other small business owners, Korean merchants could also become dissatisfied with government's *failure* to act. The prosperity of the 1980s gave commercial landlords license to raise rents to the maximum, much to the distress of small business owners throughout the city. Koreans joined with their non-Korean counterparts to push for commercial rent control—to no avail.

Although Italians and Jews have largely deserted petty retail trade, they have remained in wholesaling, where the businesses are larger and profits more sizable. Thus Jewish and Italian fruit and vegetable or fish wholesalers have acquired a substantial Korean trade. The encounter has not always been a happy one, as Illsoo Kim recounted in his pathbreaking book: "Especially in their first years of emergence into the fruit and vegetable business, Koreans reported many incidents at the Hunts Point [wholesale] Market. The incidents ranged from unfair pricing and sale of poor-quality produce by the Italian and Jewish wholesalers, to physical threats and beatings administered by competing white retailers."[28] Such conflicts sparked the first mass demonstration by Koreans ever in New York. Although Kim reports that Koreans were subsequently accepted by the wholesaling community, there have been continued incidents and protests, including a recent boycott by Koreans of one of the city's largest fish wholesalers.[29]

In New York, as in almost every other major American city, black neighborhoods have provided new immigrants from Asia and the Middle East with an important economic outlet. To some extent, Koreans and other immigrants have simply replaced older white groups that had long sold to blacks and were now eager to bail out of an increasingly difficult and tense situation. By opening stores in black neighborhoods Koreans were also filling the gap left by the departure of large, nonethnic chain stores, which were steadily eliminating the low-margin, high-cost operations involved in serving a ghetto clientele. Selling to black customers proved fraught with conflict. Small protests erupted in the late 1970s. In 1981 a boycott erupted along 125th Street, Harlem's main commercial thoroughfare, with black leaders calling Korean shop owners "vampires" who came to Harlem to "suck black consumers dry."[30]

Repeated security problems as well as more organized clashes led Korean store owners to establish neighborhood prosperity associations, in addition to those organizations that grouped merchants in a particular retail branch. Thus, alongside groups like the Korean Produce Association or the Korean Apparel Contractors Associations, one finds neighborhood groups like the Korean Merchant Association of the Bronx or the Uptown Korean Merchants Association, which seek "to improve Korean merchants' relations with local residents or communities" while lobbying local police for more effective support.[31]

In 1990 antagonism between black shoppers and Korean merchants erupted in picket lines set up in front of two Korean stores in the Flatbush section of Brooklyn. The clash started with a dispute between a Korean store owner and a black Haitian customer who charges assault; that claim then provoked black activist groups—of fairly dubious repute[32]—to establish a boycott that targeted not only the offending owner, but a neighboring Korean merchant against whom no injury was ever charged.

The boycott lasted for months, choking off business at both stores. Although customers disappeared, the two stores were kept alive by contributions from the organized Korean community, which perceived a broader danger to its economic viability should the boycott succeed. As time went on, government officials were inevitably involved. The boycott became a crisis for Mayor Dinkins, who was widely criticized for not actively seeking an end to the dispute.

The boycott ground to a halt, and a court threw out the legal suit brought by the aggrieved Haitian shopper.

Other, fortunately short-lived boycotts were started in New York even while the Flatbush dispute lingered on. A clash in a nearby Brooklyn area between blacks and a small group of Vietnamese refugees—possibly mistaken for Koreans—showed how quickly tensions generated in one arena could move to another.

Conclusion

The story of New York's Irish, Jews, blacks, and Koreans is richer and more complicated than the occupational histories I've recounted in the preceding pages. But if the [reading's] deliberately one-sided focus provides only a partial account, it reminds us of ethnicity's continuing importance, and not simply because of feelings for one's own kind or animosities toward outsiders. Rather, ethnicity's centrality stems from its role as the mechanism whereby groups of categorically different workers have been sorted into an identifiably distinct set of jobs. In this sense, the ethnic division of labor has been the central division of labor in modern New York. Now, as in the past, distinctive roles in the ethnic division of labor impart a sense of "we-ness" and group interest—ensuring the persistence of ethnic fragmentation and conflict.

Seeing the Big Picture   **Who's Got the "Good" Jobs and Why?**
Look at Section VIII on Occupations in the Appendix. Which racial and ethnic groups monopolize which occupations? How might these trends reflect Waldinger's thesis concerning control of occupations and upward mobility?

---

33 "There's No Shame in My Game": Status and Stigma among Harlem's Working Poor

Katherine S. Newman • Catherine Ellis

KATHERINE S. NEWMAN is professor and director of Princeton's Institute for International and Regional Studies. Her 1999 book, *No Shame in My Game: The Working Poor in the Inner City,* won both the Sidney Hillman Book Prize and the Robert F. Kennedy Book Award.

CATHERINE ELLIS is a consulting producer for American RadioWorks®, the documentary unit of American Public Media. She holds a PhD in anthropology from Columbia University.

IN THE EARLY 1990S, THE MCDONALD'S corporation launched a television ad campaign featuring a young black man named Calvin, who was portrayed sitting atop a Brooklyn stoop in his Golden-Arches uniform while his friends passed by to hard-time him about holding

Questions to Consider   Katherine Newman and Catherine Ellis ask us to imagine what life is like working a "McJob." How do individuals maintain self-respect working at a job that provides little in the way of social status? Is it possible for these workers to find employment that pays a living wage (about $16 an hour in New York City)? What does "No Shame in My Game" mean, and what does this phrase suggest about our attitude toward work?

down a "McJob." After brushing off their teasing with good humor, Calvin is approached furtively by one young black man who asks, *sotto voce,* whether Calvin might help him get a job. He allows that he too could use some earnings and that, despite the ragging he has just given Calvin, he thinks the uniform is really pretty cool—or at least that having a job is pretty cool.

Every fast-food worker we interviewed for this study knew the Calvin series by heart: Calvin on the job; Calvin in the street; Calvin helping an elderly woman cross the street on his way to work; Calvin getting promoted to management. They knew what McDonald's was trying to communicate to young people by producing the series in the first place. Fast-food jobs are burdened by a lasting stigma, but one that can be overcome in time. Eventually, so the commercial suggests, the public "dissing" will give way to private admiration as the value of sticking with a job eclipses the stain of a burger flipper's lowly reputation.

One of the moral maxims of American culture is that work defines the person. We carry around in our heads a rough tally that tells us what kinds of jobs are worthy of respect or of disdain, a pyramid organized by the income attached to a particular job, the educational credentials it demands, and the social characteristics of an occupation's incumbents. We use this system of **stratification** (ruthlessly at times) to boost the status of some and humiliate others.[1]

Given our tradition of equating moral value with employment, it stands to reason that the most profound dividing line in our culture is that which separates the working person from the unemployed.[2] Only after this line has been crossed do we begin to make the finer gradations that distinguish a white-collar worker from his blue-collar counterpart, a CEO from a secretary. A whole host of moral virtues—discipline, personal responsibility, pragmatism—are ascribed to those who have found and kept a job, almost any job, while those who have not are dismissed in public discourse as slothful and irresponsible.[3]

We inhabit an unforgiving culture that fails to acknowledge the many reasons some people cross that employment barrier and others are left behind. We may remember, for a time, that unemployment rates are high;

that particular industries have downsized millions of workers right out of their jobs; or that racial barriers or negative attitudes toward teenagers make it harder for some people to get jobs than others. Yet in the end American culture wipes out these background truths in favor of a simpler dichotomy: the worthy and the unworthy, the working folk and the lazy deadbeats.

For those on the positive side of the divide, those who work for a living, the rewards are far greater than a paycheck. The employed enter a social world in which their identities as mainstream Americans are shaped, structured, and reinforced. The workplace is the main institutional setting—and virtually the only one after one's school career is over—in which individuals become part of the collective American enterprise that lies at the heart of our culture: the market. We are so divided in other domains—race, geography, family organization, **gender roles,** and the like—that common ground along almost any other lines is difficult to achieve. For our diverse and divided society, participation in the world of work is the most powerful source of social integration.

It is in the workplace that we are most likely to mix with those who come from different backgrounds, are under the greatest pressure to subordinate individual idiosyncrasy to the requirements of an organization, and are called upon to contribute to goals that eclipse the personal. All workers have these experiences in common, even as segregation constrains the real mix of workers, conformity is imposed on some occupations more than others, and the goals to which we must subscribe are often elusive, unreachable, or at odds with personal desire.

The creation of a workplace identity is rarely the task of the self-directed individualist, moving along some preordained path. It is a miracle worked by organizations, firms, supervisors, fellow workers, and by the whole long search that leads from the desire to find a job to the endpoint of landing one. This transformation is particularly fraught for ghetto youth and adults, for they face a difficult job market, high hurdles in convincing employers to take a chance on them, and relatively poor rewards—from a financial point of view—for their successes. But the crafting of an identity is an important developmental process for them, just as it is for their more privileged counterparts.

---

stratification How a society ranks its members within a social hierarchy. In the United States, class, power, and social status are the primary sorting mechanisms.

gender roles Beliefs, attitudes, expectations, and behaviors that a society links to one's sex.

Powerful forces work to exclude African-Americans, Latinos, and other minorities from full participation in American society. From the schools that provide a substandard education for millions of inner-city kids, to an employment system rife with discrimination, to a housing market that segregates minority families, there is almost no meaning to the notion that Americans all begin from the same starting line.[4] Precisely because this is the case, blasting one's way through the job barrier and starting down that road of acquiring a common identity as mainstream worker is of the greatest importance for black and brown youth in segregated communities. It may be one of the few accessible pipelines into the core of American society and the one with the greatest payoff, symbolic and material.

This paper draws upon a two-year study of fast-food workers and job seekers in central and northern Harlem. Two hundred African-American and Latino workers participated in this study by participating in face-to-face interviews. Sixty of them completed extensive life histories, and a smaller group contributed yearlong personal diaries and permitted the members of our research group to spend extensive periods of time with them, their family members, and their friends. We draw upon all of these data here to explore the nature of values among the working poor in the inner city.

The Social Costs of Accepting Low-Wage Work

While the gainfully employed may be honored over those who stand outside the labor force, all jobs are not created equal. Fast-food jobs, in particular, are notoriously stigmatized and denigrated. "McJob" has become a common epithet meant to designate work without redeeming value. The reasons for this heavy valence are numerous and worthy of deconstruction, for the minority workers who figure in this study have a mountain of stigma to overcome if they are to maintain their self-respect. Indeed, this is one of the main goals of the organizational culture they join when they finally land a job in the restaurant chain we will call "Burger Barn."

Fast-food jobs epitomize the assembly line structure of deskilled service jobs: they are highly routinized, and appear to the untutored observer to be entirely lacking in discretion—almost military in their scripted nature. The symbolic capital of these routinized jobs can be measured in negative numbers. They represent the opposite of the autonomous entrepreneur who is lionized in popular culture (from *Business Week* to hip-hop).

Burger Barn workers are told that they must, at all cost to their own dignity, defer to the public. Customers can be unreasonably demanding, rude, and demeaning, and workers must count backwards from one hundred in an effort to stifle their outrage. Servicing the customer with a smile is music to management's ears because making money depends on keeping the clientele happy, but it can be an exercise in humiliation for inner-city teenagers. It is hard for them to refrain from reading this public nastiness as another instance of society's low estimation of their worth. But if they want to hold on to these minimum-wage jobs, they soon realize that they have to tolerate comments that would almost certainly provoke a fistfight outside the workplace.

It is well known among ghetto consumers that fast-food crew members have to put up with whatever verbiage comes across the counter. That knowledge occasionally prompts nasty exchanges designed explicitly to anger workers, to push them to retaliate verbally. Testing those limits is an outlet for customers down on their luck, and a favorite pastime of teenagers in particular. This may be the one opportunity they have to put someone else down in public, knowing there is little the worker can do in return.

It is bad enough to be on the receiving end of this kind of abuse from adults, especially white adults, for that has its own reading along race lines. It is, in some respects, even worse to have to contend with it from minority peers, for there is much more personal honor at stake, more pride to be lost, and an audience whose opinion matters more. This no doubt is why harassment is a continuous problem for fast-food workers. It hurts. Their peers, with plenty of anger bottled up for all kinds of reasons extraneous to the restaurant experience, find counterparts working the cash register convenient targets for venting.

Roberta Sampson[5] is a five-year veteran of Burger Barn who has worked her way up to management. A formidable African-American woman, Roberta has always prided herself on her ability to make it on her own. Most of Roberta's customers have been perfectly pleasant people; many have been long-time repeat visitors to her restaurant. But she has also encountered many who radiate disrespect.

> Well, I had alcoholics, derelicts. People that are aggravated with life. I've had people that don't even have jobs curse me out. I've dealt with all kinds.
>
> Sometimes it would get to me. If a person yelled out [in front of] a lobby full of people, "Bitch, that's why you work at Burger Barn," I would say [to myself], "I'm probably making more than you and your mother." It hurts when people don't even know what you're making and they say those things. Especially in Harlem, they do that to you. They call you all types of names and everything.

Natasha Robins is younger than Roberta and less practiced at these confrontations. But she has had to contend with them nevertheless, especially from age-mates who are (or at least claim to be) higher up the status hierarchy than she is. Hard as she tries, Natasha cannot always control her temper and respond the way the firm wants her to:

> It's hard dealing with the public. There are good things, like old people. They sweet. But the younger people around my age are always snotty. Think they better than you because they not working at Burger Barn. They probably work at something better than you.
>
> *How do you deal with rude or unfriendly customers?* They told us that we just suppose to walk to the back and ignore it, but when they in your face like that, you get so upset that you have to say something. . . . I got threatened with a gun one time. 'Cause this customer had threw a piece of straw paper in the back and told me to pick it up like I'm a dog. I said, "No." And he cursed at me. I cursed at him back and he was like, "Yeah, next time you won't have nothing to say when I come back with my gun and shoot your ass." Oh, *excuse* me.

Ianna Bates, who had just turned sixteen the summer she found her first job at Burger Barn, has had many of the same kinds of problems Natasha Robins complains of. The customers who hard-time her are just looking for a place to vent their anger about things that have nothing to do with buying lunch. Ianna recognizes that this kind of thing could happen in any restaurant, but believes it is a special problem in Harlem, for ghetto residents have more to be angry about and fewer accessible targets for one-upmanship. Cashiers in fast-food shops catch the results:

> What I hate about Burger Barn is the customers, well, some of them that I can't stand. . . . I don't want to stereotype Harlem . . . , but since I only worked in Harlem that's all I can speak for. Some people have a chip on their shoulders. . . . Most of the people that come into the restaurant are black. Most of them have a lot of kids. It's in the ghetto. Maybe, you know, they are depressed about their lifestyles or whatever else that is going on in their lives and they just. . . . I don't know. They just are like *urff!*
>
> And no matter what you do you cannot please them. I'm not supposed to say anything to the customer, but that's not like me. I have a mouth and I don't take no short from nobody. I don't care who it is, don't take anybody's crap.

Despite this bravado, Ianna well knows that to use her mouth is to risk her job. She has had to work hard to find ways to cope with this frustration that do not get her into trouble with management:

> I don't say stuff to people most of the time. Mostly I just look at them like they stupid. Because my mother always told me that as long as you don't say nothin' to nobody, you can't never get in trouble. If you look at them stupid, what are they going to do? If you roll your eyes at somebody like that, I mean, that's really nothing [compared to] . . . cursing at them. Most of the time I try to walk away.

As Ianna observes, there is enough free-floating fury in Harlem to keep a steady supply of customer antagonism coming the way of service workers every day of their work lives. The problem is constant enough to warrant official company policies on how Burger Barn's crew members should respond to insults, what managers should do to help, and the evasive tactics that work best to quell an incendiary situation without losing business.[6] Management tries to minimize the likelihood of such incidents by placing girls on the registers rather than boys, in the apparent belief that young men will attract more abuse and find it harder to quash their reactions than their female counterparts.

Burger Barn does what it can to contend with these problems on the shop floor. But the neighborhood is beyond its reach and there too fast-food workers are often met with ridicule from the people they grew up with. They have to learn to defend themselves against the criticism that they have lowered themselves in taking these jobs coming from people they have known all their lives. Stephanie Harmon, who has worked at Burger Barn for over a year, explains that here too she leans on the divide between the worker and the do-nothing:

> People I hang out with, they know me since I was little. We all grew up together. When they see me comin', they laugh and say, "Here come Calvin, here come Calvin sister." I just laugh and keep on going. I say, "You're crazy. But that's OK cause I got a job and you all standing out here on the corner." Or I say, "This is my job, it's legal." Something like that. That Calvin commercial show you that even though his friends tease him and he just brushed them off, then he got a higher position. Then you see how they change toward him.

As Stephanie indicates, the snide remarks of peers and neighbors when a worker first dons a Burger Barn uniform are often replaced with requests for help in getting hired and a show of respect when that worker sticks with the job, shows up with money in her pockets and, best of all, moves into management. Still, the scorn is a burden to endure.

Tiffany Wilson, also a teen worker in a central Harlem Burger Barn, thinks she knows why kids in her community who don't work give her such a hard time. They don't want her to succeed because if no one is making it, then no one needs to feel bad about failing. But if someone claws their way up and looks like they have a chance to escape the syndrome of failure, it must mean everyone could, in theory, do so as well. The teasing, a thinly veiled attempt to enforce conformity, is designed to push would-be success stories back into the fold:

> What you will find in any situation, more so in the black community, is that if you are in the community and you try to excel, you will get ridicule from your own peers. It's like the "crab down" syndrome. . . . If you put a bunch of crabs in a big bucket and one crab tries to get out, what do you think the other crabs would do now? According to my thinking, they should pull him up or push him or help him get out. But the crabs pull him back in the barrel. That's just an analogy for what happens in the community a lot.

Keeping everyone down prevents any particular person from feeling that creeping sense of despair that comes from believing things could be otherwise but aren't.

Swallowing ridicule would be a hardship for almost anyone in this culture, but it is particularly hard on minority youth in the inner city. They have already logged several years' worth of interracial and cross-class friction by the time they climb behind a Burger Barn cash register.

More likely than not, they have also learned from peers that no self-respecting person allows themselves to be "dissed" without striking back. Yet this is precisely what they must do if they are going to survive on the shop floor.

This is one of the main reasons why these jobs carry such a powerful stigma in American popular culture: they fly in the face of a national attraction to autonomy, independence, and the individualist's right to respond in kind when their dignity is threatened. In ghetto communities, this stigma is even more powerful because—ironically—it is in these enclaves that this mainstream value of independence is elaborated and embellished. Film characters from the Superfly variety to the political version (e.g., Malcolm X), rap stars, and local idols base their claims to notoriety on standing above the crowd, going their own way, being beyond the ties that bind ordinary mortals. There are white parallels, to be sure, but this is a powerful genre of icons in the black community, not because it is a disconnected subculture, but because it is an intensified version of a perfectly recognizable American middle- and working-class fixation.

It is therefore noteworthy that thousands upon thousands of minority teens, young adults, and even middle-aged adults line up for jobs that will subject them, at least potentially, to a kind of character assassination. They do so not because they start the job-hunting process with a different set of values, one that can withstand society's contempt for fast-food workers. They take these jobs because in so many inner-city communities, there is nothing better in the offing. In general, they have already tried to get better jobs and have failed, landing instead at the door of Burger Barn as a last resort.

The stigma of these jobs has other sources beyond the constraints of enforced deference. Low pay and poor prospects for mobility matter as well. Fast-food jobs are invariably minimum-wage positions.[7] Salaries rise very little over time, even for first-line management. In ghetto areas, where jobs are scarce and the supply of would-be workers chasing them is relatively large, downward pressure keeps these jobs right down at the bottom of the wage scale.[8]

The public perception (fueled by knowledge of wage conditions) is that there is very little potential for improvement in status or responsibility either. Even though there are Horatio Algers in this industry, there are no myths to prop up a more glorified image. As a result, the epithet "McJob" develops out of the perception that a fast-food worker is not likely to end up in a prestigious position as a general manager or restaurant owner; she is going to spend her whole life flipping burgers.

As it happens, this is only half true. The fast-food industry is actually very good about internal promotion. Shop floor management is nearly always recruited from the ranks of entry-level workers. Carefully planned training programs make it possible for people to move up, to acquire transferable skills, and to at least take a shot at entrepreneurial ownership. Industry leaders, like McDonald's, are proud of the fact that half of their present board of directors started out on the shop floor as crew members. One couldn't say as much for most other Fortune 500 firms.

Nevertheless, the vast majority of workers never even get close to management. The typical entry-level worker cycles through the job in short order, producing an industry average job tenure of less than six months. Since this is just an average, it suggests that a large number of employees are there and gone in a matter of weeks. It is this pattern, a planned operation built around low skills and high turnover, that has given fast-food jobs such a bad name. Although it is quite possible to rise above the fray and make a very respectable living in fast-food management, most crew members remain at the entry level and leave too soon to see much upward movement. Observing this pattern on such a large scale—in practically every town and city in the country—Americans naturally conclude that there is no real future in a job of this kind and anyone with more on the ball wouldn't be caught dead working behind the counter.

The stigma also stems from the low socioeconomic status of the people who hold these jobs. This includes teenagers, immigrants who often speak halting English, those with little education, and (increasingly in affluent communities afflicted with labor shortages) the elderly. To the extent that the prestige of a job refracts the social characteristics of its average incumbents, fast-food jobs are hobbled by the perception that people with better choices would never purposively opt for a McJob. We argue that entry-level jobs of this kind don't merit this scorn: a lot more skill, discretion, and responsibility are locked up in a fast-food job than meets the public eye. But this truth hardly matters where public perception is concerned. There is no faster way to indicate that a person is barely deserving of notice than to point out that they hold a "chump change" job in Kentucky Fried Chicken

or Burger King. We "know" this is the case just by looking at the age, skin color, or educational credentials of the people already on the job: the tautology has a staying power that even the most expensive public relations campaign cannot shake.

It is hard to know the extent to which this stigma discourages young people in places like central Harlem from knocking on the doors of fast-food restaurants in search of employment. It is clear that the other choices aren't much better and that necessity drives thousands, if not millions, of teens and older job seekers to repudiate the stigma associated with fast-food work or learn to live with it.[9] But no one comes into the central Harlem job market without having to contend with the social risks to their identity that come with approaching stigmatized ground.

Tiffany Wilson started working in the underground economy bagging groceries when she was little more than ten years old because her mother was having trouble supporting the family, "checks weren't coming in," and there was "really a need for food" in the family. She graduated to summer youth by the time she was fourteen and landed a job answering phones in a center that dealt with domestic violence cases, referring terrified women to shelters. By the time she was sixteen, Tiffany needed a real job that would last beyond the summertime, so she set about looking—everywhere. As a black teenager, she quickly discovered there wasn't a great deal open to her. Tiffany ended up at Burger Barn in the Bronx, a restaurant two blocks from her house and close enough to her high school to make after-school hours feasible.

> The first Burger Barn I worked at was because nobody else would take me. It was a last resort. I didn't want to go to Burger Barn. You flip burgers. People would laugh at you. In high school, I didn't wanna be in that kind of environment. But lo and behold, after everything else failed, Martin Paints, other jobs, Burger Barn was welcoming me with open arms. So I started working there.

Tiffany moved to Harlem when she finished high school and found she couldn't commute back to the Bronx. Reluctant to return to the fast-food business, Tiffany tried her luck at moving up, into a service job with more of a white-collar flavor. She looked everywhere for a position in stores where the jobs are free of hamburger grease and hot oil for French fries, stores where clerks don't wear aprons or hair nets. Nothing panned out, despite her best efforts:

> I'm looking at Lerners and Plymouth [clothing stores] and going to all these stores and lo and behold Burger Barn is there with open arms because I had two years of experience by then.

The new Burger Barn franchise was right in the middle of Harlem, not far from the room she rents over a store-front church. It had the additional appeal of being a black-owned business, something that mattered to Tiffany in terms of the "more cultural reasons why [she] decided to work there." But she confesses to a degree of disappoint-ment that she was not able to break free of entry-level fast-food jobs. With a high-school diploma in hand, Tiffany was hoping for something better.

William Johnson followed a similar pathway to Burger Barn, graduating from summer youth jobs in the middle of high school and looking for something that would help pay for his books and carfare. The Department of Labor gave him a referral to Burger Barn, but he was reluctant at first to pursue it:

> To go there and work for Burger Barn, that was one of those real cloak-and-dagger kind of things. You'll be coming out [and your friends say], "Yo, where you going?" You be, "I'm going, don't worry about where I'm going." And you see your friends coming [to the restaurant] and see you working there and now you be [thinking], "Now, the whole [housing] project gonna know I work in Burger Barn." It's not something I personally proclaim or pride and stuff. . . . If you are a crew member, you really aren't shit there. . . . You got nothing there, no benefits, nothing. It was like that [when I was younger] and it's like that now.

William tried every subterfuge he could think of to con-ceal his job from the kids he knew. He kept his uniform in a bag and put it on in the back of the restaurant so that it would never be visible on the street. He made up fake jobs to explain to his friends where his spending money was coming from. He took circuitous routes to the Barn and hid back by the gigantic freezer when he spotted a friend coming into the store. The last thing William wanted was to be publicly identified as a shift worker at Burger Barn.

In this, William was much like the other teen and young adult workers we encountered. They are very sensi-tive to stigma, to challenges to their status, and by taking low-wage jobs of this kind they have positioned themselves to receive exactly the kind of insults they most fear. But the fact is that they do take these risks and, in time, latch onto other "narratives" that undergird their legitimacy.

Breaking the Stigma

One of the chief challenges of an organization like Burger Barn is how to take people who have come to them on the defensive and turn them into workers who at least appear on the surface, if not deep in their souls, to enjoy their work. Customers have choices; they can vote with their feet. If ordering french fries at Burger Barn requires them to run a gauntlet of annoyance, rudeness, or diffidence from the person who takes their order, they can easily cross the street to a competitor the next time. It is clearly in the company's interest to find ways to turn the situation around. Ideally, from the industry's viewpoint, it would be best if the whole reputation of these jobs could be reversed. This is what McDonald's had in mind when it launched the Calvin series. But for all the reasons outlined earlier in this chapter, that is not likely to happen, for the conditions that give rise to the stigma in the first place—low wages, high turnover, enforced deference—are not likely to change. Beyond publicizing the opportunities that are within reach, much of which falls on deaf ears, there is little the industry can do to rehabilitate its workers in the eyes of the public and thereby dampen the tension across the counter.

Yet behind the scenes, managers and workers, and peers working together in restaurant crews, do build a moral defense of their work. They call upon timeless American values, values familiar to many, including con-servatives, to undergird their respectability. Pointing to the essential virtues of the gainfully employed, Burger Barn workers align themselves with the great mass of men and women who work for a living. "We are like them," they declare, and in so doing separate themselves from the people in their midst who are not employed.

They have plenty of experience with individuals who don't work, often including members of their own fami-lies: beggars who come around the restaurants looking for handouts every day; fast-talkers who come into Burger Barn hoping for free food; and age-mates who prefer to deal drugs. In general, these low-wage workers are far less forgiving, and far less tolerant, of these people than are the liberals who champion the cause of the working poor. Since they hold hard, exhausting, poorly paid jobs, they see little reason why anyone ought to get a free ride. What the indigent should do, on this account, is to follow their example: get a job, any job.

Ianna Bates is an articulate case in point. She has had to confront the social degradation that comes from holding a "low job" and has developed a tough hide in response. Her dignity is underwritten by the critique she has absorbed about the "welfare dependent":

> I'm not ashamed because I have a job. Most people don't and I'm proud of myself that I decided to get up and do something at an early age. So as I look at it, I'm not on welfare. I'm doing something.
>
> I'm not knocking welfare, but I know people that are on it that can get up and work. There's nothing wrong with them. And they just choose not to. . . . They don't really need to be on [welfare]. They just want it because they can get away with it. I don't think it's right because that's my tax dollars going for somebody who is lazy, who don't wanna get up. I can see if a woman had three children, her husband left her and she don't have no job cause she was a housewife. OK. But after a while, you know, welfare will send you to school. Be a nurse assistant, a home attendant, something!
>
> Even if you were on welfare, it should be like, you see all these dirty streets we have? Why can't they go out and sweep the streets, clean up the parks. I mean, there is so much stuff that needs to be done in this city. They can do that and give them their money. Not just sit home and not do anything.

Patricia Hull, a mother of five children in her late thirties, couldn't agree more. Patty has worked at Burger Barn for five years now, having pulled herself off of welfare by the sheer determination to be a decent role model for her children. One might imagine that she would be more tolerant of **AFDC** recipients, since she has been there. She moved up to the Big Apple from Tennessee after her husband walked out on her, hoping to find more job opportunities than the few that were available in the rural south. It took a long time for her to get on her feet and even Patty would agree that without "aid" she would not have made it this

AFDC Aid to Families with Dependent Children: assistance provided by the federal government to families in economic need.

far. Still, having finally taken the hard road to a real job, she sees no reason why anyone else should have an easier ride:

> There's so much in this city; it's always hiring. It may not be what you want. It may not be the pay you want. But you will always get a job. If I can work at Burger Barn all week and come home tired and then have to deal with the kids and all of that, and be happy with $125 a week, so can you. Why would I give quarters [to bums on the street]? My quarter is tax-free money for you! No way.

Or, in a variation on the same theme, Larry Peterson reminds us that any job is better than no job. The kids who would dare to hard-time Larry get nothing but a cold shoulder in return because Larry knows in his soul that he has something they don't have: work for which he gets paid.

> I don't care what other people think. You know, I just do not care. I have a job, you know. It's my job. You ain't puttin' *no* food on my table; you ain't puttin' *no* clothes on my back. I will walk tall with my Burger Barn uniform on. Be proud of it, you know.

These views could have come straight from the most conservative Republicans in the country, bent on justifying draconian cuts in the welfare budget. For they trade on a view held by many of the ghetto-based working poor: that work equals dignity and no one deserves a free ride. The difference between them is simply that the working poor know whereof they speak: they have toiled behind the hot grease pits of french-fry vats, they have stood on their feet for eight or nine hours at a stretch, all for the magnificent sum of $4.25 an hour. Virtually all they have to show for their trouble is the self-respect that comes from being on the right side of that gaping cavern that separates the deserving (read working) and the undeserving (read nonworking) poor (Katz 1989).

Other retorts to status insults emerge as well. Flaunting financial independence often provides a way of lashing back at acquaintances who dis young workers for taking Burger Barn jobs. Brian Gray, born in Jamaica but raised in one of Harlem's tougher neighborhoods, knows that his peers don't really think much of his job. "They just make fun," he says. "Ah, you flipping burgers. You gettin' paid $4.25. They'd go snickering down the street." But it wasn't long after Brian started working that he picked up some serious money, serious at least for a teenager in his neighborhood.

What I did was made Sam [the general manager] save my money for me. Then I got the best of clothes and the best sneakers with my own money. Then I added two chains. Then [my friends] were like, "Where you selling drugs at?" And I'm like, "the same place you said making fun of me, flipping burgers. That's where I'm getting my money from. Now, where are you getting yours from?" They couldn't answer.

Contrary to public perception, most teenagers in Harlem are afraid of the drug trade and won't go near it. They know too many people who are six feet under, in jail, or permanently disabled by the ravages of drugs. If you aren't willing to join the underground economy, where are you going to get the money to dress yourself, go out on the town, and do the other things teens throughout the middle class do on Mom and Dad's sufferance? Most of Harlem's youth cannot rely on their parents' financial support to meet these needs. Indeed, this is one of the primary pressures that pushes young people out into the labor market in the first place, and at an early age. Most workers we interviewed had their first job by the age of fourteen.

What Brian does, then, is to best his mates at their own game by showing them that he has the wherewithal to be a consumer, based on his own earnings. He derives no small amount of pleasure from turning these tables, upending the status system by outdoing his friends on style grounds they value as much as he does.

It might be comforting to suggest that these hard-working low-wage workers were, from the very beginning, different from their nonworking counterparts, equipped somehow to withstand the gauntlet of criticism that comes their way when they start out on the bottom of the labor market. It would be comforting because we would then be able to sort the deserving, admirable poor (who recognize the fundamental value of work and are willing to ignore **stigma**) from the undeserving (who collapse in the face of peer pressure and therefore prefer to go on the dole). This is too simplistic. Burger Barn workers of all ages and colors fully admit that their employment is the butt of jokes and that it has subjected them to ridicule. Some, like Larry Peterson, argue that they don't care what other people think, but even these

stigma A social mark of disgrace that prevents a person from entering mainstream society. For example, society stigmatizes ex-felons and pedophiles.

brave souls admit that it took a long time for them to build up this confidence.

Where, then, does the confidence come from? How do ghetto residents develop the rejoinders that make it possible to recapture their dignity in the face of peer disapproval? To some degree, they can call on widely accepted American values that honor working people, values that float in the culture at large.[10] But this is not enough to construct a positive identity when the reminders of low status—coming from customers, friends, and the media—are abundant. Something stronger is required: a workplace culture that actively works to overcome the negatives by reinforcing the value of the work ethic. Managers and veteran employees on the shop floor play a critical role in the reinforcement process by counseling new workers distressed by bad-mouthing.

Kimberly Sampson, a twenty-year-old African-American woman, began working at Burger Barn when she was sixteen and discovered firsthand how her "friends" would turn on her for taking a low-wage job. Fortunately, she found a good friend at work who steadied her with a piece of advice:

> Say it's a job. You are making money. Right? Don't care what nobody say. You know? If they don't like it, too bad. They sitting on the corner doing what they are doing. You got to work making money. You know? Don't bother with what anybody has to say about it.

Kim's advisor, a workplace veteran who had long since come to terms with the insults of his peers, called upon a general status hierarchy that places the working above the nonworking as a bulwark against the slights. His point was later echoed by Kim's manager in the course of a similar episode, as she explained:

> Kids come in here . . . they don't have enough money. I'll be like, "You don't have enough money; you can't get [the food you ordered]." One night this little boy came in there and cursed me out. He [said], "That's why you are working at Burger Barn. You can't get a better job. . . ."
>
> I was upset and everything. I started crying. [My manager] was like, "Kim, don't bother with him. I'm saying, *you got a job.* You know. It is a *job.*"

Absorbing this defensive culture is particularly important for immigrant workers in Harlem who often find fast-food jobs the first venue where they have sustained interaction with African-Americans who resent the fact that they have jobs at all, much less jobs in their community. Marisa Gonzalez, a native of Ecuador, had a very difficult time when she first began working as a hostess at Burger Barn. A pretty, petite nineteen-year-old, she was selected for the job because she has the kind of sparkle and vivaciousness that any restaurant would want customers to see. But some of her more antagonistic black customers saw her as an archetype: the immigrant who barely speaks a word of English who snaps up a job some native-born English speaker ought to have. Without the support of her bilingual, Latino manager, she would not have been able to pull herself together and get on with the work:

> I wasn't sent to the grill or the fries [where you don't need to communicate with customers]. I was sent to the cash register, even though the managers knew I couldn't speak English. That was only one week after my arrival in the United States! So I wasn't feeling very well at all. Three weeks later I met a manager who was Puerto Rican. He was my salvation. He told me, "Marisa, it's not that bad." He'd speak to me in English, even though he knows Spanish. He'd tell me, "Don't cry. Dry off those tears. You'll be all right, you'll make it." So he encouraged me like no other person in that Burger Barn, especially when the customers would curse at me for not knowing English. He gave me courage and after that it went much better.

Among the things this manager taught Marisa was that she should never listen to people who give her a hard time about holding a job at Burger Barn. Having been a white-collar clerical worker in her native country, it did bother Marisa that she had slipped down the status hierarchy—and it still does. She was grateful, nevertheless, to have a way to earn money and her family was desperate for her contribution. When customers would insult her, insinuating that someone who speaks limited English was of lowly status, she turned to management for help. And she found it in the form of fellow Latino bosses who told her to hold her head up because she was, after all, working, while her critics on the whole were not.

Once these general moral values are in place, many Burger Barn workers take the process one step further: they argue their jobs have hidden virtues that make them more valuable than most people credit. Tiffany Wilson, the young black woman who reluctantly settled for a Burger Barn job when none of the clothing stores she wanted to work for would take her, decided in the end that there was more substance to her job than she credited initially:

> When I got in there, I realized it's not what people think. It's a lot more to it than flipping burgers. It's a real system of business. That's when I really got to see a big corporation at play. I mean, one part of it, the foundation of it: cashiers, the store, how it's run. Production of food, crew workers, service. Things of that nature. That's when I really got into it and understood a lot more.

Americans tend to think of values as embedded in individuals, transmitted through families, and occasionally reinforced by media images or role models. We tend not to focus on the powerful contribution that institutions and organizations make to the creation and sustenance of beliefs. Yet it is clear that the workplace itself is a major force in the creation of a rebuttal culture among these workers. Without this line of defense it would be very hard for Burger Barn employees to retain their dignity. With the support of fellow workers, however, they are able to hold their heads up, not by defining themselves as separate from society, but by calling upon the values they hold in common with the rest of the working world.

This is but one of the reasons why exclusion from the society of the employed is such a devastating source of social isolation. We could hand people money, as various guaranteed income plans of the past thirty years have suggested. But we can't hand out honor. For a majority of Americans, honor comes from participation in this central setting in our culture and from the positive identity it confers.

Franklin Roosevelt understood this during the Great Depression and responded with the creation of thousands of publicly funded jobs designed to put people to work building the national parks, the railway stations, the great highways that criss-cross the country, and the murals that decorate public walls from San Francisco to New York. Social scientists studying the unemployed in the 1930s showed convincingly that people who held **WPA** jobs were far happier and healthier than those who were on the dole, even when their incomes did not differ significantly. WPA workers had their dignity in the midst of poverty;

WPA Works Progress Administration: a New Deal program from the 1930s to provide jobs for the unemployed.

those on the dole were vilified and could not justify their existence or find an effective cultural rationale for the support they received.

This historical example has its powerful parallels in the present. Joining the workforce is a fundamental, transforming experience that moves people across barriers of subculture, race, gender, and class. It never completely eradicates these differences and in some divisive settings it may even reinforce consciousness of them—through glass ceilings, discriminatory promotion policies, and the like. But even in places where pernicious distinctions are maintained, there is another, overarching identity competing with forms that stress difference: a common bond within the organization and across the nation of fellow workers. This is what makes getting a job so much more than a means to a financial end. It becomes a crucial developmental hurdle, especially for people who have experienced exclusion before, including minorities, women, the elderly, and teenagers. Any experience that can speak back to the stigma that condemns burger flippers as the dregs, resurrecting them as exemplars of the American work ethic, has extraordinary power.

Those who choose to earn a living in the legitimate job market receive few material rewards for their effort, but they can claim moral legitimacy from the traditional American work ethic. They can't flash large rolls of cash before the eyes of their neighbors, but they can pride themselves on "doing the right thing," avoiding the dangers of the drug trade and the sloth of welfare recipients. While they understand that some people have a legitimate need to receive government assistance, they don't see the payoff of dealing drugs, and this is not an opinion they keep to themselves. Workers with friends or family in the drug trade often implore them to get out, warning them of the dangers, and reasoning that they each make about the same amount of money in a week, while the one involved with drugs has to work longer hours.

Nadine Stevens has worked at Burger Barn since graduating from high school five years ago. By all accounts she lives in one of the most dangerous neighborhoods in Harlem. Her apartment building is the home of an active drug trade and, indeed, the mailboxes were recently removed from the building by police because they were being used for drug transactions. She knows most of the drug dealers who sit on her stoop every day and night, having grown up with them. She and her mother and sister, whose

ground-floor apartment faces the street, have seen many young women they know wasted by drugs, and young men killed in their hallway.

Nadine tries to convince the dealers she knows to get out of the trade, and to shoot for getting into management at Burger Barn. She and her sister, Rachael, with whom she works at Burger Barn, recently accosted a young teen they knew on the street whom they suspected of drug running. They told her that if she was desperate for money they'd get her a job at Burger Barn. Sensing the girl's reluctance, Nadine cried, "There's no shame in my game! Come work with me."

The dealers they know argue that the Burger Barn employee is working in a poorly paid, demeaning job and that, furthermore, they couldn't get hired there if they tried. Although their work is dangerous, illegal, and despised by neighbors, they brandish the accoutrements of success glorified in the United States: expensive cars, stylish clothes, and lots of cash. Their honor is measured in dollars, a common American standard that competes for the attention of people otherwise destined to earn little more than the minimum wage.

Anthony Vallo has had to choose on which side of the law to work and, once he secured his Burger Barn job, had to decide what to do about his friends and acquaintances who chose the wrong side. Two of his best friends are in jail. Another friend is dealing drugs and probably isn't far from a jail term himself. What Anthony does is try to maintain a cordial relationship with these guys, but to put as much distance between himself and them as he can without giving offense:

> This friend of mine is selling and stuff like that, but he's my friend. We used to go to school back then. He was like, "Damn, you still doin' that Burger Barn shit? I can get you a real job!" I think he respects me; at least he don't criticize me behind my back. But I try to avoid him, you know.

Drug dealers are not the only problem cases with which Harlem workers must contend. At least until welfare reform began to force women on AFDC back into the labor force, many young mothers working low wage jobs were faced with the fork in the road that led either to a job at a place like Burger Barn or public assistance. Since most know a fair number of women who have elected, or had no choice but to opt for, the latter, it takes no small amount of fortitude to go for a minimum-wage job.[11] Indeed, given that AFDC offered greater financial benefits—when health coverage, food stamps, and subsidized housing are part of the package—than these jobs provide, it takes a strong attachment to the work ethic and a willingness to sacrifice elements of one's financial well-being in favor of the dignity that goes with holding a real job.

The Importance of Going to Work

Although having a well-paid, respected career is prized above all else in the United States, our culture confers honor on those who hold down jobs of any kind over those who are outside of the labor force. Independence and self-sufficiency—these are virtues that have no equal in this society. But there are other reasons why we value workers besides the fact that their earnings keep them above water and therefore less in need of help from government, communities, or charities. We also value workers because they share certain common views, experiences, and expectations. The work ethic is more than an attitude toward earning money—it is a disciplined existence, a social life woven around the workplace.

For all the talk of "family values," we know that in the contemporary period, family often takes a backseat to the requirements of a job, even when the job involves flipping burgers. What we are supposed to orient toward primarily is the workplace and its demands. This point could not be made more forcefully than it is in the context of the welfare reform bills of 1996. Public policy in the late 1990s makes clear that poor women are now supposed to be employed even if they have young children. With a majority of women with children, even those under a year of age, in the labor force, we are not prepared to cut much slack to those who have been on welfare. They can and should work like the rest of us, or so the policy mantra goes. This represents no small change in the space of a few decades in our views of what honorable women and mothers should do. But it also reflects the growing dominance of work in our understanding of adult priorities.

We could think of this increasingly work-centered view of life as a reflection of America's waning economic position, a pragmatic response to wage stagnation,

downsizing, and international competition: we must work harder. And this it may be. But it is also part of a secular transformation that has been ongoing for decades as we've moved away from home-centered work lives in the agricultural world to employment-centered lives outside the domestic sphere altogether. The more work departs from home, the more it becomes a social system of its own, a primary form of integration that rivals the family as a source of identity, belonging, and friendship. Women like Antonia Piento are not content only to take care of children at home. They want a life that is adult centered, where they have peers they can talk to. Where they might once have found that company in the neighborhood, now they are more likely to find it on the shop floor. Those primary social ties are grounded in workplace relations, hence to be a worker is also to be integrated into a meaningful community of fellow workers, the community that increasingly becomes the source of personal friends, intimate relations and the worldview that comes with them.

Work is therefore much more than a means to a financial end. This is particularly the case when the work holds little intrinsic satisfaction. No one who gets paid for boiling french fries in hot oil thinks they are playing a world-shattering role. They know their jobs are poorly valued; they can see that in their paychecks, in the demeanor of the people whom they serve across the counter, even among some managers. But what they have that their nonworking counterparts lack is both the dignity of being employed and the opportunity to participate in a social life that increasingly defines their adult lives. This community gives their lives structure and purpose, humor and pleasure, support and understanding in hard times, and a backstop that extends beyond the instrumental purposes of a fast-food restaurant. It is the crucible of their values, values that we have argued here are decidedly mainstream.

The working poor sit at the bottom of the occupational structure and feel the weight of disapproval coming down upon their shoulders from better paid, more respectable employees. Yet they stand at the top of another pyramid and can look down the slope toward people they know well who have taken another pathway in the world.

34   Sweatshops in Sunset Park: A Variation of the Late-Twentieth-Century Chinese Garment Shops in New York City

Xiaolan Bao

The late XIAOLAN BAO was a professor of history at California State University Long Branch. She is the author of *Holding Up More Than Half the Sky: Chinese Women Garment Workers in New York City, 1948–1992.*

Questions to Consider   Imagine working twelve hours a day, seven days a week, under physical conditions that are brutal: exposure to lint, physical confinement, sleep deprivation, and chemicals that constantly burn your throat. Your take-home pay at the end of an eighty-four-hour week is about $55. This is not a Jacob Riis description of New York City in 1890 but New York City one hundred years later in the 1990s. Bao's ethnography documents the modern sweatshop and the new immigrants who supply the labor and large profits to the entrepreneurs who are quick to take advantage of young women new to the United States.

O N MARCH 12, 1995, THE *NEW YORK TIMES* carried a report on the Chinese garment shops in the Sunset Park area of Brooklyn, a neighborhood that houses the new Chinese garment production center in New York City. Unlike most of the Chinatown garment shops in Manhattan, many of the Chinese shops in Sunset Park are not unionized. The weak influence of organized labor and law enforcement agencies in the area had virtually turned the industry there into a safety valve for some Chinese employers to extract quick profits while not complying with any labor laws. Incidents of exploitation increased with the expansion of the Chinese garment shops in the area.

The report in the *New York Times,* written by reporter Jane H. Lii, largely confirmed the above observation. The vivid description of life in the shops, based on the reporter's firsthand experience, gripped the hearts of its readers. According to Lii, the shop she worked in for an entire week was "typical of the small, new shops outside Manhattan":

> The steel doors opened into a dim, dusty warehouse. Red and blue rags covered the four windows, shutting out all natural light. Bundles of cut cloth sat piled in haphazard mounds, some stacked taller than a worker. Under fluorescent lights swinging from chains, rows of mid-aged Chinese women hunched over sewing machines, squinting and silent.

Were the working conditions there as horrific as those that splashed across the headlines in city newspapers? Lii's reply indicated that there was "something more complex at work." What, then, was the complexity? Lii reported that the owner of the shop was "actually benevolent, albeit in a harsh way." "She does not pay minimum wage, but she serves her workers tea. She makes them work until midnight, but she drives them home afterward. She uses child laborers, but she fusses over them, combing their ponytails, admiring their painted fingernails, even hugging them." According to Lii, the boss had opened the business only to save her family's honor, for her brother had, among many things, absconded with close to $80,000 owed to his workers in back wages. The shop also was reopened, according to its present owner, in order to provide jobs for those who came from the same region in China and whom she called "our people."

As Lii reported, the situation of the workers in the shop was also complicated. They "sewed virtually non-stop" because they wanted to make money and had no other alternatives without speaking English. They brought their children into the shop to care for them while working. Several children, however, toiled by their mothers' sides to supplement their incomes. It was said that their mothers wanted to instill in them a work ethic by allowing them to do so.

Lii reported that both the employer and her workers considered American labor laws ideal and laudable, but impractical. The workers considered their employer a good boss "precisely because she was willing to violate labor laws and allow their children to work by their sides." The situation was, therefore, "a miserable complicity born of necessity in an insular, immigrant world" or, simply, "a grim conspiracy of the poor," as the reporter concluded. No wonder that the result of working at Sunset Park was pitiful:

> Seven days later, after 84 hours of work, I got my reward, in the form of a promise that in three weeks I would be paid $54.24 or 65 cents an hour (minimum wage is $4.25). I also walked away from the lint-filled factory with aching shoulders, a stiff back, a dry cough and a burning sore throat.

How representative is Lii's seven-day experience in the shops, and how valid is her analysis? In what ways are the conditions in the Sunset Park Chinese shops similar to the union shops in Manhattan's Chinatown, the hub of the Chinese industry in New York City? In what ways are they different? To what extent are the conditions in Sunset Park similar to those of the city's garment shops at the turn of the twentieth century? What are the factors that have led to these similarities and differences? In the era of globalization, what can the conditions in Sunset Park Chinese garment shops tell us about the impact of globalization in the U.S.? This study attempts to answer these questions.

This article is primarily based on the author's historical research of the Chinese garment industry in New York City over the last ten years, her visits to a number of shops in Sunset Park in the late 1990s, and her interviews with several dozen workers in the area.[1] It gives a brief account of the working conditions in the shops and discusses several highly controversial issues in the Sunset Park Chinese community that relate to the garment industry. By presenting a more differentiated picture of the industry,

it argues that while labor organizing and law enforcement remain important ways to address labor abuse in the industry, it is imperative for law enforcement agencies, organized labor, and all concerned individuals to understand the complexity embedded in the highly competitive structure of the garment industry, the multidimensional impact of labor legislation and law enforcement, and the need to develop new forms of labor organizing that are informed and responsive to the challenges of the time. Without such an understanding, any effort to curb the sweating phenomenon is likely to be sporadic and without lasting effect on the industry.

Working Environments

The shop where Jane Lii worked and reported is, in large part, typical of the Chinese garment shops in the Sunset Park area. Many of them are housed in former warehouses or converted garages. Because these shops are often hidden behind a steel door and have no sign on the front, one can hardly tell from the outside the nature of the activities inside the shops or, simply, whether there is any activity at all.

Sunset Park offers the Chinese garment industry many advantages. First, the former warehouses and the converted garages there are spacious. Even though they do not provide comfortable working conditions, they offer much more production space than industrial lofts in Manhattan's Chinatown.[2] The 1983 Chinatown Garment Industry Study reports that in 1981, Chinese shops with about 30 sewing machines occupied an average of 6,070 square feet in Soho. These shops were and are still the largest garment shops in the Chinatown area.[3] However, shops in Sunset Park with a similar number of sewing machines can cover as much as 10,000 square feet.[4] The spacious environment of the shops not only allows an effective flow of production, but also provides shop owners with enough space to expand their businesses.

In addition, rents and maintenance fees for buildings in Sunset Park are relatively inexpensive. In the spring of 1998, for example, the owner of a shop, located between Fort Hamilton Parkway and 43rd Street and covering more than 10,000 square feet, told me that she paid only $2,500 a month for a space that accommodates forty workers. For the same money, she could afford only a 4,000-square-foot shop in Manhattan's Chinatown. Maintenance fees are also low. For an additional yearly payment of $100 to $200, the gas and other equipment and utility lines would be checked by the building owner.[5]

There are, however, many characteristics that Sunset Park shops share with their counterparts in Manhattan's Chinatown. Besides bundles of cut cloth piled up in haphazard mounds in almost any open floor space, there are severe problems with ventilation. Shops that were converted from former warehouses and garages have very few or virtually no windows at all. Conditions are even worse when the employers cover the few windows with rags or newspapers or simply lock the main entrance to conceal operations. In these shops the air is stifling and filled with lint and dust, while workers sew under fluorescent lights in the daytime.[6]

However, unlike Chinatown shops that generally suffer from space limitations, the physical size and working conditions of Sunset Park shops are not all the same. There are shops that have more than thirty workers and cover a space of over 10,000 square feet. There are also shops packed with a dozen sewing machines and piles of cut garments but covering less than 4,000 square feet. These small and big shops are located side by side. However, regardless of the differences, they have something in common. Like their counterparts in Manhattan's Chinatown, there is virtually no space reserved for workers' activities other than sewing. Even in the relatively spacious shops, workers eat their lunch at their sewing machines or at the desks where they work.

Division of Labor

Although the shops in Sunset Park, like those in Manhattan's Chinatown, work on various lines of garments from manufacturers or other contractors, workers mostly produce sportswear and other low-priced women's apparel. The division of labor in the shops varies according to the size of the shop and the line of the garments they produce, but there are in general five kinds of workers on the floor: the sorter, the foreperson, machine operators, pressers, and floor workers.

Garment production starts with the sorter, who separates the cut-up fabrics according to the style of the garments and decides where the work should begin. The cut fabrics are then sent to the machine operators for either sewing or hemming. Machine operators include those workers who sew minor parts of the garments, such as zippers, collars, cuffs and pockets. The garment then passes to the hands of the foreperson, who checks the quality of the sewed or hemmed garments. A quality garment will be sent to buttoners and trimmers who attach buttons, sew buttonholes, and trim extra threads. In its final stage, the garment will be sent to floor workers who hang tags, eliminate irregularities, and put the garments in a transparent plastic bag for shipping.

Like its counterparts elsewhere in the city, the Chinese garment industry in Sunset Park is characterized by its gender hierarchy. The rationale used to justify it is always inconsistent and contradictory. For example, the sorter and pressers, the two highest paid jobs on the shop floor, are almost invariably men. Trimmers, the lowest paid workers, are virtually all women. This arrangement is said to have its basis in women's lack of physical strength to move the bundles of cut-up materials around, and women's intellectual inability to sort the cut-up pieces and to lay out a workable schedule for production. Women are also believed to be too weak to operate the heavy pressing machines and endure the heat generated by them. As a result, they are denied the opportunity to work as a sorter or a presser. What is forgotten in this ungrounded rationale for the gender division of labor on the floor is the duration of strength, which the Chinese call *yin li,* and the extraordinary wisdom to figure out the way to sew the garments with their ever-changing styles. Both of these are necessary qualities of machine operators, who are overwhelmingly women.

It is said that women constitute the majority of machine operators in the shops because the flexible work hours, made possible by the piece-rate system and the larger number of operators in the shops, allow them to fulfill their family responsibilities while working in the shops. This justification ignores the highly competitive environment among the large number of machine operators that is generated by the piece-rate system. Since garment production is seasonal and work tends to be limited in most of the shops, in order to make ends meet, women workers are most likely to utilize every minute available to compete with one another in seizing work and to produce as many garments as they can. This work atmosphere is likely to deprive them of the flexibility that the piece-rate system is supposed to offer.

In addition, as known in the shops, workers' earnings depend not only on the piece rates and the speed at which they work, but also on the kind of work they do. The more mechanical and simple the work is, the faster they can produce, and the more money they can earn. There is no denying that pressers work under extremely stressful conditions, because there are usually only two or three of them in a shop of thirty or more machines and they have to press all the finished garments within a given time. However, their work is simpler than that of machine operators, so they can easily speed up their work after they become used to the structure of the garments and thus increase their incomes. Because there are only a few pressers in a shop, they are protected from the frenetic competition that is a routine part of the lives of machine operators.[7]

Unlike the pressers, machine operators' incomes fluctuate a great deal. Since styles are transient due to the unpredictable nature of fashion, it tends to take much longer for machine operators to get familiar with their work before they can speed up their production. The unpredictable nature of their work also creates more opportunities for their employers to keep wages low by constantly changing their piece rates, which are allegedly based on styles.

Family wages are always invoked to justify not only the higher pay of some traditionally men's work, but also the special payment arrangements in such sections as buttoning and bagging (putting the finished garments into bags). Since piece rates in these two sections are much lower than other sections, employers would subcontract the entire workload to one or two married male workers and allow them to complete the work with the assistance of their families. It used to be said that this arrangement was made to help the men fulfil their traditional gender roles as "rice winners" and to respect Chinese traditional culture. However, this rationale was cast aside in the early 1990s when the male workers left for higher paying jobs and women replaced them in these sections.

As Nancy Green and Susan Glenn have cogently argued, the gender division of labor in the garment industry has never been static.[8] Take the operation of sewing machines for example. Although most sewing machine operators are women, an increasing number of undocumented male workers have taken over these positions in Sunset Park over the last few years. Gender remains at work, however. The recently arrived men could easily take over the traditionally female jobs from women, but the

gender identity of their jobs continued to subject them to a position inferior to those in the traditionally men's sections. They are generally believed to be less skilled, physically weak, and hence less manly than the rest of the male workers in the shops.

Fluidity between class and gender lines, generated by the structural flexibility of the garment industry, does not preclude opportunities for upward mobility for female as well as male workers, albeit in different ways and to different degrees. Although most Chinese employers are men and had been workers themselves, an increasing number of women workers have become owners of the garment shops in recent years. This was the case in the shop where reporter Lii worked. Many women employers learned English by attending the free language classes offered by their union or other public institutions. Speaking from fair to good English, they operate their businesses successfully, without the assistance of men. Their past experience as workers and their gender identity may enable them to better understand their women employees. However, this does not guarantee that they will be benevolent bosses, as implied in Lii's report. Recent cases of labor law violations in the Chinese garment shops owned by women have demonstrated that, situated in a highly competitive and marginal position in the city's industry, women employers can be as unscrupulous as their male counterparts.[9]

Wages and Hours

Workers' wages in the Sunset Park garment shops fluctuate greatly, contingent upon the type of work they produce, the level of skill, and the quality and adequacy of work their employer provides. A new hand may earn practically nothing for the first day, while a skilled long-stitch machine operator can earn as much as $600 a week in the high season. In general, as in the case of most Chinatown shops in Manhattan, the sorter, the foreperson, the cleaner(s), and the floor workers are paid by the hour. My interviews show that in 1998 a full-time foreperson or a sorter earned an average of more than six dollars per hour, and the finished garment checkers and cleaners, about three dollars. The rest of the workers in the shops are paid at piece rates. Their incomes vary greatly, ranging from weekly averages of $600 to $700 for a presser; $400 to $500 for a hemmer; $300 to $400 for a single machine operator and buttoner; $250 to $300 for a general machine operator; and $150–$200 for a trimmer. Compared with the union's minimum wages, the above wages of the Sunset Park Chinese garment workers may appear desirable. However, most of these weekly wages are in fact the result of workers' working ten to twelve hours a day. Their work hours are even longer during the busy seasons, with competition mounting in recent years.

Forms of payment are also factors that affect workers' incomes. Like their counterparts in Manhattan's Chinatown, most employers in Sunset Park issue payments in a combination of checks and cash. The portion of the payment received by check is determined by the worker's status or need. For union members, whose number is small in the area, employers tailor the amount of their checks strictly according to the union minimum income requirement for benefit eligibility. However, for nonunion workers, who form the overwhelming majority of the workforce in Sunset Park, the amounts of their checks are either kept below the poverty threshold so that they can maintain eligibility for welfare benefits, or kept in line with the US Immigration and Naturalization Service's basic requirement for financial eligibility for sponsoring the immigration of their family members or relatives into the United States. Working underground, undocumented workers are paid invariably by cash.

Chinese employers argue that workers themselves request various forms of payment. However, my interviews reveal that all workers, regardless of their status, are forced to accept a reduction in their wages, because checks are issued with a deduction of a five to seven percent "handling fee." The same is true for cash payments. Furthermore, piece rates are often not announced before the completion of work and in some shops employers reserve their rights to reduce workers' wages if they consider the wages to be too high.

Researcher Mark Levitan reports that in 1990, 72 percent of the reported incomes of less-skilled blue-collar workers, apparel workers included, were below the poverty threshold for a family of four ($12,674).[10] Underreporting might be a factor in leading to the low-income status of some workers' families. However, what Levitan reported did not appear to be far from reality in the case of Chinese garment workers in New York. My interviews suggest that in the late 1990s the actual average annual income of most Sunset Park Chinese garment workers

was only about $20,000.[11] To sustain their families, many have to work long hours, in violation of U.S. labor laws.

In the shops where the employers still bother to concern themselves with the investigations of law enforcement agencies, workers were required to punch their work cards to show that they were working eight hours a day, even before they start their day's work. My interviews, however, reveal that 90 percent of the workers employed in Sunset Park are working ten to twelve hours a day. During the busy seasons or when orders have to be rushed out, it is not unusual for workers to work unusually long hours, or as Lii indicated, even labor around the clock.

Long hours of work, coupled with the hazardous environment of the shops severely damages workers' health. What happened to Bao Zhi Ni is, indeed, not an isolated case. Her written testimony at a public hearing held by the New York State Assembly Subcommittee on Sweatshops on October 2, 1997, is illustrative of workers' situations:

> My name is Bao Zhi Ni. I am a garment worker. I have worked in the garment factories for close to ten years. For many long hours, I work without proper safety equipment, and under filthy conditions. I work at least ten to twelve hours everyday, but because the bosses depress the wages so low we can only make $20, $30 a day, even though we're working over ten hours . . .
>
> For many long hours I sit at the sewing machine repeating the same motions. I also have to handle heavy bundles of garments every day. Each day at work is an exhausting day. My eyes are tired, and my vision is blurry. My fingers, wrists, shoulders, neck, back, spine, all these parts of my body are inflicted with pain. I started feeling the pain in my lower back five years ago, but I continued to work in the sweatshops. I have no medical benefits.
>
> My shoulders and back hurt constantly. Because I have been forced to work for such long hours, the cartilage between the bones in my back has rubbed away, and I have a pinched nerve. With the pain and the numbness in my left leg, I know that I have muscular and nervous problems. My fingers and wrists hurt. Now, even after just one or two hours of work, my back aches so much that I can barely stand straight. . . . In order to make a living I have no choice but to force myself to work through this pain. Sometimes I can't do it, but I have no choice but to take one or two days off.
>
> Sometimes I have to take one or two weeks off. When I take this time off to heal just a little, my boss

gets angry. The boss will call my house to scold me and say that I'm lazy, tell me that I must go back to work as soon as possible.[12]

My interviews reveal that almost all the garment workers who worked in the industry for more than five years have various health problems. Deng Ying Yi, a long-time labor activist at the Workers Center in Brooklyn run by the Union of Needletrades, Industrial and Textile Employees (UNITE!), is virtually disabled after working in the garment industry for more than ten years, with her nervous system partially damaged. Her case is not unique among workers in Sunset Park. However, most of these nonunionized workers are not covered by any form of health insurance.

To survive in their new homeland, nonunionized workers have to develop their own system to cope with the situation. Many rely heavily on their family ties and community networks. The experience of a Mr. Zhang, who had been a middle-rank official in Guangzhou but who became a finished garment checker in a Sunset Park Chinese garment shop, is indicative of this phenomenon:

> I was already fifty-two when I immigrated to this country. I worked in a garment shop as *cha yi* (Cantonese: a finished garment checker) and my wife *jin sin* (Cantonese: a trimmer). Together, we earned an average of less than $400 a week and we still had to raise a daughter, our youngest daughter who was in her teens and was eligible to come with us when we immigrated to this country. She had to eat, to dress and to go to school. In addition, we had to save money in order to sponsor our two older children to come to the United States. How did we manage to do all this? Well, we relied on our family....
>
> I came with my other five siblings under the sponsorship of a brother. Each of us came with his or her own family. Altogether, it was more than twenty of us who came to New York City on the same day on the same plane. We rented three two-bedroom apartments in this part of Brooklyn because the brother who came earlier told us that rents are much less expensive in this area. Each apartment was shared by two families. My family and my brother's family shared a two-bedroom apartment and we paid a total of $700 for rent and utilities but we ate separately. My family spent a little more than $100 each month on groceries. How did we manage to do this? We bought the cheapest possible food at the market, say, the thirty-nine-cent-a-pound chicken

on sale at Key Foods and the four-head-for-one-dollar broccoli at the street stands in this neighborhood. In addition, my wife and I also picked up empty soda cans and other stuff on our way home from work. If we were lucky, the monthly income from that part of our labor could cover our groceries for an entire week.

> For eight years after we came to this city, we never ate out and never stopped working, eleven to twelve hours a day and seven days a week. Whenever we did not have work to do in our shop my wife and I went to work in another shop.[13]

While family ties are important resources for immigrant workers who came with their families, community networks are the most important assets for undocumented immigrant workers, most of whom did not come with their families. For example, undocumented workers from Wenzhou have contributed money to establish their own "mutual funds." These funds can be used by any member in time of need. This practice has proved to be the most effective way for these workers to survive in time of adversity, since they are denied any social services and benefits in the United States.

As elsewhere in the world, the gendered definitions of roles in the Sunset Park Chinese garment shops, their hierarchical order, and the rationale applied to justify them are shaped by the flexible but highly competitive structure of the garment industry, and have been inherently unstable. This fluidity generates dynamics in the industry, but has also taken a toll on those who labor in the industry. It is by exhausting human resources among the workers and in their community that the nonregulated segment of the garment industry has managed to thrive. Sunset Part is a case in point.

"Co-Ethnic Conspiracy?"

One major aspect of the Chinese garment industry in New York that has generated great interest among some scholars is its co-ethnic nature. Although in recent years more and more garment shops in New York have employers and workers who do not share the same ethnic identity, this is not the case with many of the Chinese garment shops in Manhattan's Chinatown and Brooklyn's Sunset Park. Most Chinese employers continue to hire only workers from major Chinese settlements.

As many studies have pointed out, this co-ethnic nature of the industry has benefited both workers and management.[14] Like their Eastern European counterparts at the turn of the twentieth century, Chinese workers do not have to learn to speak or understand English to work in a garment shop. They can also learn the trade on site and from scratch. In truth, without the industry, many working-class Chinese immigrant families may not have been able to survive.

The co-ethnic nature of the industry is also said to have simplified and humanized management of the shops. Many studies have discussed the particular recruitment pattern of the Chinese shops. Although in recent years a growing number of new immigrant workers have begun to seek employment through advertisements in community newspapers or the help-wanted signs posted in the front of the shops, most employers continue to rely on the recommendations of their workforce for new recruits, and most new immigrant workers obtain their first jobs through their families, friends, and relatives. Some employers also hire job applicants on the spot, without giving them much of a background check. New recruits, especially those who are employed with the recommendations from workers already in the shop, are allowed to use the facilities in the shop to receive on-site training.

Workers can maintain their cultural practices at their workplaces. They celebrate major Chinese festivals in the shops. They also share Chinese food and cooking with one another, listen to the blasting of the closed-circuit Chinese radio broadcasts, and share news about their homeland while working. As Lii noted, although employers in most Chinese shops do not offer their employees overtime payments when they expect workers to work long hours or on weekends, they offer them free rice and water, or even tea in some shops, to eat and drink with their lunch. They also provide lunch or afternoon tea to compensate workers' working on weekends. It is also widely known that most employers in Sunset Park will drive their employees home if their work ends after 11:00 P.M.

Workers who are unfamiliar with the labor laws and their rights in the United States feel obligated to work hard for their employers if their employers are willing to accommodate their needs. The undocumented workers feel particularly grateful to their employers if their employers have offered them any form of protection during immigration or other law enforcement raids. Employers in Sunset Park are known to cover workers up with piles of cut-garments scattered on the floor, or allow them to use the ladder in the shop to climb to the skylight. These gestures foster gratitude on the workers' part, which they feel obligated to reciprocate.

Many workers find it easy to identify with their employers if they are immigrants and have been workers themselves. Workers who desire upward social mobility look up to their employers as role models, a mirror of their future in the land of opportunity. Workers' empathy with their employers' situation, generated by a mixture of gratitude, fear, and admiration, has often led to their acquiescence to their employers' unscrupulous practices on the shop floor. In some cases this relationship of empathy has become so entrenched that law enforcement agents from outside the Chinese community and Chinese union organizers find it difficult to break. No wonder observers of the industry, like reporter Lii, do not hesitate to call the Sunset Park shop "a miserable complicity born of necessity in an insular, immigrant world." However, this conspiracy theory is too simplistic to explain the complex interdependent relationship between the workers and their employers in the ethnic enclave economy of the United States. It also fails to highlight the imbalance of power embedded in this relationship. Failing to locate the ultimate beneficiaries of this relationship, this theory cannot explain fully the causes of sweated labor in the shops.

Clearly, employers' various forms of accommodation benefit themselves rather than the workers. Let's take the special form of recruitment, for example. Since workers' incomes are based on the work they have accomplished, it will only hurt the new recruits if they are slow to learn their routine of work. However, on-site training allows employers to strengthen their personal ties with the newly hired as well as those who are already in the shop. Paying wages in a mixture of cash and checks or simply by cash also enables the employers to avoid paying taxes, the amounts of which are likely to be much larger than their workers'. A closer investigation of the situation in the industry also reveals that accommodations offered by employers are not unconditional. They are given only to workers who follow the rules they set. Those who refuse to do so are fired, blacklisted, physically assaulted, or subjected to other forms of retaliation.

Most Chinese employers do not force their workers to work long hours. However, production is organized in such a way that workers who do not stay as long as the rest will find themselves in an extremely disadvantageous position. Since there is no limit on work hours in most of the shops and workers who are willing to maximize their work hours can work as long as they wish, those who refuse to do so will end up having only "pork neckbones" (a slang in the Chinatown garment industry, referring to garments difficult to sew), or simply no garments to work on the next morning when they return.

Similar situations occur if a worker is ill and takes sick leave, or refuses to work on Sunday. Employers will hire a replacement worker almost immediately after a laborer fails to show up. Employers will also distribute "chickens in soy sauce" (another slang in the Chinatown garment industry, referring to work easy to sew) or paychecks on Sunday. Under these situations, workers who take a sick day are likely to lose their jobs, and those who do not work on Sunday will miss not only an important opportunity to increase their incomes, but also to get paid in a timely manner. Since workers' wages tend to be withheld by their employers for months in Sunset Park, failing to be present on payday will mean another indefinitely long delay in getting paid. It's no wonder that workers in Sunset Park tend to lament, "We have the option to die but we don't have the option to take a sick day or a rest."

Some employers have also blatantly taken advantage of their workers' acquiescence to maximize their profit. Instances of *zhen jia lao ban* (real and fake bosses) and *yi guo liang zhi* (one country, two systems), stories told by labor activist Deng Ying Yi, are indications of how far employers would go.[15] As Deng recalled, one day workers of a shop came to the UNITE! Workers' Center to seek assistance in collecting their wages. It turned out that their employer had closed the shop after owing them several hundred thousands of dollars in back wages and had vanished without a trace. However, when the State Department of Labor finally undertook this case, the department found it difficult to file charges against the real owner of the shop. The owner, an undocumented immigrant himself, had registered the shop with the name and social security number of an elderly worker and had been signing all the legal documents under this worker's name without informing him. Filing charges against the owner of the shop would mean charges against this worker, who was not the real owner of the shop.[16]

The story of "one country, two systems" is about a peculiar phenomenon in some unionized shops in Sunset Park. According to Deng, although union contracts stipulate that all workers in a union shop are union members and entitled to union benefits, employers of some unionized shops refuse to register their new recruits as union members and keep their wages in the books. Consequently, there are both union and nonunion members in the same shop who are working under very different systems of employment.

My interviews further reveal other forms of discrimination on the floor. For example, some employers offer different piece rates to workers of different immigration status and from different regions in China. Cantonese immigrant workers, who form the majority of the workforce, tend to receive higher piece rates and work relatively regular hours, while non-Cantonese or undocumented workers are denied all these "privileges." Discriminatory treatments have taken a different form in a small number of shops that hire several skilled workers from other ethnic groups. The non-Chinese workers are offered wages and other working conditions that comply with labor laws, while their Chinese fellow workers, who work side by side with them, have to struggle against the grim reality of low pay and long hours of work.[17]

Chinese employers have been so reckless in exploiting workers in their own community that it reinforces the stereotypical image of Chinese workers as the docile "willing slaves" in the Sunset Park area. This image of the workers subjects them to exploitation not only by Chinese employers, but also by shop owners of other ethnic groups. In 1997, the *Sing Tao Daily* reported that seven Chinese workers from a Jewish-owned garment shop came to seek help from the UNITE! Workers' Center. They complained that they had been discriminated against by their Jewish employer who had closed the shop and refused to pay them according to labor laws, as he did to his Hispanic workers.[18]

The most common problem workers face, however, is the failure to receive compensation for their work in a timely manner. Employers benefit tremendously from withholding their workers' wages. Community labor activists estimate that a shop of average size in Sunset Park has thirty-five workers and the lowest wage of garment workers in the area is about $150 per week. If the owner of a shop withholds his/her employees' wages for eight weeks, which is not uncommon in the area, the employer will have more than $40,000 in hand by the end of the eighth week, even if workers in the shop earned the lowest wage in the area. With this $40,000, an employer can open another shop without having to pay interest as they would if borrowing money from a bank.

Regrettably, as union organizers and law enforcement agencies have pointed out, workers tend not to take any legal action against their employers until their employers close down the shops. The reasons are varied. One major reason is the workers' lack of knowledge about their rights and the political operation in their new homeland. With few employment alternatives, many immigrant workers fear that any form of cooperation with law enforcement agencies or organized labor will cost them their jobs. This was particularly the situation before the signing of the Hot Goods Bill by the New York State governor in 1996.[19] Prior to the adoption of this bill, law enforcement agencies had difficulty in helping workers retrieve their back wages if a shop was closed and the employer was hard to locate. As a result, the longer wages were withheld, the more reluctant workers were to report their cases. They feared that their reporting would lead their employers to close the shop for good.

Workers' reluctance to report labor violations on the floor is also compounded by a lack of understanding about the U.S. income tax system. Many are afraid that the amount of money they receive will be reduced by paying taxes if they seek assistance from law enforcement agencies and have to report their back wages to the Internal Revenue Service. Understandably, undocumented workers have additional concerns. Working underground, they fear that a visit from the Department of Labor to their work place will bring in a raid by the Immigration and Naturalization Service.

While workers are often reluctant to take action against their employers, employers are not hesitant to take advantage of workers' fear. According to longtime observers of the community, many employers in the garment industry engage in speculative financial activities with the money they have withheld from their workers, such as gambling or buying high-return but high-risk stocks. Since most of these activities will not lead to their expected outcomes, the employers close down their shops to avoid payments they owe their employees.

There are also employers who simply try to extract larger profits by closing down operations, absconding with the money they have withheld from their employees, and reopening their business under a different name. This

was the case where reporter Lii worked. Hence, labor violations are widespread and the turnover rate of many Sunset Park Chinese garment shops is at a record high.[20] This highly unstable situation makes it even more difficult to enforce labor laws in the area, especially in recent years when most of these agencies are understaffed.

Tensions and exploitation in many Chinese garment shops in Sunset Park lay bare the limits of ethnic solidarity in the garment industry. Relegated to the same ethnic economic sector, Chinese employers have to rely on workers in their own community to run their businesses and accommodate workers' needs. However, situated in a marginal position of a highly competitive industry, many employers also do not hesitate to exploit their community ties to maintain their competitive edge in the industry. As in the case with their predecessors in the city's industry, the garment industry offers new Chinese immigrant workers many advantages in working among their own, but it also makes them more vulnerable to exploitation by management on all levels. The degree of labor violation in many Chinese garment shops demonstrates not only the limits of ethnic solidarity but also the devastating impact of the frenetic search for cheap labor on the Chinese community. This impact, as well as the limited nature of ethnic solidarity, will be further explored in the following section.

"The Cantonese vs. the Fujianese"?

One major issue that surfaced constantly during my interviews with workers is their concern about the increasing number of undocumented workers in the industry, most of whom are believed to be from Fuzhou, a major city in the province of Fujian in southeastern China. These newcomers, who speak their own dialect, are often blamed for worsening labor conditions on the shop floor and deteriorating living standards in Sunset Park. They also are charged with undermining workers' solidarity in the industry. Many Cantonese workers believe that there is no way for them to get along well with the Fujianese.

In the course of interviewing workers in Sunset Park, however, I came to know many Cantonese and Fujianese workers who are good friends. I also came to see that although a large number of undocumented workers came from Fuzhou, Fuzhou is not the only place that has sent undocumented Chinese immigrants to the United States.

Undocumented Chinese workers also come from Wenzhou, Guangdong, and almost all the coastal areas of China. There are also some from Malaysia and other Southeast Asian countries. Nevertheless, there is a pronounced tendency in New York's Chinese community to identify all undocumented workers as Fujianese. Stories about how fanatically hardworking they are became a recurring theme in the narratives of almost all the non-Fujianese workers. Fujianese workers were said to be so money-crazy that they would bring their rice cookers to the shops, cook and eat there while working, and even spend the night in the shops if they found any work there.

These undocumented workers are also blamed for having eroded the image of the Chinese in the Sunset Park area. It is said that since they spend so many hours at work, they could even do without a place to stay. It is a general belief in the Sunset Park Chinese community that several dozen immigrants from Fuzhou would share a single one-bedroom apartment, either only spending the night there or using it just for bathing and other purposes while spending their nights in the garment shops. I heard little sympathy for their plight in my interviews with non-Fujianese workers.

Anecdotal as these stories are, recycled repeatedly, they have fostered a profound prejudice against workers from Fuzhou. This prejudice is so prevalent that it often blinds non-Fujianese workers to class conflicts on the shop floor. For example, I came across a group of Cantonese workers who had just been fired by their employer for refusing to work as many hours as he wanted. Rather than blaming their unscrupulous employer, they blamed their unemployment on the workers from Fuzhou whom their employer had hired for lower rates and longer hours of work.

Although all prejudices are unjustified, factors that have contributed to the prejudice against Fujianese workers are worth exploring. My conversation with a Mrs. Deng, a Taishanese worker and a staunch opponent of "those hateful Fujianese," is revealing:[21]

A: As you know, the Chinese garment shops in Sunset Park have a bad name as sweatshops these days. Our lives are miserable. It was all because of those hateful Fujianese. They have taken our jobs. The bosses love them because they don't have family responsibilities and can work twenty-four hours a day in the shop. They are very greedy. What is in their eyes is only money, money, money. Recently we Cantonese have been losing ground in my shop. The Fujianese are taking over. They are everywhere in my shop.

Q: Could you tell me how many workers from Fuzhou are exactly in your shop?

A: Well, I never counted them, but, never mind, let me try. There are a total of about forty machine operators in my shop, one, two, three, yes, three are Cantonese, three are Mandarin speaking from Shanghai and Wuhan, and . . . [It turned out that only eight out of a total of thirty-five workers in her shop were from Fuzhou and only five out of the nine undocumented workers in her shop came from Fuzhou.]

Q: So the majority in your shop is not Fujianese and the undocumented workers in your shop are not all from Fuzhou.

A: Yes, you are right. My impression was wrong. But still I am nervous about them. Let me tell you something, actually, there are also undocumented workers from Taishan. A village in Taishan is now almost empty, you know, because they had a smuggler in that village, and he had connections with those snakeheads in New York City. The conditions of the undocumented workers from that village are deplorable. I always think that my situation is already miserable enough. [She was collecting welfare benefits at the time of this interview. Her husband just had a surgery and could not work and she had four schoolchildren to raise.] But theirs are even worse. However, I have been told that compared with those from Fuzhou, they seem to be doing fine because many of them have family members or relatives in New York. Those from Fuzhou don't seem to have this advantage and they owe the snakeheads much more money than those from Taishan. Anyway, I should admit that I don't know very much about them because I don't talk to them and they don't talk to me either.

Q: What then made you so angry with them?

A: They work too hard! Whenever there is some work in the shop, especially the easy jobs, they are there. Very often we don't have any work left when we return in the morning. They have finished all the work at night! But we can't do this. We have to go home at night to take care of our families and to have a little rest. We are human beings, you know. But work is money. They have taken away all our money. They are so hateful!

Q: Did your boss ever close the door of the shop at a time like that?

A: No, how could you expect them to do so? Of course not; for the bosses, the sooner they can get the work done the better. So they love those illegal immigrants from Fuzhou. In the past, many garment shop owners had signs on the gates of their shops, saying "Cantonese only," because they were afraid that they would be harassed by the Fujianese gangsters, who are well known for their fearlessness, if they had Fujianese workers in their shops. But now they don't care. They need workers who can work twenty-four hours a day. So the sign on their gates has also changed. It reads "Fujianese only."

The situation has made me really mad. To be honest, who doesn't need money? I too wish that I could work around the clock, if I did not have a family to take care of. I need money too. I don't mind working hard. I was a peasant in China. Rain or shine, I worked outdoors, under conditions much worse than sewing in a garment shop. I wish I could make more money for my family.

But, wait a minute, I sense something wrong with myself in answering your questions. Haven't I somewhat misjudged those undocumented workers from Fuzhou? Yes, I think I have.

Obviously, tension among the workers, ignited by the highly competitive nature of garment organization and accelerated by the manipulation of management, has led to their misjudgment of reality in the shop.

Ungrounded as the stories about undocumented workers from Fuzhou are, generated by a mixture of myth and reality, they take a toll on all workers from the same place. This can be seen in the response of a Ms. Wong:

> I think we immigrants from Fuzhou have been treated very unfairly by our own Chinese community. I am not an illegal immigrant. I came with all the papers as a legal immigrant. In addition, unlike the majority of illegal immigrants from the Fuzhou area, I came from the city and with my family. But still, I am looked at as an illegal immigrant because I came from Fuzhou.
>
> I don't speak Cantonese, so I could not find a job in a restaurant or other place. That's how I ended up working in a garment shop.
>
> My husband and I had a hard time looking for a place for our family to stay when we first came. Landlords from other parts of China refused to rent to us, because we are from Fuzhou. People in the community

said we lived like pigs, with several dozen people usually packed in one apartment but registered under only one or two names. So the landlords were scared. Landlords from Fuzhou did not treat us well either. They charged us much higher rents because they knew that we had no choice.

> My husband and I finally got to rent this place because we decided to speak Mandarin and pretended to be from other parts of China when we first met our landlady, who is Cantonese. Yes, now, she knows that we are from Fuzhou but she doesn't care anymore because we have become very good friends, and she says we are the best tenants she has ever had.[22]

Many immigrant workers from Fuzhou whom I interviewed shared her experience. Although almost all immigrant workers from Fuzhou have been affected by the prejudice against them, the undocumented ones among them are the most victimized. A Mr. Dong's response was typical:

> I don't understand why we should be treated like this! We are human beings too! Yes, we work very hard, because we need money to pay back our debts! Yes, many of us share an apartment, because we want to save money. Do we enjoy our lives in this country? Of course not. We are separated from our families and working underground. We are bullied by our bosses, even including those from Fuzhou. They make us work long hours but pay us much less than other workers in the shops. I don't think anyone would like to live a life like ours! But, still, we are not going to give up because we are working for a better life for our families.
>
> My family lives in a village along the Ming River, and I was a fisherman in the village before I came to the United States. I left my home village because the water there was so seriously polluted that there were no edible fish left. I could not make a living for my family by fishing.
>
> Some people ask, "Why don't you go home if life is so hard for you?" But can we? My family has borrowed a lot of money to send me here. My wife and my kids have pinned their hopes on me, yearning for me to bring them to *meiguo* [the beautiful land, which refers to the United States].
>
> In addition, what will folks in my village say if I return home penniless? I remember when I was in the village, I envied those who returned home from the United States. They looked so successful, squandering money like dirt. I wished I could be like them one day. Of course, after I came to the United States, I got to

know that many of them too had been working in a sweatshop, as I do now. If they can make it, I can make it, too. So, I work hard. It is none of anyone's business if I don't eat, don't sleep, and work nonstop.[23]

The strong desire to improve the well-being of their families, reinforced by a degree of vanity for a glamorous return, led the undocumented workers to leave their native land and fall prey to the sweating system in the United States. Although the living conditions of their native land have "pushed" them out of China, it was the underground economy in the United States that has "pulled" them in and lured them to violate U.S. immigration laws.

The experience of the Fujianese garment workers in Sunset Park reminds one of what has happened to each group of newcomers in New York's garment industry. While the constant search for cheap labor brings in different groups of ethnic workers at different points in history, newcomers are always blamed for the cutthroat competition in the industry. This "finger pointing" takes place even within the same ethnic group. As national characteristics were used in the past as a convenient way of explaining the deterioration of working conditions, today regional and dialectal differences, immigration status, and even the location of one's family have become indexes in the Chinese garment industry for differentiating the old from the new, the "human" from the "inhuman," and thereby the excusers from the excused.[24] Labor solidarity in the community is thus undermined by conflicts of interest among workers, as well as elements in the cultural repertoire of the community.

Will Too Much Law Enforcement Kill the Chinese Garment Industry in New York City?

In the late 1990s, a number of Chinese employers in Sunset Park began to react strongly when the New York State Apparel Industry Task Force carried out its mission to enforce labor laws in the city's garment industry. In October 1996, after the task force completed its investigation and charged many Chinese garment shops with labor violations, Chinese employers in Sunset Park launched a massive demonstration to protest the state operation. They called it "adding salt to the wound." Claiming that the law enforcement agency had unjustly labeled all Chinese shops as "sweatshops," Chinese employers held the state

investigation accountable for causing the further decline of Chinese garment industry in the city by providing manufacturers with the justification for withdrawing their work from the Chinese community.

According to the Chinese employers, manufacturers should be blamed for the deteriorating working conditions in the Chinese shops. Since they suppressed piece rates to such an intolerable degree and demanded such quick production and delivery of finished garments, Chinese employers were forced to reduce the piece rates they offered to their workers and expect them to work longer hours in order to remain competitive. In addition, since manufacturers frequently delayed payments for finished work, Chinese employers had to withhold wages to their own workers. Labor law enforcement will kill the Chinese garment industry, they asserted, because only by reducing wages and extending work hours could the industry survive in the highly competitive environment of garment production in New York.[25]

The Chinese employers' accusation against manufacturers is not entirely groundless, given manufacturers' frantic efforts to reduce the costs of labor in recent years. However, as many concerned individuals in the community have rightly pointed out, even though the Chinese garment industry has been hit hard by the outflow of garment production from the city, the sweatshop conditions in the industry are what allow the manufacturers to put a human face on their move from the city.[26]

What has happened since the State Department of Labor established its Apparel Industry Task Force in 1987? Did the efforts of the Task Force lead to the decline of the Chinese garment industry in New York City? Did the industry really decline?

Statistics show that despite the shrinking of the city's share in the U.S. garment industry, the absolute numbers of Chinese shops and their workforce in the past decade or more did not suggest any sign of decline; indeed, they grew. In the early 1980s, there were approximately 500 Chinese shops in the city, largely concentrated in Manhattan's Chinatown and employing an estimated 25,000 Chinese workers. In 1998, there was an estimate of more than 800 Chinese shops, scattered in various parts of the city and employing more than 30,000 Chinese workers.[27]

One specific segment of the Chinese garment industry has declined significantly in recent years, however. It is the number of the unionized shops in Manhattan's

Chinatown. Between 1992 and 1997 the number of garment shops in Manhattan's Chinatown dropped from 608 to 555 and employment declined from 21,015 to 14,887, a loss of more than 6,000 jobs.[28] The decline in the Manhattan's Chinatown garment industry coincided with the rapid growth of the Chinese garment shops in other parts of the city, in particular, Sunset Park in Brooklyn. Although Manhattan's Chinatown remains the center of the Chinese garment industry in New York, with about 500 Chinese shops still clustered in this area, its importance has been significantly reduced by the rapid growth of the Chinese garment industry in other boroughs.

The decline of Manhattan's Chinatown shops has also led to the weakening of union influence on the entire Chinese garment industry in New York City. In the early 1980s, when shops in Chinatown represented an overwhelming majority of the Chinese garment shops in New York City, more than 90 percent of them were unionized. By the end of the 1990s, it is estimated that the UNITE! Local 23-25 represented only half of the Chinese garment shops in the city.[29] The union's influence has declined even in Manhattan's Chinatown, with the percentage of Chinese union shops dropping from more than 90 percent in the early 1980s to fewer than 80 percent by 1997.[30] As a result, membership of the UNITE! Local 23-25—the largest local of the union, with an 85 percent Chinese membership—dropped from 28,083 in 1992 to 22,995 in 1996, a loss of more than 5,000 members.[31]

Despite problems embedded in the unionization of the Chinatown garment industry in earlier years, there are still many significant differences in working conditions between union and nonunion shops. The shrinking percentage of union shops in the Chinese garment industry indicates that more and more Chinese garment workers have been deprived of the benefits and protection to which union members are entitled. It should, therefore, come as no surprise that labor violations are rampant in many nonunion Chinese shops, which have, in turn, undercut working conditions in the union shops.

There is little doubt that manufacturers and retailers should be held accountable for the deteriorating working conditions in the city's garment industry. However, many individuals in the community are also correct in pointing out that it is the sweating system in some Chinese garment shops that has provided them with the most convenient excuse to pull production out of New York City. This is particularly true when politicians of all stripes have recognized a political advantage in promoting the elimination of sweatshops in the U.S., and manufacturers and retailers have also been pressured by consumer groups as well as labor to distance themselves from contract shops labeled as sweatshops.

The Chinese employers' argument that "too much law enforcement will kill the Chinese garment industry in New York City" reminds one of the situations at the turn of the twentieth century. As Nancy Green has noted, during that time when progressive reformers, labor leaders, and state legislators endeavored to improve labor conditions by passing new legislation and enforcing laws, manufacturers also argued that too many constraints would make the landscape of the garment industry disappear altogether from the city.[32] However, the garment industry remains in New York City, and so will the Chinese garment industry, at least for the decade to come.

Some Reflections

Driven by the search for cheap nonunion labor, runaway shops and sweated labor are not unique to the Chinese garment industry, nor are they new in the history of the city's industry. As early as the 1920s the dispersion of garment shops from Manhattan into various parts of the city already became a peculiar aspect in the landscape of New York's garment industry.[33] The Chinese garment industry, as a major part of the city's industry, is no exception in these regards.

The experience of Chinese workers is in many ways similar to that of their predecessors in the city's garment industry, but there are also differences. Particularly in the 1980s and 1990s, these differences were caused by the challenge of the times rather than simply by the cultural characteristics of the Chinese workers. Garment workers in the first half of the twentieth century were able to enjoy improved working conditions, thanks to the strong influence of labor unions and the continuous growth of the city's garment industry. However, Chinese workers in the late twentieth century were increasingly subjected to abusive labor conditions as the city's industry declined rapidly. Their union, plagued by its entrenched bureaucratic culture, could hardly respond to their needs.

As in the case of the city's garment industry in the early twentieth century, law enforcement and labor organizing remain the two most powerful ways to address the problems in the Chinese garment industry. Both law enforcement agents and labor organizers face the challenge of how to understand the complex reality of the garment industry beyond the highly politicized representations of it in political arenas. However, they also have to address different issues in their own realms.

As Mark Levitan has aptly put it, one of the major factors that has undermined significantly the efforts to eliminate sweated labor in the city is that "there are not enough cops on the beat." Despite the growth of sweated labor in the city's garment industry and the politicians' highly emotional pledges to eliminate it, both New York State and federal investigation teams are severely understaffed. According to Levitan, in 1998, there were only twenty-three investigators in the federal office of the Wage and Hour Division that had responsibility for the entire New York City metropolitan area, and only twenty-three out of thirty-four positions in New York City's Apparel Industry Task Force were filled.[34] As a result, in addition to improving their understanding of the dynamics generated by the highly competitive structure of the garment industry, the history and culture of each ethnic group, and the multifaceted impact of their operations, law enforcement agents still have to battle the shortage of hands in carrying out their tasks, a difficult situation that is indeed not of their own making.

Organized labor faces another type of challenge. Never before has UNITE!, the major labor union of the U.S. garment industry, been under so much pressure to reform itself. The parochialism and the culture of business unionism that UNITE! shares with other traditional trade unions have proved to be impotent in this new age of the global economy. Today, with the impressive growth of the community-based labor organizations in New York's Chinatown and other ethnic communities, the question UNITE! faces is no longer whether it is willing to change but whether the change is adequate to maintain its legitimacy as a labor union in the industry.[35] In this era when capital has already globalized its search for inexpensive labor, how can we develop effective organizing strategies that are not only responsive to the needs of U.S. workers but also allow them to join forces with workers in other parts of the world? This is a question very much on the agendas of trade unions as well as concerned individuals in the Chinese community and the city.

35 Hispanics in the American South and the Transformation of the Poultry Industry

William Kandel • Emilio A. Parrado

WILLIAM KANDEL is a sociologist with the Economic Research Service of the U.S. Department of Agriculture, where he conducts research on the geographic dispersion of immigrants and minorities in rural areas and the role of industrial restructuring in demographic change.

EMILIO A. PARRADO is an associate professor of sociology at the University of Pennsylvania.

FINDINGS FROM THE 2000 CENSUS INDICATE two important trends affecting the Hispanic population. The first is the extraordinarily high rate of Hispanic population increase outside of urban areas over the past decade, with growth rates exceeding both metropolitan and nonmetropolitan growth rates for all other racial and ethnic groups (Cromartie 1999; Pérez 2001). In addition, for the first time in U.S. history, half of all nonmetropolitan Hispanics currently live outside the five southwestern states of Arizona, California, Colorado, New Mexico, and Texas (Cromartie and Kandel 2002). The diversity of new rural areas raises questions about forces outside of the Southwest that are attracting migrants, the Hispanic population's assimilation patterns into communities unaccustomed to dealing with immigration, and the connection between structural economic change and Hispanic population growth.

The main objective of this chapter is to link changes in the poultry industry with the growth of the Hispanic population in nonmetropolitan counties in nine southeastern states: Alabama, Arkansas, Georgia, Louisiana, Mississippi, North Carolina, South Carolina, Tennessee, and Virginia. We document the restructuring of the poultry industry and spatially correlate poultry production and areas of Hispanic settlement. Next, given the impact of these population changes on local communities, we examine two case studies to elaborate more directly on the implications of Hispanic growth for the culture, organization, and everyday life of two nonmetropolitan counties in Virginia

Questions to Consider   In 2000, half our nation's foreign-born were from Latin America. This segment represents only about 10 percent of the total U.S. population—less than the 15 percent of the population made up of foreign-born individuals in 1890, but there is an important difference. Early migrations to the United States consisted of mostly white people from Europe. The most recent waves of immigrants are Latino and Asian. Another major difference from past migration patterns is that Latinos from Mexico and Central America are no longer concentrated only in the states that border Mexico. William Kandel and Emilio Parrado examine the ways Latino migration to the southeastern part of the United States has invigorated regions that had been in economic decline, noting that the economic resurgence has resulted largely from the creation of jobs that are dangerous, dirty, unregulated, and exploitive. Do these jobs present new immigrants with a path toward upward mobility or a life of poverty wages?

and North Carolina. Finally, we derive implications for further research to address relations between Hispanics and other minority groups.

New Destinations in Nonmetropolitan America

The degree to which Hispanic residential settlement has expanded outside of traditional migrant-receiving states can be illustrated with 1990 and 2000 Census data. Table 1

TABLE 1   Nonmetropolitan State Populations Ranked by Hispanic Population Growth

Rank	State	Nonmetro Hispanic Population			Nonmetro Population			Hispanic Share (%)	
		1990	*2000*	*% Change*	*1990*	*2000*	*% Change*	*1990*	*2000*
1	North Carolina	16,714	98,846	491	2,252,775	2,612,257	16	1	4
2	Delaware	1,221	6,915	466	113,229	156,638	38	1	4
3	Alabama	5,198	26,155	403	1,330,857	1,453,233	9	0	2
4	South Carolina	5,830	27,853	378	1,064,088	1,205,050	13	1	2
5	Georgia	26,270	124,296	373	2,126,654	2,519,789	18	1	5
6	Tennessee	7,119	32,737	360	1,579,336	1,842,679	17	0	2
7	Arkansas	9,559	36,504	282	1,310,724	1,434,529	9	1	3
8	Virginia	8,136	28,258	247	1,407,096	1,550,447	10	1	2
9	Mississippi	7,774	24,321	213	1,797,542	1,932,670	8	0	1
10	Minnesota	11,283	34,860	209	1,364,205	1,456,119	7	1	2
11	Iowa	11,807	35,611	202	1,576,857	1,600,191	1	1	2
12	Indiana	12,260	36,921	201	1,581,713	1,690,582	7	1	2
13	Kentucky	8,479	24,465	189	1,905,535	2,068,667	9	0	1
14	Nebraska	16,641	44,564	168	791,050	811,425	3	2	5
15	Wisconsin	11,098	28,893	160	1,560,597	1,723,367	10	1	2
16	Missouri	10,822	27,807	157	1,626,202	1,800,410	11	1	2
17	Pennsylvania	11,004	27,403	149	1,798,645	1,889,525	5	1	1

Sources: U.S. Bureau of the Census 1990, 2000.

Note: Shaded rows are the eight southeastern states highlighted in the study.

presents state-level nonmetropolitan population in absolute and percentage terms for the top seventeen states, sorted by Hispanic population growth rate. Eight of the nine southeastern poultry-producing states appear among the ten states with the fastest-growing nonmetropolitan Hispanic populations; the remaining seven include midwestern states with large beef and pork meatpacking industries.

While Hispanics continue to be overwhelmingly located in metropolitan areas, during the 1990s their nonmetropolitan growth of 70.4 percent exceeded their metropolitan growth rate of 60.4 percent (Cromartie and Kandel 2002). By the decade's end, according to Census 2000 data, Hispanics represented approximately 5.5 percent of the nonmetropolitan population, but had accounted for over 25.0 percent of its growth during the decade. Moreover, Hispanic population growth during the 1990s surpassed total population growth in nonmetropolitan areas in every state except Hawaii.

Widespread media attention on Hispanics in new destinations, however, owes more to their geographic concentration. In 2000, over a third of the 3.2 million rural Hispanics lived in just 109 of all 2,288 nonmetropolitan counties (Cromartie and Kandel 2002).

Since the 1990s, a number of ethnographic studies have documented the immigrants' reception in relatively small communities with few foreign-born residents (Griffith 1995; Guthey 2001; Hernández-León and Zúñiga 2000). The growing nonmetropolitan presence of Hispanics can be attributed to several concurrent trends. First, increased enforcement policies by the Immigration and Naturalization Service to reduce undocumented immigration, ironically, have pushed undocumented migrants away from the traditional migrant-receiving states of California, Arizona, and Texas and into southeastern and midwestern states that previously had few Hispanic migrants (Durand, Massey, and Charvet 2000).

Second, several informants and anecdotal accounts describe labor market saturation in the traditional migrant gateway cities of Los Angeles, Houston, and Chicago and suggest that growing numbers of "pioneer migrants" are seeking employment in new parts of the country. Hispanic settlement in nonmetropolitan areas also was facilitated by an economic recession in the early 1990s in the urban Southwest and other U.S. metropolitan centers. In addition to looking for employment opportunities in nonmetropolitan areas, many Hispanic immigrants may seek to escape problems associated with urban settings, such as poor schools, youth gangs, violence, and expensive and crowded housing.

Third, immigrants are also moving to nontraditional areas because of employers' recruiting efforts to sustain the number of workers needed in industries with less-than-desirable jobs (Johnson-Webb 2002). Consequently, the proportion of Hispanics in industries with low wages and harsh working conditions—meat processing, carpet manufacturing, oil refining, and forestry, to name a few—has increased dramatically since the 1990s (Broadway 1994; Engstrom 2001; Gouveia and Stull 1995; Hernández-León and Zúñiga 2000; Díaz McConnell forthcoming; McDaniel 2002). Because the U.S. Department of Labor does not classify these positions as temporary or highly skilled, firms cannot use special immigration provisions, such as the **H2A** or H2B **visas,** to obtain foreign workers. Information on recruitment practices consists of mostly qualitative journalistic accounts that, nevertheless, describe a host of practices that firms use to recruit workers (Carlin 1999; Katz 1996a, 1996b; Smothers 1996; Taylor and Stein 1999).

An influx of immigrants and newcomers into rural communities often generates conflicting feelings among local residents. Hispanic population growth in many nonmetropolitan places coincides with revived economic activity and reversals of stagnant or declining demographic patterns of previous decades (Broadway 1994; Brown 1993). Nevertheless, immigrant population growth may challenge the ability of rural communities to meet increased demands for social services, particularly schooling for immigrant children, and often increases poverty rates and income inequality (Reed 2001). While immigrants undoubtedly hold the least-desirable and most poorly paid jobs, their presence may exert downward wage pressure on native-born residents working in other low-skilled industries (Massey, Durand, and Malone 2002). Ethnic diversity is viewed by many Americans as a public good that introduces different cultures, languages, and cuisines to native-born residents and reinforces America's cherished self-image as a nation built on the energy and hopes of immigrants (Lapinski et al. 1997). Yet, popular reports suggest a significant level of social conflict in and municipal response from communities that have experienced influxes of immigrants in a relatively short time (Grey 1995; Guthey 2001; Studstill and Nieto-Studstill 2001). We return to these oppositional perspectives that use qualitative descriptions of poultry-producing communities below.

Trends in Poultry Consumption

To see how Hispanic migration to new regions in the southeastern U.S. is related to industrial restructuring, we first consider changes in one of the region's dominant low-skill industries, poultry processing. The poultry industry has been a mainstay in the Southeast for many decades, but since the 1970s, a number of trends have aggregated to influence the demand for labor and, consequently, the settlement patterns of Hispanics. These include (1) increased consumption; (2) increased demand for value-added production; (3) industry consolidation and vertical integration, leading to larger firms; (4) increasing location of production facilities in the Southeast; and (5) the relative attractiveness of meat-processing jobs.

The impetus for changes in the poultry industry began with three consumption trends that strongly influenced the demand for labor. The first was domestic consumption, which grew as the result of two somewhat contradictory trends. In 1977, when beef consumption far exceeded poultry consumption, widely publicized findings from the Framingham Study explicitly outlined health risks associated with red meat in the diet (Dawber 1980). The report's implications were not lost on the American public, which began to eat less beef and more poultry. Per capita poultry consumption doubled between 1977 and 1999, while beef consumption dropped 30 percent over the same period (Figure 1).

Yet, while the Framingham Study represents a milestone event, increasing consumption of fast food in the United States coincided with the growing demand for convenience food. Growth in fast-food franchises such as Kentucky Fried Chicken and marketing through nontraditional outlets such as McDonald's created an enormous

---

H2A visa A visa granted to a foreign national for temporary or agricultural work in the United States.

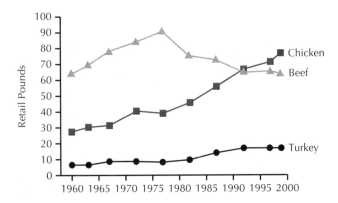

FIGURE 1   Per Capita Consumption of Chicken, Turkey, and Beef, 1960–1999. *Source:*U.S. Department of Agriculture 1960–2000.

demand for a wide variety of chicken products. Within a little over a decade, per capita consumption of poultry surpassed that of beef for the first time since World War II (U.S. Department of Agriculture [USDA] 1960–2000).

The second consumption trend, growth in poultry exports, paralleled domestic demand. Following domestic consumer demand for further-processed products, poultry firms began supplementing their slaughtering plants with production facilities that cut up chickens and packaged the parts for different segments of the market. Breasts and other white meat met domestic consumption preferences, and dark meat was reserved for the export market. By the mid-1970s, chicken exports had increased significantly, and between 1987 and 2002, they skyrocketed, from 500 million to 6.5 billion pounds (USDA 1960–2000).

The demand for more convenient prepared food generated a precipitous increase in the sale of cut-up poultry and an equally precipitous decline in the sale of whole birds. In 1963, the poultry product mix sold in American supermarkets consisted of 85 percent whole birds and 15 percent cut-up poultry products; by 1997, that proportion was exactly the reverse (Ollinger, MacDonald, and Madison 2000). Consequently, many poultry producers appended "cut-up" operations to their meat-processing plants. The structural shift of value-added production from the retail sector (supermarkets) to the production sector (meat-slaughtering and -processing plants) has had profound consequences for labor demand, and, consequently, for labor supply.

Poultry Industry Concentration and Consolidation

Significant increases in both industry concentration and average poultry plant size have accompanied the trend toward increased consumption. Industrial concentration can often be measured using the "four firm concentration ratio," the proportion of total production controlled by the four largest firms (Ollinger, MacDonald, and Madison 2000). For the slaughter of chickens, this ratio more than doubled, from 14 percent to 41 percent, between 1963 and 1992; for turkey slaughter, the ratio increased from 23 percent to 45 percent over the same period. Concentration of poultry-processing firms fluctuated, but it also shows an upward trend during the same period. Data after 1992 are not available, but industry reports suggest that this trend continued throughout the 1990s.

Beginning in the late 1940s, firms began to realize greater scale economies by integrating all facets of operation. Under this mode of production, firms contract out to formerly independent chicken farms and provide the chicks, feed, medicines, veterinary services, and other inputs; contracted growers later return grown birds of consistent size and quality to the plant for slaughter (Bugos 1992). Slaughter operations also became more complex as firms responded to increasingly varied consumer and industry demands by adopting cut-up operations and packaging their products in ready-to-sell containers. By controlling all phases of poultry production, such vertically integrated firms could increase their overall profitability while lowering prices; in real terms, the price of poultry dropped by just over 50 percent between 1960 and 1999 (USDA 1960–2000).

Industry consolidation and production have led to larger plants. To measure the extent of industry consolidation, we use proportion of production from firms with four hundred or more employees, a widely used measure developed by the U.S. Bureau of the Census. Beginning in 1967, the proportion of chicken produced by such large plants tripled; by 1992, they accounted for three-quarters of all poultry slaughter and processing (Ollinger, MacDonald, and Madison 2000).

Increased consumer demand, growing exports, and industry consolidation trends have combined to expand the demand for labor in the poultry industry. Figure 2 presents employment figures in both the poultry industry and the red meat industry for comparison. The above-noted trends in industry consolidation and plant size also occurred to roughly the same extent in the red meat–processing industry (MacDonald et al. 2000). Yet, as Figure 2 demonstrates, employment in the red meat industry has not grown at all since 1970. In contrast, employment in the poultry industry has grown by 150 percent during the same period, and today it actually exceeds that of the beef industry (U.S. Department of Labor [DOL] 1972–2001).

Hispanics in the Poultry Industry

Attracting workers to the poultry industry is a growing challenge. Nationwide, wages paid in the industry are significantly higher than the minimum wage. However, at $7.39 an hour as of 1997, they had not changed in real terms in more than thirty years and remained among the lowest for manufacturing and food industry employment (Hetrick 1994; U.S. Department of Commerce [DOC] 1967–1997). The wage data we used do not specify region, but wages in southern states were probably below the average. Unionization rates, never high in the South in general, have remained well below 5 percent in meat-processing industries since the early 1980s, according to the Current Population Survey. Poultry processing, like other meat processing, is a relatively hazardous and unattractive occupation, with harsh working conditions that have been continually exposed as bad in media and scholarly accounts (Bjerklie 1995; Sun and Escobar 1999). Moreover, economic growth that began in the early 1980s and continued for almost two decades created employment options that diminished relative incentives for working in the poultry industry.

Under these circumstances, it is not surprising that the poultry industry in the southeastern states has experienced difficulty finding a sufficient supply of local workers willing to accept their wages and working conditions. Consequently, the industry's expansion and concentration

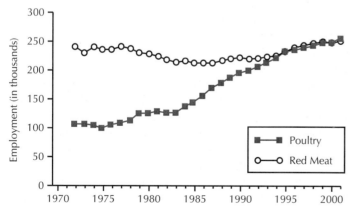

FIGURE 2   Employment in Poultry and Red Meat Products Industry, 1972–2001. *Source:* U.S. Department of Labor, 1972–2001.

within a geographic region whose economic development was already creating an immense demand for low-skilled workers forced the sector to look elsewhere.

As with other low-skill, low-wage industries, the poultry business began actively recruiting immigrants, most coming from Mexico and Central America. Numerous reports have documented the extreme lengths firms have gone to recruit workers for their plants (Barboza 2001). For a region that had low absolute numbers of Hispanics, the size of the poultry-processing workforce has grown significantly.

The results of these recruiting efforts can be seen in Figure 3, which maps the confluence of the location of significant poultry production with Hispanic settlement within the nine southeastern states. Areas denoted by dark gray represent counties in these states which, according to the U.S. Census of Agriculture, ranked, in 1987, 1992, and 1997, within the top 100 chicken-producing counties in the nation. Areas denoted by light gray represent rapid-growth nonmetropolitan Hispanic counties, defined as those in which the Hispanic population grew in absolute and percentage terms by one thousand persons and 150 percent, respectively, between 1990 and 2000. Combining the two patterns yields counties that overlap, shown

in solid color. Note that while the rapid Hispanic growth counties are nonmetropolitan, the poultry-growing counties include nonmetropolitan as well as metropolitan counties. Since the Census of Agriculture data refer to where poultry is raised, as opposed to where it is slaughtered and processed, we would expect most of the poultry counties to be in rural, nonmetropolitan areas. Moreover, because of the economics of poultry transportation, we can reasonably assume that most are close to poultry-processing facilities. Thus, contiguous counties in Figure 3 account for a significant number of all counties highlighted.

The proximity of the Hispanic population to poultry-producing regions is unmistakable, and when combined with the qualitative evidence on recruiting practices, it provides a clear picture of the close connection between the poultry industry and Hispanic population growth. Duplin County in North Carolina, for example, has seen its Hispanic population increase by almost seven thousand since the 1990s, owing in no small part to the demand for labor in its Carolina Turkey, Nash Johnson, and Butterball Turkey plants. The Hispanic population in Hall County, Georgia, has grown by twenty-three thousand, not only because of its proximity to Atlanta, but also because of the poultry plants

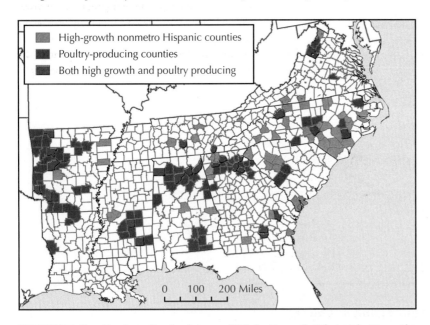

FIGURE 3 **Poultry-Producing and High-Growth Hispanic Counties, Nine Southeastern States, 1990–2000.** *Sources:* U.S. Department of Agriculture, 1987, 1992, 1997; U.S. Bureau of the Census 1990, 2000.

in the town of Gainsville. Marshall County in Alabama employs over three thousand poultry workers, owing to a Tyson Poultry plant in Guntersville, and its Hispanic population has grown by forty-three hundred in the same period.

We have argued that the transformations in this industry correlate with Hispanic population growth in the area. As such, we would expect important changes in the racial and ethnic composition of the labor force working in the poultry industry (see Fugure 4). The National Agricultural Workers Survey, considered the most representative survey of farmworkers, places the Hispanic composition of the agricultural farmworker population at more than double the proportion estimated by the CPS.

Labor Market and Demographic Impacts

A central question driving most arguments in favor of or against immigration is the extent to which Hispanic inflows displace or complement local workers. Particularly important is the interaction between Hispanic employment and labor-market outcomes of other minority groups, especially African Americans. While this question well exceeds the scope of this chapter, we contend that labor-market compositional shifts are intertwined with industrial transformations. When such shifts are applied to the poultry industry, we can expect growth in product demand, industrial concentration, and production variability to facilitate demand for Hispanic workers. In this process, Hispanic population inflows do not necessarily imply worker displacement, because all three macrotrends create additional employment.

Some of these expectations are confirmed by our two case studies. Despite very rapid population growth, the unemployment rate declined in Accomack and Duplin Counties, from 9.6 percent to 4.2 percent, and from 8.6 percent to 5.0 percent, respectively, between 1992 and 2000 (DOC 2002). In fact, in 2001, the unemployment rates in both counties were much lower than the nationwide nonmetropolitan average. In addition, when asked why poultry companies were increasingly hiring Hispanic workers, our informants consistently replied that new jobs were opening up and that nobody else wanted them. This is especially true in Duplin County, with its large, new Carolina Turkeys processing plant. In such a context, the expectation of worker displacement may not be reasonable.

Moreover, informants acknowledged the creation of many skilled positions in, for example, administrative, government, or educational employment for which Hispanics do not qualify. Overall, evidence suggests that while industrial transformations in the poultry industry expanded the demand for low-skilled workers and thus attracted Hispanics, the concomitant and multiplicative effect of economic growth and population increase also facilitated upward occupational mobility and better employment for more educated local residents.

In addition to their racial and ethnic impact on the labor market, Hispanic inflows change the demography

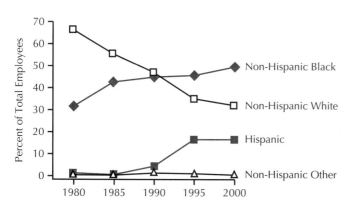

FIGURE 4   **Racial and Ethnic Composition of Meat-Processing Industry Employees, Nine Southeastern States, 1980–2000.** *Source:* U.S. Department of Commerce, 1963–1997.

of Accomack and Duplin Counties in other ways. Two changes are particularly relevant: gender composition and age distribution.

Gender ratios in these counties vary significantly by racial and ethnic group. According to the 2000 Census, the number of men per 100 women in Accomack County is 94 for whites, 85 for blacks, and 166 for Hispanics. In Duplin County, the gender ratio is 95 for whites, 84 for blacks, and 156 for Hispanics. For the United States as a whole, the gender ratio for Hispanics is 105 men per 100 women. Clearly, the two counties are anomalies within the United States, reflecting the predominantly male component of recent immigration there.

In addition, differences in gender ratios highlight a diverging pattern between Hispanics and blacks. The relative undersupply of women in the Hispanic case contradicts their relative oversupply among African Americans. Studies have found that gender ratios have significant importance in marriage patterns, particularly among blacks, making it more difficult for individuals to find partners in contexts of unbalanced gender markets (Lichter, LeClere, and McLaughlin 1991; Lichter et al. 1992). It is unclear how these patterns will affect the marriage behavior of single Hispanic men and women (Oropesa and Lichter 1994; Parrado and Zenteno in press). If Hispanic men try to find partners in the United States, the relative undersupply of Hispanic women may promote interracial marriage. Alternatively, to the extent that marriage is still constrained across racial and ethnic lines, single men may be forced to return to their local communities to find a partner (Parrado 2002). In this scenario, gender imbalances can also affect patterns of return migration. Given their cultural background, forming a union is still a central personal objective among Hispanics, particularly Mexicans. Conversations with immigrants in these communities suggest that gender imbalances and the difficulties in finding a partner, above and beyond economic success, critically affect settlement decisions.

In addition, gender imbalances have an effect on broader sexual behaviors. Immigrant communities are particularly vulnerable to the proliferation of prostitution and other forms of sexually risky behaviors. Use of prostitutes is particularly prevalent among single and married migrants who leave their families behind, which increases the risk of spreading sexually transmitted diseases, including AIDS. In fact, researchers have hypothesized that

migration to the United States is a central contributor to the diffusion of the AIDS epidemic in Mexico, even in rural areas (McQuiston and Parrado 2002; Mishra, Conner, and Magaña 1996). Within the guidelines of the Healthy People objectives established by the U.S. Department of Health and Human Services, Latino organizations in Duplin County have begun to address sexually risky behavior by developing training programs and educational campaigns promoting condom use and AIDS prevention.

The other demographic trait with striking community impacts, age distribution, varies similarly across racial and ethnic groups. Figure 5 plots the percentage of the population in different age groups by race and ethnicity in Duplin County; patterns for Accomack County are very similar. Hispanics represent a much younger population than either blacks or whites. If we look at migration dynamics, the Hispanic percentage peaks very early, at zero to nine years old and again at twenty to twenty-four; it declines at older ages. The two peaks reflect the fact that labor migration is initiated in the early twenties, while children migrate early on or are born following their parents' settlement. The age distribution of blacks and whites is more even, with relatively higher proportions above age forty.

The age distribution of the Hispanic population has affected local communities in these counties in two ways. First, the rapid arrival of school-aged children has increased demand for educational facilities and contributed to school overcrowding. In addition, given the lack of knowledge of English among students and their parents, their arrival has suddenly increased the need for English as a second language (ESL) classes as well as interpreters to facilitate parent-teacher communication. The challenges that immigrants pose for public education systems are particularly relevant; some schools in Duplin County have become 50 percent Hispanic within the space of just a few years. Educators in both counties often find that the new arrivals have little educational background or familiarity with the U.S. educational system. Financing is particularly problematic. In Duplin County, for instance, Carolina Turkeys has recognized the tremendous burden that ESL classes impose on school budgets and now provides financial assistance for their provision.

Second, younger populations increase the prevalence of certain risk behaviors, including crime, alcoholism, and motor vehicle accidents. The higher representation of Hispanics in younger groups makes them particularly

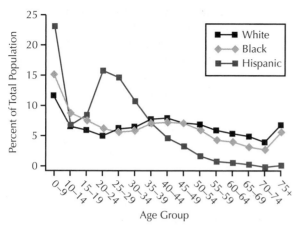

FIGURE 5   **Age Distribution, by Race and Ethnicity, Duplin County, North Carolina, 2000.**
Source: U.S. Bureau of the Census 2000.

vulnerable to such problems, and special programs to address these issues might be required. In addition, age can also affect racial and ethnic relations. Research on neighborhood transitions in cities like Chicago shows that resistance to ethnic change stems not only from the different ethnicity of the arriving population but also from its youth (Flippen 2001). Elderly residents, in particular, may feel threatened by the arrival of younger groups, who they sense can disrupt their way of life or increase their vulnerability to crime. Such feelings can fuel anti-immigrant sentiments among native residents.

Community Impacts and Reaction

Signs of a Hispanic influx into Accomack County in the 1990s generally appeared muted, with only an occasional store sign in Spanish to suggest the presence of Hispanics. From the perspective of social-service delivery, however, indications of a Hispanic presence have cropped up in many small ways. The county court now has a certified court interpreter; previously, anyone with some bilingual ability would be asked to volunteer a translation for defendants. The two health clinics in the area now have Spanish-speaking personnel. The local hospital now uses a commercial phone service to automatically translate conversations. Some county schools have begun canvassing other districts for Spanish-speaking teachers. Employees at the Virginia Employment Commission frequently help Hispanic workers find new or better-paying jobs and often provide emergency

food aid, a benefit frequently requested by those just arriving. However, other services, such as securing a driver's license or alcohol counseling, still require people to find their own translator or interpreter. At the community level, Hispanics now enjoy soccer matches all day each Sunday, a local weekly radio program in Spanish, a small Spanish-language newspaper, and church services in Spanish.

In Duplin County, where community impacts are more noticeable, several institutions have emerged that specifically attend to the needs of the Hispanic population and facilitate assimilation and incorporation into U.S. society. Latinos Unidos, for example, provides information about health and legal issues, offers ESL classes, and trains community members to serve local communities. County government has also adapted to the growing Latino community. A leadership program offered through a local college to promote entrepreneurship is now being reformatted into Spanish, an effort that has had a measurable impact on the emergence of Hispanic businesses. Small grocery, video, and music stores cater directly to the Hispanic community and can easily be identified when visiting the counties. In addition, Carolina Turkeys donated two lots to local Hispanic residents on which to construct churches.

Not surprisingly, Hispanic growth is changing the cultural landscape of these communities, from the types of food and consumer goods being sold in stores to the festivities that are celebrated. These changes sometimes occur in conjunction with shifts within the companies that hire Hispanics.

For instance, in September 2000, workers from Carolina Turkeys in Duplin County organized an international festival to recognize the growing diversity of the county's Hispanic population. During the successful Semana de la Hispanicidad (Hispanic Heritage Week) in 2001, flags from every Latin American country were posted throughout the company's hallways. Following their lead, black employees decided to celebrate African-American Week in January 2002. In 2002, Carolina Turkeys invited the Mexican consul to give a speech in Duplin County, a widely publicized event that drew over three hundred people, garnered media attention for the Latino population, and created closer links with other groups. Many hope these kinds of initiatives will increase awareness and understanding of the growing diversity of Duplin County's population.

None of the informants we interviewed in Accomack and Duplin Counties suggested that the growth of the Hispanic population had caused concern among community residents, and they offered several reasons for the amenable reception. As part of the Delmarva region, Accomack County has been accustomed for decades to hosting migrants who work in the area's vegetable and grain farms. Moreover, the growth of the Hispanic population here was never as dramatic as it has been in some southeastern towns, such as Siler City, North Carolina, or Dalton, Georgia, where large numbers of Hispanics have recently settled in areas with relatively smaller base populations. In addition, there is increasing recognition of the contribution of the Hispanic population to the local economies. As one informant acknowledged, "We understand that without them, our vegetables wouldn't be picked because we don't have domestic workers that can do the job—or that would want to do the job."

When pressed, however, some of our informants mentioned hearing gripes about job competition between the Hispanic migrant workers and local blacks. Another issue that disturbs local residents in both counties is the trafficking in false driver's licenses, particularly because some of the recipients have little or no driving experience. Hispanic residents, on the other hand, are worried about crime and being targeted for robbery, in particular, because they often carry their money with them or keep their savings in their houses instead of in banks.

Racial and ethnic inequalities in access to housing also create tension. In Accomack County, 82 percent of white households live in owner-occupied housing units, compared with 63 percent of black households, and only 36 percent of Hispanic households. Figures for Duplin County are almost identical. In addition, Hispanics tend to live in overcrowded conditions in both counties, with an average household size of 4.5 persons compared with 2.5 for blacks and whites. Management at Carolina Turkeys in Duplin County and the Tyson and Perdue plants in Accomack County recognize the companies' role in providing adequate rental housing for Hispanic workers and have built homes or purchased house trailers close to their plants.

Conclusions and Policy Implications

In this chapter, we have presented evidence to illustrate how industrial restructuring correlates with changes in labor force composition and, by implication, with patterns of international migration and settlement. If similar trends in industrial development occur in other industries, we can expect them to generate further migration and population change. The visibility of prominent manufacturing firms will require greater attention by policy makers to labor-recruitment practices and the growing number of proposals for changing current immigration policies.

Seeing the Big Picture   **How Is Upward Mobility Linked to Education, Occupation, and Immigration?**

In the Appendix, examine the high school dropout rates for Latinos in the Education section (Section I), then look at the occupations where Latinos are clustered, shown in the Occupations section (Section VIII). What does a "good" job require in a postindustrial service economy, and what might this mean for Latino immigrants?

36 Racism and Popular Culture[1]

Danille Dirks • Jennifer Mueller

DANILLE DIRKS is a doctoral candidate at the University of Texas at Austin.

JENNIFER MUELLER is a doctoral candidate at Texas A&M.

Exemplifying the ill will, oppression, and domination of blacks by whites, the merchants of popular culture have used these icons to shackle our psyches as deftly as enslavers once used real chains to shackle our bodies.

—TURNER, 1994, XV

To pretend (as we all do from time to time) that film or television, for example, is a neutral vessel, or contentless, mindless, or unpersuasive, is sheer denial. It is, for better and frequently for worse, one of the major forces in the shaping of our national vision, a chief architect of the modern American sense of identity.

—WILLIAMS, 1996, 194

IN 2002, THE BOARD GAME GHETTOPOLY WAS released, promising "playas" the amusement of "buying stolen properties, pimpin' hoes, building crack houses and projects, paying protection fees, and getting car jacked" (Ghettopoly, 2002). Invoking stereotypical images that implicitly implicate the cultural deficiency of African Americans, the game pieces included a pimp, a hoe, a machine gun, a 40-ounce malt liquor beverage, a marijuana leaf, a basketball, and a piece of crack rock. The game garnered significant positive attention, advertised as a great way to entertain and introduce "homies," coworkers, and children to "ghetto life." Yet, this game must be grasped beyond simple considerations of entertainment

Questions to Consider   It is easy to think that we have moved beyond the extremely racist images that were a mainstay of television's early years. The mammy stereotype of Aunt Jemima selling pancakes, the Mexican Frito Bandito criminal advertising corn chips, and the heavily accented Chinese dry cleaner selling laundry soap seem like antiquated relics of television's past. Dirks and Mueller argue that although the extremely offensive racist imagery once so common on television may have been discarded, it has been replaced with equally problematic images that in turn shape how individuals view popular culture. What is more problematic is that many of these racist and stereotypical images are now so ingrained in popular culture that they appear to be normal representations of these groups. Think for a moment of the shows, sports mascots, television characters, or advertisements that draw on stereotypes to convey a particular message. To what extent are those images now such a part of popular culture that these stereotypes seem to be an accurate depiction of an entire group?

or play. Ghettopoly must be added to the wide array of popular culture productions that exist as contemporary reflections of the continual distortion and misappropriation of so-called blackness by dominant groups in the United States. In this paper, we seek to illustrate the many ways in which racist popular culture images persist today, and how their continued existence reflects a white thirst for blackness that seems unquenchable. We adopt the view that marks popular culture as pedagogical and, against the backdrop of this assumption, consider what the racial lessons are that we learn from popular culture.

The concept of race in American social life is a concept under constant contestation, giving it no single fixed meaning in defining racial boundaries, hierarchies, and images (Guerrero, 1993). Despite this fluidity, both historically and today, ideas about race have dictated notions about white superiority as much as they have about black inferiority. Although ideas about race are in their rawest forms fictions of our collective imagination, they have real and meaningful consequences—economic, psychological, and otherwise. Popular culture has had a centuries-old history of communicating racist representations of blackness in Western societies, giving it the power to distort, shape, and create reality, often blurring the lines between reality and fiction (Baudrillard, 1981, 1989; Pieterse, 1992). We argue that these productions do not exist without consequences—they permeate every aspect of our daily lives.

Popular culture has served as part of the ideological and material apparatus of social life for as long as it has existed. Most cultural theorists today disavow the polarities of popular culture as merely pure and innocent entertainment or as an uncontested instrument for executing top-down domination, adopting instead, as Kellner (1995) does, the model of media cultural texts as complex artifacts that embody social and political discourses. The power of popular culture lies in its ability to distort, shape, and produce reality, dictating the ways in which we think, feel, and operate in the social world (Kellner). And while popular culture certainly exists in many ways as a contested terrain in the sense that Kellner asserts, it has been frequently used hegemonically, as an effective pedagogical tool of dominant classes in Western culture, supporting the lessons that keep structural inequalities safely in place (hooks, 1996).

As theorists like Kellner (1995) and Guerrero (1993) have asserted, this is the promise and predicament of

popular culture. Contemporary media culture certainly provides a form for the reproduction of power relations based in racism (and classism and sexism), yet its very fluidity and contestation provide some space and resource for struggle and resistance. This is the sole reason why challenging racist representations—in their various recycled and newer transformations—is crucial if we are truly, vigorously devoted to making social change a reality.

Historical Background

In the United States, popular culture has assisted in the maintenance of a white supremacist racial hierarchy since its American inception. We provide a brief history of American popular culture's racist past to show that there is nothing creative about present-day images, ideas, or material goods manufactured by today's merchants of culture. Antiblack images are central to our historical analysis because, as Guerrero (1993) has contended, "Blacks have been subordinated, marginalized, positioned, and devalued in every possible manner to glorify and relentlessly hold in place the white-dominated order and racial hierarchy of American society" (p. 2). This is certainly not to deny a long history of exploitation and domination for other groups in the United States, particularly among popular culture ideas and images; yet we see antiblack ideology and iconography as structurally embedded in every aspect of American social life—historically and today. In many respects, this ideology contains the racial "yardstick" by which other groups have been and continue to be measured, and elevated or devalued. We hope to show that contemporary popular cultural ideas and images are recycled products and remnants of dominant ideologies past—ideologies that exploited, distorted, and oppressed people of color historically and continue to do so today. As popular culture is constantly reinventing itself under the guise of innovation, a historical understanding of these ideas and images is crucial to deconstructing their continued existence today as simply reformations of such deeply rooted ideologies, rather than truly novel inventions.

Contemptible Collectibles

Although the sale of actual African Americans ended in 1865 with the official demise of the state-supported U.S. slavery system, the consumption of blackness through popular culture ideas, images, and material goods marked an easy, if figurative, transition in the postbellum South. From black-faced caricatures found on postcards, children's toys, and household items to 19th-century minstrelsy, these examples provide only a smattering of the racist iconography and ideology found throughout Western culture. As such, images of coons, pickaninnies, mammies, bucks, and Uncle Toms were born, to live out lives distorting the image of black Americans for centuries to come.

In the United States, popular racist stereotypes of the Jim Crow era easily became the faces of mass-produced lawn ornaments, kitchen items, postcards, and children's toys such as noisemakers, dolls, and costumes. Many of the material goods depicting black personas from this time, such as the mammy or pickaninny, have been mistakenly called "Black Americana," suggesting that these items come from the creative endeavors of black Americans themselves. However, this description is as incorrect as it is insulting, leading one author to more accurately describe them as "contemptible collectibles" (Turner, 1994). Perversely, these items have become immensely popular among collectors, with some originals of the era fetching several thousands of dollars apiece.

Manufacturers of everything from coffee, hair products, and detergents plastered the insidious iconography on virtually every type of household product available. Particularly prevalent was the image of the "coon," who, in addition to being depicted as unreliable, lazy, stupid, and child-like, was known for his "quaking," superstitious nature, making him an ideal target. Similar characterizations included the wide-eyed pickaninny and the image of the mammy (Skal, 2002). Mammy—the rotund, smiling, benevolent, uniformed black woman—is by far the most popularly disseminated contemptible collectible of all. Today she continues to happily oversee our pancakes and waffles as Aunt Jemima. For all of her popularity, no other image has been so historically identified as a fiction of white imagination than she. Social historians have pointed out that the existence of any "real" mammies in the antebellum South would have been very few and far between; her being overweight would be equally implausible given the severe rationing of food for slaves (Clinton, 1982; Turner, 1994). Yet the image of this obsequious and docile black woman has survived only to become immortalized through the mass production (and reproduction) of thousands of household and kitchen items made for "sufficiently demented homemakers" (Turner, 42).

Postcards depicting black Americans in various states of childishness and need have provided some of the most interesting snapshots of white thinking and imagination of the time. As if it were an aesthetic rule, adults and children were regularly depicted in print media coupled with watermelons. Even more disturbing is the vast collection of alligator-themed postcards and "artwork" depicting small black children and infants being chased or ready to be devoured by the toothy creatures. Apparently both alligators and their white American counterparts have an insatiable appetite for distorted images of society's most vulnerable members. Consumption here, in the Freudian and an all-too-literal sense, cannot be understated among this genre of "memorabilia."

Racist artifacts of the time were not limited to the enjoyment of adults, however, as children's toys represent some of the more pernicious forms of transmission of racist thought and belief. Dress-up items for children allowed them to "play at being a 'Negro'," including wigs, masks, and a "Negro make-up outfit," described in a 1912 Sears display as "the funniest and most laughable outfit ever sold" (Wilkinson, 1974, 105). Indeed, blackface Halloween masks and costumes are among the numerous racist artifacts created and marketed during the 19th-century Jim Crow era, and popularly collected as Americana memorabilia today (Pilgrim, 2001).

The Only True American Drama

Many 19th-century Americans proudly boasted of minstrelsy as the first distinct form of American entertainment, laying claim to it as "our only original American institution" (Pilgrim, 2000; Toll, 1974, v). In many respects, it might be considered the earliest form of American popular culture. Despite the romantic sound of such historicized ideas, to most people such entertainment was more simply referred to as "nigger minstrelsy" or "coon shows." The typical minstrel show was put on by a troupe of white men in burnt cork blackface makeup, performing song, dance, and comedy claiming to be authentically "Negro." Such minstrels created extreme caricatures through heavy mocking dialect, bulging eyes, and gaping lips, easily reinforcing and popularizing beliefs that blacks were inherently lazy, dim-witted, subhuman, inferior, and unworthy of integration, to their almost exclusively white audiences (Feagin, 2000; Pilgrim, 2000; Toll, 1974).

Minstrel shows swept the nation in the 1840s, even performing for the "Especial Amusement of the President of the United States" (including Abraham Lincoln and John Tyler's inauguration), making them one of the most popular forms of entertainment in the country for over half a century (Roediger, 1991; Toll, 1974).

Toward the later half of the 19th century, black Americans began replacing white minstrels in order to make a living on the stage, blackening their own faces and engaging in similarly exaggerated performances. This tragic and ironic twist greatly enhanced the credibility of minstrel images of black Americans, as white audiences perceived black minstrels as "genuine Negroes" displaying what were simply "natural impulses" (Toll, 1974, 202). Clearly, the degrading and dehumanizing minstrel portrayals set up ideas that were as much about whiteness as blackness, highlighting white virtue against the clear contrast of the inferior black (Feagin, 2000). As Toll explains, characterizations of blacks as indolent, improvident, immature, and unintelligent were "the very antithesis of what white men liked to believe about themselves," and as such served not only as "ego-boosting scapegoats for whites" but also as confirmation that blacks could not play a constructive role in society and should remain segregated (p. 71).

Historical Images Today

In 1987, independent filmmaker Marlon Riggs completed *Ethnic Notions,* an award-winning documentary on contemptible collectible objects and other minstrelsy media with the premise that: "Contained in these cultural images is the history of our national conscience: a conscience striving to reconcile the paradox of racism in a nation founded on human equality—a conscience coping with this profound contradiction through caricature" (*Ethnic Notions,* 1987). It begs an answer to the questions, why did such images exist in the first place: Who made them and why they have enjoyed such immense popularity both historically and continuing into contemporary society? And, what does their continued popularity say about racial relations in the United States today?

During early American history, popular culture reflected and supported an ideology that sought to romanticize conditions of slavery—particularly when its eradication came into focus. As people worked to dismantle the U.S. slavery system, the rise of dehumanizing images such as the contented Sambo and coon

served to whitewash the depravity of plantation life and ease white consciences. These caricatures mirrored the prevailing belief that slaves were not human, therefore not deserving of full and free citizenship. Over time researchers have assigned additional functions to the continually expanding dehumanizing characterizations, suggesting, for instance, that they assuaged white male economic insecurity or created solidarity for the KKK by asserting the image of black male rapist (Gayle, 1976; Guerrero, 1993).

In probing the historical rationales underlying the creation and maintenance of such racist iconography, it is highly significant to consider the continued popularity of their original forms during an age where blacks are no longer slaves or non-citizens. These images continue to be manufactured, and the reproduction and sale of contemptible collectibles are in full swing. Our own eBay search using the terms "nigger" and "mammy" in the early weeks of 2006 found thousands of items—original and reproduction—of jolly nigger banks, mammy salt and pepper shakers, and postcards with watermelons and pickaninnies in every shape and style imaginable. Apparently, as Turner (1994) writes, "We still live in a world eager to develop new reasons and rationales for commodifying African Americans—past and present" (p. 30).

Indeed, other authors have turned to identifying what they consider contemporary examples of recycled racial themes. For instance, Grindstaff (2004) points to daytime talk shows, and Lhamon (1998), hip hop, as examples of modern-day minstrelsy. Similarly, Bogle (2000 [1973]) in tracing black representations in movies from 1903's *Uncle Tom's Cabin* through the end of the 20th century, notes the regular resurfacing of the old racial stereotypes among contemporary characters, even in the face of seeming progress.

Present-Day Realities

Despite the advances made during the Civil Rights movement, we live in a post–Civil Rights era where social progress has been co-opted to help deny the existence of racism today. We view contemporary forms of racist popular culture as dangerous not only for the same reasons they were in the past, but also because we live in a slippery, self-congratulatory era where we can easily look back at popular images of the past with such disdain, that it temporarily blinds most from its subtle, yet equally egregious, forms today. Delgado and Stephancic (1992) suggest that "We acquiesce in today's version with little realization that it is wrong, that a later generation will 'How could they?' about us. . . . [Racism] of our own time strikes us, if at all, as unexceptional, trivial, or well within literary license" (p. 1278).

Yet racism in popular culture has not gone uncontested, and in recent years well-organized and successful protests have risen up in various forms against corporations, athletic organizations, and other purveyors of racialized popular media. However, for as many successful protests, decades-long battles continue today to end the dehumanizing portrayals of marginalized groups in the United States. We begin by focusing on some recent successes gained in fighting against distorted and dangerous images as exemplary of the context of contestation that has and can exist in contemporary media culture. As others have asked, if future generations are to look back on the images and iconography current today, what will they have to say? And what we will say about our own roles in rallying against them?

Contested Images

Corporate entities, in their push for profits, have misappropriated images of the racialized Other for as long as they have existed. Yet these images have not gone uncontested, and social organizing around these movements has been swift and well-organized, despite severe corporate foot dragging in recent decades. One example comes from Frito-Lay's 1967 introduction of the Frito Bandito—a greasy, pudgy character who would steal Anglos' Frito corn chips at gunpoint (Noriega, 2000). The company launched several commercials depicting the corporate mascot singing: "Ayiee, yie-yie-yieeee/I am dee Frito Bandito/I love Frito's Corn Chips/I love dem I do/I love Frito's Corn Chips/I take dem from you."

Chicano groups such as the National Mexican-American Anti-Defamation Committee and Involvement of Mexican-Americans in Gainful Endeavors organized and appealed to Frito-Lay on moral grounds to remove the negative image and replace it with a more positive one. In response, Frito-Lay "sanitized" the *bandito*, deciding to remove his gun and his gold tooth, making him less grimacing—an utter disregard for the moral pleas that the image was damaging to Mexican Americans. It was only after the threat of a class action anti-defamation lawsuit

on behalf of the 6.1 million Mexican Americans in the United States at the time that Frito-Lay dropped the corporate mascot, after four years of immense profiteering (Carrillo, 2003; Noriega, 2000).

More recently in 2003 retail giant Abercrombie and Fitch launched a line of T-shirts featuring screen printed images of slant-eyed, smiling caricatures donning rice hats. Shirts with slogans such as "Wong Brothers Laundry Service: Two Wongs Make It White" led to swift online activism and organizing among Asian American and student groups across the United States. In response to the massive protests—both online letter and petition campaigns and on-site protesting across American shopping malls—Abercrombie and Fitch finally agreed to pull the shirts from stores. However, this reluctant action was taken with a weak non-apology by the company spokesperson: "We personally thought Asians would love this T-shirt. We are truly and deeply sorry we've offended people. . . . We never single out anyone group to poke fun at. We poke fun at everybody, from women to flight attendants to baggage handlers, to football coaches, to Irish Americans to snow skiers. There's really no group we haven't teased" (Strasburg, 2002). An explanation such as this reveals an utter disregard for persons of Asian descent by attempting to level the racial playing field, effectively dismissing the exploited and often tragic existence of Asian Americans in the United States. By providing a list of groups also allegedly targeted (openly revealing sexist and classist notions), it suggests that any group who takes offense simply cannot take a joke, deflecting any wrongdoing away from the company itself. Yet this attempt at racial innocence became even more thinly veiled in 2005, when the company was ordered to pay $40 million in a class action settlement for the company's widespread racial, ethnic, and gender hiring discrimination (Lieff, Cabniser, Heimann, & Bernstein, 2005).

Some of the most widely contested and long-standing controversies over dehumanizing and degrading images are those surrounding athletic team mascots. American Indians have been widely targeted with the naming of teams, such as the Washington Redskins, Cleveland Indians, and Atlanta Braves. Images of so-called Indianness are inaccurate and inappropriate cultural fictions of the white imagination that are disturbing on several levels. First, these images continue today despite decades-long fights over their use. Second, like blackface, they perpetuate a perverse means by which whites can "play Indian" during halftime spectacles (Deloria, 1998). Third, these images relegate Native Americans to the "mascot slot," denying them a meaningful sociopolitical identity in American public life (Strong, 2004; Trouillot, 1991). Overall, the continued existence of these racist representations—despite other images that have been resisted and retired—indicate that white America is so deeply invested in these cultural inventions, that they are unconcerned if the images bear any resemblance to reality as long as they can still "participate" in the mythologized dances, rituals, and movements they have come to love so dearly. Whites' resistance reflects an unjust sense of entitlement to "owning" these images, as well as their devotion to profit from the continued use of these racist representations.

Social movements against Native American mascot images remain some of the most visible and arguably most successful examples of American Indian activism and sociocultural resurgence, and over 1,000 mascot images have been retired as a result (King & Springwood, 2001). Much of this protest has invoked comparison among other marginalized groups, stating that groups such as the "Pittsburgh Negroes, the Kansas City Jews, and the San Diego Caucasians" would cause outrage, asking why these logos continue to exist for Native Americans (Strong, 2004, 81). Using this logic, a University of Northern Colorado intramural basketball team called themselves "The Fighting Whities," in protest of a local high school team, The Fighting Reds. In one year, they raised over $100,000 for scholarships for American Indians, selling clothing items with their name and mascot, a 1950s-style caricature of a middle-aged white man in a suit, bearing the phrase "Every thang's gonna be all white!" (Rosenberg, 2002).

Despite these successes, there is clear evidence that the critical evaluation and challenge of racist representations is more often the exception than the rule—both in real life as well as on screen. In the next section, we trace the twisted fate depicted in Spike Lee's film *Bamboozled* (2000) and the tumultuous, real-life events leading to the demise of black comedian Dave Chappelle's wildly successful Comedy Central sketch show. We offer this examination because their deep connection provides an excellent example of the boundaries of reality colliding and blurring with fiction.

Satire Appropriated: Bamboozled *and* Chappelle's Show

Released in 2000, Spike Lee's *Bamboozled* satirically restages minstrelsy to show that contemporary white America has no interest in seeing black Americans portrayed on television as anything more than buffoons.[2] Lee's film challenges modern racial ideology that encourages the belief that we have progressed far beyond the days of black-faced minstrel shows. The film is posthumously narrated by the main character, Pierre Delacroix, an African American television network executive "**buppie**" recklessly determined to get fired from his job at a major network where they are looking to improve a ratings slump by creating something "dope, sexy, and funny." Seeking to be laid off, he pitches what he thinks is an outrageously offensive and racist pilot, *Mantan: The New Millennium Minstrel Show,* to his white boss, Thomas Dunwitty. To his surprise, Dunwitty jumps on the idea, quickly turning the pilot into a show about "two real coons" who are "keepin' it real."

Dunwitty, who boasts being blacker than Delacroix because he has an African American wife and two biracial children, sets *Mantan: The New Millennium Minstrel Show* in a watermelon (or "nigger apple") patch with a house band, The Alabama Porch Monkeys. The show, like its historical minstrel predecessors, chronicles the dull-witted and unlucky antics of tap-dancing Mantan and his sidekick, Sleep 'n' Eat. The live-audience sitcom garners a wildly successful following across America, and by the end of the film, audience members of all races don blackface, exclaiming they are "real niggers." Quickly the satire is lost—if it ever existed—and Delacroix is loved by all for his "creative genius" and the fact that "the show can't be racist because he's black." Finally unshackled to laugh freely at some of the most degrading images of black Americans of all time, America becomes obsessed with *Mantan,* delighting in and restaging a nostalgic era where, "a man could be a man, a woman could be a woman, and a nigger knew his place."

Interestingly, before *Bamboozled* had been released, *The New York Times* blocked its ad of a watermelon-eating pickaninny, perhaps over concern that the satire would be lost on its readers. Blending real life with fiction, the allure of *Bamboozled* is its seamless juxtaposition of

Buppie Black Urban Professional

historical reality with a fictional sociopolitical future fantasy. Weaving images of *Ethnic Notions* (1987) throughout, *Bamboozled* reminds its viewers that these racist icons from the not-so-distant past can, and have been, resurrected with relative ease. Ironically, if not surprisingly, *Bamboozled's* art-imitating-life approach was brought to fruition with the tremendous success of African American comedian Dave Chappelle's Comedy Central Network program, *Chappelle's Show.*

With sketches like "The Racial Draft," "The Niggar Family," and "The Life of Clayton Bigsby" (a blind white supremacist unaware that he is a black man), *Chappelle's Show* tackled American racial issues head-on with satire and humor—enjoying two wildly successful seasons of episodes dealing with race, sex, and celebrity. Having signed a $50-million contract with Comedy Central, fans were shocked when the third season was delayed indefinitely in early 2005 amidst rumors that Chappelle had become drug addicted and mentally unstable. During this time of delay and uncertainty, it became clear how much white America had come to "love"—and *need*—*Chappelle's Show.* To be sure, *Chappelle's Show* enjoyed a multiracial audience, and white fans were not the only ones bemoaning its absence. Chappelle's smart satire provided black Americans an outlet for expressing common racial frustration. White audiences had an arguably different attraction to the material, however, as the program not only provided white America with the license to play out their black alter egos while exclaiming, "I'm Rick James, bitch!" but also finally created a space where white Americans could safely—and openly—laugh at some of their most inner thoughts on race and racism.[3]

Perhaps, then, it is unsurprising to learn that these were the precise reasons Chappelle had come to question his role in bringing sharp-witted satire into millions of white American homes only to have the message destroyed upon delivery. In a revealing interview done to dismiss rumors of his disappearance, Chappelle described one of his last tapings, where he played the role of a black-faced pixie trying to get other black pixies to act in stereotypical ways. Discussing his reaction to one spectator, a white man laughing too loudly, Chappelle revealed, "When he laughed, it made me uncomfortable. As a matter of fact, that was the last thing I shot . . . because my head almost exploded" (Farley, 2005).

Comedy Central and Chappelle's long-time, white writing partner, Neal Brennan, failed to understand the underlying reasons for concern over how the show was being received. Brennan said, "We'd write it. He'd love it, say, 'I can't wait to do it.' We'd shoot it, and then at some point he'd start saying, 'This sketch is racist, and I don't want this on the air.' And I was like, 'You like this sketch. What do you mean?' There was this confusing contradictory thing: he was calling his own writing racist." Similar to the fate of *Bamboozled's* Delacroix, white America renders black artists incapable of determining the artistic or problematic merits of their own work. White America takes on a paternalistic role in deciding what is racist and not and are least likely to make these types of judgments fairly and without their own best interests—psychological or economic—at heart. The fictional Delacroix and the real Dave Chappelle both clearly came to understand the difficult lesson pinpointed by critical film analyst, Armond White (1995): "A Black filmmaker can take nothing for granted" (p. 62).

To be sure, this lesson extends to people of color in most if not all genres of popular media production. And ultimately, as Chappelle himself noted, in the multinational media outlet, those not willing to tow the line are replaceable when it is the message, and perhaps more importantly, the dollar hanging in the balance. Reflecting on the end of the second season, the actor portended his own fate, "I was replaceable. I'm still replaceable now. That's what's so crazy about show business". In *Bamboozled,* when Mantan and Sleep 'n' Eat finally decide to walk away from the degrading show, their characters are quickly replaced by another desperate actor waiting in the wings, Honey Cut. Comedy Central, too, has attempted to fill the gap left by Chappelle with a new show, *Mind of Mencia.* This program features Latino comic Carlos Mencia, who shares his own brand of racial humor with the Comedy Central audience. As the show's Web page promises, consumers can "enter Carlos Mencia's mind and immerse themselves in his unique, unflinching take on the world." While *Mind of Mencia* attempts to work within the racial satire formula that made Chappelle famous, its execution is much less analytical and nuanced, relying on blatant stereotypes to make fun of everyone from Mexican immigrants to the disabled. And, indeed, this show appeals to the fans of *Chappelle* who missed the point of his smart satire.

Beyond *Mencia,* at the time of this writing, Comedy Central had promised its viewers a third season of *Chappelle's Show*—with or without Chappelle (who traditionally introduced each show to a live audience following a monologue), highlighting yet again the economic interests at stake. Literally scrapping together pieces from unused filming from the previous two seasons, the network is giving the show a life of its own to feed the Chappelle-hungry white audiences. Here, we see the fates of *Mantan* and *Chappelle's Show* end the same: the show taking on a life of its own, supported only by a white thirst for the laughter and the expense at which it tolls black Americans in real life, even in the absence of its creators. With or without Chappelle, it appears as if he will be just fine, reflecting, "I want to make sure I'm *dancing and not shuffling*. . . . Your soul is priceless" (Farley, 2005).

Addressing Race in Film

Analysts like Bogle (2000 [1973]), Kellner (1995), Vera and Gordon (2003), White (1995), and others have each taken on the important task of critically addressing the varied ways in which race is portrayed, often problematically, in the popular media of film. While it is beyond the scope of this paper to recite their important contributions here, we wish to consider two very recent examples of race in film that present arguably new formats for conveying recycled ideas. For many years following the Civil Rights movements of the 1960s, a politically correct discourse pushed frank talk about race into the corners of popular culture. This was precisely what made the classic *Guess Who's Coming to Dinner?* (1967) such a seemingly groundbreaking work for its time. In many respects, and as *Chappelle's Show* demonstrated for TV media, it appears that we have moved into a new post–Civil Rights era where it has become fashionable to talk about race, as a more "genuine" proof that we are a progressive society. In this way, 2005's feature film *Crash* is for movies what *Chappelle's Show* is for television.

The Oscar award–winning motion picture drama *Crash* (2005) was hailed by critics and audiences alike for its seemingly forthright treatment of race in America. It marked itself unafraid to take on the explicit bigotry of whites, from the heinous abuses of a racist white cop to the purse-clutching prejudices of a wealthy white woman. Perhaps more importantly, however, was *Crash's* seeming

equal-opportunity-racism message—not only were the white characters regular espousers of racist dialogue, but the many characters of color were as well. Nearly all characters in this movie, including African Americans, Latino Americans, Asian Americans, and Arab Americans, participated in interpersonal interactions that are traditionally labeled racist. The net effect is a leveling of the racial playing field. White moviegoers certainly made uncomfortable by the white characters' forthrightness with their prejudices can be comforted in the notion that racism is not a white problem, but rather a human problem. We all must fight against our tendencies to stereotype—whites are no longer the lonely oppressors, but rather engaged in a common struggle against the detached evil of racism.

While *Crash* undoubtedly addresses race in a more candid way than is traditionally done in Hollywood, it is precisely its claim of being progressive that marks it dangerous. What appears to be an enlightened take is in many respects a new form of whitewashing. Liberal whites, in particular, will feel validated by their brave willingness to face the uncomfortable. In another 2005 film, we see the same ideas offered through humor. The remake of *Guess Who's Coming to Dinner* (1967), offers a racial role reversal in *Guess Who.* Similar to its predecessor, *Guess Who* portrays a middle-class black family unwilling to accept their daughter's white boyfriend.

Laughter is the vehicle that makes this film—and its messages about race—appear innocuous at best, hardly as controversial as its predecessor. Yet, with the portrayal of a black father unwittingly prejudiced against a white boyfriend, it levels the racial playing field—teaching us that black people are just as racist and prejudiced as white people, a problematic message that resonates well among those who believe that "reverse discrimination" and "reverse racism" are alive and well. Here, historical issues regarding racism are shallowly presented and go unchallenged (Vera & Gordon, 2005). Films like *Crash* and *Guess Who* that focus on interpersonal interactions, and present equal-opportunity-racism themes, effectively dismiss the long, structured, systemic legacy of white supremacy in the United States. These new forms of erasure make certain histories—and people—invisible, and this is particularly problematic for the future of racial relations not only in the United States, but globally as well.

Something Old, Something New, Something Borrowed, Something . . .

Under critical historical examination, images of "blackness" found in popular culture today have shifted very little from their historical counterparts. Yet, as Patricia Hill Collins (2004) explains, "In modern America, where community institutions of all sorts have eroded, popular culture has increased in importance as a source of information and ideas" (p. 121). This is particularly problematic for black American youth, as popular culture has come to authoritatively fill the void where other institutions that could "help them navigate the challenges of social inequality" are beginning to disappear (p. 121).

Although whites have appropriated black popular culture throughout history, in recent decades it has reached new heights of global commodification—circulating problematic ideas about race, class, gender, and sexuality domestically and globally. Black women's roles in popular culture have been limited to mammies, matriarchs, jezebels, or welfare queens, yet we have seen these images being repackaged for contemporary consumption and global exportation (Collins, 2001). Contemporary hip hop portrays black women—lyrically and visually—as golddiggers and sexualized bitches who like to "get a freak on," an updated form of the jezebe1 (Collins, 2004).

Sexualized images of black men have also been repackaged for contemporary popular consumption as well, being touted as a way of life for many black American young men. Bell Hooks (2004) writes that, "Gangsta culture is the essence of patriarchal masculinity. Popular culture tells young black males that only the predator will survive" (p. 27). Today's *criminal-blackman* is not much different from the historical stereotype of bucks who are "always big, baadddd niggers, oversexed and savage, violent and frenzied as they lust for white flesh" (Bogle, 2000 [1973], 13; Russell, 2001). Currently, sexualized images of black femininity and black masculinity have become highly marketable yet remain historically rooted in an intersectional racialized sexism. "These controlling images are designed to make racism, sexism, poverty, and other forms of injustice appear to be natural, normal, and inevitable parts of everyday life" (Collins, 2001, 69). Such lessons are not only learned all too well domestically, but globally as well, with their continued popularity and exportation.

The Future of Racism and Popular Culture

Pieterse (1992) tells us, "The racism that [has] developed is not an American or European one, but a Western one" (p. 9). With the global exportation of Western popular culture, it is no surprise that racist Western iconography and ideology have enjoyed immense popularity as well. The Hollywood film industry is a prime example of this problematic globalization of images, with U.S. studios controlling three-quarters of the distribution market outside the United States (Movie Revenues, 2006). When Disney's Uncle Remus tale, *Song of the South* (1946), was highly contested for its "this is how the niggers sing" jubilant portrayal of plantation life, its distribution was blocked in the United States after serious protest (Bernstein, 1996; Neupert, 2001; Schaffer, 1996; Vera & Gordon, 2003). However, the film was quickly made available for global distribution, making it the highest-grossing film in 1946 with $56.4 million in worldwide sales (World Wide Box Office, 2006).

Not to let the fantastic lore of Uncle Remus' tales be forgotten, in 1992 Walt Disney World resurrected Critter Country to create the animated roller coaster ride Splash Mountain (Schaffer, 1996). Children and adults 40 inches and taller from all over the world can "hop a hollowed-out log to follow Brer Rabbit's mischievous escapades as he tries to flee the clutches of Brer Fox and Brer Bear until you plunge five stories off Chick-a-pin Hill! 'It's the truth. It's actual. Everything is satisfactual. It's a zip a dee doo dah day!'" (Walt Disney World, 2006). Like other stories manufactured under the Disneyfication project, *Song of the South* and Splash Mountain serve to disguise the horrors of American slavery from visitors to Disney World and Disneyland in the United States, but also from visitors to Tokyo Disneyland and, in 2006, Hong Kong Disneyland (Walt Disney World, 2006; Wasko, 2001). While the antebellum American South may be far off the radars of visitors to such spectacles, *Song of the South* and Splash Mountain represent the height of Baudrillard's (1992) sense of whitewashed and sanitized American **simulacra,** to be sure.

Global recycling of contested antiblack images and ideas has been found in numerous other examples. In

---

Simulacra a diluted or superficial representation of something else (i.e. Main street in Disneyworld).

2003, the Bubble Sisters, an all-female quartet in Korea, made headlines when they used a "blackface gimmick" to gain popularity among pop music fans. Performing in black-face makeup, afros, grotesquely caricatured rubber lips, and dancing in pajamas, the group received airtime from several sources, including MTV Korea, leading to swift protests against the Bubble Sisters and their producers (Hodges, 2003). In response, Bubble Sister Seo Seung-hee explained the group "loved music by black people," and "we happened to have black makeup. With the makeup we felt good, natural, free and energized. In taking the real album cover photos, we finally decided to go for it" (KOCCA, 2003). Similar to other contemporary examples of people who have reported "accidentally" donning blackface, blackface appears to just spontaneously happen to people.[4] After severe backlash, their manager reported, "To the 1 percent of people who were offended by this, we're really sorry. . . . We won't be performing with black faces" (Hodges, 2003).

In Japan, *Chikibura Samba* (or "Little Black Sambo" in English), a children's book with a long history of controversy over its racial caricatures and stereotypes, was re-released in 2005, 17 years after Japanese booksellers agreed to pull it from shelves following a U.S.-led campaign against its racist imagery and language. Its contemporary re-release sold over 100,000 copies, making it a national bestseller in Japan. The book publisher's president, Tomio Inoue, announced that, "Times have changed since the book was removed. Black people are more prominent in politics and entertainment, so I don't think this book can be blamed for supporting racial stereotypes. We certainly had no intention of insulting black people" (McCurry, 2005). Like other corporate apologies, this one invokes a colorblind racial story of progress to try to minimize their actions in the name of profits. And this apology does not appear to address whether this racial progress has occurred in the United States or Japan (a country with an even smaller population of black persons), and still delineates black people's roles to entertainers, a stereotypical post invoked to cite progress among the entire population of black people.

With new technologies and the continued globalization of American popular culture, we can only imagine that these images will find their ways into more and more spaces—problematically defining blackness across the globe. As one study found with interviews of rural Taiwanese who had never traveled to the United States, they "knew" about race and black Americans in the United States from watching U.S. movies. Like other immigrants who come to the United States, their exposure to U.S. movies undoubtedly shaped their stereotypical views and acceptance of racist ideas about black Americans. As popular culture's global audience grows, so do the lessons it provides about race and racism in the United States today. Without a critical resistance against these images, we can have no hope for racial equality in the United States or globally.

Conclusion

> On any typical day, one could feasibly rise and dress in their Abercrombie and Fitch "Wok n Bowl" T-shirt, eat breakfast with Aunt Jemima. Get ready for lunch with, "Yo quiero Taco Bell!" Have dinner with Uncle Ben, before retiring to the television to watch the Indians, Redskins, or Braves (and don't forgot to throw down your "tomahawk chop" in an important moment of collective consciousness). After a leisurely game of "Ghettopoly" before heading to bed, you finally watch the late night news to get a daily dose of Arab and Muslim terrorists and criminal-blackmen bedtime stories.

As Noriega (2001) has argued, race in popular culture is in many ways a paradox—its representation has become regular in our media culture, while the profound ways it affects the real-life chances of individuals and groups remain hidden. And indeed, as Noriega notes, while popular media cannot be implicated as the "cause" of racism, neither does it offer a value-free medium for the exchange of ideas and information. The problem with the stranglehold popular culture has over dictating the way that the populace "knows" people of color is that for people who have very little real, interpersonal experience with individuals from these groups, they can believe in an essentialist vision composed of every stereotype and myth promoted. In today's world of mass information, it is easy to see how the very ubiquity of such images makes keeping pace with them nearly impossible. As addressed above, this is the promise and predicament of popular culture. The deep need for a critical cultural studies is clear, one that seeks to understand the tools available, how they have been used in support of the dominant ideology, and how they might challenge such ideologies and offer counter-cultural solutions.

37 The Media as a System of Racialization: Exploring Images of African American Women and the New Racism

Marci Bounds Littlefield

MARCI BOUNDS LITTLEFIELD is an assistant professor of sociology at Indiana University–Purdue University, Indianapolis.

Questions to Consider

In this reading, Littlefield makes the point that "the media produce and circulate images that determine our beliefs and attitudes and that inform our behaviors." What might the link be between our attitudes toward race, gender, and sexuality and the sexist and racist ways individuals behave toward women and racial minorities? Is it possible that how the media present black women in rap videos shapes the way these women are treated? How might negative images of women of color translate in their objectification or result in discrimination? Could one argue that these images are merely entertainment and have no bearing on how women are treated?

HISTORICALLY, THE MEDIA PERPETUATE IDEAS about race and ethnicity that place African American women at a clear disadvantage. Beginning with the welfare queen image during the Reagan administration and moving to the porno chick represented in current videos, society views a daily discourse on race, gender, and class that continues to reproduce dominant and distorted views of African American womanhood and sexuality. The overabundance of this portrayal in popular culture raises serious implications associated with linking sexual promiscuity to the nature and identity of African American women. These popular representations of African American women and men are mostly unchallenged by larger society and the African American community. This article discusses the media as a system of racialization and proposes to challenge this system as a method of social justice and social change.

As a society, America was fashioned and born out of binary ethnocentric, oppressive, sexual notions of race. These notions of race informed the early colonists; they described Africans as beasts with animal passions prone to lasciviousness (Jordan, 1968). The initial reactions of the colonists to the Africans foreshadowed the experience of Africans in American society, and the sexual depictions of the African women functioned as a catalyst igniting the politics of race. American society became the living epitome of hypocrisy as it struggled with creating a pluralistic society.

Pluralism, a pattern of racial integration, represented the American ideology—a nation that would accept and celebrate racial and ethnic differences while affirming its allegiance to the larger society (Schaefer, 2005). In practice, American pluralism enforced Anglo conformity and created an American identity that excludes all groups outside the norm and realm of Whiteness. This binary distinction among the races created a hierarchy in which Anglo perceptions about race and ethnicity dominated the social structure, and other non-White groups were placed in the Other category, which translated into inferior social status. Rather than fashion a society that embraces difference, we instead live in one that punishes, dehumanizes, and alienates difference in every form of social life.

In theory, racial and ethnic difference should create the impetus and premise for a just society. However, this difference in American society translates into social policies, laws, customs, and norms that justify all forms of oppression and a social structure that promotes inequality and domination based on class, race, and gender. The prevalent and permanent systems of racialization that inform our lived experiences as a society and divide us in spite of civil rights, affirmative action, and diversity initiatives are multiple. These systems of racialization must be interrogated to disrupt a society that has developed and prospered at the expense of the oppressed. Although many vehicles inform the hegemonic social structure, the media are the primary agent of socialization in which participants are seduced, educated, and transformed by ideas concerning race, gender, and class on a global level, and these ideas often support White supremacist capitalist patriarchy.[1]

As I scrutinize the profound impact of the media in their transformative possibilities, it is disturbing to witness the popular portrayal of the values of our youth, which do not extend beyond sex, drugs, and money, as portrayed in the ever-so-popular hip-hop videos. This genre has been referred to as the voice of the youth but, today, clearly represents the impact of a capitalist White patriarchal society that supports images that degrade minorities to sell music. Thus, like slavery, the bodies, talent, and potential of minority youth are commodified and objectified to promote an industry that marginally benefits the artists but continues to send the message that race is a defining factor in American society.

On first glance, it appears that American society is accepting of its minorities: Popular representations of youth culture are represented in a variety of media outlets, diversity initiatives are supported in most government agencies, and businesses embrace ideas about multiculturalism. International viewers have sufficient examples to conclude that minorities have obtained a piece of the American dream, given the representation of African Americans in politics, sports, and music. This, however, is the logic behind the *new racism,* which Collins (2004) describes as being predicated on inclusion and containment, which hides behind the notion of a color-blind society. This new racism assumes that the social changes that took effect during the civil rights movement benefited African Americans and that, consequently, America has lived up to its promise of equality. Current strategies that highlight diversity initiatives but do not single out problems faced by Black Americans dilute the real issues and needs of African Americans. Therefore, any social justice paradigm has to include an analysis of the hegemonic

structure of American society and the role of the media as an agent that enforces historical ideas about African American sexuality and perpetuates inequality. This article analyzes the concomitant effects of the media as a system of racialization and proposes a social justice framework that interrogates this system and proposes methods for change.

Mass Media

The media have historically perpetuated ideas about race and ethnicity that place African American women at a clear disadvantage. The overabundant portrayal of the African American woman stereotype, as **Jezebel** in popular culture, raises serious questions concerning the state of race in America and the persistence of linking sexual promiscuity to the nature and identity of African American women. Despite the changes and understanding of race as a social concept with no biological meaning, race is still a factor in the lives of African American women who, since slavery, have been consistently portrayed as the sexual prowler. The media perpetuate this image, popularize it, and present it as the defining characteristic of African American women, thus leaving our communities with images that are damaging, demeaning, and injurious to race relations.

Although the idea of race and its definition are constantly changing, the effects of race are still present and so persist in the areas of employment, education, poverty, and health care, to name a few. Although this is clearly the nature of social stratification in American society, the systems that perpetuate racism are not definitively identified as a factor in perpetuating the hegemonic ideas concerning race and gender. Consequently, popular representations of African American women in videos and the acceptance of these representations by the African American community and larger society suggest that African American women are still society's sexual scapegoat. These popular representations of African American women and men go largely unchallenged by larger society and by the African American community, which accepts these images without recognizing their power to disrupt an oppressive cycle of commodification.

The media have transformed the ways that we are able to communicate as a society, and these methods of

Jezebel A racist stereotype depicting black women as hypersexual and promiscuous.

communication make it easy to transfer ideas in a global context. The media strategically remake our picture of reality by controlling the images and the information that we receive. This process of selective reporting affects the ability of the populace to make objective, informed decisions because the information presented is biased and controlled (Murray, Schwartz, & Lichter, 2001). The media serve as a tool that people use to define, measure, and understand American society. For that reason, the media serve as a system of racialization in that they have historically been used to perpetuate the dominant culture's perspective and create a public forum that defines and shapes ideas concerning race and ethnicity. This is clearly evident in the representation of African Americans in various media. The power of the media to define and create attitudes that inform behavior is a crucial strategy of the new racism because the media are used to reproduce and disseminate the ideologies needed to justify racism (Collins, 2004).

Scholars suggest that the media produce and circulate images that determine our beliefs and attitudes and that inform our behaviors (Collins, 1991; Schiller, 1973). This is evident in studies that draw a correlation between television and violence/aggression in children (Baker & Ball, 1969) and infer television as an agent of socialization (Berger & Luckmann, 1967), and as a source for providing role models that affect children's attitudes, beliefs, and behavior (Comstock, Chaffee, Katzman, McCombs, & Roberts, 1978). The media are also suggested as being a factor in shaping, processing, and defining self-identity for young viewers (Milkie, 1999), whereas the media's negative stereotypical images may damage young girls' self-image as well (McRobbie, 1982). Symbolic interactionist approaches consider how viewers interpret media representations. They are concerned with how meaning is created, and this meaning varies according to the viewers' social, cultural, and historical group perspective (Blumer, 1969). This group perspective is shared among members of the same *interpretive community* because of similar cultural experiences that may not be shared by different groups (Fish, 1980). Therefore, the way that African Americans interpret popular media representations and the way that they believe other groups perceive these representations can be an important factor in shaping their identity.

Again, the context in which the media shape our ideas concerning race is an important discussion as we consider the current generation. Born in the eighties and afterward, this generation has been bombarded with negative controlling images of African Americans. Beginning with the welfare queen image during the Reagan administration to the strip-club porno chick represented in current videos, the media of the new generation broadcast a daily discourse on race, gender, and class that continues to reproduce dominant and distorted views of African American womanhood and sexuality. Thus, the media have historically operated as an agent constructing racial ideology.

Historical Representations

Historical representations of African American women help us to see the permanence and persistence of stereotypical images that justify the treatment of African American women as society's Other. African American women were described by English slave traders as "hot constitution's ladies' . . . making no scruple to prostitute themselves to the Europeans . . . so great is their inclination to white men" (Jordan, 1968, p. 35). These notions of African American women as sexual predators defined their sexuality in the 16th and early 17th century and became the standard in which they were measured. Slavery defined African American women as society's Other, which placed them in a category different from that of White women and suggested that they were not true women. Consequently, a number of stereotypes emanated, one of which depicted African American women as the Jezebel, an insatiable sexual being unable to control her sexuality (Collins, 1991). These images created a context for African American women that defined their sexuality and made it impossible to violate their identity. African American women were described as lustful and impudent, and this became a justification for the rape and commodification of their bodies in the 19th century. This commodification during slavery objectified African American women, and this objectification continues to be defined by the media in music videos and in other popular representations of African American culture.

During the era of King Cotton, early American culture produced a society in which race defined social interactions with African Americans. The slave trade and the cultural ethos of slavery defined African American women in pluralistic terms of property, commodities, breeders, concubines, servants, and laborers (Collins, 1991, 2004).

This view of African American women represented the interpretation of the hegemonic culture, and it was maintained through a system of educational, psychological, economic, and physical degradation. This system insisted that these women not consider themselves as women but as sexual animals whose purpose was to satisfy the needs of the oppressor. Hence, the stereotypes used to justify racial oppression included lazy, unintelligent, sexual, and sinister, and African American men and women were both viewed in this context.

Early Portrayal of African American Women in the Media

The stereotypical representation of Blacks in the media began with the release of W. Griffith's film *The Birth of a Nation* in 1915. This film was released during reconstruction, and it played on Southern fears of racial equality. Southerners believed that equality for African Americans would ultimately lead to miscegenation and political disaster. In response, the film fed Southern racism by using common stereotypes of African Americans as savages. *Birth of a Nation* ran for 44 consecutive weeks, sparked the revival of the KKK, and fueled the lynching campaign (*Slavery and the Making of America*, 2004). African American men and women were represented in spaces that relegated them to a persona of servitude, crime, savagery, inferiority, and animalism (Diawara, 1993). Through this forum, the media participated in a public discourse on race that had a direct impact on the lives of African Americans. This film also led to further representations of African Americans in the public sphere that summarized the context in which African Americans had been defined since slavery.

Portraying stereotypical images of African American women in a way that dehumanizes them is not a new one; it stems from a societal need to place a group of people in the Other category, which objectifies their existence and suggests that they are not really human and so deserve the unfair treatment that they receive (Collins, 2004). Relegating African American women to the Other category set historical precedence for viewing them through a prism of difference, whereas everyone outside that prism is viewed as normal. Collins (1991) suggests that this binary relationship is a natural part of human society's tendency to make distinctions, which attributes good and bad in its schematic arrangement and to which African American

women have consistently been placed in the Other category. Thus, maintaining images of African American women as the Other provides ideological justification for race, gender, and class oppression. DuCille (1996) labels this constant portrayal of African American women in the Other category as the "occult of true Black womanhood."

The portrayal of African Americans in the media in these representations served to perpetuate the racial inferiority that was part of the Southern mentality and transformed into an American way of thinking about African Americans. This ideology posited African Americans as inferior beings who did not warrant any social justice and were deserving of their ill treatment. Earlier attempts to rectify social injustice during reconstruction were superseded by the country's desire to pacify the South and restore it a measure of autonomy and power that the Civil War undermined. African Americans were relegated to an inferior position, and the historic *Plessey v. Ferguson* case of 1896, the Black codes, and the lynching campaign ensured that African Americans would not experience equal opportunity. As such, the ideas about race were developed during this era, and the media disseminated an ideology of African American inferiority.

Current Representations

Today, the images of African American women carry an almost identical resemblance to their original characterizations as sexually insatiable creatures. The most recent objections include the "Tip Drill" video, which displays African American women as nameless objects whose sexuality is for sale. The alarming image of Nelly swiping his credit card through the buttocks of a African American woman serves as rallying cry for the community of students, scholars, and others to open a public debate concerning the pornographic and misogynist representations of African American women in music videos and the meaning of these representations for the viewers. As this debate continues, this video is one of many popular representations of African American women that perpetuate an age-old ideology that their sexuality and their bodies should be used for public profit. Accordingly, the media

Plessey v. Ferguson The U.S. Supreme Court decision that held that blacks and whites could be legally segregated as long as both were treated equally. Commonly known as the separate but equal doctrine.

perpetuate these controlling images and inform African American women's reality by creating stereotypical images that perpetuate a system of domination that links sex, race, and gender to the sexuality of African American women.

The crucial problem with the negative images of African American women in today's society is not merely the overabundance of these images but rather the absence of equal amounts of alternative, positive images. These images are damaging because they limit African American women's choices by excluding other options. Therefore, the representations of these women in the music videos depict the oversexual, deviant image of the African American woman which society crafted during slavery and has systematically perpetuated. When considering the popular representation of these women in the media and especially in the music industry, the question becomes, are there enough positive images to combat the sexually insatiable representations of African American women that inundate our culture?

When these images were first presented in the early 19th century, African American club women sought to influence and redefine the images of African American women through public work centered on racial uplift and through education and public service (Pough, 2004). The 19th century bore African American women as social leaders in the public sphere and challenged the common representations of African American women as sexual deviants. Women such as Maria Stewart, Mary Shad Clary, Margaret Murray Washington, and Anna Julia Cooper ensured that African American women were viewed in ways that uplifted the race and presented African American women in a positive light. Scholars suggest that a few female rappers are the modern-day equivalent of these 19th-century female revolutionaries—that is, they are willing to challenge the male space that has consumed the rap industry and in doing so present an alternative female voice (Emerson, 2002; Pough, 2004; Rose, 1994). Although this argument may have some merit, the limited examples of positive women rappers are not sufficient to alter the negative representations of African American women; unlike the club women, current female rappers do not appear to have a real purpose, a group perspective, or a common goal.

Today the media inundate the populace with the body politics of African American womanhood, where women's bodies are exploited as they were for cheap labor during slavery—in each case, the institution reinforces the

images of African women as hypersexual workhorses used for profit whether by slave owners or recording producers. These sexually insatiable images are detrimental for the African American woman because they have a life of their own and take shape and meaning to viewers of these images. Although images alone cannot create behavior, they can certainly inform behavior (which is essentially what happened during reconstruction) and become the fabric of an American way of life. According to Collins (1991), stereotypes of African American women create barriers for them to succeed in areas of employment outside the traditional occupations relegated to them. The idea that African American women are not capable of intellectual thought and direction has become the way of thinking about African American women. Today the continued use of their bodies for profit makes rape and other forms of violence against women an acceptable norm.

New Racism

When we see images of African American sexuality portrayed in the media, they are viewed through this new lens of difference, which suggests that diversity exists but which denies the context for which racial definitions and categorizations create social inequality. On one hand, our society accepts racial labels and distinctions, but it does not accept policies initiated to create a just society and, in reality, does not foster real inclusion of minority groups. This new racism is precisely the context in which the melting pot metaphor originally defined American society as a pluralistic society that professes racial justice and egalitarian principles of equality while, in practice, promoting Anglo conformity.

Clearly, the state of American society in the 19th century and the obvious need to join in the battle for racial uplift defined the social agenda of African Americans. Today the need to participate in a racial uplift campaign is unclear. As of 2007, this agenda is not clearly defined and has been represented as a class problem and not a race problem. Inequality has been redefined to discuss issues around class, whereas race is presented as an issue that has been "solved" by the civil rights movement, by affirmative action, and by the legal precedents that have favored African Americans. This is the crux of the new racism that has convinced the populace that multiculturalism, diversity, and equality have been accounted for in American society. The African American distinction becomes no more meaningful than any other minority distinction, and African Americans continue to experience institutional discrimination and live in communities with disparities that affect their life chances. Meanwhile, oversexed depictions of African American women justify the problems that overwhelmingly affect the African American community—namely, the increase in unwed childbirths, AIDS, teenage pregnancy, decline in marriage among African Americans—and thus create the same paradigm of blaming the victim that has characterized dominant-minority relations in the United States.

Pedagogy and Social Justice

Any social justice strategy that seeks to understand and respond to the current issues surrounding the media as a system of racialization has to first address methods of pedagogy. As educators, we have to address the pedagogy of how people define the continuing effects of racism and understand the extent of the hegemonic domination as part of our social structure that permeates and controls the minds of the oppressed. Any social justice paradigm has to include an understanding of the system and the current context in which all actors have a role in promoting misogynist ideology.

In the African American community, there seems to be an overall resistance to the reality of its resident sexism. Accordingly, when it views music videos and other media representations of African American women and men, its conclusion is that the youth have gone astray and that the missing value structure defines their decisions, rather than a comprehensive understanding of the oppressive social structure, which is committed to patriarchy and capitalism. Consequently, the decisions of music artists are seen in a vacuum, outside a social context, which dismisses the community's role in not addressing the issues. Hence, an attention to community education that educates young Black women, Black men, and the overall community is the only context that will have any meaning for social justice. Every actor in the social system must take responsibility for the way that he or she perpetuates the media as a source of racialization by directly participating in the music industry and by not demanding change. As a result, change is possible only when all participants understand their own agency and respond. As long as the traditional blame-the-victim scenario defines our understanding of popular culture and the media, then the actors will never be challenged to change or make different choices.

There has to be a cultural context for African American men to think differently about gender and a reason to reject the hypermasculine images presented in popular culture that reward sexual violence, criminality, and deviant lifestyles. African American men need to understand their role in replicating an ideology that dehumanizes African American women and uses their talent as a way to make an industry richer at their expense. African American women have to understand the impact of the choices that they make in playing in stereotypical roles. The women who are portrayed in the videos are explained away by "choice," by free will, which places the blame solely on the women who supposedly make this free choice. However, there is no discussion of the social context in which this choice is made, and there is no consideration that African American women's bodies have historically been used to economically prosper the capitalist system of social inequality. During slavery, African American women were stripped of their agency, and their bodies were commodified in a way in which choice never existed. Many African American women protested this lack of choice: Some killed their babies and performed abortions; others ran away. True freedom did not exist under slavery. Today this free choice is still diluted because ideas about sexuality and how sex is used in the African American community create a paradigm that defines the reality of African Americans. Unfortunately, what is absent is a forum to have these conversations, which would educate young African American women and thus create a new way of thinking about media images and choices.

Community organizations and other businesses need to develop alternate choices for young men and women—an alternative to buying into the stereotypical images portrayed by the media necessary to make it in the world of music and television. The old ideas of self-help that defined the social context for African Americans in the early 20th century created a generation of people who left a strong legacy for African Americans in business, education, and other industries who did not allow a capitalist social system to define their choices and their life chances. Alternative methods of "making it" have to be considered so that our youth will have other viable choices.

Popular and expressive culture can create a space for resisting stereotypical images and for creating a context where social justice means challenging the media as a source of racialization and an agent of racism. Ideas about race and ethnicity are transferred to the public through images and public presentations of racial groups, and until these presentations are filtered and challenged, racial identity and understanding will constantly be viewed through the lens of capitalism. That is, until minority groups play an active role in self-definition and reject the presentations of minorities by producers who are motivated by the dollar, then media representations will continue to define minority groups. Until African American women and men understand their respective roles in the portrayal of race and are challenged to make different choices, then we will always need public spaces to define and discuss racial issues.

38 Black and White in Movies: Portrayals of Black-White Biracial Characters in Movies

Alicia Edison • George Yancey

ALICIA EDISON is a Graduate Student at the University of North Texas. Her research focuses on race and ethnicity, biracial identity formation, and the perpetuation of racial stereotypes within the media.

GEORGE A. YANCEY is a Professor of Sociology at the University of North Texas. His work has focused on interracial families and multiracial churches. His latest book is *Interracial Families: Current Concepts and Controversies.*

CONGRATULATIONS! YOU ARE A BIRACIAL American and your life story is being made into a major motion picture. In addition, you have been hired as the casting director. Who will you choose to play you? Will it be Julia Roberts, Denzel Washington, or Thandie Newton? Will your decision be influenced by which actor resembles you most in appearance? Will your decision be based on the economic class of your character in the movie? This research examines the relationship between social class and the portrayals of Blacks and Black/White biracial individuals in movies. Lights . . . Camera . . . Action!

We suggest that race is predictive of the socioeconomic class of the roles assigned to different actors. In general, the media tend to portray individuals with light skin with positive attributes and individuals with dark skin with negative attributes (Wade and Bielitz, 2005; Frisby, 2006). Light skin is associated with a higher socioeconomic class than dark skin (Hunter, 2007;

Questions to Consider In the U.S. Census of 2010, about seven million Americans reported they were of mixed race; that is, they chose to describe themselves as being more than one race on the decennial census. There have of course been "mixed race" individuals in the United States for hundreds of years. However, the combination of individuals crossing the color line in romance and having mixed race children and celebrities acknowledging their mixed race background has resulted in a general acceptance of "being" mixed race in America. Edison and Yancey argue that representations of mixed race individuals in films reflect a hierarchy in which race and social class intersect. Think for a moment of light- and dark-skinned movie stars and the various roles they have played. Do any patterns emerge concerning how light- or dark-skinned an actor is and the roles he or she gets in Hollywood movies?

Hunter, 2002; Jones, 2000). Thus, biracial characters are more likely to be of a higher economic class than black characters.

Race and Skin Color

The most prominent physical characteristic that differentiates Blacks from Whites is skin color (Goldsmith et al., 2007; Wade and Bielitz, 2005; Jones, 2000; Beaudoin and Thorson, 2006). In many instances, individuals are labeled as members of a particular race by their appearance, most particularly their skin color (Goldsmith et al., 2007). White skin is tied to privilege, intelligence, and refinement, while darker skin associated with poverty, violence, and lack of intelligence (Jones, 2000; Hunter, 2007; Wade and Bielitz, 2005; Keith, 2009). These racial stereotypes are perpetuated when African Americans appear in the media (Littlefield, 2008; Jones, 2000). In many movies, actors and actresses with light skin are portrayed with positive characteristics and belong to middle or upper social classes. Actors and actresses with dark skin do not regularly play characters with such positive characteristics. They play roles associated with negative characteristics and as belonging to working or lower social classes (Jones, 2000; Margolis, 1999).

Historically, skin tone has been a predictor of socioeconomic status (Herring and Keith, 2004). In particular, light skin color is correlated with higher socioeconomic status among Blacks. Light skin color is also associated with integrated housing options, higher levels of self-esteem, and fewer mental health problems Bowman et al., 2003; Keith, 2009; Wade and Bielitz, 2005). Darker skin color is associated with lower status, but with more ethnic authenticity (Hunter, 2007; Goldsmith et al., 2007; Rockquemore and Brunsma, 2001).

Racial Identity, Appearance, and Social Class

Many biracial individuals have fluid racial identities that change from place to place and from time to time (Rockquemore and Brunsma, 2001). However, a biracial individual's ability to maneuver between racial identities is constrained by their phenotype (Rockquemore and Brunsma, 2001). It is less likely for a biracial person with a dark complexion to have a White or biracial identity recognized by other individuals. Conversely, biracial individuals with light skin are able to move between racial identities and have their racial identities validated.

Social class is an additional component that affects how individuals perceive biracial individuals. Biracial individuals living in middle- and upper-class environments are more likely to be perceived as biracial (rather than Black) than those living in working- and lower-class environments (Brunsma, 2005). However, regardless of socioeconomic status, dark-skinned biracial individuals are likely to be recognized as being Black (Harvey et al., 2005).

Media and Identity

Media sources also affect racial identity. For example, television and movies are powerful tools of socialization in the United States that impact how people view themselves. American children spend much of their time exposed to visual forms of media, especially television. American children between the ages of two and six view about two hours of television each day. Children from ages six to eleven years old watch, on average, twenty-three hours of television a week. Those between the ages of twelve and seventeen watch more than twenty-one hours a week (Outley, 2006). Media inform, entertain, and influence how we, and especially youth, self-identify and interact with others (Littlefield, 2008; Wilson and Gutierrez, 1995; Larson, 2006). Therefore, how we see ourselves, including how we identify racially, is influenced, in part, by the media (Gruber and Thau, 2003; Jones, 2000; Huntemann and Morgan, 2001; Thornton, 2009).

The consumption of media is a form of self-socialization (Huntemann and Morgan, 2001). Viewers tend to pay the most attention to characters who share their age, race, and gender and those they wish they could be like (Beaudoin and Thorson, 2006; Comstock and Scharrer, 2001). Young audiences learn lessons from these characters and emulate them (Littlefield, 2008; Huntemann and Morgan, 2001). Identification with certain characters tends to increase when those characters are labeled as belonging to the same social group as the viewer (Beaudoin and Thorson, 2006).

Media also influence how we develop our understanding of race and other racial groups (Kellner, 2003). Children learn social prejudices and practices by observing patterns in society (Littlefield, 2008; Berry and Asamen, 2001). Children are especially affected by media representations of minority groups (Wilson and Gutierrez, 1995). Media images are usually the first impression children have of groups outside of their immediate family. Often, these images are imprinted in children's minds without any discussion or explanation and leave a powerful and lasting impression (Wilson and Gutierrez, 1995).

Media and Social Control

Media are not only tools of socialization; they can also be tools of domination and social control. Media can be used by the powerful to force subordinate groups to internalize exploitative demands (Huntemann and Morgan, 2001). An ideology is a set of beliefs, values, and meanings that reflect and justify the views of a particular group in society. Racial ideologies are used to evaluate members of racial groups and to uphold the prevailing racial hierarchy. When maintained by the racial group with the most power over the media, these evaluations are infused into mainstream culture and become part of the social structure (Thornton, 2009). In the United States, media are used by members of the dominant racial group, or Whites, to retain power, wealth, and status by promoting an ideology that justifies the current racial hierarchy (Lull, 2003; Wilson and Gutierrez, 1995).

When an ideology becomes part of the social structure, it can be effectively used to control subordinate groups. The dominant group define and determine what is reality, not only for themselves but also for subordinate groups. The subordinate group accept the philosophies of the dominant group as their reality (Littlefield, 2008). Because of this, media that reach mass audiences can be considered forms of social control.

Through media, the dominant group is able to reinforce the status quo by justifying inequality and/or by denying the existence of inequality (Littlefield, 2008; Larson, 2006). The media, in particular certain movies, tend to deny racial inequality by focusing on individual behavior and neglecting social structures. This message informs viewers that race does not matter and is a thing of the past. Our society is often portrayed as "color-blind," a place in which racism does not exist, and where race is not important (Gallagher, 2006; Thornton, 2009). Examples of such cases can be seen in interracial buddy movies,

such as *Silver Streak, Forty-Eight Hours, Beverly Hills Cop,* and *Lethal Weapon* and movies with a token black (Donaldson, 2006). On the other hand, other movies demonize Blacks and thus justify their inferior status (Larson, 2006). Blacks are depicted as criminals in movies such as *Set It Off* and *New Jack City.* Violence is another characteristic of Blacks in movies like *New Jack City.* In addition, Blacks are demonized as sexually promiscuous. This is prevalent in *Jungle Fever, The Best Man, Boomerang,* and *Two Can Play That Game.*

Biracial Identity and Media

Biracial individuals are judged and scrutinized not only by Whites but also by Blacks. While some biracial Americans are looked at with suspicion by Blacks as not being "Black enough," colorism also exists. Colorism is the practice by which Blacks who are relatively light-skinned and/or have other physical indications of White ancestry, such as a narrow nose or straight/wavy hair, are given favored status by other Blacks, as well as Whites (Hunter, 2007). It has its roots in colonization and enslavement by Europeans (Hunter, 2002). Colorism is the reinforcement of Eurocentric phenotypical standards and one of the ways a stigmatized group internalizes the oppressive ideologies of the dominant group.

Positive portrayals of light-skinned Black and biracial characters and negative portrayals of darker-skinned characters in movies support colorism. The latter uphold the present racial hierarchy by spreading images that reinforce negative racial stereotypes about Blacks while the former tend to support the color-blind perspective that race no longer matters. Disproportionate portrayals of Black characters as negative support and help spread harmful racial stereotypes while, at the same time, "color-blind" portrayals of middle- and upper-class Black and biracial characters support the notion that race no longer matters (at least for middle- and upper-class people).

Seeing the Big Picture   **How the Media Shapes Perceptions of Race and Occupations**

Section VIII in the Appendix shows that racial minorities are underrepresented in most white collar occupations. Think for a moment about some of your favorite television shows. Are racial minorities over or underrepresented as lawyers or doctors or CEO on television? Are the facts in the appendix regarding occupations by race consistent with what you see on television? What are the societal implications of having racial minorities over or underrepresented in the media.

39 Winnebagos, Cherokees, Apaches, and Dakotas: The Persistence of Stereotyping of American Indians in American Advertising and Brands

Debra Merskin

DEBRA MERSKIN is an associate professor at the University of Oregon. Her research interests focus on the representation of women and minorities in media, historical studies, and the social influences of the media.

FROM EARLY CHILDHOOD ON, WE HAVE all learned about "Indianness" from textbooks, movies, television programs, cartoons, songs, commercials, fanciful paintings, and product logos.[1] Since the turn of the century, American Indian images, music, and names have been incorporated into many American advertising campaigns and product images. Whereas patent medicines of the past featured "coppery, feather-topped visage of the Indian" (Larson, 1937, p. 338), butter boxes of the present show the doe-eyed, buckskin-clad Indian "princess." These stereotypes are pervasive, but not necessarily consistent—varying over time and place from the "artificially idealistic" (noble savage) to present-day images of "mystical environmentalists or uneducated, alcoholic bingo-players confined to reservations" (Mihesuah, 1996, p. 9). Yet today a trip down the grocery store aisle still reveals ice cream bars, beef jerky, corn meal, baking powder, malt liquor, butter, honey, sour cream, and chewing tobacco packages emblazoned with images of American Indians. Companies that use these images of Indians do so to build an association with an idealized and romanticized notion of the past through the process of branding (Aaker & Biel, 1993). Because these representations are

Questions to Consider

Driving your Winnebago recreational vehicle (fully loaded 2001 Chieftain model) with Jeep Cherokee in tow, you pull into the Navajo National Park in New Mexico for your much-needed vacation. You sit down, light up a Natural American Spirit Cigarette, open a forty-ounce bottle of Crazy Horse Malt Liquor, and get ready to watch the World Series match between the Atlanta Braves (with their "Tomahawk Chop") and the Cleveland Indians. Each of these products draws on extremely stereotypical imagery of American Indians. Why, according to Debra Merskin, do these stereotypes continue, and what effect do these images have on the way individuals view American Indians?

so commonplace (Land O' Lakes maiden, Jeep Cherokee, Washington Redskins logo), we often fail to notice them, yet they reinforce long-held stereotypical beliefs about Native Americans.

Trade characters such as Aunt Jemima (pancake mix), Uncle Rastus (Cream of Wheat), and Uncle Ben (rice) are visual reminders of the subservient occupational positions to which Blacks often have been relegated (Kern-Foxworth, 1994). Similarly, Crazy Horse Malt Liquor, Red Chief Sugar, and Sue Bee Honey remind us of an oppressive past. How pictorial metaphors on product labels create and perpetuate stereotypes of American Indians is the focus of this study. McCracken's (1993) Meaning Transfer Model and Barthes's (1972) semiotic analysis of brand images serve as the framework for the analysis of four national brands. The following sections discuss how stereotypes are constructed and how they are articulated in, and perpetuated through, advertising.

To understand how labels on products and brand names reinforce long-held stereotypical beliefs, we must consider beliefs already in place that facilitated this process. Goings (1994), in his study of African American stereotypes, points out that "Racism was not a byproduct of the Civil War; it had clearly been around since the founding of the nation" (p. 7). Similarly, anti-Indian sentiments did not begin with the subjugation and dislocation efforts of the 1800s. Racial and ethnic images, part of American advertising for more than a century, were created in "less enlightened times" but have become a part of American popular culture and thought (Graham, 1993, p. 35) and persist today. The system of representation thereby becomes a "stable cultural convention that is taught and learned by members of a society" (Kates & Shaw-Garlock, 1999, p. 34).

Part of the explanation for the persistent use of these images can be found in the power and persuasiveness of popular culture representations. Goings's (1994) analysis of Black collectibles and memorabilia from the 1880s to the 1950s is a useful analogy for understanding the construction of Native American stereotypes in popular culture. He suggests that "collectible" items such as salt and pepper shakers, trade cards, and sheet music with images of happy Sambos, plump mammies, or wide-eyed pickaninnies served as nonverbal articulations of racism made manifest in everyday goods. By exaggerating the physical features of African American men and women, and making them laughable and useable in everyday items, these household objects reinforced beliefs about the place of Blacks in American society. Aunt Jemima, the roly-poly mammy; and Uncle Rastus, the happy slave chef (ironically both remain with us today) helped make Whites feel more comfortable with, and less guilty about, maintenance of

distinctions on the basis of race well after Reconstruction. These items were meant for daily use, hence constantly and subtly reinforcing stereotypical beliefs.

Similarly, Berkhofer (1979) suggests that "the essence of the white image of the Indian has been the definition of American Indians in fact and in fancy as a separate and single other. Whether evaluated as noble or ignoble, whether seen as exotic or downgraded, the Indian as image was always alien to white" (p. xv). White images of Native Americans were similarly constructed through children's games, toys, tales, art, and theater of the 1800s. Whereas "Little Black Sambo" tales reinforced the construction of racist beliefs about Blacks, songs such as "Ten Little Indians" or "cowboy and Indian" games similarly framed Indian otherness in the White mind. Goings (1994) makes an important point about the source of the construction of objects that represent this way of thinking:

> It is important to note that Black memorabilia are figures from white American history. White Americans developed the stereotypes; white Americans produced the collectibles; and white American manufacturers and advertisers disseminated both the images and the objects to a white audience. (p. xix)

The maintenance of these kinds of beliefs satisfies the human need for psychological equilibrium and order, finding support and reinforcement in ideology. Defined as "typical properties of the 'social mind' of a group" (van Dijk, 1996, p. 56), ideologies provide a frame of reference for understanding the world. *Racist* ideologies serve several social functions operating to reproduce racism by legitimating social inequalities, thereby justifying racially or ethnically constructed differences. Racist ideology is used to (1) organize specific social attitudes into an evaluative framework for perceiving otherness, (2) provide the basis for "coordinated action and solidarity among whites," and (3) define racial and ethnic identity of the dominant group (van Dijk, 25–27). These beliefs and practices are thereby articulated in the production and distribution of racist discourse.

To every ad they see or hear, people bring a shared set of beliefs that serve as frames of reference for understanding the world around them. Beyond its obvious selling function, advertising images are about making meaning. Ads must "take into account not only the inherent qualities and attributes of the products they are trying to sell, but also the way in which they can make those properties mean something to us" (Williamson, 1978, p. 12).

Barthes (1972) describes these articulations as myth, that is, "a type of speech" or mode of signification that is conveyed by discourse that consists of many possible modes of representation including, but not limited to, writing, photography, publicity, and advertising. Myth is best described by the process of semiology (Barthes, 1972). Semiology "postulates a relation between two terms, a signifier and a signified" (Barthes, 1972, p. 112). The correlation of the terms *signifier, signified,* and *sign* is where associative meaning is made. What we see in an advertisement or product label, at first glance, are basic elements composed of linguistic signs (words) and iconic signs (visuals). Barthes (1972) uses a rose, for example, as a symbol of passion. Roses are not passion per se, but rather the roses (signifier) + concept of passion (signified) = roses (sign). He states that "the signifier is empty, the sign is full, it is a meaning" (Barthes, 1972, p. 113). Another example that involves race is the use of Aunt Jemima for maple syrup. We see the representation of a bandana-clad Black woman who suggests the mammy of the Deep South (signified). When placed on the bottle of syrup (sign), meaning is transferred to the otherwise ambiguous product—care giving, home cooking, and food sharing. The sign is formed at the intersection between a brand name and a meaning system that is articulated in a particular image. Quite simply, a sign, whether "object, word, or picture," has a "particular meaning to a person or group of people. It is neither the thing nor the meaning alone, but the two together" (Williamson, 1978, p. 17).

McCracken (1993, p. 125), who defines a brand as a "bundle or container of meaning," expanded on the Barthesian analysis and developed a framework for understanding the cultural relationship that brands have within society. His anthropological model . . . illustrates the meanings of brands. McCracken shows how brands assume meaning through advertising, combined with consumption behavior, and the nature of common knowledge that consumers bring to this system. The present study expands on this process by adding a reinforcement loop from consumer back to the culture where stereotypes are experienced and recirculated through the system.

A brand can have gendered meaning (maleness/ femaleness), social standing (status), nationality (country

meaning), and ethnicity/race (multicultural meaning). A brand can also stand for notions of tradition, trustworthiness, purity, family, nature, and so on. McCracken (1993) uses the Marlboro man as an example of these components with which a simple red and white box came to signify freedom, satisfaction, competence, maleness, and a quintessentially American, Western character. The product becomes part of the constellation of meanings that surrounds it and thereby "soaks up" meanings. When the rugged Marlboro man is situated on his horse, on the open plain, almost always alone, the meanings of the constellation become clear—freedom, love of the outdoors, release from the confines of industrialized society—he is a "real man," self-sufficient and individualistic. These meanings become part of a theme made up of prototypical content while simultaneously being "idealizations and not reality itself" (Schmitt & Simonson, 1997, p. 124).

Advertisements are created in such a way as to boost the commodity value of brand names by connecting them to images that resonate with the social and cultural values of a society. These images are loaded with established ideological assumptions that, when attached to a commodity, create the commodity sign. Tools of branding are thereby used to create a particular image in the mind of the consumer. According to van Dijk (1996), this pattern often serves to present an US versus THEM dichotomy, with US being White, "positive, tolerant, modern," and THEM being minorities who are "problematic, deviant and threatening" (pp. 26–27). Hence, attitudes, beliefs, and behavior that are racist serve to support a dominant ideology that focuses on difference and separatism.

These ideas and values are articulated through the construction, maintenance, and perpetuation of stereotypes. Stereotypes are overgeneralized beliefs that

> get hold of the few simple, vivid, memorable, easily grasped, and widely recognized characteristics about a person, reduce everything about the person to those traits, exaggerate and simplify them, and fix them without change or development to eternity. (Hall, 1997, p. 258)

An example is the way the "Indian problem" of the 1800s has been shown in "cowboy and Indian" films. In his analysis of the representation of Indians in film, Strickland (1998, p. 10) asks, "What would we think the American Indian was like if we had only the celluloid Indian from which to reconstruct history?" (Strickland, 1998, p. 10). The cinematic representation includes the Indian as a

> bloodthirsty and lawless savage; the Indian as enemy of progress; the Indian as tragic, but inevitable, victim; the Indian as a lazy, fat, shiftless drunk; the Indian as oil-rich illiterate; the Indian as educated half-breed unable to live in either a white or Indian world; the Indian as nymphomaniac; the Indian as noble hero; the Indian as stoic and unemotional; the Indian as the first conservationist. (Strickland, 1998, p. 10)

Champagne's (1994) analysis of Indians in films and theater suggests that the longevity of James Fenimore Cooper's *Last of the Mohicans,* evidenced by its many film treatments, demonstrates that "Hollywood prefers to isolate its Indians safely within the romantic past, rather than take a close look at Native American issues in the contemporary world" (p. 719).

Natty Bumppo, in James Fenimore Cooper's *Deerslayer,* is a literary example of the male who goes from a state of "uncultured animality" to a state of "civilization and culture" (Green, 1993, p. 327). Larson (1937) describes how this stereotype was translated into a tool for marketing patent medicines:

> No sooner had James Fenimore Cooper romanticized the Indian in the American imagination in his novels than patent-medicine manufacturers, quick to sense and take advantage of this new enthusiasm, used the red man as symbol and token for a great variety of ware. How the heart of the purchaser—filled, like as not, with the heroic exploits of Cooper's Indians—must have warmed as he gazed at the effigy, symbolic of "Nature's Own Remedy." (p. 338)

The female savage becomes an Indian princess who "renounces her own family, marries someone from the dominate culture and assimilates into it" (Green, 1993, p. 327), for example, Pocahontas. From this perspective, Indians are thought of as childlike and innocent, requiring the paternalistic care of Whites; that is, they are tamable. In her study of Indian imagery in *Dr. Quinn, Medicine Woman,* Bird (1996, p. 258) suggests that what viewers see is a White fantasy filled with White concerns around "guilt and retrospective outrage." Green's (1993) analysis of the use of male Indian images in ads posits that Natives continue to be portrayed according to stereotypical images: (1) noble savage (the stoic, innocent, child of nature), (2) civilizable savage (redeemable, teachable), and (3) bloodthirsty savage (fierce, predatory,

cultureless, animalistic). Taken together, these studies suggest that historically constructed images and beliefs about American Indians are at the essence of stereotypical thinking that are easily translated into product images.

To study the articulation of racist ideology in brand images, four currently available national products (Land O' Lakes butter, Sue Bee Honey, Big Chief [Monitor] Sugar, and Crazy Horse Malt Liquor) were analyzed according to Barthes's (1972) semiotic analysis. First, the material object was identified (signifier); second, the associative elements were identified (signified); and, third, these were brought together in what we as consumers recognize as the sign. Company Web sites, press releases, and product packages were used for visual and textual information. Several attempts to communicate directly with the companies yielded no response. Through this method of analysis we can see how these meanings are transferred to the different products on the basis of both race and gender.

The following section presents a descriptive analysis of Land O' Lakes, Sue Bee Honey, Big Chief (Monitor) Sugar, and Crazy Horse Malt Liquor brand images.

Land O' Lakes

Although not the first national manufacturer to draw on the mystique of Indianness (that honor goes to Red Man Tobacco in 1904), Land O' Lakes is certainly one of the more prominent. In 1921, the Minnesota Cooperative Creameries Association opened for business in Arden Hills, Minnesota. This company served as the central shipping agent for a small group of small, farmer-owned dairy cooperatives (Morgan, 1986, p. 63). In 1924, the group wanted a different name and solicited ideas from farmers. Mrs. E. B. Foss and Mr. George L. Swift came up with the winning name—Land O' Lakes, "a tribute to Minnesota's thousands of sparkling lakes" (p. 63). The corporate Web site opens with a photograph of a quiet lake amid pine trees and blue sky. The copy under the photograph reads:

> Welcome to Land O' Lakes. A land unlike anywhere else on earth. A special place filled with clear, spring-fed lakes. Rivers and streams that dance to their own rhythms through rich, fertile fields. It's the land we call home. And from it has flowed the bounty and goodness we bring to you, our neighbors and friends.
>
> (Land O' Lakes, 2000)

In addition, "The now famous Indian maiden was also created during the search for a brand name and trademark. Because the regions of Minnesota and Wisconsin were the legendary lands of Hiawatha and Minnehaha, the idea of an Indian Maiden took form" (Land O' Lakes, 2000). A painting was sent to the company of an Indian maiden facing the viewer, holding a butter carton with a background filled with lakes, pines, flowers, and grazing cows.

At the Land O' Lakes corporate Web site, the director of communications includes a statement about the maiden image, where he agrees that the logo, the "Indian Maiden," has powerful connotations (Land O' Lakes). Hardly changed since its introduction in the 1920s, he says that Land O' Lakes has built on the "symbolism of the purity of the products" (Burnham, 1992). The company "thought the Indian maiden would be a good image. She represents Hiawatha and the Land of Gitchygoomee and the names of Midwest towns and streets that have their roots in the American Indian population" (Burnham, 1992).

The signifier is thereby the product, be it butter, sour cream, or other Land O' Lakes products. The Indian woman on the package is associated with youth, innocence, nature, and purity. The result is the generic "Indian maiden." Subsequently, the qualities stereotypically associated with this beaded, buckskinned, doe-eyed young woman are transferred to the company's products. Green's "noble savage" image is extended to include the female stereotype.

Sue Bee Honey

The Sioux Honey Association, based in Sioux City, Iowa, is a cooperative of honey producers, yielding 40 million pounds of honey annually (Sioux Honey Association, 2000). Corporate communications describe a change of the product name in 1964 from Sioux Bee to Sue Bee, "to reflect the correct pronunciation of the name" (Sioux Honey Association, 2000). The brand name and image are reinforced on trucks (both real and toys), on the bottles and jars in which the honey is sold, and through collectibles such as coffee mugs and recipe books.

Sue Bee Honey also draws upon the child-of-nature imagery in an attempt to imbue qualities of purity into their products. If we were to view Sue Bee in her full form (as she is shown on many specialty items such as mugs, glasses, and jars) we would see that she is an Indian maiden on top, with braided hair and headband, and a bee below the waist. Changing the spelling of her name from "Sioux Bee" to "Sue Bee" could be interpreted in a variety of ways—possibly simply as a matter of pronunciation, as the company asserts, or as an effort to draw attention away from the savage imagery stereotypically attributed to members of this tribe and more toward the little girlishness of the image. In this case, the product is honey, traditionally associated with trees and forests and natural places. This association works well with the girl–child Indian stereotype. By placing the girl bee on the package of honey, consumers can associate the innocence, purity, and naturalness attributed to Native American females with the quality of the product.

In the tradition of Pocahontas, both the Land O' Lakes and the Sue Bee maidens symbolize innocence, purity, and virginity—children of nature. The maiden image signifies a female "Indianness." She is childlike, as she happily offers up perhaps honey or butter (or herself) that "is as pure and healthy as she is" (Dotz & Morton, 1996, p. 11). The maiden's image is used to represent attempts to get back to nature, and the association is that this can be accomplished through the healthy, wholesome products of Land O' Lakes. Both images are encoded with socially constructed meanings about female Indian sexuality, purity, and nature.

Monitor Sugar Company

Founded in 1901, the Monitor Sugar Company processes approximately 4% of U.S. beet production into sugar (granulated, powdered, brown, and icing; Monitor Sugar Company, 2000). For 60 years, the company has been producing sugar from beets, relying on the image of an American Indian in full headdress to sell the sugar goods. The products are available on grocery store shelves and in bulk for institution, delivered by trucks with the Big Chief logo emblazoned on the sides.

So, who is this Chief said to represent? Is he a bona fide tribal leader or a composite Indian designed to communicate naturalistic characteristics associated with Indians with the sugar? Green's (1993) savage typology suggests that this individual is a combination of the noble savage (natural) and the bloodthirsty savage (ferocious). He is proud, noble, and natural and yet he is wearing a ceremonial headdress that communicates strength and stoicism.

Crazy Horse Malt Liquor

A 40-ounce beverage that is sold in approximately 40 states (Metz & Thee, 1994), Crazy Horse Malt Liquor is brewed by the Heilman Brewing Company of Brooklyn, New York. Crazy Horse Malt Liquor employs the image of Tasunke Witko (Crazy Horse) on the label of its malt liquor. On the front of the bottle is an American Indian male wearing a headdress that appears to be an eagle feather bonnet, and there is a symbol representing a medicine wheel—both sacred images in Lakota and other Native cultures (Metz & Thee, 1994).

Image analysis shows that the sign is that of an actual Indian chief. Signified, however, are beliefs about Indians as warriors, westward expansion, how mighty the consumer might be by drinking this brand, and wildness of the American Western frontier.

This brand, perhaps more than any other, has come under public scrutiny because it is the image of a particular person. A revered forefather of the Oglala Sioux tribe of South Dakota, Crazy Horse died in 1877 (Blalock, 1992). The labels feature the prominent image of Chief Crazy Horse, who has long been the subject of stories, literature, and movies. Larger than life, he has played a role in American mythology.

Signifying Green's (1993) bloodthirsty savage image, Crazy Horse Malt Liquor makes use of American myths through image and association. Ironically, Crazy Horse objected to alcohol and warned his nation about the destructive effects of liquor (Specktor, 1995). As a sign, Crazy Horse represents a real symbol of early American life and westward expansionism. He was, according to the vice president of the Oglala Sioux Tribe, a "warrior, a spiritual leader, a traditional leader, a hero who has always been and is still revered by our people" (Hill, 1992; Metz & Thee, 1994, p. 50). This particular image brings together some interesting aspects of branding. Not only is the noble and bloodthirsty savage stereotype brought together in a proud, but ultimately defeated, Indian chief, but also this is an image of a real human being. The association of alcohol with that image, as well as targeting the Indian population, draws on assumptions of alcohol abuse.[2]

Although there are dozens of possible examples of Native images on product labels, ranging from cigarette packages to sports utility vehicles, the examples discussed above illustrate the principles behind semiotics. The four presented here are significant examples of national brands employing stereotypical representations. When people are made aware of these products, they see how these images are consistently found in many products that employ Indian stereotypes either in product names or in their logos.

Many of these signs and symbols have been with us so long we no longer question them. Product images on packages, in advertisements, on television, and in films are nearly the only images non-Indians ever see of Native Americans. The covers of romance novels routinely feature Indian men sweeping beautiful non-Indian women off their feet as their bodices are torn away. These stereotypical representations of American Indians denies that they are human beings, and presents them as existing only in the past and as single, monolithic Indians (Merskin, 1998).

American Indians are certainly not the only racial or ethnic group to be discriminated against, overtly or covertly. Aunt Jemima and Rastus certainly have their origins in dehumanizing, one-dimensional images based on a tragic past. Yet, like Betty Crocker, these images have been updated. Aunt Jemima has lost weight and the bandana, and the Frito Bandito has disappeared (Burnham, 1992). But the Indian image persists in corporate marketing and product labeling.

These are highly visible and perhaps more openly discussed than images that appear on the products we see in grocery store aisles. An Absolut Vodka ad shows an Eskimo pulling a sled of vodka and a GreyOwl Wild Rice package features an Indian with braids, wearing a single feather, surrounded by a circle that represents (according to GreyOwl's distribution manager) the "oneness of nature" (Burnham, 1992). A partial list of others includes Apache helicopter, Jeep Cherokee, Apache rib doormats, Red Man Tobacco, Kleek-O the Eskimo (Cliquot Club ginger ale), Dodge Dakota, Pontiac, the Cleveland Indians, Mutual of Omaha, Calumet Baking Powder, Mohawk Carpet Mills, American Spirit cigarettes, Eskimo pies, Tomahawk mulcher, Winnebago Motor Homes, Indian Motorcycles, Tomahawk missiles, many high school sports teams, and the music behind the Hamm's beer commercials that begins "From the land of sky blue waters." And the list goes on.

Change is coming, but it is slow. For one thing, American Indians do not represent a significant target audience to advertisers. Representing less than 1% of the population, and the most economically destitute of all ethnic minority populations, American Indians are not particularly useful to marketers. Nearly 30% live below the official poverty line, in contrast with 13% of the general U.S. population (Cortese, 1999, p. 117). Without the population numbers or legal resources, it is nearly impossible for the voices of Natives to be heard, unlike other groups who have made some representational inroads. According to Westerman (1989), when minority groups speak, businesses are beginning to listen: "That's why Li'l Black Sambo and the Frito Bandito are dead. They were killed by the very ethnic groups they portrayed" (p. 28).

Not only does stereotyping communicate inaccurate beliefs about Natives to Whites, but also to Indians. Children, all children, are perhaps the most important recipients of this information for it is during childhood that difference is first learned. If, during the transition of adolescence, Native children internalize these representations that suggest that Indians are lazy, alcoholic by nature, and violent, this misinformation can have

a life-long impact on perceptions of self and others. As Lippmann (1922/1961) wrote,

> The subtlest and most pervasive of all influences are those which create and maintain the repertory of stereotypes. We are told about the world before we see it. We imagine most things before we experience them. (p. 89)

By playing a game of substitution, by inserting other ethnic groups or races into the same situation, it becomes clear that there is a problem. Stereotypical images do not reside only in the past, because the social control mechanisms that helped to create them remain with us today.

Future research should continue to examine how the advertising and marketing practice of branding contributes to the persistent use of racist images on product labels. This study adds to the sparse literature on media representations of Native Americans in general and adds to Green's (1993) typology by including female counterparts to the male savage stereotypes. Future research could explore more images of Native Americans in ads and on products. Qualitative research with members of different tribes would add depth to this area of study.

Seeing the Big Picture   The Tomahawk Chop: Racism in Image and Action

Look though the Appendix and notice the relative quality-of-life measures of American Indians. What is the link between this group's socioeconomic standing and the way they are portrayed in the media?

40   Sport in America: The New Racial Stereotypes
Richard E. Lapchick

RICHARD E. LAPCHICK is the DeVos Eminent Scholar Chair and director of the Business Sports Management graduate program in the College of Business Administration at the University of Central Florida.

> **Questions to Consider**   Richard Lapchick asks why athletes are subject to such an intense level of scrutiny by the press. What argument does he make that links race, stereotypes, and celebrity culture to the attitudes most Americans have about student and professional athletes?

Athletes and Crime

The beginning of the twenty-first century brought the hope that many social injustices would be rectified. However, surveys taken throughout the 1990s indicated that many inaccurate perceptions persisted such as the majority of whites surveyed continuing to believe that most African-Americans are less intelligent, more prone to drug use, more violent, and more inclined towards violence against women than whites are.

Sport culture, as it is currently interpreted, now provides whites with the chance to talk about athletes in a way that reinforces these stereotypes of African-Americans. Because African-Americans dominate the most popular sports, whites tend to "think black" when they think about the major sports.

Each time any athlete gets into trouble, I receive many calls from writers and television producers seeking comments. After a fight involving a basketball or football player, the interrogation invariably includes, "What makes football or basketball players more inclined to get into fights?" I have never been asked this question of a hockey or baseball player, despite the fact that there are as many game fights in those sports.

After a reported incident of domestic violence involving a basketball or football player, the inevitable question is, "What makes football or basketball players more inclined to abuse women?" Equal numbers of hockey and baseball players are accused of domestic violence, yet I have never been asked this question about them.

Each year during the professional drafts in each sport I am asked, "What do you think about colleges and even high school football and basketball players jumping to the pros and missing their chance for an education?" I have never been asked that question about baseball or hockey, tennis or golf players who put higher education on hold to pursue athletic careers.

Shawn Fanning left Northeastern University early to turn pro and earn millions; he was called a genius for founding Napster. The Dean of Northeastern University's School of Engineering told me that one of his biggest problems comes from companies attempting to lure away his top students each year. They leave for the money.

I believe that at least part of the systematic coupling of athletes and crime revolves around racial stereotyping. The media have persistently and consistently suggested that basketball and football players, who happen to be overwhelmingly African-American, are more violent than athletes in other sports and people in society in general. The result is that nearly everyone, including the police, women, fans, the media, sports administrators, and athletes themselves, believes that certain athletes, especially basketball or football players, are more inclined to be violent in general and violent against women in particular.

Rosalyn Dunlap, an African-American who was a five-time All American sprinter who now works on social issues involving athletes, including gender violence prevention, said, "perpetrators are not limited to any category or occupation. The difference is that athletes who rape or batter will end up on television or in the newspapers. Such images of athletes in trouble create a false and dangerous mindset with heavy racial overtones. Most other perpetrators will be known only to the victims, their families, the police, and the courts."

Once, while speaking to a group of distinguished international fellows at an elite academic institution, I asked members of the audience to write down five words that they would use to describe American athletes. In addition to listing positive adjectives, not one missed including one of the following words: dumb, violent, rapist or drug-user. I regularly meet with NBA and NFL players, as well as with college student-athletes on dozens of campuses. There are a lot of angry athletes who are convinced the public is stereotyping them because of the criminal acts of a few.

Many American men have grown to dislike athletes. A typical man might crave the money and the fame that a pro athlete enjoys, but he recognizes that such athletic success is unattainable for him. After reading all the negative press about athletes, he doesn't want to read that Mike Tyson felt he was treated unfairly by the justice system, knowing full well that Tyson made a reported hundred million dollars in his post-release rehabilitation program. He has little sympathy for the large number of pro athletes signing contracts worth more than ten million dollars a year. He is a micro-thought away from making egregious stereotypes about the "other groups" perceived as stealing his part of the American pie.

Big-time athletes fit the "other groups" category. Whether it is an African-American athlete or coach, or a white coach of African-American athletes, when something goes wrong with a player, a national reaction is likely to be immediate. Tom "Satch" Sanders, who helped the Boston Celtics win eight world championships, is now vice president for player programs for the NBA. His office encourages and guides players to finish their education, prepare for careers after basketball, and adjust to all the attention that NBA stars attract. Sanders presents a view complementary to Dunlap's. He proposes that the public has made a link between the stereotypes for athletes and African-Americans: "Everyone feels that athletes have to take the good with the bad, the glory with the negative publicity. However, no one appreciates the broad-brush application that is applied in so many instances. Of the few thousand that play sports on the highest level, if four

or five individuals in each sport—particularly if they are black—have problems with the law, people won't have long to wait before some media people are talking about all those athletes."

APBnews.com released two revealing studies in 2000. The first was a study of NFL players on two teams that made it to the 2000 Super Bowl. The second was a study of the sixteen NBA teams in the 2000 playoffs. In the NFL study, 11 percent of the players had a criminal history. That stood in dramatic contrast to the 35 to 46 percent lifetime arrest rate (taken from extensive studies in California and New York) for adult males under thirty, the same age group as most NFL players. Most NFL players are between 18 and 30 years old although most of those are between the ages of 21 and 30. In the study of NBA players, the arrest rate of those on the sixteen playoff teams was 18 percent, again a fraction of the national figures for their comparable age group of males.

Jeff Benedict's book *Pros and Cons* created a sensation in 1998 by saying that 21 percent of NFL players had arrest records. In an article he coauthored in 1999 for the statistics journal *Chance,* he said that the lifetime arrest rates for the NFL players he documented in *Pros and Cons* was less than half the arrest rate in the general population.

Fans build stereotypes of athletes from media coverage of the athletes and the games. Fans, who are mostly white, observe sport through a media filter that is created by an overwhelming number of white men. There are 1,600 daily newspapers in America employing only nineteen African-American sports columnists. There are only two African-American sports editors who work on newspapers in a city that has professional sports franchises. The fact that the number of sports columnists, as reported in the 2000 conference of the National Association of Black Journalists, has almost doubled from 11 since 1998 is a positive sign. However, there are no African-American sports writers on 90 percent of the 1,600 daily newspapers.

I am not suggesting, nor would I ever suggest, that most or even many of the white news writers are racist. However, they were raised in a culture in which many white people have strong beliefs about what it means to be African-American. The obvious result is that their reporting provides reinforcement of white stereotypes of African-American athletes. According to the National Opinion Research Center Survey, sponsored by the National

Science Foundation for the University of Chicago, whites surveyed share the following attitudes:

- Fifty-six percent of whites think African-Americans are more violent.
- Sixty-two percent of whites think African-Americans do not work as hard as whites.
- Seventy-seven percent of whites think most African-Americans live off welfare.
- Fifty-three percent think African-Americans are less intelligent.

Some white writers may have picked up these stereotypes in their own upbringing. When they write about an individual African-American athlete or several African-American athletes who have a problem, it becomes easy to unconsciously leap to the conclusion that fits the stereotype. Sanders said, "Blacks in general have been stereotyped for having drugs in the community as well as for being more prone to violence, However, now more than ever before, young black athletes are more individualistic and they resist the 'broad brush.' They insist on being judged as individuals for everything." But even that resistance can't be misinterpreted by the public and by the writers as off-the-court trash talking.

The athletes of the twenty-first century come from a generation of despairing youth cut adrift from the American dream. When the Center for the Study of Sport in Society started in 1984, one of its primary missions was to help young people balance academics and athletics. Since 1990, its mission has been extended to help young people lead healthy and safe lives.

Today our colleges are recruiting athletes:

- who have witnessed violent death. If an American child under the age of sixteen is killed every two hours with a handgun, then there is a good chance that young athletes will have a fallen family member or friend.
- who are mothers and fathers when they arrive at our schools. There are boys who helped 900,000 teenage girls get pregnant each year. Some student-athletes will leave after four years of college with one or more children who are four or five years old.
- who have seen friends or family members devastated by drugs.
- who have seen battering in their homes. An estimated 3 percent of American men are batterers and an estimated 3 million women are battered each year.

- who were victims of racism in school. Seventy-five percent of all students surveyed by Lou Harris reported seeing or hearing about racially or religiously motivated confrontations with overtones of violence very or somewhat often.
- who grew up as latchkey kids. Either a single parent or two working parents head 57 percent of American families, black and white alike.

Not enough campuses or athletic departments have the right people to help guide these young men and women into their adult lives. College campuses desperately need professionals that can deal with these nightmarish factors.

Academic Issues in College Sport

The amount of media coverage devoted to student-athlete literacy problems seem unique to athletes. The media rarely report that 30 percent of *all* entering freshmen must take remedial English or mathematics. The same holds true for the media's portrayal of student-athlete graduation rates. Although college athletic departments should strive to increase the number of student-athletes who graduate, graduation rates for the student body as a whole have changed. Only 14 percent of entering freshmen graduated in four years. If an athlete does not graduate in four years, some call him dumb; others say the school failed him. Few note that he may be typical of college students.

Don McPherson nearly led Syracuse University to a national championship when he was their quarterback in the 1980s. After seven years in the NFL and CFL, McPherson worked until 1999 directing the Mentors in Violence Prevention (MVP) Program, the nation's largest program using athletes as leaders to address the issue of men's violence against women.

McPherson reflected on the image that associates athletes with a lack of intelligence: "When whites meet an uneducated black athlete who blew opportunities in college or high school, they think he is dumb. They don't question what kind of school he may have had to attend if he was poor, or how time pressures from sport may have affected him. If they don't make it as a pro athlete, they're through without a miracle. I met lots of 'Trust Fund Babies' at Syracuse. They blew opportunities. No one called them dumb, just rich. We knew they would not need a miracle to get a second chance. I played at Syracuse at a time when being a black quarterback had become more acceptable. But the stereotypes still remained. As a player, people still remember me as a great runner and scrambler. I had not dented their image of the physical vs. intelligent black athlete."

McPherson led the nation in passing efficiency over Troy Aikman and won many awards, including the Maxwell Award, but he was most proud of being the quarterback with the highest passing efficiency rating in the nation. "I should have shattered the image of the athletic and mobile black quarterback and replaced it with the intelligent black quarterback. Unfortunately, stereotypes of football players, mostly black, still prevail. They make me as angry as all the stereotypes of black people in general when I was growing up."

McPherson wore a suit to class and carried the *New York Times* under his arm. But McPherson said that those whites that recognize his style were "surprised and said I was 'a good black man,' as if I were different from other black men. Most students assumed I was poor and that football was going to make me rich. Like many other blacks on campus, I was middle class. My father was a detective and my mother was a nurse."

Irrespective of color or gender, student-athletes graduate at higher rate than non-student-athletes, yet it is difficult to get accurate reporting of this in the press. According to the NCAA's 1999 report:

- Fifty-eight percent of white male Division I student-athletes graduated vs. 57 percent of white male nonathletes. Forty-two percent of African-American male Division I student-athletes graduated vs. 33 percent of African-American male nonathletes.
- Seventy-one percent of white female Division I student-athletes graduated compared to 61 percent of white female nonathletes. Fifty-seven percent of African-American female Division I student-athletes graduated vs. only 43 percent of African-American female nonathletes.

Some disparities do appear when we compare white student-athletes to African-American student-athletes:

- Fifty-three percent of white male Division I basketball student-athletes graduated versus 37 percent of African-American male Division I basketball student athletes.
- Seventy percent of white female Division I basketball student-athletes graduated compared to only 56 percent of African-American female Division I basketball student-athletes.

College sport does not own problems of illiteracy and low graduation rates. They belong to higher education in general and its inheritance of the near bankruptcy of secondary education in some communities.

The publication of graduation rates, long feared by athletic administrators, reveals scandalous rates, but it also shows poor graduation rates specifically for students of color. The predominantly white campuses of most colleges and universities are not welcoming environments for people of color. African-American student-athletes arrive on most campuses and see that only 10 percent of the student body, 3 percent of the faculty, and less than 5 percent of top athletics administrators and coaches look like them. Unless there is a Martin Luther King Center or Boulevard, all of the buildings and streets are named after white people.

In many ways, the publication of graduation rates for student-athletes helped push the issue of diversity to the forefront of campus-wide discussions of issues of race, ethnicity, and gender. Educators finally recognized how they were failing students of color by not creating a conducive, welcoming educational environment.

Drugs and Alcohol Use Among Athletes

A common stereotype depicts athletes as abusing drugs and alcohol. Some athletes do use drugs. CNN Headline news broadcasts stories about famous athletes caught with drugs. Repeated exposure to such reports inflates the size of the problem, but the facts do not reveal widespread abuse among athletes at the professional, college, or even high school level.

According to an extensive 1995 *Los Angeles Times* survey of athletes and the crimes they committed, a total of twenty-two professional and college athletes and three coaches were accused of drug use or a drug-related crime that year. On average, the media reported a story about a new sports figure with a drug problem every two weeks. Center estimates now put the number of sports figures accused of drug-related crimes at fifty per year or one media story per week on average.

Stories about athletes accused of drug use or drug-related crime are and should be disturbing. But those stories are rarely, if ever, put in the context of the 1.9 million Americans who use cocaine each month or the 12.1 million who use heroin throughout their lives. A total of 13 million individuals (6 percent of the American population) use some illicit drug each month, and 17 percent of men in the eighteen-to-twenty-five age group are drug users. Whether it is twenty-two or fifty, athletes who use drugs make up a small fraction of a single percent of the more than 400,000 athletes who play college and professional sports in America.

The NBA's drug policy, which leaves open the possibility of a lifetime ban for any athlete who is caught using drugs, is generally recognized as a model for the sports world. The policy may have stopped a substance abuse problem that predated its inception. According to an APBnews.com report, *Crime in the NBA,* released in June 2000, forty-one players were charged, booked, or arrested in eighty-two instances of crimes more serious than traffic tickets over the course of their time on the rosters of the sixteen NBA playoff teams. The story noted that "it is perhaps a credit to the NBA's antidrug policy that none of the eighty-two incidents noted in the APBnews.com study were related to hard drugs." (Marijuana was cited in six cases.) The forty-one players put the NBA's arrest rate at 18 percent. APB News.com reported that, "By way of comparison, the lifetime arrest rate of the general population as measured in four different studies ranges from 31 percent to 50 percent."

On the subject of alcohol abuse, the same 1995 *Los Angeles Times* survey of athletes and the crimes they committed, reported that twenty-eight college and professional athletes and four coaches were charged with alcohol-related infractions. None of these thirty-two cases were put in the context of the 13 million Americans who engage in binge drinking at least five times per month. Yet we read about a new athlete with an alcohol problem every eleven days. Such images can fuel an exaggerated sense of crisis in athletics when they are not viewed in full social context.

McPherson remembered being "shocked" when he arrived on Syracuse's campus at how much drinking went on each night among the student body. He felt compelled to call football players he knew on other campuses. "It was the same everywhere. Now when I go to speak on college campuses I always ask. It is worse today. Athletes are part of that culture, but insist that practice and academics crowd their schedules too much to be in bars as often as other students." Student personnel administrators on college campuses acknowledge that abusive drinking is the number one issue on college campuses today.

Athletes and Violence

Media coverage of professional, college, and even high school athletes consistently implies that the violence of sport makes its participants more violent in society.

Are sports any more violent today than they were twenty years ago when no one would have made such an assertion? I don't think so. But the streets and schools across America surely are more violent than they were twenty years ago—there are 2,000 assaults in schools across the nation every hour of every day. The number of American children killed by guns in the 1900s has exceeded the total number of soldiers who died in the Vietnam War. Gun violence obeys no boundaries of race, class, or geography. School shootings occurred in Pearl (Mississippi), Paduka (Kentucky), Jonesboro (Arkansas), and Littleton (Colorado). Violence seems part of the school day.

If one were to put together a lowlights tape of the fights in sports that the public best remembers, I guarantee that most people would list Kermit Washington hitting Rudy Tomjanovich, Latrell Sprewell choking P. J. Carlesimo, and Roberto Alomar spitting at umpire John Hirschbeck. Fear of men of color attacking whites in our society is part of the culture. There is no doubt that the treatment afforded to Washington, Sprewell, and Alomar was measurably different than that given Denver Bronco Bill Romanowski, who is white, after he spit in the face of a black player in 1999.

Most of the stories written about specific athletes who are violent or gender violent are about African-American athletes. Stories about them that appear without appropriate filters of what is going on in society reinforce racial stereotyping.

Athletes and Gender Violence

In the wake of the O. J. Simpson case, any incident involving an athlete assaulting a woman has received extraordinary publicity. The individual cases add up to another stereotype of the new millennium: athletes, especially basketball and football players, are more inclined to be violent towards women than nonathletes are.

Joyce Williams-Mitchell has worked extensively in this field, most recently as the executive director of the Massachusetts Coalition of Battered Women's Service Groups. As an African-American woman, she abhors the image of athletes being more prone to violence against women. "It is a myth. The facts do not bear this out. All the studies of patterns of batterers defined by occupation point to men who control women through their profession. We hear about police, clergy, dentists, and judges. I only hear about athletes as batterers when I read the paper. They are in the public's eye. Men from every profession have the potential to be batterers."

There have been, of course, too many cases of athletes committing assaults on girls and women. As I wrote this section, I received a voice mail message from a reporter: "Have you heard that Corey Dillion is the latest case of an athlete hitting a woman? I guess that depends on when you pick up the message. There may have already been another case!" His message implied that attacks on women by athletes took place hourly.

However, there has never been a thorough, scientific study conclusively showing that athletes are more inclined to violence. Jeffrey Benedict, Todd Crossett, and Mark McDonald wrote the only study that comes close. It was based on sixty-five cases of assault against women that took place on ten Division I campuses over a three year period. Thirteen of the cases involved athletes; seven of the athletes were basketball or football players.

Despite the authors' acknowledgment of both the small number of cases revealed and the fact that the survey did not control for alcohol and tobacco use or the man's attitude toward women (then three main predictors of a male's inclination to gender violence), the press regularly quoted their study without qualification. Media reports never stated that the study came up with only thirteen abusive athletes over three years. They simply said that the study concluded that student-athletes, in particular basketball or football players, committed nearly 20 percent of all campus assaults. Rosalyn Dunlap pointed out that, "This is a racially loaded conclusion. When I was a student-athlete at the University of Missouri, I never thought of keeping myself safe from a 260-pound football player any more than any other man on the street. In fact, male athletes on campus protected me."

The following is a list of data usually missing in the debate about athletes and violence against women.

- In 1994, 1,400 men killed their significant others. In that year, O. J. Simpson was the only athlete accused of murder.

- In 1998, an estimated 3 million women were battered and close to one million were raped. According to various reports in the press in the five years between 1995 and 2000, between seventy and one hundred athletes and coaches were accused of assault against a woman each year.

- The 1999 *Chronicle of Higher Education*'s annual campus crime survey showed that there were a total of 1,053 forcible sex offenses reported in 1997. Fewer than thirty-five student-athletes were arrested in conjunction with these crimes.

Gender violence is a serious problem among American men. The cost of crime to America is pegged at $500 billion per year, according to a National Institute for Justice research report for the Justice Department released in March 1996. Gender assault and child abuse accounted for $165 billion—more than one third of that total.

Rosalyn Dunlap, who worked with The National Consortium for Academics and Sport to create more awareness about the issue, said, "There are no men who should be exempted from being educated about the issue of gender violence although many believe they are. It is a problem for naval commanders, daycare providers, fraternities, guys in a bar, in corporations, in halls of higher education and, yes, on athletic teams. But no more so on athletic teams."

There have been numerous cases in which women brought suits against corporations from harassment and/or assault. The *Boston Globe* gave extensive coverage in the late 1990s to the case against Astra USA, Inc., a chemical company, where women lodged sixteen formal complaints for incidents ranging from sexual harassment to rape. Twenty-nine women brought suit against Mitsubishi for the same reasons. None of the press about Astra suggested that working in a chemical company produced a climate of sexual aggression. At Mitsubishi, no one suggested any relationship between the manufacturing process and gender assault. So why do stories about athletes imply such a linkage to athletics? Does it fit white America's racial imagery?

McPherson believes it does: "Football and basketball mean black. When the public talks about gender violence and athletes, it talks black. No one discusses the problems of golfer John Daly or Braves manager Bobby Cox. Warren Moon was another story altogether. Problems about athletes hit the papers and people think they detect a pattern because of the seeming frequency. But no one else's problems get in the papers. How do we make legitimate comparisons? With Astra and Mitsubishi, we look at the corporate climate and don't generalize about individuals. But with athletes, especially black athletes, we look at players and look for patterns to add up."

Some observers say athletes are trained to be violent and that we can expect that training to carry over into their homes. If this is true, then what about the training in lethal force we give the police, the Army, the Air Force, the Navy, and the Marines? Will these men also come home and kill? McPherson adds, "There is no logic to connect these cases, but we do fit our stereotypes of African-Americans with such images when we carry through the implication for athletes."

With all the recent publicity about the horrors of gender violence, it would be easy to forget that it was America's big, dirty secret until the O. J. Simpson case made it a notorious subject. Before that trial, few Americans were willing to talk about gender violence. The same unwillingness to confront racism diminishes society's ability to eradicate it. But the situation will never change if it remains unconfronted.

Athletes should take a leadership role on this issue, just as they have on drug abuse and educational opportunity. The MVP Program, organized in 1992 by Northeastern University's Center for the Study of Sport in Society and now headed by Jeff O'Brien, a former football player, has worked on more than sixty-five campuses training male and female athletes to be spokespeople on the issue of gender violence. Each of those schools has become proactive on an issue that has hurt so many women and their families.

Don McPherson insists that "we have to do more to help our youth survive by including our athletes rather than excluding them in helping our youth. The stereotyping of our athletes does not help. We need to be ready with facts to dispute the easy labels."

McPherson and Tom Sanders both argue vigorously that America's athletes not only don't fit the emerging stereotypes about athletes and crime, but the vast majority of professional athletes are extremely positive role models. Sanders said, "when I look at the many NBA players who have their own foundations and who are very involved with giving back to the communities where they play and where they came from, I know they are hurt by the stereotypes." McPherson asserts that "most of the players in the NFL are

deeply religious, family-centered men who are constantly giving back to their communities with time and money."

Rosalyn Dunlap wonders when the public and the media will stop being cynical about athletes. "I hear so many people say that if athletes do something in the community that they do it for publicity. Why can't we accept that athletes want to help? Sport and those who play it can help educate us and sensitize us. While we can't ignore the bad news, we should also focus on the overwhelming good news of what athletes do to make this a better world."

I do not believe the stereotypes. However, I do believe the high profile of all professional sports makes it incumbent on those involved to call on sports institutions to demand a higher standard for athletes. Athletes, once challenged, have played a leading role in the battle to educate our children; in the life and death fight against alcohol and drug abuse; and in the attempt to resolve conflicts with reason and not with fists or weapons. Now it is time to challenge them to fight the long overdue battle against gender violence.

The challenge to athletes involved a starting point of confronting the behavior of an individual athlete. Some universities had to make star athletes academically ineligible or expel them from school to convince others that they were serious about education and would not tolerate either poor academic records or athletes violating social norms.

After the tragic death of Len Bias, the nation was forced to recognize that cocaine was not "recreational," but lethal. Schools began random drug testing; the NBA promised to uphold a lifetime ban for players who ignored league drug policies. This ban was necessary to show players as well as their young fans that there could be no tolerance for the use of life-threatening drugs.

The ban will always seem unfair to the player caught with drugs. I am sure Michael Ray Richardson, who was the first NBA player banned for life, still looks in the mirror and asks, "Why me? There were other guys." But the discipline had to start somewhere. What was unfortunate for Richardson was fortunate for the NBA and for society. Action, no matter how symbolic, was critical.

Likewise, when street violence began to invade our rinks, courts, and fields, sport had to take a stand with automatic and serious sanctions that cost players money and cost teams their playing services. No commissioner or director of a players association wanted their entire league and all of its athletes branded as thugs because of those who acted out during the game.

The New England Patriots bit the bullet for all professional sports and decided not to sign draftee Christian Peter, the University of Nebraska's highly acclaimed football player, who carried numerous criminal charges on his record. It was a milestone decision. Patriot owner Robert Kraft felt compelled to take a strong stand immediately after they drafted Peter, despite the fact that he would lose dollars in the draft and could have faced lawsuits from Peter's representatives. The importance of his decision was not only that players would see clear consequences for their actions, but also that children who idolize those players would also see such consequences as relevant to their own choices in life.

Sports figures are in a unique position to effect change. Keith Lee, a six-year NFL veteran who is now the chief operating officer of the National Consortium for Academics and Sport, works to improve race relations among young people. He states, "We need positive role models who can help young people to believe in what they cannot yet see. We need them now more than ever."

Seeing the Big Picture   **Television's Interrracial Images: Some Fact, Mostly Fiction**

Think for a moment of your three favorite television shows. Now think about watching your two favorite sports teams. Is your social world as integrated as the programming you watch on TV?

HOW AMERICA'S COMPLEXION CHANGES

A NATIONALLY DISTRIBUTED, FULL-PAGE magazine advertisement placed by IBM depicts nine of its employees at a business meeting. The employees, presumably managers, are focusing on a white-haired man who is pointing to a chart. The activity depicted is rather mundane—meetings of this type take place thousands of times every business day. What makes this ad exceptional is what it is selling. In large letters across the top of the page, the text of the ad announces "Diversity Works." The employees shown in the hand-drawn advertisement consist, in order, of an older white woman, a black woman, an Asian woman, a white man, an older black man with white hair, two men of ambiguous racial identity, and a white woman in a wheelchair. The racial and ethnic makeup of the cartoon characters in this ad is intended to convey to readers that IBM, as the supporting text tells us, "values individual differences." What is particularly interesting is the lack of white men in this rendering of the inner workings of a large corporation.

IBM may indeed value diversity, but the reality is that the upper ranks of corporate management are still the domain of white men. The bipartisan Glass Ceiling Commission found that white men "hold about 95 of every 100 senior management positions, defined as vice president or above." How corporate America presents its workforce to the public and how diverse the organization actually is, especially as one moves up the occupational ranks, is a contradiction. Perhaps there is a reason this advertisement was a drawing and not an actual photograph of a diverse work environment. What occupations or organizations can you name in which high-status positions reflect the racial, ethnic, and gender composition of the United States? Think about the racial and ethnic composition of members of Congress, or the CEOs of the Fortune 500 companies, or the fifty state governors, or tenured college professors. What is the race and gender of your university or college president? What about the racial or ethnic background

of sports or entertainment celebrities? What patterns emerge, and what do they mean?

We are an incredibly diverse nation. We are reminded of this by advertisements promoting diversity from corporations like IBM, McDonald's, Texaco, Denny's, and Du Pont. We are reminded of this when we are repeatedly told that by the year 2050, about half of U.S. residents will be white and the other half will be black, Asian, and Latino. We are reminded of this when we debate the relative merits of affirmative action, bilingual education, or immigration quotas.

In the public imagination, the idea of ethnic and racial diversity seems to be simultaneously celebrated, feared, and reviled. The United States is promoted as the land of opportunity, but some groups have had more opportunity than others. Why? The United States is defined as a country of immigrants, yet many citizens are fearful that the "new wave" of immigrants will radically change "American" culture. Why? The United States is proclaimed as a color-blind nation, yet inequities based on race and ethnicity are still the norm for a sizable part of the population. If we are a color-blind nation, why is it very likely you will marry someone from the same racial background?

The readings in Part IV examine these contradictions. The four readings in the first section of Part IV, **Race, Ethnicity, and Immigration** focus on the changing complexion of the United States. Stephen Steinberg calls into question the assertion that the United States is a melting pot by pointing out that some groups have

319

never been "melted" into the stew because they were not allowed in the pot.

John Logan documents the rise of black immigrants from Africa and the Caribbean and the unique immigration experiences of these groups. This exceptionally diverse group often gets "lumped" by the media with African Americans or Latinos, but Logan demonstrates that such groupings would be a mistake.

Michael Suleiman examines a community that until very recently received very little attention from the mainstream media. Suleiman describes the ebb and flow of Arab immigrants to the United States and their socioeconomic success relative to other immigrant groups. Mary Waters examines mobility and racial identity construction to explore how race, ethnicity, and opportunity shape the experiences of Afro-Caribbeans in New York City.

The second section, **Race and Romance: Blurring Boundaries,** explores historical and contemporary trends in interracial marriage. Roland Fryer examines both historical trends and current patterns in interracial marriage. His research suggests that falling in love, even across the color line, reflects patterns that privilege one racial minority over another.

Law Professor Randall Kennedy uses popular representations of interracial couples in the media to examine just how much progress we have made in the area of interracial romance. Heather Dalmage explains how and why "racial borders" are patrolled in order to promote racial endogamy.

Kimberly McClain DaCosta examines how the color line is being redrawn within the context of the rise of multiracial families and individuals who define themselves as occupying more than one racial identity.

Finally, Charles Gallagher suggests ten things we can do to ameliorate racism as we go about our day. ✳

41 The Melting Pot and the Color Line
Stephen Steinberg

STEPHEN STEINBERG is the assistant chair of day studies and a sociologist in the Urban Studies Department at Queens College.

"EVERY NATION, UPON EXAMINATION, TURNS out to have been a more or less successful melting pot." So wrote Robert Park, the founder of the famed Chicago School of Sociology, in 1930. It is a testament to Park's prescience that he was able to imagine the melting pot at a time when the United States was ethnically more diverse, and more fragmented, than ever before. During the previous half-century, the nation had absorbed some 24 million immigrants, mostly from Eastern and Southern Europe. These "new immigrants"—Italians, Poles, Russian Jews, Ukrainians, Hungarians and others, far removed geographically and culturally from the people who settled the United States during its first century—were widely believed to be "unassimilable." In Chicago, for example, 70 percent of the population consisted of immigrants and the children of immigrants, and the city was divided into a patchwork of ethnic neighborhoods. In 1921 and 1924, Congress responded with legislation that cut the volume of immigration and instituted national quotas biased against further immigration from Southern and Eastern Europe.

Against this background, Park's dictum provided reassurance that the intermingling of peoples was a universal process and that America's ethnic discord would resolve itself over time. This optimism was shared by Chicago sociologists W. Lloyd Warner and Leo Srole, who conducted field studies of immigrant communities in the 1940s. Warner and Srole argued that appearances were

Questions to Consider

According to the theory of the melting pot, diverse ethnic and racial groups will be thrown together and meld into a new American amalgam that represents the finest cultural aspects of each community. Food is perhaps the easiest way to understand the melting pot perspective. Salsa, not ketchup, is now the number one condiment. There are almost 64,000 pizzerias, almost 7,000 Taco Bells, and 30,000 Asian restaurants in the United States, according to experts in the food industry. But as sociologist Stephen Steinberg argues, not everyone has been allowed into the pot. He suggests "America's melting pot has been inclusive of everybody but blacks." Is his statement about black exclusion from the melting pot justified when we consider African American contributions to popular culture?

deceptive, that the ethnic enclave, though it seemed to nurture isolation and separatism, actually functioned as a decompression chamber, helping immigrants adjust to their new surroundings and preparing the next generation to venture into the mainstream. Whatever its original raison d'etre, the ethnic community actually functioned as an instrument of assimilation.

But if early sociologists were confident about assimilation, a later generation rejected the idea of the melting pot. Ironically, many of these scholars were themselves children of immigrants who have risen to the top of the academic ladder. Their revisionist view of the melting pot can be seen as part of a broader trend among second-generation immigrants: assimilation breeds nostalgia. First-generation immigrants, who are most authentically steeped in ethnic culture, tend to throw it away, often with both hands, as they pursue the opportunities that led them to come to America in the first place. Decades later, their largely assimilated children engage in desperate, but usually futile, efforts to recover the very culture that their parents relinquished. As the children of immigrants entered the ranks of social science, they brought this same nostalgia to their analysis of ethnic trends.

The turning point came with the publication of *Beyond the Melting Pot* in 1970. Scholars Nathan Glazer and Daniel Patrick Moynihan, who had each ascended from immigrant poverty to the ivory tower, concluded from their study of New York City that "the most important thing about the melting pot was that it did not happen." The syntax of this much-quoted passage warrants a moment's reflection. To say that the melting pot "did not happen" is not the same as saying that it was not happening. After all, Park and other theorists of assimilation never claimed that the melting pot was a fait accompli; nor did they project a deadline for the completion of this evolutionary process. Nevertheless, the book's title and argument found a receptive audience. Aside from selling over half a million copies, *Beyond the Melting Pot* marked the beginning of a paradigm shift in the study of ethnicity.

Other books soon appeared that trumpeted the survival of ethnicity over the sinister forces of assimilation. Their titles celebrated *The Decline of the WASP* (1971) and *The Rise of the Unmeltable Ethnics* (1971). A year later, an article in the *New York Times Magazine* proclaimed, "America Is NOT a Melting Pot." Indeed, these writers contended that the United States was undergoing an "ethnic revival" that would resuscitate immigrant cultures. Again, there is a striking historical irony. When ethnic groups were intact and cultural differences pronounced, leading sociologists held that assimilation was inevitable. Several decades later, when these groups had undergone profound transformation, forsaking major elements of their ancestral cultures and assuming comfortable identities as Americans, the prevailing view was that the melting pot had "never happened."

But such attempts to turn back the clock of assimilation would prove difficult. With the exception of Native Americans, ethnic groups in America are transplanted peoples, far removed in time and space from their original homelands. The necessity of adapting to life in America made assimilation, in Park's words, "progressive and irreversible." By the late 1970s, a number of scholars, myself among them, had begun to argue that the so-called ethnic revival was in fact a symptom of decline, a dying gasp of ethnic consciousness. In fact, all the long-term trends suggested that the melting pot was working as predicted: during the twentieth century, immigrants largely lost their original language and culture, ethnic enclaves dispersed as economic and occupational mobility increased, and the rate of ethnic and religious intermarriage accelerated.

It may be that some observers deny the evident fact of assimilation simply because of the ambiguous terminology that we use to describe it. "Melting pot" conjures up an image of a bubbling cauldron into which immigrants descend—whether they jump or are pushed is another matter—and are quickly dissolved into oblivion. Though rhetorically effective, this imagery obscures the evolutionary nature of assimilation. Correctly understood, it is a process that occurs incrementally across generations. To argue that ethnicity is still an active force in American life—as Glazer and Moynihan did in 1970 and other scholars have repeated ever since—is to beg the crucial question. Just because assimilation isn't complete doesn't mean that it isn't taking place.

How we view assimilation also depends on our conception of culture. Revisionists argue that the melting pot theory is based on a static view, in which the original culture of an immigrant's homeland is simply replaced by American culture. Such critics concede that Italian-Americans, for example, bear little resemblance to Italians in Italy, but they argue that Italian-Americans are nevertheless a distinct community, forged on American soil, complete with its own identity and subculture.

Yet melting pot theorists also realize that immigrant cultures evolve and take new forms as newcomers adapt to life in America. The crucial issue is not whether change occurs, but rather the direction and the end result of that change. The key question is this: will the ethnicity of formerly hyphenated Americans endure, or is it merely a transitional stage in a long-term assimilation? My position has long been that, even if we assume a greater tolerance for diversity than actually exists in American society, the conditions were never promising for a genuine and lasting pluralism.

· · ·

Today there is an emerging consensus that the descendants of the great waves of European immigration have reached an advanced stage of assimilation. The most striking evidence is provided by the soaring rates of intermarriage across ethnic lines. According to a 1990 study by sociologist Richard Alba, the percentage of white ethnics aged twenty-five to thirty-four who married outside their own groups was as follows: Germans, 52 percent; Irish, 65 percent; English, 62 percent; Italians, 73 percent; French, 78 percent; Scots, 82 percent; Poles, 84 percent. Even in the case of Jews, for whom intermarriage was historically low, the figure is now thought to approach 50 percent. The conclusion seems inescapable that the melting pot, in the most literal sense, is a reality for groups of European ancestry.

Indeed, sociologists now lump these groups together under the rubric of "Euro-American," thus resolving with a single word the assimilation question that was debated for half a century. It is now conceded that the various nationalities of European descent have become simply "white." As a result, ethnic pluralists and opponents of the melting pot have retreated to a new position: the melting pot does exist, but it is "for whites only." On this view, the common "whiteness" of the Irish, Italians, Poles, Jews and other groups destined them to "melt," even though they were once regarded as distinct races whose cultural and genetic differences rendered them unassimilable. A new genre of "whiteness studies" has documented the process through which these erstwhile pariahs were incorporated into the white majority. The core argument is encapsulated in the titles of several recent books, including *How the Irish Became White, How Jews Became White Folks* and *Whiteness of a Different Color.*

But this argument goes on to hold that the current wave of immigrants, composed mainly of "people of color" from Asia, Latin America and the Caribbean, will not be able to follow in the footsteps of the white ethnics. The fault line dividing ethnic groups in America is no longer nationality or religion, but race. Indeed, a number of scholars have declared that "assimilation theory is dead," since its Eurocentric bias renders it useless for understanding the condition and destiny of people of color.

Aside from racism, the new ethnic pluralists cite several positive factors that, they argue, will spare the new immigrants from the dreaded melting pot. Today's immigrants enter a society that is far more tolerant of ethnic diversity. The ideology of multiculturalism extols ethnic difference and provides institutional mechanisms, such as bilingual education, for the preservation of immigrants' language and culture. As a result, the Asians, Latinos and Caribbeans who make up the new immigration have formed cohesive ethnic communities with flourishing economies and foreign-language media, including cable television, that provide institutional anchorage for language and culture. Furthermore, compared to earlier immigrants, the new immigrants have easy access to their homelands, thanks to telecommunications and cheap airfare. And finally, many new immigrants arrive with education and skills, and often capital as well, and therefore are not forced to compromise their ethnic identities for the sake of economic survival. Indeed, in today's global economy, it is not a handicap but an asset to be multilingual and multicultural.

These are all valid points. The question is whether they add up to the conclusion that assimilation is dead, and that the new immigrants will not "melt" as did their predecessors from Europe. It must be conceded that this is a possible scenario, given what we know about racism as a divisive force in America history. One cannot immediately discount the argument that the melting pot is "for whites only," and that today's immigrants will be prevented from assimilating.

In fact, however, this proposition receives little empirical support from the large body of research on today's immigrants. Indeed, the most compelling evidence leads to the conclusion that, notwithstanding their racial difference, the new immigrants are not only assimilating but are doing so at an even faster rate than did earlier immigrants from Europe.

In retrospect, an early indicator of the eventual assimilation of European immigrants was the rapidity with which they lost their native languages. A pattern emerges with stubborn consistency. Immigrants, of course, retained their native tongues; their children typically were bilingual; and by the third generation, the vast majority were monolingual in English. The virtual eradication of languages in only two generations shows just how fragile culture is, at least once it loses its "survival value" and is severed from the institutions that nourish it. Needless to say, immigrants and their bilingual children were not indifferent to the snuffing out of their native language. But the lesson of history is that sentiment—even passionate loyalty—is not enough to withstand the powerful forces of assimilation.

This process is being reenacted—if anything, at an accelerated pace—among the new immigrants. In a study of Los Angeles based on 1990 census data, David Lopez found that, among Asians, the shift to English monolingualism was nearly universal by the third generation. Consider what this means for family relations. Unless the immigrant grandparents acquire a basic fluency in English, which often is not the case, then grandchildren cannot converse with their grandparents except through the mediation of their bilingual parents.

The picture is somewhat more complex among Latinos, though the overall pattern is still one of rapid language loss. If retention of Spanish were to occur anywhere in the United States, it would be in Los Angeles. Not only do most L.A. Latinos live in predominantly Latino neighborhoods, but the city also has a thriving ethnic press and electronic media. Furthermore, Los Angeles has had an official policy of promoting multiculturalism, including bilingual education and bilingual ballots. Yet Lopez found that 57 percent of third-generation Latinos spoke only English at home. Closer examination of the data revealed that Spanish was retained mainly in households where a foreign-born person—presumably that all-important immigrant grandparent—was present. In the case of Mexican-American youth living in households with no immigrants, only 20 percent spoke Spanish at home.

A study of Cubans in South Florida also found that most young people preferred to speak English at home, even when they were bilingual. Nor was this true only of the middle classes. Among second-generation youth who classified themselves as working class or poor, three-quarters preferred to speak English. Clearly, even though today's society is nominally more conducive to language retention, the new immigrants are moving very rapidly to English monolingualism.

If loss of a native language marks the beginning of the assimilation process, marriage across ethnic lines represents the last (or next to last) stage. Here again, the data do not support either the assumptions or the hopes of the new ethnic pluralists. A study based on the 1990 census found that 40 percent of Asians born in the United States married non-Asians—and these are mostly the children,

not even the grandchildren, of immigrants. The figures ranged from 22 percent among Vietnamese to 31 percent among Japanese, 38 percent among Asian Indians, 46 percent among Chinese, 65 percent among Filipinos and 72 percent among Koreans. These figures are so high that they call into question the very category of race in describing Asian-Americans. Indeed, the level of marriage between Asians of different nationalities is strikingly low, suggesting that they do not see themselves as members of a pan-ethnic Asian "race." Rather, most Asians who intermarry do so with whites, giving rise to speculation that Asians are in the process of "becoming white."

Rates of intermarriage for Latinos are lower than for Asians, but they are high nevertheless. Almost one-third of U.S.-born Hispanics between the ages of twenty-five and thirty-four are married to non-Hispanic whites. Indeed, marriage across racial lines has become so commonplace that some commentators have raised the possibility of a "mestizo America"—a racial mixture that blurs the boundaries among ethnic groups. On this view, it is not a question of minorities being absorbed into the white majority, but rather of a fusing of these diverse peoples into a new amalgam. This is the literal meaning of a "melting pot," and a fulfillment of Robert Park's prescient observation that every nation is a "more or less successful melting pot." Like it or not, and the dissent of the ethnic pluralists is clear, assimilation does appear to be progressive and irreversible, the inexorable by-product of forces put into motion by the very act of immigrating.

• • •

Admittedly, this sweeping conclusion, while it captures the main thrust of American ethnic history, does not tell the whole story: in particular, it does not account for the African-American experience. Here we speak of a group that came to America in slave ships, not immigrant steamers. While successive waves of immigrants flowed into the country, first to settle the land and later to provide labor for burgeoning industries, blacks were trapped in the South in a system of feudal agriculture. Even in the North, a rigid color line excluded them from the manufacturing sector. In short, the Industrial Revolution was "for whites only," depriving blacks of the jobs and opportunities that delivered Europe's huddled masses from poverty.

This was the historic wrong that was supposed to be remedied by landmark civil rights legislation in the 1960s.

But by the time most blacks arrived in Northern cities, the manufacturing sector was undergoing a permanent decline, reflecting the impact of labor-saving technology and the export of jobs to low-wage countries. Not only did blacks encounter far less favorable opportunities than did immigrants, not only did they suffer from the economic consequences of past discrimination, and not only did they encounter pervasive racism in the world of work, but they also experienced intense labor competition from yet another huge wave of immigrants, which began in the 1960s and continues to this day.

Though these new immigrants are conspicuous for their "racial" difference, they are not subjected to the all-encompassing system of racial discrimination that was the legacy of slavery. Furthermore, many of these immigrants arrived with education and skills—and sometimes capital as well—that accelerated their mobility and social integration. As noted earlier, Asians and Latinos already display a far greater degree of "residential assimilation" than blacks. And at a time when marriage across racial lines is soaring for Asians and Latinos, it has inched up only slightly for blacks, again indicating that a fundamentally different dynamic is at work. The conclusion is unavoidable: America's melting pot has been inclusive of everybody but blacks.

This is not to deny the obvious fact that there has been enormous progress over the past half-century. Jim Crow is a thing of the past, thanks largely to the black protest movement. The emergence of a large black middle class is another encouraging development, though in my view this does not reflect the deracialization of labor markets so much as the favorable impact of affirmative action policy over several decades. Finally, there has been an unmistakable shift in America's fundamental attitudes toward race. The prominence of blacks among the nation's elites, as well as its pantheon of folk heroes, is stark proof that skin color is no longer a badge of inferiority.

Nevertheless, ours is still a society riven by race. Claims of "progress" invariably depend on comparing the situation today to a retrograde past. The problem here, as James Baldwin observed, is that the crimes of the past are used to gloss over the crimes of the present. When comparisons are made between blacks and whites today, a far less sanguine picture emerges. For example, blacks today earn only three-fifths as much as whites. Furthermore, although the income gap between blacks and whites closed

somewhat in the 1960s, there has been little or no progress since the mid-1970s. So long as nearly a quarter of blacks, and half of black youth, live below the poverty line, these class factors will continue to engender and reinforce racial division.

Even more germane to the question of whether America is a melting pot, black and white Americans are as residentially segregated as ever. Nor is this true only of inner-city blacks. Middle-class blacks also encounter pervasive discrimination in housing, and their arrival into white suburbs usually triggers white flight, resulting in resegregation. It is a mark of the melting pot's failure that African-Americans, whose roots go back to the founding of the nation, are more segregated than even recent immigrants from Asia and Latin America.

In short, despite "progress," ghettoization is still a fact of life. And here we confront a great historical paradox—for these ghettos, the enforced "home" of the nation's racial pariahs, also nourished a vibrant African-American subculture. As sociologist Bob Blauner has observed, while immigrant ghettos "functioned as way stations on the road to acculturation and assimilation," the black ghetto has been permanent, "a continuing crucible for ethnic development and building." And unlike immigrants, who clung to vestiges of cultures ripped from their moorings in distant places, black culture evolved out of the lived experience of black people in America. Instead of isolated fragments selected precisely because they did not interfere with mainstream American culture, black culture is an integral part of the everyday lives of black people. As a result, black culture displays a vitality and dynamism that is generally lacking among the ossifying cultures of the nation's immigrant groups.

Ironically, generations of sociologists have taken precisely the opposite position, on the one hand celebrating the cultures of the nation's immigrant groups and, on the other, holding that blacks were merely "white Americans in black skin," lacking a culture of their own. In the same book where they declared that the melting pot "never happened," Glazer and Moynihan wrote that "it is not possible for Negroes to view themselves as other ethnic groups viewed themselves because—and this is the key to much in the Negro world—the Negro is only an American and nothing else. He has no values and culture to guard and protect." Under a barrage of criticism, Glazer subsequently explained that he meant blacks had no *foreign* culture to guard or protect. However, this only compounds the error, since these foreign cultures—and precisely because they were foreign—were destined to a gradual but inexorable decline. On the other hand, as an indigenous product of the American experience, black culture continues not only to thrive in segregated black communities but also to exert a powerful influence on mainstream American culture.

·   ·   ·

Throughout this essay, I have emphasized that the melting pot is still at work and that, like past immigrants, today's immigrants from outside the Western Hemisphere will also be fully assimilated at some indeterminate point in the future. The problem, of course, is that we live in the present. It may be our national destiny to become a melting pot, but today the United States is a remarkably polyglot society in which ethnicity flourishes. Despite an overriding trend toward assimilation, ethnic loyalties and attachments remain strong even among segments of older immigrant groups. New immigrants, freshly arrived on American soil, are only at the early stages of the assimilation process. To turn a blind eye to these realities by focusing on long-term trends runs the risk of blotting out the lives and sensibilities of entire communities.

Nor does this warning apply only to ideologues on the political right who, in the name of the melting pot, have waged a relentless crusade against bilingualism, multicultural education and affirmative action. In recent years, a left discourse has emerged that looks "beyond race" and "beyond ethnicity," imagining a post-ethnic future where people are not defined by genes or ancestry. This vision promotes intermarriage across racial and ethnic lines as a way of eliminating, once and for all, the dissonances and conflicts attending racial and ethnic diversity.

For example, historian Gary Nash, a pioneer of multicultural education, has published an essay titled "The Hidden History of Mestizo America," in which he argues that we "need new ways of transcending America's Achilles' heel of race, now that a certain amount of progress has been achieved in living up to our own credo." Like Nash, sociologist Orlando Patterson advocates miscegenation as the ultimate solution to America's intractable race problem. Never mind that African-Americans—not to speak of other ethnic groups—may not wish to miscegenate themselves out of existence. Never mind that it would take generations, if not centuries, to produce the hybrid nation that they envision. Instead of confronting the urgent problems of race in America and addressing the challenges of a multicultural society, these visionaries are throwing in the towel. They use a utopian vision of the melting pot as a façade for moral capitulation.

Let me be clear. There is compelling evidence that the United States will one day become a melting pot, and that this day is approaching faster than ethnic pluralists are willing to acknowledge. From a moral standpoint, however, it is imperative that this melting pot evolve through the operation of historical forces rather than through public policy interventions. It is wrong—to continue the metaphor—to turn up the temperature under the melting pot, or to nudge, cajole or push people into the bubbling cauldron. Any use of state power to undermine ethnicity or to force assimilation is incompatible with democratic principles and violates the rights of ethnic minorities to hold onto their languages and cultures.

The irony of the matter is that, like earlier waves of immigrants, today's newcomers will find their way to the melting pot in due course. So, presumably, will African-Americans, but not until the structures of American apartheid are thoroughly dismantled and the persistent inequalities are resolved. These groups will pursue the personal and social integration that is the promise of the melting pot. But they must do so of their own accord, and not on somebody else's timetable. Here we can take another lesson from history: the carrot, not the stick, has always been the more effective instrument of assimilation.

Seeing the Big Picture   Who Is Allowed to "Melt" in the Pot? Who Wants To?

In Section X of the Appendix, do rates of intermarriage support the assertion that the United States is a melting pot? What does the popularity of hip-hop and rap say about the theory of the melting pot?

42 Who Are the Other African Americans? Contemporary African and Caribbean Immigrants in the United States

John R. Logan

JOHN R. LOGAN is professor of sociology at Brown University. Dr. Logan is co-author, along with Harvey Molotch, of *Urban Fortunes: The Political Economy of Place.* His most recent, edited book, *The New Chinese City: Globalization and Market Reform,* was published by Blackwell in 2001.

A S QUICKLY AS THE HISPANIC AND ASIAN populations in the United States have grown, there has been nearly equal growth among black Americans with recent roots in Africa and the Caribbean. The number of black Americans born in sub-Saharan Africa nearly tripled during the 1990s. The number identifying a Caribbean ancestry increased by over 60 percent. Census 2000 shows that Afro-Caribbeans in the United States number over 1.5 million—more than some more visible national-origin groups, such as Cubans and Koreans. Africans number over six hundred thousand. In some major metropolitan regions, these "new" black groups amount to 20 percent or more of the black population. And, nationally, nearly 25 percent of the growth of the black population between 1990 and 2000 was due to people arriving from Africa and the Caribbean.

This [reading] summarizes what is known about these "new" black Americans: their numbers, social backgrounds, and residential locations in metropolitan areas. It makes the following key points:

- It is well known that the socioeconomic profile of non-Hispanic blacks is unfavorable compared to whites, and Asians. There is also striking variation within America's black population. The social and economic profile of Afro-Caribbeans and Africans is far above that of African Americans and even better than that of Hispanics.
- Afro-Caribbeans are heavily concentrated on the East Coast. Six out of ten live in the New York, Miami, and

Questions to Consider The national narrative on immigration usually focuses on immigrants from Mexico and Central and South America, but there has been a sizable increase in the number of black immigrants from Africa and the Caribbean. There is also a tendency to lump the socioeconomic status and life experiences of new black immigrants from Africa and the Caribbean with African Americans. Professor Logan's research shows that there are some similarities between these populations (e.g., levels of segregation from whites), but these groups are exceptionally diverse. How and in what ways do the experiences of these new groups differ from those of African Americans? Is it the case that the experiences of black African and Caribbean immigrants are similar to those of Latinos? Why and how?

Ft. Lauderdale metropolitan regions. More than half are Haitian in Miami; Haitians are well represented, but outnumbered by Jamaicans, in New York and Ft. Lauderdale.

- America's African population, on the other hand, is much more geographically dispersed. The largest numbers are in Washington, D.C., and New York. In both places, the majority are from West Africa, especially Ghana and Nigeria. East Africa, including Ethiopia and Somalia, is the other main region of origin.
- Like African Americans, Afro-Caribbeans and Africans are highly segregated from whites. But these black ethnic groups overlap only partly with one another in the neighborhoods in which they live. Segregation among

black ethnic groups reflects important social differences among them.

• In the metropolitan areas where they live in largest
numbers, Africans tend to live in neighborhoods with a
higher median income and education level than African
Americans and Afro-Caribbeans. In these metro areas,
Afro-Caribbeans tend to live in neighborhoods with a
higher percentage of homeowners than either African
Americans or Africans.

Counting Non-Hispanic Blacks in America

The Census Bureau provides different ways of identifying these black populations, depending on the data source
that is used.

For data on individuals, the 1990 5 percent Public Use
Microdata Sample (1990 PUMS) data files and the Census
2000 1 percent Public Use Microdata Sample (2000 PUMS)
make it possible to count the number of African Americans,
Afro-Caribbeans, and Africans by combining information
on their race, birth, and ancestry. Among non-Hispanic
blacks, this study classifies those reporting their ancestry,
country of birth, or both in the predominantly black islands
of the Caribbean (including such places as Jamaica and Trinidad, but not Guyana) as "Afro-Caribbean." . . .

The Size and Regional Distribution of the Black Population

Census 2000 counted over thirty-five million non-Hispanic
blacks, as shown in Table 1. This represents over 12 percent
of the U.S. population. The non-Hispanic black population
grew by over six million people, a growth rate of almost
21 percent, since the last decennial census. More than nine
out of ten of these were African American (based on our
classification of persons using 2000 PUMS), but the percentage of other black groups is growing rapidly (from 4 percent
in 1990, based on 1990 PUMS data, to 6.1 percent in 2000).

Over 1.5 million blacks can now be classified as
Afro-Caribbeans, and over 600,000 can be classified as
African. The Afro-Caribbean population grew by more
than 618,000 (almost 67 percent), and Africans grew by
more than 383,000 (a growth rate of almost 167 percent,
approaching a tripling of the African population). These
two groups combined, despite being much smaller than

the African-American population, contributed about
17 percent of the six-million-person increase in the non-
Hispanic black population during the 1990s. Although not
an often recognized part of the American ethnic mosaic,
both of these groups are emerging as large and fast-
growing populations. Afro-Caribbeans now outnumber
and are growing faster than such well-established ethnic
minorities as Cubans and Koreans.

Analysis of all 331 metropolitan regions reveals distinct residential patterns for African Americans, Afro-
Caribbeans, and Africans. Consider the ten metropolitan
regions with the largest representation of the latter two
groups. These are listed in Tables 2 and 3. New York, Boston,
Washington, D.C., and Atlanta are the metros represented
in both tables.

Like African Americans, who are present in large numbers in many metro areas, Africans are dispersed throughout
the country. Only a quarter of Africans live in one of the ten
largest metropolitan regions, and these metro areas are geographically dispersed. This dispersion, in combination with
their smaller numbers, may help explain the "invisibility" of
African immigrants in the United States (Arthur 2000). In
contrast, Afro-Caribbeans are heavily concentrated in just
a few metro areas, all on the East Coast. Six out of ten live
in the New York, Miami, and Ft. Lauderdale metro areas;
nearly six hundred thousand live in New York alone.

All of the top ten metro regions for Afro-Caribbean
populations show growth rates of at least 40 percent
since 1990, but four metro areas more than doubled the
size of this population. Atlanta saw a fourfold increase
in its Afro-Caribbean population, while Orlando nearly
tripled its population of this group. With the exceptions
of Washington, D.C., and Atlanta, the percentage of the
non-Hispanic black population accounted for by Afro-
Caribbeans in these top metropolitan regions is quite
striking. For instance, over one-quarter of the non-
Hispanic black population in the New York and Boston
metro areas is Afro-Caribbean.

Jamaicans and Haitians are the two major sources
of Afro-Caribbeans in all ten areas shown in Table 2. A
majority in Miami (61 percent), West Palm Beach (62 percent), and Boston (57 percent) and a near majority in Newark (49.8 percent) are of Haitian ancestry. Jamaicans are
the larger group in Ft. Lauderdale (46 percent), New York
(40 percent), Nassau-Suffolk (39 percent), Washington,
D.C. (49 percent), and Atlanta (53 percent).

TABLE 1 Composition and Growth of the Non-Hispanic Black Populations of the U.S., 1990–2000

Group	Population 1990	Population 2000	Percentage of Black Population 1990	Percentage of Black Population 2000	Percentage of Total Population 1990	Percentage of Total Population 2000	Growth 1990–2000
African American	28,034,275	33,048,095	96.0	93.9	11.3	11.7	17.9
Afro-Caribbean	924,693	1,542,895	3.2	4.4	0.4	0.5	66.9
African	229,488	612,548	0.8	1.7	0.1	0.2	166.9
Non-Hispanic white	188,013,404	194,433,424			75.6	69.1	3.4
Non-Hispanic black	29,188,456	35,203,538			11.7	12.5	20.6
Hispanic	21,836,851	35,241,468			8.8	12.5	61.4
Asian	6,977,447	10,050,579			2.8	3.6	44.0
United States Total	248,709,873	281,421,906			100.0	100.0	13.2

Washington, D.C., and New York have the largest African-born populations (80,281 and 73,851, respectively). The 1990–2000 growth rates exceed 100 percent in all the top metro areas for this population (save Los Angeles–Long Beach at 53.5 percent). Minneapolis–St. Paul saw a 628.4 percent increase in its African population, largely due to refugees from East Africa. In Minneapolis–St. Paul, Africans contribute over 15 percent of the non-Hispanic black population; in Boston, Africans account for nearly 10 percent of non-Hispanic blacks.

In the ten metro areas in Table 3, most Africans were born in West Africa (mainly Nigeria and Ghana) or East Africa (Ethiopia or Somalia). East Africans are the larger source in Minneapolis (61 percent), and they approximately equal West Africans in Los Angeles–Long Beach (37 percent) and Dallas (40 percent). Elsewhere, West Africans predominate: Washington, D.C. (53 percent), New York (69 percent), Atlanta (48 percent), Boston (60 percent), Houston (61 percent), Chicago (58 percent), and Philadelphia (53 percent).

TABLE 2 Metros with Largest Afro-Caribbean Population, 2000

Metro Area	Afro-Caribbean 1990	Afro-Caribbean 2000	Percentage of Black Total 1990	Percentage of Black Total 2000	Percentage of Metro Total 1990	Percentage of Metro Total 2000	Growth 1990–2000
New York, NY	403,198	566,770	20.3	25.7	4.7	6.1	40.6
Miami, FL	105,477	153,255	28.5	34.4	5.4	6.8	45.3
Fort Lauderdale, FL	55,197	150,476	29.6	43.4	4.4	9.3	172.6
Boston, MA–NH	40,825	62,950	20.6	25.6	1.3	1.8	54.2
Nassau–Suffolk, NY	32,210	60,412	17.7	25.5	1.2	2.2	87.6
Newark, NJ	29,818	55,345	7.3	12.1	1.6	2.7	85.6
West Palm Beach–Boca Raton, FL	20,441	49,402	19.8	30.3	2.4	4.4	141.7
Washington, DC–MD–VA–WV	32,440	48,900	3.1	3.7	0.8	1.0	50.7
Orlando, FL	14,872	42,531	10.4	18.4	1.2	2.6	186.0
Atlanta, GA	8,342	35,308	1.1	2.9	0.3	0.9	323.3

TABLE 3   Metros with Largest African-Born Population, 2000

Metro Area	African Born		Percentage of Black Total		Percentage of Metro Total		Growth
	1990	2000	1990	2000	1990	2000	1990–2000
Washington, DC–MD–VA–WV	32,248	80,281	3.0	6.1	0.8	1.6	148.9
New York, NY	31,532	73,851	1.6	3.4	0.4	0.8	134.2
Atlanta, GA	8,919	34,302	1.2	2.9	0.3	0.8	284.6
Minneapolis–St. Paul, MN–WI	3,788	27,592	4.3	15.4	0.1	0.9	628.4
Los Angeles–Long Beach, CA	16,826	25,829	1.8	2.7	0.2	0.3	53.5
Boston, MA–NH	11,989	24,231	6.0	9.8	0.4	0.7	102.1
Houston, TX	9,882	22,638	1.6	3.1	0.3	0.5	129.1
Chicago, IL	8,738	19,438	0.6	1.2	0.1	0.2	122.5
Dallas, TX	7,373	19,134	1.8	3.6	0.3	0.5	159.5
Philadelphia, PA–NJ	5,098	16,344	0.6	1.6	0.1	0.3	220.6

Social and Economic Characteristics of America's Black Populations

We know that the socioeconomic profile of non-Hispanic blacks does not compare favorably to those of whites and Asians. Table 4 offers a comparison based on the 1990 and 2000 PUMS. Less recognized is the diversity within the black population. African Americans have lower educational attainment and median household income and higher unemployment and impoverishment than Afro-Caribbeans and Africans. Afro-Caribbeans and Africans generally compare favorably to America's Hispanic population, while African Americans fare worse. There has been considerable debate about the source of these differences (see, especially, Sowell 1978 and a review of critiques of Sowell's conclusions by James 2002). Thomas Sowell suggests that they are due to cultural gaps, where the thrift and work ethic of immigrants operate in favor of the newer black groups. Mary Waters (1999) reports that Afro-Caribbean immigrants tend to agree with this thesis and that they often seek to distance themselves from an African-American identity; however, she also finds that employers favor Afro-Caribbean workers, in part because they are perceived to be more compliant and more willing to accept inferior wages and working conditions. Winston James (2002) argues that most differences in outcomes are due to immigrant selectivity (see also Takyi 2002a) and that black immigrants, like African Americans and unlike most other immigrant groups, are strongly affected by racial discrimination in the United States.

In sum, Table 4 makes the following points:

- *Nativity:* Over two-thirds of the Afro-Caribbean and nearly 80 percent of the African population is foreign born. The percentage of foreign born in these groups is higher than that of Asians. Not surprisingly, the percentage of foreign born among the group we define as African American is small.

- *Education:* Educational attainment of Africans (14.0 years) is higher than Afro-Caribbeans (12.6 years) or African Americans (12.4 years); indeed, it is higher even than that of whites and Asians.

- *Income:* Median household income of African Americans is lower than that of any other group in the table, lower even than that of Hispanics. Africans and Afro-Caribbeans have much higher median incomes (about $43,000), though these are still well below those of whites and Asians.

- *Unemployment and poverty:* Africans and Afro-Caribbeans also have the lowest rates of unemployment and impoverishment among blacks, comparing favorably to Hispanics. Their position is substantially worse than that of Asians and whites, but Africans' unemployment is not far from that of these two groups.

The social and economic profile of all three black groups generally improved during the 1990s, though the gain in median household income of Afro-Caribbeans was marginal, and the average educational attainment of Africans slipped. Gains for African Americans somewhat

TABLE 4 Social and Economic Characteristics of Non-Hispanic Black Populations in Comparison with Major U.S. Racial and Ethnic Groups, 1990 and 2000

Group	Population	Foreign Born (%)	Years of Education	Median Household Income ($)	Unemployed (%)	Below Poverty (%)
1990						
African American	28,034,275	1.8	11.7	29,251	12.5	32.8
Afro-Caribbean	924,693	72.4	12.1	42,927	9.4	17.8
African	229,488	72.1	14.3	35,041	8.5	24.7
Non-Hispanic white	188,013,404	3.9	12.9	47,481	4.7	11.3
Non-Hispanic black	29,188,456	4.7	11.7	29,850	12.3	32.3
Hispanic	21,836,851	42.7	10.2	35,041	9.9	27.0
Asian	6,977,447	67.5	13.1	54,508	5.0	15.9
2000						
African American	33,048,095	2.2	12.4	33,790	11.2	30.4
Afro-Caribbean	1,542,895	68.3	12.6	43,650	8.7	18.8
African	612,548	78.5	14.0	42,900	7.3	22.1
Non-Hispanic white	194,433,424	4.2	13.5	53,000	4.0	11.2
Non-Hispanic black	35,203,538	6.4	12.5	34,300	11.0	29.7
Hispanic	35,241,468	40.9	10.5	38,500	8.8	26.0
Asian	10,050,579	66.5	13.9	62,000	4.6	13.9

diminished their gap with other non-Hispanic black populations. Very substantial differences in the average socioeconomic standing of these groups remain, though it is unclear how these various characteristics are interrelated. Some studies have shown, for example, that among employed males, there are no differences among black groups in work intensity and motivation to work (Dodoo 1999). There are also additional differences among Africans with different national origins (Takyi 2002b; Kollehlon and Eule 2003).

Residential Patterns within Metropolitan Regions

Another way to evaluate and compare the experiences of these black populations is to look at the degree to which their neighborhoods are segregated from those of other groups and from one another. It was shown above that the socioeconomic conditions of Afro-Caribbeans and Africans are different from those of African Americans; are their residential surroundings also distinct?

This question can be studied through the summary files in which Afro-Caribbeans are identified by ancestry and Africans by country of birth. The 1990 and 2000 population censuses provide the counts necessary to calculate levels of group isolation (the percentage of same-group members in the census tract where the average group member lives); exposure to all non-Hispanic blacks and exposure to whites (defined as the percentage of non-Hispanic blacks and non-Hispanic whites, respectively, in the census tract where the average group member lives); and segregation (the Index of Dissimilarity) from non-Hispanic whites and other black groups (the scores show the percentage of a given group that would have to move to another tract in order for the two groups to be equally distributed). These are indicators of the extent to which a group has developed its own residential enclaves in metropolitan areas. These figures have been calculated by computing levels of isolation, exposure, and dissimilarity in every metropolitan area, then taking a weighted average, giving more weight to areas with more group members.

Table 1 showed that African Americans make up just under 12 percent of the population in the United States, while Afro-Caribbeans and Africans account for 0.5 percent and 0.2 percent, respectively. Thus, if these non-Hispanic black groups were distributed randomly (without regard to in-group preferences or discrimination), their isolation index values would be about 12, 0.5, and 0.2, respectively. Likewise, the exposure scores would match the population percentages of non-Hispanic blacks and whites in Table 1. Dissimilarity is a measure of evenness and thus captures how equally members of a given group are distributed across tracts compared to another group. A dissimilarity score of less than 30 is generally thought to indicate low segregation, scores between 30 and 55 indicate moderate segregation, and scores above 55 indicate high segregation.

Table 5 shows that exposure to whites is low and declining for each black group. Africans have the highest exposure to whites (in 2000, just under half of the people in the neighborhood where an average African person lived was white); Afro-Caribbeans now have the lowest exposure to whites (29.9 percent) among black groups. Conversely, dissimilarity scores indicate high, though

slightly declining, segregation of all non-Hispanic black groups from whites. All dissimilarity scores from non-Hispanic whites are in excess of 60 percent.

The percentage of African Americans in the neighborhood where an average African American person lives declined from 54.3 percent in 1990 to 49.4 percent in 2000. Because of their smaller size, other black groups have much lower isolation scores, though these were on an upward trajectory in the 1990s. While they live in neighborhoods where their own group tends to be a small minority, Afro-Caribbeans' neighborhoods are, on average, close to 50 percent black. Africans, on the other hand, live in neighborhoods where blacks are outnumbered by whites (though they did increase their exposure to blacks from 23.3 percent to 28.3 percent).

Segregation of black groups from one another, as measured by the Index of Dissimilarity, is declining, but it is strikingly high. (Note that these average values are not symmetrical because the average segregation of group *x* from group *y* is weighted by the number of group *x* residents; segregation of group *y* from group *x* is weighted by the number of group *y* residents.) Caution should be exercised in interpreting these figures, however. Because

TABLE 5   **Segregation of Black Populations, National Metro Averages**

		African Americans	Afro-Caribbeans	African Born
Exposure to whites	1990	33.4%	33.5%	56.7%
	2000	33.3	29.9	46.3
Segregation from whites	1990	68.6	74.1	69.6
	2000	65.0	71.8	67.8
Isolation (exposure to own group)	1990	54.3	12.5	1.8
	2000	49.4	15.3	3.3
Exposure to blacks	1990	56.1	47.3	23.3
	2000	51.8	47.3	28.3
Segregation from African Americans	1990	—	46.6	68.9
	2000	—	42.5	59.2
Segregation from Afro-Caribbeans	1990	62.3	—	66.7
	2000	56.3	—	60.3
Segregation from Africans	1990	75.8	66.1	—
	2000	66.7	60.0	—

Africans and Afro-Caribbeans are found in very small numbers in many metropolitan areas, the national averages include many values for metro areas where the score is unreliable. It will be more revealing to assess dissimilarity scores among black groups in places like New York, Washington, D.C., and Atlanta, where all three are found in larger numbers. These data are shown in Tables 6 and 7.

Table 6 describes residential patterns for Afro-Caribbeans in the ten largest metropolitan areas for this population. Segregation from whites is very high in all of them, increasing in some areas, while declining in others. Exposure to whites, however, varies greatly—from living in neighborhoods that are less than a quarter white and majority black (New York, Miami, and Newark) to living in neighborhoods where whites make up as much as 40 percent of the population (Boston, West Palm Beach, and Orlando). Segregation from African Americans is only in the moderate range (35–45), indicating that Afro-Caribbeans' neighborhoods overlap substantially with those of African Americans. Segregation from Africans is substantially higher, though it remains within the moderate range. New York is the one case where both Afro-Caribbeans and Africans are present in large numbers, and segregation between these two groups is in the high range.

Table 7 shows segregation measures in the ten largest metropolitan areas for the African born. Exposure of Africans to whites declined significantly in all ten regions; it was extremely low in New York (17.0 percent) and near or above 50 percent only in Minneapolis–St. Paul, Boston, Dallas, and Philadelphia. Segregation from whites is in the high range in all cases, though falling in some of them. At the same time, Africans' exposure to blacks is growing, though it is much lower for Africans than for Afro-Caribbeans.

The table generally confirms the national pattern in which Africans are surprisingly segregated from African Americans and Afro-Caribbeans, though these values generally declined during the last decade. Washington, D.C., and Atlanta offer the possibility that where their populations are larger, Africans' neighborhoods may overlap more with those of other blacks. However, the case of New York shows that such a tendency is not inevitable.

Blacks' Neighborhood Characteristics

Non-Hispanic black groups are residentially segregated from whites and from each other. Do they also live in neighborhoods of different quality? (For research on this same question in the 1970–1980 period, see Adelman et al. 2001.) This final section of this [reading] analyzes selected neighborhood characteristics for the average group member: the neighborhood's median household income (in constant dollars for 1990 and 2000), the percentage of group

TABLE 6   Segregation of the Ten Metro Regions with Largest Afro-Caribbean Population in Census 2000

Metro Area	Exposure to whites		Segregation from whites		Exposure to blacks		Segregation from African Americans		Segregation from Africans	
	1990	2000	1990	2000	1990	2000	1990	2000	1990	2000
New York, NY	15.4%	11.8%	81.8%	82.7%	62.2%	64.0%	40.2%	39.2%	62.6%	57.7%
Miami, FL	23.9	15.0	66.6	68.1	49.6	54.1	50.6	47.3	66.1	59.0
Fort Lauderdale, FL	52.8	36.6	56.1	57.2	36.3	43.6	44.4	34.6	69.8	67.5
Boston, MA–NH	42.7	40.7	76.4	73.2	42.8	39.3	41.3	34.9	63.4	54.5
Nassau–Suffolk, NY	45.5	36.7	76.8	75.2	38.0	38.7	40.8	36.4	68.7	48.8
Newark, NJ	26.2	22.9	79.8	78.0	60.8	60.0	40.5	37.8	59.7	47.7
West Palm Beach–Boca Raton, FL	46.1	47.3	69.7	60.2	41.5	34.6	42.7	44.0	83.0	74.4
Washington, D.C.–MD–VA–WV	40.8	34.6	67.0	64.6	43.0	43.3	55.2	48.4	44.9	42.5
Orlando, FL	62.8	42.4	52.9	58.1	26.0	32.6	49.1	40.2	67.3	65.4
Atlanta, GA	48.8	36.2	69.0	61.8	46.6	52.3	53.6	39.8	56.8	48.2

TABLE 7   Segregation of the Ten Metro Regions with Largest African-Born Population in Census 2000

Metro Area	Exposure to whites 1990	Exposure to whites 2000	Segregation from whites 1990	Segregation from whites 2000	Exposure to blacks 1990	Exposure to blacks 2000	Segregation from African Americans 1990	Segregation from African Americans 2000	Segregation from Afro-Caribbeans 1990	Segregation from Afro-Caribbeans 2000
Washington, D.C.–MD–VA–WV	47.7%	37.5%	62.7%	63.1%	34.6%	36.7%	62.9%	58.2%	44.9%	42.5%
New York, NY	29.9	17.0	71.6	78.0	38.4	47.0	62.1	48.5	62.6	57.7
Atlanta, GA	53.1	39.4	67.2	63.6	39.7	43.2	57.4	54.0	56.8	48.2
Minneapolis–St. Paul, MN–WI	78.0	59.2	73.0	68.4	11.2	21.9	66.1	50.0	79.3	73.5
Los Angeles–Long Beach, CA	44.7	34.4	59.4	59.9	17.1	19.9	68.3	60.6	65.8	61.1
Boston, MA–NH	55.5	47.5	68.2	63.7	22.4	26.6	64.7	48.9	63.4	54.5
Houston, TX	46.8	33.0	68.2	67.9	23.7	27.3	71.3	64.7	61.6	54.8
Chicago, IL	51.7	45.1	78.0	72.7	29.1	31.0	80.5	71.2	73.2	66.3
Dallas, TX	66.4	49.0	64.8	60.0	15.5	19.6	74.3	64.2	72.9	66.4
Philadelphia, PA–NJ	56.8	49.2	78.1	70.2	34.5	38.7	72.2	61.9	68.0	58.8

members who own their homes, and the percentage of residents (over age twenty-five) with a college education. These are characteristics of the neighborhoods in which an average group member lives, rather than of the groups themselves (these were shown previously in Table 4).

Table 8 shows that non-Hispanic blacks, regardless of ethnicity, live in worse neighborhoods, on average, than do non-Hispanic whites, with one exception—Africans exceed whites in the educational attainment of their neighbors.

More relevant here are the differences among black populations:

- *Income:* The average African American lives in a census tract with a median income of $35,679, while the

average Afro-Caribbean lives in a census tract with a median income of $41,328. Africans live in more advantaged neighborhoods with a median income of $45,567 (though this is still more than $7,000 below the neighborhood median income of an average non-Hispanic white).

- *Homeownership:* The average African American lives in a tract where 53.1 percent of the residents own their homes. This is higher than the other black groups, and to some extent it reflects the advantage of having lived for more generations in the United States. The average Afro-Caribbean lives in a tract where 49.8 percent of the residents own homes. Although

TABLE 8   Neighborhood Characteristics of the Average Group Member, National Metro Averages

Group	Median Household Income ($) 1990	Median Household Income ($) 2000	Percentage Homeowners 1990	Percentage Homeowners 2000	Percentage College Educated 1990	Percentage College Educated 2000
African American	31,548	35,679	49.8	53.1	14.0	17.5
Afro-Caribbean	39,970	41,328	44.1	49.8	17.5	20.3
African born	44,715	45,567	44.7	47.2	28.8	29.3
Non-Hispanic white	47,683	52,637	67.6	70.7	23.8	29.0

lower than the national average for African Americans, this deficit is largely due to their concentration in the New York area, where this group is mainly found in inner-city neighborhoods. Regional comparisons of this neighborhood characteristic show that Afro-Caribbeans fare much better than African Americans in New York and somewhat better in Washington, D.C., and Atlanta. The average African lives in a tract where 47.2 percent of neighbors are homeowners.

- *Education:* The average African lives in a neighborhood where 29.3 percent of residents have a college education, compared to 29 percent for an average non-Hispanic white. This reflects the very high educational attainment of the Africans who have been able to immigrate to the United States. By contrast, the average African American lives in a neighborhood where 17.5 percent of residents have a college education, while 20 percent of an average Afro-Caribbean person's neighbors have a college education.

Table 9 provides a closer look at the metro areas where Afro-Caribbeans are most numerous. Homeownership in their neighborhoods, as noted above, is especially low in New York (and Newark and Boston as well, where they also are concentrated in the inner city).

Their neighborhoods are relatively less affluent and less educated in New York. In other metro areas in the table, homeownership in their neighborhoods is actually well above the national average for African Americans. Afro-Caribbeans live in relatively affluent neighborhoods in Nassau–Suffolk (which is all suburban), Washington, D.C., and Atlanta and in neighborhoods with a relatively high education level in Washington, D.C., Atlanta, and Boston.

Similar information is given in Table 10 for the top ten metro areas of Africans. Their neighborhoods have especially high levels of education in Washington, D.C., but in several other metro areas, the percentage of neighbors with a college degree is higher than the national average for whites' neighborhoods: Atlanta, Los Angeles–Long Beach, Houston, Chicago, and Dallas. Exceptionally low are the education levels in New York and Philadelphia. Africans also live in especially affluent neighborhoods in Washington, D.C., with a median income of over $57,000—again, well above the national average for whites' neighborhoods. These income levels are lowest in New York and Minneapolis. Finally, Philadelphia stands out for high homeownership in Africans' neighborhoods (over 60 percent), while in New York, homeownership is exceptionally low (less than 25 percent).

TABLE 9 Neighborhood Characteristics of the Average Afro-Caribbean Resident

Metro Area	Median Household Income ($)		Percentage Homeowners		Percentage College Educated	
	1990	*2000*	*1990*	*2000*	*1990*	*2000*
New York, NY	39,410	38,758	31.0	35.1	15.5	18.2
Miami, FL	33,665	33,873	53.8	58.1	13.9	15.0
Fort Lauderdale, FL	35,403	39,621	59.2	64.3	13.3	17.0
Boston, MA–NH	40,825	42,463	36.9	42.3	22.5	26.1
Nassau–Suffolk, NY	63,190	64,241	73.7	75.9	21.4	23.5
Newark, NJ	44,036	45,216	39.6	41.9	17.9	20.5
West Palm Beach–Boca Raton, FL	33,061	38,114	54.9	62.2	12.5	17.5
Washington, DC–MD–VA–WV	53,864	57,218	51.9	57.6	31.5	35.7
Orlando, FL	38,210	39,252	59.6	60.0	17.2	18.1
Atlanta, GA	46,267	50,911	57.9	61.9	27.1	29.9

TABLE 10   Neighborhood Characteristics of the Average
African-Born Resident

Metro Area	Median Household Income ($)		Percentage Homeowners		Percentage College Educated	
	1990	2000	1990	2000	1990	2000
Washington, DC–MD–VA–WV	55,784	57,143	47.0	50.4	37.5	39.5
New York, NY	40,145	35,243	24.3	24.2	22.7	20.3
Atlanta, GA	43,049	48,614	45.1	49.8	30.0	30.5
Minneapolis–St. Paul, MN–WI	36,321	37,679	46.4	44.0	31.2	27.9
Los Angeles–Long Beach, CA	49,075	47,009	41.9	42.9	26.9	29.8
Boston, MA–NH	43,138	42,925	37.9	40.2	27.3	28.2
Houston, TX	41,298	46,531	39.2	48.8	30.9	30.9
Chicago, IL	40,700	45,509	41.0	47.4	30.7	34.3
Dallas, TX	45,671	49,347	38.2	43.6	35.0	33.1
Philadelphia, PA–NJ	43,811	41,647	60.2	60.7	25.4	23.1

Conclusion: The Increasing Diversity of America's Black Populations

All of these analyses point in a similar direction. Black Americans of all ethnic backgrounds are highly segregated from whites and disadvantaged in comparison to them. Yet, beneath this communality born of the color line are substantial differences between the majority of blacks with historical origins in the United States and new, growing minorities from the Caribbean and Africa. Nearly 17 percent of recent growth in the black population is due to increases in these new groups. Particularly in metro areas where they constitute 20 percent or more of the black population, an increasingly urgent social and political question is whether common problems associated with race will outweigh differences linked to national origins (Logan and Mollenkopf 2003). Scholars generally agree that the differences are substantial and that black immigrants have limited prospects of assimilation either into mainstream American society or into the African-American minority (Kasinitz 1992; Ho 1991). In some places with a long history of black ethnic diversity, such as New York City, the differences have appeared to be divisive in political

races (Rogers 2004). But some studies have shown that majority-black institutions are capable of successfully incorporating newcomers (Foerster 2004).

The newcomers have numerous advantages compared to African Americans. Their own education levels and incomes tend to be higher. Not only do they typically live in somewhat different neighborhoods, but in most metro areas, these neighborhoods have a higher socioeconomic standing.

Comparable diversity has been documented among Hispanics (particularly contrasting South Americans and Cubans with Mexicans, Central Americans, and Dominicans) and Asians (among whom Indians and Filipinos present a very different profile than Chinese or Koreans). The American public is used to thinking in terms of the broader racial and ethnic categories—Hispanic, Asian, black. Certainly in the history of black-white relations in this country, the distinctions between blacks of different social class or national origin have paled in comparison to their common treatment. We may nevertheless be moving into an era when those distinctions become more salient and when we must think not only in terms of majority and minority groups but in terms of a nation of many minorities.

43

The Arab Immigrant Experience

Michael W. Suleiman

MICHAEL W. SULEIMAN is University Distinguished Professor in the Department of Political Science at Kansas State University. He has written and co-edited numerous works in the field of Arab American studies, including *U.S. Policy on Palestine from Wilson to Clinton* and *Arab Americans: Continuity and Change.*

Introduction

In 1977, William E. Leuchtenburg, the prominent American historian, remarked, "From the perspective of the American historian, the most striking aspect of the relationship between Arab and American cultures is that, to Americans, the Arabs are a people who have lived outside of history."[1] Professor Leuchtenburg could have just as accurately made the same observation about Arabs in America.

Ignorance about Arab Americans among North Americans at large means that, before looking at more detailed accounts of the Arab-American experience, we may benefit from a quick overview of Arab immigration to North America and what the Arab-American communities here have been like.

There have been two major waves of Arab immigration to North America. The first lasted from the 1870s to World War II and the second from World War II to the present. Members of the two waves of immigrants had somewhat different characteristics and faced different challenges in the social and political arena. Any examination of the immigrant communities must take into account these differences. As we shall see, the two communities began to come together in the 1960s, especially after the 1967 Arab-Israeli war,[2] and this rapprochement must also be taken into account.

The term "Arab Americans" refers to the immigrants to North America from the Arabic-speaking countries of the Middle East and their descendants. The Arabic-speaking countries today include Algeria, Bahrain, Egypt, Iraq, Jordan, Kuwait, Lebanon, Libya, Mauritania, Morocco,

Questions to Consider   Since 9/11 the media seem to have discovered the Arab American population in the United States, but this group has had significant presence in this country for almost 150 years. In this article Suleiman maps Arab migration to the United States and the "Americanization" process this group, like almost all immigrant groups to this country, has experienced. He suggests that an ambiguous racial status and racism were used to deny citizenship to Arab immigrants. How and why did this happen?

Oman, pre-1948 Palestine and the Palestinians, Qatar, Saudi Arabia, Sudan, Syria, Tunisia, United Arab Emirates, and Yemen. Somalia and Djibouti are also members of The League of Arab States and have some Arabic-speaking populations. Most Arab immigrants of the first wave came from the Greater Syria region, especially present-day Lebanon, and were overwhelmingly Christian; later immigrants came from all parts of the Arab world, but especially from Palestine, Lebanon, Syria, Egypt, Iraq, and Yemen, and had large numbers of Muslims among them. Although most Muslim Arab immigrants have been Sunni (reflecting the population in the region), there is a substantial Shi'a minority. Druze started immigrating in small numbers late in the nineteenth century.

Immigrants from the Arabic-speaking countries have been referred to and have referred to themselves by different names at different times, including Arabs or Arabians, but until World War II the designation Syrian or Syrian-Lebanese was used most often. The changeability of the name may indicate the absence of a definite and enduring identity, an issue that is discussed later. For the purposes of this [reading], the various names are used interchangeably, but the community primarily is referred to as Arab or Arab American.[3]

It is impossible to determine the exact number of Arab immigrants to North America, because U.S. and Canadian immigration officials have at different times used different classification schemes. Until 1899 in the United States, for instance, immigration statistics lumped the Arabs with Greeks, Armenians, and Turks. For this and other reasons, only estimates can be provided.

According to U.S. immigration figures, which generally are considered to be low, about 130,000 Arabs had immigrated to the United States by the late 1930s.[4] Estimates of the size of the Arab-American community by scholars and community leaders vary widely. A conservative estimate is that there were approximately 350,000 persons of Arab background in the United States on the eve of World War II.[5] In the 1990s, the size of the Arab community in the United States has been estimated at less than one million to the most frequently cited figure of two and one-half to three million.[6]

Numerous reasons have been given for the first wave of Arab immigration to America, which began in large numbers in the 1880s, but the reasons usually fall into two categories: push and pull factors, with the push factors accorded greater weight.

Most scholars argue that the most important reasons for emigration were economic necessity and personal advancement.[7] According to this view, although the economy in geographic or Greater Syria (a term encompassing the present-day countries and peoples of Syria, Lebanon, the Palestinians, Israel, Jordan, and possibly Iraq) registered some clear gains in the late nineteenth and early twentieth centuries, this progress was uneven in its impact and did not manifest itself in a sustained manner until "after emigration to the New World began to gather momentum."[8] The economy of Mount Lebanon suffered two major crippling blows in the mid-1800s. The first was the opening of the Suez Canal, which sidetracked world traffic from Syria to Egypt and made the trip to the Far East so easy and fast that Japanese silk became a major competitor for the Lebanese silk industry. The second blow came in the 1890s, when Lebanese vineyards were invaded by phylloxera and practically ruined.[9]

Also contributing to the economic stress in the Syrian hinterland was a rapid increase in population without a commensurate increase in agricultural or industrial productivity. Many families found that the subsistence economy could support only one child, who eventually inherited the farm or household. Other male children had to fend for themselves, and emigration to a New World of great wealth became an irresistible option.[10]

Many Lebanese Christians, who constituted most of the early Arab arrivals in North America, emphasize religious persecution and the lack of political and civil freedom as the main causes of their emigration from lands ruled by an oppressive **Ottoman** regime.[11] Under Ottoman rule, Christians in the Syrian province were not accorded equal status with their Muslim neighbors. They were subjected to many restrictions on their behavior and often suffered persecution. These oppressive conditions worsened and discriminatory actions occurred more often as the Ottoman rulers became weaker and their empire earned the title of the "Sick Man of Europe." As the power of the sultan declined, the local rulers began to assert greater authority and power, which they at times used to suppress and oppress further their subjects, particularly Christians. In part, this persecution took place in response to the increased power and prestige of "Christian" Europe and the encroachment of its rulers on Ottoman sovereignty. This effect, combined with the Christian population's desire for greater equality, threatened the Muslim public's sense of security. Like the "poor white trash" of the American South at the time of the Civil War and the Civil Rights Movement, the Muslim population in the Syrian province was poor and oppressed—but it still enjoyed a social status that was superior to that of the non-Muslims, particularly the Christians. The threat of losing that "high" status made many Muslims susceptible to suggestions from local Ottoman rulers that their Christian neighbors were the cause of rather than companions in their troubles. The worsened social and economic conditions in Syria in the mid-1800s and the beginning of the disintegration of feudalism, especially among the Druze, produced social turmoil that erupted in sectarian riots in which thousands of Christians perished.[12] Many Christian Lebanese, especially Maronites, cite the 1860 disturbances and

Ottoman Empire An empire covering parts of Europe, Asia, and Africa that dominated that region from the thirteenth century until World War I.

massacres as the main factor contributing to the exodus from their homeland.

In addition to the economic, political, and social causes of the early Arab immigration to North America, some incidental factors should be cited. Among these are improved transportation and communication facilities worldwide, development of steam navigation that made the sea voyage safer and shorter, and aggressiveness of agents of the steamship companies in recruiting new immigrant passengers. Although American missionaries often actively discouraged Syrians or Arabs from migrating to the United States, their very presence as model Americans, their educational activities, and their reports about American life ignited a desire, especially among the graduates of American schools and colleges in Syria, to emigrate to America.

After the feasibility and profitability of immigration to the United States and to "America" in general were well established, chain migration became the norm, with immigrants making it possible for the ambitious and the disgruntled in the old homeland to seek newer horizons. Those wanting to escape military service in the Ottoman army and those craving freedom from oppression and the liberty to speak and publish without censorship or reprisal left their homeland quickly and stealthily and sought what they thought would be a temporary refuge in America.

The Early Arab Community in America

Before World War II, most Arabs in America were Christians who came from the Mount Lebanon region of geographic Syria. Especially until the turn of the century, these travelers were mainly poor, uneducated, and illiterate in any language. They were not trained for a particular profession. As unskilled workers, after they learned the rudiments of the English language, they could work in factories and mines. However, such jobs were taxing and monotonous and, most importantly, did not offer opportunities for the fast accumulation of wealth, which was the primary objective of these early Arab arrivals. Farming presented them with the added hardships of isolation, loneliness, and severe weather conditions. Peddling therefore was an attractive alternative. It did not require much training, capital, or knowledge of English. With a few words of English learned on the run, a suitcase (*Kashshi*)

full of notions (e.g., needles, thread, lace) provided by a better-established fellow Lebanese or other Arab supplier, probably a relative who helped bring them to the New World, many new arrivals often were on the road hawking their wares only a day or so after they landed in America. Success in peddling required thrift, hard work, very long hours, the stamina to endure harsh travel conditions (mostly walking the countryside on unpaved roads), and not infrequently, the taunting and insults from children or disgruntled customers. These conditions were made tolerable for most early Arab arrivals by their vision of a brighter economic future and the concomitant prestige they and their families would eventually acquire in the old country. When they could afford to do so, they switched to the "luxury" of a horse and buggy and later to a dry-goods store.[13]

Before World War I, Arabs in North America thought of themselves as sojourners, as people who were in, but not part of, American society. Their politics reflected and emulated the politics of their original homeland in substance and style, because they were only *temporarily* away from home. In New York, *Kawkab America* (*Kawkab Amirka*), the first Arabic-language newspaper established in North America, declared in its very first issue its unequivocal support for the Ottoman sultan, whose exemplary virtues it detailed at length.[14] All other newspapers had to define in one way or another their attitude toward and their relationship with the Ottoman authorities. Although *Kawkab America* was pro-Ottoman, at least initially, *Al-Ayam* (*al-Ayyam*) was the most vehement opponent of the Ottoman authorities, a role it later shared with *Al-Musheer* (*al-Mushir*).[15] It excoriated the cruelty and corruption of Ottoman rulers, especially in the Mount Lebanon region. It also called for rebellion against the Turkish tyrants and urged its readers to exercise their freedom in America to call for freedom back home. Other newspapers, including *Al-Hoda* (*al-Huda*) and *Meraat-ul-Gharb* (*Mir'at al-gharb*), fell between these two extremes of total support or clear rejection of Ottoman authority.

The orientation of early Arab Americans toward their homeland meant that their political activities were also focused on issues that were important in their country or village of origin. There was communal solidarity, but the community was a collective of several communities. The sectarian and regional disputes that separated the Arabs back home were also salient in this "temporary" residence. The newspapers they established were in the main socializing agencies conveying the messages of their sectarian leadership. Because the Orthodox already had their *Kawkab America, Al-Hoda* was set up to represent and speak for the Maronites. Later, *Al-Bayan (al-Bayan)* proclaimed itself the newspaper of the Druze.[16] Within each community there were rivalries and competing newspapers, each claiming to be the best defender or representative of its sect.

World War I was a watershed event for Arabs in North America, cutting them off from their people back home. This separation from the homeland became almost complete with the introduction of very restrictive quota systems in the United States and Canada after World War I, which practically cut off emigration from Arab regions. These developments intensified the community's sense of isolation and separation, simultaneously enhancing its sense of solidarity. One consequence was a strengthening of the assimilationist trend—a trend already reinforced by the American-born children of these Arab immigrants.

The substance and style of the Arab community's politics changed after the war, with a clear realization that they had become part of American society. Intersectarian conflicts became less intense and fewer in number. Calls for unity were heeded more often. For instance, Syrian-Lebanese clubs formed regional federations that joined together to form a national federation.[17] A process of socialization into American politics resulted in greater participation in voting and party membership and in public and political service at local or state levels. "Syrian" Republican and Democratic Clubs were formed in the United States, and the arena for political competition changed as the Arab community became part of the American body politic. There also emerged a clear change in matters of style—generally for the better. By the 1930s and 1940s, conflicts became fewer and somewhat less personal, and the language of discourse became much less offensive.

Whereas first-generation Arabs in America managed as best they could in an alien environment, their children were thoroughly immersed in American society and culture—and their first or only language was English. Consequently, English-language newspapers and journals were established to cater to young Americans of Arab heritage.[18] Eastern churches began to translate some of the liturgy and conduct part of the services in English to prevent the loss of members,[19] although many members left the church nonetheless. Some intellectuals, including some of the most celebrated Arab-American writers and poets, took advantage of the blessings of freedom and democracy in North America to attack the tyranny and corruption of the clergy, especially in the old homeland but also in America. Some also expressed atheistic or agnostic views, and others left their old churches and joined new ones.[20]

As Arabs assimilated in American society, they also worked harder for a better image of themselves and their people in the old homeland. More effort was spent on campaigns to inform Americans about the rich Arab heritage. In the political arena, especially in the United States, there were many, serious efforts to get the government to support foreign policy positions favored by the Arab community, especially in regard to Palestine. During World War I and its aftermath, the main political preoccupation of the Arabic-speaking groups in North America was to achieve the liberation of their homelands from Ottoman rule and to provide economic assistance to their starving relatives, especially in the Mount Lebanon region. To accomplish these objectives, their leaders set up relief committees, raised funds, and sent money and supplies whenever it was possible to do so. They also urged Arab young men in the United States to join the American armed forces to help their new country and to liberate their old homeland.[21] Leaders organized campaigns to have their people buy American Liberty bonds to help with the war effort.[22]

After the war, the Arabs in America were divided over the destiny of the regions liberated from Ottoman rule. In general, there was a strong sentiment among the Maronites to support French control over Syria and Lebanon under the League of Nations' Mandate.[23] Others argued for complete independence, viewing France as a new occupying power.[24] On the question of Palestine, there was general agreement in support of the Palestinian-Arab population and for eventual, if not immediate, independence. There was widespread opposition to Zionism as a movement bent on establishing a Jewish state there.[25] Arabs in America showed their support for the Palestinians through lectures, publications, fund raising, and political lobbying, especially with U.S. government officials.[26]

Until World War I, Arabs in North America may be considered sojourners exhibiting many traits of a middleman minority—a community whose members primarily engage in one particular specialized activity such as migrant farm work or peddling. Substantial numbers of Arabs in America engaged in commerce, most often beginning as peddlers commissioned by their own countrymen. Their objective was to make the greatest amount of money in the shortest possible time to help their families in the old country and eventually to retire in comfort in their village or neighborhood. In the meantime, they spent as little as possible of their income in America, often living in crowded tenements and, while on the road, in barns or shacks to avoid expensive hotel costs. They did not live rounded lives, allowing themselves no luxuries and finding contentment and solace in family life. Because they could pull up stakes anytime, they sought liquidity in their economic enterprises. Long-term investments were avoided. For that reason, in addition to other advantages, they preferred peddling, dry goods stores, restaurants, the professions, and a cottage industry in lace and needlework. In all of these activities, their primary contacts were with other Arab Americans, especially relatives or people from the same town, religious sect, or geographic region.[27] They developed few lasting relationships with "Americans." *Al-Nizala,* the term the Arab-American community used to refer to itself, is a name that clearly describes its status and purpose. It means a temporary settlement, and it was used in contrast to "the Americans" to indicate the alien or stranger status of Arabs in America. At first, Arabs in America formed their own residential colonies, especially in New York and Boston. Even when they did not, they encouraged within-group marriage, frequently praising its virtues and especially pointing out the disadvantages of marrying "American" girls. In other words, they resisted assimilation, even after their intellectuals began to urge acculturation to life in America.[28]

Arabs in America, sharing an attitude common to other middleman or sojourner communities, were charged with being "clannish, alien, and unassimilable."[29] Such attitudes were fairly common among influential American journalists and public officials, who also viewed Arabs as inferior to whites. In the economic field, Arabs were sometimes seen as parasites, because they allegedly did not engage in any productive industry, merely being engaged in trade. They were sometimes attacked as a drain on the American economy, because they sent part of their income back home.[30]

The Process of Americanization

Arab immigrants soon found out that the land of opportunity was also strewn with hardship and an "unwelcome" mat. In response to insults and charges of inferiority, they did occasionally defend themselves.[31] However, to add injury to insult, the U.S. and Canadian authorities began to claim that Arabs had no right to naturalization and citizenship because they allegedly were Asian and did not belong to the white race.[32] This problem of racial identification and citizenship traumatized the Arabic-speaking community. In their attempt to resolve this crisis, the "Syrians" searched for their roots and found them in their *Arab* background, which ensured them Caucasian racial status and therefore eligibility for U.S. citizenship—or so they argued.[33] Beginning in 1909, Arabic-speaking individuals from geographic Syria began to be challenged in their citizenship petitions. It was not until 1914, however, that George Dow was denied a petition to become a U.S. citizen because, as a "Syrian of Asiatic birth," he was not a free white person within the meaning of the 1790 U.S. statute.[34] In 1915, the Dow decision was reversed based on the argument that the pertinent binding legislation was not that of 1790 but the laws of 1873 and 1875, and in accordance with these, Syrians "were so closely related to Europeans that they could be considered 'white persons."[35] Despite this precise and authoritative language, "Syrians" in the United States continued to be challenged and to feel insecure about their naturalization status until the period of 1923 to 1924.[36]

Even during World War II, the status of Arabs remained unclear. In 1942, a Muslim Arab from Yemen was denied U.S. citizenship because "Arabs as a class are not white and therefore not eligible for citizenship," especially because of their dark skin and the fact that they are "part of the Mohammedan world," separated from Christian Europe by a wide gulf.[37] On the other hand, in 1944, an "Arabian" Muslim was granted citizenship status under the 1940 Nationality Act, because "as every schoolboy knows, the Arabs have at various times inhabited parts of Europe, lived along the Mediterranean, been contiguous to European nations and been assimilated culturally and otherwise by them."[38]

Apart from the legal battles to ensure they were allowed to reside in their new homelands, especially in the United States, Arabic-speaking persons had to figure out what identity best fit their indeterminate status. They knew who they were and had a very strong sense of personal identity centered first and foremost in the family. There were, however, other lesser but still important identities related to clan, village, or sect. Because these identities were strong, a "national" identity could remain amorphous or at least indeterminate, shifting from one orientation to another with relative ease and without much psychological dislocation. In practical terms, the Arabic-speaking people in North America functioned as a collective of communities whose bonds of solidarity beyond the family were mainly related to sect or country, such as Maronite, Orthodox, Muslim, Druze, and Palestinian affiliations. Before World War II, the primary or most acceptable designation for the group was "Syrian." However, when Lebanon emerged as a country in the 1920s, some Maronites, especially N. Mokarzel, the editor and publisher of *Al-Hoda,* spearheaded a campaign to get the community to change its name to Lebanese, because Lebanon was where most of its members originally came from.[39] The campaign was not a big success, although many of the clubs did change their name to Syrian-Lebanese.[40]

Another and more important identity crisis occurred when these peripatetic sojourners realized that they had to decide whether to become "settlers" or return to the old homeland. It had become increasingly difficult for them to function as temporary aliens. After World War I, it became clear to large numbers of Arabs in North America that it was not possible to go "home" again and that the United States and Canada were their homes.[41] This change from sojourner to permanent settler necessitated and was accompanied by other changes in the way Arabs in America thought and in the way they behaved. The substantial investments they had made in homes, property, and real estate in the old country lost their original purpose, and much more attention was paid to material improvements and investments in their new countries. In the United States, one manifestation was the migration by substantial numbers of the New York Arab community from the rundown and extremely crowded tenements of Manhattan to the nicer environment of South Ferry in Brooklyn and beyond.[42]

Arabs in America saw that they had to become full-fledged Americans. Assimilation became strongly and widely advocated, and citizenship training and naturalization were greatly encouraged. Although outmarriage was still not favored, some now claimed that success in such situations was possible if the American partner (usually female) was a "good" person who behaved in a conservative or traditional manner.[43] Along the same lines, Arab women were told to retain the modesty code of the old homeland.[44]

Although Arab women in America constituted a major asset to their kinfolk, they also presented the community with many difficulties, primarily related to issues of honor and modesty. This problem was most acute among the Druze, some of whom asked to restrict or totally ban the immigration of Druze women to America. Among Christians, women peddlers were a big concern. The complaints and areas targeted for reform included the act of peddling itself, the personal appearance and dress of the woman peddler, the distance she covered and whether she had to stay away from home overnight, and her demeanor or behavior. These problems were viewed as especially serious because large numbers had decided to stay in America and wanted to become "acceptable" to the host society. The preference was for Arab women to help their kinfolk by crocheting or sewing at home or by minding their family's store. Work in factories was also acceptable, although not favored, especially among the rising middle-class Arab Americans.[45]

The decision to settle in America meant setting a higher priority on children's education for boys and girls. This was viewed as more important than any contribution the children might make to the family's economic welfare. The result was a marked improvement in women's education and an increase in the number of male and female graduates from universities and professional institutions.

Another consequence of the decision to stay in America was that parents and children had to learn to be good Americans, and they flocked to citizenship classes. Parents attended English-language classes and studied the American governmental system in preparation for their new role as American citizens. Americanization was seen as a process of shedding old loyalties, the traditional culture, and the Arabic language. The children therefore grew up barely aware of their Arabic heritage.

Although the assimilationist approach began to gain favor and was encouraged by the leadership, it was not presented in ideological terms. Often, it took the form of a suggestion that Arabs should no longer feel like strangers in their new country and that they should make a positive contribution to American society.[46] Nevertheless, in the heyday of the melting pot approach to assimilation, the Arabs in America strove to remove any differences, except perhaps food and music, that separated them from the general American population. They also neglected or chose not to teach their children Arabic or to instill into them much pride of heritage.[47] The result was that, by World War II, Arabs in North America were, for all practical purposes, an indistinguishable group from the host society. It took a second wave of immigration and other developments to rekindle interest in their Arab heritage and to revive them as an ethnic community.

Post–World War II Immigration

The second wave of Arab immigration brought to North America a much more diverse population, one that differed greatly from the early pioneering group. Whereas the first-wave immigrants came almost exclusively from the area of Greater Syria and were overwhelmingly Lebanese, the new immigrants came from all parts of the Arab world, including North Africa. Unlike early arrivals, who were predominantly Christian, the new immigrants were Christians and Muslims.

The two groups' reasons for immigration were also somewhat different. In addition to economic need and the attraction of a major industrial society, new immigrants often were driven out of their homes as a result of regional conflicts (e.g., Palestine-Israel, Arab-Israeli, Iraq-Iran, Iraq-Kuwait) or civil wars (e.g., Lebanon, Yemen) or as a consequence of major social and political changes in the homeland that made life difficult, especially for the wealthy or the middle class in Egypt, Iraq, Syria, and other countries. The search for a democratic haven, where it is possible to live in freedom without political or economic harassment and suppression by the government was a strong motivation, even more so than during the earlier period, that affected much larger numbers of individuals. To these political and economic motivations can be added a psychological one. The great improvements in transportation and communication facilitated the process of immigration, and by making the world seem smaller, they made it much easier for people to accept the notion of migration to other parts of the world, especially to the United States and Canada.

Whereas the early Arab immigrants were mainly uneducated and relatively poor, the new arrivals included large numbers of relatively well-off, highly educated professionals: lawyers, professors, teachers, engineers, and doctors. Many of the new immigrants began as students at American universities who decided to stay, often as a result of lack of employment opportunities back home or because of the unstable political conditions in the homeland—conditions that often threatened imprisonment or death for returnees.[48] Besides these comparatively affluent immigrants, especially in the 1990s, relatively large numbers of semieducated Arabs, primarily engaged in commerce, came to North America as political refugees or as temporary residents to escape the wars and violence of the Middle East region.

An important difference between members of the two immigration waves is the way each group thought of itself in terms of American society and politics. First-wave immigrants were viewed and thought of themselves as mere sojourners staying in the United States on a temporary basis with the primary or sole purpose of making a fortune they could enjoy back home. This orientation remained dominant at least until World War I and probably well into the 1920s. Such a stance meant that they avoided participation in American society beyond taking care of basic needs such as commerce. They were "Syrians" or "Arabians" and sought to establish their own churches, clubs, or newspapers. They sought (and preached to their people) not to "meddle" in the affairs of the host society. They were anxious not to offend their hosts, not to break the law, and not to behave in a manner offensive to Americans, but they also tried not to imitate American social customs (i.e., Americanize), not to mix socially with Americans, and not to intermarry. Although most did not participate in politics much beyond voting, they nevertheless expressed pride in the occasional Arab who was able to make it as a city alderman, political party functionary, or a candidate for local political office.

The change from these conditions came slowly and as a result of changes in the world around them, especially World War I, the Ottomans' oppressive treatment of their subjects in the Syria-Lebanon region, and the success of Zionism in securing Western, especially British and

American, support for its objective of establishing a Jewish homeland in Palestine.

Immigrants who arrived after World War II came with a well-defined view of democracy and the role of citizens in it—ideas they had learned in their homeland but that had originally been imported from Europe and America. Their higher level of education and social status gave them greater confidence about participating in American politics almost as soon as they arrived in their new country. Even when they thought about returning to their Arab homeland, they were anxious to live full and productive lives in the United States or Canada for themselves and their children. The Arab-American community today constitutes a combination of the diversities of the early and more recent immigrants. In addition to the sectarian and mainly social clubs that the early immigrants formed, new political organizations were gradually established. In the United States, Syrian Democratic and Syrian Republican clubs were formed in the 1920s and 1930s. These were, as the Arab Democratic and Arab Republican clubs are today, adjuncts to the main two major parties designed to encourage political participation and to integrate Arabs into the American body politic. What was new and significant was the establishment of bona fide Arab-American pressure groups and voluntary associations whose main function has been to protect themselves against harassment from private groups or public agencies and to influence policy in the United States and Canada concerning different parts of the Arab World or Middle East.

As World War I had marked a watershed for the early Arab immigrants, the 1967 Arab-Israeli war did for the entire community. The older and newer Arab-American communities were shocked and traumatized by the 1967 war. In particular, they were dismayed and extremely disappointed to see how greatly one-sided and pro-Israeli the American communications media were in reporting on the Middle East.[49] The war itself also produced soul-searching on the part of many Arab Americans, old and new, and often reinforced or strengthened their Arab identity. This group included many members already active in various Palestinian, Syrian, and Lebanese clubs, which were mainly social in nature.

By 1967, members of the third generation of the early Arab immigrants had started to awaken to their own identity and to see that identity as Arab, not "Syrian." Elements of this third generation combined with politically sophisticated immigrants to work for their ethnic community and the causes of their people in the old homelands. The result was establishment of the Association of Arab-American University Graduates (AAUG) in late 1967, which was the first post–World War II national, credible, nonsectarian organization seeking to represent diverse elements of the Arab-American community and to advance an Arab rather than regional or country orientation.

To the AAUG, however, American hostility to "Arabs" and the concept of Arabism was so extreme and so widespread among policy makers and the general public that influencing the political process or public policy, especially in the United States, seemed futile. The Republican and Democratic parties were almost completely and solidly one-sided in their support of Israel and in their hostility to Arab causes, even though the United States had huge economic and military assets in the region and was on the friendliest terms with most leaders and countries of the Arab world. The AAUG sought support from or identified with other individuals and groups. Among these were a few politicians such as Senator William Fulbright and others who were courageous enough to voice criticism of U.S. policy in the Middle East, other minority or disenfranchised groups in American society, and some intellectuals who began to criticize the administration and its policies.

The AAUG's first priority was the need to provide accurate information about the Arab world and Arabs in North America and to distribute this literature to the public at large, wherever access was possible. It sought to educate the Arab countries and people about the true nature of the problems facing the region and to educate Arab intellectuals and political leaders about U.S. and Canadian policies and the American political process. While the AAUG sought mainly to inform and educate, it also performed other tasks, because no other organizations existed to perform them. Among the tasks to which the AAUG devoted some time and effort were political lobbying, attacks against defamation of and discrimination against Arabs and Arab Americans, and activism among Arab Americans to get them to participate in politics.

These ancillary tasks were later championed and performed by newer organizations. The National Association of Arab Americans (NAAA) was formed in 1972 in the United States to act as a political lobby to defend and advance Arab-American interests and causes. In 1980, in response to the continuing slanders and attacks against Arabs and Arab Americans, the American-Arab Anti-Discrimination Committee (ADC) was established and quickly drew widespread support from the varied elements of the Arab community. In 1985, the Arab American Institute (AAI) was formed, primarily to encourage Arab Americans to become active in the American political arena.[50]

Building a New Future

To get a feel for how the Arab community has fared in America, it is useful to review some of the challenges and concerns that Arabs have faced in their new homeland and how they have coped with building a new future. Among the most important issues with which Arabs in America have had to wrestle is the definition of who they are, their sense of identity as a people, especially as they encountered and continue to encounter bias and discrimination in their new homeland.

Although Arabs in the United States and Canada constitute an ethnic group, they were not an ethnic minority in their old homeland. Their new identity has been shaped by many factors but especially by continuing interactions between conditions in the old and new homelands and by the interplay between their perceptions of themselves and how others see them. The early immigrants spoke Arabic and came from a predominantly Arabic culture and heritage, but they did not think of themselves as "Arabs." The main bond of solidarity among them at that time was based on familial, sectarian, and village- or region-oriented factors. The plethora of names by which they were known in the New World reflects their lack of "national" identity and ignorance or confusion on the part of the host society. Another factor in this process was the American, especially U.S., obsession with the idea of race and the various attempts early in this century to classify every immigrant group, no matter how small, by its racial composition.[51] The early Arabic-speaking groups were called Asians, "other Asians," Turks from Asia, Caucasian, white, black, or "colored."

Although immigration officials and the general press looked down on Arabic-speaking peoples, they nevertheless viewed them as part of the "white race," at least for the first thirty years or so of their presence in North America. These authorities then decided those immigrants were not white. With their very identity questioned and maligned, the reaction of the early Arab Americans was to try to refute what they saw as demeaning and untrue charges. They argued that they were very much part of the white race.[52] Stung by accusations of inferiority in terms of scientific and technological accomplishments, Syrian-Arab Americans developed a two-cultures thesis long before C. P. Snow discussed it.[53] Their argument, which became popular in the community, especially among Arab literati, was that, although America was the most advanced country in the world in science, technology, and industrialization, the East was spiritually superior.[54] Coming from the Holy Land, they offered themselves as guides and instructors to Americans in their search for and desire to experience the life and times of Jesus—where he was born, preached, was crucified, and rose from the dead.[55] Arab Americans spoke and wrote about the "spiritual" East in terms that suggested perpetuity: it was always so and would always be so. By accident or not, these writers in essence condemned the East to an absence of material progress and desire to produce such for all time.

The emphasis on Eastern spirituality, although useful in making Arabs feel good about themselves compared with "materialist" Americans, still left Arabs in America with little cultural heritage to offer their American-born children. The result often was to ignore their Arab heritage and, especially beginning in the 1920s, to emphasize almost full assimilation in American society. As the children grew up immersed in American society and culture while simultaneously exposed to a smattering of Arabic words at home and some Arabic food and music, they often found themselves experiencing an identity crisis of some kind, mainly resulting in rootlessness, ambiguity, and a fractionalized personality.[56] These were the reactions of some of the Arab-American literati of the post–World War II period. The very culture of their own country denied them the privilege of being openly proud of their heritage. They sometimes dealt with this awkward situation by complaining about American prejudice and discrimination against Arabs and by simultaneously denigrating their own people and heritage—if only to ingratiate themselves with their readers, their fellow Americans.[57]

The 1967 war changed the situation radically. Israel, in the short period of seven days, defeated the Arab armies. The Arab people generally felt let down and humiliated. Arabs in America, both newcomers and third-generation descendants of the early pioneers, deeply resented the extreme partisanship America and Americans (especially the U.S. government and people) showed toward Israel and the occasional hostility toward Arabs. The consequence was for Arab Americans to shake off their malaise and to organize. Their first goal was to fight against the negative stereotyping of Arabs. Their second was to help modify American policy toward the Middle East and make it more balanced. In the process, sectors of the well-established older community de-assimilated. They began openly to call themselves Arab and to join political groupings set up to defend Arab and Arab-American causes.[58] Arab Americans also began to organize conferences and publish journals and books in defense of their cause. They wrote fiction, poetry, and memoirs declaring pride in and solidarity with Arabs and the Arab community in America.

Open Arab-American pride in their heritage and activism on behalf of their cause does not, however, mean that prejudice against them ceased. On the contrary, many in the community feel that prejudice and discrimination have increased. Different reasons have been advanced to explain the prejudice and discrimination that Arabs encounter in North America, and different individuals and groups have emphasized what they believe to be the main cause or the one most pertinent to their situation.

The most popular explanation for the negative stereotypes Americans hold about Arabs is that they are ignorant of the truth because they have not read or have read inaccurate and false reports about Arabs and have not come into contact with Arabs. According to this view, the stereotypes are mainly the result of propaganda by and on behalf of Zionist and pro-Israeli supporters. The primary objective of this propaganda has been to deprive Arabs, especially Palestinians, from presenting their case to the American public and the American political leadership.[59]

In this view, the attempt to deny Arabs and Arab Americans a public voice also extends to the political arena. In this way, it becomes a "politics of exclusion" in an attempt to prevent debate on any issues that reflect poorly on Zionists or Israel. It also smears and defames Arab candidates for political office to defeat them and exclude them from effective participation in political decision making. This "political racism" is presumed to be ideological in nature and not necessarily directed against Arabs or Arab Americans as a people or as an ethnic community.[60]

Another view sees hostility and violence against Arabs and Arab Americans as anti-Arab racism. This hostility is seen as part of the native racist attitudes and is believed to be present in all sectors of American society, not just among fringe groups. Somewhat related to this view is "jingoistic racism," which is directed at whatever foreign enemy is perceived to be out there.[61] Because of the many recent conflicts in the Middle East in which the United States directly or indirectly became involved and where incidents of hijacking and hostage taking occurred, many Americans reacted negatively against a vaguely perceived enemy next door, often not distinguishing between Arabs and Muslims or between Arabs and any foreigner who "looks" Arab.[62]

Still another view of negative Arab stereotypes, at least in the United States, argues that these ideas are "rooted in a core of hostile archetypes that our culture applies to those with whom it clashes."[63] According to this argument, most of the elements that constitute the Arab image in America are not unique to Arabs but also have been applied to other ethnic groups, especially blacks and Jews in the form of racism and anti-Semitism. These negative stereotypes have been transferred to a new group, the Arabs or Arab Americans.

Part of the negative stereotyping and hostility many Americans harbor toward Arabs is based on the latter's alleged mistreatment of their women. It is rather ironic, therefore, that Arab-American women find themselves the subject of prejudice, discrimination, and hostility at the hands of American men and women. This is often the result of hostility based on race, color, or religion.[64]

Arab-American women have had more problems than their male counterparts in defining an acceptable or comfortable identity. The problem is multifaceted and affects different sectors differently. Women who have come from the most traditional countries of the Arab world have experienced a greater restriction of their freedom in the United States. This is primarily the result of an inability on the part of traditional husbands, fathers, and brothers to deal with the nearly complete freedom accorded to women in American society. Just as important is the inability of the women to participate fully in the United States because they do not know the language, lack the necessary education, and are unfamiliar with American customs. They are not psychologically ready to countenance, let alone internalize, certain mores pertaining to the public display of affection and male-female interaction. Because many cannot drive and probably do not have a car, they find themselves much more isolated than they were back home, where they often had a vibrant and full life, albeit within the confines of the family and female friends.[65]

Among middle-class, first-generation Arab-American women, there is perhaps not much adjustment necessary. They usually follow the somewhat liberal mores they brought with them from the old homeland. On the other hand, Arab girls reaching their adolescence in the United States are likely to experience more problems as a result of the potential clash between traditional child-rearing practices and the freer atmosphere found in North America.[66]

Among better-educated, young Arab-American women, the issue of identity is both more subtle and more openly discussed. Like their male Arab-American counterparts, these women suffer from and are offended by the hostility against Arabs and Arab Americans. They also find American views of how women are allegedly treated in the Arab world to be inaccurate and grotesque. Nevertheless, they would like to expand the rights of Arab women and to improve the quality of their lives. They resent and reject any attempt on the part of Arab-American men to define what their role should be in maintaining Arab culture and mores in North America. In particular, they want to reject the notion that family honor resides in women and that the way a woman behaves, especially concerning her modesty and sexuality, can bring honor or dishonor to the family. They do not wish to be the conveyors or transmitters of tradition and culture—at least not as these are defined by men or as they prevail in the old homeland.[67]

Women and men in the Arab-American community of the 1990s find that the "white" racial classification that the early Syrian-Arab community worked so hard to attain is flawed. In practical daily interactions, Arabs in America are often treated as "honorary whites" or "white but not quite."[68] In reaction to this situation, at least four different orientations have been advocated. For the majority, especially among the older and well-established Christian community, there is some disgruntlement but general passivity about the discrimination and the prejudice that accompany their "white but not quite" status, and they work to remove these negative attitudes. Others, especially the Arab American Institute, have argued

for a special designation of Arabs in the United States as a minority (e.g., the Hispanics) or as a specific census category encompassing all peoples of the Middle East.[69] Still others, especially some young, educated Arab-American women, have expressed a preference for the designation "people of color."[70] This would place them as part of a larger category that includes most of the federally recognized minorities in the United States. There are also those who resent being boxed into one category. Their sense of identity is multifaceted; they are men or women; Arab, American, Muslim or Christian; white or dark skinned; and so on. They think of themselves in different ways at different times or in different contexts, and they argue for getting rid of such categories or for the use of more descriptive categories that recognize different aspects of their background, culture, or physical appearance.[71]

The search for an adequate or comfortable identity for Arabs in America has been guided and perhaps complicated by the need to feel pride in their heritage and simultaneously avoid prejudice and discrimination in their new homeland. For most, the search is neither successful nor final. They continue to experience marginality in American society and politics, and they try to overcome this in various ways. Some resort to ethnic denial; they de-emphasize their Arab or Islamic background by claiming a connection with what they believe is a more acceptable appearance in America. Instead of proclaiming their Arabism, for instance, they claim that they are Lebanese or Egyptian. Some may even deny their heritage altogether, claiming to be Greek or Italian. Some new arrivals instead choose ethnic isolation. They are unwilling to change themselves and do not believe they can change the host society.

Among those who want full integration or assimilation into American society, especially middle-class Arab Americans, many emphasize the strong cultural link between Arabs and Americans. They refuse to give up and continue to work hard to show where the dominant American view is wrong. For most, accommodation is the easiest and most comfortable stance. These men and women consciously or subconsciously act in ways that reduce their difference from the American dominant group. They attempt "to pass."[72] Others, especially those who seek material success, especially those who are in public professions (e.g., television, radio, movies), often give in and convert to the prevailing view. Not infrequently, the very individuals who are looked down on by the Arab-American community are selected to speak for and represent the Arabs in America.[73]

The Arab-American Community in the 1990s

After more than a century of immigration, it is clear that the basic reasons Arabs came are no different from those that drove or attracted other groups to come here. They came because of the promise of a quick fortune and a sense of adventure; the threat of war or economic disaster; education, training, technology; and the thrill of living in a free democratic system. Whatever their reasons, true integration and full assimilation have eluded them. In part, this is the result of the many developments leading to the debunking of the notion of a melting pot and the greater tolerance of a multicultural society. The more important reason, however, has been the hostility the host society has shown toward Arab immigrants.[74]

Nevertheless, Arabs in America have done very well. Since the 1960s, there has always been at least one representative of Arab background in the U.S. Congress (e.g., James Abourezk, Mary Rose Oakar, Mark Joe [Nick] Rahall II). Others have served as state governors (e.g., Victor Atiyeh, OR) or on the White House staff (e.g., John H. Sununu). Similarly, individuals of Arab descent have been elected to the Canadian parliament (e.g., Mac Harb, Mark Assad) and to provincial legislatures. Many of these individuals have faced difficulties in attaining their positions because they were of Arab background. Some have found it useful to de-emphasize or deny that background to get or maintain their positions. Most also have not been strong or vocal supporters of Arab or Arab nationalist causes.

Nonetheless, ethnic pride is more openly displayed by an increasing number of political candidates at local, state, and national levels.[75]

Arab Americans have done well and fared better economically than the general population average in many areas. The 1980 and 1990 U.S. census data show that Arab Americans reach a higher educational level than the American population as a whole. According to the 1990 census, 15.2 percent of Arab Americans have "graduate degrees or higher"—more than twice the national average of 7.2 percent. Household income among Arab Americans also tends to be higher than the average. Arab Americans have also done well in professional, management, and sales professions.[76]

Although many Arabs in America have reached the highest level of their profession in almost all professions,[77] the American media primarily highlight the negative achievements of Arabs and Muslims. Quite often, the media announce the Arab or Islamic origin or affiliation of anyone accused of a terrorist act—even before they know whether the perpetrator is Arab or Muslim. In the case of positive role models such as Michael DeBakey or Ralph Nader, the media often never mention their Arab background. One reason is that "some [too many] have found it necessary to hide their origins because of racism."[78] Lists of prominent Arab Americans occasionally are published in the press to inform the public about the community's accomplishments, but the fact that such lists are compiled indicates that Arab Americans feel the sting of negative stereotyping and try to correct the bad publicity. Despite the fact that Arabs have lived in America for more than a century and despite their major successes, they are still struggling to be accepted in American society. Full integration and assimilation will not be achieved until that happens.[79]

44 Ethnic and Racial Identities of Second-Generation Black Immigrants in New York City

Mary C. Waters

MARY C. WATERS is a professor of sociology at Harvard University. She is the author of *Ethnic Options: Choosing Identities in America* and the co-author of *From Many Strands: Ethnic and Racial Groups in Contemporary America.*

Questions to Consider   Based on her research of West Indians and Haitian Americans in New York City, Mary Waters found that first-generation black immigrants "tended to distance themselves from American blacks." Why? What does this "distancing" strategy say about the way American blacks are perceived by new immigrant groups? How is racism *within* a racial group possible?

THE GROWTH OF NONWHITE VOLUNTARY immigrants to the United States since 1965 challenges the dichotomy that once explained different patterns of American inclusion and assimilation—the ethnic pattern of assimilation of European immigrants and the racial pattern of exclusion of America's nonwhite peoples. The new wave of immigrants includes people who are still defined racially in the United States but who migrate voluntarily and often under an immigrant preference system that selects for people with jobs and education that put them well above their coethnics in the economy. Do the processes of immigration and assimilation for nonwhite immigrants resemble the processes for earlier white immigrants? Or do these immigrants and their children face very different choices and constraints because they are defined racially by other Americans?

This [reading] examines a small piece of this puzzle—the question of the development of an ethnic identity among the second generation of black immigrants from the Caribbean. While there has been a substantial amount of interest in the identities and affiliations of these immigrants, very little research has been conducted on the identities of their children. The children of black immigrants in the United States face a choice about whether to identify as black American or whether to maintain an ethnic identity reflecting their parents' national origins. First-generation black immigrants to the United States have tended to distance themselves from American blacks, stressing their national origins and ethnic identities as Jamaican or Haitian or Trinidadian, but they also face overwhelming pressures

in the United States to identify only as blacks (Foner 1987; Kasinitz 1992; Stafford 1987; Sutton and Makiesky 1975; Woldemikael 1989). In fact, they have been described as "invisible immigrants," because rather than being contrasted with other immigrants (for example, contrasting how Jamaicans are doing relative to Chinese), they are compared with black Americans. The children of black immigrants, because they lack their parents' distinctive accents, can choose to be even more invisible as ethnics than their parents. Second-generation West Indians in the United States most often will be seen by others as merely "American"—and must actively work to assert their ethnic identities.

The types of racial and ethnic identities adopted by a sample of second-generation West Indians[1] and Haitian Americans in New York City are explored here, along with subjective understandings these youngsters have of being American, being black American, and being their ethnic identity. After a short discussion of current theoretical approaches to understanding assimilation among the second generation, three types of identities adopted by the second generation are described and the different experiences of race relations associated with these identities are traced. Finally this [reading] suggests some implications for future patterns of identity development. . . .

Interviews with first-generation immigrants and their American coworkers reveal a great deal of tension between foreign-born and American-born blacks in both the working-class and the middle-class work sites. Long-standing tensions between newly arrived West Indians and American blacks have left a legacy of mutual stereotyping. (See Kasinitz 1992.) The immigrants see themselves as hardworking, ambitious, militant about their racial identities but not oversensitive or obsessed with race, and committed to education and family. They see black Americans as lazy, disorganized, obsessed with racial slights and barriers, with a disorganized and laissez-faire attitude toward family life and child raising. American blacks describe the immigrants as arrogant, selfish, exploited in the workplace, oblivious to racial tensions and politics in the United States, and unfriendly and unwilling to have relations with black Americans. The first generation believes that their status as foreign-born blacks is higher than American blacks, and they tend to accentuate their identities as immigrants. Their accent is usually a clear and unambiguous signal to other Americans that they are foreign born.

The dilemma facing the second generation is that they grow up exposed to the negative opinions voiced by their parents about American blacks and to the belief that whites respond more favorably to foreign-born blacks. But they also realize that because they lack their parents' accents and other identifying characteristics, other people, including their peers, are likely to identify them as American blacks. How does the second generation handle this dilemma? Do they follow their parents' lead and identify with their ethnic identities such as Jamaican or Haitian or West Indian? Or do they try to become "American" and reject their parents' ethnic immigrant identities? . . .

Theoretical Approaches to Assimilation

Theories derived from the experiences of European immigrants and their children in the early twentieth century predicted that the more time spent in the United States, the more likely second-generation youths were to adopt an "American identity" and to reduce ties to the ethnic identities and culture of their parents. This "straight-line" assimilation model assumes that with each succeeding generation, the groups become more similar to mainstream Americans and more economically successful. For instance, Warner and Srole's (1945) study of ethnic groups in Yankee City (Newburyport, Massachusetts) in the early 1930s describes the generational march from initial residential and occupational segregation and poverty to residential, occupational, and identificational integration and Americanization.

However, the situation faced by immigrant blacks in the 1990s differs in many of the background assumptions of the straight-line model. The immigrants do not enter a society that assumes an undifferentiated monolithic American culture but rather a consciously pluralistic society in which a variety of subcultures and racial and ethnic identities coexist. In fact, if these immigrants assimilate, they become not just Americans but black Americans. The immigrants generally believe that it is higher social status to be an immigrant black than to be an American black. Second, the economic opportunity structure is very different now from what it was at the beginning of the twentieth century. The unskilled jobs in manufacturing that enhanced job mobility for immigrants' children at the turn of the century have been lost as economic restructuring in the United States has shifted to a service economy (Gans 1992). The immigrants also are quite varied in the skills they bring with them. Some arrive with advanced educations and professional qualifications to take relatively well-paying jobs, which put them ahead of native American blacks (for example, Jamaican nurses). Others are less skilled and face difficulties finding work in the United States. Finally, the degree of residential segregation faced by blacks in the United States, whether foreign born or American born, has always been, and continues to be, of a much higher order than the segregation faced by foreign-born white immigrants (Lieberson 1980; Massey 1990). Thus, even with occupational mobility, it is not clear that blacks would be able to move into higher-status neighborhoods in the orderly progression that Warner and Srole (1945) describe in their Yankee City study of European ethnic succession. A further complication for the black second generation is that part of being a black American involves dealing with American racism. Because immigrants and black Americans report a large difference in the perception and expectation of racism in American society, part of becoming American for the second generation involves developing a knowledge and perception of racism and its subtle nuances. . . .

Patterns in the Second Generation

The interviews suggest that while the individuals in this study vary a great deal in their identities, perceptions, and opinions, they can be sorted into three general types: identifying as Americans, identifying as ethnic Americans with some distancing from black Americans, or identifying as an immigrant in a way that does not reckon with American racial and ethnic categories.

A black American identity characterized the responses of approximately 42 percent of the eighty-three second-generation respondents interviewed. These youngsters identified with other black Americans. They did not see their "ethnic" identities as important to their self-image. When their parents or friends criticized American blacks or described what they perceived as fundamental differences between Caribbean-origin people and American blacks, these youngsters disagreed. They tended to downplay a national-origin identity and described themselves as American.

Another 30 percent of the respondents adopted a very strong ethnic identity that involved a considerable amount of distancing from American blacks. It was important for these respondents to stress their ethnic identities and for other people to recognize that they were not American blacks. These respondents tended to agree with parental judgments that there were strong differences between Americans and West Indians. This often involved a stance that West Indians were superior to American blacks in their behaviors and attitudes.

A final 28 percent of respondents had an immigrant attitude toward their identities, as opposed to American-identified youth or ethnic-identified youth. Most, but not all, of these respondents were more recent immigrants themselves. A crucial factor for these youngsters is that their accents and styles of clothing and behavior clearly signaled to others that they were foreign born. In a sense, their identity as an immigrant people precluded having to make a "choice" about what kind of American they were. These respondents had a strong identity, such as Jamaican or Trinidadian, but did not evidence much distancing from American blacks. Rather their identities were strongly linked to their experiences on the islands, and they did not worry much about how they were seen by other Americans, white or black.

A number of factors influence the type of identity the youngsters develop. They include the class background of the parents, the social networks in which the parents are involved, the type of school the child attends, and the family structure. All of these factors affect the ability of parents and other family members to shield children from neighborhood peer groups that espouse antischool values.

The type of identity and outlook on American race and ethnic relations that the youngsters developed was strongly related to their social class and its trajectory. The ethnic-identified youngsters were most likely to come from a middle-class background. Of the eighty-three second-generation teens and young adults interviewed, 57 percent of the middle-class teens identified ethnically, whereas only 17 percent of the working-class and poor teens identified ethnically.[2] The poorest students were the most likely to be immigrant or American identified. Only one out of the twelve teens whose parents were on public assistance identified ethnically. The American identified, perhaps not surprisingly, were also more likely to be born in the United States—67 percent of the American identified were born in the United States, as opposed to only 13 percent of the immigrant identified and 42 percent of the ethnically identified.

Parents with more education and income were able to provide better schools for their offspring. Among the respondents, some of the middle class had moved from the inner-city neighborhoods they had originally settled in to middle-class neighborhoods in the borough of Queens or to suburban areas where the schools were of higher academic quality and more likely to be racially integrated. Other middle-class parents sent their children to Catholic parochial schools or to citywide magnet schools such as Brooklyn Tech or Stuyvesant. Thus, the children were far more likely to attend schools with other immigrant children and with other middle-class whites and blacks, although some of the Catholic high schools were all black in enrollment.

The children of middle-class parents who did attend the local high schools were likely to be recent immigrants who had an immigrant identity. Because of their superior education in the West Indies, these students were the best in the local high schools, attended honors classes, and were bound for college. The children of middle-class parents who identified as American and were pessimistic about their own future opportunities and adopted antischool ideologies were likely to have arrived early in their lives and to have attended New York City public schools in inner-city areas from an early age.

The social networks of parents also influenced the type of identity the children developed. Regardless of social class, parents who were involved in ethnic voluntary organizations or heavily involved in their churches seemed to instill a strong sense of ethnic identity in their children. Parents whose social networks transcended neighborhood boundaries seemed to have more ability to provide guidance and social contacts for their children.

The two neighborhood schools where we interviewed the teenagers were among the five most dangerous schools in New York City—they were inadequate facilities with crumbling physical buildings, high dropout rates, and serious problems with violence. Both schools were all minority, with over 90 percent of the student body composed of black students, both American and foreign born. The students who attended these schools and were not in the separate honors track (which was overwhelmingly filled with newly arrived immigrants) faced very limited future options, even if they managed to graduate.

Finally, the family structure and the experience of migration itself have a profound effect on the degree of control parents have over teenage children. Many families are composed of single working mothers and children. These mothers have not been able to supervise their children as much as they would like, and many do not have any extended family or close friends available to help with discipline and control. Even families with two spouses present often have been apart for long periods because one spouse preceded the family in migration. Often children have been left in the islands or sent ahead with relatives to New York, with the parents often struggling to reassert authority after the family reunites. The generational conflict that ensues tends to create greater pressure for students to want to be "American" to differentiate themselves from parents.

Ethnic Response

All of the teenage respondents reported comments by their parents about American blacks that were very similar to those recorded in our interviews with the first generation. The differences were in how the teens interpreted what their parents were saying. In general, the ethnic-identified teens agreed with their parents and reported seeing a strong difference between themselves and black Americans, stressing that being black is not synonymous with being black American. They accept their parents' and the wider society's negative portrayals of poor blacks and wanted to avoid any chance that they will be identified with them. They described the culture and values of lower-class black Americans as lacking discipline, a work ethic, good child-rearing practices, and respect for education. They contrast these failures with the values of their parents' ethnic groups, which include an emphasis on education, strict discipline for children, a strong work ethic, and social mobility. They try to impress that they are Jamaican or Haitian and most definitely not black American. This allows them less dissonance with their parents' negative views of American blacks. They do not reject their parents' culture and identities but rather reject the American social system that would identify them as black American and strongly reject the African American peer group culture to which they would be assigned by whites and others if they did not consciously transmit their ethnic identities.

Although society may define the second generation on the basis of skin color, the second-generation ethnic teens believed that being black American involves more than merely having black skin. One young woman criticized American blacks in this way:

> Some of them [black Americans] think that their heritage includes not being able to speak correctly or walk correctly, or act loud and obnoxious to make a point. I don't think they have to do that. Just when I see black Americans, it depends on how I see you on the street. Walking down the street with that walk that moves a little bit too much. I would say, I'd think you dropped out of high school.

These teens also differentiated themselves from black Americans in terms of their sensitivity to racism, real or imagined. Some of the ethnic-identified second generation echo the feelings we heard from the first generation that American blacks are too quick to use race as an explanation or excuse for not doing well:

> There was a time back in the, '40s and, '50s and, '60s or whenever when people was actually trying to keep down black people and stuff like that. But, you know, some black people now, it's like they not actually trying to make it better, you know? Some are just like, people are like, oh, this place is trying to keep me down, and they sulk and they cry about it, and they're not really doing that much to help themselves.

. . . It's just like hyping the problem if they keep [saying] everything is racial, everything is racial.

The second-generation teens who are doing well try to understand how it is that they are so successful when black Americans are not—and often they chalk it up to family values. They say that their immigrant families have close-knit family values that stress education. Aware of, and sometimes sharing, the negative images of black Americans that the whites they encounter believe, the second generation also perceives that whites treat them better when they realize they are not "just" black Americans. When asked if they benefited ever from their ethnicity, they responded "yes": "It seems white Americans don't tend to put you in the same category as black Americans." Another respondent said:

The West Indians tend to go that extra step because they, whites, don't usually consider them really black Americans, which would be working class. They don't consider them, I guess, as black. They see them as a person.

The dilemma for the second generation is that while they have a strong sense of their own identities as very different from black Americans, this was not clear to other people. Often both whites and blacks saw them as just black Americans and did not notice that they were ethnically different. When people did comment on their ethnic difference it was often because of the way they talked and the way they walked. These two characteristics were cited as reasons that whites and other blacks gave for thinking those of the second generation were not "really black." Whites tend to let these children know that they think of them as exceptions to the rule, with the rule being that most blacks are not good people. However, these young people also know that unless they tell people of their ethnicity, most whites have no idea they are not black Americans.

Many of these teens coped with this dilemma by devising ways to telegraph their identities as second-generation West Indians or Haitians. One girl carried a Guyanese map as part of her key chain so that when people looked at her keys they would ask her about it and she could tell them that her parents were from Guyana. One young woman described having her mother teach her an accent so that she could use it when she applied for a job or a place to live. Others just try to work it into conversation

when they meet someone. This means that their self-identification is almost always at odds with the identifications others make of them in impersonal encounters in American society and that, as a result, they must consciously try to accentuate their ethnic identity:

Q: When a form or survey asks for your race what do you put down?

A: Oh boy, that is a tough one. It's funny because, you know, when we fill applications I never know what to check off, you know. I'm serious. 'Cause they have Afro-American, but they never have like Caribbean. They do have white, Chinese. To tell the truth, I would like to be called Caribbean, West Indian. Black West Indian.

The teens who were around many black Americans felt pressure from their peers to be part of the group and identify as black American. These teens would consciously talk about passing for American at some points and passing for Haitian or Jamaican at others by changing the way they talked or acted:

When I'm at school and I sit with my black friends and, sometimes I'm ashamed to say this, but my accent changes. I learn all the words. I switch. Well, when I'm with my friends, my black friends, I say I'm black, black American. When I'm with my Haitian-American friends, I say I'm Haitian. Well, my being black, I guess that puts me when I'm with black Americans, it makes people think that I'm lower class. . . . Then, if I'm talking like this [regular voice] with my friends at school, they call me white.

American-Identified Second Generation

The American-identified second-generation teenagers differed in how little they stressed their immigrant or ethnic identities to the interviewers. They follow a path that is more similar to the model posed in the straight-line theory. They stress that they are American because they were born here, and they are disdainful of their parents' lack of understanding of the American social system. Instead of rejecting black American culture, it becomes their peer culture, and they embrace many aspects of it. This brings them in conflict with their parents' generation, most especially with their parents' understandings of American blacks. They most definitely assimilate to black America; they speak black English with their peers, they listen to rap music, and they accept the peer culture of their black American friends. They are aware of the fact that they are considered black American by others and that they can be accused of "acting white" if they don't speak black English and behave in particular ways. Most included their ethnic identities as background, but none of them adopted the stance that they were not, in a major sense, black American. When asked about ethnic background and how other people think of it, one respondent replied:

Q: What is your ethnic background?

A: I put down American because I was born up here. I feel that is what I should put down. . . .

Q: What do other people think you are?

A: Black American because if I don't say. . . . Like if they hear my parents talk or something they always think they are from Jamaica. . . . But they just think I am black American because I was born up here.

Many of these teens discuss how they do not control how others see them:

A: Some people just think I am American because I have no accent. So I talk like American people. I don't talk Brooklynese. They think I am from down south or something. . . . A lot of people say you don't look Haitian. I think I look Haitian enough. I don't know, maybe they are expecting us to look fresh off the boat. I was born here and I grew up here, so I guess I look American and I have an American accent.

Q: If people think you are black American do you ever do anything about it?

A: No, I don't. If they ask me if I am American, I say yes. If they ask me where my parents are from, I tell them Haiti.

In fact, they imply that being a black American is more stylish and "with it" than being from the islands:

A: I consider myself a black American. When I think of a black American I don't think of them as coming from the West Indies.

Q: Any characteristics that come to mind?

A: I would not think of someone in a suit. I would think of a regular teenager. I would think of a regular person. I think of someone that is in style.

Q: What about someone from the islands?

A: Jamaicans. They dress with neon colors. Most of the girls wear gold and stuff like that.

Some of the young people told us that they saw little if any difference between the ethnic blacks and the American blacks. Many stressed the Caribbeanization of black New York and described how all the Americans were interested in being Caribbean now:

A: It use to be Jamaicans and American blacks did not get along because everyone was afraid of Jamaicans. But now I guess we are closer now. You tell an American that you are Jamaican and it is no big deal. Americans are acting more like Jamaicans. Jamaicans are acting like Americans.

Q: What do you mean by acting like each other?

A: Sure there are a lot of Americans out there speaking patois. And then all the Jamaicans are coming over here and they are like "Yo, what's up" and they are like that. Pretty soon you can't really tell who is Jamaican and who is American.

However, the parents of the American-identified teens have expressed to their children the same negative impressions of American blacks that the ethnic-identified teens reported. These teenagers report many negative appraisals of American blacks by their parents:

> They always say Haiti is better in this way or in that way. They say the kids here have no respect. The kids here are brought up without any supervision. My father is always talking about they [American blacks] be hanging out on the corner. And he says you won't find Haitians doing that. My mom always says you will marry a Haitian. Why are you talking to those American boys?

This young Haitian American teen tries to disagree with her mother and to temper her mother's interpretations of American blacks:

Q: Are there any characteristics or traits that come to mind about Haitian Americans?

A: Not really. I don't really—cause most people are Haitian American if they are born here. . . . Like me, I don't know if I act like a Haitian or do I have Haitian characteristics, but I'm mostly—like everything I do or like is American. My parents, they do not like American blacks, but they feel that they are lazy. They don't want to work and stuff like that from what they see. And I feel that, um, I feel that way too, but sometimes it won't be that person's fault, so I try to stick up for them. And my mother is like, yeah, you're just too American.

In marked contrast to the ethnic-identified teens, though, the American-identified teens disagreed with their parents' statements about American blacks, reluctantly agreed with some of it but provided qualifications, or perhaps, most disturbingly, accepted the appraisals as true of American blacks in general and themselves as American blacks. This young Trinidadian American swallows her parents' stereotypes and applies them directly to herself:

Q: How close do you feel in your ideas about things to West Indians?

A: Not very close. My feelings are more like blacks than theirs. I am lazy. I am really lazy and my parents are always making comments and things about how I am lazy. They are always like, in Trinidad you could not be this lazy. In Trinidad you would have to keep on working.

The fact that the teens are identifying as American and that their parents have such negative opinions of Americans causes some conflict. The teens either adopt a negative opinion of themselves or disagree with their parents' assessments of American blacks. But it is not just their parents who criticize black Americans. These youngsters are very aware of the generalized negative view of blacks in the wider culture. In answer to the question, "Do whites have an image of blacks?" all of them responded that whites have a negative view of blacks, seeing them as criminal, lazy, violent, and uncaring about family. Many of the teenagers prefaced their remarks by saying that they did not know any whites but that they knew this is what whites thought through the mass media and through the behaviors of whites they encountered in buses, trains, and stores. This mostly involved incidents such as whites protecting their handbags when the teenagers arrived or store clerks following them and expecting them to shoplift. This knowledge that the society in which they live devalues them because of their skin color and their identity affected these teens deeply.

Immigrant-Identified Teens

The more recently arrived young people who still identify as immigrant differed from both the ethnic- and the American-identified youth. They did not feel as much pressure to "choose" between identifying with or distancing from black Americans as did either the American or the ethnic teens. Strong in their national-origin identities, they were neutral toward American distinctions between ethnics and black Americans. They tended to stress their nationality or their birthplace as defining their identity. They also pointed to their experiences growing up and attending school in a different country. This young man had dreadlocks and a strong Jamaican accent. He stresses his African roots and lets his Jamaican origin speak for itself:

Q: What is your ethnicity? For example, when forms or surveys ask what your ethnic group or ancestry is what do you put?

A: African.

Q: Do you ever put Jamaican or anything?

A: No, not really. Only where Jamaican comes up is if someone asks where you're from. I'll say I am from Jamaica.

Q: What do people usually think you are?

A: They say I am Jamaican.

Q: They know that immediately?

A: Yeah.

Q: How do they know?

A: I change my voice. I don't have to tell them. I think it's also because of my locks sometimes and the way I carry myself, the way I dress.

While an ethnic-identified Jamaican American is aware that she might be seen by others as American and thus actively chooses to present herself as Jamaican, an immigrant-identified Jamaican could not conceive of herself as having a choice, nor could she conceive of being perceived by others as American. While an ethnic-identified teen might describe herself as Jamaican American, for the immigrant teen Jamaican would be all the label needed. Most teens in this category were recent immigrants. The few U.S.-born teens classified as immigrant identified had strong family roots on the islands, were frequent visitors to the islands, and had plans to return to live there as adults. A crucial factor that allows these youngsters to maintain this identity is that their accents and styles of clothing and behavior clearly signaled to others that they were foreign born.

Q: How important is it to you that your friends think of you in terms of your ethnicity?

A: Oh, very important. You know, I try hard not to lose my roots, you know, when I come to the United States. A lot of people who come here try to lose their accent, you know. Even in the workplace, you know, because they fear what other people might think of them. Even in the workplace. Me, I never try to change, you know, the way I am. I always try to, you know, stay with them, the way of my culture.

Q: So it's something you want people to recognize?

A: Yeah, definitely, definitely, absolutely.

Q: Why?

A: Why? I'm proud of who I am, you know. I'm proud of where I'm from and I'm not going to change because somebody might not like the way I walk, talk or dress, you know.

The importance of birthplace was stressed repeatedly by the immigrant identified as they stressed their difference from American-born coethnics:

Q: What would you put on a form or survey that asked about your ethnicity?

A: I'll say I'm Jamaican. You gotta say where you come from.

Q: And do you think of yourself more as a Jamaican or more as an American?

A: I think of more of a Jamaican' 'cause it's, I wasn't born here. I was born in Jamaica and was there for fourteen years.

Q: And what about kids who are born in America, but their parents were born in Jamaica?

A: Well, you see that is the problem. You see, kids whose parents are Jamaican, they think that, well, they are Jamaican. They need to recheck that they're Americans 'cause they was born in the country and they wasn't born outside the country. So I think they should, you know, know more about American than Jamaican.

Some who adopt this strong identity with the immigrant country were born in the United States, but the combination of strong family roots on the island, frequent visits, and plans to go live there when they are older allows them to think of themselves as not really American at all. This is especially easy to do in the public high schools where there are large numbers of freshly arrived youngsters from the islands.

Q: What do you think your race is?

A: Well, I'm black. I consider myself black. I don't consider myself black American, Afro-American and stuff like that because it's hard to determine, you know, for a person as an individual to determine himself to be Afro-American. . . . I'll be more a Guyanese person because certain things and traditions that I am accustomed to back home, it's still within the roots of me. And those things have not changed for a long period of time, even though you have to adapt to the system over here in order to get ahead and cope with what is going on around you.

While the ethnics tended to describe people as treating them better when they described their ethnic origins, and the Americans tended to stress the antiblack experiences they have had and the lack of difference between the foreign born and the American, the immigrant teens spoke about anti-immigrant feelings and discrimination and responded with pride in their national origins.

Contrasting Identities

In some sense one can see each of these identities as an embrace of one identity and an opposition to another. The American-identified youth are assimilating, in fact, to the American black subculture in the neighborhood. They are adapting to American black cultural forms, and they do so in distinction to their parents' ethnic identities and the wider mainstream white identities. These students adopt some of the "oppositional" poses that American black teenagers show toward academic achievement, the idea of America, the idea of opportunity, and the wider society (Fordham 1988; Ogbu 1990; Portes and Zhou 1993). They also are opposed to their parents' outlooks and ideas, stressing that what worked as a life strategy and a child-raising technique in the islands does not work in the United States. These teens tend to adopt a peer culture of racial solidarity and opposition to school authorities. What is clear from the interviews is that this stance is in part a socialized response to a peer culture, but the vast majority of it comes about as a reaction to their life experiences. Most specifically, the teens respond to their experiences with racial discrimination and their perceptions of blocked social mobility. The lives of these youngsters basically lead them to reject their parents' immigrant dream of individual social mobility and to accept their peers' analysis of the United States as a place with blocked social mobility where they will not move far.

The American-identified teens do not seem aware of the scholarly literature and the perceptions among ethnic- and immigrant-identified youngsters that the foreign born are of higher social status than the American born. In the peer culture of the neighborhood and the school, these teenagers describe a situation in which being American offers higher social status than being ethnic. For instance, several youngsters described "passing" as black American in order not to be ridiculed or picked on in school:

> I used to be scared to tell people that I was Haitian. Like when I was in eighth grade there were lots of Haitians in the ESL classes, and people used to beat them up. They used to pick on them. I said to myself I am going to quiet down, say I am American.

When asked about the images others held of being from the islands, most of the teens described neutral attributes, such as styles of dress. However, many who identified as Americans also described negative associations with the immigrants' identities. The Jamaicans said most people thought of drug dealers when they thought of Jamaicans. A few of the teens also intimated that people from the islands were backward in not knowing how to live in a big city, both in appreciating the wonders of the city and being street smart to avoid crime and hassles with other people. In terms of the former attribute, the teens described people from the islands who were not accustomed to shopping in big malls or having access to a wide variety of consumer goods.

Not one of the American-identified teens voiced the opinion of the overwhelming majority of the ethnic teens that whites were more likely to like the foreign born. In part, this reflected the differences the groups had in their contact with whites. Most of the inner-city ethnic-identified teens had almost no contact with whites, except for teachers. They also are in schools where the vast majority of the students are foreign born or second generation. The larger number of middle-class teens who were ethnic-identified were more likely to have white classmates in citywide magnet high schools, in parochial schools, or in suburban schools or workplaces.

The inner-city American-identified teens also voiced more positive appraisals of black Americans than did the immigrant- or the ethnic-identified teens. Their descriptions reflect the reality of living in neighborhoods where there is crime and violence. A majority of the American-identified teens said that a good trait of black Americans is that they work hard and they struggle. These are the very same children whose parents describe black Americans

primarily as lazy and unwilling to take advantage of the opportunities available to them. The children seem to be perceiving a reality that the parents cannot or will not.

Many of these teens live in neighborhoods that are all black and also attend schools that are all black. So, aside from teachers, these young people have almost no contact with white Americans. This does not stop them from absorbing the fact that whites have negative stereotypic views of blacks. But unlike the middle-class blacks who come in contact with whites who tell them that they are "good blacks," these youths live in the urban areas associated with crime, they dress like the typical black urban youth, and they talk with Brooklyn accents and black American slang. When they do encounter whites in public places, the whites do not ask about their parents' backgrounds.

Q: Have you ever experienced any discrimination or hostility in New York?

A: From being Trinidadian no. But because of being black, you know, everybody stereotypes. And they say "blacks, they tend to steal, and stuff like that." So, like, if I am walking down the street and a white lady go by and they smile and I smile. They put their bag on the other side.

The parents of these teens grew up in situations where blacks were the majority. The parents do not want their children to be "racial" in the United States. They define "being racial" as being overly concerned with race and with using race as an excuse or explanation for lack of success at school or on the job. The first generation tends to believe that, while racism exists in the United States, it can be overcome or circumvented through hard work, perseverance, and the right values and attitudes. The second generation experiences racism and discrimination constantly and develops perceptions of the overwhelming influence of race on their lives. These teens experience being hassled by police and store owners, not being given jobs, even being attacked on the streets if they venture into white neighborhoods. The boys adopt black American culture in their schools, wearing flattops, baggy pants, and certain types of jewelry. This contributes to the projection of the "cool pose," which in turn causes whites to be afraid of them. This makes them angry and resentful. The media also tell these youngsters that blacks are disvalued by American society. While parents tell their children to strive for upward mobility and to work harder in the face of discrimination, the American-identified teens think the rewards for doing so will be very slim.

This causes a wide gulf between the parents and their children. These parents are absolutely terrified of their children becoming Americans. For the children, to be American is to have freedom from the strict parental controls of the immigrant parents. This is an old story in the immigrant saga, one visible in novels and movies about conflicts between Jewish and Italian immigrants and their children. But the added dimension here is that these parents are afraid of the downward social mobility that becoming an American black represents to them. And this idea is reinforced constantly to these parents by whites who tell them that they are better than American blacks.

One question about how things had changed since the civil rights movement shows the different perceptions of the teens about race in American society. The ethnically identified gave answers I suspect most white Americans would give. They said that things are much better for blacks now. They state that blacks now can ride at the front of the bus and go to school with whites. The irony, of course, is that I was sitting in an all black school when they told this story. The vast majority of the American-identified teens state that things are not better since the civil rights movement; the change is that discrimination now is "on the down low," covered up, more crafty. Some pointed out that we were in an all-black school. The result of these different world views is that the parents' view of an opportunity structure that is open to hard work is systematically undermined by their children's peer culture and, more important, by the actual experience of these teens.

On the other hand, the ethnic-identified teens, whose parents are more likely to be middle class and doing well or who attend parochial or magnet schools, see clearer opportunities and rewards ahead, despite the existence of racism and discrimination. Their parents' message that hard work and perseverance can circumvent racial barriers does not fall on unreceptive ears. The ethnic-identified youngsters embrace an identity derived directly from their parents' immigrant identity. Such an identity is in opposition to their peers' identities and in solidarity with their parents' identities. These youngsters stress that they are Jamaican Americans and that, while they may be proud of their racial identity as black, they see strong differences between themselves and black Americans. They specifically see their ethnic identities as keys to upward social mobility, stressing, for instance, that their parents' values of hard work and strict discipline help them to succeed in the United States when black Americans fail. This ethnic identity is very much an American-based identity—it is in the context of American social life that these youngsters base their assumptions of what it means to be Jamaican or Trinidadian. In fact, the pan-ethnic identities of Caribbean or West Indian often are the most salient label for these youngsters, as they see little differences among the groups and it is more important to differentiate themselves as second-generation Americans. The distancing that these teens show from black Americans often leads them to accept many negative stereotypes of black Americans. These youngsters tend to have ethnic friends from a West Indian background, white American friends, and very few, if any, black American friends.

The immigrant-identified teens are different from either of the other two, because of how they think about who they are not as well as how they think about who they are. These teens have a strong identity as Jamaican or Trinidadian, but this identity tends to be related to their interactions with other Jamaicans or Trinidadians rather than their interactions with black or white Americans. These youngsters identify with their homelands or their parents' homelands, but not in opposition to black Americans or in opposition to white Americans. They tend to be immersed in the immigrant community, to have friends who are all the same ethnicity or from other islands. They tend to be more recent arrivals. Unlike the ethnically identified, however, they do not distance themselves from American blacks, and they have neutral or positive attitudes and relations with them. At the same time, they see themselves as different from, but not opposed to, black Americans.

These identities are fluid and change over time and in different social contexts. We found cases of people who describe identifying very strongly as black American when they were younger and who became more immigrant identified when they reached high school and found a large immigrant community. Most new arrivals to the United States start out as immigrant identified, and the longer they stay in the United States, the more they begin to think of themselves in terms of American categories. The kind of social milieu the child faces, especially the school environment, has a strong influence on the outcome. A school with many black Americans creates pressure to identify racially; likewise a neighborhood and school with many immigrants makes it possible to avoid thinking much about American categories. In the face of much pressure not to follow the rules and not to succeed academically, youngsters who are doing well in school and do value education increasingly come to stress their ethnic backgrounds as an explanation for their ambition and success.

The American racial classification system that pushes toward an either/or—"black or white"—designation of people makes the immigrant option harder to hold onto. When others constantly identify the individual as black and refuse to make distinctions based on black ethnicity, pressure builds for the individual to adapt his or her identity to that outside identification—either to say "Yes, I am black," and to accept categorization with black Americans or to resent the characterization and strongly make an ethnic identification as Trinidadian American. The American myopia about ethnic differences within the black community makes the middle-ground immigrant identity unstable. Because every young person is aware of the negative images held by whites and the wider society of black Americans, the acceptance of an American black identity also means the acceptance of the oppositional character of that identity. Oppositional identities, as Ogbu (1990) clearly argues, are self- and group-affirming identities for stigmatized groups—defining as good and worthy those traits and characteristics that are the opposite of those valued by the majority group. This tends to draw the aspirations of the teens downward.

Implications of the Patterns

Some of the distancing shown by the ethnic-identified teens vis-à-vis underclass black identity is the same as that exhibited by middle-class black Americans. Elijah Anderson (1990) has noted that middle-class blacks in a gentrifying neighborhood in Philadelphia use various verbal and nonverbal strategies to convey to others that they are not from the ghetto and that they disapprove of the ghetto-specific behaviors of the blacks who live

there. Being an ethnic black in interactions with whites seems to be a shorthand way of conveying distance from the ghetto blacks. Thus, the second generation reserves their ethnic status for use as an identity device to stress their distance from poor blacks and to stress their cultural values, which are consistent with American middle-class values. This same use of an ethnic identity is present among first-generation immigrants of all social classes, even those in racially segregated poor neighborhoods in New York.

The second generation in the segregated neighborhoods, with little chance for social mobility, seems to be unaware that status as a black ethnic conveys higher social status among whites, in part because they have not had much contact with whites. The mass media convey to them the negative image of American blacks held by whites but do not convey to them the image among intellectuals, middle-class whites, and conservative scholars, such as Thomas Sowell, that they have cultural capital by virtue of their immigrant status. They do get the message that blacks are stereotyped by whites in negative ways, that the all-black neighborhoods they live in are violent and dangerous, and that the neighborhoods of whites are relatively safe. They also encounter a peer culture that values black American cultural forms. The immigrant culture of struggle, hard work, and educational success that their parents try to enforce is experienced in negative ways by these youngsters. They see their parents denying them privileges that their American peers enjoy and, unlike the middle-class youth, they do not automatically associate hard work, lack of dating and partying, and stress on scholastic achievement with social mobility. In the peer culture of the school, immigrant- and ethnic-identified teens tend to be the best students. In the neighborhood inner-city schools, newly arrived immigrants who have attended better schools in the islands tend to outperform the students who have spent their lives in substandard New York City public schools. This tends to reinforce the association between ethnicity and school success—and the more American-identified teens adopt an adversarial stance toward school.

Warner and Srole (1945), in their study of Yankee City in the 1930s, report that it is the socially mobile white ethnics whose ties to the ethnic group and the ethnic identity decline. In their work, those individuals stuck in the lower classes turned to their ethnic identities and groups as a sort of consolation prize:

> Our class system functions for a large proportion of ethnics to destroy the ethnic subsystems and to increase assimilation. The mobile ethnic is much more likely to be assimilated than the nonmobile one. The latter retains many of the social characteristics of his homeland. . . . Some of the unsuccessfully mobile turn hostile to the host culture, develop increasing feelings of loyalty to their ethnic traditions, become active in maintaining their ethnic subsystems, and prevent others from becoming assimilated. But, generally speaking, our class order disunites ethnic groups and accelerates their assimilation. (p. 284)

It could be that the process will be exactly the opposite for black immigrants and black ethnics. In this case, the more socially mobile cling to ethnic identity as a hedge against their racial identity. The less mobile blacks see little advantage to stressing an ethnic identity in the social worlds in which they travel, which are shared mostly with black Americans. Stressing an ethnic identity in that context risks being described as "acting white," being seen as rejecting the race and accepting the white stereotypes, which they know through their everyday lives are not true.

The changes in race relations in the United States since the 1960s are very complicated and most surely involve a mixing of class and race. Some white Americans are trying to see the difference between ghetto inner-city blacks, whom they fear and do not like, and middle-class blacks, whom they do not fear and with whom they would like to have contact, if only to prove to themselves that they are not racist or, in a more formal sense, to meet their affirmative goals.

Middle-class blacks realize this and try to convey their class status in subtle and not so subtle ways (Feagin 1991). The immigrants also utilize the fact that New Yorkers tend to use foreign-born status as a proxy for the class information they are seeking. The white New Yorkers we interviewed do notice differences among blacks, and they use ethnic differences as clues for class differences. If the association found here between social class and ethnic identity is widespread, this perception could become a self-fulfilling prophesy. It could be that the children of poor parents will not keep an ethnic identity and the children whose parents achieve social mobility will keep the ethnic identity. This will reinforce the image in the minds of whites that the "island people" are "good blacks," thus giving the edge in employment decisions and the like to ethnic blacks over American blacks.

On the other hand, it remains to be seen how long the ethnic-identified second generation will continue to identify with their ethnic backgrounds. This also is related to the fact that whites tend to make racial judgments about identity when it comes to blacks. The second generation does not have an accent or other clues that immediately telegraph their ethnic status to others. They are aware that, unless they are active in conveying their identities, they are seen as black Americans, and that often in encounters with whites, the status of their black race is all that matters. It could be that by the time they have children, they will have decided that the quest not to be seen as a black American will be a futile one.

Seeing the Big Picture   Is a Nonethnic Racial Identity Possible?

The four readings in this section recall a saying appropriate to this material: "You can change your ethnicity, but you can't change your race." Is this expression true or false? Why?

RACE AND ROMANCE ~
Blurring Boundaries

45   Guess Who's Been Coming to Dinner? Trends in Interracial Marriage over the 20th Century
Roland G. Fryer Jr.

ROLAND G. FRYER JR. is assistant professor of economics, Harvard University, and Faculty Research Fellow, National Bureau of Economic Research, both in Cambridge, Massachusetts. His e-mail address is rfryer@fas.harvard.edu.

WHILE BLACK–WHITE PARITY HAS NOT YET been achieved in the United States, many gauges relating to economic and political empowerment have shown extraordinary convergence. Over the past 40 years, for instance, the black–white ratio of median earnings for male full-time workers increased from .50 to .73 (Welch, 2003) and the racial disparity in life expectancy decreased from 6.8 years to 5.3 years (author's calculations using data from the National Center of Health Statistics). For the first time, recent cohorts of black and white children with similar backgrounds enter school on equal footing (Fryer and Levitt, 2004).

But in the most intimate spheres of life—religion, residential location, marriage, and cohabitation—far less convergence has occurred. Martin Luther King Jr. famously noted in a number of his speeches that "the 11 o'clock hour on Sunday is the most segregated hour in American life" (for example, see King, 1956). Today, an estimated 90 percent of Americans worship primarily with members of their own race or ethnicity (Stodgill and Bower, 2002). Residential segregation, though lower today than in 1970, remains remarkably high. In a typical American city, 64 percent of blacks would have to change neighborhoods to ensure an even distribution of blacks across the city (Cutler, Glaeser, and Vigdor, 1999). Even friendship networks within seemingly integrated public schools are

Questions to Consider   In *Loving v. Virginia* (1967) the U.S. Supreme Court ruled that antimiscegenation laws were unconstitutional. Simply put, the Court argued that the federal government had no right to intervene in or prohibit matters of intimacy between consenting adults. One would expect that almost fifty years later people would have married in considerable numbers across the color line. It is true that the number of interracial marriages has increased considerably, but the number is still relatively small (about 7 percent of all marriages). What is most interesting from a sociological perspective is that marriages across the color line are not random. Some racial groups are more likely to marry across the color line than others. Which groups tend to engage in exogamy or marry "out" of their race more than the others, and why? What's the basis for your answer?

remarkably segregated; the typical student has .7 friends of a different race (Echenique and Fryer, forthcoming).

Historically, there was a distinction between economic and political equality on one side and social equality on the other (Woodward, 1955). Courts often stated that blacks would be made equal under the law but remain subordinate in informal, intimate spheres of life. In

Plessy v. Ferguson (163 U.S. 537 [1896]), the U.S. Supreme Court argued that integration in schools, parks, railroads, and courts could not be mandated because they were private, social concerns. The last civil rights to be granted pertained to the laws governing social interactions, like whom to marry and where to live.

In this paper, I focus on one aspect of social intimacy—marriages across black, white, and Asian racial lines. The paper begins with a brief history of the regulation of race and romance in America. Then, using census data from 1880 to 2000, an analysis of interracial marriage uncovers a rich set of cross-section and time-series patterns.

Marrying across racial lines is a rare event, even today. Interracial marriages account for approximately 1 percent of white marriages, 5 percent of black marriages, and 14 percent of Asian marriages. Among married whites, 0.4 percent choose to marry blacks and 0.6 percent choose to marry Asians. Among married blacks, 4.6 percent intermarry with whites and 0.5 percent with Asians. Asians intermarry almost exclusively with whites—white spouses comprise 13.2 percent of all Asian marriages and blacks roughly 1 percent.

The data are most consistent with a Becker-style marriage market model [Becker, 1973] in which objective criteria of a potential spouse, his/her race, and the social price of intermarriage are central. The evidence in favor of the classic Becker model is far from overwhelming and hinges on several plausible (but untestable) assumptions. Yet it is the only hypothesis I test that does not contradict the data in important ways, after testing a range of theories, including a social exchange theory of marriage that dominates the sociology literature and a marriage theory based on random search and social interactions.

Ultimately, social intimacy is a way of measuring whether or not a majority group views a minority group on equal footing. In most information-based theories of discrimination, stereotyping, stigma, and inequality, social intimacy leads to less discrimination and improved outcomes for racial minority groups (for example, Fryer and Jackson, 2003; Rosch, 1978; see also Loury, 2002, for a conceptual discussion of racial stigma). Relatedly, Patterson (1982) argues that "social death," the treating of individuals as less than full persons, is the real historical tragedy of racial relations in the United States.

The primary motivation for this paper was to explore the division between political and social inequality in the unlovely history of *black–white* relations in America and how interracial intimacy may be a more appropriate barometer for the closing of the divide than labor market statistics, but some of the more interesting patterns in the data concern *Asian* intermarriage. As a group, Asians did not face the intensity or longevity of social ostracism endured by blacks, but for many years the U.S. placed strict quotas on immigrants from Asia. This legacy may explain why the time-series patterns look so similar to those for blacks. The civil rights movement was liberating for all racial groups.

A Brief History of Romance, Regulation, and Race

When slavery replaced indentured servitude as the primary source of labor in the upper regions of the South during the last decades of the seventeenth century, whites began to work in close contact with blacks. In some cases, coworkers became intimate and blurred the color line (Moran, 2003). Antimiscegenation laws (laws that forbade marrying across racial lines) became a way to draw a distinction between black and white, slave and free. The Chesapeake colonies, now Maryland and Virginia, were the first to enact statutes that punished whites for racial mixing. In Virginia, the law instructed that a white spouse be banished from the colony within three months of an interracial wedding. This penalty was increased to six months in jail in 1705. In Maryland, if a white woman married a black man she became a slave to her husband's master. Interracial marriage laws also ensured that blacks could not have access to inheritance. Over time, bans on interracial marriage and corresponding social taboos were also directed at Asian groups like Chinese, Japanese, and Filipinos—especially in Western states. However, miscegenation has always been legal for Native Americans and Hispanics.

Table 1 provides dates for the permanent repeal of antimiscegenation laws, by state. The first column shows the twelve states that never had laws against black–white marital unions. The second column shows states that repealed such laws before 1900. The third column shows states that repealed such laws after 1900, but before the 1967 U.S. Supreme Court decision in *Loving v. Virginia* (388 U.S. 1), which held such laws to be unconstitutional. The final column shows the states that repealed their laws only after the Supreme Court ruling.

Looking back, one obvious question is why more states didn't drop their bans on interracial marriage after the passage of the 14th Amendment to the U.S. Constitution

TABLE 1 **Permanent Repeals of Antimiscegenation Laws, by State**

Never had such laws	*Repealed before 1900*	*Repealed after 1900, before* **Loving**	*Repealed after* **Loving**
Alaska	Illinois (1874)	Arizona (1962)	Alabama
Connecticut	Iowa (1851)	California (1948)	Arkansas
Hawaii	Maine (1883)	Colorado (1957)	Delaware
Kansas[a]	Massachusetts (1843)	Idaho (1959)	Florida
Minnesota	Michigan (1883)	Indiana (1965)	Georgia
New Hampshire	Ohio (1887)	Maryland (1967)	Kentucky
New Mexico[a]	Pennsylvania (1780)	Montana (1953)	Louisiana
New Jersey	Rhode Island (1881)	Nebraska (1963)	Mississippi
New York[b]		Nevada (1959)	Missouri
Vermont		North Dakota (1955)	North Carolina
Washington[a]		Oregon (1951)	Oklahoma
Wisconsin		South Dakota (1957)	South Carolina
		Utah (1963)	Texas
		Wyoming (1965)	Tennessee
			Virginia
			West Virginia

[a]Had laws, but repealed them before statehood.
[b]Had a law against interracial sex when it was a Dutch colony (New Amsterdam).

in 1868, which attempted to make sure that slaves would receive the rights of citizens by requiring "equal protection of the laws." Indeed, six states in the North, Midwest, and West repealed antimiscegenation laws at about this time, and a few Southern states temporarily dropped bans on interracial marriage. But the Southern states soon reversed course.

For instance, in an Alabama 1872 state Supreme Court decision, *Burns v. State* (48 Alabama 195), the court dropped bans on interracial marriage by appealing to the Civil Rights Act of 1866 and the 14th Amendment to argue that marriage was a contract and blacks now had the right to enter contracts with whites. But immediately following the removal of the Northern troops from the South, officials began to delineate sharply between political equality and social equality. Political equality was the formal access to governmental processes, whereas social equality involved informal relations between neighbors, friends, and family. In 1877, the Alabama Supreme Court reversed its decision in *Green v. State* (58 Alabama 190), concluding that the Civil Rights Act of 1866 was not meant to overturn antimiscegenation laws. The court rejected the idea that marriage was simply a contract between individuals. Instead, the court insisted that "homes are nurseries of the states" and that public officials were entitled to regulate marriage to promote the general good. The court argued that equal-protection laws were not violated so long as both parties were equally punished, and the court also declared that it was "under no obligation to promote social equality."

Even the famous 1954 school desegregation decision in *Brown v. Board of Education of Topeka Kansas* (347 U.S. 483), which was a fundamental breakthrough on the road to civil rights, did not bring an end to bans on interracial marriage. Six months after the *Brown* decision, the Supreme Court, without dissent, refused to hear an appeal by Linnie Jackson who was convicted under an Alabama statute barring interracial marriage. Alabama argued that *Brown* did not apply to antimiscegenation because the ruling only involved public services and facilities. One justice described the court's view on desegregation and antimiscegenation at this time by saying (as quoted in Moran, 2003), "One bombshell at a time, please!"

It was at the intersection of sexual freedom and civil rights that antimiscegenation laws would finally be eliminated. In the 1965 case of *Griswold v. Connecticut* (381 U.S. 479), the Supreme Court struck down a Connecticut statute that limited the use of contraception by married couples. The decision declared that marriage was an institution "intimate to the degree of being sacred." Two years later, the case of *Loving v. Virginia* held that all bans on interracial marriages were unconstitutional—forcing 16 states to allow interracial marriage.

Trends in Interracial Marriage over the Twentieth Century

To study the patterns of interracial marriage over time, I use data from the Integrated Public Use Microdata Series based on U.S. Census Data for 1880–2000. Interracial pairings are made using the "spouse location" variable which allows one to search through a census household to identify a given person's spouse, and then to identify demographic data about the spouse. An interracial marriage is defined as a marriage between two individuals who report a different race when the census is taken. Three racial groups are analyzed: Asians, blacks, and whites. All other racial groups and individuals without valid responses to race are dropped from the sample. Other racial categories were omitted because their definitions have not remained constant over time and very often the sample of intermarriages involving these groups is too small. Unless otherwise specified, the denominator used to calculate the rates of intermarriage for a racial group is the number of married persons within that group.

Racial Intermarriage Relative to All Marriage

Figure 1 shows trends in interracial marriage for whites, blacks, and Asians over time. Panel A documents the trends in interracial marriage among whites. In 1880, interracial marriages among whites and blacks or Asians were extremely rare (less than 0.1 percent of all white marriages). Whites were more likely to intermarry with blacks than Asians, though this trend eventually reversed. For the first 100 years of the time series, the share of white male–black female marriages remained under 0.1 percent, trended up from 1980 through 2000, and peaked in the latter years at 0.2 percent. White female–black male unions increased from 0.10 percent in 1970 to 0.45 percent in 2000.

White intermarriages with Asians follow a very different pattern. White male–Asian female matches were quite rare from 1880 to 1960. In 1960, this level was rising dramatically. These marriages continued to increase nearly

ten-fold over the next 40 years, and today are the most common interracial marriage. White female marriages with Asian men followed a similar, though less pronounced, trajectory.

Black males and females have similar trends of miscegenation across the twentieth century, though the level of interracial mixing is quite different, as shown in Panel B of Figure 1. Rates of interracial marriage between blacks and other racial groups remained flat from 1880 to 1970. Between 1970 and 2000, black men exhibit an almost six-fold increase in intermarriage with whites. Currently, almost 6 percent of black male marriages are with whites. Black females exhibit similar trends, although the timing of the increase is later and the raw prevalence of interracial marriages is less for black females. Roughly 2.9 percent of black female marriages are to white men. Black men and women are equally unlikely to marry Asians.

In 1880, approximately 1 percent of Asian men intermarried with whites. Rather than increase monotonically over time, the share of Asian men intermarrying with whites rises until 1940 and then decreases. Asian females exhibit the opposite pattern, showing dramatic increases in intermarriage with whites until 1980 and then a slow decrease. Until 1960, Asian men were more likely than Asian women to intermarry with whites. By the 2000 census, however, this trend had reversed. Asian women are almost twice as likely to marry a white person as Asian men.

In our sample, Asians comprise 1.4 percent, blacks 11.3 percent, and whites the remainder. It is quite remarkable, in a purely statistical sense, that white males and Asian females are the most prevalent interracial marriage. However, the fact that black–Asian intermarriage occurs so rarely could theoretically be due to their relatively small shares of the population, and need not imply negative preferences for one another—later we explore this possibility—but unadjusted means of interracial marriages need to be interpreted with care.

Figure 1 calculates intermarriage rates relative to all married people. However, the propensity of racial groups to marry has fluctuated substantially over time. If rates of intermarriage are divided by all people, not just by individuals who are married, some different patterns emerge.

Overall marriage rates have declined in recent decades. For instance, between 1962 and 2004 the marriage rate for black women has declined steadily from

(A) Whites

(B) Blacks

(C) Asians

FIGURE 1   **Percent of Whites (A), Blacks (B), and Asians (C) Marrying Out of Race, Excluding Foreign-Born, Counting All Persons** *(as a percent of all marriages).*

62 percent to 36 percent (based on author's calculations using the Current Population Survey). Marriage rates among whites have decreased from 84 percent to 64 percent.

If rates of intermarriage are divided by all people, then white men and white women show essentially similar trends as in Panel A of Figure 1: a low level of intermarriage until 1960—typically less than 0.05 percent—followed by a sharp increase in all categories of miscegenation. By 2000, 0.4 percent of white men had married an Asian female and 0.1 percent had married a black female, while 0.2 percent of white women had married a black male and 0.15 percent had married an Asian male. Asians and blacks also exhibit remarkably similar time-series patterns to that displayed in Figures IB and IC, though the magnitudes are substantially smaller because the denominator contains all persons rather than only married persons.

Intermarriage by Education Level

There seems to be some conventional wisdom that interracial marriages are concentrated among those with lower levels of education. But while this claim used to be true several decades ago, the pattern has reversed itself. Interracial marriages are now more concentrated among the those with higher levels of education.

For this analysis, I divide education level into four categories: high school dropout (less than 12 years of education), high school degree, some college (enrolled in college but not graduated), and college degree or more. Individuals without valid educational attainment responses were dropped from the sample. The analysis is also limited to the period between 1940 and 2000, because detailed data on educational attainment are only available in the census after 1940. (Before 1940, the census only asks whether or not a person is literate, not their educational attainment.)

From 1940 to 1960, whites with less than a high school level of education were the most likely to intermarry, at a rate of about 0.1 percent of all marriages, while intermarriage among higher-educated groups was essentially zero. In the 1960s and 1970s, whites with higher education levels begin to show a marked increase in miscegenation rates while intermarriage rates among the least-educated tailed off just a bit. In 2000, white men with some college education or more than a college education had

intermarriage rates above 0.4 percent, and white women in these education categories had intermarriage rates above 0.25 percent.

The pattern for Asians is similar to that of whites. From 1940 to 1960, about 8–12 percent of the marriages of Asian men with less than a high school education were outside the race. For Asian men with higher levels of education, the rate of intermarriage was typically 1–2 percent in these years. But the rate of intermarriage for low-educated Asian men has since plummeted to 1 percent in 1990 and almost zero by 2000, while the rate of intermarriage for Asian men with college education or more had risen above 4 percent by 1980. Asian women show a similar pattern, although the timing is a little different. Asian women of all education levels were very unlikely to intermarry in 1940, with all education levels having intermarriage rates under 2 percent. But from 1950 to 1980, Asian women with a high school education or less were more likely to intermarry than those with more education, at rates of 8–10 percent. But by 2000, intermarriage rates for Asian women with less than a high school education had dropped again, to 2 percent, while intermarriage rates for Asian women with a college education or more had risen to 8 percent.

Blacks follow this same general pattern, with a twist. Between 1940 and 1960, the least educated blacks were the most likely to intermarry, with intermarriage rates typically between 0.6 percent and 1.0 percent of all marriages. But during the 1960s and 1970s, the prevalence of intermarriage rates among this education group changed little, while those with more education increased intermarriage rates. By 2000, blacks with some college education were the most likely to intermarry, with an intermarriage rate of 2.5 percent for black men and 1.1 percent for black women (who are generally less likely to intermarry than black men). However, blacks are also much less likely than whites or Asians to possess a college or higher-level degree. Adjusting for the relative numbers of individuals in each educational category, more-educated blacks experience a sharper increase in their intermarriage rates than their less-educated counterparts. With this adjustment, the patterns of racial intermarriage by level of education are strikingly similar across all racial groups.

Military Service and Intermarriage

Soldiers are forced to interact and trust individuals of various ethnic and racial groups; the price for not doing so can be large. Romano (2003) provides a detailed historical description of interracial mixing in America since World War I, emphasizing the role of the military and of war in shaping preferences towards interracial marriage. To date, there has been no statistical analysis of members of the military versus civilians in the proclivity to intermarry. The data collected for this paper show that while military service seems to have had little effect on rates of intermarriage from 1940 to 1960, black and white veterans have had higher rates of intermarriage than nonveterans since then.

From 1940 to 1960, white veterans and nonveterans had very similar rates of racial intermarriage at 0.1–0.2 percent. As rates of intermarriage rise, the rate of intermarriage for white veterans rose faster than for nonveterans. By 2000, the intermarriage rate of white veterans was 1.3 percent versus a rate of 0.9 percent for nonveterans. Similarly, black veterans and nonveterans have very similar rates of intermarriage from 1940 to 1960, at about 1 percent. But as rates of racial intermarriage rise for both groups, the increase is faster for black veterans. By 2000, black veterans had an intermarriage rate of 6.9 percent, compared to 4.3 percent for black nonveterans.

In this area, Asians do not follow a similar pattern to blacks or whites. From 1940 to 1970, the intermarriage rate for Asian veterans was similar to that of nonveterans in the range of 10–15 percent. However, when rates of intermarriage increased for both groups in the 1970s, the rate for Asian nonveterans increased more quickly. By 2000, the racial intermarriage rate was 35 percent for nonveteran Asians versus only 24 percent of veteran Asians.

With the current data, it is impossible to distinguish between selection (individuals who enter the military are those who would be more inclined to intermarry) and treatment (the military experience cultivates a demand for interracial intimacy). The latter possibility is bolstered by the fact that the time-series variation fits with historical data on the integration of military units (MacGregor, 1985). The Armed Forces were fully segregated through World War II. President Harry Truman ordered an end to racial segregation in the late 1940s, and racially integrated units started during the Korean War. The trend has continued since. The military is currently believed to be as racially integrated as any U.S. institution, although blacks may still lag in officer representation, especially at the highest ranks (MacGregor, 1985).

Fitting Theories of the Family to Facts about Interracial Marriage

A number of facts emerged from the analyses in the preceding sections. White male–Asian female marriages are the most common interracial marriage, comprising 20 percent of all Asian female marriages and 35 percent for domestic-born Asian women. White female–black male is the second most common pairing, constituting 6 percent of black male marriages. Asian–black marriages are virtually nonexistent. Adjusting for the relative supply of each racial group in the population provides a different portrait of interracial marriage—particularly for intermarriage with Asians whose small numbers can make the raw calculations deceiving. Intermarriage rates differ substantially by education, geographic considerations, and veteran status. The most striking patterns are those concerning the reversal in the role of education in intermarriage. In the middle of the twentieth century, the least educated were more likely to be in an interracial marriage, but by the end of the century, the most educated were the most likely to intermarry.

In this section, we investigate the extent to which three theories of interracial marriage can account for this rich set of facts. The first theory is the most well known in sociology: social exchange theory (Merton, 1941). The remaining two are economic models: a search model and a Becker-style marriage-market model (Becker, 1973).

Social Exchange Theories

The leading theory in sociology for explaining intermarriage between racial groups is social exchange theory. This approach was originally laid out in Merton (1941); Blau (1964) and Kalmijn (1993) offer some interesting extensions of the basic model. The ideas are similar to some models of hedonic pricing in economics (Rosen, 1974).

Let individuals be represented by a vector of characteristics: attractiveness, sense of humor, height, weight, race, gender, family wealth, criminal record, and so on. Suppose the value of a person in a marriage market depends on that person's objective value, given a person's vector of characteristics, and the societal cost of marrying an individual with such characteristics. Further, assume that all else equal, marrying across racial lines is a cost.

The predictions of the social exchange theory are clear. For whites, given they are believed to be on top of the social hierarchy, interracial marriage will always come at a social cost, though interracial marriage with whites is a benefit to other groups. In equilibrium, then, whites must be compensated for their higher social status by intermarrying with racial minorities who possess more redeeming qualities. In minority–white marriages, the minorities will have superior objective characteristics—like being more attractive or intelligent—than their white mates. Thus, the social exchange model refers to a trade between objective characteristics and social status.

Social exchange theory is successful at capturing some elements of the data. For example, if one assumes that the societal cost of intermarriage fell sharply during the 1960s, then one can explain the increase in miscegenation after that time. If one further assumes that the societal cost of marrying Asians differs (in specific ways) from intermarrying with blacks, the relative magnitudes of Asian and black intermarriage with whites can be obtained. Further, a more general model of social exchange in which societal costs of interracial marriage decrease as objective value increases picks up further subtleties in the data.

However, this theory fails to explain the characteristics of who marries whom in interracial unions, which is really the key prediction. If anything, the average education of blacks who chose to intermarry is less than the average education of those who intramarry (despite the fact that higher-educated blacks are the most likely to intermarry—they are outnumbered by blacks with less education). This is a direct contradiction of the theory.

---

46 Captain Kirk Kisses Lieutenant Uhura: Interracial Intimacies—The View from Hollywood
Randall L. Kennedy

RANDALL L. KENNEDY is a professor of law at Harvard Law School. His areas of research and interest include the intersection of racial conflict and legal institutions in American life. He is author of *Interracial Intimacies: Sex, Marriage, Identity and Adoption* (2003) and *Race, Crime, and the Law (1997)*.

> **Questions to Consider** How many television shows and movies can you name in which the love interests are interracial couples? Now list the number of those interracial couples that were a black man and a white woman. Is it still true, as law Professor Randall Kennedy suggests, that the only way Hollywood would pair a black man, even a superstar like Denzel Washington, with a white woman, would be for him to be "paralyzed from the waist down" as in the movie *The Bone Collector* (1999)?

IN 1960 THERE WERE ABOUT 51,000 BLACK-WHITE married couples in the United States; in 1970, 65,000; in 1980, 121,000; in 1991, 213,000; and in 1998, 330,000. In other words, between 1960 and 2000, black-white mixed marriages increased more than six-fold. But not only are mixed marriages becoming more numerous; they are also becoming more common among people who are younger and more fertile. Previously, participants in such marriages tended to be older than other brides and grooms. Frequently they were veterans of divorce, embarking on second or third marriages. In recent years, though, interracial couples have been marrying at younger ages than their pioneering predecessors, and have shown a greater inclination to raise children and pursue all of the other "normal" activities that married life offers.

Given the low historical baselines against which trends today are measured, it is easy to exaggerate the scope of black-white marital integration. It should therefore be stressed that mixed marriages remain remarkably rare, comprising a mere .6 percent of the total marriages in 1998, for instance, when 330,000 couples out of 55,305,000 overall had one black and one white partner. Moreover, blacks' racial isolation on the marriage market appears to eclipse that of other people of color. The percentages of Native Americans and Asian Americans marrying whites are much larger than the percentage of blacks doing the same.[1] Professor Nathan Glazer is correct, then, in stating that "blacks stand out uniquely among the array of ethnic and racial groups in the degree to which marriage remains within the group." Among the complex reasons for this social isolation are aggregate subjective evaluations of marriageability, beauty, personality, comfort, compatibility, and prestige that favor certain groups over others. At the dawn of the twenty-first century, a wide array of social pressures continue to make white-black marital crossings more difficult, more costly, and thus less frequent than other types of interethnic or interracial crossings.

Still, even taking into account the peculiar persistence of the black-white racial divide, the trajectory of this form of **miscegenation** is clear: through turbulent times and in the face of considerable opposition, the number of black-white marriages has been increasing consistently (albeit slowly) for at least forty years. Reinforcing this growth is the fact that interracial marriage has become compatible with lofty ambitions across a variety of fields—not only entertainment but government service, scholarship, the philanthropic sector, business, and the professions. The Thomas-Lamp marriage is indicative of this trend. So, too, are the unions of William Cohen (former senator from Maine and secretary of defense in the Clinton administration) and his black wife; Peter Norton (inventor of widely used computer software) and his black wife;[2] and Franklin Raines (former director of the Office of Management and Budget and chief executive officer of Fannie Mae) and his white wife. Furthermore, despite the substantial influence of the black-power

miscegenation The "mixing" of different racial groups—that is, marrying, cohabiting, having sexual relations and children with a partner from outside of one's racially or ethnically defined group.

backlash, some African Americans whose positions make them directly dependent upon black public opinion have managed to marry whites without losing their footing. A good example is Julian Bond, the chairman of the board of directors of the NAACP, whose wife is white.

There are other signs, too, that black-white interracial romance has become more broadly accepted and even, in certain contexts, quite fashionable. One such indicator is advertising. Advertisers seek to persuade people to buy goods and services by increasing awareness of them and associating them with imagined pleasures. In the past, advertisers targeting general audiences with the lure of romance have typically—indeed, overwhelmingly—used couples of the same race. But these days, at least occasionally, interracial couples are being deployed as enticements to shop at Nordstrom's, Club Monaco, or Walmart, or to purchase furniture from IKEA, jeans from Guess, sweaters from Tommy Hilfiger, cologne from Calvin Klein, shampoo from Procter & Gamble, or watches from Gucci.

Television programming also signals important changes in sexual attitudes. Prior to the 1960s, portrayals or even insinuations of black-white interracial romance were virtually nonexistent on TV. The November 22, 1968, episode of the popular science-fiction series *Star Trek* marked a breakthrough in showing a kiss shared by the legendary (white) Captain James T. Kirk and (black) Lieutenant Uhura. Remarkably, however, the characters were not portrayed as actively *wanting* to kiss each other; instead they were *forced* to do so by a villain who captured Kirk's vessel, the starship *Enterprise,* and usurped the will of its crew. Not until 1975 did network television portray a married black-white couple, Tom and Helen Willis, who occupied a prominent place on the popular sitcom *The Jeffersons.* The show, a spinoff of Norman Lear's *All in the Family,* was about an eponymous black family whose patriarch, the hardworking but obnoxious George Jefferson, was obsessed with upward mobility, or what the theme song referred to as "movin' on up." The Willises lived in the same expensive apartment building as the Jeffersons. Although George constantly taunted the couple, calling them zebras, the families ultimately merged when the Jeffersons' son married the Willises' daughter.[3] Since the 1970s, depictions of interracial intimacies have remained rare on commercial television, though they do surface occasionally. In 1989 the short-lived *Robert Guillaume Show* presented viewers with a romance between a divorced black marriage counselor and his white secretary. The following year, the upstart Fox television network reluctantly aired *True Colors,* a situation comedy centered on the marriage of a black dentist (with two teenage sons) and a white schoolteacher (with a live-in mother and a teenage daughter). According to the show's creator, executives at the three older networks (ABC, CBS, and NBC) expressly stated that they were afraid the interracial marriage would alienate potential advertisers and dissuade at least some local affiliates from broadcasting the program. Notwithstanding cold feet at the top, writers have in the last decade or so succeeded in convincing television executives to air more entertainment fare featuring, or at least noting the existence of, interracial intimacy. Indeed, several of the most popular and influential shows of the 1990s portrayed transracial romances. Sometimes the racial aspect of the relationship was highlighted, as in *L.A. Law's* dramatization of a black lawyer feeling that he must choose between his white lover and his job as an elected representative of a mainly black constituency. Sometimes it was ignored, as on *Ally McBeal,* where race matters seldom if ever arose in conversations between the white woman attorney and the black male physician with whom she was infatuated. On occasion, on-screen interracial relationships failed. The producers of *ER,* for example, terminated a romance between a black male doctor and a white colleague, not in deference to viewer opposition but because the black actor involved objected. He complained that whereas his character had always been obnoxious in his dealings with black women, he was now being shown as sympathetic in his treatment of the white woman. On other programs, interracial romance was permitted to blossom. In 1994, for example, on *In the Heat of the Night,* the white sheriff of a town in the Deep South married a black woman on-screen,[4] and in 1997, a network production of *Cinderella* paired a black actress in the title role with a Filipino Prince Charming, to great popular acclaim.[5]

In some venues, nonfictional portrayals of interracial intimacy have been sensationally negative, as on confessional talk shows that, for a while at least, uniformly depicted transracial relationships as troubled, weird,

or pathological.[6] In other contexts, however, television programs have acknowledged the gamut of personalities and emotions to be found among those who happen to be involved in interracial intimacies. In the fall of 1999, the Public Broadcasting System (PBS) aired *An American Love Story,* a ten-hour documentary film by Jennifer Fox that chronicled the lives of an interracial family: Bill Sims, a black man; Karen Wilson, a white woman; and their two daughters, Cecily and Chaney. Wilson and Sims first met in 1967, at a resort where he was playing piano in a rhythm-and-blues band and she was vacationing with her parents. He was the son of a cleaning woman and a steelworker who was also a Baptist minister; her father was a machinist, and her mother was a grocery clerk. When their courtship began, Bill was eighteen and Karen seventeen. Neither set of parents objected to the relationship, and both urged the couple to marry after Wilson got pregnant (though they in fact did not do so until the child was six years old).

Whites in Wilson's hometown of Prospect, Ohio, strongly condemned her romance with Sims. Her supposed friends ostracized the couple, and the local sheriff jailed Sims on several occasions for no other reason than to harass him. In 1972 they moved with their baby daughter to Columbus, but even in this larger, less isolated locale, they encountered overt hostility. They suspected bigots of killing their dog and setting their car afire in a successful campaign to frighten them away. They moved again, this time to Flushing, New York, where they hoped to find a more openminded community.

Over the years, the Wilson-Sims family subsisted largely on Karen's reliable earnings as a manager, supplemented by Bill's spotty wages as, among other things, a carpenter, mail carrier, and musician. At the price of some tedium, *An American Love Story* shows its subjects engaged in all the quotidian tasks of daily life—cooking, cleaning, resting, seeking comfort, venting frustration—that have little or nothing to do with racial differences. It also shows them facing various nonracial crises, including Karen's hysterectomy and Bill's alcoholism. Almost inevitably, though, racial difficulties surface to menace the couple and their children. Among the most poignant segments of the series are wrenching scenes from Cecily's years as an undergraduate at Colgate College, where tyrannical black classmates tell her, essentially, that if she wants to be their friend, she must refuse to join a predominantly white sorority and, more generally, defer to their black-separatist sensibilities. She declines their terms, and they retaliate; she is hurt. Throughout, the television audience is privy to the conflict.[7]

The creators of *An American Love Story* wanted to document an interracial marriage that spanned the final decades of the twentieth century. Its subjects, for their part, wanted to change perceptions through education; this ambition constituted the principal explanation offered by the Sims-Wilson clan for permitting their family life to be examined in such a public manner. Education was also the primary aim cited by the program's director, Jennifer Fox, a white woman who credited her own love affair with a black man with opening her eyes to important areas of American life to which she had previously been blind.[8]

On the big screen, too, recent years have seen an increase in both the number and the quality of depictions of interracial intimacy. There was a time, not so long ago, when the scarcity of such portrayals made keeping track of them easy; now, because of their increasing numbers and variety, that task is much more difficult. True, the fear of an adverse audience response can still cause cautious film producers to suppress interracial romance, not only through their choice of projects but even in their handling of plot points. In John Grisham's novel *The Pelican Brief* (1992), for instance, the protagonists become lovers, but in the screen version (1993), there is no romance; the relationship remains resolutely platonic. The reason for this alteration is obvious: the male lead is played by a black actor (Denzel Washington), and the female lead by a white actress (Julia Roberts). There are, moreover, scores of other examples of black actors apparently being singled out for Hollywood's cold shoulder treatment lest they mirror real-life interracial erotic excitement. Prominent among these desexualized roles are Will Smith's character in *Men in Black* (1997) and Wesley Snipes's in *Murder at 1600* (1997). This approach led one wag to remark, in reference to *The Bone Collector* (1999), that the only way Denzel Washington would ever be shown "getting the girl" was if he played a man paralyzed from the waist down. That being said, a number of major motion pictures released in the past decade have followed actors

and actresses of all complexions in their pursuit of sexual pleasures across color lines, and have done so with a boldness that probably would not have been tolerated in the environment that generated *Guess Who's Coming to Dinner?* Examples include the explicit erotic grapplings of Lawrence Fishburne and Ellen Barkin in *Bad Company* (1995), Wesley Snipes and Natassia Kinski in *One Night Stand* (1997), Reese Witherspoon and Bookeem Woodbine in *Freeway* (1996), Warren Beatty and Halle Berry in *Bulworth* (1998), Tom Cruise and Thandie Newton in *Mission: Impossible 2* (2000), Julia Stiles and Sean Patrick Thomas in *Save the Last Dance* (2000), and Halle Berry and Billy Bob Thornton in *Monster's Ball* (2001).[9] In increasing numbers of films, moreover, interracial intimacy has been emerging as simply one part of a larger story in which racial difference is of little or no significance. This is an important development because presuming the normalcy of interracial intimacy—treating it as "no big deal"—may be more subversive of traditional norms than stressing the racial heterodoxy of such relationships. Although examples of this presumption can be found in several films (e.g., *Pulp Fiction* [1994], *Cruel Intentions* [1999], and *Mystery Men* [1999]), the most significant was the blockbuster *The Bodyguard* (1992), which starred Kevin Costner and Whitney Houston.

• • •

Perhaps the most potent influence in creating new possibilities for interracial intimacy is that wielded by individuals engaged in (or born of) transracial dating, marriage, and parenting. This population, numbering in the hundreds of thousands, exhibits tremendous variety. One generalization that can properly be made about it, however, is that it is becoming increasingly vocal. There was a time, not so long ago, when the vast majority within this group sought invisibility; now, by contrast, many of its members seek recognition and are establishing or joining advocacy organizations devoted to publicizing their views and institutionalizing their presence. Announcing the formation of the Association of Multi-Ethnic Americans (AMEA) in November 1988, Carlos Fernandez declared:

> We who embody the melting pot . . . stand up, not merely as neutrals in interethnic conflicts, but as intolerant

participants against racism from whatever quarter it may come. . . . We are the faces of the future. Against the travails of regressive interethnic division and strife, we can be a solid core of unity bonding the peoples of all cultures together in the common course of human progress.

People involved in interracial intimacies used to voice quiet requests for simple protection against intimidation and violence. Now their demands are becoming more ambitious. One of these has to do with racial labeling. Many interracial couples object to standardized forms that compel them to designate their children either merely "black" or merely "white." Similarly, many who identify themselves as "mixed"—or "mulatto" or "half-and-half" or "multiracial"—bridle at classificatory regimes that impose singular racial identifications, as if everyone must be *only* white *or* black *or* Latino *or* Asian (etc., etc.). Prior to the census of 2000, the United States Census Bureau counted individuals according to that assumption. But after a good deal of prodding by AMEA and similar groups, the bureau decided to broaden the menu boxes available for indicating racial affiliation. Rather than being limited to only one box, respondents are now authorized to check whatever boxes they deem applicable, though the census bureau continues to decline to offer a separate "multiracial" box.[10] One complaint leveled against the traditional "check one box" regime is that it fosters confusion and inaccuracy—describing as "black," for example, people who are also partly white or partly Native American or partly Asian. Susan Graham, the (white) founder of Project RACE (Reclassify All Children Equally) notes that her "child has been white on the U.S. Census, black at school, and multiracial at home, all at the same time." Beyond the issue of statistical inaccuracy, the system has more personal ramifications, in that it compels mixed individuals to select for recognition only one aspect of their composite background, and thereby subordinate all the other aspects.

The census bureau's multiple-box-checking initiative addresses some but by no means all of the objections raised by critics.[11] Some contend that even the option of checking several boxes indicates, in effect, that multiracial individuals are only parts of other communities, rather than constituent members of a distinct multiracial community of their own. Some observers

protest, moreover, the continuation of *any* racial scheme of classification, however it may be supplemented or repackaged. Whatever one may think of the ideas propounded by these various dissidents, it is clear that they are flexing their political muscles as never before and affecting hearts and minds in fundamental ways. They are not content to accept inherited conventions but insist instead on adding their own preferences to America's cultural mix. Professor Maria P. P. Root has demanded a Bill of Rights for racially mixed people, which would include the rights to identify one's race differently in different situations, to change one's racial identity over a lifetime (and more than once), to have loyalties to and identifications with more than one racial group, and to be able freely to choose whom to befriend and love. The winner of the 1995 Miss USA beauty pageant objected to being pegged as "black." "If people are going to know me," Chelsi Smith explained, "it's important for them to know that I'm black and white and that it hasn't been a disadvantage." Tiger Woods likewise does not enjoy being referred to as the first "black" or "African American" golf superstar, believing that those labels obscure other aspects of his ancestry that are just as important to him. He has therefore coined the term "'Cablinasian'—[for] Caucasian, Black, Indian, Asian"—to describe himself.[12] The coinage has proved controversial.[13] Many people, mainly blacks, have accused him of wanting to flee an African American identity that whites will impose upon him regardless of his preferences. ("When the black truck comes around," one observer quipped, "they're gonna haul his ass on it.") Such reactions notwithstanding, the real point here is that Root, Smith, Woods, and tens of thousands more like them have felt sufficiently self-assured to speak up, and have received substantial support in doing so. Their conduct mirrors and strengthens a new force in America: the will of people engaged in or born of multiracial relationships, who have begun to insist upon public recognition of the full complexity of their lives.

Across the country, scores of interracial support groups have sprung up, among them MOSAIC (Multiethnics of Southern Arizona in Celebration); A Place for Us (North Little Rock, Arkansas); I-Pride (Interracial

Intercultural Pride, Berkeley, California); MASC (Multiracial Americans of Southern California, Los Angeles, California); F.C. (Families of Color) Communiqué (Fort Collins, Colorado); Interracial Family Alliance (Augusta, Georgia); Society for Interracial Families (Troy, Michigan); 4C (Cross Cultural Couples & Children, Plainsboro, New Jersey); the Interracial Club of Buffalo; the Interracial Family Circle of Washington, D.C.; and HONEY (Honor Our New Ethnic Youth, Eugene, Oregon). On college campuses, students can join organizations such as FUSION (Wellesley), Kaleidoscope (University of Virginia), Students of Mixed Heritage and Culture (SMHAC, Amherst), Half 'n' Half (Bryn Mawr), and Mixed Plate (Grinnell). These groups offer forums in which people can meet others in their situation, disseminate relevant information, debate, and organize. Although most of these organizations lack deep roots, many display a vigor and resourcefulness that suggest they will survive into the foreseeable future. They stem from and represent a community in the making. It is a community united by a common demand that the larger society respect and be attentive to people who either by descent or by choice fall outside the conventional racial groupings—people who are partners in interracial couples, parents of children whose race is different from their own, and children whose race differs from their parents'. The members of this community want whites to cease viewing them as products or agents of an alarming mongrelization. They want blacks to stop regarding them as inauthentic and unstable in-betweeners. They want security amid the established communities from which they have migrated. They want to emerge from what the writer Lise Funderberg has aptly called the "racial netherworld." They want to enjoy interaction with others without regret or fear, defensiveness or embarrassment. They want respect.

Seeing the Big Picture   Love May Be Blind, but It's Not Color-Blind

Look at Section X in the Appendix. All things being equal, one would think that if people choose to marry across the color line these unions would be randomly distributed—that is, we would observe similar marriage rates across racial categories. But we don't. What do these data suggest about intergroup relations?

47   Discovering Racial Borders
Heather M. Dalmage

HEATHER M. DALMAGE is an associate professor of sociology at the School of Policy Studies at Roosevelt University, Chicago. She is the author of *Tripping on the Color Line: Black–White Multiracial Families in a Racially Divided World* (2000) and a national expert on interracial relationships. She is editor of *The Multiracial Movement: The Politics of Color* (2003).

Questions to Consider   Heather M. Dalmage explains how racial borders are "policed" to discourage individuals from falling in love across the color line. How and in what ways (if any) were racial borders enforced in your own life so that dating across the color line was not very likely to happen? How would your family react if your new romantic partner was from a racial category different from your own? Given that such unions are often stigmatized, what strategies do interracial couples employ, according to Dalmage, to dismiss such views and normalize their own relationship?

Border Patrolling

The belief that people ought to stick with their own is the driving force behind efforts to force individuals to follow prescribed racial rules. Border patrollers often think (without much critical analysis) that they can easily differentiate between insiders and outsiders. Once the patroller has determined a person's appropriate category, he or she will attempt to coerce that person into following the category's racial scripts. In *Race, Nation, Class: Ambiguous Identities*, Etienne Balibar and Immanuel Wallerstein observe that "people shoot each other every day over the question of labels. And yet, the very people who do so tend to deny that the issue is complex or puzzling or indeed anything but self-evident."[1] Border patrollers tend to take race and racial categories for granted. Whether grounding themselves in essentialist thinking or hoping to strengthen socially constructed racial categories, they believe they have the right and the need to patrol. Some people, especially whites, do not recognize the centrality and problems of the color line, as evinced in color-blind claims that "there is only one race: the human race" or "race doesn't really matter any more." Such thinking dismisses the terror and power of race in society. These individuals may patrol without being aware of doing so. In contrast, blacks generally see patrolling the border as both problematic and necessary.

While border patrolling from either side may be scary, hurtful, or annoying, we must recognize that blacks and whites are situated differently. The color line was imposed by whites, who now have institutional means for maintaining their power; in contrast, blacks must consciously and actively struggle for liberation. Repeatedly, people in multiracial families have told me, "The one thing that David Duke and Louis Farrakhan agree on is that we should not exist." What is not analyzed are the different historical legacies that bring both men to the same conclusion. The only form of borderism in which blacks engage is border patrolling, although they can act on prejudicial feelings and discriminate. After centuries of systemic control, only whites can be racist. As Joe Feagin and Hernán Vera explain, "black racism would require not only a widely accepted racist ideology directed at whites, but also the power to systematically exclude whites from opportunities and rewards in major economic, cultural, and political institutions."[2] White and black border patrollers may both dislike interracial couples and multiracial families, but their dislike comes from different historical and social perspectives. Moreover, border patrolling tends to take place intraracially: whites patrol whites, and blacks patrol black and multiracial people.

White Border Patrolling

Despite the institutional mechanisms in place to safeguard whiteness, many whites feel both the right and the obligation to act out against interracial couples. If a white person wants to maintain a sense of racial superiority, then he or she must attempt to locate motives and explain the actions of the white partner in the interracial couple. A white person who crosses the color line threatens the assumption that racial superiority is essential to whites. The interracially involved white person is thus often recategorized as inherently flawed—as "polluted."[3] In this way, racist and **essentialist** thinking remains unchallenged.

Frequently white families disown a relative who marries a person of color, but several people have told me that their families accepted them again once their children were born. The need to disown demonstrates the desire to maintain the facade of a pure white family.[4] By the time children are born, however, extended family members have had time to shift their racial thinking. Some grant acceptance by making an exception to the "rule," others by claiming to be color-blind. Neither form of racial thinking, however, challenges the color line or white supremacy. In fact, both can be painful for the multiracial family members, who may face unending racist compliments such as "I'll always think of you as white."

The myth of purity is maintained by controlling white women's wombs. Thus, white women are patrolled more harshly than white men are. The regulations women face have not always been overtly displayed but have developed within the culture's conception of the *family ethic,* an ideal extant since the arrival of the early settlers that has influenced perceptions of proper work and home roles for white, middle-class family members.[5] The proper family should have a male breadwinner and patriarch and a female who makes her husband and obedient children her life's central work. According to Mimi Abramowitz, the family ethic "has made [women] the guardians of family and community morality, expected them to remain pious and chaste and to tame male sexuality, and defined them as weak and in need of male protection and control."[6] Ultimately, the family ethic has kept white women under the control of white men. In *Whiteness Visible: The Meaning of Whiteness in American Literature and Culture,* Valerie Babb notes that images depicting white women as helpless and in need of white men's protection grew against a backdrop of a developing patriarchy. White women faced particularly harsh regulations because the "loss of sexual purity through intercourse with other races endangers visible race difference, a key driving force behind an ideology of whiteness that gives political, economic, and social advantage to those with 'appropriate' race lineage."[7] The myth of white racial purity required white women to give birth to the offspring of white men—and only white men. Unfortunately, many white women have played active roles in maintaining this myth of purity. For instance, in 1897 one wrote: "If it takes lynching to protect women's dearest possession from drunken, ravening beasts, then I say lynch a thousand a week if it becomes necessary."[8] Today many white women who give birth to children of color give them up for adoption, fearing that as mothers of children of color they will become pariahs in their families and society at large.[9] Such complicity has worked to strengthen the color line and white-supremacist abuses.

It has been argued that white women should be protected because they are the gatekeepers of racial purity.[10] Any white woman who would trade in her white privilege and connections to white male power must be dismissed as unnaturally bad and bizarre. Julie, a white mother recently divorced from her black husband, has contended with white border patrolling and its underlying images. One incident (although not the only one) occurred while she was on a date with a white physician:

> He asked to see a picture of my daughter. I handed it to him. He was very clever; he asked, "Is her dad from the U.S.?"
>
> I think he was praying her dad was Spanish, and he could deal with that, anything but black. I could tell it bothered him, so I said, "Listen, I can see by the look on your face that there is obviously a problem here, so why don't we just talk about it right now."
>
> He said, "You want to know the truth? Well, I have a real problem with the fact that you slept with a black man." Then he went on with the whole, "You're such a pretty and intelligent woman; why would you marry a black man?"

Her date was drawing on the interlocking imagery of race and sex and what it means to be a good white

essentialism The false idea that individuals or groups have an immutable fundamental nature that exists outside of society. An essentialist statement would be that all women are nurturing.

woman. In his attempt to explain away Julie's behavior, he searched for motives, implying that only unattractive, unintelligent white women sleep with and marry black men. Further, the fact that she slept with a black man removed her eligibility as a white woman. She is assumed to be fundamentally and essentially changed. Perhaps he feared that his white purity would be contaminated with blackness through this bad white woman. Perhaps he felt threatened because he could not immediately detect her racial flaw. He may have begun to discover the mutability of race, which could undermine his own sense of racial superiority. While all people of color face some form of racist imagery in a white racist society, Julie notes the centrality and power given to racist images directed specifically against black people and interracially involved whites and blacks: "I think he was praying her dad was Spanish, and he could deal with that, anything but black."

Black men are seen "as a constant threat" to patriarchal whiteness.[11] Abby Ferber writes: "A photograph of a white woman with an Asian American man, for example, does not have the same symbolic power. The image of interracial sexuality between a white woman and a black man is pregnant with meaning in the American imagery. Powerful enough to serve as a symbol of all interracial sexuality."[12] White women who enter into interracial relationships with black men are often treated as aberrant, misguided white trash who are in this relationship solely for sex or rebellion. Barbara gained forty pounds because she "got tired of being mistaken for a prostitute." She explains, "It's assumed that the only reason you're involved in the relationship is because you're sexually depraved. . . that you've got to be the dregs of society to get involved or you want to hurt somebody." Women may be explained away as money or status seekers.[13] Often when we are out, people will ask Philip what he does for work. After learning he's an attorney, they don't bother to ask me what I do. This could be a gender issue; in a **patriarchal** world men are seen as the subjects, women the objects. But I often wonder how much it has do with assumptions about uncovering the motive behind our relationship—that I have traded my white status for his occupational and class status.[14]

The strength of racist images is manifested in the comments directed at women who are assumed to be good,

upstanding white women. June, a businesswoman who is raising two biracial sons in suburban New Jersey, commented, "I think America still hates [white] women who sleep with black men. And when they see you with these children, they want to believe you adopted them, which is usually the first question people will ask: 'Did you adopt them?' I always just say, 'No, I slept with a black man.'"

June's comments highlight a few issues. First, she does not specify who constitutes "America." Whites may hate these women because they threaten the color line that maintains white privilege and power. At the same time, blacks may hate them because they threaten the unity of African Americans. Second, several white women talked to me about the frequency of the adoption question—one more attempt to explain their behavior. If women who appear to be good turn out to be polluted, white border patrollers become nervous. Their inability to tell "us" from "them" calls into question their own racial identity. The more the border patroller clings to an identity of racial superiority, the more he or she looks for ways to explain away these aberrant white women. Third, like June, many interracially married white women resist allowing whites to recategorize them in an attempt to regain or maintain a sense of superiority. "No, I used the good-old fashioned method" is a common retort to such questioners.

Not all white women resist border patrollers. Many succumb to the hostility and end their relationships with black men. Several white women told me they had temporarily ended their interracial relationship, each citing border patrolling as the reason. For instance, Barbara, the woman who gained forty pounds to avoid being seen as a prostitute, said:

> When I met my husband, he was the sweetest, kindest—he was a wonderful human being, everything I was looking for except for the color and at one point I was really apprehensive about it. The race thing really bothered me 'cause I didn't like being stared at and I didn't like people hating me. I didn't like how black women viewed me, and to white men I was a possession. It's like, "you crossed the line." You know the feeling, like you have to be the lowest of the low to be with an African American. "Who are you trying to hurt?" It was just really sick. So I went away for a while.

Although she did eventually marry this "wonderful human being," she needed time away to think about race on a

---

patriarchal Refers to a society organized so that men dominate women.

more sophisticated level—time to question her internalization of racist images and the color line.

The stereotype of black male sexuality converges with the myth of the chaste and virtuous good white woman, making white female–black male relationships the ones most patrolled by whites.[15] White men contend with a different type of border patrolling in a society that privileges both whiteness and maleness. Historically, white men who interracially marry were reported to come from lower economic classes and were at times designated as crazy.[16] Today the more common image that white interracially married men face is of being in the relationship solely for sex. These men may be seen as committing an individual transgression but are not held responsible for protecting whiteness. In her study of white supremacist publications, Abby Ferber found that "while relationships between white women and black men are condemned, and described as repulsive, relationships between white men and black women were common and remain beyond condemnation."[17] The lack of imagery about white male–black female relations reflects a history of silence among whites concerning their complicity in the rape of black women. Moreover, in a society in which whiteness (and maleness) represents power, privilege, and unearned advantage, many white men view their privilege in the world as normal. They risk "outing" these taken-for-granted privileges when they talk about race.[18]

The white men with whom I spoke were split about the importance of—even the existence of—border patrolling. Unlike black men, black women, and white women, they did not consistently talk about the effects of racialized images. When I asked, "As an interracially married white man, how do you think others view you?" responses were split: half the men spoke of border patrollers; the other half denied the importance of race in their lives and society. The first few times I heard white men deny or disregard the importance of racism and border patrolling, I was surprised. It took me some time and several more interviews to make sense of this.

Joe, the first interracially married white man I interviewed, lived in a predominantly white, upper-class community about an hour from New York City. With his infant daughter on his lap and a tape recorder on the table, he began to unfold the details of his life. I asked how he thinks others view him. He responded, "I can't worry about what other people think. For a long time my wife worried, but once she got over that, we had a big wedding. . . . It took a lot to convince her that's how we should think about it, and I think she's more comfortable with that." He said that they do not have problems as an interracial couple, that everything is smooth. We were chatting after the interview when his wife walked into the room. She began to cite several problems they had faced because of their interracial relationship. When she referred to each incident, he nodded in agreement.

Several months later I interviewed Raymond, a white interracially married man living on Chicago's north side. Drinking coffee in a local café, he discussed the meaning of race in his life. When I asked him about how others view him, he replied staunchly, "I don't know, and I don't care. I never thought about it. I don't think about it. What do they think when they see my wife and me together? Pardon my language, but I don't give a shit what they think; I just don't give a shit. I go for months, and that never occupies my mind."

These men may be proving masculinity through a show of strength, rugged individualism, and disinterest and thus verbally disregard border patrolling and racial images. Each, however, repeatedly claimed that race does not matter. Instead, they believed the focus "should be on ethnic backgrounds" or on the fact that "we are all Americans." Men who did not want to recognize racial images tended not to recognize the privilege associated with whiteness, drawing instead on notions of meritocracy. Whether or not they recognized differences, they did not recognize power. Nevertheless, they used their power as white males to create a racial discussion with which they felt comfortable. For instance, Joe's comfort came from not having to hear any racially derogatory comments: "If somebody would make a derogatory comment, I would just say, 'My wife is black.' Usually I wouldn't even have to say, 'I don't want to hear comments like that'—they would just stop." Whiteness is about privilege and power. It is a privilege to be able to set the parameters of racial discussions and expect that others will comply. Moreover, the power of these professional white men overrides the power that white border patrollers may have to influence them.

In addition to proving masculinity, these men may be attempting to downplay the prevalent stereotype that interracial couples are together for sexual reasons only. For instance, Raymond repeatedly stated that his relationship was not about "jungle fever," a phrase that filmmaker Spike Lee popularized to suggest that interracial couples are attracted only because of sexual curiosity. At the end of our interview I asked Raymond if there was anything else he wanted to say. He answered, "Let people know that this is not about jungle fever. Race does not matter. I love my wife." His repeated references to jungle fever reflected his awareness of border patrolling despite his claim of color blindness. Rather than critically thinking about race and the origins of such stereotypes, he defensively dismisses the significance of race.

Some white men did recognize and address the importance of racial images, border patrollers, and the relationship between race and power. The common thread for these men was that they had friendships and networks with black males before meeting their spouse. Through these male friends they began to recognize the privileges that remain invisible to so many other white men. The importance of friendships with black males cannot be understated. White men sit in a position of power because of both their race and sex. When sex differences are removed as a factor in their relationships, they can understand more clearly the ways in which race mediates power relations. This is not as obvious to white men who are introduced to blackness (and thus whiteness) through intimate relations with a woman.

Clancy, a fifty-year-old white man who grew up outside Chicago, had black roommates and friends in college. By the time he met his wife he understood from his buddies the effects of racism in society. He spoke in detail about the border patrolling he faced from the white teachers at the Chicago elementary school where he taught after getting married: "My wife and I walked into a meeting with the white teachers and the people from the neighborhood, and it sent those people into conniptions. I won't forget that. It was my first year teaching there, and from then on it was like, 'God have mercy on my soul,' I was a dead person in that school and that stayed with me for seventeen years—the whole time I was there." In this case, Clancy's teaching position was continually threatened by white border patrollers.

Peter, a white minister living on Chicago's South Side, had graduated from a black seminary in the southern United States. As the only white in many situations, he was immersed in black culture. The privileges and power bestowed on whites in a system of whiteness and the richness of black culture became visible to him. Like Clancy, he recognized and addressed the border patrolling he encountered from whites. In the following case, Peter had just been named the pastor of a white church in a white working-class neighborhood in Cleveland: "I had gotten moved to a white church. That turned out to be two years from hell. The church did not want me to be appointed there. They actually had a special meeting after they got wind of who was coming; 95 percent of the church did not want me there because I was interracially married. The first church meeting I was at, the chair asked for further motions. One person said, 'I make a motion that the reverend resign from this church.'" Peter laughed about the absurdity of the situation and then continued: "The first sermon, attendance was over one hundred; everyone came out to see the show. From then on, attendance never got above sixty, so basically about forty people boycotted the whole time I was there. I had people who still attended but resigned all their offices." In addition, church members began a letter-writing campaign to the bishop accusing Peter of various wrongdoings—for example, claiming he had taken all the Bibles out of the church. Peter and his family eventually moved to a black church in Chicago. The Ohio church members who had resigned their offices returned to them after he left.

Privileges granted to people with white skin have been institutionalized and made largely invisible to the beneficiaries. With overwhelming power in society, why do individual whites insist on border patrolling? As economic insecurity heightens and demographics show that whites are losing numerical majority status, the desire to scapegoat people of color, especially the poor, also heightens. As whites lose their economic footing, they claim white skin as a liability. Far from recognizing whiteness as privilege, they become conscious of whiteness only when defining themselves as innocent victims of "unjust" laws, including affirmative action.[19] In their insecurity they cling to images that promote feelings of superiority. This, of course, requires a racial hierarchy and a firm essentialist color line. Border patrolling helps to maintain the myth of purity and thus a color line created to ensure that whites maintain privileges and power.

Black Border Patrolling

Some blacks in interracial relationships discover, for the first time, a lack of acceptance from black communities. Others experienced border patrolling before their marriage, perhaps because of hobbies and interests, class, politics, educational goals, skin tone, vernacular, or friendship networks. Patrolling takes on new proportions, however, when they go the "other way" and marry a white person. While all relationships with individuals not seen as black are looked down on, relationships with whites represent the gravest transgression. Interracially married black women and men often believe they are viewed as having lost their identity and culture—that they risk being seen as "no longer really black." Before their interracial marriage, most called black communities their home, the place from which they gained a sense of humanity, where they gained cultural and personal affirmation. During their interracial relationship many discovered black border patrolling. Cathy Cohen suggests that "those failing to meet indigenous standards of blackness find their life chances threatened not only by dominant institutions or groups, but also by their lack of access to indigenous resources and support."[20] Interracially involved blacks needed to carefully weigh their decision to cross the color line.

George, a black man, lives with his wife, Dorothy, a white woman, and their two young children in Montclair, New Jersey, a racially mixed suburb of New York City. I drove along the town's big, clean, tree-lined streets one Sunday morning to meet with George in his home. During our interview he explained that he had dated a white girl in high school and was aware of how blacks and whites respond to such a relationship. Nonetheless, a recent event at his Manhattan workplace troubled him. Bill, a black male coworker, told him:

> "I couldn't marry a white woman. How about you?"
>
> I said, "I am married to a white woman."
>
> "You joking me, George! Big strong handsome brother like you!"
>
> I said, "Yo, man, I don't know what all that handsome stuff you comin' with."
>
> He said, "All jokes aside, George, you telling me you went the other way?"
>
> I said, "There's nothing wrong with that."
>
> And he's like "Oh, George, I don't believe it."

> He was just solemn after that and looked down, so I said, "Bill, does that mean we're not going to be friends anymore?"
>
> He goes, "No, man, you still my man."
>
> He gave me the ole handshake; I said, "Bill, no, man, you frontin' now."
>
> He said, "I'm just surprised, you know. You never told me about your wife."

The implication here is that a "strong brother" would not sell out his community like this; only weak men would do that. Before this confrontation George had been an integral part of many conversations at work about race, racism, and black culture. After it he found "they'll be talking about something totally in the black culture. I come into the room and be listening; and when I would put my opinion in, the conversation would end—just like that. The room goes empty. . . . because I'm married to a white woman, blacks figure my culture is gone; it's shot." He is accused of having lost connectedness to African Americans, being weak, and marrying a white woman to escape his blackness.

Blacks in interracial relationships defend themselves against accusations of weakness, neurosis, and betrayal. In *Black Skin, White Masks,* Frantz Fanon writes about black men in interracial relationships: "I marry white culture, white beauty, white whiteness. When my restless hands caress those white breasts, they grasp white civilization and dignity and make them mine."[21] In his psychoanalytic interpretation of the effects of **colonization** and racism, Fanon suggests that many black men who intermarry suffer from neurosis created in a world in which black men are not valued and thus do not value themselves. They think that a relationship with a white woman will validate them—that is, whiten them. Of black women, Fanon writes, "It is because the Negress feels inferior that she aspires to win admittance into the white world."[22] Without acknowledging the pain caused by border patrolling and the desire many interracially married blacks have to maintain strong ties with other blacks, Fanon labels black men and black women in interracial relationships as pathological and neurotic.

---

colonization When one country controls another in order to seize resources, such as land, gold, timber, or ivory, or to enslave its population.

More recently, Paul Rosenblatt and his colleagues conducted a study of forty-two multiracial couples in the Minneapolis–St. Paul area. They conclude that many African Americans feel that "it is inappropriate to choose as a partner somebody from the group that has been oppressing African Americans."[23] Many black border patrollers have an overriding concern about loyalty to the race. If an individual is not being loyal, then he or she is explained away as weak, acting in ways that are complicit with the oppression of other black Americans. In "Essentialism and the Complexities of Racial Identity," Michael Eric Dyson suggests, "Loyalty to race has been historically construed as primary and unquestioning allegiance to the racial quest for freedom and the refusal to betray that quest to personal benefit or the diverting pursuit of lesser goals. Those who detour from the prescribed path are labeled 'sellouts,' 'weak,' 'traitors,' or 'Uncle Toms.'"[24] Thus, black men and women face differing social realities and forms of patrolling.

An overwhelming percentage of black-white couples involve a black male and a white female at a time when there are "more single women in the black community than single men."[25] Many black men are hindered by a racist educational system and job market that make them less desirable for marriage. Many others are scooped into the prison industrial complex. High-profile athletes and entertainers who marry white women confirm for many that black men who are educated and earn a good living sell out, attempting to buy white status through their interracial relationship.[26] Beyond issues of money and status, many black women see black male–white female interracial relationships "as a rejection of black women's beauty, [and] as a failure to acknowledge and reward the support that black women give black men."[27] In *Rooted against the Wind*, Gloria Wade-Gayles writes about the pain and feeling of rejection that black women experience when they see black men with white women:

> We see them, and we feel abandoned. We feel abandoned because we have been abandoned in so many ways, by so many people, and for so many centuries. We are the group of women furthest removed from the concept of beauty and femininity which invades almost every spot of the planet, and as a result, we are taught not to like ourselves, or, as my student said, not to believe that we can ever do enough or be enough to be loved or desired.[28]

Black women and men may both feel a sense of rejection when they see an interracial couple, but for each that sense of rejection comes from a different place. In a society in which women's worth is judged largely by beauty—more specifically, **Eurocentric** standards of beauty—black women are presumed to be the farthest removed from such a standard. Men's worth is judged largely by their educational and occupational status, two primary areas in which black men are undermined in a racist system. Black men with few educational and job opportunities lack status in the marriage market. Thus, when black men see a black woman with a white man, they may be reminded of the numerous ways in which the **white-supremacist** system has denied them opportunities. The privilege and power granted to whites, particularly to white males, is paraded in front of them; and they see the black women in these relationships as complicit with the oppressor.

I met Parsia, a successful businesswoman and a black interracially married mother living in Connecticut, through a family friend. Having grown up in a close-knit African American community, she was uncertain if she wanted to marry interracially and risk losing the support of that community. Now happily married and the mother of a beautiful little girl, she is still very aware of border patrolling. For this reason she prefers not to bring her husband to some areas in Harlem and to black-centered events:

> African Americans do view blacks in interracial relationships as turncoats. There is a pervasive belief in the African American community that it is much more difficult to maintain your identity in an interracial relationship. I believe that once blacks see me as part of an interracial couple, it changes their perception of me right away. They disrespect me as another black person, and then they just disregard my belonging to the community, and suddenly I become the outsider—an outsider because I am with him.

Eurocentric The view that European culture is superior to all other cultures in the world; implies that European culture should be the yardstick by which all other cultures are measured.
white supremacist A person who believes in the supremacy of the white race.

Her fears are not unfounded. One day she and her husband were walking in Philadelphia when a young black man accosted them:

> If I had been alone and this young brother was hassling me in any way, I would have stopped, turned around, and said, "Look, why are you bothering me? What's the deal here?" But I didn't feel at all that I could have this conversation with this young man. He was so hostile, and the source of his hostility was totally his perception of black-white relationships, and there was nothing I could say to change that perception.

This young border patroller may be responding to a belief that Parsia is a race traitor. She is no longer an insider worthy of respect but an outsider who signifies neurosis in the form of self-hate and community betrayal—perhaps the highest form of betrayal. The prospect of rejection by other African Americans is enough for many blacks to deny, hide, or avoid interracial relationships. Border patrolling from other blacks, racism from whites, and the prospect of struggling alone in a racist society seem too high a price; so many who enter interracial relationships end them in a short time.

Today there are no longer legal sanctions against interracial marriage, but de facto sanctions remain. At times, family and friends exert pressure to end the interracial relationship; at other times, pressure may come from the border patrolling of strangers. Even if the relationship is clandestine, thoughts of how friends, family members, coworkers, employers, and the general public might respond can deter people from moving forward in a relationship. In each of the following cases the couples did get back together eventually, but all the black women took some time away from the relationship to make this choice.

Lisa met her white husband when she was a college student at a historically black college in the South.

> [I was] the only female in the jazz orchestra, [so] there were all these [black] guys saying, "Why are you with this white guy?" And one band member would make racial comments about "Don't marry whitey, don't trust whitey, don't do this for whitey." This guy in the band tried to talk me out of marrying Peter. I had some apprehension, so I broke up with him and told him I did not want to develop a relationship.

Parsia explains why she temporarily ended her relationship before finally deciding to marry her white husband, Joe:

> When I met Joe, I was really resistant to dating across racial lines. No way would I do that. It took me a very long time to get over that and deal with those feelings, biases, and expectations. I expected friends would feel very uncomfortable socializing with us. I still do believe that there is a certain language that blacks have when we are apart from other races, when we are alone socially. That's a very important part of my life, and I expected that I might lose that, and that was a very fearful thing for me. The more I felt him getting closer, the more I started seeing the possibility of longevity in the relationship, the more afraid I got. I was terrified that I would be in an interracial relationship for the rest of my life, so I pulled back in a big way and we broke up. There was definitely a shame and a guilt I had to get over because I felt that by dating interracially I was betraying black men.

Her fear reflects her reliance on other African Americans for mutual support in a white-supremacist system. Moreover, her observation that "there is a certain language that blacks have when we are apart from other races" indicates a shared cultural identity that creates and demands the enforcement of borders.

In some cases parents and family reinforce reservations about crossing over. Quisha, like Parsia, broke up with her white boyfriend, Raymond, because she needed time to think about what life would be like in an interracial relationship. "I was really excited about him and told my mom, and she just had a heart attack because he was white. I totally did not expect this from her. She would call everyday and was just hammering it into me to just forget this—and so I really badly and abruptly broke it off with Raymond. He was a real gentleman; he kept calling to find out what happened, and I totally blew him off." She explained her underlying fears as she discussed how she handles people staring at her: "I can feel my grandmother and my mother and my aunts disapproving in those stares, so that's intimidating." Lisa, Parsia, and Quisha all married the men they had left, but they needed time to think about risks, their own understandings of race and community, and what it means to be a black woman in the United States.

They are three of the many black women in inter-racial relationships who challenge the idea that white men are responsible for the low number of black female–white male interracial marriages. Theorists attempting to explain motives behind interracial marriages have often pointed to the low number of these marriages as evidence that white men are choosing not to marry black women.[29] These theorists suggest that white men are least likely to intermarry with black women because they would gain nothing in these marriages: no money, no status. My research, however, demonstrates the power of black women. The stories they share directly challenge long-held motive myths that imply that black women would marry white men if only white men would choose them. On the contrary, in each of the relationships just discussed, the black woman instigated a breakup. Perhaps their understanding of what it means to be strong, dedicated, and connected to black communities is responsible for the lower numbers of black female–white male marriages.

Border patrolling plays a central role in life decisions and the reproduction of the color line. As decisions are made to enter and remain in an interracial relationship, the color line is challenged and racial identities shift. Many blacks spoke of the growth they experienced because of their interracial relationship and border patrolling. Parsia explains, "I used to be real concerned about how I would be perceived and that as an interracially married female I would be taken less seriously in terms of my dedication to African American causes. I'm not nearly as concerned anymore. I would hold my record up to most of those in single-race relationships, and I would say, 'Okay, let's go toe to toe, and you tell me who's making the biggest difference,' and so I don't worry about it anymore." Identities, once grounded in the presumed acceptance of other black Americans, have become more reflective. Acceptance can no longer be assumed. Definitions of what it means to be black are reworked. Likewise, because of border patrolling, many whites in interracial relationships began to acknowledge that race matters. Whiteness becomes visible in their claims to racial identity.

Conclusion

Unlike transracially adopted and multiracial people who are raised across the color line, people in interracial relationships discover borderism when they decide to cross the line. This unique form of discrimination, grounded in a racist and segregated society, is always at work even when multiracial family members are not present. Yet by examining the experiences of multiracial family members, we can see the myriad ways in which the color line is both reproduced and resisted. Because interracially married people are often raised in single-race worlds, they have internalized borderism. Thus, part of the decision to become involved interracially includes the need to overcome internalized borderist thoughts. Most of them begin questioning color-blind and essentialist perspectives and learn to understand race as more fluid and complex. Skin color and physical features become just one set of criteria used to think about community and belonging. Many of the people I interviewed referred to this growth process (although not all interracially married people accept the invitation to rethink race).

In a society that often rejects people who cross the color line, individuals involved in such relationships have much to consider before making a permanent commitment. Given the significance of race in our society, a basic choice that all couples contend with is whether or not to stay together in the face of borderism. A few individuals claimed that there was no decision; they fell in love, and that was it. For most others, however, a life across the color line and facing borderism did not look all that inviting and in fact was enough to cause some to terminate their relationships.[30] While the number of people involved in interracial relationships is not known, we do know that in 1995 the census bureau estimated that there were only 246,000 black-white interracial marriages in the United States.[31] This is quite a small percentage considering that in the same year there were more than 50 million total marriages.[32] Borderism and its various components are strong and painful enough to keep black-white interracial marriages the least common marriage pattern for both blacks and whites.

48 Redrawing the Color Line? The Problems and Possibilities of Multiracial Families and Group Making

Kimberly McClain DaCosta

KIMBERLY MCCLAIN DACOSTA is interested in the intersection of cultural ideas about race and the family and is currently completing a book on efforts to create a multiracial collective identity in the United States, based on interviews and fieldwork with members of organizations for interracial families and people of mixed descent. She is currently associate dean of students and an associate professor at the Gallatin School of Individualized Study at New York University.

It is my belief that the next generation's principal task will be the hard and painful one of destroying color-caste in the United States.
—W. LLOYD WARNER [1]

AFTER TIGER WOODS WON THE 1997 MASTERS Tournament, he quickly became the poster boy of multiracialism—the well-adjusted, hugely successful, mixed race child with two devoted, loving, and *married* parents. Woods's rising public profile mirrored and symbolized the increasingly public profile of mixed descent persons. By the 1990s, multiracial families and multiracial identity were given more attention in the media, portrayed in such a positive way that one could be excused if one forgot the powerful stigma previously heaped upon intermarried couples and their families. Woods's success and embrace by the American public lent credibility to assertions that multiraciality was "old news"—that this had been going on for centuries (by which people usually meant interracial sex, not family), and that Americans were no longer shocked by this anymore.

Yet the emergence of multiracial families represents a significant historical shift, particularly when we consider the efforts made to prevent and conceal family ties across racial boundaries. The emergence of a multiracial identity as the expression of such family ties is a major shift

Questions to Consider   In 2000 the U.S. Census Bureau allowed individuals to check more than one racial category in the decennial census. Although there is a long history of "multiracials" in the United States, the effect of institutionalizing the mixed race or multiracial category has carved out a distinct social identity that challenges the way we typically think about racial categories. Within the context and acceptance of a multiracial movement one can now claim, as Professor DaCosta points out, a "Japanese and Mexican" or a "black and Irish" identity. How might these "new" identities redraw the color line? How might you respond when someone explains to you they are "black, white, and little bit Latina" or "Italian, Asian, and Puerto Rican"?

as well. Given that race as a mark of identity (rather than an uncomplicated descriptor of a biological reality) only developed in the twentieth century, and that the major period of growth in marriages across racial categories did not begin until the 1960s, this shift has taken place in a relatively short period of time. In the last decade, the idea of "multiracial community" has developed a social and cultural presence in the United States. Since the struggle over the census in the 1990s, references to "multiracials" regularly appear in the popular press, in academic literature, and in the marketplace, and the creation of multiracial organizations has continued unabated. Due to the efforts of people in those organizations, in conjunction with increasing rates of intermarriage, the multiracial family is no longer a contradiction in terms. Rather than "melting" into traditional racial groups, people of mixed race are elaborating a distinct sense of groupness as "multiracial." At the same time, they are asserting specific mixed ethnoracial identifications such as "Japanese and Mexican" or "black and Irish."

How then should we evaluate the impact and significance of multiracial group making? How is the color line being redrawn? The definition of race—a basic concept for describing social differences and inequalities in the United States—is in the process of changing. But in what ways and with what impact?

It is impossible to evaluate the impact of multiracial politics without attention to historical and social contexts. Without such contexts, it is tempting to conclude, as many have, that the collective efforts of multiracials are inherently progressive, inherently regressive, or even irrelevant. Appearing on the Oprah Winfrey show, for example, a black/white woman explains to the audience that as a multiracial person she can be a bridge to promote understanding between racial groups. In hearings over changes to racial classification, opponents to the possibility of the state enumerating mixed descent persons invoke the specter of **apartheid** South Africa, suggesting that new categories will create an escape hatch from blackness. At around the same time, some scholars claim that Asian outmarriage reflects Asian self-hatred and is an attempt to leave behind a stigmatized group. Still others state that the issue is "old news," not important enough to waste time commenting on it.

The social and historical contexts will allow us to make sense of what multiracials are doing today and that make such blanket assessments of multiracial politics less defensible. For the multiracial movement is about race and family—cultural categories, not static institutions—the meanings of which depend on context. This being the case, there can be no definitive answer to the question "are multiracial politics progressive or regressive?" Such evaluations will differ according to individual identities and political intentions. More useful than evaluations of the logic of racial categories or intermarriage in the abstract, then, are historically grounded and ethnographically

parsed accounts that show us what is different between now and the past and that ask what these categories mean to the people who feel invested in organizing around them.

Family Matters

According to Drake and Cayton (1993 [1945]), "Social segregation is maintained, in the final analysis, by **endogamy**—the rule that Negroes must marry Negroes, and whites must marry whites—and by its corollary that when an intermarriage does "accidentally" occur, the child must automatically be classed as a Negro no matter how white his skin color."[2]

In order to understand multiracial group making—its rise, shape, contents, and possible impact—one must not only denaturalize race but denaturalize the family, for the construction of the American family and race are joint historical and cultural processes that are mutually determinative. Racial classifications and antimiscegenation policies facilitated the creation of sharp divisions between social groups, defined them as racially different, and in so doing shaped the cultural common sense in which racial difference and the division of families along racial lines appears to be natural. Despite the possibility of legal marriage across racial boundaries, the normative family is still monoracial, and racial affiliation exacts a kind of loyalty that disqualifies intimate connections across racial categories. The realization that they are misfits in this context motivates multiracial actors to challenge the prevailing race/family nexus.

This struggle is apparent in the stories told by my respondents. While the interracial unions in my respondents' families were legally sanctioned, some struggled with the discretionary acts of disowning by their monoracial parents that mimicked the economic impacts that antimiscegenation laws once had. For most intermarried couples and families, however, what is at stake lies in the terrain of relatedness, emotional connection, the sense of cultural loss and gain, and the recognized reflection of the self in one's child—all structured by the racial dimension of the normative family.

apartheid The state-sanctioned and legally enforced policy of racial segregation instituted by South Africa.

endogamy The custom of marrying only within one's racial, ethnic, or social group.

The legalization of intermarriage, along with popular representations of multiracial families as heterosexual and nuclear leads to interpretations of multiracial families as an interesting "flavor" of the normative family. While it is clear that the heterosexual nuclear family is accorded material and social privilege in U.S. society, and that most of the contemporary discussion of multiracial families concerns heterosexual couplings, it misses the point to see multiracial families as an interesting variation on the theme of the heterosexual nuclear family. Rather, multiracial families—and multiracial politics broadly conceived—should be understood as part of an historical transformation in kinship, ideology, and social relations that have come about as the result of conflict, contradiction, and struggle.

Yet just how far we have come is a matter of debate. Although antimiscegenation laws are unconstitutional, intermarriage remains rare, especially so between blacks and whites. Moreover, a nontrivial percentage of people (of all racial groups) still disapprove of intermarriage. While the social climate for intermarried couples and families has certainly improved in the last several decades, Drake and Cayton's observations of Chicago in the 1930s describe all too well the state of intermarriage today, especially for blacks. They found that while blacks had made gains in governmental and economic areas, only "very moderate" gains had been made in "spatial and family relations." They concluded that while intermarriage is legally permitted, "it is generally discouraged." "[I]nformal social controls among both Negroes and whites," they wrote, "keep the number of such marriages small despite the fact there are no legal prohibitions against them" (1993 [1945], 127).

Of course, the same degree of separation is not found between Asians and whites and Latinos and whites. Intermarriage rates with whites for Asians, Latinos, and Native Americans are comparable to those of Southern and Eastern European immigrants in the early twentieth century who, through intermarriage with American-born whites, expanded the definition of who is white. With each generation in the United States and as income and education levels rise, Latinos and Asians are more likely to marry whites. This has prompted Roger Sanjek (1994) to argue that we may be seeing a "race-to-ethnicity" conversion for Hispanics and Asians, but not for African Americans.

Despite very low intermarriage rates for blacks, which testify to a firmer racialized boundary separating blacks from other groups, assertions by multiracials—even those of African descent—that they are not "just black" confounds that once defining feature of the color line to which DuBois ([1903] 1996) referred a century ago. Multiracial activists' demand for a recognition of mixedness challenges the categorical nature of the American racial classification system which, until 1997, recognized membership in only one category. As such, it is in direct opposition to the logic of the one-drop rule—the key mechanism that maintained that color line. Moreover, their efforts disrupt what the one-drop rule firmly established, namely the racial basis of kinship in which relatedness across racial boundaries is not socially recognized.

In everyday life, not just in official categories, the definition of blackness (and consequentially of white, Asian, Indian, and Latino identities) is shifting as well. So while in the 1930s Drake and Cayton (1993 [1945]) observed that the "children of mixed matings" are "always defined as Negroes," an understanding that prevailed through the 1980s, this is no longer as certain as it once was. Mariah Carey, for example, is not understood (or marketed) as a black singer, despite being of African descent, just as respondents with an ambiguous physical appearance and who lack cultural credentials are not necessarily accepted by blacks as (authentically) black, nor are they necessarily seen as sharply different by nonblacks despite knowledge of their African ancestry.

Racial Options?: Choice and the Limits of Choice

Twenty-six years ago, in the conclusion of her study on the Lumbee Indians of Robeson County, North Carolina, Karen Blu stated that "there is no 'right' to choose one's 'racial' ancestry, as race is currently conceived, but if race and ethnicity become progressively intertwined in a new way, it is possible that being Black will, in years to come, be more a matter of individual choice and less a matter of assignment by others" (1980, 210). Students of race and ethnicity in the United States often note that a key difference between the ways Americans experience ethnic and racial identities is the degree of choice one has to identify (or not) in ethnic or racial terms. This distinction is based on the historical experience of European immigrants. As the voluntary and involuntary factors that held together European immigrant ethnic communities (for example, residential segregation, discrimination, prejudice, religious affiliation) have declined, so too has the salience of ethnicity in the lives of their descendants (Alba 1990; Gans 1979; Lieberson 1985; Waters 1990). For these white ethnics, ethnicity is chosen rather than ascribed and expressions of ethnic identity are largely symbolic in content.

In her often-cited book *Ethnic Options: Choosing Identities in America,* Mary Waters (1990) found that not only did her white respondents choose which ethnicity to be, but also whether to be ethnic *at all.* Moreover, ethnic identity held few negative consequences for her respondents. It did not limit whom they could marry, determine where they could live, their employment prospects, or who their friends were. In contrast, the literature is replete with examples showing the continued prevalence and salience of ethnoracial ascription for nonwhites. The third and fourth generation Japanese and Chinese Americans Mia Tuan studied report that "others consistently expect them to identify ethnically (e.g., as Chinese or Japanese) or racially as Asian and be knowledgeable about Chinese or Japanese 'things' and express dissatisfaction when they are not" (Tuan 1998, 156). Attributions of racial difference are consequential for African Americans whether or not they choose to assert a racial identity, even for middle-class blacks who conform to white middle-class norms of behavior (Bell 1992; Cose 1992; Fordham 1997).[3] Racial options—the ability to choose whether to identify or be identified in racial terms—have been elusive.

Events of the last decade, however, suggest that we need to revisit the question of whether or not "racial options" are in the making. The institutionalized option to choose multiple racial affiliations in official race counts represents a racial option "on paper." The flexibility exhibited by respondents in how they describe, display, and perform their ethnoracial identities makes clear that indeed racial identification and categorization are somewhat malleable. But how much can this be said to approximate the kind of symbolic ethnicity found among white ethnics?

In all the ways ethnic identity did not matter for Waters's respondents, racial identity *did* matter for mine. Regardless of how much they chose to identify themselves as mixed, they faced resistance from institutions, peers, and even family members. When they wished not to have to identify themselves in racial terms, others *did* classify them in racial terms, and not necessarily in the ways they wished to be classified. Moreover, *how* they looked mattered very much in what types of identity expressions were likely to be authenticated by others. The dark-skinned person who identifies as white—or even mixed—must still work very hard to get others to treat him as such. In other words, not all heritages can equally be chosen or discarded at will. That their efforts have been met with suspicion and resistance is telling of lingering opposition to treating what are considered racial distinctions as just another form of ethnicity.

A key aspect of the optional character of white ethnicity is its costlessness. Unlike the ethnic identifications of white ethnics, for my respondents "being" mixed race or marrying someone of a different race had significant costs. Some intermarried respondents were "disowned" by their parents. For others, racial difference within the family was sometimes a source of tension that distorted emotional connections between family members. Moreover, for mixed descent respondents, asserting a mixed racial identification threatened their belonging within ethnic communities.

Yet while racial identification for multiracials is not entirely voluntary or costless, there is a way in which multiracial identification looks like the symbolic ethnicity of whites. Waters (1990) explains the apparent paradox that while ethnicity is a matter of choice, relatively costless and inconsequential in her respondents' lives, her respondents "cling tenaciously to their ethnic identities." They do so, she argues, because symbolic ethnicity actually reconciles two contradictory impulses in the American character—the desire for both individuality *and* conformity. "Having an ethnic identity is something that makes you both special and simultaneously part of a community. It is something that comes to you involuntarily through heredity, and at the same time it is a personal choice. And it allows you to express your individuality in a way that does not make you stand out as in any way different from all kinds of other people" (Waters, 1990, 150).

Similarly, the idea that racial identity can be freely chosen appeals to the high value Americans place on individualism. The novelty of a mixed racial identity makes one stand out against dominant modes of identification. At the same time, the elaboration of a sense of multiracial group identity makes one feel as if one belongs to a community where one is, if only in one's perceived marginality, just like everyone else. The irony here is that while the discourse of choice in racial identification suggests we as individuals are determining for ourselves who we want to be, in fact we are "choosing" within a given set of epistemological, social, and political conditions that make only certain choices possible.

Scholars have sometimes described the trajectory of white ethnicity from a consequential group affiliation to a largely symbolic one as a transition from "being" to "feeling" ethnic (Bakalian 1993). "People desperately wish to 'feel' ethnic," Steinberg argues, "precisely because they have all but lost the prerequisites of 'being' ethnic." (1989, 63). In this respect, the multiracial example is perhaps best understood as a move in the opposite direction. Elaborations of multiracial collective identification represent an attempt to move *from* "feeling" *to* "being" multiracial. For some of my respondents, that feeling of being mixed race was largely a feeling of not fitting into any ethnoracial community. For others it was based on a feeling of being a part of both. The construction of multiracial organizations, the push for official designation of mixed race status—these are moves to make multiracials appear more real in a culture that elevates ethnicity and race as primary markers of personhood—to not only feel multiracial, but also to "be" multiracial in civic and social life.

The dividing line between what constitutes racial versus ethnic difference in the United States has always fallen fairly close to the line marking whom one would consider marrying and what ancestry one would publicly claim. Yet according to this barometer, some racialized distinctions—particularly American Indian status—have also been treated as "ethnic" ones—interesting "decorations" to the family tree that have little consequence in everyday life. Of course, the symbolic aspect of American Indian identity has only been inconsequential for persons of mixed background, whose native ancestry is generations removed, and who do not live on reservations. While to date visible non-European ancestry has been consequential, particularly for persons of African descent, one can certainly imagine a time in the not too distant future where being Asian, Mexican, and even black will increasingly be treated and *experienced* (much like American Indian ancestry is currently treated by whites who claim it)—symbolically. As this generation of mixed descent persons have children of their own, who may cross even more racialized boundaries, they are likely to encourage their children to "embrace" all of their ancestry. As such, the proliferation of racial identifiers that individuals use is

likely to expand. The consequences of such racial identifications and the nature of the connections to those racialized communities, however, will largely depend on where they live, whom they live with, and what they look like.

The Future of Multiracial Group Making

I have discussed in detail how the multiracial example draws our attention to the hegemonic, yet hidden assumptions about the American family—namely that families are monoracial—and how racial homogeneity has been fundamental to how families are constructed. But what does the multiracial example teach us about ethnoracial group making? In the process of elaborating what they share with each other, and seeking public recognition for themselves, multiracials make the mixed position a socially recognizable one. As the idea that multiracials exist is further institutionalized, it is appropriate to evaluate in what sense this "group" will come to be like traditional ethnoracial groups.

Like panethnic formations among Latinos, Asian Americans, and American Indians in the United States, the construction of multiracial community is profoundly shaped by state policies. These panethnic formations arose out of a context in which the state "lumped" together groups who consider themselves to be distinct on some basis deemed salient (such as shared language or presumed racial similarity). In response, these distinct cultural and linguistic groups began to assert a common identification (Espiritu 1992; Nagel 1995; Omi and Winant 1994). Collective identification, generally speaking, followed categorization.

The assertion of a collective identification among "multiracials" emerges out of a different relationship to the state. Unlike Latinos, Asians, and American Indians, "multiracials" have not been lumped together for the purposes of racial classification or the administration of social policies. Neither were they counted separately in racial statistics nor was social policy developed to deal with them as a class of people. Multiracials began to coalesce in response to social and cultural pressures that defined them as misfits and that stigmatized interracial families. They *sought* a state classification as a remedy to those grievances.

Now that the state classifies mixed race people as such, one of the key factors motivating multiracial mobilization in the 1990s is no longer available. Additionally, the prejudice and stigma associated with interracial marriage and families have declined significantly. Even in the absence of those initial motivating factors, however, it seems likely that collective mobilization around multiracial identification will continue for the foreseeable future.

First, mixed race organizations have become increasingly institutionalized. The Mavin Foundation has professionalized what began as grassroots, minimally organized community building efforts. Matt Kelley, its founder and president, has assembled a paid staff that operates a Web site, runs community outreach activities, and acts as a kind of clearinghouse for information on mixed race people and issues of race and social justice. The foundation publishes a quarterly magazine (*Mavin: The Mixed Race Experience*), the production values of which rival those of most national monthlies—a far cry from the photocopied newsletters irregularly produced by local community organizations in the 1990s. Moreover, through its Campus Awareness and Compliance Initiative, sponsored jointly with HIF, AMEA, and the Level Playing Field Institute, it aims to ensure that the MOOM [mark one or more] option is fully institutionalized in federal agencies.[4]

Groups like Mavin, as well as campus organizations and academic classes, focused on mixed race people are manifestations of ongoing attempts to create and sustain mixed race community. Once established, people have vested interests in maintaining them, as they provide jobs, income, and a public platform for members. These venues for expressing and exploring multiracial identity are likely to thrive, as the "two or more races" population is expected to grow significantly in the next decade. Recent population estimates show the "two or more races" population was the third fastest growing group between 2003 and 2004 (behind Hispanics and Asians) (Files 2005). While demographic statistics cannot predict whether multiracial collective identification will be meaningful to this population, the ongoing institutionalization of mixed race identity will encourage such an identification. For example, schools are required to ask students if they are "of two or more races," and given the opportunity to identify themselves this way, many people will. With statistics on this population, school administration will likely craft programs for such students, further encouraging such an

identification. Indeed this is already happening. In 1988 when students at Harvard formed a discussion group for mixed race students, they knew of no other such group. By 2005, the ninth annual Pan-Collegiate Mixed Race Conference took place while one of the largest professional associations of student affairs personnel inaugurated a standing committee on multiracial student affairs, alongside its committees for Asian, African American, Latino, and Native American students.[5]

While the educational arena will likely encourage multiracial identification, so too will the market. The juggernaut of consumer capitalism has taken up multiracialism. As long as mixed race retains its air of hipness and authenticity, marketers will continue to exploit it. As long as the population that identifies itself as mixed race continues to grow, business will court "it," developing products to meet its putative needs and helping to make multiracials in the process. Five years after Census 2000, multiracial community is increasingly translocal, Web based, and media driven. The advent of high-speed global communications technology in the 1990s has allowed those previously isolated by geography to "come together" virtually. These virtual communities are cheap to start up and to run and so will likely continue. Not incidentally, the low cost and wide reach of Web communications has greatly facilitated the creation of companies selling mixed race consumer products. Increasingly, mixed race organizations, Web communities, and entrepreneurs engage in a symbiotic relationship, with each Web site giving links to each other, and in so doing reinforcing their raison d'etre.

While mixed racial identifications have become further institutionalized through state codification, it is not clear to what extent "multiracials" will make demands on the state on behalf of multiracials as a group. To date, self-appointed spokespersons for multiracials limit themselves to ensuring that federal agencies collect multirace data and to calls to investigate the extent to which multiracials have unique health care needs.[6] At this time, the multiple race population is not a protected class for the purposes of antidiscrimination efforts, which may be the next battle multiracial activists wage. The political commitments of younger organized multiracials, however, appear to be left leaning. Participants in Mavin, the leaders of Mixed Media Watch, and my respondents largely consider themselves to be politically progressive and anti-racist. They are skeptical of the claims that race does not matter by conservatives who point to their multiple racial identifications as proof of its irrelevance. There is a strong impulse among these respondents to avoid essentializing a set of differences that distinguish multiracials from others. Yet through the debate over official classification and the organizations in which they explore what they share as a group, racial mixedness is constituted as an adequate principle upon which to act.

There is an inescapable irony of group making that in seeking to undermine the foundations of American racial thinking, they reaffirm racial thinking as well. While activists and parents describe their use of multiple terms for indicating their racial identity as "revolutionary" or simply "accurate," it is also true that the logic of mixed race stems from the same underlying logic that preceded it—that individuals have race, and when they combine sexually we get "racial mixture." Both ideas assume there is race, it is carried in the body, and it's mixed through sexual reproduction.

While those who fought official enumeration of mixed race status challenged the prevailing way that race was categorized, they stopped short of challenging the principle of racial classification itself. While seeming to challenge the racial state, multiracial activists *affirmed* the right of the state to label individuals in racial terms by arguing that it has a *duty* to label them in ways that fully recognize the possibility of boundary crossing. This can only entrench the underlying notion that individuals are made of "racial stuff" (albeit of more than one type) and that their racial composition ought to be recognized by that ultimate symbolic agency—the state. Their activism recognizes, indeed *welcomes* the right of the state to record a race for each of its members (even if individuals "self-identify"). This is a striking acceptance of the racial state, in and through which the category of race was created and through which it is reproduced.

Yet this irony is not limited to this movement. "The reproduction of ethnicity and the reinforcement of its pragmatic salience," writes Comaroff, "is as much a function of efforts directed at its erosion as it is of activities that assert its positive value" (Comaroff 1987, 315). If race is where you locate your difficulties, race is where you look for solutions. "Race" seems like an efficacious basis upon which to act.

The construction of multiracial community, like pan-ethnic constructions and movements for ethnic renewal, is a flexible, sometimes strategic and sometimes contradictory phenomenon. It creates new racial subjects while conforming to the preexisting U.S. racial order, as it provides a crucial consciousness-raising tool with which to make demands on the state. It undermines rigid modes of racial thinking in the United States while multiplying the available ways of naming racial difference. While mixed race people may identify *with* each other, they eschew the notions of racial sameness that racial identity usually entails. While a collective mixed race identity is potentially subversive, it may be readily absorbed into the existing racial order, in which multiraciality comes to be seen as simply another racial category, robbed of its critical content.[7] The meaning of multiracial will be affected by the political alignments, demographics, and economic pressures of all other groups.

Critics of the group-making project among multiracials claim that "the multiracial community" is a fabrication. After all, mixed race people come in a variety of "mixes." As such, as a group they share no ancestry in common. Nor do they necessarily share language, religion, or culture. They are not, in other words, a "real" ethnic group. Yet the fabricated aspect of multiracial group making that its critics find so troubling is precisely what makes studying this phenomenon so valuable. The notion of "fabrication" has a double meaning, signifying both an act of creation (which captures the constructed nature of groups) and a *deception,* in which the ways we tend to perceive groups in everyday life (as durable, real, substantial entities) masks the reality that groups do not exist as such, but rather are the products of a complex work of *group making.* All ethnoracial groups are constructed. In the project of making multiracials, however, the ways in which such construction proceeds are just more obvious.

The Family's Role in Racial Change

Multiracial activists have used the state as a means through which to gain symbolic recognition not only of their racial identity, but of their families as well. The multiracial family, some believe, serves as proof that America's racial problems can be overcome. I dub this the "family thesis," inspired by Benjamin DeMott's critique of contemporary racial politics. In his book, *The Trouble with Friendship,* DeMott (1998 [1995]) critiques what he calls "the friendship thesis" that underlies many putative solutions offered in culture and politics for healing racial division. According to DeMott, embedded within the "friendship thesis" is the "certainty that one-on-one, black-white relations can be relied on to resolve race problems." In a similar vein, the "family thesis" suggests that if we all just intermarried and had children together our problems would be resolved.

Historical and cross-cultural analyses show the problems with such an idea. First, rather than bringing about social equality, intermarriage tends to follow other indicators of social equality (such as educational achievement) between groups. But more to the point, it is questionable that personal relations can resolve what is wrought institutionally with the help of the state, no matter how intimate and caring those personal relations are. The hierarchies of relatedness that my respondents hold, which structure their sense of trust, affinity, and beliefs about others (despite growing up in interracial families), suggest that more than intimate and empathetic relations between individuals is needed to bring about social change. Empathy is limited in its capacities to bring about social change, since people can cultivate empathy for specific individuals while keeping intact their basic (negative) beliefs about the categories of people from which those individuals come. This is why assertions that people in intermarriages and multiracial individuals are less prejudiced natural bridges across the racial divide are problematic. It is easy to make exceptions for one's kin, marking them as the exception to the negative rule for others of a particular group, thus leaving the line of demarcation intact.

The complexities of interracial intimacy revealed through the stories of my respondents are cautionary tales with implications for how we interpret intermarriage statistics as barometers of racial change. In his influential study of white ethnicity Richard Alba writes, "By far the most impressive evidence of the diminishing power of ethnicity among whites is the rising tide of interethnic marriage. Marriage is a sensitive barometer of social integration because it involves great social intimacy" and links together members of families in regular contact (1990, 11–12). In contemporary interpretations of intermarriage patterns, families are assumed to engage in regular contact and to be intimate—to care for one another in a variety of ways (physically, financially, and emotionally). In the process, children are assimilated into one ethnic group (usually the dominant one) or act as bridges between those of their parents. This formulation imagines intermarriage as the sine qua non of assimilation: a cultural merger that produces children who embody that merging.

While interracial families are imagined as sites where racial differences meet and melt (away), racialized differences among family members create variable experiences for the members of such families. The family, as feminist scholars have argued for decades, is not a monolithic unit, and members within families have divergent and competing interests. For my respondents, race often formed the ground of those competing interests. In other words, while intermarriage may be common for some groups, it does not follow that it is either preferred or without controversy for either the partners in a marriage or their children, to say nothing of the ethnoracial communities with which they are engaged.

While invaluable for helping us understand changes in identification and marriage patterns, such statistics are very crude instruments for understanding meaning and tell us very little about practice—how and why people think of themselves in such terms and how they behave on the basis of them. When we rely on demographics to tell our stories we are merely recording and elaborating the preconstructed categories of the state and of social movements and are unable to say anything about whether and in what ways such categories are meaningful.

My point here is both methodological and epistemological. We need qualitative ethnographic work to understand meaning and process and we also need to question on what basis the assortment of people who marked boxes on the census can be considered a social group. Analyzing the statistics on racial identification tells us about patterns, but before we begin to make inferences about what those patterns say about group boundaries, the existence of groups, or the "groupness" of groups, we need to know something about meaning and practice.

Family's Radical Potential

All this is not to say that interracial kinship lacks a radical *potential.* Though I am cautious about interpreting multiracial identification and rising rates of intermarriage as signs of fading ethnoracial boundaries, I do believe that these developments, along with a growing public discussion of interracial intimacy, reflect and signal significant changes in the nature of racial division in the United States. The attempt to obtain some form of multiracial classification grew out of a desire to make visible those bonds that are easily elided—a recognition of not only a varied racial heritage, but of *relationships*. The MOOM option institutionalizes and records in statistical form a trace of those relationships.

For many of my respondents, parenting mixed race kids provided a powerful means through which they were able to extend their sense of obligation, empathy, and likeness beyond the circle of their ethnic group of origin. The notion that one can change one's people, to embrace the "other," is a potentially powerful tool to begin healing social divisions because it says that such social boundaries are artificial, and despite the very real consequences of those boundaries, through love and work they can be overcome.

The experience of living within interracial families allowed many of my respondents to overcome the racial categories that have almost always served to mark others outside one's moral domain, emphasizing the difference, and even the inhumanity, of the Other. It strikes me that the multiracial movement has its most radical potential in this vein. Presentations of multiracial family *as* families lessen the presumed distance across racial categories. Kinship symbolically bridges the imagined distance between racial groups. I am reminded of Patricia Williams's observation of a white woman suckling a black child. She writes:

> Is there not something unseemly in our society about the spectacle of a white woman mothering a black child? A white woman giving totally to a black child; a black child totally and demandingly dependent for everything, sustenance itself, from a white woman. The image of a white woman suckling a black child . . . Such a picture says, there is no difference; it places the hope of continuous generation of immortality of the white self in a little black face.

Given the pitfalls of family imagery mentioned earlier, images of the family are only truly transformative if they extend the cultural obligation to care for and about others *outside* the limits of both genealogical relatives *and*

racial groups. One respondent tried to put into words how he saw this potential:

> The way that a multiracial person sees the world—we come in so many different shades that I realize I can't look at someone and tell what they are any more. They could be black and white. They could be the same mixture that I am and look totally different or look very similar. So walking down the street, I can't look at someone and immediately conclude that I'm not related to them in some way, maybe not immediately but somewhere back in history we probably had some common ancestors, you know. Who knows? I really don't know. I can't say as a fact. So in a sense you start walking down the street and you look at everyone and see everyone as being related to you. Now, if you do that how can you discriminate against someone if you acknowledge that they're related to you? You can't discriminate against your brother or sister. What line, what rules—what lines of demarcation are you going to use to say this is us, this is them, these are the haves, these are the have-nots. You start to break them down. So the people can then start seeing or recognizing that—we are talking about the whole idea of one common humanity, you know, and I think that's a part of multiracial identity. The more you learn about multiracial people you just see multiracial people. This is what they look like. They're not so different as I thought. You know, so-and-so might not be so different. So that's why I really like to promote a multiracial outlook.

Seeing oneself in the other, as Jessica Benjamin (1988) argued, opposes the breakdown of mutual recognition that allows members of one category to see themselves as apart and above (or below) that leads to domination. It is this sense—that they are visible yet not seen—that motivates the action of the people who have been most involved in the multiracial movement. An acknowledgment of their social existence is something they understand to be crucial to eroding the color line. The issue is as much emotional as it is structural.

Understanding the emergence of multiracial families as a politicization of kinship helps clarify, if not the political implications of multiracial politics, then how multiracials understand the meaning of the actions in which they are engaged. The meaning of multiracial movement for its participants cannot be grasped merely at the cognitive level, where analysts of multiracial politics insist on grounding their critiques (for example, chastizing notions of racial accuracy or the use of fractional language as a reification of race). The notion of racial coherence put forth by respondents and evident in the idea that multiracial identification is expressive of a "whole self," should be understood not as a ground of politics, but as its effect—a response to the social conditions that create, sustain, and reproduce racial division.

The opposition between race and mixed race reaffirms boundaries between categories (white/black/Asian and so forth) even as the vocabulary of kinship brings together categories of bodies previously isolated outside of the sphere of family. So while multiracialism may rescribe racial thinking by leaving intact the idea of race, it also calls attention to the peculiar history of the United States that denies social and sexual mixing across boundaries and helps us understand the role of such denial in supporting white domination.

The notion that one can choose one's racial identification disrupts the notion of genealogical descent as well. Such a notion says that people can choose *not* to identify with one of their ancestors' categories, or may choose to identify with a group to which none of their ancestors belonged, as did Mandy Rodriguez. Moreover, while some people might claim a multiracial identity, their children might not necessarily retain such an understanding of themselves.

While perhaps not revolutionary, the emergence of multiracial families as such represents a significant transformation in the logic (or illogic) underpinning dominant American racial discourse. The increasing prevalence and acceptance of intermarriage is a redefinition of permissible objects of sexual passion, as well as a redefinition of kinship. Multiracial families (and multiracial politics more broadly) do not necessarily challenge the biologistic and genealogical logic of race or family. Instead, they undercut the twin pillars of racial formation—hypodescent and antimiscegenation—creating the space by which the racialized family and familized notions of race are undermined.

While the multiracial family has long been a cultural contradiction in terms, that is no longer the case. The formation of collective organizations for multiracial families and their assertions that they are indeed families challenges a fundamental feature of American racial domination, yet its implications are not entirely clear. Intermarriage patterns and the political and cultural response to them and to mixed racial identity have always been linked to the broader system of racial domination that demarcates white from black (and less rigidly, white from other ethnoracial groups), and the fates of those of African descent (whether one is putatively "mixed" or not) have always been linked. While the possibility exists that the greater visibility of multiracial families will lead to more acceptability of all kinds of relations across racial boundaries—beginning with intimate and familial ones and corresponding with spatial and social ones—this does not mean, of course, that the problem that defined America in the twentieth century—the color line—has not followed us into the twenty-first.

Seeing the Big Picture   **Interracial Marriage and the Blurring of the Color Line**
Look at Figure 35 "Interracial Married Couples" in the Appendix. Why is it that so few individuals marry across the color line? What would it take for these numbers to radically change?

49   Policy Steps toward Closing the Gap

Meizhu Lui, Bárbara J. Robles, Betsy Leondar-Wright, Rose M. Brewer, and Rebecca Adamson

MEIZHU LUI is the executive director of United for a Fair Economy (UFE).

BÁRBARA J. ROBLES taught Latino public policy at the LBJ School of Public Affairs at the University of Texas at Austin from 1998 to 2005. She has a PhD in economics from the University of Maryland at College Park.

BETSY LEONDAR-WRIGHT is UFE's communications director. A longtime economic justice organizer and researcher, she is the author of *Class Matters: Cross-Class Alliance Building for Middle-Class Activists* (New Society Publishers, 2005).

ROSE M. BREWER, is associate professor and Morse Alumni Distinguished Teaching Professor of African American & African Studies at the University of Minnesota and a contributing editor to *Souls,* an interdisciplinary journal of the Institute for Contemporary Black History at Columbia.

REBECCA ADAMSON, a Cherokee, is founder and president of First Nations Development Institute (1980) and founder of First Peoples Worldwide (1997).

Questions to Consider The authors provide a number of proposals for achieving socioeconomic equality between the races. How and in what ways does everyone benefit from living in a society where there is greater social equality? As you read each suggestion, ask yourself if you believe that these calls for greater social justice are politically possible. Would most Americans sign on to these plans to create a more just society? If it seems as though their proposal might be too difficult to implement, what would you do to convince the public that achieving racial equality would benefit all of society?

THIS LIST IS BY NO MEANS COMPREHENSIVE, but perhaps it can spark more energy to tackle the issue of wealth building for communities of color, and for all those currently without economic security.

First Steps: Human Assets

Education has been an important tool in creating white advantage. It was a crime to teach African slaves to read and write; Latinos have been disadvantaged by English-only classrooms; Native Americans were forced into assimilationist school settings, and Asians had to sue to go to school with whites.

In today's economy, more than ever, you need an education to get ahead. Even for a menial job, a high school diploma is often required. Current mechanisms for public school funding—largely local property taxes—enable wealthier families in white suburbs who pay more property taxes to have more dollars invested in their public schools. Disparity in funding produces disparities in educational outcomes, and perpetuates a class and race divide. The infusion of federal dollars to invest more in communities that are poor could help close the gap.

As unionized jobs in manufacturing have shrunk, higher education has become an even more important ticket to a job at a decent wage with benefits. Professor Hubie Jones, former dean of the Boston University School of Social Work and a longtime community activist, grew up with his single mom in Harlem, New York. Without the possibility and promise of free higher education at the City College, he says, he would not have had the motivation to work hard in school in order to get that ticket up and out. Gangs and drugs would have been the only option.

Free public universities came about in 1862, the same year as the Homestead Act, when the Morrill Act established land-grant colleges in every state. Their purpose was to provide knowledge and skills to the newly landed masses.[1] Public institutions of higher education were the ticket out of poverty for many people of color who could not afford tuition at private colleges. Today, affordable higher education is moving out of reach for many of our children.

The federal government spends $55 billion on student aid, but the mix has been changing. Seventy-seven percent of that aid is in loans, not grants, a reversal of past policies. With tax cuts mostly for the wealthy, and the resulting budget shortfalls, states have been spending less on their public colleges, and tuitions have been growing at a faster rate than family income. The new welfare policies set in 1996 have led to a decline in enrollment of low-income women in college. Before the Temporary Assistance for Needy Families (TANF) program, forty-two states allowed women to count college attendance as employment in order to qualify for benefits: after TANF, only twenty-six states still allowed this option.[2] We can change the mix back again, and raise new taxes to invest in public colleges. A well-educated populace is the cornerstone of democracy, and the cornerstone is crumbling.

For those who don't speak English as their first language, English classes are the first stepping-stones to success. It is not possible to get a decent job without English skills. Some immigrants are not literate in their native language and need extended classes. Some come with degrees from other countries, and can learn English quickly. For all of them, long waiting lists for free or affordable classes prevent them from obtaining this skill so essential for entry of limited English speakers into the U.S. workforce. On the other hand, so that non–English

speakers do not get cheated out of their assets, or miss out on the benefits of programs for which they qualify, English-only policies must be rejected.

One big health problem can wipe out a lifetime of savings. The cost of care for a premature baby in a neonatal intensive care unit can be $500,000. In 1999, one quarter of the families that filed for bankruptcy cited health problems and the related costs as the reason.[3]

A 2000 study found that people of color are more likely to be uninsured than non-Hispanic whites, and are less likely to have job-based health insurance.[4] Thirty percent of Latinos, 25 percent of African Americans, 20 percent of Asian Americans and Pacific Islanders, and 17 percent of Native Americans are uninsured.[5] (The relatively low percentage rate of uninsured Native Americans is mostly due to their access to Indian Health Services as opposed to private or Medicaid coverage.[6]) Medicaid, which cares for the poor in inner cities and rural areas, is increasingly underfunded, as states face budget crises.

Universal coverage is possible. In 1983, Hawaii received permission from the federal government to require all employers to provide insurance to employees. In 1993, they were able to pool all their public dollars to create one big statewide insurance system. Not only were they able to provide health, dental, and mental health coverage for all, but the system was also able to save public dollars through a competitive bidding system.[7]

Hitting a Stride: Income Assets

One of the main reasons that nonwhite people were shut out of asset building was because they were restricted to no wage or low-wage jobs. From African slaves in the South to Latino day laborers on the street corners of Los Angeles, people of color have been denied fair compensation for their labor power. They have been limited to jobs that whites did not and do not want, were excluded from unions, paid taxes to work, and have always been the last hired and the first fired.

Jobs are needed that provide the cash income to cover day-to-day needs, *with something left over to build savings,* the basis for financial wealth. Today, income disparity lays the groundwork for future wealth disparities. Thomas Shapiro, in *The Hidden Cost of Being African American: How Wealth Perpetuates Inequality,* analyzed the impact of income on wealth. Once basic living expenses are met, each additional dollar of annual income generates $3.26 in net worth over a person's lifetime. Wealth disparity grows because of differences in income. For example, the difference in net worth between someone making $30,000 a year and someone making $60,000 a year is nearly $100,000.[8] Income includes not just wages and salaries based on working, but cash supports for those who are unemployed, retired, or parents of small children.

In Bárbara Robles's class at the LBJ school at the University of Texas in Austin, students simply did not believe her when she told them that the minimum wage means a family must live on $10,000 a year. Over 27 million workers make less than $8 dollars an hour; of these workers, 16.8 million are adults twenty-five and over; more than 16 million are women; 22 million are white; 4.2 million are black; and more than 17.5 million work full-time.[9] The present federal minimum wage of $5.15 an hour translates into an annual income of $10,712. The Economic Policy Institute has done several studies that reveal that an increase in the minimum wage would primarily benefit full- and part-time workers of low-income families,[10] which are disproportionately headed by single women of color. It would require raising the minimum wage to at least $8.10 an hour as of 2004 for a family of four to move above the official poverty line.[11] Around the country, people are organizing for more than the minimum wage: they are demanding a living wage. Since the cost of living varies across the country, communities are calculating costs particular to their cities. For example, in San Francisco voters approved a city living wage of $8.50 an hour in 2003; this will put over $100 million per year into the pockets of roughly fifty-four thousand workers.

And what about a maximum wage? In most countries, the ratio of CEO pay to worker pay has been around 40 to 1. In the United States in 2004, the ratio of CEO pay to the average worker's pay was 431 to 1.[12] Rep. Martin Sabo of Minnesota wants to curb that excess. His Proposed Income Equity Act would prevent corporations from claiming tax deductions on any executive pay that totals over 25 times what a company's lowest paid workers are earning.

The poorest group in the United States is women of color and their children. As Miami resident Thelma Brown puts it, "[C]ertified nursing assistants in Miami start at $5.75 an hour with no benefits. Day care costs ninety to one hundred dollars every two weeks per kid;

then you have to pay rent, electricity, food, and everything else. A single mom can't live on one job at that rate."[13] They require government help to survive. For many years, it was mainly white women who received welfare payments. Attieno Davis, a longtime African American activist, remembers how empowering it was for black women in the 1960s to realize that they were *entitled* to these benefits, too. Latinos also were underenrolled, since no outreach was conducted in Spanish, nor were there Spanish-speaking workers in welfare offices. However, President Reagan's caricature of "welfare queens," stereotyped as a woman of color, created backlash. In 1996, the program changed to Temporary Assistance to Needy Families. To quality for the meager payments, women cannot have assets of more than $1,000 in some states.

One positive tax provision for the poor is the Earned Income Tax Credit (EITC). It was born out of the welfare debates in the late 1960s and early 1970s. At the time, President Nixon was proposing a guaranteed income to all families with children, regardless of whether the parent(s) worked. It is amazing today to remember that Nixon was proposing such a progressive policy. But Democratic senator Russell Long of Louisiana felt that the Nixon proposal would discourage people from working. His alternate proposal provided tax relief to low-income workers, rather than guaranteed income for all. The EITC was passed in 1975. Its annual budget rose from $2 billion to $12 billion between 1980 and 1992. According to the 2001 Census, forty-three million people were living in low-income working families with children, and two out of every three poor families with children had at least one parent working. The EITC has lifted more families with children out of poverty than any other government program.[14]

Low-wage workers use the money they receive from the EITC for investments in education and savings, as well as to help them pay daily living expenses.[15] In order to encourage savings. Ray Boshara from the New America Foundation suggests that a portion of EITC refunds could be channeled directly into a basic savings account.[16] The Center on Budget and Policy Priorities found that EITC funds are often spent locally, serving as an economic development tool for low-income neighborhoods.[17]

Decent pay and accumulation of assets is hard to come by if you are not allowed citizenship. As we have seen, immigrant status has been a major barrier to economic equality for people of color. Jeannette Huezo, a political refugee from El Salvador, has lived and worked in Boston for fifteen years. However, she had to leave four of her children behind when she fled, and they are not allowed to reunite; she has been sending money home to support them. Salvadorans in the United States send remittances back home that now amount to half of the Salvadoran economy. Being forced into low-paying jobs because of their tenuous legal status, coupled with the need to send money home, makes it difficult to build assets in either country. The National Coalition for Dignity and Amnesty developed a proposal for a federal Freedom Act. It would legalize undocumented immigrants currently living in the United States and create a status of "temporary residency" for future migrants, who would be eligible for permanent residency after three years.

People of color should be hired into jobs for which they are qualified and [enabled] to rise to the level of their capabilities. Affirmative action, won through the Civil Rights Movement, did bring many more people of color into middle-income jobs where they could begin to save, buy homes, and build wealth. However, the gap is still not closed. Over their working lifetime, African Americans with a college degree can expect to earn $500,000 less than equally qualified white people.[18] Asians do fine getting in on the ground floor and moving up, but then encounter glass ceilings: an Asian with a college degree had median annual earnings in 1993 of $36,844; comparably qualified whites made $41,094.[19] The need for affirmative action and government enforcement of non-discrimination laws is far from over.

Going the Distance: Financial Assets

Over the course of history, the federal government has used public resources to create wealth-building starter kits as well as continuing subsidies for whites, and has removed assets from people of color and denied them the benefits given to whites. In recent years, the white middle class has taken a hit: overall, it's shrinking, and general economic inequality has reached the levels of the Gilded Age at the turn of the last century. As a result, more and more academics, advocates, foundations, and public officials are recognizing that income alone is not enough to lift a family out of poverty. While this attention is not mainly because of wide recognition of the racial wealth gap, there is an opportunity to bring race into the conversation.

It's not that there aren't federal asset policies currently in place. The government spends approximately $355 billion a year in direct outlays and tax expenditures (allowing tax breaks for certain kinds of income). However, they are not named as asset policies, and they disproportionately benefit those who already have assets.[20] As we have seen, the net worth of people of color is far below that of whites.

While there are many ways to group asset-building opportunities, the Asset Policy Initiative of California has designed a framework that is simple and user-friendly. They see that strategies in four areas are needed. *Asset accumulation* is about policy strategies that encourage families to save; *asset leveraging* policies help low-wealth families use their limited savings to get loans for larger assets such as home and business ownership. Unfortunately, if there are not *asset preservation* assistance programs, often low-wealth people lose everything they have to predatory lenders. And finally, "*asset creation*" goes beyond individual strategies; communities can gain control over development in their own neighborhoods and rural communities.

Asset Accumulation

New thinking on how to help low-income people save money has been inspired by Michael Sherradan's groundbreaking book *Assets and the Poor: A New American Welfare Policy.* Sherradan and others recognize that income-support programs do not foster asset accumulation.[21]

Individual Development Accounts (IDAs) are nontaxable matching funds savings accounts that can be used—and used *only*—toward purchasing a home, retirement, education, starting a business, or other asset-accumulating endeavors. The outside matching source comes either from the public or private sector. Generally, the program has been targeted to the working poor, those who have a low but stable income in which some money can be set aside. Foundations and local banks have both provided funding to augment savings on the part of the poor. There are about 250 neighborhoods participating in IDA programs across the country, many in communities of color. The National Council of La Raza and the First Nations Development Institute have developed projects for Latinos and Native peoples.

Pilot IDA programs funded privately have encouraged policy change. According to the Corporation for

Enterprise Development (CFED), since 1993, twenty-nine states and the District of Columbia have passed laws in support of IDAs. Thirty-two states have included IDA initiatives in their welfare reform programs and seven states have instituted state-funded IDA programs. In 1998, a federal pilot program of savings incentives for the poor was enacted, with $125 million over five years set aside for matching individual savings. While on the one hand this legislation helps to make the IDA idea more visible, it is not on a scale to be truly transformative.[22]

Another promising idea involves investing in our future: our nation's children. It is every parent's dream to leave their child a nest egg. And wouldn't it be great if everyone could be born with a trust fund! An impossible dream? Just such a program was instituted in England, sponsored by Prime Minister Tony Blair's Labor Party. In 2003, the British Parliament established what has become known as "baby bonds," a small child trust fund for each newborn in the country. Modest amounts of public funds will be deposited and invested for each newborn infant, and made available for withdrawal at the age of eighteen. If a child is given an initial deposit of $1,000, and then the parent makes a yearly contribution of $500, matched by another $500 from an outside source, this would translate into $40,000 available to eighteen-year-olds to use toward education, starting a business, or putting a down payment on a home.[23]

In 2005, a bill to create a similar program was introduced in Congress by an unusual alliance of conservative Republicans and progressive Democrats. The America Saving for Personal Investment, Retirement, and Education Act (the ASPIRE Act of 2005) proposed that a $500 KIDS Account be established for every newborn child. Children in households earning below the national median income would be eligible for a supplemental government contribution of up to $500. Additional benefits would include tax-free earnings, matched savings for lower income families, and financial education. Here is a program that provides a double incentive for lower income people to save: no taxes on the savings account, and matched government contributions for the poor.

Whether such new asset subsidiary programs should be universal or targeted to people of color is a strategic question. In any case, additional resources for outreach, translation, and other mechanisms to ensure inclusion must be part of the program.

Asset Leveraging

When you have some savings, you can either keep them, or use them to leverage more assets through making bigger investments.

Rotating savings and credit associations (ROSCA) have been an important strategy utilized by immigrant households in order to start a small business, purchase a home, or pay for a child's education. This strategy has origins in many different ethnic groups from East Asia, Latin America, the Caribbean, the Near East, and Africa. The Vietnamese ROSCA is called a *hui,* the Ethiopian is *ekub,* Jamaican is *partners,* Dominican, *san,* Korean, *keh,* and Cambodian *tong-tine.*[24]

A ROSCA is formed among family members, friends, and kin groups. They require participants (usually five or more people) to pay in a monthly sum agreed upon by the group. A participant can make a request to borrow the month's pool of money, or there may be an agreed-upon sequence for withdrawal—tax- and interest-free, since these transactions take place outside of the mainstream economic structure. This continues until all members have had access to the funds. The system is based on trust and social pressure. Thus, if members do not return the money at some point, their reputation in the community is tainted, something they are usually not willing to risk.

A *Philadelphia Inquirer* reporter sat in on a ROSCA meeting. "A Vietnamese *hui* group listened as one member asked to break the payout schedule and let her have that month's collection. . . . [T]he group sat in judgment on her needs, then let her take the tax-free, no-interest pot of $14,000." But because ROSCAs are part of an unregulated, unprotected financing system, they have no recourse in case of theft. While sometimes immigrants do not trust banks, banks also do not make it easy to deposit ROSCA dollars. They treat deposits as belonging to an individual or household, and have no category to accommodate this unique form of savings. They report any deposit of more than $10,000 to the Internal Revenue Service. Without a financial institution to hold the money, one member has to keep the mounting dollars under his or her bed. A policy that recognized ROSCAs as a micro lending system, and allowed the money to be banked and borrowed tax-free, would build on existing community customs and help rather than hinder these activities.

Another way to use your small savings to leverage larger loans without worrying about a financial institution charging excessive fees and interest is to join a community credit union. The credit union movement was essentially a response to mainstream financial institutions' neglect of marginalized groups. Community Development Credit Unions (CDCU) provide basic financial services such as check cashing and small loans at fair rates to their members within a restricted area or community.[25] They are member based and member governed; some are based in churches or community organizations. One of the problems plaguing poor communities is that the meager resources present in poor communities tend to flow out of them.[26] In response to this problem, CDCUs keep local money in the community, as well as draw in outside money.[27] The resources accrued from CDCUs are then channeled back into the community and are used to respond to its various needs.

Usually, the first asset leveraged from savings is a home to live in. Expanding opportunities for home ownership are critical in closing the racial wealth divide. Home equity is one of the first building blocks for wealth, and is the most significant source of assets for people of color. For blacks, 62 percent of their net worth is held in homes; for Latinos, 51 percent. For white families, housing accounts for only 32 percent of their net worth. Given the history of federal subsidies for home ownership for whites, targeted funding for people and communities of color is now needed.

The Community Reinvestment Act of 1977 (CRA) came out of community struggles demanding access to banks and mortgage companies. Evidence was compiled showing that financial institutions engaged in discriminatory lending practices based on race, age, and location, instead of on an applicant's creditworthiness. These discriminatory practices had contributed to the decline of low-income and minority neighborhoods. The CRA required banks to lend in low-income communities, and federal banking regulators were mandated to maintain a close watch on financial institutions to ensure that they were meeting the needs of local communities. Communities of color were successful in getting the federal government to use its powers to stop private industry from providing affirmative action in lending to whites.

Through the CRA, significant strides were made during the 1990s as major banking institutions increase lending toward affordable housing and economic development to assist low-income people.[28] Over $20 billion has been invested in low-income neighborhoods and communities of color thanks to the CRA.[29]

Asset Preservation

Home ownership has been a double-edged sword for many home owners of color. It is a struggle first to gain access to fair loan terms, and another to try and keep the home. If we were to dig beneath the home ownership figures, which provide only a snapshot in time, we would find a lot more turnovers of home ownership among people of color than among whites. Lending predators target the weak—those unfamiliar with the rules of the game.

ACORN's Mary Gaspar described her ordeal: "Here's how my nightmare started: I got a check in the mail from Household Finance with an offer to refinance our home. . . . Household was misleading and dishonest. I received my first bill and it was $13,000 more than I thought it was going to be! I have seen how Household preys on people who are economically desperate as well as middle-class people like us." ACORN (Association of Community Organizations for Reform Now) responded by putting public pressure on Household Finance by holding demonstrations at their annual shareholder meetings. They were joined in their efforts by members of United for a Fair Economy's Responsible Wealth project. Proxy votes given to ACORN members by Responsible Wealth members who owned shares allowed Mary to tell her story—*inside* the halls of wealth, usually barred to the people of color whose hard-earned homes were being stolen from them. Having shareholders and ACORN members speaking with one voice brought Household to the table to discuss changing its behavior.[30]

Mortgage foreclosure has been another impediment to maintaining home ownership. A report done by the Family Housing Fund in Minneapolis found that the major reason home owners default on mortgage payments is job loss or a significant reduction in income; other causes include health emergencies and separation or divorce. While home ownership rates have increased, so have instances of foreclosure.

Foreclosure prevention is an important tool in stabilizing home owners at risk of losing their homes and neighborhoods by preventing houses from becoming vacant and boarded up. Between 1991 and 1997, the Mortgage

Foreclosure Program (MFP) carried out by the Family Housing Fund assisted close to seventeen hundred home owners and helped to reinstate the mortgages of over half of them within the St. Paul and Minneapolis area.[31] Foreclosure prevention counseling provides a more affordable way for home owners to stabilize their home ownership, compared to going through a mortgage insurer. It costs an average of $2,800 to help a home owner reinstate a mortgage, while with a mortgage insurer it could cost $10,000 to $28,000, depending on the insurer and the location of the home.[32] Ana Moreno, a housing consultant who conducted the study, contends that "[p]rograms that promote home ownership for households with very low incomes need to be linked to the full continuum of homeownership support services—pre-purchase education and counseling, financial assistance, post-purchase support, and delinquency and foreclosure prevention."[33]

Even with a home, you can spend your final years in poverty, if you have no retirement account from which to draw. Social security was invented to protect U.S. workers from this risk: it is the country's most successful insurance program. While 10 percent of those over age sixty-five live in poverty today, without social security that rate would be almost 50 percent.[34] Occupations held mostly by African Americans and Latinos were excluded initially, but all employment sectors were included beginning in 1950. Social security was also expanded to include not only retirement benefits, but also benefits to disabled workers and the families of workers who have died.

Because people of color have less income from stock holdings or capital gains than whites, social security is especially important to them: it is the sole source of income for 40 percent of elderly African Americans. The shorter life span of African American men means that both survivor and disability benefits go disproportionately to African Americans. While African Americans make up 12 percent of the U.S. population, 23 percent of children receiving social security survivor benefits are African American, as are about 17 percent of disability beneficiaries.[35]

Private pension plans are also an important asset. They provide retirement income, often as an employment benefit. The loss of unionized manufacturing jobs in the 1990s led to the loss of this asset for many. Laid off from auto and steel jobs which opened up to them during World War II, African Americans in particular have had to shift to jobs in the low-wage service sector, which do not provide employer-sponsored pension plans. In 2001, the mean value of the retirement account of a black family was $12,247, compared to $10,206 for a Latino family and $65,411 for a white family.[36]

For those who are fortunate to have jobs with pensions, there has been a change from defined benefit plans, in which workers receive a defined percentage of their wages, based on age and years of service, to defined contribution plans, in which employers and/or employees contribute a defined amount of money into a plan, but they do not guarantee that the money will still be there when you retire. The risk has been shifted to the worker. The AFL-CIO news related the story of Wanda Chalk, an African American employee at Enron. She had worked at Enron for fifteen years and had stock options worth $150,000, which were to generate income for her retirement. But due to Enron's fraudulent dealings, when Enron crashed, so did she. She lost her job, her stock value dropped to zero, and her retirement security went up in smoke.

Privatizing social security could produce the same effect. Preservation of assets, not risky schemes that could fail when you need the money most, needs to remain the cornerstone of retirement plans. As a society, we should not revert to a pre-Depression system, where our elders are at risk of dying in poverty.

Asset Creation

Even if a few individuals of color hold greater assets, that will not be enough to close the racial wealth divide. Just because in 2004 Bill Cosby was worth $540 million in assets, and just because the Unanues, owners of Goya Foods, were worth $700 million, it doesn't help those members of their racial groups who are stuck at the bottom. Assets need to be utilized to expand wealth for the community as a whole.

For example, Native land was given away to railroad owners and, in 1887, tribal land was broken into individual plots. Over the years, more and more Native owners lost their plots, resulting in a checkerboard pattern of landownership in what should have been tribally owned territory. In 2002, the Northwest Area Foundation, funded by heirs of James J. Hill, head of the Great Northern Railroad, who grew rich from the displacement of Ojibwes in Minnesota, made voluntary reparations. They gave $20 million in seed money for a buyback. Now millions of acres are back under tribal control.

In the 1970s, the inner city of Battle Creek, Michigan, became an economically depressed area, due to the closing of a military base nearby; by 1990, there were fifty recognized crack houses within a mile of downtown. Battle Creek Neighborhoods Incorporated, a community development financial institution, stepped in. Their approach has been to focus on lending to people who are willing to buy particular community blocks rather than to buyers of housing units scattered throughout the city. Their loans come with a requirement to improve the property and to participate in improving the quality of life on the block. For example, they sponsor "best of neighborhood" contests—Best Front Porch, Best Back Yard, Best Group Effort—that encourage home maintenance and improvement. Brenda Sue Woods wasn't going to participate in the Porch contest at first, but then decided to try. When she took first place, "I was just screaming like I won something on The Price Is Right." The emphasis on neighborhoods will enable housing values to rise in the area.

The Hawai'i Alliance for Community-Based Economic Development, a statewide nonprofit organization, provides loans not to individuals, but to groups. For example, a group of young people put in a proposal with the goal of "reconnection with their elders." One of the ways they used the loan was for a community van to transport those elders to needed services.

In a variety of locations, nonprofit organizations and government entities are experimenting with wealth-creation frameworks that are "inclusive, community-driven, and action oriented, protecting community, cultural, and environmental concerns while shielding individual private rights."[37] These efforts are road signs to the future.

---

50   Ten Things You Can Do to Improve Race Relations

Charles A. Gallagher

CHARLES A. GALLAGHER is professor and chair of the Department of Sociology, Social Work and Criminal Justice at La Salle University in Philadelphia. His research focuses on racial and social inequality, immigration, urban sociology, and the ways in which the media, the state, and popular culture construct, shape, and disseminate ideas of race. He has published articles on the sociological functions of color-blind political narratives, how racial categories expand and contract within the context of interracial marriages, race theory, racial innumeracy, and how one's ethnic history shapes perceptions of privilege.

Questions to Consider   Photocopy and pass along my "Ten Things You Can Do to Improve Race Relations" to family, friends, teachers, spiritual leaders, brothers, and sisters. Please contact me with any additions you might have for my list. I can be reached at gallagher@lasalle.edu.

THE STUDY OF RACE AND ETHNIC RELATIONS in the United States can be a rather depressing and disempowering undertaking. Ongoing institutional racism in education, employment, housing, lending, and law enforcement; continued wealth and income disparities between racial groups; and the persistence of racial prejudice and discrimination in most spheres of social life may leave one with the impression that nothing can be done to improve race relations. The modern civil rights movement was three hundred years in the making, and while movement toward racial equality has been substantial, racism and racial inequality still infect our nation and poison civic life. Such prejudice and inequality persist in part because changing the institutional barriers that allocate occupational and educational opportunity is a slow and difficult task. Upward mobility for different racial and ethnic groups is typically measured in generations rather than decades or years. One is tempted to throw one's hands in the air and yell, "There is nothing I can do!!!" But there is. You have the power to influence your family, friends, and peers by discussing the topics raised in this class. At the individual, interpersonal, and community level you can engage in activities to promote equal opportunity while building bridges between people from different racial backgrounds. Understanding the root causes of ethnic and racial inequality in the United States and examining in this class the facts, theories, evidence, and examples that pertain to such inequality will allow you to explain to others why racism and racial and ethnic inequality remain so stubbornly part of our culture. You now have the sociological tools to calmly, intelligently, and rationally engage in conversations with other adults about racism in America and what individuals, institutions, and the government *could* and *should* do to fashion a society where equal opportunity exists for all groups. Following are ten simple things you can do as you go about your day to raise your own and other people's consciousness about race relations and racial justice in America.

1. Talk to Your Family

Respectfully engage your friends and family in what you learned in this class. If you have family members that are racist or use stereotypes, ask them politely and nonjudgmentally why they harbor such animosity towards a whole group of people. Did they have a bad experience with someone from that group? Ask them if they have ever been the target of animosity or hatred because of their race, ethnic background, religion, or nationality. How did such an encounter make them feel? Were their parents or grandparents ever subject to such prejudice or discrimination? Why? Ask them if they think their prejudice or racism violates the American creed of equal treatment and opportunity for all regardless of group membership. If they believe in the American creed, how do they reconcile their racism or prejudice? Ask them if they believe in the golden rule that states "do unto others as you would have them do unto you."

2. Avoid Sterotypical Language

Be mindful that certain words or phrases typically mean the person is about to use stereotypes to describe a group. When you hear someone say "All black people do this . . . ,"

or "Latinos always like to . . . ," or "I never met a white person who could . . . ," a red flag should go up that stereotypes are in use. Politely ask if they are referring to an individual encounter with someone from another group or if they mean to speak for thirty-eight million blacks, forty million Latinos, ten million Asians, two hundred million whites, or 2.5 million American Indians in this country. Ask the person if they really believe *all people* in that group actually share the same behaviors and attitudes. Is it possible that certain behaviors or beliefs only appear in one racial or ethnic group and not another?

3. Racism Isn't Funny

Don't tolerate racist jokes. If you hear a joke being told that disparages someone because of his or her group membership, stop the person from telling the joke. If they insist on finishing, ask them why they don't like black people or white people or Asians or Catholics or whomever they are ridiculing in their attempt at humor. You have many retorts to such simplistic and retrograde behavior. You might say "Hey, I don't think putting down other people is funny," or "I have gay friends, I don't want to hear you trashing them," or "My brother-in-law is black (or white or Asian or Catholic or Jewish, etc.) and I think he's great." Be willing to "take the stand" about what is appropriate public discourse. If you do not speak up and let the person know that such remarks are socially inappropriate, you are condoning their beliefs and behavior. Inaction is a form of action.

4. Be Introspective

Think back to reading 17, in which Robert Merton discussed the unprejudiced nondiscriminator. This person was not prejudiced, nor did she discriminate against anyone in any way. How can we live our lives so social or peer pressure does not push us toward racist, prejudiced, or bigoted beliefs or actions? If you find yourself being a prejudiced nondiscriminator (fair-weather illiberal) or an unprejudiced discriminator (fair-weather liberal), ask yourself how you got there. Be introspective and honest about why you acted or behaved a certain way toward someone from a different ethnic or racial group. What scared you about the situation that made you deviate from your core beliefs or values? Did you overreact? Were you defensive? If you could relive that experience, what would you do differently? Is it possible you were socialized or taught to react the way you did? What role did peer pressure play in your actions? The most important thing you can do is to think critically about the root causes of your anxieties, attitudes, and actions. Be introspective and be willing to change how you think about groups different from your own.

5. Be a Good Citizen—Vote

Vote in every election. Take the time to find out candidates' positions on policies that have implications for race relations. Do not support a politician whose campaign rhetoric is racially divisive or attempts to win votes by manipulating racial (or class) fears. Knowing what the issues are (and are not) requires reading a newspaper every day.

6. TV, Rap, Rock: Appeals to the Lowest Common Denominator

When you watch television, realize that you are under constant bombardment by the most simplistic and stereotypical images of ethnic and racial groups. Ask yourself which racial and ethnic groups are on prime time and how those groups are represented. Are whites, blacks, Asians, Latinos, or American Indians in a wide range of roles, or are some groups more likely to be maids, gangbangers, exotics, or lawyers? Why? What you watch on television is not just entertainment. The mass media provide the images, symbols, and narratives that shape the way we understand society. The media cement existing stereotypes and construct expectations about where groups should be placed in America's racial hierarchy. The television industry uses stereotypes to make racial inequality look like the "normal" order of society. How are you are being manipulated by the programs you watch?

7. Learn Your Family's History

Take time to talk to the elderly people in your life. Ask your parents, aunts and uncles, neighbors, and spiritual leaders in your community about how race relations have changed since they were children. Ask your parents, grandparents, and other relatives about the *Brown* decision, the Civil Rights movement, Martin Luther King, Jr.'s assassination, the American Indian Movement (AIM),

La Raza, and the L.A. riots. How do they explain these events? What were they doing as these monumental events unfolded? Your elders are resources. Talk to them about the past and the present.

8. Teach through Example

Be a positive role model to all the younger people in your life. If you are of college age or older, you probably have a number of children and young adults who look up to you for moral guidance. If they hear you use foul language, then in all likelihood they will too. If you speak and act in a racist manner, they will learn your racism. Explain to those who view you as a role model what it means to live in a multiracial, multiethnic society. Explain to them what the American creed and the "golden rule" mean.

9. Step Out of Your Comfort Zone

Involve yourself in activities that place you in an environment where you will be exposed to people from different racial and ethnic backgrounds. Think about attending museums, music events, ethnic festivals, restaurants, supermarkets, shops, or any other public place where you will share space with people different from yourself.

10. Know Thyself

Did you grow up in a community that was racially homogenous? Was your house of worship pretty much composed of people who looked like you? Are your best friends all of the same race? Was your elementary school segregated? How about your high school? What did it look like in terms of racial composition? Do you think being raised in a segregated environment shapes racial attitudes? How? How do you think being the only racial minority in most social settings might shape a person's views of race relations? Have your ideas about race changed since you were fifteen years old? How and why? Reflect on these questions and write your answers as an essay. Circulate what you write to your friends and family. Set up a meeting to have a discussion on what you wrote and what their views on race relations in the United States are.

"If You're Not Part of the Solution, You're Part of the Problem."

RACE BY THE NUMBERS ~
America's Racial Report Card

Introduction

How are the race categories used in Census 2000 defined?

"White" refers to people having origins in any of the original peoples in Europe, the Middle East, or North Africa. It includes people who indicated their race or races as "White" or wrote in entries such as Irish, German, Italian, Lebanese, Near Easterner, Arab, or Polish.

"Black or African American" refers to people having origins in any of the black racial groups of Africa. It includes people who indicated their race or races as "Black, African Am., or Negro" or wrote in entries such as African American, Afro American, Nigerian, or Haitian.

"American Indian and Alaska Native" refers to people having origins in any of the original peoples of North and South America (including Central America), and who maintain tribal affiliation or community attachment. It includes people who indicated their race or races by marking this category or writing in their principal or enrolled tribe, such as Rosebud Sioux, Chippewa, or Navajo.

"Asian" refers to people having origins in any of the original peoples of the Far East, Southeast Asia, or the Indian subcontinent. It includes people who indicated their race or races as "Asian Indian," "Chinese," "Filipino," "Korean," "Japanese," "Vietnamese," or "Other Asian," or wrote in entries such as Burmese, Hmong, Pakistani, or Thai.

"Native Hawaiian and Other Pacific Islander" refers to people having origins in any of the original peoples of Hawaii, Guam, Samoa, or other Pacific Islands. It includes people who indicated their race or races as "Native Hawaiian," "Guamanian or Chamorro," "Samoan," or "Other Pacific Islander," or wrote in entries such as Tahitian, Mariana Islander, or Chuukese.

"Some other race" was included in Census 2000 for respondents who were unable to identify with the five Office of Management and Budget race categories. Respondents who provided write-in entries such as Moroccan, South African, Belizean, or a Hispanic origin (for example, Mexican, Puerto Rican, or Cuban) are included in the Some other race category (U.S. Census 2000).

Compare total U.S. population to trends shown in Appendix figures.

Compare the size of the total population at the bottom of the page to the trends observed in figures in the Appendix. Is the group overrepresented? For example, Figure 26 shows us that 89% of all lawyers are white although whites make up 74% of the total U.S. population. Whites are overrepresented in the field of law. Or is it the case that a group is underrepresented? Figure 27 shows us that 5% of all physicians are Latinos but Latinos make up 15% of the total U.S. population. Latinos are underrepresented as physicians.

The U.S. population is 74% white (including Latinos who define themselves as white). The total U.S. population comprises: non-Hispanic white, 67%; black, 12.4%; Latino, 14.8%; Asian, 4.4%; and American Indian, 0.8%.

FIGURE 1 Changes to Race and Ethnicity Categories on the U.S. Census, 1790–2000.

Year	Categories included	Categories eliminated
1790	Free White male/female, Non-taxed Indian, Slaves (3/5 of a person)	
1870	White, Black, mulatto, quadroon, octoroon, Indian	Non-taxed Indian, slaves, free White
1890	White, Black, mulatto, quadroon, octoroon, Indian, Japanese, Chinese	
1900	Black, White, Japanese, Chinese, Indian	Mulatto, quadroon, octoroon
1910	Black, White, Japanese, Chinese, Indian, mulatto	
1930	White, Black, Japanese, Chinese, Indian, Hindu, Korean, Mexican	Mulatto
1940	White, Black, Japanese, Chinese, Indian, Hindu, Korean	Mexican
1950	White, Black, Japanese, Chinese, American Indian	Hindu, Korean
1960	White, Black, Japanese, Chinese, American Indian, Hawaiian, part-Hawaiian, Aleut, Eskimo	
1980	White, Black or African American, American Indian and Alaska Native, Asian, Native Hawaiian and Other Pacific Islander	
2000	"check all that apply" system implemented	

Source: Dispatches from the Color Line: The Press and Multiracial America. Suny Press 2007 Catherine R. Squires.

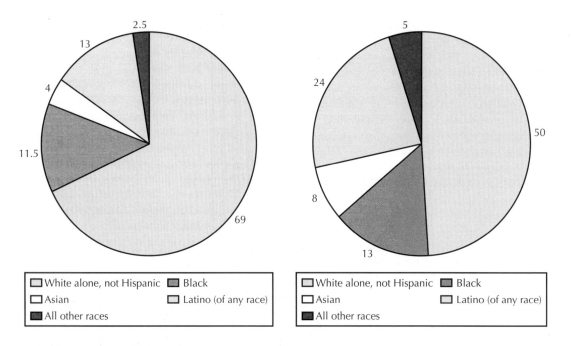

FIGURE 2 Population of the U.S. 2000 and Projected 2050. *Source:* Data from U.S. Census Bureau, 2004, "U.S. Interim Projections by Age, Sex, Race, and Hispanic Origin," http://www.census.gov/ipc/www/usinterimproj/.

The U.S. population is 74% white (including Latinos who define themselves as white). The total U.S. population comprises: non-Hispanic white, 67%; black, 12.4%; Latino, 14.8%; Asian, 4.4%; and American Indian, 0.8%.

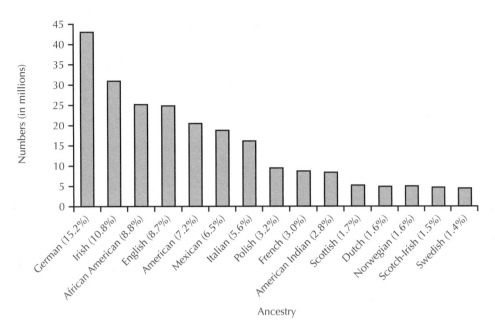

FIGURE 3 **Fifteen Largest Ancestries.** *Source:* Data from U.S. Census Bureau, Census 2000 special tabulation. *Note:* Percent of total population in parenthesis. Data based on sample.

Section I: Education

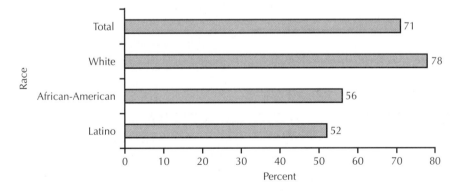

FIGURE 4 **High School Graduation Rates for 2002.** *Source:* Data from Manhattan Institute, Education Working Paper No. 8, February 2005.

The U.S. population is 74% white (including Latinos who define themselves as white). The total U.S. population comprises: non-Hispanic white, 67%; black, 12.4%; Latino, 14.8%; Asian, 4.4%; and American Indian, 0.8%.

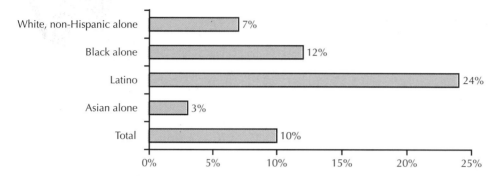

FIGURE 5 **High School Dropout Rates for 2004.** *Source:* Data from Child Trends'
calculations of U.S. Census Bureau, *School Enrollment—Social and Economic Characteristics of Students: October 2004:
Detailed Tables:* Table 1.

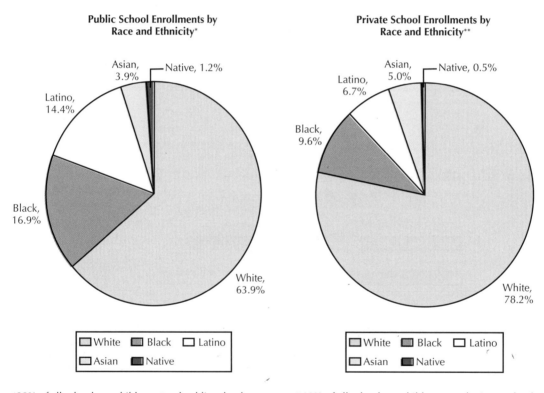

*90% of all school age children attend public school.   **10% of all school age children attend private school.

FIGURE 6 **Racial Composition of Public and Private Schools.** *Source:* Data from Common
Core of Data, 1997–98 and Private School Survey, 1997–98.

The U.S. population is 74% white (including Latinos who define themselves as white). The total U.S. population
comprises: non-Hispanic white, 67%; black, 12.4%; Latino, 14.8%; Asian, 4.4%; and American Indian, 0.8%.

FIGURE 7   Degrees Conferred.

Racial/Ethnic Group	BA	MA	Law	MD	PhD
White	70.0	60.3	83.0	68.6	81.0
Black	8.7	7.8	4.4	6.7	7.0
Latino	6.3	4.4	6.6	6.4	5.0
Asian	6.2	4.8	7.4	15.6	6.0
Native American	0.7	0.5	0.5	1.4	<1

Source: Data from U.S. Department of Education, National Center for Education Statistics, Integrated Postsecondary Education Data System (IPEDS), Fall 2003, National Postsecondary Student Aid Study (NPSAS; 2000), and NSF/NIH/USED/USDA/NASA, Survey of Earned Doctorates by U.S. Citizens, 2003.

Section II: Housing

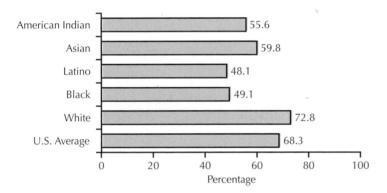

FIGURE 8   Homeownership Rates for 2003. *Source:* Data from
U.S. Bureau of the Census: Home Ownership Rates by Race and Ethnicity of Householder, Annual Statistics 2003.

FIGURE 9   Index of Dissimilarity for the USA.

	Black	Latino	Asian	Native American
Dissimilarity Index 2000 (weighted averages)	64	51	41	33

Source: Data from U.S. Bureau of the Census, 2000 Summary File 1.
Note: A zero on this index would mean that racial groups are evenly integrated throughout a city. A score of one hundred means complete racial segregation among groups.

The U.S. population is 74% white (including Latinos who define themselves as white). The total U.S. population comprises: non-Hispanic white, 67%; black, 12.4%; Latino, 14.8%; Asian, 4.4%; and American Indian, 0.8%.

Figure 10 Segregation from Whites in the Largest 10 Metropolitan Areas.

Metropolitan Area	Population (millions)	Black	Latino	Asian
Los Angeles—Long Beach	9.5	67.5	63.2	48.3
New York	9.3	81.8	66.7	50.5
Chicago	8.3	80.8	62.1	44.4
Philadelphia	5.1	72.3	60.2	43.8
Washington, DC	4.9	63.1	48.4	39.0
Detroit	4.4	84.7	45.7	45.9
Houston	4.2	67.5	55.7	49.4
Atlanta	4.1	65.6	52.5	45.2
Dallas	3.5	59.4	54.1	45.0
Boston	3.4	65.7	58.8	44.9

Source: Data from John R. Logan, Brian Stults, and Reynolds Farley. 2004. "Segregation of Minorities in the Metropolis: Two Decades of Change" Demography 41: 1–22. For more information, see http://browns4.dyndns.org/cen2000_s4.

Note: A zero on this index would mean that racial groups are evenly integrated throughout a city. A score of one hundred means complete racial segregation among groups.

Section III: Health

FIGURE 11 Health Disparities by Race.

	White	Black	Latino	Asian	AI/NA
Heart disease (%)	26.9	40.1	27.7	5.4	n/a
Premature deaths (%)	14.7	31.5	23.5	n/a	36.0
High blood pressure (%)	31.1	43.2	18.6	16.3	20.7
Overweight and obesity rate (%)	55.3	65.8	57.6	35.9	61.6
Birthrate (births/1000)	11.7	16.1	22.6	16.5	13.8
Infant mortality (death/1000)	5.7	13.5	5.4	4.7	9.7
Rate of teen births (births/1000)	28.5	68.3	83.4	18.3	53.8
Cases of HIV (rates 100K)	12.3	18.4	39.7	8.6	16.9
Distribution of new AIDS cases (%)	31.1	48.2	18.5	1.3	0.5
Tuberculosis (rates 100K)	1.5	12.6	10.4	27.8	6.8
Cigarette smoking (%)	23.3	21.7	18.5	13.7	38.4

Source: Data from U.S. Bureau of the Census, updated July 2005.

The U.S. population is 74% white (including Latinos who define themselves as white). The total U.S. population comprises: non-Hispanic white, 67%; black, 12.4%; Latino, 14.8%; Asian, 4.4%; and American Indian, 0.8%.

FIGURE 12 Percentage of Americans Uninsured by Race.

	Uninsured Non-Elderly	Uninsured Children
White	13%	6%
Black	21%	9%
Latino	34%	20%
Other	19%	15%
USA	16%	10%

Source: Data from National Health Interview Survey, 2003.

Section IV: Crime

FIGURE 13 Percentage of Crime in the U.S. by Race and Ethnicity.

	White	Black	Asian	Native American
Murder & non-negligent manslaughter	42.5	55.4	1.4	0.7
Forcible rape	58.7	38.7	1.5	1.1
Robbery	42.8	55.4	1.2	0.6
Aggravated assault	61.7	36.0	1.3	1.0
Burglary	67.2	30.8	1.1	0.9
Larceny-theft	67.9	29.2	1.6	1.4
Motor vehicle theft	57.4	39.8	1.8	0.9
Arson	74.7	23.6	0.8	0.9
Violent crime	57.5	40.3	1.3	0.9
Property crime	66.9	30.4	1.5	1.2

Source: Data from U.S. Bureau of Justice Statistics, 2002.

The U.S. population is 74% white (including Latinos who define themselves as white). The total U.S. population comprises: non-Hispanic white, 67%; black, 12.4%; Latino, 14.8%; Asian, 4.4%; and American Indian, 0.8%.

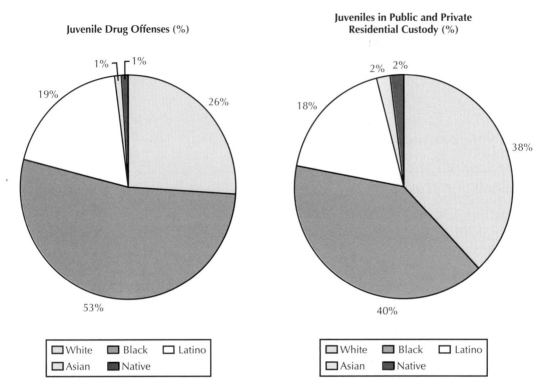

Juvenile Drug Offenses (%)

1% ⌐1%
19%
26%
53%

White Black Latino
Asian Native

Juveniles in Public and Private Residential Custody (%)

2% 2%
18%
38%
40%

White Black Latino
Asian Native

FIGURE 14 **Juvenile Crime Statistics.** *Source:* Data from U.S. Bureau of Justice Statistics, 2002.

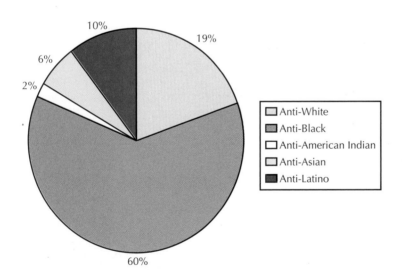

10%
19%
6%
2%
60%

Anti-White
Anti-Black
Anti-American Indian
Anti-Asian
Anti-Latino

FIGURE 15 **Hate Crimes by Race.** *Source:* FBI's Uniform Crime Report, 2003.

The U.S. population is 74% white (including Latinos who define themselves as white). The total U.S. population comprises: non-Hispanic white, 67%; black, 12.4%; Latino, 14.8%; Asian, 4.4%; and American Indian, 0.8%.

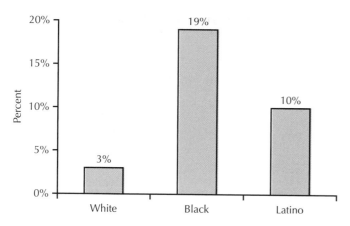

FIGURE 16 Lifetime Chances of Going to Prison.
Source: Data from U.S. Bureau of Justice Statistics, 2001.

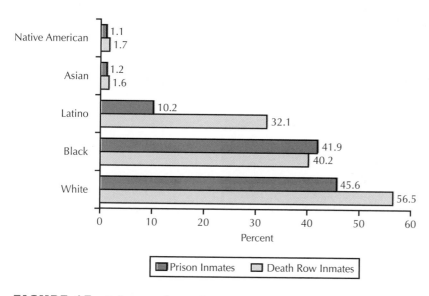

FIGURE 17 **Prison and Death Row Inmates.** *Source:* Data from U.S. Department of Justice and Death Row USA Spring 2004.

The U.S. population is 74% white (including Latinos who define themselves as white). The total U.S. population comprises: non-Hispanic white, 67%; black, 12.4%; Latino, 14.8%; Asian, 4.4%; and American Indian, 0.8%.

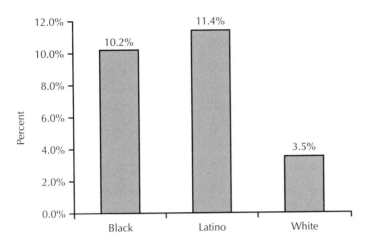

FIGURE 18 **Likelihood of Being Searched during a Traffic Stop.** *Source:* Data from U.S. Bureau of Justice Statistics, 2002.

Section V: Computers

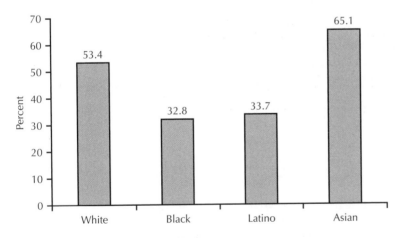

FIGURE 19 **Families Who Own Computers (Income $15–30K, 2000).** *Source:* Data from U.S. Bureau of the Census.

The U.S. population is 74% white (including Latinos who define themselves as white). The total U.S. population comprises: non-Hispanic white, 67%; black, 12.4%; Latino, 14.8%; Asian, 4.4%; and American Indian, 0.8%.

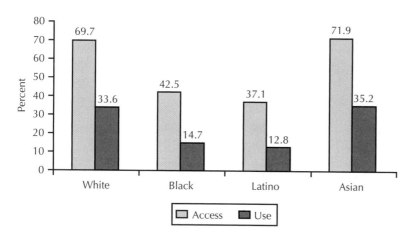

FIGURE 20 Computer Access and Use by Children 3–17 Years Old.

Source: Data from U.S. Bureau of the Census, 2000.

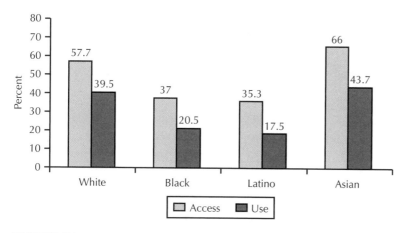

FIGURE 21 Computer Access and Use by Persons 18 and Older.

Source: Data from U.S. Bureau of the Census, 2000.

Section VI: Income, Weath, and Poverty

FIGURE 22 Median Household Income, 2007.

White	Black	Latino	Asian
$54,920	$33,916	$38,679	$66,103

Source: http://www.census.gov/Press-Release/www/releases/archives/income_wealth/012528.html.

The U.S. population is 74% white (including Latinos who define themselves as white). The total U.S. population comprises: non-Hispanic white, 67%; black, 12.4%; Latino, 14.8%; Asian, 4.4%; and American Indian, 0.8%.

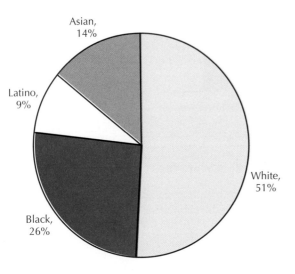

The Poor: Households with Incomes
between $2500 and $4999

Asian,
14%

Latino,
9%

White,
51%

Black,
26%

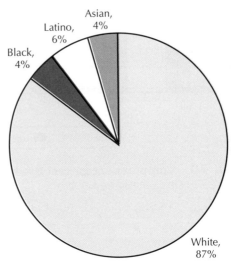

The Rich: Households with Incomes
over $250,000

Asian,
4%

Latino,
6%

Black,
4%

White,
87%

FIGURE 23   Who Is Rich, Who Is Poor.

Source: U.S. Census current population survey, 2006.

FIGURE 24   Poverty in the United States.

	White	Black	Latino	Asian
% of population living in poverty (2002)	17.6	29.9	13.4	24.5
Related kids under 18 in families living in poverty (2001)	8.9	30.0	27.4	11.1
Working poor (%) (1998)	6.9	13.6	19.2	n/a
Poverty (%) (2003)	8.2	24.3	22.5	11.8

Source: Data from U.S. Bureau of the Census, 2001–2003.

The U.S. population is 74% white (including Latinos who define themselves as white). The total U.S. population comprises: non-Hispanic white, 67%; black, 12.4%; Latino, 14.8%; Asian, 4.4%; and American Indian, 0.8%.

Section VII: Employment

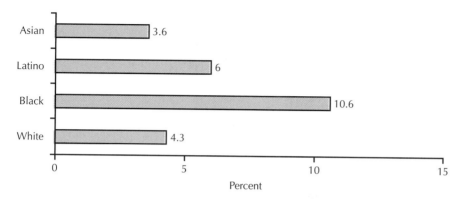

FIGURE 25 **Unemployment Statistics.** *Source:* U.S. Bureau of Labor Statistics, 2004–2005.

Section VIII: Occupations

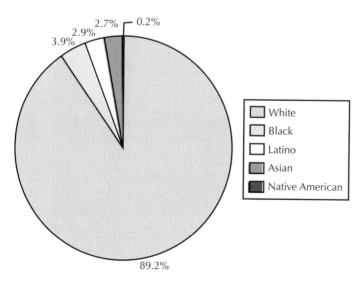

FIGURE 26 **Lawyers by Race and Ethnicity.** *Source:* Data from U.S. Census Bureau 1 Percent Public Use Microdata Sample Surveys, 201, 2000. *Note:* Numbers are the percent of the population.

The U.S. population is 74% white (including Latinos who define themselves as white). The total U.S. population comprises: non-Hispanic white, 67%; black, 12.4%; Latino, 14.8%; Asian, 4.4%; and American Indian, 0.8%.

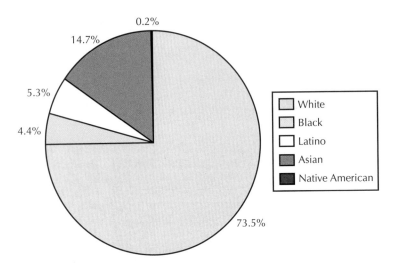

FIGURE 27 **Physicians and Surgeons by Race and Ethnicity.** *Source:* Data from U.S. Census Bureau 1 Percent Public Use Microdata Sample Surveys, 201, 2000. *Note:* Numbers are the percent of the population.

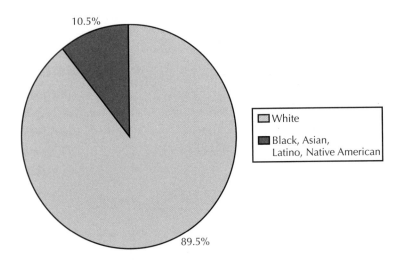

FIGURE 28 **Washington D.C. National Press Corps Reporters and Editor by Race and Ethnicity.** *Source:* Data from Unity, 2004. *Note:* Numbers are the percent of the population.

The U.S. population is 74% white (including Latinos who define themselves as white). The total U.S. population comprises: non-Hispanic white, 67%; black, 12.4%; Latino, 14.8%; Asian, 4.4%; and American Indian, 0.8%.

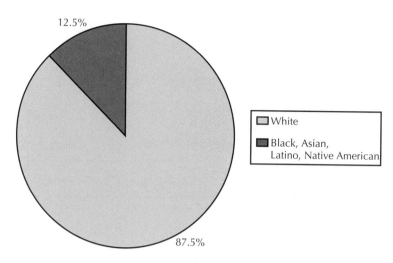

12.5%

87.5%

White
Black, Asian, Latino, Native American

FIGURE 29 **Newsrooms Nationwide by Race and Ethnicity.**
Source: Data from Unity, 2004. *Note:* Numbers are the percent of the population.

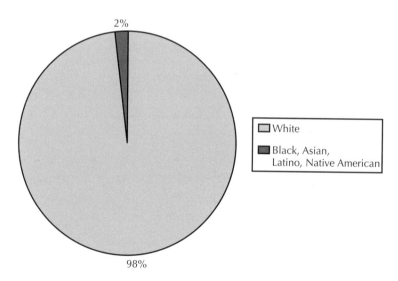

2%

98%

White
Black, Asian, Latino, Native American

FIGURE 30 **CEOs of Fortune 500 Companies by Race and Ethnicity.** *Source:* Data from Christian Science Monitor, October 31, 2005. *Note:* Numbers are the percent of the population.

The U.S. population is 74% white (including Latinos who define themselves as white). The total U.S. population comprises: non-Hispanic white, 67%; black, 12.4%; Latino, 14.8%; Asian, 4.4%; and American Indian, 0.8%.

FIGURE 31   Other Occupations by Race and Ethnicity.

	White	Black	Latino	Asian	Native American
Registered Nurses	80.4	8.9	3.4	5.5	0.4
Engineers	80.9	4.2	3.9	9.2	0.3
Police Supervisors	81.4	9.5	6.1	0.5	0.9
Police/Detectives	76.6	11.4	8.5	1.4	0.7
College Instructors	79.7	5.6	4.5	8.1	0.4
Judges/Hearing Examiners/JPs/some Arbitrators	82.1	12.0	3.4	1.4	0.9
Clergy	81.8	8.4	3.9	4.1	0.7
Information Technology	73.8	7.6	5.1	11.4	0.3
School Teachers	81.8	9.0	5.7	1.8	0.5

Source: Data from U.S. Census Bureau 1 Percent Public Use Microdata Sample Surveys, 201, 2000.

Section IX: Government

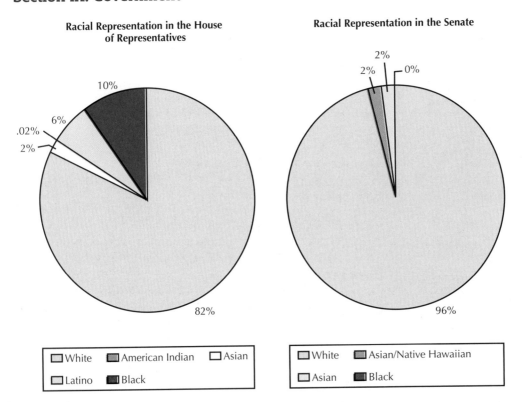

Racial Representation in the House of Representatives

10%
6%
.02%
2%
82%

□ White   ▨ American Indian   □ Asian
□ Latino   ▧ Black

Racial Representation in the Senate

2%
2%   0%
96%

□ White   ▨ Asian/Native Hawaiian
□ Asian   ▧ Black

FIGURE 32   Racial/Ethnic Representation in the 112th Congress. *Source:* Data from U.S. House of Representatives, House Press Gallery; U.S. Senate, Daily Press Gallery, Minority Senators, 2010.

The U.S. population is 74% white (including Latinos who define themselves as white). The total U.S. population comprises: non-Hispanic white, 67%; black, 12.4%; Latino, 14.8%; Asian, 4.4%; and American Indian, 0.8%.

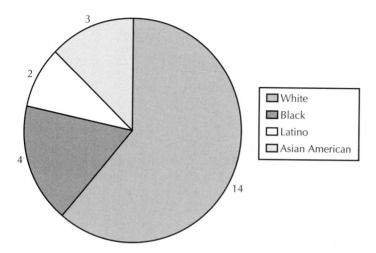

FIGURE 33 **Racial Representation in the Presidential Cabinet 2011.**

Source: House Press Gallery: *The President's Cabinet;* The White House.

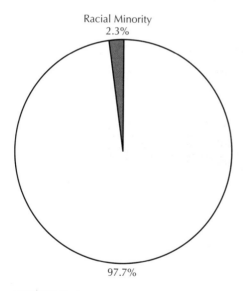

FIGURE 34 **Race of Presidents as of 2011.**

The U.S. population is 74% white (including Latinos who define themselves as white). The total U.S. population comprises: non-Hispanic white, 67%; black, 12.4%; Latino, 14.8%; Asian, 4.4%; and American Indian, 0.8%.

Section X: New Boundaries: Immigration and Interracial Couples

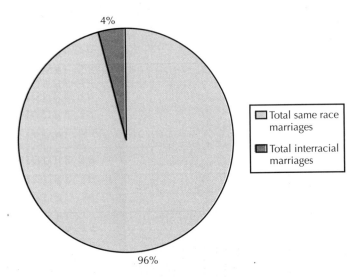

4%

96%

Total same race marriages

Total interracial marriages

FIGURE 35 **Interracial Married Couples 2003.**

Source: Data from U.S. Census Bureau, *Statistical Abstract of the United States: 2004–2005.*

FIGURE 36 **Ten Largest Cities and Their Multiracial Populations 2000.**

Place	Total population		Two or more races population		
	Rank	Number	Rank	Number	Percent
New York, NY	1	8,008,278	1	393,959	4.9
Los Angeles, CA	2	3,694,820	2	191,288	5.2
Chicago, IL	3	2,896,016	3	84,437	2.9
Houston, TX	4	1,953,631	4	61,478	3.1
Philadelphia, PA	5	1,517,550	10	33,574	2.2
Phoenix, AZ	6	1,321,045	8	43,276	3.3
San Diego, CA	7	1,223,400	5	59,081	4.8
Dallas, TX	8	1,188,580	12	32,351	2.7
San Antonio, TX	9	1,144,646	9	41,871	3.7
Detroit, MI	10	951,270	18	22,041	2.3
Honolulu, HI	46	371,657	6	55,474	14.9
San Jose, CA	11	894,943	7	45,062	5.0

Source: Data from U.S. Census Bureau, Census 2000 Restricting Data (Public Law 94–171) Summary File, Table PL1.

The U.S. population is 74% white (including Latinos who define themselves as white). The total U.S. population comprises: non-Hispanic white, 67%; black, 12.4%; Latino, 14.8%; Asian, 4.4%; and American Indian, 0.8%.

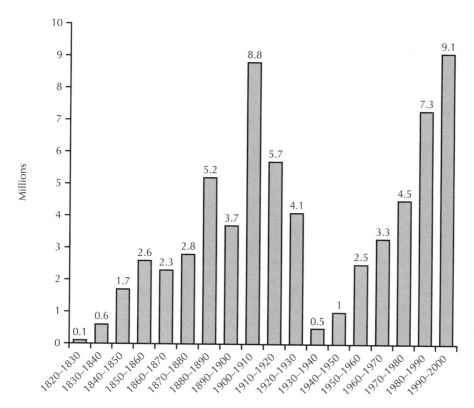

FIGURE 37   Total Immigration to the United States from 1820 to 2000, by Decade. *Source:* Data from U.S. Immigration and Naturalization Service.

The U.S. population is 74% white (including Latinos who define themselves as white). The total U.S. population comprises: non-Hispanic white, 67%; black, 12.4%; Latino, 14.8%; Asian, 4.4%; and American Indian, 0.8%.

FIGURE 38   Settlement Patterns of Immigrants.

		Immigrants		Share of Population	
		2000	*1990*	*2000*	*1990*
1	Los Angeles–Long Beach	3,449,444	2,892,456	36.2%	32.7%
2	New York, NY	3,139,647	2,285,024	33.7%	26.8%
3	Chicago, IL	1,425,978	885,081	17.2%	11.9%
4	Miami, FL	1,147,765	874,569	50.9%	45.1%
5	Houston, TX	854,669	440,321	20.5%	13.3%
6	Orange County, CA	849,899	575,108	29.9%	23.9%
7	Washington, DC	832,016	489,641	16.9%	11.6%
8	Riverside–San Bernardino, CA	612,359	360,643	18.8%	13.9%
9	San Diego, CA	606,254	428,810	21.5%	17.2%
10	Dallas, TX	591,169	234,522	16.8%	8.8%
11	Oakland, CA	573,144	337,435	24.0%	16.2%
12	San Jose, CA	573,130	347,201	34.1%	23.2%
13	San Francisco, CA	554,819	441,290	32.0%	27.5%

Source: Data from John R. Logan. 2006. "Settlement Patterns of Immigrants in Metropolitan America" in Mary Waters and Reed Ueda (eds.), *The New Americans: A Handbook to Immigration Since 1965*. Harvard University Press, 2007.

The U.S. population is 74% white (including Latinos who define themselves as white). The total U.S. population comprises: non-Hispanic white, 67%; black, 12.4%; Latino, 14.8%; Asian, 4.4%; and American Indian, 0.8%.

Notes and References

READING 2

References

Aptheker, Herbert, ed. 1974. *A Documentary History of the Negro People in the United States.* Secaucus, NJ: Citadel.

Boskin, Joseph. 1966. *Into Slavery: Radical Decisions in the Virginia Colony.* Philadelphia: Lippincott.

Catterall, Helen. 1937. *Judicial Cases Concerning American Slavery and the Negro.* 5 vols. Washington, DC: Negro University Press.

Davidson, Basil. 1961. *The African Slave Trade.* Boston: Little, Brown.

Donnan, Elizabeth, ed. 1965. *Documents Illustrative of the History of the Slave Trade to America.* 4 vols. New York: Octagon.

Elkins, Stanley. 1976. *Slavery: A Problem in American Institutional and Intellectual Life.* Chicago: University of Chicago Press.

Federal Writers Project. 1969. *The Negro in Virginia.* New York: Arno.

Franklin, John Hope. 1974. *From Slavery to Freedom: A History of American Negroes.* New York: Knopf.

Jordan, Winthrop. 1968. *White over Black: American Attitudes toward the Negro, 1550–1812.* Chapel Hill: University of North Carolina Press.

Morgan, Edmund S. 1975. *American Slavery, American Freedom: The Ordeal of Colonial Virginia.* New York: Norton.

Mullin, Gerald. 1974. *Flight and Rebellion: Slave Resistance in Eighteenth-Century Virginia.* New York: Oxford University Press.

Mullin, Michael, ed. 1975. *American Negro Slavery: A Documentary History.* New York: Harper & Row.

Phillips, Ulrich B. 1966. *American Negro Slavery: A Survey of the Supply, Employment and Control of Negro Labor as Determined by the Plantation Regime.* Baton Rouge: Louisiana State University Press.

Redding, J. Saunders. 1973. *They Came in Chains.* Philadelphia: Lippincott.

Stampp, Kenneth M. 1956. *The Peculiar Institution.* New York: Knopf.

Tannenbaum, Frank. 1963. *Slave and Citizen: The Negro in the Americas.* New York: Random House.

READING 3

Notes

1. *San Francisco Chronicle,* 14 September 1982, 19 May 1983. Ironically, the 1970 Louisiana law was enacted to supersede an old Jim Crow statute which relied on the idea of "common report" in determining an infant's race. Following Phipps's unsuccessful attempt to change her classification and have the law declared unconstitutional, a legislative effort arose which culminated in the repeal of the law. See *San Francisco Chronicle,* 23 June 1983.

2. The Mormon church, for example, has been heavily criticized for its doctrine of black inferiority.

3. Thomas F. Gossett notes:

   Race theory . . . had up until fairly modern times no firm hold on European thought. On the other hand, race theory and race prejudice were by no means unknown at the time when the English colonists came to North America. Undoubtedly, the age of exploration led many to speculate on race differences at a period when neither Europeans nor Englishmen were prepared to make allowances for vast cultural diversities. Even though race theories had not then secured wide acceptance or even sophisticated formulation, the first contacts of the Spanish with the Indians in the Americas can now be recognized as the beginning of a struggle between conceptions of the nature of primitive peoples which has not yet been wholly settled. (Thomas F. Gossett, *Race: The History of an Idea in America* [New York: Schocken Books, 1965], p. 16.)

   Winthrop Jordan provides a detailed account of early European colonialists' attitudes about color and race in *White over Black: American Attitudes Toward the Negro, 1550–1812* (New York: Norton, 1977 [1968]), pp. 3–43.

4. Pro-slavery physician Samuel George Morton (1799–1851) compiled a collection of 800 crania from all parts of the world which formed the sample for his studies of race. Assuming that the larger the size of the cranium translated into greater intelligence, Morton established a relationship between race and skull capacity. Gossett reports that:

   In 1849, one of his studies included the following results: The English skulls in his collection proved to be the largest, with an average cranial capacity of 96 cubic inches. The Americans and Germans were rather poor seconds, both with cranial capacities of 90 cubic inches. At the bottom of the list were the Negroes with 83 cubic inches, the Chinese with 82, and the Indians with 79. (Ibid., p. 74.)

On Morton's methods, see Stephen J. Gould, "The Finagle Factor," *Human Nature* (July 1978).

5. Definitions of race founded upon a common pool of genes have not held up when confronted by scientific research which suggests that the differences *within* a given human population are greater than those between populations. See L. L. Cavalli-Sforza, "The Genetics of Human Populations," *Scientific American,* September 1974, pp. 81–89.

6. Arthur Jensen, "How Much Can We Boost IQ and Scholastic Achievement?" *Harvard Educational Review* 39 (1969):1–123.

7. Ernst Moritz Manasse, "Max Weber on Race," *Social Research* 14 (1947):191–221.

8. Quoted in Edward D. C. Campbell, Jr., *The Celluloid South: Hollywood and the Southern Myth* (Knoxville: University of Tennessee Press, 1981), pp. 168–70.

9. Marvin Harris, *Patterns of Race in the Americas* (New York: Norton, 1964), p. 56.

10. Ibid., p. 57.

11. After James Meredith had been admitted as the first black student at the University of Mississippi, Harry S. Murphy announced that he, and not Meredith, was the first black student to attend "Ole Miss." Murphy described himself as black but was able to pass for white and spent nine months at the institution without attracting any notice (Ibid., p. 56).

12. A. Sivanandan, "From Resistance to Rebellion: Asian and Afro-Caribbean Struggles in Britain," *Race and Class* 23(2–3) (Autumn–Winter 1981).

13. Gordon W. Allport, *The Nature of Prejudice* (Garden City, NY: Doubleday, 1958), pp. 184–200.

14. We wish to use this phrase loosely, without committing ourselves to a particular position on such social psychological approaches as symbolic interactionism, which are outside the scope of this study. An interesting study on this subject is S. M. Lyman and W. A. Douglass, "Ethnicity: Strategies of Individual and Collective Impression Management," *Social Research* 40(2) (1973).

15. Michael Billig, "Patterns of Racism: Interviews with National Front Members," *Race and Class* 20(2) (Autumn 1978):161–79.

16. "Miss San Antonio USA Lisa Fernandez and other Hispanics auditioning for a role in a television soap-opera did not fit the Hollywood image of real Mexicans and had to darken their faces before filming." Model Aurora Garza said that their faces were bronzed with powder because they looked too white. "'I'm a real Mexican [Garza said] and very dark anyway. I'm even darker right now because I have a tan. But they kept wanting me to make my face darker and darker" (*San Francisco Chronicle,* 21 September 1984). A similar dilemma faces Asian American actors who feel that Asian character lead roles inevitably go to white actors who make themselves up to be Asian. Scores of Charlie Chan films, for example, have been made with white leads (the last one was the 1981 *Charlie Chan and the Curse of the Dragon Queen*). Roland Winters, who played in six Chan features, was asked by playwright Frank Chin to explain the logic of casting a white man in the role of Charlie Chan: "'The only thing I can think of is, if you want to cast a homosexual in a show, and get a homosexual, it'll be awful. It won't be funny . . . and may be there's something there . . .'" (Frank Chin, "Confessions of the Chinatown Cowboy," *Bulletin of Concerned Asian Scholars* 4(3) (Fall 1972)).

17. Melanie Martindale-Sikes, "Nationalizing 'Nigger' Imagery Through 'Birth of a Nation,'" paper prepared for the 73rd Annual Meeting of the American Sociological Association, 4–8 September 1978, San Francisco.

18. Jordan, *White over Black,* p. 95; emphasis added.

19. Historical focus has been placed either on particular racially defined groups or on immigration and the "incorporation" of ethnic groups. In the former case the characteristic ethnicity theory pitfalls and apologetics such as functionalism and cultural pluralism may be avoided, but only by sacrificing much of the focus on race. In the latter case, race is considered a manifestation of ethnicity.

20. The degree of antipathy for these groups should not be minimized. A northern commentator observed in the 1850s: "An Irish Catholic seldom attempts to rise to a higher condition than that in which he is placed, while the Negro often makes the attempt with success." Quoted in Gossett, op. cit., p. 288.

21. This analysis, as will perhaps be obvious, is essentially DuBoisian. Its main source will be found in the monumental (and still largely unappreciated) *Black Reconstruction in the United States, 1860–1880* (New York: Atheneum, 1977 [1935]).

22. Alexander Saxton argues that:

North Americans of European background have experienced three great racial confrontations: with the Indian, with the African, and with the Oriental. Central to each transaction has been a totally one-sided preponderance of power, exerted for the exploitation of nonwhites by the dominant white society. In each case (but especially in the two that began with systems of enforced labor), white workingmen have played a crucial, yet ambivalent, role. They have been both exploited and exploiters. On the one hand, thrown into competition with nonwhites as enslaved or "cheap" labor they suffered economically; on the other hand, being white, they benefited by that very exploitation which was compelling the nonwhites to work for low wages or for nothing. Ideologically they were drawn in opposite directions. *Racial identification cut at right angles to class consciousness.* (Alexander Saxton, *The Indispensable Enemy: Labor and the Anti-Chinese Movement in California* [Berkeley and Los Angeles: University of California Press, 1971], p. 1; emphasis added.)

23. Selig Perlman, *The History of Trade Unionism in the United States* (New York: Augustus Kelley, 1950), p. 52; emphasis added.

24. Whether southern blacks were "peasants" or rural workers is unimportant in this context. Some time during the 1960s blacks attained a higher degree of urbanization than whites. Before World War II most blacks had been rural dwellers and nearly 80 percent lived in the South.

25. See George Gilder, *Wealth and Poverty* (New York: Basic Books, 1981); Charles Murray, *Losing Ground* (New York: Basic Books, 1984).

26. A brilliant study of the racialization process in Britain, focused on the rise of "mugging" as a popular fear in the 1970s, is Stuart Hall et al., *Policing the Crisis* (London: Macmillan, 1978).

27. The case of Vincent Chin, a Chinese American man beaten to death in 1982 by a laid-off Detroit auto worker and his stepson who mistook him for Japanese and blamed him for the loss of their jobs, has been widely publicized in Asian American communities. On immigration conflicts and pressures, see Michael Omi, "New Wave Dread: Immigration and Intra–Third World Conflict," *Socialist Review* 60 (November–December 1981).

READING 4

References

Anderson, Margo J. 1988. *The American Census: A Social History.* New Haven: Yale University Press.

Blumenbach, Johann Friedrich. 1776. *On the Natural Varieties of Mankind.* New York: Bergman, 1969.

Cavalli-Sforza, Luigi Luca. 2001. *Genes, Peoples, and Languages.* Berkeley: University of California Press.

Erlich, Paul, and Marcus Feldman. 2003. Genes and Cultures: What Creates Our Behavioral Phenome? *Current Anthropology* 44:87-107.

Fredrickson, George M. 2002. *Racism: A Short History.* Princeton, NJ: Princeton University Press.

Gould, Stephen Jay. 1996. *The Mismeasure of Man.* New York: W. W. Norton.

McKee, James B. 1993. *Sociology and the Race Problem: The Failure of a Perspective.* Urbana: University of Illinois Press.

Office of Management and Budget (OMB). 1977. *Directive No. 15, Race and Ethnic Standards for Federal Statistics and Administrative Reporting.* Washington, DC: United States Office of Management and Budget.

Omi, Michael, and Howard Winant. 1994. *Racial Formation in the United States: From the 1960s to the 1990s.* New York: Routledge Press.

Peterson, William. 1980. Concepts of Ethnicity. In *Harvard Encyclopedia of American Ethnic Groups,* edited by Stephan Thernstrom. Cambridge, MA: Harvard University Press.

Simpson, George Eaton, and J. Milton Yinger. 1953. *Racial and Cultural Minorities: An Analysis of Prejudice and Discrimination.* New York: Harper & Bros.

Snipp, C. Matthew. 1989. *American Indians: The First of This Land.* New York: Russell Sage Foundation.

———. 2003. Racial Measurement in the American Census: Past Practices and Implications for the Future. *Annual Review of Sociology* 29: 563-588.

READING 5

Notes

1. All racialized social systems operate along white supremacist lines. See Charles W. Mills, *Blackness Visible* (Ithaca, NY: Cornell University Press, 1998).

2. I make a distinction between race and ethnicity. Ethnicity has a primarily sociocultural foundation, and ethnic groups have exhibited tremendous malleability in terms of who belongs. In contrast, racial ascriptions (initially) are imposed externally to justify the collective exploitation of a people and are maintained to preserve status differences. The distinction I make was part of a debate that appeared recently in the *American Sociological Review.* For specialists interested in this matter, see Bonilla-Silva, "The Essential Social Fact of Race," *American Sociological Review* 64, no. 6 (1999): 899–906.

3. Herbert Blumer was one of the first analysts to make this argument about systemic rewards received by the races ascribed the primary position in a racial order. See Herbert Blumer, "Reflections on Theory of Race Relations," pp. 3–21 in *Race Relations in World Perspective,* edited by A. W. Lind (Honolulu, HI: University of Hawaii Press, 1955). Du Bois's argument about the psychological wages of whiteness has been used recently by Manning Marable, *How Capitalism Underdeveloped Black America;* and by David Roediger, *The Wages of Whiteness.*

4. This point has been made by Michel Omi and Howard Winant, *Racial Formation in the United States;* Winant, *Racial Conditions.*

5. I am referring to cases such as Haiti. Nonetheless, recent research has suggested that even in such places, the abolition of slavery did not end the racialized character of the social formation. See Michel-Rolph Troillot, *Haiti, State Agency Nation: Origins and Legacy of Duvalierism* (New York: Monthly Review Press, 1990).

6. For a similar argument, see Floya Anthias and Nira Yuval-Davis, *Racialized Boundaries: Race, Nation, Gender, Colour, and the Anti-Racist Struggle* (London, England: Tavistock, 1992).

7. For an early statement on this matter, see Hubert M. Blalock, Jr., *Toward a Theory of Minority-Majority Group Relations* (New York: John Wiley and Sons, 1967). For a more recent statement, see Susan Olzack, *The Dynamics of Ethnic Competition and Conflict* (Stanford, CA: Stanford University Press, 1992).

8. Nineteenth-century nation-building processes throughout Latin America included the myth of racial democracy and color- or race-blindness. This facilitated the struggles for independence and the maintenance of white supremacy in societies wherein white elites were demographically insignificant. For discussions pertinent to this argument see the excellent collection edited by Michael Hanchard, *Racial Politics in Contemporary Brazil* (Durham and London: Duke University Press, 1999).

9. See my "The Essential Social Fact of Race," *American Sociological Review* 64, no. 6 (December 1999): 899–906.

10. On this point, see Warren Whatley and Gavin Wright, *Race, Human Capital, and Labor Markets in American History,* Working Paper #7 (Ann Arbor, MI: Center for Afroamerican and Africa Studies, University of Michigan, 1994). For an incisive discussion, see Samuel L. Meyers, Jr., "Measuring and Detecting Discrimination in the Post–Civil Rights Era," pp. 172–197 in *Race and Ethnicity in Research Methods,* edited by John H. Stanfield II and Rutledge M. Dennis (London: Sage Publications, 1993).

11. Michael Reich, "The Economics of Racism," in *Racial Conflict, Discrimination, and Power: Historical and Contemporary Studies,* edited by William Barclay, Krishna Kumar, and Ruth P. Simms (New York: AMS Press, 1976), p. 224.

12. Omi and Winant, *Racial Formation in the United States,* 64.

13. On the invention of the white race, see Theodore W. Allen, *The Invention of the White Race,* Vol. I (London: Verso, 1994). On the invention of the "Indian" race, see Robert E. Berkhoffer, *The White Man's Indian* (New York: Vintage, 1978). On the invention of the black and white races, see Winthrop Jordan, *White over Black.*

14. A classic book on the ideological binary construction of the races in the United States is Thomas Gossett, *Race: The History of an Idea in America* (Dallas, TX: Southern Methodist University Press, 1963). For an analysis of an earlier period in the Americas, see Tzevetan Todorov, *The Conquest of America: The Question of the Other* (New York: Harper Colophon, 1984).

15. On this matter, I stated in my recent debate in the pages of the *American Sociological Review* with Mara Loveman that "'race,' like 'class' or 'gender,' is *always contingent* but is also *socially real.* Race operates 'as a shuttle between socially constructed meanings and practices, between subjective and lived, material reality' (Hanchard 1994:4)." (901). Michael G. Hanchard, *Orpheus and Power* (Princeton, NJ: Princeton University Press, 1994).

16. This last point is an extension of Nicos Poulantzas' view on class. Races—as classes—are not an "empirical thing"; they denote racialized social relations or racial practices at all levels. Poulantzas, *Political Power and Social Classes* (London: Verso, 1982), p. 67.

17. For a full discussion, see my "The Essential Social Fact of Race." For a similar argument, see Teresa Amott and Julie Matthaei, *Race, Gender, and Work: A Multicultural Economic History of Women in the United States* (Boston, MA: South End Press, 1996).

18. Frederick Barth, "Introduction," pp. 9–38 in *Ethnic Groups and Boundaries: The Social Organization of Culture Difference,* edited by F. Barth (Bergen, Norway: Universitetsforlaget, 1969).

19. For the case of the Jews, see Robert Miles, *Racism After "Race Relations"* (London: Routledge, 1993). For the case of the Irish, see Allen, *The Invention of the White Race.*

20. For a recent excellent discussion on ethnicity with many examples from the United States, see Stephen Cornell and Douglas Hartmann, *Ethnicity and Race: Making Identities in a Changing World* (London: Pine Forge Press, 1998).

21. Roediger, *The Wages of Whiteness.* See also Noel Ignatiev, *How the Irish Became White* (New York: Routledge, 1995).

22. For identity issues among Caribbean immigrants, see the excellent edited collection by Constance R. Sutton and E. M. Chaney, *Caribbean Life in New York City: Sociocultural Dimensions* (New York: Center for Migration Studies of New York, 1987).

23. Barth, "Introduction," 17.

24. A few notable discussions on this matter are Ira Berlin, *Slaves Without Masters: The Free Negro in Antebellum South* (New York: Pantheon, 1975); John Hope Franklin, *From Slavery to Freedom: A History of the Negro Americans* (New York: Alfred Knopf, 1974); August Meir and Elliot Rudwick, *From Plantation to Ghetto* (New York: Hill and Wang, 1970).

25. The motivation for racializing human relations may have originated in the interests of powerful actors, but after social systems are racialized, all members of the dominant race participate in defending and reproducing the racial structure. This is the crucial reason why Marxist analysts

(e.g., Cox, Reich) have not succeeded in successfully analyzing racism. They have not been able to accept the fact that after the phenomenon originated with the expansion of European capitalism into the New World, it acquired a life of its own. The subjects who were racialized as belonging to the superior race, whether or not they were members of the dominant class, became zealous defenders of the racial order.

26. Hillel Ticktin, *The Politics of Race: Discrimination in South Africa* (London: Pluto, 1991), p. 26.

27. The classic book on this is Paula Giddings, *When and Where I Enter: The Impact of Black Women on Race and Sex in America* (New York: Bantam, 1984). See also Nancy Caraway, *Segregated Sisterhood: Racism and the Politics of American Feminism* (Knoxville, TN: University of Tennessee Press, 1991).

28. This argument is not new. Analysts of the racial history of the United States have always pointed out that most of the significant historical changes in this country's race relations were accompanied by some degree of overt violence. See Harold Cruse, *Rebellion or Revolution* (New York: William Morrow, 1968); Franklin, *From Slavery to Freedom;* and James W. Button, *Blacks and Social Change: Impact of the Civil Rights Movement in Southern Communities* (Princeton, NJ: Princeton University Press, 1989).

29. This point is important in literature on revolutions and democracy. On the role of violence in the establishment of bourgeois democracies, see Barrington Moore, Jr., *Social Origins of Dictatorship and Democracy* (Boston, MA: Beacon Press, 1966). On the pivotal role of violence in social movements, see Frances Fox Piven and Richard A. Cloward, *Poor People's Movements: Why They Succeed, How They Fail* (New York: Vintage, 1979).

30. The notion of relative autonomy comes from the work of Poulantzas (*Power and Social Classes*) and implies that the ideological and political levels in a society are partially autonomous in relation to the economic level; that is, they are not merely expressions of the economic level.

31. Paul Gilroy, *"There Ain't No Black in the Union Jack": The Cultural Politics of Race and Nation* (Chicago, IL: University of Chicago Press, 1991), p. 17.

32. See Ellis Cose, *The Rage of a Privileged Class: Why Are Black Middle Class Angry? Why Should America Care?* (New York: HarperCollins, 1993); Lawrence Otis-Graham, *Member of the Club: Reflections on Life in a Racially Polarized World* (New York: HarperCollins, 1995).

33. In addition to the work by Joe R. Feagin and Hernán Vera already cited, see Lawrence Bobo, J. Kluegel, and R. Smith, "Laissez Faire Racism: The Crystallization of a Kinder, Gentler, Antiblack Ideology," and, particularly, Mary R.

Jackman, *Velvet Glove: Paternalism and Conflict in Gender, Class and Race Relations* (Berkeley, CA: University of California Press, 1994).

34. Curiously, historian Eugene Genovese made a similar argument in his book *Red and Black*. Although he still regarded racism as an ideology, he stated that once it "arises it alters profoundly the material reality and in fact becomes a partially autonomous feature of that reality." *Red and Black: Marxian Explorations in Southern and Afroamerican History* (New York: Pantheon, 1971), p. 340.

35. Stuart Hall, "Race Articulation and Societies Structured in Dominance," in *Sociological Theories: Race and Colonialism,* edited by UNESCO (Paris: UNESCO, 1980), p. 336.

36. Actions by the Ku Klux Klan have an unmistakably racial tone, but many other actions (choosing to live in a suburban neighborhood, sending one's children to a private school, and opposing government intervention in hiring policies) also have racial undertones.

READING 6
References

Acevedo-Garcia Dolores, Lochner K. A., Osypuk T. L., Subramanian S. V. 2003. "Future Directions in Residential Segregation and Health Research: A Multilevel Approach." *American Journal of Public Health* 93:215–21.

Akresh Ilana R., Frank Reanne. 2008. "Health Selection among New Immigrants." *American Journal of Public Health* 98:2058–64.

Alegria Margarita, Mulvaney-Day Norah, Torres Maria, Polo Antonio, Cao Zhun, Canino Glorisa. 2007. "Prevalence of Psychiatric Disorders across Latino Subgroups in the United States." *American Journal of Public Health* 97:68–75.

American Sociological Association. 2003. "The Importance of Collecting Data and Doing Social Scientific Research on Race." Washington, DC: American Sociological Association.

Angel Jacqueline L., Angel Ronald J. 2006. "Minority Group Status and Healthful Aging: Social Structure Still Matters." *American Journal of Public Health* 96:1152–59.

Angel Jacqueline L., Buckley Cynthia J., Finch Brian Karl. 2001. "Nativity and Self-Assessed Health among Pre-Retirement Age Hispanics and Non-Hispanic Whites." *International Migration Review* 35:784–803.

Bierman Alex. 2006. "Does Religion Buffer the Effects of Discrimination on Mental Health? Differing Effects by Race." *Journal for the Scientific Study of Religion* 45:551–65.

Blauner Robert. 1972. *Racial Oppression in America.* New York: Harper and Row.

Bonilla-Silva Eduardo. 1997. "Rethinking Racism: Toward a Structural Interpretation." *American Sociological Review* 67:465–80.

Braveman Paula A., Cubbin Catherine, Egerter Susan, Williams David R., Pamuk Elsie. 2010. "Socioeconomic Disparities in Health in the United States: What Can We Learn from the Patterns?" *American Journal of Public Health* 100:S186–S196.

Bullard Robert. 2000. *Dumping in Dixie: Race, Class, and Environmental Quality*. Boulder, CO: Westview Press.

Bullard Robert D., Johnson Glenn S. 2000. "Environmental Justice: Grassroots Activism and Its Impact on Public Policy Decision Making." *Journal of Social Issues* 56:555–78.

Clinton William J. 1994. "Federal Actions to Address Environmental Justice in Minority Populations and Low-Income Populations." Executive Order 12898. *Federal Register* 59:FR7629.

Conley Dalton. 1999. *Being Black, Living in the Red: Race, Wealth, and Social Policy in America*. Berkeley: University of California Press.

Cooper Richard S., Kaufman Jay S., Ward Ryk. 2003. "Race and Genomics." *New England Journal of Medicine* 348:1166–70.

Du Bois William E. B. [1899] 1967. *The Philadelphia Negro: A Social Study*. New York: Schocken Books.

Duster Troy, Garrett Karen. 1984. "A Social Frame for Biological Knowledge." Pp. 1–40 in *Cultural Perspectives on Biological Knowledge*. Norwood, NJ: Ablex Publishing.

Ellison Christopher G., Musick Marc A., Henderson Andrea K. 2008. "Balm in Gilead: Racism, Religious Involvement, and Psychological Distress among African-American Adults." *Journal for the Scientific Study of Religion* 47:291–309.

Engels Frederick. [1844] 1984. *The Condition of the Working Class in England*. Chicago, IL: Academy Chicago.

Farmer Melissa M., Ferraro Kenneth F. 2005. "Are Racial Disparities in Health Conditional on Socioeconomic Status?" *Social Science and Medicine* 60:191–204.

Feagin Joe R., McKinney K. D. 2003. *The Many Costs of Racism*. Lanham, MD: Rowman and Littlefield Publishers.

Ferraro Kenneth F., Farmer Melissa M. 1996. "Double Jeopardy to Health Hypothesis for African Americans: Analysis and Critique." *Journal of Health and Social Behavior* 37:27–43.

Finch Brain K., Frank Reanne, Vega William A. 2004. "Aculturation and Acculturation Stress: A Social-Epidemiological Approach to Mexican Migrant Farmworkers' Health." *International Migration Review* 38:236–62.

Frank Reanne. 2005. "International Migration and Infant Health in Mexico." *Journal of Immigrant Health* 7:11–22.

Frank Reanne. 2008. "Functional or Futile?: The (In)utility of Methodological Critiques of Genetic Research on Racial Disparities in Health. A Commentary on Kaufman's 'Epidemiologic Analysis of Racial/Ethnic Disparities: Some Fundamental Issues and a Cautionary Example.'" *Social Science and Medicine* 66:1670–74.

Frazier E. Franklin. 1947. "Sociological Theory and Race Relations." *American Sociological Review* 12:265–71.

Frisbie W. Parker, Forbes Doulgas, Hummer Robert A. 1998. "Hispanic Pregnancy Outcomes: Additional Evidence." *Social Science Quarterly* 79:149–69.

Guo Guang, Roettger Michael E. 2008. "The Integration of Genetic Propensities into Social- Control Models of Delinquency and Violence among Male Youths." *American Sociological Review* 73:543–68.

Hauser Robert M. 1994. "Measuring Socioeconomic Status in Studies of Child Development." *Child Development* 65:1541–45.

Hayward Mark D., Miles Toni P., Crimmins Eileen M., Yang Yu. 2000. "The Significance of Socioeconomic Status in Explaining the Racial Gap in Chronic Health Conditions." *American Sociological Review* 65:910–30.

Heron Melonie, Hoyert Donna L., Murphy Sherry L., Xu Jiaquan, Kochanek Kenneth D., Tejada-Vera Betzaida. 2009. "Deaths: Final Data for 2006." *National Vital Statistics Reports* 57:1–135.

Hummer Robert A. 1996. "Black-White Differences in Health and Mortality: A Review and Conceptual Model." *The Sociological Quarterly* 37:105–25.

Hummer Robert A., Rogers Richard G., Nam Charles B., LeClere Felicia B. 1999. "Race/Ethnicity, Nativity, and U.S. Adult Mortality." *Social Science Quarterly* 80:136–53.

Jaynes Gerald David, Williams Robin M. 1989. *A Common Destiny: Blacks and American Society*. Washington, DC: National Academy Press.

Krieger Nancy. 1987. "Shades of Difference: Theoretical Underpinnings of the Medical Controversy on Black/White Differences in the United States, 1830–1870." *International Journal of Health Services* 17:259–78.

Kuzawa Christopher W., Sweet Elizabeth. 2009. "Epigenetics and the Embodiment of Race: Developmental Origins of U.S. Racial Disparities in Cardiovascular Health." *American Journal of Human Biology* 21:2–15.

LaVeist Thomas A. 1989. "Linking Residential Segregation and Infant Mortality Race Disparity in U.S. Cities." *Sociology and Social Research* 73:90–94.

LaVeist Thomas A., Gaskin Darrell J., Richard Patrick. 2009. "The Economic Burden of Health Inequalities in the United States." Washington, DC: Joint Center for Political and Economic Studies.

Link B. G., Phelan J. 1995. "Social Conditions as Fundamental Causes of Disease." *Journal of Health and Social Behavior* 35:80–94.

Malone N., Baluja K. F., Costanzo J. M., Davis C. J. 2003. *The Foreign-Born Population: 2000*. Washington, DC: U.S. Census Bureau.

Markides Kyriakos S., Coreil J. 1986. "The Health of Hispanics in the Southwestern United States: An Epidemiologic Paradox." *Public Health Reports* 101:253.

Markides Kyriakos S., Eschbach Karl. 2005. "Aging, Migration, and Mortality: Current Status of Research on the Hispanic Paradox." *Journals of Gerontology: Series B* 60B:68–75.

Massey Douglas S. 2004. "Segregation and Stratification: A Biosocial Perspective." *Du Bois Review: Social Science Research on Race* 1:7–25.

Massey Douglas S., Denton Nancy A. 1993. *American Apartheid: Segregation and the Making of the Underclass*. Cambridge, MA: Harvard University Press.

Mechanic David. 2002. "Disadvantage, Inequality, and Social Policy." *Health Affairs* 21:48–59.

Miranda Jeanne, McGuire Thomas G., Williams David R., Wang Philip. 2008. "Mental Health in the Context of Health Disparities." *American Journal of Psychiatry* 165:1102–1108.

Morenoff Jeffrey D. 2003. "Neighborhood Mechanisms and the Spatial Dynamics of Birth Weight." *American Journal of Sociology* 108:976–1017.

Mossakowski Krysia N. 2003. "Coping with Perceived Discrimination: Does Ethnic Identity Protect Mental Health?" *Journal of Health and Social Behavior* 44:318–31.

Murphy Sherry L. 2000. "Deaths: Final Data for 1998." *National Vital Statistics Reports* 56:4–26.

Navarro Vincente. 1990. "Race or Class Versus Race and Class: Mortality Differentials in the United States." *Lancet* 336:1238–40.

Oliver Melvin L., Shapiro Thomas M. 2006. *Black Wealth, White Wealth: A New Perspective on Racial Inequality*. New York: Routledge.

Omi Michael, Winant Howard. 1994. *Racial Formation in the United States: From the 1960s to the 1990s*. New York City: Routledge.

Orzechowski Shawna, Sepielli Peter. 2003. *New Worth and Asset Ownership of Households: 1998 and 2000*. Washington, DC: U.S. Census Bureau.

Risch Niel, Burchard Esteban, Ziv Elad, Tang Hua. 2002. "Categorization of Humans in Biomedical Research: Genes, Race and Disease." *Genome Biology* 3:1–12.

Rumbaut Ruben G. 1996. "Origins and Destinies: Immigration, Race, and Ethnicity in Contemporary America." Pp. 21–42 in *Origins and Destinies: Immigration, Race, and Ethnicity in America*, edited by Pedraza S., Rumbaut R. G. Belmont, CA: Wadsworth Publishing Co.

Sampson Robert J., Wilson William J. 1995. "Toward a Theory of Race, Crime, and Urban Inequality." Pp. 37–54 in *Crime and Inequality*, edited by Hagan J., Peterson R. D. Stanford, CA: Stanford University Press.

Schulz Amy J., Mullings Leith. 2006. *Gender, Race, Class and Health*. San Francisco, CA: Jossey-Bass.

Schulz Amy J., Williams David R., Israel Barbara A., Lempert Lora B. 2002. "Racial and Spatial Relations as Fundamental Determinants of Health in Detroit." *The Milbank Quarterly* 80:677.

Serre David, Paabo Svante. 2004. "Evidence for Gradients of Human Genetic Diversity within and among Continents." *Genome Research* 14:1679–85.

Shields Alexandra E., Fullerton Stephanie M., Olden Kenneth. 2009. "Genes, Environment, and Cancer Disparities." Pp. 49–82 in *Toward the Elimination of Cancer Disparities*, edited by Koh H. K. New York: Springer Publishing.

Singh Gopal K., Miller Barry A. 2004. "Health, Life Expectancy, and Mortality Patterns among Immigrant Populations in the United States." *Canadian Journal of Public Health* 95:I14–I21.

Singh Gopal K., Yu Stella M. 1996. "Adverse Pregnancy Outcomes: Differences between U.S. and Foreign-Born Women in Major U.S. Racial and Ethnic Groups." *American Journal of Public Health* 86:837–43.

Smedley Brian D., Stith Adrienne Y., Nelson Alan R. 2002. *Unequal Treatment: Confronting Racial and Ethnic Disparities in Health Care*. Washington, DC: National Acadamies Press.

Smelser Neil J., Wilson William J., Mitchell Faith. 2001. *America Becoming: Racial Trends and their Consequences*. Washington, DC: National Academy Press.

Takeuchi David T., Zane Nolan, Hong Seunghye, Chae David H., Gong Fang, Gee Gilbert C., Walton Emily, Sue Stanley, Alegria Margarita. 2007. "Immigration-Related Factors and Mental Disorders among Asian Americans." *American Journal of Public Health* 97:84–90.

Wilkinson Doris Y., King Gary. 1987. "Conceptual and Methodological Issues in the Use of Race as a Variable: Policy Implications." *The Milbank Quarterly* 65:56–71.

Williams David R. 1997. "Race and Health: Basic Questions, Emerging Directions." *Annals of Epidemiology* 7:322–33.

Williams David R., Collins Chiquita. 1995. "U.S. Socioeconomic and Racial Differences in Health: Patterns and Explanations." *Annual Review of Sociology* 21:349–86.

Williams David R., Collins Chiquita. 2001. "Racial Residential Segregation: A Fundamental Cause of Racial Disparities in Health." *Public Health Reports* 116:404–16.

Williams David R., Costa Manuela V., Odunlami Adebola O., Mohammed Selina A. 2008. "Moving Upstream: How Interventions that Address the Social Determinants of Health Can Improve Health and Reduce Disparities." *Journal of Public Health Management and Practice* 14 (Supplement): S8–S17.

Williams David R., Gonzalez Hector M., Neighbors Harold, Nesse Randolph, Abelson Jamie M., Sweetman Julie, Jackson James S. 2007a. "Prevalence and Distribution of Major Depressive Disorder in African Americans, Caribbean Blacks, and Non-Hispanic Whites: Results from the National Survey of American Life." *Archives of General Psychiatry* 64:305–15.

Williams David R., Haile Rahwa, Gonzalez Hector M., Neighbors Harold, Baser Raymond, Jackson James S. 2007b. "The Mental Health of Black Caribbean Immigrants: Results from the National Survey of American Life." *American Journal of Public Health* 97:52–59.

Williams David R., McClellan Mark B., Rivlin Alice M. 2010. "Beyond the Affordable Care Act: Achieving Real Improvements in Americans' Health." *Health Affairs* 29:1481–88.

Williams David R., Mohammed Selina A. 2008. "Poverty, Migration, and Health." Pp. 135–69 in *The Colors of Poverty*, edited by Lin A. C., Harris D. R. New York: Russell Sage Foundation.

Williams David R., Mohammed Selina A. 2009. "Discrimination and Racial Disparities in Health: Evidence and Needed Research." *Journal of Behavioral Medicine* 32:20–47.

Williams David R., Mohammed Selina A., Leavell Jacinta, Collins Chiquita. 2010. "Race, Socioeconomic Status and Health: Complexities, Ongoing Challenges and Research Opportunities." *Annals of the New York Academy of Sciences* 1186:69–101.

Wilson William J. 1990. *The Truly Disadvantaged: The Inner City, the Underclass, and Public Policy*. Chicago: University of Chicago Press.

READING 7

Notes

1. Most particularly and influential, Steele's book *The Content of Our Character: A New Vision of Race in Race,* published in 1990; and Thernstrom's 1997 book, *America in Black and White: One Nation, Indivisible.*

2. Mary Patillo-McCoy's book, *Black Picket Fences,* traces the development of the black middle class.

3. Data from this section, as well as a fuller discussion of the details, can be found in *The Hidden Cost of Being African American.*

4. William Julius Wilson makes this case, especially for jobs, in his 1987 book *The Truly Disadvantaged.* Christopher Jencks and Meredith Phillips present the black-white education gap argument in *The Black-White Test Score Gap,* 1998.

5. The full multiple regression results can be found in *The Hidden Cost of Being African American.*

6. *The Wealth of Hispanic Households: 1996 to 2002.* Kochhar, Rakesh. The Pew Hispanic Center. October, 2004.

READING 8

References

Adams, R. 1969. "The Unorthodox Race Doctrine of Hawaii." Pp. 81–90 in *Comparative Perspectives on Race Relations,* edited by M. Tumin. Boston: Little, Brown.

Ballhatchet, K. 1980. *Race, Sex, and Class Under the Raj.* London: Camelot.

Bennett, L., Jr. 1962. *Before the Mayflower: A History of the Negro in America, 1619–1962.* Chicago: Johnson.

Berry, B. 1963. *Almost White.* New York: Macmillan.

———. 1965. *Race and Ethnic Relations,* 3rd ed. New York: Houghton Mifflin.

Bilbo, T. G. 1947. *Take Your Choice: Separation or Mongrelization.* Poplarville, MS: Dream House Publishing.

Blalock, H. M., Jr. 1967. *Toward a Theory of Minority-Group Relations.* New York: Capricorn Books.

Blaustein, A. P., and C. C. Ferguson, Jr. 1957. *Desegregation and the Law.* New Brunswick, NJ: Rutgers University Press.

Burma, J. G. 1946. "The Measurement of Passing." *American Journal of Sociology* 52: 18–22.

Cannon, P. 1956. *A Gentle Knight: My Husband. Walter White.* New York: Rinehart.

Catterall, H. T., ed. 1926–1937. *Judicial Cases Concerning American Slavery and the Negro.* Vols. 1–5. Washington, DC: Carnegic Institute.

Daniel, G. R. 1992. "Beyond Black and White: The New Multiracial Consciousness." Pp. 333–341 in *Racially Mixed People in America,* edited by M. P. P. Root. Newbury Park, CA: Sage.

———. 2000. *More Than Black: Multiracial Identity and the New Racial Order.* Philadelphia: Temple University Press.

Davis, F. J. 1991. *Who Is Black? One Nation's Definition.* University Park: Pennsylvania State University Press.

———. 1995. "The Hawaiian Alternative to the One-Drop Rule." Pp. 115–131 in *American Mixed Race: The Culture of Microdiversity,* edited by Naomi Zack. Lanham, MD: Rowman and Littlefield.

Day, D. 1979. *The Adoption of Black Children: Counteracting Institutional Discrimination.* Lexington, MA: Lexington Books.

Domínguez, V. R. 1986. *White by Definition: Social Classification in Creole Louisiana.* New Brunswick, NJ: Rutgers University Press.

Durkheim, E. 1960. *The Division of Labor in Society.* Translated by G. Simpson. New York: Free Press.

Eckard, E. W. 1947. "How Many Negroes Pass?" *American Journal of Sociology* 52: 498–503.

Fernandez, C. A. 1995. "Testimony of the Association of Multiethnic Americans Before the Subcommittee on Census, Statistics, and Postal Personnel of the U.S. House of

Representatives." Pp. 191–210 in *American Mixed Race: The Culture of Microdiversity,* edited by Naomi Zack. Lanham, MD: Rowman and Littlefield.

Foster, E. 1998. "Jefferson Fathered Slave's Last Child." *Nature,* November 5, pp. 27–28.

Gist, N. P., and R. Dean. 1973. *Marginality and Identity.* Leiden: Brill.

Graham, S. R. 1995. "Grassroots Advocacy." Pp. 185–189 in *American Mixed Race: The Culture of Microdiversity,* edited by N. Zack. Lanham, MD: Rowman and Littlefield.

Grosz, G. 1989. "From Sea to Shining Sea: A Current Listing of Interracial Organizations and Support Groups Across the Nation." *Interrace* 1: 24–28.

Gwaltney, J. L. 1980. *Drylongso: A Self-Portrait of Black America.* New York: Vintage.

Haizlip, S. T. 1994. *The Sweeter the Juice: A Family Portrait in Black and White.* New York: Simon and Schuster.

Haley, A. 1976. *Roots: The Saga of an American Family.* Garden City, NY: Doubleday.

Haley, A., and D. Stevens. 1993. *Queen.* New York: Avon.

Harris, M. 1964. *Patterns of Race in the Americas.* New York: Walker.

Hoetink, H. 1967. *Caribbean Race Relations: A Study of Two Variants.* London: Oxford University Press.

Howard, A. 1980. "Hawaiians." Pp. 449–452 in *Harvard Encyclopedia of American Ethnic Groups,* edited by S. Themnstrorn. Cambridge, MA: Harvard University Press.

Jorge, A. 1979. "The Black Puerto Rican Woman in Contemporary American Society." Pp. 134–141 in *The Puerto Rican Woman,* edited by Edna Acosta-Belén. New York: Praeger.

Ladner, J. A. 1977. *Mixed Families: Adopting Across Racial Boundaries.* Garden City, NY: Anchor/Doubleday.

Lew, J. 2000. "Guidance on Aggregation and Allocation of Data on Race for Use in Civil Rights Monitoring and Enforcement." OMB Bulletin No. 00-02. Washington, DC: Office of Management and Budget.

Myrdal, G., R. Sterner, and A. M. Rose. 1944. *An American Dilemma.* New York: Harper and Row.

Nakashima, C. L. 1992. "An Invisible Monster: The Creation and Denial of Mixed-Race People in America." Pp. 162–178 in *Racially Mixed People in America,* edited by M. P. P. Root. Newbury Park, CA: Sage.

Nicholls, D. 1981. "No Hawks or Pedlars: Levantines in the Caribbean." *Ethnic and Racial Studies* 4: 415–431.

Ottley, R. 1943. *New World A-Coming.* Cleveland: World Publishing.

Page, C. 1996. *Showing My Color.* New York: Harper and Collins.

Reed, T. E. 1969. "Caucasian Genes in American Negroes." *Science* 165: 762–768.

Rose, A. M. 1956. *The Negro in America.* Boston: Beacon Press.

Russell, K., M. Wilson, and R. Hall. 1992. *The Color Complex: The Politics of Skin Color Among African Americans.* Orlando, FL: Harcourt Brace.

Solaun, M., and S. Kronus. 1973. *Discrimination Without Violence.* New York: John Wiley.

Stoddard, E. R. 1973. *Mexican Americans.* New York: Random House.

Trillin, Calvin. 1986. "American Chronicles: Black or White." *New Yorker,* April 14, pp. 62–78.

Valverde, K-L. C. 1992. "From Dust to Gold: The Vietnamese Amerasian Experience." Pp. 144–161 in *Racially Mixed People in America,* edited by M. P. P. Root. Newbury Park, CA: Sage.

Van Den Berghe, P. L. 1971. "Racial Segregation in South Africa: Degrees and Kinds." Pp. 37–49 in *South Africa: Sociological Perspectives,* edited by H. Adam. New York: Oxford University Press.

Vander Zanden, J. W. 1972. *American Minority Relations,* 3rd ed. New York: Ronald.

Wagley, C., ed. 1963. *Race and Class in Rural Brazil,* 2nd ed. Paris: UNESCO.

Watson, G. 1970. *Passing for White: A Study of Racial Assimilation in a South African School.* London: Tavistock.

White, W. 1948. *A Man Called White: The Autobiography of Walter White.* New York: Viking.

Williams, G. H. 1995. *Life on the Color Line: The True Story of a White Boy Who Discovered He Was Black.* New York: Dutton.

Williams, T. K. 1996. "Race as Process: Reassessing the 'What Are You?' Encounters of Biracial Individuals." Pp. 191–210 in *The Multiracial Experience,* edited by M. P. P. Root. Newbury Park, CA: Sage.

Williamson, J. 1980. *New People: Miscegenation and Mulattoes in the United States.* New York: Free Press.

READING 9

Notes

1. U.S. Congress, *American Indian Policy Review Commission: Final Report,* vol. 1 (Washington, D.C.: Government Printing Office, 1977), 3.

2. See, e.g., Haunani-Kay Trask, *From a Native Daughter: Colonialism and Sovereignty in Hawai'i* (Monroe, Maine: Common Courage, 1993) and Roger MacPherson Furrer, ed., *He Alo á He Alo (Face to Face): Hawaiian Voices on Sovereignty* (Honolulu, Hawaii: American Friends Service Committee—Hawai'i, 1993).

3. 3528 U.S. 495 (2000).

4. Http://www.doi.gov/nativehawaiians/.

5. See S. James Anaya, "The Native Hawaiian People and International Human Rights Law: Toward a Remedy for Past and Continuing Wrongs," *Georgia Law Review* 28 (1994), 309–64.

6. Vine Deloria Jr., "The American Indian Image in North America," *Encyclopedia of Indians of the Americas*, vol. 1 (St. Clair Shores, Mich.: Scholarly Press, 1974), 43.

7. Paula D. McClain and Joseph Stewart Jr., *"Can We All Get Along?" Racial and Ethnic Minorities in American Politics* (Boulder, Colo.: Westview, 1998), 6, citing John Higham, *Strangers in the Land: Patterns of American Nativism, 1860–1925* (Westport, Conn.: Greenwood, 1963).

8. 180 U.S. 261 (1901).

9. Felix S. Cohen, *Handbook of Federal Indian Law,* reprint ed. (Albuquerque: University of New Mexico Press, 1972), 268.

10. Jack Utter, *American Indians: Answers to Today's Questions* (Lake Ann, Mich.: National Woodlands, 1993), 30–31.

11. William Quinn Jr., "Federal Acnowledgment of American Indian Tribes? The Historical Development of a Legal Concept," *American Journal of Legal History* 34 (October 1990): 331–63.

12. 56 *Federal Register* 47, 325 (1991).

13. 25 Code of Federal Regulations 83.7 (a)–(g) (1991).

14. 25 *U.S.C.* chapter 1, section 1, 961.

15. 25 *U.S.C.* chapter 1, 962.

16. William W. Quinn Jr., "Federal Acknowledgment of American Indian Tribes: Authority, Judicial Interposition, and 25 C.F.R. Sec. 83," *American Indian Law Review* 17 (Fall 1992): 48.

17. Quinn, "Federal Acknowledgment of American Indian Tribes," 52.

18. Felix Cohen, "The Erosion of Indian Rights, 1950–1953: A Case Study in Bureaucracy," *Yale Law Journal* 62 (February 1953): 352.

19. Letter from Carol A. Bacon, acting director of the Office of Tribal Services, Bureau of Indian Affairs, 3 December 1991. The author has a copy of the letter.

20. 108 Stat., 709.

21. See U.S. Congress, House, "A Bill to Provide for Administrative Procedures to Extend Federal Recognition to Certain Indian Groups, and for Other Purposes," 105th Cong., 2d sess., 1998, H. Rept. 1154. As of this writing—May 1999—none of these bills has become law.

22. Ellen Barry, "Agency Willing to Relinquish Power to Recognize Tribes," *Boston Globe,* 26 May 2000, B1.

23. 118 U.S. 948 (1998).

24. See, e.g., Trask, *From a Native Daughter,* and Anaya, "The Native Hawaiian People," 309.

25. Allogan Slagle, "Unfinished Justice: Completing the Restoration and Acknowledgment of California Indian Tribes," *American Indian Journal* 13, no. 4 (Fall 1989): 325–45.

26. William W. Quinn Jr., "The Southeast Syndrome: Notes on Indian Descendant Recruitment Organizations and Their Perceptions of Native American Culture," *American Indian Quarterly* 14, no. 2 (Spring 1990): 147–54.

27. Jackie J. Kim, "The Indian Federal Recognition Procedures Act of 1995: A Congressional Solution to an Administrative Morass," *The Administrative Law Journal of the American University* 9, no. 3 (Fall 1995): 899–932.

28. See http://www.doi.gov/bia/bar/indexq.htm for statistical details of the acknowledgment project's efforts.

29. Donald Fixico, *Termination and Relocation: Federal Indian Policy, 1945–1960* (Albuquerque: University of New Mexico Press, 1986).

30. 67 Stat., B132.

31. 110 Stat., 130.

32. N.C. Public Laws, 1953, chapter 874, p. 747.

33. 70 Stat., 254.

34. David E. Wilkins, "Breaking into the Intergovernmental Matrix: The Lumbee Tribe's Efforts to Secure Federal Acknowledgment," *Publius: The Journal of Federalism* 23 (Fall 1993): 123–42.

35. McClain and Stewart, *"Can We All Get Along?"* 6.

36. Bart Vogel, "Who Is an Indian in Federal Indian Law?" in *Studies in American Indian Law,* ed. Ralph Johnson (Pullman: Washington State University, 1970), 53.

37. C. Matthew Snipp, *American Indians: The First of This Land* (New York: Russell Sage Foundation, 1989), 34.

38. Snipp, *First of This Land,* 33.

39. Cohen, *Handbook,* 2.

40. Snipp, *First of This Land,* 33.

41. 29 Stat., 321.

42. Abdul G. Kahn, *Report on the Indian Definition Study* (Washington, D.C.: Department of Education, 1980).

43. Kahn, *Indian Definition Study,* 56.

44. Joane Nagel, *American Indian Ethnic Renewal: Red Power and the Resurgence of Identity and Culture* (New York: Oxford University Press, 1996), 243.

45. Brian Stackes, "Planned Bureau of Indian Affairs Regulations Stir Concerns Among Tribal Leaders," *Indian Country Today,* 18 August 2000, 1.

46. Russell Thornton, "Tribal Membership Requirements and the Demography of 'Old' and 'New' Native Americans," in *Changing Numbers, Changing Needs: American Indian Demography and Public Health,* ed. Gary D. Sandefur, Ronald R.

Rindfuss, and Barney Cohen (Washington, D.C.: National Academy Press, 1996), 110–11.

47. See, e.g., Francis Paul Prucha, *American Indian Treaties: The History of a Political Anomaly* (Berkeley, Calif.: University of California Press, 1994) and Robert A. Williams Jr. *Linking Arms Together: American Indian Treaty Visions of Law and Peace, 1600–1800* (New York: Oxford University Press, 1997).

48. 16 Stat., 566.

49. 7 Stat., 391.

50. 7 Stat., 391.

51. Cesare Marino, "Reservations," in *Native America in the Twentieth Century: An Encyclopedia,* ed. Mary B. Davis (New York: Garland Publishing, Inc., 1996), 544–56.

52. Vine Deloria Jr. and Clifford M. Lytle, *American Indians, American Justice* (Austin: University of Texas Press, 1983), 58.

53. Deloria and Lytle, *American Indians,* 58.

54. John H. Moore, "The Enduring Reservations of Oklahoma," in *State & Reservation: New Perspectives on Federal Indian Policy,* ed. George Pierre Castile and Robert L. Bee (Tucson: University of Arizona Press, 1992), 92–109.

55. See Robert F. Heizer, *The Destruction of California Indians* (Lincoln: University of Nebraska Press, 1993) for a first-rate account of what these nations experienced from 1847 to 1865.

56. Title 18, *U.S. Code,* section 1151.

57. Council of Economic Advisers, *Changing America: Indicators of Social and Economic Well-Being by Race and Hispanic Origin* (Washington, D.C.: Government Printing Office, 1998), 4.

58. www.census.gov/prod/2001 pubs.

59. Russell Thornton, *American Indian Holocaust and Survival: A Population History Since 1492* (Norman: University of Oklahoma Press, 1987).

60. www.census.gov/prod/2001pubs.

61. Russell Thornton, "What the Census Doesn't Count," *New York Times,* 23 March 2001, A21.

62. C. Matthew Snipp, "The Size and Distribution of the American Indian Population: Fertility, Mortality, Migration, and Residence," in *Changing Numbers, Changing Needs: American Indian Demography and Public Health,* ed. Gary D. Sandefur, Ronald R. Rindfuss, and Barney Cohen (Washington, D.C.: National Academy Press, 1996), 42–43.

63. Snipp, "The Size and Distribution," 39.

64. Snipp, *The First of This Land,* 171.

65. Snipp, *The First of This Land,* 165.

66. Lawrence H. Fuchs, *The American Kaleidoscope* (Hanover, N.H.: Wesleyan University Press, 1990), 329.

READING 10

Notes

1. For an extended discussion of the critical transnational approach to immigration, see Espiritu (2003). Certainly, I am not the first scholar to apply a critical transnational framework to the study of Asian Americans. Oscar Campomanes (1997), Sucheta Mazumdar (1990), Shirley Hune (1989), and others have written persuasively on the importance of conducting Asian American studies through an "international" frame.

2. For a detailed account of the disputes over the classification of Asian Americans in the 1980 and 1990 censuses, please see Espiritu (1992, ch. 5).

3. According to the 2000 census, 10.2 million people reported that they were *only* Asian. An additional 1.7 million people reported that they were Asian and at least one other race (Barnes and Bennett 2002, 3).

4. In 1990 the Japanese American share of the Asian American population was 12 percent, and the five largest Asian American groups were Chinese (23 percent), Filipino (19 percent), Asian Indian (11 percent), Korean (11 percent), and Vietnamese (8 percent).

5. According to the 2000 U.S. census, approximately 850,000 people reported that they were Asian and white, and 360,000 people reported that they were two or more Asian groups (Barnes and Bennett 2002, table 4). The debate over the classification of multiracials in the 2000 census often posed the interests of multiracial Asian Americans—the right to claim their full heritage—in opposition to the civil rights needs of pan-Asian America—the possible loss of political clout that is tied to numbers (see Espiritu 2001, 31). Refusing this "splitting," Asian American multiracial organizations rejected the "stand-alone multiracial" category and endorsed the "check more than one" format because the latter would allow them to identify as multiracial *and* "still be counted with their Asian American brethren and sisters" (King 2000, 202). This stance suggests that multiracial Asian and pan-Asian identities need not be mutually exclusive.

References

Barnes, Jessica, and Claudette E. Bennett. 2002. *The Asian Population 2000.* Washington: U.S. Department of Commerce.

Blauner, Robert. 1972. *Racial Oppression in America.* New York: Harper & Row.

Campomanes, Oscar. 1997. "New Formations of Asian American Studies and the Questions of U.S. Imperialism." *Positions* 5(2): 523–50.

Daniels, Roger. 1988. *Asian America: Chinese and Japanese in the United States Since 1850.* Seattle: University of Washington Press.

Davis, Angela. 1997. "Interview with Lisa Lowe—Angela Davis: Reflections on Race, Class, and Gender in the USA." In *The Politics of Culture in the Shadow of Capital,* edited by Lisa Lowe and David Lloyd. Durham, N.C.: Duke University Press.

Espiritu, Yen Le. 1992. *Asian American Panethnicity: Bridging Institutions and Identities.* Philadelphia: Temple University Press.

———. 2001. "Possibilities of a Multiracial Asian America." In *The Sum of Our Parts: Mixed Heritage Asian Americans,* edited by Teresa Williams-Leon and Cynthia L. Nakashima. Philadelphia: Temple University Press.

———. 2003. *Home Bound: Filipino American Lives Across Cultures, Communities, and Countries.* Berkeley: University of California Press.

Espiritu, Yen Le, Dorothy Fujita Rony, Nazli Kibria, and George Lipsitz. 2000. "The Role of Race and Its Articulations for Asian Pacific Americans." *Journal of Asian American Studies* 3(2): 127–37.

Hayano, David. 1981. "Ethnic Identification and Disidentification: Japanese-American Views of Chinese Americans." *Ethnic Groups* 3(2): 157–71.

Hossfeld, Karen. 1994. "Hiring Immigrant Women: Silicon Valley's 'Simple Formula.' " In *Women of Color in U.S. Society,* edited by Maxine Baca Zinn and Bonnie Thornton Dill. Philadelphia: Temple University Press.

Hune, Shirley. 1989. "Expanding the International Dimension of Asian American Studies." *Amerasia Journal* 15(2): xix–xxiv.

Ichioka, Yuji. 1988. *The Issei: The World of the First Generation Japanese Americans, 1885–1924.* New York: Free Press.

Iwasaki, Naomi. 1999. "Pan-Asian What?" *Asian American Revolutionay Movement Ezine,* http://www.aamovement.net/narratives/panasian.html (accessed December 4, 2003).

Kang, Laura Hyun Yi. 1997. "Si(gh)ting Asian/American Women as Transnational Labor." *Positions* 5(2): 403–37.

King, Rebecca Chiyoko. 2000. "Racialization, Recognition, and Rights: Lumping and Splitting Multiracial Asian Americans in the 2000 Census." *Journal of Asian American Studies* 3(2): 191–217.

Kurashige, Scott. 2000. "Panethnicity and Community Organizing: Asian Americans United's Campaign Against Anti-Asian Violence." *Journal of Asian American Studies* 3(2): 163–90.

Lim, Linda Y. C. 1983. "Capitalism, Imperialism, and Patriarchy: The Dilemma of Third-World Women Workers in Multinational Factories." In *Women, Men, and the International Division of Labor,* edited by June Nash and Maria Patricia Fernandez-Kelly. Albany: State University of New York Press.

Ling, Susie Hsiuhan. 1984. "The Mountain Movers: Asian American Women's Movement in Los Angeles." M.A. thesis, University of California at Los Angeles.

Liu, William. 1976. "Asian American Research: Views of a Sociologist." *Asian Studies Occasional Report* 2: whole issue.

Lott, Juanita. 1976. "The Asian American Concept: In Quest of Identity." *Bridge* (November): 30–34.

Lowe, Lisa. 1991. "Heterogeneity, Hybridity, Multiplicity: Marking Asian American Differences." *Diaspora* 1 (1, Spring): 25–44.

———. 1996. *Immigrant Acts: On Asian American Cultural Politics.* Durham, N.C.: Duke University Press.

Mazumdar, Sucheta. 1990. "Asian American Studies and Asian Studies: Rethinking Roots." In *Asian Americans: Comparative and Global Perspectives,* edited by Shirley Hune et al. Pullman: Washington State University Press.

Misir, Deborah N. 1996. "The Murder of Navroze Mody: Race, Violence, and the Search for Order." *Amerasia Journal* 22(2): 55–76.

Nguyen, Viet Thanh. 2002. *Race and Resistance: Literature and Politics in Asian America.* New York: Oxford University Press.

Omatsu, Glenn. 1994. " 'The Four Prisons' and the Movements of Liberation: Asian American Activism from the 1960s to the 1990s." In *The State of Asian America: Activism and Resistance in the 1990s,* edited by Karin Aguilar-San Juan. Boston: South End.

Omi, Michael. 1993. "Out of the Melting Pot and into the Fire: Race Relations Policy." In *The State of Asian Pacific Americans: Policy Issues to the Year 2000.* Los Angeles: LEAP Asian Pacific American Public Policy Institute and UCLA Asian American Studies Center.

Omi, Michael, and Howard Winant. 1986. *Racial Formation in the United States: From the 1960s to the 1980s.* New York: Routledge & Kegan Paul.

Ong, Aihwa. 1996. "Citizenship as Subject Making: New Immigrants Negotiate Racial and Ethnic Boundaries." *Current Anthropology* 25(5): 737–62.

Ong, Paul. 1989. "California's Asian Population: Past Trends and Projections for the Year 2000." Los Angeles: Graduate School of Architecture and Urban Planning.

———. 2000. "The Asian Pacific American Challenge to Race Relations." In *The State of Asian Pacific Americans: Transforming Race Relations,* edited by Paul Ong. Los Angeles: LEAP Asian Pacific American Public Policy Institute and UCLA Asian American Studies Center.

Ong, Paul, and Suzanne J. Hee. 1993. "The Growth of the Asian Pacific American Population." In *The State of Asian Pacific Americans: Policy Issues to the Year 2000.* Los Angeles: LEAP Asian Pacific American Public Policy Institute and UCLA Asian American Studies Center.

———. 1994. "Economic Diversity." In *The State of Asian Pacific Americans: Economic Diversity, Issues, and Policies,* edited by Paul Ong. Los Angeles: LEAP Asian Pacific American Public Policy Institute and UCLA Asian American Studies Center.

Sacks, Karen, and Nancy Scheper-Hughes. 1987. "Introduction." *Women's Studies* 13(3): 175–82.

Saito, Leland. 1998. *Race and Politics: Asian Americans, Latinos, and Whites in a Los Angeles Suburb.* Urbana and Chicago: University of Illinois Press.

Shah, Bindi. 2002. "Making the 'American' Subject: Culture, Gender, Ethnicity, and the Politics of Citizenship in the Lives of Second-Generation Laotian Girls." Ph.D. diss., University of California at Davis.

Shankar, Rajiv. 1998. "Foreword: South Asian Identity in Asian America." In *A Part, Yet Apart: South Asians in Asian America,* edited by Lavina Dhingra Shankar and Rajini Srikanth. Philadelphia: Temple University Press.

Shinagawa, Larry Hajime, and Gin Yong Pang. 1996. "Asian American Panethnicity and Intermarriage." *Amerasia Journal* 22(2): 127–52.

Smith, James P., and Barry Edmonston, eds. 1997. *The New Americans: Economic, Demographic, and Fiscal Effects of Immigration.* Washington, D.C.: National Academy Press.

Strobel, Leny Mendoza. 1996. " 'Born-Again Filipino': Filipino American Identity and Asian American Panethnicity." *Amerasia Journal* 22(2): 31–54.

Takaki, Ronald. 1989. *Strangers from a Different Shore: A History of Asian Americans.* Boston: Little, Brown.

U.S. Department of Commerce. U.S. Census Bureau. 2002. "Coming to America: A Profile of the Nation's Foreign Born (2000 Update)." *Census Briefs: Current Population Survey, February 2002.* Washington: U.S. Census Bureau.

U.S. Immigration and Naturalization Service (USINS). 1997. *Statistical Yearbook of the Immigration and Naturalization Service, 1995.* Washington: U.S. Government Printing Office.

Wong, Paul. 1972. "The Emergence of the Asian-American Movement." *Bridge* 2(1): 33–39.

Zhou, Min. 1999. "Coming of Age: The Current Situation of Asian American Children." *Amerasia Journal* 25(1): 1–27.

Zhou, Min, and James V. Gatewood. 2000. "Introduction: Revisiting Contemporary Asian America." In *Contemporary Asian America: A Multidisciplinary Reader,* edited by Min Zhou and James V. Gatewood. New York: New York University Press.

READING 11

References

Bean, Frank D., and Gillian Stevens. *America's Newcomers and the Dynamics of Diversity.* New York: Russell Sage Foundation, 2003. This book explores the significance of immigration for America, including its implications for loosening racial and ethnic boundaries.

Davis, F. James. *Who Is Black? One Nation's Definition.* University Park, PA: Pennsylvania State University Press, 1991. Davis details the history of the "one-drop rule" in the United States.

Gerstle, Gary. "Liberty, Coercion, and the Making of Americans." In *The Handbook of International Migration,* edited by Charles Hirschman, Philip Kasinitz, and Josh DeWind. New York: Russell Sage Foundation, 1991. A history of racial categories and how they have changed.

Loewen, James. *The Mississippi Chinese: Between Black and White.* Cambridge, MA: Harvard University Press, 1971. Loewen shows how Chinese immigrants changed their racial classification from almost black to almost white.

Nobles, Melissa. *Shades of Citizenship: Race and the Census in Modern Politics.* Stanford, CA: Stanford University Press, 2000. A history or racial categories in the Census in the United States.

Perlmann, Joel, and Mary C. Waters, eds. *The New Race Question: How the Census Counts Multiracial Individuals.* New York: Russell Sage Foundation, 2002. This anthology examines the history of racial enumeration, the likely effects of the Census change in the race question, and possible policy implications for the future.

Qian, Zhenchao. "Breaking the Racial Barriers: Variations in Interracial Marriage Between 1980 and 1990." *Demography* 34, 2 (1997), 263–276. This study illustrates the growing trends in interracial marriage.

Waters, Mary C. "Multiple Ethnicities and Identity in the United States." In *We Are a People: Narrative and Multiplicity in Constructing Identity,* edited by Paul Spikard and W. Jeffrey Burroughs. Philadelphia: Temple University Press, 2000. Water examines the different ways interracial couples identify their children.

READING 12

Notes

1. FUBU (For Us By Us) is a black-owned manufacturer of urban, hip-hop style clothing.

2. For an excellent overview of how the media construct a view of race relations that is overly optimistic, see Benjamin DeMott, *The Trouble with Friendship: Why Americans Can't Think Straight About Race* (New York: The Atlantic Monthly Press, 1995).

3. The Gallup Organization, "Black/White Relations in the U.S." (June 10, 1997): 1–5; David Shipler, *A Country of Strangers: Blacks and Whites in America* (New York: Vintage Books, 1998).

4. For an insightful discussion of how neoconservative writers like Dinesh D'Souza distort history and contemporary race

relations, see David Theo Goldberg, "The New Segregation," *Race and Society* 1, no. 1 (1998).

5. Dinesh D'Souza, *The End of Racism: Principles for a Multiracial Society* (New York: Free Press, 1995); Ellis Cose, *Color-Blind: Seeing Beyond Race in a Race-Obsessed World* (New York: Harper Collins, 1997).

6. David Moore, "Americans Most Important Sources of Information: Local News," *The Gallup Poll Monthly,* 2–5 September 1995; David Moore and Lydia Saad, "No Immediate Signs That Simpson Trial Intensified Racial Animosity," *The Gallup Poll Monthly,* 2–5 October 1995; Kaiser Foundation, *The Four Americas: Government and Social Policy Through the Eyes of America's Multi-Racial and Multi-Ethnic Society* (Menlo Park, CA: Kaiser Family Foundation, 1995).

7. A. C. Nielsen, *Information Please Almanac* (Boston: Houghton Mifflin, 1997).

8. John Lewis and Sut Jhally, "Affirming Inaction: Television and the New Politics of Race," in *Marxism in the Postmodern Age: Confronting the New World Order,* edited by A. Callari, S. Cullenberg, and C. Biewener (New York: Guilford Press, 1995).

9. For an outstanding discussion of how color blindness is used politically by neoconservatives, see Amy Ansell, *New Right, New Racism: Race and Reaction in the United States* (New York: New York University Press, 1997); Howard Winant, *Racial Conditions: Politics, Theory, Comparisons* (Minneapolis: University of Minneapolis Press, 1994); Stephen Steinberg, *Turning Back: The Retreat from Racial Justice in American Thought and Policy* (New York: Beacon Press, 1995); Eduardo Bonilla-Silva, *White Supremacy and Racism in the Post–Civil Rights Era* (Boulder: Lynne Rienner Publishers); and Michael Omi, "Racism," in *The Making and Unmaking of Whiteness,* edited by Birget Brander Rasmussen, Eric Klineberg, Irene J. Nexica, and Matt Wray (Durham: Duke University Press, 2001).

10. Ruth Frankenberg, "The Mirage of an Unmarked Whiteness," in *The Making and Unmaking of Whiteness,* edited by Birget Brander Rasmussen, Eric Klineberg, Irene J. Nexica, and Matt Wray (Durham: Duke University Press, 2001).

11. David Theo Goldberg, *Racial Subjects: Writing on Race in America* (Thousand Oaks, CA: Routledge, 1997), 55; see also Charles Jaret, *Contemporary Racial and Ethnic Relations* (New York: Harper Collins, 1995), 265–270.

12. Leslie G. Carr, *Color-Blind Racism* (Thousand Oaks, CA: Sage Publications, 1997), 108; see also David Carroll Cochran, *The Color of Freedom: Race and Contemporary American Liberalism* (New York: State University of New York Press, 1999).

13. Mary Waters, *Ethnic Options: Choosing Identities in America* (Berkeley: University of California Press, 1990); Charles A. Gallagher, "Playing the Ethnic Card: Using Ethnic Identity to Negate Contemporary Racism," in *Deconstructing Whiteness, Deconstructing White Supremacy,* edited by Ashley Doane and Eduardo Bonilla-Silva (Lynne Rienner Publishers, forthcoming 2002).

14. Ashley W. Doane Jr., "Dominant Group Identity in the United States: The Role of 'Hidden' Ethnicity in Intergroup Relations," *The Sociological Quarterly* 38, no. 3 (1997): 378.

15. Joe Feagin and Melvin Sikes, *Living With Racism: The Black Middle Class Experience* (Boston: Beacon Press, 1994).

16. The Gallup Organization, "Black/White Relations in the U.S.," 10 June 1997, 1–5.

17. Kaiser Foundation, 1995.

18. Howard Schuman et al. (1997), 193.

19. U.S. Bureau of the Census, *Housing Vacancies and Home Ownership Annual Statistics* (Washington D.C.: U.S. Government Printing Office, 1999).

20. U.S. Bureau of the Census, *Asset Ownership of Households* (Washington D.C.: U.S. Government Printing Office, 1993); see also *Black Wealth/White Wealth: A New Perspective on Racial Inequality* (New York: Routledge, 1995).

21. John J. Macionis, *Sociology,* 7th ed. (Saddle River, NJ: Prentice Hall, 1999).

22. Diana B. Henriques, *New York Times,* 4 July, 2001, p. A1.

23. U.S. Department of Health and Human Services, *National Center for Chronic Disease Prevention and Health Promotion,* 1998; Centers for Disease Control and Prevention, National Center for Health Statistics, *Monthly Vital Statistics Report* 46 (2001).

24. Feagin, 2000.

25. Karen Gullo, *The Atlanta Journal and Constitution,* 12 March 2001, p. A7.

26. Jim Abrams, *The Atlanta Journal and Constitution,* 2 December 2000, p. A9.

27. Laura Parker and Peter Eisler, *USA Today,* 6–8 April 2001, p. A1.

28. Frankenberg (2001), p. 76.

29. Lawrence Bobo and James R. Kluegel, "Status, Ideology, and Dimensions of Whites' Racial Beliefs and Attitudes: Progress and Stagnation," in *Racial Attitudes in the 1990s: Continuity and Change,* edited by Steven A. Tuch and Jack K. Martin (Westport, CT: Praeger, 1997), p. 95.

30. Carr (1997), p. x.

31. David Roediger, *The Wages of Whiteness: Race and the Making of the American Working Class* (New York: Verso Press, 1991), p. 137.

32. Cited in David Roediger, "The White Question," *Race Traitor* (Winter 1993): 104.

READING 14

Notes

I am grateful for comments on earlier drafts of this paper from Margaret Chin, Jennifer Lee, an anonymous reviewer—and from my fellow authors in this volume.

1. These categories are constructions, but they also contain populations experiencing all the pleasures and pains of being located in a hierarchy. And although I am often discussing constructions, I will forgo the practice of putting all racial, national, and related names and labels between quotes, except for unusual racial stereotypes.

2. The two races may not be called that openly, but ambiguous pejoratives have long been part of the American vocabulary, for example *underclass* now, and *pauper* a century earlier (Gans 1995). Since races are social constructions, their names will depend in large part on who does the naming—and whose names become dominant in the public vocabulary.

3. Puerto Ricans are still often described as immigrants, even though they have been American citizens for a long time and their move from the island to the mainland is a form of interstate mobility. Racial, class, and linguistic considerations have undoubtedly influenced this labeling. The same dominant-race thinking led Irving Kristol and other neo-conservatives to argue in the 1960s that blacks were similar enough to the white European immigrants to be able to adopt and act on immigrant values. They also assumed that blacks would then assimilate like immigrants, ignoring such facts as that blacks had originally come as slaves, not immigrants; had been here several centuries; and had not yet been allowed by whites to assimilate. Thirty years later, many whites ignore the same facts to propose the newest immigrants as role models for blacks.

4. Much less is said about black Hispanics, including Puerto Ricans, who suffer virtually all of the discriminatory and other injustices imposed on African-Americans.

5. Some highly placed whites are already worrying, for example in a *Time* cover story by William Henry III (1990), but then similar whites worried a century earlier what the then arriving Catholic and Jewish newcomers would do to *their* country. The current worries are as meaningless as the old ones, since they are based on extrapolations of current patterns of immigration, not to mention current constructions of (nonwhite) race and (Hispanic) ethnicity.

6. Hacker (1996) notes, for example, that the term "white trash" is no longer in common use. Indeed, for reasons worth studying, the more popular term of the moment is "trailer trash," which nonetheless seems to be applied solely to poor whites.

7. In this respect, the United States differs from many other countries in the Western hemisphere, where blacks who have managed to become affluent are treated, within limits, as whites.

8. Not only might they perceive it more angrily than I am here doing, but they might be angrier about it than about the present hierarchy, simply because it is new but no great improvement. One result could be their constructions of new racial identities for themselves that depart drastically from the ones future nonblacks consider reasonable.

9. Being far fewer than Asians in number, South Asians are nationally not very visible now. Moreover, for religious and other reasons, South Asian immigrants have so far often been able to discourage their children from intermarrying.

10. My observations on multiracial constructions and people have benefited from many conversations with Valli Rajah.

11. Between 1970 and 1994, the number of people in interracial marriages grew from 676,000 to more than three million (Fletcher 1997). In 1990, biracial children made up 4 percent of all children, increasing from half a million in 1970 to about two million that year. The largest number were Asian-white children, followed by Native American–white and African American–white ones (Harrison and Bennett 1995).

12. Some observers currently estimate that 70 percent of all Japanese and Japanese-Americans are intermarried, mostly with whites. Since they came to the United States as families long before 1965, this estimate may supply a clue about what will happen to second-, third-, and later-generation descendants of other Asian-American populations.

13. Presumably class position will affect how other descendants of old Southern mulatto and creole populations (Dominguez 1986) will be classified.

14. In the political debates over the racial categories to be used in the Year 2000 Census, vocal multiracials preferred to be counted as and with various people of color. African-Americans and other officially recognized racial groups also indicated their opposition to a multiracial category, being reluctant to reduce the power of their numbers or the federal benefits that now go to racial minorities (e.g., Holmes 1996).

15. Kohne (1996) reports that light-skinned biracial Columbia University students who identify as whites also apply for scholarships as blacks. But then, four decades earlier, I met Italian-Americans in Boston's West End who took Irish names in order to obtain jobs in Irish-dominated city hall.

16. The practice of quantifying racial bloods has a long history in Europe and the United States, thanks to both eugenics and slavery. Perhaps it will disappear when enough people have to start counting three or more races. However, people also still use blood fractions when they marry across

religions, so that the notion of racial, ethnic, or religious "blood" is by no means obsolete.

17. They are also different, for "one and the same person may be considered white in the Dominican Republic or Puerto Rico . . . 'colored' in Jamaica, Martinique, or Curacao . . . [and] a 'Negro' in Georgia" (Hoetink 1967, xii).

18. This account is based mainly on the data summarized in Fiola 1990 and Skidmore 1992, the classic analysis of the Brazilian racial system in Skidmore 1993, Adamo's 1983 case study of race and class in Rio de Janeiro, and the socio-political analyses by Marx (1995, 1996). I am indebted to Anthony Marx for guiding me into the literature on Brazil, although there is still precious little social research, especially with current data, in English.

19. No one has so far paid much attention to who is constructed as exotic and why, except the multiracial people, mostly women, to whom it is applied. Some of them benefit because they are sought by industries that hire workers with exotic facial features; but women without these occupational interests resent such labeling because it turns them into sexual objects. Industries that employ workers with exotic features, facial and otherwise, such as the fashion and entertainment industries, play an interesting, and probably unduly influential, role in the country's public racial construction.

20. Even now, at the close of the twentieth century, whites who argue that America is a "Christian" nation are pursuing a politics of identity as much as of religious dominance.

21. I am indebted to my Columbia University colleague, biologist Robert Pollack, for my understanding of this phenomenon.

22. Originally, people drew on nineteenth-century and earlier comparisons of apes and humans, with those determined to be closer to apes in facial appearance being thought inferior. Brain size was also used, at least until scientific research debunked its relevance, and the researchers also discovered that it did not correlate with status. The final blow was the discovery that the much maligned Neanderthalers had larger brains than *Homo sapiens.*

23. Ears have served mainly as anchors for adornment, although protruding ones have sometimes been brought surgically closer to the head.

24. Now that some young women show their navels or wear bathing suits with uncovered buttocks, these could become eligible for racial typing.

25. Constructionists in the social sciences and the humanities have so far mainly emphasized that races, like other human notions, are socially constructed, but social scientists have paid little attention to the actual construction process and its participants. What we know about that process comes mostly from scholars who analyze racial images over time, in literature or the popular culture, and have collected process information as part of their work.

26. Forced Chinese labor was also recruited for the cotton plantations, but the Chinese workers turned out to be inefficient cotton pickers and thus managed to avoid becoming slaves.

27. I am indebted to Roderick Harrison and especially Manuel de la Puente of the U.S. Bureau of the Census for materials that clarified this set of responses.

28. Social scientists on the staff of the Census Bureau and the Bureau of Labor Statistics spend part of their time analyzing the large number of private races that people supply in answer to open-ended questions to produce the small number of public ones reported by the federal government.

29. For some similar practices by Jews in post-Holocaust Germany, see Rapaport 1997, 166–67.

30. For example, one of Waters's respondents explained that she traced her bad moods to "the Irish in me," while "all of the good things" were Italian (Waters 1990, 25). Embryo clinics are asked by some of their customers to supply sperm and egg donors of similar ethnic origin, in one case to obtain an "Irish background, or at least light hair and light eyes" (Kolata 1997, 34). As a result, ethnicity may be so racialized that it is not very voluntary, although voluntary ethnicity may also be used to achieve voluntarily chosen racial features.

31. Needless to say, traumatic and long-lasting economic decline is a more likely cause for a public recognition of class in America.

References

Adamo, Samuel C. 1983. "The Broken Promise: Race, Health and Justice in Rio de Janeiro, 1890–1940." Ph.D. diss., University of New Mexico.

Alba, Richard D. 1990. *Ethnic Identity.* New Haven: Yale University Press.

Dominguez, Virginia R. 1986. *White by Definition.* New Brunswick: Rutgers University Press.

Feagin, Joe R., and Michael P. Sykes. 1994. *Living with Racism.* Boston: Beacon.

Fields, Barbara J. 1990. "Slavery, Race and Ideology in the United States of America." *New Left Review* 15:95–108.

Fiola, Jan. 1990. "Race Relations in Brazil: A Reassessment of the 'Racial Democracy' Thesis." Occasional Papers Series no. 34. University of Massachusetts Latin American Studies Program, Amherst.

Fletcher, Michael A. 1997. "More Than a Black-White Issue." *Washington Post National Weekly Edition,* May 26, 34.

Frey, William H. 1996. "Immigration, Domestic Migration and Demographic Balkanization in America." *Population and Development Review* 22:741–63.

Gans, Herbert J. 1992. "Second Generation Decline: Scenarios for the Economic and Ethnic Futures of the post-1965 American Immigrants." *Ethnic and Racial Studies* 15:173–92.

———. 1995. *The War against the Poor.* New York: Basic.

Gerber, Eleanor, and Manuel de la Puente. 1996. "The Development of and Cognitive Testing of Race and Ethnic Origin Questions for the Year 2000 Census." In Bureau of the Census, *1996 Annual Research Conference.* Washington: Government Printing Office.

Gitlin, Todd. 1995. *The Twilight of Common Dreams.* New York: Metropolitan.

Gordon, Milton M. 1964. *Assimilation in American Life.* New York: Oxford University Press.

Hacker, Andrew. 1996. Foreword to *The Coming Race War?* by Richard Delgado. New York: New York University Press.

Harrison, Roderick J., and Claudette Bennett. 1995. "Racial and Ethnic Diversity." In *State of the Union: America in the 1990s,* vol. 2, *Social Trends,* edited by Reynolds Farley. New York: Russell Sage Foundation.

Henry, William, III. 1990. "Beyond the Melting Pot." *Time,* April 9, 29–32.

Hoetink, Harry. 1967. *The Two Variants in Caribbean Race Relations.* London: Oxford University Press.

Holmes, Steven. 1996. "Census Tests New Category to Identify Racial Groups." *New York Times,* December 4, A25.

Ignatiev, Noel. 1995. *How the Irish Became White.* New York: Routledge.

Kalmijn, Matthijs. 1991. "Status Homogamy in the United States." *American Journal of Sociology* 93:496–523.

Kohne, Natasha G. 1996. "The Experience of Mixed-Race Women: Challenging Racial Boundaries." Unpublished senior thesis, department of sociology, Columbia University, New York.

Kolata, Gina. 1997. "Clinics Selling Embryos Made for 'Adoption.'" *New York Times,* November 23, 1, 34.

Loewen, James W. 1988. *The Mississippi Chinese.* 2d ed. Prospect Heights, Ill.: Waveland.

Marris, Peter. 1996. *The Politics of Uncertainty.* New York: Routledge.

Marx, Anthony W. 1995. "Contested Citizenship: The Dynamics of Racial Identity and Social Movements." *International Review of History* 40, supplement 3: 159–83.

———. 1996. "Race-Making and the Nation-State." *World Politics,* January, 180–208.

Mintz, Sidney W. 1989. *Caribbean Transformations.* New York: Columbia University Press.

Morganthau, Tom. 1995. "What Color Is Black?" *Newsweek,* February 12, 63–67.

Newman, Katherine. 1993. *Declining Fortunes.* New York: Basic.

Rapaport, Lynn. 1997. *Jews in Germany after the Holocaust.* Cambridge: Cambridge University Press.

Rodriguez, Clara E. 1989. *Puerto Ricans: Born in the U.S.A.* Boston: Unwin Hyman.

Roediger, David R. 1991. *Wages of Whiteness.* London: Verso.

Rumbaut, Ruben G. 1997. "Ties That Bind: Immigration and Immigrant Families in the United States." In *Immigration and the Family,* edited by Alan Booth, Ann C. Crouter, and Nancy Landale. Mahwah, N.J.: Erlbaum.

Sanjek, Roger. 1994. "Intermarriage and the Future of the Races in the United States." In *Race,* edited by Steven Gregory and Roger Sanjek. New Brunswick: Rutgers University Press.

Skidmore, Thomas L. 1992. "Fact and Myth: Discovering a Racial Problem in Brazil." Working paper 173. Helen Kellogg Institute for International Studies, University of Notre Dame.

———. 1993. *Black into White.* Durham: Duke University Press.

Stonequist, Everett V. 1937. *The Marginal Man.* New York: Scribner's.

Waters, Mary. 1990. *Ethnic Options: Choosing Identities in America.* Berkeley: University of California Press.

READING 16

Notes

1. *Grutter v. Bollinger,* 539 U.S. (2003).

2. Presumably, the reason O'Connor thought that race-based affirmative action would no longer be needed once her educational requirement had been met is that then, through the regular admission process, minorities would no longer be underrepresented in higher education. Diversity would be secured in that way.

3. Terence Pell, "The Nature of Claims about Race and the Debate over Racial Preferences," *International Journal of Applied Philosophy* 18 (2004): 23.

4. With the exception of outreach affirmative action under some, possibly restricted, interpretation.

5. A corollary of this approach is to have the government stop gathering data on racial and sexual disparities in society, which, of course would make it difficult to assess the degree to which people are suffering from racial and sexual discrimination. Ward Connerly tried, but failed, to get a referendum (Prop. 54) in California passed to that effect in 2003.

6. Mitchell Chang, Daria Witt, James Jones, and Kenji Hakuta, *Compelling Interest* (Stanford: Stanford University Press, 2003), 98.

7. Maria Krysan, "Recent Trends in Racial Attitudes" (2002), http://tigger.cc.uic.edll.

8. Jamillah Moor, *Race and College Admissions* (Jefferson, NC: McFarland, 2005), 100.

9. Jody David Armour, "Hype and Reality in Affirmative Action," *University), of Colorado Law Review* 68 (1997): 1173.

10. Ibid.

11. Howard Schuman, Charlotte Steeh, Lawrence Bobo, and Maria Krysan, *Racial Attitudes in America: Trends and Interpretations,* rev. ed. (Cambridge: Harvard University Press, 1997). Virtually the same percentage of whites continued to hold this view from 1962 through 2002. See http://tigger.cc.uic.edu/~krysan/writeup.htm.

12. Derrick Bell, *Silent Covenants* (New York: Oxford University Press, 2004), 96.

13. See Michael Brown et al., *White-Washing Race* (Berkeley: University of California Press, 2005), chapters 2 and 5; Todd Michael Furman, "A Dialogue Concerning Claim Jumping and Compensatory Justice," *Teaching Philosophy* 21 (1998): 131-51: Deborah Jones. "The Future of Bakke: Will Social Science Matter?" *Ohio State Law Joumal* 59 (1998): 1054-67; Gerald Jaynes and Robin Williams, eds., *A Common Destiny* (Washington, DC: National Academy Press, 1989); Andrew Hacker, *Two Nations* (New York: Ballantine Books, 1992); Gertrude Ezorsky, *Racism and Justice* (Ithaca: Cornell University Press, 1991); *Hunger 1995: Fifth Annual Report on the State of World Hunger* (Silver Spring, MD: Bread for the World Institute, 1995).

14. Judy Lichtman et al., "Why Women Need Affirmative Action," in *The Affirmative Action Debate,* ed. George Curry, 175-83 (Reading, MA: Perseus Books, 1996).

15. Leonard Steinhorn and Barbara Diggs-Brown, *By the Color of Our Skin* (New York: Dutton, 1999), 47.

16. J. Tom L. Beauchamp, "Goals and Quotas in Hiring and Promotion," in *Ethical Theory and Business* by Tom L. Beauchamp and Norman Bowie, 5th ed., 379ff (Upper Saddle River, NJ: Prentice-Hall, 1996).

17. Bryan Grapes, ed., *Affirmative Action* (San Diego: Greenhaven Press, 2000), Introduction.

18. Ibid.

19. Ibid.

20. M. V. Lee Badgett, *Economic Perspectives on Affirmative Action* (Washington, DC: Joint Center for Political and Economic Studies, 1995), 5.

21. LeAnn Lodder et al., *Racial Preference and Suburban Employment Opportunities* (Chicago: Legal Assistance Foundation and the Chicago Urban League, April 2003).

22. Devah Pager and Bruce Western, "Race at Work: Realities of Race and Criminal Record in the New York City Job Market" (2005), http://www.nyc.govlhtml!cchrlpdf/race_reporcweb.pdf; Salim Muwakkil, "Have We Put Racism behind Us? Don't Kid Yourselves," *Wall Street Journal,* September 29, 2003.

23. The Impact Fund, Berkeley, California, www.impactfund.org.

24. Richard Tomasson et al., *Affirmative Action* (Washington, DC: American University Press, 1996).

25. T. Hsien and F. H. Wu, "Beyond the Model Minority Myth," in *Affirmative Action Debate,* ed. G. E. Curry (Cambridge, MA: Perseus, 1998).

26. Claude S. Fischer et al., *Inequality by Design* (Princeton: Princeton University Press, 1996), 164-65.

27. S. G. Stolberg, "Race Gap Seen in Health Care of Equally Insured Patients," *New York Times,* March 21, 2002.

28. Faye Crosby, *Affirmative Action Is Dead; Long Live Affirmative Action* (New Haven: Yale University Press, 2004), 200.

29. Muwakkil, "Have We Put Racism behind Us?"

30. Ibid.

31. Steven R. Donziger, *The Real War 011 Crime* (New York: HarperCollins, 1999), 99.

32. "Five Reasons to Oppose the Death Penalty," Campaign to End the Death Penalty (pamphlet, 2006), http://nodeath.server269.com/dowllloads/583fivereasollS.pdf.

33. Marcia Coyle, "When Movements Coalesce," *National Law Journal,* September 21, 1992. See also B. J. Goldman, *Not Just Prosperity: Achieving Sustainability with Environmental Justice* (Washington, DC: National Wildlife Federation, 1993.)

34. Coyle, "When Movements Coalesce."

35. Ibid.

36. Ibid.

37. Ibid.

38. Ibid.

39. For a summary and a critique of Farrell's views, see Warren Farrell and James P. Sterba, *Does Feminism Discriminate Against Men?—A Debate* (New York: Oxford University Press, 2008).

40. Jean-Marie Navetta, "Gains in Learning, Gaps in Earning," *AAUW Outlook* (Spring 2005): 12.

41. Joan Williams, *Unbending Gender: Why Family and Work Conflict and What to Do About It* (New York: Oxford University Press, 2000), 274.

42. Tom L Beauchamp. "In Defense bf Affirmative Action," *Journal of Ethics* 2 (1998): 143-58.

43. Lichtman, "Why Women Need Affirmative Action."

44. Ibid.

45. Ibid.

46. Cherly Gomez-Preston, *When No Means No* (New York: Carol, 1993), 35-36. The problem is international as well as national. A three-year study of women in Estonia, Finland,

Sweden, and the Soviet Union showed that nearly 50 percent of all working women experience sexual harassment. A survey released in 1991 by the Santama Group to Consider Sexual Harassment at Work showed that about 70 percent of Japanese women say they have experienced some type of sexual harassment on the job. See Teresa Webb, *Step Forward* (New York: Master Media, 1991), xiv, xvii.

47. Ellen Bravo and Ellen Cassedy, *The 9-5 Guide to Combating Sexual Harassment* (New York: John Wiley, 1992),4-5.

48. Gomez-Preston, *When No Means No.*

49. Ibid.

50. *New York Times,* November 11, 1996 and February 4, 1997.

51. Linda Bird Francke, *Ground Zero* (New York: Simon & Shuster, 1997), 157.

52. Diana Schemo, "Rate of Rape at Academy Is Put at 12 Percent in Survey," *New York Times,* August 29, 2003.

53. U.S. Department of Defense, "Armed Forces Survey 2002 Sexual Harassment Survey," Defense Technical Information Center, Ft. Belfort, Virginia. In 2002 the Department of Defense excluded "unwanted sexual behavior" as part of the measure for sexual harassment, which reduced the frequency of sexual harassment in 1995 to 45 percent and to 24 percent in 2002. But why was unwanted sexual behavior removed from the measure of sexual harassment? The 2002 survey provides no explanation for this change. Could it have been done to just reduce the overall figure for sexual harassment?

54. Evelyn Murphy with E. J. Graff, *Getting Even* (New York: Simon & Shuster, 2005), 90-91.

55. Londa Schiebinger, "Women's Health and Clinical Trials," *Journal of Clinical Investigations* 112 (2003): 973-77.

56. Londa Schiebinger, *Has Feminism Changed Science* (Cambridge: Harvard University Press, 2001), 113-25.

57. Ibid.

READING 19

Notes

1. Raphael Tardon, "Richard Wright Tells Us: The White Problem in the United States," *Action,* 24 Oct. 1946. Reprinted in Kenneth Kinnamon and Michel Fabre, *Conversations with Richard Wright* (Jackson, Miss., 1993), 99. Malcolm X and others used this same formulation in the 1960s, but I believe that it originated with Wright, or at least that is the earliest citation I have found so far.

2. This is also Toni Morrison's point in *Playing in the Dark: Whiteness in the Literary Imagination* (Cambridge, Mass., 1992).

3. Richard Dyer, "White," *Screen* 29 (fall 1988): 44.

4. I thank Michael Schudson for pointing out to me that since the passage of civil rights legislation in the 1960s whiteness dares not speak its name, cannot speak in its own behalf, but rather advances through a color-blind language radically at odds with the distinctly racialized distribution of resources and life chances in American society.

5. Walter Benjamin, "Madame Ariane: Second Courtyard on the Left," from *One-Way Street* (London, 1969), 98–99.

6. Richard Slotkin, *Gunfighter Nation: The Myth of the Frontier in Twentieth Century America* (New York, 1992); Eric Lott, *Love and Theft* (New York, 1993); David Roediger, *Wages of Whiteness* (New York, 1992); Michael Rogin, "Blackface White Noise: The Jewish Jazz Singer Finds His Voice," *Critical Inquiry* 18 (spring 1992).

7. Robin Kelley, *Hammer and Hoe* (Chapel Hill, N.C., 1990); Lizabeth Cohen, *Making a New Deal* (Cambridge, 1991); George Sanchez, *Becoming Mexican American* (New York, 1993); Edmund Morgan, *American Slavery, American Freedom* (New York, 1975); John Hope Franklin, *The Color Line: Legacy for the Twenty-first Century* (Columbia, Mo., 1993).

8. Alexander Saxton, *The Rise and Fall of the White Republic* (New York, 1992); Roediger, *Wages;* Michael Rogin, *Ronald Reagan, the Movie: And Other Episodes in Political Demonology* (Berkeley, 1987); Michael Rogin, "Blackface"; Michael Rogin, "'Democracy and Burnt Cork': The End of Blackface, the Beginning of Civil Rights," presented at the University of California Humanities Research Institute Film Genres Study Group, November 1992.

9. See Kenneth Jackson, *Crabgrass Frontier: The Suburbanization of the United States* (New York, 1985); and Douglas S. Massey and Nancy A. Denton, *American Apartheid: Segregation and the Making of the Underclass* (Cambridge, Mass., 1993).

10. I thank Phil Ethington for pointing out to me that these aspects of New Deal policies emerged out of political negotiations between the segregationist Dixiecrats and liberals from the North and West. My perspective is that white supremacy was not a gnawing aberration within the New Deal coalition but rather an essential point of unity between southern white and northern white ethnics.

11. Records of the Federal Home Loan Bank Board of the Home Owners Loan Corporation. City Survey File, Los Angeles, 1939, Neighborhood D-53, National Archives, Washington, D.C., box 74, records group 195.

12. Massey and Denton, *American Apartheid,* 54.

13. John R. Logan and Harvey Molotch, *Urban Fortunes: The Political Economy of Place* (Berkeley, 1987), 182.

14. Ibid., 114.

15. Ibid., 130.

16. See Gary Gerstle, "Working-Class Racism: Broaden the Focus," *International Labor and Working Class History* 44 (fall 1993): 36.

17. Logan and Molotch, *Urban Fortunes,* 168–69.

18. Troy Duster, "Crime, Youth Unemployment, and the Black Urban Underclass," *Crime and Delinquency* 33 (Apr. 1987): 308.

19. Ibid., 309.

20. Massey and Denton, *American Apartheid,* 55.

21. Logan and Molotch, *Urban Forunes,* 113.

22. Robert D. Bullard, "Environmental Justice for All," in *Unequal Protection: Environmental Justice and Communities of Color,* ed. Robert Bullard (San Francisco, 1994), 9–10.

23. Massey and Denton, *American Apartheid,* 61.

24. Gertrude Ezorsky, *Racism and Justice: The Case for Affirmative Action* (Ithaca, N.Y., 1991), 25.

25. Logan and Molotch, *Urban Fortunes,* 116.

26. Jim Campen, "Lending Insights: Hard Proof That Banks Discriminate," *Dollars and Sense* 191 (Jan.–Feb. 1991): 17.

27. Mitchell Zuckoff, "Study Shows Racial Bias in Lending," *The Boston Globe,* 9 October 1992, 1, 77, 78.

28. Paul Ong and J. Eugene Grigsby III, "Race and Life-Cycle Effects on Home Ownership in Los Angeles, 1970 to 1980," *Urban Affairs Quarterly* 23 (June 1988): 605.

29. Massey and Denton, *American Apartheid,* 108.

30. Gary Orfield and Carol Ashkinaze, *The Closing Door: Conservative Policy and Black Opportunity* (Chicago, 1991), 58, 78.

31. Logan and Molotch, *Urban Fortunes.*

32. Campen, "Lending Insights," 18.

33. Gregory Squires, "'Runaway Plants,' Capital Mobility, and Black Economic Rights," in *Community and Capital in Conflict: Plant Closings and Job Loss,* ed. John C. Raines, Lenora E. Berson, and David McI. Gracie (Philadelphia, 1982), 70.

34. Gertrude Ezorsky, *Racism and Justice: The Case for Affirmative Action* (Ithaca, N.Y., 1991), 15.

35. Orfield and Ashkinaze, *The Closing Door,* 225–26.

36. McClatchy News Service, "State Taxes Gouge the Poor, Study Says," *Long Beach Press-Telegram,* 23 April 1991, A1.

37. "Proposition 13," *UC Focus* (June–July 1993): 2.

38. William Chafe, *The Unfinished Journey* (New York, 1986), 442; Noel J. Kent, "A Stacked Deck: Racial Minorities and the New American Political Economy," *Explorations in Ethnic Studies* 14 (Jan. 1991): 11.

39. Kent, "Stacked Deck," 13.

40. Melvin Oliver and James Johnson, "Economic Restructuring and Black Male Joblessness in United States Metropolitan Areas," *Urban Geography* 12 (Nov.–Dec. 1991); Gerald David Jaynes and Robin M. Williams, Jr., eds., *A Common Destiny: Blacks and American Society* (Washington, D.C., 1989); Reynolds Farley and Walter R. Allen, *The Color Line and the Quality of Life in America* (New York, 1987); Melvin Oliver and Tom Shapiro, "Wealth of a Nation: A Reassessment of Asset Inequality in America Shows at Least 1/3 of Households Are Asset Poor," *Journal of Economics and Sociology* 49 (Apr. 1990); Jonathan Kozol, *Savage Inequalities: Children in America's Schools* (New York, 1991); Cornell West, *Race Matters* (Boston, 1993).

41. Orfield and Ashkinaze, *Closing Door,* 46.

42. Ibid., 206.

43. Bart Landry, "The Enduring Dilemma of Race in America," in Alan H. Wolfe, *America at Century's End* (Berkeley, 1991), 206; Franklin, *Color Line,* 36–37.

44. Kathleen Hall Jamieson, *Dirty Politics: Deception, Distraction, and Democracy* (New York, 1992), 100.

45. Mary Edsall and Thomas Byrne Edsall, *Chain Reaction* (New York, 1991).

46. Nathan Glazer makes this argument in *Affirmative Discrimination* (New York, 1975).

47. I borrow the term "overdetermination" here from Louis Althusser, who uses it to show how dominant ideologies become credible to people in part because various institutions and agencies independently replicate them and reinforce their social power.

48. Rogena Schuyler, "Youth: We Didn't Sell Them into Slavery," *Los Angeles Times,* 21 June 1993, B4.

49. Ibid.

50. Jim Newton, "Skinhead Leader Pleads Guilty to Violence, Plot," *Los Angeles Times,* 20 Oct. 1993, A1, A15.

51. Antonin Scalia, quoted in Cheryl I. Harris, "Whiteness as Property," *Harvard Law Review,* 106 (June 1993): 1767.

52. Ibid.

53. The rise of a black middle class and the setbacks suffered by white workers during deindustrialization may seem to subvert the analysis presented here. Yet the black middle class remains fragile, far less able than other middle-class groups to translate advances in income into advances in wealth and power. Similarly, the success of neoconservatism since the 1970s has rested on securing support from white workers for economic policies that do them objective harm by mobilizing counter-subversive electoral coalitions against busing and affirmative action, while carrying out attacks on public institutions and resources by representing "public" space and black space. See Oliver and Shapiro, "Wealth of a Nation." See also Logan and Harvey, *Urban Fortunes.*

54. Johnny Otis, *Upside Your Head! Rhythm and Blues on Central Avenue* (Hanover, N.H., 1993).

55. Mobilizations against plant shutdowns, for environmental protection, against cutbacks in education spending, and for reproductive rights all contain the potential for pan-ethnic antiracist organizing, but, too often, neglect of race as a

central modality for how issues of employment, pollution, education, or reproductive rights are experienced isolates these social movements from their broadest possible base.

56. Walter Benjamin, "Madame Ariane: Second Courtyard on the Left," from *One-Way Street* (London, 1969), 98, 99.

READING 20

References

Blumer, Herbert. 1958. "Racial Prejudice as a Sense of Group Position." *Pacific Sociological Review* 1: 3–7.

Bobo, Lawrence D. 1988. "Attitudes Toward the Black Political Movements: Trends, Meaning, and Effects on Racial Policy Attitudes." *Social Psychology Quarterly* 51(4): 287–302.

————. 1999. "Prejudice as Group Position: Microfoundations of a Sociological Approach to Racism and Race Relations." *Journal of Social Issues* 55(3): 445–72.

————. 2000. "Reclaiming a DuBoisian Perspective on Racial Attitudes." *Annals of the American Academy of Political and Social Science* 568: 186–202.

Bobo, Lawrence, and James R. Kluegel. 1997. "Status, Ideology, and Dimensions of Whites' Racial Beliefs and Attitudes: Progress and Stagnation." In *Racial Attitudes in the 1990s: Continuity and Change,* edited by Steven A. Tuch and Jack K. Martin. New York: Praeger.

Bobo, Lawrence, James R. Kluegel, and Ryan A. Smith. 1997. "Laissez-Faire Racism: The Crystallization of a Kinder, Gentler Antiblack Ideology." In *Racial Attitudes in the 1990s: Continuity and Change,* edited by Steven Tuch and Jack K. Martin. New York: Praeger.

Bobo, Lawrence D., and Ryan A. Smith. 1998. "From Jim Crow Racism to Laissez-Faire Racism: The Transformation of Racial Attitudes." In *Beyond Pluralism: The Conception of Groups and Group Identities in America,* edited by Wendy F. Katkin, Ned Landsman, and Andrea Tyree. Urbana, Ill.: University of Illinois Press.

Bobo, Lawrence D., and Mia Tuan. Forthcoming. *Prejudice in Politics: Group Position, Public Opinion, and the Wisconsin Treaty Rights Controversy.* Cambridge, Mass.: Harvard University Press.

Bobo, Lawrence, and Camille L. Zubrinsky. 1996. "Attitudes on Residential Integration: Perceived Status Differences, Mere In-group Preference or Racial Prejudice?" *Social Forces* 74(3): 883–909.

Bonilla-Silva, Edward. 2001. *White Supremacy and Racism in the Post–Civil Rights Era.* Boulder, Colo.: Lynne Rienner.

Charles, Camille Z. 2000. "Neighborhood Racial-Composition Preferences: Evidence from a Multiethnic Metropolis." *Social Problems* 47(3): 379–407.

————. 2003. "The Dynamics of Racial Residential Segregation." *Annual Review of Sociology* 29: 67–107.

Cohen, Cathy J. 1999. *The Boundaries of Blackness: AIDS and the Breakdown of Black Politics.* Chicago: University of Chicago Press.

Dawson, Michael C. 1994. *Behind the Mule: Race and Class in African American Politics.* Princeton, N.J.: Princeton University Press.

————. 2000. "Slowly Coming to Grips with the Effects of the American Racial Order on American Policy Preferences." In *Racialized Politics: The Debate on Racism in America,* edited by David O. Sears, James Sidanius, and Lawrence D. Bobo. Chicago: University of Chicago Press.

————. 2001. *Black Visions.* Chicago: University of Chicago Press.

Dawson, Michael C., and Ravana Popoff. 2004. "Reparations: Justice and Greed in Black and White." *Du Bois Review* 1: 47—92.

Farley, Reynolds, Charlotte Steeh, Maria Krysan, Tara Jackson, and Keith Reeves. 1994. "Stereotypes and Segregation: Neighborhoods in the Detroit Area." *American Journal of Sociology* 100(3): 750–80.

Feagin, Joe R. 2001. *Racist America: Roots, Current Realities, and Future Reparations.* New York: Routledge.

Fields, Barbara J. 1982. "Ideology and Race in American History." In *Region, Race, and Reconstruction: Essays in Honor of C. Vann Woodward,* edited by J. Morgan Kousser and James M. McPherson. New York: Oxford University Press.

Gans, Herbert J. 1999. "The Possibility of a New Racial Hierarchy in the Twenty-first-Century United States." In *The Cultural Territories of Race: Black and White Boundaries,* edited by Michele Lamont. New York: Russell Sage Foundation.

Holt, Thomas, 2000. *The Problem of Race in the Twenty-first Century.* Cambridge, Mass.: Harvard University Press.

Jackman, Mary R. 1994. *The Velvet Glove: Paternalism and Conflict in Gender, Class, and Race Relations.* Berkeley: University of California Press.

Kim, Claire Jean. 2000. *Bitter Fruit: The Politics of Black-Korean Conflict in New York City.* New Haven, Conn.: Yale University Press.

Kinder, Donald R., and Lynn M. Sanders. 1996. *Divided by Color: Racial Politics and Democratic Ideals.* Chicago: University of Chicago Press.

Klinkner, Philip, and Rogers Smith. 1999. *The Unsteady March: The Rise and Decline of Racial Equality in America.* Chicago: University of Chicago Press.

Kluegel, James R., and Lawrence D. Bobo. 2001. "Perceived Group Discrimination and Policy Attitudes: The Sources and Consequences of the Race and Gender Gaps." In *Urban Inequality: Evidence from Four Cities,* edited by Alice O'Connor, Chris Tilly, and Lawrence D. Bobo. New York: Russell Sage Foundation.

Kluegel, James R., and Eliot R. Smith. 1986. *Beliefs About Inequality: Americans' Views About What Is and What Ought to Be.* New York: Aldine de Gruyter.

Krysan, Maria. 2000. "Prejudice, Politics, and Public Opinion: Understanding the Sources of Racial Policy Attitudes." *Annual Review of Sociology* 26: 135–68.

Lamont, Michele. 2000. *The Dignity of Working Men: Morality and the Boundaries of Race, Class, and Immigration.* Cambridge, Mass.: Harvard University Press.

Lee, Taeku. 2002. *Mobilizing Public Opinion: Black Insurgency and Racial Attitudes in the Civil Rights Era.* Chicago: University of Chicago Press.

Sears, David O., Collette van Laar, and Rick Kosterman. 1997. "Is It Really Racism?" The Origins of White Americans' Opposition to Race-Targeted Policies." *Public Opinion Quarterly* 61: 16–53.

Smith, Eliot R. 1993. "Social Identity and Social Emotions: Toward New Conceptualizations of Prejudice." In *Affect, Cognition, and Stereotyping: Interactive Processes in Group Perception,* edited by Diane M. Mackie and David L. Hamilton. New York: Academic Press.

Sniderman, Paul M., and Thomas Piazza. 1993. *The Scar of Race.* Cambridge: Harvard University Press.

Thernstrom, Stephan, and Abigail Thernstrom. 1997. *America in Black and White: One Nation, Indivisible.* New York: Simon & Schuster.

Thompson, J. Phillip. 1998. "Universalism and Deconcentration: Why Race Still Matters in Poverty and Economic Development." *Politics and Society* 26: 181–219.

Waters, Mary C. 1999. *Black Identities: West Indian Immigrant Dreams and American Realities.* Cambridge, Mass.: Harvard University Press.

Yinger, John. 1998. "Housing Discrimination Is Still Worth Worrying About." *Housing Policy Debate* 9: 893–927.

Zuberi, Tukufu. 2001. *Thicker Than Blood: How Racial Statistics Lie.* Minneapolis: University of Minnesota Press.

Zubrinsky, Camille L., and Lawrence Bobo. 1996. "Prismatic Metropolis: Race and Residential Segregation in the City of Angels." *Social Science Research* 24: 335–74.

READING 21

References

Allport, G. 1958. *The Nature of Prejudice.* Garden City, N.Y.: Doubleday Anchor.

Almgren, G., A. Guest, G. Imerwahr, and M. Spittel. 1998. Joblessness, family disruption, and violent death in Chicago: 1970–1990. *Social Forces* 76: 1465–1494.

Anderson, E. 1990. *Streetwise: Race, Class, and Change in an Urban Community.* Chicago: University of Chicago Press.

Bertram, S. 1988. *An Audit of the Real Estate Sales and Rental Markets of Selected Southern Suburbs.* Homewood, Ill.: South Suburban Housing Center.

Blalock, H.M., Jr. 1967. *Toward a Theory of Minority-Group Relations.* New York: Wiley.

Bobo, L., H. Schuman, and C. Steeh. 1986. Changing racial attitudes toward residential integration. Pp. 152–169 in *Housing Desegregation and Federal Policy,* ed. Chapel Hill: University of North Carolina Press.

Bobo, L., and C. Zubrinsky. 1996. Attitudes on residential integration: Perceived status differences, mere in-group preference, or racial prejudice? *Social Forces* 74:883–909.

Brooks-Gunn, J., G. Duncan, and J. Aber, eds. 1997. *Neighborhood Poverty: Context and Consequences for Children.* New York: Russell Sage.

Brooks-Gunn, J., G. Duncan, P. Klebanov, and N. Sealand. 1993. Do neighborhoods influence child and adolescent development? *American Journal of Sociology* 99:353–395.

Clark, W. 1991. Residential preferences and neighborhood racial segregation: A test of the Schelling segregation model. *Demography* 28:1–19.

Corcoran, M., R. Gordon, D. Laren, and G. Solon. 1989. Effects of family and community background on men's economic status. Working Paper 2896, National Bureau of Economic Research, Cambridge, Mass.

Crane, J. 1991. The epidemic theory of ghettos and neighborhood effects on dropping out and teenage childbearing. *American Journal of Sociology* 96:1226–1259.

Danziger, S., and P. Gottschalk. 1995. *America Unequal.* Cambridge: Harvard University Press and the Russell Sage Foundation.

Datcher, L. 1982. Effects of community and family background on achievement. *The Review of Economics and Statistics* 64:32–41.

Demerath, N., and H. Gilmore. 1954. The ecology of southern cities. Pp. 120–125 in *The Urban South,* R. Vance and N. Demerath, eds. Chapel Hill: University of North Carolina Press.

Denton, N. 1994. Are African Americans still hypersegregated? Pp. 49–81 in *Residential Apartheid: The American Legacy,* R. Bullard, J. Grigsby III, and C. Lee, eds. Los Angeles: CAAS Publications, University of California.

Denton, N., and D. Massey. 1988. Residential segregation of Blacks, Hispanics, and Asians by socioeconomic status and generation. *Social Science Quarterly* 69:797–817. 1989. Racial identity among Caribbean Hispanics: The effect of double minority status on residential segregation. *American Sociological Review* 54:790–808. 1991. Patterns of neighborhood transition in a multiethnic world. *Demography* 28:41–64.

Duncan, O., and B. Duncan. 1957. *The Negro Population of Chicago: A Study of Residential Succession.* Chicago: University of Chicago Press.

Farley, R. 1977. Residential segregation in urbanized areas of the United States in 1970: An analysis of social class and racial differences. *Demography* 14:497–518.

Farley, R., S. Bianchi, and D. Colasanto. 1979. Barriers to the racial integration of neighborhoods: The Detroit case. *Annals of the American Academy of Political and Social Science* 441:97–113.

Farley, R., H. Schuman, S. Bianchi, D. Colasanto, and S. Hatchett. 1978. "Chocolate city, vanilla suburbs": Will the trend toward racially separate communities continue? *Social Science Research* 7:319–344.

Farley, R., C. Steeh, M. Krysan, T. Jackson, and K. Reeves. 1994. Stereotypes and segregation: Neighborhoods in the Detroit area. *American Journal of Sociology* 100:750–780.

Feins, J., R. Bratt, and R. Hollister. 1981. *Final Report of a Study of Racial Discrimination in the Boston Housing Market.* Cambridge: Abt Associates.

Fix, M., G. Galster, and R. Struyk. 1993. An overview of auditing for discrimination. Pp. 1–68 in *Clear and Convincing Evidence: Measurement of Discrimination in America,* M. Fix and R. Struyk, eds. Washington, D.C.: The Urban Institute Press.

Frey, W., and R. Farley. 1994. Changes in the segregation of Whites from Blacks during the 1980s: Small steps toward a more integrated society. *American Sociological Review* 59:23–45. 1996. Latino, Asian, and Black segregation in U.S. metropolitan areas: Are multiethnic metros different? *Demography* 33:35–50.

Furstenburg, F. Jr., S. Morgan, K. Moore, and J. Peterson. 1987. Race differences in the timing of adolescent intercourse. *American Sociological Review* 52:511–518.

Guest, A., G. Almgren, and J. Hussey. 1998. The ecology of race and socioeconomic distress: Infant and working age mortality in Chicago. *Demography* 35:23–34.

Hakken, J. 1979. *Discrimination Against Chicanos in the Dallas Rental Housing Market: An Experimental Extension of the Housing Market Practices Survey.* Washington, D.C.: Office of Policy Development and Research, U.S. Department of Housing and Urban Development.

Harrison, R., and D. Weinberg. 1992. Racial and ethnic residential segregation in 1990. Paper presented at the annual meeting of the Population Association of America, Denver, April 13.

Helper, R. 1969. *Racial Policies and Practices of Real Estate Brokers.* Minneapolis: University of Minnesota Press.

Hintzen, H. 1983. *Report of an Audit of Real Estate Sales Practices of 15 Northwest Chicago Real Estate Sales Offices.* Chicago: Leadership Council for Metropolitan Open Communities.

Hochschild, J. 1995. *Facing up to the American Dream: Race, Class, and the Soul of the Nation.* Princeton: Princeton University Press.

Hogan, D., and E. Kitagawa. 1985. The impact of social status, family structure, and neighborhood on the fertility of Black adolescents. *American Journal of Sociology* 90:825–855.

Hwang, S., and S. Murdock. 1982. Residential segregation in Texas in 1980. *Social Science Quarterly* 63:737–748.

Jackson, P. 1981. Paradoxes of Puerto Rican segregation in New York. Pp. 109–126 in *Ethnic Segregation in Cities,* C. Peach, V. Robinson, and S. Smith, eds. London: Croom Helm.

Jackson, T. 1994. The other side of the residential segregation equation: Why Detroit area Blacks are reluctant to pioneer integration. Paper presented at the Russell Sage Foundation Multi-City conference.

James, F., and E. Tynan. 1986. Segregation and discrimination against Hispanic Americans. Pp. 83–98 in *Housing Discrimination and Federal Policy,* J. Goering, ed. Chapel Hill: University of North Carolina Press.

Jencks, C., and S. Mayer. 1990. The social consequences of growing up in a poor neighborhood. Pp. 111–186 in *Inner City Poverty in the United States,* L. Lynn, Jr., and M. McGeary, eds. Washington, D.C.: National Academy of Sciences.

Kantrowitz, N. 1973. *Ethnic and Racial Segregation in the New York Metropolis.* New York: Praeger.

Kasarda, J. 1993. Inner city concentrated poverty and neighborhood distress: 1970–1990. *Housing Policy Debate* 4(3):253–302.

Krivo, L., and R. Kaufman. 1999. How low can it go? Declining Black-White segregation in a multi-ethnic context. *Demography* 36:93–110.

Krivo, L., and R. Peterson. 1996. Extremely disadvantaged neighborhoods and urban crime. *Social Forces* 75:619–648.

Krivo, L., R. Peterson, H. Rizzo, and J. Reynolds. 1998. Race segregation, and the concentration of disadvantage: 1980–1990. *Social Problems* 45:61–80.

Levy, F. 1995. Incomes and income inequality. Pp. 1–58 in *State of the Union: America in the 1990s,* Farley, ed. New York: Russell Sage.

Lieberson, S. 1980. *A Piece of the Pie: Blacks and White Immigrants Since 1880.* Berkeley: University of California Press.

Lopez, M. 1981. Patterns of interethnic residential segregation in the urban Southwest, 1960 and 1970. *Social Science Quarterly* 62:50–63.

Massey, D. 1979. Effects of socioeconomic factors on the residential segregation of Blacks and Spanish Americans in United States urbanized areas. *American Sociological Review* 44:1015–1022. 1981. Hispanic residential segregation: A comparison of Mexicans, Cubans, and

Puerto Ricans. *Sociology and Social Research* 65:311–322. 1985. Ethnic residential segregation: A theoretical synthesis and empirical review. *Sociology and Social Research* 69:315–350. 1990. American apartheid: Segregation and the making of the underclass. *American Journal of Sociology* 96:329–358.

Massey, D., and B. Bitterman. 1985. Explaining the paradox of Puerto Rican segregation. *Social Forces* 64:306–331.

Massey, D., G. Condran, and N. Denton. 1987. The effect of residential segregation on Black social and economic well-being. *Social Forces* 66:29–57.

Massey, D., and N. Denton. 1987. Trends in the residential segregation of Blacks, Hispanics, and Asians. *American Sociological Review* 52:802–825. 1988. The dimensions of residential segregation. *Social Forces* 67:281–315. 1989a. Residential segregation of Mexicans, Puerto Ricans, and Cubans in U.S. metropolitan areas. *Sociology and Social Research* 73:73–83. 1989b. Hypersegregation in U.S. metropolitan areas: Black and Hispanic segregation along five dimensions. *Demography* 26:373–393. 1992. Racial identity and the spatial assimilation of Mexicans in the the United States. *Social Science Research* 21:235–260. 1993. *American Apartheid: Segregation and the Making of the Underclass.* Cambridge: Harvard University Press.

Massey, D., and M. Eggers. 1990. The ecology of inequality: Minorities and the concentration of poverty, 1970–1980. *American Journal of Sociology* 95:1153–1189.

Massey, D., and M. Fischer. 1999. Does rising income bring integration? New results for Blacks, Hispanics, and Asians in 1990. *Social Science Research* 28:316–326. 2000. How segregation concentrates poverty. *Ethnic and Racial Studies* 23:670–691.

Massey, D., and E. Fong. 1990. Segregation and neighborhood quality: Blacks, Hispanics, and Asians in the San Francisco metropolitan area. *Social Forces* 69:15–32.

Massey, D., and A. Gross. 1991. Explaining trends in residential segregation 1970–1980. *Urban Affairs Quarterly* 27:13–35.

Massey, D., A. Gross, and M. Eggers. 1991. Segregation, the concentration of poverty, and the life chances of individuals. *Social Science Research* 20:397–420.

Massey, D., and K. Shibuya. 1995. Unraveling the tangle of pathology: The effect of spatially concentrated joblessness on the well-being of African Americans. *Social Science Research* 24: 252–366.

Massey, D., M. White, and V. Phua. 1996. The dimensions of segregation revisited. *Sociological Methods and Research.* 25:172–206.

Morenoff, J., and R. Sampson. 1997. Violent crime and the spatial dynamics of neighborhood transition: Chicago, 1970–1990. *Social Forces* 76:31–64.

Morris, M., A. Bernhardt, and M. Hancock. 1994. Economic inequality: New methods for new trends. *American Sociological Review* 59:205–219.

Moskos, C., and J. Butler. 1996. *All That We Can Be: Black Leadership and Racial Integration the Army Way.* New York: Basic Books.

Patillo, M. 1998. Sweet mothers and gangbangers: Managing crime in a Black middle-class neighborhood. *Social Forces* 76:747–774.

Saltman, J. 1979. Housing discrimination: Policy research, methods, and results. *Annals of the American Academy of Political and Social Science.* 441:186–196.

Schelling, T. 1971. Dynamic models of segregation. *Journal of Mathematical Sociology* 1:143–186.

Schneider, M., and J. Logan. 1982. Suburban racial segregation and Black access to local public resources. *Social Science Quarterly* 63: 762–770.

Schroeder, A. 1985. *Report on an Audit of Real Estate Sales Practices of Eight Northwest Suburban Offices.* Chicago: Leadership Council for Metropolitan Open Communities.

Schuman, H., and L. Bobo. 1988. Survey-based experiments on White racial attitudes toward residential integration. *American Journal of Sociology* 2:273–299.

Schuman, H., C. Steeh, and L. Bobo. 1985. *Racial Attitudes in America: Trends and Interpretations.* Cambridge: Harvard University Press.

Schuman, H., C. Steeh, L. Bobo, and M. Krysan. 1998. *Racial Attitudes in America: Trends and Interpretations.* Cambridge: Harvard University Press.

Simkus, A. 1978. Residential segregation by occupation and race in ten urbanized areas, 1950–1970. *American Sociological Review* 43:81–93.

Sniderman, P., and T. Piazza. 1993. *The Scar of Race.* Cambridge: Harvard University Press.

Taylor, M. 1998. The effect of racial composition on racial attitudes of Whites. *American Sociological Review* 63:512–535.

Turner, E. and J. Allen. 1991. *An Atlas of Population Patterns in Metropolitan, Los Angeles and Orange Counties.* Occasional Publication in Geography No. 8. Northridge, Calif.: Center for Geographical Studies, California State University at Northridge.

U.S. Bureau of the Census. 1979. The Social and Economic Status of the Black Population in the United States: An Historical View, 1790–1978. Current Population Reports, Special Studies Series P–23, No. 80. Washington, D.C.: U.S. Government Printing Office.

Wilson, W. 1987. *Truly Disadvantaged: The Inner City, the Underclass, and Public Policy.* Chicago: University of Chicago Press.

Yinger, J. 1986. Measuring racial discrimination with fair housing audits: Caught in the act. *American Economic Review* 76:991–993. 1985. The racial dimension of urban housing markets in the 1980s. Pp. 43–67 in *Divided Neighborhoods:*

Changing Patterns of Racial Segregation, G.A. Tobin, ed. Newbury Park, Calif.: Sage Publications. 1989. Measuring discrimination in housing availability. Final Research Report No. 2 to the U.S. Department of Housing and Urban Development. Washington, D.C.: The Urban Institute. 1995. *Closed Doors, Opportunities Lost: The Continuing Costs of Housing Discrimination.* New York: Russell Sage.

Zubrinsky, C., and L. Bobo. 1996. Prismatic metropolis: Race and residential segregation in the City of Angels. *Social Science Research* 25: 335–374.

READING 23

Notes

1. Robert D. Bullard, 1994, *Dumping in Dixie: Race, Class and Environmental Quality.* Boulder, CO: Westview Press.

2. Robert D. Bullard, "Solid Waste Sites and the Black Houston Community," *Sociological Inquiry* 53 (Spring 1983): 273–288.

3. U.S. General Accounting Office (1983), *Siting of Hazardous Waste Landfills and Their Correlation with Racial and Economic Status of Surrounding Communities,* Washington, DC: Government Printing Office.

4. Commission for Racial Justice (1987), *Toxic Wastes and Race in the United States,* New York: United Church of Christ.

5. Charles Lee, 1992, *Proceedings: The First National People of Color Environmental Leadership Summit,* New York: United Church of Christ Commission for Racial Justice.

6. Dana Alston, "Transforming a Movement: People of Color Unite at Summit against Environmental Racism," *Sojourner* 21 (1992), pp. 30–31.

7. William K. Reilly, "Environmental Equity: EPA's Position," *EPA Journal* 18 (March/April 1992): 18–19.

8. R. D. Bullard and B. H. Wright, "The Politics of Pollution: Implications for the Black Community," *Phylon* 47 (March 1986): 71–78.

9. Robert D. Bullard, "Race and Environmental Justice in the United States," *Yale Journal of International Law* 18 (Winter 1993): 319–335; Robert D. Bullard, "The Threat of Environmental Racism," *Natural Resources & Environment* 7 (Winter 1993): 23–26, 55–56.

10. Louis Sullivan, "Remarks at the First Annual Conference on Childhood Lead Poisoning," in Alliance to End Childhood Lead Poisoning: Final Report, Washington DC: Alliance to End Childhood Lead Poisoning, October, 1991, p. A-2.

11. Bill Lann Lee, "Environmental Litigation on Behalf of Poor, Minority Children, *Matthews v. Coye:* A Case Study," paper presented at the Annual Meeting of the American Association for the Advancement of Science, Chicago (February 9, 1992).

12. Ibid., p. 32.

13. Ibid.

14. Robert D. Bullard, "The Environmental Justice Framework: A Strategy for Addressing Unequal Protection," paper presented at Resources for the Future Conference on Risk Management, Annapolis, MD (November 1992).

15. Paul Mohai and Bunyan Bryant, "Race, Poverty, and the Environment," *EPA Journal* 18 (March/April 1993): 1–8; R. D. Bullard, "In Our Backyards," *EPA Journal* 18 (March/April 1992): 11–12; D. R. Wernette and L. A. Nieves, "Breathing Polluted Air," *EPA Jounal* 18 (March/April 1992): 16–17; Patrick C. West, "Health Concerns for Fish-Eating Tribes?" *EPA Journal* 18 (March/April 1992): 15–16.

16. Marianne Lavelle and Marcia Coyle, "Unequal Protection," *National Law Journal* (September 21, 1992): S1–S2.

17. Robert D. Bullard, ed., *Confronting Environmental Racism: Voices from the Grassroots,* Boston: South End Press, 1993, chapter 1; Robert D. Bullard, "Waste and Racism: A Stacked Deck?" *Forum for Applied Research and Public Policy* 8 (Spring 1993): 29–35; Robert D. Bullard (ed.), *In Search of the New South—The Black Urban Experience in the 1970s and 1980s* (Tuscaloosa, AL: University of Alabama Press, 1991).

18. Florence Wagman Roisman, "The Lessons of American Apartheid: The Necessity and Means of Promoting Residential Racial Integration," *Iowa Law Review* 81 (December 1995): 479–525.

19. Joe R. Feagin, "A House Is Not a Home: White Racism and U.S. Housing Practices," in R. D. Bullard, J. E. Grigsby, and Charles Lee, eds., *Residential Apartheid: The American Legacy,* Los Angeles: UCLA Center for Afro-American Studies Publication, 1994, pp. 17–48.

20. Eric Mann, *L.A.'s Lethal Air: New Strategies for Policy, Organizing, and Action,* Los Angeles: Labor/Community Strategy Center, 1991, p. 31.

21. Jim Motavalli, "Toxic Targets: Polluters That Dump on Communities of Color Are Finally Being Brought to Justice," *E Magazine,* 4 (July/August 1997): 29–41.

22. Joe Bandy, "Reterritorializing Borders: Transnational Environmental Justice on the U.S./Mexico Border," *Race, Gender, and Class* 5 (1997): 80–103.

23. Bunyan Bryant and Paul Mohai, *Race and the Incidence of Environmental Hazards* (Boulder, CO: Westview Press, 1992); Bunyan Bryant, ed., *Environmental Justice,* pp. 8–34.

24. R. Pinderhughes, "Who Decides What Constitutes a Pollution Problem?" *Race, Gender, and Class* 5 (1997): 130–152.

25. Diane Takvorian, "Toxics and Neighborhoods Don't Mix," *Land Use Forum: A Journal of Law, Policy and Practice* 2 (Winter 1993): 28–31; R. D. Bullard, "Examining the Evidence of Environmental Racism," *Land Use Forum: A Journal of Law, Policy, and Practice* 2 (Winter 1993): 6–11.

26. For an in-depth examination of the Houston case study, see R. D. Bullard, 1987, *Invisible Houston: The Black Experience in Boom and Bust.* College Station, TX: Texas A&M University Press, pp. 60–75.

27. Ruth Rosen, "Who Gets Polluted: The Movement for Environmental Justice," *Dissent* (Spring 1994): 223–230; R. D. Bullard, "Environmental Justice: It's More than Waste Facility Siting," *Social Science Quarterly* 77 (September 1996): 493–499.

28. Commission for Racial Justice, *Toxic Wastes and Race in the United States,* pp. xiii–xiv.

29. U.S. General Accounting Office, *Siting of Hazardous Waste Landfills and Their Correlation with Racial and Economic Status of Surrounding Communities,* Washington, DC: U.S. General Accounting Office, 1983, p. 1.

30. Robert D. Bullard, ed., *Confusing Environmental Racism: Voices from the Grassroots,* Boston: South End, 1993; Robert D. Bullard, "The Threat of Environmental Racism," *Natural Resources & Environment* 7 (Winter 1993): 23–26; Bunyan Bryant and Paul Mohai, eds., *Race and the Incidence of Environmental Hazards,* Boulder, CO: Westview Press, 1992; Regina Austin and Michael Schill, "Black, Brown, Poor and Poisoned: Minority Grassroots Environmentalism and the Quest for Eco-Justice," *The Kansas Journal of Law and Public Policy* 1 (1991): 69–82; Kelly C. Colquette and Elizabeth A. Henry Robertson, "Environmental Racism: The Causes, Consequences, and Commendations," *Tulane Environmental Law Journal* 5 (1991); 153–207; Rachel D. Godsil, "Remedying Environmental Racism," *Michigan Law Review* 90 (1991): 394–427.

31. Bullard and Feagin, "Racism and the City," pp. 55–76; Robert D. Bullard, "Dismantling Environmental Racism in the USA," *Local Environment* 4 (1999): 5–19.

32. W. J. Kruvant, "People, Energy, and Pollution," in D. K. Newman and Dawn Day, eds., *The American Energy Consumer,* Cambridge, Mass.: Ballinger, 1975, pp. 125–167; Robert D. Bullard, "Solid Waste Sites and the Black Houston Community," *Sociological Inquiry* 53 (Spring 1983): 273–288; United Church of Christ Commission for Racial Justice, *Toxic Wastes and Race in the United States,* New York: Commission for Racial Justice, 1987; Dick Russell, "Environmental Racism," *The Amicus Journal* 11 (Spring 1989): 22–32; Eric Mann, *L.A.'s Lethal Air: New Strategies for Policy, Organizing, and Action,* Los Angeles: Labor/Community Strategy Center, 1991; D. R. Wernette and L. A. Nieves, "Breathing Polluted Air: Minorities are Disproportionately Exposed," *EPA Journal* 18 (March/April 1992): 16–17; Bryant and Mohai, *Race and the Incidence of Environmental Hazards;* Benjamin Goldman and Laura J. Fitton, *Toxic Wastes and Race Revisited,* Washington, DC: Center for Policy Alternatives, NAACP, and United Church of Christ, 1994.

33. Myrick A. Freedman, "The Distribution of Environmental Quality," in Allen V. Kneese and Blair T. Bower (eds.), *Environmental Quality Analysis,* Baltimore: Johns Hopkins University Press for Resources for the Future, 1971; Michael Gelobter, "The Distribution of Air Pollution by Income and Race," paper presented at the Second Symposium on Social Science in Resource Management, Urbana, Illinois (June 1988); Gianessi et al., "The Distributional Effects of Uniform Air Pollution Policy in the U.S.," *Quarterly Journal of Economics* (May 1979): 281–301.

34. Patrick C. West, J. Mark Fly, and Robert Marans, "Minority Anglers and Toxic Fish Consumption: Evidence from a State-Wide Survey in Michigan," in Bryant and Mohai, *Race and the Incidence of Environmental Hazards,* pp. 100–113.

35. Robert D. Bullard, "Solid Waste Sites and the Black Houston Community," *Sociological Inquiry* 53 (Spring 1983): 273–288; Robert D. Bullard, *Invisible Houston: The Black Experience in Boom and Bust,* College Station, TX: Texas A&M University Press, 1987, chapter 6; Robert D. Bullard, "Environmental Racism and Land Use," *Land Use Forum: A Journal of Law, Policy & Practice* 2 (Spring 1993): 6–11.

36. United Church of Christ Commission for Racial Justice, *Toxic Wastes and Race;* Paul Mohai and Bunyan Bryant, "Environmental Racism: Reviewing the Evidence," in Bryant and Mohai, *Race and the Incidence of Environmental Hazards;* Paul Stretesky and Michael J. Hogan, "Environmental Justice: An Analysis of Superfund Sites in Florida," *Social Problems* 45 (May 1998): 268–287.

37. Marianne Lavelle and Marcia Coyle, "Unequal Protection: The Racial Divide in Environmental Law," *National Law Journal,* September 21, 1992.

38. Agency for Toxic Substances Disease Registry, *The Nature and Extent of Lead Poisoning in Children in the United States: A Report to Congress,* Atlanta: U.S. Department of Health and Human Resources, 1988, pp. 1–12.

39. J. Schwartz and R. Levine, "Lead: An Example of the Job Ahead," *EPA Journal* 18 (March/April 1992): 32–44.

40. Centers for Disease Control and Prevention, "Update: Blood Lead Levels—United States, 1991–1994," *Mortality and Morbidity Weekly Report* 46, no. 7 (February 21, 1997): 141–146.

41. James L. Pinkle, D. J. Brody, E. W. Gunter, R. A. Kramer, D. C. Paschal, K. M. Glegal, and T. D. Matte, "The Decline in Blood Lead Levels in the United States: The National Health and Nutrition Examination Survey (NHANES)," *Journal of the American Medical Association* 272 (1994): 284–291.

42. Arnold W. Reitze, Jr., "A Century of Air Pollution Control Law: What Worked; What Failed; What Might Work," *Environmental Law* 21 (1991): 1549.

43. For an in-depth discussion of transportation investments and social equity issues, see R. D. Bullard and G. S. Johnson, eds., *Just Transportation: Dismantling Race and Class Barriers to Mobility.* Gabriola Island, BC: New Society Publishers, 1997.

44. Sid Davis, "Race and the Politics of Transportation in Atlanta," in R. D. Bullard and G. S. Johnson, *Just Transportation,* pp. 84–96; Environmental Justice Resource Center, *Sprawl Atlanta: Social Equity Dimensions of Uneven Growth and Development,* a report prepared for the Turner Foundation, Atlanta: Clark Atlanta University (January 1999).

45. D. R. Wernette and L. A. Nieves, "Breathing Polluted Air: Minorities Are Disproportionately Exposed," *EPA Journal* 18 (March 1992): 16–17.

46. CDC, "Asthma—United States, 1982–1992." *MMWR* 43 (1995): 952–955.

47. CDC, "Asthma Morality and Hospitalization among Children and Young Adults—United States, 1980–1993." *MMWR* 45 (1996): 350–353.

48. Anna E. Pribitkin, "The Need for Revision of Ozone Standards: Why Has the EPA Failed to Respond?" *Temple Environmental Law & Technology Journal* 13 (1994): 104.

49. CDC/NCHS, *Health United States* 1994, DHHS Pub. No. (PHS) 95-1232, Tables 83, 84, 86, 87.

50. CDC, "Asthma—United States, 1982–1992." *MMWR* 43 (1995): 952–955.

51. CDC, "Disabilities among Children Aged Less Than or Equal to 17 years—United States, 1991–1992." *MMWR* 44 (1995): 609–613.

52. U.S. EPA, "Review of National Ambient Air Quality Standards for Ozone, Assessment of Scientific and Technical Information," OAQPS Staff Paper, Research Triangle Park, NC: EPA, 1996; Haluk Ozkaynk, John D. Spengler, Marie O'Neil, Jianping Xue, Hui Zhou, Kathy Gilbert, and Sonja Ramstrom, "Ambient Ozone Exposure and Emergency Hospital Admissions and Emergency Room Visits for Respiratory Problems in Thirteen U.S. Cities," in American Lung Association, *Breathless: Air Pollution and Hospital Admissions/Emergency Room Visits in 13 Cities,* Washington, DC: American Lung Association, 1996; American Lung Association, *Out of Breath: Populations-at-Risk to Alternative Ozone Levels,* Washington, DC: American Lung Association, 1995.

53. Centers for Disease Control and Prevention, National Center for Environmental Health, Division of Environmental Hazards and Health Effects, Air Pollution and Respiratory Branch, "Asthma Mortality and Hospitalization Among Children and Young Adults—United States, 1980–1993," *Morbidity and Mortality Weekly Report,* 45 (1996).

54. Centers for Disease Control, "Asthma: United States, 1980–1990," *MMWR* 39 (1992): 733–735.

55. Mary C. White, Ruth Etzel, Wallace D. Wilcox, and Christine Lloyd, "Exacerbations of Childhood Asthma and Ozone Pollution in Atlanta," *Environmental Research* 65 (1994): 56.

56. R. D. Bullard, "The Legacy of Apartheid and Environmental Racism," *St. John's Journal of Legal Commentary* 9 (Spring 1994): 445–474.

57. Donald Schueler, "Southern Exposure," *Sierra* 77 (November/December 1992): 45.

58. Robert D. Bullard, "Ecological Inequities and the New South: Black Communities Under Siege." *Journal of Ethnic Studies* 17 (Winter 1990): 101–115; Donald L. Bartlett and James B. Steele, "Paying a Price for Polluters," *Time* (November 23, 1998), pp. 72–80.

59. Schueler, "Southern Exposure," p. 46.

60. Ibid., pp. 46–47.

61. James O'Byrne and Mark Schleifstein, "Drinking Water in Danger," *The Times Picayune,* February 19, 1991, p. A5.

62. Conger Beasley, "Of Poverty and Pollution: Keeping Watch in Cancer Alley," pp. 39–45.

63. Bartlett and Steele, "Paying a Price for Polluters," p. 77.

64. Conger Beasley, "Of Pollutions and Poverty: Deadly Threat on Native Lands," *Buzzworm,* 2 (5) (1990): 39–45; Robert Tomsho, "Dumping Grounds: Indian Tribes Contend with Some of the Worst of America's Pollution," *The Wall Street Journal* (November 29, 1990); Jane Kay, "Indian Lands Targeted for Waste Disposal Sites," *San Francisco Examiner* (April 10, 1991); Valerie Taliman, "Stuck Holding the Nation's Nuclear Waste," *Race, Poverty & Environment Newsletter* (Fall 1992): 6–9.

65. Bradley Angel, *The Toxic Threat to Indian Lands: A Greenpeace Report.* San Francisco: Greenpeace, 1992; Al Geddicks, *The New Resource Wars: Native and Environmental Struggles Against Multinational Corporations,* Boston: South End Press, 1993.

66. Jane Kay, "Indian Lands Targeted for Waste Disposal Sites," *San Francisco Examiner* (April 10, 1991).

67. Ward Churchill and Winona la Duke, "Native America: The Political Economy of Radioactive Colonialism," *Insurgent Sociologist* 13 (1) (1983): 61–63.

68. Greenpeace, "The Logic Behind Hazardous Waste Export," *Greenpeace Waste Trade Update* (First Quarter 1992): 1–2.

69. Dana Alston and Nicole Brown, "Global Threats to People of Color," pp. 179–194 in R. D. Bullard, ed., *Confronting Environmental Racism: Voices from the Grassroots,* Boston: Southend Press, 1993.

70. Roberto Sanchez, "Health and Environmental Risks of the Maquiladora in Mexicali," *Natural Resources Journal* 30(1) (1990): 163–186.

71. Beatriz Johnston Hernandez, "Dirty Growth," *The New Environmentalist* (August 1993).

72. T. Barry and B. Simms, *The Challenge of Cross Border Environmentalism: The U.S. Mexico Case,* Albuquerque, NM: The Inter-Hemispheric Education Resource Center, 1994.

READING 24

Notes

1. Boston, John. 2003. "At Long Last, Going to Church Finally Pays." Online [cited 7 August 2003]. Available from http://www.the-signal.com/News/ViewStory.asp?storyID-2906.

2. Olson, Ted. 2004. "Fred Caldwell: Paying the Price for Unity." *Today's Christian,* July/August.

3. Excerpted from Emerson, Michael O. 2006. *People of the Dream: Multiracial Congregations in the United States.* Princeton, NJ: Princeton University Press, Chapter 2.

4. Hamilton, David L., and Tina K. Trolier. 1986. "Stereotype and Stereotyping: An Overview of the Cognitive Approach." In *Prejudice, Discrimination, and Racism,* eds. John F. Davidio and Samuel L. Gaertner, 127–63, Orlando, FL: Academic Press, p. 188.

5. These seven biases are the result of several research works. See Hewstone, Miles, Jos Jaspers, and Mansur Lalljee. 1992. "Social Representations, Social Attribution and Social Identity: The Intergroup Images of 'Public' and 'Comprehensive.' " *European Journal of Social Psychology* 12:241–69; Hogg, Michael A., and Dominic Abrams. 1988. *Social Identifications: A Social Psychology of Intergroup Relations and Group Processes.* London: Routledge; Howard, John W., and Myron Rothbart. 1980. "Social Categorization and Memory for In-group and Out-group Behavior." *Journal of Personality and Social Psychology* 38:301–10; Linville, Patricia W., Peter Salovey, and Gregory W. Fischer. 1986. "Stereotyping and Perceived Distributions of Social Characteristics: An Application to Ingroup-Outgroup Perception." In *Prejudice, Discrimination, and Racism,* eds. John F. Dovidio and Samuel L. Gaertner, 165–208, Orlando, FL: Academic Press; Tajfel, Henri. 1978. "Social Categorization, Social Identity and Social Comparison." In *Differentiation Between Social Groups: Studies in the Social Psychology of Intergroup Relations,* ed. Henri Tajfel, 61–76, London: Academic Press; Taylor, S. E. 1981. "A Categorization Approach to Stereotyping." In *Cognitive Processes in Stereotyping and Intergroup Behavior,* ed. D. L. Hamilton, 83–114, Hillsdale, NJ: Erlbaum; Wilder, D. A. 1981. "Perceiving Persons as a Group: Categorization and Ingroup Relations." In *Cognitive Processes in Stereotyping and Intergroup Behavior,* ed. D. L. Hamilton, 213–57, Hillsdale, NJ: Erlbaum.

6. Niebuhr, Reinhold. 1932. *Moral Man and Immoral Society: A Study in Ethics and Politics.* New York & London: C. Scribner's.

7. Niebuhr 1932:xxii–xxiii.

8. Hechter, Michael. 1987. *Principles of Social Solidarity.* Berkeley: University of California Press, p. 41.

9. This section was excerpted from Emerson, Michael O., and Christian Smith. 2000. *Divided by Faith: Evangelical Religion and the Problem of Race in America.* New York: Oxford University, Chapter 8.

10. Hollinger, David. 1995. *Postethnic America: Beyond Multiculturalism.* New York: Basic Books.

11. Much but not all of this section is excerpted from Emerson, Michael O. 2006. *People of the Dream,* Chapters 4 and 7.

READING 25

Notes

1. National Center for Health Statistics, Centers for Disease Control and Prevention. Deaths—leading causes. Available at: http://www.cdc.gov/nchs/fastats/lcod.htm. Accessed February 13, 2004.

2. Fried VM, Prager K, MacKay AP, Xia H. Chartbook on trends in the health of Americans. In: *Health, United States, 2003.* Hyattsville, Md: National Center for Health Statistics, 2003.

3. Jemal A, Thomas A, Murray T, Thun M. Cancer statistics, 2002. *CA Cancer J Clin.* 2002;52:23–47.

4. Ries Lag, Eisner MP, Kosary CL, et al., eds. SEER cancer statistics review, 1973–1999. Bethesda, Md: National Cancer Institute; 2002. Available at: http://seer.cancer.gov/csr/1973–1999. Accessed February 13, 2004.

5. *Healthy People 2010: Understanding and Improving Health.* Washington, DC: US Dept of Health and Human Services, 2001. Also available at: http://web.health.gov/healthypeople/document. Accessed January 1, 2005.

6. Fitzpatrick K, LaGory M. *Unhealthy Places: The Ecology of Risk in the Urban Landscape.* New York, NY: Routledge; 2000.

7. Lillie-Blanton M, LaVeist T. Race/ethnicity, the social environment, and health. *Soc Sci Med.* 1996;43:83–91.

8. Macintyre S, Maciver S, Sooman A. Area, class, and health: should we be focusing on places or people? *J Soc Policy.* 1993;22:213–234.

9. Yen J, Syme SL. The social environment and health: a discussion of the epidemiologic literature. *Annu Rev Public Health.* 1999;20:287–308.

10. Ellen I, Mijanovich GT, Dillman K. Neighborhood effects on health: exploring the links and assessing the evidence. *J Urban Aff.* 2001;23:391–408.

11. Pickett KE, Pearl M. Multilevel analyses of neighborhood socioeconomic context and health outcomes: a critical review. *J Epidemiol Community Health.* 2000;55:111–122.

12. Robert SA. Socioeconomic position and health: the independent contribution of community socioeconomic context. *Annu Rev Sociol* 1999;25:489–516.

13. Diez Roux AV. Investigating neighborhood and area effects on health. *Am J Public Health*. 2001;91:1783–1789.

14. Hillemeier MM, Lynch J, Harper S, Casper M. Measuring contextual characteristics for community health. *Health Serv Res*. 2004;38:1645–1717.

15. Macintyre S, Ellaway A, Cummins S. Place effects on health: how can we conceptualize, operationalize, and measure them? *Soc Sci Med*. 2002;55:125–139.

16. Mantovani RE, Daft L, Macaluso TF, Welsh J, Hoffman K. *Authorized Food Retailers' Characteristics and Access Study*. Alexandria, Va: US Dept of Agriculture, 1997.

17. Cheadle A, Psaty BM, Curry S, et al. Community-level comparisons between the grocery store environment and individual dietary practices. *Prev Med* 1991;20:250–261.

18. Cohen NL, Stoddard AM, Sarouhkhanians S, Sorensen G. Barriers toward fruit and vegetable consumption in a multiethnic worksite population. *J Nutr Educ*. 1998;30:381–386.

19. Drewnowski A, Specter SE. Poverty and obesity: the role of energy density and energy costs. *Am J Clin Nutr* 2004;79:6–16.

20. French SA, Story M, Jeffery RW. Environmental influences on eating and physical activity. *Annu Rev Public Health*. 2001;22:309–335.

21. Furst T, Connors M, Bisogni CA, Sobal J, Falk LW. Food choice: a conceptual model of the process. *Appetite*. 1996;26:247–266.

22. Glanz K, Basil M, Mailbach E, Goldberg J, Snyder D. Why Americans eat what they do: taste, nutrition, cost, convenience, and weight control concerns as influences on food consumption. *J. Am Diet Assoc*. 1998;98:1118–1126.

23. Huang K. Role of national income and prices. In: Frazao E, ed. *America's Eating Habits: Changes and Consequences.* US Dept of Agriculture, 1999;161–171. Agriculture Information Bulletin No. 750.

24. Reicks M, Randall J, Haynes B. Factors affecting vegetable consumption in low-income households. *J Am Diet Assoc*. 1994;94:1309–1311.

25. Race and place matter for major Chicago area grocers. Chicago, Ill: Metro Chicago Information Center: Available at http://www.mcic.org. Accessed January 3, 2005.

26. Morland K, Wing S, Diez Roux A, Poole C. Neighborhood characteristics associated with the location of food stores and food service places. *Am J Prev Med*. 2002;22:23–29.

27. Alwitt LF, Donley TD. Retail stores in poor urban neighborhoods. *J Consum Aff*. 1997;31:139–164.

28. Chung C, Myers SL. Do the poor pay more for food? An analysis of grocery store availability and food price disparities. *J Consum Aff*. 1999; 33:276–296.

29. Cotterill RW, Franklin AW. *The Urban Grocery Store Gap*. Storrs, Conn: Food Marketing Policy Center, University of Connecticut, 1995.

30. Cummins S, Macintyre S. A systematic study of an urban foodscape: the price and availability of food in Greater Glasgow. *Urban Stud*. 2002;39:2115–2130.

31. Cummins S, Macintyre S. "Food deserts"—Evidence and assumption in health policy making. *BMJ*. 2002; 325:436–438.

32. Jones SJ. *The Measurement of Food Security at the Community Level: Geographic Information Systems and Participating Ethnographic Methods* [dissertation]. Chapel Hill, NC. University of North Carolina at Chapel Hill, 2002.

33. Donohue RM. *Abandonment and Revitalization of Central City Retailing: The Case of Grocery Stores* [dissertation]. Ann Arbor, Mich: University of Michigan, 1997.

34. The business case for pursuing retail opportunities in the inner city. Boston, Mass: The Boston Consulting Group and The Initiative for a Competitive Inner City, 1988. Available at: http://www.icic.org. Accessed January 3, 2005.

35. The changing models of inner city grocery retailing. Boston, Mass: The Initiative for a Competitive Inner City, 2002. Available at: http://www.icic.org. Accessed January 3, 2005.

36. Jargowsky PA. *Poverty and Place: Ghettos, Barrios, and the American City*. New York, NY: Russell Sage Foundation, 1997.

37. Massey DS, Denton NA. *American Apartheid: Segregation and the Making of the Underclass*. Cambridge, Mass: Harvard University Press, 1993.

38. Massey, DS, Fischer MJ. How segregation concentrates poverty. *Ethn Racial Stud*. 2000;23:670–691.

39. Sugrue TJ. *The Origins of the Urban Crisis: Race and Inequality in Postwar Detroit*. Princeton, NJ: Princeton University Press, 1996.

40. Wilson WJ. *The Truly Disadvantaged: The Inner City, the Underclass, and Public Policy*. Chicago, Ill: University of Chicago Press, 1987.

41. Farley R, Danziger S, Holzer HJ. *Detroit Divided*. New York, NY: Russell Sage Foundation, 2000.

42. Geronimus AT. To mitigate, resist, or undo: addressing structural influences on the health of urban populations. *Am J Public Health*. 2000;90:867–872.

43. Schulz A, Williams DR, Israel B, Lempert LB. Racial and spatial relations as fundamental determinants of health in Detroit. *Milbank Q*. 2002;80:677–707.

44. Darden JT, Hill RC, Thomas J, Thomas R. *Detroit: Race and Uneven Development.* Philadelphia, Pa: Temple University Press, 1987.

45. Collins CA, Williams DR. Segregation and mortality: the deadly effects of racism. *Social Forum.* 1999;14:495–523.

46. Thomas JM. *Redevelopment and Race: Planning a Finer City in Postwar Detroit.* Baltimore, Md: The Johns Hopkins University Press, 1997.

47. Williams DR, Collins CA. Racial residential segregation: a fundamental cause of racial disparities in health. *Public Health Rep.* 2001;116:404–416.

48. *Michigan Metropolitan Information Center 2000 Census Demographic Characteristics.* Detroit, Mich: The Center for Urban Studies, Wayne State University. Available at: http://www.cus.wayne.edu/census/censuspubs.aspx. Accessed January 3, 2005.

49. Iceland J, Weinberg DH, Steinmetz E. *Racial and Ethnic Residential Segregation in the United States: 1980–2000.* Washington, DC: US Government Printing Office, 2002. US Census Bureau, Series CENSR-3.

50. Kieffer E, Willis S, Odoms-Young A, et al. Reducing disparities in diabetes among African American and Latino residents of Detroit: the essential role of community planning focus groups. *Ethn Dis.* 2004;14:S1-27–S1-37.

51. Laraia BA, Siega-Riz AM, Kaufman JS, Jones SJ. Proximity to supermarkets is positively associated with diet quality index for pregnancy. *Prev Med.* 2004;39:869–875.

52. Morland K, Wing S, Diex Roux A. The contextual effect of the local food environment on residents' diets: the atherosclerosis risk in communities study. *Am J Public Health.* 2002;92:1761–1767.

53. Wrigley N, Warm D, Margetts B, Whelan A. Assessing the impact of improved retail access on diet in a "food desert": a preliminary report. *Urban Stud.* 2002;39:2061–2082.

54. Zenk SN. *Neighborhood Racial Composition, Neighborhood Poverty, and Food Access in Metropolitan Detroit: Geographic Information Systems and Spatial Analysis* [dissertation]. Ann Arbor, Mich: University of Michigan, 2004.

55. Hartigan J. *Racial Situations: Class Predicaments of Whiteness in Detroit.* Princeton, NJ: Princeton University Press, 1999.

56. McWhirter C. Life of one street mirrors city's fall: racial fears trigger white flight in '50s. *The Detroit News.* June 17, 2001. Available at: http://www.detnews.com/specialreports/2001/elmhurst. Accessed January 5, 2005.

57. Metzger K, Booza J. *African Americans in the United States, Michigan, and Metropolitan Detroit.* Detroit, Mich: Center for Urban Studies, Wayne State University, 2002. Center for Urban Studies Working Paper Series, No. 8.

58. McWhirter C. 1967 Riot sent street into wrenching spiral: once stable block withers as property owners desert. *The Detroit News.* June 18, 2001. Available at: http://www.detnews.com/specialreports/2001/elmhurst. Accessed January 5, 2005.

59. *1990 Census Subcommunity Profiles for the City of Detroit.* Detroit, Mich: Southeast Michigan Census Council, 1993.

60. *2000 Census Subcommunity Profiles for the City of Detroit.* Detroit, Mich: United Way Community Services, 2001.

61. Israel BA, Schulz AJ, Parker EA, Becker AB. Review of community-based research: assessing partnership approaches to improve public health. *Annu Rev Public Health.* 1998;19:173–201.

62. James SA. Primordial prevention of cardiovascular disease among African Americans: a social epidemiological perspective. *Prev Med.* 1999;29:S84–S89.

63. Pothukuchi K. Attracting supermarkets to inner city neighborhoods: economic development out of the box. *Econ Dev Q.* In press.

64. *The African American Grocery Shopper 2000.* Washington DC: Food Marketing Institute; 2000.

65. Pothukuchi K, Kaufman JL. Placing the food system on the urban agenda: the role of municipal institutions in food system planning. *Agric Human Values.* 1999;16:213–224.

66. Ashman L, Vega J, Dohan M, Fisher A, Hipper R, Romain B. *Seeds of Change: Strategies for Food Security for the Inner City.* Los Angeles, Calif: University of California Los Angeles; 1993.

67. Gottlieb R, Fisher A, Dohan M, O'Connor L, Parks V. *Homeward Bound: Food-Related Transportation Strategies for Low Income and Transit Dependent Communities.* Los Angeles, Calif: University of California Transportation Center, 1996. Available at: http://www.foodsecurity.org/homewardbound.pdf. Accessed February 13, 2004.

68. Cohen HW, Northridge ME. Getting political: racism and urban health. *Am J Public Health* 2000;90:841–842.

READING 26

Notes

1. Jim Newton, "Judges Voice Anger over Mandatory U.S. Sentences," *L.A. Times,* 21 August 1993, A1.

2. As of 1995, there were 14,000 people in prison for federal crack convictions, 80 percent of whom were black. Ronald Smothers, "Wave of Prison Uprisings Provokes Debate on Crack," *N.Y. Times,* 24 October 1995, A18.

3. H. R. Rep. No. 104-272 at 20 (1995), reprinted in 1995 U.S.C.C.A.N. 335,353 (citing U.S. Sentencing Commission study).

4. *United States v. Armstrong,* 517 U.S. 456 (1996) (Stevens, J., dissenting) (citing United States Sentencing Commission,

Special Report to Congress: *Cocaine and Federal Sentencing Policy,* 39, 161, 1995).

5. *United States v. Clary,* 846 F. Supp. 768, 787 (E. D. Mo. 1994); see also *United States v. Walls,* 841 F. Supp. 24, 28 (D.D.C. 1994).

6. *State v. Russell,* 477 N.W.2d 886, 887 n.1 (Minn. 1991). In the Eastern District of Missouri, 98.2 percent of defendants convicted of crack cocaine charges from 1988 to 1992 were black. *United States v. Clary,* 846 F. Supp. at 786.

7. See, e.g., *United States v. Richardson,* 130 F.3d 765 (7th Cir. 1997); *United States v. Andrade,* 94 F.3d 9 (1st Cir. 1996); *United States v. Teague,* 93 F.3d 81 (2d Cir. 1996), *cert. denied,* 117 S. Ct. 708 (1997); *United States v. Lloyd,* 10 F.3d 1197 (6th Cir. 1993), *cert. denied,* 513 U.S. 883 (1994); *United States v. Jackson,* 67 F.3d 1359 (8th Cir. 1995), *cert. denied,* 517 U.S. 1192 (1996).

8. United States Sentencing Comm., Special Report to the Congress, *supra* note 4.

9. In 1997, the Sentencing Commission recommended reducing rather than eliminating the disparity, and the Clinton Administration supported the proposal. As of this writing, Congress has not acted on the recommendation.

10. *Stephens v. State,* 1995 WL 116292 (Ga. S. Ct. Mar. 17, 1995).

11. *Stephens v. State,* 456 S.E.2d 560 (Ga. 1995).

12. American Bar Association, *The State of Criminal Justice,* 9 (February 1993) (23 percent minority increase, 10 percent nonminority).

13. Id.

14. Jerome G. Miller, *Search and Destroy: African American Males in the Criminal Justice System,* 81 (New York: Cambridge Univ. Press, 1996).

15. Marc Mauer & Tracy Juling, The Sentencing Project, *Young Black Americans and the Criminal Justice System: Five Years Later,* 12 (1995).

16. David J. Rothman, "The Crime of Punishment," *New York Rev. of Books,* 17 February 1994, 34, 37.

17. Jerome G. Miller, *Search and Destroy, supra* note 14.

18. Id.

19. Id.

20. Marc Mauer, *Intended and Unintended Consequences: State Racial Disparities in Imprisonment,* 10 (Sentencing Project, Jan. 1997).

21. Human Rights Watch, *Cruel and Unusual: Disproportionate Sentences for New York Drug Offenders,* 2 (March 1997).

22. Dep't of Justice, Bureau of Justice Statistics Bulletin, *Prisoners in 1994,* 10, Table 13 (1995).

23. Id. at 11, Table 14 (state prisoners incarcerated on drug offenses increased from 19,000 in 1980 to 186,000 in 1993).

24. American Bar Association, *State of Criminal Justice, supra* note 12.

25. Office of Juvenile Justice and Delinquency Programs, *Juvenile Court Statistics 1991,* 25, Table 35, 71, Table 114 (May 1994). In this source, Hispanic youth were included in the "white" racial category.

26. 13,800 black juveniles were detained for drug violations, as compared to 7,400 white juveniles. Id. at 74, Table 118, 28, Table 39.

27. Id. at 29, Table 40.

28. Id. at 25, Table 37.

29. National Center on Institutions and Alternatives, *Hobbling a Generation: Young African American Males in the Criminal Justice System of America's Cities: Baltimore, Maryland* (September 1992).

30. See, e.g., Randall Kennedy, "The State, Criminal Law, and Racial Discrimination: A Comment," 107 Harv. L. Rev. 1255 (1994). For a detailed response, see David Cole, "The Paradox of Race and Crime: A Comment on Randall Kennedy's 'Politics of Distinction,'" 83 Geo. L.J. 2547 (1995); see also Randall Kennedy, "A Response to Professor Cole's 'Paradox of Race and Crime,'" 83 Geo. L.J. 2573 (1995).

31. National Institute of Justice, Department of Justice, *Three Strikes and You're Out: A Review of State Legislation,* 1 (September 1997); Tom Rhodes, "Third Strike and Pizza Thief Is Out for 25 Years," *The Times,* 4 April 1996 (available on NEXIS).

32. Maura Dolan & Tony Perry, "Justices Deal Blow to '3 Strikes,'" *L.A. Times,* 31 June 1996, A1.

33. Id.; see also The President's Radio Address, Weekly Comp. Pres. Doc. 1493 (July 16, 1994) (supporting "three strikes and you're out" provision in federal crime bill).

34. Rhodes, *supra* note 31.

35. Daniel B. Wood, "Softer Three-Strikes Law Brings Wave of Appeals," *Christian Science Monitor,* 24 June 1996, 3.

36. Christopher Davis, Richard Estes, and Vincent Schiraldi, *"Three Strikes": The New Apartheid* (Report of the Center on Juvenile and Criminal Justice, San Francisco, March 1996).

37. Fox Butterfield, "Tough Law on Sentences Is Criticized," *N.Y. Times,* 8 March 1996, A14.

38. See, e.g., Andy Furillo, "Most Offenders Have Long Criminal Histories," *Sacramento Bee,* 31 March 1996, A1.

39. Id.

40. William Spelman, *Criminal Incapacitation,* 15 (New York: Plenum Press, 1994) ("the typical criminal career lasts only 5 to 10 years"); 1 *Criminal Careers and Career Criminals,* 94 (Alfred Blumstein et al., eds.) (Washington, D.C.: National Academy Press, 1986) (same).

41. Daniel B. Wood, "LA Police Lash Out Against Three Strikes," *Christian Science Monitor,* 29 March 1996, 3.

42. Fox Butterfield, *supra* note 37.

43. Id.

44. Ian Katz, "Bull Market in Prisons and Knee-Jerk Politics," *The Guardian,* 25 May 1996 (available on NEXIS).

45. Bureau of Justice Statistics, *Sourcebook of Criminal Justice Statistics—1995,* Table 6.11 (1996).

46. Ann Golenpaul, ed., *Information Please Almanac,* 829 (Boston: Houghton Mifflin, 1997).

47. Ian Katz, *supra* note 44.

48. Christopher Davis, et al., *supra* note 36.

49. Douglas C. McDonald & Kenneth E. Carlson, *Sentencing in the Federal Courts: Does Race Matter? The Transition to Sentencing Guidelines, 1986–90: Summary,* 1–2 (Washington, D.C.: Bureau of Justice Statistics, 1993).

50. Id. at 13–17.

51. Id. at 16–17.

52. See, e.g. Stephen Klein, Joan Petersilia, and Susan Turner, "Race and Imprisonment Decisions in California," 247 *Science* 812–16 (Feb. 16, 1990) (studying California sentences and concluding that race did not improve the accuracy of predicting what type of punishment offenders would receive); Alfred Blumstein, "On the Racial Disproportionality of United States Prison Populations," 73 J. of Crim. L. & Crim. 1259 (1983) (finding little evidence of racial bias in incarceration for serious crimes); but see Jerome Miller, *Search and Destroy, supra* note 14 (reviewing studies finding evidence of racial discrimination); Crutchfield, et. al, "Analytical and Aggregation Biases in Analysis of Imprisonment: Reconciling Discrepancies in Studies of Racial Disparity," 31 J. of Res. In Crime & Delinquency 178 (1994) (critiquing prior studies for aggregating information in a way that might conceal discrimination; finding evidence of discrimination).

53. Michael H. Tonry, *Malign Neglect: Race, Crime, and Punishment in America,* 29 (New York: Oxford Univ. Press, 1995).

54. Barbara S. Meierhoefer, "Individualized and Systemic Justice in the Federal Sentencing Process," 29 Am. Crim. L. Rev. 889, 891 (1992).

55. William Wilbanks, *The Myth of a Racist Criminal Justice System* (Monterey, CA: Brooks/Cole, 1986).

56. Stephen P. Klein, *Racial Disparities in Sentencing Decisions,* 5 (Santa Monica, CA: Rand, 1991).

57. Unless otherwise indicated, the information in the next two paragraphs is drawn from Bonnie Whitebread, "Marijuana Prohibition," 56 U. Va. L. Rev. 983 (1970).

58. Whitebread, 56 Va. L. Rev. at 1096.

59. Gertrude Samuels, "Pot, Hard Drugs, and the Law," *N.Y. Times Magazine,* 15 February 1970, 14.

60. Richard J. Bonnie, "The Meaning of 'Decriminalization': A Review of the Law," Contemporary Drug Problems 277, 278 (Fall 1981).

61. Id. at 279; see also Bureau of Justice Statistics, U.S. Dept of Justice, *Drugs, Crime and the Justice System,* 84–85 (1992) (reporting that when large numbers of white middle-class youth were arrested for marijuana possession in the late 1960s and early 1970s, public complaints led Congress and eleven states to decriminalize or reduce substantially the penalties for that crime).

READING 27

Notes

1. *Frontline:* The Plea, at www.pbs.org/wgbh/pages/frontline/shows/plea/four/patt.html; and Angela Davis, *Arbitrary Justice: The Power of the American Prosecutor* (New York: Oxford University Press, 2007), 50–52.

2. American Civil Liberties Union, *Stories of ACLU Clients Swept Up in the Hearne Drug Bust of November 2000* (Washington, DC: American Civil Liberties Union, Nov. 1, 2002), www.aclu.org/DrugPolicy/DrugPolicy.cfm?ID=11160&c=80.

3. Human Rights Watch, *Punishment and Prejudice: Racial Disparities in the War on Drugs,* HRW Reports, vol. 12, no. 2 (May 2000).

4. Ibid.

5. Jeremy Travis, *But They All Come Back Facing the Challenges of Prisoner Reentry* (Washington, DC: Urban Institute Press, 2002), 28.

6. Ibid.

7. Ibid.

8. Marc Mauer and Ryan S. King, *Schools and Prisons: Fifty Years After Brown v. of Education* (Washington, DC: Sentencing Project, Apr. 2004), 3.

9. Marc Mauer, *The Changing Racial Dynamics of the War on Drugs* (Washington, DC: Sentencing Project, Apr. 2009).

10. See, e.g., U.S. Department of Health and Human Services, Substance Abuse and Mental Health Services Administration, *Summary of Findings from the 2000 National Household Survey on Drug Abuse,* NHSDA series H-I3, DHHS pub. no. SMA 01-3549 (Rockville, MD: 2001), reporting that 6.4 percent of whites, 6.4 percent of blacks, and 5.3 percent of Hispanics were current illegal drug users in 2000; *Results from the 2002 National Survey on Drug Use and Health: National Findings,* NSDUH series H-22, DHHS pub. no. SMA 03-3836 (2003), revealing nearly identical rates of illegal drug use among whites and blacks, only a single percentage point between them; *Results from the 2007 National Survey on*

Drug Use and Health: National Findings, NSDUH series H-34, DHHS pub. no. SMA 08-4343 (2007), showing essentially the same findings; and Marc Mauer and Ryan S. King, *A 25-Year Quagmire: The War on Drugs and Its Impact on American Society* (Washington, DC: Sentencing Project, Sept. 2007), 19, citing a study suggesting that African Americans have slightly higher rates of illegal drug use than whites.

11. See, e.g., Howard N. Snyder and Melissa Sickman, *Juvenile Offenders and Victims: 2006 National Report,* U.S. Department of Justice, Office of Justice Programs, Office of Juvenile Justice and Delinquency Prevention (Washington, DC: 2006), reporting that white youth are more likely than black youth to engage in illegal drug sales; Lloyd D. Johnson, Patrick M. O'Malley, Jerald G. Bachman, and John E. Schulenberg, *Monitoring the Future, National Survey Results on Drug Use, 1975–2006, vol. 1, Secondary School Students,* U.S. Department of Health and Human Services, National Institute on Drug Abuse, NIH pub. no. 07-6205 (Bethesda, MD: 2007), 32, stating "African American 12th graders have consistently shown lower usage rates than White 12th graders for most drugs, both licit and illicit"; and Lloyd D. Johnston, Patrick M. O'Malley, and Jerald G. Bachman, *Monitoring the Future: National Results on Adolescent Drug Use: Overview of Key Findings 2002,* U.S. Department of Health and Human Services, National Institute on Drug Abuse, NIH pub, no. 03-5374 (Bethesda, MD: 2003), presenting data showing that African American adolescents have slightly lower rates of illicit drug use than their white counterparts.

12. National Institute on Drug Abuse, *Monitoring the Future, National Survey Results on Drug Use, 1975–1999, vol. 1, Secondary School Students* (Washington, DC: National Institute on Drug Abuse, 2000).

13. U.S. Department of Health, *National Household Survey on Drug Abuse, 1999* (Washington, DC: Substance Abuse and Mental Health Services Administration, Office of Applied Studies, 2000), table G, p, 71, www.samhsa.gov/statistics/statistics.html.

14. Bruce Western, *Punishment and Inequality* (New York: Russell Sage Foundation. 2006), 47.

15. Ibid.

16. See Lynn Lu, "Prosecutorial Discretion and Racial Disparities in Sentencing: Some Views of Former U.S. Attorneys," *Federal Sentencing Reporter* 19 (Feb. 2007).

17. Douglas S. Massey and Nancy A. Denton, *American Apartheid: Segregation and the Making of the Underclass* (Cambridge, MA: Harvard University Press, 1993), 2.

18. For a discussion of possible replacement effects, see Robert MacCoun and Reuter, *Drug War Heresies: Learning from Other Vices, Times, and Places* (New York: Cambridge University Press, 2001).

19. See Katherine Beckett, Kris Nyrop, Lori Pfingst, and Melissa Bowen, "Drug Use, Drug Possession Arrests, and the Question of Race: Lessons from Seattle," *Social Problems* 52, no. 3 (2005): 419–41; and Katherine Beckett, Kris Nyrop, and Lori Pfingst, "Race, Drugs and Policing: Understanding Disparities in Drug Delivery Arrests," *Criminology* 44, no. 1 (2006): 105.

20. Beckett, "Drug Use," 436.

21. Ibid.

22. Ibid.

23. David Cole, *No Equal Justice: Race and Class in the American Criminal Justice System* (New York: The New Press, 1999), 161.

24. Ibid., 162.

25. *City of Los Angeles v. Lyons,* 461 U.S. 95, 105 (1983).

26. See *United States v. Brignoni-Ponce,* 422 U.S. 873 (1975); and *United States v. Martinez-Fuerte,* 428 U.S. 543 (1976).

27. See Massey, *American Apartheid.*

28. For a thoughtful overview of these studies, see David Harris, *Profiles in Injustice: Why Racial Profiling Cannot Work* (New York: The New Press, 2002).

29. *State v. Soto,* 324 N.J. Super. 66, 69–77, 83-85, 734 A.2d 350, 352-56, 360 (N.J. Super. Ct. Law Div. 1996).

30. Harris, *Profiles in Injustice,* 80.

31. Ibid.

32. Jeff Brazil and Steve Berry, "Color of Drivers Is Key to Stops on I-95 Videos," *Orlando Sentinel,* Aug. 23, 1992; and David Harris, "Driving While Black and All Other Traffic Offenses: The Supreme Court and Pretextual Traffic Stops," *Journal of Criminal Law and Criminology* 87 (1997): 544, 561–62.

33. ACLU, *Driving While Black: Racial Profiling on our Nation's Highways* (New York: American Civil Liberties Union, 1999) 3, 27–28.

34. See www.aclunc.org, press release, "Oakland Police Department Announces Results of Racial Profiling Data Collection," May 11, 2001.

35. Al Baker and Emily Vasquez, "Number of People Stopped by Police Soars in New York," *New York Times,* Feb. 3, 2007.

36. Office of the Attorney General of New York State, *Report on the New York City Police Department's "Stop & Frisk" Practices* (New York: Office of the Attorney General of New York State, 1999), 95, 111, 121, 126.

37. Ibid., 117 n. 23.

38. Baker and Vasquez, "Number of People Stopped by Police Soars."

39. Ryan Pintado-Vertner and Jeff Chang. "The War on Youth," *Colorlines 2,* no. 4 (Winter 1999–2000), 36.

40. *Alexander v. Sandoval,* 532 U.S. 275 (2001).

READING 28

References

Beckett, Katherine, Kris Nyrop, and Lori Pfingst. 2006. Race, Drugs, and Policing: Understanding Disparities in Drug Delivery Arrests. *Criminology* 44: 105–138.

Beckett, Katherine, Kris Nyrop, Lori Pfingst, and Melissa Bowen. 2005. Drug Use, Drug Possession Arrests, and the Question of Race: Lessons from Seattle. *Social Problems* 52: 419–441.

Blumstein, Alfred. 2001. Race and Criminal Justice. In *America Becoming: Racial Trends and Their Consequences,* vol. 2, eds. N. J. Smelser, W. J. Wilson, and F. Mitchell, 21–31. Washington, DC: National Academy Press.

Garland, David. 2001. Introduction: The Meaning of Mass Imprisonment. In *Mass Imprisonment: Social Causes and Consequences,* ed. D. Garland, 1–3. Thousand Oaks, CA: Sage.

Irwin, John. 2007. *The Warehouse Prison: Disposal of the New Dangerous Class.* Los Angeles: Roxbury.

Jacobs, David, and Jason T. Carmichael. 2002. The Political Sociology of the Death Penalty: A Pooled Time-Series Analysis. *American Sociological Review* 67: 109–131.

Jacobs, David, and Daniel Tope. 2007. The Politics of Resentment in the Post–Civil Rights Era: Minority Threat, Homicide, and Ideological Voting in Congress. *American Journal of Sociology* 112: 1458–1494.

Lauritsen, Janet, and Robert J. Sampson. 1998. Minorities, Crime, and Criminal Justice. In *The Handbook of Crime and Punishment,* ed. M. J. Tonry, 58–84. New York: Oxford University Press.

Marable, Manning. 2002. *The Great Wells of Democracy: The Meaning of Race in American Life.* New York: Norton.

Mauer, Marc, and Ryan Scott King. 2004. Schools and Prisons Fifty Years after *Brown v. Board of Education.* The Sentencing Project. www.sentencingproject.org/pdfs/brownvboard. pdf.

New York Times. 2008. Prison Nation. March 10. http://www. nytimes.com2008/01/10/opinion/10mon1.html (accessed April 22, 2009).

Pew Center on the States. 2008. *One in 100: Behind Bars in America 2008.* Washington, DC: Pew Charitable Trusts.

Ruth, Henry S., and Kevin R. Reitz. 2003. *The Challenge of Crime: Rethinking Our Response.* Cambridge: Harvard University Press.

READING 29

Notes

1. For discussions of the effect of incarceration, see, e.g., J. Grogger, "The Effect of Arrests on the Employment and Earnings of Young Men," *Quarterly Journal of Economics* 110 (1995): 51–72; B. Western, "The Impact of Incarceration on Wage Mobility and Inequality," *American Sociological Review* 67, no. 4 (2002): 526–46.

2. This research is reported in D. Pager, "The Mark of a Criminal Record," *American Journal of Sociology* 108, no. 5 (2003): 937–75. IRP thanks the University of Chicago Press for permission to summarize the article.

3. See, for example, D. Neal and W. Johnson, "The Role of Premarket Factors in Black-White Wage Differences," *Journal of Political Economy* 104, no. 5 (1996): 869–95; S. Steele, *The Content of Our Character: A New Vision of Race in America* (New York: Harper Perennial, 1991).

4. The method of audit studies was pioneered in the 1970s with a series of housing audits conducted by the Department of Housing and Urban Development, and was modified and applied to employment by researchers at the Urban Institute in the early 1990s. M. Turner, M. Fix, and R. Struyk, *Opportunities Denied, Opportunities Diminished: Racial Discrimination in Hiring* (Washington, DC: Urban Institute Press, 1991).

5. Bureau of Labor Statistics, Local Area Unemployment Statistics. Last accessed March 2003. http://www.bls.gov/lau/ home.htm.

6. Over 90 percent of recent, entry-level job openings in Milwaukee were located in the outlying counties and suburbs, and only 4 percent in the central city. J. Pawasarat and L. Quinn, "Survey of Job Openings in the Milwaukee Metropolitan Area: Week of May 15, 2000," Employment and Training Institute Report, University of Wisconsin–Milwaukee, 2000.

7. M. Bendick, Jr., C. Jackson, and V. Reinoso, "Measuring Employment Discrimination through Controlled Experiments," *Review of Black Political Economy* 23 (1994): 25–48.

READING 30

Notes

1. Susanne B. Haga, "Policy Implications of Defining Race and More by Genetic Profiling," *Genomics, Society and Policy* 2, no. 1 (2006): 57–71, quotation at 64.

2. Troy Duster, "Behavioral Genetics and Explanations of the Link Between Crime, Violence, and Race," in *Wrestling with Behavioral Genetics: Science, Ethics, and Public Conversation,* ed. Erik Parens, Audrey R. Chapman, and Nancy Press

(Baltimore: Johns Hopkins University Press, 2006), 158. See also Troy Duster, "Selective Arrests, an Ever-Expanding DNA Forensic Database, and the Specter of an Early Twenty-First Century Equivalent of Phrenology," in *DNA and the Criminal Justice System: The Technology of Justice,* ed. David Lazer (Cambridge, MA: MIT Press, 2004), 315–334.

3. Alex R. Piquero and Robert W. Brame, "Assessing the Race-Crime and Ethnicity-Crime Relationship in a Sample of Serious Adolescent Delinquents," *Crime and Delinquency,* February 29, 2008, 390–422.

4. Michael Risher, "Racial Disparities in Databanking of DNA Profiles," *Gene-Watch* 22, nos. 3–4 (July–August 2009), http://www.councilforresponsiblegenetics.org/Gene Watch/GeneWatchPage.aspx?pageId=204 (accessed May 23, 2010).

5. Troy Duster, *Backdoor to Eugenics,* 2nd ed. (New York: Routledge, 2003), 150–151.

6. Barbara S. Meierhoefer, "The Role of Offense and Offender Characteristics in Federal Sentencing," *Southern California Law Review* 66 (November 1992): 367–398, at 388, http://www.lexisnexis.com/hottopics/lnacademic/ (accessed April 26, 2010).

7. Harry Levine, Jon Gettman, Craig Reinarman, and Deborah Peterson Small, "Drug Arrests and DNA: Building Jim Crow's Database" (paper presented at the Forum on Racial Justice Impacts of Forensic DNA Databanks, New York University, June 19, 2008), citing U.S. Department of Health and Human Services, SAMHSA, Office of Applied Studies, *2005 National Survey on Drug Use and Health,* Detailed Tables, Table 1.80B, "Marijuana Use in Lifetime, Past Year, and Past Month Among Persons Aged 18 to 25, by Racial/Ethnic Subgroups: Percentages, Annual Averages Based on 2002–2003 and 2004–2005," http://www.oas.samhsa.gov/NSDUH/2k5NSDUH/tabs/Sect1peTabs67to132, htm#Tab1,80B (accessed April 26, 2010).

8. Levine et al., "Drug Arrests and DNA."

9. Vincent Schiraldi and Jason Ziedenberg, "Race and Incarceration in Maryland" (Washington, DC: Justice Policy Institute, October 23, 2003), 1–29, at 1, http://www.justicepolicy.org/images/upload/03-10_REP_MD RaceIncarceration_AC-MD-RD.pdf (accessed April 26, 2010).

10. Justice Policy Institute, *Vortex,* 8.

11. Justice Mapping Center, *NYC Analysis–October 2006,* Slide #7, "Men Admitted to Prison: New York City," http://www.justicemapping.org/expertise/ (accessed May 23, 2010). The Justice Mapping Center uses computer mapping and other graphical depictions of quantitative data to analyze and communicate social policy information.

12. Pilar Ossorio and Troy Duster, "Race and Genetics," *American Psychologist* 60, no. 1 (January 2005): 115–128, at 122.

13. Risher, "Racial Disparities in Databanking of DNA Profiles."

14. Aleksandar Tomic and Jahn K. Hakes, "Case Dismissed: Police Discretion, and Racial Differences in Dismissals of Felony Charges," *American Law and Economics Review* 10, no. 1 (2008): 110–141.

15. Justice Policy Institute, *Vortex,* 3.

16. Data obtained from Stephen Saloom, policy director, the Innocence Project, May 30, 2007.

17. Rick Weiss, "Vast DNA Bank Pits Policing vs. Privacy," *Washington Post,* June 3, 2006, A1.

18. Duster, "Selective Arrests," 329.

19. Pew Center on the States, *One in 100: Behind Bars in America, 2008* (Washington, DC: Pew Charitable Trusts, 2008), 6, http://www.pewcenteronthestates.org/uploadedFiles1 One%20in%20100.pdf (accessed April 26, 2010). See also N. C. Aizenman, "New High in U.S. Prison Numbers," *Washington Post,* February 29, 2008, A1.

20. Brett E. Garland, Cassia Spohn, and Eric J. Wodahl, "Racial Disproportionality in the American Prison Population: Using the Blumstein Method to Address the Critical Race and Justice Issue of the 21st Century," *Justice Policy Journal* 5 (Fall 2008): 1–42, at 4.

21. Henry T. Greely, Daniel P. Riordan, Nanibaa A. Garrison, and Joanna L. Mountain, "Family Ties: The Use of DNA Offender Databases to Catch Offenders' Kin," *Journal of Law, Medicine and Ethics* 34, no. 2 (Summer 2006): 248–262, quotation at 258.

22. CODIS, "Measuring Success," http://www.fbi.gov/hq/lab/codis/clickmap.htm (accessed May 28, 2010). The National DNA Index (NDIS) contains over 8,201,707 offender profiles and 315,789 forensic profiles as of April 2010. Ultimately, the success of the CODIS program will be measured by the crimes it helps to solve. CODIS's primary metric, the "Investigation Aided," tracks the number of criminal investigations where CODIS has added value to the investigative process. As of April 2010 CODIS has produced over 116,200 hits assisting in more than 114,000 investigations. The CODIS Web site statistics are updated every month.

23. Ibid., 454.

24. Greely et al., "Family Ties," 259.

25. B. Leapman, "Three in Four Young Black Men on the DNA Database," *Sunday Telegraph,* November 5, 2006, http://www.telegraph.co.uk/news/uknews/ 1533295/Three-in-four-young-black-men-on-the-DNA-database.html (accessed April 26, 2010).

READING 32

Notes

1. Stephen Erie, *Rainbow's End* (Berkeley: University of California Press, 1988), 88–89.

2. Thomas Kessner, *Fiorella H. LaGuardia* (New York: McGraw-Hill, 1989); Charles Garrett, *The LaGuardia Years* (New Brunswick, NJ: Rutgers University Press, 1961).

3. A survey of the surviving members of the class indicates that 38 percent were Catholic and 36 percent Jewish, with Russia and Ireland the leading countries of origin of the respondents' grandparents (Richard Herrnstein et al., "New York City Police Department Class of 1940: A Preliminary Report" [unpublished manuscript, Department of Psychology, Harvard University, n. d.]).

4. Nathan Glazer and Daniel P. Moynihan, *Beyond the Melting Pot* (Cambridge, MA: MIT Press, 1969).

5. Data on the ethnic composition of the fire department are from *Equal Employment Opportunity Statistics: Agency Full Report* (New York: New York City Department of Personnel, 1990); data on the religious composition are from Center for Social Policy and Practice in the Workplace, *Gender Integration in the Fire Department of the City of New York* (New York: Columbia University School of Social Work, 1988), p. 41.

6. Roger Waldinger, *Through the Eye of the Needle* (New York: New York University Press, 1986).

7. Heywood Broun and George Britt, *Christians Only* (New York: Vantage Press, 1931), 244.

8. Dominic Capeci, *The Harlem Riot of 1943* (Philadelphia: Temple University Press, 1977), 172.

9. Waldinger, *Through the Eye of the Needle,* 109–10. Employment data calculated from the census apply to employed persons twenty-five to sixty-four years old only. "Blacks" refers to native-born African Americans only. Data calculated from the Public Use Microdata Samples (U.S. Bureau of the Census, *Census of Population, 1940,* Public Use Microdata Samples [Computer file] [Washington, DC: U.S. Dept. of Commerce, Bureau of the Census, producer, 1983; Ann Arbor, MI: Inter-university Consortium for Political and Social Research, distributor, 1984]; U.S. Bureau of the Census, Census of Population, 1950, Public Use Microdata Samples [computer file] [Washington, DC: U.S. Dept. of Commerce, Bureau of the Census, and Madison: University of Wisconsin, Center for Demography and Ecology, producers, 1984; Ann Arbor, MI: Inter-university Consortium for Political and Social Research, distributor, 1984]).

10. Hasia Diner, *In the Almost Promised Land* (Westport, CT: Greenwood Press, 1977), presents a favorable account of the response among the Jewish trade union elite to the black influx into the garment industry; see chap. 6. Herbert Hill has offered a far more critical account in numerous writings, most important, "The Racial Practices of Organized Labor: The Contemporary Record," in *Organized Labor and the Negro,* edited by Julius Jacobson (New York: Doubleday, 1968), 286–337. For a judicious balancing of the issues, see Nancy Green, "'Juifs et noirs aux etats-unis: La rupture d'une 'alliance naturelle,'" *Annales, E.S.C.,* 2(March–April 1987): 445–64.

11. Diane Ravitch, *The Great School Wars* (New York: Basic Books, 1974).

12. Roger Waldinger, "The Making of an Immigrant Niche," *International Migration Review* 28(1)(1994).

13. "The Debate Goes On," *Alumnus: The City College of New York* 87(1)(Winter 1992):8–11.

14. Emmanuel Tobier, "Population," in *Setting Municipal Priorities,* edited by Charles Brecher and Raymond Horton (New York: New York University Press, 1981), 24.

15. Data are from U.S. Bureau of the Census, *Occupations at the 1900 Census* (Washington, DC: GPO, 1904). See also Herman Bloch, *The Circle of Discrimination* (New York: New York University Press, 1969).

16. Data are from the U.S. Bureau of the Census, *Census of Population, 1940.*

17. Calculated from the U.S. Bureau of the Census, *Census of Population and Housing, 1990,* Public Use Microdata Sample (a Sample): 5-Percent Sample (computer file) (Washington, DC: U.S. Dept. of Commerce, producer, 1993; Ann Arbor, MI: Inter-university Consortium for Political and Social Research, distributor, 1993).

18. Colored Citizens' Non-Partisan Committee for the Re-election of Mayor Walker, *New York City and the Colored Citizen* (n.d. [1930?]), LaGuardia Papers, Box 3530, New York Municipal Archives.

19. Calculated from U.S. Bureau of the Census, *Census of Population, 1940,* Public Use Microdata Samples. Also see Edwin Levinson, *Black Politics in New York City* (New York: Twayne, 1974).

20. Ira Katznelson, *Black Men, White Cities* (New York: Oxford University Press, 1973), 82.

21. For a more detailed discussion of the Lindsay period, see Roger Waldinger, "The Ethnic Politics of Municipal Jobs," working paper no. 248, UCLA Institute of Industrial Relations, Los Angeles, 1993.

22. Raymond Horton, "Human Resources," in *Setting Municipal Priorities,* edited by Charles Brecher and Raymond Horton (New York: New York University Press, 1986). See also Roger Waldinger, "Changing Ladders and Musical Chairs," *Politics and Society* 15(4) (1986–87):369–402, and "Making of an Immigrant Niche."

23. City of New York, Citywide Equal Employment Opportunity Committee, *Equal Employment Opportunity in New York City Government, 1977–1987* (New York: Citywide Equal Employment Opportunity Committee, 1988), 6.

24. Data are from unpublished EEOC reports from the New York City Department of Personnel, New York Board of Education, New York City Transit Authority, and New York City Health and Hospitals Corporation.

25. City of New York, Mayor's Commission on Hispanic Concerns, *Report* (New York: Mayor's Commission on Hispanic Concerns, 1986), 109.

26. *1991 Korean Business Directory* (Long Island City, NY: Korean News, 1991).

27. Roger Waldinger, "Structural Opportunity or Ethnic Advantage: Immigrant Business Development in New York," *International Migration Review* 23(1)(1989):61.

28. Illsoo Kim, *The New Urban Immigrants* (Princeton, NJ: Princeton University Press, 1981), 51.

29. Pyong Gap Min, "Cultural and Economic Boundaries of Korean Ethnicity: A Comparative Analysis," *Ethnic and Racial Studies* 14(2) (1991):235.

30. Lucie Cheng and Yen Espiritu, "Korean Businesses in Black and Hispanic Neighborhoods," *Sociological Perspectives* 32(4) (1989):521.

31. Illsoo Kim, "The Koreans: Small Business in an Urban Frontier," in *New Immigrants in New York,* edited by Nancy Foner (New York: Columbia University Press, 1987), 238.

32. Tamar Jacoby, "Sonny Carson and the Politics of Protest," *NY: The City Journal* 1(4)(1991): 29–40.

READING 33

Notes

1. The research for this chapter was made possible by generous grants from the Russell Sage, Ford, Rockefeller, Spencer, and William T. Grant Foundations. A revised version of this chapter appears in Newman 1999.

2. There are further shades of gray below the line of the employed that distinguish those who are searching for work and those who have accepted their fate as nonworkers, with the latter suffering the greatest stigma of all.

3. For more on the moral structure associated with work and achievement of the American dream, see Hochschild 1995.

4. See Wilson 1996, Massey and Denton 1993, Hacker 1992, and Urban Institute 1991.

5. All names and identifying information have been changed to protect confidentiality.

6. Hochschild 1983 documents similar attempts in the airline industry. One airline holds a mandatory seminar for flight attendants to teach them "anger-desensitization" when dealing with rude and demeaning customers.

7. In areas experiencing exceptionally tight labor markets—including much of the Midwest in the late 1990s—wages for these jobs are climbing above the minimum-wage line.

8. This is one of the many reasons why increasing the minimum wage is so important. Ghettos have such impoverished job bases to begin with that they are almost always characterized by slack labor markets. Only when the labor supply outside ghetto walls has tightened down to almost impossible levels do we begin to see this tide lift inner-city boats. Eventually employers do turn to the workers who are low on their preference queues (as we learned in the 1980s during the Massachusetts miracle), but these conditions are, sadly, rare and generally short-lived.

9. Indeed, over a five-month period in 1993 there were fourteen job applicants for every job opening at two different Burger Barns in Harlem (Newman and Lennon 1995).

10. The fact that Harlem residents rejected for these jobs hold these values is some evidence for the preexisting nature of this mind-set—although these rejects had already piled up work experience that may have contributed to the sharpening of this alternative critique.

11. It should be noted that women on welfare and women in low-wage jobs are not necessarily two distinct groups. Many women find it necessary to go back and forth between holding a low-wage job and relying solely on welfare, and many supplement one form of income with the other (not to mention other income from friends, family, and unreported work), since neither source alone provides enough money to support a family (see Edin 1994).

References

Edin, Kathryn. 1994. "The Myths of Dependency and Self-Sufficiency: Women, Welfare, and Low-Wage Work." Unpublished paper. Department of Sociology and Center for Urban Policy Research, Rutgers University.

Hacker, Andrew. 1992. *Two Nations.* New York: Ballantine.

Hochschild, Arlie. 1983. *The Managed Heart.* Berkeley: University of California Press.

Hochschild, Jennifer L. 1995. *Facing Up to the American Dream.* Princeton: Princeton University Press.

Katz, Michael. 1989. *The Undeserving Poor.* New York: Pantheon.

Massey, Douglas S., and Nancy A. Denton. 1993. *American Apartheid.* Cambridge: Harvard University Press.

Newman, Katherine S. 1999. *No Shame in My Game: The Working Poor in the Inner City.* New York: Knopf/Russell Sage Foundation.

Newman, Katherine S., and Chauncy Lennon. 1995. "The Job Ghetto." *American Prospect,* summer, 66–67.

Urban Institute. 1991. *Opportunities Denied, Opportunities Diminished.* Report 91–9. Washington: Urban Institute Press.

Wilson, William Julius. 1996. *When Work Disappears.* New York: Knopf.

READING 34

Notes

1. Unless otherwise noted, the following discussion is primarily based on these sources and the information provided by Liang Huan Ru, the former veteran union organizer in Brooklyn.

2. I use "Manhattan's Chinatown" because new Chinatowns have recently emerged in other boroughs of New York City, such as Queens and Brooklyn.

3. Abeles, Schwartz, Haechel & Silverblatt, Inc., *The Chinatown Garment Industry Study* (hereafter *Study*) (New York: International Ladies' Garment Workers' Union Local 23–25 and the New York Skirt and Sportswear Association, 1983), 55. For the sizes of the shops in Manhattan's Chinatown, see *Study*, 49–59.

4. See for example, the weekly special issue of the *Sing Tao Daily* (hereafter *STD*), March 8, 1998, 7.

5. My visit to the shop and interview with the shop owner.

6. One woman worker told me in an interview that it was so hot inside her shop in summer that sometimes she simply could not help crying while trying to rush out her work.

7. Experienced pressers began to lose this advantage in more and more Chinese garment shops in recent years, largely due to the increased competition from undocumented male workers. Unable to compete with the low wages accepted by the latter, they too had to face economic insecurity in the industry. I am indebted to a reminder from Liang Huan Ru, an organizer of UNITE! Local 23–25, and May Ying Chen, vice president of UNITE!, for this piece of information. What, however, must be kept in mind is that while competition has mounted among pressers in recent years, women machine operators also faced competition from undocumented workers.

8. See Susan Glenn, *Daughters of the Shtetl: Life and Labor in the Immigrant Generation* (Ithaca, New York: Cornell University Press, 1990), 90–131, and Nancy Green, *Ready-to-Wear and Ready-to-Work: A Century of Industry and Immigrants in Paris and New York* (Durham: Duke University Press, 1997), 161–87.

9. The most recent case was the one at 446 Broadway in November 1997, in which a young woman employer closed her shop after withholding a large sum of money in back wages from her employees. The case was covered by most major newspapers inside and outside the Chinese community. See, for example, *New York Times,* December 14, 1997.

10. See "Opportunity at Work: The New York City Garment Industry" (New York: Community Service Society of New York, 1998), 39.

11. This observation has been supported by recent coverage in Chinese community newspapers. For example, as covered in *World Journal* (hereafter *WJ*) in 1996, the monthly income of an elderly couple who worked in a Chinese garment shop was $1,800 and $2,200, respectively. Given the depressed piece rates in the last two years and the seasonal nature of the industry, this observation, based on interviews with workers in Sunset Park, does not seem to be far away from reality.

12. Directly quoted from "Behind Closed Doors: A Look into the Underground Sweatshop Industry," a report by the New York State Assembly Sub-Committee on Sweatshops (New York, November 1997), 59–61.

13. Interview by the author on April 13, 1998.

14. See, for example, Bernard Wong, "The Role of Ethnicity in Enclave Enterprises: A Study of the Chinese Garment Factories in New York City," *Human Organization* 46 (2), 1987: 120–9.

15. "One country, two systems" is the Chinese state policy in Hong Kong after the former British colony was returned to China in 1997.

16. Cases like this are not unheard of in the Chinese garment industry in Manhattan's Chinatown as well as other boroughs of the city. See, for example. The Chinese Staff and Workers Association, *Zhi Gong Zhi Sheng* (January 1994).

17. I was told that this small number of workers from other ethnic groups were likely to have worked for the former owner of the shop and the Chinese employer employed them as part of the deal when he/she purchased the business. I was also told that some Chinese employers deliberately kept these workers to protect their businesses from harassment by Chinese gangsters, who tended not to attack shops with non-Chinese workers for fear that their illicit activities would be known beyond the Chinese community.

18. *STD,* December 19, 1997.

19. The "Hot Goods Bill" was signed into law on July 2, 1996. This bill has established "additional methods of obtaining restitution for unpaid apparel industry workers from contractors, manufacturers, and retailers." For a further discussion of this bill, see "Behinds Closed Doors," 4.

20. The *Study* has reported that at the end of 1981, 28 percent of all Chinese shops in Chinatown had been in business for less than one year and close to half of them had been in operation for less than two years (p. 68). However, in the late 1990s, as many workers have pointed out, the Chinese garment shops in Sunset Park are often opened and closed down within months.

21. Taishan is a county in Guangdong Province. Immigrants from this county are also generally called "Cantonese."

22. Interview by the author on July 2, 1998.

23. Interview by the author on June 21, 1998.

24. Immigration status and whether one is living with their family have become important indexes because much of the Chinese community has chosen to believe that legal immigration and family life are the norms throughout the history of the community, however invalid this belief is.

25. For a summary of their arguments, see *STD*, April 22, 1998.

26. For different voices in the community, see, for example, the weekly special issues of *STD*, May 17, 1998 and June 28, 1998.

27. The estimate of 800 Chinese shops is based on an adding of the approximate 500 shops in Manhattan and the more than 300 shops in Brooklyn and other boroughs. More than 30,000 workers were estimated by the community press in the end of 1997. See *STD*, December 22, 1997.

28. These statistics are provided by the Research Department of the New York State Department of Labor.

29. In 1997, when the union signed a new contract with Chinese employers, the three Chinese contractors' associations represented only 406 shops in the city. This was later reported in most Chinese community newspapers. See, for example, *STD*, February 23, 1998.

30. This percentage of Chinatown union shops in 1997 is based on a comparison of the number of garment shops in the Chinatown area provided by the state labor department, which is not classified according to ethnicity, and the estimate of Chinatown union organizers and the Chinese newspapers. See, for example, *STD*, December 22, 1997 and April 29, 1998 and *WJ*, February 28, 1998.

31. These statistics are provided by the UNITE! Research Department. The estimated percentage of the local's Chinese membership in this study is consistent with the numbers provided by the local.

32. Green, *Ready-to-Wear,* 50.

33. See Nancy Green, "Sweatshop Migrations: The Garment Industry between Home and Shop," in *The Landscape of Modernity: Essays on New York City, 1900–1940,* eds. David Ward and Olivier Zunz (New York: Russell Sage Foundation, 1992), 213–32.

34. Mark Levitan, *Opportunity at Work: The New York City Garment Industry* (New York: Community Service Society of New York, 1998), 59.

35. One of the most active community-based labor organizations in New York's Chinatown in the last two decades is the Chinese Staff and Workers' Association.

READING 35

References

Barboza, David. 2001. "Meatpackers' Profits Hinge on Pool of Immigrant Labor." *New York Times* (Dec. 21).

Bjerklie, Steve. 1995. "On the Horns of a Dilemma: The U.S. Meat and Poultry Industry." In *Any Way You Cut It: Meat Processing and Small-Town America,* ed. D. D. Stull, M. J. Broadway, and D. Griffith, 41–60. Lawrence: University Press of Kansas.

Broadway, Michael J. 1994. "Hogtowns and Rural Development." *Rural Development Perspectives* 9: 40–46.

Brown, Dennis. 1993. "Changes in the Red Meat and Poultry Industries: Their Effect on Nonmetropolitan Employment." *Agricultural Economic Report* 665. Washington, DC: Economic Research Service, U.S. Department of Agriculture.

Bugos, G. E. 1992. "Intellectual Property Protection in the American Chicken-Breeding Industry." *Business History Review* 66: 127–168.

Carlin, Michael. 1999. "Even Tougher on Farm Labor?" *Raleigh News and Observer* (July 28).

Cromartie, John. 1999. "Race and Ethnicity in Rural Areas." *Rural Conditions and Trends* 9 (2): 9–19.

———, and William Kandel. 2002. "Did Residential Segregation in Rural America Increase with Recent Hispanic Population Growth?" Poster presented to the Meetings of the Population Association of America, Atlanta, GA, May 8–11.

Dawber, Thomas. 1980. *The Framingham Study.* Cambridge, MA: Harvard University Press.

Díaz McConnell, Eileen E. Forthcoming. "Latinos in the Rural Midwest: Historical Context and Contemporary Challenges." In *Apple Pie and Enchiladas: Latino Newcomers and the Changing Dynamics of the Rural Midwest,* ed. J. Chapa, A. Millard, and R. Saenz. Austin: University of Texas Press.

Durand, Jorge; Douglas S. Massey; and Fernando Charvet. 2000. "The Changing Geography of Mexican Immigration to the United States: 1910–1996." *Social Science Quarterly* 81: 1–16.

Engstrom, James. 2001. "Industry and Immigration in Dalton, Georgia." In *Latino Workers in the Contemporary South,* ed. A. Murphy, C. Blanchard, and J. A. Hill, 44–56. Athens: University of Georgia Press.

Flippen, Chenoa. 2001. "Neighborhood Transition and Social Organization: The White to Hispanic Case." *Social Problems* 48 (3): 299–321.

Gouveia, Lourdes, and Donald D. Stull. 1995. "Dances with Cows: Beefpacking's Impact on Garden City, Kansas, and Lexington, Nebraska." In *Any Way You Cut It: Meat Processing and Small-Town America,* ed. D. D. Stull, M. J. Broadway, and D. Griffith, 85–108. Lawrence: University Press of Kansas.

Grey, Mark A. 1995. "Pork, Poultry, and Newcomers in Storm Lake, Iowa." In *Any Way You Cut It: Meat Processing and Small-Town America,* ed. D. D. Stull, M. J. Broadway, and D. Griffith, 109–128. Lawrence: University Press of Kansas.

Griffith, David. 1995. "Hay Trabajo: Poultry Processing, Rural Industrialization, and the Latinization of Low-Wage Labor." In *Any Way You Cut It: Meat Processing and Small-Town America,* ed. D. D. Stull, M. J. Broadway, and D. Griffith, 129–152. Lawrence: University Press of Kansas.

Guthey, Greig. 2001. "Mexican Places in Southern Spaces: Globalization, Work and Daily Life in and around the North Georgia Poultry Industry." In *Latino Workers in the Contemporary South,* ed. A. Murphy, C. Blanchard, and J. A. Hill, 57–67. Athens: University of Georgia Press.

Hernández-León, Rubén, and Víctor Zúñiga. 2000. "'Making Carpet by the Mile': The Emergence of a Mexican Immigrant Community in an Industrial Region of the U.S. Historic South." *Social Science Quarterly* 81: 49–66.

Hetrick, Ron L. 1994. "Why Did Employment Expand in Poultry Processing Plants?" *Monthly Labor Review* (June): 31–34.

Johnson-Webb, Karen D. 2002. "Employer Recruitment and Hispanic Labor Migration: North Carolina Urban Areas at the End of the Millennium." *Professional Geographer* 54 (3): 406–421.

Katz, Jesse. 1996a. "The Chicken Trail: How Migrant Latino Workers Put Food on America's Table." *Los Angeles Times* (Nov. 10).

———. 1996b. "Poultry Industry Imports Labor to Do Its Dirty Work." *Los Angeles Times* (Dec. 8).

Lapinski, John S., et al. 1997. "Trends: Immigrants and Immigration." *Public Opinion Quarterly* 61: 356–383.

Lichter, Daniel T.; F. B. LeClere; and D. K. McLaughlin. 1991. "Local Marriage Market and the Marital Behavior of Black and White Women." *American Journal of Sociology* 96: 843–867.

Lichter, Daniel T., et al. 1992. "Race and the Retreat from Marriage: A Shortage of Marriageable Men?" *American Sociological Review* 57 (6): 781–799.

MacDonald, James, et al. 2000. "Consolidation in U.S. Meatpacking." *Agricultural Economic Report* 322–785. Washington, DC: Economic Research Service, U.S. Department of Agriculture.

Massey, Douglas S.; Jorge Durand; and Nolan Malone. 2002. *Beyond Smoke and Mirrors: Mexican Immigration in an Era of Economic Integration.* New York: Russell Sage.

McDaniel, Josh M. 2002. "Immigrants and Forest Industries in Alabama: Social Networks and Pioneer Settlements." Paper presented to the Immigration and America's Changing Ethnic Landscapes Conference, Athens, GA, Apr. 12–14.

McQuiston, Chris, and Emilio A. Parrado. 2002. "Migration and HIV Risks among Mexicans: Evidence from Participatory Action Research." Unpublished manuscript.

Mishra, Shiraz I.; Ross F. Conner; and J. Raúl Magaña, eds. 1996. *AIDS Crossing Borders.* Boulder, CO: Westview Press.

Ollinger, Michael; James MacDonald; and Milton Madison. 2000. *Structural Change in U.S. Chicken and Turkey Slaughter.* Agricultural Economic Report 787. Washington, DC: Economic Research Service, U.S. Department of Agriculture.

Oropesa, R. S., and D. Lichter. 1994. "Marriage Markets and the Paradox of Mexican American Nuptiality." *Journal of Marriage and the Family* 56: 889–908.

Parrado, Emilio A. 2002. "International Migration and Men's Marriage in Mexico." Unpublished Manuscript.

———, and René Zenteno. In press. "Gender Differences in Union Formation in Mexico: Evidence from Marital Search Models." *Journal of Marriage and Family.*

Pérez, Laura. 2001. "The Changing Geography of Latinos: Evidence from Census 2000." Paper presented to the American Sociological Association Meetings, Anaheim, CA.

Reed, Deborah. 2001. "Immigration and Males' Earnings Inequality in the Regions of the United States." *Demography* 38: 363–373.

Smothers, Ronald. 1996. "Unions Head South to Woo Poultry Workers." *New York Times* (Jan. 30).

Studstill, John D., and Laura Nieto-Studstill. 2001. "Hospitality and Hostility: Latin Immigrants in Southern Georgia." In *Latino Workers in the Contemporary South,* ed. A. Murphy, C. Blanchard, and J. A. Hill, 68–81. Athens: University of Georgia Press.

Sun, Lena H., and Gabriel Escobar. 1999. "On Chicken's Front Line." *Washington Post* (Nov. 28–Dec. 1).

Taylor, Marisa, and Steve Stein. 1999. "Network Helps Recruit Immigrants for U.S. Job Market." *Fort Worth Star-Telegram* (July 4).

U.S. Bureau of the Census. 1990. *Census of Population.* Summary Tape File 3. Washington, DC.

———. 2000. *Census of Population.* Summary Tape File 1. Washington, DC.

U.S. Department of Agriculture. Economic Research Service (USDA.ERS). *Poultry Yearbook,* 1960–2000, various issues. Washington, DC.

U.S. Department of Commerce (DOC). 1963–1997. *Current Population Survey.* Earnings Supplement, various years. Washington, DC.

———. 1967–1997. *Census of Manufactures.* Industry Series, various years. Washington, DC.

———. 2002. *Local Area Unemployment Statistics.* Washington, DC. http://www.bls.gov/lau

U.S. Department of Labor (DOL). 1972–2001. *Occupational Employment Statistics.* Washington, DC.

———. Bureau of International Labor Affairs. 1989. *The Effects of Immigration on the U.S. Economy and Labor Market.* Washington, DC.

READING 36

Notes

1. The authors are grateful to Glenn Bracey, Katisha Greer, and Krisen Lavelle for their helpful and insightful comments.

2. For two longer reviews of *Bamboozled,* see Barlowe (2003) and Epp (2003).

3. This quote is taken from the sketch, *Charlie Murphy's True Hollywood Stories,* "In the first (and easily the most popular sketch in the show so far—one that catapulted Chappelle to the level of phenomenon within days after airing), Charlie Murphy (Eddie Murphy's real-life brother) recounts supposed altercations between himself and the late funk musician Rick James, which took place during the height of his popularity in the early 1980s. Chappelle intersperses Murphy's retelling of his story with reenacted excerpts in which Chappelle plays the young Rick James and Murphy plays his younger self" (Wikipedia, 2005).

4. There have been numerous incidents of blackface parties at colleges across the United States (Muelier, Dirks, and Picca, forthcoming). One Swarthmore student stated, "I figured (obviously jokingly), that if I painted my face black, I would thus gain some super powers that would enable me to dance," explaining that dressing in blackface was a "spur of the moment thing." A Swarthmore history professor responded, "You don't inadvertently put on blackface, you inadvertently bang your shoulder on the way out the door'" (Nelson, 2002).

References

Barlowe, J. (2003). "You must never be a misrepresented people": Spike Lee's *Bamboozled. Canadian Review of American Studies, 33,* 1–16.

Baudrillard, J. (1981). *Simulacra and Simulation.* Ann Arbor, MI: University of Michigan Press.

Baudrillard, J. (1989). *America.* Translated by C. Turner. London: Verso.

Bernstein, M. (1996). Nostalgia, ambivalence, irony: *Song of the South* and race relations in 1946 Atlanta. *Film History, 8,* 219–236.

Bogle, D. (2005 [1973]). *Toms, Coons, Mulattoes, Mammies, and Bucks: An Interpretive History of Blacks in American Films.* New York: Continuum.

Carrillo, K. J. (2003). Highly offensive: Karen Juanita Carrillo examines the ongoing currency of racist curios. Retrieved November 6, 2005 from: http://www.ferris.edu/news/jimcrowllinks/neWSliStlOffensive.htm.

Clinton. C. (1982). *The Plantation Mistress: Woman's World in the Old South.* New York: Pantheon.

Collins, P. H. (2001). *Black Feminist Thought: Knowledge, Consciousness, and the Politics of Empowerment.* New York: Routledge.

Collins, P. H. (2004). *Black Sexual Politics: African Americans, Gender, and the New Racism.* New York: Routledge.

Comedy Central (Producer). (2003). *Chappelle's Show* [Television series]. United States: Comedy Central.

Delgado, R. & Stephancic, J. (1992). Images of the outsider in American law and culture: Can free expression remedy systemic social ills? *Cornell Law Review, 77,* 1258–1297.

Deloria, P. J. (1998). *Playing Indian.* New Haven, CT: Yale University Press.

Ebay, Inc. (2006). Offensive material. Retrieved January 7, 2006 from: http://pages.ebay.com/help/policies/offensive.html.

Epp, M. H. (2003). Raising minstrelsy: Humour, satire and the stereotype in *The Birth of a Nation* and *Bamboozled. Canadian Review of American Studies, 33,* 17–35.

Farley, C. J. (2005, May 15). On the beach with Dave Chappelle. *Time Online Edition.* Retrieved October 19, 2005 from: http://www.time.com/tirne/arts/printoutl0,8816.1061415,00.html.

Feagin, J. R. (2000). *Racist America: Roots, Current Realities, and Future Reparations.* New York: Routledge.

Gayle, A., Jr. (1976). *The Way of the New World: The Black Novel in America.* New York: Doubleday Anchor.

Ghettopoly. (2002). *Ghettopoly.* Retrieved October 7, 2005 from: http://www.ghettopoly.com.

Grindstaff, L. (2004). *Reviving blackface: Talk shows as modem-day minstrelsy.* Paper presented at the International Communication Association meeting, May 27–31, New Orleans, LA.

Guerrero, E. (1993). *Framing Blackness: The African American Image in Film.* Philadelphia, PA: Temple University Press.

Haggis, P. (Director). (2005). *Crash* [Motion picture]. United States: Lions Gate Films.

Hodges, M. (2003, February 27). Bubble rap: How not to package a band. *Digital Korea Herald.* Retrieved November 6, 2005 from: http://wk.koreaherald.co.kr/SITE/datahtml_dir12003/021271200302270007.asp.

Hooks, B. (1996). *Reel to Real: Race, Sex, and Class at the Movies.* New York: Routledge.

Hooks, B. (2004). *We Real Cool: Black Men and Masculinity.* New York: Routledge.

Kellner, D. (1995). *Media Culture: Cultural Studies, Identity and Politics between the Modern and the Postmodern.* New York: Routledge.

King, C. R. & Springwood, C. F. (2001). *Team Spirits: The Native American Mascots Controversy.* Lincoln, NE: University of Nebraska Press.

KOCCA (Korea Culture and Content Agency). (2003, February 25). Trouble bubbles up around pop group's look. Retrieved November 6, 2005 from: http://www.kocca.or.kr/ctnews/eng/SITE/datahtml_dir12003/02/251200302250128.html.

Kramer, S. (Director). (1967). *Guess Who's Coming to Dinner?* [Motion picture]. United States: Stanley Kramer Productions.

Lee, S. (Director). (2000). *Bamboozled* [Motion picture]. United States: 40 Acres and a Mule Filmworks.

Lhamon, W. T., Jr. (1998). *Raising Cain: Blackface Performance from Jim Crow to Hip Hop.* Cambridge, MA: Harvard UP.

Lieff, Cabraser, Heimann & Bernstein, LLP. (2005). *$40 million paid to class members in December 2005 in Abercrombie & Fitch discrimination lawsuit settlement.* Retrieved January 10, 2006 from: http://www.afjustice.coml.

McCurry, J. (2005, June 15). Japanese publisher defies Little Black Sambo protest. *The Guardian.* Retrieved January 7, 2006 from: http://books.guardian.co.uklnews/articles/0,6109,1506576,00.html.

Movie Revenues. (2006). Global film industry. Retrieved January 7,2006 from: http://www.factbook.net/wbglobal_rev.htm.

Mueller, J. C., Dirks D. & Picca, L. H. (forthcorning). Unmarking racism: Halloween costuming and engagement of the racial other. *Qualitative Sociology.*

Nelson, G. (2002, November 14). Collection on blackface raises larger race issues. *The Phoenix Online.* Retrieved June 1, 2004 from: http://www.sccs.swarthmore.edu/org/phoenix/2002/2002-11-07/news/l24l0.php.

Neupert, R. (2001). Trouble in watermelon land: George Pal and the Little Jasper cartoons. *Film Quarterly,* 55, 14–26.

Noriega, C. (2000). *Shot in America: Television, the State and the Rise of Chicano Cinema.* Minneapolis: University of Minnesota Press.

Noriega, C. (2001). *Race matters, media matters.* Viewing Race Project. Retrieved January 11, 2006 from: http://www.viewingrace.org/content.php?sec=essay&sub=1.

Pieterse, J. N. (1992). *White on Black: Images of Africa and Blacks in Western Popular Culture.* New Haven, CT: Yale University Press.

Pilgrim, D. (2000). Who was Jim Crow? The Jim Crow Museum of Racist Memorabilia. Retrieved June 1, 2004 from: http://www.ferris.edu/jimcrow/who.htm.

Pilgrim, D. (2001). New racist forms: Jim Crow in the 21st century. The Jim Crow Museum of Racist Memorabilia. Retrieved August 28, 2004 from: http://www.ferris.edu/jimcrow/newforms/.

Riggs, M. (Director). (1987). *Ethnic Notions* [Motion picture]. United States: Marlon Riggs.

Roediger, D. (1991). *The Wages of Whiteness: Race and the Making of the American Working Class.* New York: Verso.

Rosenberg, M. (2002, June 10). Take that, paleface! *The Nation.* Retrieved online January 6, 2006 from: http://www.thenation.com/doc/20020610/editors2.

Russell, K. K. (2001). *The Color of Crime: Racial Hoaxes, White Fear, Black Protectionism, Police Harassment, and Other Macroaggressions.* New York: New York University Press.

Schaffer, S. (1996). Disney and the imagineering of histories. *Postmodern Culture,* 6, 3. Retrieved January 7, 2006 from the ProjectMuse database.

Skal, D. J. (2002). *Death Makes a Holiday: A Cultural History of Halloween.* New York: Bloomsbury.

Strasburg, J. (2002, April 19). Abercrombie recalls T-shirts many found offensive. *San Francisco Chronicle.* Retrieved January 6, 2005 from: http://www.sfgate.com/cgi-bin/article.cgi?file=/c/a/2002/04/19/MN102999.DTL.

Strong, P. T. (2004). The mascot slot: Cultural citizenship, political correctness, and pseudo-Indian sports symbols. *Journal of Sport & Social Issues,* 28, 79–87.

Toll, R. C. (1974). *Blacking Up: The Minstrel Show in Nineteenth-Century America.* New York: Oxford University Press.

Trouillot, M. R. (1991). Anthropology and the savage slot: The poetics and politics of otherness. In R. G. Fox (ed.), *Recapturing Anthropology: Working in the Present.* Santa Fe, NM: School of American Research Press.

Turner, P. A. (1994). *Ceramic Uncles and Celluloid Mammies: Black Images and Their Influence on Culture.* New York: Anchor.

Vera, H. & Gordon, A. M. (2003). *Screen Saviors: Hollywood Fictions of Whiteness.* Lanham, MD: Rowman & Littlefield.

Vera, H. & Gordon, A. M. (2005). On how to dissolve racial taboos. [Review of the motion picture *Guess Who?*] *Contexts,* 4, 68–69.

Walt Disney World. (2006). Splash Mountain. Retrieved January 7, 2006 from: http://disneyworld.disney.go.com/wdw/parks/attractionDetail?id=SplashMountain AttractionPage&bhcp=1.

Wasko, J. (2001). Is it a small world, after all? In J. Wasko, M. Phillips & E. R. Meehan (eds.), *Dazzled by Disney?: The Global Disney Audiences Project* (pp. 3–30). London: Leicester University Press.

White, A. (1995). *The Resistance: Ten Years of Pop Culture That Shook the World.* New York: Overlook Hardcover.

Wilkinson, D. Y. (1974). Racial socialization through children's toys: A sociohistorical examination. *Journal of Black Studies,* 5, 96–109.

Williams, P. J. (1996). Metro Broadcasting, Inc. v. FCC: Regrouping in singular times. In K. Crenshaw, N. Gotanda, G. Peller & K. Thomas (eds.), *Critical Race Theory: The Key Writings That Formed the Movement.* New York: New Press.

World Wide Box Office. (2006). *Song of the South* worldwide sales. Retrieved January 6, 2006 from: http://worldwide boxoffice.com.

READING 37

Note

1. Term developed by bell hooks (1995) to describe the interlocking nature of domination and oppression.

References

Baker, R. K., & Ball, S. I. (Eds.). (1969). *Violence and the media.* Washington, DC: Government Printing Office.

Berger, P. L., & Luckmann, T. (1967). *The social construction of reality.* New York: Doubleday.

Blumer, H. (1969). *Symbolic interaction: Perspective and method.* Upper Saddle River, NJ: Prentice Hall.

Collins, P. H. (1991). *Black feminist thought: Knowledge, consciousness, and the politics of empowerment.* New York: Routledge.

Collins, P. (2004). *Black sexual politics: African Americans, gender, and the new racism.* New York: Routledge.

Comstock, G. A., Chaffee, S., Katzman, N., McCombs, M., & Roberts, D. (1978). *Television and human behavior.* New York: Columbia University Press.

Diawara, M. (1993). *Black American cinema.* New York: American Film Institute.

duCille, A. (1996). *Skin trade.* Cambridge, MA: Harvard University Press.

Emerson, R. A. (2002). "Where my girls at?" Negotiating Black womanhood in music videos. *Gender & Society, 16,* 115–135.

Fish, S. (1980). *Is there a text in this class? The authority of interpretive communities.* Cambridge, MA: Harvard University Press.

Hooks, B. (1995). *Killing rage, ending racism.* New York: Holt.

Jordan, W. (1968). *White over Black: American attitudes toward the Negro, 1550–1812.* Chapel Hill: University of North Carolina Press.

McRobbie, A. (1982). Jackie: An ideology of adolescent femininity. In B. Waites, T. Bennet, & G. Martin (Eds.), *Popular culture: Past and present* (pp. 263–283). London: Open University Press.

Milkie, M. A. (1999). Social comparisons, reflected appraisals, and mass media: The impact of pervasive beauty images on Black and White girls' self-concepts. *Social Psychology Quarterly, 62,* 190–210.

Murray, D., Schwartz, J., & Lichter, S. R. (2001). *It ain't necessarily so: How the media remake our picture of reality.* New York: Penguin Books.

Pough, G. D. (2004). *Check it while I wreck it: Black womanhood, hip-hop culture, and the public sphere.* Boston: Northeastern University Press.

Rose, T. (1994). *Black noise rap music and Black culture in contemporary America.* New York: Wesleyan University Press.

Schaefer, R. T. (2005). *Race and ethnicity in the United States* (3rd ed.). Upper Saddle River, NJ: Prentice Hall.

Schiller, H. L. (1973). *The mind managers.* Boston: Beacon.

Slavery and the making of America. (2004). [Film]. New York: Ambrose.

READING 38

References

Beaudoin, C. E., and Thorson, E. 2006. "The Social Capital of Blacks and Whites: Differing Effects of the Mass Media in the United States," *Human Communication Research 32:* 157–77.

Berry, G. L., and Asamen, J. K. 2001. "Television, Children and Multicultural Awareness: Comprehending the Medium in a Complex Multimedia Society," in D. S. Singer and J. L. Singer (eds.) *Handbook of Children and the Media.* Thousand Oaks, CA: Sage Publications, pp. 359–74.

Bowman, P. J., Muhammad, R., and Ifatunji, M. 2003. "Skin Tone, Class, and Racial Attitudes among African Americans," in C. Herring, V. Keith, and H. D. Horton (eds.) *Skin Deep: How Race and Complexion Matter in the "Color-Blind" Era.* Urbana, IL: University of Illinois at Chicago, pp. 128–58.

Brunsma, D. L. 2005. "Interracial Families and the Racial Identification of Mixed-Race Children: Evidence from the Early Childhood Longitudinal Study," *Social Forces 84 (2):* 1131–57.

Comstock, G., and Scharrer, E. 2001. "Use of Television and other Film-Related Media," in D. G. Singer and J. L. Singer (eds.) *Handbook of Children and the Media.* Thousand Oaks, CA: Sage Publications, pp. 47–72.

Donaldson, M. B. 2006. *Masculinity in the Interracial Buddy Film.* Jefferson, NC: McFarland.

Frisby, C. M. 2006. "'Shades of Beauty': Examining the Relationship of Skin Color to Perceptions of Physical Attractiveness," *Facial Plastic Surgery 22 (3):* 175–9.

Gallagher, C. A. 2006. "Color Blindness: An Obstacle to Racial Justice?" in D. L. Brunsma (ed.) *Mixed Messages: Doing Race in the "Color-Blind" Era.* Boulder, CO: Lynne Rienner, pp. 103–16.

Goldsmith, A. H., Hamilton, D., and Darity, W., Jr. 2007. "From Dark to Light: Skin Color and Wages among African-Americans," *Journal of Human Resources 42 (4):* 701.

Gruber, E., and Thau, H. 2003. "Sexually Related Content on Television and Adolescents of Color: Media Theory, Psychological Development, and Psychological Impact," *Journal of Negro Education 72 (4):* 438–56.

Harvey, R. D., LaBeach, N., Pridgen, E., and Gocial, T. M. 2005. "The Intragroup Stigmatization of Skin Tone among Black Americans," *Journal of Black Psychology 31 (3):* 237.

Herring, C., and Keith, V. M. (eds). 2004. *Skin Deep: How Race and Complexion Matter in the "Color-Blind" Era*. Chicago: University of Illinois Press.

Huntemann, N., and Morgan, M. 2001. "Mass Media and Identity Development," in D. G. Singer and J. L. Singer (eds.) *Handbook of Children and the Media*. Thousand Oaks, California: Sage Publications, pp. 309–23.

Hunter, M. L. 2002. "'If You're Light You're Alright': Light Skin Color as Social Capital for Women of Color," *Gender and Society* 16 (2): 175–93.

Hunter, M. 2007. "The Persistent Problem of Colorism: Skin Tone, Status, and Inequality," *Sociology Compass* 1 (1): 237–54.

Jones, T. 2000. "Shades of Brown: The Law of Skin Color," *Duke Law Journal* 49 (6): 1487–557.

Keith, V. M. 2009. "A Colorstruck World: Skin Tone, Achievement, and Self-Esteem among African American Women," in E. N. Glenn (ed.) *Shades of Difference: Why Skin Color Matters*. Stanford, CA: Stanford University Press, pp. 25–39.

Kellner, D. 2003. "Cultural Studies, Multiculturalism, and Media Culture," in G. Dines and J. M. Humez (eds.) *Gender, Race, and Class in Media: A Text-Reader*. Thousand Oaks, CA: Sage Publications, pp. 9–20.

Larson, S. G. 2005. *Media and Minorities: The Politics of Race in News and Entertainment*. Lanham, MD: Rowman and Littlefield.

Littlefield, M. B. 2008. "The Media as a System of Racialization: Exploring Images of African American Women and the New Racism," *American Behavioral Scientist* 51 (5): 675.

Lull, J. 2003. "Hegemony," in G. Dines and J. M. Humez (eds.) *Gender, Race, and Class in Media: A Text-Reader*. Thousand Oaks, CA: Sage Publications, pp. 61–7.

Margolis, H. (1999). "Stereotypical Strategies: Black Film Aesthetics, Spectator Positioning, and Self-directed Stereotypes in *Hollywood Shuffle* and *I'm Gonna Git You Sucka*," *Cinema Journal* 38 (3): 50–66.

Outley, C. W. 2006. "A Content Analysis of Health and Physical Activity Messages Market to African American Children during After-School Television Programming," *Archives of Pediatrics and Adolescent Medicine* 160: 432–5.

Rockquemore, K. A., and Brusma, D. L. 2001. *Beyond Black: Biracial Identity in America*. Thousand Oaks, CA: Sage Publications.

Thornton, M. C. 2009. "Policing the Borderlands: White—and Black—American Newspaper Perceptions of Multiracial Heritage and the Idea of Race, 1996–2006," *Journal of Social Issues* 65 (1): 105–27.

Vincent, C., Ball, S. J., and Braun, A. 2008. "'It's Like Saying Coloured': Understanding and Analyzing the Urban Working Classes," *Sociological Review* 56 (1): 61–77.

Wade, T. J., and Bielitz, S. 2005. "The Differential Effect of Skin Color on Attractiveness, Personality Evaluations, and Perceived Life Success of African Americans," *Journal of Black Psychology* 31: 215–36.

Wilson, C. C. I., and Gutierrez, F. 1995. *Race, Multiculturalism, and the Media: From Mass to Class Communication*, 2nd ed. Thousand Oaks, CA: Sage Publications.

READING 39

Notes

1. Many people have preferences about terms used to describe America's indigenous peoples. "American Indian" is commonly used, as is "Native American, Native, and Indian." These terms are used interchangeably in recognition of individual preferences, without disregarding the weight each word carries.

2. Lawsuits are currently underway to limit Heilman Breweries' use of the name Crazy Horse Liquor (Specktor, 1995). Several states have outlawed the sale of the beverage (Specktor, 1995). Also under review are important legal issues such as a tribe's sovereign power to exercise civil jurisdiction and the Witko family's right to protect the image of their ancestor.

References

Aaker, D., & A. L. Biel. (1993). *Advertising's role in building strong brands*. Mahwah, NJ: Lawrence Erlbaum.

Barthes, R. (1972). *Mythologies*. New York: The Noonday Press.

Berkhofer, R., Jr. (1979). *The white man's Indian: Images of the American Indian from Columbus to the present*. New York: Vintage Books.

Bird, S. E. (1996). Not my fantasy: The persistence of Indian imagery in *Dr. Quinn, Medicine Woman*. In S. E. Bird (Ed.), *Dressing in feathers: The construction of the Indian in American popular culture* (pp. 245–262). Boulder, CO: Westview Press.

Blalock, C. (1992). Crazy Horse controversy riles Congress: Controversies over Crazy Horse Malt Liquor and Black Death vodka. *Beverage Industry, 83*(9), 1–3.

Burnham, P. (1992, 27 May). Indians can't shake label as guides to good buys. *The Washington Times*, p. E1.

Champagne, D. (1994). *Native America: Portrait of the peoples*. Detroit: Visible Ink.

Cortese, A. J. (1999). *Provocateur: Images of women and minorities in advertising*. New York: Rowman & Littlefield Publishers, Inc.

Dotz, W., & Morton, J. (1996). *What a character! 20th century American advertising icons*. San Francisco: Chronicle Books.

Goings, K. W. (1994). *Mammy and Uncle Mose: Black collectibles and American stereotyping.* Bloomington, IN: Indiana University Press.

Graham, R. (1993, 6 January). Symbol or stereotype: One consumer's tradition is another's racial slur. *The Boston Globe,* p. 35.

Green, M. K. (1993). Images of American Indians in advertising: Some moral issues. *Journal of Business Ethics, 12,* 323–330.

Hall, S. (1997). *Representation: Cultural representations and signifying practices.* London: Sage.

Hill, R. (1992). The non-vanishing American Indian: Are the modern images any closer to the truth? *Quail* (May), 35–37.

Kates, S. M., & Shaw-Garlock, G. (1999). The ever-entangling web: A study of ideologies and discourses in advertising to women. *Journal of Advertising 28*(2), 33–49.

Kern-Foxworth, M. (1994). *Aunt Jemima, Uncle Ben, and Rastus: Blacks in advertising yesterday, today, and tomorrow.* Westport, CT: Praeger.

Land O' Lakes. (2000). [On-line]. Available: http://www.landolakes.com.

Larson, C. (1937). Patent-medicine advertising and the early American press. *Journalism Quarterly, 14*(4), 333–339.

Lippmann, W. (1922/1961). *Public opinion.* New York: Macmillan & Company.

McCracken, G. (1993). The value of the brand: An anthropological perspective. In D. Aaker & A. L. Biel (Eds.), *Brand equity is advertising: Advertising's role in building strong brands.* Mahwah, NJ: Lawrence Erlbaum.

Merskin, D. (1998). Sending up signals: A survey of American Indian media use and representation in the mass media. *The Howard Journal of Communications, 9,* 333–345.

Metz, S., & Thee, M. (1994). Brewers intoxicated with racist imagery. *Business and Society Review, 89,* 50–51.

Mihesuah, D. A. (1996). *American Indians: Stereotypes and realities.* Atlanta, GA: Clarity Press.

Monitor Sugar Company. (2000) [On-line]. Available: http://members.aol.com/asga/mon.htm.

Morgan, H. (1986). *Symbols of America.* New York: Penguin Books.

Schmitt, B., & Simonson, A. (1997). *Marketing aesthetics: The strategic management of brands, identity, and image.* New York: The Free Press.

Sioux Honey Association. (2000). [On-line]. Available: http://www.suebeehoney.com.

Specktor, M. (1995, January 6). Crazy Horse exploited to peddle liquor. *National Catholic Reporter, 31*(10), 3.

Strickland, R. (1998). The celluloid Indian. *Oregon Quarterly* (Summer), 9–10.

van Dijk, T. A. (1996). *Discourse, racism, and ideology.* La Laguna: RCEI Ediciones.

Westerman, M. (1989, March). Death of the Frito bandito: Marketing to ethnic groups. *American Demographics, 11,*28–32.

Williamson, J. (1978). *Decoding advertisements: Ideology and meaning in advertising.* New York: Marion Boyars.

READING 42

References

Adelman, Robert M., Hui-shien Tsao, Stewart E. Tolnay, Kyle D. Crowder. 2001. "Neighborhood Disadvantage among Racial and Ethnic Groups: Residential Location in 1970 and 1980." *Sociological Quarterly* 42: 603–32.

Arthur, John A. 2000. *Invisible Sojourners: African Immigrant Diaspora in the United States.* New York: Praeger.

Dodoo, F. Nii-Amoo. 1999. "Black and Immigrant Labor Force Participation in America." *Race and Society* 2: 69–82.

Foerster, Amy. 2004. "Race, Identity, and Belonging: 'Blackness' and the Struggle for Solidarity in a Multiethnic Labor Union." *Social Problems* 51: 386–409.

Ho, Christine. 1991. *Salt-Water Trinnies: Afro-Trinidadian Immigrant Networks and Non-assimilation in Los Angeles.* New York: AMS Press.

James, Winston. 2002. "Explaining Afro-Caribbean Social Mobility in the United States: Beyond the Sowell Thesis." *Comparative Studies in Society and History* 44: 218–62.

Kasinitz, Philip. 1992. *Caribbean New York.* Ithaca, NY: Cornell University Press.

Kollehlon, Konia T., and Edward E. Eule. 2003. "The Socioeconomic Attainment Patterns of Africans in the United States." *International Migration Review* 37: 1163–90.

Logan, John R., and John Mollenkopf. 2003. *People and Politics in America's Big Cities.* New York: Drum Major Institute for Public Policy.

Rogers, Reuel R. 2004. "Race-Based Coalitions among Minority Groups: Afro-Caribbean Immigrants and African-Americans in New York City." *Urban Affairs Review* 39: 283–317.

Sowell, Thomas. 1978. "Three Black Histories." In *Essays and Data on American Ethnic Groups,* ed. Thomas Sowell. Washington, DC: Urban Institute.

Takyi, Baffour K. 2002a. "Africans in the Diaspora: Black-White Earnings Differences among America's Africans." *Ethnic and Racial Studies* 25: 913–41.

———. 2002b. "The Making of the Second Diaspora: On the Recent African Immigrant Community in the United States of America." *Western Journal of Black Studies* 26: 32–43.

Waters, Mary. 1999. *Black Identities: West Indian Immigrant Dreams and American Realities.* Cambridge, MA: Harvard University Press.

READING 43

Notes

1. See William E. Leuchtenburg, "The American Perception of the Arab World." In George N. Atiyeh, ed., *Arab and American Cultures* (Washington, DC: American Enterprise Institute for Public Policy Research, 1977), p. 15.

2. Although it is possible to speak of several waves of Arab immigration to North America (e.g., 1880s to World War I, World War I to World War II, 1945 to 1967, 1968 to the present), there have been two main waves: from the 1880s to World War II and from World War II to the present. The major differences in the character and composition of the immigrant populations can be detected primarily between these two groups.

3. Unless otherwise indicated, references to the Arab community include the Arabs in Canada and those in the United States. Because of the much smaller numbers of Arabs in Canada, leadership on major issues usually has come from the Arab community in the United States.

4. See appendixes 1 and 2 in Gregory Orfalea, *Before the Flames: Quest for the History of Arab Americans* (Austin, TX: University of Texas Press, 1988), pp. 314–15. There were about 11,000 Arabs in Canada in 1931. For more on the subject of Arab immigration to Canada, see Baha Abu-Laban, *An Olive Branch on the Family Tree: The Arabs in Canada* (Toronto: McClelland and Stewart, 1980).

5. This is the official U.S. government figure cited in Philip Hitti's "The Emigrants," published in the 1963 edition of the *Encyclopedia of Islam* and reproduced in *Al-Hoda, 1898–1968* (New York: Al-Hoda Press, 1968), p. 133. A much larger estimate of 800,000 (Lebanese) was given by Ashad G. Hawie, *The Rainbow Ends* (New York: Theo. Gaus' Sons, 1942), pp. 149, 151.

6. This figure does not include the Arab community in Canada, which has fewer than 400,000 persons today. For estimates of Arab immigration to Canada, see Baha Abu-Laban, *An Olive Branch on the Family Tree: The Arabs in Canada* (Toronto: McClelland and Stewart, 1980) and Ibrahim Hayani's chapter in Michael Suleiman, ed., *Arabs in America: Building a New Future* (Philadelphia: Temple University Press, 1999). Philip M. Kayal gave the low estimate in 1974 for Arabs in the United States but provided a revised estimate much closer to the generally accepted figure in 1987. See his "Estimating Arab-American Population," *Migration Today* 2, no. 5 (1974): 3, 9, and "Report: Counting the 'Arabs' Among Us," *Arab Studies Quarterly* 9, no. 1 (1987): 98–104.

7. See Philip K. Hitti, *The Syrians in America* (New York: George H. Doran, 1924), p. 48; Alixa Naff, *Becoming American: The Early Arab Immigrant Experience* (Carbondale, IL: Southern Illinois University Press, 1985), p. 83; Samir Khalaf, "The Background and Causes of Lebanese/Syrian Immigration to the United States before World War I," in Eric J. Hooglund, ed., *Crossing the Waters: Arabic-Speaking Immigrants to the United States before 1940* (Washington, DC: Smithsonian Institution Press, 1987), pp. 17–35; and Charles Issawi, "The Historical Background of Lebanese Emigration: 1800–1914," in Albert Hourani and Nadim Shehadi, eds., *The Lebanese in the World: A Century of Emigration* (London: I.B. Tauris, 1992), pp. 13–31. See also Baha Abu-Laban, "The Lebanese in Montreal," in Albert Hourani and Nadim Shehadi, eds., *The Lebanese in the World: A Century of Emigration* (London: I.B. Tauris, 1992), pp. 227–42.

8. Charles Issawi, "The Historical Background of Lebanese Emigration: 1800–1914." In Albert Hourani and Nadim Shehadi, eds., *The Lebanese in the World: A Century of Emigration* (London: I.B. Tauris, 1992), p. 22.

9. Philip K. Hitti, *The Syrians in America* (New York: George H. Doran, 1924), pp. 49–50. See also Akram Fouad Khater, "'House' to 'Goddess of the House': Gender, Class, and Silk in 19th-Century Mount Lebanon," *International Journal of Middle East Studies* 28, no. 3 (1996): 325–48.

10. For an informed and intelligent discussion on this and related issues, see Louise Seymour Houghton's series of articles entitled "Syrians in the United States," *The Survey* 26 (1 July, 5 August, 2 September, 7 October, 1911), pp. 480–95, 647–65, 786–803, 957–68.

11. For an early account of Arab immigration to the United States and to North America in general, which cites religious persecution as the reason for migration, see Basil M. Kherbawi, "History of the Syrian Emigration," which is part seven of Kherbawi's *tarikh al-Wilayat al-Muttahida (History of the United States)* (New York: al Dalil Press, 1913), pp. 726–96, published in Arabic.

12. See Leila Tarazi Fawaz, *An Occasion for War: Civil Conflict in Lebanon and Damascus in 1860* (Berkeley, CA: University of California Press, 1995). See also, Mikha'il Mishaqa, *Murder, Mayhem, Pillage and Pluder: The History of Lebanon in the 18th and 19th Centuries.* Translated by Wheeler M. Thackston, Jr. (Albany, NY: State University of New York Press, 1988).

13. See Louise Seymour Houghton's series of articles entitled "Syrians in the United States," *The Survey,* 26 (1911), pp. 480–95; and Alixa Naff, *Becoming American: The Early Arab Immigrant Experience* (Carbondale, IL: Southern Illinois University Press, 1985), pp. 128–200. For Canadian statistics, see Baha Abu-Laban, *An Olive Branch on the Family Tree: The Arabs in Canada* (Toronto: McClelland and Stewart, 1980).

14. *Kawkab America* (15 April 1892): 1, English section. The English titles of Arabic newspapers cited here are provided as originally used. The titles in parentheses are the transliterations used by the Library of Congress.

15. Even though *Kawkab America* was published for about seventeen years, only copies of the first four years are available; the others have been lost.

16. See Motaz Abdullah Alhourani, "The Arab-American Press and the Arab World: News Coverage in Al-Bayan and Al-Dalil" (master's thesis, Kansas State University, Manhattan, KS, 1993).

17. For a history of the organizational and political activities of Arabic-speaking groups in the United States during this period, see James Ansara, "The Immigration and Settlement of the Syrians" (master's thesis, Harvard University, Cambridge, MA, 1931).

18. Among these, the most important journal was *The Syrian World,* published and edited by Salloum Mokarzel. A useful publication is the *Annotated Index to the Syrian World, 1926–1932* by John G. Moses and Eugene Paul Nassar (Saint Paul, MN: Immigration History Research Center, University of Minnesota, 1994).

19. See Philip M. and Joseph M. Kayal, *The Syrian-Lebanese in America: A Study in Religion and Assimilation* (Boston, MA: Twayne Publishers, 1975).

20. A good account of the most prominent of these writers is provided by Nadira Jamil Sarraj, *Shu'ara' al-Rabitah al-Qalamiyah* (Poets of the Pen League) (Cairo, Egypt: Dar al-Ma'arif, 1964), published in Arabic.

21. See, for instance, Ameen Rihani, "To Syrians in the [American] Armed Forces," *As-Sayeh* (*al-Sa'ih*) (16 September 1918): 2, published in Arabic.

22. Advertisements and editorials in support of American Liberty bonds were found in most Arabic publications of that period, including *Al-Hoda* and *Meraat-ul-Gharb.*

23. See, in particular, *Syria Before the Peace Conference* (New York: Syrian-Lebanese League of North America, 1919).

24. This was the view often voiced after French entrenchment in Syria and Lebanon in the late 1920s and the 1930s.

25. For a summary of these views, see "Editors and Arabian Newspapers Give Opinions on Zionism," *The Jewish Criterion* (5 July 1918): 16–17.

26. Among the more active participants in public lectures and writings on this issue were Ameen Rihani and F. I. Shatara. The Arab National League was established in 1936, and members spoke out on Palestine and other issues. For coverage of these and other activities related to the Palestine issue, see *Palestine & Transjordan* for that period. See also "A Communique from the Arab National League," *As-Sayeh* (6 August 1936): 9.

27. On the occupations of emigrant Arabs, especially in North America and specifically about those engaged in commerce, see Salloum Mokarzel, *Tarikh al-tijara al-Suriyya fi al-mahajir al-Amrikiyya* (*The History of Trade of Syrian Immigrants in the Americas*) (New York: Syrian-American Press, 1920), published in Arabic. On peddling activity, see Alixa Naff, *Becoming American: The Early Arab Immigrant Experience* (Carbondale, IL: Southern Illinois University Press, 1985), pp. 128–200.

28. The Arabic press of the period was replete with such advice.

29. Edna Bonacich, "A Theory of Middleman Minorities," *American Sociological Review* 38 (1973): 591.

30. Prejudice against Arabs in America was widespread, and there was also some discrimination, especially in the southern United States. See, for instance, Nancy Faires Conklin and Nora Faires, " 'Colored' and Catholic: The Lebanese in Birmingham, Alabama." In Eric J. Hooglund, ed., *Crossing the Waters: Arabic-Speaking Immigrants to the United States before 1940* (Washington, DC: Smithsonian Institution Press, 1987), pp. 69–84.

31. See, for instance, H. A. El-Kourie, "Dr. El-Kourie Defends Syrian Immigrants," *Birmingham Ledger* (20 September 1907) and "El-Kourie Takes Burnett to Task," *Age-Herald* (Birmingham, AL) (20 October 1907): 6.

32. In 1908, Canada issued the Order-in-Council, P.C. 926, which severely restricted Asiatic immigration. Negative attitudes about "Syrians," mistaking them for "Turks," also were a factor in reducing the level of Arab immigration to Canada. See Baha Abu-Laban, "The Lebanese in Montreal." In Albert Hourani and Nadim Shehadi, eds., *The Lebanese in the World: A Century of Emigration* (London: I.B. Tauris, 1992), p. 229.

33. See Kalil A. Bishara, *The Origins of the Modern Syrian* (New York: Al-Hoda Publishing House, 1914), published in English and Arabic.

34. See *Ex Parte Dow,* 211 F. 486 (E.D. South Carolina 1914) and *In Re Dow,* 213 F. 355 (E.D. South Carolina 1914).

35. *Dow v. United States et al,* 26 F. 145 (4th Cir. 1915).

36. See Joseph W. Ferris, "Syrian Naturalization Question in the United States: Certain Legal Aspects of Our Naturalization Laws," Part II, *The Syrian World* 2, no. 9 (1928): 18–24.

37. *In Re Ahmed Hassan,* 48 F. Supp. 843 (E.D. Michigan 1942).

38. *Ex Parte Mohriez,* 54 F. Supp. 941 (D. Massachusetts 1944).

39. See the Arabic edition of *Al-Hoda, 1898–1968* (New York: Al-Hoda Press, 1968).

40. *The Syrian Voice* changed its name to *The Syrian and Lebanonite Voice* in the late 1930s.

41. See M[ichael A.] Shadid, "Syria for the Syrians," *Syrian World* 1, no. 8 (1927): 21–24, and see " 'Syria for the Syrians' Again: An Explanation and a Retraction," *Syrian World* 3, no. 4 (1928): 24–28.

42. For an excellent early study of New York Arabs, see Lucius Hopkins Miller, "A Study of the Syrian Communities of Greater New York," *Federation* 3 (1903): 11–58.

43. This was the message often presented in *Al-Akhlaq* (*al-Akhlaq*) (*Character*) in the 1920s.

44. See the various articles in the Arabic press by Afifa Karam and Victoria Tannous.

45. This issue occupied the Arab community for a long time and was almost a weekly subject in the main newspapers until peddling activity dwindled in the late 1920s. See, for instance, Afifa Karam's (untitled) article about women peddlers and the *Kashshi* in *Al-Hoda* (14 July, 1903): 2.

46. See, for instance, Habib I. Katibah, "What Is Americanism?" *The Syrian World* 1, no. 3 (1926): 16–20; W. A. Mansur, "The Future of Syrian Americans," *The Syrian World* 2, no. 3 (1927): 11–17, and see "Modern Syrians' Contributions to Civilization," *The Syrian World* 4, no. 5 (1930): 7–14.

47. The question about whether to teach Arabic to their children was a controversial issue in the 1920s and hotly debated in two main journals, *The Syrian World* and *Al-Akhlaq*.

48. See Michael W. Suleiman, "A Community Profile of Arab-Americans: Major Challenges and Concerns," *Arab Perspectives* (September 1983): pp. 6–13.

49. See Ibrahim Abu-Lughod, ed., *The Arab-Israeli Confrontation of June, 1967: An Arab Perspective* (Evanston, IL: Northwestern University Press, 1970).

50. Michael W. Suleiman, "Arab-Americans and the Political Process." In Ernest McCarus, ed., *The Development of Arab-American Identity* (Ann Arbor, MI: University of Michigan Press, 1994), pp. 37–60.

51. See "Dictionary of Races or Peoples." In *United States Reports of the Immigration Commission* (Washington, DC: Government Printing Office, 1911).

52. The details of these appeals are discussed in Michael W. Suleiman, "Early Arab-Americans: The Search for Identity." In Eric J. Hooglund, ed., *Crossing the Waters: Arabic-Speaking Immigrants to the United States before 1940* (Washington, DC: Smithsonian Institution Press, 1987), pp. 37–54.

53. C. P. Snow, *The Two Cultures and the Scientific Revolution* (Cambridge, England: Cambridge University Press, 1961).

54. This became a popular theme among many Arab-American writers. See, for instance, Abraham Mitry Rihbany, *A Far Journey* (Boston, MA: Houghton-Mifflin, 1914).

55. Abraham Mitrie Rihbany, *The Syrian Christ* (Boston, MA: Houghton-Mifflin, 1916).

56. See Evelyn Shakir, "Pretending to Be Arab: Role-Playing in Vance Bourjaily's 'The Fractional Man,'" MELUS 9, no. 1 (1982): 7–21. See also Vance Bourjaily, *Confessions of a Spent Youth* (New York: Bantam Books, 1961).

57. See, for instance, William Peter Blatty, *Which Way to Mecca, Jack?* (New York: Bernard Geis Associates, 1960).

58. See Ali Shteiwi Zaghel, "Changing Patterns of Identification among Arab Americans: The Palestine Ramallites and the Christian Syrian-Lebanese" (Ph.D. diss., Northwestern University, 1977).

59. Much has been written in this vein. For a lengthy bibliography, see Michael W. Suleiman, *The Arabs in the Mind of America* (Brattleboro, VT: Amana Books, 1988). For a Canadian-Arab activist's view, see Sheikh Muhammad Said Massoud, *I Fought as I Believed* (Montreal: Sheikh Muhammad Said Massoud, 1976).

60. Helen Hatab Samhan, "Politics and Exclusion: The Arab American Experience," *Journal of Palestine Studies* 16, no. 2 (1987): 11–28.

61. Nabeel Abraham, "Anti-Arab Racism and Violence in the United States." In Ernest McCarus, ed., *The Development of Arab-American Identity* (Ann Arbor, MI: University of Michigan Press, 1994), pp. 155–214.

62. For documentation, see, for instance, *1990 ADC Annual Report on Political and Hate Violence* (Washington, DC: American-Arab Anti-Discrimination Committee, 1991). For Canadian statistics, see Zuhair Kashmeri, *The Gulf Within: Canadian Arabs, Racism and the Gulf War* (Toronto: James Lorimer & Co., 1991).

63. Ronald Stockton, "Ethnic Archetypes and the Arab Image." In Ernest McCarus, ed., *The Development of Arab-American Identity* (Ann Arbor, MI: University of Michigan Press, 1994), p. 120.

64. See the various essays and poems in Joanna Kadi, ed., *Food for Our Grandmothers: Writings by Arab-American and Arab-Canadian Feminists* (Boston, MA: South End Press, 1994).

65. See Louise Cainkar, "Palestinian Women in the United States: Coping with Tradition, Change, and Alienation" (Ph.D. diss., Northwestern University, 1988).

66. See Charlene Joyce Eisenlohr, "The Dilemma of Adolescent Arab Girls in an American High School" (Ph.D. diss., University of Michigan, 1988).

67. For an excellent study on Arab-American women, see Evelyn Shakir, *Bint Arab: Arab and Arab American Women in the United States* (Westport, CT: Praeger, 1997).

68. Joseph Massad, "Palestinians and the Limits of Racialized Discourse," *Social Text* 11, no. 1 (1993): 108.

69. The attempt has failed, at least so far. See the 16 September 1997 letter to Katherine K. Wellman of the Office of Management and Budget sent on Arab American Institute (AAI) stationery and signed by Helen Hatab Samhan (AAI), Samia El Badry (Census 2000 Advisory Committee), and Hala Maksoud, American-Arab Anti-Discrimination Committee.

70. Lisa Suhair Majaj, "Two Worlds: Arab-American Writing," *Forkroads* 1, no. 3 (1996): 64–80. See also different entries in Joanna Kadi, ed., *Food for Our Grandmothers: Writings by Arab-American and Arab-Canadian Feminists* (Boston, MA: South End Press, 1994).

71. See, for instance, Pauline Kaldas, "Exotic." In Joanna Kadi, ed., *Food for Our Grandmothers: Writings by Arab-American and*

Arab-Canadian Feminists (Boston, MA: South End Press, 1994), pp. 168–69.

72. See Nabeel Abraham, "Arab-American Marginality: Mythos and Praxis." In Baha Abu-Laban and Michael W. Suleiman, eds., *Arab Americans: Continuity and Change* (Belmont, MA: AAUG Press, 1989), pp. 17–43.

73. See Michael W. Suleiman, "American Views of Arabs and the Impact of These Views on Arab Americans," *Al-Mustaqbal Al-Arabi* 16 (1993): 93–107, published in Arabic.

74. Milton Gordon states that the absence of a hostile attitude on the part of the host society is a key factor in the integration and assimilation of immigrants. See his *Assimilation in American Life: The Role of Race, Religion, and National Origins* (New York: Oxford University Press, 1964).

75. These attitudes were evident in a 1998 survey of Arabs active in U.S. politics, an analysis of which I plan to publish.

76. For analyses of some of the 1980 and 1990 U.S. census data, see John Zogby, *Arab America Today: A Demographic Profile of Arab Americans* (Washington, DC: Arab American Institute, 1990), and Samia El-Badry, "The Arab-American Market," *American Demographics* (January 1994): 22–27, 30. See also "CPH-L-149 Selected Characteristics for Persons of Arab Ancestry: 1990," U.S. Bureau of the Census, 1990 Census of Population and Housing, C-P-3-2, Ancestry of the Population in the United States: 1990.

77. Examples include Michael DeBakey in medicine (heart surgery); Elias Corey in chemistry (1990 Nobel Prize winner); Casey Kasem, Danny Thomas, and Paula Abdul in entertainment; Helen Thomas in journalism; Doug Flutie in sports (1984 Heisman Trophy winner); and Ralph Nader in consumer advocacy.

78. Casey Kasem, "We're Proud of Our Heritage," *Parade* (*Kansas City Star*) (16 January 1994): 1.

79. See Lisa Suhair Majaj, "Boundaries: Arab/American." In Joanna Kadi, ed., *Food for Our Grandmothers: Writings by Arab-American and Arab-Canadian Feminists* (Boston, MA: South End Press, 1994), pp. 65–84.

READING 44

Notes

1. The families of the teens were from twelve different countries including Jamaica (31 percent); Trinidad (21 percent); Guyana (16 percent); Barbados (10 percent); Haiti (10 percent); Grenada (5 percent); and a few each from the smaller islands of Montserrat, Saint Thomas, Anguilla, Saint Lucia, Dominica, and Nevis.

2. Middle class was defined as having at least one parent with a college degree or a professional or business position. Working class was defined as a parent with a low-skill job; poor were students whose parents were not currently employed.

References

Anderson, E. 1990. *Streetwise: Race, Class, and Change in an Urban Community.* Chicago: University of Chicago Press.

Feagin, J. R. 1991. "The Continuing Significance of Race—Antiblack Discrimination in Public Places." *American Sociological Review* 56(1): 101–116.

Foner, N. 1987. "The Jamaicans: Race and Ethnicity Among Migrants in New York City." In *New Immigrants in New York,* edited by N. Foner. New York: Columbia University Press.

Fordham, S. 1988. "Racelessness as a Factor in Black Students' School Success: Pragmatic Strategy or Pyrrhic Victory?" *Harvard Education Review* 58(1) (February).

Gans, H. J. 1992. "Second-Generation Decline: Scenarios for the Economic and Ethnic Futures of Post-1965 American Immigrants." *Ethnic and Racial Studies* 15 (April): 173–192.

Kasinitz, P. 1992. *Caribbean New York: Black Immigrants and the Politics of Race.* Ithaca, NY: Cornell University Press.

Lieberson, A. 1980. *A Piece of the Pie: Blacks and White Immigrants Since 1980.* Berkeley: University of California Press.

Massey, D. 1990. "American Apartheid: Segregation and the Making of the Underclass." *American Journal of Sociology* 96(2) (September): 329–357.

Ogbu, J. U. 1990. "Minority Status and Literacy in Comparative Perspective." *Daedalus* 119(2) (Spring): 141–168.

Portes, A., and M. Zhou. 1993. "The New Second Generation: Segmented Assimilation and Its Variants." *Annals of the American Academy of Political and Social Sciences* 530 (November): 74–96.

Stafford, S. B. 1987. "Language and Identity: Haitians in New York City." In *Caribbean Life in New York City: Sociocultural Dimensions,* edited by C. R. Sutton and E. M. Chaney. New York: Center for Migration Studies.

Sutton, C. R., and S. P. Makiesky. 1975. "Migration and West Indian Racial and Ethnic Consciousness." In *Migration and Development: Implications for Ethnic Identity and Political Conflict,* edited by H. I. Safa and B. M. Du Toit. Paris: Mouton.

Warner, W. L., and L. Srole. 1945. *The Social Systems of American Ethnic Groups.* New Haven, CT: Yale University Press.

Woldemikael, T. M. 1989. *Becoming Black American: Haitian and American Institutions in Evanston, Illinois.* New York: AMS Press.

READING 45

References

Becker, Gary. 1973. "A Theory of Marriage: Part I." *Journal of Political Economy,* 81(4): 813–46.

Blau, Peter M. 1964. *Exchange and Power in Social Life.* New York: Wiley.

Cutler, David, Edward Glaeser, and Jacob Vigdor. 1999. "The Rise and Decline of the American Ghetto." *Journal of Political Economy,* 107(3): 455–506.

Echenique, Federico, and Roland Fryer. Forthcoming. "A Measure of Segregation Based on Social Interactions." *Quarterly Journal of Economics.*

Fryer, Roland, and Mathew Jackson. 2003. "Categorical Cognition: A Psychological Model of Categories and Identification in Decision Making." National Bureau of Economic Research Working Paper 9579.

Fryer, Roland, and Steven Levitt. 2004. "Understanding the Black–White Test Score Gap in the First Two Years of School." *Review of Economics and Statistics,* 86(2): 447–64.

Kalmijn, Matthijs. 1993. "Trends in Black/White Intermarriage." *Social Forces,* 72(1): 119–46.

King, Martin Luther, Jr. 1956. "Paul's Letter to American Christians." Sermon delivered at Dexter Avenue Baptist Church, Montgomery, Alabama, on November 4, 1956. In *Knock at Midnight: Inspiration from the Great Sermons of Reverend Martin Luther King, Jr.,* ed. Clayborne Carson and Peter Holloran. New York: Warner Books, 1998.

Loury, Glenn. 2002. *The Anatomy of Racial Inequality.* Cambridge, MA: Harvard University Press.

MacGregor, Morris. 1985. *Integration of the Armed Forces 1940–1965.* Defense Studies Series. Washington, DC: Center of Military History, United States Army.

Merton, Robert K. 1941. "Intermarriage and the Social Structure: Fact and Theory." *Psychiatry,* August, 4(8): 361–74.

Moran, Rachel. 2003. *The Regulation of Race and Romance.* Chicago: University of Chicago Press.

Patterson, Orlando. 1982. *Slavery and Social Death: A Comparative Study.* Cambridge, MA: Harvard University Press.

Romano, Renee. 2003. *Race Mixing: Black–White Marriage in Postwar America.* Cambridge: Harvard University Press.

Rosch, Eleanor. 1978. "Principles of Categorization." In *Cognition and Categorization,* ed. E. Rosch and B.B. Lloyd, 27–48. Hillsdale, NJ: Erlbaum.

Rosen, Sherwin. 1974. "Hedonic Prices and Implicit Markets: Product Differentiation in Pure Competition." *Journal of Political Economy,* 82(1), 34–55.

Stodgill, Ron, and Amanda Bower. 2002. "Welcome to America's Most Diverse City." *Time,* in partnership with CNN, August 25. http://www.time.com/time/nation/printout/0,8816,340694,00.html.

Welch, Finis. 2003. "Catching Up: Wages of Black Men." *American Economic Review,* 93(2): 320–25.

Woodward, C. Vann. 1955. *The Strange Career of Jim Crow.* New York: Oxford University Press.

READING 46

Notes

1. "Over 93 percent of whites and of blacks marry within their own groups, in contrast to about 70 percent of Asians and of Hispanics and less than one-third of American Indians." Roderick J. Harrison and Claudette E. Bennett, "Racial and Ethnic Diversity," in Reynolds Farley, ed., *State of the Union: America in the 1990s—Vol. Two: Social Trends* (1995), 165.

   When people of Latino and Asian ancestry marry exogamously, "their spouses are very likely to be white; interracial marriages in the United States [have seldom] involved the mixing of two minority groups" (Ibid.).

2. Reflecting on his marriage, Peter Norton once mused, "Other than sex itself, why do you want to spend your life in the company of a woman as opposed to a best male friend? Part of the answer has to do with the wonderful, bizarre, inexplicable differences between male psychology and female psychology. Well, in the same vein, why would you want to spend your life with a person from the same ethnic background? You miss the frisson" (quoted in David Owen, "The Straddler," *The New Yorker,* January 30, 1995).

3. Roxie Roker, the black actress who played Helen Willis, was herself married to a white man. The popular musician Lenny Kravitz is their son. See Lynn Norment, "Am I Black, White, or in Between?," *Ebony,* August 1995; "Roxie Roker, 66, Who Broke Barrier in Her Marriage on TV's *Jeffersons,*" *New York Times,* December 6, 1995.

4. Denise Nicholas, who played the character whom the sheriff married, actively shaped the public image of her role, particularly with respect to the interracial relationship. Nicholas felt that the characters "should either break [the relationship] off or get married because oftentimes, historically, interracial relationships were back-alley affairs, hidden and lied about, particularly in the South. It became really important to me that the [characters] do something dignified; I didn't want my character to be cheap" ("Denise Nicholas and Carroll O'Connor Wed on TV Drama 'In the Heat of the Night,'" *Jet,* May 9, 1994). It should be recalled that the basis for the television series was the film of the same name (1967), which featured a thoroughly bigoted white sheriff (played by Rod Steiger, in an Academy Award–winning performance).

5. ABC's hugely successful musical production starred Brandy as Cinderella and Paolo Montalban as the prince. Taking the role of Prince Charming's mother, the queen, was a black actress, Whoopi Goldberg, while the king was played by a white actor, Victor Garber. See Veronica Chambers, "The Myth of Cinderella," *Newsweek,* November 3, 1997; "Cinderella

TV Music Special Produces Spectacular Rating for ABC," *Jet*, November 24, 1997.

6. Such depictions were no accident. When television producers sought guests for these programs, they advertised for people who had had *bad* experiences in or on account of interracial relationships. It was this bias that gave rise to episodes such as "Woman Disowned by Her Family for Dating a Black Man" on *Jenny Jones* and "Blacks and Blondes: White Girls Dating Black Guys for Sex, Style, and Status" on *Geraldo*.

7. Several months after *An American Love Story* aired, Cecily Wilson married a white union organizer whom she had met on a blind date. See "Weddings: Cecily Wilson, Gregory Speller," *New York Times*, May 7, 2000.

8. Fox has stated that she was surprised by some of her relatives' negative reactions to her interracial relationship, and surprised, too, by the regularity of the racial mistreatment her black lover suffered. In retrospect, she observes, "it was almost like I was deluded or something; I thought I was living in a different world than I was living in" (quoted in Paula Span, "Modern Family Life in Black and White: PBS Documentary Chronicles an Interracial Marriage," *Washington Post*, September 9, 1999).

9. Two excellent coming-of-age films that evoke the hazards and rewards of teenage interracial dating in the 1950s are Robert De Niro's *A Broux Tale* (1993) and Barry Levinson's *Liberty Heights* (2000).

10. Although they failed to persuade the United States Census Bureau to offer the "multiracial" box for the 2000 census, multiracialist reformers have succeeded in convincing a number of state governments—including those of Georgia, Illinois, Florida, Indiana, Michigan, and Ohio—to require that such a box be provided on state forms that collect racial data. They have also managed to convince several important private institutions, among them Harvard University, to add a "multiracial" category alongside the other, more familiar and established, choices. See Tanya Kateri Hernandez, "'Multiracial' Discourse: Racial Classifications in an Era of Color-Blind Jurisprudence," *Maryland Law Review* 57 (1998): 97, 98 n. 4.

11. When the racial-classification issue was decided for the 2000 census, the person in charge of the supervisory agency was Franklin Raines, a black man married to a white woman. Franklin and Wendy Raines had two children who themselves faced this classification dilemma. See Julia Malone, "Facing the Racial Question: More Categories in the Census," *The Atlanta Journal and Constitution*, October 15, 1997.

12. Woods made his views known on Oprah Winfrey's television show soon after he won the prestigious Masters golf tournament. See Greg Couch, "Woods: I'm More Than Black," *Chicago Sun-Times*, April 22, 1997, p. 1.

13. In a satirical essay entitled "The Mulatto Millennium," Danzy Senna facetiously defined "Cablinasian" thus:

A rare exotic breed found mostly in California. This is the mother of all mixtures. . . . A show mulatto, with great performance skills, the Cablinasian will be whoever the crowd wants him to be, and can switch at the drop of a dime. Does not, however, answer to the name Black. . . . Note: If you spot a Cablinasian, please contact the Benetton Promotions Bureau. [In Claudine Chiawei O'Hearn, ed., *Half and Half: Writers on Growing Up Biracial and Bicultural* (1998), 26.]

For a powerful defense of Woods's position, see Gary Kamiya, "Cablinasian like Me," Salon.com, April 1997. For a critique, see Leonard Pitts, "Is There Room in This Sweet Land of Liberty for Such a Thing as 'Cablinasian'? Face It, Tiger: If They Say You're Black, Then You're Black," *Baltimore Sun*, April 29, 1997.

READING 47

Notes

1. Etienne Balibar and Immanuel Wallerstein, *Race, Nation, Class: Ambiguous Identities* (New York: Verso, 1991), 71.

2. Joe Feagin and Hernán Vera, *White Racism* (New York: Routledge, 1995), ix–x.

3. Abby L. Ferber, *White Man Falling: Race, Gender and White Supremacy* (New York: Roman and Littlefield, 1998), 100.

4. Naomi Zack, *Race and Mixed Race* (Philadelphia: Temple University Press, 1994).

5. Mimi Abramowitz, *Regulating the Lives of Women: Social Welfare Policy from Colonial Times to the Present* (Boston: South End Press, 1996).

6. Ibid., 3.

7. Valerie Babb, *Whiteness Visible: The Meaning of Whiteness in American Literature and Culture* (New York: New York University Press, 1998), 76.

8. Grace Elizabeth Hale, *Making Whiteness: The Culture of Segregation in the South, 1890–1940* (New York: Vintage Books, 1998), 109.

9. See, for instance, Gail Folaron and McCartt Hess, "Placement Considerations for Children of Mixed African American and Caucasian Parentage," *Child Welfare League of America* 72, 3 (1993): 113–135.

10. See for instance, Ferber, *White Man Falling*.

11. Ibid.

12. Ibid., 104.

13. Robert Merton, "Intermarriage and the Social Structure: Fact and Theory," *Psychiatry* 4 (1941): 361–374; see also Matthijs Kalmijn, "Trends in Black/White Intermarriage," *Social Forces* 72, 1 (1996): 119–146.

14. Merton, "Intermarriage"; Kingsley Davis, "Intermarriage in Caste Societies," *American Anthropologist* (September 1941): 388–395.

15. Ferber, *White Man Falling.*

16. Zack, *Race and Mixed Race;* Joel Williamson, *New People: Miscegenation and Mulattoes in the United States* (New York: New York University Press, 1984).

17. Ferber, *White Man Falling,* 103.

18. Kate Davy, "Outing Whiteness." *Theatre* 47, 2 (1995): 189–205.

19. Charles Gallagher, "White Reconstruction in the University," *Socialist Review* 24, 1 and 2 (1995): 165–188.

20. Cathy J. Cohen, "Contested Membership: Black Gay Identities and the Politics of AIDS," in *Queer Theory/Sociology,* ed. Steven Seidman (Cambridge, Mass.: Blackwell, 1996), 365.

21. Frantz Fanon, *Black Skins, White Masks* (New York: Grove), 83.

22. Ibid., 60.

23. Paul C. Rosenblatt, Terri A. Karis, and Richard D. Powell, *Multiracial Couples: Black and White Voices* (Thousand Oaks, Calif.: Sage, 1995), 155.

24. Michael Eric Dyson, "Essentialism and the Complexities of Racial Identity," in *Multiculturalism: A Critical Reader,* ed. David Theo Goldberg (Cambridge, Mass.: Blackwell, 1994), 222.

25. Rosenblatt et al., *Multiracial Couples,* 150.

26. Ibid., 151.

27. Ibid.

28. Gloria Wade-Gayles, *Rooted against the Wind* (Boston: Beacon, 1996), 110.

29. David Heer, "Negro-White Marriages in the United States," *Journal of Marriage and the Family* 28 (1966): 262–273; Kalmijn, "Trends"; Merton, "Intermarriage"; Davis, "Intermarriage in Caste Societies."

30. Although many people break up permanently, I interviewed individuals who eventually made the decision to commit to an interracial marriage.

31. Claudette Bennett, "Interracial Children: Implications for a Multiracial Category" (paper presented at the annual meeting of the American Sociological Association, Washington, D.C., 1995).

32. Rosenblatt et al., *Multiracial Couples,* 5.

READING 48

Notes

1. "A Methodological Note" in Drake and Cayton (1993) [1945].

2. *Black Metropolis,* p. 127.

3. The strength and consequences of the tendency to racialize those of African descent in the United States is underscored by the persistent attempts of immigrants of African descent from the Caribbean and African continent to *emphasize* their cultural and linguistic differences from African Americans so as to escape the consequences of such racialization (Waters 1999).

4. OMB Directive 15 guidelines mandated federal agency compliance by 2003. As of 2006, the Education Department had not yet implemented the MOOM option. In August 2006, however, Education Department officials released a proposal for a plan to allow students to mark multiple racial categories that, if adopted, would comply with the federal guidelines.

5. The American College Personnel Association has an estimated 8,000 members.

6. Mavin Foundation has been quite involved in expanding the tracking and donation of bone marrow by mixed race people. They assert that mixed race people in need of bone marrow have difficulty finding matches because they are of mixed race.

7. Winant (1994) contrasts hegemony with domination. Rather than being silenced or repressed, hegemony incorporates opposition and difference (with modification) into the social order, as it robs opposition of its critical content.

References

Alba, R. (1990). *Ethnic Identity: The Transformation of White America.* New Haven, CT, Yale University Press.

Bakalian, A. (1993). *Armenian-Americans: From Being to Feeling Armenian.* New Brunswick, NJ, Transaction Publishers.

Bell, D. (1992). *Faces at the Bottom of the Well.* New York, Basic Books.

Blu, K. (1980). *The Lumbee Problem: The Making of an American Indian People.* Cambridge, UK, Cambridge University Press.

Comaroff, J. L. (1987). "Of Totemism and Ethnicity: Consciousness, Practice and the Signs of Inequality." *Ethnos* 52: 301–323.

Cose, E. (1992). *Rage of a Privileged Class: Why Do Prosperous Blacks Still Have the Blues?* New York, Harper Perennial.

DeMott, B. (1998 [1995]). *The Trouble with Friendship: Why Americans Can't Think Straight about Race.* New Haven, Yale University Press.

Drake, S. C. and H. Cayton. (1993 [1945]). *Black Metropolis: A Study of Negro Life in a Northern City.* Chicago, University of Chicago Press.

DuBois, W. E. B. ([1903] 1996). *The Souls of Black Folk. The Oxford W. E. B. DuBois Reader.* E. J. Sundquist. New York and Oxford, MI, Oxford University Press.

Espiritu, Y. L. (1992). *Asian American Panethnicity: Bridging Institutions and Identities.* Philadelphia, Temple University Press.

Files, J. (June 10, 2005). Report Describes Immigrants as Younger and More Diverse. *The New York Times:* 12.

Fordham, S. (1997). *Blacked Out.* Chicago, University of Chicago Press.

Gans, H. J. (1979). "Symbolic Ethnicity: The Future of Ethnic Groups and Cultures in America." *Ethnic and Racial Studies* 2: 1–20.

Lieberson, S. (1985). Unhyphenated Whites in the United States. *Ethnicity and Race in the U.S.A.: Toward the Twenty-first Century.* R. D. Alba. New York, Routledge: 159–180.

Nagel, J. (1995). "American Indian Ethnic Renewal: Politics and the Resurgence of Identity." *American Sociological Review* 60(6): 947–965.

Omi, M. and H. Winant. (1994). *Racial Formation in the United States: From the 1960s to the 1990s.* New York, Routledge.

Sanjek, R. (1994). Intermarriage and the Future of Races in the United States. *Race.* S. Gregory and R. Sanjek. New Brunswick, NJ, Rutgers University Press: 103–130.

Steinberg, S. (1989). *The Ethnic Myth: Race, Ethnicity, and Class in America.* Boston, Beacon Press.

Tuan, M. (1998). *Forever Foreigners or Honorary Whites? The Asian Ethnic Experience Today.* New Brunswick, NJ, Rutgers University Press.

Waters, M. (1990). *Ethnic Options: Choosing Ethnic Identities in America.* Berkeley, University of California Press.

Waters, M. C. (1999). *Black Identities: West Indian Immigrant Dreams and American Realities.* Cambridge, MA, Harvard University Press.

Winant, H. (1994). Racial Formation and Hegemony: Global and Local Developments. *Racism, Modernity and Identity on the Western Front.* A. Rattansi and S. Westwood. Cambridge, UK, Polity Press. 266–289.

READING 49

Notes

1. Brown, 9.
2. Price, 2003.
3. Sklar et al., 2001, 122.
4. Henry J. Kaiser Family Foundation, 1.
5. Ibid., 2.
6. Ibid., 4.
7. U.S. Department of Health and Human Services.
8. Shapiro, *Hidden Cost,* 2004, 52.
9. Sklar et al., 2001, 90.
10. Collins and Yeskel, 2000, 182.
11. Ibid.
12. Anderson et al., 2005, 1.
13. Root Cause, 2003.
14. Sklar et al., 2001, 118.
15. Phillips, 2001.
16. Boshara et al., 2004, 1.
17. Sklar et al., 2001, 118.
18. Muhammad et al., 2004, 7.
19. Woo, 2000, 104.
20. Shapiro, PowerPoint, 2004.
21. Sherradan, 1991, 3–7.
22. Brown, 17.
23. Shapiro, *Hidden Cost,* 2004, 185.
24. Ginsberg and Ochoa, 2003, B1.
25. Isbister, 1994, 2.
26. Ibid., 5.
27. Ibid.
28. Policy Link, 2003.
29. Ibid.
30. United for a Fair Economy, 2002.
31. Moreno, 1998, 6–7.
32. Ibid., 1.
33. Ibid., 17.
34. Orr, 2004, 14.
35. Spriggs, 2004, 18.
36. Muhammad et al., 2004, 17.
37. Agres, 2005, 37.

References

Agres, Bob. "Community Building in Hawai'i," in *The Nonprofit Quarterly,* Summer 2005.

Anderson, Sarah, John Cavanagh, Scott Klinger, and Liz Stanton, *Executive Excess 2005.* Boston and Washington, DC: Institute for Policy Studies and United for a Fair Economy, 2005. http://www.faireconomy.org/press/2005/EE2005.pdf (accessed September 8, 2005).

Boshara, Ray, Reid Cramer, and Leslie Parrish. *Policy Options to Encourage Savings and Asset Building by Low-Income Americans,* New America Foundation, Discussion Draft. January 28, 2004. www.newamericafoundation.org.

Brown, Michael K. "Race in the American Welfare State: The Ambiguities of 'Universalistic' Social Policy Since the New

Deal." *Without Justice for All: The New Liberalism and Our Retreat from Racial Equality.* Adolph L. Reed, editor. Boulder, CO: Westview Press, 1999.

Collins, Chuck, and Felice Yeskel. *Economic Apartheid in America: An Economic Primer on Economic Inequality and Insecurity.* New York: The New Press, 2000.

Ginsberg, Thomas, and Paola Ochoa (contributor). "Immigrants Pool Money, Find Success." *Philadelphia Inquirer,* Nov. 17, 2003.

Henry J. Kaiser Family Foundation. "New Report Provides Critical Information About Health Insurance Coverage and Access for Racial and Ethnic Minority Groups." Washington, DC, Aug. 1, 2000. http://www.kff.org/uninsured/upload/13342_1.pdf (accessed December 16, 2004).

Isbister, John. *Thin Cats: The Community Development Credit Union Movement in the United States.* Davis, CA: Center for Cooperatives, University of California, 1994.

Moreno, Ana. *Mortgage Foreclosure Prevention: Program and Trends.* Minneapolis: Family Housing Fund, December 1998.

Muhammad, Dedrick, Attieno Davis, Meizhu Lui, and Betsy Leondar-Wright. *The State of the Dream 2004: Enduring Disparities in Black and White.* Boston: United for a Fair Economy, 2004.

Orr, Doug. "Social Security Isn't Broken." *Dollars & Sense,* 256 (2004).

Phillips, Katherin Ross. *Who Knows About the Earned Income Tax Credit?* Washington, DC: Urban Institute, Jan. 1, 2001. http://www.urban.org/UploadedPDF/anf_b27.pdf, p. 1.

Policy Link. "Community Reinvestment Act: Why use the tool?" http://www.policylink.org/EquitableDevelopment/content/tools/56/20-all? (Accessed December 4, 2003).

Price, Derek, Lumina Foundation for Education, *Inequality in Higher Education: The Historic and Continuing Significance of Race,* panel on Colorlines Conference, Harvard Law School Civil Rights Project, Aug. 30, 2003.

Root Cause. *Community Impact Report.* Miami, FL: November 11, 2003. http://users.resist.ca/~mangus/CIR_eng.pdf (accessed 1/8/05).

Shapiro, Thomas. *The Hidden Cost of Being African American: How Wealth Perpetuates Inequality.* New York: Oxford University Press, 2004.

Shapiro, Thomas. PowerPoint presentation at Center for American Progress panel on wealth inequality, September 23, 2004.

Sherradan, Michael. *Assets and the Poor: A New American Welfare Policy.* Armonk, NY: M. E. Sharpe, 1991.

Sklar, Holly, Laryssa Mykyta, and Susan Wefald. *Raise the Floor Wages: Wages and Policies That Work for All of Us.* New York: Ms. Foundation for Women, 2001.

Spriggs, William E. "African Americans and Social Security: Why the Privatization Advocates Are Wrong," *Dollars & Sense,* 256 (2004): 18.

United for a Fair Economy, *Annual Report.* 2002.

U.S. Department of Health and Human Services, Substance Abuse and Mental Health Services Administration, *National Household Survey on Drug Abuse.* Rockville, MD: 1998. http://oas.samhsa.gov/nhsda/NHSDAsumrpt.pdf (accessed December 19, 2004).

Woo, Deborah. *Glass Ceilings and Asian Americans: The New Face of Workplace Barriers,* Walnut Creek, CA: AltaMira Press, 2000.

Credits

READING 1

Harris, Marvin "How Our Skins Got Their Color" (pp. 112–14) from OUR KIND. Copyright © 1989 by Marvin Harris. Reprinted by permission of HarperCollins Publishers.

READING 2

Zinn, Howard "Drawing the Color Line" (pp. 23–38) from A PEOPLE'S HISTORY OF THE UNITED STATES: 1492–PRESENT by HOWARD ZINN. Copyright © 1980 by Howard Zinn. Reprinted by permission of HarperCollins Publishers.

READING 3

Omi, Michael and Howard Winant "Racial Formations" from *Racial Formation in the United States: From the 1960s to the 1990s* by Michael Omi. Copyright © 1994. Reproduced with permission of TAYLOR & FRANCIS GROUP LLC – BOOKS in the format Textbook via Copyright Clearance Center.

READING 4

Snipp, C. Matthew. "Defining Race and Ethnicity: The Constitution, the Supreme Court, and the Census" from DOING RACE: 21 ESSAYS FOR THE 21st CENTURY, edited by Hazel Rose Markus & Paula M. L. Moya. © 2010 by W.W. Norton & Company, Inc. Used by permission of W.W. Norton & Company, Inc.

READING 5

"Racialized Social System Approach to Racism" by Eduardo Bonilla-Silva, from *White Supremacy and Racism in the Post-Civil Rights Era* by Eduardo Bonilla-Silva. Copyright © 2001 by Lynne Rienner Publishers. Used by permission of the publisher.

READING 6

Williams, David and Michelle Sternthal. "Understanding Racial-ethnic Disparities in Health: Sociological" Courtesy of *Journal of Health and Social Behavior* 51, no. 1 suppl (November 2010): S15–S27.

READING 7

"Transformative Assets, the Racial Wealth Gap, and the American Dream" by Thomas Shapiro. Reprinted by permission of the National Urban League.

READING 8

"Defining Race: Comparative Perspectives" by F. James Davis from *Mixed Messages: Multiracial Identities in the "Color-Blind" Era*, edited by David Brunsma. Copyright © 2006 by Lynne Rienner Publishers. Used with permission by the publisher.

READING 9

"A Tour of Indian Peoples and Indian Lands" by David E. Wilkins, from *American Indian Politics and the American Political System*, pp. 11–40. Copyright © 2002. Reprinted by permission of Rowman & Littlefield Publishers, Inc.

READING 10

Yen, Le Espiritu. "Asian American Panethnicity: Contemporary National and Transnational Possibilities" in *Not Just Black and White: Historical and Contemporary Perspectives on Immigration, Race, and Ethnicity in the United States*. Copyright © 2004 Russell Sage Foundation, 112 East 64th Street, New York, NY 10021. Reprinted by permission.

READING 11

Lee, Jennifer and Frank Bean. "Beyond Black and White: Remaking Race in America" *American Sociological Association* 2, no. 3 (2003): 26–33. Sage journals Online free http://ctx.sagepub.com/content/2/3/26.abstract.

READING 12

"Color-Blind Privilege: The Social and Political Functions of Erasing the Color Line in Post-Race America" by Charles A. Gallagher, from the RCG JOURNAL SPECIAL EDITION ON PRIVILEGE, Abby L. Ferber and Dena R. Samuels, co-editors, Vol. 10, No. 4, 2003.

READING 27

Alexander, Michelle. Excerpt from *The New Jim Crow*. Copyright © 2010 by Michelle Alexander. Reprinted by permission of The New Press, www.thenewpress.com.

READING 28

Bobo, Lawrence D. & Victor Thompson. "Racialized Mass Incarceration: Poverty, Predjudice, and Punishment" from DOING RACE: 21 ESSAYS FOR THE 21st CENTURY, edited by Hazel Rose Markeu & Paula M.L.Moya. © 2010 by W.W. Norton & Company, Inc. Used by permission of W.W. Norton & Company, Inc.

READING 29

Pager, Devah. "The Mark of a Criminal Record" from IN FOCUS, The Newsletter for the Institute for Research on Poverty 23, no. 2 (Summer 2004). Copyright © 2004 by the Regents of the University of Wisconsin. Reprinted with permission.

READING 30

"Using DNA for Justice: Colorblind or Biased?" from *Genetic Justice: Data Banks, Criminal Investigations, and Civil Liberties* by Sheldon Krimsky and Tania Simoncelli. Copyright ©2010. Columbia University Press. Reprinted with permission of the publisher.

READING 31

"Kristen v. Aisha; Brad v. Rasheed: What's in a Name and How It Affects Getting a Job" by Amy Braverman Puma, from "Why Brad and Kristen Beat Out Jermaine and Ebony." UNIVERSITY OF CHICAGO MAGAZINE 95 no. 3 (February 2003). Reprinted with permission.

READING 32

Waldinger, Robert, "When the Melting Pot Boils Over" in Michael Peter Smith and Joseph R. Feagin (eds) *The Bubbling Cauldron* (University of Minnesota Press, 1995) pp. 265–281. Copyright 1995 by the Regents of the University of Minnesota. Reprinted by permission.

READING 33

Newman, Katherine S. & Catherine Ellis "'There's No Shame in My Game': Status and Stigma among Harlem's Working Poor" Reprinted from THE CULTURAL TERRITORIES OF RACE edited by Michele Lamont. Copyright © 1999 University of Chicago and the Russell Sage Foundation. Reprinted by permission of the University of Chicago Press.

READING 34

Bao, Xiaolan. "Sweatshops in Sunset Park: A Variation of the Late Twentieth-Century Chinese Garment Shops in New York City" from *International Labor and Working-Class History*, Vol. 61, (April 2002), pp. 69–90. Copyright © 2002 The International Labor and Working-Class History Society. Reprinted with the permission of Cambridge University Press.

READING 35

Kandel, William & Emilio A. Parrado. "Hispanics in the American South and the Transformation of the Poultry Industry" from HISPANIC SPACES, LATINO PLACES: COMMUNITY AND CULTURAL DIVERSITY IN CONTEMPORARY AMERICA, edited by Daniel D. Arreola. Copyright © 2004. By permission of the University of Texas Press.

READING 36

Dirks, Danielle and Jennifer Mueller "Racism and Popular Culture" With kind permission from Springer Science+Business Media: *Handbook of the Sociology of Racial and Ethnic Relations* edited by Hernan Vera and Joe Feagin. Copyright © Springer Press 2007.

READING 37

Littlefield, Marci Bounds. "The Media as a System of Racialization: Exploring Images of African American Women and the New Racism" from *American Behavioral Scientist* 51, no. 5 (Jan. 2008): 675–685. Republished with permission from Sage Publications. Permission conveyed through Copyright Clearance Center, Inc.

READING 38

"Biracials in the Movies" by Alicia Edisaon and George Yancey in *Multiracial Americans and Social Class* edited by Kathleen Odell Korgen (Routledge 2010)

READING 39

Merskin, Debra. "Winnebagos, Cherokees, Apaches, and Dakotas: The Persistence of Stereotyping of American Indians in American Advertising and Brands" Copyright 2001. From *Howard Journal of Communications* 12 issue 3 (2001): 156–169. Taylor & Francis Online free www.tandfonline.com/doi/abs/10.1080/106461701753210439.